You
Ic

for 1996!

Includes both
U.S. & Canadian budget motels!

New and **exclusive** GUARANTEED motel room rates!
See details inside on how motels will *guarantee* **room rates**
to holders of this book!

Rooms for **$48** for **two persons** overnight at budget motels.
Listings give **prices** for individual motels, including ranges,
and seasonal fluctuations.

Discounts! See types and amounts!

Budget motel **locations** by city or area.

Telephone numbers, toll-free
numbers, and faxes

Extras such as pool, cable or satellite TV, videotape player,
exercise room, sauna, morning coffee, or mini-breakfasts

Credit cards you can use at
the motel you choose

Everything you need
to find the budget motel you want
while you are on the road
on vacation or for business

Reviews

"Why pay more if this will serve your needs? There are tips on best buys & money-saving discounts, toll-free numbers & more.."
—Quick Trips Travel Letter

"If you are sick of paying $60 for a room only to find that there was one just as good five miles down the road for $19.95, do yourself a big favor and order up a copy of the *State by State Guide to Budget Motels*."
—Motorcycle Consumer News

"For a listing of **low-cost** accommodations, try the *State by State Guide to Budget Motels*."
—Travel-Holiday magazine

"A nationwide **no-frills** listing of motels ...with a run-down on their facilities."
—Publishers Weekly

"*The State by State Guide to Budget Motels* ...is a reference which **any** budget traveler will find **invaluable**... (and)...will save money."
—The Midwest Book Review

"One book that is almost guaranteed to save you a lot of money on the road."
—The Shoestring Traveler

"If you have ever made the mistake of stopping at what appeared to be a low-cost motel and found yourself in...an overpriced and mislabeled motel, this book can **save you**."
—Rider magazine

"*The State by State Guide to Budget Motels*, 1995, includes... rates, phone numbers, discounts and facilities for nearly 4,000 motels (and) arranged by state (or Canadian province) and city."
—Travel Smart

"A practical travel book to use over and over again. An ideal reference for any library travel guide shelf.."
—Wisconsin Bookwatch

Note: In 1995, *The State by State Guide to Budget Motels* was presented a special award "for Distinguished Service to The Lodging Industry" by Budget Host Inns.

1996 STATE BY STATE GUIDE TO
BUDGET MOTELS

Your national guide to
the best low-cost lodgings

Loris G. Bree

MARLOR PRESS, INC.

1996 STATE BY STATE GUIDE TO

BUDGET MOTELS

1996 State by State Guide to Budget Motels. Published by Marlor Press, Inc. All rights reserved. No part of this book may be reproduced in any form without the written permission of the publisher, Marlor Press, Inc.

Copyright 1996 by Loris G. Bree

ISBN 0-943400-84-8

Distributed to the book trade by Contemporary Books Inc, Chicago

First Edition / January / 1996

Printed in the United States of America

Loris G. Bree, Editor
Lori Stone, Assistant to the Editor

Disclaimer: Prices, facilities, and services are subject to change at any time. Information presented in this book is based on reports from the motels and/or their organizations. The author and the publisher have made best efforts to secure current data from the selected motels at presstime. To assure themselves of up to date and pertinent information at the time they use this book, customers should double-check prices, facilities, and services, etc., to determine that these will meet their own needs. Those rates listed as "guaranteed rates" are rates reported by the motels to this publication and "guaranteed" by the motel to publication holders and are valid only during the dates registered, and, certain exclusions may apply. In any event, Marlor Press, Inc., and the author, are not responsible for price changes, rates of any kind, schedules, services, reservations, availability, facilities, agreements, or loss or injury of any kind.

Maps are from *Ready to Use Outline Maps of U.S. States and Regions*, by Phillip Runquist, copyright 1994 Dover Publications, Inc., and used courtesy of the publisher.

MARLOR PRESS, INC.

4304 Brigadoon Drive
Saint Paul, Minnesota 55126

CONTENTS

Introduction, VI
How to use this guide, VII
Where to get discounts, VIII
Toll-free numbers, VIII
Guaranteed rates, X
Guide to abbreviations, XI

Budget motels by state (U.S.A.)

Alabama, 1	Montana, 165
Arizona, 6	Nebraska, 168
Arkansas, 13	Nevada, 175
California, 19	New Hampshire, 177
Colorado, 49	New Jersey, 178
Connecticut, 57	New Mexico, 180
Delaware, 59	New York, 186
District of Columbia, 60	North Carolina, 192
Florida, 59	North Dakota, 201
Georgia, 79	Ohio, 204
Hawaii, 90	Oklahoma, 212
Idaho, 91	Oregon, 216
Illinois, 94	Pennsylvania, 219
Indiana, 104	Rhode Island, 226
Iowa, 109	South Carolina, 227
Kansas, 115	South Dakota, 234
Kentucky, 121	Tennessee, 240
Louisiana, 126	Texas, 250
Maine, 128	Utah, 268
Maryland, 130	Vermont, 273
Massachusetts, 134	Virginia, 275
Michigan, 136	Washington, 288
Minnesota, 145	West Virginia, 292
Mississippi, 153	Wisconsin, 295
Missouri, 156	Wyoming, 303

Budget motels (Canada)

Alberta, 309	Nova Scotia, 312
British Columbia, 310	Ontario, 313
Manitoba, 311	Prince Edward Island, 319
New Brunswick, 311	Quebec, 319
	Saskatchewan, 321

Introduction

About budget motels

You can save as much as **50 percent** per night by staying in a budget motel as compared to a higher priced inn or hotel.

To be included in this book, a motel must charge **$48 or less** for a double occupancy overnight.

Who uses budget motels?

About **25 percent** of all business travelers these days favor budget motels.

Surveys show **no difference** between lodging users. Most travelers who use budget motels are similar to those who reside in the higher-priced hotels.

The average household income of those who stay at budget motels is $69,656, according to one national survey. This figure ranks only slightly lower than that of those persons who stay at the full-service hotels. Both groups were about equally divided in professional positions.

Also they seemed to carry about the same type and number of credit cards. They did about the same amount of travel by air and by car.

Both groups were about equally well educated: a high percentage of each had college degrees.

Comparisons:

What is the difference between a hotel room and a budget motel room?

Actually, very little.

You get about **as much space** in a budget motel room as you do in a typical large-city hotel room, though you sometimes pay almost twice the price for the hotel room.

In a hotel, your room will be large enough for a bed, clean bathroom, color television set, desk, easy chair and dresser.

Out on the freeway, away from downtown, you will undoubtedly find any number of budget motels convenient to your automobile travel. These will probably have fewer rooms than the larger hotels and the room will probably be only two or three feet shorter than the downtown room. Like the hotel, it will have the bed, TV set, desk and easy chair.

But what you probably won't get is a fancy lobby, an expensive dining room, or lots of extra staff. The no-frills motel lobby will be smaller and dedicated to checking in and out. You'll park your own car, close to your own room, and handle your own luggage.

The main difference is price. Here the budget motel is a clear winner at prices around $48 for two persons overnight, and, less for a single person.

Budgets: the best buy

For travelers of all kinds, including both business and vacationers, it's no wonder that budget motels are the **fastest growing segment** of the travel lodging industry.

Travel editors today rank budget motels as the **"best buy"** for vacationing or business lodging.

About 20 percent of all lodgings are now budget motels.

How to use this Guide

About the Guide

The *State by State Guide to Budget Motels* is **completely revised** each year just prior to press time. Only motels that provided accurate and updated information for the coming year, as well as provide quality control assurance, are included.

Cost Ranges

In these pages, you'll find budget motels with rooms costing no more than **$48** a night for **two people**. The motel must offer this price at least six months of the year.

There may be seasonal adjustments, or special event price increases, in some areas. These are shown by **Higher spec event rates**. When you reserve, confirm the price.

Organization

Motels are organized **alphabetically** by state and then by city. Turn to the state you are visiting, then look for the city, also listed alphabetically. The motels are listed alphabetically.

Listings

Each motel listing is followed by:

Street and mailing address, so you can write for reservations and to help you locate the motel when you're arriving.

Telephone numbers, direct dial (see the toll-free listings, if you're calling long distance) as well as fax numbers.

Credit cards accepted. These are indicated by the following symbols

AE-American Express; **V**-Visa; **M**- Master Card; **D**-Discover; **DC**-Diners Club; **CB**-Carte Blanche.

Directions to find the motel from the nearest highway or city center. Note "Also see" for other motels in this area.

Facilities, such as swimming pool, exercise room, non-smoking rooms or other services, such as free morning coffee, continental breakfast, daily newspaper, cribs, or cable or satellite TV.

Prices per day, for one person, and for two.

Discounts offered and when applicable.

Note: Some listings are in **bold face.** This indicates that a motel has selected an "enhanced listing" to bring its information and facilities to a traveler's attention.

How to find the best buys

You can check the listings to find the budget motel that **best suits** your needs, price range, and location In off-seasons, some individual motels will offer a *special rate* or *special discount* if you ask for them. Check for these as well as other standard discounts offered.

Check for rates

We suggest you specifically *ask at the desk* for the **rates** for your stay. Rates can change with changing circumstances. In some tourist areas, or during special events, rates do go up. We try to provide information about these changes, if possible.

Toll-Free Numbers

Many of the major chains and reservation services offer toll-free numbers so that you may make reservations at no expense to you. Listed below are numbers for sites that are listed in this guide. Unless otherwise indicted, numbers are available throughout the U.S. Some, but not all, are also available in Canada. These numbers are for reservations only. The operators usually will be able to provide information about rates and discounts but will not have any other information about the motels.

Best Inns	(800) BEST-INN
Best Western	(800) 528-1234
Budget Host	(800) BUD-HOST
Clarion	(800) CLARION
Comfort Inns	(800) 228-5150
Cross County Inns	(800) 621-1429
Days Inn	(800) DAYS INN
Daystop	(800) DAYS INN
Econo Lodges	(800) 55-ECONO
Exel Inns	(800) 356-8013
Friendship	(800) 453-4511
HoJo Inns	(800) IGO HOJO
Howard Johnson	(800) IGO HOJO
IMA	(800) 341-8000
Kelly Inns	(800) 635-3559
National 9 Inns	(800) 524-9999
Quality Inns	(800) 228-5151
Ramada Inns	(800) 2-RAMADA
Rodeway Inns	(800) 228-2000
Sandman Inns	(800) 726-3626
Scotsman Inns	(800) 667-7268
Sleep Inns	(800) 62-SLEEP
Super 8 Motels	(800) 800-8000
Vagabond Inns	(800) 522-1555
Wellesley Inns	(800) 444-8888
Wilson Inns	(800) WILSONS

Special Numbers:

Hearing Impaired TTY Phone for Clarion, Comfort, Econo, Friendship, Quality, Rodeway, and Sleep Hotels 800-228-3393
French Language number for the above motels 800-BO-REVES
Super 8 TDD/ Telecommunication Device for the Deaf 800-533-6634
Best Western TDD 800-528-2222
Best Western French Language Reservations 800-528-1234
Best Western Spanish Language Reservations 800-528-1234
Motel 6 toll number 505-891-6161
Motel 6 TDD 505-891-6160

Where to Get Discounts & Amenities

Ask about discounts at the motel desk or when you call for reservations.

Although we have, in the past, tried to list discounts under each individual motel, some of the major chains are offering so many discounts that we don't have room to list them all. Many also offer discounts that need further explanation.

Look for discounts to be listed after independent motels and look here for discounts offered by many chains. Since the lodgings that make up these chains are frequently independently owned franchises, you can expect that they will offer some, but not all of the discounts listed here.

Be sure to ask when you make reservations or check in to see if you qualify for a discount.

Many properties that offer government discounts also include the military in these discounts. Military personnel and their families should inquire about discounts when making reservations.

Best Inns give a *senior citizen* discount of anyone 50 years old or older. *Children* under 18 stay free with a parent.

Best Western participating motels may offer a discount to *senior* citizens, *government and military* personnel, and *frequent travelers.* Members of the *Young Traveler's Club* 16 and under stay free with a parent. They pay a commission to *travel agents. Business* members of the Corporate Rate Program get special rates. They also offer personalized service to people planning *reunions, meetings* and *group* travel. Members of the Best Western Seniority and Young Traveler's Club receive points to be redeemed for special awards.

Budget Host Many motels offer discounts to *senior citizens, AARP* and *AAA members, commercial travelers, truckers* and/or a commission to *travel agents.*

Choice Hotels including **Comfort Inn, Quality Inn, Clarion Resort, Econo Lodge, Rodeway Inn, Friendship Inn** and **Sleep Inns** have a *Family Plan* allowing children under 18 to stay free in parent's or grandparent's room, *Prime Time* and *Senior Saver* for people aged 50 and over and members of AARP allow a 10% discount at all hotels, or a 30% discount at some hotels when you call (800) 328-2211 and ask for Prime Time Senior Saver. At participating motels, *business travelers* received discounted room rats and special amenities, *government, active and retired military* get per diem rates. Any guest currently registered in a Choice property can receive a 10% discount on *future reservations* when you ask a desk clerk to make a reservation for you. Other discounts include a 10% discount to members of the *American Automobile Association* and the *Canadian Automobile Association*; a discounted rate for weekend reservations through *the Weekender* program.

Cross County Inns give a discount of 25% off the posted room rate to all *persons 60 years old* or better.

Days Inns and **Daystops/** have several special travel clubs with discounts to qualified members. The *September Day's Club* offers 15% to 50% savings on room rates to travelers over 50 (membership fee). A 10% *Senior Citizen Discount* will be given to any senior who presents a valid membership for any senior organization. Holders of an *Inn-Credible* card are business people who receive 10% to 30% discounts. The *Government/ Military Rates Program* and the *USA Days Program* are free plans for government and military employees and cost-reimbursed contractors, offering per diem rates. The *Kids Stay Free* program allows children 12 and under to stay free in an adult's room. The *Sports Plus Club* is a free club for sports teams and coaches; the *School Days Club* is a free club for teachers and school administrators; both offer special benefits and rates. All of the above are available at every Days Inn.

Exel Inns and **American Budget Inns** allow *kids 18 and under* to stay free with a parent. With an *Insider's Card*, frequent travelers may stay free on the 13th night.

Howard Johnson and **HoJo Inns** offer a *senior citizen* discount at many locations. Members of the *Golden Years Travel Club* receive 15% off standard room rates at all locations plus many bonus savings. Under the *Family Plan*, children under 18 stay free when staying in the same room as an adult and using existing beds. They also have a *Government Rate Program* for federal, state and local government employees and active military personnel traveling on government business. The *Corporate Rate Program* offers special rates to companies and business travelers who regularly reserve rooms. All locations carry a supply of "most forgotten items" for last minute emergency. Contact the front desk for a complimentary item.

IMA (Independent Motels of America) offers an *IMA Travel Card* which is honored at most IMA affiliated properties. The card allows the guest to receive a $10 cash bonus on their 6th night of lodging at any property accepting the card. At many of the properties *children* sleep free and *seniors* receive a discount.

Motel 6 allows *children* 17 and under to stay free in the same room with a parent.

Ramada Inns offer, at participating inns, *Best Years Club* for senior travelers and *children* 18 and under stay free when sharing a room with an adult. At many midwest locations the *business class* offers a complimentary breakfast, newspaper and local calls for business travelers.

Sandman Hotels and Inns have a *55 Plus Program* for seniors of 55 or more years. Ask for a free card at any Sandman. With the *Lucky 13 card*, available at all inns, the 13th night stayed at one of the inns is free.

Super 8 Motels *VIP Club*: Guaranteed reservations, discounted rates at all locations and other special privileges for frequent travelers. Most offer a commission to *travel agents*. Some motels may also offer discounted rates to *government* employees, *groups*, members of the *military, senior citizens,* and *truck drivers*. Many locations allow *children 12 and under* to stay free in a parent's room.

Wellesley Inns offer *ALL USERS OF THIS BOOK* a special rate. To receive the rate quoted here (10% off the regular rate), call their toll-free reservation number (800-444-8888) and request the *Wellesly Club* rate or call ahead at the motel of your choice and request the Wellesley Club rate.

Wilson Inns offer a 10% discount to *members of the AARP.* hildren 19 and under stay free when sharing a room with a parent. *Travel agents* receive a 10% commission at all hotels and inns.

Non-smoking rooms

Many chains and independents have some rooms in **every motel** that are used only by non-smokers.

The rooms are assigned, as requested, and not be available to late arriving guests. Occasionally a motel may be restricted entirely to non-smokers or have only a few rooms for smokers.

Pets

We have tried to indicate where pets are not allowed (No pets). Most motels require that you request permission before bringing your pet into a room.

Many charge a special rate for pets, some require a deposit (pets w/d) and some may provide a kennel for your pet while staying at the motel.

Guaranteed rates

In some listings you will note that the motel has guaranteed that holders of the *1996 State by State Guide to Budget Motels* will not be charged more than the maximum rates shown.

To receive these rates you must identify yourself as an owner of a copy of this directory and request the guaranteed rate when you make reservations. You may be asked to show the directory when you register.

You should also verify the rates when registering. *These rates are only valid during January through December, 1996.* Note that certain **exclusions** to these guaranteed rates may apply, as noted below.

Exclusions: Special events, holidays or special weekends may cause the lodgings to temporarily increase their rates.

During these times the guaranteed rates do not apply. The motels may also have special rooms with special amenities for which they charge more. These might include larger beds, more beds, kitchens, whirlpool rooms or other features.

What happened to "Mom and Pop" Motels?

We frequently hear from readers who want more independent motels and fewer chains. We, too, would like to have more independent "Mom and Pop" motels listed in the book.

Unfortunately, most people are more willing to stay at a name they recognize and therefore it is more profitable for a motel to have a "brand name." Many of the so-called chain motels are owned by independent owners who pay a franchise fee to have the name, the reservation service, the advertising and, often, the business advice of the franchiser.

That means that although there are fewer and fewer motels that appear to be independent, most of those "name brands" are owned by an individual owner, often the person who greets you at the desk.

Awards

We would like to draw your attention to a new trend in the large franchise groups and/or chains that we heartily endorse. Although all of the chains listed in the *State by State Guide to Budget Motels* have high quality standards and regularly inspect their franchised properties, there are obviously some individual motels that give you higher quality than others.

Several of the chains have decided to recognize motels in their group who achieve highest standards. Whenever we are aware of a property that has received an award, we mention it in our listing.

Among the awards are:

Pride Award, Motel of the Year, Manager of the Year, Top 8 Quality Award: **Super 8 Motels**

Inn of the Year, Gold Hospitality Award: Choice Motels **(Clarion, Quality, Comfort, Sleep, Econo, Rodeway, Friendship)**

Gold Key Award: **Ramada**

Premier Award: **Motel 6**

Of course, we continue to show motels that have been inspected and received approval by the American or Canadian Automobile Association (AAA, CAA) or by the Mobile travel guides (Mobil).

What to look for in a listing

This is an ENHANCED LISTING

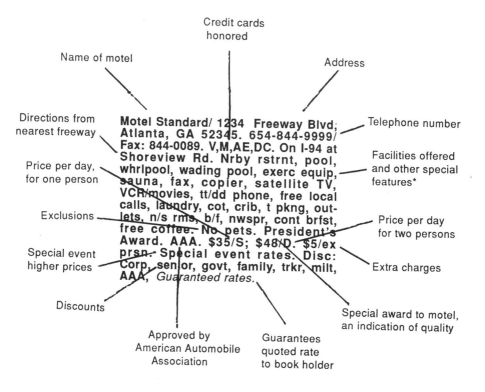

*See **Guide to Abbreviations**, p. XI

Guide to Abbreviations

Below are abbreviations and their meanings that are used in the motel listings

AAA	approved by the American Automobile Association
AARP	discount to American Association of Retired Persons members
add	additional
AE	American Express
adj	adjacent
alt	alternate
approx	approximate
Apr	April
arpt	airport
apt	apartment
Aug	August
av	avenue
b pkng	bus parking
b/f	barrier free rooms that allow wheel chair access
bdrm	bedroom
bet	between
blk	block
blvd	boulevard
bnd	bound
brfst	breakfast
bsns	business
CAA	Canadian Automobile Association
CB	Carte Blanche
chg	charge
clr	circle
cntr	center
co	county
comm	commercial
conn rms	connecting rooms
cont	continental
cot	rollaway or other temporary bed
ct	court
cr	credit
crd	card
cvd	covered
D	Discover
/D	double (2 people)
DC	Diners Club
dd	direct dial
Dec	December
disc	discount
dntn	downtown
dr	drive
E	east
ER	enroute
Ebnd	eastbound
eff	efficiency
exerc equip	exercise equipment
expwy	expressway
facil	facility
fax	facsimile machine
Feb	February
frwy	freeway
ft	fort
govt	government
grnd	ground
grp	group
hr	hour
hwy	highway
IMA	Independent Motels of America
immed	immediate
Indr	indoor
Intl	international
isl	island
Jan	January
jct	junction

Jun	June	rv pkng	parking for recreational vehicles
Jul	July		
l/s	length of stay	/S	single (one person)
ln	lane	S	south
lrg	large	Sbnd	southbound
lt	left	seas	season
M	Master Card	Sep	September
Mar	March	serv	service
mi	miles	spec	special
milt	military	Spr	Spring
min	minimum	SR	state route
movies	rental movies, video cassettes for VCR	st	saint/street
		Sum	Summer
Mt	Mount	t pkng	truck parking
mtg	meeting	TA	travel agent
mtl	motel	thru	through
N	north	tr	trail
Nbnd	northbound	trans	transportation
n/s rms	rooms for non smokers	trav	traveler
		t pkng	truck parking
No pets	no pets allowed	trkr	trucker
Nov	November	trnpk	turnpike
nrby	nearby	tt	touch tone
ntl	national	TDD	telecommunications device for the hearing impaired
nwspr	newspaper		
Oct	October	US	United States
outlets	outdoor electrical outlets	V	Visa
pk	park	W	west
pkng	parking	Wbnd	westbound
pkwy	parkway	whrlpool	whirlpool
pl	place	Win	Winter
playgrnd	playground	wknd	weekend
prem	premises	yr	year
prsn	person		
rd	road		
refrig	refrigerator		
reserv	reservation		
rm	room		
rstrnt	restaurant		
rt	right		
rte	route		

XIV

ALABAMA

Alabama

Alexander City
Super 8 Motel/ 1104 280 Bypass, Alexander City AL 35010. 205-329-8858/ Fax: Ext 403. D,AE,DC,CB,M,V. US 280 Bypass. B/f, n/s rms, b/rv pkng, outlets, cable TV, mtg rm, cot. Free local calls, crib. No pets. $37/S; $42-44/D; $5/ex prsn. Discs.

Anniston
Super 8 Motel/ 6220 McLellan Blvd, Anniston AL 36206. 205-820-1000/ Fax: Ext 302. M,V,D,CB,AE,DC. I-20 (Exit 185) to Hwy 21, N 5 mi. From Hwy 431 to Hwy 21, N pass 4 traffic lights. B/f, n/s rms, pool, laundry, cont brfst, b pkng, copier, kitchenette, VCR/ movies, refrig, cot, crib. Free local calls. $33-37/S; $35-45/D; $4/ex prsn. Discs.

Also see Oxford.

Bessemer (Birmingham area)
Econo Lodge/ 1021 9th Av SW, Bessemer AL 35023. 205-424-9780. V,AE,M,DC. 12 mi SW of Birmingham, US 11 S at 9th Av. Rstrnt/ lounge, pool, mtg rm, fax, cable TV, t pkng, n/s rms. No pets. $36-39/S; $39-45/D; $5/ex prsn. Discs.

Motel 6/ 1000 Shiloh Ln, Bessemer AL 35020. 205-426-9646/ Fax: 426-9305. V,M,DC,D,AE. I-20/59 (Exit 108) to Academy Dr, SE of US 11/Tuscaloosa Hwy, lt on Shiloh Ln. Nrby rstrnt, cable TV, laundry, pool, t pkng. $27/S; $33/D; $6/ex prsn. 4/29-5/5: $40/S; $46/D. Higher spec event rates. Disc.

Birmingham
Best Southern Inn/ 2224 5th Av N, Birmingham AL 35203. 205-324-6107. V,M,AE,DC. I-20 to 22nd St to 5th Av N. Cable TV. Free local calls, fax. AAA/ National 9. $30/S; $30-39/D; $5/ex prsn. Disc: Corp.

Howard Johnson/ 275 Oxmoor Rd, Birmingham AL 35209. 205-942-0919/ Fax: Ext. 404. V,M,DC,AE,D,CB. I-65 S (Exit 256B) at Oxmoor Rd. N/s rms, pool, t/b pkng, fax, cable TV. Free local calls, cont brfst. $33-43/S; $39-49/D. Disc.

Super 8 Motel/ 1813 Crestwood Blvd, Birmingham AL 35210. 205-956-3650/ Fax: Ext 361. M,V,D,CB,AE,DC. I-20 (Exit 133) at US 78. N/s rms, pool. Free local calls. $36/S; $41/D; $5/ex prsn. Higher spec event rates. Discs.

Also see Bessemer, Homewood, Moody.

Brewton
Days Inn/ 217 Hwy 31 S, Brewton AL 36426. 334-867-9999/ Fax: 867-5594. AE,D,DC,V,M,CB,JDB. US 29 & 31. Nrby rstrnt, pool, whrlpool, mtg rm, b/f, t pkng, arpt trans, cable TV, microwave, refrig. Free cont brfst. Chairman's Award. $50-55/S; $50-65/D; $5/ex prsn. 4/1-9/30: $40-45/S; $48-60/D. Discs.

Camden
Days Inn/ Hwy 10 Bypass, Camden AL 36726. 205-682-4555/ Fax: 682-4801. V,AE,M,DC,CB,D,JCB. On Hwy 10 Bypass, N of I-41. Nrby rstrnt, pool, b/f, t pkng, boat pkng, cable TV. Free cont brfst. $39-45/S; $43-62/D; $5/ex prsn. Discs.

Childersburg
Days Inn/ 33669 US Hwy 280, Childersburg AL 35044. 205-378-6007/ Fax: 378-3535. V,AE,M,DC,CB,D,JCB. On US 280, E of Hwy 76. Nrby rstrnt/ lounge, pool, b/f, t pkng, rm serv. Chairman's Award. $39-45/S; $43-50/D; $6/ex prsn. Discs.

ALABAMA

Clanton
Friendship Inn/ 2301 7th St S, Clanton AL 35045. 205-755-4049. V,M,DC,AE. I-65, Exit 205. Nrby rstrnt, pool, fax, cable TV, n/s rms. $28-35/S; $31-38/D; $3/ex prsn. Discs.

Collinsville
HoJo Inn/ I-59 & Hwy 68, Collinsville AL 35961. 205-524-2114. V,M,DC, AE, D,CB. I-59 (Exit 205) at SR 68. N/s rms, pool, t/b pkng, cable TV, fax, nrby rstrnt. Gold Medal Winner. $33-46/S; $35-50/D. Discs.

Cullman
Comfort Inn/ 5917 SR 157 NW, Cullman AL 35057. 205-734-1240. V,M,AE,D,DC. On SR 157, 1 blk E of I-65. Nrby rstrnt, pool, mtg rm, cable TV, t pkng, n/s rms. Free cont brfst. No pets. $44-49/S; $40-60/D; $5/ex prsn. Discs.

Howard Johnson Lodge/ Box 267, Cullman AL 35056. 205-737-7275/ Fax: 734-8336. V,M,DC,AE,CB,D. At jct I-65 (Exit 308) & US 278 W. N/s rms, mtg rm, rstrnt, pool, t pkng, cable TV, fax, copier. $36-50/S; $42-58/D. Discs.

Super 8 Motel/ Hwy 157 & I-65, Cullman AL 35055. 205-734-8854/ Fax: 739-9284. V,M,DC,AE,D,CB. Hwy 157 & I-65, Exit 310. B/f, n/s rms, nrby rstrnt, pool, whrlpool, t/b/rv pkng, outlets, copier, cable TV, refrig, mtg rm, cot, crib. $35-38/S; $39-43/D; $5/ex prsn. Discs.

Daleville
Econo Lodge/ 241 Daleville Av, Daleville AL 36322. 334-598-6304. V, AE,M,DC. On SR 85, 1 mi from Ft Rucker. Nrby rstrnt, pool, b/f, cable TV, n/s rms, eff. Free local calls. $35-45/S; $40-55/D; $5/ex prsn. Discs.

Decatur
HoJo Inn/ 440 Johnston St SE, Decatur AL 35601. 205-355-8504. V,M,DC, AE,CB,D. I-65 (Exit 340-A) to Hwy 20 - Alt 72, W to US 31, S to mtl. On 31 S, 5 mi from I-65. N/s rms, pool, t pkng, cable TV, mtg rm, laundry. Free cont brfst, local calls. $33-39/S; $36-43/D. Discs.

Dothan
Days Inn/ 2841 Ross Clark Circ, Dothan AL 36301. 334-793-2550/ Fax: 793-7962. V,AE,M,DC,CB,D,JCB. US 231 bet Wesley Way and Fortner St. Nrby rstrnt, pool, b/f, exerc equip, t pkng, picnic area, cot. Free crib. $31-38/S; $36-45/D; $5/ex prsn. Discs.

Howard Johnson Lodge/ 2244 Ross Clark Cir, Dothan AL 36301. 205-792-3339/ Fax: 793-1254. V,M,DC, AE,D,CB. On SR 210 (Ross Clark Cir), just W of US 231. N/s rms, b/f, adj rstrnt, pool, t pkng, cable TV, fax, copier, laundry, whrlpool. Free cont brfst. No pets. Gold Medal Winner. $33-43/S; $37-47/D. Disc.

Motel 6/ 2907 Ross Clark Cir SW, Dothan AL 36301. 334-793-6013/ Fax: 793-2377. V,M,DC,AE,D. Hwy 231: Sbnd, take Ross Clark Cir S 2 mi to mtl; Nbnd, take Ross Clark Cir NW 2 mi. Nrby rstrnt, cable TV, pool, n/s rms. Free local calls. $27/S; $33/D; $6/ex prsn. Disc.

Enterprise
Ramada Inn/ 630 Glover Av, Enterprise AL 36330. 334-347-6262/ Fax: 347-8378. V,AE,M. On SR 134, W of Hwy 167. Pool, b/f, n/s rms, rstrnt/ lounge, cable TV, mtg rm, cot. Gold Key Award. $40-45/S; $45-50/D; $5/ex prsn. Discs.

Evergreen
Days Inn/ 901 Liberty Hill Dr, Evergreen AL 36404. 205-578-2100. V,AE,M, DC,CB,D,JCB. I-65 (Exit 96) at SR 83, turn W to mtl. Nrby rstrnt, b/f, t pkng, cable TV, micro/fridge, cot. $35-48/S; $38-60/D; $5/ex prsn. Discs.

Econo Lodge/ Bates Rd, Box 564, Evergreen AL 36401. 334-578-4701. AE,V,M,DC. I-65 (Exit 96) & Hwy 83. Nearby rstrnt/ lounge, pool, fax, b/f, cable TV, t pkng, n/s rms. Free local calls. $30-45/S; $36-52/D; $4/ex prsn. Disc.

Florence
HoJo Inn/ 1241 Florence Blvd, Florence AL 35630. 205-764-5421/ Fax: Ext 192. V,M,DC,AE,D,CB. Hwy 72, 1.9 mi E of dntn and 1.9 mi W of Hwy 133 (Cox Creek Pkwy). N/s rms,

b/f, rstrnt, pool, t pkng, rm serv, valet,fax. Free cont brfst, nwspr. $32-39/S; $35-45/D. Discs.

Super 8 Motel/ Box 1457, Florence AL 35631. 205-757-2167/ Fax: 757-1282. M,V,D,CB,AE,DC. Hwy 72 & 43 E. N/s rms, pool, outlets, b/t pkng, copier, cable TV. Free local calls. $35/S; $39-41/D; $2/ex prsn. Discs.

Fort Payne
Quality Inn/ Box 655, Ft Payne AL 35967. 205-845-4013. AE,V,M,DC. I-59 (Exit 218) to SR 35, W. Rstrnt, pool, mtg rm, fax, b/f, cable TV, t/b pkng, laundry, n/s rms. Free local calls, coffee. No pets. AAA. $38-43/S; $43-48/D; $5/ex prsn. Discs.

Gadsden
Friendship Inn/ 2110 Rainbow Dr, Gadsden AL 35901. 205-547-9033. M,V,D,AE. I-59, exit 182 to I-759, exit 4A, US 411 S, 1 1/2 mi on lt. Nrby rstrnt, cable TV, n/s rms. Free cont brfst. $35-85/S; $45-85/D; $5/ex prsn. Discs.

Greenville
Econo Lodge/ 946 Ft Dale Rd, Greenville AL 36037. 334-382-3118. V,AE,M,DC. I-65 (Exit 130) & SR 185. Nrby rstrnt, b/f, cable TV, t pkng. $35-38/S; $41-45/D; $4/ex prsn. Disc.

Heflin
HoJo Inn/ Rte 2, Box 44T, Heflin AL 36264. 205-463-2900. M,V,D,CB, AE, DC. I-20 (Exit 199) rt at Shell station. N/s rms, b/f, t pkng, cable TV. Free cont brfst. $32-45/S; $35-50/D. Discs.

Homewood (Birmingham area)
Super 8 Motel/ 140 Vulcan Rd, Homewood AL 35209. 205-945-9888/ Fax: 945-9928. D,AE,DC,CB,M,V. I-65 (Exit 256) at Oxmoor Rd. B/f, n/s rms, b pkng, cable TV, mtg rm, cot. Free local calls, crib. No pets. $37/S; $42-45/D; $4/ex prsn. Discs.

Huntsville
Comfort Inn/ 3788 University Dr, Huntsville AL 35805. 205-533-3291. V,M,DC,AE. I-65 to US 72, E to mtl. Nrby rstrnt, pool, mtg rm, fax, b/f, cable TV, t pkng, exerc equip, n/s rms. Free cont brfst, local calls. No pets. $44-50/S; $48-54/D; $4/ex prsn. Discs.

Econo Lodge/ 3772 University Dr, Huntsville AL 35816. 205-534-7061. V,AE,M,DC. I-65, exit US 72 E (University). Nrby rstrnt/ lounge, pool, fax, b/f, cable TV. Free cont brfst, local calls. $32-36/S or D. Discs.

Executive Lodge Suite Hotel/ 1535 Sparkman Dr, Huntsville AL 35816. 205-830-8600/ Fax: 830-8899/ 800-248-4722. V,M,AE,D,DC,CB. I-565 (Exit 15) to Sparkman Dr, go underneath overpass, through traffic light. Nrby rstrnt, pool, n/s rms, exerc equip, satellite TV, VCR/ movies, playgrnd, arpt trans, tt/dd phones, mtg rm, fax, copier, laundry, refrig, microwave, cot, crib, t/b/rv pkng, eff, b/f. Free cont brfst, local calls. AAA. $40-53/S or D. *Guaranteed rates.*

HoJo Inn/ 4404 University Dr, Huntsville AL 35816. 205-837-3250/ Fax: Ext 7160. M,V,D,CB,AE,DC. Hwy 72 W. N/s rms, pool, t pkng, cable TV, fax. Free cont brfst. $30-37/S; $40-46/D. Discs.

Motel 6/ 3200 W University Dr, Huntsville AL 35816. 205-539-8448/ Fax: 539-6015. M,V,AE,DC,D. On US 72 (University Dr) E of Jordan Ln. Nrby rstrnt, cable TV, pool, n/s rms. t pkng, elevator. Free local calls. $23-24/S; $27-28/D; $4/ex prsn. Disc.

Super 8 Motel/ 3803 University Dr, Huntsville AL 35805. 205-539-8881/ Fax: 533-5322. D,AE,DC,CB,M,V. Hwy 565 E to Jordan Ln, turn lt to University, rt to mtl. B/f, n/s rms, pool, t/b/rv pkng, cable TV, cot. Free local calls, crib. No pets. $32/S; $38/D; $3/ex prsn. Discs.

Villager Lodge/ 3100 University Dr, Huntsville AL 35816. 205-533-0610/ Fax: 533-9849. V,M,AE,D,DC. 1 blk E of jct Hwy 72 & Hwy 53. Nrby rstrnt/ lounge, pool, n/s rms, satellite TV, TDD, tt/dd phone, mtg rm, fax, copier, laundry, refrig, microwave, cot, crib, eff, conn rms, b/f. $26/S; $31/D; $3/ex prsn. Disc: Senior, bsns, govt, milt, l/s, family.

Also see Madison.

ALABAMA

Jasper

Days Inn/ 101 Sixth Av N, Jasper AL 35501. 205-221-7800/ Fax: 221-4941. V,AE,M,DC,CB,D,JCB. On US 78 bet Hwys 195 & 69. Nrby rstrnt, pool, b/f, t pkng, refrig, microwave, cable TV, boat pkng, outlets, t/b pkng. $38-60/S; $43-65/D; $5/ex prsn. Discs.

Lanette

Econo Lodge/ 12 E 22nd St, Lanette AL 36863. 334-768-3500. V,AE,M,DC. I-85 (Exit 79) to US 29, S to mtl. Nrby rstrnt, fax, b/f, cable TV, dd phone. Free local calls, coffee. No pets. $36-43/S; $43-47/D; $4/ex prsn. 1/1-4/30: $43-59/S; $59-69/D. Discs.

Madison (Huntsville area)

Howard Johnson Park Square Inn/ 8721 Hwy 20 W, Madison AL 35758. 205-772-8855/ Fax: 464-0783. AE,V,M,D. I-565 (Exit 8) to Hwy 20 (follow signs), turn rt for 1/2 mi to mtl. N/s rms, b/f, rstrnt/ lounge, pool, exerc equip, mtg rm. Free arpt trans. Gold Medal Winner. $45-125/S; $45-130/D. Discs.

Motel 6/ 8995 Hwy 20, Madison AL 35758. 205-772-7479/ Fax: 772-9771. V,M,DC,AE,D. I-565 (Exit 8) N on Wall-Triana Hwy, lt on Hwy 20 to mtl. Nrby rstrnt, cable TV, pool, n/s rms, t pkng. Free local calls. Premier Award. $26/S; $30/D; $4/ex prsn. Disc.

Mobile

Best Inns/ 156 Beltline Hwy S, Mobile AL 36608. 334-343-4911. AE,D,CB,M,V,DC. I-65 (Exit 3) at Arpt Blvd/Frontage Rd. Nrby rstrnt, indr pool, mtg rm, n/s rms, dd/tt phone, fax, b/f. Free Special K brfst, coffee, crib, local calls. AAA. $40-46/S; $47-53/D; $6/ex prsn. Higher spec event rates. Discs.

Comfort Inn/ 5650 Tillman's Corner Pkwy, Mobile AL 36619. 205-666-6604. V,M,AE,D,DC. I-10 (Exit 15B) at US 90. 3 mi W of I-65 & I-10. Nrby rstrnt, pool, mtg rm, fax, b/f, cable TV, n/s rms, microwave, refrig. Free cont brfst. No pets. $45-80/S or D; $5/ex prsn. Discs.

Econo Lodge/ 1 S Beltline Hwy, Mobile AL 36606. 334-479-5333. M,V,D, CB, AE. I-65 & Dauphin St, Exit 4. Located in Spring Hill Medical & bsns district. Nrby rstrnt, fax, b/f, cable TV. Free coffee, nwspr, local calls. AAA. $39-49/S; $40-51/D; $4/ex prsn. Discs.

Motel 6/ 400 S Beltline Hwy, Mobile AL 36608. 334-343-8448/ Fax: 343-7502. M,V,AE,DC,D. I-65, take W Exit 3B, at Airport Blvd, N on W frontage rd. Nrby rstrnt, cable TV, pool, n/s rms, elevator. Free local calls. $28-30/S; $32-34/D. $4 ex/prsn. Disc.

Motel 6/ 5488 Inn Rd/ I-10 Service Rd, Mobile AL 36619. 334-660-1483/ Fax: 660-7832. V,M,DC,D,AE. I-10 to US 90/ Tillman's Corner Pkwy (Exit 15B), rt to traffic signal, lt then immed lt on Service Rd for 1/2 mi. Nrby rstrnt, cable TV, laundry, pool, n/s rms, t pkng. Free local calls. $29-32/S; $33-36/D; $4/ex prsn. Disc.

Motel 6/ 1520 Matzenger Dr, Mobile AL 36605. 334-473-1603/ Fax: 473-4682. V,M,DC,D,AE. I-10: Ebnd, to Exit 22; Wbnd, Exit 22A. N on Dauphin Island Pkwy, lt on McVay Dr, lt on Matzenger Dr. Cable TV, laundry, pool, n/s rms, t pkng. Free local calls. $26-27/S; $30-31/D; $4/ex prsn. Disc.

Monroeville

Days Inn/ Rte 1, Box 195, Monroeville AL 36460. 334-743-3297/ Fax: 743-2920. V,AE,M,DC,CB,D,JCB. Hwy 84 & SR 21. Nrby rstrnt, pool, whrlpool, mtg rm, b/f, cable TV, refrig, microwave, cot. Free crib. Chairman's Award. $40-44/S; $44-48/D; $4/ex prsn. Discs.

Econo Lodge/ 1750 S Alabama Av, Monroeville AL 36460. 334-575-3312. V,AE,M,DC. On US 84. Nrby rstrnt, pool, fax, b/f, cable TV, t pkng, outlets, n/s rms. Free local calls, cont brfst. No pets. $35-48/S; $39-50/D; $5/ex prsn. Discs.

Montgomery

Econo Lodge/ 4135 Troy Hwy, Montgomery AL 36116. 334-284-3400. V,M,DC,AE. I-85, exit Eastern bypass to US 231 S. Nrby rstrnt/ lounge, fax, whrlpool, cable TV, t pkng. Free cont brfst. AAA. $37-43/S; $38-47/D; $2-4/ex prsn. 4/1-4/30: $39-44/S; $40-48/D. Discs.

ALABAMA

Motel 6/ 1051 Eastern Bypass, Montgomery AL 36117. 334-277-6748/ Fax: 277-9195. V,M,DC,D,AE. From I-85 (Exit 6) to E Blvd (US 80-231 Bypass) N. On Access Rd N of Exit 6. Nrby rstrnt, cable TV, pool, n/s rms. Free local calls. $30-32/S; $34-36/D; $4/ex prsn. Higher spec event rates. Disc.

Super 8 Motel/ 1288 W South Blvd, Montgomery AL 36108. 205-284-1900. V,M,DC,AE,D,CB. I-65 to S Blvd (US 80), W 1 blk at jct I-80, 82, & 231. N/s rms, pool, t/b/rv pkng, copier, cable TV, in-rm coffee, cot, crib. Free local calls. No pets. $33/S; $37-40/D; $3/ex prsn. Discs.

Rodeway Inn/ 7725 Mobile Hwy, Box 231351, Montgomery/ Hope Hull AL 36123. 334-281-7151. AE,V,M,D. I-65 (Exit 164) to US 31 S. Rstrnt, pool, fax, b/f, cable TV, t pkng, n/s rms. Free full brfst. No pets. $24-40/S; $29-47/D; $4/ex prsn. Discs.

Moody
Super 8 Motel/ 2451 Moody Pkwy, Moody AL 35004. 205-640-7091. D, AE,DC,CB,M,V. 1/2 mi N of I-20 on US 411. B/f, n/s rms, cont brfst, copier, cable TV, cot, crib. Free local calls. No pets. $35/S; $38-40/D; $4/ex prsn. Discs.

Moulton
Days Inn/ 12701 Hwy 157, Moulton AL 35650. 205-974-1214/ Fax: 974-1582. V,AE,M,DC,CB,D,JCB. Hwy 157 & Hwy 24. Nrby rstrnt, pool, whrlpool, mtg rm, b/f, t pkng, cable TV. Free local calls, crib. AAA. $36-42/S; $42-47/D; $5/ex prsn. 3/1-12/31: $35-49/S; $45-58/D. Discs.

Muscle Shoals
Econo Lodge/ 2807 Woodward Av, Muscle Shoals, AL 35661. 205-381-0236. V,AE,M,DC. On US 72 & US 43. Rstrnt, pool, fax, b/f, whrlpool, cable TV, t pkng, outlets. Free cont brfst. No pets. $40-60/S; $43-64/D; $3/ex prsn. Discs.

Opelika
Motel 6/ 1015 Columbus Pkwy, Opelika AL 36801. 334-745-0988/ Fax: 745-2589. V,M,AE,D,DC. I-85 (Exit 62) at US 280. Nrby rstrnt, cable TV, laundry, pool, n/s rms, t pkng. Free local calls. $25-26/S; $29-30/D; $4/ex prsn. Football wknds: $40/S; $44/D. Higher spec event rates. Disc.

Orange Beach
Sleep Inn/ 25400 Perdido Beach Blvd, Orange Beach AL 36561. 334-981-6722. M,V,D,AE. I-10 (Exit 44) to SR 59, S to SR 182, W 6 mi to mtl. Nrby rstrnt, pool, mtg rm, fax, b/f, cable TV, t pkng, n/s rms. Free cont brfst. No pets. $45-109/S or D; $5-10/ex prsn. 5/1-5/31, 9/4-10/31: $79-109/S or D. 6/1-9/3: $89-119/S or D. Higher spec event rates. Discs.

Oxford (Anniston area)
Econo Lodge/ 25 Elm St, Oxford AL 36203. 205-831-9480. M,V,D,CB,AE. I-20, exit 185. Nrby rstrnt, pool, mtg rm, fax, b/f, cable TV, t pkng, food crt. Free cont brfst. $42/S; $47/D; $5/ex prsn. 7/18-7/21: $80/S; $85/D. Discs.

Howard Johnson Lodge/ Box 3308, Oxford AL 36203. 205-835-3988/ Fax: 835-1056. M,V,D,CB,AE,DC. I-20 (Exit 185) N 2 blks, turn rt at intersection. N/s rms, b/f, pool, rm serv, whrlpool, playgrnd, game rm, laundry, valet, cable TV, in-rm coffee, refrig. Free cont brfst, local calls. Gold Medal Winner. $32-42/S or D.

Motel 6/ 202 Grace St, Oxford AL 36203. 205-831-5463/ Fax: 831-5628. V,M,DC,D,AE. I-20 (Exit 185) at SR 21, S to mtl. Nrby rstrnt, cable TV, pool, n/s rms,. t pkng. Free local calls. $23-24/S; $27-28/D; $4/ex prsn. 4/29-5/5: $50/S or D. Higher spec event rates. Disc.

Prattville
Econo Lodge/ 2605 Cobbs Ford Rd, Prattville AL 36067. 334-285-5022. V,M,D,AE,DC. I-65, Exit 179, turn W to mtl. Nrby rstrnt, t pkng. Free cont brfst. $37/S; $43/D; $5/ex prsn. Discs.

Scottsboro
Comfort Inn/ 23518 John T Reid Pkwy, Scottsboro AL 35768. 800-221-2222 — opening soon. V,M,AE,D,DC. At US 72. Nrby rstrnt, pool, mtg rm, cable TV, t pkng, n/s rms. Free cont brfst. No pets.

ALABAMA / ARIZONA

$39-50/S; $42-60/D; $5/ex prsn.

Sylacauga
Super 8 Motel/ 40770 Hwy 280, Box 46, Sylacauga AL 35150. 205-249-4321/ Fax: 245-7473. V,M,AE, D, DC, AE. 2 mi W of Sylacauga dntn cntr. B/f, n/s rms, pool, t/b/rv pkng, copier, cable TV, mtg rm, cot, crib. Free local calls. AAA. $34/S; $38/D; $4/ex prsn. Discs.

Thomasville
Best Western Inn/ 1200 Mosley Dr, Thomasville AL 36784. 334-636-0614. V,M,AE,D,DC,CB. I-65, Exit 43N. I-20, exit E onto 43S. Nrby rstrnt, pool, n/s rms, cable TV, tt/dd phone, mtg rm, fax, copier, laundry, refrig, microwave, cot, crib, outlets, t/b pkng, eff, b/f. Free local calls, cont brfst, coffee, tea. AAA. $37/S; $41-45/D; $4/ex prsn. 6/1-8/31: $39/S; $41-48/S. Disc: Senior, bsns, TA, l/s, family, trkr, milt. *Guaranteed rates.*

Troy
Comfort Inn/ 811 US 231, Box 486, Troy AL 360081. 334-566-7799. M,V,D,AE. On US 231. Nrby rstrnt, pool, fax, b/f, cable TV, t pkng. Free cont brfst. AAA. $43-64/S; $48-69/D; $5/ex prsn. Discs.

Econo Lodge/ 1013 US Hwy 231, Box 1086, Troy AL 36081. 334-566-4960. AE,M,V,DC. On US 231. Nrby rstrnt, pool, fax, b/f, cable TV, t pkng, n/s rms. Free local calls. $36-46/S; $41-51/D; $5/ex prsn. Discs.

Tuscaloosa
Motel 6/ 4700 McFarland Blvd E, Tuscaloosa AL 35405. 205-759-4942/ Fax: 759-1093. V,M,DC,D,AE. I-20/I-59, Exit 73, S on McFarland Blvd (US 82) 1 blk. Nrby rstrnt, cable TV, laundry, n/s rms, pool, t pkng. Free local calls. $28-29/S; $34-35/D; $6/ex prsn. Higher spec event rates. Disc.

Super 8 Motel/ 4125 McFarland Blvd E, Tuscaloosa AL 35405. 205-758-8878/ Fax: 758-2602. V,M,DC,AE,D,CB. Jct Hwys 59 & 82. From I-20/59, exit at McFarland Blvd. From Hwy 82, Exit 73. B/f, n/s rms, cable TV, cot, crib. Free local calls. No pets. $35/S; $39/D; $5/ex prsn. Discs.

Arizona

Bullhead City (Laughlin area)
Econo Lodge/ 1717 SR 95, Bullhead City AZ 86442. 520-758-8080. V, M, DC,AE. S of Las Vegas, across river from Laughlin, NV on SR 95. Nrby rstrnt, pool, fax, b/f, cable TV, n/s rms. Free cont brfst, local calls. No pets. $22-95/S; $28-95/D; $6/ex prsn. 5/1-5/31: $32-95/S; $38-95/D. Discs.

Motel 6/ 1616 Hwy 95, Bullhead City AZ 86442. 520-763-1002/ Fax: 763-3868. V,M,DC,D,AE. SR 95 at Karlis Dr to mtl. Cable TV, pool, n/s rms, nrby rstrnt. Free local calls. Premier Award. Sun-Thurs: $22-24/S or D. Fri-Sat, holiday, spec events: $30-32/S or D. Disc.

Camp Verde
Comfort Inn/ Box 3430, Camp Verde AZ 86322. 800-221-2222 - opening soon. M,V,D,AE. I-17 (Exit 287), E 100 yds, turn S on Industrial Dr. Nrby rstrnt, pool, mtg rm, fax, b/f, whrlpool, cable TV, n/s rms. Free cont brfst. $40-56/S; $46-62/D; $6/ex prsn. 2/1-3/31, 5/1-10/31: $42-58/S; $48-64/D. 4/1-4/30: $52-68/S; $58-74/D. Discs.

Casa Grande
Motel 6/ 4965 N Sunland Gin Rd, Casa Grande AZ 85222. 520-836-3323/ Fax: 421-3094. V,M,AE,D,DC. I-10 (Exit 200) at I-8. Cable TV, laundry, pool, n/s rms, t pkng. Free local calls. Premier

ARIZONA

Award. $33-35/S; $39-41/D; $6/ex prsn. Higher spec event rates. Disc.

Douglas
Motel 6/ 111 16th St, Douglas AZ 85607. 520-364-2457/ Fax: 364-9332. V,M,AE,D,DC. US 80/16th St at N "J" Av. Cable TV, laundry, pool, n/s rms, t pkng. Free local calls. $26-28/S; $32-34/D; $6/ex prsn. Disc.

Flagstaff
Budget Host Saga Motel/ 820 W Hwy 66, Flagstaff AZ 86001. 520-779-3631. AE,DC,D,M,V. I-40 Bsns Loop at Rioroan Rd. Cable TV, dd phones, in-rm coffee, n/s rms, rstrnt/ lounge, pool, playgrnd, picnic area, t pkng across st, cot, crib. AAA. $30/S; $34-46/D; $4/ex prsn. 5/8-9/10: $46/S; $46-57/D. Higher spec event rates. Discs.

Comfort Inn/ 914 S Milton Rd, Flagstaff AZ 86001. 602-774-7326. V,M,AE, D,DC. On US 89 Alt, 1 mi N of I-40 & I-17 (Exit 195B). Nrby rstrnt, pool, fax, b/f, cable TV, n/s rms. Free cont brfst. Hospitality Award. $38-57/S; $41-57/D; $5/ex prsn. 5/1-6/8: $54-77/S; $56-77/D. 6/9-9/3: $63-88/S; $65-88/D. 9/4-10/28: $53-74/S or D. Discs.

Econo Lodge/ 1601 E. Lockett Rd, Flagstaff AZ 86011. 520-527-1477. V,M,DC,AE. I-40 (Exit 201) to Bsns 40/ SR180/ SR 66, rt on Lockett Rd to mtl. Nrby rstrnt, fax, b/f, whrlpool, cable TV, laundry, family rms, n/s rms. Free coffee. No pets. AAA. $30-45/S or D; $5/ex prsn. 3/11-4/30, 8/27-10/31: $39-65/S or D. 5/1-8/26: $55-99/S or D. Higher spec event, holiday, wknd rates.

Econo Lodge/ 2355 S Beulah Blvd, Flagstaff AZ 86001. 520-774-2225. M,V,D,CB,AE. I-40 & I-17, Exit 195B. Nrby rstrnt, pool, fax, b/f, whrlpool, cable TV. Free coffee. No pets. AAA. $37-56/S; $40-58/D; $5/ex prsn. 3/1-4/30, 5/1-6/8: $45-65/S; $48-68/D. 6/9-9/30: $45-89/S; $48-92/D. Discs.

Econo Lodge/ 2480 E Lucky Lane, Flagstaff AZ 86001. 520-774-7701. M,V,D,CB,AE. I-40 E or W, Exit 198 at Butler, rt on Lucky Lane. Nrby rstrnt, indr pool, fax, b/f, outlets, laundry. Free cont brfst. No pets. AAA. $32-42/S; $44-64/D; $5/ex prsn. 5/1-8/26: $54-98/S or D. 8/27-10/31: $49-89/S or D. 11/1-12/31: 39-49/S; $44-64/D. Discs.

HoJo Inn/ 3300 E Hwy 66, Flagstaff AZ 86004. 520-526-1826/ Fax: 527-1872. V,M,DC,AE,CB,D. I-40, Exit 201. I-17 to I-40 E, Exit 201. N/s rms, b/f, rstrnt, t/b/rv pkng, dd phone. Free local calls. No pets. $35-50/S; $40-60/D. Discs.

Motel 6/ 2500 E Lucky Ln, Flagstaff AZ 86004. 520-779-6184/ Fax: 774-2249. V,M,DC,AE,D. I-40 (Exit 198) to Butler, N to Lucky Ln, rt. Cable TV, pool, n/s rms. Free local calls. $27-30/S; $33-36/D; $6/ex prsn. 5/25-12/21: $34/S; $40/D. Disc.

Motel 6/ 2010 E Butler Av, Flagstaff AZ 86004. 520-774-1801/ Fax: 774-1987. V,M,DC,D,AE. From I-40 (Exit 198) to Butler, W to mtl. Cable TV, laundry, pool, n/s rms. Free local calls. $28-32/S; $34-38/D; $6/ex prsn. 5/25-9/27: $37/S; $43/D. Disc.

Motel 6/ 2440 E Lucky Ln, Flagstaff AZ 86004. 520-774-8756/ Fax: 774-2067. V,M,D,AE,DC. I-40 (Exit 198) to Butler, W to Lucky Lane, turn rt. Cable TV, pool, n/s rms. Free local calls. $27-30/S; $33-36/D; $6/ex prsn. 5/25-9/27: $34/S; $40/D. Disc.

Motel 6/ 2745 S Woodlands Village, Flagstaff AZ 86001. 520-779-3757/ Fax: 774-2137. V,M,DC,D,AE. Near jct of I-17 & I-40. I-40 (Exit 195) to US 89A, N on Milton Rd 3 blks, lt at light on Forest Meadows St, 2 blks to Woodlands Village Rd, lt. Cable TV, laundry, pool, n/s rms. Free local calls. $30-32/S; $36-38/D; $6/ex prsn. 5/25-10/11: $39/S; $45/D. Di

Fort Huachuca
See Sierra Vista.

Fredonia
Shiprock Motel/ 337 S Hwy 89A, Fredonia AZ 86022. 602-643-7355. V,M,AE,DC. 89 A to N Rim of Grand Canyon. DD phones. National 9. $30/S; $32-38/D; $45/3 prsn; Family unit: $2/ex prsn.

ARIZONA

Goodyear (Phoenix area)
Super 8 Motel/ 1710 N Dysart Rd, Goodyear AZ 85338. 602-932-9622/ Fax: 932-4685. V,M,AE,DC,CB,D. Dysart Rd, immediately S of I-10, Exit 129. B/f, n/s rms, pool, nrby rstrnt/ lounge, hot tub, t pkng, cable TV. Free local calls. $43/S; $47/D; $2/ex prsn. Discs.

Holbrook
Budget Host Inn/ 235 W Hopi Dr, Holbrook AZ 86025. 602-524-3809/ Fax: 524-3072. V,AE,CB,D,DC,M. I-40 (Exit 285) to Hopi Dr, W to mtl. Nrby rstrnt, n/s rms, exerc equip, cable TV, tt/ dd phone, fax, laundry, refrig, microwave, t pkng, conn rms. Free local calls, coffee. AAA. $20-24/S; $24-30/D; $4/ex prsn. 6/1-9/15: $22-26/S; $26-34/D.c

Days Inn/ 2601 Navajo, Holbrook AZ 86025. 520-524-6949/ Fax: 524-6665. V,AE,M,DC,CB,D,JCB. I-40 (Exit 289) at SR 77, turn W to mtl. Nrby rstrnt, indr pool, whrlpool, b/f, t/b/rv pkng, refrig, microwave, cable TV, laundry, cot. Free cont brfst. Chairman's Award. $38-42/S; $42-50/D; $6/ex prsn. 4/1-5/15: $38-50/S; $46-60/D. 5/15-9/30: $42-60/S; $46-68/D. 10/1-10/31: $40-50/S; $50-58/D. Discs.

Econo Lodge/ 2596 Navajo Blvd, Holbrook AZ 86025. 520-524-1448. V,M,DC,AE. I-40 (Exit 289) to E Navajo Blvd, 1/2 mi to mtl. Rstrnt, pool, fax, b/f, cable TV, t pkng, n/s rms. AAA. $30-40/S; $38-48/D; $5/ex prsn. 5/1-9/30: $39-44/S; $42-50/D. Discs.

Motel 6/ 2514 Navajo Blvd, Holbrook AZ 86025. 520-524-6101/ Fax: 524-1806. V,M,DC,D,AE. I-40 (Exit 289) to Navajo Blvd/ Bsns 40, W 1/2 mi. Nrby rstrnt, cable TV, laundry, pool, n/s rms, t pkng. Free local calls. $27-30/S; $31-34/D; $4/ex prsn. Disc.

Rainbow Inn/ 2211 E Navajo Blvd, Holbrook AZ 86025. 520-524-2654/ 800-551-1923. V,M,AE,D,DC,CB. I-40 (Exit 289); W 1 1/2 mi on Navajo Blvd. Nrby rstrnt/ lounge, n/s rms, cable TV, TDD, tt/dd phone, fax, copier, laundry, refrig, microwave, cot, t/b/rv pkng. Free local calls, coffee, tea. AAA/ Mobil. $26-39/S; $28-47/D; $4/ex prsn. 6/1-10/1: $30-39/S; $32-43/D. Disc: Senior, TA, govt, family, trkr, milt. *Guaranteed rates.*

Super 8 Motel/ 1989 Navajo Blvd, Holbrook AZ 86025. 520-524-2871/ Fax: 524-3514. M,V,AE,D,DC,CB. I-40 (Exits 286 or 289) to Hwy 77. NW of frwy. B/f, n/s rms, pool, whrlpool, laundry, toast bar, t/b/rv pkng, in-rm coffee, copier, cot, crib. Free local calls. No pets. $37-41/S; $41-48/D; $3/ex prsn. Discs.

Comfort Inn/ 2602 E Navajo Blvd, Holbrook, AZ 86025. 520-524-6131/ Fax: 524-2281. AE,V,MC,DC,D. I-40 (Exit 289) to E Navajo Blvd, W 1/2 mi to mtl. Rstrnt, pool, fax, b/f, cable TV, t pkng, n/s rms. Free cont brfst. $42-50/S; $44-54/D; $5/ex prsn. 5/1-9/30: $44-60/S; $48-68/D. Discs.

Kingman
Motel 6/ 3351 E Andy Devine Av, Kingman AZ 86401. 520-757-7151/ Fax: 757-2438. V,M,DC,AE,D. I-40/US Hwy 93 (Exit 53) to Hwy 66/Andy Devine Av, NE to mtl. Nrby rstrnt, pool, n/s rms. Free local calls. $28-30/S; $32-36/D; $6/ex prsn. Disc.

Motel 6/ 424 W Beale St, Kingman AZ 86401. 520-753-9222/ Fax: 753-4791. V,M,DC,D,AE. I-40/ US 93 (Exit 48) to W Beale St, E to mtl. Nrby rstrnt, cable TV, pool, n/s rms, t pkng. Free local calls. Premier Award. $30-34/S; $34-38/D; $4/ex prsn. Disc.

Motel 6/ 3270 E Andy Devine Av, Kingman AZ 86401. 520-757-7121/ Fax: 757-0387. V,M,DC,D,AE. I-40/ US 93, Exit 53, NE on Hwy 66/ Andy Devine Av to mtl. Nrby rstrnt, cable TV, pool, n/s rms, t pkng. Free local calls. $28-30/S; $32-34/D; $4/ex prsn. Disc.

Super 8 Motel/ 3401 E Andy Devine Av, Kingman AZ 86401. 520-757-4808/ Fax: Ext 324. M,V,AE,D,DC,CB. I-40 (Exit 53) at Hwy 66, lt on Andy Devine Hwy 3 blks. B/f, n/s rms, t/b/rv pkng, elevator, cable TV, mtg rm, TDD. Free local calls, crib. Excellence Award. $33-34/S; $40-46/D; $5/ex prsn. Discs.

Lake Havasu City
Howard Johnson Lodge and Suites/

ARIZONA

335 London Bridge Rd, Lake Havasu City AZ 86403. 602-453-4656. M,V,D,CB,AE,DC. From Hwy 95 S, turn rt on S Palo Verde Blvd, turn lt on London Bridge Rd. N/s rms, b/f, pool, t/rv pkng, boat pkng, whrlpool, cable TV, dd phone. Free cont brfst. No pets. Gold Medal. $40-70/S or D. 2/1-4/30: $45-75/S; $50-79/D. Discs.

Super 8 Motel/ 305 London Bridge Rd, Lake Havasu City AZ 86403. 602-855-8844/ Fax: 855-7132. M,V,AE,D,DC,CB. SR 95W, on London Bridge Rd. B/f, n/s rms, pool, t/b/rv pkng, boat pkng, whrlpool. Free local calls. $36/S; $40-46/D; $5/ex prsn. Higher spec event, wknd rates. Dis

Laughlin

See Bullhead City.

Mesa (Phoenix area)

Motel 6/ 630 W Main St, Mesa AZ 85201. 602-969-8111/ Fax: 655-0747. V, M,DC,AE,D. I-10 to Superstition Frwy (SR 60), E to Alma School Rd (Exit 7), N 2 mi to Main St, rt 3/4 mi. Pool, n/s rms. Free local calls. $30-32/S; $36-38/D; $6/ex prsn. 1/18-4/17: $35/S; $41/D. Higher spec event rates. Disc.

Motel 6/ 336 W Hampton Av, Mesa AZ 85210. 602-844-8899/ Fax: 969-6749. V,M,DC,D,AE. I-10 to SR 60 (Superstition Frwy), E to Country Club Dr, N 1/2 blk to W Hampton Av, turn E. Nrby rstrnt, cable TV, laundry, pool, n/s rms. Free local calls. $32/S; $38/D; $6/ex prsn. 1/18-4/10: $38/S; $44/D. Higher spec event rates. Disc.

Motel 6/ 1511 S Country Club Dr, Mesa AZ 85210. 602-834-0066/ Fax: 969-6313. V,M,DC,D,AE. I-10 to SR 60 (Superstition Frwy) to Country Club Rd/Dr, N 1/2 blk, turn rt. Nrby rstrnt, cable TV, pool, n/s rms, t pkng. Free local calls. $32-34/S; $38-40/D; $6/ex prsn. 1/18-4/10: $40/S; $46/D. Disc.

Rodeway Inn/ 5700 E Main St, Mesa AZ 85205. 602-985-3600. AE,V,M,DC. I-10 S to US 60 E (Superstition Frwy) 17 mi, lt on Higley Rd, rt on Main St, 1 mi to mtl. Rstrnt/ lounge, pool, mtg rm, cable TV, t pkng, n/s rms. Free cont brfst. $36-89/S; $39-99/D; $5/ex prsn. Discs.

Nogales

Motel 6/ 141 W Mariposa Rd, Nogales AZ 85621. 520-281-2951/ Fax: 281-9592. V,M,DC,D,AE. I-19, take 1st Nogales exit (8), E on Hwy 189/W Mariposa Rd. Cable TV, pool, n/s rms, t pkng. Free local calls. $33/S; $39/D; $6/ex prsn. Disc.

Page

Econo Lodge/ 121 S Lake Powell Blvd, Box 3557, Page AZ 86040. 520-645-2488. M,V,D,CB,AE,DC. SR 98, US 89 S or US 89 N to mtl. Nrby rstrnt, pool, family rms. No pets. $40-60/S or D; $5/ex prsn. 11/1-3/31: $35-50/S or D. 5/1-9/30: $70-90/S or D. Discs.

Phoenix

Comfort Inn/ 4120 E Van Buren Pkwy, Phoenix AZ 85008. 602-275-5746. V,M,DC,AE. I-10 W to SR 143 (Exit 153A) to Washington, lt to 44th St, rt to Van Buren, lt to mtl. Nrby rstrnt, pool, mtg rm, t pkng, n/s rms. Free cont brfst. $39-48/S; $41-53/D; $5-12/ex prsn. 1/19-3/31: $43-54/S; $48-59/D. 5/1-12/28: $28-34/S; $33-38/D. Discs.

Days Inn/ 1550 52nd Dr, Phoenix AZ 85043. 602-484-9257/ Fax: 484-0513. V,AE,M,DC,CB,D,JCB. I-10 to 51st St, N to 52nd Dr, turn E & follow dr to mtl. Nrby rstrnt, pool, b/f, t pkng, cot. Free local calls, cont brfst, crib. $36-45/S; $40-55/D; $10/ex prsn. Discs.

Motel 6/ 1530 N 52nd Dr, Phoenix AZ 85043. 602-272-0220/ Fax: 278-4210. V,M,DC,D,AE. I-10 (Exit 139) at 51st Av, N 1 blk to Willeta St, lt. From I-17, take I-10 W and follow above directions. Cable TV, pool, n/s rms. Free local calls. $43/S; $49/D; $6/ex prsn. 4/11-12/20: $36-37/S; $42-43/D. Higher spec event rates. Disc.

Motel 6/ 2330 W Bell Rd, Phoenix AZ 85023. 602-993-2353/ Fax: 548-3461. V,M,DC,D,AE. I-17 (Exit 212A) to Bell Rd, E 1/2 mi to mtl. Cable TV, laundry, pool, n/s rms. Free local calls. $43/S; $49/D; $6/ex prsn. 4/11-12/20: $33/S; $39/D. Higher spec event rates. Disc.

ARIZONA

Motel 6/ 2323 E Van Buren St, Phoenix AZ 85006. 602-267-7511/ Fax: 231-8701. V,M,DC,D,AE. I-10 (Exit 148) to Jefferson St, E to 24th St, lt 1/4 mi to Van Buren St, lt 1/8 mi to mtl. Rstrnt, cable TV, pool, n/s rms. Free local calls. $32/S; $38/D; $6/ex prsn. 4/11-12/20: $27-28/S; $33-34/D. Disc.

Motel 6/ 5315 E Van Buren St, Phoenix AZ 85008. 602-267-8555/ Fax: 231-9115. V,M,DC,D,AE. I-10 to Loop 202/Red Mountain Frwy, E to 52nd St (Exit 4), rt 1/4 mi to Van Buren. Cable TV, pool, n/s rms. Free local calls. $35/S; $41/D; $6/ex prsn. 4/11-12/20: $28-30/S; $34-36/D. Higher spec event rates. Disc.

Motel 6/ 2548 W Indian School Rd, Phoenix AZ 85017. 602-248-8881/ Fax: 230-2371. V,M,D,AE,DC. I-17 (Exit 202) to Indian School Rd, W 1/8 mi to mtl. Nrby rstrnt, cable TV, pool, laundry, n/s rms, elevator. Free local calls. $33/S; $39/D; $6/ex prsn. 4/11-5/22: $38/S; $44/D. 12/21-4/10: $42/S; $48/D. Higher spec event rates. Discs.

Motel 6/ 4130 N Black Canyon Hwy, Phoenix AZ 85017. 602-277-5501/ Fax: 274-9724. V,M,DC,AE,D. I-17 (Exit 202) to Indian School Rd, W. Cable TV, pool, n/s rms, t pkng, whrlpool. Free local calls. $35/S; $41/D; $6/ex prsn. 4/11-5/22: $31-32/S; $37-38/D. Higher spec event rates. Disc.

Motel 6/ 214 S 24th St, Phoenix AZ 85034. 602-244-1155/ Fax: 231-0043. V,M,DC,AE,D. I-10 (Exit 148) at Jefferson St, E to 24th St, rt 1/4 mi. Pool, n/s rms. Free local calls. $26-$31/S; $32-37/D; $6/ex prsn. 12/21-4/10: $35/S; $41/D. Higher spec event rates. Discs.

Motel 6/ 2735 W Sweetwater Av, Phoenix AZ 85029. 602-942-5030/ Fax: 548-3483. V,M,DC,D,AE. I-17 (Sbnd, Exit 210; Nbnd, Exit 209/Cactus) to Thunderbird Rd, W to service rd, lt to Sweetwater Av, rt to mtl. Cable TV, pool, n/s rms, t pkng. Free local calls. $31-38/S; $37-44/D; $6/ex prsn. Higher spec event rates. Discs.

Motel 6/ 8152 N Black Canyon Hwy, Phoenix AZ 85051. 602-995-7592/ Fax: 995-9592. V,M,D,AE,DC. I-17 at Northern Av. Inn is just N of K-Mart. Nrby rstrnt, cable TV, pool, n/s rms, elevator, t pkng. Free local calls. $30/S; $36/D; $6/ex prsn. 12/21-4/10: $42/S; $48/D. 4/11-5/22: $38/S; $44/D. Higher spec event rates. Disc.

Quality Inn/ 3541 E Van Buren Pkwy, Phoenix AZ 85008. 602-273-7121. V,M,DC,AE. SR 143 (Exit 13A) to Washington, lt to 44th St, rt to Van Buren, lt to mtl. Rstrnt/ lounge, pool, mtg rm, fax, t pkng, n/s rms. $41-57/S; $46-61/D; $6-7/ex prsn. 1/19-3/31: $45-65/S; $50-69/D. 5/1-12/28: $29-36/S; $33-40/D. Discs.

Sleep Inn/ 2621 S 47th Pl, Phoenix AZ 95034. 800-221-2222 — opening soon. M,V,D,AE. SR 143 to University Dr, turn lt to mtl. Nrby rstrnt, pool, fax, b/r, whrlpool, cable TV. Free cont brfst. No pets. $40-50/S; $50-60/D; $5/ex prsn. 5/1-10/1: $40/S; $35-45/D. 10/2-12/30: $36-46/S; $40-50/D.

Super 8 Motel/ 4021 N 27th Av, Phoenix AZ 85017. 602-248-8880/ Fax: 241-0234. V,M,AE,DC,CB,D. I-17, Indian School exit, 1 blk W, 1/2 blk S on 27th Av. B/f, n/s rms, pool, laundry, cont brfst, t/b/rv pkng, copier, cable TV, cot, crib. Free local calls, trans. No pets. AAA. $41-45/S; $44-51/D; $4/ex prsn. Higher spec event rates. Discs.

Also see Goodyear, Mesa, Scottsdale, Tempe.

Prescott

Motel 6/ 1111 E Sheldon St, Prescott AZ 86301. 520-776-0160/ Fax: 445-4188. V,M,DC,D,AE. US 89 to Truck Rte US 89 (E Sheldon St), W to just past E Gurley St. Nrby rstrnt, cable TV, laundry, pool, n/s rms. Free local calls. $37-39/S; $43-45/D; $6/ex prsn. Disc.

Safford

Comfort Inn/ 1578 W Thatcher Blvd, Safford AZ 85546. 520-428-5851. M,V,D,AE. On US 70 W side of Safford. Nrby rstrnt, pool, fax, b/f, cable TV, t pkng. Free cont brfst. AAA. $42-56/S; $44-64/D; $5/ex prsn. Discs.

Scottsdale (Phoenix area)

Motel 6/ 6848 E Camelback Rd, Scottsdale AZ 85251. 602-946-2280/ Fax: 949-7583. V,M,DC,D,AE. On Camelback Rd 2 blks W of Scottsdale Rd. Nrby rstrnt, cable TV, pool, laundry, n/s rms. Free local calls. $34-38/S; $40-44/D; $6/ex prsn. 12/21-4/10: $47/S; $53/D. Higher spec event rates. Disc.

Show Low

Super 8 Motel/ 1941 E Deuce of Clubs, Show Low AZ 85901. 602-537-7694/ Fax: 537-1373. M,V,D,CB,AE,DC. E side of tn on Hwy 60. B/f, n/s rms, cable TV, cot, crib. Free local calls. AAA. $36/S; $40-42/D; $2/ex prsn. Discs.

Sierra Vista (Ft Huachuca area)

Motel 6/ 1551 E Fry Blvd, Sierra Vista AZ 85635. 520-459-5035/ Fax: 458-4046. V,M,AE,D,DC. Hwy 92 to Fry Blvd, W to mtl. Cable TV, laundry, pool, n/s rms. Free local calls. $28-30/S; $34-36/D; $6/ex prsn. Disc.

Super 8 Motel/ 100 Fab Av, Sierra Vista AZ 85635. 602-459-5380/ Fax: 459-6052. V,M,DC,AE,D,CB. Hwy 90 to Fry Blvd, E 1 blk. B/f, n/s rms, pool, nrby rstrnt, cont brfst, cable TV, refrig, cot, crib. Free local calls. $41/S; $46-51/D; $5/ex prsn. Higher spec event, wknd rates. Discs.

Springerville

Super 8 Motel/ W US 60, Springerville AZ 85938. 602-333-2655/ Fax: 333-5149. V,M,AE,D,DC,AE. Western edge of Springerville on Hwy 60. B/f, n/s rms, cable TV, cot, crib. Free local calls. AAA. $36/S; $39-41/D; $2/ex prsn. Di

Sun City

See Youngtown.

Tempe (Phoenix area)

Comfort Inn/ 5300 S Priest St, Tempe AZ 85283. 602-820-7500. M,V,D,AE. I-10 to Baseline Rd., E 1 blk to Priest St. Nrby rstrnt, pool, mtg rm, fax, whrlpool, t pkng, n/s rms. Free cont brfst. AAA. $45-65/S; $55-75/D; $5/ex prsn. 1/16-4/30: $55-80/S; $65-90/D. 5/1-9/30: $35-60/S; $40-70/D. 10/1-12/27: $40-60/S; $45-70/D. Discs.

Econo Lodge/ 2101 E Apache Blvd, Tempe AZ 85281. 602-966-5832/ Fax: 921-2648. V,AE,M,DC. I-10, to Superstition Frwy (SR 60), E to Price Rd exit, N to Apache Blvd, W 1 blk. Pool, fax, b/f, cable TV, laundry, copier, n/s rms. Free cont brfst. No pets. AAA. $45-75/S; $55-90/D, $5/ex prsn. 5/1-8/31, 11/1-12/15: $33-45/S; $40-50/D; 9/1-10/31: $46-56/S; $50-65/D. 12/16-4/30: Discs.

Motel 6/ 513 W Broadway Rd, Tempe AZ 85282. 602-967-8696/ Fax: 929-0814. V,M,DC,AE,D. I-10 (Exit 153) to Broadway Rd, E 1 mi. Pool, n/s rms. Free local calls. $31-32/S; $37-38/D; $6/ex prsn. 1/18-4/10: $37/S; $43/D. Higher spec event rates. Disc.

Motel 6/ 1720 S Priest Dr, Tempe AZ 85281. 602-968-4401/ Fax: 929-0810. V,M,D,AE,DC. I-10 (Exit 153) to Broadway, E to Priest, lt 1 blk. Cable TV, pool, n/s rms, t pkng, elevator. Free local calls. $33-34/S; $39-40/D; $6/ex prsn. 1/18-4/10: $39/S; $45/D. Higher spec event rates. Disc.

Motel 6/ 1612 N Scottsdale Rd/ Rural Rd, Tempe AZ 85281. 602-945-9506/ Fax: 970-4763. V,M,DC,AE,D. I-10 (Exit 153) to Broadway Rd, E 2 1/2 mi to Rural Rd, N (lt) 2 1/2 mi to mtl. Pool, n/s rms. Free local calls. $30-32/S; $36-38/D; $6/ex prsn. 1/18-4/10: $37/S; $43/D. Higher spec event rates. Disc.

Tucson

Comfort Inn/ 715 W 22nd St, Tucson AZ 85713. 520-791-9282. V,M,DC,AE. I-10 to 22nd St, W 1 blk. Pool, whrlpool, cable TV, n/s rms. Free cont brfst. No pets. $35-80/S; $40-100/D; $5/ex prsn. Discs.

Econo Lodge/ 1165 N Stone Av, Tucson AZ 85705. 520-622-7763. AE,V,M,D,DC. I-10 (Exit 257) to Speedway Blvd, E 1/2 mi to Stone Av, lt to mtl. Nrby rstrnt, pool, fax, cable TV, n/s rms. Free cont brfst. No pets. AAA. $39-44/S; $44-49/D; $6-8/ex prsn. 2/1-2/29: $79-89/S; $89-99/D. 3/1-4/30: $44-49/S; $54-59/D. 5/1-9/30: $34-39/S; $39-44/D. Discs.

Econo Lodge/ 3020 S 6th Av, Tucson AZ 85713. 520-623-5881. V,M,AE,D,

ARIZONA

DC. I-10, exit to 6th Av. Rstrnt, pool, whrlpool, n/s rms, satellite TV, tt/ dd phone, fax, laundry, cot, crib, t/b/rv pkng, conn rms, b/f. Free local calls. No pets. $27-70/S; $37-80/D; $5/ex prsn. Discs.

Motel 6/ 4950 S Outlet Center Dr, Tucson AZ 85706. 520-746-0030/ Fax: 741-7403. V,M,DC,D,AE. I-10: (Wbnd, Exit 264 to Irvington Rd; Ebnd, Exit 264B to Palo Verde Rd, N to Irvington Rd;) From Irvington Rd lt on Outlet Center Dr to mtl. Cable TV, laundry, pool, n/s rms, t pkng. Free local calls. Premier Award. $34-36/S; $40-42/D; $6/ex prsn. 1/18-4/10: $44/S; $50/D. Disc.

Motel 6/ 1222 S Frwy, Tucson AZ 85713. 520-624-2516/ Fax: 624-1697. V,M,D,AE,DC. I-10 (Exit 259) to 22nd St, W to mtl. Cable TV, pool, laundry, n/s rms, t pkng, elevator. Free local calls. $31-32/S; $37-38/D; $6 ex/prsn. 1/18-4/10: $42/S; $48/D. Disc.

Motel 6/ 960 S Frwy, Tucson AZ 85745. 520-628-1339/ Fax: 624-1848. V,M,DC,D,AE. I-10 (Exit 258) to Congress St; Sbnd, continue across Congress on frontage rd 3/4 mi; Nbnd, turn W under frwy, then lt on frontage rd 3/4 mi. Nrby rstrnt, cable TV, pool, n/s rms, t pkng, laundry. Free local calls. $31-32/S; $37-38/D; $6/ex prsn. 1/18-4/10: $42/S; $48/D. Disc.

Motel 6/ 755 E Benson Hwy, Tucson AZ 85713. 520-622-4614/ Fax: 624-1584. V,M,DC,AE,D. I-10: Wbnd, exit Benson Hwy; Ebnd, exit Park Av, lt, then rt on Benson Hwy to mtl. Nrby rstrnt, pool, n/s rms. Free local calls. $28-30/S; $34-36/D; $6/ex prsn. 1/18-4/10: $39/S; $45/D. Disc.

Motel 6/ 1031 E Benson Hwy, Tucson AZ 85713. 520-628-1264/ Fax: 624-1731. V,M,DC,D,AE. I-10 (Exit 262): Ebnd, cross over Park Av to mtl; Wbnd, lt on Park Av, lt on Benson Hwy. Nrby rstrnt, cable TV, pool,laundry, n/s rms, t pkng. Free local calls. $29-30/S; $35-36/D; $6/ex prsn. 1/18-4/10: $39/S; $45/D. Disc.

Motel 6/ 4630 W Ina Rd, Tucson AZ 85741. 520-744-9300/ Fax: 744-2439. V,M,DC,D,AE. I-10 (Exit 248) to Ina Rd. Cable TV, laundry, pool, n/s rms, t pkng, elevator. Free local calls. Premier Award. $36-38/S; $42-44/D; $6/ex prsn. 1/18-4/10: $44/S; $50/D. Disc.

Rodeway Inn/ 810 E Benson Hwy, Tucson AZ 85713. 520-884-5800. AE, V, M, D. I-10 E at Exit 262. Nrby rstrnt, pool, fax, cable TV, t pkng, arpt trans, n/s rms. Free cont brfst. AAA. $38-42/S; $42-47/D; $5/ex prsn. 12/28-1/27, 2/16-4/30: $50-64/S; $56-68/D. 1/28-2/15: $88-99/S; $94-99/D. Discs.

Super 8 Motel/ 1248 N Stone St, Tucson AZ 85705. 602-622-6446/ Fax: Ext 224. M,V,AE,D,DC,CB. I-10 (Exit 257) to Speedway Blvd, E 1 mi to Stone, N 2 blks. B/f, n/s rms, pool, t pkng, laundry, cable TV. No pets. $35-45/S; $42-55/D; $3/ex prsn. 1/25-2/12: $85/S; $85-90/D. Discs.

Willcox

Econo Lodge/ 724 N Bisbee Av, Willcox AZ 85643. 520-384-4222. M,V,D,CB, AE,DC. I-10, Exit 340. Nrby rstrnt, pool, fax, b/f, cable TV, t pkng, VCRs. $40-68/S; $46-78/D; $5/ex prsn. Discs.

Motel 6/ 921 N Bisbee Av, Willcox AZ 85643. 520-384-2201/ Fax: 384-0192. V,M,AE,D,DC. I-10 (Exit 340) at Rex Allen Dr. E on R Allen Dr, N on Bisbee Av. Nrby rstrnt, cable TV, laundry, pool, n/s rms, t pkng. Free local calls. $28-29/S; $34-35/D; $6/ex prsn. Disc.

Williams

Budget Host Inn/ 620 W Bill Williams Av, Williams AZ 86046. 520-635-4415/ Fax: 635-4781/ 800-745-4415. V,M,D,AE,DC. I-40 (Exits 161, 163, 165) S to Bill Williams Av. Bet 6th & 7th St. Rstrnt, n/s rms, cable TV, tt phone, fax. Free local calls. AAA. $25/S; $45/D; $5/ex prsn. 5/1-10/31: $40/S; $48/D. *Guaranteed rates.c*

Days Inn/ 2488 W Bill Williams Av, Williams AZ 86046. 520-635-4051/ Fax: 635-4411. V,AE,M,DC,CB,D,JCB. SE corner of I-40 (Exit 151) & Hwy 64. Nrby rstrnt, indr pool, whrlpool, mtg rm, b/f, t pkng, laundry, cot. Free crib. $39-66/S; $46-76/D; $10/ex prsn. 4/1-9/30: $39-75/S; $50-85/D. Discs.

ARIZONA / ARKANSAS

Econo Lodge/ 302 E Bill Williams Av, Williams AZ 86046. 520-635-4085. AE,V,M,D,DC. I-40 (Exit 161 or 165) to E Bill Williams Av, lt 1/2 mi to mtl. Nrby rstrnt, cable TV, t pkng, dd phone, n/s rms. No pets. $28-69/S; $39-95/D; $10/ex prsn. Higher spec event rates. Discs.

Norris Motel/ 1001 W Bill Williams Av, Williams AZ 86046. 520-635-2202/ Fax: 635-9202. V,M,AE,D. 1/3 mi from railway depot on B Williams Av. Cable TV, dd phone, arpt/ train trans, refrig, crib. AAA/ IMA. $26-32/S; $28-38/D; $5/ex prsn. 4/1-5/14, 9/8-10/31: $48/S; $48-52/D. 5/15-9/7: $62/S; $62-66/D. Disc: TA, IMA, AAA ex holiday and wknds.

Super 8 Motel/ 2001 E Bill Williams Av, Williams AZ 86046. 602-635-4700. M,V,D,CB,AE,DC. I-40 (Exit 165) at Grand Canyon Exit. B/f, n/s rms, pool, t/b/rv pkng, cable TV, cot, crib. $35-50/S; $35-60/D; $5/ex prsn. Higher spec event rates. Discs.

Winslow

Comfort Inn/ 520 Desmond St, Winslow AZ 86047. 602-289-9581. V,M,DC,AE. I-40 (Exit 253) to N Park Dr, W to mtl. Nrby rstrnt, indr pool, fax, b/f, whrlpool, cable TV, n/s rms. Free cont brfst. AAA. $44-54/S; $48-58/D; $5/ex prsn. 6/1-9/30: $52-62/S; $58-68/D. Discs.

Econo Lodge/ 1706 N Park Dr, Winslow AZ 86047. 520-289-4687. V,M,D,AE, DC. I-40 (Exit 253) at Park Dr. Pool, fax, b/f, cable TV, n/s rms. Free coffee. $32-45/S; $36-49/D; $5/ex prsn. Discs.

Super 8 Motel/ 1916 W Third St, Winslow AZ 86047. 602-289-4606. M, V,AE,D,DC,CB. I-40 (Exit 252) to Bsns 40, E 2 blks. B/f, n/s rms, nrby rstrnt, cont brfst, outlets, b/t pkng, trans, cable TV, cot, crib. Free local calls. $35-41/S; $39-45/D; $4/ex prsn. Discs.

Youngtown (Sun City area)

Motel 6/ 11133 Grand Av, Youngtown AZ 85363. 602-977-1318/ Fax: 977-7749. V,M,DC,D,AE. US 60/89/93 (Grand Av) at AZ Loop 101. From I-10 (Exit 133) take 99th Av, go N 9 mi to Grand Av (Exit 11), lt 2 1/2 mi. Cable TV, pool, nrby rstrnt, n/s rms. Free local calls. $36-37/S; $42-43/D; $6/ex prsn. 12/21-4/10: $45/S; $51/D. Higher spec event rates. Disc.

Yuma

Motel 6/ 1445 E 16th St, Yuma AZ 85365. 520-782-9521/ Fax: 343-4941. V,M,DC,D,AE. I-8 (Exit 2) to US 95/ 16th St, E to mtl. Nrby rstrnt, cable TV, laundry, pool, n/s rms, t pkng. Free local calls. $27-28/S; $33-34/D; $6/ex prsn. 1/18-4/10: $37/S; $43/D. Disc.

Motel 6/ 1640 S Arizona Av, Yuma AZ 85364. 520-782-6561/ Fax: 343-4923. V,M,DC,D,AE. I-8 (Exit 2) to US 95/ 16th St, W to Arizona Ave. Nrby rstrnt, cable TV, laundry, pool, n/s rms, t pkng. Free local calls. $25-26/S; $31-32/D; $6/ex prsn. 1/18-4/10: $32/S; $38/D. Disc.

Arkansas

Arkadelphia

Econo Lodge/ 106 Crystal Palace Dr, Box 420, Arkadelphia AR 71923. 501-246-8026. V,AE,M,DC. I-30 (Exit 78) & SR 7. Nrby rstrnt, cable TV, t pkng, n/s rms. Free coffee, local calls. $38-41/S; $40-46/D; $2/ex prsn. Discs.

Quality Inn/ Box 420, Arkadelphia AR 71923. 501-246-5855. V,M,DC,AE. I-30 (Exit 78) to SR 7/ S Ouachita St. I-30 & SR 7. Nrby rstrnt, pool, fax, cable TV, t pkng, n/s rms. AAA. $40-60/S or D; $4/ex prsn. 3/1-4/30: $44-65/S or D. 5/1-8/19: $42-60/S; $44-60/D. Discs.

Super 8 Motel/ 118 Valley, Arkadelphia AR 71923. 501-246-8585/ Fax: Ext 224. M,V,AE,DC,CB. I-30, Exit 78, turn S. B/f, n/s rms, cont brfst, copier, cable TV, cot, crib. Free local calls. $39/S; $42-45/D; $3/ex prsn. Higher spec

ARKANSAS

event rates. Discs.

Batesville
Super 8 Motel/ 1287 N St Louis St, Batesville AR 72501. 501-793-5888. V,M,DC,AE,D,CB. Hwy 167 N. at jct SR 69/25. B/f, n/s rms, t/b/rv pkng, copier, cable TV, cot, crib. Free local calls. No pets. Pride award. $40/S; $47-49/D; $3/ex prsn. Discs.

Benton (Little Rock area)
Days Inn/ 1501 I-30, Benton AR 72087. 501-776-3200/ Fax: 776-0906. AE,M,V,DC,D. I-30, Exit 118, cross over and continue W on Service Rd. Nrby rstrnt, pool, cable TV. Free nwspr. $35-40/S; $40-48/D; $5/ex prsn. Discs.

Econo Lodge/ 1221 Hot Springs Rd, Benton AR 72015. 501-776-1515/ Fax: 776-0247. V,AE,M,DC. I-30, Exit 117, next to Waffle house. Adj rstrnt, fax, b/f, cable TV, n/s rms. AAA. $28-34/S; $35-40/D; $4/ex prsn. Discs.

Ramada Inn/ 16732 I-30, Benton AR 72015. 501-776-1900/ Fax: 776-2084. V,AE,M. I-30 (Exit 117) at SR 35. Pool, b/f, n/s rms, rstrnt, cot. Gold Key Award. $35-47/S; $40-52/D; $7/ex prsn. Discs.

Blytheville
Comfort Inn/ Box 1408, Blytheville AR 72316. 501-763-7081. V,M,DC,AE. I-55 & SR 18 E, 3 mi S of MO state line. Rstrnt/ lounge, pool, mtg rm, fax, cable TV, t pkng, n/s rms. Free cont brfst. AAA. $40-45/S; $44-50/D; $6/ex prsn. Discs.

Brinkley
Days Inn/ I-40 & US 49, Brinkley AR 72021. 501-734-1052. V,AE,M,DC,CB, D,JCB. Nrby rstrnt, pool, b/f, t pkng, cable TV, cot. Free cont brfst. $32-34/S; $38-40/D; $4/ex prsn. 4/1-9/30: $34-38/S; $42-45/D. Discs.

Econo Lodge/ Box 428, Brinkley AR 72021. 501-734-2035. V,AE,M,DC. I-40 (Exit 216) & SR 49 NE. Rstrnt, cable TV, t pkng, n/s rms. Free coffee. $32-45/S; $36-50/D; $3/ex prsn. 5/1-10/31: $36-48/S; $40-52/D. Discs.

Super 8 Motel/ I-40 & US 49, Brinkley AR 72021. 501-734-4680/ Fax: 734-3623. M,V,AE,D,DC,CB. I-40 (Exit 216) at US 49. B/f, n/s rms, cable TV, pool, laundry, copier, outlets, mtg rm, cot, crib. Free local calls, cont brfst. $36/S; $40-44/D; $4/ex prsn. Discs.

Cabot
Days Inn/ 114 W Main, Cabot AR 72023. 501-843-0145/ Fax: 843-0098. V,AE,M,DC,CB,D,JCB. Hwy 167/ 67 to Hwy 89, turn E to mtl. Nrby rstrnt, pool, whrlpool, mtg rm, b/f, t pkng, refrig, microwave, cable TV, cot. Free cont brfst. $40-55/S; $45-65/D; $5/ex prsn. Discs.

Clarksville
Days Inn/ 2600 W Main St, Clarksville AR 72830. 501-754-8555/ Fax: 754-2045. V,AE,M,DC,CB,D,JCB. I-40 (Exit 55) at US 64. Rstrnt, pool, b/f, t pkng, cable TV, refrig, cot. $32-38/S; $38-42/D; $4/ex prsn. Discs.

Super 8 Motel/ 1238 S Rogers Av, Clarksville AR 72830. 501-754-8800/ Fax: 754-2294. AE,M,V,DC,CB,D. I-40 (Exit 58) at SR 103. B/f, n/s rms, laundry, pool, outlets, cot. Free local calls, coffee. $36/S; $41-43/D; $4/ex prsn. Discs.

Comfort Inn/ 1167 S Rogers Av, Clarksville, AR 72830. 501-754-3000. AE,V,MC,DC,D. I-40 (Exit 58) at SR 103. Nrby rstrnt, pool, b/f, cable TV, t pkng, n/s rms. Free cont brfst. AAA. $38-50/S; $45-60/D; $5/ex prsn. 5/1-10/31: $42-57/S; $47-65/D. Discs.

Conway
Days Inn/ 1002 E Oak St, Conway AR 72032. 501-450-7575. V,AE,M,DC,CB, D,JCB. I-40 (Exit 127) at US 64 E. Nrby rstrnt, pool, whrlpool, mtg rm, b/f, cable TV, cot. Free local calls, cont brfst. Chairman's Award. $40-45/S; $45-55/D; $5/ex prsn. 5/1-11/30: $45-55/S; $50-65/D. Discs.

Motel 6/ 1105 Hwy 65 N, Conway AR 72032. 501-327-6623/ Fax: 327-2749. V,M,DC,D,AE. I-40 (Exit 125) SW on Hwy 65B to mtl. Cable TV, pool, n/s rms. Free local calls. $27-28/S $31-32/D; $4/ex prsn. Disc.

ARKANSAS

Dardanelle

Western Frontier Motel/ Box 490, Dardanelle AR 72834. 501-229-4118. V,M,AE,D. I-40 (Exit 81) to Hwy 7S, 6 mi to Jct 7 & 22. Rstrnt, pool, n/s rms, cable TV, tt/dd phones, mtg rm, fax, cot, crib, t/b pkng, conn rms. Free local calls. AAA. $34/S; $44/D; $5/ex prsn. Disc: Senior, bsns, govt, trkr, milt. *Guaranteed rates.*

Dumas

Days Inn/ 501 Hwy 65 S, Dumas AR 71639. 501-382-4449. V,AE,M,DC,CB, D,JCB. On US 65 at Dumas. Nrby rstrnt, pool, whrlpool, b/f, t pkng, cable TV, laundry. Free local calls, executive brfst. Chairman's Award. $40/S; $45/D; $5/ex prsn. Discs.

Eureka Springs

Country Music Inn/ Rte 6, Box 241, Eureka Springs AR 72632. 501-253-7625. M,V,D. On Hwy 23 S, 1 blk S jct Hwy 62. Nrby rstrnt, n/s rms, cable TV, tt/dd phone, crib, outlets, t/rv pkng. Free local calls, coffee. No pets. AAA. $20-36/S; $20-38/D; $5/ex prsn. 5/1-10/31: $24-75/S; $24-82/D; $6/ex prsn. Higher spec event/ holiday/ wknd rates. Disc: Senior, govt, trkr, milt, l/s, AARP, AAA. *Guaranteed rates*

Econo Lodge/ Rt 1, Box 287, Eureka Springs AR 72632. 501-253-7111. V,M,D,AE,DC. On US 62 E, 1 mi S of SR 23. Nrby rstrnt, b/f, cable TV, t pkng, n/s rms. Free cont brfst. $34-38/S; $38-42/D; $6/ex prsn. 5/1-6/15, 9/1-9/30: $44-48/S; $48-52/D. 6/16-8/31, 10/1-10/27: $56-60/S; $60-64/D. Higher spec event rates. Disc.

Fayetteville

Motel 6/ 2980 N College Av, Fayetteville AR 72703. 501-443-4351/ Fax: 444-8034. V,M,DC,D,AE. On the N side of tn on US 71B. From US 71, follow US 71B. Nrby rstrnt, cable TV, pool, n/s rms. Free local calls. $30/S; $34/D; $4/ex prsn. Disc.

Sleep Inn/ 720 Milsap Rd, Fayetteville AR 72703. 800-221-2222 — opening soon. V,M,AE,D,DC. US 71, exit at North College to Milsap Rd, to mtl. Nrby rstrnt, fax, b/f, cable TV, n/s rms. Free cont brfst. $42-60/S; $47-70/D; $5/ex prsn. Discs.

Forrest City

Comfort Inn/ 115 Barrow Hill Rd, Forrest City AR 72335. 501-633-0042. V,M,DC,AE. I-40 to Wynne exit at SR 1, N 2 blks to mtl. Nrby rstrnt, pool, fax, b/f, cable TV, t pkng, n/s rms. Free cont brfst. No pets. AAA. $37-43/S; $39-48/D; $4/ex prsn. Discs.

Fort Smith

Days Inn/ 3600 Grinnell Av, Ft Smith AR 72903. 501-646-5100/ Fax: 646-4598/ 800-613-1114. V,M,AE,D,DC,CB. I-540 (Exit 12) to Hwy 71, S 1/2 mi. Nrby rstrnt/ lounge, pool, n/s rms, cable TV, arpt trans, tt phone, mtg rm, fax, copier, nwspr, cot, crib, t/b pkng, b/f. Free cont brfst, local calls, coffee, tea, cocoa. No pets. AAA. $48/S; $48-49/D; $5/ex prsn. Disc: Senior, bsns, govt, milt, family. *Guaranteed rates.*

Motel 6/ 6001 Rogers Av, Ft Smith AR 72903. 501-484-0576/ Fax: 484-9054. V,M,DC,D,AE. From I-540 take Rogers Av exit. Located at the NW corner of I-540 and Hwy 22. Cable TV, laundry, pool, n/s rms. Free local calls. $30-32/S; $36-38/D; $6/ex prsn. Disc.

Budgetel Inn/ 2123 Burnham Rd, Ft Smith AR 72903. 501-484-5770/ Fax: 484-0579/ 800-428-3438. V,M,AE,D, DC,CB. I-540 (Exit 8A) to Rogers Av, W to Burnham Rd, N to mtl. Nrby rstrnt/ lounge, pool, n/s rms, satellite TV, TDD, tt/dd phone, mtg rm, fax, copier, elevator, crib, conn rms, b/f. Free local calls, cont brfst, coffee. $38-40/S; $43-45/D. Disc: Senior, govt, family. *Guaranteed rates.*

Glenwood

Quachita Mountain Inn/ Box 32, Glenwood AR 71943. 501-356-3737/ Fax: 356-4804. V,M,AE,D. I-30 to Hwy 8, N to Hwy 70, rt, 1/2 mi. Nrby rstrnt, pool, n/s rms, cable TV, VCR/ movies, tt phone, fax, copier, cot, t/b/rv pkng, conn rms, b/f. Free cont brfst, local calls, coffee. No alcohol. AAA. $33/S; $38/D; $5/ex prsn. 3/1-10/1: $34/S; $39/D. Disc: Senior, bsns, family. *Guaranteed rates.*

ARKANSAS

Harrison

Comfort Inn/ 1210 US 62/65 N, Box 1158, Harrison AR 72601. 501-741-7676. M,V,D,AE. At jct of US 62 & 65. Nrby rstrnt, pool, mtg rm, fax, b/f, cable TV, t pkng, n/s rms. Free cont brfst. No pets. AAA. $43-48/S; $48-65/D; $7/ex prsn. 5/1-11/4: $49-54/S; $54-80/D. Discs.

Super 8 Motel/ 1330 Hwy 62/65 N, Harrison AR 72601. 501-741-1741/ Fax: 741-8858. AE,M,V,DC,CB,D. Hwy 62/65 N at Hester Dr. B/f, n/s rms, pool, game rm, outlets, cont brfst, t/b/rv pkng, copier, cable TV, cot. Free popcorn, local calls, crib. $44-50/S; $44-55/D. Discs.

Top Of The Hill Resort Motel/ 401 S Main, Harrison AR 72601. 501-743-1000/ Fax: 743-1100. V,M,AE,D. Hwys 62/65 Bypass to 65B (Main St). Nrby rstrnt, pool, n/s rms, cable TV, playgrnd, fax, refrig, micro-wave, cot, t/b/rv pkng, conn rms. Free cont brfst, local calls. AAA. $30/S; $34-37/D; $1/ex prsn. Disc: Senior, bsns, TA, govt, l/s, trkr, milt. *Guaranteed rates.*

Hazen

Super 8 Motel/ I-40 & Hwy 11, Hazen AR 72064. 501-255-3563. M,V,D,CB,AE,DC. I-40 (Exit 193) to Hwy 11, at SE corner of jct. B/f, n/s rms, pool, laundry, cont brfst, t/b/rv pkng, satellite TV, cot. Free crib. $33/S; $35-38/D; $4/ex prsn. Higher spec event rates. Discs.

Heber Springs

The Lake & River Inn/ 2322 Hwy 25B, Heber Springs AR 72543. 501-362-3161/ 800-362-5578. V,M,AE,D. On Greers Ferry Lake. Nrby rstrnt, pool, whrlpool, n/s rms, cable TV, playgrnd, arpt trans, tt/dd phone, nwspr, refrig, microwave, cot, outlets, t/b/rv pkng, eff, conn rms. Free local calls, coffee. AAA. $27-30/S; $35-40/D. 5/1-10/15: $35-40/S; $45-50/D. Holidays $5 extra. Disc: Senior, bsns, TA, govt, milt, trkr, l/s. *Guaranteed rates.*

Henderson

Rodeway Inn/ US 62 N E, Rt 1, Box CC, Henderson AR 72544. 501-488-5144. M,V,D,AE. US 62/412 E to Lake Norfork, cross bridge to E side of lake.

Mtl 8 mi E of Mtn Home. Rstrnt/ lounge, indr pool, mtg rm, whrlpool, sauna, whirlpool, cable TV, t pkng, n/s rms. $30-74/S; $35-74/D; $5/ex prsn. Discs.

Hope

Days Inn/ 1500 N Hervey, Hope AR 71801. 501-722-1904/ Fax: 777-1911. V,M,DC,AE,D. I-30 (Exit 30) at Hwy 4, S to mtl. Rstrnt, pool, mtg rm, b/f, t pkng, cable TV, cot, crib. $35-45/S; $40-60/D; $5/ex prsn. Discs.

Quality Inn/ I-30 & SR 29, Hope AR 71801. 501-777-0777. V,M,DC,AE. I-30 (Exit 31) to SR 29, N to mtl. Rstrnt, pool, mtg rm, fax, b/f, cable TV, t pkng, n/s rms. AAA. $30-35/S; $35-40/D; $5/ex prsn. 3/1-9/1: $34-44/S; $44-54/D. Discs.

Hot Springs

Econo Lodge/ 4319 Central Av, Hot Springs AR 71913. 501-525-1660. V,M,DC,AE. SR 7 S, 3 1/2 mi S of jct US 70 & US 270. Rstrnt, pool, mtg rm, fax, b/f, whrlpool, cable TV, t pkng, n/s rms. No pets. $35-40/S; $38-45/D; $5/ex prsn. 1/20-4/30: $45-57/S; $52-61/D. 5/1-9/15: $40-48/S; $42-51/D. Discs.

Super 8 Motel/ 4726 Central Av, Hot Springs AR 71913. 501-525-0188. AE, M,V,DC,CB,D. Hwy 7, S at Central Av. B/f, n/s rms, nrby rstrnt, elevator, cable TV, cot. Free local calls, crib. No pets. $39-43/S; $45-49/D; $5/ex prsn. Discs.

Jonesboro

Comfort Inn/ 2904 Phillips Dr, Jonesboro AR 72401. 501-972-8686. M, V, D,AE. SW corner of jct US 63 (J N Martin Expwy) & Hwy 49 (Stadium Blvd). Nrby rstrnt, pool, mtg rm, fax, cable TV, n/s rms. Free cont brfst. No pets. $40-50/S; $45-60/D; $5/ex prsn. Discs.

Motel 6/ 2300 S Caraway Rd, Jonesboro AR 72401. 501-932-1050/ Fax: 935-3421. V,M,DC,D,AE. On S Caraway Rd N of US 63 and S of SR 18. Nrby rstrnt, cable TV, pool, n/s rms. Free local calls. $25/S; $29/D; $4/ex prsn. Disc.

Ramada Limited/ 3000 Apache Dr, Jonesboro AR 72401. 501-932-5757/ Fax: 933-8760. V,AE,M. US 63 to US 49, N to Apache Dr, turn E. Indr pool,

ARKANSAS

arpt trans, b/f, n/s rms, mtg rm, cable TV, laundry. Free executive cont brfst. Gold Key Award. $41-56/S; $48-68/D; $7/ex prsn. Discs.

Super 8 Motel/ 2500 S Caraway Rd, Jonesboro AR 72401. 501-972-0849/ Fax: 972-0464. AE,M,V,DC,CB,D. US 63 N Bypass to Caraway Rd, 1/2 mi N. B/f, n/s rms, laundry, outlets, t/b/rv pkng, cont brfst, cable TV, cot. Free local calls, crib. $31/S; $35-38/D; $6/ex prsn. Discs.

Wilson Inn/ 2911 Gilmore Dr, Jonesboro AR 72401. 501-972-9000. AE,V,M,D,DC,CB. I-55, N on Hwy 63 to Jonesboro, exit at Caraway Rd, turn rt, rt on Phillips Rd, follow signs. N/s rms, refrig, fax, cable TV, microwave, mtg rm, whrlpool, exerc equip. Free local calls, cont brfst, popcorn. AAA. $40/S; $45-50/D; $5/ex prsn. Disc: Senior, AAA, corp, govt, milt, family.

Little Rock

Comfort Inn/ 3200 Bankhead Dr, Little Rock AR 72206. 501-490-2010/ Fax: 490-2229. M,V,D,AE. I-440 at Bankhead Dr (Arpt exit). Nrby rstrnt, pool, mtg rm, fax, b/f, cable TV, t pkng, exerc equip, n/s rms. Free local calls, cont brfst. $40-67/S; $45-72/D; $5/ex prsn. 8/1-9/30: $38-65/S; $43-68/D. Discs.

Motel 6/ 7501 Interstate 30, Little Rock AR 72209. 501-568-8888/ Fax: 568-8355. V,M,AE,D,DC. I-30 (Exit 134) at Scott Hamilton Dr. Cable TV, laundry, pool, n/s rms. Free local calls. Premier Award. $30-32/S; $36-38/D; $6/ex prsn. Disc.

Motel 6/ 10524 W Markham St, Little Rock AR 72205. 501-225-7366/ Fax: 227-7426. V,M,DC,AE,D. I-30 to I-430, N to Markham St (Exit 6). Cable TV, laundry, pool, n/s rms. Free local calls. $32/S; $38/D; $6/ex prsn. Disc.

Super 8 Motel/ I-40 & Prothro Jct, Little Rock AR 72117. 501-940-0141/ Fax: 945-7224. V,M,AE,D,DC,AE. I-40, Exit 157. B/f, n/s rms, pool, nrby rstrnt, laundry, outlets, b/t pkng, trans, copier, cot. Free local calls, crib. $41/S; $47/D; $2/ex prsn. Discs.

Wilson Inn/ 4301 E Roosevelt, Little Rock AR 72206. 501-376-2466. AE, M, V, CB,DC,D. I-440, Exit 3. Near airport. Mtg rm, whrlpool, exerc equip, fax, refrig, work desks. Free cont brfst, local calls, popcorn. AAA. $41/S; $41-80/D. Disc: AAA, AARP, TA, senior, fami

Also see Benton, North Little Rock.

Malvern

Super 8 Motel/ Rte 8, Box 719-6, Malvern AR 72104. 501-332-5755. AE,M,V,DC,CB,D. Hwy 270 W & I-30. N/s rms, pool, outlets, t/b/rv pkng, cable TV, cot. Free local calls, crib. $35-39/S; $39-45/D; $3/ex prsn. Discs.

Monticello

Days Inn/ 317 Hwy 425 N, Monticello AR 71655. 501-367-1881. V,AE,M,DC, CB, D,JCB. On US 425N, just N of US 4. Nrby rstrnt, pool, whrlpool, mtg rm, b/f, laundry, cot. Free cont brfst. $42-46/S; $47-52/D; $5/ex prsn. Discs.

Morrilton

Econo Lodge/ 1506 N SR 95, Morrilton AR 72110. 501-354-5101. V,AE,M,DC. I-40 (Exit 107) SR 95, S to mtl. Rstrnt, pool, whrlpool, cable TV, t pkng, n/s rms. Free coffee, local calls. $34-48/S; $40-52/D; $5/ex prsn. Disc.

Super 8 Motel/ Box 333, Morrilton AR 72110. 501-354-8188/ Fax: 354-6474. V,M,AE,DC,CB,D. I-40, Exit 108, at SR 9. SE corner of intersection. Rstrnt, pool, n/s rms, game rm, laundry, cont brfst, fax, copier, t pkng, cable TV, mtg rm, refrig, cot, crib. Free local calls. Pride award. $36/S; $36-40/D; $4/ex prsn. Discs.

North Little Rock
(Little Rock area)

Days Inn/ 5800 Pritchard Dr, N Little Rock AR 72117. 501-945-4100/ Fax: 945-4142. V,AE,M,DC,CB,D,JCB. I-40 (Exit 157) at SR 161, turn S to mtl. Nrby rstrnt, whrlpool, b/f, t pkng, cable TV, cot. Free local calls, cont brfst. $35-50/S; $45-60/D; $5/ex prsn. Discs.

Motel 6/ 400 W 29th St, N Little Rock AR 72114. 501-758-5100/ Fax: 758-26 34. V,M,DC,D,AE. I-40: Ebnd, Exit 153A (Hwy 107); Wbnd, Exit 152 (Hwy 176E). On 29th & Willow, S of I-40. Cable TV, pool, n/s rms. Free local

ARKANSAS

calls. $29-30/S; $35-36/D; $6/ex prsn. Disc.

Ozark
Budget Host Ozark Motel/ 1711 W Commercial, Ozark AR 72949. 501-667-2166. AE,CB,DC,M,V,D. Jct Hwy 64 & 23 N. Cable TV, dd phone, adj rstrnt/ mtg rms, arpt trans, family rm, in-rm coffee, t pkng, cot. AAA. $28-32/S; $30-38/D; $4/ex prsn.

Pine Bluff
Super 8 Motel/ 4101 W Barraque St, Pine Bluff AR 71602. 501-534-7400. AE,M,V,DC,CB,D. SW corner of jct US 65 & US 79. B/f, n/s rms, laundry, t/b/rv pkng, cable TV, cot, crib. Free local calls. No pets. $40/S; $40-45/D; $3/ex prsn. Discs.

Prescott
Comfort Inn/ Rte 5, Box 236, Prescott AR 71857. 501-887-6641. V,M,DC,AE. I-30 (Exit 44) to SR 24, E 1 blk to mtl. Rstrnt, pool, fax, cable TV, t pkng, n/s rms. Free cont brfst. $34-42/S; $38-46/D; $4/ex prsn. 5/1-10/31: $36-44/S; $40-48/D. Discs.

Russellville
Comfort Inn/ 3091 E D St, Box 1754, Russellville AR 72801. 501-967-7500. V,M,DC,AE. I-40, Exit 84. Nrby rstrnt, pool, mtg rm, fax, b/f, cable TV, t pkng, n/s rms. Free cont brfst. AAA. $40-50/S; $43-51/D; $5/ex prsn. 5/1-11/1: $43-50/S; $48-55/D. Discs.

Motel 6/ 215 W Birch St, Russellville AR 72801. 501-968-3666/ Fax: 890-5207. V,M,DC,D,AE. I-40 (Exit 81) N on Hwy 7, lt on Birch St to mtl. Cable TV, pool, n/s rms, t pkng. Free local calls. $25-26/S; $29-30/D; $4/ex prsn. Disc.

Super 8 Motel/ 2404 N Arkansas, Box 2436, Russellville AR 72801. 501-968-8898. V,M,AE,DC,CB,D. I-40 & SR 7. B/f, n/s rms, outlets, brfst, t/b/rv pkng, copier, VCR/ movies, cable TV, cot, crib. Free local calls. Pride Award. $38/S; $45-47/D; $3/ex prsn. Discs.

Searcy
Comfort Inn/ 107 S Rand Dr, Searcy AR 72143. 501-279-9100. V,M,AE,DC. US 67/167 (Exit 46) to Race St, W 1/4 mi to mtl. Nrby rstrnt, pool, fax, cable TV, n/s rms. Free cont brfst. No pets. $40-60/S; $45-60/D; $5/ex prsn. Discs.

Springdale
Econo Lodge/ 2001 S Thompson Av, Springdale AR 72764. 501-756-1900. V,AE,M,DC. US 71 to US 412, E to US 71 Bsns, S 6/10 mi on lt. Rstrnt/ lounge, pool, fax, cable TV, t pkng, n/s rms. Free cont brfst. No pets. $35-100/S; $45-125/D; $4/ex prsn. Higher spec event rates. Discs.

Texarkana
Budgetel Inns/ 5102 N Stateline Rd, Texarkana AR 75502 501-773-1000/ Fax: 773-5000. V,M,D,AE,DC,CB. I-30 (Exit 223B) at US 59 & 71/ Stateline Rd N. N/s rms, b/f, nrby rstrnt, pool, fax. Free cont brfst, in-rm coffee, local calls. AAA. $30-43/S; $37-50/D. 2/5-6/8: $34-45/S; $41-52/D. 6/9-12/31: $36-47/S; $43-54/D. Discs.

Howard Johnson Lodge/ 200 Realtor Rd, Texarkana AR 75502. 501-774-31 51. V,M,AE,D. I-30 (Exit 223A) to State Line Av at Hwys 71/ 59. N/s rms, b/f, pool, t/b pkng, cable TV, fax. Free cont brfst, arpt trans. Gold Medal Winner. $33-42/S; $37-46/D. Discs.

Motel 6/ 1924 Hampton Rd, Texarkana AR 75501. 903-793-1413/ Fax: 793-58 31. V,M,AE,D,DC,AE. I-30 (Exit 222) to Summerhill Rd, N to Hampton Rd, rt to mtl. Cable TV, pool, n/s rms. Free local calls. $25/S; $31/D; $6/ex prsn. Disc.

Motel 6/ 900 Realtor Av, Texarkana AR 75502. 501-772-0678/ Fax: 773-2359. V,M,DC,D,AE. I-30 (Exit 1) to Jefferson, S to Realtor/ Frontage Rd, turn rt. Cable TV, laundry, pool, n/s rms, t pkng. Free local calls. $25/S; $31/D; $6/ex prsn. Disc.

Super 8 Motel/ 325 E 51st St, Texarkana AR 75502. 501-774-8888/ Fax: 773-4653. AE,M,V,DC,CB,D. NE corner of I-30 and US 71. B/f, n/s rms, pool, game rm, outlets, cont brfst, t/b/rv pkng, copier, elevator, satellite TV, cot. Free local calls, nwspr, crib. $31/S; $37-41/D; $6/ex prsn. Discs.

Van Buren
Motel 6/ 1716 Fayetteville Rd, Van

Buren AR 72956. 501-474-8001/ Fax: 474-8294. V,M,AE,D,DC. I-40 (Exit 5) at SR 59. Cable TV, laundry, pool, n/s rms, t pkng, rstrnt. Free local calls. Premier Award. $30-32/S; $36-38/D; $6/ex prsn. Disc.

Super 8 Motel/ 106 N Plaza Ct, Van Buren AR 72956. 501-471-8888/ Fax: 471-8728. V,M,AE,DC,CB,D. I-40 & Hwy 59. B/f, n/s rms, pool, laundry, outlets, t/b/rv pkng, cable TV, mtg rm, cot. Free local calls, brfst. $40-42/S; $42-45/D; $1/ex prsn. Higher spec event rates. Discs.

West Memphis
(Memphis TN area)

Econo Lodge/ 2315 S Service Rd, W Memphis AR 72301. 501-732-2830. V,AE,M,DC. I-40/I-55 (Exit 279) at Ingram Blvd. Rstrnt, fax, cable TV, t pkng, casino trans, n/s rms. Free local calls, coffee. $33-40/S; $38-40/D; $4/ex prsn. Discs.

Motel 6/ 2501 S Service Rd, W Memphis AR 72301. 501-735-0100/ Fax: 735-4661. V,M,DC,D,AE. I-55/I-40 (Exit 279) to Ingram Blvd, turn S. Nrby rstrnt, cable TV, laundry, pool, n/s rms, t pkng. Free local calls. $29-33/S; $35-39/D; $6/ex prsn. Disc.

California

Alturas

Super 8 Motel/ 511 N Main St, Alturas CA 96101. 916-233-3545/ Fax: 233-3305. M,V,D,CB,AE,DC. On I-395 (Main St). N/s rms, fax, copier, cable TV, ADD, cot, crib. Free local calls. Pride Award. AAA. $41-46/S; $45-55/D; $4/ex prsn. Discs.

Anaheim
(Los Angeles - Disneyland area)

Comfort Inn/ 2200 S Harbor Blvd, Anaheim CA 92802. 714-750-5211/ Fax: 750-2226. V,M,DC,AE. I-5 (Santa Ana Frwy) to SR 57 (Harbor Blvd), S on Harbor to Orangewood Av. Rstrnt, pool, fax, b/f, whrlpool, cable TV, n/s rms. Free full brfst, tea, trans to Disneyland. No pets. $39-89/S or D; $5/ex prsn. 6/1-9/3: $44-94/S or D. Discs.

Days Inn/ 1111 S Harbor Blvd, Anaheim CA 92805. 714-533-8830/ Fax: 758-0573. V,AE,M,D,DC,CB,JCB. I-5 at Harbor Blvd. Fax, n/s rms, nrby rstrnt, pool, whrlpool, b/f, arpt trans, cable TV, in-rm safe, laundry. Free deluxe cont brfst, Disney trans. $39-59/S; $39-75/D; $10/ex prsn. 5/27-9/30: $49-65/S; $49-79/D. Discs.

Days Inn/ 1604 S Harbor Blvd, Anaheim CA 92802. 714-635-3630/ Fax: 520-3290. V,AE,M,D,DC,CB,JCB. I-5 at Harbor Blvd, turn S. Across from Disneyland. Fax, n/s rms, rstrnt, pool, whrlpool, b/f, arpt trans, in-rm coffee, refrig, microwave, laundry. $36-58/S; $36-85/D; $6/ex prsn. 12/25-12/31: $46-68/S; $46-95/D. Discs.

CALIFORNIA

Econo Lodge/ 837 S Beach Blvd, Anaheim CA 92804. 714-952-0898. V,AE,M,DC. I-5, exit Lincoln Av, 1/2 mi W to Beach Blvd. SR 91, exit Beach Blvd, S 1 1/2 mi to mtl. Nrby rstrnt, pool, fax, b/f, cable TV, n/s rms. Free cont brfst. No pets. AAA. $32-38/S; $35-40/D; $5/ex prsn. 9/16-10/31: $32-34/S; $40-45/D. Discs.

Econo Lodge/ 1570 S Harbor Blvd, Anaheim CA 92802. 714-772-5721. AE,V,M,D. I-5 to Harbor Blvd, turn S. Across st from Disneyland. Rstrnt, pool, fax, cable TV. Free cont brfst. No pets. AAA. $39-54/S or D; $5-8/ex prsn. 5/1-8/25: $52-89/S; $59-89/D. 12/24-1/2: $54-92/S or D. Discs.

Friendship Inn/ 705 S Beach Blvd, Anaheim CA 92804. 714-761-4200. V,AE,M,DC. Beach Blvd (SR 39), 2 mi S of SR 91. Nrby rstrnt, indr pool, whrlpool, cable TV, n/s rms. $32-35/S; $35-38/D; $3/ex prsn. Discs.

Knights Inn Anaheim/ 10301 Beach Blvd, Anaheim CA 90680. 714-826-6060/ Fax: 828-6856/ 800-843-5644. V,M,AE,D,DC,CB. I-5 or 91 to Beach Blvd S. I-22 or 405 to Beach Blvd N. Nrby rstrnt/ lounge, n/s rms, cable TV, VCR/ movies, arpt trans, tt/dd phone, fax, copier, nwspr, refrig, microwave, cot, crib, outlets, t/b/rv pkng, eff, conn rms, b/f. Free cont brfst, local calls, coffee, tea, cocoa. No pets. AAA. $34-38/S; $34-42/D; $5/ex prsn. Disc: Senior, bsns, TA, govt, l/s, family, trkr, milt, grp. *Guaranteed rates.*

Motel 6/ 1440 N State College, Anaheim CA 92806. 714-956-9690/ Fax: 956-5106. M,V,DC,D,AE. Hwy 91 at State College exit; N of 91, E of St College. Nrby rstrnt, cable TV, laundry, n/s rms. Free local calls. $32-34/S; $36-38/D; $4/ex prsn. 12/21-5/22: $29/S; $35/D. Disc.

Motel 6/ 100 W Freedman Way, Anaheim CA 92801. 714-520-9696/ Fax: 533-7539. V,M,DC,AE,D. I-5, exit Katella Av. Cable TV, laundry, pool, nrby rstrnt, game rm, n/s rms, whrlpool, elevator. Free local calls. $35-36/S; $39-40/D; $4/ex prsn. Higher spec event rates. Disc.

Rodeway Inn/ 1030 W Ball Rd, Anaheim CA 92802. 714-520-0101. M,V,D,AE. I-5: N, exit Harbor Blvd, rt to Ball Rd; S, exit Ball Rd. Nrby rstrnt, pool, fax, b/f, cable TV, n/s rms. Free cont brfst. $35-45/S or D; $5/ex prsn. 5/1-5/30, 12/21-1/4: $39-59/S or D. 5/31-9/1: $39-64/S or D. Discs.

Super 8 Motel/ 415 W Katella Av, Anaheim CA 92802. 714-778-6900/ Fax: 535-5659. V,M,AE,D,DC,CB. I-5 to Katella, 2 blks W. 1 blk from Disneyland Park entrance. Nrby rstrnt, lounge, pool, whrlpool, n/s rms, fax, copier, laundry, cot, crib, t/b/rv pkng. Free local calls, cont brfst, Disney trans. AAA. $39/S; $39-44/D. 6/1-9/4, 12/22-1/3: $46/S; $56/D. Discs.

Super 8 Motel/ 915 S West St, Anaheim CA 92802. 714-778-0350/ Fax: 778-3878. AE,V,M,DC,CB,D. I-5 to Harbor Blvd, N to Ball Rd, W to West St, turn rt. B/f, n/s rms, pool, whrlpool, cont brfst, laundry, elevator. Free Disney trans. No pets. $39-45/S; $39-55/D. Higher spec event/ holiday rates. Discs.

Arcadia (Los Angeles area)

Motel 6/ 225 Colorado Pl, Arcadia CA 91007. 818-446-2660/ Fax: 821-1060. V,M,AE,D,DC,AE. I-10 to Santa Anita exit, N to Huntington Dr, lt to Colorado Pl, bear rt to mtl. Nrby rstrnt, cable TV, pool, n/s rms. Free local calls. $35-36/S; $39-40/D; $4/ex prsn. Higher spec event rates. Disc.

Arcata

Comfort Inn/ 4701 Valley W Blvd, Arcata CA 95521. 707-826-2827. M, V, D, AE. US 101, exit Guintoli Lane to Valley W Blvd. Nrby rstrnt, fax, b/f, whrlpool, cable TV, copier, movies, n/s rms. Free cont brfst. AAA. $40-50/S; $45-55/D; $6/ex prsn. 5/1-5/31: $45-55/S; $50-60/D. 6/1-9/14: $65-80/S; $70-85/D. Discs.

Motel 6/ 4755 Valley W Blvd, Arcata CA 95521. 707-822-7061/ Fax: 822-4827. M,V,DC,D,AE. US 101: Nbnd, Giuntoli Ln/ Janes Rd exit, rt to Valley W Blvd, rt to mtl; Sbnd, Janes Rd exit, turn lt, cross over frwy, rt to Valley W Blvd, rt. Nrby rstrnt, cable TV, pool, n/s rms. Free local calls. $30/S; $36/D; $6/ex prsn. 5/23-9/28: $38/S; $44/D. Disc.

CALIFORNIA

National 9 Suites/ 2255 Alliance Rd, Arcata CA 95521. 707-822-4651. V,M, AE,DC. Hwy 101: Nbnd, Exit 14th St, rt on Alliance Rd; Sbnd, Exit Janes Rd-Spear Av, rt to Alliance. Cable TV, putting green, laundry, kitchens, dd phone, family units, cot. AAA. $34/S; $38-62/D; $8/ex prsn. Summer: $38/S; $42-52/D.

Super 8 Motel/ 4887 Valley W Blvd, Arcata CA 95521. 707-822-8888/ Fax: 822-2513. AE,V,M,DC,CB,D. Hwy 101 at Giuntoli Ln. B/f, n/s rms, cont brfst, t/b/rv pkng, copier, cable TV, cot. Free crib. AAA. $39-42/S; $44-47/D. Higher spec event rates. Discs.

Atascadero

Motel 6/ 9400 El Camino Real, Atascadero CA 93422. 805-466-6701/ Fax: 466-5836. M,V,DC,D,AE. US 101 to Santa Rosa Rd exit, turn E to El Camino Real (next to frwy). Cable TV, laundry, pool, n/s rms. Free local calls. $27/S; $33/D; $6/ex prsn. Disc.

Super 8 Motel/ 6505 Morro Rd, Atascadero CA 93422. 805-466-0794. V, M,AE,D,DC,AE. Hwy 101 (Exit 41) at W Morro Bay. B/f, n/s rms, nrby rstrnt, t/b/rv pkng, cable TV, cot, crib. Free local calls. AAA. $39-65/S; $44-80/D; $3/ex prsn. Higher wknd, holiday, spec event rates. Disc.

Auburn

Country Squire National 9 Inn/ 13480 Lincoln Way, Auburn CA 95603. 916-885-7025. V,M,AE,DC. 1.25 mi off I-80 via Foresthill Rd-Auburn Raven exit. Suites. National 9. Sun-Thurs: $36/S; $38-42/D; $2/ex prsn. Fri-Sat: $38/S; $40-44/D.

Bakersfield

Comfort Inn/ 830 Wible Rd, Bakersfield CA 93304. 805-831-1922. V,M,DC,AE. SR 99 to Ming Av, N on Wible. Nrby rstrnt, pool, whrlpool, cable TV, laundry, refrig, dd phone, n/s rms. Free cont brfst. No pets. $38-60/S; $43-60/D; $5/ex prsn. Discs.

Comfort Inn/ 2514 White Ln, Bakersfield CA 93304. 805-833-8000. V,M,DC,AE. SR 99 at White Ln, turn E. Rstrnt, pool, mtg rm, fax, b/f, cable TV, t pkng, refrig, dd phone, n/s rms. Free full brfst. No pets. $34-42/S; $40-50/D; $5/ex prsn. 5/1-10/31: $38-46/S; $40-50/D. Discs.

Econo Lodge/ 200 Trask St, Bakersfield CA 93312. 805-764-5221. V,AE, M,DC. I-5 & Stockdale Hwy. Nrby rstrnt, pool, fax, b/f, cable TV, n/s rms. $35-44/S; $44-59/D; $5/ex prsn. Discs.

Motel 6/ 2727 White Ln, Bakersfield CA 93304. 805-834-2828/ Fax: 834-3923. M,V,DC,D,AE. Hwy 99: White Ln Exit, E to mtl. Hwy 58: exit to Hwy 99, S to White Ln. Nrby rstrnt, cable TV, pool, n/s rms, t pkng. Free local calls. $26-29/S; $32-35/D; $6/ex prsn. Disc.

Motel 6/ 1350 Easton Dr, Bakersfield CA 93309. 805-327-1686/ Fax: 327-2337. V,M,DC,AE,D. Hwy 99 to California Av, E to Easton Dr, turn rt. Adj rstrnt, pool, n/s rms. Free local calls. $25/S; $31/D; $6/ex prsn. Disc.

Motel 6/ 5241 Olive Tree Crt, Bakersfield CA 93308. 805-392-9700/ Fax: 392-0223. M,V,DC,D,AE. Hwy 99 to Olive Dr, W to Knudsen Dr, rt to Olive Tree Crt. Cable TV, laundry, pool, nrby rstrnt, n/s rms. Free local calls. $22-23/S; $26-27/D; $4/ex prsn. Disc.

Motel 6/ 8223 E Brundage Ln, Bakersfield CA 93307. 805-366-7231/ Fax: 366-8834. M,V,DC,D,AE. Hwy 58 to 184/Weed Patch Hwy, N to 1st light, rt to mtl. Nrby rstrnt, cable TV, pool, n/s rms, t pkng. Free local calls. $26-27/S; $32-33/D; $6/ex prsn. Disc.

Quality Inn/ 1011 Oak St, Bakersfield CA 93304. 805-325-0772/ Fax: 325-4646. M,V,D,AE. SR 99 to California Av E, rt on Oak St to mtl. Rstrnt, pool, mtg rm, fax, b/f, sauna, whrlpool, cable TV, t pkng, exerc equip, laundry, n/s rms. Free cont brfst. AAA. $42-49/S; $44-49/D; $5/ex prsn. Discs.

Quality Inn/ 4500 Pierce Rd, Bakersfield CA 93308. 805-324-5555/ Fax: 325-0106. V,M,AE,D,DC. SR 99: Sbnd, exit at Golden State Hwy to Pierce Rd; Nbnd, exit At Airport Dr to Pierce Rd. At Airport Dr & Pierce Rd. Rstrnt/ lounge, pool, mtg rm, fax, b/f, sauna, whrlpool, cable TV, t pkng, laundry, trans, n/s rms. $44/S or D; $5/ex prsn. Discs.

CALIFORNIA 22

Townhouse National 9 Inn/ 505 Union Av, Bakersfield CA 93307. 805-325-3326. V,M,AE,DC. Hwy 58 to Union Av; 2 mi W of SR 99. Cable TV, dd phone, pool, playgrnd, adj rstrnt, n/s rms, crib. $22/S; $25-27/D; $5/ex prsn.

Baldwin Park (Los Angeles area)

Motel 6/ 14510 Garvey Av, Baldwin Park CA 91706. 818-960-5011/ Fax: 813-0334. M,V,DC,D,AE. I-10: Wbnd, to Puente Av, turn lt; Ebnd, to Puente Av, rt on Dalewood St 1/2 mi, rt on Puente. Cable TV, pool, nrby rstrnt, n/s rms, t pkng. Free local calls. $29/S; $33/D; $4/ex prsn. Disc.

Banning

Hacienda National 9 Inn/ 1240 W Ramsey St, Banning CA 92220. 714-849-4636. V,M,AE,DC. Adj to I-10, 1/2 mi NW of 8th St exit. Cable TV, pool, whrlpool, bbq pits, picnic area, n/s rms, kitchenettes, cont brfst. No pets. $30/S; $35-40/D; $5/ex prsn. Kitchenettes: $5 extra.

Super 8 Motel/ 1690 W Ramsey St, Banning CA 92220. 909-849-6887/ Fax: 922-9157. V,M,D,DC,DB,AE. I-10 to 22nd St, turn N to Ramsey, E 1/4 mi to mtl. B/f, n/s rms, cont brfst, b/rv pkng, copier, cable TV, cot. Free crib. AAA. $36-39/S; $41-47/D; $5/ex prsn. Higher spec event rates. Discs.

Barstow

Econo Lodge/ 1230 E Main St, Barstow CA 92311. 619-256-2133. V,M,DC,AE. I-15 or I-40, exit E Main St, W to mtl. Nrby rstrnt, pool, fax, b/f, cable TV, t pkng, n/s rms. $27-43/S; $30-56/D; $5/ex prsn. Discs.

Motel 6/ 150 N Yucca Av, Barstow CA 92311. 619-256-1752/ Fax: 256-9110. V,M,DC,AE,D. I-40, Wbnd and I-15, N or Sbnd, exit E Main St, N to Yucca Av, rt to mtl. Nrby rstrnt, pool, n/s rms. Free local calls. $24/S; $28/D; $4/ex prsn. Disc.

Motel 6/ 31951 E Main St, Barstow CA 92311. 619-256-0653/ Fax: 252-8323. M,V,DC,D,AE. I-40, to Marine Crps Logistics Center exit, E to mtl. I-15 Sbnd, Barstow/Needles Exit, lt on Main St to I-40E, follow above directions. Cable TV, pool, n/s rms. t pkng. Free local calls. $23/S; $27/D; $4/ex prsn. Disc.

Super 8 Motel/ 170 Coolwater Ln, Barstow CA 92311. 619-256-8443/ Fax: 256-0997. M,V,D,CB,AE,DC. I-15 or I-40 to E Main, W to Coolwater Ln. N/s rms, pool, cable TV, in-rm coffee, cot. Free local calls, crib. $39/S; $43-46/D; $3/ex prsn. Discs.

Beaumont

Budget Host Golden West Motel/ 625 E 5th St, Beaumont CA 92223. 714-845-2185. AE,M,V,D,DC,CB. Adj I-10, exit Beaumont Av, 1 blk E on 5th St. Satellite TV, dd phone, family rms, nrby rstrnt, pool, t pkng, crib. AAA/ Mobil. $28-32/S; $32-40/D; $3/ex prsn. Discs.

Bellflower (Los Angeles area)

Motel 6/ 17220 Downey Av, Bellflower CA 90706. 310-531-3933/ Fax: 529-8571. V,M,DC,D,AE. Hwy 91/ Artesia Frwy to Downey Av, turn S. E of I-710. Cable TV, laundry, pool, n/s rms. Free local calls. $35-36/S; $39-40/D; $4/ex prsn. Disc.

Belmont

Econo Lodge/ 630 El Camino Real, Belmont CA 94002. 415-593-5883. V, M,DC,AE. US 101, exit Ralston Av, rt on El Camino 2 blks. Nrby rstrnt, b/f, cable TV, n/s rms, eff, VCR. No pets. $38-48/S or D; $2/ex prsn. Discs.

Big Bear

Motel 6/ 42899 Big Bear Blvd, Box 132 806, Big Bear CA 92315. 909-585-6666/ Fax: 585-6685. M,V,DC,D,AE. Hwy 18 & Division Rd. Cable TV, laundry, pool, n/s rms. Free local calls. $38/S; $44/D; $4/ex prsn. Fri, Sat, Holidays & Spec Events: $46/S; $52/D. Disc.

Blythe

Motel 6/ 500 W Donlon St, Blythe CA 92225. 619-922-6666/ Fax: 921-8469. M,V,DC,D,AE. I-10: exit to Lovekin Blvd. Motel is SE of exit, on Donlon St. Cable TV, laundry, pool, n/s rms. t pkng. Free local calls. $27/S; $33/D; $6/ex prsn. Disc.

Buellton

Econo Lodge/ 630 Av of Flags, Buellton

CALIFORNIA

CA 93427. 805-688-0022. V,M,DC,AE. US 101: Sbnd, exit Av of the Flags; Nbnd, exit Solvang-Lompoc/SR 246, rt on Av of Flags. Nrby rstrnt, fax, b/f, cable TV, t pkng, food crt, eff, n/s rms. $30-60/S; $40-70/D; $8/ex prsn. Spec events: $50-80/S; $60-90/D. Discs.

Motel 6/ 333 McMurray Rd, Box 1670, Buellton CA 93427. 805-688-7797/ Fax: 686-0297. M,V,DC,D,AE. US 101 to Hwy 246, Solvang exit, E 1 blk to McMurray, lt on McMurray. Cable TV, pool, n/s rms, t pkng. Free local calls. $33-36/S; $39-44/D; $6/ex prsn. Higher spec event rates. Disc.

Buena Park (Los Angeles - Disneyland area)

Best Western Buena Park/ 8580 Stanton Av, Buena Park CA 90620. 714-828-5211/ Fax: 826-3716/ 800-646-1629. V,M,AE,D,DC,CB. I-91 W to Beach, S 2 mi to Stanton, turn rt. Nrby rstrnt/ lounge, pool, whrlpool, n/s rms, cable TV, tt phone, mtg rm, fax, copier, nwspr, refrig, elevator, microwave, cot, crib, outlets, b pkng, conn rms. Free cont brfst, coffee. AAA. $32/S; $36/D; $4/ex prsn. 5/26-9/9, 12/28-12/31: $38/S; $42/D. Higher spec event/ holiday/ wknd rates. Disc: Senior, bsns, TA, govt, l/s, family, trkr, milt, sports teams. *Guaranteed rates.*

Colony Inn/ 7800 Crescent Av, Buena Park CA 90620. 714-527-2201/ Fax: 826-3826/ 800-982-6566. V,M,AE,D, DC,CB. I-5 or 91 to Beach Blvd S, turn rt on Crescent. Nrby rstrnt, pool, sauna, whrlpool, satellite TV, tt phone, fax, laundry, cot. AAA/ Mobil. $32-39/S or D; $10/ex prsn. 5/24-8/19: $36-45/S or D. Disc: Senior, bsns, TA, govt, trkr, milt, AAA, l/s. *Guaranteed rates.*

Motel 6/ 7051 Valley View, Buena Park CA 90620. 714-522-1200/ Fax: 562-8978. M,V,DC,D,AE. Hwy 91 at Valley View; N of 91. Rstrnt, cable TV, laundry, pool, n/s rms, t pkng. Free local calls. $32-33/S; $38-39/D; $6/ex prsn. 12/21-5/22: $29/S; $33/D; $4/ex prsn. Disc.

Ramada Inn/ 7555 Beach Blvd, Buena Park CA 90620. 714-522-7360/ Fax: 523-2883. V,AE,M,D,DC,CB,JCB. Hwy 91 (Riverside Frwy) at Beach Blvd S. Pool, n/s rms, rstrnt, sauna, whrlpool, exerc equip. Free cont brfst, scheduled Disney trans. $44/S or D. Discs.

Super 8 Motel/ 7930 Beach Blvd, Buena Park CA 90620. 714-994-6480/ Fax: 994-3874. M,V,D,CB,AE,DC. I-91 or I-5 to Beach Blvd, S to mtl. N/s rms, pool, whrlpool, laundry, cont brfst, b/rv pkng, copier, satellite TV, mtg rm. Free cot, crib. AAA. $36/S; $38-40/D; $3/ex prsn. Discs.

Burbank

Bahia Motel/ 3400 W Olive Av, Burbank CA 91505. 818-841-9000/ Fax: 566-8874. V,M,AE,D,DC,CB. I-5: N, to Olive Av, W 1 mi; S, to Hollywood Way, S 1 mi, lt on Olive. Nrby rstrnt/ lounge, pool, n/s rms, satellite TV, tt/dd phone, fax, refrig, microwave, cot, crib, outlets. Free coffee. No pets. AAA. $40/S; $44/D; $5/ex prsn. 12/27-1/2: $45/S; $52/D.

Buttonwillow

Motel 6/ 20638 Tracy Av, Box 897, Buttonwillow CA 93206. 805-764-5153/ Fax: 764-6876. V,M,DC,AE,D. I-5, Exit Hwy 58/ Bakersfield. Nrby rstrnt, cable TV, pool, n/s rms, t pkng. Free local calls. $21-22/S; $27-28/D; $6/ex prsn. Disc.

Motel 6/ 3810 Tracy Av, Box 818, Buttonwillow CA 93206. 805-764-5207/ Fax: 764-6875. M,V,DC,D,AE. I-5 to Hwy 58, Bakersfield exit. Tracy Av is parallel to I-5 on NE side. Nrby rstrnt, cable TV, laundry, pool, n/s rms, t pkng. Free local calls. $21-22/S; $27-28/D; $6/ex prsn. Disc.

Super 8 Motel/ 20681 Tracy Av, Box 921, Buttonwillow CA 93206. 805-764-5117/ Fax: 764-6676./ 800-800-8000. V,M,AE,D,DC,CB. I-5 at Hwy 58, on frontage rd E of I-5, N of Hwy 58. Nrby rstrnt/ lounge, pool, whrlpool, n/s rms, satellite TV, tt/dd phone, fax, nwspr, laundry, refrig, microwave, crib, t/b/rv pkng, conn rms, b/f. Free local calls, coffee. AAA. $31/S; $36-41/D; $4/ex prsn. 4/1-9/30: $33/S; $38-43/D. Disc: Senior, bsns, TA, govt, l/s, family, trkr, milt. *Guaranteed rates.*

Camarillo

Motel 6/ 1641 E Daily Dr, Camarillo CA

CALIFORNIA 24

93010. 805-388-3467/ Fax: 388-8037. M,V,DC,D,AE. Hwy 101/ Ventura Frwy to Carmen Dr exit, E to Daily, rt to mtl. Cable TV, pool, n/s rms. Free local calls. $32-34/S; $38-40/D; $6/ex prsn. Disc.

Campbell (San Jose area)
Motel 6/ 1240 Camden Av, Campbell CA 95008. 408-371-8870/ Fax: 879-0236. V,M,DC,AE,D. Hwy 17 at Camden Av Exit, SE to mtl. Nrby rstrnt, n/s rms. Free local calls. $39/S; $45/D; $6/ex prsn. Disc.

Carlsbad
Motel 6/ 6117 Paseo del Norte, Carlsbad CA 92009. 619-438-1242/ Fax: 931-7958. V,M,DC,AE,D. I-5, exit Palomar Arpt Rd, E to Paseo del Norte, rt. Nrby rstrnt, pool, n/s rms. Free local calls. $27-28/S; $33-34/D; $6/ex prsn. Disc.

Motel 6/ 1006 Carlsbad Village Dr, Carlsbad CA 92008. 619-434-7135/ Fax: 730-0159. M,V,DC,D,AE. I-5 at Carlsbad Village Dr exit (Elm). Nrby rstrnt, cable TV, n/s rms. Free local calls. $28-30/S; $34-36/D; $6/ex prsn. Disc.

Motel 6/ 750 Raintree Dr, Carlsbad CA 92009. 619-431-0745/ Fax: 431-9207. M,V,DC,AE,D. I-5, to Poinsettia Ln, W to Avenida Encinas, rt on Raintree Dr. Nrby rstrnt, cable TV, pool, n/s rms. Free local calls. $27-28/S; $33-34/D; $6/ex prsn. 5/23-9/27: $30/S; $36/D. Disc.

Carpinteria (Santa Barbara area)
Motel 6/ 4200 Via Real, Carpinteria CA 93013. 805-684-6921/ Fax: 566-0387. M,V,DC,D,AE. US 101: Nbnd, to Santa Monica Rd Exit, lt on Via Real to mtl; Sbnd, to Santa Claus Ln Exit, lt at end of exit under frwy, then rt on Via Real. Cable TV, laundry, pool, n/s rms. Free local calls. $31-33/S; $37-39/D; $6/ex prsn. 12/21-5/22: $36/S; $42/D. Disc.

Motel 6/ 5550 Carpinteria Av, Carpinteria CA 93013. 805-684-8602/ Fax: 566-9097. V,M,DC,AE,D. US 101 to Casitas Pass Rd Exit, SW to Carpinteria Av, lt. Cable TV, pool, nrby rstrnt, n/s rms. Free local calls. $31-33/S; $37-39/D; $6/ex prsn. Disc.

Castaic
Econo Lodge/ 31410 Castaic Rd, Castaic CA 91384. 805-295-1070. AE,V, M,D,DC. I-5: Nbnd, exit Parker Rd E to Castaic, turn S to mtl; Sbnd, exit Lake Hughes Rd, rt to Old Road, rt at Castaic. Nrby rstrnt, pool, whrlpool, cable TV, n/s rms. Free cont brfst. No pets. $35-59/S; $37-69/D. Discs.

Chico
Motel 6/ 665 Manzanita Crt, Chico CA 95926. 916-345-5500/ Fax: 894-2846. M,V,DC,D,AE. Hwy 99 to Cohasset Rd exit SW to Manzanita Crt. Nrby rstrnt, cable TV, pool, n/s rms. t pkng. Free local calls. $30-31/S; $36-37; $6/ex prsn. Disc.

Vagabond Inn/ 630 Main St, Chico CA 95928. 916-895-1323/ Fax: 343-2719. V,AE,M. Just off Hwy 32 in Chico. Hwy 99 to Hwy 32, W to 8th St, lt to Main St, rt to mtl. Pool, nrby rstrnt, mtg rm, family rm, in-rm coffee, cable TV, secretarial serv. $42/S; $47/D.

Chino
Motel 6/ 12266 Central Av, Chino CA 91710. 909-591-3877/ Fax: 590-8319. M,V,DC,D,AE. Hwy 60 at Central Av exit, N on Central. Nrby rstrnt, cable TV, pool, n/s rms. Free local calls. $29/S; $33/D; $4/ex prsn. Disc.

Chowchilla
Safari National 9 Inn/ 220 E Robertson Blvd, Chowchilla CA 93610. 209-665-4821. V,M,AE,DC. On Hwy 99 S of Merced, N of Fresno. Cable TV, pool, dd phone, adj rstrnt, t pkng, movies, kitchenettes, cot, crib. $24-32/S; $26-38/D; $3/ex prsn. National 9.

Chula Vista
Motel 6/ 745 "E" St, Chula Vista CA 91910. 619-422-4200/ Fax: 585-8944. M,V,DC,D,AE. I-5 at "E" St. Nrby rstrnt, cable TV, pool, n/s rms. Free local calls. $29-32/S; $33-36/D; $4/ex prsn. Disc.

Rodeway Inn/ 778 Broadway, Chula Vista CA 92010. 619-476-9555. M, V, D,AE. I-5, "J" St exit, E to Broadway, rt 3 blks. Nrby rstrnt, pool, mtg rm, b/f, whrlpool, cable TV, t pkng, refrig, microwave, n/s rms. Free coffee. No

CALIFORNIA

pets. AAA. $42-47/S; $48-56/D; $5/ex prsn. 6/16-9/15: $47-52/S; $55-65/D. Discs.

Claremont (Los Angeles area)
Howard Johnson Lodge/ 721 S Indian Hill Blvd, Claremont CA 91711. 714-626-2431/ Fax: 624-7051. AE,V,MC,DC,CB,D. I-10 (San Bernadino Frwy) & Indian Hill Blvd. Mtg rm, rstrnt, pool, trans, t pkng, laundry. $40-65/S or D. Disc.

Clearlake
Days Inn/ 13865 Lakeshore Dr, Clearlake CA 95422. 707-994-8982/ Fax: 994-0613. V,AE,M,D,DC,CB,JCB. Hwy 29 to SR 53, N 3 mi to Lakeshore Dr, 3 1/2 mi to mtl. Fax, n/s rms, rstrnt, pool, b/f, laundry, dock. Free cont brfst. No pets. AAA. On the lake. $35-65/S; $45-65/D; $5/ex prsn. Discs.

Coalinga
Motel 6/ 25008 W Dorris Av, Coalinga CA 93210. 209-935-1536/ Fax: 934-0814. V,M,DC,AE,D. I-5 to Hwy 198/ Hanford-Lemoore Exit, W 1/2 mi to mtl. Nrby rstrnt, cable TV, pool, n/s rms. Free local calls. $27/S; $33/D; $6/ex prsn. Disc.

Motel 6/ 25278 W Dorris, Coalinga CA 93210. 209-935-2063/ Fax: 934-0813. M,V,DC,D,AE. I-5 to Hwy 198 (Hanford-Lemoore) exit; W 1/2 mi. Nrby rstrnt, cable TV, laundry, pool, n/s rms. Free local calls. $27/S; $33/D; $6/ex prsn. Disc.

Corona
Motel 6/ 200 N Lincoln Av, Corona CA 91720. 909-735-6408/ Fax: 340-2123. M,V,DC,D,AE. SR 91 at Lincoln Av exit. Nrby rstrnt, cable TV, pool, n/s rms. Free local calls. $26/S; $30/D; $4/ex prsn. Disc.

Costa Mesa (Newport Beach area)
Comfort Inn/ 2430 Newport Blvd, Costa Mesa CA 92626. 714-631-7840. M,V,D,AE. I-405 (San Diego Frwy) to SR 55, exit at Del Mar/ Fair Dr, 3 blks SW to Santa Isabel, lt to Newport Blvd. Nrby rstrnt, pool, fax, b/f, sauna, cable TV, n/s rms. Free cont brfst. No pets. $42-52/S; $45-55/D; $5/ex prsn. 5/16-9/15: $45-55/S; $48-58/D. Discs.

Days Inn/ 2100 Newport Blvd, Costa Mesa CA 92627. 714-642-2670/ Fax: 642-2677. V,M,AE,D,DC,CB. I-55 S to 22nd St, go straight, u-turn at Bay St. Pool, tt/dd phone, fax, refrig, cot, crib. Free cont brfst. No pets. AAA. $42-48/S; $46-48/D; $4/ex prsn. 5/1-9/30: $48-54/S; $52-56/D. Holidays: $56-60/S or D. Disc: Senior, bsns, govt, milt.

Motel 6/ 1441 Gisler Av, Costa Mesa CA 92626. 714-957-3063/ Fax: 979-8257. V,M,DC,AE,D. I-405 at Harbor Blvd, exit S, lt on Gisler Av. Nrby rstrnt, pool, n/s rms. Free local calls. $31-32/S; $35-36/D; $4/ex prsn. Disc.

Super 8 Motel/ 2645 Harbor Blvd, Costa Mesa CA 92626. 714-545-9471/ Fax: 432-8129. AE,V,M,DC,CB,D. 1 mi S of I-405 Harbor Blvd exit. B/f, n/s rms, nrby rstrnt whrlpool, sauna, cont brfst, cable TV, nwspr, cot, crib. Free local calls. $44/S; $47-49/D; $5/ex prsn.

Crescent City
Days Inn/ 220 "M" St, Crescent City CA 95531. 707-464-9553. V,AE,M,D,DC,CB,JCB. Hwy 101 N bet 2nd and 3rd St. Fax, n/s rms, nrby rstrnt, cable TV, dd phone, in-rm coffee, cot. $30-36/S; $30-38/D; $5/ex prsn. 4/1-6/30, 9/3-9/30: $35-45/S; $39-55/D. 7/1-9/2: $52-57/S; $59-69/D. Disc.

Econo Lodge/ 119 L St, Crescent City CA 95531. 707-464-2181. V,M,DC,AE. Located bet US 101N & US 101S. Nrby rstrnt, fax, cable TV, n/s rms. Free cont brfst. No pets. AAA. $30-40/S; $35-45/D; $5/ex prsn. 5/1-6/30, 9/8-10/31: $35-45/S; $40-50/D. 7/1-9/7: $50-55/S; $55-70/D. Discs.

Super 8 Motel/ 685 Hwy 101 S, Crescent City CA 95531. 707-464-4111. M,V,D,CB,AE,DC. On US 101/ Redwood Hwy, across from Crescent City Harbor at Citizens Dock Rd. B/f, n/s rms, t/rv pkng, cable TV, in-rm coffee. Free local calls. Pride Award. AAA. $43/S; $45-50/D; $3/ex prsn. Discs.

Davis
Econo Lodge/ 221 D St, Davis CA 95616. 916-756-1040. M,V,D,CB,AE,DC. I-80 E or W, take Davis exit onto

CALIFORNIA 26

Richards Blvd to dntn. On "D" St bet 2nd & 3rd St. Nrby rstrnt, fax, b/f, cable TV. $39-46/S; $42-48/D; $5/ex prsn. Discs.

Motel 6/ 4835 Chiles Rd, Davis CA 95616. 916-753-3777/ Fax: 753-0569. M,V,DC,D,AE. I-80 at Mace Blvd exit. Nrby rstrnt, cable TV, pool, laundry, n/s rms, arpt trans. Free local calls. $30-31/S; $36-37/D; $6/ex prsn. Disc.

Desert Hot Springs (Palm Springs area)

Motel 6/ 63950 20th Av, Desert Hot Springs CA 92258. 619-251-1425/ Fax: 251-0494. V,M,AE,D,DC. I-10: Wbnd, exit to Indian Av, turn rt, lt to motel; Ebnd, exit to Indian Av, turn lt, lt on 20th Av to motel. Adj rstrnt, cable TV, pool, laundry, n/s rms, t pkng. Free local calls. Premier Award. $33-37/S; $37-41/D; $4/ex prsn. Higher spec event rates. Disc.

Disneyland

See Anaheim, Buena Park, Orange, Stanton.

Downey (Los Angeles area)

Comfort Inn/ 9438 E Firestone Blvd, Downey CA 90241. 310-803-3555. V, M,AE,D,DC. I-605 to Firestone Blvd, W 1 mi to mtl. Nrby rstrnt, fax, b/f, whrlpool, cable TV, n/s rms. Free cont brfst. No pets. AAA. $39-69/S; $44-74/D; $5/ex prsn. 1/16-4/30, 9/16-10/31: $44-72/S; $49-79/D. Discs.

Duarte (Los Angeles area)

Rodeway Inn/ 1533 E Huntington Dr, Duarte CA 91010. 818-303-4544. AE, V,M,D. I-605 to Huntington Dr, turn W. I-210, exit Mount Olive, turn lt on Huntington. Nrby rstrnt, fax, b/f, cable TV, outlets, n/s rms. Free cont brfst. No pets. AAA. $42-45/S; $45-50/D; $6/ex prsn. 12/29-1/1: $80-90/S; $95-99/D. Discs.

Dunnigan

Value Lodge/ 3930 County Rd 89, Box 740, Dunnigan CA 95937. 916-724-3333/ Fax: 724-4233. V,M,AE. Just off I-5 at Dunnigan, 2 mi N of I-505 jct. Pool, satellite TV, dd phone, laundry, b/f, n/s rms, cont brfst, refrig, nrby rstrnt/ lounge. Free cot, crib. AAA/ IMA. $39/S; $45-48/D. 5/24-9/30: $44/S; $49-55/D. Disc: AAA, senior, AARP, TA, IMA, trkr, family.

El Cajon (San Diego area)

El Cajon Downtown National 9 Inn/ 425 W Main St, El Cajon CA 92020. 619-442-5536. V,M,AE,DC. Adj to I-80. Cable TV, dd phone, adj rstrnt, n/s rms, coffee. No pets. $25/S; $30-35/D; $5/ex prsn.

Howard Johnson Lodge/ 1274 Oakdale Av, El Cajon CA 92021. 619-442-0651/ Fax: 697-0874. M,V,D,CB,AE,DC. I-8 (Exit 54) at 2nd St. Pool, t pkng, rm serv, rstrnt, cable TV, fax. Free cont brfst, coffee, local calls. No pets. $34-69/S; $38-69/D. Discs.

Motel 6/ 550 Montrose Ct, El Cajon CA 92020. 619-588-6100/ Fax: 588-1973. M,V,DC,D,AE. I-8 at Magnolia St Exit; S on Magnolia. Cable TV, pool, laundry, n/s rms. Free local calls. $28-29/S; $34-35/D; $6/ex prsn. Disc.

Super 8 Motel/ 588 N Mollison Av, El Cajon CA 92021. 619-579-1144/ Fax: 579-1787. M,V,D,CB,AE,DC. I-8 at Mollison Av. N/s rms, pool, whrlpool, cont brfst, b/t pkng, cable TV, mtg rm. Free local calls. $32/S; $32-37/D; $5/ex prsn. Discs.

El Centro

Motel 6/ 395 Smoketree Dr, El Centro CA 92243. 619-353-6766/ Fax: 337-1123. M,V,DC,D,AE. I-8 to 4th St/Hwy 86 exit, turn N on 4th St (Hwy 86) to Smoketree, turn rt. Nrby rstrnt, cable TV, pool, laundry, n/s rms, t pkng. Free local calls. $26-28/S; $32-34/D; $6/ex prsn. Disc.

El Monte (Los Angeles area)

Motel 6/ 3429 Peck Rd, El Monte CA 91731. 818-448-6660/ Fax: 279-5664. M,V,DC,D,AE. I-10 to N Peck Rd/ Valley Blvd exit, go N on Peck Rd. Cable TV, pool, n/s rms. Free local calls. $29/S; $33/D; $4/ex prsn. Disc.

Encinitas

Friendship Inn/ 410 N Hwy 101, Encinitas CA 92024. 619-436-4999/ Fax:

943-9321. V,M,AE,D,DC,CB. I-5 to Encinitas Blvd, W to Hwy 101, N 1 mi, turn lt. Nrby rstrnt, fax, b/f, cable TV, refrig, microwave, VCR. Free cont brfst. No pets. 1994 Inn of the Year. $35-40/S; $45/D; $5/ex prsn. 2/1-6/15: $40-45/S; $45-55/D. 6/16-10/15: $45-55/S; $60-65/D. Discs.

Escondido

Motel 6/ 900 N Quince St, Escondido CA 92025. 619-745-9252/ Fax: 745-4203. M,V,DC,D,AE. I-15 at Hwy 78 at Centre City Pkwy S exit; S to Mission Av, rt on Mission, rt on Quince. Nrby rstrnt, cable TV, pool, laundry, elevator, n/s rms. t pkng. Free local calls. $29/S; $33/D; $4/ex prsn. Disc.

Super 8 Motel/ 528 W Washington Av, Escondido CA 92025. 619-747-3711/ Fax: 747-8385. M,V,D,CB,AE,DC. I-15 to Hwy 78, E to Center City Pkwy, S to 2nd light/ Washington Av, rt 1 blk. I-5, take 78 E to Escondido, exit at Centre city Pkwy, S to 2nd light/ Washington Av. B/f, n/s rms, pool, whrlpool, laundry, cont brfst, elevator, cable TV, t/b/rv pkng, cot, crib. Pride Award. AAA. $35/S; $40-45/D; $5/ex prsn. Discs.

Eureka

Budget Host Town House/ 933 4th St, Eureka CA 95501. 707-443-4536/ Fax: 444-2099/ 800-445-6888. V,M,AE, D,DC,CB. US 101 at corner of 4th & K Sts, dntn. Nrby rstrnt/ lounge, n/s rms, cable TV, tt phones, fax, refrig, microwave, cot, crib. Free coffee. AAA. $32-36/S; $40-44/D; $6/ex prsn. 5/16-6/30, 9/2-9/30: $38-42/S; $44-54/D. 7/1-9/1: $42-45/S; $50-59/D. Disc: Senior, bsns, TA, govt, trkr, milt, AAA. *Guaranteed rates.*

Budget Host Inn Town House/ 933 4th St, Eureka CA 95501. 707-443-4536. V, M,D,DC,CB,AE. On US 101 Sbnd, dntn at 4th & K Sts. Cable TV, dd phone, in-rm coffee, family rms, n/s rms, nrby rstrnt, t pkng, cot, crib. AAA. $32-36/S; $36-44/D; $6/ex prsn. 5/1-5/31, 10/1-10/31: $36-42/S; $40-48/D. 6/1-9/30: $40-55/S; $44-59/D. Spec Events: $40-85. Discs.

Comfort Inn/ 2014 Fourth St, Eureka CA 95501. 707-444-0401. V, M,AE,D, DC. US 101 to "V" St, turn E. Nrby rstrnt, fax, cable TV, copier, n/s rms. Free cont brfst. No pets. AAA. $40-90/S; $45-95/D; $6/ex prsn. 5/1-10/1: $45-90/S; $50-95/D. Discs.

Friendship Inn/ 2832 Broadway, Eureka CA 95501. 707-441-8442. V,M,D,AE. On US 101. Nrby rstrnt, fax, cable TV, n/s rms. No pets. $30-40/S; $35-50/D; $5/ex prsn. 5/1-6/30, 9/11-10/31: $35-45/S; $40-55/D. 7/1-9/10: $40-50/S; $50-65/D. Discs.

Motel 6/ 1934 Broadway, Eureka CA 95501. 707-445-9631/ Fax: 444-3217. V,M,DC,AE,D. US Hwy 101/ Broadway, between Del Norte and Hawthorne Sts. N/s rms, t pkng. Free local calls. $30/S; $36/D; $6/ex prsn. 5/23-9/28: $38/S; $44/D. Disc.

Sea Breeze National 9 Inn/ 2846 Broadway, Eureka CA 95501. 707-443-9381. V,M,AE,DC. 1 blk N of Bayshore Mall on Broadway. DD phones. No pets. AAA. $28-36/S; $34-52/D; $4-6/ex prsn. Spec events $6 extra.

Super 8 Motel/ 1304 Fourth St, Eureka CA 95501. 707-443-3193. M,V,D,CB, AE,DC. 8 blks N on US 101 at "N" St, turn W. N/s rms, pool, whrlpool, sauna, mtg rm, cot, crib. No pets. Pride Award. AAA. $38/S; $45-46/D; $4/ex prsn. Discs.

Fairfield

Motel 6/ 1473 Holiday Ln, Fairfield CA 94533. 707-425-4565/ Fax: 435-9232. M,V,DC,D,AE. I-80 at Travis Blvd. Nrby rstrnt, cable TV, pool, n/s rms. Free local calls. $30-34/S; $36-40/D; $6/ex prsn. Disc.

Motel 6/ 2353 Magellan Rd, Fairfield CA 94533. 707-427-0800/ Fax: 435-9209. M,V,DC,D,AE. I-80, W Texas St/Rockville Rd exit, E on W Texas, S on Beck Av, E on Magellan Rd. Cable TV, pool, n/s rms, t pkng. Free local calls. $26-29/S; $32-35/D; $6/ex prsn. Disc.

Fontana

Comfort Inn/ 16780 Valley Blvd, Fontana CA 92335. 909-822-3350. V, M, DC,AE. I-10 to Sierra Av, N to Valley Blvd, W to mtl. Nrby rstrnt, pool, fax, b/f, cable TV, t pkng, laundry, n/s rms.

CALIFORNIA

No pets. AAA. $40-50/S; $45-55/D; $4/ex prsn. Discs.

Motel 6/ 10195 Sierra Av, Fontana CA 92335. 909-823-8686/ Fax: 829-3150. M,V,DC,D,AE. I-10, exit at Sierra Av, N to mtl. Nrby rstrnt, cable TV, pool, n/s rms, t pkng. Free local calls. $30/S; $34/D; $4/ex prsn. Disc.

Fortuna

Mission Motel/ 819 Main St, Fortuna CA 95540. 707-725-5136. V,M,AE,DC. Hwy 101 at Main St, turn rt. Cable TV, dd phone, adj rstrnt, family rms, n/s rms, cot, crib. AAA/ National 9. $30-34/S; $34-48/D.

Super 8 Motel/ 1805 Alamar Way, Fortuna CA 95540. 707-725-2888/ Fax: Ext 123. V,AE,M. Hwy 101 to Kenmar Rd, W to Almar Way, rt to mtl. B/f, n/s rms, nrby rstrnt, cont brfst, laundry, t/b/rv pkng, cable TV, VCR movies, cot, crib. Free local calls. Pride Award. $42/S; $46-50/D; $5/ex prsn. Discs.

Fremont

Econo Lodge/ 46101 Warm Springs Blvd, Fremont CA 94539. 510-656-2800/ Fax: 659-0325. V,AE,M,DC. I-880 to Mission Blvd, N to Warm Springs Blvd, W to mtl. Near I-680. Nrby rstrnt, fax, b/f, cable TV. No pets. Free cont brfst. $37-59/S; $39-63/D; $5/ex prsn. Discs.

Motel 6/ 46101 Research Av, Fremont CA 94539. 510-490-4528/ Fax: 490-5937. M,V,DC,D,AE. I-680, exit at Mission Blvd. S of frwy on Brown Rd/Research Av. Cable TV, pool, n/s rms. Free local calls. $30-32/S; $36-38/D; $6/ex prsn. Disc.

Motel 6/ 34047 Fremont Blvd, Fremont, CA 94536. 510-793-4848/ Fax: 791-8170. M,V,DC,D,AE. I-880 at Fremont/Alvardo Blvd exit; turn E on Fremont, rt at Lucky's Supermarket, return to mtl. Nrby rstrnt, cable TV, n/s rms, t pkng. Free local calls. $30-32/S; $36-38/D; $6/ex prsn. Disc.

Fresno

Motel 6/ 4080 N Blackstone Av, Fresno CA 93726. 209-222-2431/ Fax: 229-8491. V,M,DC,AE,D. SR 41, to Ashlan Av, W 2 blks to Blackstone Av, lt 1 blk. Rstrnt, cable TV, pool, n/s rms, t pkng. Free local calls. $27-28/S; $33-34/D; $6/ex prsn. Disc.

Motel 6/ 445 N Parkway Dr, Fresno CA 93706. 209-485-5011/ Fax: 498-0560. V,M,DC,D,AE. Hwy 99 to Belmont Av exit, W on Belmont, S on N Parkway Dr. Cable TV, pool, n/s rms, t pkng. Free local calls. $26/S; $32/D; $6/ex prsn. Disc.

Motel 6/ 1240 Crystal Av, Fresno CA 93728. 209-237-0855/ Fax: 497-5869. V,M,DC,AE,D. Hwy 99, exit Olive Av off-ramp W, rt on Crystal Av. Nrby rstrnt, cable TV, pool, n/s rms, t pkng. Free local calls. $24-26/S; $30-32/D; $6/ex prsn. Disc.

Motel 6/ 4245 N Blackstone Av, Fresno CA 93726. 209-221-0800/ Fax: 224-8298. M,V,DC,D,AE. Hwy 41 at Ashlan Av, W 2 blks to Blackstone Av, turn rt. Nrby rstrnt, cable TV, pool, laundry, n/s rms. Free local calls. $30-32/S; $36-38/D; $6/ex prsn. Disc.

Motel 6/ 933 N Parkway Dr, Fresno CA 93728. 209-233-3913/ Fax: 498-8526. M,V,DC,D,AE. Hwy 99 to Olive St exit, W on Olive St, S on Parkway Dr. Nrby rstrnt, cable TV, elevator, n/s rms, t pkng. Free local calls. $24-25/S; $30-31/D; $6/ex prsn. Disc.

Rep's National 9 Inn/ 3876 N Blackstone Av, Fresno CA 93726. 209-222-8623. V,M,AE,DC. 3-1/2 mi N on SR 41. SR 99: Sbnd, exit Shaw Av; Nbnd, exit Clinton Av. Cable TV, pool, refrig, adj rstrnt, eff. No pets. $28-34/s; $32-42/D; $3/ex prsn.

Super 8 Motel/ 1087 N Parkway Dr, Fresno CA 93728. 209-268-0741. M, V, D,CB,AE,DC. Hwy 99 & Olive, W of 99, S of Olive. N/s rms, pool, cable TV, fax, cont brfst, pm coffee and snacks, cot. Free local calls. Pride Award. $36-40/S; $39-50/D; $5/ex prsn. Discs.

Fullerton (Disneyland area)

Motel 6/ 1415 S Euclid St, Fullerton CA 92632. 714-992-0660/ Fax: 992-0375. V,M,DC,AE,D. Hwy 91/ Riverside Frwy to Euclid St, N 1/4 mi to mtl. Nrby rstrnt, n/s rms. Free local calls. $29-30/S; $33-34/D; $4/ex prsn. Disc.

CALIFORNIA

Gilroy

National 9 Inn/ 5530 Monterey Rd, Gilroy CA 95020. 408-842-6464. V, M, AE, DC. Hwy 101, Monterey St exit. T pkng, pool, refrig, microwave, in-rm coffee, satellite TV, suites. $27-67/S; $30-75/D; $5/ex prsn; $40-100/suites.

Rodeway Inn/ 611 Leavesley Rd, Gilroy CA 95020. 408-847-0688. AE,V,M,D. US 101 to Leavesley Rd, E to mtl. Nrby rstrnt, pool, fax, b/f, cable TV, t pkng, n/s rms. Free cont brfst. No pets. AAA. $35-65/S; $40-75/D; $5/ex prsn. Discs.

Super 8 Motel/ 8435 San Ysidro Av, Gilroy CA 95020. 408-848-4108/ Fax: 848-2651. V,M,D,DC,DB,AE. Hwy 101 at Leavesley Rd. B/f, n/s rms, pool, cont brfst, t/b/rv pkng, copier, fax, elevator, satellite TV. Free local calls, crib. AAA. $39/S; $42-45/D; $4/ex prsn. 6/15-9/15: $43/S; $47/D. Higher spec event, Apr-Sept wknds. Discs.

Glendale (Los Angeles area)

Econo Lodge/ 1437 E Colorado St, Glendale CA 91205. 818-246-8367. M,V,D,CB,AE,DC. I-5, exit Colorado St E, or SR 2, exit Colorado St W. Nrby rstrnt, fax, b/f, whrlpool, cable TV. Free cont brfst. No pets. $45-55/S; $48-60/D; $5/ex prsn. 12/30-1/2: $70-85/S; $75-95/D. Discs.

Friendship Inn/ 200 W Colorado St, Glendale CA 91204. 818-246-7331. M, V,D,AE. I-5, exit Colorado St E. SR 134 (Ventura Frwy), exit Central Av S, lt on Colorado St. Nrby rstrnt, pool, cable TV, suites, coffee. No pets. $42-46/S; $46-50/D; $4/ex prsn. 12/30-12/31: $58-62/S; $64-68/D. Discs.

Goleta (Santa Barbara area)

Motel 6/ 5897 Calle Real, Goleta CA 93117. 805-964-3596/ Fax: 683-0647. M,V,DC,D,AE. US 101 at Fairview exit, N 1 blk to Calle Real, rt 1 blk. Nrby rstrnt, cable TV, pool, laundry, n/s rms. Free local calls. $40-42/S; $46-48/D; $6/ex prsn. Disc.

Hacienda Heights (Los Angeles area)

Motel 6/ 1154 S Seventh Av, Hacienda Heights CA 91745. 818-968-9462/ Fax: 968-8184. V,M,DC,AE,D. Hwy 60/ Pomona Frwy at 7th Av. Pool, rstrnt, n/s rms, t pkng. Free local calls. $29-30/S; $33-34/D; $4/ex prsn. Disc.

Harbor City (Los Angeles area)

Motel 6/ 820 W Sepulveda Blvd, Harbor City CA 90710. 310-518-2034/ Fax: 835-2840. M,V,DC,D,AE. I-110 at Sepulveda Blvd; W on Sepulveda. Cable TV, n/s rms. Free local calls. $35/S; $39/D; $4/ex prsn. Disc.

Hayward (San Francisco area)

Motel 6/ 30155 Industrial Pkwy SW, Hayward CA 94544. 510-489-8333/ Fax: 489-1748. V,M,DC,AE,D. I-880 at Whipple Rd. N/s rms, nrby rstrnt. Free local calls. $29-32/S; $35-38/D; $6/ex prsn. Disc.

Super 8 Motel/ 21800 Foothill Blvd, Hayward CA 94544. 510-733-5012. M,V,D,CB,AE,DC. Hwy 580 at Foothill Blvd Exit to Hwy 238. B/f, n/s rms, copier, crib. $38/S; $42-44/D. Discs.

Super 8 Motel/ 2460 Whipple Rd, Hayward CA 94544. 510-489-3888/ Fax: 489-4070. V,M,DC,AE,D,CB. I-880, exit Whipple Rd E. B/f, n/s rms, pool, elevator, cont brfst, satellite TV, fax, copier, cot, crib. Free local calls. $39-40/S; $45-50/D; $5/ex prsn. Higher spec event, wknd rates. Discs.

Hemet

Super 8 Motel/ 3510 W Florida, Hemet CA 92343. 714-658-2281/ Fax: 925-6492. V,M,AE,DC,CB,D. Hwy 74 (Florida Av), 1/2 blk W of Sanderson Av. B/f, n/s rms, pool, whrlpool, cont brfst, t/b/rv pkng, elevator, cable TV, mtg rm, mtg rm, refrig, cot. Free crib. $39/S; $43-47/D; $4/ex prsn. Higher spec event rates. Discs.

Hesperia (Victorville area)

Days Suites/ 14865 Bear Valley Rd, Hesperia CA 92345. 619-948-0600/ Fax: 956-8645. V,AE,M,D,DC,CB,JCB. I-15 to Bear Valley Rd, turn E to mtl. Fax, n/s rms, rstrnt, whrlpool, mtg rm, b/f, exerc equip, t pkng, refrig, cable TV. Free local calls, cont brfst. $39-45/S; $45-55/D; $5/ex prsn. Discs.

Super 8 Motel/ 12033 Oakwood Av, Hesperia CA 92345. 619-949-3231. AE,

CALIFORNIA

V,M,DC,CB,D. I-15 to Bear Valley Rd, E to Mariposa Rd, turn S to Oakwood. B/f, n/s rms, pool, laundry, cable TV. No pets. $35/S; $40-42/D; $3/ex prsn. Discs.

Highland (Los Angeles area)
Super 8 Motel/ 26667 E Highland Av, Highland CA 92346. 909-864-0100/ Fax: 425-0612. V,M,AE,DC,CB,D. Hwy 215 to SR 30, E approx 4 mi to Highland Av, turn L. B/f, n/s rms, pool, cot, crib. Free local calls. No pets. AAA. $36/S; $38-41/D; $2/ex prsn. Discs.

Hollywood (Los Angeles Area)
Econo Lodge/ 777 N Vine St, Hollywood CA 90038. 213-463-5671. V,AE,M,DC. US 101: Sbnd, exit Vine; Nbnd, exit Melrose. Nrby rstrnt, pool, cable TV, laundry, n/s rms. Free cont brfst. No pets. $39-45/S; $45-50/D; $6/ex prsn. Discs.

Friendship Inn/ 5333 Hollywood Blvd, Hollywood CA 90027. 213-466-1691. V,AE,M,DC. US 101 (Hollywood Frwy), exit Hollywood Blvd E 1/4 mi. Nrby rstrnt, pool, eff, coffee, n/s rms. No pets. $36-40/S; $38-44/D; $4/ex prsn. Discs.

Hollywood Downtowner Motel/ 5601 Hollywood Blvd, Hollywood CA 90028. 213-464-7191/ Fax: 467-5863. V,M, AE, D,DC,CB. On Hollywood Blvd, 3 blks E of the Hollywood Frwy (101). Nrby rstrnt, pool, dd phone, fax, copier, cot, conn rms. Free coffee. No pets. $38-40/S; $40-42/D; $2/ex prsn. 6/15-10/15: $40/S; $42-44/D. Disc: TA, l/s. *Guaranteed rates.*

Huntington Beach (Los Angeles area)
Howard Johnson Lodge/ 17251 S Beach Blvd, Huntington Beach CA 92647. 714-375-0250/ Fax: 375-0251. M,V,D,CB,AE,DC. Frwy 405 to Beach Blvd S. Mtg rm, b/f, pool, t pkng, whrlpool, laundry, fax, copier. Free local calls, cont brfst. Gold Medal Winner. $42-65/S; $42-70/D. Discs.

Friendship Inn/ 18112 Beach Blvd, Huntington Beach, CA 92648. 714-841-6606. M,V,D,AE. I-405 (San Diego Frwy) Beach Blvd exit S to mtl. Nrby rstrnt, pool, fax, n/s rms, in-rm/lobby coffee, eff. No pets. AAA. $46-56/S; $48-62/D; $7/ex prsn. 6/1-9/15: $48-58/S; $52-67/D. Discs.

Indio
Motel 6/ 82195 Indio Blvd, Indio CA 92201. 619-342-6311/ Fax: 342-4157. M, V,DC,D,AE. I-10 to Monroe St, S to Indio Blvd, turn lt. Hwy 111 to Monroe St, N to Indio Blvd, turn rt. Nrby rstrnt, cable TV, laundry, pool, n/s rms, t pkng. Free local calls. $31-33/S; $35-37/D; $4/ex prsn. 12/21-5/22: $28/S; $32/D. Disc.

Inglewood (Los Angeles area -- near airport)
Econo Lodge/ 4123 W Century Blvd, Inglewood CA 90304. 310-672-7285. V,M,DC,AE. I-405, exit Century Blvd, E to mtl. Nrby rstrnt, fax, b/f, cable TV, n/s rms. AAA. $40-47/S; $42-50/D; $5/ex prsn. Discs.

Motel 6/ 5101 W Century Blvd, Inglewood CA 90304. 310-419-1234/ Fax: 677-7871. V,M,AE,D,DC. I-405 at Century Blvd. Near the airport. Cable TV, pool, n/s rms, arpt trans, mtg rm, elevator, rstrnt. Free local calls. Premier Award. $42/S; $48/D; $6/ex prsn. Higher spec event rates. Disc.

Rodeway Inn/ 3940 W Century Blvd, Inglewood CA 90241. 310-672-4570. M,V,D,AE. I-405, exit Century Blvd E. Nrby rstrnt, fax, b/f, cable TV, t pkng, n/s rms. Free cont brfst. No pets. $38-43/S; $40-45/D; $5/ex prsn. 5/1-9/30: $40-45/S; $45-50/D. Discs.

Super 8 Motel/ 4238 W Century Blvd, Inglewood CA 90303. 310-672-0740/ Fax: 672-1904. V,M,AE,DC,CB,D. Hwy 405 to Century Blvd, E to mtl. Hwy 110 to Century, W to mtl. Near LAX. B/f, n/s rms, cont brfst, elevator, elevator. No pets. AAA. $40-43/S; $40-51/D; $3/ex prsn. Higher spec event rates. Discs.

Irvine
Motel 6/ 1717 E Dyer Rd, Irvine CA 92705. 714-261-1515/ Fax: 261-1265. V,M,AE,D,DC. Hwy 55 at Dyer Rd, S of I-5. Rstrnt, cable TV, laundry, pool, arpt trans, n/s rms, whrlpool, t pkng. Free local calls. Premier Award. $38/S;

CALIFORNIA

$44/D; $6/ex prsn. Disc.

Jackson
El Campo Casa Resort Motel/ 12548 Kennedy Flat Rd, Jackson CA 95642. 209-223-0100. V,M,AE. Jct Hwys 49 & 88, bet Jackson & Sutter Creek. Nrby rstrnt, pool, playgrnd, cot, crib, conn rms. Free coffee, tea. AAA. $33-49/S; $38-60/D; $5/ex prsn. 5/1-9/30: $38-51/S; $42-70/D. Disc: Senior, bsns, TA, govt, trkr, milt.

King City
Motel 6/ 3 Broadway Cir, King City CA 93930. 408-385-5000/ Fax: 385-0943. M, \V,DC,D,AE. US 101 to Broadway exit, W to Broadway Cir. Cable TV, laundry, pool, n/s rms, t pkng. Free local calls. $26/S; $32/D; $6/ex prsn. Disc.

La Habra (Los Angeles area)
Motel 6/ 870 N Beach Blvd, La Habra CA 90631. 310-694-2158/ Fax: 691-8381. V,M,DC,AE,D. I-5/ Ventura Frwy take Beach Blvd/ Hwy 39 N 6 mi to Whittier Blvd to mtl. N/s rms, nrby rstrnt. Free local calls. $29/S; $33/D; $4/ex prsn. Disc.

La Jolla
Andrea Villa Inn/ 2402 Torrey Pines Road, La Jolla CA 92037. 619-459-3311/ 800-La Jolla. V,M,AE,D,DC. I-5: N, to Ardith Rd, rt to mtl; S, take La Jolla Village Dr to Torrey Pines, lt. Nrby rstrnt/ lounge, pool, whrlpool, n/s rms, cable TV, tt/dd phones, mtg rm, fax, copier, nwspr, laundry, refrig, microwave, cot, crib, outlets, eff, conn rms. Free cont brfst, coffee, tea, cocoa. AAA. $48/S or D; $10/ex prsn. Rates are for Sept-May. *Guaranteed rates.*

Inn at La Jolla/ 5440 La Jolla Blvd, La Jolla CA 92037. 619-454-6121/ Fax: 459-1377/ 800-525-6552. V,M,AE,D,DC,CB. I-95 to Grand/ Garnett, W to Mission Blvd, lt on La Jolla Blvd, 1 mi on lt. Nrby rstrnt/ lounge, pool, whrlpool, n/s rms, cable TV, tt phone, fax, copier, nwspr, refrig, cot, crib, b pkng, conn rms. Free cont brfst, coffee, tea, cocoa. AAA. $48-79/S or D; $10/ex prsn. 6/1-9/30: $69-99/S or D. Disc: Senior, bsns, TA.

La Jolla Shores Inn/ 5390 La Jolla Blvd, La Jolla CA 92037. 619-454-0175/ 800-525-6552. V,M,AE,D,DC,CB. I-95 to Garnett/ Grand, W to Mission Blvd, lt on La Jolla Blvd 1 mi. Nrby rstrnt/ lounge, pool, whrlpool, n/s rms, cable TV, tt phone, fax, copier, nwspr, refrig, cot, crib, b pkng, conn rms. Free cont brfst, coffee, tea, cocoa. AAA. $48-79/S or D; $10/ex prsn. 6/1-9/30: $69-99/S or D. Disc: Senior, bsns, TA, AAA.

La Mesa (San Diego area)
Days Inn/ 7475 El Cajon Blvd, La Mesa CA 91941. 619-697-9005/ Fax: 461-2121. V,AE,M,D,DC,CB,JCB. I-8 to 70th St, turn S to El Cajon Blvd. Fax, n/s rms, rstrnt, pool, whrlpool, mtg rm, b/f, kitchen, cable TV. Free cont brfst. All rooms are suites. $39-44/S; $44-49/D; $5/ex prsn. Disc.

Motel 6/ 7621 Alvarado Rd, La Mesa CA 92041. 619-464-7151/ Fax: 466-3859. V,M,DC,AE,D. I-8: Ebnd, exit Fletcher Pkwy, turn rt; Wbnd, exit 70th St, lt, lt on Alvarado Rd (frontage rd), E 3/4 mi. N/s rms, nrby rstrnt. Free local calls. $27/S; $33/D; $6/ex prsn. Disc.

Laguna Beach
Econo Lodge/ 1661 S Coast Hwy, Laguna Beach CA 92651. 714-494-9717. M,V,D,CB,AE,DC. On SR 1. Nrby rstrnt, pool, cable TV. Free cont brfst. No pets. $41-100/S or D; $10/ex prsn. 5/27-9/17: $60-130/S or D. Discs.

Lancaster
Motel 6/ 43540 17th St W, Lancaster CA 93534. 805-948-0435/ Fax: 940-0657. V,M,DC,AE,D. Hwy 14 at Av K, turn W to 17th St. Nrby rstrnt, pool, n/s rms. Free local calls. $28/S; $32/D; $4/ex prsn. Disc.

Lemon Grove
Oak National 9 Inn/ 8429 Broadway, Lemon Grove CA 92138. 619-463-9353. V,M,AE,DC. Hwy 94, exit Spring St. Adj rstrnt, laundry, pool, copier, fax, kitchens, cot, crib. All suites. No pets. $31-35/S; $33-45/D; $5/ex prsn.

Livermore
Motel 6/ 4673 Lassen Rd, Livermore CA 94550. 510-443-5300/ Fax: 606-

CALIFORNIA 32

9347. V,M,DC,AE,D. I-580 to Springtown Blvd, N to Lassen Rd, turn lt. Nrby rstrnt, pool, n/s rms. Free local calls. $32-33/S; $38-39/D; $6/ex prsn. Disc.

Lompoc

Motel 6/ 1521 N "H" St, Lompoc CA 93436. 805-735-7631/ Fax: 736-0537. V,M,DC,AE,D. Hwy 1 to Ocean Av, rt on "H" St. Cable TV, pool, nrby rstrnt, n/s rms. Free local calls. $24/S; $30/D; $6/ex prsn. Disc.

Lone Pine

Trails National 9 Inn/ 633 S Main St, Lone Pine CA 93545. 619-876-5555. V,M,AE,DC. On Hwy 395, in tn across from Mt Whitney Ranger Station. Pool, adj rstrnt, n/s rms, cable TV, refrig, microwave, in-rm coffee, fax. AAA. $45-59/S or D; $4/ex prsn. $60/suite. Spec events, holidays: Add $10.

Long Beach (Los Angeles area)

Friendship Inn/ 50 Atlantic Av, Long Beach CA 90802. 310-435-8369. V,M,DC,AE. I-405 (San Diego Frwy), exit Atlantic Av, S to Ocean Blvd. I-710 S, exit Dntn to Shoreline Dr, lt on Ocean Blvd, rt on Atlantic Av 1/2 blk. Nrby rstrnt, fax, cable TV, in-rm coffee, refrig, VCR, brfst, n/s rms. No pets. $36-46/S; $39-49/D; $5/ex prsn. 5/1-9/30: $39-49/S; $39-56/D. Discs.

Motel 6/ 5665 E 7th St, Long Beach CA 90804. 310-597-1311/ Fax: 597-2741. V,M,DC,AE,D. I-405: Sbnd, take Bellflower Blvd S 2 mi, rt on 7th St 1/2 blk; Nbnd, take 7th St Exit, W 3 mi to mtl. Nrby rstrnt, n/s rms. Free local calls. $34/S; $38/D; $4/ex prsn. Disc.

Vagabond Inn/ 150 Alamitos Av, Long Beach CA 90802. 310-435-7621/ Fax: 436-4011. V,AE,M. Hwy 710 (Long Beach Frwy) S to Alamitos Av (end of frwy) pass Ocean Blvd, N 1 blk to inn. Pool, nrby rstrnt, kitchenette, cable TV, conn rms. $44/S or D.

Los Angeles

Econo Lodge/ 11933 Washington Blvd W, Los Angeles CA 90066. 310-398-1651. AE,V,M,D,DC. I-405: Nbnd, exit Washington/Venice, rt on Sepulveda, rt on Washington Blvd; Sbnd, exit Venice, lt on Sawtelle, rt on Washington. Nrby rstrnt, cable TV, n/s rms. No pets. $40-55/S; $45-55/D; $5/ex prsn. Discs.

Econo Lodge/ 3400 W 3rd St, Los Angeles, CA 90020. 213-385-0061. AE, V, M, DC. US 101 to Vermont Av, S to mtl. I-110 N to US 101. Rstrnt, pool, mtg rm, fax, cable TV, n/s rms, t pkng. Free cont brfst. AAA. $39-49/S; $42-54/D; $5/ex prsn. 6/16-9/10: $42-54/S; $47-59/D. Discs.

Quality Inn/ 5410 Hollywood Blvd, Los Angeles, CA 90027. 213-463-7171. AE,V,MC,DC,D. From Hollywood Frwy (US 101) take Hollywood Blvd exit, S 2 blks to mtl. Rstrnt, pool, fax, b/f, t pkng, n/s rms. Free cont brfst. No pets. $45-80/S or D; $6/ex prsn. Discs.

Also see Anaheim, Arcadia, Baldwin Park, Bellflower, Buena Park, Claremont, Downey, Duarte, El Monte, Glendale, Hacienda Heights, Harbor City, Highland, Hollywood, Huntington Beach, Inglewood, La Habra, Long Beach, Norco, Norwalk, Orange, Pasadena, Pomona, Rosemead, Rowland Heights, San Dimas, Santa Ana, Santa Fe Springs, Sepulveda, Stanton, Sylmar, Upland, Westminster, Whittier.

Los Banos

Islander National 9 Inn/ 1620 Pacheco Blvd, Los Banos CA 93635. 209-826-3045. V,M,AE,DC. 6 mi E of I-15 on Hwy 152. Cable TV, pool, adj rstrnt, t pkng. $20-22/S; $25-32/D.

Lost Hills

Motel 6/ 14685 Warren St, Box 305, Lost Hills CA 93249. 805-797-2346/ Fax: 797-2976. M,V,DC,D,AE. I-5 to Hwy 46 (Lost Hills) exit, W to Warren St, turn N. Cable TV, laundry, pool, n/s rms, t pkng. Free local calls. $23/S; $29/D; $6/ex prsn. Disc.

Mammoth Lakes

Motel 6/ 3372 Main St, Box 1260, Mammoth Lakes CA 93546 619-934-6660/ Fax: 934-6989. V,M,AE,D,DC. US 395 to SR 203/ Mammoth Lakes Exit, W on Main St to cntr of Town to mtl. Nrby rstrnt, cable TV, laundry, pool, n/s rms. Free local calls. $39-44/S; $43-48/D; $4/ex prsn. Higher spec event rates. Disc.

CALIFORNIA

Marina (Monrerey area)
Motel 6/ 100 Reservation Rd, Marina CA 93933. 408-384-1000/ Fax: 384-0314. V,M,DC,D,AE. Hwy 1 to Reservation Rd exit, E to mtl. Adj rstrnt, cable TV, n/s rms. Free local calls. $38/S; $44/D; $6/ex prsn. 12/21-5/22: $33/S; $39/D. Disc.

Mariposa
Comfort Inn/ 4994 Bullion St, Box 1066, Mariposa CA 95338. 800-221-2222 --opening soon. M,V,D,AE. SR 99 to SR 140 E to Mariposa. Nrby rstrnt, pool, mtg rm, fax, b/f, whrlpool, cable TV, n/s rms. Free cont brfst. No pets. $48-72/S or D; $6/ex prsn. Discs.

Martinez (San Francisco area)
National 9 Motel/ 3999 Alhambra Av, Martinez CA 94553. 415-228-7471. V,M,AE,DC. Hwy 4 to Alhambra Av. Cable TV, pool, sauna, adj rstrnt. $39/S; $44/D; $7/ex prsn. Disc: Family.

Super 8 Motel/ 4015 Alhambra Ave, Martinez CA 94553. 510-372-5500/ Fax: 228-8830. V,M,AE,D,DC,AE. From Hwy 80 take SR 4 E, exit Alhambra Av, lt at traffic light. From Hwy 680, take SR 4 W, exit Alhambra, turn rt. B/f, n/s rms, cont brfst, cable TV, microwave, refrig. No pets. $43-46/S; $45-58/D; $5/ex prsn. Discs.

McFarland
Oasis National 9 Inn/ 855 2nd St, McFarland CA 93250. 805-792-2151. V,M,AE,DC. Elmo/ Perkins Exit, turn lt. Cable TV, dd phone, rstrnt/ lounge, pool. No pets. $22/S; $25-28/D.

Merced
Motel 6/ 1215 "R" St, Merced CA 953-40. 209-722-2737/ Fax: 723-6672. V, M,DC,AE,D. Hwy 99 at "R" St, W 1/2 blk. Nrby rstrnt, n/s rms. Free local calls. $25-26/S; $31-32/D; $6/ex prsn. Disc.

Motel 6/ 1410 "V" St, Merced CA 953-40. 209-384-2181/ Fax: 722-2152. M, V,DC,D,AE. Hwy 99 at Hwy 140/ Sonora-Gustin Exit, turn E to mtl. Cable TV, pool, n/s rms, t pkng. Free local calls. $27-28/S; $33-34/D; $6/ex prsn. Disc.

Milpitas (San Jose area)
Super 8 Motel/ 485 S Main St, Milpitas CA 95035. 408-946-1615/ Fax: 262-6128. M,V,D,CB,AE,DC. I-680 to Hwy 237, W to Main St exit, S to Corning. I-880 to Hwy 237, E to Serra Way, rt to Main St, 2nd rt. B/f, n/s rms, laundry, cont brfst, t/b/rv pkng, cot, crib. No pets. $42-45/S; $47-52/D; $4/ex prsn. Discs.

Modesto
Blue Mill National 9 Inn/ 1672 Herndon Rd, Modesto CA 95307. 209-537-4821. V,M,AE,DC. Hwy 99 S, exit Hatch Rd, rt on Herndon. Cable TV, in-rm coffee, pool, t pkng, VCR, b/f, n/s rms, cot. AAA. $38-42/S; $38-50/D; $7/ex prsn.

Motel 6/ 722 Kansas Av, Modesto CA 95351. 209-524-3000/ Fax: 578-1250. M,V,DC,D,AE. Hwy 99 to Kansas Av exit. Motel is just W of 99. Cable TV, pool, n/s rms. Free local calls. $28-29/S; $32-33/D; $4/ex prsn. Disc.

Motel 6/ 1920 W Orangeburg Av, Modesto CA 95350. 209-522-7271/ Fax: 578-0188. V,M,DC,AE,D. Hwy 99 exit Briggsmore E, follow Carpenter Rd to W Orangeburg, rt 1/4 mi. Nrby rstrnt, pool, n/s rms, t pkng. Free local calls. $29/S; $33/D; $4/ex prsn. Disc.

Mojave
Friendship Inn/ 15620 Sierra Hwy, Mojave CA 93501. 805-824-4523. V, AE,M,DC. Jct of SR 14 & SR 58. Nrby rstrnt, pool, fax, cable TV, eff, dd phone, n/s rms. $28-35/S; $35-45/D; $6/ex prsn. Discs.

Motel 6/ 16958 SR 58, Mojave CA 93501. 805-824-4571/ Fax: 824-8306. M,V,DC,D,AE. At jct of SR 58 & 14, N edge of town. Nrby rstrnt, cable TV, laundry, pool, n/s rms, t pkng. Free local calls. $25/S; $29/D; $4/ex prsn. Disc.

Vagabond Inn/ 2145 Hwy 58, Mojave CA 93501. 805-824-2463/ Fax: 824-9508. V,AE,M. At jct of Hwys 14 & 58 in Mojave, turn rt on 58 into Mojave to 2nd light, lt 2 blks to mtl. Nrby rstrnt, pool, t/b pkng, conn rms, refrig, cable TV. $40/S; $45/D.

CALIFORNIA

Monterey

Comfort Inn 1252 Munras Av, Monterey CA 93940. 408-372-2908. M,V,D,AE. SR 1 to Munras Av exit, turn NW to mtl. Nrby rstrnt, pool, fax, cable TV, n/s rms. Free cont brfst. No pets. $46-59/S; $48-59/D; $5/ex prsn. 5/1-6/30, 9/1-10/31: $56-75/S; $58-75/D. 7/1-8/31: $69-99/S or D. Discs.

Comfort Inn/ 1262 Munras Av, Monterey CA 93940. 408-372-8088. M,V,D,AE. SR 1 to Munras Av, turn NE to mtl. Nrby rstrnt, pool, fax, cable TV, n/s rms. Free cont brfst. No pets. $46-59/S or D; $5/ex prsn. 5/1-6/30, 9/1-10/31: $58-78/S or D. 7/1-8/31: $69-110/S or D. Discs.

Motel 6/ 2124 N Fremont St, Monterey CA 93940. 408-646-8585/ Fax: 372-7429. M,V,DC,D,AE. Hwy 1: Sbnd, to Casa Verde Exit, SE to Fremont; Nbnd, to Fremont Blvd/ Seaside exit. Nrby rstrnt, cable TV, pool, laundry, n/s rms. Free local calls. Sun-Thurs: $40/S or D. Fri, Sat, Holiday, Spec Event: $46/S or D. 5/23-11/1: $50/S or D. Higher spec event rates. Disc.

Super 8 Motel/ 2050 N Fremont St, Monterey CA 93940. 408-373-3081. M, V,D,CB,AE,DC. Hwy 1: Nbnd, take N Fremont St exit; Sbnd, take Casa Verde exit, lt then rt at signal. N/s rms, pool, whrlpool, sauna, cont brfst, cable TV, VCR/ movies, cot. Free local calls. No pets. AAA. $42-46/S; $42-52/D. Discs.

Also see Marina.

Moreno Valley (Riverside area)

Econo Lodge/ 24810 Sunnymead Blvd, Moreno Valley CA 92553. 909-247-8582/ Fax: 242-0949. V,AE,M,DC. SR 60 (Pamona Frwy), exit Perris, rt on Sunnymead Blvd. Rstrnt, pool, mtg rm, fax, cable TV. $35-40/S; $40-48/D; $3/ex prsn. Discs.

Motel 6/ 24630 Sunnymead Blvd, Moreno Valley CA 92553 909-243-0075/ Fax: 247-1349. V,M,DC,AE,D. Hwy 60 at Perris Blvd Exit. Adj rstrnt, cable TV, laundry, elevator, pool, n/s rms. Free local calls. $29/S; $33/D; $4/ex prsn. Disc.

Motel 6/ 23581 Alessandro Blvd, Moreno Valley CA 92553. 909-656-4451/ Fax: 653-0418. M,V,DC,D,AE. Hwy 60, Heacock St exit to Alessandro Blvd, turn W. Nrby rstrnt, cable TV, pool, n/s rms. Free local calls. $26/S; $30/D; $4/ex prsn. Disc.

Morro Bay

Econo Lodge/ 1100 Main St, Morro Bay CA 93442. 805-772-5609. V,M,D,AE, DC. Hwy 1 N, exit Main St, rt 1/2 mi. Adj rstrnt, nrby lounge, b/f, cable TV, n/s rms. No pets. $36-95/S; $38-99/D; $5/ex prsn. 5/27-7/31: $42-105/S; $44-115/D. 8/1-9/30: $56-115/S; $60-130/D. Discs.

Motel 6/ 298 Atascadero Rd, Morro Bay CA 93442. 805-772-5641/ Fax: 772-3233. M,V,DC,D,AE. From Hwy 1 take Atascadero Rd (Hwy 41) exit, W to mtl. Cable TV, pool, laundry, n/s rms, t pkng. Free local calls. $34/S; $40/D; $6/ex prsn. Higher spec event rates. Disc.

Mount Shasta

Swiss Holiday Lodge/ 2400 S Mt Shasta Blvd, Box 335, Mount Shasta CA 96067. 916-926-3446. V,M,AE,D,DC. Hwy 89 & I-5. Nrby lounge, pool, whrlpool, n/s rms, exerc equip, cable TV, playgrnd, arpt trans, tt/dd phone, refrig, cot, crib, outlets, t/b/rv pkng, conn rms. Free local calls, cont brfst, coffee, tea, cocoa. AAA/ Mobil. $35-41/S; $39-59/D; $4/ex prsn. Disc: Senior, bsns, TA. *Guaranteed rates.*

National City (San Diego area)

Econo Lodge National City/ 1640 E Plaza Blvd, National City CA 91950. 619-474-9202/ Fax: 474-6447. V, AE, M,DC. I-805 to Plaza Blvd, W 2 blks. From I-5: (S, exit 8th St, N, exit Plaza Blvd), E 1 mi to Palm Av. Nrby rstrnt, pool, n/s rms, cable TV, tt/dd phone, fax, copier, laundry, refrig, elevator, cot, conn rms, b/f. Free cont brfst, coffee. No pets. AAA. $29/S; $32-35/D; $3-6/ex prsn. Disc: Senior, bsns, TA, govt, l/s, milt. *Guaranteed rates.*c

Needles

Motel 6/ 1420 "J" St, Needles CA 92363. 619-326-3399/ Fax: 326-3857. M,V,DC,D,AE. I-40/US 66 to "J" St exit,

CALIFORNIA

turn S. Adj rstrnt, cable TV, pool, t pkng, n/s rms. Free local calls. $25/S; $29/D; $4/ex prsn. Disc.

Motel 6/ 1215 Hospitality Ln, Needles CA 92363. 619-326-5131/ Fax: 326-3854. V,M,DC,AE,D. I-40/ US 66 at "J" St exit. Cable TV, pool, n/s rms. Free local calls. $25/S; $29/D; $4/ex prsn. Disc.

Super 8 Motel/ 1102 E Broadway, Needles CA 92363. 619-326-4501/ Fax: 326-2054. V,M,AE,D,DC,AE. I-40 to US 95 S (Blythe Hwy)/ E Broadway. N/s rms, pool, laundry, outlets, cont brfst, t/b/rv pkng, cable TV, crib. Free local calls. No pets. Pride Award. $35/S; $40/D; $5/ex prsn. Higher wknd, spec event rates. Discs.

Newark

Motel 6/ 5600 Cedar Crt, Newark CA 94560. 510-791-5900/ Fax: 793-6273. M,V,DC,D,AE. I-880/Nimitz frwy to Mowry Av, W to Cedar Blvd, N to Cedar Crt. Nrby rstrnt, cable TV, laundry, pool, n/s rms, t pkng. Free local calls. $29-32/S; $35-38/D; $6/ex prsn. Disc.

Newbury Park (Thousand Oaks area)

Motel 6/ 2850 Camino Dos Rios, Newbury Park CA 91320. 805-499-0585/ Fax: 375-0977. M,V,DC,D,AE. US 101 at Wendy Dr Exit, NE to Camino Dos Rios. Cable TV, pool, n/s rms, t pkng. Free local calls. $29-30/S; $35-36/D; $6/ex prsn. Disc.

Newport Beach

See Costa Mesa.

Norco (Los Angeles area)

Howard Johnson Lodge/ 1685 Hammer Av, Norco CA 91760. 909-278-8886. AE,V,MC,DC,CB,D. I-15 to 2nd St, W to Hammer Av, turn lt. Mtg rm, b/f, pool, laundry. Free cont brfst. No pets. $40-60/S; $45-65/D. Disc.

North Highlands (Sacramento area)

Motel 6/ 4600 Watt Av, N Highlands CA 95660. 916-973-8637/ Fax: 971-9793. M,V,DC,D,AE. I-80 at Watt Av, turn N on Watt. Nrby rstrnt, cable TV, n/s rms. Free local calls. $34-36/S; $40-42/D; $6/ex prsn. Disc.

Rodeway Inn/ 3425 Orange Grove Av, N Highlands CA 95660. 916-488-4100. V,M,D,AE. I-80, exit Watt Av N, lt on Orange Grove Av. Nrby rstrnt, pool, mtg rm, b/f, cable TV, t pkng, laundry, n/s rms. Free arpt trans, cont brfst. $40-60/S; $45-65/D; $6/ex prsn. Discs.

Norwalk (Los Angeles area)

Comfort Inn/ 12512 Pioneer Blvd, Norwalk CA 90650. 310-868-3453. V,M, DC,AE. I-5 N, exit Imperial hwy, W on Pioneer Blvd to mtl. In dntn. Rstrnt, fax, b/f, whrlpool, cable TV, t pkng, n/s rms. Free cont brfst. No pets. $39-54/S; $44-69/D; $5/ex prsn. Discs.

Econo Lodge/ 12225 E Firestone Blvd, Norwalk CA 90650. 310-868-0791. V, AE,M,DC. I-5, exit Firestone Blvd N to mtl. Nrby rstrnt, pool, cable TV, n/s rms. Free cont brfst. $39/S; $44-49/D; $5/ex prsn. Discs.

Motel 6/ 10646 E Rosecrans Av, Norwalk CA 90650. 310-864-2567/ Fax: 864-0531. V,M,DC,AE,D. I-605 at Rosecrans Av, W to mtl. Rstrnt, n/s rms, t pkng. Free local calls. $30/S; $34/D; $4/ex prsn. Disc.

Oakland

Motel 6/ 8480 Edes Av, Oakland CA 94621. 510-638-1180/ Fax: 568-7501. M,V,DC,D,AE. I-880 at Hegenberger/ Coliseum exit, rt on Edes Av, at 1st light. Nrby rstrnt, cable TV, laundry, pool, n/s rms. Free local calls. Sun-Thurs: $36-40/S; $42-46/D. Fri, Sat, Holiday, Spec Events: $39-42/S; $45-48/D. 5/23-9/6: $42/S; $48/D. Higher spec event rates. Disc.

Oceanside

Motel 6/ 3708 Plaza Dr, Oceanside CA 92056. 619-941-1011/ Fax: 941-5608. M,V,DC,D,AE. I-5 to SR 78; go E to Plaza Dr, turn rt. Cable TV, pool, n/s rms. Free local calls. $30/S; $36/D; $6/ex prsn. Disc.

Motel 6/ 1403 Mission Av, Oceanside CA 92054. 619-721-6662/ Fax: 757-5192. M,V,DC,D,AE. I-5 to Mission Av exit. Just E of jct. Nrby rstrnt, cable TV, pool, n/s rms, t pkng. Free local calls. $30-32/S; $36-38/D; $6/ex prsn. Disc.

Comfort Inn/ 1440 Mission Av, Ocean-

CALIFORNIA

side, CA 92054. 619-967-4100. AE,V,MC,DC,D. I-5, exit to Mission Av (SR 76), E 1/2 blk to mtl. Nrby rstrnt, mtg rm, cable TV, n/s rms. Free cont brfst. No pets. $38-65/S or D; $10/ex prsn. Discs.

Ontario

Comfort Inn/ 2301 S Euclid Av, Ontario CA 91762. 909-986-3556. V,M,DC,AE. SR 60, Pomona Frwy, exit Euclid Av. Nrby rstrnt, pool, mtg rm, fax, b/f, whrlpool, cable TV, kitchenettes, n/s rms. No pets. $37-49/S; $39-50/D; $3/ex prsn. Higher spec event rates. Discs.

Motel 6/ 1515 N Mountain Av, Ontario CA 91762. 909-986-6632/ Fax: 460-9219. M,V,DC,D,AE. I-10 (San Bernardino Frwy) to Mountain Av exit S. Pomona Frwy (60) to Mountain Av N. Cable TV, pool, n/s rms. Free local calls. $29-31/S; $33-35/D; $4/ex prsn. Disc.

Motel 6/ 1560 E Fourth St, Ontario CA 91764. 909-984-2424/ Fax: 984-7326. M,V,DC,D,AE. I-10 at Fourth St exit; E on Fourth. Cable TV, pool, n/s rms. Free local calls. $29/S; $33/D; $4/ex prsn. Disc.

Ramada Limited/ 1120 E Holt Blvd, Ontario CA 91761. 909-984-9655/ Fax: 984-6355. V,AE,M,D,DC,CB,JCB. Hwy 10 to Holt Blvd, E on Holt Blvd to mtl. Pool, trans, b/f, n/s rms, rstrnt/ lounge. Free cont brfst. $33/S; $38-40/D; $6/ex prsn. Discs.

Super 8 Motel/ 514 N Vineyard Ave, Ontario CA 91764. 714-983-2886/ Fax: 988-2115. M,V,AE,D,DC,CB. Jct I-10 & Vineyard. B/f, n/s rms, pool, rstrnt/ lounge, whrlpool, cont brfst, copier, laundry. Free local calls, crib. No pets. $40-46/S; $44-49/D; $3/ex prsn. Discs.

Orange (Los Angeles - Disneyland area)

HoJo Inn/ 1930 E Katella, Orange CA 92667. 714-639-1121/ Fax: 639-3264. V,M,DC,AE,CB,D. Costa Mesa Frwy (US 55) at Katella exit. Rstrnt, pool, t pkng, cable TV, refrig, n/s rms. Gold Medal Winner. $35-55/S; $40-100/D. Discs.

Motel 6/ 2920 W Chapman Av, Orange CA 92668. 714-634-2441/ Fax: 634-0127. M,V,DC,D,AE. I-5 to Chapman Av, E to mtl. Cable TV, laundry, pool, rstrnt, n/s rms, t pkng. Free local calls. $29/S; $35/D; $6/ex prsn. Disc.

Oroville

Econo Lodge/ 1835 Feather River Blvd, Oroville CA 95965. 916-533-8201. AE,V,M,D,DC. SR 70, exit at Oro Dam, lt at Feather River Blvd. Nrby rstrnt, pool, fax, cable TV, t pkng, n/s rms. Free cont brfst. $32-48/S; $38-52/D; $7/ex prsn. Discs.

Motel 6/ 505 Montgomery St, Oroville CA 95965. 916-532-9400/ Fax: 534-7653. M,V,DC,D,AE. SR 70 to Montgomery St exit, E to Feather River Blvd. Cable TV, laundry, pool, rstrnt, n/s rms, t pkng. Free local calls. $27-29/S; $33-35/D; $6/ex prsn. Disc.

Oxnard

Friendship Inn/ 1012 S Oxnard Blvd, Oxnard CA 93030. 805-486-8381. M, V, D,AE. SR 1, 3 mi S of US 101. Adj rstrnt/ lounge, pool, mtg rm, fax, cable TV, t pkng, n/s rms. $40-45/S; $45-58/D; $8/ex prsn. 2/1-4/30: $42-49/S; $44-52/D. 5/1-12/31: $38-42/S; $43-46/D; $8/ex prsn. Spec events: $50-58/S; $58-88/D. Discs.

Palm Desert (Palm Springs area)

Motel 6/ 78100 Varner Rd, Palm Desert CA 92211. 619-345-0550/ Fax: 772-5027. M,V,DC,D,AE. I-10, to Washington St exit, N to Varner Rd, lt to mtl. Nrby rstrnt, cable TV, pool, n/s rms, t pkng. Free local calls. $30-33/S; $34-37/D; $4/ex prsn. Disc.

Palm Springs

Budget Host Inn/ 1277 S Palm Canyon Dr, Palm Springs CA 92264. 619-325-5574/ Fax: 327-2020. V,M,D,CD, CB,AE. 1/2 mi S of dntn on Hwy 111. Satellite TV, dd phone, in-rm coffee, refrig, n/s rms, nrby rstrnt/ lounge, pool, whrlpool, laundry, t pkng. No pets. $39-59/S; $45-69/D; $6/ex prsn. 2/1-4/15: $45-65/S; $49-75/D. 10/1-12/25: $35-45/S; $39-55/D. Spec Events: $89-99. Discs.

Howard Johnson/ 701 E Palm Canyon

Dr, Palm Springs CA 92264. 619-320-2700/ Fax: 322-5354. V,AE,M,D, DC, CB,JCB. I-10 to Indian Ave, S to Palm Canyon Dr, S to mtl. Lounge, pool, trans, t pkng, wading pool, whrlpool, fax, laundry, safe Deposit boxes. Gold Medal Winner. $46-86/S or D. Disc.

Motel 6/ 660 S Palm Canyon Dr, Palm Springs CA 92262. 619-327-4200/ Fax: 320-9827. M,V,DC,D,AE. I-10: Ebnd, take Hwy 111/ Palm Canyon Dr, go SE to mtl; Wbnd, Ramon Rd exit, go SW to Hwy 111/ E Palm Canyon Dr. Nrby rstrnt, cable TV, pool, laundry, elevator, whrlpool. Free local calls. Sun-Thurs: $32-37/S; $36-41/D; $4/ex prsn. Fri, Sat, Holidays, Spec Events: $36-38/S; $40-42/D. Higher spec event rates. Disc.

Motel 6/ 595 E Palm Canyon Dr, Palm Springs CA 92264. 619-325-6129/ Fax: 320-9304. M,V,DC,D,AE. I-10: Ebnd, Hwy 111 (Palm Canyon Dr) to mtl; Wbnd, Ramon Rd, SW to S Palm Canyon Dr/ Hwy 111, turn lt. Nrby rstrnt, cable TV, laundry, pool, n/s rms. Free local calls. Sun-Thurs: $32-35/S; $36-39/D; $4/ ex prsn. Fri, Sat, Holiday, Spec Events: $36-39/S; $40-43/D. Higher spec event rates. Disc.

Quality Inn/ 1269 E Palm Canyon Dr, Palm Springs CA 92264. 619-323-2775/ Fax: 323-4234. M,V,D,AE. ON SR 111. Rstrnt/ lounge, pool, mtg rm, whrlpool, cable TV, n/s rms. No pets. $39-155/S or D; $5/ex prsn. Discs.

Also see Desert Hot Springs, Palm Desert and Rancho Mirage.

Palmdale

Motel 6/ 407 W Palmdale Blvd, Palmdale CA 93551. 805-272-0660/ Fax: 272-8935. M,V,DC,D,AE. Antelope Valley Frwy (Hwy 14) to Palmdale Blvd, go NW to mtl. Nrby rstrnt, cable TV, laundry, pool, n/s rms. Free local calls. $26-29/S; $30-33/D; $4/ex prsn. Disc.

Super 8 Motel/ 200 W Palmdale Blvd, Palmdale CA 93550. 805-273-8000/ Fax: 266-4521. V,M,D,DC,DB,AE. Hwy 14 at Palmdale Blvd. B/f n/s rms, pool, cont brfst, whrlpool, cable TV, fax, copier, t/b/rv pkng, nrby rstrnt. No pets. AAA. $40-46/S; $44-49/D; $3/ex prsn. Discs.

Palo Alto

Motel 6/ 4301 El Camino Real, Palo Alto CA 94306. 415-949-0833/ Fax: 941-0782. M,V,DC,D,AE. US 101 (Bayshore Frwy), take San Antonio Rd S 1 1/2 mi to El Camino Real, turn rt 3 blks. Nrby rstrnt, cable TV, pool, elevator, n/s rms. Free local calls. $40/S; $46/D; $6/ex prsn. 12/21-4/10: $36/S; $42/D. 4/11-5/22: $43/S; $49/D. Higher spec event rates. Disc.

National 9 Inn/ 3339 El Camino Real, Palo Alto CA 94306. 415-493-2521. V, M,AE,DC. Hwy 101, exit Embarcadero Rd to Oregon Express, follow to El Camino, lt past 2nd light, on lt by China Lion. Cable TV, dd phone, microwave, refrig, nrby rstrnt, arpt trans. Free local calls, cont brfst. No pets. $32-35/S; $37-50/D.

Pasadena (Los Angeles area)

Econo Lodge/ 2860 E Colorado, Pasadena CA 91107. 818-792-3700. V,AE,M,DC. I-210, exit Sierra Madre Blvd S to Colorado Blvd E to mtl. Nrby rstrnt, fax, b/f, cable TV, n/s rms. Free cont brfst. No pets. $35-55/S; $40-60/D; $5/ex prsn. 12/28-1/2: $95-125/S; $105-145/D. Discs.

Paso Robles

Motel 6/ 1134 Black Oak Dr, Paso Robles CA 93446. 805-239-9090/ Fax: 238-6254. V,M,DC,AE,D. US 101 to Hwy 46, turn W. Nrby rstrnt, pool, n/s rms. Free local calls. $30/S; $36/D; $6/ex prsn. Disc.

Petaluma

Motel 6/ 1368 N McDowell Blvd, Petaluma CA 94952. 707-765-0333/ Fax: 765-4577. V,M,DC,AE,D. US 101: (Nbnd, Old Redwood Hwy/ Penngrove exit; Sbnd, Petaluma Blvd exit) N to Old Redwood Hwy, rt at 1st light to McDowell Blvd, N. Cable TV, pool, n/s rms, t pkng. Free local calls. $30-32/S; $36-38/D; $6/ex prsn. Disc.

Pico Rivera

Econo Lodge/ 8477 Telegraph Rd, Pico Rivera CA 90660. 310-869-9588. V,AE,M,DC. I-5 exit Rosemead, N to Telegraph Rd, W to mtl. From I-605, exit Telegraph Rd, W to Rosemead. Nrby rstrnt, fax, b/f, whrlpool, cable TV,

CALIFORNIA

n/s rms. Free cont brfst. No pets. $35-55/S; $40-59/D; $5/ex prsn. 5/1-9/7: $39-59/S; $44-65/D. 12/31-1/2: $69-99/S or D. Disc.

Pinole
Motel 6/ 1501 Fitzgerald Dr, Pinole CA 94564. 510-222-8174/ Fax: 262-9435. M,V,DC,D,AE. I-80 at Appian Way; S to Fitgerald Dr, turn W. Nrby rstrnt, cable TV, laundry, pool, n/s rms. Free local calls. $38-40/S; $44-46/D; $6/ex prsn. Disc.

Pismo Beach
Motel 6/ 860 4th St, Pismo Beach CA 93449. 805-773-2665/ Fax: 773-0723. M,V,DC,D,AE. US 101 at 4th St exit, turn S to mtl. Cable TV, laundry, pool, n/s rms, t pkng. Free local calls. Sun-Thurs: $26/S; $30/D; $4/ex prsn. Fri, Sat, Holiday, Spec Events: $30/S; $34/D. 5/23-9/6: $33/S; $37/D. Higher spec event rates. Disc.

Pittsburg
Motel 6/ 2101 Loveridge Rd, Pittsburg CA 94565. 510-427-1600/ Fax: 432-0739. M,V,DC,D,AE. Hwy 4 to Loveridge Rd exit, S to mtl. Nrby rstrnt, cable TV, pool, n/s rms, t pkng. Free local calls. $28-30/S; $34-36/D; $6/ex prsn. Disc.

Pleasanton
Motel 6/ 5102 Hopyard Rd, Pleasanton CA 94588. 510-463-2626/ Fax: 225-0128. V,M,DC,AE,D. I-580 at Hopyard Rd. Pool, n/s rms, t pkng. Free local calls. $33-36/S; $39-42/D; $6/ex prsn. Disc.

Pomona (Los Angeles area)
Motel 6/ 2470 S Garey Av, Pomona CA 91766. 909-591-1871/ Fax: 591-6674. V,M,DC,AE,D. Hwy 60 at Garey Av. Cable TV, pool, n/s rms, nrby rstrnt. Free local calls. $29/S; $33/D; $4/ex prsn. Disc.

Porterville
Motel 6/ 935 W Morton Av, Porterville CA 93257. 209-781-7600/ Fax: 782-9219. M,V,DC,D,AE. Rte 65 to Henderson Av, turn W to Porter, S to Morton, lt to mtl. Cable TV, laundry, pool, nrby rstrnt, n/s rms. Free local calls. $23/S; $27/D; $4/ex prsn. Disc.

Rancho Cordova (Sacramento area)
Comfort Inn/ 3240 Mather Field Rd, Rancho Cordova CA 95670. 916-363-3344. V,M,AE,D,DC. US 50 to Mather Field AFB, turn rt 1/4 mi to mtl. Nrby rstrnt, pool, mtg rm, fax, b/f, whrlpool, cable TV, t pkng, n/s rms. Free cont brfst. AAA. $45-74/S; $45-79/D; $10/ex prsn. Discs.

Motel 6/ 10271 Folsom Blvd, Rancho Cordova CA 95670. 916-362-5800/ Fax: 362-2753. M,V,DC,D,AE. US 50 to Mather AFB/Rancho Cordova exit, then N to Folsom Blvd. Nrby rstrnt, cable TV, pool, n/s rms. Free local calls. $28-29/S; $34-35/D; $6/ex prsn. Disc.

Motel 6/ 10694 Olson Dr, Rancho Cordova CA 95670. 916-635-8784/ Fax: 852-1469. V,M,DC,AE,D. Hwy 50, exit Zinfandel Drive N to Olson Dr. Nrby rstrnt, n/s rms. Free local calls. $29-30/S; $35-36/D; $6/ex prsn. Disc.

Rancho Mirage (Palm Springs area)
Motel 6/ 69-570 Hwy 111, Rancho Mirage CA 92270. 619-324-8475/ Fax: 328-0864. V,M,DC,AE,D. I-10 to Date Palm Dr, S to Hwy 111, turn lt. Adj rstrnt, pool, n/s rms, whrlpool. Free local calls. Sun-Thurs: $29-33/S; $33-37/D; $4/ex prsn. Fri, Sat, Holidays and Spec Events: $34-37/S; $38-41/D. Higher spec event rates. Disc.

Red Bluff
Motel 6/ 20 Williams Av, Red Bluff CA 96080. 916-527-9200/ Fax: 528-1219. M,V,DC,D,AE. I-5 to SR 36/ 99E, E to Sale Ln, turn rt to mtl. Nrby rstrnt, cable TV, pool, n/s rms, t pkng. Free local calls. $28-32/S; $34-38/D; $6/ex prsn. Disc.

Super 8 Motel/ 203 Antelope Blvd, Red Bluff CA 96080. 916-527-8882/ Fax: 527-5078. V,M,D,DC,AE. I-5 to Hwy 36 & 99, E to mtl. B/f, n/s rms, t/b/rv pkng, copies, satellite TV, cot. Free crib. Pride Award. AAA. $42-44/S; $47-52/D; $5/ex prsn. Higher spec event rates. Discs.

Value Lodge/ 30 Gilmore Rd, Red Bluff CA 96080. 916-529-2028/ Fax: 527-1702. V,M,AE,D. Pool, n/s rms, cable

TV, dd phone, laundry, cot, crib, nrby rstrnt, in rm coffee. AAA/ IMA. $37-39/S; $41-45/D; $4/ex prsn. 5/24-9/30: $41-43/S; $45-49/D. Disc: Family, AAA, senior, TA, IMA, st govt, comm.

Redding

Colony Inn/ 2731 Bechelli Ln, Redding CA 96002. 916-223-1935/ 800-354-5222. V,M,AE,D,DC,CB. I-5 to Cypress, W to Bechelli Ln, S 2 blks. Pool, n/s rms, cable TV, tt phones, fax, copier, b/f. Free local calls, cont brfst. No pets. AAA. $36/S; $44/D; $5/ex prsn. Disc: Senior, bsns, TA, govt, l/s, family, trkr, milt. *Guaranteed rates.*

Motel 6/ 2385 Bechelli Ln, Redding CA 96002. 916-221-0562/ Fax: 222-0458. V,M,DC,AE,D. I-5 at Cypress Av Exit, W to Bechelli Ln. Nrby rstrnt, pool, n/s rms. Free local calls. $32-36/S; $38-42/D; $6/ex prsn. Disc.

Motel 6/ 1250 Twin View Blvd, Redding CA 96003. 916-246-4470/ Fax: 246-4268. M,V,DC,D,AE. I-5 at Twin View Blvd, turn E. Cable TV, laundry, pool, n/s rms, t pkng. Free local calls. $38/S; $44/D; $6/ex prsn. 12/21-5/22: $32/S; $38/D. Disc.

Motel 6/ 1640 Hilltop Dr, Redding CA 96001. 916-221-1800/ Fax: 221-6175. M,V,DC,D,AE. I-5 to SR 44, exit E to Hilltop Dr, turn S 1 blk to mtl. Nrby rstrnt, cable TV, pool, laundry, n/s rms. Free local calls. $40/S; $46/D; $6/ex prsn. 5/21-5/22: $36/S; $42/D. Disc.

Super 8 Motel/ 5175 Churn Creek Rd, Redding CA 96002. 916-221-8881/ Fax: Ext 300. V,M,D,DC,AE. I-5 & Churn Creek Rd (SE corner). B/f, n/s rms, pool, whrlpool, sauna, b/t pkng, copier, cable TV, cot, crib. Free local calls. No pets. Pride Award. AAA. $42/S; $46-48/D; $4/ex prsn. Discs.

Redwood City

Super 8 Motel/ 2526 El Camino Real, Redwood City CA 94061. 415-366-0880/ Fax: 367-7958. M,V,D,CB,AE,DC. US 101 to Hwy 84/ Woodside Rd Exit, W to El Camino S. N/s rms. $39/S; $44-49/D. Discs.

Richmond

Super 8 Motel/ 1598 Carlson Blvd, Richmond CA 94804. 510-256-2665/ Fax: 428-4472. M,V,D,CB,AE,DC. I-80 at Carlson Blvd. N/s rms, cable TV, crib. Free local calls. No pets. $39/S; $42-55/D; $8/ex prsn. Discs.

Ridgecrest

Econo Lodge/ 201 Inyo-Kern Rd, Ridgecrest CA 93555. 619-446-2551. M,V,D,CB,AE,DC. US 395, exit SR 178E (Inyo-Kern Rd) 6 mi to motel. Nrby rstrnt, fax, cable TV, t pkng, dd phone, refrig. Free coffee. No pets. AAA. $44-50/S; $46-50/D; $2/ex prsn.

Motel 6/ 535 S China Lk Blvd, Ridgecrest CA 93555. 619-375-6866/ Fax: 375-8784. M,V,DC,D,AE. Hwy 395 at SR 178/ Ridgecrest exit, E about 8 mi to China Lk Blvd, S for 2 mi. Nrby rstrnt, cable TV, laundry, pool, n/s rms, t pkng. Free local calls. $26/S; $30/D; $4/ex prsn. Disc.

Riverside

Econo Lodge/ 1971 University Av, Riverside CA 92507. 909-684-6363. V,M,DC,AE. I-215/SR 60 to University, W to mtl. SR 91 to University, SE to mtl. Nrby rstrnt, pool, mtg rm, fax, cable TV, eff, n/s rms. $35-45/S; $38-48/D; $4/ex prsn. Discs.

Motel 6/ 1260 University Av, Riverside CA 92507. 909-784-2131/ Fax: 784-1801. V,M,DC,AE,D. I-215/ Hwy 91 at University Av. Nrby rstrnt, n/s rms. Free local calls. $26/S; $30/D; $4/ex prsn. Disc.

Motel 6/ 3663 La Sierra Av, Riverside CA 92505. 909-351-0764/ Fax: 687-1430. M,V,DC,D,AE. Hwy 91 at La Sierra Av exit, N to Diana Av. Adj rstrnt, cable TV, laundry, pool, n/s rms, t pkng. Free local calls. $26/S; $30/D; $4/ex prsn. Disc.

Also see Moreno Valley.

Rohnert Park

Motel 6/ 6145 Commerce Blvd, Rohnert Park CA 94928. 707-585-8888/ Fax: 585-3443. V,M,AE,D,DC. US 101 at Rohnert Park Expwy. Nrby rstrnt, cable TV, laundry, pool, n/s rms, t pkng. Free local calls. $30/S; $36/D; $6/ex prsn. Disc.

CALIFORNIA

Rosemead (Los Angeles area)
Motel 6/ 1001 S San Gabriel Blvd, Rosemead CA 91770. 818-572-6076/ Fax: 280-6992. M,V,DC,D,AE. Hwy 60 to San Gabriel Blvd N. I-10 (San Bernardino Frwy) to Walnut Grove S. Nrby rstrnt, cable TV, laundry, pool, n/s rms. Free local calls. $34/S; $38/D; $4/ex prsn. Disc.

Rowland Heights (Los Angeles area)
Motel 6/ 18970 E Labin Court, Rowland Heights CA 91748. 818-964-5333/ Fax: 912-2124. M,V,DC,D,CB. Hwy 60 at Nogales Av, S on Nogales. Nrby rstrnt, cable TV, laundry, pool, n/s rms, t pkng. Free local calls. $29-30/S; $33-34/D; $4/ex prsn. Disc.

Sacramento
Econo Lodge Sacramento/ 711 16th St, Sacramento CA 95814. 916-443-6631/ Fax: 442-7251/ 800-409-9595. V,M,AE,D,DC,CB. I-5 to "J" St, lt on 16th. 50/80 Wbnd, to 16th, rt 1 mi. 80 Bsns Ebnd, to 15th, lt on 16th, 1 mi. Nrby rstrnt, n/s rms, satellite TV, tt/dd phone, fax, refrig, elevator, microwave, cot, crib, b/f. Free cont brfst, coffee, tea, cocoa. No pets. AAA. $36/S; $40/D; $6/ex prsn. 5/24-9/2: $38/S; $42/D. Disc: Senior, govt, l/s, milt, AAA, AARP.

Gold Star Inn/ 6610 Stockton Blvd, Sacramento CA 95691. 916-399-8077. V,M,AE,DC. Hwy 99 S to Nbnd exit on Stockton Blvd. From Reno, exit 47th E (7th Ave). Cable TV, b/f, dd phone, kitchens. No pets. AAA/ National 9. $35-40/S; $40-50/D; $5/ex prsn.

Motel 6/ 7780 Stockton Blvd, Sacramento CA 95823. 916-689-9141/ Fax: 689-7340. V,M,AE,DC. Hwy 99 at Mack Rd Exit. Nrby rstrnt, cable TV, n/s rms. Free local calls. $30-32/S; $36-38/D; $6/ex prsn. Disc.

Motel 6/ 5110 Interstate Av, Sacramento CA 95842. 916-331-8100/ Fax: 339-2241. V,M,DC,AE,D. I-80 at Madison Av, E to mtl. N/s rms. Free local calls. $32-36/S; $38-42/D; $6/ex prsn. Disc.

Motel 6/ 7850 College Town Dr, Sacramento CA 95826. 916-383-8110/ Fax: 386-0971. M,V,DC,D,AE. US 50 at Howe Av/ Power Inn Exit; turn N on Howe to College Tn Dr. Nrby rstrnt, cable TV, pool, n/s rms. Free local calls. $32-34/S; $38-40/D; $6/ex prsn. Disc.

Motel 6/ 7407 Elsie Av, Sacramento CA 95828. 916-689-6555/ Fax: 689-6495. M,V,DC,D,AE. Hwy 99 at Mack Rd, E on Mack Rd, past Stockton Blvd to Elsie. Nrby rstrnt, cable TV, pool, n/s rms, t pkng. Free local calls. $30-32/S; $36-38/D; $6/ex prsn. Disc.

Motel 6/ 1415 30th St, Sacramento CA 95816. 916-457-0777/ Fax: 454-9814. M,V,DC,D,AE. Hwy 99 at I-80 Bsns exit, N to "N" or "J" St exits, immed N of jct with Hwy 99. Nrby rstrnt, cable TV, laundry, pool, n/s rms. Free local calls. $36-38/S; $42-44/D; $6/ex prsn. Disc.

Motel 6/ 227 Jibboom St, Sacramento CA 95814. 916-441-0733/ Fax: 446-5941. V,M,DC,AE,D. I-5/ Hwy 99 at Richards Blvd, W to mtl. Pool, nrby rstrnt, n/s rms, t pkng. Free local calls. $32-34/S; $38-40/D; $6/ex prsn. Disc.

Super 8 Motel/ 7216 55th St, Sacramento CA 95823. 916-427-7925/ Fax: 424-9011. V,M,DC,AE,D,CB. Hwy 99 at Florin Rd E. B/f, n/s rms, pool, t/b/rv pkng, copier, elevator, satellite TV, cot, crib. Free local calls. $40/S; $42-48/D; $4/ex prsn. Discs.

Also see North Highlands, Rancho Cordova.

Salinas
Motel 6/ 1010 Fairview Av, Salinas CA 93905. 408-758-2122/ Fax: 424-4781. M,V,DC,D,AE. US 101: NBnd, to Fairview exit; Sbnd, to 2nd Monterey Peninsula/ Sanborn Rd exit, lt under frwy, rt on Fairview. Cable TV, pool, n/s rms. Free local calls. $28-29/S; $34-35/D; $6/ex prsn. Disc.

Motel 6/ 140 Kern St, Salinas CA 93901. 408-753-1711/ Fax: 424-5187. V,M,DC,AE,D. Hwy 101, Market St Exit, E to Kern. Nrby rstrnt, pool, n/s rms, t pkng. Free local calls. $27-29/S; $33-35/D; $6/ex prsn. Disc.

Motel 6/ 1257 De La Torre Blvd, Salinas CA 93905. 408-757-3077/ Fax: 424-5185. M,V,DC,D,AE. Hwy 101 at Airport Blvd Exit, turn SE on De La

CALIFORNIA

Torre to mtl. Cable TV, laundry, pool, n/s rms, t pkng. Free local calls. $28-30/S; $34-36/D; $6/ex prsn. Higher spec event rates. Disc.

Salinas National 9 Inn/ 109 John St, Salinas CA 93901. 408-424-4801. V,M,AE,DC. US 101 bypass, exit John St. Cable TV, pool, family rms. $28/S; $30-36/D; $48/family unit. Wknds: $10 higher.

Super 8 Motel/ 1030 Fairview Av, Salinas CA 93905. 408-422-6486. M,V,D,CB,AE,DC. Hwy 101 to Sanborn Rd/ Monterey Peninsula, S on Sanborn, rt to Fairview. B/f, n/s rms, cont brfst. Free local calls, maps. AAA. $34-36/S; $39-40/D; $5/ex prsn. Discs.

San Bernardino

Motel 6/ 111 Redlands Blvd, San Bernardino CA 92408. 909-825-6666/ Fax: 872-1104. M,V,DC,D,AE. I-10 to Waterman Av. Cable TV, pool, n/s rms, nrby rstrnt/ t stop. Free local calls. $27-30/S; $31-34/D; $4/ex prsn. Disc.

Motel 6/ 1960 Ostrem's Way, San Bernardino CA 92407. 909-887-8191/ Fax: 880-9231. M,V,DC,D,AE. I-215 to University Pkwy exit, W to Hallmark Pkwy, turn lt to mtl. Adj rstrnt, cable TV, laundry, pool, n/s rms, t pkng. Free local calls. $29-31/S; $33-35/D; $4/ex prsn. Disc.

Super 8 Motel/ 777 W 6th St, San Bernardino CA 92410. 909-889-3561/ Fax: 884-7127. V,M,AE,DC,CB,D. I-215 to 5th St, turn E 1/4 blk. N/s rms, pool, whrlpool, cont brfst, t/b/rv pkng, cable TV, nwspr, refrig, laundry. Free local calls. No pets. $38/S; $41/D; $4/ex prsn. Discs.

San Diego

Comfort Inn/ 4610 DeSoto St, San Diego CA 92109. 619-483-9800. V, M, DC,AE. I-5: Sbnd, exit Balboa/ Garnet, turn lt at 2nd light to Damon St; Nbnd, exit Grand/ Garnet, turn rt at Santa Fe to mtl. Rstrnt, pool, whrlpool, cable TV, n/s rms. Free cont brfst. No pets. $39-79/S or D; $7/ex prsn. Discs.

Comfort Inn/ 1955 San Diego Av, San Diego CA 92110. 619-543-1130. M, V, D,AE. I-5 to Old Town Av, rt on San Diego Av, 1/2 mi to mtl. Nrby rstrnt, fax, b/f, whrlpool, cable TV, t pkng. Free cont brfst, trans. No pets. AAA. $40-60/S; $47-67/D; $7/ex prsn. Discs.

Econo Lodge/ 3880 Greenwood St, San Diego CA 92110. 619-543-9944. V, M,DC,AE. I-5 S or I-8 W, exit Rosecrans, rt on Hancock, rt on Greenwood. Rstrnt, fax, b/f, cable TV, t pkng, n/s rms. Free cont brfst. No pets. AAA. $39-59/S or D; $5/ex prsn. 7/1-9/4: $44-69/S or D. Discs.

Motel 6/ 2424 Hotel Cir N, San Diego CA 92108. 619-296-1612/ Fax: 543-9305. M,V,DC,D,AE. I-5 to I-8/ Taylor St Exit, go 1/2 mi E on I-8 to Taylor St & Hotel Cir Exit. Cable TV, pool, laundry, n/s rms, elevator, nrby rstrnt. Free local calls. $35-38/S; $39-42/D; $4/ex prsn. Disc.

Motel 6/ 5592 Clairemont Mesa Blvd, San Diego CA 92117. 619-268-9758/ Fax: 292-0832. M,V,DC,D,AE. I-805 at Clairemont Mesa Blvd; W. Nrby rstrnt, cable TV, n/s rms, t pkng. Free local calls. $35-36/S; $39-40/D; $4/ex prsn. Disc.

Quality Inn/ 2901 Nimitz Blvd, San Diego CA 92106. 619-224-3655. M, V, D,AE. I-5 or I-8, exit Rosecrans. Go 1 mi, lt on Nimitz Blvd, 1/2 blk on rt. Rstrnt/ lounge, pool, mtg rm, fax, b/f, cable TV, t pkng, n/s rms. No pets. AAA. $45-55/S or D; $6/ex prsn. 5/1-9/3: $45-60/S; $52-70/D. Discs.

Super 8 Motel/ 4540 Mission Bay Dr, San Diego CA 92109. 619-274-7888/ Fax: Ext 118. M,V,D,CB,AE,DC. I-5: Sbnd, to Balboa/ Garnet exit, go straight, pass 4 lights; Nbnd, to Grand/ Garnet exit, go straight, pass 2 lights. B/f, n/s rms, pool, cont brfst, laundry, b pkng, cable TV, TDD, refrig, copier, fax. Free trans. $35-38/S; $38-48/D; $4/ex prsn. Discs.

Super 8 Motel/ 1835 Columbia St, San Diego CA 92101. 619-544-0164/ Fax: 237-9940. M,V,AE,D,DC,CB. I-5; Sbnd, exit Front St, rt on Cedar, 2 blks to State, rt; Nbnd, exit Hawthorn St, lt on Columbia. B/f, n/s rms, cont brfst, cable TV, elevator. $42/S; $45-48/D; 36/ex prsn. Discs.

CALIFORNIA 42

Also see Chula Vista, El Cajon, La Mesa, National City, Spring Valley.

San Dimas (Los Angeles area)

Motel 6/ 502 W Arrow Hwy, San Dimas CA 91773. 909-592-5631/ Fax: 394-5909. M,V,DC,D,CB. I-210 at Arrow Hwy, turn SE on Arrow for 1/2 mi. Nrby rstrnt, cable TV, laundry, n/s rms. Free local calls. $30/S; $34/D; $4/ex prsn. Disc.

San Francisco

See Hayward, Martinez.

San Jose

Motel 6/ 2081 N First St, San Jose CA 95131. 408-436-8180/ Fax: 441-1656. M,V,DC,D,AE. US 101 at N First St exit, turn N on First St. Nrby rstrnt, cable TV, laundry, n/s rms. Free local calls. $39-40/S; $45-46/D; $6/ex prsn. Higher spec event rates. Disc.

Motel 6/ 2560 Fontaine Rd, San Jose CA 95121. 408-270-3131/ Fax: 270-6235. M,V,DC,D,AE. US 101 Bayshore Frwy to Tully Rd E Exit, turn rt on Alvin and immediately rt on Fontaine Rd. Nrby rstrnt, cable TV, laundry, pool, n/s rms, t pkng. Free local calls. $37-40/S; $41-46/D; $4-6/ex prsn. Disc.

Also see Campbell, Milpitas.

San Luis Obispo

Motel 6/ 1433 Calle Joaquin, San Luis Obispo CA 93401. 805-549-9595/ Fax: 544-2826. M,V,DC,D,AE. Hwy 101 to Los Osos Valley Rd exit, W to Calle Joaquin, rt to mtl. Cable TV, pool, n/s rms. Free local calls. Sun-Thurs: $30/S; $34/D; $4/ex prsn. Fri, Sat, Holidays, Spec Events: $33/S; $39/D; $6/ex prsn. Higher spec event rates. Disc.

Motel 6/ 1625 Calle Joaquin, San Luis Obispo CA 93401. 805-541-6992/ Fax: 547-1152. V,M,DC,AE,D. US Hwy 101 at Los Osos/ Baywood Pk Exit. Nrby rstrnt, pool, n/s rms. Free local calls. Sun-Thurs: $30/S; $34/D; $4/ex prsn. Fri, Sat, Holidays, Spec Events: $33/S; $37/D. 5/23-12/20: $29-31/S; $33-35/D. Disc.

Super 8 Motel/ 1951 Monterey St, San Luis Obispo CA 93401. 805-544-7895. V,M,D,DC,AE. Hwy 101 to Monterey St, turn S. B/f, n/s rms, pool, cable TV, nrby rstrnt, microwave, refrig. Free local calls, cont brfst. No pets. AAA. $41-49/S; $43-55/D; $3/ex prsn. Higher spec event, wknd, holiday rates. Discs.

San Mateo

Rancho Dolores National 9 Inn/ 2110 S El Camino Real, San Mateo CA 94403. 415-341-9231. V,M,AE,DC. On SR 82, 2 blks S of Jct SR 92. Cable TV, pool. No pets. $30-36/S; $36-48/D; $6/ex prsn.

San Miguel

National 9 Mission Inn/ 1099 K St, Box 327, San Miguel CA 93451. 805-467-3674. V,M,AE,DC. Hwy 101 exit 10th St. Cable TV, t pkng. No phones. $40/S; $45-50/D; $5/ex prsn.

San Rafael

Rainbow National 9 Inn/ 855 Francisco Blvd, San Rafael CA 94901. 415-456-8620. V,M,AE,DC. From 101 & 580, take Francisco Blvd exit. T pkng, n/s rms, dd phone, in-rm coffee, suites. No pets. $40-50/S; $45-60/D; $65/suites.

San Simeon

Motel 6/ 9070 Castillo Dr, San Simeon CA 93452. 805-927-8691/ Fax: 927-5341. V,M,AE,D,DC. Hwy 1 at Vista Del Mar. Rstrnt, cable TV, laundry, pool, n/s rms. Free local calls. Premier Award. Sun-Thurs: $40/S or D. Fri, Sat, Holidays, Spec Events: $46/S or D. Higher spec event rates. Disc.

San Ysidro

Motel 6/ 160 E Calle Primaro, San Ysidro CA 92173. 619-690-6663/ Fax: 690-1949. M,V,DC,D,AE. I-5 to Via de San Ysidro Blvd, W to Calle Primaro, S to mtl. Nrby rstrnt, cable TV, laundry, pool, n/s rms. Free local calls. $25-26/S; $31-32/D; $6/ex prsn. Disc.

Santa Ana (Los Angeles area)

Howard Johnson Lodge/ 939 E 17th St, Santa Ana CA 92701. 714-558-3700/ Fax: 568-1641. AE,V,MC,DC,CB,D. I-5 (Santa Ana Frwy), at 17th St Exit; E 1 blk. Hwy 55 to 17th St, 2 mi W. Mtg rm,

CALIFORNIA

b/f, pool, trans, t pkng, whrlpool, sauna, rstrnt. $42-45/S; $47-52/D. Discs.

Motel 6/ 1623 E First St, Santa Ana CA 92701. 714-558-0500/ Fax: 558-1574. M,V,DC,D,AE. I-5 at First St. Cable TV, n/s rms, whrlpool, nrby rstrnt, family suite. Free local calls. $30/S; $36/D; $6/ex prsn. Disc.

Santa Barbara

Motel 6/ 3505 State St, Santa Barbara CA 93105. 805-687-5400/ Fax: 569-5837. M,V,DC,D,AE. US 101 to Las Positas Rd, E to State St, lt 2 blks to mtl. Cable TV, pool, n/s rms. Free local calls. $42-47/S; $46-53/D; $4-6/ex prsn. Disc.

Also see Carpenteria, Goleta.

Santa Clara

Motel 6/ 3208 El Camino Real, Santa Clara CA 95051. 408-241-0200/ Fax: 243-8237. M,V,DC,D,AE. US 101 at Lawrence Expwy, go SW 2 1/2 mi to El Camino Real, lt 1/2 mi. Cable TV, pool, n/s rms. Free local calls. $34-37/S; $40-43/D; $6/ex prsn. Higher spec event rates. Disc.

Santa Cruz

Days Inn/ 325 Pacific Av, Santa Cruz CA 95060. 408-423-8564. V,AE,M,D, DC,CB,JCB. Hwy 17 or Hwy 1 to Ocean St, S to Soquel, rt to Front St, lt to Pacific Av, continue on Pacific to mtl. Fax, n/s rms, rstrnt, pool, b/f, family kitchens. Free cont brfst. $48-98/S or D; $6/ex prsn. Discs.

Econo Lodge/ 550 Second St, Santa Cruz CA 95060. 408-426-3626/ Fax: 458-3603. V,M,DC,AE. SR 17 S or SR 1 N, exit Ocean St, rt on San Lorenzo Blvd, lt on Riverside, rt on Second St. Nrby rstrnt, pool, fax, cable TV, eff, n/s rms. Free cont brfst. No pets. $28-95/S; $30-110/D; $10/ex prsn. 5/1-6/15: $38-110/S; $45-125/D. 6/16-9/15: $55-150/S; $65-175/D. 9/16-10/31: $32-95/S; $35-110/D. Disc.

Friendship Inn/ 505 Riverside Av, Santa Cruz CA 95060. 408-426-2899. V, M,D,AE. SR 17 S to Ocean St Beaches exit, follow Beach & Boardwalk sign. Nrby rstrnt, fax, cable TV, n/s rms. Free cont brfst. No pets. $26-75/S; $28-85/D; $10/ex prsn. 5/1-9/15: $52-130/S; $62-150/D. 3/1-4/30: $32-75/S; $42-85/D. Discs.

Super 8 Motel/ 338 Riverside Av, Santa Cruz CA 95060. 408-426-3707. V, M, DC, AE,D,CB. Hwy 1: Sbnd, to Laurel, rt to San Lorenzo, rt to Riverside, turn rt; Nbnd, to Ocean St to San Lorenzo, rt to Riverside, lt to mtl. B/f, n/s rms, pool, cont brfst, cable TV, refrig, microwave, cot, crib. Pride Award. $37/S; $41-43/D; $4/ex prsn. Higher wknd, spec event rates. Discs.

Super 8 Motel/ 321 Riverside Av, Santa Cruz CA 95060. 408-423-9449. M,V, D,CB,AE,DC. Hwy 1: Sbnd, rt on Laurel, rt on San Lorenzo, rt on Riverside; Nbnd, exit Ocean St, rt on San Lorenzo, lt on Riverside. B/f, n/s rms, pool, whrlpool, cont brfst, cable TV, cot, crib. Pride Award. $35/S; $39-43/D; $4/ex prsn. Discs.

Santa Fe Springs (Los Angeles area)

Motel 6/ 13412 Excelsior Dr, Santa Fe Springs CA 90670. 310-921-0596/ Fax: 926-2351. V,M,DC,AE,D. I-5 at Carmenita Rd Exit. N/s rms, nrby rstrnt. Free local calls. $29-30/S; $33-34/D; $4/ex prsn. Disc.

Santa Maria

Howard Johnson Lodge/ 210 S Nicholson Av, Santa Maria CA 93454. 805-922-5891/ Fax: 928-9222. M,V,D,CB, AE,DC. Hwy 101 to Main St, E to Nicholson Av, turn rt. Mtg rm, b/f, rstrnt, pool, t/b pkng, laundry, whrlpool, kiddie pool, fax, play area. Free coffee. $39-79/S or D. Discs.

Motel 6/ 2040 N Preisker Ln, Santa Maria CA 93454. 805-928-8111/ Fax: 349-1219. M,V,DC,D,AE. US 101 to Broadway St (Rte 135); S on Broadway to N Preisker Ln; lt to mtl. Cable TV, pool, n/s rms. Free local calls. $28-29/S; $32-33/D; $4/ex prsn. Disc.

Santa Nella

Motel 6/ 12733 S Hwy 33, Santa Nella CA 95322. 209-826-6644/ Fax: 827-1524. M,V,DC,D,AE. I-5 to Rte 33 exit, S on 33. Cable TV, pool, laundry, n/s rms, t pkng. Free local calls. $32-34/S;

CALIFORNIA 44

$38-40/D; $6/ex prsn. Disc.

Santa Rosa

Econo Lodge/ 1800 Santa Rosa Av, Santa Rosa CA 95407. 707-523-3480. V,AE,M,DC. US 101: Sbnd, exit Corby/ Santa Rosa, over the overpass, rt on Santa Rosa. lt on Colgan; Nbnd, exit Baker Av/ Santa Rosa. Nrby rstrnt, cable TV, t pkng, n/s rms. Free coffee. No pets. $36-51/S; $41-66/D; $5/ex prsn. Discs.

Motel 6/ 2760 Cleveland Av, Santa Rosa CA 95403. 707-546-1500/ Fax: 527-8070. M,V,DC,D,AE. US 101 at Steele Ln exit, W to Cleveland, rt 2 blks. Nrby rstrnt, cable TV, laundry, pool, n/s rms. Free local calls. $33/S; $39/D; $6/ex prsn. 5/23-11/1: $36/S; $42/D. Disc.

Motel 6/ 3145 Cleveland Av, Santa Rosa CA 95403. 707-525-9010/ Fax: 528-2761. V,M,DC,AE,D. US 101 at Steele Ln Exit, W to Cleveland Av, turn rt 1/2 mi. Nrby rstrnt, pool, n/s rms. Free local calls. $33/S; $39/D; $6/ex prsn. Disc.

Ramada Limited/ 866 Hopper Av, Santa Rosa CA 95403. 707-575-4600/ Fax: 575-0945. V,AE,M,D,DC,CB,JCB. Hwy 10: S, exit Hopper, SE to mtl; N, exit Mendocino Av, rt over frwy, rt onto Cleveland, N to Hopper, E to mtl. Pool, b/f, n/s rms, cable TV, refrig, adj rstrnt. Free cont brfst. Gold Key Award. $43-75/S; $47-85/D; $7/ex prsn. Disc.

Selma

Super 8 Motel/ 3142 S Highland Av, Selma CA 93662. 209-896-2800/ Fax: 896-7244. V,M,D,DC,CB,AE. Hwy 99 at Floral Av. B/f, n/s rms, pool, t/b/rv pkng, copier, cable TV, cot. Free crib. Pride Award. $43-46/S; $48-54/D; $5/ex prsn. Discs.

Sepulveda (Los Angeles area)

Comfort Inn/ 8647 Sepulveda Blvd, Sepulveda CA 91343. 818-893-3776. M,V,D,AE. I-405, Roscoe exit W to Sepulveda Blvd, turn N to mtl. Nrby rstrnt, pool, fax, b/f, cable TV, n/s rms. Free cont brfst. No pets. $38-48/S; $40-50/D; $5/ex prsn. 5/1-5/31: $35-43/S; $40-48/D. 6/1-10/31: $43-55/S; $50-65/D. Discs.

Motel 6/ 15711 Roscoe Blvd, Sepulveda CA 91343. 818-894-9341/ Fax: 894-2467. V,M,DC,AE,D. I-405 at Roscoe Blvd Exit. Pool, nrby rstrnt, n/s rms. Free local calls. $34/S; $40/D; $6/ex prsn. Disc.

Simi Valley

Motel 6/ 2566 N Erringer Rd, Simi Valley CA 93065. 805-526-3533/ Fax: 579-1664. M,V,DC,D,AE. Hwy 118/ Simi Valley Frwy at Erringer Rd exit, turn S on Erringer. Cable TV, pool, n/s rms. Free local calls. $38/S; $44/D; $6/ex prsn. Disc.

South Lake Tahoe

Motel 6/ 2375 Lake Tahoe Blvd, S Lake Tahoe CA 96150. 916-542-1400/ Fax: 542-2801. M,V,DC,D,AE. US 50 at SR 89, 4 mi W of CA/NV border. Nrby rstrnt, cable TV, pool, n/s rms. Free local calls. Sun-Thurs: $30-32/S; $32-36/D; $6/ex prsn. Fri, Sat, Holidays, Spec Events: $39-40/S; $40-45/D. 5/23-9/28: $43/S; $49/D. Higher spec event rates. Disc.

National 9 Inn/ 3901 Pioneer Trail, S Lake Tahoe CA 96157. 916-541-2119. V,M,AE,DC. On Hwy 50 at Pioneer Tr. Cable TV, pool, whrlpool, dd phone, t pkng, nrby rstrnt. $22-38/S; $28-47/D; $5/ex prsn. 6/1-9/17: $35-80/S; $45-95/D. 12/31-1/1: $95/S; $110/D; $10/ex prsn. Higher spec events, wknd rates.

Rodeway Inn/ 4082 Lake Tahoe Blvd, S Lake Tahoe CA 96150. 916-541-7900. M,V,D,AE. US 50 from Sacramento turns into Lake Tahoe Blvd in Lake Tahoe. Rstrnt, pool, fax, b/f, whrlpool, cable TV, t pkng, n/s rms. Free cont brfst. $44-62/S or D; $6/ex prsn. 5/1-6/30: $35-55/S or D. 7/1-9/30: $48-78/S or D. 10/1-1/1: $35-109/S or D. Discs.

Spring Valley (San Diego area)

Super 8 Motel/ 9603 Campo Rd, Spring Valley CA 91977. 619-589-1111/ Fax: 460-7561. V,M,AE,D,DC,AE. I-8: Ebnd, to Spring St, lt on Campo Rd 1 mi; Wbnd, to 125, S 1.5 mi to Spring St, lt on Campo Rd. N/s rms, pool, cont brfst, laundry, copier, VCR, kitchenettes. Free local calls, crib, cot, movies. AAA. $32-37/S; $38-49/D. Higher spec event/ holiday/ wknd rates. Disc.

Stanton (Los Angeles - Disneyland area)

Comfort Inn/ 11632 Beach Blvd, Stanton CA 90680. 714-891-7688. V,M,DC,AE. I-5, SR 91, SR 22 or I-405, exit Beach Blvd. Bet Orangewood & Chapman on Beach Blvd (SR 39). Nrby rstrnt, pool, b/f, whrlpool, cable TV, t pkng, outlets, n/s rms. No pets. $44-59/S; $48-64/D; $4/ex prsn. 5/1-6/15, 9/5-12/21: $38-54/S; $42-59/D. Discs.

Motel 6/ 7450 Katella Av, Stanton CA 90680. 714-891-0717/ Fax: 373-6537. M,V,DC,D,AE. I-5 to Artesia/ Knott Ave Exit, S on Knott 4.7 mi to Katella Av, E 1/2 mi to mtl. Cable TV, pool, nrby rstrnt, n/s rms, t pkng. Free local calls. $25/S; $29/D; $4/ex prsn. Disc.

Stockton

Econo Lodge/ 2210 S Manthey Rd, Stockton CA 95206. 209-466-5741. V,AE,M,DC. I-5, exit 8th St. Nrby rstrnt, fax, pool, b/f, cable TV, laundry, eff, n/s rms. Free coffee. No pets. AAA. $36-38/S; $38-46/D; $5/ex prsn. 5/1-10/31: $36-40/S; $38-48/D. Spec events: $55-75/S; $65-80/D. Discs.

Motel 6/ 6717 Plymouth Rd, Stockton CA 95207. 209-951-8120/ Fax: 474-3829. V,M,DC,AE,D. I-5 to Benjamin Holt Drive Exit, E, lt on Plymouth Rd. Pool, n/s rms, nrby rstrnt. Free local calls. $28-30/S; $34-36/D; $6/ex prsn. Disc.

Motel 6/ 1625 French Camp Turnpike Rd, Stockton CA 95206. 209-467-3600/ Fax: 464-2659. M,V,DC,D,AE. I-5, exit Eighth St, go E, 1st lt on French Camp Tnpk Rd, about 1 mi. Cable TV, laundry, pool, n/s rms, t pkng. Free local calls. $27-28/S; $33-34/D; $6/ex prsn. Disc.

Motel 6/ 817 Navy Dr, Stockton CA 95206. 209-946-0923/ Fax: 464-3948. V,M,DC,AE,D. I-5 at Charter Way Exit, turn W to Navy Dr. Nrby rstrnt, pool, n/s rms, t pkng. Free local calls. $27-28/S; $33-34/D; $6/ex prsn. Disc.

Sunnyvale

Motel 6/ 775 N Mathilda Av, Sunnyvale CA 94086. 408-736-4595/ Fax: 738-2271. M,V,DC,D,AE. US 101 at Mathilda Av/ So Sunnyvale exit, just W of 101. Cable TV, laundry, elevator, pool, n/s rms. Free local calls. $40-42/S; $46-48/D; $6/ex prsn. Higher spec event rates. Disc.

Motel 6/ 806 Ahwanee Av, Sunnyvale CA 94086. 408-720-1222/ Fax: 720-0630. M,V,DC,D,AE. US 101 at Mathilda Av/ So Sunnyvale Exit, S to mtl. Adj rstrnt, cable TV, pool, n/s rms. Free local calls. $35-37/S; $41-43/D; $6/ex prsn. Higher spec event rates. Disc.

Sylmar (Los Angeles area)

Friendship Inn/ 12783-87 San Fernando Rd, Sylmar CA 91342. 818-367-1223. V,AE,M,DC. I-405/ I-5, exit Roxford St E, Sylmar to San Fernando Rd. Sbnd I-210, Roxford St W to San Fernando Rd, S. Nrby rstrnt, pool, fax, b/f, cable TV, n/s rms. No pets. $38-40/S; $42-44/D; $6/ex prsn. 5/1-5/25, 9/5-12/28: $36-38/S; $40-42/D. 5/26-9/4: $42/S; $45-52/D. Discs.

Motel 6/ 12775 Encinitas Av, Sylmar CA 91342. 818-362-9491/ Fax: 364-6914. M,V,DC,D,AE. I-5/I-210 at Roxford St exit. Bet I-5 & I-210. Cable TV, laundry, pool, nearby rstrnt, n/s rms. Free local calls. $30-35/S; $36-41/D; $6/ex prsn. Disc.

Super 8 Motel/ 14955 Roxford St, Sylmar CA 91342. 818-367-0141/ Fax: 367-2236. M,V,D,CB,AE,DC. I-5: Sbnd, to I-210, E to Roxford St, exit; Nbnd, to I-5 to I-210, E to Roxford St. B/f, n/s rms, pool, whrlpool, copier, cont brfst, mtg rm, elevator. $38-40/S; $41-48/D; $3/ex prsn. Discs.

Tahoe Vista

Cedar Glen Lodge/ 6589 N Lake Blvd, Box 188, Tahoe Vista CA 96148. 916-546-4281/ Fax: 546-2250. V,M,D,AE. Lodge overlooking Lake Tahoe. Pool, nrby rstrnt, cable TV, dd phone, whrlpool, sauna, playgrnd, refrig, in-rm coffee, n/s rms. Free cont brfst, nwspr. AAA/ IMA. Sun-Thurs: $43/S; $48/D; $8/ex prsn. Fri, Sat, 1/12-1/15, 2/15-2/19: $50/S; $55-68/D. 2 or 3 night minimum may apply. 4/19-5/23: $39-40/S; $40-50/D. Disc: TA, IMA.

Temecula

Motel 6/ 41900 Moreno Dr, Temecula CA 92590. 909-676-7199/ Fax: 676-

CALIFORNIA

2619. M,V,DC,D,AE. I-15 at Rancho California Rd; W to Front St, lt to Moreno Dr. Nrby rstrnt, cable TV, pool, n/s rms. Free local calls. $29-30/S; $35-36/D; $6/ex prsn. Disc.

Thousand Oaks
Econo Lodge/ 1425 Thousand Oaks Blvd, Thousand Oaks CA 91362. 805-496-0102/ Fax: 494-1295. V,AE,M,DC. US 101, exit Rancho Rd, rt on Thousand Oaks Blvd. SR 23, exit Thousand Oaks Blvd. Nrby rstrnt, pool, fax, b/f, cable TV, t pkng. Free coffee, cont brfst. No pets. AAA. $36-50/S; $42-58/D; $10/ex prsn. 5/1-9/30: $42-52/S; $50-65/D. Discs.

Motel 6/ 1516 Newbury Rd, Thousand Oaks CA 91320. 805-499-0711/ Fax: 375-0887. V,M,DC,AE,D. US Hwy 101 at Ventu Park Rd Exit, S to Newbury Rd, W to mtl. Nrby rstrnt, cable TV, pool, n/s rms. Free local calls. $30/S; $36/D; $6/ex prsn. Disc.

Also see Newbury Park.

Tracy
Motel 6/ 3810 Tracy Blvd, Tracy CA 95376. 209-836-4900/ Fax: 833-1949. M,V,DC,D,AE. I-205 at Tracy Blvd. W of I-5. Cable TV, laundry, pool, n/s rms, t pkng, nrby rstrnt. Free local calls. $29/S; $33/D; $4/ex prsn. Disc.

Tulare
Friendship Inn/ 26442 SR 99, Tulare CA 93274. 209-688-0501. V,AE,M,DC. SR 99, Tagus exit. Nrby rstrnt, pool, cable TV, t pkng, n/s rms. Free cont brfst. $30-35/S; $35-40/D; $3/ex prsn. 2/12-2/15: $45-50/S; $55-60/D. 5/1-10/31: $35-40/S; $40-45/D. Discs.

Motel 6/ 1111 N Blackstone Dr, Tulare CA 93274. 209-686-1611/ Fax: 686-6374. M,V,DC,D,AE. Hwy 99 N, take Hillman St/ Prosperity Av exit, lt on Prosperity Av. From 99 S, take Prosperity Av/Blackstone Dr exit, lt on Blackstone Dr. Nrby rstrnt, cable TV, pool, n/s rms. Free local calls. $27-29/S; $33-35/D; $6/ex prsn. Disc.

Turlock
Motel 6/ 250 S Walnut Av, Turlock CA 95380. 209-667-4100/ Fax: 667-8306. M,V,DC,D,AE. Hwy 99: Patterson/W Main or Main St exit; W on Main to S Walnut Rd, turn S. Cable TV, laundry, pool, n/s rms, t pkng, nrby rstrnt. Free local calls. $27-28/S; $33-34/D; $6/ex prsn. Disc.

Twentynine Palms
Motel 6/ 72562 Twentynine Palms Hwy, Twentynine Palms CA 92277. 619-367-2833/ Fax: 367-4965. V,M,DC,AE,D. Twentynine Palms Hwy at 49 Palms Rd, in Twentynine Palms. Rstrnt, cable TV, pool, n/s rms, t pkng. Free local calls. Premier Award. $32-33/S; $36-37/D; $4/ex prsn. Disc.

Ukiah
Cottage Inn Motel/ 755 State St, Ukiah CA 95402. 707-462-8509. V,M,AE,DC. Whrlpool, indr pool, dd phone, coffee, cot, crib, suites. National 9. $29-38/S; $33-45/D; $5/ex prsn. $56-95/suites. Higher spec event rates.

Motel 6/ 1208 S State St, Ukiah CA 95482. 707-468-5404/ Fax: 462-8405. M,V,DC,D,AE. Hwy 101: Talmage Rd Exit W to State St, turn S to mtl. Nrby rstrnt, cable TV, pool, n/s rms. Free local calls. $30/S; $36/D; $6/ex prsn. 5/23-9/28: $35/S; $41/D. Disc.

Super 8 Motel/ 1070 S State St, Ukiah CA 95482. 707-462-6657/ Fax: 468-8665. AE,V,M,DC,CB,D. Hwy 101 to Talmage Rd exit, W to State S, rt. B/f, n/s rms, pool, arpt trans, nrby rstrnt/lounge, b/t pkng, cable TV, cont brfst, cot, refrig. Free local calls. $40-46/S; $44-56/D; $4/ex prsn. Higher spec event, wknd rates. Discs.

Upland (Los Angeles area)
Comfort Inn/ 1282 W 7th St, Upland CA 91786. 714-985-8115/ Fax: 985-9136. V,M,DC,AE. I-10 to Mountain Av, N to 7th St, W 1 blk to mtl. Nrby rstrnt, pool, fax, b/f, cable TV, n/s rms. Free cont brfst. No pets. AAA. $36-46/S; $40-50/D; $2-3/ex prsn. 2/1-10/31: $38-48/S; $42-52/D. Discs.

Vacaville
Motel 6/ 107 Lawrence Dr, Vacaville CA 95687. 707-447-5550/ Fax: 447-7625. M,V,DC,D,AE. I-80 at I-505 Winters /Redding Exit. Nrby rstrnt, cable TV,

pool, laundry, n/s rms, t pkng. Free local calls. $28-32/S; $34-38/D; $6/ex prsn. Disc.

Super 8 Motel/ 101 Allison Court, Vacaville CA 95688. 707-449-8884/ Fax: 449-9132. V,M,DC,AE,D,CB. I-80 at Monte Vista to Allison Court. B/f, n/s rms, pool, fax, copier, cont brfst, satellite TV, cot, crib. Free local calls. $40/S; $45-50/D; $5/ex prsn. Discs.

Vallejo

Motel 6/ 597 Sandy Beach Rd, Vallejo CA 94590. 707-552-2912/ Fax: 645-9324. V,M,DC,AE,D. I-80 E, exit Sonoma Blvd. I-80 W, exit Maritime Academy Rd. Cable TV, pool, n/s rms, t pkng. Free local calls. $28-30/S; $34-36/D; $6/ex prsn. Disc.

Motel 6/ 1455 Marine World Pkwy, Vallejo CA 94589. 707-643-7611/ Fax: 554-0138. V,M,DC,AE,D. I-80 at Hwy 37/San Rafael, W 1 1/2 mi to mtl. Nrby rstrnt, n/s rms. Free local calls. $29-30/S; $35-36/D; $6/ex prsn. Disc.

Motel 6/ 458 Fairgrounds Dr, Vallejo CA 94589. 707-642-7781/ Fax: 647-7231. M,V,DC,D,AE. I-80 at Redwood St, W of I-80. Cable TV, laundry, elevator, pool, n/s rms. Free local calls. $30-32/S; $36-38/D; $6/ex prsn. Disc.

Royal Bay Inn/ 44 Admiral Callaghan Lane, Vallejo CA 94591. 707-643-1061/ Fax: 643-4719. V,M,D,DC,CB,JCB. I-80 Sbnd, Exit Tennessee St E; Nbnd: exit Tennessee St W. Admiral Callaghan Ln at Tennessee St. Rstrnt/ lounge, b/f, pool, fax, laundry, cable TV, t pkng, cont brfst, n/s rms, cot. Free local calls. AAA/ IMA Sun-Thurs: $30-44/S; $37-53/D; $7/ex prsn. Fri-Sat: $37-51 /S; $37-53/D; $4/ex prsn. Disc: TA, IMA. Senior and AAA discounts may apply.

Ventura

Motel 6/ 3075 Johnson Dr, Ventura CA 93003. 805-650-0080/ Fax: 339-0926. M,V,DC,D,AE. US 101 at Johnson Dr Exit, NE on Johnson. Cable TV, laundry, pool, elevator, n/s rms, whrlpool. Free local calls. $36/S; $40/D; $4/ex prsn. Disc.

Motel 6/ 2145 E Harbor Blvd, Ventura CA 93001. 805-643-5100/ Fax: 643-4519. M,V,DC,D,AE. US 101 at Seaward Av Exit, S on Seaward to Harbor Blvd, turn rt. Cable TV, pool, n/s rms, t pkng. Free local calls. $33-34/S; $37-38/D; $4/ex prsn. Disc.

Victorville

Motel 6/ 16901 Stoddard Wells Rd, Victorville CA 92392. 619-243-0666/ Fax: 243-2554. M,V,DC,D,AE. I-15 at Stoddard Wells Exit. Nbnd, 1st exit; Sbnd, 2nd exit. Nrby rstrnt, cable TV, pool, n/s rms, t pkng. Free local calls. $24/S; $28/D; $4/ex prsn. Disc.

Also see Hesperia.

Visalia

Econo Lodge/ 1400 S Mooney Blvd, Visalia CA 93277. 209-732-6641. V, M, D,AE,DC. SR 198, exit Mooney Blvd, rt to mtl. Rstrnt, pool, fax, cable TV, n/s rms. Free cont brfst. No pets. AAA. $39-45/S; $41-49/D; $5/ex prsn. 5/1-10/31: $41-51/S; $45-55/D. Discs.

Walnut Creek

Motel 6/ 2389 N Main St, Walnut Creek CA 94596. 510-935-4010. V,M,D, DC, CB,AE. Hwy 24 to I-680 N, Exit Main St, SE. Cable TV, nrby rstrnt, n/s rms, pool. Free local calls. Sun-Thurs: $40/S; $46/D; $6/ex prsn. Fri, Sat, Holidays, Spec Events: $44/S; $50/D. S; $46-48/D. 5/23-9/6: $44/S; $50/D. Higher spec event rates.

Watsonville

Motel 6/ 125 Silver Leaf Dr, Watsonville CA 95076. 408-728-4144/ Fax: 722-1173. V,M,DC,D,AE. SR 1 to Green Valley Rd, E to Silver Leaf Dr. Nrby rstrnt, cable TV, pool, elevator, n/s rms. Free local calls. $35-39/S; $41-45/D; $6/ex prsn. Disc.

Weed

Motel 6/ 466 N Weed Blvd, Weed CA 96094. 916-938-4101/ Fax: 938-2436. M,V,DC,D,AE. I-5 at Hwy 97/ N Weed Exits. Cable TV, laundry, pool, n/s rms. Free local calls. $29-34/S; $35-40/D; $6/ex prsn. Disc.

West Sacramento

Motel 6/ 1254 Halyard Dr, W Sacramento CA 95691. 916-372-3624/ Fax:

CALIFORNIA 48

372-0849. V,M,DC,AE,D. I-80: Wbnd, exit Harbor Blvd S, rt on Halyard; Ebnd, exit Harbor Blvd. Pool, n/s rms, nrby rstrnt. Free local calls. $29-30/S; $35-36/D; $6/ex prsn. Disc.

Westley

Days Inn/ 7144 McCracken Rd, Westley CA 95387. 209-894-5500/ Fax: 894-3291. V,AE,M,D,DC,CB,JCB. I-5 at Westley exit. Fax, n/s rms, nrby rstrnt, pool, whrlpool, b/f, t pkng, cot. $38-45/S; $42-48/D; $5/ex prsn. Disc.

Westminster (Los Angeles area)

Motel 6/ 6266 Westminster Av, Westminster CA 92683. 714-891-5366/ Fax: 373-4287. M,V,DC,D,AE. I-405 at Westminster Av Exit. Cable TV, pool, nrby rstrnt, n/s rms. Free local calls. $32/S; $38/D; $6/ex prsn. Disc.

Motel 6/ 13100 Goldenwest, Westminster CA 92683. 714-895-0042/ Fax: 894-3423. V,M,DC,D,AE. SR 22/ Garden Grove Freeway to Goldenwest Exit, S to mtl. Cable TV, pool, nrby rstrnt, n/s rms. Free local calls. $30/S; $34/D; $4/ex prsn. Disc.

Super 8 Motel/ 15559 Beach Blvd, Westminster CA 92683. 714-895-5584. V,M,DC,AE,D,CB. 1 blk N of I-405, Beach Blvd exit. B/f, n/s rms, pool, elevator, cable TV, cot, crib. No pets. $35-38/S; $37-45/D; $3/ex prsn. Discs.

Whittier (Los Angeles area)

Days Inn/ 14330 Telegraph Rd, Whittier CA 90604. 310-944-4760/ Fax: 944-4376. V,AE,M,D,DC,CB,JCB. Frwy 605 to Telegraph Rd, E to mtl. Frwy 5 to Valley View, rt to Telegraph Rd, rt to mtl. Fax, n/s rms, nrby rstrnt, pool, whrlpool, mtg rm, b/f, t pkng, cable TV, cot. Free cont brfst. $40-43/S; $45-58/D; $5/ex prsn. Discs.

Motel 6/ 8221 S Pioneer Blvd, Whittier CA 90606. 310-692-9101/ Fax: 908-9561. M,V,DC,D,AE. I-605, at Washington Blvd/ Slauson Exits. E of 605. Cable TV, pool, nrby rstrnt, n/s rms, t pkng. Free local calls. $29-30/S; $33-34/D; $4/ex prsn. Disc.

Williams

Motel 6/ 455 4th St, Williams CA 95987. 916-473-5337/ Fax: 473-5132. M,V,DC,D,AE. I-5 at Bsns Rte 20; W of I-5, N of Hwy 20. Nrby rstrnt, cable TV, laundry, pool, nrby rstrnt, n/s rms, t pkng. Free local calls. $30-32/S; $36-38/D; $6/ex prsn. Disc.

Willows

Days Inn/ 475 N Humboldt, Willows CA 95988. 916-934-4444/ Fax: 934-0222. V,AE,M,D,DC,CB,JCB. I-5 at Willows Hwy 162 exit. Fax, n/s rms, rstrnt, pool, whrlpool, b/f, t pkng, microwave, refrig, cable TV. $32-50/S; $36-64/D; $5/ex prsn. Discs.

Super 8 Motel/ 457 Humboldt Av, Willows CA 95988. 916-934-2871/ Fax: 934-5512. V,M,D,DC,CB,AE. I-5 & Hwy 162 at Humboldt Av. B/f, n/s rms, t/b/rv pkng, outlets, cont brfst, cable TV, cot. Free crib. $39-43/S; $44-50/D; $5/ex prsn. Higher spec event rates. Discs.

Woodland

Motel 6/ 1564 Main St, Woodland CA 95776. 916-666-6777/ Fax: 668-4367. M,V,DC,D,AE. I-5 at Main St/Woodland Exits, W to mtl. Cable TV, pool, n/s rms, nrby rstrnt. Free local calls. $30-34/S; $36-40/D; $6/ex prsn. Disc.

Yreka

Motel 6/ 1785 S Main St, Yreka CA 96097. 916-842-4111/ Fax: 842-7864. M,V,DC,D,AE. I-5 at Ft Jones Exit, W to Main St, turn rt. Nrby rstrnt, cable TV, laundry, pool, n/s rms. Free local calls. $34/S; $40/D; $6/ex prsn. 12/21-5/22: $29/S; $35/D. Disc.

Yuba City

Motel 6/ 700 N Palora Av, Yuba City CA 95991. 916-674-1710/ Fax: 755-4378. M,V,DC,D,AE. Hwy 99 at Bridge St Exit, 1/2 mi S of jct with SR 20. Cable TV, pool, n/s rms, t pkng. Free local calls. $30-32/S; $36-38/D; $6/ex prsn. Disc.

Yucca Valley

Super 8 Motel/ 57096 29 Palms Hwy, Yucca Valley CA 92284. 619-228-1773/ Fax: 365-7799. V,M,D,DC,CB,AE. Hwy 62 at Barberry Av. B/f, n/s rms, t/b/rv pkng, cable TV, cot. Free crib. Pride Award. $41-43/S; $46-50/D; $5/ex prsn. Higher spec event rates. Discs.

COLORADO

Colorado

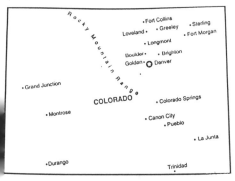

Alamosa
Super 8 Motel/ 2505 W Main, Alamosa CO 81101. 719-589-6447/ Fax: 589-4167. AE,V,M,D,CB,DC. W end of Alamosa, Hwy 160 (Main), next to Burger King. B/f, n/s rms, cont brfst, copier, hot tub, laundry, mtg rm, cable TV, suites. Free local calls. AAA. $41/S; $45-49/D; $6/ex prsn. 5/21-10/31: $46/S; $51-56/D. Higher spec event rate. Discs.

Brighton (Denver area)
Super 8 Motel/ 1020 Old Brighton Rd, Brighton CO 80601. 303-659-6063/ Fax: 659-9367. V,M,AE,DC,CB,D. US 85 at Bromley Ln. B/f, n/s rms, outlets, t/b/rv pkng, cable TV, suites, cot, crib. Free local calls. $31-37/S; $35-40/D; $3/ex prsn. Discs.

Brush
Budget Host Empire Motel/ 1408 Edison, Brush CO 80723. 303-842-2876. AE,D,M,V. I-76 (Exit 90A) to SR 71, S to US 34, rt 1 mi. Cable TV, dd phone, n/s rms, cot, t pkng across st. Free crib. AAA. $28-32/S; $34-43/D; $3/ex prsn. Disc.

Buena Vista
Alpine Lodge/ 12845 Hwy 24 & 285, Buena Vista CO 81211. 719-395-2415. V,M,AE. Hwys 24 & 285, 2 mi S of Buena Vista on the Arkansas River. Nrby rstrnt/ lounge, n/s rms, playgrnd, arpt trans, tt/dd phone, microwave, cot, crib, outlets, b/f pkng, conn rms, b/f. No pets. AAA. $28-62/S; $32-62/D; $5/ex prsn. 5/1-10/1: $37-70/S or D. Disc: Senior, AAA. Guaranteed rates.

Burlington
Chaparral Budget Host/ 405 S Lincoln, Burlington CO 80807. 719-346-5361/ Fax: 346-8502. AE,M,V,D,DC,CB. 1 blk off I-70 & Hwy 385, Exit 437. Cable TV, dd phone, conn rms, n/s rms, pool, hot tub, adj rstrnt, t pkng, outlets, cot, crib. AAA/ Mobil. $28-34/S; $30-38/D; $4/ex prsn. 6/1-9/15: $33-43/S; $34-44/D. Discs.

Super 8 Motel/ 2100 Fay, Burlington CO 80807. 719-346-5627. V,M,AE,DC,CB,D. I-70 (Exit 437) at US 385, N 2 blks. B/f, n/s rms, outlets, t/b/rv pkng, cable TV, cot, suites. Free local calls, crib. Pride Award. $35/S; $39-41/D; $3/ex prsn. Discs.

Canon City
Super 8 Motel/ 209 N 19th St, Canon City CO 81212. 719-275-8687/ Fax: Ext 121. D,M,V,AE,DC,CB. Hwy 50 & 19th St. B/f, n/s rms, laundry, outlets, b/t pkng, copier, cable TV, cot, crib. Free local calls. $29-31/S; $31-34/D; $4/ex prsn. 5/1-10/31: $39-50/S; $45-50/D. Higher spec event rate. Discs.

Castle Rock
Super 8 Motel/ 1020 Park St, Castle Rock CO 80104. 303-688-0880. V,M, AE,DC,CB,D. I-25 (Exit 182) to Wolfensberger Rd, W 1 blk to Park St. B/f, n/s rms, b pkng, cable TV, fax, mtg rm, cot. Free local calls, crib. $37-44/S; $40-51/D; $3/ex prsn. Discs.

Colorado Springs
Dale Downtown Motel/ 620 W Colorado Av, Colorado Springs CO 80905. 719-636-3721/ Fax: 636-9049/ 800-456-3204. V,M,AE,D,DC,CB. I-25 (Exit 142) to Bijou, W 2 blks to Walnut, S 4 blks to Colorado, W 1 blk to mtl. Nrby rstrnt/ lounge, pool, n/s rms, cable TV, tt/dd phone, fax, copier, refrig, cot, crib, outlets, t/b pkng, eff, conn rms, b/f. No pets. AAA. $29/S; $36/D; $5/ex prsn. 5/15-9/15: $40/S; $48/D. Guaranteed rates.

Comfort Inn/ 8280 SR 83, Colorado Springs CO 80920. 719-598-6700. V,M, AE,DC. I-25 (Exit 150A) to Black Forest/ Academy Blvd to SR 83. Nrby rstrnt, pool, mtg rm, fax, b/f, cable TV, n/s rms. Free cont brfst. AAA. $40/S;

COLORADO

$45/D; $5/ex prsn. 5/1-9/30: $59/S; $65/D. 10/1-12/31: $35/S; $39/D. Discs.

Days Inn/ 4610 Rusina Rd, Colorado Springs CO 80907. 719-598-1700/ Fax: 592-9029. V,M,AE,D,CB,DC,JCB. I-25 (Exit 146) at Garden of the Gods Rd. Fax, n/s rms, rstrnt/ lounge, pool, mtg rm, b/f, t pkng, laundry, cot. Free cont brfst. $39-60/S; $44-65/D; $5/ex prsn. 5/26-9/6: $68-120/S; $75-125/D. 9/7-9/30: $50-85/S; $55-90/D. Discs.

Econo Lodge/ 714 N Nevada Av, Colorado Springs CO 80903. 719-636-3385. V,M,AE,DC. I-25 (Exit 143) Uintah St to Nevada, rt 4 blks. Nrby rstrnt, pool, fax, cable TV, coffee, eff, n/s rms. $32-58/S; $35-69/D; $5/ex prsn. Discs.

Econo Lodge/ 1623 S Nevada Av, Colorado Springs CO 80906. 719-632-6651. V,M,D,AE,DC. I-25 N, exit 140A; I-25 S, exit 140B. Nrby rstrnt, pool, mtg rm, b/f, cable TV, kitchen, playgrnd, suites, n/s rms. No pets. $35-55/S; $40-65/D; $5/ex prsn. Discs.

Howard Johnson/ 5056 N Nevada Av, Colorado Springs CO 80918. 719-598-7793/ Fax: 531-6831. AE,V,M,DC, CB,D. I-25, Exit 148A. N/s rms, b/f, pool, t pkng, cable TV, laundry, picnic area, t/b/rv pkng. Free local calls, cont brfst. No pets. $40-110/S or D. Discs.

Motel 6/ 3228 N Chestnut St, Colorado Springs CO 80907. 719-520-5400/ Fax: 630-0377. V,M,D,AE,DC. I-25, take Fillmore St (Exit 145) W to Chestnut (Frontage Rd). Cable TV, pool, laundry, n/s rms. Free local calls. $30-34/S; $36-40/D; $6/ex prsn. 5/2-10/11: $42/S; $48/D. Higher spec event rates. Disc.

Quality Inn/ 555 W Garden of Gods Rd, Colorado Springs CO 80907. 719-593-9119. V,M,D,AE. I-25 (Exit 146) at Garden of Gods Rd, W 1 blk. Nrby rstrnt, pool, mtg rm, fax, b/f, cable TV, t pkng, exerc equip, n/s rms. Free cont brfst, pm snacks. $39-75/S or D; $5/ex prsn. 5/26-9/5: $72-125/S or D. Discs.

Rodeway Inn/ 2409 E Pikes Peak, Colorado Springs CO 80909. 719-471-0990. V,M,D,AE. I-25: N, (Exit 143) to Uintah, W to Union, S to Pikes Peak, W to mtl; S, (Exit 135) to Academy, N to Pikes Peak, E to mtl. Nrby rstrnt, pool, mtg rm, fax, cable TV, n/s rms, family rms. AAA. $40-43/S; $43-45/D; $6/ex prsn. 5/1-9/16: $47-58/S; $56-65/D. Discs.

Super 8 Motel/ 605 Peterson Rd, Colorado Springs CO 80915. 719-597-4100. V,M,AE,DC,CB,D. NE corner of US 24 & Peterson Rd. B/f, n/s rms, outlets, t/b/rv pkng, cont brfst, cable TV, cot, crib. Free local calls. No pets. AAA. $35/S; $39/D; $4/ex prsn. 5/16-9/30: $45/S; $49-50/D. Higher spec event rate. Discs.

Also see Woodland Park.

Cortez

Arrow Motor Inn National 9/ 440 S Broadway, Cortez CO 81321. 970-565-3755/ Fax: 565-7214/ 800-727-7692. V,M,AE,D,DC. On US 160 & 666 in Cortez. Pool, whrlpool, n/s rms, cable TV, dd phone, fax, laundry, refrig, microwave, cot, crib, t/b pkng. Free coffee, tea. AAA/ National 9. $36/S; $39-46/D; $4/ex prsn. 5/23-9/4: $44-48/S; $44-58/D. Disc: Trkr, AAA.

Super 8 Motel/ 505 E Main St, Cortez CO 81321. 970-565-8888/ Fax: 565-6595. AE,DC,D,M,V,CB. 5 blks E of City Ctr on Hwy 160. B/f, n/s rms, in-rm coffee, laundry, outlets, t/b/rv pkng, toast bar, cable TV, suites, cot, crib. Free local calls. No pets. $39/S; $43-46/D; $2/ex prsn. 5/13-10/29: $47-56/S; $51-60/D. Higher spec event rate. Discs.

Craig

Super 8 Motel/ 200 Hwy 13 S, Craig CO 81625. 303-824-3471. V,M,AE,DC, CB,D. 1/2 mi S of US 40. B/f, n/s rms, toast bar, t/b/rv pkng, outlets, cable TV, cot, crib. Free local calls. $29-32/S; $34-39/D; $4-7/ex prsn. 10/12-11/18: $45/S; $49-56/D. Higher spec event rate. Discs.

Denver

Howard Johnson Lodge/ 4765 Federal Blvd, Denver CO 80211. 303-433-8441/ Fax: 458-0863. AE,V,M,DC,CB,D. I-70 W (Exit 277) to Federal Blvd. 2 mi W of I-25/ I-76 Exit at Federal Blvd, S 2 mi. N/s rms, mtg rm, b/f, rstrnt/ lounge, pool, t pkng, cable TV. No pets. $35-

65/S; $40-70/D. 5/1-9/30: $45-90/S; $50-95/D. Discs.

Motel 6/ 3050 W 49th Av, Denver CO 80221. 303-455-8888/ Fax: 433-2218. V,M,D,AE,DC. I-70 (Exit 272) to Federal Blvd, N to 49th Av, lt on 49th. Nrby rstrnt, cable TV, indr pool, n/s rms, t pkng, elevator. Free local calls. $28-32/S: $34-38/D; $6/ex prsn. Disc.

Motel 6/ 12020 E 39th Av, Denver CO 80239. 303-371-1980/ Fax: 375-7763. M,V,DC,D,AE. I-70 (Exit 281) to Peoria St, S to 39th Av, turn rt on frontage rd. Cable TV, laundry, pool, nrby rstrnt, n/s rms, t pkng. Free local calls. $32-34/S; $38-40/D; $6/ex prsn. Disc.

Super 8 Motel/ 2601 Zuni St, Denver CO 80211. 303-433-6677/ Fax: 455-1530. D,M,V,AE,DC,CB. I-25 at (Exit 212B) Speer Blvd N. Pool, nrby rstrnt, game rm, cable TV, suites. Free local calls. $35/S; $37-40/D; $2/ex prsn. Higher spec event rate. Discs.

Super 8 Motel/ 5888 N Broadway, Denver CO 80216. 303-296-3100/ Fax: 296-0786. AE,V,M,D,DC,CB. I-25 (Exit 215) at 58th St. On W side of I-25. B/f, n/s rms, pool, laundry, cable TV, t/b/rv pkng, cot. Free local calls, crib. $39/S; $41-43/D; $3/ex prsn. Higher spec event rate. Discs.

Also see Brighton, Englewood, Greenwood Village, Henderson, Lakewood, Thornton, Westminster, Wheat Ridge.

Dove Creek

Country Inn Motel/ 442 W Hwy 666, Box 521, Dove Creek CO 81324. 303-677-2234. V,M,AE,DC. Cable TV, dd phone. National 9. $25/S; $28-30/D; $3/ex prsn. 4/1-11/30: $34/S; $36-42/D.

Durango

Comfort Inn/ 2930 N Main Av, Durango CO 81301. 303-259-5373. V,M,D,AE. US 160 N to Main Av, N 1 mi. Nrby rstrnt, pool, fax, b/f, whrlpool, cable TV, n/s rms. Free cont brfst. No pets. Hospitality Award. AAA. $40-79/S; $45-90/D; $5/ex prsn. 5/1-6/17: $50-84/S; $52-93/D. 6/18-8/18: $78-84/S; $84-93/D. 8/19-10/18: $60-84/S; $74-93/D. Discs.

Econo Lodge/ 2002 Main Av, Durango CO 81301. 303-247-4242. V,M,D,AE,DC. US 160, N on Camino Del Rio to Main Av. Nrby rstrnt, pool, whrlpool, cable TV, t pkng, outlets, n/s rms, family rms, kitchens, VCR. No pets. $29-34/S; $32-39/D; $4/ex prsn. 5/1-5/18, 10/8-10/31: $39-56/S; $49-66/D. 5/19-9/10: $62-72/S; $66-82/D. 6/16-9/10: $72-86/S; $79-94/D. 9/11-10/7: $58-68/S; $64-74/D.Discs.

Englewood (Denver area)

Super 8 Motel/ 5150 S Quebec St, Englewood CO 80111. 303-771-8000/ Fax: 771-0058. V,M,D,AE,DC,CB. I-25 to Belleview, W on Belleview to Quebec, lt on Quebec. In the Denver Tech Cntr. N/s rms, elevator, nrby rstrnt/ lounge. Free local calls. $43/S; $47-49/D; $4/ex prsn. Discs.

Evans (Greeley area)

Motel 6/ 3015 8th Av, Evans CO 80620. 303-351-6481/ Fax:353-3024. M,V,DC, D,AE. US 85: Sbnd, to Denver exit, go 2 blks S; Nbnd, to 31st St, turn lt then rt to mtl. Cable TV, laundry, pool, n/s rms, t pkng. Free local calls. $27-30/S; $33-36/D; $6/ex prsn. Disc.

Florence

Riviera Motel/ 136 E Front St, Florence CO 81226. 719-784-6716. V,M,AE,DC. On US Hwy 115 S from Colorado Springs, 5 mi off Hwy 50. Microwave, refrig, hot tub. Free coffee. No pets. National 9. $28-35/S; $30-50/D; $5/ex prsn.

Fort Collins

Budget Host Inn/ 1513 N College Av, Ft Collins CO 80524. 303-484-0870/ Fax: 224-2998. AE,D,M,V. 1 mi N of dntn on US 287. Cable TV, tt phone, in-rm coffee, n/s rms, family rms, kitchens, adj rstrnt, hot tub, picnic area, cot. Free crib. No pets. AAA. Winter: $35/S; $43-46/D; $5/ex prsn. Summer: $46/S; $46-53/D. Spec events: $66.

Days Inn/ 3625 E Mulberry, Ft Collins CO 80524. 970-221-5490/ Fax: 482-4826. V,M,AE,D,CB,DC,JCB. I-25 at I-14, turn E along 14 to mtl. Fax, n/s rms, nrby rstrnt, b/f, t pkng, arpt trans, cable TV, in-rm coffee. Free local calls, cont brfst. $30-42/S; $35-45/D; $5/ex

COLORADO

prsn. 4/1-5/11: $37-44/S; $42-49/D. 5/12-9/30: $42-49/S; $47-54/D. Discs.

Motel 6/ 3900 E Mulberry, Ft Collins CO 80524. 303-482-6466/ Fax: 493-8189. M,V,DC,D,AE. I-25 (Exit 269B), W on Hwy 14, rt on 1st frontage rd. Nrby rstrnt, cable TV, laundry, pool, n/s rms, t pkng. Free local calls. $27-32/S; $33-38/D; $6/ex prsn. Disc.

National 9 Inn/ 3634 E Mulberry St, Ft Collins CO 80524. 303-482-1114. V,M,AE,DC. I-25, Exit 269 B. Adj rstrnt, laundry, cable TV. No pets. $40/S; $40-60/D; $5/ex prsn.

Sleep Inn/ 3808 Mulberry St, Ft Collins CO 80524. 303-484-0814. V,M,D,AE. I-25 (Exit 269 B) to Mulberry St, W 1/4 mi to mtl. Nrby rstrnt, cable TV, n/s rms. Free cont brfst. $32-39/S; $38-48/D; $5/ex prsn.

Super 8 Motel/ 409 Centro Way, Ft Collins CO 80524. 970-493-7701/ Fax: Ext 300. AE,V,MC,DC,CB,D. I-25 (Exit 269B) at Hwy 14. B/f, n/s rms, whrlpool, sauna, laundry, outlets, t/b/rv pkng, cable TV, suite, mtg rm, TDD, cot. Free local calls, crib. $37-44/S; $42-51/D; $5/ex prsn. Discs. 7/23-8/2: $44/S; $49-51/D. Discs.

Fort Morgan

Econo Lodge/ 1409 Barlow Rd, Ft Morgan CO 80701. 303-867-9481. V,AE,M,DC. At I-76 (Exit 82) & Barlow Rd. Rstrnt/ lounge, pool, mtg rm, fax, cable TV, t pkng, n/s rms. AAA. $38-78/S; $43-83/D; $5/ex prsn. Discs.

Super 8 Motel/ 1220 N Main, Ft Morgan CO 80701. 303-867-9443/ Fax: 867-8658. V,M,AE,DC,CB,D. I-76 (Exit 80) to Hwy 52. Enter through Arby's lot. B/f, n/s rms, laundry, b/t pkng, cable TV, cot. Free local calls. Pride Award. $38/S; $41-44/D; $3/ex prsn. Higher spec event rate. Discs.

Fountain

1st Interstate Inn/ 650 Champlin Dr, Box 457, Fountain CO 80817. 719-382-5615. V,M,AE,D,DC. I-25 (Exit 128) at Hwys 85 & 87. Nrby rstrnt, cable TV, dd phone, arpt trans, outlets, laundry, n/s rms, cot, crib. $27-29/S; $29-34/D; $2/ex prsn. 5/1-10/31: $32-34/S; $34-44/D. Spec events: $37-39/S; $42-49/D; $5/ex prsn. Disc: Senior, TA, family, comm.

Frisco

New Summit Inn/ 1205 N Summit Blvd, Box 540, Frisco CO 80443. 970-668-3220/ Fax: 668-0188/ 800-745-1211. V,M,AE,D,DC,CB. 2 blks from I-70, Exit 203. Nrby rstrnt/ lounge, whrlpool, exerc equip, cable TV, video games, arpt trans, tt phone, fax, copier, nwspr, laundry, refrig, microwave, cot, crib, outlets, t/b/rv pkng, conn rms, b/f. Free cont brfst, local calls. AAA. $38-48/S; $43-48/D; $5/ex prsn. 5/24-9/2: $60-65/S; $65-70/D; 2/16-4/1: $90-95/S or D. 12/20-1/1: $95-100/S or D. Higher holiday wknd rates. Disc: Family, I/s. *Guaranteed rates.*

Georgetown

Super 8 Motel/ 1600 Argentine St, Georgetown CO 80444. 303-569-3211. AE,DC,D,M,V. I-70, Exit 228 on S side of I-70. B/f, n/s rms, nrby rstrnt, whrlpool, game rm, t/b/rv pkng, copier, cable TV, cot. Free local calls, crib. $41/S; $45-48/D; $4/ex prsn. 12/22-3/31: $45/S; $49-52/D. Higher spec event rates. Discs.

Glenwood Springs

Budget Host Budget 8 Motel/ 51429 Hwy 6 & 24, Glenwood Springs CO 81601. 303-945-5682. AE,M,V,D. I-70 (Exit 114) at Hwys 6 & 24. W side of tn. N/s rms, t/rv pkng, cable TV, dd phone, suites, family rms, kitchens, conn rms, pool, picnic area, mtg rm. Free crib. Winter: $29-43/S; $37-53/D; $5/ex prsn. Summer: $49-57/S; $53-66/D. Discs.

Grand Junction

Budget Host Inn/ 721 Horizon Dr, Grand Junction CO 81506. 970-243-6050/ Fax: 243-0310. V,AE,CB,DC,D,M. I-70 at Arpt Exit 31. T pkng, n/s rms, cable TV, dd/tt phone, pool, playgrnd, laundry. Free crib. No pets. AAA/ Mobil. Winter: $35-39/S; $39-43/D; $6/ex prsn. Summer: $39-43/S; $43-49/D. Discs.

Days Inn of Grand Junction/ 733 Horizon Dr, Grand Junction CO 81506.

COLORADO

970-245-7200/ Fax: 243-6709. V,AE,M,DC. I-70 (Exit 31) at Horizon Dr. Rstrnt, pool, mtg rm, b/f, t pkng, arpt trans, cable TV, n/s rms. Free local calls, coffee, nwspr. $42-48/S; $48-52/D; $6/ex prsn. 6/1-9/10: $48-52/S; $54-58/D. Higher spec event rates.

Howard Johnson Lodge 752 Horizon Dr, Grand Junction CO 81506. 303-243-5150/ Fax: 242-3692. AE,V,M,DC, CB,D,JCB. I-70 (Exit 31) at Horizon Dr; on N side of I-70. N/s rms, mtg rm, b/f, rstrnt, pool, trans, laundry, valet, game rm, tennis. Free trans. AAA. Gold Medal Winner. $39-49/S or D. 5/1-5/26, 10/1-10/31: $40-49/S; $45-54/D. 5/27-9/30: $54-64/S; $59-69/D. Discs.

Motel 6/ 776 Horizon Dr, Grand Junction CO 81506. 970-243-2628/ Fax: 243-0213. M,V,DC,D,AE. I-70, Exit 31: Ebnd, Airport-Mesa College exit; Wbnd, Horizon Dr exit, go NE on Horizon. Nrby rstrnt, cable TV, pool, laundry, n/s rms. Free local calls. $27-37/S; $33-43/D; $6/ex prsn. Disc.

Super 8 Motel/ 728 Horizon Dr, Grand Junction CO 81506. 303-248-8080. V,M,AE,DC,CB,D. I-70, Exit 31. Hwy 6/50, follow signs for arpt & Horizon Dr. B/f, n/s rms, pool, laundry, elevator, cot, crib. Free local calls. $35/S; $40/D; $5/ex prsn. 3/1-11/30: $40/S; $45/D. Higher spec event rate. Discs.

Greeley

Super 8 Motel/ 2423 29th St, Greeley CO 80631. 970-330-8880/ Fax: 330-1895. AE,DC,D,M,V,CB. On Hwy 34 Bypass to 23rd Av, S 1 blk to 29th St. B/f, n/s rms, toast bar, copier, cable TV. Free local calls. No pets. $39/S; $45/D; $4/ex prsn. Higher spec event/ wknd rate. Discs.

Also see Evans.

Greenwood Village (Denver area)

Motel 6/ 9201 E Arapahoe Rd, Greenwood Village CO 80112. 303-790-8220/ Fax: 799-3405. M,V,DC,D,AE. I-25 (Exit 197) to Arapahoe Rd, E 1 blk, lt on Boston St. Nrby rstrnt, cable TV, pool, n/s rms, elevator. Free local calls. Premier Award. $35-37/S; $41-43/D; $6/ex prsn. Disc.

Gunnison

A-B-C Motel/ 212 E Tomichi Av, Gunnison CO 81230. 970-641-2400/ Fax: 641-6342. V,M,AE,D. On US 50. Nrby rstrnt, cable TV, dd phone, arpt trans, outlets, whrlpool, b/f. n/s rms, cot, crib. No pets. AAA/ IMA. $32/S; $38-42/D; $2-4/ex prsn. 5/2-9/15, 12/21-1/2: $43-45/S; $49-58/D. Disc: IMA.TYPE[IMA

Super 8 Motel/ 411 E Tomichi, Gunnison CO 81230. 970-641-3068. V,M, D,AE,DC,CB. 3 blks E of Main St on Hwy 50. N/s rms, t/b/rv pkng, trans, cable TV, cot, crib. No pets. $38-47/S; $38-53/D; $4/ex prsn. Discs.

Henderson (Denver area)

Super 8 Motel/ 9051 I-76, Henderson CO 80640. 303-287-8888/ Fax: 287-8881. AE,V,M,D,DC,CB. I-76 at 88th Av. N on W Frontage Rd. B/f, n/s rms, t/b/rv pkng, laundry, outlets, cont brfst, elevator, satellite TV, suite, crib, cot. Free local calls. No pets. $37/S; $41-43/D; $3/ex prsn. 4/1-9/30: $39/S; $42/D. Higher spec event rate. Discs.

Hotchkiss

Hotchkiss Inn/ 406 Hwy 133, Hotchkiss CO 81419. 970-872-2200. V,M,D,AE. Hwy 92 from Delta, 20 mi, 1/2 mi on 133. Nrby rstrnt, n/s rms, cable TV, tt phone, laundry, t/b/rv pkng, conn rms. AAA. $42/S; $48/D; $6/ex prsn. 10/15-11/15, holidays: $53/S/ $59/D. Disc: Senior.

Idaho Springs

6 & 40 National 9 Inn/ 2920 Colorado Blvd, Idaho Springs CO 80452. 303-567-2691. V,M,AE,DC. Jct I-70 to Bsns Rte US 6 & 40, Exit 241 A. Cable TV, dd phone, barbeque grill. No pets. $32/S; $38-45/D; $4/ex prsn.

La Junta

Quality Inn/ 1325 E 3rd St, Box 1180, La Junta CO 81050. 719-384-2571. V,M,AE,D,DC,AE. US 50 at E edge of city. Rstrnt/ lounge, pool, mtg rm, fax, whrlpool, cable TV, t pkng, outlets, n/s rms. $40-45/S; $42-49/D; $2/ex prsn. 5/1-10/31: $45-49/S; $47-54/D. Discs.

Super 8 Motel/ 27882 Frontage Rd, La Junta CO 81050. 719-384-4408/ Fax: ᴑ84-2236. V,M,D,AE,DC,CB. W side of tn on Hwy 50. N/s rms, t/b/rv pkng, copier, cable TV. Free local calls. AAA. $37/S; $43-47/D; $6/ex prsn. Discs.

Lakewood (Denver area)

Comfort Inn/ 3440 S Vance St, Lakewood CO 80227. 303-989-5500. V,M,D,AE. NE corner of US 285 (Hampden Av) & Wadsworth Blvd, 1 blk E of Wadsworth on Vance St. Nrby rstrnt, pool, mtg rm, fax, whrlpool, cable TV, t pkng, exerc equip, n/s rms. Free cont brfst. Hospitality Award. AAA. $39-85/S or D; $6-8/ex prsn. 5/1-9/29: $45-85/S; $53-85/D. Discs.

Econo Lodge/ 715 Kipling St, Lakewood CO 80215 303-232-5000. V,AE,M,DC. I-25 to 6th Av, W to Kipling. Nrby rstrnt, pool, fax, b/f, cable TV, laundry, n/s rms. Free cont brfst, in-rm coffee. No pets. AAA. $42-50/S or D; $5/ex prsn. 5/1-5/31: $40-45/S or D. 6/1-8/31: $45-60/S or D. Discs.

Motel 6/ 480 Wadsworth Blvd, Lakewood CO 80226. 303-232-4924/ Fax: 274-4621. M,V,DC,D,AE. At US 6 & Wadsworth Blvd. I-25: take 6th Av W to Wadsworth S Exit. Nrby rstrnt, cable TV, pool, n/s rms. Free local calls. $29-32/S; $35-38/D; $6/ex prsn. Disc.

Rodeway Inn/ 7150 W Colfax Av, Lakewood CO 80215. 303-238-1251. V,M,D,AE. I-25 (Exit 210) to Colfax Ave E, 3 1/2 mi to mtl. Rstrnt/ lounge, pool, mtg rm, fax, b/f, cable TV, t pkng, n/s rms. Free cont brfst. $42-58/S or D; $6/ex prsn. 5/1-5/31: $40-55/S or D. 6/1-8/31: $45-65/S or D. 9/1-11/30: $40-60/S or D. Discs.

Lamar

El Mar Budget Host Motel/ 1210 S Main St, Lamar CO 81052. 719-336-4331/ Fax: 336-7931. V,M,AE,D,DC, CB. Jct Hwys 50, 287 & 385 dntn Lamar, 1 mi S on Hwy 287/385. Nrby rstrnt, pool, n/s rms, cable TV, arpt trans, tt phone, fax, copier, cot, crib, t/b/rv pkng, eff. Free local calls, coffee, tea, cocoa. No pets. AAA. $28-34/S; $36-39/D; $4/ex prsn.

Super 8 Motel/ 1202 N Main, Lamar CO 81052. 719-336-3427/ Fax: Ext 223. D,M,V,AE,DC,CB. Hwy 50, N side of Lamar. B/f, n/s rms, laundry, b/t pkng, outlets, cont brfst, copier, cable TV, suites, cot, crib. Free local calls. $31-36/S; $34-43/D; $3/ex prsn. Higher spec event, wknd rate. Discs.

Limon

Econo Lodge/ Box 925, Limon CO 80828. 719-775-2867. V,AE,M,DC. I-70 & US 24. Nrby rstrnt, fax, cable TV, n/s rms. Free coffee. $31-44/S; $39-48/D; $4/ex prsn. 3/1-4/30: $38-48/S; $43-53/D. 5/1-9/15: $41-56/S; $49-64/D. Discs.

Super 8 Motel/ Box 1202, Limon CO 80828. 719-775-2889/ Fax: 775-2055. V,M,AE,DC,CB,D. I-70 (Exit 359) at Hwy 24. B/f, n/s rms, cont brfst, outlets, t/b/rv pkng, cable TV, cot, crib. $34-40/S; $39-44/D; $4/ex prsn. Higher spec event rate. Discs.

Longmont

1st Interstate Inn/ 3940 Hwy 119, Longmont CO 80504. 303-772-6000. V, M, AE,D,DC. I-25, Exit 240. Nrby rstrnt, cable TV, dd phone, arpt trans, outlets, cot, crib, n/s rms. $32/S; $37-39/D; $2/ex prsn. 5/1-10/31: $37/S; $42-47/D; $3/ex prsn. Spec events: $40/S; $49/D; $5/ex prsn. Disc: Senior, TA, comm, family.

Briarwood Inn Motel/ 1228 N Main, Longmont CO 80501. 303-776-6622/ Fax: 772-7453. V,M,AE,D,DC,CB. I-25, exit Longmont Hwy 119, 6 mi W to Hwy 287 or Main St, rt 9 blks. Nrby rstrnt/ lounge, whrlpool, n/s rms, cable TV, tt/dd phone, nwspr, laundry, refrig, microwave, cot, crib, eff, conn rms, b/f. Free local calls, coffee, tea. No pets. AAA. $43/S; $47-50/D; $5/ex prsn. 5/1-9/30: $57/S; $60-65/D. Disc: Senior, bsns, govt, l/s. *Guaranteed rates.*

Budget Host Inn/ 3815 Hwy 119 & I-25, Longmont CO 80501. 303-776-8700. AE,M,V,D,DC,CB. I-25 (Exit 240) at Hwy 119. Cable TV, dd phone, rstrnt, mtg rm, indr pool, wading pool, laundry, t pkng, cot, crib. AAA/ Mobil. Winter: $30-39/S; $39-53/D; $5/ex prsn. Summer: $39-53/S; $49-65/D. Discs.

Comfort Inn/ I-25 & SR 119, Longmont CO 80504. 800-221-2222 — opening soon. V,M,D,AE. I-25 (Exit 240) at SR 119, turn W to mtl. Nrby rstrnt, indr

COLORADO

pool, b/f, whrlpool, cable TV, n/s rms. Free full brfst. No pets. $43-70/S; $47-80/D; $5/ex prsn. Discs.

Super 8 Motel/ 10805 Turner Blvd, Longmont CO 80504. 719-772-0888/ Fax: 772-3717. V,M,AE,DC,CB,D. I-25 (Exit 240) at Hwy 119. B/f, n/s rms, laundry, outlets, b/t pkng, showers for trkrs, outlets, copier, cable TV, cot. Free local calls, crib. $39/S; $41-47/D; $2/ex prsn. Higher spec event rate. Discs.

Super 8 Motel/ 2446 N Main St, Longmont CO 80501. 303-772-8106. V,M,AE,DC,CB,D. Jct of Hwy 66 & Hwy 287. 6 mi W of I-25, Exit 243. B/f, n/s rms, outlets, cable TV, suites, mtg rm, cot. Free local calls, crib. $43-46/S; $47-53/D; $5/ex prsn. Higher spec event rate. Discs.

Loveland

Budget Host Exit 254 Inn/ 2716 SE Frontage Rd, Loveland CO 80537. 303-667-5202. AE,M,V,D,DC,CB. 3 mi S of US 34 on I-25. T pkng, outlets, dd phone, in-rm coffee, family rms, n/s rms, mtg rm, pool, playgrnd, picnic area, arpt trans, cot. Free crib. No pets. AAA/ Mobil. $28-40/S; $30-46/D; $4/ex prsn. Summer: $32-49/S; $36-59/D. Discs.

Super 8 Motel/ 1655 E Eisenhower Blvd, Loveland CO 80537. 303-663-7000. V,M,AE,DC,CB,D. I-25 (Exit 257B) at US 34 W. N/s rms, nrby rstrnt, laundry, outlets, t/b pkng. Free local calls. $35-40/S; $38-47/D; $4/ex prsn. 6/10-9/5: $47/S; $47-56/D. Higher spec event/ holiday rate. Discs.

Manitou

Villa Motel/ 481 Manitou Av, Manitou CO 80829. 719-685-5492. V,AE,D,DC, DC. On Bsns Hwy 24. Pool, cable TV, dd phone, n/s rms, laundry, whrlpool, cot, crib, conn rms, kitchenettes. No pets. AAA/ IMA. $39-47/S or D. 4/26-5/16, 9/3-9/28: $49-55/S or D. 5/17-9/2: $72-80/S or D. Higher rates for kitchenettes. Disc: Senior, TA, family.

Montrose

San Juan Inn/ 1480 Hwy 550 S, Montrose CO 81401. 970-249-6644/ Fax: 249-9314. V,M,AE,D,DC,CB. Main St, turn S on Hwy 550. Nrby rstrnt, indr pool, whrlpool, n/s rms, cable TV, playgrnd, arpt trans, tt/dd phone, fax, nwspr, laundry, cot, crib, outlets, t/b/rv pkng. Free local calls, coffee. AAA. $44-52/S; $49-62/D; $5/ex prsn. 4/1-5/31, 11/16-3/31: $38-43/S; $41-49/D. Disc: Bsns, govt, family, milt. *Guaranteed rates.*

Super 8 Motel/ 1705 E Main, Montrose CO 81401. 970-249-9294/ Fax: Ext 334. V,M,AE,DC,CB,D. Hwy 50. B/f, n/s rms, hot tub, outlets, t/b/rv pkng, copier, cable TV, toaster bar, cot, crib. Free local calls. $35-38/S; $43-50/D; $4/ex prsn. Higher spec event rate. Discs.

Pagosa Springs

Super 8 Motel/ 34 Piedra Rd, Pagosa Springs CO 81147. 303-731-4005. V,M,D,AE,DC,CB. 2 1/2 mi W of tn on Hwy 160. B/f, n/s rms, outlets, t pkng, cable TV, cot, crib. Free local calls. $37-46/S; $43-53/D; $5/ex prsn. Discs.

Parachute

Super 8 Motel/ 252 Green St, Parachute CO 81635. 970-285-7936/ Fax: 285-9538. V,M,AE,DC,CB,D. I-70, Exit 75. B/f, n/s rms, laundry, t/b/rv pkng, outlets, copier, cable TV, mtg rm. Free local calls. $38/S; $43/D; $4/ex prsn. Higher spec event rate. Discs.

Pueblo

Days Inn/ 4201 N Elizabeth, Pueblo CO 81008. 719-543-8031/ Fax: 546-1317. V,M,AE,D,CB,DC,JCB. I-25 to US 50, E to Elizabeth St, turn N to mtl. Fax, n/s rms, nrby rstrnt, indr pool, whrlpool, t pkng, cable TV, n/s rms. Free cont brfst. $43-65/S; $46-85/D. Discs.

Motel 6/ 960 Hwy 50 W, Pueblo CO 81008. 719-543-8900/ Fax: 543-5515. M,V,AE,CB,D. I-25 (Exit 101) to US 50, W 1 blk. Nrby rstrnt, cable TV, pool, n/s rms. elevator. Free local calls. $29-34/S; $35-40/D; $6/ex prsn. Disc.

Motel 6/ 4103 N Elizabeth St, Pueblo CO 81008. 719-543-6221/ Fax: 546-9612. M,V,DC,D,AE. From I-25/ US 85 & US 87 (Exit 101) to US 50, W 1/2 mi. Nrby rstrnt, cable TV, laundry, pool, n/s rms. Free local calls. $29-34/S; $35-40/D; $6/ex prsn. Disc.

COLORADO

Rambler Motel/ 4400 N Elizabeth St, Pueblo CO 81008. 719-543-4173. V,M,AE,DC. I-25 N, Exit 101 or 102. Pool, in-rm coffee, t pkng, cable TV. No pets. AAA/ National 9. Winter: $25/S; $31-34/D; $6/ex prsn. Summer: $32/S; $43-54/D.

Super 8 Motel/ 1100 Hwy 50 W, Pueblo CO 81008. 719-545-4104. V,M,AE,DC, CB,D. I-25 (Exit 101) to Hwy 50, 1/4 mi W. B/f, n/s rms, b/t pkng, satellite TV, crib, cot. Free local calls. $33-48/S; $36-55/D; $3/ex prsn. Higher spec event rate. Discs.

Salida

Aspen Leaf Lodge/ 7350 W Hwy 50, Salida CO 81201. 719-539-6733/ 800-759-0338. V,M,AE,D,DC,CB. On US Hwy 50, 2 blks W of Hot Springs pool. Nrby rstrnt, whrlpool, n/s rms, cable TV, playgrnd, arpt trans, tt/dd phone, fax, copier, refrig, microwave, cot, crib, outlets, t/b pkng, conn rms. Free local calls, coffee. No alcohol. AAA. $33-43/S; $33-47/D; $3-5/ex prsn. 1/1-1/2, 3/9-3/24, 5/18-9/14: $48-53/S; $48-63/D. Disc: Senior, bsns, TA, govt, l/s, family, trkr, milt. *Guaranteed rates.*

Circle R Motel/ 304 W Rainbow, Salida CO 81201. 719-539-6296/ 800-755-6296. V,M,AE,D. 5 mi E of Hwy 50 & 285 on US 50, across from Wal-Mart. Nrby rstrnt, whrlpool, n/s rms, cable TV, playgrnd, tt/dd phone, laundry, outlets, eff, conn rms, b/f. Free local calls, coffee, tea, cocoa. AAA. $30/S; $33-37/S; $3/ex prsn. 5/26-9/9: $43/S; $45-49/D; $5/ex prsn. 12/24-1/1, 3/10-3/31: $40/S; $43-47/D. *Guaranteed rates.*

Days Inn/ 407 E Hwy 50, Salida CO 81201. 719-539-6651/ Fax: 539-6240. V,M,AE,D,CB,DC,JCB. Hwy 50 on E side of tn. Fax, n/s rms, nrby rstrnt, b/f, cable TV. Free cont brfst. $34-44/S; $37-47/D; $6/ex prsn. 5/15-9/30: $45-55/S; $54-69/D. Discs.

Salida Motel/ 1310 E Hwy 50, Salida CO 81201. 719-539-2895. V,M,AE,DC. On E Hwy 50. Cable TV, dd phone, mtg rm, t pkng, hot tub, crib. Free coffee, local trans. No pets. National 9. $30-55/S; $35-75/D; $5/ex prsn.

Super 8 Motel/ 525 W Rainbow, Salida CO 81201. 719-539-6689/ Fax: 539-7018. AE,V,M,D,CB,DC. On Hwy 50 (Rainbow), just E of Hwy 285. B/f, n/s rms, pool, nrby rstrnt, whrlpool, cable TV. Free local calls. Pride Award. AAA. $37-45/S; $37-57/D; $5/ex prsn. Higher spec event, wknd rate. Discs.

Sterling

1st Interstate Inn/ 20930 Hwy 6, Box 1692, Sterling CO 80751. 970-522-7274. V,M,AE,D,DC. I-76, Exit 125. Nrby rstrnt, cable TV, dd phone, outlets, n/s rms, laundry, cot, crib. AAA. $27-29/S; $29-34/D; $4/ex prsn. 5/1-10/31: $32-36/S; $34-42/D. Spec events: $37-39/S; $42-44/D; $5/ex prsn. Disc: Senior, TA, comm, family.

Super 8 Motel/ 12883 Hwy 61, Sterling CO 80751. 970-879-5230/ Fax: 879-3341. D,M,V,AE,DC,CB. I-76, at Exit 125. B/f, rstrnt/ lounge, indr pool, laundry, cable TV, t/b/rv pkng, mtg rm, outlets, cot. Free local calls, crib. $39/S; $39-43/D; $3/ex prsn. Higher spec event rate. Discs.

Thornton (Denver area)

Motel 6/ 6 W 83rd Place, Thornton CO 80221. 303-429-1550/ Fax: 427-7513. V,M,D,AE,DC. I-25 (Exit 219) to 84th Av Exit, go W to Acoma Way, lt on Acoma, lt on W 83rd Pl. Nrby rstrnt, cable TV, laundry, pool, n/s rms, t pkng. Free local calls. $28-32/S; $34-38/D; $6/ex prsn. Disc.

Trinidad

Budget Host Trinidad/ 10301 Santa Fe Tr Dr, Trinidad CO 81082. 719-846-3307. AE,M,V,D,DC,CB. I-25 (Exit 11) E side of frwy. Satellite TV, dd phone, in-rm coffee, n/s rms, nrby rstrnt, picnic area, laundry, t/rv pkng, cot, crib. AAA/ Mobil. $28-32/S; $35-45/D; $6/ex prsn. 5/16-9/14: $36-40/S; $40-70/D. Discs.

Budget Summit Inn/ 9800 Santa Fe Trail Dr, Trinidad CO 81082. 719-846-2251/ Fax: Ext 30. V,M,AE,D,DC,CB. I-25, Exit 11, S 1/8 mi on Frontage Rd. E side of freeway. Whrlpool, n/s rms, satellite TV, arpt trans, tt/dd phone, mtg rm, fax, copier, nwspr, laundry, refrig, microwave, cot, crib, outlets, t/b/rv pkng, eff, b/f. Free cont brfst. No pets, smoking or alcohol. AAA/ Mobil. $30-40/S; $40-48/D; $6/ex prsn. 5/15-9/15: $48/S or D. Disc: Senior, bsns, l/s, milt.

Super 8 Motel/ 1924 Freedom Rd, Trinidad CO 81082. 719-846-8280/ Fax: 846-3323. AE,DC,D,M,V,CB. I-25 (Exit 15) at Goddard Av, next to Wal-Mart. B/f, n/s rms, nrby rstrnt, laundry, toast bar, b/t pkng, cable TV, copier, suites. Free local calls, crib. Pride Award. $37/S; $44-48/D; $5/ex prsn. Higher spec event/ wknd rate. Discs.

Walsenburg

Budget Host Country Host Motel/ 553 US 85, 87, Box 190, Walsenburg CO 81089. 719-738-3800. AE,M,V,D, DC,CB. I-25, Exit 52. Satellite TV, dd phone, nrby rstrnt, t pkng, cot. Free crib. Winter: $27-39/S; $35-49/D; $3/ex prsn. Summer: $39-45/S; $47-59/D. Discs.

Westminster (Denver area)

Super 8 Motel/ 12055 Melody Dr, Westminster CO 80234. 303-451-7200/ Fax: Ext 350. AE,V,M,DC,CB,D. I-25 (Exit 223) at 120th Av, 1/4 mi W of I-25. B/f, n/s rms, whrlpool, sauna, toast bar, copier, elevator, mtg rm, cable TV, exerc equip, micro-refrig, TDD, cot. Free local calls, crib. $35/S; $40-48/D; $4/ex prsn. Higher spec event/ wknd rate. Discs.

Wheat Ridge (Denver area)

Motel 6/ 10300 S I-70 Frontage Rd, Wheat Ridge CO 80033. 303-467-3172/ Fax: 431-5896. M,V,DC,D,AE. I-70 (Exit 267) to Kipling St, S to Frontage Rd; rt to mtl. Cable TV, laundry, pool, n/s rms. Free local calls. $28-32/S; $34-38/D; $6/ex prsn. Disc.

Motel 6/ 9920 W 49th Av, Wheat Ridge CO 80033. 303-424-0658/ Fax: 431-2196. V,M,D,AE,DC. I-70 (Exit 267) to Kipling St, N to 49th, turn rt. Nrby rstrnt, cable TV, laundry, n/s rms. Free local calls. $28-32/S; $34-40/D; $6/ex prsn. Disc.

Super 8 Motel/ 10101 W 48th Av, Wheat Ridge CO 80033. 303-424-8300/ Fax: Ext 303. AE,V,M,DC,CB,D. I-70 (Exit 267) at Kipling St. B/f, n/s rms, pool, whrlpool, sauna, t/b/rv pkng, copier, elevator, cable TV, mtg rm, cot. Free local calls, crib. No pets. $35/S; $39-43/D; $4/ex prsn. Higher spec event rate. Discs.

Woodland Park (Colorado Springs area)

Rodeway Inn/ 19253 E US 24, Woodland Park CO 80863. 719-689-8732. V,M,D,AE. I-25 to US 24, 17 mi on US 24 to Inn at city limits of Woodland Park. Nrby rstrnt, b/f, whrlpool, n/s rms. Free cont brfst. $40-46/S; $44-48/D; $6/ex prsn. 5/1-9/30: $48-58/S; $54-62/D. Discs.

Connecticut

Branford (New Haven area)

Motel 6/ 320 E Main St, Branford CT 06405. 203-483-5828/ Fax: 488-4579. M,V,DC,D,AE. I-95 (Exit 55) to Hwy 1/ E Main St, SW to 2nd light. Rstrnt, cable TV, n/s rms, t pkng. Free local calls. Premier Award. $36-39/S; $42-45/D; $6/ex prsn. Disc.

Cromwell

Super 8 Motel/ 1 Industrial Park Rd, Cromwell CT 06416. 203-632-8888. AE,V,MC,D,DC,CB. I-91, Exit 21. N/s rms, cont brfst, cable TV, in-rm coffee, suites, mtg rm, elevator. Free cribs. $41/S; $46-48/D; $5/ex prsn. Higher spec event, wknd rate. Discs.

East Hartford (Hartford area)

Econo Lodge/ 927 Main St, E Hartford CT 06108. 203-289-7781. V,AE,M,DC. I-84 (Exit 56) to Governor St E, rt on Main St (US 5 S) to mtl. Nrby rstrnt, mtg rm, cable TV, n/s rms, t pkng. No pets. $30-35/S; $38-45/D; $5/ex prsn. Discs.

Wellesley Inn/ 333 Roberts St, E Hartford CT 06108. 203-289-4950/ Fax: 289-9258. AE,M,D,DC,CB,V. Cable TV,

CONNECTICUT

microwave, refrig. Free cont brfst. $45/S or D; $5/ex prsn. *Spec rates - see discount section in front of book.

Enfield (Hartford area)

Motel 6/ 11 Hazard Av, Enfield CT 06082. 860-741-3685/ Fax: 741-5539. V,M,D,AE,DC. I-91 (Exit 47E, Hazardville/Somers) to Hazard, E to Phoenix Av, lt into Enfield Square Mall. Nrby rstrnt, cable TV, laundry, n/s rms, t pkng. Free local calls. $27-30/S; $33-36/D; $6/ex prsn. Disc.

Super 8 Motel/ 1543 King St, Enfield CT 06082. 203-741-3636. V,M,D,AE, DC,CB. I-91, Exit 46. B/f, n/s rms, nrby rstrnt, laundry, cont brfst, copier, fax, cable TV, mtg rm. Free local calls, crib. $36/S; $43-48/D; $5/ex prsn. Discs.

Groton (Mystic area)

Econo Lodge/ 425 Bridge St, Groton CT 06340. 203-445-6550. V,AE,M,DC. I-95 (N, Exit 85; S, Exit 86) rt at 1st stoplight. Nrby rstrnt, fax, b/f, cable TV, n/s rms, t pkng. No pets. $35-40/S; $45-50/D; $10/ex prsn. 5/1-6/30: $50-55/S; $60-65/D. 7/1-9/30: $60-70/S; $70-80/D. 10/1-10/31: $55-60/S; $60-65/D. Discs.

Quality Inn/ 404 Bridge St, Groton CT 06340. 203-445-8141. V,M,D,AE. I-95 (N, Exit 85; S, Exit 86) S to Thames St/ Bridge Rd. Rstrnt/ lounge, pool, mtg rm, fax, cable TV, t pkng, exerc equip, laundry, n/s rms. No pets. AAA. $45-65/S or D; $10/ex prsn. 5/16-10/31: $80-95/S; $95-105/D. Discs.

Hartford

Super 8 Motel/ 57 W Service Rd, Hartford CT 06120. 203-246-8888. D,M,V,AE,DC,CB. I-91, Exit 33. B/f, n/s rms, rm serv, satellite TV, suites, mtg rm, cot, crib. AAA. $38/S; $40-42/D; $4/ex prsn. Higher spec event/wknd rate. Discs.

Also see East Hartford, Enfield, Southington, Weathersfield, Windsor Locks.

Mystic

See Groton.

New Haven

See Branford.

New London

Oakdell Motel/ 983 Hartford Turnpike, New London/ Waterford CT 06385. 860-442-9446/ 800-676-REST. V, M,AE,D. I-95, Exit 82. I-395, Exit 77. Pool, cable TV, dd phone, refrig, microwave, cot, crib, t pkng. Free cont brfst. AAA. $40-48/S; $45-48/D; $5/ex prsn. 5/1-9/30: $48-75/S; $48-85/D.

Also see Niantic.

Niantic

Motel 6/ 269 Flanders Rd, Niantic CT 06357. 203-739-6991/ Fax: 691-1828. V,M,D,AE,DC. I-95 (Exit 74) to Flanders Rd, S to mtl. Cable TV, laundry, pool, nrby rstrnt, n/s rms, t pkng. Free local calls. $30/S; $36/D; $6/ex prsn. 5/23-10/29: $43/S; $49/D. Higher spec event rates. Disc.

Old Saybrook

Heritage Motor Inn/ 1500 Boston Post Rd, Old Saybrook CT 06475. 860-388-3743. V,M,AE. 1/2 mi E of I-95, Exit 66. Nrby rstrnt, pool, cable TV, conn rms. No pets. AAA/ Mobil. $45-55/S or D; $5/ex prsn. 5/13-10/13: $55-80/S or D. Spec event/ holiday/ wknd rates: $80/S or D. *Guaranteed rates.*

Plainville

Howard Johnson Lodge/ 400 New Britain Av, Plainville CT 06062. 203-747-6876/ Fax: 747-9747. V,M,D, AE, DC,CB. I-84 (Exit 34) at Crooked St. N/s rms, mtg rm, b/f, rstrnt/ lounge, pool, t/b pkng, in-rm coffee, cable TV, fax, laundry. $39-59/S; $44-64/D. Discs.

Southington (Hartford area)

Motel 6/ 625 Queen St, Southington CT 06489. 860-621-7351/ Fax: 620-0453. V,M,D,AE,DC. I-84 (Exit 32) to Queen St, NW to mtl. Rstrnt, cable TV, laundry, n/s rms, t pkng. Free local calls. $28-30/S; $34-36/D; $6/ex prsn. Disc.

Waterbury

Howard Johnson Lodge/ 2636 S Main

St, Waterbury CT 06706. 203-746-7961. V,M,D,AE,DC,CB. I-84 (Exit 19) to SR 8, N to (Exit 29) S Main St. N/s rms, mtg rm, b/f, rstrnt/ lounge, pool, t/b pkng, valet serv, VCR/ movies. Free cont brfst. $40-50/S; $42-60/D. Discs.

Wethersfield

Motel 6/ 1341 Silas Deane Hwy, Wethersfield CT 06109. 860-563-5900/ Fax: 563-1213. V,M,D,AE,DC. I-91 (Exit 24/ Weathersfield-Rocky Hill) to Silas Deane Hwy, W to mtl. Nrby rstrnt, cable TV, laundry, n/s rms, t pkng. Free local calls. $28-30/S; $34-36/D; $6/ex prsn. Disc.

Windsor Locks (Hartford area)

Motel 6/ 3 National Dr, Windsor Locks CT 06096. 860-292-6200/ Fax: 623-1821. V,M,D,AE,DC. Hwy 20 to Hwy 75/ Turnpike Rd, N to mtl. Cable TV, pool, n/s rms, t pkng. Free local calls. $28-30/S; $34-36/D; $6/ex prsn. Disc.

Wolcott

Wolcott Motor Inn/ 1273 Wolcott Rd, Rte 69, Wolcott CT 06716. 203-879-4618/ 800-424-9466. V,M,AE,DC. I-84, Exit 23, rt on Rte 62, 7 mi to mtl. Nrby rstrnt/ lounge, n/s rms, cable TV, tt phone, refrig, microwave, cot, t/b/rv pkng, eff, conn rms. Free coffee, tea, cocoa. No pets. AAA. $40-80/S; $45-85/D; $5/ex prsn. Disc: Senior, govt, l/s, family. *Guaranteed rates.*

Delaware

Dover

Howard Johnson Lodge/ 561 N Dupont Hwy, Dover DE 19901. 302-678-8900/ Fax: 678-2245. V,M,D,AE,DC,CB. I-495, I-295, NJ Tnpk to US 13 S. On US 13 in Dover. N/s rms, mtg rm, b/f, rstrnt/ lounge, pool, t pkng, satellite TV, fax, laundry. Free cont brfst, coffee. No pets. $43-53/S; $48-58/D. Discs.

New Castle (Wilmington area)

Econo Lodge/ 232 S Dupont Hwy, New Castle DE 19720. 302-322-4500. V,AE,M,DC. I-95 (Exit 5) to SR 141, S l/2 mi to US 13, S 2 mi to mtl. Nrby rstrnt, fax, b/f, cable TV, dd phone, AM coffee, family rms, n/s rms. Free cont brfst. No pets. $38-60/S or D; $5-10/ex prsn. 5/1-11/30: $38-110/S or D. Discs.

Econo Lodge/ SR 9 & I-295, New Castle DE 19720. 302-654-5400. V,AE,M,DC. I-295 N, exit SR 9N (last exit before DE Memorial Bridge). From NJ, 1st exit after DE Mem Bridge. Nrby rstrnt, cable TV, t pkng, dd phone, coffee, n/s rms. Free cont brfst. $32-48/S; $36-52/D; $5/ex prsn. Discs.

Motel 6/ 1200 West Av, New Castle DE 19720. 302-571-1200/ Fax: 571-1310. V,M,D,AE,DC. I-295 (New Castle Av/ Wilmington Exit) to SR 9 (New Castle Av), NE 1 blk to West Av, rt to mtl. Cable TV, laundry, pool, nrby rstrnt, n/s rms, t pkng. Free local calls. $27-30/S; $33-36/D; $6/ex prsn. Disc.

Super 8 Motel/ 215 Dupont Hwy, New Castle DE 19720. 302-322-9480/ Fax: Ext 404. AE,V,MC,DC,CB,D. US 13/40/301, E of I-95 on Hwy 273; S of I-295 or I-495 on Hwys 13 & 40. B/f, n/s rms, toast bar, cable TV, laundry, elevator, suites, mtg rm, rv pkng, cot. Free local calls, crib. $38-40/S; $43-45/D; $6/ex prsn. 4/1-5/31: $40/S; $45/D. Wknds, 4/1-5/31: $44/S; $48/D. Discs.

Rehoboth Beach

Econo Lodge/ 4361 SR 1, Rehoboth Beach DE 19971. 302-227-0500. V,M,AE. On SR 1, 1 mi N of Rehoboth Beach. Rstrnt/ lounge, pool, mtg rm, fax, b/f, cable TV, n/s rms. Free local calls, coffee. No pets. $35-45/S; $40-50/D; $5/ex prsn. 5/1-5/25: $38-70/S; $45-70/D. 5/26-9/3: $75-125/S or D.

DELAWARE / D.C./ FLORIDA

9/4-10/8: $40-70/S; $45-70/D. Dis

Wilmington

See New Castle.

District of Columbia

Washington
See Camp Springs, MD College Park, MD Gaithersburg, MD Laurel, MD Silver Spring, MD Alexandria, VA Fairfax, VA Woodbridge, VA Manassas, VA

Florida

Alachua (Gainesville area)
Comfort Inn/ Rte 1, Box 230-C, Alachua FL 32615. 904-462-2414. V,AE,M,DC. I-75 (Exit 78E) to US 441, dntn. Nrby rstrnt, pool, fax, b/f, cable TV, laundry, n/s rms. Free cont brfst. No pets. AAA. $40-50/S; $45-55/D; $5/ex prsn. Discs.

Days Inn/ Rte 1, Box 225, Alachua FL 32615. 904-462-3251. V,M,AE,D,CB, DC,JCB. I-75 (Exit 441) at US 441. Fax, n/s rms, nrby rstrnt, pool, mtg rm, t pkng, arpt trans, cable TV, laundry, cot, crib. Free cont brfst. $42-99/S; $48-99/D; $4/ex prsn. Disc.

Atlantic Beach (Jacksonville area)
Comfort Inn Mayport/ 2401 Mayport Rd, Atlantic Beach FL 32233. 904-249-0313/ Fax: 241-2155. V,AE,M,DC. On A1A (Mayport Rd), 2 mi from Intercoastal Waterway. Nrby rstrnt/ lounge, pool, fax, b/f, cable TV, t pkng, n/s rms. Free cont brfst. No pets. AAA. $39-90/S; $44-95/D; $5/ex prsn. Discs.

Avon Park
Econo Lodge/ 2511 US 27 S, Avon Park FL 33825. 813-453-2000. V,M,AE. On US 27. Nrby rstrnt, pool, fax, b/f, cable TV, t pkng, laundry, dd phone, n/s rms. Free cont brfst. $39-49/S; $45-55/D; $5/ex prsn. 2/1-3/31: $49-99/S; $59-99/D. Disc.

Bonifay
Econo Lodge/ 2210 S Waukesha St, Bonifay FL 32425. 904-547-9345. V,M,D,AE. Jct I-10 & SR 79. Nrby rstrnt, fax, b/f, cable TV, t pkng, n/s rms. Free local calls. $32-65/S; $38-80/D; $5/ex prsn. Discs.

Bonita Springs
Econo Lodge/ 28090 Quail's Nest Ln, Bonita Springs FL 33923. 813-947-3366. V,AE,M,DC. I-75, Exit 18. Rstrnt, pool, mtg rm, fax, b/f, cable TV, t pkng, n/s rms. Free coffee, nwspr. $59-69/S or D; $4/ex prsn. 1/17-4/30: $65-75/S; $75-85/D. 5/1-10/31: $38-48/S; $42-52/D; 11/1-12/19: $40-50/S; $44-54/D. Discs.

Bradenton (Sarasota area)
Days Inn/ 644 67th St Cir E, Bradenton FL 34208. 941-746-2505/ Fax: 745-1839. V,M,AE,D,CB,DC,JCB. I-75 (Exit 42) to SR 64, turn W to mtl. Fax, n/s rms, nrby rstrnt, pool, cable TV, fridge, cont brfst, laundry. $28-45/S or D; $5/ex prsn. 1/16-3/31: $35-75/s or D. Disc.

Econo Lodge/ 6727 14th St W, Bradenton FL 34207. 813-758-7199. V,AE, M,DC. I-75 (Exit 41) to SR 70, lt on US 41. Nrby rstrnt, pool, fax, cable TV, t pkng, n/s rms. Free cont brfst. AAA. $40-56/S; $43-60/D; $5/ex prsn. 2/1-4/30: $56-80/S; $56-90/D. 5/1-12/24: $30-43/S; $30-46/D. Discs.

Econo Lodge/ 607-67th St Cir E, Bradenton FL 34208. 813-745-1988. V,AE,M,DC. I-75 (Exit 42) at SR 64, turn rt at Citgo gas station. Nrby rstrnt,

FLORIDA

pool, b/f, cable TV, t pkng, n/s rms. Free coffee. No pets. AAA. $39-51/S; $41-53/D; $4/ex prsn. 2/1-4/15: $55-75/S; $55-85/D. 4/16-12/24: $32-42/S; $36-46/D. Discs.

Motel 6/ 660 67th St Cir E, Bradenton FL 34208. 941-747-6005/ Fax: 745-1388. M,V,DC,D,AE. I-75 (Exit 42) to SR 64; W to 66th St/ Travelers Oasis Pk, rt on 6th Av E. Nrby rstrnt, cable TV, laundry, pool, n/s rms, elevator. Free local calls. $28-30/S; $32-34/D; $4/ex prsn. 1/25-4/10: $40/S; $44/D. Disc.

Bradenton Beach

Pelican Post Motel/ 202 1st St N, Bradenton Beach FL 34217. 941-778-2833/ Fax: 778-4207/ 800-315-0212. V,M,D. I-75, Exit 42, go 15 mi to Anna Maria Island, lt 2 mi, lt on 1st St N. Nrby rstrnt/ lounge, cable TV, tt/dd phones, fax, refrig, microwave, cot, eff. Free local calls, coffee, tea, cocoa. $50-62/S or D. 2/1-4/15: $65-75/S or D. 4/16-9/5: $40-50/S or D. 9/6-12/19: $35-45/S or D; $6/ex prsn. Disc: Family, l/s. *Guaranteed rates.*

Brandon (Tampa area)

Budgetel Inns/ 602 S Faulkenburg Rd, Brandon FL 33619. 813-684-4007/ Fax: 681-3042. V,M,D,AE,DC,CB. I-75 (Exit 51) to SR 60 (Brandon Blvd), W to Faulkenburg Rd, N to mtl. N/s rms, b/f, fax, rstrnt, pool. Free cont brfst, in-rm coffee, local calls. AAA. $43-53/S; $50-60/D. 1/26-2/17: $53-63/S or D. 2/18-4/16: $45-55/S; $52-62/D. 4/7-12/30: $37-47/S; $44-54/D. Spec rates may apply. Discs.

Callahan

Friendship Inn/ Box 628, Callahan FL 32011. 904-879-3451. V,AE,M,DC. 1 mi N of Callahan on US 301/1/23. Rstrnt, pool, fax, b/f, t pkng, n/s rms, dd phone. Free local calls, coffee. $33/S; $36/D; $4/ex prsn. Discs.

Clearwater

Econo Lodge/ 21252 US 19 N, Clearwater FL 34625. 813-799-1569. V,M,AE.On US 19, just N of Hwy 60. Rstrnt/ lounge, pool, mtg rm, fax, b/f, whrlpool, cable TV, t pkng. AAA. $44/S or D; $5/ex prsn. 2/1-4/7: $65/S or D. Discs.

Also see Palm Harbor.

Clearwater Beach

Beach Ambassador/ 656 Bayway Blvd, Clearwater Beach FL 34630. 813-442-6606. V,M,AE,DC. 3/4 mi S on Bay. Cable TV, kitchens, laundry, pool, dock fishing. No pets. National 9. $32-56/S; $32-59/D; $5/ex prsn.

Cocoa

Econo Lodge/ 3220 N Cocoa Blvd, Cocoa FL 32926. 407-632-4561. V,AE,M,DC. At US 1 & SR 528. I-95, exit 76/E or 77/E, then E to US 1. Rstrnt/ lounge, pool, mtg rm, fax, b/f, cable TV, t pkng, micro-fridge, laundry, n/s rms. AAA. $40-60/S; $45-65/D; $5/ex prsn. 1/27-4/30: $45-65/S; $50-70/D. 5/1-12/21: $35-55/S; $40-60/D. Discs.

Cocoa Beach

Motel 6/ 3701 N Atlantic Av, Cocoa Beach FL 32931. 407-783-3103/ Fax: 868-0875. M,V,DC,D,AE. Hwy 520 at Atlantic Av (A1A). Nrby rstrnt, cable TV, pool, laundry, n/s rms, t pkng. Free local calls. Premier Award. $34-39/S; $38-43/D; $4/ex prsn. 1/25-4/3: $45/S; $49/D. Higher spec event rates. Disc.

Coral Springs

Wellesley Inn/ 3100 N University Dr, Coral Springs FL 33065. 305-344-2200/ Fax: 344-7885. AE,M,D,DC,CB,V. Cable TV, pool, fax, microwave, refrig, in-rm coffee. Free cont brfst. $62/S or D; $5/ex prsn. 4/9-12/20: $42/S or D. *Spec rates - see discount section in front of book.

Crestview

Econo Lodge/ 3107 S Ferdon Blvd, Crestview FL 32536. 904-682-6255. V,AE,M,DC. I-10 (Exit 12) & SR 85. Nrby rstrnt, b/f, cable TV, t pkng, n/s rms. Free cont brfst, local calls. No pets. $35-43/S; $40-53/D; $5/ex prsn. Discs.

Super 8 Motel/ 3925 S Ferdon Blvd, Crestview FL 32539. 904-682-9649/ Fax: Ext 172. AE,V,MC,D,DC,CB. I-10 (Exit 12) to Hwy 85, turn S. B/f, n/s rms, cable TV, cont brfst, some t pkng, kitchenette, cot. Free local calls, crib. Pride Award. AAA. $33/S; $38/D; $5/ex

FLORIDA

prsn. Higher spec event/ wknd rate. Discs.

Cross City

Carriage Inn Motel/ Box 1360, Cross City FL 32628. 904-498-3910/ Fax: 498-5054. V,M,AE,D. I-75 (Exit 76) to Hwy 26, W to 19 N. US Hwys 19, 98, Alt 27, Rstrnt, pool, n/s rms, cable TV, arpt trans, tt/dd phone, mtg rm, fax, copier, cot, crib, t/b pkng, conn rms. AAA. $30/S; $35/D; $4/ex prsn. Disc: Senior, govt, milt. *Guaranteed rates.*

Dania Beach

Motel 6/ 825 E Dania Beach Blvd, Dania Beach FL 33004 305-921-5505/ Fax: 920-0591. M,V,DC,D,AE. I-95 (Exit 25) to Stirling Rd, E to US 1, turn S then E on Dania Beach Blvd. Nrby rstrnt, cable TV, laundry, pool, n/s rms, t pkng. Free local calls. $40/S; $44/D; $4/ex prsn. 1/25-4/10: $46/S; $50/D. 4/11-12/20: $34/S; $38/D. Disc.

Davenport (Orlando area)

Motel 6/ 5620 US 27 N, Davenport FL 33837. 941-424-2521/ Fax: 424-0582. V,M,DC,D,AE. I-4 (Exit 23) to US 27, N to mtl. Nrby rstrnt, cable TV, laundry, pool, n/s rms. Free local calls. $24-27/S or D. Higher spec event rates. Disc.

Daytona Beach

Budget Host Inn Candelight/ 1305 S Ridgewood Av, Daytona Beach FL 32114. 904-252-1142. AE,M,V. On US 1, near jct with Hwy 400 (Beeville Rd). Cable TV, dd phone, conn rms, kitchens, n/s rms, nrby rstrnt/ lounge, picnic area, laundry, t pkng, cot. AAA. $24-34/S; $28-38/D; $5-10/ex prsn. 5/1-6/30, 9/3-12/16: $22-26/S; $26-32/D. Spec events: $70-145. Discs.

Econo Lodge/ 301 S Atlantic Av, Daytona Beach FL 32118. 904-255-6421. V,M,AE. I-95 (Exit 87A) at US 92. Rstrnt, pool, cable TV, t pkng, n/s rms. No pets. $36-165/S or D. $10/ex prsn. Discs.

HoJo Inn/ 2015 S Atlantic Av, Daytona Beach FL 32118. 904-255-2446/ Fax: 673-6260. V,M,D,AE,DC,CB. I-95 (Exit 87) to US 1, S to US 92, E to A1A, S 1 1/2 mi. N/s rms, b/f, pool, cable TV, in-rm safe, laundry, eff. No pets. $37-55/S or D. 2/9-4/10: $65-130/S or D. Discs.

Howard Johnson Plaza Hotel/ 701 S Atlantic Av, Daytona Beach FL 32118. 904-258-8522/ Fax: 257-9122. V,M,AE,D,DC,CB. I-95 to US 92, E 7 mi to Atlantic Av (A1A), S 1/2 mi. Rstrnt/ lounge, pool, exerc equip, whrlpool, kitchens, n/s rms. $45-115/S or D. Discs.

Quality Inn/ 1615 S Atlantic Av, Daytona Beach FL 32118. 904-255-0921. V,M,D,AE. I-95 (Exit 87) to US 92, E to A1A, S 1 mi to mtl. Rstrnt/ lounge, pool, mtg rm, fax, b/f, cable TV, kiddie pool. No pets. $35-70/S or D; $10/ex prsn. 5/1-8/20: $45-108/S or D. Spec events: $106-139/S or D. Discs.

Rodeway Inn/ 1299 S Atlantic Av, Daytona Beach FL 32118. 904-255-4545. V,AE,M,DC. US 92 to SR A1A, 1/2 mi S. Rstrnt, pool, fax, cable TV, n/s rms. No pets. $30-65/S or D; $10/ex prsn. 2/1-4/30: $50-132/S or D. 5/1-5/31: $35-70/S or D. 6/1-9/41: $45-100/S or D. Discs.

Super 8 Speedway/ 2992 W International Speedway Blvd, Daytona Beach FL 32124. 904-253-0643/ Fax: 238-5436/ 800-303-3297. V,M,AE,D. I-95, Exit 87. Nrby rstrnt/ lounge, pool, n/s rms, cable TV, tt/dd phone, fax, copier, laundry, refrig, microwave, cot, crib, t/b/rv pkng, conn rms. Free cont brfst, coffee, tea. AAA. $40/S or D; $5/ex prsn. Spec events: $40-170/S or D. Disc: Senior, govt, l/s, family, trkr, milt. *Guaranteed rates.*

Also see Ormond Beach.

DeFuniak Springs

Comfort Inn/ 1326 S Freeport Rd, DeFuniak Springs FL 32433. 904-892-1333. V,AE,M,DC. I-10 (Exit 14) to US 331, N to mtl. Nrby rstrnt, pool, mtg rm, fax, b/f, cable TV. Free cont brfst. AAA. $35-150/S; $40-150/D; $5/ex prsn. Discs.

DeLand

Quality Inn/ 2801 E New York Av, DeLand FL 32724. 904-736-3440. V, M, D, AE. I-4 to SR 44, W 1/4 mi. Rstrnt/ lounge, pool, mtg rm, fax, b/f, cable TV, t pkng, VCR, n/s rms. Free cont brfst. $35-90/S; $40-90/D; $5-20/ex prsn. 2/9-4/30: $45-160/S; $50-160/D. 5/1-6/29: $35-60/S; $40-60/D. 6/30-7/2: $85-105/S; $95-105/D. Discs.

Deerfield Beach (Ft Lauderdale area)

Comfort Suites/ 1040 E Newport Center Dr, Deerfield Beach FL 33442. 305-570-8887. V,M,D,AE. I-95 (Exit 36C) to Sawgrass Expwy, W 1/4 mi to Newport Executive Cntr. Rstrnt/ lounge, pool, mtg rm, fax, b/f, whrlpool, cable TV, t pkng, n/s rms. Free cont brfst. No pets. AAA. $89-149/S or D; $10/ex prsn. 1/4-3/31: $79-149/S or D. 4/1-4/30: $49-119/S or D. 5/1-12/22: $39-109/S or D. Discs.

Wellesley Inn/ 100 SW 12th Av, Deerfield Beach FL 33442. 305-428-0661/ Fax: 427-6701. AE,M,D,DC,CB,V. Cable TV, pool, fax, microwave, refrig, in-rm coffee. Free cont brfst. $54/S or D; $5/ex prsn. 4/9-12/20: $39/S or D. *Spec rates - see discount section in front of book.

Destin

Sleep Inn/ 50000 Emerald Coast Pkwy, Destin FL 32541. 904-654-7022. V,M,D,AE. On new US 98. Nrby rstrnt, pool, fax, b/f, cable TV, t pkng, n/s rms. Free cont brfst. No pets. AAA. $39-45/S; $43-50/D; $5/ex prsn. 3/7-4/30: $53-62/S; $57-67/D. 5/1-9/6: $60-70/S; $64-75/D. Discs.

Fern Park (Orlando area)

Comfort Inn 8245 US 17/92, Fern Park FL 32730. 407-339-3333. V,M,D,AE. I-4 to Maitland Blvd, E to US 17/ 92, N 3/4 mi to mtl. Nrby rstrnt, pool, fax, b/f, whrlpool, cable TV, t pkng. Free cont brfst. No pets. AAA. $44-64/S; $46-69/D; $6/ex prsn. 2/1-4/30: $46-99/S; $49-99/D. 5/1-12/14: $44-74/S; $46-74/D. 12/15-12/31: $46-89/S; $49-89/D. Discs.

Florida City

Comfort Inn/ 333 SE 1st Av, Florida City FL 33034. 305-248-4009. V, M,DC,AE. On US 1 near SW 344th St. Nrby rstrnt, b/f, cable TV, n/s rms. Free cont brfst. AAA. $59-70/S or D; $10/ex prsn. 3/22-12/23: $40-50/S or D. 12/24-12/31: $80/S or D. Discs.

Rodeway Inn/ 815 N Krome Av, Florida City FL 33034. 305-248-2741. V,M,D, AE. FL Trnpk S to US 1, rt on Palm Dr (SR 9336), rt on Krome Av (SR 997), 1/2 mi on rt. Nrby rstrnt, pool, b/f, cable TV, n/s rms. Free cont brfst. No pets. AAA. $42-50/S or D; $10 ex prsn. 2/1-3/20, 12/24-12/31: $60-70/S or D. 5/1-12/23: $36-40/S or D. Discs.

Fort Lauderdale

Motel 6/ 1801 SR 84, Ft Lauderdale FL 33315. 305-760-7999/ Fax: 832-0653. M,V,DC,D,AE. I-95 (Exit 27) to SR 84, E to mtl. Nrby rstrnt, cable TV, pool, laundry, n/s rms, t pkng. Free local calls. $40/S; $44/D; $4/ex prsn. 1/25-4/10: $46/S; $50/D. 4/11-12/20: $36/S; $40/D. Disc.

Wellesley Inn/ 5070 N State Rd 7, Ft Lauderdale FL 33319. 305-484-6909/ Fax: 731-2374. AE,M,D,DC,CB,V. Cable TV, pool, fax, microwave, refrig, in-rm coffee. Free cont brfst. $53/S or D; $5/ex prsn. 4/9-12/20: $40/S or D. *Spec rates - see discount section in front of book.

Wellesley Inn/ 4800 NW 9th Av, Ft Lauderdale FL 33309. 305-776-6333/ Fax: 776-3648. AE,M,D,DC,CB,V. Cable TV, pool, fax, microwave, refrig, in-rm coffee. Free cont brfst. $50/S or D; $5/ex prsn. 4/9-12/20: $39/S or D. *Spec rates - see discount section in front of book.

Also see Deerfield Beach, Hollywood.

Fort Myers

Days Inn/ 11435 S Cleveland Av, Ft Myers FL 33907. 941-936-1311/ Fax: 936-7076. V,M,AE,D,CB,DC,JCB. On US 41 (Cleveland Av) bet Colonial Blvd & Beacon Manor Dr. Fax, n/s rms, nrby rstrnt, pool, t pkng, arpt trans, in-rm safes. $45-95/S; $51-111/D; $6/ex prsn. 4/16-12/15: $39-60/S; $44-65/D. Discs.

Econo Lodge/ 13301 N Cleveland, Ft Myers FL 33903. 813-995-0571. V,AE,M,DC. I-75 (Exit 26) to SR 78, W to US 41, S 3 mi. Nrby rstrnt, pool, fax, b/f, cable TV, laundry, micro-fridge, n/s rms. Free cont brfst. AAA. $45-65/S;

$50-70/D; $5/ex prsn. 1/19-4/30: $55-75/S; $60-80/D. 5/1-12/14: $35-50/S; $40-55/D. Discs.

Motel 6/ 3350 Marinatown Ln, Ft Myers FL 33903. 941-656-5544/ Fax: 656-6276. M,V,DC,D,AE.DIR[IUS 41 at Marinatown Ln. Nrby rstrnt, cable TV, pool, n/s rms. Free local calls. Premier Award. $35/S; $39/D; $4/ex prsn. 1/25-4/10: $47/S; $51/D. 4/11-12/20: $29-30/S; $33-34/D. Disc.

Taki-ki Motel/ 2631 First St, Ft Myers FL 33916. 941-334-2135/ Fax: 332-1879. V,M,AE,D,DC,CB. 4 1/2 mi W of I-75, Exit 25. Pool, n/s rms, cable TV, tt/dd phone, fax, refrig, microwave, cot, crib, eff, conn rms. Free local calls, coffee. AAA. $48/S; $58/D; $5/ex prsn. 4/15-12/15: $30/S; $35/D; $3/ex prsn. Disc: Govt, l/s. *Guaranteed rates.*

Wellesley Inn/ 4400 Ford St Extension, Ft Myers FL 33916. 941-278-3949/ Fax: 278-3670. AE,M,D,DC,CB,V. Cable TV, pool, fax, microwave, refrig, in-rm coffee. Free cont brfst. $62/S or D; $5/ex prsn. 4/9-12/20: $40/S or D. *Spec rates - see discount section in front of book.

Fort Pierce

Econo Lodge/ 7050 Okeechobee Rd, Ft Pierce FL 34945. 407-465-8600. V,M,AE. I-95 (Exit 65) to SR 70 W. FL Trnpk (Exit 152) to SR 70 E. Nrby rstrnt, cable TV, t pkng, n/s rms. No pets. $50-65/S; $55-65/D; $5/ex prsn. 5/1-11/15: $34-45/S; $40-45/D. Discs.

Motel 6/ 2500 Peters Rd, Ft Pierce FL 34945. 407-461-9937/ Fax: 460-9472. M,V,DC,D,AE. I-95 (Exit 65) to Hwy 70-Okeechobee Rd, lt to Peters Rd, rt to mtl. Nrby rstrnt, cable TV, pool, n/s rms, t pkng. Free local calls. $26-28/S; $30-32/D; $4/ex prsn. 1/25-4/10: $37/S; $41/D. Disc.

Fort Walton Beach

Econo Lodge/ 1284 Marler Dr, Ft Walton Beach FL 32548. 904-243-7123/ Fax: 243-7109. V,M,D,AE. US 98, exit N Santa Rosa Blvd to mtl. Nrby rstrnt, fax, b/f, cable TV, n/s rms. Free cont brfst. $31-37/S; $40-49/D; $5/ex prsn. 3/1-4/30: $35-70/S; $70-90/D. 5/1-9/5: $35-42/S; $45-80/D. 9/6-10/31: $42/S; $59/D. Discs.

Howard Johnson Lodge/ 314 Miracle Strip Parkway, Ft Walton Beach FL 32548. 904-243-6162/ Fax: 664-2735. V,M,AE,D,DC,CB. S on SR 85 to US Hwy 98, W approx 2 mi. Mtg rm, b/f, rstrnt, pool, t pkng, laundry, valet serv, boat dock & ramp, kiddie pool. $40-50/S; $45-62/D. Discs.

Super 8 Motel/ 333 Miracle Strip Pkwy SW, Ft Walton Beach FL 32548. 904-244-4999/ Fax: 243-5657. D,M,V, AE, DC,CB. 1 mi W of SR 85 on US 98. B/f, n/s rms, pool, nrby rstrnt, cable TV, kitchenettes, cot. Free local calls, crib. No pets. AAA. $38-48/S; $42-56/D; $6/ex prsn. Higher holiday/spec event rate. Discs.

Gainesville

Comfort Inn/ 2435 S West 13th St, Gainesville FL 32608. 904-373-6500. V, M,AE,DC. US 441, N of Hwy 331, S of University Av. Nrby rstrnt, pool, fax, b/f, whrlpool, cable TV, laundry, n/s rms. Free cont brfst. No pets. AAA. $42-46/S; $48-52/D; $6/ex prsn. Discs.

Econo Lodge/ 700 NW 75th St, Gainesville FL 32607. 904-332-2346. V,AE,M,DC. I-75 & SR 26 (Newberry Rd), to 2nd stop light. Nrby rstrnt, cable TV, n/s rms. Free AM coffee. No pets. $34-89/S; $42-89/D; $5/ex prsn. Discs.

Econo Lodge/ 2649 SW 13th St, Gainesville FL 32608. 904-373-7816. V,AE,M,DC. On US 441 (SW 13th St). I-75, Exit 74, E 2 mi to US 441 N. Nrby rstrnt, fax, b/f, cable TV, micro-fridges, n/s rms. Free cont brfst. AAA. $35-75/S; $40-80/D; $5/ex prsn. Discs.

HoJo Inn/ 1900 SW 13th St, Gainesville FL 32608. 904-372-1880/ Fax: 335-6862. V,M,D,AE,DC,CB. I-75 (Exit 75) to SR 24, NE to US 441, S to mtl. N/s rms, rstrnt/ lounge, pool, t/b pkng, laundry, cable TV, dd phone, fax, copier. Free cont brfst, trans. $30-38/S; $33-45/D. Discs.

Motel 6/ 4000 SW 40th Blvd, Gainesville FL 32608. 904-373-1604/ Fax: 335-8314. M,V,DC,D,AE. I-75 (Exit 75) to Archer Ave (SR 24), NE to SW 40th Blvd, turn rt. Nrby rstrnt, cable TV, laundry, pool, t pkng, n/s rms. Free

FLORIDA

local calls. $26-28/S; $30-32/D; $4/ex prsn. Football wknds: $50/S; $54/D. Higher spec event rates. Disc.

Super 8 Motel/ 4202 SW 40th Blvd, Gainesville FL 32608. 904-378-3888/ Fax: Ext 404. V,M,DC,CB,AE,D. I-75 (Exit 75) at Archer Rd, turn E to SW 40th Blvd, turn S. B/f, n/s rms, cable TV, suite, micro-fridge, TDD, cot. Free local calls, crib. $36/S; $42/D; $5/ex prsn. Higher spec event rate. Discs.

Also see Alachua.

Haines City

Econo Lodge/ 1504 US 27 S, Haines City FL 33844. 813-422-8621. V,M,AE. I-4 (Exit 23) to US 27, S 10 mi to mtl. Rstrnt/ lounge, pool, mtg rm, fax, cable TV, t pkng, n/s rms. AAA. $50-60/S; $60-70/D; $5/ex prsn. 5/1-12/25: $40-45/S; $45-50/D. Discs.

Hollywood (Ft Lauderdale area)

Days Inn Ft Lauderdale - Hollywood Airport/ 2601 N 29th Av, Hollywood FL 33020. 954-923-7300/ Fax: 921-6706. V,M,AE,D. I-95 (Exit 24) to Sheridan St, W 1 blk. Nrby rstrnt/ lounge, pool, whrlpool, n/s rms, exerc equip, cable TV, arpt trans, tt phone, mtg rm, fax, copier, nwspr, laundry, refrig, elevator, cot, crib, outlets, conn rms, b/f. Free coffee, tea. No pets. AAA. $65/S or D. 4/15-12/15: $48/S or D. Holiday, spec events: $75. Disc: Senior, bsns, TA, govt, milt.

HoJo Inn/ 2900 Polk St, Hollywood FL 33020. 305-923-1516/ Fax: 929-2579. D,M,V,AE,DC,CB. I-95 or FL Turnpike to Hollywood Blvd, E to 28th Av, lt 1 blk to Polk St, lt. N/s rms, rstrnt, pool, t/b pkng, cable TV. Free coffee. $41-70/S or D. 12/16-3/31: $54-88/S or D. Higher spec event rates. Discs.

Homestead

Howard Johnson Lodge/ 1020 N Homestead Blvd, Homestead FL 330-30. 305-248-2121/ Fax: 248-9772. V, M,AE,D,DC,CB. FL Turnpike extension to Homestead exit, W to US 1, rt 1 blk. From 41, take US 27 (997) to 11th St, E to US 1, S 1 blk. Rstrnt, pool, t pkng, rm serv, laundry, valet serv. Free wake-up coffee. Outstanding Achievement Award. $44-60/S; $48-68/D. Discs.

Jacksonville

Best Inns/ 8220 Dix Ellis Trail, Jacksonville FL 32256. 904-739-3323. AE,DC,CB,M,V,D. I-95, Exit 100 W on Baymeadows to Freedom Commerce Pkwy, then S on Dix Ellis Tr. N/s rms, dd/tt phone, fax, b/f, t pkng, pool. Free local calls, cont brfst, pm coffee, crib. AAA. $40-46/S; $47-53/D; $6/ex prsn. Higher spec event rates. Discs.

Budgetel Inns/ 3199 Hartley Rd, Jacksonville FL 32257. 904-268-9999/ Fax: 268-9611. V,M,D,AE,DC,CB. I-295, Exit 2 (Hwy 13) N, E on Hartley Rd. N/s rms, b/f, fax, rstrnt, pool. Free cont brfst, in-rm coffee, local calls. AAA. $39-50/S; $46-57/D. Higher spec event rates. Discs.

Comfort Inn/ 6237 Arlington Expwy, Jacksonville FL 32211. 904-725-5093. V,M,D,AE. I-95 (Exit 117) to Union St, E across Mathews Bridge to beaches. Rstrnt/ lounge, pool, mtg rm, fax, whrlpool, cable TV, n/s rms. Free cont brfst. No pets. $40-75/S; $45-80/D; $6/ex prsn. Spec Events: $70-100/S; $125-150/D. Discs.

Comfort Inn/ 3233 Emerson St, Jacksonville FL 32207. 904-398-3331. V,M,D,AE. I-95 (Exit 104) to Emerson St, turn SW. Rstrnt, pool, mtg rm, fax, b/f, cable TV, t pkng, n/s rms. Free cont brfst. $35-40/S or D; $5/ex prsn. Discs.

Econo Lodge/ 5221 University Blvd W, Jacksonville FL 32216. 904-737-1690. V,M,D,AE. I-95 (S, Exit 103A; N, Exit 102) at University Blvd. Rstrnt, pool, mtg rm, fax, cable TV, t pkng, n/s rms. $33-75/S; $36-75/D. 9/1-4/30: $33-36/S; $36-39/D. Discs.

Motel 6/ 6107 Youngerman Cir, Jacksonville FL 32244. 904-777-6100/ Fax: 779-2223. M,V,DC,D,AE. I-295 (Exit 4) to SR 21 (Blanding Blvd), S to Youngerman Circle, rt. Cable TV, laundry, pool, nrby rstrnt, t pkng, n/s rms. Free local calls. $29-30/S; $33-34/D; $4/ex prsn. Disc.

Motel 6/ 8285 Dix Ellis Trail, Jacksonville FL 32256. 904-731-8400/ Fax: 730-0781. M,V,DC,D,AE. I-95 (Exit 100) to Baymeadows Rd, W to Dix Ellis Trail, S to mtl. Nrby rstrnt, cable TV, pool, n/s rms. Free local calls. Premier

FLORIDA

Award. $30-33/S; $34-37/D; $4/ex prsn. Disc.

Motel 6/ 10885 Harts Rd, Jacksonville FL 32218. 904-757-8600/ Fax: 757-2072. M,V,DC,D,AE. I-95 (Exit 125) to SR 104/ Dunn Ave/ Busch Dr, W on Dunn Av, rt on Harts Rd. Nrby rstrnt, cable TV, laundry, pool, n/s rms. Free local calls. $28-30/S; $32-34/D; $4/ex prsn. Disc.

Quality Inn/ 4660 Salisbury Rd, Jacksonville FL 32256. 904-281-0900. V,M,D,AE. I-95 (Exit 101) to J Turner Butler, E on Salisbury Rd. Rstrnt, pool, mtg rm, fax, b/f, sauna, cable TV, n/s rms. Free cont brfst. No pets. AAA. $45-99/S or D. Discs.

Quality Inn/ 510 S Lane Av, Jacksonville FL 32254. 904-786-0500. V, M, D, AE. I-10 (Exit 54) at Lane Av. Nrby rstrnt/ lounge, pool, mtg rm, fax, b/f, cable TV, t pkng, n/s rms. Free full brfst. $39-65/S; $45-65/D; $10/ex prsn. Discs.

Super 8 Motel/ 10901 Harts Rd, Jacksonville FL 32218. 904-751-3888/ Fax: Ext 402. V,M,DC,CB,AE,D. I-95 (Exit 125) to Dunn Av, turn E to Harts Rd, turn N. B/f, n/s rms, t/b/rv pkng, cable TV, TDD, cot. Free local calls, crib. $35/S; $40/D; $5/ex prsn. Higher spec event/ wknd rate. Discs.

Super 8 Motel/ 5929 Ramona Blvd, Jacksonville FL 32205. 904-781-2878/ Fax: 693-3146. V,M,AE,D,CB,DC. Lane Av & I-10, 3/4 mi E of Loop 295 & I-10. N/s rms, b/f, pool, nrby rstrnt, cont brfst, outlets, laundry, copier, fax. b/t pkng, cot. Free AM coffee, crib. $33/S; $33-39/D; $5/ex prsn. Higher spec event rates. Discs.

Also see Atlantic Beach, Orange Park.

Jennings

Econo Lodge/ Rt 1, Box 222, Jennings FL 32053. 904-938-5500. V,M,AE. I-75 (Exit 87) to SR 143, W to mtl. Nrby rstrnt, pool, fax, b/f, cable TV, t pkng, n/s rms. Free cont brfst. No pets. $25-30/S; $30-35/D; $6/ex prsn. Discs.

Jupiter

Wellesley Inn/ 34 Fishermans Wharf, Jupiter FL 33477. 407-575-7201/ Fax: 575-1169. AE,M,D,DC,CB,V. Cable TV, pool, fax, microwave, refrig, in-rm coffee. Free cont brfst. $62/S or D; $5/ex prsn. 4/9-12/20: $42/S or D. *Spec rates - see discount section in front of book.

Kissimmee
(Orlando - Walt Disney World)

Best Western Kissimmee/ 2261 E Bronson Hwy, Kissimmee FL 34744. 407-846-2221/ Fax: 846-1095. V,M,AE,D,DC,CB. FL Trnpk, Exit 244. Rstrnt/ lounge, pool, n/s rms, satellite TV, video games, playgrnd, tt/dd phone, mtg rm, fax, copier, nwspr, laundry, refrig, elevator, cot, crib, t/b/rv pkng, eff, conn rms, b/f. No pets. Mobil. $27/S or D. 2/10-3/31, 6/11-8/19: $37/S or D. 1/1-1/2, 2/12-2/18, 4/1-4/15, 7/1-7/8, 12/22-12/31: $49/S or D.*Guaranteed rates.*

Comfort Inn/ 7571 W Irlo Bronson Hwy, Kissimmee FL 34747. 407-396-7500. V, AE,M,DC. 1 mi W of Walt Disney World/ EPCOT Ctr on US 192 W. Rstrnt/ lounge, pool, fax, b/f, cable TV, t pkng, trans, n/s rms. AAA. $27-51/S or D. 2/9-4/30: $27-65/S or D. 6/9-8/13, 12/22-1/1: $41-65/S or D. Discs.

Comfort Suites/ 4018 W Irlo Bronson Hwy, Kissimmee FL 34741. 407-870-2000. V,M,D,AE. I-4 (Exit 25A) to US 192, E 5 mi to mtl. Rstrnt/ lounge, pool, fax, b/f, whrlpool, cable TV, attraction trans, n/s rms. Free cont brfst. No pets. AAA. $42-128/S or D; $8/ex prsn. 5/1-8/18, 12/26-1/2: $68-128/S or D. Discs.

Days Inn East of the Magic Kingdom/ 5840 W Bronson Hwy, Kissimmee FL 34746. 407-396-7969/ Fax: 396-1789/ 800-327-9126. V,M,AE,D,CB,DC. I-4 (Exit 25A) to US 192, E 1/2 mi. Rstrnt/ nrby lounge, pool, n/s rms, cable TV, video games, playgrnd, arpt trans, TDD, tt/dd phone, mtg rm, fax, copier, nwspr, laundry, cot, crib, outlets, t/b/rv pkng, conn rms, b/f. $31/up to 4 people. 2/9-4/13, 6/7-8/24, 12/23-12/31: $41/up to 4 people. Disc: Senior, bsns, family, TA, trkr, govt, milt.

Days Suites East of the Magic Kingdom/ 5820 W Bronson Hwy, Kissimmee FL 34746. 407-396-7900/ Fax:

FLORIDA

396-1789/ 800-327-9126. V,M,AE,D, CB,DC. I-4 (Exit 25A) to US 192, E 1/2 mi. Rstrnt/ nrby lounge, pool, n/s rms, cable TV, video games, playgrnd, arpt trans, TDD, tt/dd phone, mtg rm, fax, copier, nwspr, laundry, refrig, microwave, cot, crib, outlets, t/b/rv pkng, conn rms, b/f. $43/Suite; 2/9-4/13, 6/7-8/24, 12/23-12/31: $73/Suite. Disc: Senior, bsns, family, TA, govt, trkr, milt.

Econo Lodge/ 7514 W Bronson Hwy, Kissimmee FL 34746. 407-396-2000. V,M,AE. I-4 (Exit 25B) to US 192. 1 mi W of W Disney World. Rstrnt/ lounge, pool, mtg rm, b/f, whrlpool, cable TV, kiddie pool, game rm, n/s rms. Free Disney trans. No pets. AAA. $29-59/S or D; $5/ex prsn. Discs.

Econo Lodge/ 4311 W Bronson Hwy, Kissimmee FL 34746. 407-396-7100. V,M,AE. US 192 (Exit 25A). Nrby rstrnt, pool, fax, b/f, cable TV, t pkng, kiddie pool, game rm, n/s rms. Free Disney trans. No pets. AAA. $29-49/S or D; $3/ex prsn. Discs.

Econo Lodge/ 8620 W Bronson Hwy, Kissimmee FL 34747. 407-396-9300. AE,V,M,DC. I-4 (Exit 25B) to US 192. Rstrnt/ lounge, pool, fax, b/f, whrlpool, cable TV, game rm, VCR/ movies. No pets. AAA. $39-79/S or D; $9/ex prsn. 5/1-12/20: $29-69/S or D. 12/21-12/31: $59-79/S or D. Discs.

Friendship Inn/ 4669 W US 192, Kissimmee FL 34746. 407-396-1890. V, M, D,AE. I-4, exit 25A, 5 1/2 mi on lt. Tnpk, exit 244, rt, 8 mi. Nrby rstrnt/ lounge, pool, fax, b/f, cable TV, t pkng, n/s rms. $22-35/S; $25-35/D; $5/ex prsn. 12/24-1/2: $50/S or D. Discs.

HoJo Inn/ 6051 W Bronson Hwy, Kissimmee FL 34747. 407-396-1748/ Fax: 649-8642. AE,V,M,DC,CB,D. I-4 (Exit 25A) to US 192, E 1 mi. N/s rms, b/f, rstrnt, pool, fax, playgrnd, kiddie pool, whrlpool. Free coffee. No pets. Gold Medal Winner. $30-75/S or D. Discs.

Howard Johnson Hotel/ 8660 W Bronson Hwy, Kissimmee FL 34747. 407-395-4500/ Fax: 396-8875. V,M,AE,D, DC,CB. I-4 (Exit 258) to US 192, W 4.5 mi to mtl. N/s rms, b/f, rstrnt/ lounge, pool, basketball, tennis, in-rm safe, VCR, cable TV. Free Disney trans. No pets. $39-79/S or D. 12-24-1/1: $59-99/S or D. Discs.

Howard Johnson Lodge/ 2323 Hwy 192 E, Kissimmee FL 32743. 407-846-4900. AE,V,M,DC,CB,D. FL Trnpk (Exit 244) at US 192, turn W to mtl. N/s rms, b/f, rstrnt/ lounge, pool, t pkng, game rm, trans, fax, in-rm safe, laundry, bi-lingual staff and linguist phones. $25-84/S; $29-89/D. Discs.

Howard Johnson Lodge/ 4643 W Hwy 192, Kissimmee FL 34706. 407-396-1340/ Fax: 396-1347. V,M,D,DC, CB,AE. I-4 (Exit 25A) to US 192, E 5 mi to mtl. FL Turnpike (Exit 244) at US 192, W 9 mi. N/s rms, b/f, pool, arpt trans, t pkng, laundry, refrig, fax, microwave. Free cont brfst. No pets. $25-35/S; $28-60/D. Discs.

Howard Johnson Plaza Hotel/ 5150 W US 192, Kissimmee FL 34746. 407-396-1111/ Fax: 396-1607. V,M,D,AE, DC,CB. I-4 (Exit 25A) to US 192, E to mtl. Fl turnpike (Exit 244) to US 192, W 12 mi. N/s rms, b/f, rstrnt/ lounge, pool, hot tub, sauna, playgrnd, tennis, shuf-fleboard, lake, rm serv, trans, laundry. No pets. $39-95/S or D. Discs.

Knights Inn Maingate/ 7475 W Irlo Bronson Mem Hwy, Kissimmee FL 34746. 407-396-4200/ Fax: 396-8838/ 800-944-0062. V,M,AE,D,DC,CB. I-4 E 1 1/2 mi. Nrby rstrnt/ lounge, pool, n/s rms, satellite TV, video games, tt/dd phones, fax, copier, laundry, refrig, cot, crib, eff, conn rms, b/f. Free coffee. No pets. AAA. $27/S or D. 2/10-3/31, 6/11-8/19: $37/S or D. 1/1-1/2, 2/12-2/18, 4/1-4/15, 7/1-7/8, 12/22-12/31: $49/S or D. Disc: Senior, bsns, TA, govt, family, milt. *Guaranteed rates.*

Motel 6/ 5731 W Bronson Hwy, Kissimmee FL 34746. 407-396-6333/ Fax: 396-7715. M,V,DC,D,AE. I-4 (Exit 25A) to US 192, E 2 mi. Nrby rstrnt, cable TV, laundry, pool, n/s rms, t pkng. Free local calls. $20-22/S; $24-26/D; $4/ex prsn. 1/25-5/22: $26/S; $30/D. Higher spec event rates. Disc.

Motel 6/ 7455 W Bronson Hwy, Kissimmee FL 34747. 407-396-6422/ Fax: 396-0720. M,V,DC,D,AE. I-4 (Exit 25B) to US 192 W/ Irlo Bronson Hwy, W 2 mi

FLORIDA

to mtl. Nrby rstrnt, cable TV, laundry, pool, n/s rms. Free local calls. $30/S or D; $4/ex prsn. 1/25-5/22, 12/21-1/1: $35/S or D. 5/23-6/12, 9/5-12/19: $26/S; $30/D. 6/13-9/4: $34/S; $38/D. Higher spec event rates. Disc.

Quality Inn and Suites/ 2039 E Irlo Bronson Hwy, Kissimmee FL 34744. 407-846-7814. V,M,D,AE. At US 192 & Florida Trnpk (Exit 244). Nrby rstrnt, pool, mtg rm, fax, b/f, whrlpool, cable TV, t pkng, n/s rms. No pets. AAA. $29-97/S or D. Discs.

Quality Inn/ 4944 W Irlo Bronson Hwy, Kissimmee FL 34746. 407-396-4455. V, M,AE,DC. I-4 (Exit 25A) to US 192, E 4 mi to mtl. At jct SR 535. Rstrnt/ lounge, pool, cable TV, t pkng, n/s rms. No pets. $45-65/S or D; $5/ex prsn. Discs.

Rodeway Inn/ 5245 W Irlo Bronson Hwy, Kissimmee FL 34746. 407-396-7700. V,AE,M,DC. I-4 (Exit 25A) E 3 mi. Rstrnt/ lounge, pool, mtg rm, fax, b/f, cable TV, t pkng, fame rm. No pets. $29-64/S or D. 5/1-6/15, 8/28-12/21: $29-43/S or D. 6/16-8/27: $39-53/S or D. Discs.

Sleep Inn/ 8536 W Irlo Bronson Hwy, Kissimmee FL 34746. 407-396-1600. V, AE,M,DC. I-4 (Exit 25B) to US 192, W to mtl. Nrby rstrnt, pool, fax, b/f, cable TV, t pkng, n/s rms. Free cont brfst. No pets. AAA. $29-40/S or D; $5/ex prsn. 6/18-8/31: $49-79/S or D. 12/22-12/31: $79-140/S or D. Discs.

Super 8 Motel/ 4880 W Bronson Hwy, Kissimmee FL 34746. 407-396-1144/ Fax: 396-4389/ 800-325-4872. V, M, AE,D,CB,DC. I-4 (Exit 25A) to Hwy 192 (Bronson Hwy), E 4 mi. FL Trnpk (Exit 244) to Hwy 192, rt 10 mi. N/s rms, b/f, pool, cont brfst, b/t pkng, boat rental, laundry, in-rm safe, cable TV, attraction trans, cot. Free AM coffee, crib. $26-29/S or D. 2/12-3/31: $39/S or D. Higher spec event rates. Discs.

Also see Orlando.

Lake Buena Vista

Comfort Inn/ 8442 Palm Pkwy, Lake Buena Vista FL 32836. 407-239-7300. V,M,DC,AE. I-4 to SR 535, N to Palm Pkwy, rt to mtl. Rstrnt/ lounge, pool, fax, b/f, cable TV, t pkng, n/s rms. Free Disney trans. AAA $29-69/S or D. Discs.

Lake City

Econo Lodge/ Box 430, Lake City FL 32055. 904-752-7891. V,AE,M,DC. I-75 at US 90. Rstrnt, pool, fax, b/f, cable TV, t pkng, family rms, n/s rms. Free cont brfst. $31-50/S; $35-65/D; $5/ex prsn. Discs.

Econo Lodge/ Rte 3, Box 173, Lake City FL 32055. 904-755-9311. V, AE, M,DC. I-75 & US 441, 14 mi S of Lake City. Nrby rstrnt, pool, fax, cable TV, t pkng, n/s rms. $25-34/S; $31-40/D; $4/ex prsn. Discs.

Friendship Inn/ Box 2156, Lake City FL 32056. 904-755-5203. V,AE,M,DC. I-75 (Exit 82) to US 90, E 1 blk, rt on Commerce Blvd. Rstrnt, fax, b/f, cable TV, t pkng, n/s rms. Free cont brfst. AAA. $28-32/S; $32-40/D; $5/ex prsn. Discs.

Howard Johnson Lodge/ Rte 13, Box 1082, Lake City FL 32055. 904-752-6262/ Fax: 752-8251. AE,V,M,DC, CB,D. I-75 (Exit 82) to US 90. N/s rms, mtg rm, rstrnt, pool, t pkng, laundry, shuffleboard. Free cont brfst. $32-45/S; $42-60/D. Higher spec event, holiday, wknd rates. Discs.

Motel 6/ Rte 13, Box 640, Lake City FL 32055. 904-755-4664/ Fax: 758-7753. M,V,DC,D,AE. I-75 (Exit 82) to US 90, W to mtl on Hall of Fame Dr. Nrby rstrnt, cable TV, laundry, pool, t pkng, n/s rms. Free local calls. $24/S; $28/D; $4/ex prsn. Disc.

Super 8 Motel/ I-75 & SR 47, Lake City FL 32055. 904-752-6450/ Fax: 102. D,M,V,AE,DC,CB. I-75 (Exit 81) at SR 47. B/f, n/s rms, t/b/rv pkng, cable TV, cot. Free local calls, crib. No pets. $31/S; $36/D; $5/ex prsn. Higher spec event rate. Discs.

Lakeland

Comfort Inn/ 1817 E Memorial Blvd, Lakeland FL 33801. 813-688-9221/ Fax: 687-4797. V,M,D,AE. I-4: Ebnd, (Exit 16) to US 92, E 5 mi to mtl; Wbnd, (Exit 19) to SR 33 S, lt on Memorial Blvd 1 mi to mtl. Nrby rstrnt, pool, cable TV, t pkng, n/s rms. Free cont brfst. $30-47/S; $35-55/D; $4/ex prsn. Discs.

Motel 6/ 3120 US 98 N, Lakeland FL 33809. 941-682-0643/ Fax: 686-1701. M,V,DC,D,AE. I-4 (Exit 18) to US 98, SE to Griffin Rd, turn rt. Nrby rstrnt, cable TV, laundry, elevator, pool, t pkng, n/s rms. Free local calls. $29-30/S; $33-34/D; $4/ex prsn. 1/25-4/10: $36/S; $40/D. Disc.

Wellesley Inn & Suites/ 3520 N Highway 98, Lakeland FL 33805. 941-859-3399/ Fax: 859-3483. AE,M,D,DC, CB,V. Cable TV, pool, fax, microwave, refrig, in-rm coffee. Free cont brfst. $60/S or D; $5/ex prsn. 4/9-12/20: $45/S or D. $60-75/suites. *Spec rates - see discount section in front of book.

Lantana

Motel 6/ 1310 W Lantana Rd, Lantana FL 33462. 407-585-5833/ Fax: 547-9701. M,V,DC,D,AE. I-95 (Exit 46) to Lantana Rd, E to first signal light, rt to mtl. Nrby rstrnt, cable TV, laundry, pool, n/s rms. Free local calls. $30-32/S; $34-36/D; $4/ex prsn. 1/25-4/10: $40/S; $44/D. Disc.

Leesburg

Budget Host Inn/ 1225 N 14th St, Leesburg FL 34748. 904-787-3534/ Fax: 787-0060. AE,D,M,V. Jct US 441 & 27. Cable TV, dd phone, conn rms, kitchens, nrby rstrnt/ lounge, pool, picnic area, laundry, arpt trans, t pkng, cot. No pets. AAA. $36/S or D; $4/ex prsn. 1/19-4/22: $47-48/S or D. Discs.

Super 8 Motel/ 1392 N Blvd W, Leesburg FL 34748. 904-787-6363/ Ext 402. V,M,DC,CB,AE,D. Jct of Hwys 27 & 441. B/f, n/s rms, pool, micro-fridge, elevator, cable TV, cot. Free local calls, crib. $36-41/S; $42-47/D; $6/ex prsn. Higher spec event rate. Discs.

Live Oak

Econo Lodge/ I-10 & US 129, Live Oak FL 32060. 904-362-7459. V,AE,M,DC. I-10 (Exit 40) at US 129. Rstrnt, pool, mtg rm, fax, b/f, whrlpool, cable TV, t pkng, laundry, n/s rms, micro-fridges. Free cont brfst. AAA. $37-75/S; $42-80/D; $5/ex prsn. Discs.

MacClenny

Days Inn/ 1499 S 6th St, MacClenny FL 32063. 904-259-5100. V,M,AE,D,CB, DC,JCB. I-10 (Exit 48) to SR 121, turn N to mtl. Fax, n/s rms, nrby rstrnt, pool, b/f, t pkng, cable TV, cot. Free cont brfst. $35-55/S; $40-60/D; $5/ex prsn. Discs.

Econo Lodge/ Box 425, MacClenny FL 32063. 904-259-3000. V,AE,M,DC. I-10 (Exit 48) at SR 121. Nrby rstrnt, pool, mtg rm, fax, b/f, whrlpool, cable TV, t/rv pkng, laundry, n/s rms, micro-fridges. Free cont brfst. AAA. $35-70/S; $40-75/D; $5/ex prsn. Discs.

Madison

Super 8 Motel/ Rte 1. Box 3329-F, Madison FL 32340. 904-973-6267. V,M,D,AE,DC,CB. I-10 (Exit 37) to SR 53. B/f, n/s rms, nrby rstrnt, t/b/rv pkng, copier, satellite TV, mtg rm, cot. crib. No pets. $39/S; $44/D; $4/ex prsn. Higher spec event rates. Discs.

Melbourne

Econo Lodge/ 4505 W New Haven Av, Melbourne FL 32904. 407-724-5450. V,AE,M,DC. I-95 (Exit 71) & US 192. Nrby rstrnt, cable TV, t pkng, tt phone, n/s rms. Free cont brfst. $31-49/S; $33-61/D; $6/ex prsn. Discs.

Miami Beach

Days Inn/ 7450 Ocean Terrace, Miami Beach FL 33141. 305-866-1631/ Fax: 868-4617. V,M,AE,D,CB,DC,JCB. I-95 (Exit 9) to 79th St E, 79th becomes 71st, lt to SR A1A, N to 75th St, turn rt. Fax, n/s rms, rstrnt/ lounge, pool, arpt trans, refrig, game rm. $59-99/S or D; $8/ex prsn. 2/1-3/31: $69-109/S or D. 4/1-4/15: $59-89/S or D. 4/16-12/14: $39-79/S or D. Discs.

Mount Dora

Econo Lodge/ 300 N New US 441, Mount Dora FL 32757. 904-383-2181. V,AE,M,DC. On US 441 N at Mt. Dora. Rstrnt/ lounge, pool, fax, cable TV, t pkng, kitchenettes, eff, n/s rms. Free cont brfst. No pets. AAA. $40-49/S; $45-59/D; $5/ex prsn. 5/1-6/25, 11/1-12/20: $35-40/S; $40-49/D. 6/26-10/31: $35-45/S; $40-49/D. Discs.

Naples

Budget Host Spinnaker Inn/ 6600 Dudley Dr, Naples FL 33999. 813-434-0444/ Fax: 434-0414/ 800-351-0444.

FLORIDA

AE,D,M,V. I-75, Exit 16 W, lt 1st St. Nrby rstrnt, pool, cable TV, tt/dd phone, fax, copier, nwspr, cot, crib, t/b/rv pkng, eff, conn rms, b/f. Free cont brfst, coffee, tea. AAA. $54/S; $60/D; $6/ex prsn. 4/21-12/14: $36/S; $39/D. 1/15-4/20: $75/S; $85/D. Disc: Family, l/s. *Guaranteed rates.*

Comfort Inn/ 3860 Tollgate Blvd, Naples FL 33999. 813-353-9500. V,AE,M,DC. I-75 (Exit 15) at SR 951, turn S. Nrby rstrnt/ lounge, pool, mtg rm, whrlpool, cable TV, t pkng. Free cont brfst. No pets. Hospitality Award. AAA. $64-139/S or D; $8/ex prsn. 2/1-4/30, 12/21-12/31: $89-149/S or D. 5/1-12/20: $44-119/S or D. Discs.

Days Inn/ 1925 Davis Blvd, Naples FL 33942. 941-774-3117/ Fax: 775-5333. V,M,AE,D,CB,DC,JCB. US 41 & SR 84. Fax, n/s rms, nrby rstrnt, pool, whrlpool, b/f, t pkng, cable TV, refrig, safe, picnic area, barbecue, playgrnd, laundry. Free cont brfst. Chairman's Award. $80/S or D; $5/ex prsn. 2/1-3/31: $95/S or D. 4/1-4/16: $75/S or D. 4/17-12/18: $44-50/S or D. Discs.

Wellesley Inn/ 1555 Fifth Av S, Naples FL 33942. 941-793-4646/ Fax: 793-5248. AE,M,D,DC,CB,V. Cable TV, pool, fax, microwave, refrig, in-rm coffee. Free cont brfst. 1/1-2/4, 4/1-4/8: $70/S or D; $5/ex prsn. 2/5-3/31: $90/S or D. 4/9-12/20: $42/S or D. *Spec rates - see discount section in front of book.

Naranja Lakes

Econo Lodge/ 27707 S Dixie Hwy, Naranja Lakes FL 33032. 305-245-4330. V,M,D,AE. FL Trnpk (Exit 12) to Carrivean Blvd, S on US 1 to 277th St. Nrby rstrnt, fax, cable TV, t pkng, n/s rms. $65-75/S; $75-85/D; $5/ex prsn. 3/1-4/30: $45-50/S; $50-55/D. 5/1-12/15: $30-35/S; $35-40/D; Discs.

New Port Richey

Econo Lodge/ 7631 US 19, New Port Richey FL 34652. 813-845-4990. V,AE,M,DC. SR 52 at US 19 S. Nrby rstrnt, pool, fax, cable TV, laundry, kitchenettes, n/s rms. Free coffee. $33-38/S; $36-40/D; $5/ex prsn. 2/1-4/30: $40-45/S; $46-50/D. 5/1-12/21: $30-33/S; $33-38/D. Discs.

Howard Johnson Lodge/ 6523 US 19, New Port Richey FL 34652. 813-848-3487. V,M,D,AE,DC,CB. I-75: Sbnd (Exit 59) to Hwy 52, W to Hwy 19, lt 6 mi; Nbnd (Exit 58) to Hwy 54, W to Hwy 19, rt 3 mi. N/s rms, b/f, rstrnt/ lounge, pool, t pkng, cable TV, suites. Free cont brfst. $35-60/S; $38-65/D. Discs.

New Smyrna Beach

Smyrna Motel/ 1050 N Dixie Freeway, New Smyrna Beach FL 32168. 904-428-2495/ 800-362-1841. V,M,AE,D,DC. I-95 (Exit 84) to SR 44 (Bsns 44), E to US 1, N 3 lights on lt. Nrby rstrnt, n/s rms, cable TV, playgrnd, tt phones, refrig, cot, crib, t/b pkng, conn rms. AAA. $30/S; $35/D; $5/ex prsn. 2/1-4/30, 7/1-7/31: $40-42/S; $45-48/D. Disc: Senior, TA, trkr, family. *Guaranteed Rates.*

Niceville

Comfort Inn/ 101 SR 85 N, Niceville FL 32578. 904-678-8077. V,M,D,AE. SR 85 & SR 20. Nrby rstrnt, pool, mtg rm, fax, b/f, whrlpool, cable TV, t pkng, n/s rms. Free cont brfst. Hospitality Award. $48-75/S or D; $10/ex prsn. 5/1-9/3: $58-80/S; $65-85/D. 9/4-12/31: $48-70/S or D. Discs.

Friendship Inn/ 626 John Sims Pkwy, Niceville FL 32578. 904-678-4164. V,AE,M,DC. On Hwy 20 at Niceville. Rstrnt/ lounge, pool, mtg rm, fax, cable TV, t pkng, n/s rms. $30-36/S; $36-42/D; $5/ex prsn. 5/1-9/10: $34-40/S; $50-60/D. Discs.

North Palm Beach (West Palm Beach area)

Econo Lodge/ 757 US 1 N, N Palm Beach FL 33408. 407-848-1424. V, M, D,AE,DC. I-95: S (Exit 57) E to US 1, S 1 1/2 mi; N (Exit 56) E to US 1, N. From Trnpk, exit 109 E to US 1 S. Nrby rstrnt, pool, fax, b/f, sauna, cable TV, t pkng, exerc equip, n/s rms, laundry, eff. Free cont brfst. $61-71/S or D. 1/14-4/30: $71-90/S or D. 5/1-11/30: $40-50/S or D. 12/1-12/16: $50-60/S or D. Discs.

Ocala

Budget Host Western Motel/ 4013 NW Blitchton Rd, Ocala FL 34482. 904-732-6940. AE,M,V,D. 2 blks W of jct I-

FLORIDA

75 & US 27. Cable TV, dd phones, conn rms, n/s rms, cont brfst, t pkng, cot, crib. AAA/ Mobil. $26-32/S; $34-40/D; $4-6/ex prsn. 4/15-12/15: $22-26/S; $28-32/D. Spec events: $32-52/S; $42-72/D. Discs.

Comfort Inn/ 4040 W Silver Springs Blvd, Ocala FL 34482. 904-629-8850. AE,M,V,DC. I-75 (Exit 69) at Hwy 40 (Silver Springs Rd). Rstrnt, pool, cable TV, t pkng, n/s rms. No pets. $35-60/S; $40-65/D; $5/ex prsn. Discs.

Friendship Inn/ 723 SW Pine Av, Ocala FL 34474. 904-622-1266. V,AE,M,DC. I-75 to SR 200, E to US 301/441. Nrby rstrnt, pool, cable TV, n/s rms. No pets. $22-40/S; $24-46/D; $5/ex prsn. Discs.

Friendship Inn/ 2829 NE Silver Springs Blvd, Ocala FL 34470. 904-622-7503. V,AE,M,DC. I-75 (Exit 69) to SR 40 E, 4 mi to mtl. Nrby rstrnt, pool, cable TV, n/s rms. No pets. $22-40/S; $24-46/D; $5/ex prsn. Higher spec event rates. Discs.

Quality Inn/ 3767 NW Blitchton Rd, Ocala FL 34475. 904-732-2300/ Fax: 351-0153. V,M,DC,AE. I-75 (Exit 70) at US 27. Rstrnt/ lounge, pool, mtg rm, fax, cable TV, t pkng, n/s rms. $37-49/S; $41-49/D; $6/ex prsn. 5/1-6/15, 9/17-12/14: $30-35/S; $34-39/D. 6/15-9/16: $33-38/S; $39-43/D. Discs.

Also see Silver Springs.

Orange Park (Jacksonville area)

Comfort Inn/ 341 Park Av, Orange Park FL 32073. 904-264-3297. V,AE,M,DC. I-295 (Exit 3) to US 17. Rstrnt/ lounge, pool, mtg rm, fax, cable TV, t pkng, n/s rms. Free cont brfst. No pets. AAA. $31-49/S or D. $6/ex prsn. Discs.

Wilson Inn/ 4580 Collins Rd, Orange Park FL 32073. 904-264-4466. AE, M,V,CB,D,DC. I-295, Exit 3. Pool, cable TV, refrig, microwave, fax. Free local calls, brfst bar, popcorn, punch. AAA. $40/S; $45-56/D. Disc: AARP, AAA, family, senior.

Orlando (Walt Disney World area)

Best Western Orlando West/ 2014 W Colonial Dr, Orlando FL 32804. 407-841-8600/ Fax: 843-7080/ 800-645-6386. V,M,AE,D,DC,CB. 1-1/2 mi W of I-4, Exit 41. Rstrnt/ lounge, pool, n/s rms, cable TV, tt phone, mtg rm, fax, copier, laundry, crib, t/b/rv pkng, conn rms. AAA. $39/S or D; $5/ex prsn. 2/20-4/20, 6/14-9/1: $49-59/S or D. 12/31-1/1, 2/14-2/20, Spec events: $70/S; $80/D. *Guaranteed rates.*

Comfort Inn Orlando/ 8421 S Orange Blossom Trail, Orlando FL 32809. 407-855-6060. V,M,DC,AE. US 441, S to mtl. 3rd light on rt. Rstrnt/ lounge, pool, mtg rm, cable TV, t pkng, buffet brfst, n/s rms. Free trans. No pets. AAA. $40-99/S or D; $6/ex prsn. Discs.

Comfort Inn/ 5825 International Dr, Orlando FL 32819. 407-351-4100. V,M,AE,DC. Kirkman Rd & International Dr. Nrby rstrnt, pool, b/f, cable TV, trans, n/s rms. Free cont brfst. No pets. AAA. $29-99/S or D. Discs.

Comfort Inn/ 3956 W Colonial Dr, Orlando FL 32808. 407-291-1452. V, M, D,AE. I-4 to SR 50, W 3 mi to mtl. Nrby rstrnt, pool, fax, cable TV, n/s rms. Free local calls, cont brfst. No pets. AAA. $55-85/S or D; $5/ex prsn. 5/1-6/14, 7/7-12/20: $35-65/S or D. Discs.

Days Inn Lake Buena Vista Village/ 12490 Apopka Vineland Rd, Orlando FL 32836. 407-239-4646/ Fax: 239-8469/ 800-521-3297. V,M,AE,D,CB, DC,JCB. I-4 (Exit 27) to Hwy 535, N 1 blk. Rstrnt/ lounge, pool, kiddie pool, n/s rms, cable TV, VCR/ movies, video games, arpt trans, TDD, tt/dd phone, mtg rm, fax, copier, laundry, refrig, elevator, cot, crib, outlets, t/b/rv pkng, eff, conn rms, b/f. $37/up to 4 people. 2/9-4/13, 6/7-8/24, 12/23-12/31: $69/up to 4 people. Disc: Senior, bsns, TA, govt, milt, trkr, family, l/s.

Days Inn Lakeside/ 7335 Sand Lake Rd, Orlando FL 32809. 407-859-7700/ Fax: 407-851-6266/ 800-231-5514. V, M,AE,D,CB,DC,JCB. I-4 (Exit 29) to Sand Lake Rd, 1 blk to mtl. Rstrnt/ lounge, pool, n/s rms, cable TV, video games, playgrnd, arpt trans, TDD, tt/dd phone, fax, copier, laundry, refrig, elevator, cot, crib, outlets, t/b/rv pkng, eff, b/f. No pets. AAA. $31/up to 4 people. 2/19-4/13, 6/7-8/24, 12/23-12/31: $41/up to 4 people. Disc: Senior, bsns, TA, govt, milt, trkr, family.

FLORIDA 72

Days Inn Orlando/ 2500 W 33rd St, Orlando FL 32839. 407-841-3731/ Fax: 841-0642. AE,M,V,DC,D. I-4 (Exit 32) at 33rd St. Rstrnt, pool, t pkng, arpt trans, laundry, cable TV, cot. $30-90/S or D. Discs.

Days Lodge Florida Mall/ 1851 W Landstreet Rd, Orlando FL 32809. 407-859-7700/ Fax: 851-6266/ 800-231-5514. V,M,AE,D,CB,DC,JCB. FL Trnpk (Exit 254) to Rte 441, N (Orange Blossom Tr). 5 mi from Orlando Intl Arpt via Beeline Expwy. Rstrnt/ lounge, pool, n/s rms, cable TV, video games, playgrnd, arpt trans, TDD, tt/dd phone, mtg rm, fax, copier, laundry, refrig, elevator, cot, crib, outlets, t/b/rv pkng, eff, conn rms, b/f. AAA. $25/up to 4 people. 2/9-4/13, 6/7-8/24, 12/23-12/31: $35/up to 4 people. Disc: Senior, bsns, TA, govt, milt, trkr, family.

Econo Lodge/ 3300 W Colonial Dr, Orlando FL 32808. 407-293-7221. V,AE,M,DC. FL Tnpk (Exit 267) to Colonial Dr, E 7 mi to mtl. I-4: W (Exit 41) to Hwy 408, W (rt) 2 mi to mtl; E (Exit 30B) to Kirkman Rd, N to Colonial Dr, turn E (rt) to mtl. Rstrnt/ lounge, pool, mtg rm, fax, cable TV, laundry, trans, n/s rms. AAA. $28-38/S or D; $6/ex prsn. 2/9-4/30, 6/9-9/4: $38-54/S or D. Discs.

Howard Johnson Hotel/ 6603 International Dr, Orlando FL 32819. 407-351-2900/ Fax: 352-2738. D,M,V,AE,DC,CB. I-4 (Wbnd, Exit 30A; Ebnd, Exit 29) to International Dr. N/s rms, b/f, rstrnt, pool, exerc equip, cable TV, in-rm safe, sun deck, game rm, laundry, b pkng. $40-80/S or D. Discs.

Howard Johnson Hotel/ 929 W Colonial Dr, Orlando FL 32804. 407-843-1360/ Fax: 839-3333. V,M,D,AE,DC,CB. I-4 (Exit 41) to Hwy 50, W 1/2 mi. FL Trnpk (Exit 267) to Hwy 50, E. N/s rms, mtg rm, b/f, rstrnt, pool, laundry, rm serv, cable TV, whrlpool. Free cont brfst, coffee. No pets. AAA. $35-55/S or D. Discs.

Howard Johnson Lodge/ 8700 S Orange Blossom Trail, Orlando FL 32809. 407-851-2330/ Fax: 857-6747. V,M,D,AE,DC,CB. FL Trnpk (Exit 254) to US 441, N 1/4 mi. I-4 (Exit 28) to Beeline, W to Hwy 441 (Consulate Av) N. N/s rms, b/f, rstrnt, pool, trans, t pkng, cable TV, laundry. $30-65/S; $35-75/D. Discs.

Howard Johnson Lodge/ 9956 Hawaiian Court, Orlando FL 32819. 407-351-5100/ Fax: 352-7188. V, M, AE,D,DC,CB. I-4 (Exit 28) to International Dr, turn rt, 1st lt to Hawaiian Court. Mtg rm, b/f, lounge, pool, laundry, nwspr, cable TV, rental cars, suites. Free coffee. $41-81/S or D. $59-99/suites.

Howard Johnson Resort Hotel/ 5905 International Dr, Orlando FL 32819. 407-351-2100/ Fax: 352-2991. AE,V,M,DC,CB,D. FL Trnpk to I-4 (Exit 30A), W to International Dr. N/s rms, mtg rm, rstrnt/ lounge, pool, rm serv, cable TV, laundry, game rm. $39-99/S or D. Discs.

Motel 6/ 5300 Adanson Rd, Orlando FL 32810. 407-647-1444/ Fax: 647-1016. M,V,DC,D,AE. I-4 (Exit 46) to Lee Rd, W 1/4 mi. Nrby rstrnt, cable TV, pool, n/s rms. Free local calls. $25-30/S; $29-34/D; $4/ex prsn. Higher spec event rates. Disc.

Motel 6/ 5909 American Way, Orlando FL 32819. 407-351-6500/ Fax: 352-5481. M,V,DC,D,AE. I-4 (Exit 30A) to American Way (E)/ Kirkman Rd (W), S to American Way. Nrby rstrnt, cable TV, laundry, pool, n/s rms. Free local calls. Premier Award. $33/S or D. 1/25-4/10: $36/S or D. 4/11-5/22: $25/S or D. Higher spec event rates. Disc.

Quality Inn Plaza/ 9000 International Dr, Orlando FL 32819. 407-345-8585. V,M,AE,D,DC,CB. I-4 (Exit 29) to Sand Lake Rd, rt to International Dr. Beeline Expressway to International Dr, turn rt. Rstrnt/ lounge, pool, fax, b/f, cable TV, t pkng, n/s rms, trans. $29-59/S or D. Discs.

Quality Inn/ 2601 McCoy Rd, Orlando FL 32809. 407-856-4663. V,M,AE. I-4 to Beeline Expwy E. Nrby rstrnt/ lounge, pool, fax, b/f, cable TV, t pkng, n/s rms, mini suites. Free cont brfst, attraction/ arpt trans. No pets. AAA. $40-65/S; $45-75/D. 5/1-8/15: $38-50/S; $45-60/D. 8/16-12/26: $32-40/S; $35-50/D. Discs.

FLORIDA

Quality Inn/ 7600 International Dr, Orlando FL 32819. 407-351-1600. V, M, DC,AE. I-4 to SR 482 E, N on International Dr. Rstrnt/ lounge, pool, b/f, t pkng, n/s rms, trans. $29-53/S or D. Discs.

Rodeway Inn/ 8601 S Orange Blossom Tr, Orlando FL 32809. 407-859-4100. V,AE,M,DC. SR 528 W Beeline exit, US 441 N 1/2 mi. Rstrnt, pool, b/f, cable TV, t pkng, n/s rms. No pets. AAA.$35-70/S;$40-75/D; $5/ex prsn. Discs.

Wellesley Inn/ 5635 Windhover Dr, Orlando FL 32819. 407-345-0026/ Fax: 345-8809. V,M,AE,D,CB. Cable TV, pool, fax, microwave, refrig, in-rm coffee. Free cont brfst. $40/S or D; $5/ex prsn. 2/9-4/27, 6/14-8/22: $55/S or D.

Also see Davenport, Fern Park, Kissimmee, Sanford, Winter Garden.

Ormond Beach (Daytona Beach area)

Comfort Inn/ 1567 N US 1, Ormond Beach FL 32174. 904-672-8621. V,M,D,AE. I-95 (Exit 89) to US 1. Nrby rstrnt, pool, fax, b/f, cable TV, t pkng, laundry, n/s rms. Free cont brfst. AAA. $40-46/S; $46-60/D; $6/ex prsn. 2/1-4/30: $56-150/S; $66-150/D. 5/1-7/31: $65-100/S; $70-100/D. Discs.

Days Inn Ormond Beach/ 1608 N US Hwy 1, Ormond Beach FL 32174. 904-672-7341/ 800-303-3297. V,M,AE,D. I-95 (Exit 89) at US 1. Nrby rstrnt/ lounge, pool, n/s rms, cable TV, tt/dd phone, fax, copier, laundry, cot, crib, t/b/rv pkng, conn rms. Free cont brfst, coffee, tea. AAA $40/S or D; $5/ex prsn. Spec events: $40-170/S or D. Disc: Senior, govt, milt, trkr, family, l/s. *Guaranteed rates.*

Howard Johnson Lodge/ 1633 N US 1, Ormond Beach FL 32174. 904-677-7310/ Fax: Ext 310. AE,V,M,DC,CB,D. I-95 (Exit 89) to US 1. N/s rms, b/f, pool, t pkng, playgrnd, laundry, cable TV. $30-140/S or D. Discs.

Palm Harbor (Clearwater area)

Econo Lodge/ 32000 US 19 N, Palm Harbor FL 34684. 813-786-2529. AE, V,M,DC. US 19 & 584 (Tampa Rd), 8 mi N of US 60. Rstrnt, pool, fax, b/f, cable TV, eff, n/s rms. Free cont brfst. $34-54/S; $39-54/D; $5/ex prsn. 1/26-4/30: $44-69/S; $49-74/D. 5/1-12/21: $30-44/S or D. Discs.

Panama City

Econo Lodge/ 4411 W US 98, Panama City FL 32401. 904-785-2700. V, AE, M,DC. US 98 W, 1 mi E of Hathaway Bridge. Nrby rstrnt, pool, fax, b/f, cable TV, t pkng, n/s rms. No pets. $30-90/S; $35-95/D; $6/ex prsn. Discs.

Super 8 Motel/ 207 US 231, Panama City FL 32405. 904-784-1988. V, M, DC,CB,AE,D. US 231, bet SR 77 & SR 391. B/f, n/s rms, outlets, copier, cable TV, suites, cot. Free local calls, crib. AAA. $35-38/S; $41-49/D; $5/ex prsn. Higher spec event/ wknd rate. Discs.

Panama City Beach

Quality Inn/ 15285 Front Beach Rd, Box 9160, Panama City Beach FL 32417. 904-234-6636. V,M,D,AE. US 231 to US 98, W to Alt 98 (Front Beach Rd). Mtl 7 mi past Hathaway bridge on beach side. Rstrnt/ lounge, pool, cable TV, t pkng, n/s rms. Free cont brfst. No pets. $45-125/S or D; $5-10/ex prsn. Discs.

Pensacola

Comfort Inn/ 6919 Pensacola Blvd, Pensacola FL 32505. 904-478-4499. V,M,DC,AE. I-10 (Exit 3A) to US 29, S 1/2 mi. Nrby rstrnt, pool, fax, cable TV, t pkng. Free cont brfst. $34-56/S; $38-64/D; $4/ex prsn. 5/1-5/25: $34-44/S; $38-50/D. Discs.

Econo Lodge/ 7194 Pensacola Blvd, Pensacola FL 32503. 904-479-8600. V, M,D,AE,DC. I-10 (Exit 3A) & US 29. Nrby rstrnt, pool, fax, cable TV, n/s rms. Free cont brfst. $34-50/S; $38-54/D; $4/ex prsn. 3/1-3/31: $37-56/S; $41-60/D. 5/1-9/10: $40-60/S; $44-64/D. Discs.

HoJo Inn/ 4126 Mobile Hwy, Pensacola FL 32506. 904-456-5731. D,M,V,AE, DC,CB. I-10: (Ebnd, Exit 21; Wbnd, Exit 2) to Hwy 297, S to US 90 (Mobile Hwy), continue S to mtl. N/s rms, pool, t pkng, cable TV. Free cont brfst. $28-50/S; $30-65/D. Discs.

Motel 6/ 7827 N Davis Hwy, Pensacola

FL 32514. 904-476-5386/ Fax: 476-7458. V,M,AE,DC,D. I-10 (Exit 5) turn N. Nrby rstrnt, cable TV, pool, elevator, n/s rms, t pkng. Free local calls. $30-32/S; $36-38/D; $6/ex prsn. Disc.

Motel 6/ 7226 Plantation Rd, Pensacola FL 32504. 904-474-1060/ Fax: 476-5104. M,V,DC,D,AE. S of I-10 (Exit 5) Hwy 291 on Plantation Rd in the University Mall area. Nrby rstrnt, cable TV, pool, n/s rms, t pkng. Free local calls. $28-32/S; $34-38/D; $6/ex prsn. Disc.

Motel 6/ 5829 Pensacola Blvd, Pensacola FL 32505. 904-477-7522/ Fax: 476-7126. M,V,DC,D,AE. I-10: (Ebnd, Exit 3A/ Wbnd, Exit 3B) to Hwy 29S, S 2 mi to mtl. Nrby rstrnt, cable TV, pool, n/s rms. Free local calls. $26-29/S; $30-33/D; $4/ex prsn. Disc.

Quality Inn/ 6911 Pensacola Blvd, Pensacola FL 32505. 904-479-3800. V,M,DC,AE. I-10 (Exit 3A) to US 29 (Pensacola Blvd), S 1/2 mi to mtl. Rstrnt, pool, mtg rm, t pkng, n/s rms. $32-42/S; $34-54/D; $5/ex prsn. Discs.

Rodeway Inn/ 8500 Pine Forest Rd, Pensacola FL 32534. 904-477-9150. V,M,AE. I-10 W (Exit 2) turn rt 1/10 mi to mtl. Nrby rstrnt/ lounge, pool, mtg rm, cable TV, t pkng, n/s rms. AAA. $30-38/S; $35-40/D; $4/ex prsn. 3/16-4/30: $35-40/S; $36-40/D. 5/1-9/5: $35-42/S; $40-48/D. Discs.

Super 8 Motel/ 7220 Plantation Rd, Pensacola FL 32504. 904-476-8038/ Fax: 474-6284. V,M,DC,CB,AE,D. I-10, Exit 5, turn lt at light, rt into Univ Mall; drive behind Service Mdse. B/f, n/s rms, pool, t/b/rv pkng, copier, cable TV, cot. Free local calls, crib. $34-39/S; $45-50/D; $5/ex prsn. Higher spec event/wknd, rate. Discs.

Pinellas Park

La Mark Charles Motel/ 6200 34th St N, Pinellas Park FL 34665. 813-527-7334/ Fax: 526-9294/ 800-448-6781. V,M, AE,D. I-275 (Exit 15) to Gandy Blvd, W to US 19, S 8 blocks. Nrby rstrnt/ lounge, pool, whrlpool, n/s rms, tt/dd phone, mtg rm, fax, copier, laundry, cot, crib, t/b/rv pkng, eff, conn rms. AAA/ Mobil. $60-75/S or D; $5/ex prsn. 5/1-12/21: $48/S or D. Disc: Family, l/s.

Guaranteed rates.

Pompano Beach

Motel 6/ 1201 NW 31st Av, Pompano Beach FL 33069. 305-977-8011/ Fax: 972-0814. M,V,DC,D,AE. I-95 (Exit 34) to Atlantic Blvd, W 1 1/2 mi to 31st Ave, rt 1/2 mi. Nrby rstrnt, cable TV, pool, n/s rms, t pkng. Free local calls. $32/S; $36/D; $4/ex prsn. 1/25-4/10: $37/S; $41/D. 4/11-12/20: $30/S; $34/D. Disc.

Port Charlotte

Days Inn/ 1941 Tamiami Trail, Port Charlotte FL 33948. 813-627-8900/ Fax: 743-8503. V,M,AE,D,CB,DC,JCB. On US 41 near Peachland Blvd. Fax, n/s rms, rstrnt/ lounge, pool, mtg rm, b/f, exerc equip, t pkng, refrig, cot, crib. Chairman's Award. $47-75/S; $49-85/D; $5/ex prsn. 2/8-3/31: $75-90/S; $77-100/D. 4/1-12/25: $39-49/S; $39-55/D. Discs.

Econo Lodge/ 4100 Tamiami Tr, Port Charlotte FL 33952. 813-743-2442. V,M,AE. I-75 to US 41, N 1 mi to mtl. Nrby rstrnt, cable TV, n/s rms. No pets. $28-51/S; $33-71/D; $5/ex prsn. Discs.

Quality Inn/ 3400 Tamiami Tr, Port Charlotte FL 33952. 813-625-4181. V,AE,M,DC. US 41 at Harbor Blvd. Rstrnt/ lounge, pool, mtg rm, b/f, cable TV, t pkng, n/s rms. Free cont brfst. AAA. $44-58/S; $49-70/D; $6/ex prsn. 2/1-3/31: $56-80/S; $66-95/D. 4/1-12/15: $35-49/S; $39-55/D. Discs.

Port Richey

Comfort Inn/ 11810 US 19, Port Richey FL 34668. 813-863-3336. V,M,DC,AE. On US 19 at Pt Richey. Nrby rstrnt, pool, fax, b/f, cable TV. Free cont brfst. No pets. AAA. $39-76/S or D; $5/ex prsn. 4/16-12/20: $30-56/S or D. Discs.

Punta Gorda

Howard Johnson Lodge/ 33 Tamiami Trail, Punta Gorda FL 33950. 941-639-2167/ Fax: 639-1707. V,M,D,AE, DC, CB. I-75 (Exit 29) to US 41, N to mtl. N/s rms, mtg rm, rstrnt/ lounge, pool, laundry. $37-84/S; $42-89/D. Discs.

Motel 6/ 9300 Knights Dr, Punta Gorda FL 33950. 941-639-9585/ Fax: 639-6820. M,V,DC,D,AE. I-75 (Exit 28) to

Jones Loop Rd, W to mtl. Nrby rstrnt, cable TV, pool, n/s rms, t pkng. Free local calls. Premier Award. $32/S; $36/D; $4/ex prsn. 1/25-4/10: $42/S; $46/D. 4/11-12/20: $28/S; $32/D. Disc.

Riviera Beach

Motel 6/ 3651 W Blue Heron Blvd, Riviera Beach FL 33404. 407-863-1011/ Fax: 842-1905. M,V,DC,D,AE. I-95 (Exit 55) to Blue Heron Blvd, E 1/4 mi. Cable TV, pool, n/s rms, t pkng. Free local calls. $32/S; $36/D; $4/ex prsn. 1/25-4/10: $40/S; $44/D. Disc.

Saint Augustine

Comfort Inn/ 1111 Ponce De Leon Blvd, St Augustine FL 32084. 904-824-5554. V,AE,M,DC. I-95 S (Exit 95) to US 1, S to mtl. Nrby rstrnt, pool, whrlpool, cable TV, t pkng, n/s rms. Free cont brfst. $40-100/S or D. Discs.

Comfort Inn/ 2625 SR 207, St Augustine FL 32033. 904-829-3435. V, AE, M, DC. I-95 (Exit 94) at SR 207. Nrby rstrnt, pool, fax, cable TV, t pkng. Free cont brfst. AAA. $44-99/S; $49-109/D; $6/ex prsn. 4/1-4/30, 9/4-1/1: $39-64/S; $44-69/D. 5/1-9/3: $39-74/S; $44-79/D. Discs.

Days Inn/ 2800 Ponce de Leon Blvd, St Augustine FL 32084. 904-829-6581/ Fax: 824-0135. V,M,AE,D,CB,DC,JCB. US 1 & SR 16. Fax, n/s rms, nrby rstrnt, pool, b/f. $34-56/S; $39-66/D; $5/ex prsn. 2/9-3/31: $44-57/S; $49-62/D. Discs.

Econo Lodge/ 2535 SR 16, St Augustine FL 32092. 904-829-5643. V,M,AE. I-95 (Exit 95) to SR 16 W. Rstrnt/ lounge, pool, fax, cable TV, t pkng, n/s rms. AAA. $29-89/S; $39-99/D; $5/ex prsn. 1/2-3/31: $34-89/S; $39-99/D. 5/1-9/3: $29-79/S; $36-89/D. Discs.

HoJo Inn/ 2550 SR 16, St Augustine FL 32092. 904-829-5686/ Fax: 826-0489. AE,V,M,DC,CB,D. I-95 (Exit 95) to SR 16. N/s rms, b/f, rstrnt, pool, t pkng, laundry, cable TV. Free coffee. $29-42/S; $32-49/D. Discs.

Howard Johnson Lodge/ 137 San Marco Av, St Augustine FL 32084. 904-824-6181/ Fax: 825-2774. AE,V,M, DC,CB,D. I-95 (Exit 95) to SR 16, E to San Marco Av, turn rt 3 blks to mtl. N/s rms, mtg rm, b/f, rstrnt, pool, whrlpool, nrby rstrnt, family rm, kitchenette, b pkng. Free tour trams. No pets. Gold Medal Winner. $39-89/S or D. Discs.

Howard Johnson Resort Hotel/ 300 A1A Beach Blvd, St Augustine FL 32084. 904-471-2575. AE,V,M,DC,CB,D. I-95, SR 207 (Exit 94) to SR 312, E to A1A S, 1st mtl on the ocean. N/s rms, mtg rm, rstrnt/ lounge, pool, b pkng, b/f, cable TV. AAA. $30-110/S or D. Discs.

Quality Inn/ 2445 SR 16, St Augustine FL 32092. 904-829-1999. V,M,DC,AE. I-95 (Exit 95) to SR 16, W to mtl. Rstrnt, pool, b/f, n/s rms. Free cont brfst. $29-42/S; $34-49/D; $6/ex prsn. Discs.

Super 8 Motel/ 3552 N Ponce-de-Leon Blvd, St Augustine FL 32084. 904-824-6399. V,M,D,AE,DC,CB. I-95 to SR 16, lt on US 1, N 2 blks on rt. N/s rms, pool, nrby rstrnt, laundry, cont brfst, b pkng, cot. Free crib. $29-35/S; $34-45/D; $5/ex prsn. Discs.

Saint Petersburg

Days Inn/ 650 34th St N, St Petersburg FL 33713. 813-321-2958/ Fax: 327-1625. V,M,AE,D,CB,DC,JCB. I-275 (Exit 11) to 5th Av N, W to 34th St, turn rt. Fax, n/s rms, pool, whrlpool, b/f, t pkng, arpt trans, cot. Free cont brfst. Chairman's Award. $46-51/S or D; $6/ex prsn. 2/1-4/22: $60-66/S or D. 4/23-12/19: $40-46/S or D. Discs.

Days Inn/ 6800 Sunshine Skyway Ln, St Petersburg FL 33711. 813-867-1151/ Fax: 864-4494. V,M,AE,D,CB,DC,JCB. I-275, Exit 3. Fax, n/s rms, rstrnt/ lounge, pool, whrlpool, mtg rm, b/f, t pkng,playgrnd, game rm, tennis, cot. $39-79/S or D; $10/ex prsn. 2/1-4/30: $49-99/S or D. Discs.

Empress Motel/ 1503 9th St N, St Petersburg FL 33704. 813-894-0635/ Fax: 823-1446. V,M,AE,D. I-275 (Exit 12) to 22nd Av N, E to 9th St N, 7 blks S. Pool, dd phone, fax, laundry, eff, conn rms. Free coffee, tea, cocoa. No pets. AAA. $39/S or D; $5/ex prsn. 4/16-12/15: $28/S or D. Disc: L/s. *Guaranteed rates.*

Also see Treasure Island.

FLORIDA

Sanford (Orlando area)
Super 8 Motel/ 4750 SR 46 W, Sanford FL 32771. 407-323-3445. AE,V,M,DC, CB,D. Jct I-4 (Exit 51) at SR 46. B/f, n/s rms, pool, cont brfst, cable TV, kitchenettes. $38-40/S; $43-50/D; $5/ex prsn. 2/2-3/10: $65/S or D. Higher spec event rates. Discs.

Sarasota
Comfort Inn/ 4800 N Tamiami Tr, Sarasota FL 34234. 813-355-7091. V,M,D,AE. I-75 (Exit 40) to University Pkwy, W 6 mi to US 41 (Tamiami Tr), S 1/4 mi to mtl. Pool, fax, b/f, whrlpool, cable TV, t pkng, n/s rms. Free cont brfst. $50-60/S; $60-75/D; $5/ex prsn. 1/16-4/20: $70-80/S; $80-90/D. 4/21-12/20: $45-50/S; $45-55/D. Discs.

Wellesley Inn/ 1803 N Tamiami Trail, Sarasota FL 34234. 941-366-5128/ Fax: 953-4322. AE,M,D,DC,CB,V. Cable TV, pool, fax, microwave, in-rm coffee. Free cont brfst. 1/1-1/31: $60/S or D; $5/ex prsn. 2/1-4/8: $70/S or D. 4/9-12/20: $42/S or D. *Spec rates - see discount section in front of book.

Also see Bradenton.

Sebring
HoJo Inn/ 2919 US 27 S, Sebring FL 33870. 941-385-6111. V,M,D,AE, DC, CB. On US 27 S. N/s rms, pool, t pkng, cable TV, eff, cot, crib, fax, copier. No pets. AAA. $34-54/S; $42-69/D. Discs.

Silver Springs (Ocala area)
Econo Lodge/ 5331 NE Silver Springs Blvd, Silver Springs FL 32688. 904-236-2383. V,M,D,AE,DC. I-75 (Exit 69) to SR 40 (Broadway Av), E 8 mi (Broadway becomes Silver Springs Blvd) to mtl. Nrby rstrnt, pool, cable TV, n/s rms. Free cont brfst. No pets. $30-46/S; $38-65/D; $5/ex prsn.

Howard Johnson Lodge/ 5565 E Silver Springs Blvd, Box 475, Silver Springs FL 34488. 904-236-2616/ Fax: 236-1941. AE,V,M,DC,CB,D. I-75 (Exit 69) to SR 40, E 9 mi. N/s rms, b/f, rstrnt, pool, playgrnd, eff. $38-70/S; $40-80/D. Discs.

Sun City Center
Comfort Inn/ 718 Cypress Village Blvd, Sun City Center FL 33573. 813-633-3318. V,M,D,AE. I-75 to SR 674, E 1/4 mi to mtl. Nrby rstrnt, pool, fax, b/f, sauna, cable TV, n/s rms. Free cont brfst. No pets. $50-60/S; $60-70/D; $5/ex prsn. 1/16-4/30: $65-75/S; $70-80/D. 5/1-10/31: $45-50/S; $45-55/D. Discs.

Tallahassee
Best Inns/ 2738 Graves Rd, Tallahassee FL 32303. 904-562-2378. AE, DC, CB,M,V,D. I-10, Exit 29 to US 27. N/s rms, dd/tt phone, fax, b/f, pool, fax, mtg rm. Free local calls, cont brfst, pm coffee, crib. AAA. $40-46/S; $47-53/D; $6/ex prsn. Discs.

Econo Lodge/ 2681 N Monroe St, Tallahassee FL 32303. 904-385-6155. V,AE,M,DC. I-10 (Exit 29) to US 27 (Monroe St), S 3 blks. Nrby rstrnt, fax, b/f, cable TV, conn rms, n/s rms, microfridges. Free cont brfst. $33-75/S; $38-75/D; $5/ex prsn. Discs.

Motel 6/ 2738 N Monroe, Tallahassee FL 32303. 904-386-7878/ Fax: 385-5616. V,M,AE,DC,D. I-10 (Exit 29) to N Monroe, S 1/4 mi. Cable TV, pool, n/s rms, elevator, nrby rstrnt. Free local calls. $28-30/S; $34-36/D; $6/ex prsn. Football wknds: $40/S or D. Disc.

Motel 6/ 1481 Timberlane Rd, Tallahassee FL 32312. 904-668-2600/ Fax: 894-3104. M,V,DC,D,AE. I-10 (Exit 30) to Thomasville Rd, N to Timberlane Rd, W to mtl. Cable TV, pool, laundry, nrby rstrnt, n/s rms. Free local calls. $28/S; $34/D; $6/ex prsn. Football wknds: $40/S or D. Higher spec event rates. Disc.

Motel 6/ 1027 Apalachee Pkwy, Tallahassee FL 32301. 904-877-6171/ Fax: 656-6120. M,V,DC,D,AE. I-10 (Exit 29) to US 27 (N Monroe St), S 4 mi to Apalachee Pkwy, E to mtl. Nrby rstrnt, cable TV, pool, n/s rms. Free local calls. Premier Award. $28-31/S; $34-37/D; $6/ex prsn. Football wknds: $50/S or D. Higher spec event rates. Disc.

Ramada Inn/ 1355 Apalachee Pkwy, Tallahassee FL 32301. 904-877-3171/ Fax: 942-2918. V,M,AE,D,CB,DC,JCB. Dntn, 1 mi from St Capital & bsns district. I-27 to Magnolia Rd, S to mtl.

FLORIDA

Pool, b/f, n/s rms, rstrnt/ lounge, mtg rm. Free arpt trans. $45-75/S or D; $5/ex prsn. Discs.

Super 8 Motel/ 2702 N Monroe St, Tallahassee FL 32303. 904-386-8818/ Fax: 385-9583. V,M,DC,CB,AE,D. I-10 (Exit 29) to Hwy 27 (Monroe St), turn S to mtl. B/f, n/s rms, elevator, cable TV, mtg rm, cot. Free local calls. No pets. $36/S; $40-41/D; $5/ex prsn. Higher spec event rate. Discs.

Tampa

Budget Host Tampa Motel/ 3110 W Hillsborough Av, Tampa FL 33614. 813-876-8673/ Fax: 875-2928/ 800-283-4678. V,M,AE,D,DC,CB. 2 mi W of I-275, Exit 30. 2 blks E of Dale Mabry Hwy. Nrby rstrnt/ lounge, pool, n/s rms, satellite TV, arpt trans, tt/dd phone, fax, b pkng. No pets. AAA. $28-31/S; $30-39/D; $3/ex prsn. Disc: Senior, govt, l/s, family, trkr, milt. *Guaranteed rates.*

Budget Host Tampa Motel/ 3110 W Hillsborough Ave, Tampa FL 33614. 813-876-8673/ Fax: 875-2928. V, ER, AE,CB,DC,D,M. 2 mi W of I-275, Exit 30; 2 blks E of Dale Mabry Hwy. Satellite TV, dd phone, family rms, adj rstrnt, pool, arpt trans. No pets. AAA. $28-31/S; $30-39/D; $3/ex prsn. Discs.

Budgetel Inns/ 4811 US Hwy 301 N, Tampa FL 33610. 813-626-0885/ Fax: 623-3321. V,M,D,AE,DC,CB. I-4 (Exit 6) to Hwy 301, S to mtl. N/s rms, b/f, fax, pool. Free cont brfst, in-rm coffee, local calls. $41-51/S; $48-58/D. 1/26-2/17: $64-74/S or D. 2/18-4/6: $42-52/S; $49-59/D. 4/7-12/30: $34/S; $41/D. Higher spec event rates. Discs.

Comfort Inn/ 2106 E Busch Blvd, Tampa FL 33612. 813-931-3313. V,M,D,AE. I-275 to Bush Blvd, E /2 mi. Nrby rstrnt, pool, fax, b/f, cable TV, n/s rms. Free cont brfst. No pets. AAA. $51-75/S; $56-75/D; $5/ex prsn. 5/1-9/2, 11/1-12/21: $43-75/S; $45-75/D. 9/3-10/31: $38-75/S; $43-75/D. Discs.

Days Inn/ 2901 E Busch Blvd, Tampa FL 33612. 813-933-6471/ Fax: 931-0261. V,M,AE,D,CB,DC,JCB. I-275 (Exit 33) to Busch Blvd, turn E/lt. Fax, n/s rms, rstrnt, pool, mtg rm, t pkng, laundry, cable TV, cot. Free crib. $33-59/S; $38-69/D; $5/ex prsn. Discs.

Econo Lodge/ 2905 N 50th St, Tampa FL 33619. 813-621-3541. V,AE,M,DC. I-4 (Exit 3) & 50th St. Nrby rstrnt, pool, fax, cable TV, t pkng, laundry, mtg rm, n/s rms. No pets. $35-50/S; $45-70/D; $5/ex prsn. 5/1-12/27: $30-40/S; $40-50/D. Discs.

Econo Lodge/ 1701 E Busch Blvd, Tampa FL 33612. 813-933-7681. V, AE, M,DC. I-275 (Exit 33) to Busch Blvd, E 3/4 mi to mtl. Rstrnt/ lounge, pool, mtg rm, fax, cable TV, t pkng, n/s rms. Free cont brfst. $30-40/S; $35-45/D; $5/ex prsn. 2/1-4/30: $35-45/S; $40-50/D. Discs.

Econo Lodge/ 1020 S Dale Mabry, Tampa FL 33629. 813-254-3005. V, AE, M,DC. I-275 (Exit 23B) to US 92, S to mtl. Nrby rstrnt, pool, fax, b/f, cable TV, t pkng, n/s rms. Free cont brfst, coffee. AAA. $46-54/S; $50-58/D; $4/ex prsn. 5/1-6/5, 11/1-12/25: $40-48/S; $44-50/D. 6/6-10/31: $36-40/S; $40-44/D. Discs.

Friendship Inn/ 2500 E Busch Blvd, Tampa FL 33612. 813-933-3958. V,AE,M,DC. I-275, Exit 33, E 1 mi to mtl. I-75, Exit 54, follow signs to Busch Gardens. Nrby rstrnt, pool, fax, b/f, cable TV, n/s rms. No pets. $22-35/S; $26-50/D; $5/ex prsn. Discs.

HoJo Inn/ 3314 S Dale Mabry Hwy, Tampa FL 33629. 813-832-4656/ Fax: 831-6930. V,M,D,AE,DC,CB. I-275 (Exit 23B) to Dale Mabry Hwy, S 2.5 mi, just past Bay to Bay Blvd. N/s rms, b/f, pool, rental car, cont brfst, cable TV, eff, fax, t pkng. No pets. $36-45/S; $40-52/D. Discs.

Howard Johnson Lodge/ 4139 E Busch Blvd, Tampa FL 33617. 813-988-9191/ Fax: 988-9195. V,M,D,AE,DC,CB. I-275 (Exit 33) to Busch Blvd, E 2.5 mi. Just past Busch Gardens. N/s rms, mtg rm, rstrnt/ lounge, pool, arpt trans, t pkng, rn serv, $29-58/S; $34-78/D. Discs.

Howard Johnson Lodge/ 720 E Fowler Av, Tampa FL 33612. 813-971-5150/ Fax: 971-2065. AE,V,M,DC,CB,D. I-275 (Exit 34) to Fowler Av. I-75 (Exit 54) to Fowler Av, W 5 mi. N/s rms, pool, arpt trans, t pkng, fax, kiddie pool, playgrnd.

FLORIDA

Free coffee cont brfst. No pets. $33-65/S; $35-65/D. Discs.

Motel 6/ 333 E Fowler Av, Tampa FL 33612. 813-932-4948/ Fax: 931-4577. M,V,DC,D,AE. I-275 (Exit 34) to E Fowler Av, W to mtl. Nrby rstrnt, cable TV, pool, laundry, n/s rms, t pkng. Free local calls. $26-28/S; $30-32/D; $4/ex prsn. 1/25-4/10: $30/S; $34/D. Disc.

Motel 6/ 6510 N Hwy 301, Tampa FL 33610. 813-628-0888/ Fax: 620-4899. V,M,AE,DC,D. I-4 (Ebnd, Exit 6B; Wbnd, Exit 6) to US 301, N to mtl. Nrby rstrnt, cable TV, pool, elevator, n/s rms, t pkng. Free local calls. $29-30/S; $33-34/D; $4/ex prsn. 1/25-4/10: $34/S; $38/D. Disc.

Also see Brandon.

Treasure Island (St Petersburg area)

Friendship Inn/ 11799 Gulf Blvd, Treasure Island FL 33706. 813-360-1438. V,M,AE. I-275 (Exit 11) to 5th Av, rt on Central Av, rt onto Gulf Blvd to 118th Av. Nrby rstrnt, pool, fax, cable TV, exerc equip, n/s rms. No pets. $39-69/S or D; $5/ex prsn. 2/16-4/13: $59-95/S or D. Discs.

Venice

Motel 6/ 281 US 41 N, Venice FL 34292. 941-485-8255/ Fax: 488-3005. M,V,DC,D,AE. I-75 (Exit 35) to Jacaranda Blvd, S to Venice Av, W to US 41. Nrby rstrnt, cable TV, laundry, pool, n/s rms. Free local calls. $32-33/S; $36-37/D; $4/ex prsn. 1/25-4/10: $46/S; $50/D. Disc.

Vero Beach

HoJo Inn/ 1985 90th Av, Vero Beach FL 32966. 407-778-1985/ Fax: 778-1998. V,M,D,AE,DC,CB. I-95 (Exit 68) to Hwy 60, E 1/2 mi to traffic light, turn rt at light. N/s rms, t pkng, VCR/movies, fax, laundry, refrig, nrby rstrnt. Free cont brfst. $34-50/S; $38-65/D. Discs.

Walt Disney World.

See Davenport, Kissimmee, Lake Buena Vista, Orlando, Winter Garden.

Wesley Chapel

Sleep Inn/ I-75 & SR 54, Wesley Chapel FL 33543. 800-221-222 — opening soon. V,M,D,AE. I-75 to SR 54, W 1 blk, rt on Oakley Blvd. Nrby rstrnt, pool, mtg rm, cable TV, n/s rms. Free cont brfst. No pets. $45-80/S or D; $6/ex prsn. Discs.

West Palm Beach

Comfort Inn/ 5981 Okeechobee Blvd, W Palm Beach FL 33417. 407-697-3388/ Fax: 697-2834. V,M,D,AE. FL Trnpk (Exit 99) to Okeechobee Blvd, turn E. Nrby rstrnt, pool, fax, b/f, cable TV, t pkng, n/s rms. Free cont brfst. $39-59/S or D; $7/ex prsn. 1/16-4/30, 12/16-12/31: $59-89/S or D. Discs.

Wellesley Inn/ 1910 Palm Beach Lakes Blvd, W Palm Beach FL 33409. 407-689-8540/ Fax: 687-8090. AE,M,D, DC, CB,V. Cable TV, pool, fax, microwave, refrig, in-rm coffee. Free cont brfst. $62/S or D; $5/ex prsn. 4/9-12/20: $42/S or D. *Spec rates - see discount section in front of book.

Also see North Palm Beach.

Wildwood

Super 8 Motel/ 344 E SR 44, Wildwood FL 34785. 904-748-3783/ Fax: 748-5401. V,M,AE,D,CB,DC. I-75 (Exit 66) to SR 44, turn W to mtl. N/s rms, b/f, laundry, cable TV, cont brfst, fax, t pkng. Free AM coffee. $30-36/S; $30-45/D. Higher spec event rates. Disc.

Winter Garden (Orlando area)

Super 8 Motel/ 13607 W Colonial Dr, Winter Garden FL 34787. 407-654-2020/ Fax: 654-0140. V,M,D,AE, DC, CB. From FL Tnpk (Exit 267) to SR 50, W 2 mi. B/f, n/s rms, pool, laundry, outlets, t/b/rv pkng, satellite TV, mtg rm, cot, crib. Free coffee, nwspr. $36-40/S or D; $4/ex prsn. Discs.

Winter Haven

Budget Host Driftwood Lodge/ 970 Cypress Gardens Blvd, Winter Haven FL 33880. 813-294-4229/ Fax: 293-2089. AE,M,V,D. 3 1/2 mi E on Fl Rte 540. Cable TV, dd phone, family rms, kitchens, rstrnt, pool, laundry, cot. AAA. $32-52/S; $36-68/D; $4/ex prsn. 4/21-12/18: $28/S; $32/D. Discs.

Quality Inn/ 975 Cypress Gardens Blvd,

FLORIDA / GEORGIA

Winter Haven FL 33880. 813-294-4104. V,M,D,AE. On Hwy 540, E of US 17. Nrby rstrnt, pool, b/f, cable TV, laundry, n/s rms. Free cont brfst. No pets. AAA. $50-62/S or D; $5/ex prsn. 2/1-4/20, 12/21-12/31: $62-67/S or D. 4/21-12/20: $48-53/S or D. Discs.

Yulee

Days Inn/ 3250 US Hwy 17, Yulee FL 32097. 904-225-2011/ Fax: 225-5943. V,M,AE,D,CB,DC,JCB. I-95 (Exit 130) at US 17. Fax, n/s rms, rstrnt, pool, mtg rm, b/f, t pkng, arpt trans, cot. $29-37/S; $35-47/D; $6/ex prsn. Discs.

Georgia

Note: The Summer Olympics will be held in Atlanta in 1996. Past experience, in other cities, suggests that motels will be filled for many miles surrounding the area and rates will be much higher than usual during the Olympics. If you go, don't expect to get the usual rates, and reserve a room early. We hope you have a wonderful time.

Acworth (Atlanta area)

Quality Inn/ 4980 Cowan Rd, Acworth GA 30101. 404-974-1922. V,M,AE,DC. I-75 (Exit 120) to SR 92, W to mtl. Nrby rstrnt, pool, mtg rm, fax, b/f, cable TV, t pkng, n/s rms. Free cont brfst. AAA. $38-145/S; $41-165/D; $5/ex prsn. Higher spec event rates. Discs.

Ramada Limited/ 164 N Pointway, Acworth GA 30102. 404-975-9000. V,M, AE,D,CB,DC,JCB. I-75 (Exit 120) at Hwy 92. Pool, n/s rms, nrby rstrnt, cable TV. Gold Key Award. $32-58/S;

$40-70/D; $5/ex prsn. Disc.

Adel

Days Inn I-75/ 1200 W 4th St, Adel GA 31620. 912-896-4574/ Fax: 896-4575. AE,M,V,DC,D. I-75 (Exit 10) to Hwy 37, turn W. Rstrnt, pool, mtg rm, b/f, t pkng. Free cont brfst. $30-33/S; $35-38/D; $5/ex prsn. Discs.

HoJo Inn/ 1103 W 4th St, Adel GA 31620. 912-896-2244/ Fax: 896-2245. D,M,V,AE,DC,CB. I-75, Exit 10. N/s rms, b/f, pool, t pkng, Free adult hot brfst. $28-32/S; $33-37/D. Discs.

Super 8 Motel I-75/ 1102 W 4th St, Adel GA 31620. 912-896-4523/ Fax: 896-4524. V,M,AE,D,DC,CB. I-75 (Exit 10) to W 4th St. B/f, n/s rms, pool, nrby rstrnt, cable TV, cot, crib. Free coffee. $31/S; $34/D; $3/ex prsn. Higher spec event rates. Discs.

Albany

Econo Lodge/ 1806 E Oglethorpe Blvd, Albany GA 31705 912-883-5544. V,M,AE. US 82 E. Nrby rstrnt, pool, cable TV, t pkng, n/s rms. Free cont brfst. $35-45/S; $40-50/D; $5/ex prsn. Discs.

Motel 6/ 201 S Thornton Dr, Albany GA 31705. 912-439-0078/ Fax: 439-1153. V,M,DC,D,AE. US 19/ 82/ Liberty Expwy at E Oglethorpe, E to Thornton Dr. Cable TV, pool, n/s rms. Free local calls. $24/S; $28/D; $4/ex prsn. Disc.

Super 8 Motel/ 2444 N Slappey Blvd, Albany GA 31701. 912-888-8388/ Fax: Ext 403. D,M,V,AE,DC,CB. Jct of Slappey Blvd (Bsns 19) & Palmyra RD, just S of jct of US 19/82 & SR 19. B/f, n/s rms, t/b/rv pkng, TDD, cot. Free local calls, crib. $37/S; $43/D; $6/ex prsn. Higher spec event rate. Discs.

Ashburn

Comfort Inn/ 803 Shoney's Dr, Rte 2, Box 1115, Ashburn GA 31714. 912-567-0080. V,M,AE,DC. I-75 (Exit 28) at Washington St. Rstrnt, pool, fax, b/f, cable TV, t pkng, n/s rms. Free cont brfst. No pets. AAA. $35-45/S; $38-50/D; $5/ex prsn. Discs.

Super 8 Motel/ 749 E Washington Av, Ashburn GA 31714. 912-567-4688/

Fax: 567-0248. V,M,D,AE,DC,CB. I-75 (Exit 28) to US 112, turn W. B/f, n/s rms, cable TV, t/b/rv pkng, TDD, cot. Free local calls, crib. $37/S; $43/D; $6/ex prsn. Higher spec event rates. Discs.

Athens

Econo Lodge/ 2715 Atlanta Hwy, Athens GA 30606. 706-549-1530. V, AE,M,DC. On Hwy 78, Atlanta Hwy. Rstrnt/ lounge, pool, fax, sauna, cable TV, outlets, n/s rms. Free cont brfst. No pets. $34-55/S; $39-60/D; $5 ex prsn. 9/1-11/30: $38-60/S; $44-75/D. 12/1-12/31: $30/S; $35/D. Discs.

Howard Johnson/ 2465 W Broad St, Athens GA 30606. 706-548-1111/ Fax: 354-8725. AE,V,M,DC,CB,D. US 78/29. 14 mi S of Commerce on I-85 following Hwy 441. N/s rms, rstrnt/ lounge, pool, t pkng, VCR, in-rm coffee, refrig, microwave, safe-deposit box. Free brfst, nwspr. $34-89/S; $39-90/D. Discs.

Super 8 Motel/ 3425 Atlanta Hwy, Athens GA 30606. 706-549-0251/ Fax: 549-5400. V,M,D,AE,DC,CB. .5 mi E of GA Sq Mall on Hwy 78. B/f, n/s rms, pool, kitchenettes, whrlpool, laundry, t pkng. $30-33/S; $33-38/D; $5/ex prsn. Discs.

Atlanta

Budgetel Inns/ 5395 Peachtree Industrial Blvd, Atlanta GA 30092. 770-446-2882/ Fax: 242-6882 V,M,D,AE,DC,CB. I-285, Exit 23, Peachtree Industrial Blvd, NE to mtl. N/s rms, b/f, fax, nrby rstrnt, pool. Free cont brfst, in-rm coffee, local calls. AAA. $41-53/S; $48-60/D. 5/16-7/16: $46-58/S; $53-65/D. 7/17-8/6: Spec rates apply. 8/7-9/2: $42-55/S; $49-62/D. Higher spec event rates. Discs.

Budgetel Inns/ 2480 Old National Pkwy, Atlanta GA 30349. 404-766-0000/ Fax: 763-9162. V,M,D,AE,DC,CB. I-85/I-285 to Old National Hwy S, E on Old National Pkwy. N/s rms, b/f, fax, nrby rstrnt. Free cont brfst, in-rm coffee, local calls. AAA. $39-46/S; $49-51/D. Spec rates may apply. Discs.

Econo Lodge/ 1360 Virginia Av, Atlanta GA 30344. 404-761-5201. V,AE,M,DC. I-85, Exit 19. Dntn. Nrby rstrnt, pool, fax, cable TV, arpt trans, n/s rms. Free cont brfst. No pets. AAA. $30-62/S; $30-64/D; $5/ex prsn. 5/1-9/30: $38-62/S; $38-64/D. Higher spec event rates. Discs.

Motel 6/ 3585 Chamblee-Tucker Rd, Atlanta GA 30341. 770-455-8000/ Fax: 936-8479. V,M,DC,D,AE. I-285 (Exit 27) to Chamblee-Tucker Rd, E to mtl. Nrby rstrnt, cable TV, pool, n/s rms. Free local calls. $32/S; $38/D; $6/ex prsn. Higher spec event rates. Disc.

Quality Inn/ 2960 NE Expwy, Atlanta GA 30341. 404-451-5231. V,AE,M,D. I-85 (Exit 33) at Shallowford Rd (NE Expwy). Nrby rstrnt, pool, mtg rm, fax, b/f, cable TV, t pkng, n/s rms. Free cont brfst. No pets. $49-300/S; $59-350/D. 5/1-10/31: $36-300/S; $42-350/D. Higher spec event rates. Discs.

Super 8 Motel/ 301 Fulton Industrial Cir, Atlanta GA 30336. 404-696-9713/ Fax: Ext 404. D,M,V,AE,DC,CB. I-20 (Exit 14) to Fulton Ind Blvd, W to Fulton Ind Cir, turn rt. B/f, n/s rms, t/b/rv pkng, satellite TV, suite, TDD, cot. Free local calls, crib. No pets. $33/S; $39-47/D; $5/ex prsn. 5/21-9/30: $40/S; $45-47/D. Higher spec event/wknd rate. Discs.

Also see Acworth, Calhoun, Cartersville, College Park, Conley, Decatur, Forest Park, Kennesaw, Marietta, Norcross, Stockbridge, Villa Rica.

Augusta

Amida National 9 Inn/ 434 S Bel Air Rd, Augusta GA 30907. 404-860-8173. V, M,AE,DC. I-20, Exit 63, behind Waffle House. Cable TV, dd phone, t pkng, adj rstrnt, microwave, refrig. No pets. $25/S; $25-30/D; $4/ex prsn.

Days Inn/ 3654 Wheeler Rd, Augusta GA 30909. 706-868-8610. V,M,AE,D,CB,DC,JCB. I-520 (Bobby Jones Expwy) to (Exit 2) Wheeler Rd. Fax, n/s rms, nrby rstrnt, t pkng, cot. Free cont brfst. Chairman's Award. $35-45/S or D; $5/ex prsn. Higher spec event rates. Discs.

Econo Lodge/ 2852 Washington Rd, Augusta GA 30909. 706-736-0707. V,AE,M,DC. I-20 (Exit 65) to Wash-in-

GEORGIA

gton Rd, 1 blk S. Nrby rstrnt/ lounge, fax, b/f, cable TV, t pkng, refrig, VCR, laundry, n/s rms. Free cont brfst, local calls. No pets. $30-32/S; $32-34/D; $5/ex prsn. 3/31-4/7: $150/S or D. 4/8-11/30: $34-36/S; $36-38/D. Discs.

Econo Lodge/ 4090 Belair Rd, Augusta GA 30909. 706-863-0777. V,AE,M,DC. I-20 (Exit 63) to Belair Rd. Nrby rstrnt, pool, fax, b/f, cable TV, t pkng, n/s rms. Free cont brfst, local calls. No pets. $28-35/S; $31-38/D; $4/ex prsn. 2/1-4/14: $110/S or D. Discs.

Econo Lodge/ 2051 Gordon Hwy, Augusta GA 30909. 706-738-6565. V,AE,M,DC. On US 1/ 25, 4/5 mi E of jct with I-520. Nrby rstrnt/ lounge, pool, fax, b/f, cable TV, t pkng, kitchenettes, n/s rms. Free cont brfst. No pets. $37-60/S or D; $5/ex prsn. 4/2-4/10: $100-150/S or D. Discs.

Howard Johnson Lodge/ 601 Bobby Jones Expwy, Augusta GA 30907. 706-863-2882/ Fax: Ext 118. AE,V,M,DC, CB,D. I-20 (Exit 64B) turn lt at light. N/s rms, b/f, rstrnt, pool, t pkng, cable TV, fax, refrig, microwave, conn rms. Free cont brfst. Gold Medal Winner. $30-40/S; $38-48/D. 4/1-4/10: $115-135/S; $125-145/D. Discs.

Howard Johnson/ 1238 Gordon Hwy, Augusta GA 30901. 706-724-9613/ Fax: Ext 301. D,M,V,AE,DC,CB. I-20: Ebnd (Exit 64A) to Bobby Jones Hwy 520, (Exit 4B) S to Gordon Hwy (US 25), N 8 mi; Wbnd (Exit 66) to Riverwatch Pkwy, SW to Broad St, W to Gordon Hwy, S to mtl. N/s rms, lounge, pool, t pkng, in-rm coffee, refrig, microwave, cont brfst. Free arpt trans. $29-60/S; $34-65/D. Discs.

Motel 6/ 2650 Center W Pkwy, Augusta GA 30909. 706-736-1934/ Fax: 737-8628. V,M,DC,D,AE. I-20 (Exit 65) to Washington Rd, S to Center W Pkwy, turn lt. Nrby rstrnt, cable TV, laundry, pool, n/s rms, t pkng. Free local calls. $22-23/S; $26-27/D; $4/ex prsn. 4/7-4/14: $40/S; $44/D. Higher spec event rates. Disc.

Super 8 Motel/ 954 5th St, Augusta GA 30901. 706-724-0757/ Fax: 722-7233. AE,DC,D,M,V,CB. I-20 (Exit 64) to I-520, S to (Arpt Exit 8) Douglas Barnard Pkwy, N (lt) to Gordon Hwy, W (rt) to mtl. B/f, n/s rms, pool, laundry, hot brfst, t/b/rv pkng, cable TV, suites, kitchen, VCR/ movies, in-rm coffee, cot, crib. AAA. $29/S; $33-37/D; $3/ex prsn. Higher spec event/ wknd rate. Discs.

Super 8 Motel/ 2137 Gordon Hwy, Augusta GA 30909. 706-738-5018/ Fax: Ext 400. D,M,V,AE,DC,CB. US 78/ 278 (Gordon Hwy) at I-520 (Bobby Jones Expwy), Exit 4A. B/f, n/s rms, nrby rstrnt, b/rv pkng, cable TV, suites, TDD, cot. Free local calls, crib. No pets. $32/S; $38-40/D; $6/ex prsn. Higher spec event/ wknd rate. Discs.

Austel

Knights Inn Six Flags/ 1595 Blair Bridge Road, Austell GA 30001. 770-944-0824/ Fax: 819-9739/ 800-843-5644. V,M,AE,D. I-20 W (Exit 12) to Austell-Thornton Rd, rt at 1st light on Blair Bridge, 1 blk. Rstrnt, pool, n/s rms, cable TV, TDD, tt/dd phone, fax, copier, cot, crib, eff, conn rms, b/f. Free local calls, coffee. AAA. $32-52/S; $34-54/D; $5/ex prsn. 5/1-9/30: $47-52/S; $49-54/D. Disc: Senior, bsns, l/s, trkr, milt. *Guaranteed rates.*

Baxley

Budget Host Inn/ 714 E Parker St, Rt 6, Box 4, Baxley GA 31513. 912-367-2200/ Fax: Ext 403. V,M,AE,D,DC,CB. On Hwy 341 (E Parker) off of US 1. Cable TV, dd phone, conn rms, n/s rms, nrby rstrnt, t pkng, cot, crib, refrig. AAA. $36/S; $36-45/D; $5/ex prsn. Discs.

Brunswick

Budgetel Inns/ 105 Tourist Dr, Brunswick GA 31520. 912-265-7725/ Fax: 264-6151. V,M,D,AE,DC,CB. I-95, Exit 7A to US 25/341. N/s rms, b/f, fax, nrby rstrnt, pool. Free cont brfst, in-rm coffee, local calls. AAA. $39-52/S; $44-57/D. 2/2-9/2: $39-52/S; $44-57/D. Higher spec event rates. Discs.

Howard Johnson Lodge/ I-95 & US 341, Brunswick GA 31520. 912-264-4720/ Fax: 264-5928. AE,V,M,DC, CB,D. I-95 (Exit 7A) at Brunswick, to US 341 S; follow I-95 S to mtl. On E side of I-95. N/s rms, rstrnt, pool, t pkng, valet serv, in-rm coffee, suites,

GEORGIA

Free cont brfst. No pets. Gold Medal Winner. $33-40/S; $36-48/D. Discs.

Motel 6/ 403 Butler Dr, Brunswick GA 31525. 912-264-8582/ Fax: 264-6028. V,M,DC,D,AE. I-95 (Exit 7B) at US 341, W to Butler Dr, turn S. Just W of I-95. Cable TV, pool, n/s rms, nrby rstrnt, t pkng. Free local calls. Premier Award. $28-29/S; $32-33/D; $4/ex prsn. Disc.

Quality Inn/ 125 Venture Dr, Brunswick GA 31525. 912-265-4600. V,M,D,AE. I-95 (Exit 8) to Golden Isles Pkwy, N to Perry Ln Rd. Nrby rstrnt, pool, mtg rm, fax, cable TV, t pkng, in-rm coffee, n/s rms. Free cont brfst. No pets. AAA. $41-50/S; $45-55/D; $6/ex prsn. Discs.

Quality Inn/ 3302 Glynn Av, Brunswick GA 31520. 800-221-2222 — opening soon. V,M,D,AE. I-95 (Exit 8) to Golden Isles Pkwy (Spur 25), E to US 17, S to mtl. Nrby rstrnt, mtg rm, fax, b/f, cable TV, t pkng, n/s rms. Free cont brfst. $42-62/S or D; $5/ex prsn. 5/1-9/4: $49-69/S or D. Discs.

Super 8 Motel/ 5280 New Jesup Hwy, Brunswick GA 31520. 912-264-8800. D,M,V,AE,DC,CB. I-95, Exit 7B. B/f, n/s rms, b pkng, copier, fax, cable TV, cot. Free local calls, crib. $41/S; $46-51/D; $5/ex prsn. Higher spec event/wknd rate. Discs.

Byron

Comfort Inn/ Chapman Rd, Byron GA 31008. 912-756-5200. V,M,D,AE. I-75 (Exit 46) to Hwy 49, SW to Chapman Rd, turn N. Nrby rstrnt, pool, mtg rm, fax, cable TV, t pkng, n/s rms. Free cont brfst. $40-44/S; $45-48/D; $6/ex prsn. Discs.

Econo Lodge/ Rte 1, Box 40, Byron GA 31008. 912-956-5600. V,AE,M,DC. I-75 (Exit 46) to SR 49. 10 mi S of Macon. Nrby rstrnt, pool, fax, b/f, cable TV, t pkng, n/s rms. Free cont brfst. $29-39/S; $39-49/D; $4/ex prsn. Discs.

Super 8 Motel/ 305 Hwy 49 N, Byron GA 31008. 912-956-3311/ Fax: 956-5885. V,M,D,AE,DC,CB. I-75 (Exit 46) at Hwy 49. B/f, n/s rms, pool, cont brfst, copier, cable TV, microwave, refrig. Free local calls. $36-38/S; $42-44/D; $4/ex prsn. Discs.

Calhoun (Atlanta area)

Best Western of Calhoun/ 2261 Hwy 41 NE, Calhoun GA 30701. 706-629-4521/ Fax: 629-1650/ 800-629-4521. V,M, AE,D,DC,CB. I-75, Exit 132, E side. Nrby rstrnt, pool, whrlpool, n/s rms, cable TV, copier, fax, cot, crib, conn rms. Free local calls, cont brfst. AAA. $36/S; $40/D; $4/ex prsn. Higher wknd/ olympic period rates. Disc: Senior, bsns, TA, govt, l/s, family, trkr, milt.

Days Inn/ 742 Hwy 53 SE, Calhoun GA 30701. 706-629-8271. V,M,AE,D,CB, DC,JCB. I-75 to (Exit 129) Hwy 53, turn W to mtl. Fax, n/s rms, rstrnt, pool, b/f, t pkng, mtg rm, playgrnd, cable TV. $32-65/S; $36-65/D; $5/ex prsn. Discs.

Econo Lodge/ 1438 US 41 N, Calhoun GA 30701. 706-625-5421. V,AE,M,DC. I-75 (Exit 132) to US 41. Nrby rstrnt, pool, fax, cable TV, n/s rms. Free cont brfst. No pets. AAA. $50-90/S; $60-160/D; $3 ex prsn. 5/1-8/31; $28-36/S; $38-50/D. 9/1-12/31: $33-40/S; $43-53/D. Discs.

Quality Inn/ 915 SR 53 E, Calhoun GA 30701. 706-629-9501. V,M,AE,DC. I-75 (Exit 129) to US 53 E. Rstrnt/ lounge, pool, mtg rm, fax, b/f, cable TV, t pkng, n/s rms. Free cont brfst. AAA. $34-42/S; $38-46/D; $4/ex prsn. 2/1-4/30: $38-48/S; $42-52/D. 5/1-8/31: $38-48/S; $42-52/D. Discs.

Shepherd Budget Host Inn/ Box 2407, Calhoun GA 30703. 706-629-8644. V,M,AE,DC,CB,D. On SR 53 at jct I-75, Exit 129. Cable TV, dd phone, n/s rms, rstrnt, mtg rm, pool, playgrnd, t pkng, cot. Free crib. AAA/ Mobil. $27-33/S; $30-40/D; $3/ex prsn. 7/12-8/7: $99/S or D. Higher spec event rates. Discs.

Super 8 Motel/ 1446 US 41 N, Calhoun GA 30701. 706-602-1400/ Fax: 602-1906. AE,V,M,DC,CB,D. I-75, Exit 132. B/f, n/s rms, pool, t/b/rv pkng, cable TV, cot, crib. Free local calls. AAA. $30/S; $33-35/D; $2/ex prsn. Higher spec event/ wknd rate. Discs.

Cartersville (Atlanta area)

Budget Host Inn Cartersville/ 851 Cass-White Rd NW, Cartersville GA 30120. 404-386-0350. AE,D,M,V. I-75, Exit 127, NW Quadrant. Cable TV, dd phone, n/s rms, rstrnt, pool, laundry, t pkng, cot, crib. AAA. $22-27/S; $25-50/D; $10/ex prsn. Spec events: $69. Discs.

Comfort Inn/ 28 SR 294 SE, Cartersville GA 30120. 404-387-1800. V,AE,M,DC. I-75 (Exit 125) to SR 294, E to mtl. Nrby rstrnt, pool, b/f, cable TV, n/s rms. Free cont brfst. $30-95/S; $36-160/D; $5/ex prsn. Discs.

Econo Lodge/ 26 SR 294 SE, Cartersville GA 30101. Write to Box 600, Acworth GA 30101. 404-386-3303. V,AE,M,DC. I-75N (Exit 125) to Hwy 20. Nrby rstrnt, pool, cable TV, t pkng, arpt trans, n/s rms. Free coffee. $30-105/S; $33-126/D; $5/ex prsn. Discs.

Econo Lodge/ White-Cassville Rd, Cartersville GA 30120. (Write to Box 600, Acworth GA 30101) 404-386-0700. V,AE,M,DC. I-75 N (Exit 127) to White-Cassville Rd. Rstrnt, pool, mtg rm, cable TV, t pkng, n/s rms. Free coffee, arpt trans. $30-150/S; $40-150/D; $5/ex prsn. Discs.

Howard Johnson/ 5657 Hwy 20, Cartersville GA 30120. 404-386-1449/ Fax: 386-1215. V,M,D,AE,DC,CB. I-75 (Exit 125) to Canton Hwy, E to mtl. N/s rms, b/f, pool, t pkng, cable TV, fax. $30-145/S; $35-200/D. Discs.

Quality Inn/ Box 158, Cartersville GA 30120. 404-386-0510. V,M,DC,AE. I-75 (Exit 124) to Hwy 61, W to mtl. At US 41 & Dixie Av. Rstrnt/ lounge, pool, mtg rm, fax, cable TV, t pkng, n/s rms. AAA. $33-60/S; $37-90/D; $4/ex prsn. Discs.

Super 8 Motel/ I-75 & Hwy 20, Cartersville GA 30120. 706-382-8881. D,M,V,AE,DC,CB. I-75 (Exit 125) at Hwy 20, turn E to Hwy 294, then turn S. B/f, n/s rms, t/b/rv pkng, copier, cable TV, cot. Free local calls, crib. $37/S; $41-45/D; $5/ex prsn. Higher spec event rates. Discs.

College Park (Atlanta area)

Super 8 Motel/ 2010 Sullivan Rd, College Park GA 30337. 404-991-8985/ Fax: 201. D,M,V,AE,DC,CB. I-85 (Exit 18) E on Riverdale to 1st light, rt to Sullivan Rd, turn rt. B/f, n/s rms, b/rv pkng, elevator, cable TV, mtg rm, TDD, cot. Free local calls, arpt trans, crib. No pets. $42/S; $48-54/D; $6/ex prsn. Higher spec event rates. Higher spec event rates. Discs.

Columbus

Days Inn/ 3452 Macon Rd, Columbus GA 31907. 706-561-4400. V,M,AE,D, CB,DC,JCB. I-185 (Exit 4) at Macon Rd (US 22). Fax, n/s rms, nrby rstrnt, pool, b/f, exerc equip, arpt trans, cable TV, cot. Free local calls. Chairman's Award. $44-53/S; $48-56/D; $5/ex prsn. Discs.

Econo Lodge/ 4483 Victory Dr, Columbus GA 31903. 706-682-3803. V, AE, M,DC. I-185, Exit 1. Nrby rstrnt, pool, b/f, cable TV, t pkng, n/s rms. Free local calls. $36-46/S; $40-50/D; $4/ex prsn. Discs.

Motel 6/ 3050 Victory Dr, Columbus GA 31903. 706-687-7214/ Fax: 682-2362. V,M,DC,D,AE. On US 280 (Victory Dr) between I-185 and US 80. Nrby rstrnt, cable TV, pool, n/s rms. Free local calls. $25-26/S; $29-30/D; $4/ex prsn. Disc.

Super 8 Motel/ 2935 Warm Springs Rd, Columbus GA 31909. 706-322-6580. D,M,V,AE,DC,CB. I-185 (Exit 5) to Warm Springs Rd, turn E to mtl. Near Peachtree Mall. B/f, n/s rms, b/rv pkng, copier, cable TV, cot. Free local calls, crib. $39/S; $43-47/D; $5/ex prsn. Higher spec event rates. Discs.

Commerce

HoJo Inn/ I-85 & US 441, Commerce GA 30529. 706-335-5581/ Fax: 335-7889. D,M,V,AE,DC,CB. I-85, Exit 53. N/s rms, b/f, rstrnt, pool, arpt trans, t pkng, tt phone, cable TV. $29-79/S; $34-89/D. Discs.

Conley (Atlanta area)

Econo Lodge/ 3140 Moreland Av, Conley GA 30027. 404-363-6960. V, M, D,AE. Jct I-285, I-675 & Moreland Av at Exit 39. Nrby rstrnt, pool, t pkng, exerc equip, n/s rms. Free cont brfst. $34-39/S; $37-44/D; $6/ex prsn. Higher spec event rates. Discs.

Cordele

Days Inn/ 215 S 7th St, Cordele GA 31015. 912-273-1123/ Fax: 273-3545. AE,M,V,DC,D. Jct I-75 (Exit 33) & US

GEORGIA 84

280 E. Nrby rstrnt, pool, t pkng. $37-42/S; $42-48/D; $4/ex prsn. Discs.

Friendship Inn/ 1609 16th Av E, Cordele GA 31015. 912-273-3390. V,M,D,AE. I-75 (Exit 33) to US 280, W 2 blks to mtl. Nrby rstrnt, pool, cable TV, n/s rms. $28-38/S; $35-50/D; $4/ex prsn. Discs.

Super 8 Motel/ 566 Farmers Market Rd, Cordele GA 31015. 912-273-9800/ Fax: 276-0222. V,M,D,AE,DC,CB. I-75 (Exit 35) at Farmers Market Rd. N/s rms, pool, copier, fax, t/b/rv pkng, rstrnt, cot, crib. Free local calls, cont brfst. $33/S; $37-44/D; $5/ex prsn. Higher spec event rates. Discs.

Covington

Econo Lodge/ 10101 Alcovy Jersey Rd, Covington GA 30209. 404-786-4133. V,AE,M,DC. I-20, Exit 45A, NE on Alcovy Jersey. Adj rstrnt, fax, b/f, cable TV, t pkng, n/s rms. Free full brfst. No pets. $32-37/S; $38-46/D; $3/ex prsn. Discs.

Dahlonega

Econo Lodge/ 801 N Grove St, Dahlonega GA 30533. 706-864-6191. V,AE,M,DC. Bsns 19 N to mtl. Rstrnt, pool, fax, b/f, cable TV, t pkng, n/s rms. Free cont brfst. No pets. AAA. $34-37/S; $37-45/D; $5/ex prsn. 5/1-11/11: $34-70/S; $39-70/D. Discs.

Howard Johnson/ 1010 Mountain Drive SW, Dahlonega GA 30533. 706-864-4343. AE,V,M,DC,CB,D. On US 60, in Dahlonega. N/s rms, b/f, pool, t/b pkng, cable TV, fax, micro-refrig. Free cont brfst, coffee. No pets. $34-65/S or D. Discs.

Dalton

Motel 6/ 2200 Chattanooga Rd, Dalton GA 30720. 706-278-5522/ Fax: 278-9378. V,M,DC,D,AE. I-75 (Exit 137) to US 41/ Chattanooga Rd, W to mtl. Nrby rstrnt, cable TV, n/s rms. Free local calls. No t/rv pkng. $25-26/S; $29-30/D; $4/ex prsn. Disc.

Super 8 Motel/ Box 1232, Dalton GA 30720. 706-277-9323/ Fax: Ext 104. V, M,D,AE,DC,CB. I-75 (Exit 135) Connector 3. B/f, n/s rms, pool, t pkng, cable TV, cot. Free local calls, crib. $35-39/S; $35-44/D; $5/ex prsn. Discs.

Darien

Super 8 Motel/ Box 556, Darien GA 31305. 912-437-6660/ Fax: 437-3676. V,M,D,AE,DC,CB. I-95 (Exit 10) at Hwy 251, turn W to mtl. N/s rms, pool, outlets, cable TV, b/f, cot, crib. Free local calls. AAA. $32/S; $34-38/D; $2/ex prsn. Higher spec event rates. Discs.

Decatur (Atlanta area)

Friendship Inn/ 4600 Glenwood Rd, Decatur GA 30035. 404-289-4940. V, M,D,AE. I-285 E, Exit 34. Nrby rstrnt, fax, b/f, cable TV, t pkng, n/s rms. Free cont brfst, coffee. No pets. $35-50/S or D; $5/ex prsn. 2/1-4/30: $40-200/S; $50-250/D. 5/1-9/30: $40-80/S; $45-100/D. Higher spec event rates. Discs.

Motel 6/ 2565 Wesley Chapel Rd, Decatur GA 30035. 404-288-6911/ Fax: 284-1068. V,M,DC,D,AE. I-20 (Exit 36) to Wesley Chapel Rd, N to mtl. Nrby rstrnt, cable TV, laundry, pool, n/s rms. Free local calls. Premier Award. $36/S; $42/D; $6/ex prsn. Higher spec event rates. Disc.

Douglas

Super 8 Motel/ 1610 S Peterson Av, Douglas GA 31533. 912-384-0886/ Fax: Ext 106. D,M,V,AE,DC,CB. Jct Hwys 206 & 441. B/f, n/s rms, t/b/rv pkng, cable TV, cot, TDD. Free local calls, crib. $33/S; $39/D; $6/ex prsn. Higher spec event rates. Discs.

Eastman

Days Inn/ 1126 College St SE, Eastman GA 31023. 912-374-7000/ Fax: 374-1034. V,M,AE,D,CB,DC, JCB.D US 341 S, at Eastman. Fax, n/s rms, b/f, t pkng, arpt trans, cable TV, cot. $38-40/S; $42-46/D; $5/ex prsn. Discs.

Ellijay

Budget Host Top-O-Ellijay Motel/ 10 Jeff Dr, Ellijay GA 30540. 706-635-5311/ Fax: 635-5313. V,AE,CB,DC, D,M. GA Hwy 515, Exit at Hardees, cross bridge; lt, 1500 ft on rt. Cable TV, dd phone, in-rm coffee, n/s rms, nrby rstrnt/ lounge, t pkng, outlets, cot, crib. AAA. $34-60/S; $37-80/D; $5/ex prsn. Discs.

GEORGIA

Forest Park (Atlanta area)

Days Inn Atlanta S/ 5116 Hwy 85, Forest Park GA 30050. 404-768-6400/ Fax: 767-5138. V,AE,M,DC,D. I-75 (Sbnd, Exit 80; Nbnd, Exit 78) to SR 85; make lt turn in front of Conoco Stn after passing traffic light. Nrby rstrnt, pool, n/s rms, cable TV, arpt trans, tt phone, mtg rm, fax, laundry, refrig, elevator, cot, crib, outlets, t/b/rv pkng, b/f. Free cont brfst. No pets. AAA. $43/S; $48/D; $5/ex prsn. 7/1-8/31: $80-150/S or D. 2nd wknd Mar & Nov: $80/S; $85/D. Discs. *Guaranteed rates.*

Friendship Inn/ 5060 Frontage Rd, Forest Park GA 30050. 404-363-6429. V,AE,M,DC. Jct of I-75 (Exit 78) & I-285. Nrby rstrnt, fax, b/f, cable TV, t pkng, n/s rms. No pets. $32-35/S; $35-40/D; $5/ex prsn. Higher spec event rates. Discs.

Forsyth

Super 8 Motel/ Rte 2, Box 935, Forsyth GA 31029. 912-994-9333. AE,DC, D, M, V,CB. I-75 (Exit 63) to Hwy 42 E, at Forsyth. N/s rms, pool, nrby rstrnt, laundry, t/b/rv pkng, outlets, fax, copier, cable TV, cot, crib. Free local calls. AAA. $31/S; $36-38/D; $4/ex prsn. Higher spec event rates. Discs.

Gainesville

See Oakwood.

Hartwell

Budget Inn & Suites/ 1679 Anderson Hwy, Hartwell GA 30643. 706-376-4707/ Fax: 376-6687. V,M,AE,D. I-85, Exit 59 toward Hartwell Hwy 77, 10 mi. Cable TV, VCR, tt/dd phone, fax, refrig, microwave, cot, outlets, t/b pkng, eff, conn rms. No pets. AAA. $32-35/S or D; $4/ex prsn. Higher spec event/ holiday/ wknd rates. Disc: Senior, bsns, TA, govt, l/s, family, trkr, milt.

Helen

Comfort Inn/ Edelweiss Dr, Box 1178, Helen GA 30545. 706-878-8000. V,M,AE,DC. US 129 N to SR 75, N to mtl. Nrby rstrnt, pool, mtg rm, fax, b/f, cable TV, t pkng, n/s rms. Free cont brfst. No pets. AAA. $30-89/S; $35-109/D; $5/ex prsn. 5/1-6/30: $45-99/S; $50-109/D. 7/1-8/15: $49-129/S; $59-149/D. 8/16-10/31: $69-149/S; $69-169/D. Discs.

Hinesville

Days Inn/ Hwy 84, Hinesville GA 31313. 912-368-4146. V,M,AE,D,CB, DC,JCB. I-96 to US 84, S to Gen Stuart Way, turn W. Fax, n/s rms, nrby rstrnt, pool, b/f, t pkng, cable TV, cot. Free cont brfst. $36-45/S; $40-45/D; $4/ex prsn. Discs.

Kennesaw (Atlanta area)

Rodeway Inn/ 1460 George Busbee Pkwy, Kennesaw GA 30144. 404-590-0519. V,M,D,AE. I-75 (Exit 118) to Wade Green Rd, turn N to mtl. Nrby rstrnt, pool, mtg rm, cable TV, n/s rms. Free cont brfst. $30-100/S; $37-100/D; $5/ex prsn. Higher spec event rates. Discs.

Kingsland

Quality Inn/ 985 Boone St, Kingsland GA 31548. 912-729-4363. V,M,D,AE. I-95 (Exit 2) at Hwy 40, turn rt, lt to service rd, lt on Boone St. Nrby rstrnt, pool, mtg rm, fax, b/f, cable TV, n/s rms. Free cont brfst. $37-52/S or D; $5/ex prsn. 5/1-9/4: $42-60/S or D. Discs.

Super 8 Motel/ Box 2247, Kingsland GA 31548. 912-729-6888/ Fax: Ext 402. D,M,V,AE,DC,CB. I-95 (Exit 2) at Hwy 40. B/f, n/s rms, t/b/rv pkng, cable TV, microwave, refrig, TDD, cot. Free local calls, crib. $35/S; $41/D; $6/ex prsn. Higher spec event rates. Discs.

LaGrange

Days Inn Callaway Gardens/ 2606 Whitesville Rd, LaGrange GA 30240. 706-882-8881. AE,M,V,DC,D. I-85, Exit 2, turn E and go 2 blks to mtl. Rstrnt, pool, mtg rm, b/f, t pkng. cable TV. Free cont brfst. $40-90/S; $45-100/D; $5/ex prsn. Discs.

Super 8 Motel/ 26 Pattillo Rd, La-Grange GA 30240. 706-845-9093. V, M, D,AE,DC,CB. I-85 (Exit 4) to SR 109, W 1 blk. B/f, n/s rms, b/t/rv pkng, boat pkng, outlets. $39/S; $43/D; $5/ex prsn. Discs.

Lake Park (Valdosta area)

Days Inn/ Timber Dr, Lake Park GA

GEORGIA

31636. 912-559-0229/ Fax: 559-0416. V,M,AE,D,CB,DC,JCB. I-75 (Exit 2) at SR 376. Fax, n/s rms, nrby rstrnt, pool, b/f, cot. Free cont brfst. $34-40/S; $37-40/D; $3/ex prsn. Discs.

Travelodge/ I-75, Lake Park GA 31636. 912-559-0110/ Fax: 559-0045/ 800-578-7878. V,M,AE,D,DC,CB. I-75, Exit 2, behind McDonalds. Nrby rstrnt, cable TV, tt phone, fax, copier, nwspr, laundry, refrig, cot, crib, t/b/rv pkng, eff, conn rms, b/f. Free local calls, cont brfst, coffee, tea, cocoa. AAA. $38/S; $45/D; $4/ex prsn. Aug-Sept: $45/S; $65/D; $5/ex prsn. Disc: Senior. *Guaranteed rates.*

Lavonia

Sleep Inn/ 890 Ross Pl, Box 438, Lavonia GA 30553. 706-356-2268. V,M,D,AE. I-85 (Exit 58) to Lavonia-Toccoa exit, rt 1/4 mi to mtl. Nrby rstrnt, pool, fax, b/f, cable TV, t pkng, n/s rms. Free cont brfst. No pets. $38-70/S; $42-74/D; $5/ex prsn. Discs.

Locust Grove

Super 8 Motel/ 4605 Hampton Rd, Box 613, Locust Grove GA 30248. 404-957-2936/ Fax: 957-7014. AE,V,MC,D, DC, CB. I-75 (Exit 68) Locust Grove Stop, turn W. N/s rms, pool, outlets, t/b/rv pkng, cont brfst, laundry, cable TV, cot, crib. $33-37/S; $37-45/D; $4/ex prsn. Higher spec event rate. Discs.

Macon

Comfort Inn/ 4951 Eisenhower Pkwy, Macon GA 31206. 912-788-5500. V,M,AE,DC. I-475 Bypass (Exit 1) & US 80, E to mtl. Nrby rstrnt, pool, fax, b/f, cable TV, microwave, refrig, n/s rms. Free cont brfst. No pets. AAA. $40-100/S; $45-100/D; $5/ex prsn. Discs.

Comfort Inn/ 2690 Riverside Dr, Macon GA 31204. 912-746-8855. V,AE,M,DC. I-75 (Exit 54) at Pierce Av. Nrby rstrnt/ lounge, pool, mtg rm, fax, b/f, cable TV, t pkng, laundry, n/s rms. Free cont brfst. AAA. $43-79/S; $48-89/D; $5/ex prsn. Discs.

Econo Lodge/ 4951 Romeiser Dr, Macon GA 31206. 912-474-1661. V,M,AE. I-475 (Exit 1) to US 80 E. Nrby rstrnt, pool, fax, cable TV, t pkng, n/s rms. Free cont brfst. $30-32/S; $36-45/D; $5/ex prsn. Discs.

HoJo Inn/ 4709 Chambers Rd, Macon GA 31206. 912-781-6680. D,M,V, AE,DC,CB. I-75 to I-475 Bypass & US 80, Exit 1. N/s rms, pool, t pkng, tt phone, nrby rstrnt. Free cont brfst. $33-99/S; $36-99/D. Discs.

Howard Johnson Lodge/ 2566 Riverside Dr, Macon GA 31204. 912-746-76-71. AE,V,M,DC,CB,D. I-75 (Exit 54) to Riverside Dr, turn NW to mtl. N/s rms, b/f, rstrnt/ lounge, pool, t pkng, cable TV, laundry, tt phone, game rm. Free cont brfst. $40-45/S; $45-50/D. Discs.

Motel 6/ 4991 Harrison Rd, Macon GA 31206. 912-474-2870/ Fax: 477-4889. V,M,DC,D,AE. I-475 (Exit 1) to US 80 (Eisenhower Pkwy), NE 1/4 mi. Nrby rstrnt, cable TV, pool, n/s rms. Free local calls. $25-26/S; $29-30/D; $4/ex prsn. Disc.

Quality Inn/ 4630 Chamber's Rd, Macon GA 31206. 912-781-7000. V,M,D,AE. I-475 (Exit 1) to US 80. Nrby rstrnt, pool, mtg rm, fax, sauna, whrlpool, cable TV, t pkng, exerc equip, n/s rms. Free cont brfst. $38-60/S; $45-70/D; $5/ex prsn. Discs.

Rodeway Inn/ 4999 Eisenhower Pkwy, Macon GA 31206. 912-781-4343. V,AE,M,DC. I-475 Bypass (Exit 1) to US 80, E to mtl. Nrby rstrnt, pool, fax, b/f, cable TV, outlets, n/s rms. Free cont brfst. AAA. $36-40/S; $40-48/D; $4/ex prsn. Discs.

Super 8 Motel/ 6007 Harrison Rd, Macon GA 31206. 912-788-8800/ Fax: 788-2327. AE,V,MC,DC,CB,D. I-475 (Exit 1) to US 80 & Harrison Rd. B/f, n/s rms, pool, laundry, outlets, t/b/rv pkng, copier, cable TV, mtg rm, refrig, microwave, cot, crib. AAA. $32-36/S; $38-43/D; $5/ex prsn. Higher spec event rate. Discs.

Madison

Super 8 Motel/ 2091 Eatonton Rd, Madison GA 30650. 706-342-7800/ Fax: 342-3795. V,M,D,AE,DC,CB. I-20 (Exit 51) at Hwy 441/ 129. B/f, n/s rms, laundry, outlets, t/b/rv pkng, copier, cable TV, cot. Free local calls, crib. $34-38/S; $37-45/D; $3/ex prsn. Higher spec event rates. Discs.

GEORGIA

Marietta (Atlanta area)
Howard Johnson Lodge/ 2375 Delk Rd, Marietta GA 30067. 770-951-1144/ Fax: 938-0444. V,M,D,AE,DC,CB. I-75 Delk Rd (Exit 111) to Lockheed/ Dobbins AFB exit, N of I-285. N/s rms, mtg rm, b/f, rstrnt/ lounge, indr/ outdr pool, mini-suite, refrig, microwave. Gold Medal Winner. $35-145/S; $40-165/D. Higher spec event rates. Discs.

Motel 6/ 2360 Delk Rd Marietta GA 30067. 404-952-8161/ Fax: 984-2307. V,M,DC,D,AE. I-75 (Exit 111) to Hwy 280 (Delk Rd), E to mtl. Nrby rstrnt, cable TV, laundry, pool, n/s rms, elevator. Free local calls. Premier Award. $35/S; $41/D; $6/ex prsn. Higher spec event rates. Disc.

Super 8 Motel/ 2500 Delk Rd, Marietta GA 30067. 404-984-1570/ Fax: 933-9382. V,M,D,AE,DC,CB. I-75 (Exit 111) at Marietta/ Delk Rd. B/f, n/s rms, pool, laundry, t/b/rv pkng, copier, cable TV, mtg rm, kitchenettes. Free local calls. $34/S; $39-41/D; $5/ex prsn. Higher spec event rates. Discs.

McDonough
Days Inn/ 744 SR 155 S, McDonough GA 30253. 404-957-5261/ Fax: 957-6638. V,AE,M,DC,D. I-75 (Exit 69) at SR 155, turn lt. Rstrnt, pool, t pkng, VCR/ movies, cot. Free cont brfst. $38-110/S; $44-125/D; $5/ex prsn. Discs.

HoJo Inn/ 1279 Hampton Rd, McDonough GA 30253. 404-957-2651. V,M,D,AE,DC,CB. I-75, Exit 70. N/s rms, rstrnt, pool. $35-45/S; $45-50/D. Discs.

Metter
Comfort Inn/ Box 208, Metter GA 30439. 912-685-4100. V,M,D,AE. I-16 & US 121 (Metter/ Reidsville exit). Nrby rstrnt, pool, fax, b/f, cable TV, t pkng, n/s rms. Free local calls, cont brfst. $42-53/S; $48-58/D; $6/ex prsn. Discs.

Newnan
Comfort Inn/ 1455 US 29 S, Newnan GA 30263. 404-254-0089. V,M,D,AE. I-85 (Exit 8) to US 29, N to mtl. Nrby rstrnt, pool, fax, cable TV, t pkng, microwave, refrig, n/s rms. $40-115/S; $44-135/D; $5/ex prsn. 5/1-8/31, 9/4-11/30: $44-115/S; $48-135/D. 9/1-9/3: $55-115/S; $60-135/D. Discs.

Norcross (Atlanta area)
Comfort Inn/ 5990 Western Hills Dr, Norcross GA 30071. 404-368-0218. V,M,D,AE. I-85 (Exit 37) W to Jimmy Carter Blvd, rt at third traffic light, rt on Western Hills to mtl. Nrby rstrnt, pool, fax, b/f, cable TV, t pkng,n/s rms. Free cont brfst. $37-99/S; $42-119/D; $5/ex prsn. Higher spec event rates. Discs.

Motel 6/ 6015 Oakbrook Pkwy, Norcross GA 30093. 404-446-2311/ Fax: 246-1769. V,M,DC,D,AE. I-85 (Exit 37) to Jimmy Carter Blvd, E to Live Oak Pkwy, lt 1 mi to Oakbrook Pkwy, turn lt. Nrby rstrnt, cable TV, pool, laundry, n/s rms. Free local calls. $36/S; $42/D; $6/ex prsn. Higher spec event rates. Disc.

Oakwood (Gainesville area)
Comfort Inn/ Mundy Mill Rd, Box 187, Oakwood GA 30566. 404-287-1000. V,AE,M,DC. I-985 to Hwy 53 (Mundy Mill Rd), turn S. Nrby rstrnt, pool, b/f, cable TV, t pkng, outlets, n/s rms. Free cont brfst. No pets. AAA. $40-100/S or D; $5/ex prsn. 2/16-4/30: $45-100/S or D. 5/1-9/10: $45-100/S; $49-100/D. 9/11-10/31: $49-100/S or D. Discs.

Perry
Econo Lodge/ 624 Valley Dr, Perry GA 31069. 912-987-2585. V,M,AE. I-75: Nbnd, Exit 43. Rt off ramp then lt to mtl; Sbnd, Exit 43, lt off ramp then lt after bridge to mtl. Pool, mtg rm, fax, b/f, sauna, whrlpool, exerc equip, n/s rms. Free cont brfst. No pets. $30-40/S; $33-50/D; $5/ex prsn. Discs.

Friendship Inn/ 103 Marshallville Rd, Box F, Perry GA 31069. 912-987-3200. V,M,AE. I-75, Exit 42. Nrby rstrnt, pool, fax, cable TV, t pkng, n/s rms. Free cont brfst. $28-38/S; $34-45/D; $4/ex prsn. Discs.

Quality Inn/ Drawer 1012, Perry GA 31069. 912-987-1345. V,M,DC,AE. I-75 (Exit 43) at US 341. Rstrnt/ lounge, pool, fax, cable TV, t pkng, kiddie pool, n/s rms. Free cont brfst. $45-55/S; $50-65/D; $5/ex prsn. 5/1-12/31: $35-55/S; $40-55/D. Discs.

Pine Mountain

White Columns Motel/ Box 531, Pine Mountain GA 31822. 706-663-2312/ 800-722-5083. V,M,AE,D. I-85, Exit Hwy 27 or Hwy 18 to Pine Mountain. On Hwy 27, 1 mi S of town. Cable TV, tt/dd phone, cot, crib, t/b/rv pkng. Free local calls, coffee. AAA. $33/S or D; $6/ex prsn. 3/1-11/2, 11/22-12/31:$45/S or D. Olympic period: $70/S or D. Disc: Senior, AAA.

Pooler (Savannah area)

Econo Lodge/ 500 E US 80, Pooler GA 31322. 912-748-4124. V,M,D,AE. I-95 (Exit 18) at US 80. Nrby rstrnt, pool, fax, b/f, cable TV, n/s rms. Free cont brfst. $38-48/S; $44-54/D; $6/ex prsn. 3/14-3/17: $58-68/S; $64-74/D. Discs.

Port Wentworth

Sleep Inn/ 7206 SR 21, Port Wentworth GA 31407. 912=966-9800. V,M,D,AE. I-95 (Exit 19) to SR 21, W to mtl. Nrby rstrnt, pool, mtg rm, fax, b/f, cable TV, n/s rms. Free cont brfst. No pets. AAA. $39-47/S; $45-53/D; $6/ex prsn. 3/15-3/17: $72-80/S or D. Discs.

Richmond Hill (Savannah area)

Econo Lodge/ I-95 & US 17 S, Richmond Hill GA 31324. 912-756-3312. V,AE,M,DC. I-95 (Exit 14) to Coastal Hwy (US 17), lt 2 blks. Nrby rstrnt, fax, b/f, cable TV, refrig, microwave, n/s rms. Free cont brfst. $24-38/S; $24-44/D; $5/ex prsn. Discs.

Motel 6/ I-95 & US 17, Richmond Hill GA 31324. 912-756-3543/ Fax: 756-3583. V,M,DC,D,AE. I-95 (Exit 14) to US 17, rt to mtl. Cable TV, laundry, pool, n/s rms, t pkng. Free local calls. $21-23/S; $25-27/D; $4/ex prsn. Disc.

Ringgold

Friendship Inn/ Box 405, Ringgold GA 30736. 706-965-3428. V,AE,M,DC. I-75 (Exit 139) to US 41 S. Nrby rstrnt, pool, fax, cable TV, t pkng, n/s rms, dd phone, laundry. $27-34/S; $31-38/D; $3/ex prsn. 3/3-9/4: $30-38/S; $35-48/D. Discs.

Super 8 Motel/ 401 S Hwy 151, Ringgold GA 30736. 706-965-7080/ Fax: 965-7130. AE,V,MC,DC,CB,D. I-75 (Exit 140) at Hwy 151. N/s rms, pool, outlets, b pkng, cont brfst, copier, cable TV. AAA. $40/S; $40-46/D; $3/ex prsn. Higher spec event rates. Discs.

Rome

Super 8 Motel/ 1590 Dodd Blvd SE, Rome GA 30161. 706-234-8182. D, M,V,AE,DC,CB. US 411 at Dodd Blvd, 1 mi from Rome. B/f, n/s rms, nrby rstrnt, b pkng, copier, cable TV, cot. Free local calls, crib. $37/S; $42-46/D; $5/ex prsn. Higher spec event rates. Discs.

Savannah

Budgetel Inns/ 8484 Abercorn St, Savannah GA 31406. 912-927-7660/ Fax: 927-6392. V,M,D,AE,DC,CB. I-95 (Exit 16) to Hwy 204 E; jct of Hwy 204 (Abercorn) & Montgomery Crossroads. N/s rms, b/f, fax, pool. Free cont brfst, in-rm coffee, local calls. AAA. $39-50/S; $46-57/D. 3/1-6/13, 8/9-12/31: $41-52/S; $48-59/D. 6/14-8/8: $69-80/S; $76-87/D. Spec rates may apply. Discs.

Days Inn/ 6 Gateway Blvd S, Savannah GA 31419. 912-925-9505/ Fax: 925-3495. V,M,AE,D,CB,DC,JCB. I-95 (Exit 16) at SR 204. Fax, n/s rms, nrby rstrnt, pool, b/f, t pkng, cot. Free brfst, crib. $36-69/S or D; $5/ex prsn. Discs.

Econo Lodge/ 7500 Abercorn, Savannah GA 31406. 912-352-1657. V,AE,M,DC. I-95 (Exit 16) to SR 204, E 11 mi. Nrby rstrnt, fax, b/f, cable TV, t pkng, laundry, n/s rms. Free cont brfst, local calls. No pets. $31-37/S; $35-41/D; $5/ex prsn. 3/10-3/19: $75/S or D. Discs.

Econo Lodge/ 7 Gateway Blvd W, Savannah GA 31419. 912-925-2280. AE, V,M,DC. I-95 (Exit 16) to SR 204, W 1/8 mi to mtl. Rstrnt/ lounge, pool, mtg rm, fax, cable TV, t pkng, n/s rms. AAA. $32-47/S; $37-48/D; $5/ex prsn. 3/13-3/17: $45-85/S; $50-85/D. Discs.

Howard Johnson Lodge/ 224 W Boundary St, Savannah GA 31401. 912-232-4371/ Fax: Ext 250. AE,V,M,DC,CB,D. I-16 (Exit 36) follow signs to Savannah Visitors Cntr. N/s rms, rstrnt/ lounge, pool, cable TV. No pets. $39-75/S or D. Discs.

Quality Inn/ Gateway Blvd, Savannah

GEORGIA

GA 31419. 800-221-2222 — opening soon. V,M,D,AE. I-95 (Exit 16) to Gateway Blvd (Hwy 204), turn N toward mtl. Nrby rstrnt/ lounge, indr pool, mtg rm, b/f, sauna, whrlpool, cable TV, exerc equip, n/s rms. Free cont brfst. No pets. $40-90/S; $45-95/D; $5/ex prsn. Discs.

Super 8 Motel/ 15 Ft Argyle Rd, Savannah GA 31419. 912-927-8550/ Fax: 921-0135. D,M,V,AE,DC,CB. I-95 (Exit 16) at Hwy 204, Gateway Savannah. B/f, n/s rms, pool, nrby rstrnt, cont brfst, cable TV, fax, copier, cot, crib. Free local calls. $36/S; $41-46/D; $5/ex prsn. Higher spec event rates. Discs.

Also see Pooler, Richmond Hill.

Stockbridge (Atlanta area)

Motel 6/ 7233 Davidson Pkwy, Stockbridge GA 30281. 770-389-1142/ Fax: 507-8385. V,M,DC,D,AE. I-675 (Exit 1) to SR 138, E to mtl. Nrby rstrnt, cable TV, pool, n/s rms, t pkng. Free local calls. Premier Award. $30/S; $36/D; $6/ex prsn. Higher spec event rates. Disc.

Super 8 Motel/ 1451 Hudson Bridge Rd, Stockbridge GA 30281. 404-474-5758/ Fax: 474-1297. D,M,V,AE,DC,CB. I-75 (Exit 73) at Hudson Bridge Rd, 1st exit S. B/f, n/s rms, pool, laundry, cont brfst, t/b/rv pkng, copier, cable TV, microwave, refrig, VCR, cot, crib. Free local calls, movies. No pets. $37/S; $43-46/D; $4/ex prsn. Higher spec event rates. Discs.

Thomson

Econo Lodge/ 130 N Seymour Dr, Thomson GA 30824. 706-595-7144/ Fax: 595-1219. V,AE,M,DC. I-20 (Exit 59) at US 78; turn S, rt on N Seymour Dr. Rstrnt, fax, b/f, cable TV, t pkng, outlets, n/s rms. No pets. $33-35/S; $35-40/D; $3/ex prsn. 4/7-4/14: $85/S; $95/D. Discs.

Tifton

Comfort Inn/ 1104 King Rd, Tifton GA 31794. 912-382-4410. V,M,D,AE. I-75 (Exit 19) at 2nd St, S to King Rd. Nrby rstrnt, indr pool, mtg rm, whrlpool. $40-50/S; $45-50/D; $5/ex prsn.

Quality Inn/ 1103 King Rd, Tifton GA 31794. 912-386-2100. V,M,AE,DC. I-75 & 2nd St. Nrby rstrnt, pool, mtg rm, cable TV, t pkng, n/s rms. $35-50/S; $40-50/D; $5/ex prsn. Discs.

Super 8 Motel/ I-75 & W 2nd St, Tifton GA 31793. 912-382-9500/ Fax: 382-6060. V,M,D,AE,DC,CB. I-75, Exit 19. B/f, n/s rms, pool, nrby rstrnt, cont brfst, t/b/rv pkng, copier, fax, cable TV, cot. Free crib. Pride Award. $34/S; $36/D; $2/ex prsn. Higher spec event rats. Discs.

Valdosta

Econo Lodge/ 2015 W Hill Av, Valdosta GA 31601. 912-244-4350. V,M,D,AE,DC. I-75, exit 4, US 84 E to mtl. Nrby rstrnt, pool, fax, cable TV, t pkng, n/s rms. $26-36/S; $32-42/D; $6/ex prsn. Discs.

Motel 6/ 2003 W Hill Av, Valdosta GA 31601. 912-333-0047/ Fax: 241-0998. V,M,DC,D,AE. I-75 (Exit 4) to US 84 (W Hill Av), E to mtl. Nrby rstrnt, cable TV, laundry, pool, n/s rms. Free local calls. $22-23/S; $26-27/D; $4/ex prsn. Disc.

Quality Inn South/ 1902 W Hill Av, Valdosta GA 31601. 912-244-4520. V, M, DC,AE. I-75 (Exit 4) to US 84. Rstrnt/ lounge, pool, fax, b/f, cable TV, t pkng, n/s rms. Free cont brfst. AAA. $33-40/S; $36-49/D; $4/ex prsn. Discs.

Quality Inn/ 1209 St Augustine Rd, Valdosta GA 31601. 912-244-8510. V,M,D,AE. I-75 (Exit 5) at SR 94. Rstrnt/ lounge, pool, fax, b/f, cable TV, t pkng, exerc equip, laundry, tennis, n/s rms. Free cont brfst. AAA. $40-80/S; $45-90/D; $5/ex prsn. Discs.

Also see Lake Park.

Villa Rica (Atlanta area)

Comfort Inn/ 128 SR 61 Connector, Villa Rica GA 30180. 404-459-8000. V,M,AE,DC. I-20 (Exit 5) at Hwys 61 & 101, N to mtl. Pool, fax, b/f, cable TV. Free cont brfst. $42-75/S; $45-80/D; $5-10/ex prsn. 5/1-9/11: $45-80/S; $50-85/D. Discs.

Friendship Inn/ 615 Edge Rd, Villa Rica GA 30180. 404-459-5793. V,AE,M,DC. I-20, Exit 6, rt on Edge Rd. Nrby rstrnt, pool, fax, cable TV, t pkng, outlets, n/s

GEORGIA / HAWAII

rms. No pets. $27-33/S; $33-40/D; $5/ex prsn. 3/1-4/30, 9/10-10/31: $30-36/S; $36-47/D. 5/1-9/9: $33-40/S; $40-50/D. Discs.

Super 8 Motel/ 195 Hwy 61 Connector, Villa Rica GA 30180. 404-459-8888/ Fax: 459-1211. D,M,V,AE,DC,CB. I-20 (Exit 5) & SR 61 Connector; 30 mi W of Atlanta. B/f, n/s rms, pool, cont brfst, b/t pkng, elevator, cable TV, suites, mtg rm, cot. Free local calls. $35/S; $40-45/D; $5/ex prsn. Higher spec event rates. Discs.

Warner Robins

Super 8 Motel/ 105 Woodcrest Blvd, Warner Robins GA 31093. 912-923-8600. D,M,V,AE,DC,CB. I-75 (Exit 45) to Watson Blvd, E 6 mi to Woodcrest. B/f, n/s rms, outlets, copier, cable TV, suites, cot. Free local calls, crib. $35/S; $42-46/D; $5/ex prsn. Discs.

Waycross

Super 8 Motel/ 132 Havanna Av, Waycross GA 31501. 912-285-8885/ Fax: Ext 304. D,M,V,AE,DC,CB. US 1/ 23 at Havanna Av. B/f, n/s rms, t/b/rv pkng, cable TV, suites, cot. Free local calls, popcorn, crib. No pets. $30-32/S; $35-37/D; $6/ex prsn. Higher spec event rates. Discs.

Hawaii

Island of Hawaii

Naalehu

Becky's Bed & Breakfast/ Box 673, Naalehu HI 96772. 808-929-9690/ 800-235-1233. V,M. On Hwy 11. Nrby rstrnt, whrlpool, n/s rms, cable TV, tt phone, fax, refrig, microwave, cot, crib, outlets. Free local calls, full brfst, coffee, tea, cocoa. No pets, no smoking. $45/S; $60/D; $10/ex prsn. Higher rates if staying less than 4 days. Disc: L/s. *Guaranteed rates.*

Kealakekua

Reggie's Tropical Hideaway/ Box 1107, Kealakekua HI 96750. 808-322-8888/ 800-988-2246. No credit cards. Country Farm B & B providing ocean and mountain views. Exerc equip, cable TV, VCRs, playgrnd, tt phone, nwspr, refrig, microwave, cot, b/f. Free local calls, cont brfst. $45/S or D; $10/ex prsn. Disc: Senior, l/s, family. *Guaranteed rates.*

Shirakawa Motel/ Box 467, Naalehu HI 96772. 808-929-7462. On Hwy 11, Mamalahoa Hwy. Kitchens. No pets. $30/S; $35-42/D; $8-10/ex prsn.

Island of Oahu

Honolulu

Colony's Hawaii Polo Inn/ 1696 Ala Moana Blvd, Honolulu HI 96815. 808-949-0061/ Fax: 949-4906/ 800-669-7719. V,M,AE,D,DC,CB. At entrance to Waikiki, 8 mi from arpt. Nrby rstrnt/ lounge, pool, n/s rms, cable TV, VCR/ movies, tt/dd phones, mtg rm, fax, copier, laundry, refrig, elevator, microwave, cot, crib, outlets, eff, conn rms. Free coffee, tea, cocoa. No pets. $58/S or D; $10/ex prsn. 3/15-6/15, 9/1-11/30: $48/S or D. Disc: Senior, bsns, TA, govt, l/s, milt. *Guaranteed rates.*

Makaha

Makaha Surfside/ 85-175 Farrington Hwy, B310, Makaha HI 96792. 808-696-8282/ 808-524-3455. AE. H-1 Frwy W from arpt becomes Farrington Hwy. It past Waianae High School. Next door to high school. Pool, sauna, exerc equip, cable TV, arpt trans, tt phones, laundry, refrig, elevator, microwave, crib, outlets, eff, b/f, parking, barbecue. Free local calls. No pets. $50-60/S or D. 4/1-4/30, 11/1-11/30: $45-50/S or D. 5/1-10/31: $40-45/S or D. *Guaranteed rates.*

Idaho

Boise

Econo Lodge/ 2155 N Garden St, Boise ID 83706. 208-344-4030/ Fax: 342-1635/ 800-553-2666. V,M,AE,D,DC,CB. I-84 (Exit 49) to I-184, follow toward city ctr to Fairview, turn lt under freeway to mtl. Rstrnt, nrby lounge, n/s rms, cable TV, VCR/ movies, arpt trans, tt/dd phone, fax, elevator, cot, crib, outlets, b pkng, conn rms, b/f. Free local calls, cont brfst. AAA. $32/S; $40/D; $5/ex prsn. Apr-Sep: $36/S; $42/D. Discs. *Guaranteed rates.*

Motel 6/ 2323 Airport Way, Boise ID 83705. 208-344-3506/ Fax: 344-6264. M,V,DC,D,AE. I-84 (Exit 53) to Vista Av S, lt on Arpt Way to mtl. Cable TV, pool, nrby rstrnt, n/s rms. Free local calls. $35-37/S; $41-43/D; $6/ex prsn. Disc.

Sleep Inn/ 2799 Airport Way, Boise ID 83705. 208-336-7377. V,M,D,AE. I-84 (Exit 53) to Airport Way, S to mtl. Nrby rstrnt, fax, b/f, cable TV, t pkng, n/s rms. Free cont brfst. No pets. $43-53/S; $48-58/D; $4/ex prsn. Discs.

Super 8 Motel/ 2773 Elder St, Boise ID 83705. 208-344-8871/ Fax: 344-8871. V,M,DC,D,AE. I-84 (Exit 53) at Vista Av. B/f, n/s rms, pool, copier, elevator, satellite TV, cot. Free arpt trans, crib. $41/S; $47-51/D; $5/ex prsn. Higher spec event rates. Discs.

Burley

Greenwell Motel/ 904 E Main, Burley ID 83318. 208-678-5576. V,M,AE,D,DC,CB. I-84, Exit 208 or 211 into Burley. Nrby rstrnt/ lounge, n/s rms, cable TV, arpt trans, tt/dd phone, refrig, microwave, cot, crib, outlets, t/b pkng, eff, conn rms. Free coffee. AAA/ Mobil. $30-40/S; $40-48/D; $6/ex prsn. Disc: Bsns. *Guaranteed rates.*

Coeur d' Alene

Motel 6/ 416 Appleway, Coeur d' Alene ID 83814. 208-664-6600/ Fax: 667-9446. V,M,DC,D,AE. I-90 to (Exit 12) US 95, N to Appleway, lt. Nrby rstrnt, cable TV, pool, n/s rms. Free local calls. $26/S; $32/D; $6/ex prsn. 5/23-9/28: $38/S; $44/D. 9/29-12/20: $30/S; $36/D. Disc.

El Rancho Motel/ 1915 Sherman Av, Coeur d'Alene ID 83814. 208-664-8794/ Reservations: 800-359-9791. V,M,AE,D,DC. I-90 (Exit 15) to Sherman Av, W 4 blks. Nrby rstrnt/ lounge, n/s rms, cable TV, arpt trans, tt/dd phone, refrig, microwave, cot, crib, outlets, t/b/rv pkng, conn rms. Free local calls, coffee. AAA. Winter: $33-38/S; $38-42/D; $5/ex prsn. Summer: $47-50/S; $55-59/D. Disc: Senior, bsns, TA, govt, trkr, milt, AAA.

Also see Post Falls.

Driggs

Super 8 Motel/ 133 SR 33, Box 780, Driggs ID 83422. 208-354-8888/ Fax: 354-2962. V,M,D,AE,DC,CB. ON SR 33 bet Yellowstone and Jackson, WY. B/f, n/s rms, whrlpool, laundry, t/b/rv pkng, outlets, brfst, trans, suites. Free local calls. $39-47/S; $45-51/D; $4-6/ex prsn. Higher spec event rates. Discs.

Grangeville

Monty's Motel/ 700 W Main St, Grangeville ID 83530. 208-983-2500/ Fax: 983-1458. V,M,AE,D,DC,CB. At jct Hwy 95 & 13. Nrby rstrnt/ lounge, pool, n/s rms, cable TV, arpt trans, tt/dd phone, fax, nwspr, refrig, cot, crib, outlets, t/b

IDAHO 92

pkng. Free local calls, coffee. AAA. $33-38/S; $37-43/D; $5/ex prsn.

Idaho Falls

Motel 6/ 1448 W Broadway, Idaho Falls ID 83402. 208-522-0112/ Fax: 522-7804. V,M,DC,D,AE. I-15 (Exit 118) to Broadway, 1/2 blk W to mtl. Nrby rstrnt, cable TV, pool, n/s rms. Free local calls. $30-33/S; $36-39/D; $6/ex prsn. Disc.

Quality Inn/ 850 Lindsay Blvd, Idaho Falls ID 83402. 208-523-6260. V, M, D, AE. I-15: N (Exit 119) to Lindsay Blvd, turn rt; S: (Exit 119) It on US 20 to Lindsay Blvd. Rstrnt/ lounge, pool, mtg rm, fax, whrlpool, cable TV, t pkng, outlets, n/s rms. $44-76/S; $48-80/D; $5/ex prsn. 6/1-9/30: $48-82/S; $52-86/D. Discs.

Super 8 Motel/ 705 Lindsay Blvd, Idaho Falls ID 83402. 208-522-8880/ Fax: 522-0590. D,M,V,AE,DC,CB. I-15 (Exits 118 or 119) to Lindsay Blvd. B/f, n/s rms, whrlpool, sauna, t/b/rv pkng, outlets, toast bar, copier, cable TV, suites, cot. Free local calls, crib. No pets. Pride Award. $42/S; $45-47/D; $4/ex prsn. Discs.

Jerome (Twin Falls area)

Sleep Inn/ I-84 & US 93, Jerome ID 83338. 208-324-6400. V,M,D,AE. I-84 at US 93. Nrby rstrnt, fax, b/f, whrlpool, cable TV, t pkng, n/s rms. Free cont brfst. $38-60/S; $40-65/D; $5/ex prsn. Discs.

Kamiah

Lewis Clark Resort & Motel/ Rte 1, Box 17X, Kamiah ID 83536. 208-935-2556/ Fax: 935-0366. V,M,D. 1 1/2 mi E of Kamiah on Hwy 12. Rstrnt, pool, whrlpool, n/s rms, satellite TV, VCR/ movies, playgrnd, tt/dd phone,fax, nwspr, laundry, refrig, cot, crib, outlets, t/b/rv pkng, b/f. Free local calls, full brfst, coffee. No pets. AAA. $31-35/S; $40-41/D; $6/ex prsn. 5/1-9/30: $35-39/S; $40-44/D. Disc: Senior, govt, l/s.

Lewiston

Super 8 Motel/ 3120 N South Hwy, Lewiston ID 83501. 208-743-8808. D, M,V,AE,DC,CB. Off Hwy 95 S, Missoula/Boise exit, on Hwys 12 & 95. B/f, n/s rms, laundry, outlets, t/b/rv pkng, copier, cable TV, family rms, cot. Free local calls, crib. $37-41/S; $43-52/D; $5/ex prsn. Higher spec event rates. Discs.

Montpelier

Park Motel/ 745 Washington Blvd, Montpelier ID 83252. 208-847-1911. V,M,AE,D. Cable TV. AAA. $25/S; $29/D; $4/ex prsn. 6/1-10/31: $40/S; $44/D. Guaranteed rates.

Moscow

Super 8 Motel/ 175 Peterson Dr, Moscow ID 83843. 208-883-1503/ Fax: 883-4769. D,M,V,AE,DC,CB. 1/2 blk N of Pullman Hwy & Peterson Dr. B/f, n/s rms, sauna, outlets, t/b/rv pkng, copier, cable TV, suits, mtg rm, family rm, exerc equip, cot. Free local calls, crib. No pets. $37/S; $41-45/D; $5/ex prsn. Higher spec event rates. Discs.

Mountain Home

Hilander Motel & Steak House/ 615 S 3rd W, Mountain Home ID 83647. 208-587-3311. V,M,AE,D,DC,CB. Hwy 84 (Wbnd, Exit 99; Ebnd, Exit 90) to jct with Air Base Rd. Rstrnt/ lounge, pool, n/s rms, cable TV, tt/dd phone, cot, crib, eff. Free coffee, tea, cocoa. AAA/ Mobil. $34/S; $39/D; $4/ex prsn. Disc: Senior, family. Guaranteed rates.

Sleep Inn/ 1180 US 20, Mountain Home ID 83647. 208-587-9743. V,M,AE,DC. I-84 (Exit 95) to US 20, E to mtl. Rstrnt, mtg rm, fax, b/f, cable TV, t pkng, VCR, n/s rms. Free cont brfst, local calls, nwspr. $41-46/S; $44-54/D; $5/ex person. 5/1-8/31: $45-55/S; $49-59/D. Discs.

Nampa

Super 8 Motel/ 624 Nampa Blvd, Nampa ID 83687. 208-467-2888. D, M,V,AE,DC,CB. I-84 (Exit 35) at Nampa Blvd. B/f, n/s rms, nrby t stop, laundry, t/b/rv pkng, copier, cable TV, suites, cot. Free local calls, crib. Pride Award. $37/S; $43-45/D; $4/ex prsn. Discs.

New Meadows

Hartland Inn & Motel/ 211 Norris, Box 215, New Meadows ID 83654. 208-347-2114. V,M,AE,D. On Hwy 95 at jct with Hwy 55. Nrby rstrnt, n/s rms, cable TV, fax, copier, cot. Free local calls, coffee, tea. AAA. $35-41/S; $38-45/D.

Orofino

Konkolville Motel/ 2000 Konkolville Rd, Orofino ID 83544. 208-475-5584. V,M,AE,D,DC. Hwy 12, cross bridge into Orofino, follow road to 4 way stop, go straight for 2 1/2 mi into Konkolville. Pool, whrlpool, cable TV, tt/dd phone, mtg rm, laundry, refrig, cot, crib, outlets, t/b pkng, conn rms, b/f. Free local calls, coffee, tea, cocoa. AAA. $30-34/S; $36-40/D; $2/ex prsn. Disc: Senior, bsns, l/s, family, off-season. *Guaranteed rates.*

Pocatello

Motel 6/ 291 W Burnside Av, Pocatello ID 83202. 208-237-7880/ Fax: 237-3115. V,M,DC,D,AE. I-86 (Exit 61) at Chubbuck, N on Yellowstone, lt on W Burnside Av. Nrby rstrnt, cable TV, laundry, pool, n/s rms. Free local calls. $26-27/S; $32-33/D; $6/ex prsn. Disc.

Pocatello Super 8/ 1330 Bench Road, Pocatello ID 83201. 208-234-0888/ Fax: 232-0347. D,M,V,AE,DC,CB. I-15, Exit 71, 1 blk E. B/f, n/s rms, nrby rstrnt/ lounge, toast bar, t/b/rv pkng, copier, cable TV, cot. Free local calls, crib. AAA. $39-43/S; $43-46/D; $2-3/ex prsn. Discs.

Post Falls   (Coeur d'Alene area)

Sleep Inn/ 100 Pleasant View Rd, Post Falls ID 83854. 800-221-2222 — opening soon. V,M,D,AE. I-90 to Pleasant View Rd, S 1/8 mi. Pool, mtg rm, b/f, whrlpool, cable TV, n/s rms. Free cont brfst. No pets. $35-99/S; $39-99/D; $5/ex prsn. Discs.

Rexburg

Comfort Inn/ 1513 W Main St, Rexburg ID 83440. 208-359-1311. V,M,D,AE. Jct US 20 & SR 33. Nrby rstrnt, indr pool, mtg rm, fax, whrlpool, cable TV, t pkng, outlets, exerc equip. Free cont brfst. $32-56/S; $42-66/D. 5/1-5/25: $30-54/S; $40-65/D. 5/26-9/15: $50-84/S; $60-84/D. 9/16-12/31: $34-58/S; $44-68/D. Discs.

Rexburg Super 8 Motel/ 215 W Main St, Rexburg ID 83440. 208-356-8888/ Fax: 356-8896. V,M,DC,AE,CB,D. US 20 to Rexburg/ Salmon Exit, 10 blks E. B/f, n/s rms, t/b/rv pkng, copier, cot. Free local calls, crib. No pets. Pride Award. $33-39/S; $41-48/D; $3/ex prsn. Discs.

Sandpoint

Quality Inn/ 807 N 5th Av, Box 187, Sandpoint ID 83864. 208-263-2111. V,M,AE,DC. N edge of Sandpoint on US 95, US 2, & SR 200. Rstrnt/ lounge, indr pool, mtg rm, fax, whrlpool, cable TV, outlets, n/s rms. AAA. $42-58/S; $46-68/D; $6/ex prsn. 5/1-6/30: $42-58/S; $52-76/D. 7/1-9/9: $52-78/S; $56-92/D. Discs.

Super 8 Motel/ 3245 Hwy 95 N, Sandpoint ID 83864. 208-263-2210. D,M,V,AE,DC,CB. Hwy 95, N of Sandpoint, near Bonner Mall. B/f, n/s rms, whrlpool, b/rv pkng, outlets, cable TV, family rm, cot. Free crib. AAA. $34-49/S; $40-59/D; $5/ex prsn. Higher spec event rates. Discs.

Twin Falls

Econo Lodge/ 320 Main Av S, Twin Falls ID 83301. 208-733-8770. V,M, AE,D. US 93 (Blue Lakes Blvd) S of Addison Av to 3rd St, SW on 3rd to mtl. Nrby rstrnt, pool, fax, cable TV, coffee, n/s rms. $38-45/S; $44-50/D; $4/ex prsn. 5/1-9/30: $40-47/S; $46-52/D. Discs.

Motel 6/ 1472 Blue Lake Blvd N, Twin Falls ID 83301. 208-734-3993/ Fax: 736-7368. V,M,DC,D,AE. I-84 (Exit 173) to US 93 (Blue Lake Blvd), S 3 mi to mtl. Nrby rstrnt, cable TV, laundry, pool, n/s rms. Free local calls. $30-34/S; $34-40/D; $4-6/ex prsn. Disc.

Super 8 Motel/ 1260 Blue Lakes Blvd N, Twin Falls ID 83301. 208-734-5801/ Fax: 734-7556. D,M,V,AE,DC,CB. I-84 (Exit 173) at US 93. B/f, n/s rms, nrby rstrnt, laundry, t/b/rv pkng, outlets, cable TV. Free local calls, crib. No pets. Pride Award. $45/S; $49-51/D; $5/ex prsn. Discs.

Also see Jerome.

Wallace

Stardust Motel/ 410 Pine St, Wallace ID 83873. 208-752-1213/ Fax: 753-0981/

800-643-2386. V,M,AE,D,DC. I-90 (Exit 61 or 62) to dntn Wallace, see large sign. Nrby rstrnt/ lounge, indr pool, sauna, whrlpool, n/s rms, exerc equip, cable TV, arpt trans, tt/dd phone, mtg rm, fax, copier, nwspr, cot, crib, t/b/rv pkng. Free local calls, coffee, tea, cocoa. AAA/ Mobil. $42/S; $48/D; $8/ex prsn. Disc: Senior, family, TA. No discounts 12/24-1/2 and President's week. *Guaranteed rates.*

Illinois

Alton

Super 8 Motel/ 1800 Homer Adams Pkwy, Alton IL 62002. 618-465-8885/ Fax: 465-8964. D,M,V,AE,DC,CB. Just E of Hwy 267 on Adams Pkwy. B/f, n/s rms, b/rv pkng, copier, cable TV, cot. Free crib, local calls. Pride Award. $40/S; $46-48/D; $5/ex prsn. Higher spec event rates. Discs.

Arcola

Arcola Inn Budget Host/ 236 S Jacques St, Arcola IL 61910. 217-268-4971/ Fax: 268-3525. AE,CB,DC,D,M,V. I-57 (Exit 203) at SR 133, W 1 blk. Nrby rstrnt, cable TV, tt phone, fax, cot, crib, outlets, t/b/rv pkng, conn rms. Free local calls, coffee, tea, cocoa. AAA. $29-37/S; $32-41/D; $5/ex prsn. Parents wknd, Broom Corn Festival wknd: $54/S or D. Disc: Senior, l/s. *Guaranteed rates.*

Arlington Heights (Chicago area)

Motel 6/ 441 W Algonquin Rd, Arlington Heights IL 60005. 708-806-1230/ Fax: 364-7413. M,V,DC,D,AE. I-90 at Arlington Hts, turn N on Arlington, then W on Algonquin. Cable TV, laundry, nrby rstrnt, n/s rms. Free local calls. $34/S; $40/D; $6/ex prsn. Disc.

Aurora

Motel 6/ 2380 N Farnsworth Av, Aurora IL 60504. 708-851-3600/ Fax: 978-1564. AE,DC,D,M,V. I-88/ East West Thruway, exit Farnsworth Av N to mtl. Cable TV, indr pool, nrby rstrnt, n/s rms, t pkng. Free local calls. $34/S; $40/D; $6/ex prsn. Disc.

Bloomington

Best Inns of America/ 1905 W Market, Bloomington IL 61701. 309-827-5333. V,M,AE,D,DC,CB. I-55/I-74, Exit 160A. Nrby rstrnt/ lounge, pool, n/s rms, cable TV, TDD, tt/dd phone, fax, nwspr, crib, t/b/rv pkng, conn rms. Free local calls, cont brfst, coffee, tea, cocoa. AAA/ Mobil. $37/S; $43-47/D; $6/ex prsn. Disc: Senior, family. *Guaranteed rates.*

HoJo Inn/ 401 Brock Dr, Bloomington IL 61701. 309-829-3100/ Fax: 827-4716. V,M,D,AE,DC,CB. SW side of Bloomington at the jct of SR 9 & I-55, Exit 160A. N/s rms, b/f, nrby lounge, t/b pkng, rm serv, cable TV, fax. Free local calls. $25-40/S; $29-48/D. Discs.

Super 8 Motel/ 818 IAA Dr, Bloomington IL 61701. 309-663-2388. D,M,V,AE,DC,CB. Bsns Hwy 55 to Veterans Pkwy, W on Vernon Av to IAA Dr. B/f, n/s rms, copier, cable TV, cot. Free local calls. $38/S; $46-50/D; $5/ex prsn. Higher spec event rates. Discs.

Bourbonais (Kankakee area)

Motel 6/ Rte 50 & Armour Rd, Bourbonnais IL 60914. 815-933-2300/ Fax: 933-7485. AE,DC,D,M,V. I-57 (Exit 315) to Bradley Rte 50, W 1/4 mi to Armour Rd, rt to mtl. Nrby rstrnt, cable TV, pool, n/s rms. Free local calls. $28-30/S; $34-36/D; $6/ex prsn. Disc.

Super 8 Motel/ 1390 Lock Dr, Bourbonnis IL 60914. 815-939-7888/ Fax: Ext 152. AE,DC,M,V,CB,D. I-57 (Exit 315) to Hwy 50, S 1 blk to Armour Rd, lt to Lock Dr. B/f, n/s rms, indr pool, whrlpool, laundry, outlets, b/t pkng, cable TV, suites, cot, crib. Free local calls. No pets. $45/S; $49-51/D; $6/ex prsn. Higher spec event rates. Discs.

ILLINOIS

Canton
Super 8 Motel/ 2110 Main St, Canton IL 61520. 309-647-1888. V,M,AE,D,DC, CB. On Hwy 78 N. B/f, n/s rms, t/b/rv pkng, outlets, cont brfst, cable TV, cot, crib. Free local calls. No pets. $39/S; $43-47/D; $4/ex prsn. Discs.

Carbondale
Best Inns/ 1345 E Main St, Carbondale IL 62901. 618-529-4801/ Fax: 529-7212. AE,DC,CB,M,V,D. I-57, Exit 54B/ SR 13 to Carbondale at Univ Mall/ Frontage Rd. Fax, dd/tt phone, pool, mtg rm, b/f. Free cont brfst, coffee, crib, local calls. AAA. $38-41/S; $45-48/D; $6/ex prsn. Higher spec event rates. Disc: Senior, family.

Days Inn/ 801 E Main St, Carbondale IL 62901. 618-457-3347/ Fax: 549-2897. V,M,AE,DC,D. On Hwy 13 E (Main St). W of I-57. Nrby rstrnt, whrlpool, t pkng, cot. Free cont brfst. $38-50/S; $42-50/D; $4/ex prsn. Discs.

Super 8 Motel/ 1180 E Main St, Carbondale IL 62901. 618-457-8822/ Fax: 457-4186. D,M,V,AE,DC,CB. Rt 13 & E Main St, E entrance to Carbondale. B/f, n/s rms, t/b/rv pkng, outlets, toast bar, copier, cable TV, cot. Free local calls, crib. Pride Award. $38/S; $44-46/D; $5/ex prsn. Discs.

Also see Murphysboro.

Carlinville
Carlin-Villa Motel/ RR 3, Box 7, Carlinville IL 62626. 217-854-3201/ Fax: 854-8414. V,M,AE,D,DC,CB. SR 4, 3/8 mi S of Hwy 108. Indr pool, nrby rstrnt, cable TV, dd phone, outlets, whrlpool, sauna, tanning bed, mtg rm, cot. Free cont brfst, crib. AAA/ IMA. $31-43/S; $36-50/D. Disc: Family, senior, TA, comm.

Caseyville
Best Inns/ 2423 Old Country Inn Dr, Caseyville IL 62232. 618-397-3300. AE,DC,CB,M,V,D. I-64, Exit 9 (IL 157). Pool, fax, t pkng, adj rstrnt, dd/tt phone, b/f. Free cont brfst, coffee, crib, local calls. AAA. $40-43/S; $47-53/D; $6/ex prsn. 5/9-10/12: $46-49/S; $53-59/D. Higher spec event rates. Disc: Senior, family.

Days Inn/ 8950 Tucker Dr, Caseyville IL 62232. 618-397-4200/ Fax: 397-4900. M,DC,D,V,AE,CB. I-64 to US 157, S to Tucker Dr. Fax, n/s rms, nrby rstrnt, whrlpool, b/f, cot. Free cont brfst. $40-59/S; $46-60/D; $5/ex prsn. Discs.

Champaign
Howard Johnson Lodge/ 1505 N Neil St, Champaign IL 61820. 217-359-1601/ Fax: 359-2062. M,DC,D,V,AE, CB. I-74, Neil St exit. N/s rms, mtg rm, b/f, rstrnt/ lounge, indr pool, t pkng, whrlpool, game rm, laundry. $40-64/S; $45-69/D. Discs.

Super 8 Motel/ 202 Marketview Dr, Champaign IL 61820. 217-359-2388. D, M,V,AE,DC,CB. I-74 (Exit 182 B) at Neil St N. B/f, n/s rms, b/t/rv pkng, outlets, copier, cable TV, cot. Free local calls, crib. $37/S; $43-47/D; $5/ex prsn. Higher spec event rates. Discs.

Also see Urb

Chicago
See Arlington Heights, E Hazelcrest, Elk Grove Village, Glenview, Libertyville, Palatine, Rolling Meadows, St Charles, Schiller Park, Villa Park, Waukegan, Woodstock, Hammond IN.

Clinton
Days Inn/ US 51 Bypass, Clinton IL 61727. 217-935-4140. M,DC,D,V, AE,CB. US 51 Bypass, just S of SR 54. Fax, n/s rms, nrby rstrnt, mtg rm, b/f, exerc equip, t pkng, cable TV, laundry, microwave, refrig, picnic area, playgrnd, cot. Free cont brfst. Chairman's Award. $36-44/S; $40-48/D; $5/ex prsn. Discs.

Collinsville (St Louis MO area)
Motel 6/ 295-A N Bluff Rd, Collinsville IL 62234. 618-345-2100/ Fax: 345-9160. V,M,D,AE,DC,CB. I-55/I-70 to (Exit 11) Hwy 157/N Bluff Rd, go S 2 blks. Nrby rstrnt, cable TV, pool, n/s rms, t pkng. Free local calls. $35/S; $41/D; $6/ex prsn. Disc.

Super 8 Motel/ 2 Gateway Dr, Collinsville IL 62234. 618-345-8008/ Fax: 344-7062. D,M,V,AE,DC,CB. I-55/70 (Exit 11) at SR 157, N to Eastport

ILLINOIS

Plaza Dr, W to Gateway Dr, turn N. B/f, n/s rms, b/rv pkng, toast bar, copier, cable TV, cot. Free local calls, crib. $38/S; $44-46/D; $5/ex prsn. Higher spec event rates. Discs.

Danville
Super 8 Motel/ 377 Lynch Dr, Danville IL 61832. 217-443-4499. D,M,V,AE,DC, CB. I-74 (Exit 220) to Lynch Rd, 1/4 mi N. B/f, n/s rms, b/t pkng, outlets, mtg rm, cont brfst, satellite TV, cot. $39/S; $45-47/D; $5/ex prsn. Higher spec event rates. Discs.

DeKalb
HoJo Inn/ 1321 W Lincoln Hwy, DeKalb IL 60115. 815-756-1451. AE,M,V,D,DC, CB,JCB. I-88 W to Annie Glidden Rd, N 1 mi to Lincoln Hwy, lt 1/4 mi. N/s rms, cable TV. Free local calls, cont brfst. No pets. $39-50/S; $45-56/D. Higher spec event rates. Discs.

Motel 6/ 1116 W Lincoln Hwy, DeKalb IL 60115. 815-756-3398/ Fax: 756-1687. V,M,DC,D,AE. From E-W Tollway (I-88) exit at Annie Glidden Rd, N to SR 38, turn lt. Nrby rstrnt, cable TV, pool, n/s rms. Free local calls. $26/S; $32/D; $6/ex prsn. Disc.

Decatur
Super 8 Motel/ 3141 N Water St, Decatur IL 62526. 217-877-8888. D, M, V,AE,DC,CB. I-72 (Exit 38A) to Hwy 51, S 1 3/4 mi. B/f, n/s rms, laundry, b/rv pkng, outlets, cable TV, cot. Free local calls, crib. $39/S; $46-50/D; $5/ex prsn. Higher spec event rates. Discs.

Dixon
Super 8 Motel/ 1800 S Galena Av, Dixon IL 61021. 815-284-1800/ Fax: Ext 106. AE,M,V,D,DC,CB. Jct of I-88 & SR 26. B/f, n/s rms, whrlpool, sauna, game rm, b/t pkng, outlets, cot, crib, suites. Free local calls. $41/S; $46-50/D; $6/ex prsn. Higher spec event rates. Discs.

Dwight
Super 8 Motel/ 14 E Northbrook Dr, Dwight IL 60420. 815-584-1888. V, M, D,AE,DC,CB. I-55 (Exit 220) at Hwy 47, S to mtl. N/s rms, t/b/rv pkng, outlets, toast bar, copier, satellite TV. Free local calls. Pride Award. $38/S; $44-47/D; $4/ex prsn. Discs.

East Hazelcrest (Chicago area)
Motel 6/ 17214 Halsted St, E Hazelcrest IL 60429. 708-957-9233/ Fax: 922-0610. V,M,DC,D,AE. I-80/294 to Halsted St S (SR 1), S on Halsted to mtl. Nrby rstrnt, cable TV, laundry, pool, n/s rms. t pkng. Free local calls. $34-36/S; $40-42/D; $6/ex prsn. Disc.

East Moline (Moline area)
Super 8 Motel/ 2201 John Deere Expwy, RR 2, E Moline, IL 61244. 309-796-1999. D,M,V,AE,DC,CB. I-80 (Exit 4A) to 5, W to jct of Hwy 5 & Colona Rd. B/f, n/s rms, nrby rstrnt, whrlpool, outlets, copier, cable TV, mtg rm, cot. Free local calls, crib. $38-40/S; $45-52/D; $5/ex prsn. Higher spec event rates. Discs.

East Peoria
Budget Host Country Inn/ 300 N Main St, E Peoria IL 61611. 309-694-4261/ Fax: 694-0309. V,AE,CB,DC,D,M. I-74, Exit 95A (N Main St), 1/2 blk S. Nrby rstrnt/ lounge, pool, n/s rms, cable TV, tt/dd phone, fax, copier, cot, crib, outlets, t/b/rv pkng, b/f. Free coffee, tea, cocoa. AAA. $32-39/S; $37-44/D; $5/ex prsn. Disc: Senior, bsns, TA, govt, family, trkr, milt. *Guaranteed rates.*

Motel 6/ 104 W Camp St, E Peoria IL 61611. 309-699-7281/ Fax: 694-7636. V,M,DC,D,AE. I-74 (Exit 95A) to SR 116 (N Main St), SW to Camp St, turn rt. Cable TV, pool, n/s rms. Free local calls. $30-32/S; $36-38/D; $6/ex prsn. Disc.

Super 8 Motel/ 725 Taylor St, E Peoria IL 61611. 309-698-8889/ Fax: 698-8885. AE,DC,M,V,CB,D. I-74 (Exit 96) at Washington St (Taylor). B/f, n/s rms, toast bar, b pkng, outlets, copier, elevator, cable TV, suites, mtg rm. Free local calls. Pride Award. $40/S; $46-48/D; $6/ex prsn. Higher spec event rates. Discs.

Effingham
Best Inns/ 1209 N Keller Dr, Effingham IL 62401. 217-347-5141. AE,DC,CB, M, V,D. I-57/70 (Exit 160) to Keller Dr (SR 32/33) turn lt. Pool, fax, nrby rstrnt, dd/tt phone, b/f, t pkng. Free cont brfst,

coffee, crib, local calls. AAA. $33-36/S; $40-43/D; $6/ex prsn. 5/10-10/31: $37-40/S; $44-47/D. Disc: Senior, family.

Budget Host Lincoln Lodge/ Rte 45 N, Box 634, Effingham IL 62401. 217-342-4133. AE,CB,DC,D,M,V. I-57/ I-70, Exit 162. Cable TV, dd phone, n/s rms, b/f, nrby rstrnt, t/rv pkng, cot. Free crib. AAA/ Mobil. $27/S; $32-34/D. Spec Events: $34. Discs.

Econo Lodge/ 1205 N Keller Dr, Effingham IL 62401. 217-347-7131. V, M, AE,DC. I-70/ I-57 N (Exit 160) to SR 32, N 1/4 mi. Nrby rstrnt, indr pool, mtg rm, fax, sauna, whrlpool, cable TV, t pkng, outlets, exerc area, n/s rms. Free cont brfst. AAA. $36-42/S; $42-54/D; $4/ex prsn. Discs.

Howard Johnson Lodge/ 1606 W Fayette Av, Effingham IL 62401. 217-342-4667 Fax: 342-4645. AE,M,V,D, DC,CB,JCB. I-70 or I-57 (Exit 159) at Fayette Av, rt off ramp. N/s rms, b/f, t pkng, VCR/ movies. Free cont brfst. $36-41/S; $41-46/D. Discs.

Super 8 Motel/ 1400 Thelma Keller Av, Effingham IL 62401. 217-342-6888/ Fax: 347-2863. D,M,V,AE,DC,CB. I-57/ I-70 (Exit 160) to Thelma Keller Av. B/f, n/s rms, b/t/rv pkng, outlets, cable TV, cot. Free local calls, crib. Pride Award. $37/S; $43-44/D; $4/ex prsn. Higher spec event rates. Discs.

El Paso

Days Inn/ 630 W Main St, El Paso IL 61738. 309-527-7070. M,DC,D,V,AE, CB. I-39 (Exit 14) to US 24, E to mtl. Fax, n/s rms, nrby rstrnt, indr pool, whrlpool, mtg rm, b/f, t/b pkng, laundry, cable TV, cot. Free cont brfst. $40-58/S; $45-68/D; $5/ex prsn. Discs.

Super 8 Motel/ 880 W Main, El Paso IL 61738. 309-527-4949. AE,M,V,D,DC, CB. I-39 (Exit 14) at US 24 W. B/f, n/s rms, laundry, t/b/rv pkng, outlets, cont brfst, copier, satellite TV, cot, crib. Free local calls. $38/S; $44-48/D; $4/ex prsn. Discs.

Elk Grove Village (Chicago area)

Days Inn O'Hare West/ 1920 E Higgins Rd, Elk Grove Village IL 60007. 708-437-1650/ Fax: 708-437-1679/ 800-329-7466. V,M,AE,D,DC. I-90 E to Elmhurst Rd, S to Higgins, rt 1 mi. Nrby rstrnt/ lounge, n/s rms, cable TV, tt phone, mtg rm, fax, cot, crib, outlets, t/b/rv pkng, conn rms, b/f. Free cont brfst. AAA. $48/S or D; $6/ex prsn. Disc: Senior, govt, l/s, milt. *Guaranteed rates.*

Motel 6/ 1601 Oakton St, Elk Grove Village IL 60007. 708-981-9766/ Fax: 364-6428. AE,M,V,DC,D. I-90: Wbnd, take SR 83/ Elmhurst Rd N, turn lt at 1st signal light onto Oakton St; Ebnd, to I-290, S to Higgins Rd E exit, E to corner Higgins Rd/ Oakton. Cable TV, n/s rms. Free local calls. $32/S; $38/D; $6/ex prsn. Disc.

Fairview Heights

Super 8 Motel/ 45 Ludwig Dr, Fairview Heights IL 62208. 618-398-8338/ Fax: 398-8158. D,M,V,AE,DC,CB. I-64 to SR 159, N to Ludwig. B/f, n/s rms, b/rv pkng, outlets, cont brfst bar, copier, elevator, cable TV, mtg rm, cot. Free local calls, crib. Pride Award. $40/S; $46-48/D; $5/ex prsn. Higher spec event rates. Discs.

Freeport

Super 8 Motel/ 1649 Willard Dr, Freeport IL 61032. 815-232-8800/ Fax: 232-8907. V,M,DC,AE,CB,D. SR 26 & South St. B/f, n/s rms, cont brfst, cable TV, cot, crib. Free local calls. No pets. $40/S; $46-50/D; $6/ex prsn. Discs.

Galesburg

Motel 6/ 1475 N Henderson St, Galesburg IL 61401. 309-344-2401/ Fax: 344-1960. AE,DC,D,M,V. I-74 (Exit 46A) to US 34, W 2 mi to US 150, S 1 mi to mtl. Cable TV, indr pool, n/s rms, t pkng. Free local calls. $26-28/S; $32-34/D; $6/ex prsn. Disc.

Super 8 Motel/ 260 W Main St, Galesburg IL 61401. 309-342-5174/ Fax: 343-8237. AE,M,V,D,DC,CB. I-74 (Exit 48) to Galesburg. 2 mi to mtl at jct of Main St & Academy. N/s rms, cable TV, in-rm coffee, cot. Free local calls, crib. $26-27/S; $32-44/D; $5/ex prsn. Higher spec event rates. Discs.

Genesco

Oakwood Motel/ 225 US Hwy 6 E,

ILLINOIS

Genesco IL 61254. 309-944-3696. V,M,AE,D. I-80 (Exit 19) to Hwy 82 N 1/2 mi. Rstrnt, n/s rms, cable TV, tt/dd phones, refrig, crib, t pkng, conn rms. Free local calls. AAA/ Mobil. $26/S; $34/D; $4/ex prsn. Spec events: $28/S; $37/D. Disc: Senior, bsns, TA, govt, l/s, family, trkr, milt. *Guaranteed rates.*

Gilman

Budget Host Farr's Motel/ 723 S Crescent St, Gilman IL 60938. 815-265-7261/ Fax: 265-7262. M,V,D,AE,ER. I-57 (Exit 283) to US 24/ 45, E 1/2 mi. Cable TV, dd phone, n/s rms, nrby rstrnt, t/rv pkng, outlets, cot, crib. $27-39/S; $34-55/D; $4/ex prsn. Discs.

Super 8 Motel/ 1301 S Crescent St, RR 1, Box 202-B-2, Gilman IL 60938. 815-265-7000/ Fax: Ext 329. V,M,DC, AE,CB,D. I-57, Exit 283, E 2 blks. B/f, n/s rms, nrby rstrnt, laundry, t/b/rv pkng, outlets, cont brfst, cot, crib. AAA. $42/S; $46-52/D; $4/ex prsn. Higher spec event rates. Discs.

Glenview (Chicago area)

Motel 6/ 1535 Milwaukee Av, Glenview IL 60025. 708-390-7200/ Fax: 390-0845. M,V,DC,D,AE. I-294 to Willow Rd, lt to Sanders, lt to Milwaukee, lt to mtl. Nrby rstrnt, cable TV, laundry, n/s rms. Free local calls. $32/S; $38/D; $6/ex prsn. Disc.

Greenville

Budget Host Inn/ Rte 4, Box 183, Greenville IL 62246. 618-664-1950/ Fax: 664-1960. AE,D,M,V. I-70 (Exit 45) at SR 127, N 1 1/2 blks. Cable TV, dd phone, in-rm coffee, kitchens, n/s rms, mtg rm, cont brfst, nrby rstrnt, pool, playgrnd, laundry, arpt trans, t pkng, outlets, cot. Free crib. AAA/ Mobil. Inn of the Year Award. $28-30/S; $30-37/D; $3/ex prsn. 5/1-9/30: $32-35/S; $35-45/D. Spec Events: $55-65. Discs.

Jacksonville

Motel 6/ 1716 W Morton Dr, Jacksonville IL 62650. 217-243-7157/ Fax: 243-1845. V,M,DC,D,AE. US 67 & SR 104. Nrby rstrnt, cable TV, pool, n/s rms. Free local calls. $26-27/S; $32-33/D; $6/ex prsn. Disc.

Super 8 Motel/ 1003 W Morton Rd, Jacksonville IL 62650. 217-479-0303. D,M,V,AE,DC,CB. US 67 N, lt on Morton. B/f, n/s rms, outlets, cable TV, cot, crib. Free local calls. $40/S; $47-49/D; $3/ex prsn. Higher spec event rates. Discs.

Joliet

Motel 6/ 1850 McDonough Rd, Joliet IL 60436. 815-729-2800/ Fax: 729-9528. V,M,DC,D,AE. I-80 (Exit 130B) to Larkin Av, N to 1st traffic light, lt on McDonough Rd. Cable TV, n/s rms. Free local calls. $32/S; $38/D; $6/ex prsn. D

Kankakee

See Bourbonais.

Kewanee

Super 8 Motel/ 901 S Tenney St, Kewanee IL 61443. 309-853-8800. V, M,D,AE,DC,CB. 1 mi S of jct Hwys 34 & 78. B/f, n/s rms, sauna, b/t pkng, outlets, cont brfst, copier, cable TV, mtg rm, cot, crib. Free local calls. No pets. Pride Award. $39/S; $43-47/D; $4/ex prsn. Higher spec event rates. Discs.

Lasalle

Howard Johnson Lodge/ Hwys 251 & I-80, Lasalle IL 61301. 815-224-2500/ Fax: 224-3693. M,DC,D,V,AE,CB. I-80 (Exit 75) to SR 251, N 1 blk to May Rd, W 1 blk. N/s rms, mtg rm, b/f, rstrnt, pool, rental car, t pkng, game rm, valet, cable TV. $35-48/S; $49-59/D. Discs.

Also see Peru.

Le Roy

Super 8 Motel/ 1 Demma Dr, Le Roy IL 61752. 309-962-4700/ Fax: Ext 102. AE,M,V,D,DC,CB. I-74, Exit 149. B/f, n/s rms, pool,laundry, outlets, t/b/rv pkng, cont brfst, cable TV, suites, cot, crib. Free local calls. Pride Award. $39/S; $46-50/D; $3/ex prsn. Discs.

Libertyville (Chicago area)

Best Inns/ 1809 N Milwaukee Av, Libertyville IL 60048. 708-816-8006. AE, DC,CB,M,V,D. I-94: Ebnd to SR 21, SW 3 mi to SR 137 (Buckley Rd); Wbnd to SR 137, W 3 mi. Pool, mtg rm, fax, nrby rstrnt, dd/tt phone, b/f, t pkng. Free cont brfst, coffee, crib, local calls.

AAA. $40-43/S; $47-50/D; $6/ex prsn. 6/13-8/24: $50-53/S; $57-63/D. Disc: Senior, family.

Lincoln

Super 8 Motel/ 2800 Woodlawn Rd, Lincoln IL 62656. 217-732-8886. V,M, AE,D,DC,CB. I-55, Exit 126. B/f, n/s rms, pool, t/b/rv pkng, outlets, cont brfst, cable TV. Free local calls. Pride Award. $39/S; $43-45/D; $4/ex prsn. Higher spec event rates. Discs.

Litchfield

Super 8 Motel/ Box 281, Litchfield IL 62056. 217-324-7788. D,M,V,AE,DC, CB. I-55 (Exit 52) at SR 16 W. B/f, n/s rms, t pkng, cable TV, suites, cot. Free coffee, crib. $40/S; $46-50/D; $5/ex prsn. Higher spec event rates. Discs.

Lyons

Budget Host Chalet Motel/ 8640 W Ogden Av, Lyons IL 60534. 708-447-6363/ Fax: 447-8557. AE,DC,M,V,CB, D. 1 mi W of city ctr & 2 mi N of I-55. Cable TV, dd phone, kitchens, family rms, indr pool, n/s rms, adj rstrnt. Free crib. No pets. $40/S; $40-53/D. Discs.

Macomb

Super 8 Motel/ 313 University Av, Macomb IL 61455. 309-836-8888/ Fax: 833-2646. AE,M,V,D,DC,CB. US 67 N to University Av, turn W. B/f, n/s rms, t/b/rv pkng, outlets, cont brfst, cable TV, cot, crib. Free local calls. $40/S; $47-49/D; $3/ex prsn. Higher spec event rates. Discs.

Marion

Best Inns/ Box 70, Marion IL 62959. 618-997-9421. AE,DC,CB,M,V,D. I-57 (Exit 54B) to SR 13, W 1/4 mi on rt, next to Wolohan. Pool, fax, nrby rstrnt, dd/tt phone, b/f, t pkng. Free cont brfst, coffee, crib, local calls. AAA. $37-40/S; $44-47/D; $6/ex prsn. Higher spec event rates. Disc: Senior, family.

Comfort Inn/ 2600 W Main St, Box 70, Marion IL 62959. 618-993-6221. V,M,AE,DC. I-57 (Exit 53) to Main St, W to mtl. Nrby rstrnt, pool, mtg rm, fax, b/f, cable TV, t pkng, exerc equip, n/s rms. Free cont brfst. No pets. Hospitality award. AAA. $40-51/S; $45-56/D; $5/ex prsn. Discs.

Motel 6/ 1008 Halfway Rd, Marion IL 62959. 618-993-2631/ Fax: 993-2719. AE,DC,D,M,V. I-57 (Exit 54B) to Rte 13, W to 1st traffic light, lt on Halfway Rd. Nrby rstrnt, cable TV, pool, n/s rms, t pkng. Free local calls. $26-28/S; $32-34/D; $6/ex prsn. Disc.

Super 8 Motel/ 2601 W DeYoung, Marion IL 62959. 618-993-5577/ Fax: 997-6779. D,M,V,AE,DC,CB. I-57 (Exit 54B) to SR 13, W to mtl. B/f, n/s rms, b/rv pkng, outlets, copier, cable TV, suites, cot. Free crib. $37/S; $43-44/D; $4/ex prsn. Higher spec event rates. Discs.

Marshall

Super 8 Motel/ Marshall Interstate Plaza, Marshall IL 62441. 217-826-8043. V,M,AE,D,DC,CB. I-70 (Exit 147) to Hwy 1, S then E to mtl. B/f, n/s rms, indr pool, t/b/rv pkng, outlets, cont brfst, cable TV, cot crib. Free local calls. No pets. $38/S; $43-45/D; $4/ex prsn. Higher spec event rates. Discs.

Mattoon

Howard Johnson/ Rte 2, Box 151-A, Mattoon IL 61938. 217-235-4161/ Fax: 235-5913. AE,DC,M,V,CB,D. I-57, Exit 184. N/s rms, arpt trans, t/b pkng, cable TV, laundry, fax, Free cont brfst, nwspr. No pets. $41-49/S; $41-67/D. Higher spec event rates. Discs.

Super 8 Motel/ Rte 16 E & I-57, Mattoon IL 61938. 217-235-8888/ Fax: 258-8808. D,M,V,AE,DC,CB. I-57 (Exit 190B) to SR 16, W 1/4 mi to Frontier Rd, turn rt. B/f, n/s rms, t pkng, cable TV, cable TV, suites, mtg rm. Free local calls. Pride Award. $41/S; $45-47/D; $3/ex prsn. Higher spec event rates. Discs.

McLean

Super 8 Motel/ South St & Elm St, McLean IL 61754. 309-874-2366/ Fax: Ext 400. V,M,AE,D,DC,CB. I-55, Exit 145. B/f, n/s rms, pool, whrlpool, laundry, t/b/rv pkng, outlets, cont brfst, cable TV, crib. Free local calls. Pride Award. $39/S; $46-50/D; $5/ex prsn. Discs.

Mendota

Super 8 Motel/ 508 Hwy 34 E, Box 526, Mendota IL 61342. 815-539-7429/ Fax:

ILLINOIS

Ext 103. D,M,V,AE,DC,CB. I-39 at Hwy 34, turn E. B/f, n/s rms, b/t pkng, outlets, copier, cable TV, cot, crib. Free local calls. $41/S; $46-50/D; $4/ex prsn. Discs.

Metropolis

Best Inns/ 2055 5th St, Metropolis IL 62960. 618-524-8200. AE,DC,CB,M,V, D. I-24, Exit 37. Pool, whrlpool, fax, dd/tt phone, b/f, t pkng. Free cont brfst, coffee, crib, local calls. AAA. $40-45/S; $46-51/D; $6/ex prsn. 4/1-10/31: $45-50/S; $51-56/D. Higher spec event rates. Disc: Senior, family.

Moline

Exel Inn/ 2501 52nd Av, Moline IL 61265. 309-797-5580/ Fax: 797-1561. V,M,AE,D,DC,CB. On S side of city 1/2 mi N of arpt. Nrby rstrnt, cable TV, game rm, laundry, fax, microfridge, n/s rms, arpt trans. Free cont brfst. AAA. $33-39/S; $38-47/D. Higher spec event/ wknd rates. Discs.

Motel 6/ Quad City Airport Rd, Moline IL 61265. 309-764-8711/ Fax: 762-4092. AE,DC,D,M,V. I-280/74 (Exit 5B) to Airport Rd, rt 1/2 mi. Cable TV, laundry, pool, nrby rstrnt, n/s rms, t pkng. Free local calls. $28-29/S; $34-35/D; $6/ex prsn. D

Also see East Moline.

Morton

Howard Johnson Lodge/ 128 Queenwood Rd, Morton IL 61550. 309-263-2511/ Fax: 266-7133. AE,DC,M,V,CB,D. I-74 (Exit 101) to SR 121S (Queenwood Rd Exit), turn lt. N/s rms, b/f, rstrnt/ lounge, t pkng, cable TV, fax, copier, mtg rm. Free coffee. $35/S; $45/D. Higher spec event rates. Discs.

Mount Vernon

Best Inns/ 222 S 44th St, Mount Vernon IL 62864. 618-244-4343. AE,DC,CB, M,V,D. I-57/64 (Exit 95) to SR 15, E. Pool, mtg rm, fax, nrby rstrnt, dd/tt phone, b/f, t pkng. Free cont brfst, coffee, crib, local calls. AAA $34-37/S; $41-44/D; $6/ex prsn. 5/24-9/30: $38-41/S; $45-48/D. Higher spec event rates. Disc: Senior, family.

Comfort Inn/ 201 Potomac Blvd, Mount Vernon IL 62864. 618-242-7200. V,M,D,AE. I-57 (Exit 95) to Hwy 15, W to Potomac Blvd, turn N to mtl. Nrby rstrnt, pool, mtg rm, fax, b/f, whrlpool, cable TV, t pkng, outlets, exerc equip. Free cont brfst. No pets. $45-50/S; $45-60/D; $6/ex prsn. 5/1-9/30: $50-60/S; $55-65/D. Discs.

Motel 6/ 333 S 44th St, Mount Vernon IL 62864. 618-244-2383/ Fax: 244-1697. AE,DC,D,M,V. I-57/ I-64 (Exit 95) to SR 15, E to SE frontage rd, rt. Nrby rstrnt, cable TV, pool, n/s rms, t pkng. Free local calls. $30/S; $36/D; $6/ex prsn. Disc.

Super 8 Motel/ 401 S 44th St, Mount Vernon IL 62864. 618-242-8800/ Fax: 242-8247. D,M,V,AE,DC,CB. I-57 (Exit 95) at SR 15. B/f, n/s rms, nrby rstrnt, t/b/rv pkng, outlets, copier, cable TV, suites, cot. Free local calls, crib. Pride Award. $38/S; $44-45/D; $4/ex prsn. Higher spec event rates. Discs.

Murphysboro (Carbondale area)

Super 8 Motel/ Hwy 13, Box 429, Murphysboro IL 62966. 618-687-2244. V, M, AE,D,DC,CB. W side of Carbondale on Hwy 13. Just E of SR 127. B/f, n/s rms, t/b/rv pkng, outlets, copier, cot, crib. Pride Award. $37/S; $43-44/D; $3/ex prsn. Discs.

Nauvoo

Nauvoo Family Motel/ 150 N Warsaw, Box 187, Nauvoo IL 62354. 217-453-6527. V,M,AE,D. Nrby rstrnt, cable TV, dd phone, outlets, b/f, play area, mtg rm, laundry, family rms, n/s rms, cot, crib. IMA. $38/S; $44/D; $5/ex prsn. $60-70/suites.

Normal

Motel 6/ 1600 N Main St, Normal IL 61761. 309-452-0422/ Fax: 452-2639. V,M,DC,D,AE. I-55 (Exit 165) to Bsns US 51 (N Main St), S to mtl. Cable TV, pool, n/s rms, t pkng. Free local calls. $27-32/S; $33-38/D; $6/ex prsn. Higher spec event rates. Disc.

Super 8 Motel Normal/ Two Traders Cir, Normal IL 61761. 309-454-5858/ Fax: 454-1172. V,M,AE,D,DC. I-55 (Exit 165) to Raab Rd, rt 1 blk to Traders Cir. B/f, n/s rms, whrlpool, sauna, cable TV, suites, cot, crib. Free local calls. $39-

ILLINOIS

45/S; $44-50/D; $5/ex prsn. Higher spec event rates. Discs.

Oglesby
Days Inn/ N Lewis Rd, Oglesby IL 61348. 815-883-9600/ Fax: 883-9660. M,DC,D,V,AE,CB. I-39 (Exit 54) to Ogelsby St, turn E to mtl. Fax, n/s rms, nrby rstrnt, indr pool, whrlpool, mtg rm, b/f, cable TV, copier, cot. Free cont brfst. $43-58/S; $48-63/D; $5/ex prsn. Discs.

Okawville
Super 8 Motel/ Drawer 515, Okawville IL 62271. 618-243-6525. D,M,V,AE,DC,CB. I-64 (Exit 41) at Hwy 177. B/f, n/s rms, t/b/rv pkng, outlets, copier, cable TV, cot. Free local calls, crib. $37-41/S; $42-48/D; $5/ex prsn. Higher spec event rates. Discs.

Ottawa
Comfort Inn/ 510 E Etna Rd, Ottawa IL 61350. 815-433-9600. V,M,D,AE. I-80 (Exit 90) to SR 23 S. Nrby rstrnt, indr pool, cable TV, n/s rms. Free cont brfst. No pets. $39-59/S; $47-63/D; $5/ex prsn. Discs.

Palatine (Chicago area)
Motel 6/ 1450 E Dundee Rd, Palatine IL 60067. 708-359-0046/ Fax: 358-5079. V,M,D,AE,DC. Hwy 53 at Dundee Rd. Cable TV, laundry, nrby rstrnt, n/s rms. Free local calls. $32-34/S; $38-40/D; $6/ex prsn. Disc.

Paris
Super 8 Motel/ Hwy 150, Paris IL 61944. 217-463-8888. V,M,AE,D,DC,CB. I-70 (Exit 147) to Hwy 150, N on Hwy 150/1. B/f, n/s rms, t/b/rv pkng, outlets, cont brfst, cable TV, suites. Free local calls. Pride Award. $36/S; $42-44/D; $4/ex prsn. Higher spec event rates. Discs.

Pekin
Super 8 Motel/ 3830 Kelly St, Pekin IL 61554. 309-347-8888. V,M,D,AE,DC,CB. SR 9 to Veterans Dr, N to Kelly, turn rt to mtl. B/f, n/s rms, pool, indr pool, whrlpool, cable TV, mtg rm, outlets. $45/S; $49-51/D; $6/ex prsn. Higher spec event rates. Discs.

Peoria
HoJo Inn/ 202 NE Washington St, Peoria IL 61602. 309-676-8961 Fax: Ext 213. AE,M,V,D,DC,CB,JCB. I-74, Exit 93. On river near boat works, Washington St at Hamilton St, dntn. N/s rms, mtg rm, rstrnt. Free cont brfst. No pets. AAA. $30-40/S; $40-50/D. Discs.

Peru (LaSalle area)
Comfort Inn/ 5240 Trompeter Rd, Peru IL 61354. 815-223-8585. V,M,D,AE. I-80 (Exit 75) to US 251, N to mtl. Nrby rstrnt, indr pool, cable TV, fax, copier, n/s rms. Free cont brfst. No pets. $43-59/S; $47-63/D; $4/ex prsn. Discs.

Motel 6/ 1900 May Rd, Peru IL 61354. 815-224-2785/ Fax: 224-3074. V, M, DC,D,AE. I-80 (Exit 75) to Hwy 251, N 1 blk, lt on May Rd. Nrby rstrnt, cable TV, n/s rms. Free local calls. $24-26/S; $30-32/D; $6/ex prsn. Disc.

Super 8 Motel/ 1851 May Rd, Peru IL 61354. 815-223-1848. D,M,V, AE, DC,CB. I-80 (Exit 75) to Hwy 251, N to May Rd, turn lt. B/f, n/s rms, b/rv pkng, outlets, copier, cable TV, cot. Free local calls, crib. $37/S; $44-48/D; $5/ex prsn. Higher spec event rates. Discs.

Pontiac
Super 8 Motel/ 601 S Deerfield Rd, Pontiac IL 61764. 815-844-6888/ Fax: Ext 100. D,M,V,AE,DC,CB. I-55 (Exit 197) at Hwy 116. B/f, n/s rms, toast bar, t/b/rv pkng, cable TV, suite, mtg rm, cot. Free local calls, crib. $39/S; $43-46/D; $4/ex prsn. Discs.

Princeton
Super 8 Motel/ 2929 N Main St, Princeton IL 61356. 815-872-8888/ Fax: Ext 888. V,M,AE,D,DC,CB. I-80 (Exit 56) to Hwy 26. B/f, n/s rms, pool, outlets, whrlpool, copier, cable TV, crib. Free local calls. No pets. $39-41/S; $46-50/D; $4/ex prsn. Higher spec event rates. Discs.

Prospect Heights
Exel Inn/ 540 Milwaukee Av, Prospect Heights IL 60070. 708-459-0545/ Fax: 459-8639. M,AE,V,D,DC,CB. I-294 to Willow Rd, W to Milwaukee Av, then S 2 blks. Nrby rstrnt, cable TV, game rm,

ILLINOIS

laundry, fax, microfridge, n/s rms, t pkng. Free cont brfst, health club pass. AAA. $40-49/S; $46-55/D. Higher spec event/ wknd rates. Discs.

Quincy

Super 8 Motel/ 224 N 36th, Quincy IL 62301. 217-228-8808/ Fax: Ext 404. V, M,DC,AE,CB,D. I-172 (Exit 14) to Broadway, W to 3rd traffic light (36th St), turn lt. B/f, n/s rms, toast bar, b/rv pkng, elevator, cable TV, mtg rm, suites, cot. Free local calls. $42/S; $46-48/D; $4/ex prsn. Discs.

Rantoul

Super 8 Motel/ 207 S Murray Rd, Rantoul IL 61866. 217-893-8888/ Fax: 893-9017. V,M,DC,AE,CB,D. I-57 (Exit 250) to US 136, E 2 blks to Murray Rd. B/f, n/s rms, laundry, t pkng, outlets, toast bar, copier, elevator, cable TV, mtg rm, cot. Free crib. $39/S; $43-46/D; $4/ex prsn. Higher spec event rates. Discs.

Robinson

Days Inn/ 1500 W Main St, Robinson IL 62454. 618-544-8448/ Fax: 544-8710. M,DC,D,V,AE,CB. On SR 33. W of SR 1, S of I-75. Fax, n/s rms, nrby rstrnt, mtg rm, b/f, cable TV, refrig, microwave, cot. Free cont brfst, crib. Chairman's Award. $38-48/S; $44-54/D; $6/ex prsn. Discs.

Rochelle

Super 8 Motel/ 601 E Hwy 38, Rochelle IL 61068. 815-562-2468/ Fax: Ext 102. V,M,DC,AE,CB,D. I-39 (Exit 99) to SR 38, W 3/4 mi. B/f, n/s rms, laundry, b/t pkng, outlets, copier, suites, crib. Free local calls. No pets. $41/S; $46-50/D; $4/ex prsn. Discs.

Rock Falls

Super 8 Motel/ 2100 1st Av, Rock Falls IL 61071. 815-626-8800/ Fax: 626-9522. D,M,V,AE,DC,CB. I-88 (Exit 41) to SR 88, turn N to jct of SR 88 & US 30. B/f, n/s rms, t/b/rv pkng, outlets, cont brfst, copier, cable TV, suites, mtg rm. Free local calls, crib. $37/S; $42-47/D; $2/ex prsn. Discs.

Rockford

Exel Inn/ 220 S Lyford Rd, Rockford IL 61108. 815-332-4915/ Fax: 332-3843. V,M,AE,D,DC,CB. I-90 at Bsns 20, turn lt. Nrby rstrnt, cable TV, game rm, laundry, fax, microfridge, n/s rms, t pkng. Free cont brfst. AAA. $35-40/S; $40-49/D. Higher spec event/ wknd rates. Discs.

Motel 6/ 3851 11th St, Rockford IL 61109. 815-398-6080/ Fax: 398-5816. AE,DC,D,M,V. US 20 to SR 251, S 1/4 mi to 11th St, turn W. Cable TV, indr pool, n/s rms, t pkng. Free local calls. $28/S; $32-34/D; $4-6/ex prsn. Disc.

Super 8 Motel/ 7646 Colosseum Dr, Rockford IL 61107. 815-229-5522/ Fax: 229-5547. AE,DC,M,V,CB,D. I-90 to Bsns US 20 (State St), W to Bell School Rd, turn N to Colosseum Dr. B/f, n/s rms, t/rv pkng, outlets, cont brfst, copier, cable TV, cot, crib. Free local calls. $40/S; $47-50/D; $4/ex prsn. Higher spec event rates. Discs.

Sweden House Lodge/ 4605 E State St, Rockford IL 61108. 815-398-4130/ Fax: 398-9203/ 800-886-4138. V,M,AE,D,DC,CB. I-90, exit State St/ Bsns 20, rt 3 mi. Nrby rstrnt/ lounge, indr pool, n/s rms, exerc equip, cable TV, VCRs/ movies, video games, arpt trans, tt phone, mtg rm, fax, copier, nwspr, laundry, refrig, elevator, microwave, cot, crib, t/b/rv pkng, eff, conn rms, b/f. Free local calls. AAA. $37-48/S; $39-53/D; $2/ex prsn. Wknds, 5/1-9/30: $47-58/S; $49-63/D. Disc: Senior, family. *Guaranteed rates.*

Rolling Meadows (Chicago area)

Motel 6/ 1800 Winnetka Cir, Rolling Meadows IL 60008. 708-818-8088/ Fax: 392-2940. M,V,DC,D,AE. I-90 to SR 53, N to Euclid Av, W to Hicks Rd, rt to Winnetka Av, rt to Winnetka Cir. Cable TV, pool, elevator, n/s rms. Free local calls. $32/S; $38/D; $6/ex prsn. Disc.

Saint Charles (Chicago area)

Econo Lodge/ 1600 E Main St, St Charles IL 60174. 708-584-5300. V,M,AE, DC. On North Av (SR 64) 5 mi W of SR 59. Nrby rstrnt, pool, mtg rm, fax, cable TV, n/s rms. Free cont brfst. No pets. $40-60/S; $45-65/D; $4/ex prsn. 5/1-10/31: $45-65/S; $50-70/D. 12/31: $70/S or D. Discs.

ILLINOIS

Salem
Continental Motel/ 1600 E Main, Box 370, Salem IL 62881. 618-548-3090. V,M,AE,D,DC,CB. I-57, Exit 116, lt 2.3 mi. Nrby rstrnt/ lounge, n/s rms, cable TV, tt/dd phone, cot, crib, t/b/rv pkng, conn rms, b/f. Free local calls, cont brfst, coffee, tea. AAA. $20-22/S; $23-25/D; $3/ex prsn. Disc: Senior, l/s, family. *Guaranteed rates.*

Super 8 Motel/ 118 Paragon Rd, Salem IL 62881. 618-548-5882. D,M,V,AE,DC,CB. I-57 (Exit 116) to US 50, turn W. B/f, n/s rms, laundry, breakfast bar, t/b/rv pkng, cable TV, mtg rm, cot. Free local calls, crib. Pride Award. $36/S; $41-43/D; $4/ex prsn. Higher spec event rates. Discs.

Schiller Park (Chicago area)
Motel 6/ 9408 W Lawrence Av, Schiller Park IL 60176. 708-671-4282/ Fax: 928-1752. M,V,DC,D,AE. I-294 or I-90. Follow signs to O'Hare Arpt, at arpt entry exit Mannheim Rd, S 1 mi to Lawrence Av, turn E for 1 mi. Cable TV, laundry, n/s rms. Free local calls. $36/S; $42/D; $6/ex prsn. Disc.

Springfield
Motel 6/ 6010 S 6th St, Springfield IL 62707. 217-529-1633/ Fax: 585-1271. AE,DC,D,M,V. I-55 (Exit 90) to Toronto Rd, E to mtl. Rstrnt, cable TV, n/s rms, t pkng. Free local calls. $25-27/S; $31-33/D; $6/ex prsn. Disc.

Sleep Inn/ 3470 Freedom Dr, Springfield IL 62704. 217-787-6200. V,M,AE,DC. US 36 W (Exit 93) to Springfield Chatham exit, N to mtl. Nrby rstrnt, fax, b/f, cable TV, t pkng, n/s rms. Free cont brfst. AAA. $42-60/S; $47-65/D; $5/ex prsn. Discs.

Super 8 Motel/ 1330 S Dirksen Pkwy, Springfield IL 62703. 217-528-8889/ Fax: 528-8809. D,M,V,AE,DC,CB. I-55 (Exit 96B) at S Grand Av. B/f, n/s rms, copier, elevator, cable TV, cot. Free crib. $37/S; $43-47/D; $5/ex prsn. Higher spec event rates. Discs.

Super 8 Motel/ 3675 S 6th St, Springfield IL 62703. 217-529-8898/ Fax: 529-4354. D,M,V,AE,DC,CB. I-55 (Exit 92A) to S 6th S, turn lt at light, immed rt onto access rd, N 2 blks. B/f, n/s rms, copier, elevator, cable TV, mtg rm, cot. Free crib. $37/S; $43-47/D; $5/ex prsn. Higher spec event rates. Discs.

Tuscola
Super 8 Motel/ Box 202, Tuscola IL 61953. 217-253-5488/ Fax: 253-4337. D,M,V,AE,DC,CB. I-57 (Exit 212) to Hwy 36, W to mtl. B/f, n/s rms, t pkng, cable TV, cot. Free crib. $40/S; $46-47/D; $5/ex prsn. Higher spec event rates. Discs.

Urbana (Champaign area)
Motel 6/ 1906 N Cunningham Av, Urbana IL 61801. 217-344-1082/ Fax: 328-4108. V,M,DC,D,AE. I-74 (Exit 184) to US 45, S 1 blk. Cable TV, pool, n/s rms. Free local calls. $26-30/S; $32-36/D; $6/ex prsn. Higher spec event rates. Disc.

Vandalia
Ramada Limited/ Rte 40 W, Vandalia IL 62471. 618-283-1400/ Fax: 283-3465. M,DC,D,V,AE,CB. On I-40. Pool, b/f, n/s rms, mtg rm, cot, suites. Golden Key Award. $35-45/S; $45-55/D; $8/ex prsn. Discs.

Villa Park (Chicago area)
Motel 6/ 10 W Roosevelt Rd, Villa Park IL 60181. 708-941-9100/ Fax: 941-1167. V,M,D,AE,DC. Tollway 355 to Roosevelt Rd/ Rte 38, E 5 mi. I-294: Nbnd to Roosevelt Rd, 4 mi; Sbnd, to North Av, W to Hwy 83, S to Roosevelt Rd W. Cable TV, pool, n/s rms, whrlpool. Free local calls. $34-36/S; $40-42/D; $6/ex prsn. Disc.

Washington
Super 8 Motel/ 1884 Washington Rd, Washington IL 61571. 309-444-8881. AE,DC,M,V,CB,D. US 24 to Cummings Lane, N to Washington Rd. B/f, n/s rms, cont brfst, b pkng, outlets, elevator, cable TV, cot. $37-39/S; $43-47/D; $6/ex prsn. Higher spec event rates. Discs.

Watseka
Super 8 Motel/ 710 W Walnut St, Watseka IL 60970. 815-432-6000. AE, DC, M,V,CB,D. US 24 & SR 1. B/f, n/s rms, whrlpool, laundry, cont brfst, t/b/rv

ILLINOIS / INDIANA

pkng, copier, cable TV, mtg rm, cot, crib. Pride Award. AAA. $42/S; $46-52/D; $4/ex prsn. Higher spec event rates. Discs.

Waukegan (Chicago area)

Best Inns/ 31 N Green Bay Rd, Waukegan IL 60085. 708-336-9000. AE,DC,CB,M,V,D. I-94 Nbnd, Exit SR 120 (Belvidere) at Green Bay Rd, go lt, 4/10 mi on rt; I-94 Sbnd, Exit SR 132 (Grand), go E, rt on Green Bay 3/10 mi on lt. Pool, fax, mtg rm, t pkng, dd/tt phone, b/f. Free cont brfst, coffee, crib, local calls. AAA. $40-43/S; $47-53/D; $6/ex prsn. 6/13-8/24: $52-55/S; $59-65/D. Disc: Senior, family.

Comfort Inn/ 3031 Belvidere St, Waukegan IL 60085. 708-623-1400. V, M,AE,DC. I-94/ 294 to Belvidere Rd E. Rstrnt/ lounge, mtg rm, fax, b/f, cable TV, t pkng, n/s rms. Free cont brfst. No pets. $39-70/S; $39-75/D; $6/ex prsn. 3/1-11/30: $39-80/S; $44-90/D. Discs.

Super 8 Motel/ 630 N Green Bay Rd, Waukegan IL 60085. 708-249-2388. D, M,V,AE,DC,CB. I-94, exit Hwy 132, E to Hwy 131. B/f, n/s rms, b/rv pkng, copier, cable TV, cot. Free local calls, crib. $36-43/S; $43-57/D; $5/ex prsn. Higher spec event rates. Discs.

Woodstock (Chicago area)

Super 8 Motel/ 1220 Davis Rd, Woodstock IL 60098. 815-337-8808/ Fax: 337-8815. AE,M,V,D,DC,CB. Jct of Hwys 14 & 47. Entrance on frontage rd of Hwy 47, S of 14. B/f, n/s rms, laundry, outlets, toast bar, cable TV, family rms, cot. Free crib. Pride Award. $40-43/S; $45-48/D; $5/ex prsn. Higher spec event rates. Discs.

Indiana

Anderson

Motel 6/ 5810 Scatterfield Rd, Anderson IN 46013. 317-642-9023/ Fax: 641-1186. M,V,DC,D,AE. I-69 (Exit 26) to SR 109 (Scatterfield Rd) at Anderson, W to mtl. Cable TV, pool, n/s rms, t pkng. Free local calls. $29-30/S; $35-36/D; $6/ex prsn. Higher spec event rates. Disc.

Also see Daleville.

Bloomington

Motel 6/ 126 S Franklin Rd, Bloomington IN 47401. 812-332-0337/ Fax: 332-1967. M,V,DC,D,AE. SR 37 to SR 48, turn E 1 blk, lt on Franklin. Nrby rstrnt, cable TV, pool, n/s rms. Free local calls. $26-28/S; $32-34/D; $6/ex prsn. Higher spec event rates. Disc.

Motel 6/ 1800 N Walnut St, Bloomington IN 47402. 812-332-0820/ Fax: 337-1526. M,V,DC,D,AE. SR 37 Bypass to SR 46 Bypass, E to College Av/ Walnut St, S 1 blk. Nrby rstrnt, cable TV, pool, n/s rms. Free local calls. Premier Award. $30/S; $36/D; $6/ex prsn. 5/21-12/20: $22/S; $28/D. Higher spec event rates. Disc.

Ramada Limited/ 2601 N Walnut St, Box 1030, Bloomington IN 47402. 812-332-9453/ Fax: 333-1303. M,DC,D,V, AE,CB. SR 46/45 at Walnut St. 1 mi from IN Univ. Pool, trans, n/s rms, coffee, tea, exerc equip, cable TV, laundry, microwave, refrig, mtg rm, b pkng. Free cont brfst buffet, local calls. $42-52/S; $47-57/D; $5/ex prsn. Discs.

Carlisle

Super 8 Motel/ Box 205, Carlisle IN 47838. 812-398-2500/ Fax: 398-2020. V,M,D,AE,DC,CB. On US 41, just S of SR 58. B/f, n/s rms, nearby rstrnt, game rm, laundry, t/b/rv pkng, outlets, satellite TV, cot. Free local calls, crib. Pride Award. $34/S; $39/D; $5/ex prsn. Higher spec event rates. Discs.

INDIANA

Cedar Lake
Crestview Motel/ 12551 Wicker Av, Cedar Lake IN 46303. 219-374-5434. V,M,AE,D,DC,CB. On US Hwy 41, 13 mi S of 80/ 94/ 294. Satellite TV, playgrnd, tt phone, nwspr, laundry, cot, crib, outlets, t/b/rv pkng, eff, fishing pond. Free local calls. No pets. AAA. $30/S; $35/D; $4/ex prsn. Disc: Family.

Centerville (Richmond area)
Super 8 Motel/ 2407 N Centerville Rd, Centerville IN 47330. 317-855-5461/ Fax: 855-5462. V,M,D,AE,DC,CB. I-70 at Centerville exit. N/s rms, nrby rstrnt. Free local calls. $36/S; $40-43/D; $2/ex prsn. Higher spec event rates. Discs.

Clarksville (Louisville KY area)
Econo Lodge/ 460 Auburn Av, Clarksville IN 47129. 812-288-6661. V, M,AE,D. I-65 (Exit 2) at Eastern Blvd, turn rt on Auburn Av. Nrby rstrnt, pool, mtg rm, fax, b/f, cable TV, t pkng, game rm, n/s rms. Free cont brfst. $35-70/S; $45-90/D; $5-25/ex prsn. 5/4-5/7: $140-160/S; $160-180/D. Discs.

Cloverdale
Days Inn/ 1031 N Main St, Cloverdale IN 46120. 317-795-6400/ Fax: 795-6699. M,DC,D,V,AE,CB. I-70 & SR 231. Fax, n/s rms, nrby rstrnt, mtg rm, b/f, fax, cable TV, cot. Free crib. AAA. $35-47/S; $41-50/D; $6/ex prsn. Discs.

Columbus
Super 8 Motel/ 110 Brexpark Dr, Columbus IN 47201. 812-372-8828. AE,M,V,DC,CB,D. I-65 to Hwy 46, E to Brexpark Dr. B/f, n/s rms, t/b/rv pkng, copier, satellite TV, mtg rm, cot. Free local calls, crib. $39-40/S; $46-50/D; $5/ex prsn. Higher spec event rates. Discs.

Crawfordsville
Super 8 Motel/ 1025 Corey Blvd, Crawfordsville IN 47933. 317-364-9999/ Fax: Ext 304. V,M,DC,AE,CB,D. I-74 (Exit 34) & US 231, SE corner. B/f, n/s rms, indr pool, whrlpool, laundry, t/b/rv pkng, outlets, cont brfst, copier, cable TV, cot. Free crib. AAA. $38-39/S; $45-49/D; $4/ex prsn. Higher spec event rates. Discs.

Dale
Budget Host Stone's Motel/ 410 S Washington St, Box 381, Dale IN 47523. 812-937-4448. AE,DC,CB, V,M,D. 1 1/2 mi S of I-64 on US 231. Rstrnt/ lounge, family rms, t pkng, cot, crib. No pets. AAA/ Mobil. $29-30/S; $32-44/D; $2/ex prsn.

Daleville (Anderson area)
Super 8 Motel/ I-69 & SR 67, Daleville IN 47334. 317-378-0888. AE,M,V,DC, CB,D. I-69, Exit 34. B/f, n/s rms, laundry, t/b/rv pkng, outlets, cont brfst, satellite TV, cot. Free local calls. $40/S; $44/D; $4/ex prsn. Higher spec event rates. Discs.

Decatur
Super 8 Motel/ 1302 S 13th St, Decatur IN 46733. 219-724-8888. V,M,D,AE, DC,CB. On US 27 & 33 S. B/f, n/s rms, pool, whrlpool, cont brfst, copier, t/b/rv pkng, mtg rm, cot. Free local calls, crib. Pride Award. AAA. $45/S; $50/D; $5/ex prsn. Higher spec event rates. Discs.

Elkhart
Comfort Inn/ 52137 Plaza Ct, Elkhart IN 46514. 219-264-0404. V,M,AE,DC. I-80/ I-90 (Exit 92) to Hwy 19, turn N to mtl. Nrby rstrnt, pool, whrlpool, cable TV, t pkng, n/s rms. Free cont brfst. No pets. $33-95/S; $39-95/D; $8/ex prsn. Discs.

Econo Lodge/ 3440 Cassopolis St, Elkhart IN 46514. 219-262-0540. AE, DC,M,V. I-80/ I-90 (Exit 92) at SR 19, N 1/4 mi to mtl. Nrby rstrnt, fax, b/f, cable TV, t pkng, outlets, n/s rms. AAA. $30-45/S; $40-50/D; $6/ex prsn. 5/1-10/31: $37-55/S; $49-69/D. Discs.

Super 8 Motel/ 345 Windsor Av, Elkhart IN 46514. 219-264-4457. AE,M,V, DC,CB,D. Hwy 19 (Exit 92) off IN Tollway 80 & 90. B/f, n/s rms, t/b/rv pkng, outlets, copier, cable TV, cot. Free local alls, crib. $41/S; $48-52/D; $5/ex prsn. Discs.

Evansville
Motel 6/ 4201 Hwy 41 N, Evansville IN 47711. 812-424-6431/ Fax: 424-7803. AE,DC,D,M,V. I-64 (Exit 25) to US 41, S 10 mi to mtl. Cable TV, laundry, nrby rstrnt, n/s rms, t pkng. Free local calls.

INDIANA

$30-32/S; $34-38/D; $4-6/ex prsn. Disc.

Super 8 Motel/ 4600 Morgan Av, Evansville IN 47715. 812-476-4008. AE,M,V,DC,CB,D. Hwy 41 to Morgan Av, E to jct with Green River Rd. B/f, n/s rms, b pkng, outlets, elevator, cable TV, nrby rstrnt, cot. Free crib. $43/S; $47-49/D; $3/ex prsn. Higher spec event rates. Discs.

Fort Wayne

Best Inns/ 3017 W Coliseum Blvd, Ft Wayne IN 46808. 219-483-0091. AE,DC,CB,M,V,D. I-69: (S, Exit 109B; N, Exit 109A) rt at Coliseum Blvd (1st light). Mtg rm, fax, nrby rstrnt, t pkng, dd/tt phone, b/f. Free cont brfst, coffee, crib, local calls. AAA. $37-40/S; $44-47/D; $6/ex prsn. Higher spec event rates. Disc: Senior, family.

Comfort Inn/ 2908 Goshen Rd, Ft Wayne IN 46808. 219-484-6262. V,M,AE,DC. I-69 (Exit 109A) to Goshen Rd, turn SE. US 30 & 33, exit Goshen Rd. Nrby rstrnt, pool, sauna, cable TV, n/s rms. Free cont brfst. No pets. $36-105/S; $41-115/D; $5/ex prsn. Discs.

Hometown Inn/ 6910 US Hwy 30E, Ft Wayne IN 46803. 219-749-5058/ Fax: 493-2283. V,M,AE,D,DC,CB. I-469 to Hwy 30, lt 2 1/2 mi. Nrby rstrnt, n/s rms, cable TV, VCR/ movies, video games, tt phones, mtg rm, fax, copier, laundry, microwave, cot, crib, t/b/rv pkng, eff, b/f. Free local calls, coffee, tea, cocoa. AAA. $30/S; $34/S; $4/ex prsn. Disc: Senior, bsns, govt, l/s, family, trkr, milt, AARP. *Guaranteed rates.*

Motel 6/ 3003 Coliseum Blvd W, Ft Wayne IN 46808. 219-482-3972/ Fax: 471-7205. M,V,DC,D,AE. I-69 (Exit 109A) to US 30, E 1/4 mi. Nrby rstrnt, cable TV, n/s rms, t pkng. Free local calls. $27/S; $33/D; $6/ex prsn. Higher spec event rates. Disc.

Super 8 Motel/ 522 Coliseum Blvd E, Ft Wayne IN 46805. 219-484-8326/ Fax: Ext 402. AE,M,V,DC,CB,D. I-69 (Exit 112A) to Coldwater Rd, S to Coliseum Blvd, turn rt. B/f, n/s rms, outlets, cable TV, mtg rm, TDD, cot. Free local calls, crib. $36-42/S; $48-51/D; $3/ex prsn. Higher spec event rates. Discs.

Greenfield (Indianapolis area)

Super 8 Motel/ 2100 N State St, Greenfield IN 46140. 317-462-8899/ Fax: Ext 302. AE,M,V,DC,CB,D. I-70, Exit 104. E of Indianapolis. B/f, n/s rms, indr pool, copier, t/b/rv pkng, cable TV, mtg rm, nrby rstrnt, popcorn. Free local calls, crib. No pets. Pride Award. $40/S; $43-45/D; $2/ex prsn. Discs.

Hammond (Chicago area)

Motel 6/ 3840 179th St, Hammond IN 46324. 219-845-0330/ Fax: 845-7012. M,V,DC,D,AE. I-80/ I-94 (Exit 5A) to Cline Av, S to 179th (frontage rd), rt 1/4 mi. Nrby rstrnt, cable TV, n/s rms. Free local calls. $32-34/S; $38-40/D; $6/ex prsn. Disc.

Super 8 Motel/ 3844 179th St, Hammond IN 46323. 219-844-8888/ Fax: 844-5827. AE,M,V,D,DC,CB. I-80/94 at Cline Av. B/f, n/s rms, laundry, outlets, copier, elevator, satellite TV, cot. Free crib. No pets. $42/S; $48-52/D; $6/ex prsn. Higher spec event rates. Discs.

Super 8 Motel/ 4111 Calumet Av, Hammond IN 46327. 219-932-8888/ Fax: 932-1615. AE,M,V,DC,CB,D. I-90 (Exit 5) at 141st St. B/f, n/s rms, laundry, outlets, copier, elevator, satellite TV, cot. Free crib. No pets. $42/S; $48-52/D; $6/ex prsn. Higher spec event rates. Discs.

Howe

Super 8 Motel/ 7333 N SR 9, Howe IN 46746. 219-562-2828. V,M,D,AE, DC,CB. I-80/90 (Exit 121) to SR 9, S 1/2 mi. B/f, n/s rms, outlets, b/t pkng, toast bar, copier, satellite TV, mtg rm, cot. Free local calls, crib. Pride Award. $40/S; $45/D; $5/ex prsn. Higher spec event rates. Discs.

Indianapolis

Comfort Inn/ 5040 S East St, Indianapolis IN 46227. 317-783-6711. V, M,D,AE,DC. I-465 (Exit 2B) to US 31, S 3 blks to Thompson Rd. Nrby rstrnt, pool, mtg rm, fax, b/f, cable TV, t pkng, outlets, n/s rms. Free cont brfst. No pets. $40-70/S; $46-75/D; $5/ex prsn. 5/26-5/28: $450/S or D. Discs.

Econo Lodge/ 4505 S Harding St, Indianapolis IN 46217. 317-788-9361. V,

INDIANA

M,AE,D. I-465 (Exit 4) at SR 37 S. Rstrnt/ lounge, pool, mtg rm, fax, b/f, cable TV, t pkng, exerc equip, VCR, laundry, game rm, trans, n/s rms. Free local calls. $40-80/S; $45-90/D; $5/ex prsn. 5/26-5/28: $115-140/S; $150-200/D. 5/29-9/5: $40-140/S; $45-200/D. Discs.

Econo Lodge/ 4326 Sellers St, Indianapolis IN 46226. 317-542-1031/ Fax: 542-9808. V,M,AE,D. I-465 (Exit 42) to Pendleton Pike, NE to mtl. Nrby rstrnt, fax, cable TV, t pkng, VCR, laundry, n/s rms. Free coffee. No pets. $36-55/S; $41-55/D; $5/ex prsn. 5/26-5/29: $150/S or D. 8/3-8/6: $90/S or D. Discs.

HoJo Inn/ 7050 E 21st St, Indianapolis IN 46219. 317-352-0481 Fax: 352-0194. AE,M,V,D,DC,CB,JCB. I-70 & I-465, Shadeland Exit 89. N/s rms, b/f, rstrnt, pool, t pkng, laundry, cable TV. $32-46/S; $36-50/D. Discs.

Motel 6/ 5241 W Bradbury, Indianapolis IN 46241. 317-248-1231/ Fax: 481-1728. AE,DC,D,M,V. I-465 (Exit 11A) to Airport Expwy, E to Lynhurst Dr. I-70: Ebnd to I-465 N; Wbnd, to Exit 11A/ Airport Expwy. Nrby rstrnt, cable TV, pool, n/s rms, elevator. Free local calls. $30-32/S; $36-38/D; $6/ex prsn. Higher spec event rates. Disc.

Super 8 Motel/ 4530 S Emerson Av, Indianapolis IN 46203. 317-788-0955/ Fax: Ext 132. AE,M,V,DC,CB,D. I-465/ I-74 (Exit 52) to Emerson Av, S to mtl. B/f, n/s rms, laundry, t/b/rv pkng, outlets, cont brfst, copier, cot. Free local calls, crib. $38/S; $43-45/D; $5/ex prsn. Discs.

Super 8 Motel/ 4502 S Harding St, Indianapolis IN 46217. 317-788-4774/ Fax: Ext 100. AE,M,V,DC,CB,D. I-465 & I-74, at SR 37 (Harding St). B/f, n/s rms, outlets, t/b/rv pkng, copier, cable TV, mtg rm, cot. Free local calls, crib. AAA. $36-45/S; $41-47/D; $5/ex prsn. Higher spec event rates. Discs.

Also see Greenfield, Shelbyville, Speedway.

Jeffersonville (Louisville KY area)

Motel 6/ 2016 Old Hwy 31 E, Jeffersonville IN 47129. 812-283-7703/ Fax: 280-1695. M,V,AE,D,DC. I-65 (Exit 2) to Eastern Blvd, E 1/8 mi to frontage rd, turn N. Cable TV, laundry, pool, elevator, n/s rms. Free local calls. $26-30/S; $32-36/D; $6/ex prsn. Higher spec event rates. Disc.

Kokomo

Econo Lodge/ 2040 S Reed Rd, Kokomo IN 46902. 317-457-7561. V, M, AE,D. US 31 & Blvd. Rstrnt/ lounge, pool, fax, b/f, cable TV, t pkng, outlets, n/s rms. Free AM coffee. No pets. $32/S; $37/D; $5-10/ex prsn. 5/27-5/28: $65/S; $70/D. Discs.

Motel 6/ 2808 S Reed Rd, Kokomo IN 46902. 317-457-8211/ Fax: 454-9774. V,M,D,AE,DC. US 31 at Lincoln Rd. Nrby rstrnt, cable TV, n/s rms, t pkng. Free local calls. $33/S; $39/D; $6/ex prsn. Higher spec event rates. Disc.

LaPorte

Super 8 Motel/ 438 Pine Lake Av, LaPorte IN 46350. 219-325-3808/ Fax: 324-6873. AE,M,V,DC,CB,D. 3 mi S of I-80/90, Exit 49. On Hwys 35 & 39. B/f, n/s rms, cable TV, in-rm coffee, outlets, rv pkng, cot. Free local calls, crib. $26-30/S; $36-49/D; $5/ex prsn. Higher spec event rates. Discs.

Merrillville

Motel 6/ 8290 Louisiana St, Merrillville IN 46410. 219-738-2701/ Fax: 793-9237. V,M,D,AE,DC. I-65 (Exit 253A) to Valparaiso exit, E to 1st traffic light, turn rt. Cable TV, laundry, nrby rstrnt, n/s rms. Free local calls. $34-35/S; $40-41/D; $6/ex prsn. Disc.

Super 8 Motel/ 8300 Louisiana St, Merrillville IN 46410. 219-736-8383/ Fax: Ext 403. AE,M,V,DC,CB,D. I-65 (Exit 253A) to Hwy 30, E to light, rt to 83rd, rt. B/f, n/s rms, outlets, toast bar, micro-fridge, TDD, mtg rm. Free local calls, crib. $39-42/S; $46-50/D; $6/ex prsn. Higher spec event rates. Discs.

Michigan City

Super 8 Motel/ 5724 S Franklin, Michigan City IN 46360. 219-879-0411/ Fax: 878-8909. AE,M,V,DC,CB,D. I-94 (Exit 34B) at US 421 N. B/f, n/s rms, outlets, cable TV, t pkng, in-rm coffee, cot. Free local calls, crib. No pets. $26-

INDIANA

30/S; $36-49/D; $5/ex prsn. Higher spec event rates. Discs.

Muncie

Super 8 Motel/ 3601 W Foxridge Ln, Muncie IN 47304. 317-286-4333. AE, M,V,DC,CB,D. I-69 (Exit 41) to Hwy 332, E 6 mi. B/f, n/s rms, b/t pkng, outlets, copier, cable TV, cot. Free local calls, crib. $40/S; $47-51/D; $5/ex prsn. Higher spec event rates. Discs.

Plymouth

Days Inn/ 2229 N Michigan St, Plymouth IN 46563. 219-935-4276. M, DC,D,V,AE,CB. Jct US 30 & SR 17. Fax, n/s rms, nrby rstrnt, t pkng, cable TV, cot. $39-62/S; $42-65/D; $5/ex prsn. Discs.

Motel 6/ 2535 N Michigan Av, Plymouth IN 46563. 219-935-5911/ Fax: 935-0630. M,V,DC,D,AE. US 30 at SR 17, turn N to mtl. Nrby rstrnt, cable TV, pool, n/s rms. Free local calls. $26-28/S; $32-34/D; $6/ex prsn. Higher spec event rates. Disc.

Portage

Motel 6/ 6101 Melton Rd, Portage IN 46368. 219-763-3121/ Fax: 762-5224. M,V,DC,D,AE. I-94 (Exit 19) to Hwy 249, go S to US 20, then rt to mtl. Nrby rstrnt, cable TV, pool, n/s rms, t pkng. Free local calls. $25/S; $29-31/D; $4-6/ex prsn. Disc.

Remington

Days Inn/ 4252 W US 24, Remington IN 47977. 219-261-2178/ Fax: 261-3182. M,DC,D,V,AE,CB. I-65 & US 24. Fax, n/s rms, nrby rstrnt, pool, b/f, t/rv pkng, cot. Free popcorn, crib. $41/S; $46/D; $5/ex prsn. Discs.

Richmond

Howard Johnson Lodge/ 2525 Chester Blvd, Richmond IN 47374. 317-962-7576/ Fax: 962-1063. AE,M,V,D,DC, CB,JCB. US 27 & I-70. N/s rms, b/f, pool. Free cont brfst. $32-37/S; $38-48/D. Higher spec event rates. Discs.

Also see Centerville.

Seymour

Econo Lodge/ 220 Commerce Dr, Seymour IN 47274. 812-522-8000. V, M,AE,DC. I-65 (Exit 50A) to US 50, turn E to Commerce Dr, turn rt/S. Rstrnt, pool, fax, cable TV, n/s rms. $36-45/S or D; $4/ex prsn. 5/5-5/6, 5/26-5/27, 8/4-8/5: $70/S or D. Discs.

Shelbyville (Indianapolis area)

Super 8 Motel/ 20 Rampart Dr, Shelbyville IN 46176. 317-392-6239/ Fax: Ext 101. AE,M,V,DC,CB,D. I-74 (Exit 113) to SR 9. B/f, n/s rms, sauna, laundry, cont brfst, copier, cable TV, suites, exerc equip, cot. Free crib. $42/S; $45-51/D; $5/ex prsn. Higher spec event rates. Disc.

South Bend

Best Inns/ 425 Dixie Highway N, S Bend IN 46637. 219-277-7700. AE, DC, CB,M,V,D. I-80/90 (Exit 77) to Dixie Hwy/ US 31/33, N 2 lights. Mtg rm, fax, nrby rstrnt, dd/tt phone, b/f, t pkng. Free cont brfst, coffee, crib, local calls. AAA. $39-42/S; $46-49/D; $6/ex prsn. 5/10-9/28: $45-48/S; $52-55/D. Disc: Senior, family.

Econo Lodge/ 3233 Lincoln Way W, S Bend IN 46628. 219-232-9019. V, M,AE,D. SR 20, 1/2 mi from Michiana Arpt. Nrby rstrnt, mtg rm, cable TV, n/s rms. Free coffee, local calls. $29-89/S; $33-89/D; $4/ex prsn. Higher special event rates. Disc.

Motel 6/ 52624 US 31 N, S Bend IN 46637. 219-272-7072/ Fax: 273-4475. M,V,DC,D,AE. US 33, just N of I-80/90. Cable TV, laundry, pool, n/s rms, nrby rstrnt. Free local calls. $29/S; $35/D; $6/ex prsn. Higher spec event rates. Disc.

Super 8 Motel/ 52825 US 33 N, S Bend IN 46637. 219-272-9000/ Fax: 273-0035. V,M,D,AE,DC,CB. I-80/90 IN Tollway, Exit 77, N 2 mi. B/f, n/s rms, laundry, copier, fax, kitchenettes, outlets, nrby rstrnt/ lounge. Free cont brfst, local calls, crib. $40/S; $47/D; $3/ex prsn. Discs.

Speedway (Indianapolis area)

Motel 6/ 6330 Debonair Ln, Speedway IN 46224. 317-293-3220/ Fax: 329-7644. M,V,DC,D,AE. I-465 (Exit 16A) to Speedway, rt at 1st light, then rt on Debonair. Cable TV, pool, n/s rms, t pkng. Free local calls. $28-30/S; $34-36/D; $6/ex prsn. Higher spec event rates. Disc.

Sullivan

Days Inn Sullivan/ Hwy 41 & 154, Sullivan IN 47882. 812-268-6391/ Fax: 268-4471. V,M,AE,D,DC. 23 mi S of I-70 on S 41. Nrby rstrnt, cable TV, tt/dd phone, fax, copier, nwspr, laundry, refrig, microwave, cot, crib, t/b pkng, b/f. Free local calls, cont brfst. AAA. $39/S; $45/D; $6/ex prsn. Disc: Senior, TA, govt, trkr, milt. *Guaranteed rates.*

Terre Haute

Mid Town Motel/ 400 S 3rd St, Terre Haute IN 47807. 812-232-0383. V, M, AE,D,DC,CB. I-70 (Exit 7) to US 41, 63, 150, N 2 1/2 mi. Nrby rstrnt/ lounge, n/s rms, cable TV, tt/dd phones, copier, refrig, cot, crib, eff, conn rms. Free local calls, coffee, tea, cocoa. AAA. $30-35/S; $33-40/D; $3/ex prsn. 5/24-6/2, 8/2-8/4, 10/12-10/20: $35-45/S; $45-55/D; $5/ex prsn. Disc: Senior, bsns, l/s, family, AAA. *Guaranteed rates.*

Motel 6/ 1 W Honey Creek Dr, Terre Haute IN 47802. 812-238-1586/ Fax: 238-1424. AE,DC,D,M,V. I-70 to US 41, S to Honeycreek shopping center, rt thru pkng lot. Cable TV, n/s rms, t pkng, nrby rstrnt. Free local calls. $25-29/S; $31-35/D; $6/ex prsn. Disc.

Super 8 Motel/ 3089 S 1st St, Terre Haute IN 47802. 812-232-4890/ Fax: 232-4499. AE,M,V,DC,CB,D. I-70 (Exit 7) to US 150 & 41, N to 2nd light, lt 1 blk. B/f, n/s rms, t/b/rv pkng, copier, elevator, cable TV, cot. Free crib. $37/S; $45-51/D; $5/ex prsn. Higher spec event rates. Discs.

Vincennes

Super 8 Motel/ 609 Shirlee St, Vincennes IN 47591. 812-882-5101. V,M,D, AE,DC,CB. US 41 at Hart St. B/f, n/s rms, pool, t/b/rv pkng, outlets, cont brfst, cable TV, suites, cot, crib. Free local calls. Pride Award. $39/S; $43-45/D; $4/ex prsn. Higher spec event rates. Discs.

Iowa

Algona

Burr Oak Motel/ Box 616, Algona IA 50511. 515-295-7213/ Fax: 295-2979. V, M,AE,D,CB,DC. Hwy 169 S. Rstrnt/ lounge, cable TV, dd phone, arpt trans, outlets, cot, crib, n/s rms, b/f. IMA. $29-32/S; $32-39/D; $3/ex prsn. Disc: AAA, senior, AARP, IMA.

Ames

Super 8 Motel/ 1418 S Dayton Rd, Ames IA 50010. 515-232-6510/ Fax: 232-3922. AE,M,V,DC,CB,D. I-35 (Exit 111B) to US 30, W to Dayton Rd, turn N to mtl. B/f, n/s rms, nrby rstrnt, t/b/rv pkng, outlets, cont brfst, cable TV, suites, cot, crib. Free local calls. No pets. $39/S; $43-47/D; $6/ex prsn. Discs.

Anamosa

Super 8 Motel/ 100 Grant Wood Dr, Anamosa IA 52205. 319-462-3888. V, M,AE,D,DC,CB. Jct Hwys 151 & SR 64. B/f, n/s rms, sauna, b/t pkng, outlets, cont brfst, nrby rstrnt/ lounge, copier, cable TV, mtg rm, cot, crib. Free local calls. No pets. Pride Award. $37/S; $41-46/D; $4/ex prsn. Higher spec event rates. Discs.

Atlantic

Econo Lodge/ RR 3, Box 199, Atlantic IA 50022. 712-243-4067. V,M,D,AE. I-80 (Exit 60) to US 71, S 1/2 mi. Nrby rstrnt, pool, mtg rm, fax, cable TV, t pkng, outlets, n/s rms. AAA. $35-40/S; $40-49/D; $2/ex prsn. Discs.

Burlington

Arrowhead Motel/ 2520 Mt Pleasant St, Burlington IA 52601. 319-752-6353. V, M,AE,D,DC,CB. Jct Hwys 34 & 61, N 3 blks to Mt Pleasant St, 3 blks E. N/s rms, cable TV, TDD, tt/dd phone, fax,

IOWA

laundry, refrig, cot, crib, outlets, t/b/rv pkng, eff, b/f. Free coffee, tea, cocoa. No pets. IMA. $32-38/S; $36-46/D; $4/ex prsn. 6/15-6/17, 8/31-9/3, 9/7-9/9: $40-45/S; $45-55/D; $5/ex prsn. Disc: L/s, family. *Guaranteed rates.*

Comfort Inn/ 3051 Kirkwood, Burlington IA 52601. 319-753-0000. V,M,AE,DC. US 34 to US 61, N to mtl. Nrby rstrnt, pool, fax, b/f, cable TV, t pkng, outlets, n/s rms. Free cont brfst. AAA. $40-50/S; $45-59/D; $5/ex prsn. 5/1-5/24, 10/1-10/31: $42-55/S; $50-65/D. 5/25-9/30: $45-55/S; $52-75/D. Discs.

Friendship Inn/ 2731 Mt Pleasant St, Burlington IA 52601. 319-754-7571. AE,DC,M,V. US 34 to US 61, N to Mt Pleasant, rt to mtl. Nrby rstrnt, fax, b/f, cable TV, t pkng, outlets, n/s rms. $28-40/S; $35-55/D; $5/ex prsn. 5/25-9/30: $35-55/S; $40-65/D. 10/1-10/31: $32-50/S; $38-55/D. Discs.

Super 8 Motel/ 3001 Kirkwood, Burlington IA 52601. 319-752-9806. AE,M,V,DC,CB,D. Jct of US 34 & 61; NE corner. B/f, n/s rms, t/b/rv pkng, outlets, toast bar, copier, cable TV, cot, crib. Free local calls. No pets. Pride Award. $40/S; $47-49/D; $3/ex prsn. Higher spec event rates. Discs.

Cedar Falls (Waterloo area)

Marquis Inn/ 4711 University Av, Cedar Falls IA 50613. 319-277-1412/ Fax: 268-1827/ 800-962-7784. V,M,AE,D, DC,CB. I-20, exit 58 N to University Av E. Nrby rstrnt/ lounge, sauna, whrlpool, n/s rms, cable TV, video games, arpt trans, tt phone, fax, nwspr, refrig, microwave, cot, crib, outlets. Free local calls. AAA. $29/S; $34-35/D; $5/ex prsn. Disc: Senior, TA, govt, milt, l/s.

Econo Lodge/ 4117 University Av, Cedar Falls IA 50613. 319-277-6931. V,M,AE,D. On University Av, N of US 20 & W of US 63. Rstrnt, pool, cable TV, n/s rms. Free local calls, cont brfst. $30-51/S; $35-61/D; $4/ex prsn. Discs.

Cedar Rapids

Cedar Rapids Village Inn/ 100 "F" Av NW, Cedar Rapids IA 52405. 319-366-5323/ 800-858-5511. V,M,AE,D,DC. I-380, Exit 19A from S or 20B from N. Rstrnt/ lounge, n/s rms, exerc equip, cable TV, arpt trans, tt/dd phone, mtg rm, fax, copier, nwspr, laundry, refrig, elevator, microwave, cot, crib, t/b pkng, conn rms. Free local calls, coffee. AAA. $40-46/S; $42-48/D; $5/ex prsn. Disc: Senior, bsns, TA, govt, l/s, milt.

Econo Lodge/ 622 33rd Av SW, Cedar Rapids IA 52404. 319-363-8888. V,M,AE,DC. I-380 to 33rd Av S, W 2 blks to mtl. Nrby rstrnt, indr pool, whrlpool, cable TV, n/s rms. Free cont brfst. $34-48/S; $43-90/D; $5/ex prsn. Discs.

Exel Inn/ 616 33rd Av SW, Cedar Rapids IA 52404. 319-366-2475/ Fax: 366-5712. M,AE,V,D,DC,CB. I-380 to 33rd Av, then W 2 blks. Nrby rstrnt, cable TV, game rm, laundry, fax, microfridge, n/s rms. Free cont brfst. AAA. $29-37/S; $37-46/D. Higher spec event/ wknd rates. Discs.

Centerville

Super 8 Motel/ 1021 N 18th, Centerville IA 52544. 515-856-8888. V,M,DC,AE,CB,D. On Hwy 5 (N 18th), 3/4 mi N of jct Hwys 2 & 5. B/f, n/s rms, whrlpool, sauna, t/b/rv pkng, outlets, cont brfst, cable TV, suites, mtg rm, cot, crib. Free local calls. No pets. Pride Award. $37/S; $41-46/D; $4/ex prsn. Higher spec event rates. Discs.

Chariton

Royal Rest Motel/ Box 349, Chariton IA 50049. 515-774-5961/ Fax: Ext 43. V, M,AE,D. On Hwy 34 E, 1/2 mi from Jct Hwy 14. Nrby rstrnt/ lounge, n/s rms, cable TV, arpt trans, tt/dd phone, mtg rm, fax, copier, cot, crib, outlets, t/b/rv pkng. Free local calls, coffee, tea, cocoa. No smoking. Mobil/ IMA. $28-32/S; $32-38/D; $7/ex prsn. 8/1-8/30: $38/S; $45/D. Disc: Senior, govt, l/s, family, trkr. *Guaranteed rates.*

Charles City

Hartwood Inn/ 1312 Gilbert St, Charles City IA 50616. 515-228-4352/ Fax: 228-2672/ 800-972-2335. V,M,AE,D,DC,CB. On Hwy 18 W & 218 N, 6 blks W of Main St. Pool, n/s rms, cable TV, tt/dd phone, fax, laundry, refrig, microwave, cot, crib, outlets, b/f. Free coffee. AAA/ Mobil. $33-44/S; $45-48/D; $5/ex prsn. Disc: Senior, bsns, family.

Cherokee
Super 8 Motel/ 1400 N Second St, Cherokee IA 51012. 712-225-4278/ Fax: 225-4678. AE,DC,M,V,CB,D. Jct US 59 & SR 3. B/f, n/s rms, sauna, t/b/rv pkng, outlets, copier, cable TV, exerc equip, crib. Free local calls. Pride Award. $37/S; $43-47/D; $3/ex prsn. Higher spec event rates. Discs.

Clear Lake
Super 8 Motel/ Box 340, Clear Lake IA 50428. 515-357-7521/ Fax: 357-5999. AE,M,V,DC,CB,D. I-35, Exit 193. B/f, n/s rms, b/t pkng, outlets, toast bar, satellite TV, crib. Free local calls. Pride Award. $35/S; $39-40/D; $2/ex prsn. Higher spec event awards. Discs.

Clinton
Super 8 Motel/ 1711 Lincoln Way, Clinton IA 52732. 319-242-8870. AE,M,V,DC,CB,D. On US 30/67 (Lincoln Way). B/f, n/s rms, t/b/rv pkng, outlets, toast bar, copier, cable TV, cot, crib. Free local calls. No pets. Pride Award. $40/S; $47-49/D; $3/ex prsn. Higher spec event rates. Discs.

Coralville (Iowa City area)
Econo Lodge/ 815 First Av, Coralville IA 52241. 319-354-6000. V,M,D,AE,DC. I-80, Exit 242. Nrby rstrnt, pool, fax, b/f, cable TV, t pkng, copier, n/s rms. $28-32/S; $36-41/D; $5/ex prsn. 5/1-11/30: $30-35/S; $41-46/D. Discs.

Motel 6/ 810 1st Av, Coralville IA 52241. 319-354-0030/ Fax: 338-8751. M,V,DC,D,AE. I-80 (Exit 242) at Coralville exit, go S on 1st Av 2 blks. Cable TV, pool, n/s rms. Free local calls. $28-30/S; $34-36/D; $6/ex prsn. Disc.

Council Bluffs
Motel 6/ 3032 S Expressway, Council Bluffs IA 51501. 712-366-2405/ Fax: 366-8105. AE,DC,D,M,V. I-80/ I-29 (Exit 3) to S Expwy, S to 32nd Av, rt to Frontage Rd. Nrby rstrnt, cable TV, indr pool, n/s rms, t pkng. Free local calls. $30-32/S; $34-38/D; $4-6/ex prsn. Disc.

Motel 6/ 1846 N 16th St, Council Bluffs IA 51501. 712-328-8300/ Fax: 328-1854. M,V,AE,D,DC. I-29 (Sbnd, Exit 56; Nbnd, Exit 55) at Council Bluff/ N 25th St. Cable TV, n/s rms. Free local calls. $26-28/S; $32-34/D; $6/ex prsn. Disc.

Creston
Super 8 Motel/ 804 W Taylor, Creston IA 50801. 515-782-6541. AE,M,V,DC, CB,D. Jct US 34 & SR 25. B/f, n/s rms, t/b/rv pkng, outlets, toast bar, trans, cable TV, cot, crib. Free local calls. No pets. $39/S; $46-48/D; $3/ex prsn. Higher spec event rates. Discs.

Davenport
Comfort Inn/ 7222 Northwest Blvd, Davenport IA 52806. 319-391-8222. V,M,AE,DC. I-80 (Exit 292) to SR 130 (Northwest Blvd), SE to mtl. Rstrnt/ lounge, fax, b/f, cable TV, t pkng, outlets, exerc equip, n/s rms. Free cont brfst. Hospitality Award. AAA. $41-125/S; $45-125/D; $4/ex prsn. 5/1-10/31: $43-125/S; $47-125/D. Discs.

Motel 6/ 6111 N Brady St, Davenport IA 52806. 319-391-8997/ Fax: 386-3167. M,V,DC,D,AE. I-80 (Exit 295A) to N Brady St, S 1/2 mi. Cable TV, laundry, pool, n/s rms, t pkng. Free local calls. $29-32/S; $35-38/D; $6/ex prsn. Disc.

Decorah
Super 8 Motel/ Box 465, Decorah IA 52101. 319-382-8771. AE,M,V,DC,CB,D. Hwy 9, 1 1/2 mi E of jct US 52 & SR 9. B/f, n/s rms, nrby rstrnt, whrlpool, laundry, t/b/rv pkng, outlets, toast bar, cable TV, mtg rm, cot, crib. Pride Award. $35-36/S; $44-45/D; $4/ex prsn. Higher spec event rates. Discs.

Des Moines
Budget Host Inn/ 7625 Hickman Rd, Des Moines IA 50322. 515-276-5401. V,AE,CB,DC,D,M. I-80/ I-35 (Exit 125) to Hickman Rd, E 2 mi. Cable TV, dd phone, n/s rms, cot, crib, t pkng, outlets. $35-42/S; $42-60/D; $5/ex prsn. Spec events: $40-60. Discs.

Econo Lodge/ 5626 Douglas Av, Des Moines IA 50310. 515-278-1601. V, M, AE,D. I-80 W & I-35 S (Exit 131) to Merle Hay Rd, S 1 1/2 mi, E on Douglas. Nrby rstrnt, cable TV, cable TV, t pkng. Free cont brfst. No pets. $30-45/S; $35-50/D; $4/ex prsn. Discs.

Motel 6/ 4940 NE 14th St, Box 3002,

IOWA

Des Moines IA 50316. 515-266-5456/ Fax: 266-6954. M,V,AE,D,DC. I-80/35 (Exit 136) at US 69. N of frwy on frontage rd. Nrby rstrnt, cable TV, pool, n/s rms. Free local calls. $30-34/S; $36-40/D; $6/ex prsn. Disc.

Motel 6/ 4817 Fleur Dr, Des Moines IA 50321. 515-287-6364/ Fax: 287-3909. M,V,DC,D,AE. I-35 (Exit 68) at Des Moines Arpt. E on Hwy 5 to Fleur Dr, lt 1 1/2 mi. Cable TV, n/s rms. Free local calls. $28-32/S; $34-38/D; $6/ex prsn. Disc.

Rodeway Inn/ 4995 N W Merle Hay Rd, Des Moines IA 50322. 515-278-2381/ Fax: 278-9760. V,M,AE,D. Just off I-80/I-35 (Exit 131) & Merle Hay Rd, S 1 blk. N side of Des Moines. Rstrnt, indr pool, b/f, whrlpool, cable TV, outlets, suites, laundry, mtg rm. Free cont brfst. No pets. $29-57/S; $35-63/D; $6/ex prsn. 2/21-4/30: $29-63/S; $35-69/D. 5/1-9/3: $29-85/S; $35-91/D. Discs.

Also see Urbandale.

Dubuque

Motel 6/ 2670 Dodge St, Dubuque IA 52001. 319-556-0880/ Fax: 582-0190. AE,DC,D,M,V. On US 20 W (Dodge St) W of US 52/61. Cable TV, n/s rms, nrby rstrnt, t pkng. Free local calls. $26-28/S; $32-34/D; $6/ex prsn. Disc.

Super 8 Motel/ 2730 Dodge St, Dubuque IA 52003. 319-582-8898. AE,M,V, DC,CB,D. Hwy 20 W, cntr of tn. B/f, n/s rms, t/b/rv pkng, cont brfst, cable TV, cot. Free local calls. No pets. Pride Award. $37-40/S; $42-49/D; $2/ex prsn. Higher spec event rates. Discs.

Dyersville

Super 8 Motel/ 925 15th Av SE, Dyersville IA 52040. 319-875-8885. V, M,DC,AE,CB,D. Hwy 20 to Hwy 136, N 1/2 blk to 15th, E 1/2 blk. B/f, n/s rms, whrlpool, sauna, outlets, cont brfst, t/b/rv pkng, cable TV, suites, mtg rm, cot, crib. Free local calls. No pets. Pride Award. $37/S; $41-46/D; $4/ex prsn. Higher spec event rates. Discs.

Emmetsburg

Suburban Motel/ 3536 450th Av, Emmetsburg IA 50536. 712-852-2626. V,M,AE,D. On Hwy 4 & 18, W of Emmetsburg. Nrby rstrnt/ lounge, pool, n/s rms, cable TV, tt phone, copier, microwave, cot, crib, outlets, t/b/ pkng, conn rms, b/f. Free local calls, coffee, popcorn. No pets. AAA/ Mobil/ IMA. $27-32/S; $37-41/D; $3/ex prsn. 9/1-9/20: $30-35/S; $40-45/D. Disc: IMA. *Guaranteed rates.*

Fort Dodge

Budget Host Inn/ 116 Kenyon Rd, Ft Dodge IA 50501. 515-955-8501/ Fax: 955-4968. AE,CB,DC,D,M,V. Jct Hwys 169 & Old 20. Cable TV, dd phone, n/s rms, mtg rms, rstrnt/ lounge, indr pool, whrlpool, game rm, arpt trans, t pkng, outlets, cot. Free crib. AAA. $36/S; $43/D; $5/ex prsn.

Homestead

Die Heimat Country Inn/ Amana Colonies, Homestead IA 52236. 319-622-3937. V,M,D. I-80, Exit 225 to Amana Colonies. Free full brfst. No pets. No smoking. AAA/ Mobil. $44/S or D; $5/ex prsn. Wknds: $49/S or D.

Ida Grove

Delux Motel/ 5981 Hwy 175, Ida Grove IA 51445. 712-364-3317/ Fax: 364-4076/ 800-342-0336. V,M,AE,D. Jct Hwys 59 & 175. Nrby rstrnt/ lounge, n/s rms, cable TV, tt/dd phone, fax, nwspr, microwave, crib, outlets, t pkng, conn rms, b/f. Free local calls, coffee. AAA. $30-43/S; $35-45/D; $5/ex prsn. Disc: Senior, AAA. *Guaranteed rates.*

Iowa City

See Coralville.

Iowa Falls

Super 8 Motel/ 839 S Oak, Iowa Falls IA 50126. 515-648-4618/ Fax: 649-4610. V,M,AE,D,DC,CB. 1 mi S of jct Washington Av with US 65/20. B/f, n/s rms, sauna, outlets, cont brfst, b/t pkng, copier, cable TV, mtg rm, cot, crib. Free local calls. No pets. Pride Award. $37/S; $41-46/D; $4/ex prsn. Higher spec event rates. Discs.

Kalona

Pull'r Inn Motel/ Box 200, Kalona IA 52247. 319-656-3611. V,M,AE. Jct Hwys 1 & 22. Nrby rstrnt, n/s rms, cable TV, TDD, tt/dd phone, crib, t/b pkng. Free local calls, coffee. No pets. AAA. $32/S; $39/D; $7/ex prsn. Disc: Family. *Guaranteed rates.*

Keokuk
Super 8 Motel/ 3511 Main St, Keokuk IA 52632. 319-524-3888. AE,M,V,DC,CB,D. US 218 at Plank Rd & Carbide Ln. B/f, n/s rms, nrby rstrnt, outlets, t/b/rv pkng, copier, cable TV, mtg rm, cot, crib. Free local calls. No pets. Pride Award. $40/S; $47-49/D; $3/ex prsn. Higher spec event rates. Discs.

Knoxville
Super 8 Motel/ 2205 N Lincoln, Knoxville IA 50138. 515-828-8808. AE,M,V,DC,CB,D. I mi N of Bsns jct Hwy 5, 92 & 14. B/f, n/s rms, whrlpool, laundry, outlets, t/b/rv pkng, toast bar, copier, cable TV, n/s rms, mtg rm, exerc equip, cot, crib. Free local calls. No pets. Pride Award. $36/S; $44-45/D; $4/ex prsn. Higher spec event rates. Discs.

Maquoketa
Super 8 Motel/ 10021 W Platt St, Maquoketa IA 52060. 319-652-6888. V,M,DC,AE,CB,D. On SE corner of US 61 & SR 64. B/f, n/s rms, laundry, t/b/rv pkng, cable TV, mtg rm, cot, crib. Free local calls. No pets. Pride Award. $38/S; $43-46/D; $2/ex prsn. Higher spec event rates. Discs.

Marshalltown
Comfort Inn/ 2613 S Center St, Marshalltown IA 50158. 515-752-6000. V,M,D,AE. US 30 to SR 14, N 1 mi. Nrby rstrnt, indr pool, mtg rm, fax, b/f, whrlpool, cable TV, t pkng, outlets, n/s rms. Free cont brfst. AAA. $42-54/S; $47-59/D; $5/ex prsn. Discs.

Mount Pleasant
Super 8 Motel/ US 218 N, Mount Pleasant IA 52641. 319-385-8888. AE,M,V,DC,CB,D. 1 mi N of jct Hwys 34 & 218. B/f, n/s rms, t/b/rv pkng, outlets, copier, cable TV, mtg rm, cot, crib. Free local calls. No pets. Pride Award. $40/S; $47-49/D; $3/ex prsn. Higher spec event rates. Discs.

New Hampton
Mohawk Motel/ 104 S Linn Av, New Hampton IA 50659. 515-394-3081/ Fax: 394-4808. V,M,AE,D,DC,CB. 1 blk S of Main St (Hwy 24), on US 63 & 18. Nrby rstrnt/ lounge, n/s rms, cable TV, playgrnd, tt/dd phones, fax, copier, nwspr, cot, crib, conn rms. Free local calls, coffee. No pets. IMA. $30-33/S; $38-42/D; $4/ex prsn. Disc: Senior, bsns, TA, govt, l/s, family, trkr, milt. *Guaranteed rates.*

Orange City
Dutch Colony Inn/ 706 8th St SE, Box 192, Orange City IA 51041. 712-737-3490/ Fax: 737-4181. V,M,AE,D,DC. Hwy 60 & 10 jct, 2 mi W. Nrby rstrnt, satellite TV, tt/dd phones, mtg rm, fax, refrig, microwave, cot, crib, outlets, conn rms, b/f. Free coffee. No pets, smoking. AAA. $36/S; $40/D; $2/ex prsn. 2nd, 3rd wknd in May: $41/S; $45/D; $3/ex prsn. *Guaranteed rates.*

Oskaloosa
Friendship Inn/ 1315 "A" Av E, Oskaloosa IA 52577. 515-673-8351. V,M,AE,D. SR 92 & US 63 E. Nrby rstrnt, mtg rm, cable TV, coffee, outlets, trans, n/s rms. $35-50/S; $45-60; $3/ex prsn. Discs.

Super 8 Motel/ 306 S 17th St, Oskaloosa IA 52577. 515-673-8481.AE,M,V,DC,CB,D. Jct US 63 & Hwy 92, turn S on 63 to mtl. B/f, n/s rms, t/b/rv pkng, outlets, toast bar, copier, cable TV, cot, crib. Free local calls. No pets. Pride Award. $40/S; $47-49/D; $3/ex prsn. Higher spec event rates. Discs.

Traveler Budget Inn/ 1210 A Av E, Oskaloosa IA 52577. 515-673-8333/ Fax: 673-5483. V,M,AE,D,CB,DC. US 63 & SR 92. Cable TV, n/s rms, dd phone, outlets, in-rm coffee, refrig, t pkng, cot, crib, conn rms. AAA/ IMA. $28/S; $32-34/D; $4/ex prsn. Higher spec event rates. Disc: TA.

Ottumwa
Super 8 Motel/ 2823 N Court, Ottumwa IA 52501. 515-684-5055/ Fax: 682-6622. AE,M,V,DC,CB,D. 3 mi N of jct of Hwy 34 & 63, on 63. B/f, n/s rms, indr pool, whrlpool, sauna, laundry, outlets, t/b/rv pkng, toast/ cereal bar, cable TV, mtg rm, cot, crib. Free local calls. No pets. Pride Award. $41/S; $47-52/D. Higher spec event rate. Discs.

IOWA

Perry
Super 8 Motel/ 701 26th St, Perry IA 50220. 515-465-5653. V,M,DC,AE,CB, D. 1 mi E of jct Hwys 141 & 144, at 26th St & Hwy 141. B/f, n/s rms, whrlpool, sauna, outlets, t/b/rv pkng, cont brfst, cable TV, suites, mtg rm, cot, crib. Free local calls. No pets. Pride Award. $37/S; $41-46/D; $4/ex prsn. Higher spec event rates. Discs.

Sergeant Bluff (Sioux City area)
Motel 6/ 6166 Harbor Dr, c/o Gen Del, Sergeant Bluff IA 51054. 712-277-3131/ Fax: 255-4424. M,V,DC,D,AE. I-29 (Exit 141) to Sergeant Bluff/ Arpt exit, W on Airport Rd to Harbor Dr, turn lt. Cable TV, pool, n/s rms, t pkng. Free local calls. $27-29/S; $33-35/D; $6/ex prsn. Disc.

Sibley
Super 8 Motel/ 1108 2nd Av, Sibley IA 51249. 712-754-3603/ Fax: 754-3479. AE,DC,M,V,CB,D. Hwy 60 S (2nd Av). B/f, n/s rms, laundry, t/b/rv pkng, outlets, toast bar, copier, cable TV, suites, mtg rm, cot. Free local calls, crib. Pride Award. $37/S; $43-46/D; $4/ex prsn. Higher spec event rates. Discs.

Sioux Center
Econo Lodge/ 86 - 9th St Cir NE, Sioux Center IA 51250. 712-722-4000. AE,DC,M,V. N US 75. Nrby rstrnt, whrlpool, cable TV, t pkng, n/s rms. Free cont brfst. $35-37/S; $37-40/D; $2/ex prsn. Discs.

Sioux City
Rodeway Inn/ 4230 S Lakeport St, Sioux City IA 51106. 712-274-1400. V, M,AE,DC. I-29 (Exit 144A) to US 20, E 2 1/2 mi to Lakeport Rd, 1 blk to mtl. Nrby rstrnt, fax, b/f, whrlpool, cable TV, exerc equip, n/s rms. Free cont brfst. No pets. AAA. $42-63/S; $47-68/D; $4-5/ex prsn. 5/1-6/3: $39-60/S; $44-65/D. Discs.

See Sergeant Bluff, North Sioux City, SD.

Spencer
Super 8 Motel/ 209 11th St SW, Spencer IA 51301. 712-262-8500/ Fax: Ext 125. AE,M,V,DC,CB,D. From jct US 18 and US 71, W on 18/71 to 1st Av SW, turn N to 11 St SW. B/f, n/s rms, t/b/rv pkng, outlets, cable TV, cot, crib. No pets. Pride Award. $35/S; $41-45/D; $3/ex prsn. Discs.

Storm Lake
Crossroads Motel/ 1323 Hwy 3, Storm Lake IA 50588. 712-732-1456/ Fax: 732-1198/ 800-383-1456. V,M,AE,D. Jct Hwy 3 & 71, 9 mi N of Storm Lake. Nrby rstrnt, n/s rms, satellite TV, tt phone, fax, copier, laundry, cot, crib, outlets, t/b/rv pkng, conn rms. Free local calls. $24/S; $29-31/D; $4/ex prsn. Disc: L/s. *Guaranteed rates.*

Story City
Viking Motor Inn/ 1520 Broad St, Box 198, Story City IA 50248. 515-733-4306/ 800-233-4306. V,M,AE,D. I-35, Exit 124, 2 blks W. Pool, sauna, n/s rms, cable TV, playgrnd, tt phone, copier, nwspr, refrig, microwave, cot, crib, outlets, t/b pkng, conn rms, b/f. Free local calls, laundry, cont brfst, coffee, tea, cocoa. AAA. $37-40/S; $42-48/D; $3/ex prsn. Higher spec event/ holiday/ wknd rates. Disc: Senior, bsns, govt, l/s, trkr, family, milt.

Toledo
Super 8 Motel/ Hwy 30 W, Toledo IA 52342. 515-484-5888. V,M,AE,D,DC, CB. On Hwy 30, 1 blk W of jct Hwys 63 & 30. B/f, n/s rms, whrlpool, game rm, laundry, t/b/rv pkng, outlets, toast bar, copier, satellite TV, mtg rm, cot, crib. Free local calls. Pride Award. $36/S; $41-45/D; $4/ex prsn. Higher spec event rates. Discs.

Urbandale (Des Moines area)
Econo Lodge/ 11000 Douglas Av, Urbandale IA 50322. 515-278-4601. V,M,AE,DC. I-80/I-35 (Exit 126) to Douglas Av, E 1/4 mi. Nrby rstrnt/ lounge, indr pool, mtg rm, fax, b/f, cable TV, t pkng, outlets, game rm, laundry, n/s rms. Free cont brfst. No pets. AAA. $30-45/S; $35-55/D; $5/ex prsn. 2/21-2/29: $30-60/S; $35-60/D. 5/1-9/4: $30-50/S; $35-60/D. Discs.

Walnut
Super 8 Motel/ 33647 Antique City Dr, Walnut IA 51577. 712-784-2221/ Fax: 784-3961. V,M,AE,D,DC,CB. I-80, Exit

46, N to mtl. B/f, n/s rms, outlets, t/b/rv pkng, copier, cable TV, mtg rm, cot, crib. Free local calls. Pride Award. $36/S; $44-49/D; $1/ex prsn. Disc.

Waterloo

See Cedar Falls.

Wapello

Roy-El Motel/ 405 Hwy 61 S, Wapello IA 52653. 319-523-2111/ Fax: 523-4510. V,M,AE,D. On Hwy 61. Cable TV, dd phone, arpt trans, outlets, playgrnd, t pkng, mtg rm, nrby rstrnt, cot, crib, n/s rms. Free coffee. IMA. $28/S; $34-37/D. Higher spec event rates.

Waterloo

Howard Johnson Lodge/ 300 W Mullan Av, Waterloo IA 50701. 319-234-7791/ Fax: 234-1727. M,DC,D,V,AE,CB. US 63 to First St exit, lt 1 blk on Jefferson. N/s rms, lounge, pool, t pkng, valet serv, mtg rm. Free cont brfst. $29-49/S; $34-51/D. Discs.

Waverly

Super 8 Motel/ 301 13th Av, Waverly IA 50677. 319-352-0888. V,M,DC,AE,CB, D. SR 3 to US 218, S .6 mi to 13th Av. B/f, n/s rms, whrlpool, sauna, b/t pkng, outlets, cont brfst, cable TV, suites, mtg rm, cot, crib. Free local calls. No pets. Pride Award. $37/S; $41-46/D; $4/ex prsn. Higher spec event rates. Discs.

West Liberty

Econo Lodge/ 1943 Garfield Av, Box 200, W Liberty IA 52776. 319-627-2171. V,M,AE,DC. I-80, Exit 259, to S side of interchange. Rstrnt, pool, cable TV, t pkng, outlets. $33-40/S; $36-45/D; $2/ex prsn. Discs.

Williamsburg

Crest Motel/ 340 W Evans, Williamsburg IA 52361. 319-668-1522/ Fax: 668-1872. V,M,AE,D. I-80, Exit 220, across from Tanger Outlet Mall. N/s rms, satellite TV, playgrnd, dd phone, fax, copier, nwspr, microwave, cot, crib, outlets, t/b/rv pkng, conn rms, b/f. Free local calls, coffee. AAA/ Mobil. $33/S; $38-43/D; $4/ex prsn. 5/1-11/14: $38/S; $43-48/D; $4/ex prsn. *Guaranteed rates.*

Ramada Limited/ Box 749, Williamsburg IA 52361. 319-668-1000. M,DC,D,V,AE,CB. I-80 at SR 149. 7 mi from Amana Colonies. B/f, n/s rms, nrby rstrnt, b/t pkng. Free local calls. $37-50/S; $43-66/D; $7/ex prsn. Discs.

Kansas

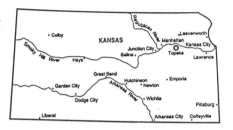

Abilene

Super 8 Motel/ 2207 N Buckeye Av, Abilene KS 67410. 913-263-4545/ Fax: 263-7448. AE,M,V,DC,CB,D. I-70 (Exit 275) at N Buckeye Av. B/f, n/s rms, toast bar, t/b/rv pkng, copier, cable TV, suites, cot. Free local calls, crib. Pride Award. $36/S; $41-44/D; $4/ex prsn. Discs.

Baxter Springs

Baxter Inn 4 Less/ 2451 Military Av, Baxter Springs KS 66713. 316-856-2106. V,M,AE. I-44, lt at 4 way stop on 166, lt again on Military, 12 blks. Nrby rstrnt, n/s rms, cable TV, fax, copier, cot, crib, outlets, t pkng. Free local calls, coffee. AAA. $32/S; $39/D; $4/ex prsn. Disc: Senior, bsns, govt, trkr, milt.

Colby

Budget Host Inn/ 1745 W 4th St, Colby KS 67701. 913-462-3338/ Fax: 462-6127. AE,DC,M,V,CB,D. 2 mi N & 6 blks W of I-70, Exit 53 on W US 24. Cable TV, dd phone, in-rm coffee, refrig, n/s rms, conn rms, pool, nrby rstrnt, arpt trans, t pkng, outlets, cot. Free crib. AAA/ Mobil. Winter: $26-36/S; $29-39/D; $4/ex prsn. Summer: $33-43/S; $36-46/D. Discs.

Econo Lodge/ 1985 S Range, Colby KS 67701. 913-462-8201. V,M,AE,D. I-70 at SR 25. Nrby rstrnt, b/f, cable TV, n/s rms. Free cont brfst. AAA. $33-40/S; $36-44/D; $3/ex prsn. 5/1-10/31: $40-50/S; $45-55/D. Discs.

KANSAS

Dodge City

Econo Lodge/ 1610 W Wyatt Earp Blvd, Box 968, Dodge City KS 67801. 316-225-0231. V,M,AE,D. On US 50, 12 blks W of Boot Hill. Rstrnt, indr pool, mtg rm, fax, b/f, sauna, whrlpool, cable TV, t pkng, laundry, outlets, n/s rms. Free arpt trans. $39-57/S; $47-57/D; $3/ex prsn. 7/29-8/7: $57-67/S; $57-72/D. Discs.

Emporia

Budget Host Inn/ 1830 E Hwy 50, Emporia KS 66801. 316-343-6922. AE,M,V,D. I-35, Exit 133. Cable TV, dd phone, family rms, n/s rms, playgrnd, picnic area, arpt trans, t pkng, outlets, cot, crib. AAA. $25-27/S; $30-34/D; $4/ex prsn. Discs.

Comfort Inn/ 2511 W 18th, Emporia KS 66801. 316-343-7750. V,M,AE,DC. I-35 (Exit 128) to Industrial St, S to 18th Av, E 1 blk. Nrby rstrnt, pool, mtg rm, fax, cable TV, t pkng, n/s rms. Free cont brfst, local calls. AAA $34-44/S; $40-48/D; $5/ex prsn. Discs.

Motel 6/ 2630 W 18th Av, Emporia KS 66801. 316-343-1240/ Fax: 343-1923. V,M,D,AE,DC. I-35 (Exit 128) to Industrial Rd, S to 18th Av, turn lt. Cable TV, n/s rms, t pkng, nrby rstrnt. Free local calls. $27-29/S; $33-35/D; $6/ex prsn. Disc.

Quality Inn/ 3021 W US 50, Emporia KS 66801. 316-342-3770. V,M,D,AE. KS Trnpk (Exit 127) to US 50, E 4 blks. Rstrnt, indr pool, mtg rm, fax, whrlpool, cable TV, t pkng, outlets, exerc equip, copier, n/s rm. Free local calls. $39-54/S; $46-57/D; $7/ex prsn. Discs.

Super 8 Motel/ 2913 W Hwy 50, Emporia KS 66801. 316-342-7567/ Fax: 343-7374. AE,M,V,DC,CB,D. I-35 (Exit 128) to Industrial St, S to US 50, then rt 1 blk. B/f, n/s rms, cable TV, fax, copier, cot, crib. Free local calls. Prime Award. $37/S; $42-48/D; $5/ex prsn. Higher spec event rates. Discs.

Garden City

Budget Host Village Inn/ 123 Honey Bee Ct, Garden City KS 67846. 316-275-0677. AE,M,V,D,CB,DC. Jct Hwy 50 & 83; E side. Cable TV, dd phone, adj rstrnt/ lounge, pool, arpt trans, baby sitters, t pkng, cot, crib. AAA. $33-37/S; $38-43/D; $3/ex prsn. Discs.

National 9 Inn/ 1502 E Fulton Av, Garden City KS 67846. 316-276-2394/ 800-333-2387. V,M,AE,DC. Hwy 50 E Bsns Rte. Pool, dd phone, cable TV, nrby rstrnt, n/s rms, refrig, suites. AAA. $34/S; $38-40/D; $3/ex prsn. $45/suites.

Goodland

Motel 6/ 2420 Commerce Rd, Goodland KS 67735. 913-899-5672/ Fax: 899-2608. M,V,AE,D,DC. I-70 (Exit 17) to SR 27, N 1/2 mi to mtl. Cable TV, laundry, pool, n/s rms, t pkng. Free local calls. $26-27/S; $32-33/D; $6/ex prsn. Disc.

Great Bend

Super 8 Motel/ 3500 10th St, Great Bend KS 67530. 316-793-8486/ Fax: 793-3816. AE,M,V,DC,CB,D. US 56, behind Western Auto Store. B/f, n/s rms, indr pool, whrlpool, laundry, cable TV, copier, cot, crib. Free local calls. Pride Award. $37/S; $42-47/D; $5/ex prsn. Higher spec event rates. Discs.

Hays

Comfort Inn/ 2810 Vine St, Hays KS 67601. 913-628-8008. V,M,D,AE. I-70 (Exit 159) to US 183, S to mtl. Nrby rstrnt, indr pool, fax, b/f, whrlpool, cable TV, n/s rms. Free full brfst. No pets. $43-70/S; $47-80/D; $5/ex prsn. Discs.

Motel 6/ 3404 Vine St, Hays KS 67601. 913-625-4282/ Fax: 625-3430. M,V,AE,D,DC. I-70 (Exit 159) to Vine St, turn S to mtl. Nrby rstrnt, cable TV, pool, t pkng, n/s rms. Free local calls. $30-34/S; $36-40/D; $6/ex prsn. Disc.

Villa Budget Host Inn/ 810 E 8th, Hays KS 67601. 913-625-2563/ Fax: 625-3967. AE,CB,DC,M,V,D,ER. 2 1/2 mi S of I-70 on Hwy 183 S. Cable TV, dd phone, in-rm coffee, nrby rstrnt, suites, family rms, n/s rms, pool, picnic area, arpt trans, cot, crib. AAA/ Mobil. $30-40/S; $34-55/D; $5/ex prsn. Spec events: $55. Discs.

Hutchinson

Quality Inn/ 15 W 4th St, Hutchinson

KANSAS

KS 67501. 316-663-1211/ Fax: 663-6636. V,M,AE,DC. US 50 to SR 96, N to 4th St, E 2 blks to mtl. Rstrnt/ lounge, pool, mtg rm, fax, b/f, cable TV, t pkng, outlets, n/s rms. AAA. $35-50/S; $44-60/D; $4/ex prsn. 3/17-3/23: $48-60/S; $58-60/D. 9/7-9/17: $85-125/S or D. Discs.

Scotsman Inn/ 322 E 4th St, Hutchinson KS 67501. 316-669-8281. V,M, AE, D,DC,CB. E 4th St, W of Hwy 61. Cable TV, dd/tt phone, data port, fax, nrby rstrnt, refrig, laundry. Free coffee, local calls. $23/S; $26-30/D; $3/ex prsn. Discs.

Independence

Super 8 Motel/ 2800 W Main, Independence KS 67301. 316-331-8288. V, M,D,AE,DC,CB. US 75 & Peter Pan Rd. B/f, n/s rms, laundry, b/t pkng, outlets, toast bar, copier, cable TV, pool, suites, cot. Free local calls, crib. No pets. Pride Award. $38/S; $43-45/D; $3/ex prsn. Higher spec event rates. Discs.

Junction City

Comfort Inn/ 1214 S Washington, Junction City KS 66441. 913-238-7887. V, M,D,AE. I-70 (Exit 296) at Washington Av. Nrby rstrnt, indr pool, fax, b/f, cable TV, n/s rms. Free cont brfst. No pets. $43-70/S; $47-80/D; $5/ex prsn. Discs.

Dreamland Motel/ 520 E Flinthill Blvd, Junction City KS 66441. 913-238-1108/ Fax: 762-4042. V,M,AE,D. I-70, Exit 300. Pool, n/s rms, cable TV, dd phone, arpt trans, outlets, b/f, kitchenettes, cot, crib. AAA/ IMA. $24/S; $28-32/D; $3-4/ex prsn. Higher spec event rates. Disc: Comm, family, senior, TA.

Econo Lodge/ 211 W Flinthills Blvd, Junction City KS 66441. 913-238-8181. V,M,AE,D. I-70, Exit 299. Nrby rstrnt, cable TV, t pkng, n/s rms. $30-35/S; $32-40/D; $3/ex prsn. Discs.

Golden Wheat Budget Host Inn/ 820 S Washington, Junction City KS 66441. 913-238-5106. AE,D,M,V. I-70, Exit 296, 3 blks N. Cable TV, dd phone, family rms, t pkng, cot, crib. No pets. AAA/ Mobil. $28-33/S; $35-45/D; $5/ex prsn. Di

Kansas City

See Lansing, Lenexa, Olathe, Overland Park.

Kingman

Budget Host Copa Motel/ 1113 E Hwy 54, Kingman KS 67068. 316-532-3118/ Fax: 532-5690. AE,DC,M,V,CB,D. E edge of tn on Hwy 54. Cable TV, dd phone, n/s rms, adj rstrnt, pool, playgrnd, cot, crib, t pkng, outlets. AAA/ Mobil. $30-33/S; $33-39/D; $3/ex prsn. Discs.

Lansing (Kansas City area)

Econo Lodge/ 504 N Main, Lansing KS 66043 913-727-2777/ Fax: 727-2862/ 800-356-0689. V,M,AE,D,DC,CB. I-70 (Exit 224) to US 73, N 9 mi. Nrby rstrnt, fax, cable TV. AAA. $32-38/S; $34-42/D; $4/ex prsn. Discs.

Lenexa (Kansas City area)

Motel 6/ 9725 Lenexa Dr, Lenexa KS 66215. 913-541-8558/ Fax: 894-8726. M,V,AE,D,DC. I-35 (Exit 224) to 95th St, turn E, then immediate rt on Lenexa Dr. Cable TV, laundry, pool, n/s rms. Free local calls. $30/S; $36/D; $6/ex prsn. Disc.

Super 8 Motel/ 9601 Westgate, Lenexa KS 66215. 913-888-8899/ Fax: 888-9204. V,M,D,AE,DC,CB. I-35 & 95th St. B/f, n/s rms, toast bar, copier, cable TV, outlets, cot, crib. Free local calls. No pets. Pride Award. $44/S; $51-53/D; $3/ex prsn. Higher spec event rates. Discs.

Liberal

Sleep Inn/ 405 E Pancake, Box 2138, Liberal KS 67901. 315-624-7113. V,M,D,AE. US 83 to US 54, E 4 blks. Nrby rstrnt, indr pool, mtg rm, fax, b/f, whrlpool, cable TV, t pkng, outlets, n/s rms. Free cont brfst. $39-44/S; $44-49/D; $4/ex prsn. Discs.

Lindsborg

Coronado Motel/ 305 N Harrison, Lindsborg KS 67456. 913-227-3943. V, M,D. I-35 Bsns Loop (Hwy 81). Pool, n/s rms, cable TV, tt/dd phone, nwspr, laundry, cot, conn rms. Free local calls, coffee. $26-35/S; $30-

KANSAS 118

45/D; $2-4/ex prsn. Disc: Senior, l/s. Highest listed rates are for spec events. *Guaranteed rates.*

Viking Motel/ 446 Harrison, Lindsborg KS 67456. 913-227-3336. V,M,AE,D, D C,CB. Bsns loop from I-135, Exit 72 or 78. 2 blks E of Bethany College. Nrby rstrnt/ lounge, pool, n/s rms, cable TV, tt/dd phones, cot, crib, t/b pkng, conn rms. Free local calls, coffee. No pets. AAA/ Mobil. $31/S; $35-39/D; $4/ex prsn. Spec event: $46/S; $50-54/D.

Manhattan

Motel 6/ 510 Tuttle Creek Blvd, Manhattan KS 66502. 913-537-1022/ Fax: 537-7307. M,V,AE,D,DC. On Tuttle Creek Blvd (US 24), N of Poyntz Av. Nrby rstrnt, cable TV, laundry, pool, n/s rms. Free local calls. $27-29/S; $33-35/D; $6/ex prsn. Disc.

Super 8 Motel/ 200 Tuttle Creek Blvd, Manhattan KS 66502. 913-537-8468. AE,M,V,DC,CB,D. Jct US 24 & SR 18. B/f, n/s rms, toast bar, copier, cable TV, cot, crib. Free local calls. No pets. Pride Award. $42/S; $49-51/D; $3/ex prsn. Discs.

McPherson

Best Western Holiday Manor/ 2211 E Kansas Av, McPherson KS 67460. 316-241-5343. V,M,AE,D,DC,CB. 1 blk W of I-135, Exit 60. Rstrnt/ lounge, pool, indr pool, sauna, whrlpool, n/s rms, cable TV, TDD, tt/dd phone, mtg rm, fax, nwspr, refrig, cot, crib, outlets, t/b/rv pkng, conn rms, b/f. Free local calls, coffee. AAA. $41/S; $47/D; $2/ex prsn. Disc: Senior, bsns, TA, govt, trkr, milt.

Newton

1st Interstate Inn/ 1515 E 1st St, Box 772, Newton KS 67114. 316-283-8850. V,M,AE,D,DC. I-35 (Exit 31) at 1st St. Nrby rstrnt, cable TV, dd phone, outlets, crib, n/s rms. $27-31/S; $29-34/D; $2/ex prsn. 5/1-10/31: $32-34/S; $34-39/D. Spec events: $37-39/S; $42-44/D; $6/ex prsn. Disc: Senior, TA, family, comm.

Super 8 Motel/ 1620 E 2nd St, Newton KS 67114. 316-283-7611/ Fax: 283-1140. AE,M,V,DC,CB,D. I-135 (Exit 31) to E 1st St, E 1 blk to Manchester, turn lt. B/f, n/s rms, cable TV, fax, copier, cot, crib. Free local calls. Pride Award. $37/S; $42-47/D; $5/ex prsn. Higher spec event rates. Discs.

Norton

Budget Host Hillcrest Motel/ Box 249, Norton KS 67654. 913-877-3343. AE, M,V,CB,DC,D. 3 blks W of jct Hwys 283 & 36, S side of hwy. Cable TV, dd/tt phone, in-rm coffee, nrby rstrnt, pool, playgrnd, arpt trans, t pkng, outlets, cot, crib. AAA/ Mobil. $29-31/S; $33-41/D; $3/ex prsn. Higher spec event/ holiday/ hunting season rates. Discs.

Oakley

1st Interstate Inn/ Box 426, Oakley KS 67748. 913-672-3203. V,M,AE,D,DC. I-70 (Exit 76) at Hwy 40. Cable TV, dd phone, arpt trans, nrby rstrnt, cot, crib, outlets. . $27-29/S; $29-34/D; $2/ex prsn. 5/1-10/31: $32-34/S; $34-39/D. Spec Events: $37/S; $42-44/D; $6/ex prsn. Disc: Senior, TA, comm, family.

Olathe (Kansas City area)

Econo Lodge/ 209 E Flaming Rd, Olathe KS 66061. 913-829-1312. V,M,D,AE. I-35 (Exit 215) to US 169, N 1/2 mi. At jct US 56 & US 169. Nrby rstrnt, fax, b/f, cable TV, t pkng, outlets, AM coffee. Free cont brfst. No pets. $36-39/S; $42-49/D; $5/ex prsn. Discs.

Ottawa

Econo Lodge/ 2331 S Cedar, Ottawa KS 66067. 913-242-3400. V,M,AE,D. Jct I-35 & US 59. Nrby rstrnt, pool, mtg rm, fax, b/f, cable TV, t pkng, dd/ tt phone, n/s rms. Free coffee. AAA. $35-40/S; $40-46/D; $4/ex prsn. Discs.

Overland Park (Kansas City area)

Econo Lodge/ 7508 Shawnee Mission Pkwy, Overland Park KS 66202. 913-262-9600. V,M,D,AE. I-35: Nbnd, Exit 228B, E 1 mi to mtl; Sbnd, to US 69, S to Shawnee Mission Pkwy, W 1 blk to mtl. Rstrnt, pool, fax, b/f, cable TV, t pkng, outlets, n/s rms. Free cont brfst, arpt trans. No pets. $36-40/S; $40-47/D; $4/ex prsn. 5/1-10/31: $39-43/S; $44-51/D. 11/7-11/13: $45-52/S; $53-56/D. Higher spec event rates. Discs.

Parsons

Super 8 Motel/ 229 E Main, Parsons

KS 67357. 316=421-8000. V,M,D,AE, DC,CB. E side of Parsons on Hwy 160. B/f, n/s rms, pool, nrby rstrnt, laundry, mtg rm, toast/ cereal bar, copier, cot, crib. Free local calls. Pride Award. $36/S; $42-44/D; $3/ex prsn. Discs.

Pittsburg

Budget Host Extra Inn/ 4023 Parkview Dr, Pittsburg KS 66762. 316-232-2800. AE,D,M,V,DC,CB. Jct Hwys 69 and 69 Bypass. Cable TV, tt/ dd phone, n/s rms, b/f, rstrnt/ lounge/ nrby mtg rms, playgrnd, picnic area, t pkng, outlets, cot. Free crib. No pets. AAA/ Mobil. $35-40/S; $41-46/D; $6/ex prsn. Spec events: $40-50/rm, 1-4 prsns.

Super 8 Motel/ 3108 N Broadway, Pittsburg KS 66762. 316-232-1881. AE, M,V,DC,CB,D. US 69, 1 blk S of jct with N Bypass. B/f, n/s rms, t/b/rv pkng, outlets, toast bar, copier, cable TV, cot, crib. Free local calls. No pets. Pride Award. $40/S; $47-49/D; $3/ex prsn. Higher spec event rates. Discs.

Pratt

Super 8 Motel/ E Hwy 54, Pratt KS 67124. 316-672-5945/ Fax: 672-2969. V,M,DC,AE,CB,D. Jct US 54 & SR 61. US 281 to US 54, E to SR 61. B/f, n/s rms, whrlpool, cable TV, suites, t pkng, cot, crib. Free local calls. Pride Award. $33/S; $38-40/D; 52/ex prsn. Higher spec event rates. Discs.

Quinter

Budget Host Q Motel/ Box 398, Quinter KS 67752. 913-754-3337. AE,M,V. Jct I-70 & Hwy 212. Cable TV, dd phone, rstrnt, mtg rms, t pkng, outlets. AAA. $30/S; $34-40/D; $3/ex prsn.

Russell

Super 8 Motel/ 1405 S Fossil, Russell KS 67665. 913-483-2488. V,M,D,AE, DC,CB. I-70 (Exit 184) at Hwy 281 N. B/f, n/s rms, nrby rstrnt, whrlpool, outlets, cont brfst, t pkng, suites. Free local calls. Pride Award. $31-35/S; $39-41/D; $3/ex prsn. Discs.

Salina

Mid America Best Western Inn/ 1846 N 9th St, Salina KS 67401. 913-827-0356/ Fax: 827-7688. V,M,AE,D, DC, CB. I-70, Exit 252, 1 blk S. Rstrnt/ lounge, pool, indr pool, sauna, whrlpool, cable TV, tt/dd phone, mtg rm, fax, copier, cot, crib, t/b/rv pkng, conn rms, b/f. Free coffee, tea, cocoa. AAA/ Mobil.PRICE[$36/S; $48/D; $3/ex prsn. 6/1-9/1: $37/S; $52/D. Disc: Senior, bsns, TA, govt, trkr, milt.*Guaranteed rates.*

Budget Host Vagabond Inn/ 217 S Broadway, Salina KS 67401. 913-825-7265/ Fax: 825-7003. AE,CB,DC,M, V,D. 2 1/2 mi S of I-70 on Broadway. Cable TV, dd phone, in-rm coffee, family rms, kitchens, n/s rms, nrby rstrnt, mtg rms, pool, t pkng, cot, crib. AAA/ Mobil. $26-45/S; $32-50/D; $4/ex prsn. Discs.

Motel 6/ 635 W Diamond Dr, Salina KS 67401. 913-827-8397/ Fax: 827-0213. M,V,DC,D,AE. I-70 (Exit 252) to 9th St, N to Diamond Dr, turn lt. Cable TV, laundry, pool, n/s rms, t pkng. Free local calls. $30-32/S; $36-38/D; $6/ex prsn. Disc.

Smith Center

US Center Motel/ 116 E Hwy 36, R2, Box 101, Smith Center KS 66967. 913-282-6611/ 800-875-6613. M,V,AE,D, DC,CB. 1/2 blk E of jct Hwys 281 & 36. Nrby rstrnt, indr pool, n/s rms, cable TV, playgrnd, tt/dd phone, crib, t pkng. Free local calls, coffee. No pets, no smoking. AAA/ Mobil. $26-30/S; $30-40/D; $4/ex prsn.

Topeka

Econo Lodge/ 1240 SW Wanamaker Rd, Topeka KS 66604. 913-273-6969. VM,AE,DC. I-470 (Exit 1) to Wanamaker Rd, N to corner of Huntoon. Nrby rstrnt, indr pool, mtg rm, fax, b/f, whrlpool, cable TV, outlets, n/s rms. Free cont brfst. AAA. $44-56/S; $46-61/D; $5/ex prsn. 5/1-10/31: $46-62/S; $48-64/D. Discs.

Motel 6/ 709 Fairlawn Rd, Topeka KS 66606. 913-272-8283/ Fax: 271-1341. M,V,AE,D,DC. I-70/ US 40: Ebnd, Exit 357A/ 6th Av, rt to Fairlawn, rt; Wbnd, Exit 357A/ Fairlawn, lt for 3 blks. Cable TV, laundry, pool, n/s rms. Free local calls. $27-30/S; $33-36/D; $6/ex prsn. Disc.

Motel 6/ 1224 Wanamaker Rd SW,

Topeka KS 66604. 913-273-9888/ Fax: 273-0665. AE,DC,D,M,V. I-470 (Exit 1B) to Wanamaker Rd, N 1/2 blk to mtl. Cable TV, laundry, pool, n/s rms, t pkng. Free local calls. $30-32/S; $36-38/D; $6/ex prsn. Disc.

WaKeeney

Budget Host Travel Inn/ Box 2B, WaKeeney KS 67672. 913-743-2121. AE,M,V,D,CB,DC. I-70 (Exit 128) at US 283. Cable TV, dd phone, family rms, nrby rstrnt/ mtg rms, pool, t pkng, outlets, cot. Free crib. Mobil. Winter: $25-26/S; $28-40/D; $3/ex prsn. Summer: $25-28/S; $30-45/D. Discs.

Wichita

Econo Lodge/ 6245 W Kellogg, Wichita KS 67209. 316-945-5261. V,M,AE,D. W US 54 (Kellogg) at Dugan Rd. Nrby rstrnt, cable TV, t pkng, n/s rms. Free cont brfst. No pets. $36-44/S; $40-48/D; $4/ex prsn. Discs.

English Village Inn/ 6727 E Kellogg, Wichita KS 67217. 316-683-5613/ Fax: 684-3530/ 800-365-8455. V,M,AE,D, DC,CB. I-35, Exit 50, 1 1/4 mi W on Hwy 54-96. Nrby rstrnt, pool, cable TV, tt/dd phone, fax, copier, nwspr, laundry, refrig, microwave, cot, crib, conn rms. Free local calls, cont brfst, coffee. No pets. AAA. $28/S; $30-34/D; $3/ex prsn. Disc: Senior, l/s, family, milt. *Guaranteed rates.*

Howard Johnson 6575 W Kellogg Dr, Wichita KS 67209. 316-943-8165/ Fax: 941-9849. M,DC,D,V,AE,CB. US 54 (Kellogg Dr) at Airport Rd exit. On Frontage Rd. N/s rms, b/f, arpt trans, cable TV, laundry, whrlpool, hot tub, cont brfst, fax, refrig, microwave. Free local calls, coffee. No pets. $38-40/S; $42-46/D. Discs.

Mark 8 Inn/ 1130 N Broadway, Wichita KS 67214. 316-265-4679. M,V,AE,DC, CB,D. Midtown, near St Francis Medical Cntr. Cable TV, dd/tt phone, dataport, fax, refrig, laundry. Free local calls, coffee. AAA. $27/S; $30/D; $3/ex prsn. $33-39/suites.

Mark 8 Lodge/ 8136 E Kellogg, Wichita KS 67207. 316-685-9415/ Fax: 683-8746. M,V,AE,D,DC,CB. Rock Rd at Kellogg. Cable TV, dd/tt phone, data ports. Free local calls, AM coffee. AAA. $32/S; $35/D; $2/ex prsn. Discs.

Motel 6/ 5736 W Kellogg, Wichita KS 67209. 316-945-8440/ Fax: 945-9895. M,V,AE,D,DC. I-235: N (Exit 7B) to US 54 (Kellogg), W to mtl; S (Exit 8) to Central, E to West St, S to Hwy 54, W to motel. Nrby rstrnt, cable TV, l pool, n/s rms, t pkng. Free local calls. $26-28/S; $30-34/D; $4-6/ex prsn. Disc.

Scotsman Inn/ 5922 W Kellogg, Wichita KS 67209. 316-943-3800/ 800-950-7268. M,V,AE,D,DC,CB. US 54 (Kellogg) and I-235 W. Cable TV, refrig, dd/tt phone, data port, n/s rms, fax. Free local calls, coffee, nwspr. AAA. $33/S; $37-38/D; $2/ex prsn. Discs.

Scotsman Inn/ 465 S Webb Rd, Wichita KS 67207. 316-684-6363/ 800-477-7268. V,M,AE,D,DC,CB. Kellogg & Webb Rd near US 54 & I-35. Cable TV, refrig, dd/tt phone, data port, laundry, fax. Free local calls, coffee, nwspr. AAA. $31/S; $35/D; $3-4/ex prsn. Discs.

Winfield

Budget Host Camelot Motor Inn/ 1710 Main St, Winfield KS 67156. 316-221-9050. V,M,AE,D,DC. On Hwy 77, 8 blks S of jct Hwy 77 & 160. Nrby rstrnt, n/s rms, cable TV, tt/dd phone, fax, crib. Free local calls, cont brfst, coffee. No pets. AAA/ Mobil. $35-38/S; $38-41/D; $3/ex prsn. 9/18-9/21, 9/27-9/28: $47-57/S or D. Disc: Senior, bsns, govt, trkr, milt.

Comfort Inn/ US 77 at Quail Ridge, Winfield KS 67156. 316-221-7529. AE, DC,M,V. On US 77 at jct with US 160. Nrby rstrnt, pool, mtg rm, fax, b/f, cable TV, t pkng, n/s rms. Free cont brfst. $47-105/S or D. Discs.

Yates Center

Townsman Motel/ 609 W Mary, Yates Center KS 66783. 316-625-2131/ Fax: 625-2133. V,M,AE,D,DC. At Jct Hwy 54 & 75, 40 mi N o f I-35. Nrby rstrnt/ lounge, n/s rms, cable TV, tt/dd phone, mtg rm, fax, copier, refrig, cot, crib, outlets, t/b pkng, conn rms, Free local calls, coffee. AAA/ Mobil. $25-26/S; $32-33/D; $4/ex prsn. Disc: Senior, l/s, family, TA, trkr, milt.

Kentucky

Ashland

Days Inn/ 12700 SR 180, Ashland KY 41101. 606-928-3600/ Fax: 928-6515. M,DC,D,V,AE,CB. I-64 (Exit 185) to US 60, N 3/4 mi to mtl. Fax, n/s rms, nrby rstrnt, pool, mtg rm, b/f, t pkng, cable TV, refrig, microwave, in-rm coffee, in-rm safe, cot. Free cont brfst. Chairman's Award. $36-45/S; $42-55/D; $5/ex prsn. Discs.

Econo Lodge/ 1010 Paint Lick Rd, Berea KY 40403. 606-986-9323. V,M,AE,DC. I-75 (Exit 76) to SR 21, W to mtl. Nrby rstrnt, fax, cable TV, t/b/rv pkng, outlets, VCR, n/s rms. Free AM coffee, cont brfst. AAA. $40-50/S; $45-55/D; $5/ex prsn. 5/1-10/31: $45-55/S; $55-65/D. Discs.

Howard Johnson Lodge/ 715 Chestnut St, Berea KY 40403. 606-986-2384. V,M,D,AE,DC,CB. I-75, Exit 76, on E side of interstate. N/s rms, b/f, t/b pkng. Free cont brfst. Gold Medal Winner. $32-42/S; $36-46D. Discs.

Bowling Green

Howard Johnson Hotel/ 523 US 31 W Bypass, Bowling Green KY 42101. 502-842-9453/ Fax: 842-0228. V,M,AE,D, DC,CB,JCB. I-65, Exit 28, take 31W S, lt on 31W bypass. N/s rms, mtg rm, b/f, lounge, indr pool, exerc equip, whrlpool, sauna, game rm. Free delux cont brfst. $35-40/S; $40-48/D. Discs.

Motel 6/ 3139 Scottsville Rd, Bowling Green KY 42101. 502-843-0140/ Fax: 782-6157. M,V,AE,D,DC. I-65 (Exit 22) to US 231, NW to mtl. Cable TV, pool, n/s rms. Free local calls. Sun-Thurs: $26/S; $32/D; $6/ex prsn. Fri, Sat, Holidays, Spec Events: $30/S; $36/D. 5/23-12/20: $26-28/S; $32-34/D. Higher spec event rates. Disc.

Brooks (Louisville area)

Comfort Inn/ 149 Willabrook Dr, Box 550, Brooks KY 40109. 502-957-6900. V,M,AE,DC. I-65, Exit 121. Indr pool, mtg rm, fax, b/f, whrlpool, cable TV, exerc equip, n/s rms. Free cont brfst. No pets. AAA. $45-65/S; $50-70/D; $6/ex prsn. 5/1-5/3, 5/7-12/31: $40-60/S; $45-65/D. 5/4-5/6: $133/S or D. Discs.

Carrolltown

Super 8 Motel/ 130 Slumber Ln, Carrollton KY 41008. 502-732-0252. V,M,D,AE,DC,CB. I-71 (Exit 44) at US 227, N 1/2 mi. N/s rms, laundry, fax, copier, nrby rstrnt. Free cont brfst, local calls. Pride Award. $44/S or D; $6/ex prsn. Discs.

Cave City

Comfort Inn/ SR 70 Service Rd, Cave City KY 42127. 502-773-2030. V, M,D,AE,DC. I-65 (Exit 53) E to SR 70, N to mtl. Nrby rstrnt, pool, fax, cable TV, n/s rms. Free cont brfst. $40-60/S; $45-65/D; $5/ex prsn. 5/1-10/31: $50-80/S; $55-85/D. Discs.

Quality Inn/ Mammoth Cave Rd, Box 547, Cave City KY 42127. 502-773-2181. V,M,AE,DC. I-65 (Exit 53) at SR 90 (Mammoth Cave Rd). Rstrnt, pool, fax, b/f, cable TV, outlets, n/s rms. Free cont brfst. AAA. $30-42/S; $42-48/D; $6/ex prsn. 5/1-5/25: $42-48/S; $48-56/D. 5/26-9/5: $48-56/S; $56-68/D. Discs.

Clarksville (Louisville area)

Howard Johnson Lodge/ 342 Eastern Blvd, Clarksville KY 47129. 812-282-7511/ Fax: 282-0252. M,DC,D,V,AE, CB. I-65 (Exit 2) at Eastern Blvd. N/s rms, lounge, pool, t pkng, fax, game rm, mtg rm. Free brfst buffet, local calls, arpt trans. $40-60/S; $46-75/D. Discs.

Danville

Super 8 Motel/ 3663 Hwy 150/127 Bypass, Danville KY 40422. 606-236-8881. AE,M,V,D,DC,CB. Jct of Hwy 127 & 150 Bypass, 1 mi E on 150 Bypass. B/f, n/s rms, t/b/rv pkng, copier, cable TV, mtg rm, laundry, microfridge, cot. Free local calls, crib. Pride Award. $36-40/S; $42-50/D; $5/ex prsn. Higher spec event rates. Discs.

KENTUCKY

Dry Ridge

Super 8 Motel/ 88 Blackburn Ln, Dry Ridge KY 41035. 606-824-3700/ Fax: 824-3801. AE,M,V,D,DC,CB. I-75 (Exit 159) at SR 22. B/f, n/s rms, t/b/rv pkng, copier, cable TV, hot brfst, baggage hndling, cot. Free local calls, nwspr, crib. No pets. Pride Award. $33-37/S; $35-45/D; $2/ex prsn. Discs.

Elizabethtown

Howard Johnson Lodge/ 708 E Dixie Av, Elizabethtown KY 42701. 502-765-2185/ Fax: 737-2065. AE,M,V,D,DC, CB,JCB. I-65, Exit 91 (Hodgenville/Paducah), bear rt to Elizabethtown, at stop sign turn rt for 1/4 mi. N/s rms, mtg rm, b/f, rstrnt, pool, t pkng, laundry. Free cont brfst. $36-40/S or D. 5/6-5/8: $60/S or D. Discs.

Motel 6/ US 62 & I-65, Elizabethtown KY 42701. 502-769-3102/ Fax: 737-5873. M,V,AE,D,DC. I-65 (Exit 94) to US 62, W on Mulberry St (US 62) 1 blk. Nrby rstrnt, cable TV, pool, n/s rms. Free local calls. $26-28/S; $32-34/D; $6/ex prsn. Higher spec event rates. Disc.

Rodeway Inn/ 656 E Dixie Av, Elizabethtown KY 42701. 502-769-2331. AE,DC,M,V. I-65 (Exit 91) & 31 W. Rstrnt, pool, fax, cable TV, t pkng, n/s rms. No pets. $31-60/S; $35-60/D; $5/ex prsn. 5/4-5/6: $110/S; $125/D. 5/7-9/4: $35-60/S; $39-60/D. Higher spec event/ some wknds rates. Discs.

Erlanger (Cincinnati OH area)

Econo Lodge/ 633 Donaldson Rd, Erlanger KY 41018. 606-342-5500. V,M,D,AE. I-75 & 71, Exit 184. Nrby rstrnt, fax, cable TV, t pkng, n/s rms. $27-35/S; $32-42/D; $5/ex prsn. Discs.

Florence (Cincinnati OH area)

Budget Host Inn/ 8075 Steilen Dr, Florence KY 41042. 606-371-0277/ Fax: 371-0286. V,M,AE,D,DC,CB. I-75 & US 42, Exit 180. Cable TV, VCR/ movies, d d phone, n/s rms, nrby rstrnt, t pkng, outlets, cot. Free crib. AAA. $31/S; $37-41/D; $6/ex prsn. 5/1-8/31: $34/S; $40-44/D. Disc: Senior, govt, milt, TA, AAA.

Cross Country Inn/ 7810 Commerce Dr, Florence KY 41042. 606-283-2030/ Fax: 283-0171. V,M,AE,D,DC. I-71 & I-75, Exit 181. Nrby rstrnt, pool, n/s rms, cable TV, TDD, tt/dd phone, fax, copier, crib, conn rms, b/f, recliner. Free local calls, coffee, tea, cocoa. No pets. AAA. $38-42/S; $45-49/D. Discs.

Motel 6/ 7937 Dream St, Florence KY 41042. 606-283-0909/ Fax: 371-8837. V,M,DC,D,AE. I-75 (Exit 180/ Union-Florence) to Hwy 42, E 1/4 mi to Dream St, lt 1/2 mi. Nrby rstrnt, cable TV, laundry, pool, n/s rms. Free local calls. Sun-Thurs: $30/S; $36/D; $6/ex prsn. Fri,Sat, Holiday, Spec events: $36/S; $42/D. 5/25-9/6: $30/S; $36/D. 9/7-12/20: $27/S; $33/D. Higher spec event rates. Disc.

Fort Campbell

See Hopkinsville.

Fort Knox

See Radcliff.

Fort Mitchell

Cross Country Inn/ 2350 Royal Dr, Ft Mitchell KY 41017. 606-341-2090/ Fax: 341-3371. V,M,AE,D,DC. I-71 & I-75, Exit 186. Nrby rstrnt, pool, n/s rms, cable TV, TDD, tt/dd phone, fax, copier, elevator, crib, conn rms, b/f, recliner. Free local calls, coffee, tea, cocoa. No pets. AAA. $38-42/S; $45-49/D. Discs.

Franklin

Comfort Inn/ 3794 Nashville Rd, Franklin KY 42134. 502-586-6100. V,M,D, A E,DC. I-65 (Exit 2) at US 31 W. Rstrnt, pool, fax, cable TV, n/s rms. Free cont brfst. AAA. $40-60/S; $44-64/D; $5/ex prsn. 5/1-10/31: $49-70/S; $54-70/D. Higher spec event rates. Discs.

Georgetown (Lexington area)

Days Inn/ I-75 & Delaplain Rd, Georgetown KY 40324. 502-863-5000/ Fax: 863-5002. M,DC,D,V,AE,CB. I-75 (Exit 129) to Delaplain Rd (SR 820), E to mtl. Fax, n/s rms, nrby rstrnt, pool, whrlpool, b/f, t pkng, cable TV, cot. Free local calls. $25-45/S; $35-50/D; $5/ex prsn. Discs.

Econo Lodge/ 3075 Paris Pike, Georgetown KY 40324. 502-863-2240.

KENTUCKY

AE,DC,M,V. I-75 (Nbnd, Exit 125; Sbnd, Exit 126) to US 460 (Paris Pike), E 1/4 mi to mtl. Nearby rstrnt, pool, fax, cable TV, t pkng, outlets, n/s rms. Free cont brfst. $27-35/S; $30-45/D; $5/ex prsn. Discs.

Ramada Limited/ 401 Delaplain, Box 926, Georgetown KY 40324. 502-863-1166/ Fax: 868-5362. M,DC,D,V,AE, CB. I-75 (Exit 129) at Delaplain. Pool, b/f, n/s rms, cable TV, mtg rm, valet serv. Free cont brfst. $36-44/S or D; $5/ex prsn. Discs.

Glasgow

Comfort Inn/ Calvery Dr at US 31 E, Glasgow KY 42141. 800-221-2222 — opening soon. V,M,D,AE. Nrby rstrnt, pool, cable TV, n/s rms. Free cont brfst. $38-49/S; $42-55/D; $6/ex prsn. Discs.

Grayson

Econo Lodge/ Rte 4, Box 440C, Grayson KY 41143. 606-474-7854. V,M,AE,D. On I-64, Exit 172, bet SR 1947 & W exit ramp to I-64. Nrby rstrnt, pool, mtg rm, fax, b/f, cable TV, t pkng, n/s rms. Free local calls, cont brfst. No pets. AAA. $33-43/S; $38-48/D; $5/ex prsn. Discs.

Hazard

Days Inn/ 359 Morton Blvd, Hazard KY 41701. 606-436-4777. M,DC,D,V,AE, CB. Daniel Boone Pkwy (W of SR 15) to Morton Blvd, turn S to mtl. Fax, n/s rms, nrby rstrnt, whrlpool, mtg rm, b/f, t pkng, cot. $42-59/S; $46-59/D; $6/ex prsn. Discs.

Super 8 Motel/ 125 Village Ln, Hazard KY 41701. 606-436-8888/ Fax: 439-0768. AE,M,V,D,DC,CB. Jct of Village Ln & Daniel Boone Pkwy, near Village Square Shopping Cntr. B/f, n/s rms, t/b/rv pkng, outlets, copier, cable TV, cot. Free local calls, crib. No pets. $43/S; $46-49/D; $5/ex prsn. Discs.

Hopkinsville (Ft Campbell area)

Econo Lodge/ 2916 Ft Campbell Blvd, Hopkinsville KY 42240. 502-886-5242. V,M,AE,DC. I-24 (Exit 86) to US 41A, N 10 mi to mtl. 8 mi from Ft. Campbell. Nrby rstrnt/ lounge, indr pool, mtg rm, fax, b/f, sauna, whrlpool, cable TV, n/s rms. Free cont brfst, local calls. $33-45/S; $38-50/D; $5/ex prsn. Discs.

Friendship Inn/ 2923 Ft Campbell Blvd, Hopkinsville KY 42240. 502-885-5242. AE,DC,M,V. I-24 (Exit 86) to US 41A (Pennyrile Pkwy), N 10 mi to Exit 7A, 2 blks on lt. Nrby rstrnt, fax, cable TV, t pkng, n/s rms. Free cont brfst. $28-33/S; $33-40/D; $4/ex prsn. Discs.

Horse Cave

Budget Host Inn/ Box 332, Horse Cave KY 42749. 502-786-2165/ Fax: 786-2168. AE,CB,DC,M,V,D. I-65 (Exit 58) to Hwy 218. Cable TV, dd phone, family rms, kitchens, rstrnt, mtg rms, pool, laundry, t pkng, outlets, cot. No pets. AAA/ Mobil. $28/S; $28-32/D; $4/ex prsn. 5/24-9/7: $32/S; $32-40/D. Discs.

Kuttawa

Days Inn/ Factory Outlet Av, Kuttawa KY 42055. 502-388-5420. M,DC,D,V, AE,CB. I-24 (Exit 40) at US 62. Fax, n/s rms, nrby rstrnt, pool, whrlpool, b/f, t pkng, cable TV, cot. Chairman's Award. $43-48/S; $48-53/D; $5/ex prsn. Discs.

Lexington

Econo Lodge North/ 925 Newtown Pike, Lexington KY 40511. 606-231-6300/ Fax: Ext 151. AE,DC,M,V. I-75/ I-64 (Exit 115) to Newton Pike, S 1 1/2 mi to mtl. Rstrnt/ lounge, pool, mtg rm, fax, cable TV, t pkng. $28-50/S; $32-55/D; $6/ex prsn. Discs.

Econo Lodge/ 5527 Athens-Boonesboro Rd, Lexington KY 40509. 606-263-5101. V,M,AE,D. I-75, Exit 104. Nrby rstrnt, fax, b/f, cable TV, t pkng, n/s rms. Free AM coffee. $28-40/S; $32-50/D; $5/ex prsn. Discs.

HoJo Inn/ 2250 Elkhorn Rd, Lexington KY 40505. 606-299-8481/ Fax: 293-2472. V,M,AE,D,DC,CB. I-75, Exit 110, approx 1/10 mi on rt side towards town. N/s rms, mtg rm, b/f, pool, t/b pkng, satellite TV, valet, fax, copier, laundry. Free cont brfst, local calls. $34-38/S; $39-47/D. Discs.

Motel 6/ 2260 Elkhorn Rd, Lexington KY 40505. 606-293-1431/ Fax: 293-8349. V,M,AE,DC,D. I-75 (Exit 110) to US 60, W to mtl. Nrby rstrnt, cable TV, pool, n/s rms, t pkng. Free local calls.

KENTUCKY

Sun-Thurs: $30/S; $36/D; $6/ex prsn. Fri, Sat, Holidays, Spec Events: $36/S; $42/D. 5/23-12/20: $26-30/S; $32-36/D. Higher spec event rates. Disc.

Quality Inn/ 1050 Newtown Pike, Lexington KY 40511. 606-233-0561. V,M, A E,DC. I-75/ I-64 (Exit 115) to SR 922, 1 mi SW to Newtown Ct. Nrby rstrnt, pool, fax, cable TV, n/s rms. Free cont brfst. AAA. $39-46/S; $44-51 /D; $5/ex prsn. 3/1-5/25: $41-51/S; $46 -56/D. 5/16-10/31: $41-61/S; $46-66/D. Discs.

Wilson Inn/ 2400 Buena Vista Dr, Lexington KY 40505. 606-293-6113. AE,V, M,DC,D,CB. I-75 at Hwy 60. Refrig, microwave, fax. Free cont brfst, local calls. AAA. $35 +/S; $40-46/D. Higher spec event rates. Disc: Sen

Also see Georgetown, Richmond.

London

Budget Host Westgate Inn/ Box 254, London KY 40741. 606-878-7330. V,AE,CB,DC,D,M. 1/4 mi W of I-75, Exit 41. Cable TV, dd phone, n/s rms, nrby rstrnt, b/f, pool, playgrnd, picnic area, t pkng, outlets, full hookup rv sites. AAA. $32/S; $34-37/D; $3/ex prsn. 5/26-10/31: $35/S; $37-40/D. Discs.

Sleep Inn/ 285 W SR 80, London KY 40741. 800-221-2222 — opening soon. V,M,D,AE. I-75 (Exit 41) to Hwys 80/229 S. Rstrnt, indr pool, mtg rm, b/f, cable TV, exerc equip, n/s rms. Free cont brfst. No pets. $40-70/S; $45-90/D; $5/ex prsn. Discs.

Louisville

Quality Inn/ 3315 Bardstown Rd, Louisville KY 40218. 502-452-1501. V,M, AE,DC. I-264 (Watterson Expwy/ Exit 16) to Bardstown Rd, S to mtl. Rstrnt, pool, mtg rm, fax, cable TV, n/s rms. $37-75/S or D; $5/ex prsn. 5/4-5/6: $115-155/S or D. Higher spec event rates. Discs.

Wilson Inn/ 3209 Kemmons Dr, Louisville KY 40218. 502-473-0000/ Fax: Ext 157. AE,V,M,DC,D,CB. I-264 at Exit 15. Microwave, refrig, work desks, fax. Free local calls, cont brfst. AAA. $35/S; $40-46/D. Disc: AARP, AAA.

Wilson Inn/ 9802 Bunsen Way, Louisville KY 40299. 502-499-0000. AE,V, M,DC,D,CB. I-64, Exit 15. Microwave, refrig, desks, fax. Free local calls, cont brfst. AAA. $35/S; $40-46/D. Disc: AARP, AAA, corp.

Also see Brooks, Clarksville, Clarksville IN, Jeffersonville IN.

Madisonville

Econo Lodge/ 1117 E Center St, Madisonville KY 42431. 502-821-0364. V,M,AE,D. US 41 (Pennyrile Pkwy, Exit 42), & SR 70 at Center St. Cable TV, t pkng, n/s rms. Free coffee. No pets. $29-35/S; $30-37/D; $6/ex prsn. Discs.

Mayfield

Super 8 Motel/ Purchase Pkwy, Mayfield KY 42066. 502-247-8899. V, M,AE,D,DC,CB. Purchase Pkwy (Exit 24) at SR 121. B/f, n/s rms, t/b/rv pkng, outlets, cable TV, suites, mtg rm, cot. Free local calls, crib. Pride Award. $37/S; $42-44/D; $5/ex prsn. Discs.

Mount Vernon

Days Inn Renfro Valley/ 1630 Richmond St, Mt Vernon KY 40456. 606-256-3300/ Fax: 256-3323/ 800-514-3194. V,M,AE,D,DC,CB. I-75, Exit 62. Rstrnt, n/s rms, cable TV, VCR movies, tt/dd phone, fax, copier, cot, crib, t/b/rv pkng, b/f. AAA. $30/S or D; $4/ex prsn. Mar-Oct wknds: $55/S; $65/D; $5/ex prsn. *Guaranteed rates.*

Econo Lodge/ Box 1106, Mount Vernon KY 40456. 606-256-4621. AE,DC,M,V. I-75 (Exit 62) at US 25. Nrby rstrnt, pool, cable TV, n/s rms. AAA. $30-45/S; $34-50/D; $5-10/ex prsn. 3/1-4/30: $34-60/S; $36-65/D. 5/1-10/31: $36-60/S; $40-65/D. Discs.

Murray

Days Inn Murray/ 517 S 12th St, Murray KY 42071. 502-753-6706/ Fax: 753-6708. AE,D,DC,M,V. US 641, S of SR 94. Nrby rstrnt, pool, n/s rms, cable TV, tt/dd phone, mtg rm, fax, copier, nwspr, refrig, microwave, cot, crib, conn rms, b/f. Free deluxe cont brfst, local calls. $44/S; $48/D; $5/ex prsn. Discs. *Guaranteed rates.*

Owensboro

Motel 6/ 4585 Frederica St, Owensboro

KENTUCKY

KY 42301. 502-686-8606/ Fax: 683-2689. M,V,AE,D,DC. US 60 Bypass/ Beltline Rd to Livermore Exit/ US 431, S 1 blk. Nrby rstrnt, cable TV, pool, n/s rms. Free local calls. $26-30/S; $32-36/D; $6/ex prsn. Disc.

Paducah

Budget Host Inn/ 1234 Broadway, Paducah KY 42001. 502-443-8401. AE,D,M,V. From dntn take Broadway to 13th. Cable TV, dd phone, adj rstrnt, t pkng. $31/S; $34-36/D.

Comfort Inn/ 5106 Old Cairo Rd, Paducah KY 42001. 502-442-1616. V, M,D,AE. I-24 (Exit 3) at SR 305. Nrby rstrnt, pool, fax, b/f, cable TV, n/s rms. Free cont brfst. No pets. $43-63/S; $47-67/D; $4/ex prsn. Discs.

Motel 6/ 5120 Hinkleville Rd, Paducah KY 42001. 502-443-3672/ Fax: 442-1412. M,V,DC,D,AE. I-24 (Exit 4) to US 60 (Hinkleville Rd), turn W. Cable TV, pool, n/s rms, t pkng, nrby rstrnt. Free local calls. Premier Award. Sun-Thurs: $36/S; $42/D; $6/ex prsn. Fri, Sat, Holidays, Spec Events: $40/S; $46/D. 5/23-12/20: $34-36/S; $40-42/D. Higher spec event rates. Disc.

Quality Inn/ 1380 S Irvin Cobb Dr, Paducah KY 42001. 502-443-8751. V,M, AE,DC. I-24 (Exit 7) to US 45, follow sign to mtl. Nrby rstrnt/ lounge, pool, mtg rm, fax, b/f, cable TV, t pkng, outlets, n/s rms. Free cont brfst. AAA. $43-53/S; $48-58/D; $5/ex prsn. Discs.

Paris

Howard Johnson Lodge/ 2011 Alverson Dr, Paris KY 40361. 606-987-0779. V,M,D,AE,DC,CB. US 27/68 Paris Bypass at Alverson Dr. N/s rms, mtg rm, b/f, arpt trans, t pkng, fax, cable TV. Free cont brfst. No pets. Gold Medal Winner. AAA. $37-52/S; $41-60/D. Discs.

Radcliff (Ft Knox area)

Econo Lodge/ 261 N Dixie Hwy, Radcliff KY 40160. 502-351-4488. V,M,AE,D. US 31 W to mtl. 1 mi from Ft Knox. Nrby rstrnt, pool, cable TV, refrig, n/s rms. Free cont brfst. AAA. $35-38/S; $40-43/D; $4-5/ex prsn. 5/5-5/6: $50-53/S or D. Discs.

Quality Inn/ 438 S Dixie Blvd, Radcliff KY 40160. 502-351-8211. AE,DC,M,V. On US 31. Nrby rstrnt, pool, fax, b/f, cable TV, VCR/ movies, game rm, n/s rms. Free cont brfst. No pets. AAA. $28-40/S; $32-45/D; $3/ex prsn. 5/1-5/4, 5/7-9/30: $32-45/S; $35-50/D. 5/5-5/6: $39-55/S; $42-60/D. Discs.

Richmond (Lexington area)

Econo Lodge/ 230 Eastern Bypass, Richmond KY 40475. 606-623-8813. V, M,AE,DC. I-75, Exit 87. Nrby rstrnt, pool, fax, cable TV, t pkng, n/s rms. $26-38/S; $34-48/D; $5/ex prsn. 5/1-11/1: $28-45/S; $32-48/D. Discs.

HoJo Inn/ 1688 Northgate Dr, Richmond KY 40475. 606-624-2612/ Fax: 624-8381. V,M,D,AE,DC,CB. I-75 (Sbnd, Exit 90A; Nbnd, Exit 90) to SR 25, W. I-64 to I-75 S. N/s rms, mtg rm, b/f, pool, t/b pkng, laundry, fax, copier. Free cont brfst, local calls. $34-38/S; $38-42/D. Discs.

Motel 6/ 1698 Northgate Dr, Richmond KY 40475. 606-623-0880/ Fax: 623-8032. M,V,AE,D,DC. I-75: (Nbnd, Exit 90; Sbnd, Exit 90A) to Hwy 421/25, SE to mtl. Nrby rstrnt, cable TV, pool, elevator, n/s rms, t pkng. Free local calls. $26/S; $32/D; $6/ex prsn. Disc.

Super 8 Motel/ 107 N Keeneland Dr, Richmond KY 40475. 606-624-1550/ Fax: 624-1553. AE,M,V,D,DC,CB. I-75 (N, Exit 90: S, Exit 90B) at US 25, W to N Keeneland Dr, N to mtl. B/f, n/s rms, t/b/rv pkng, outlets, copier, cable TV, suites, mtg rm. Free crib. Pride Award. $35/S; $40-46/D; $5/ex prsn. Discs.

Scottsville

Days Inn/ 57 Burnley Rd, Scottsville KY 42164. 502-622-7770. M,DC,D,V,AE, CB. Cumberland Pkwy to US 31E, S to mtl. Fax, n/s rms, nrby rstrnt, pool, whrlpool, b/f, t pkng, cable TV, boat pkng, cot. Free local calls. Chairman's Award. $40-46/S; $46-52/D; $6/ex prsn. Discs.

Somerset

Best Western Parkway Inn/ 125 N Hwy 27, Somerset KY 42501. 606-678-2052/ Fax: 678-8477. V,M,AE,D,DC, CB. I-75 to Mount Vernon Exit (Hwy 461), follow 461 to Hwy 80, W to Somerset. At jct Hwy 27 & 80. Nrby rstrnt, indr pool, whrlpool, n/s rms, cable TV, tt/dd phone, fax, copier, laundry, refrig, microwave, cot, crib, outlets, t/b/rv pkng, conn rms, b/f. Free local calls, cont brfst, coffee, tea, cocoa. No pets. $38/S; $44/D; $6/ex prsn. 4/1-9/30: $44/S; $50/D. Disc: Senior, bsns, govt, trkr. *Guaranteed rates.*

Williamstown

Days Inn/ 211 SR 36 W, Williamstown KY 41097. 606-824-5025/ Fax: 824-5028. M,DC,D,V,AE,CB. I-75 (Exit 154) at SR 36, turn W. Fax, n/s rms, nrby rstrnt, pool, t pkng, cot. Free coffee. Chairman's Award. $35-40/S; $40-50/D; $5/ex prsn. Discs.

HoJo Inn/ 10 Skyway Dr, Williamstown KY 41097. 606-824-7177. AE,M,V,D, DC,CB. I-75, Exit 154, Williamstown, W at top of the hill. N/s rms, rstrnt, pool, limited t pkng. Gold Medal Winner. AAA. $29-40/S; $34-49/D. Higher spec event rates. Discs.

Louisiana

Alexandria

Motel 6/ 546 MacArthur Dr, Alexandria LA 71301. 318-445-2336/ Fax: 448-33-38. M,V,DC,D,AE. US 71 at SR 28. On frontage rd. Nrby rstrnt, cable TV, laundry, pool, n/s rms, t pkng. Free local calls. $27-28/S; $31-32/D; $4/ex prsn. Disc.

Baton Rouge

Motel 6/ 10445 Rieger Rd, Baton Rouge LA 70809. 504-291-4912/ Fax: 291-8554. M,V,DC,D,AE. I-10 (Exit 163) to Siegen Ln, N to mtl. Nrby rstrnt, cable TV, laundry, pool, n/s rms, t pkng. Free local calls. No pets. $30-33/S; $36-39/D; $6/ex prsn. Football wknds: $40/S; $46/D. Higher spec event rates. Disc.

Motel 6/ 9901 Gwen Adele Av, Baton Rouge LA 70816. 504-924-2130/ Fax: 929-7150. V,M,D,AE,DC. I-12 (Exit 2B) to US 61/ Airline Dr, N to Gwen Adele Ave, rt to mtl. Nrby rstrnt, cable TV, pool, laundry, n/s rms, elevator. Free local calls. $32-34/S; $38-40/D; $6/ex prsn. Football wknds: $40/S; $46/D. Higher spec event rates. Disc.

Also see Port Allen.

Bossier City (Shreveport area)

Motel 6/ 210 John Wesley Blvd, Bossier City LA 71112. 318-742-3472/ Fax: 746-9803. M,V,DC,D,AE. I-20 (Exit 21) to Old Minden Rd, NE to John Wesley Blvd, immediately S to mtl. Cable TV, laundry, pool, n/s rms. Free local calls. No pets. Sun-Thurs: $30/S; $34/D; $4/ex prsn. Fri, Sat, Holiday, Spec events: $36/S; $40/D. 5/23-12/20: $30-32/S; $34-36/D. Disc.

Gretna (New Orleans area)

Friendship Inn/ 1411 Claire Av, Gretna LA 70053. 504-366-4311. AE,D,M,V. I-10 to Bsns US 90, W across Mississippi River Bridge (Crescent City Connection) to Westbank, exit to Lafayette S, 3rd lt on Frontage Rd, lt on Delhonde St. Rstrnt, pool, mtg rm, fax, cable TV, t pkng, n/s rms. No pets. $40-55/S; $42-60/D; $5/ex prsn. Discs.

Harvey

Quality Inn/ 3750 W Bank Expwy, Harvey LA 70058. 504-348-1262. V,M,D, AE. I-10 (E, Exit 234A; W, Exit 234C) cross Mississippi River Bridge to Westbank Expwy (Bsns US 90). Rstrnt, pool, mtg rm, fax, b/f, cable TV, n/s rms. No pets. $42-65/S; $85-105/D; $2-10/ex prsn. 3/1-4/30: $42-55/S; $45-105/D. 5/1-5/8: $79-100/S; $89-100/D. 5/9-11/23: $42-55/S; $45-65/D. Discs.

Lafayette

Lafayette Super 8 Motel/ 2224 NE Evangeline Thwy, Lafayette LA 70501. 318-232-8826/ Fax: Ext 102. V,M,AE,D. I-10 (Exit 103A) to frontage rd off US 167 S. B/f, n/s rms, t/b/rv pkng, cable TV, suites, cot. Free local calls, coffee. $27/S; $33-35/D; $4/ex prsn. Discs.

LOUISIANA

Motel 6/ 2724 NE Evangeline Thruway, Lafayette LA 70507. 318-233-2055/ Fax: 269-9267. M,V,DC,D,AE. I-10 (Exit 103B) to I-49/US 167, N to Pont de Mouton, rt to Frontage Rd, rt to mtl. Cable TV, laundry, pool, n/s rms, t pkng. Free local calls. $28/S; $32/D; $4/ex prsn. Disc.

Rodeway Inn/ 1801 N W Evangeline Thruway, Lafayette LA 70501. 318-233-5500. V,M,AE,D,DC. I-10 (Exit 103A) to US 90/I-49, S 1/4 mi. Rstrnt/ lounge, pool, mtg rm, fax, b/f, cable TV, t pkng. Free cont brfst. AAA. $33-50/S; $38-55/D; $3/ex prsn. 5/1-10/31: $35-55/S; $40-60/D. Discs.

Lake Charles

Motel 6/ 335 Hwy 171, Lake Charles LA 70601. 318-433-1773/ Fax: 497-1884. M,V,DC,D,AE. I-10 (Exits 32 or 33) at Opalousas St. Nrby rstrnt, cable TV, laundry, pool, n/s rms. Free local calls. No pets. $30-32/S; $34-36/D; $4/ex prsn. 2/1-5/22: Sun-Thurs: $32/S; $36/D. Fri, Sat, Holidays, spec events: $38/S; $42/D. Disc.

Monroe

Howard Johnson/ 5650 Frontage Rd, Monroe LA 71202. 318-345-2220/ Fax: 343-4098. V,M,AE,D,DC. I-20, Exit 120, S then lt on Frontage Rd. N/s rms, b/f, pool, t pkng, cable TV, fax. Free cont brfst. $39-43/S; $43-48/D. Discs.

Motel 6/ 1501 US 165 Bypass, Monroe LA 71202. 318-322-5430/ Fax: 388-6953. M,V,DC,D,AE. I-20 (Exit 118A) to US 165, S 1/4 mi to East St, turn E, lt to Frontage Rd. Cable TV, laundry, pool, n/s rms. Free local calls. $27-28/S; $33-34/D; $6/ex prsn. Disc.

New Orleans

Comfort Inn/ 6322 Chef Menteur Hwy, New Orleans LA 70126. 504-241-5650. V,M,DC,AE. I-10, Exit US 90 to mtl. Dn tn French Quarter. Rstrnt/ lounge, pool, fax, cable TV, t pkng, n/s rms. Free cont brfst. No pets. AAA. $45 -130/S; $48-150/D; $6-15/ex prsn. Discs.

Econo Lodge/ 4940 Chef Menteur Hwy, New Orleans LA 70126. 800-424-4777. V,M,AE. I-10: Ebnd, Exit 239B; Wbnd, Exit 239. Nrby rstrnt, pool, cable TV, t pkng, n/s rms. No pets. $45-125/S or D; $10/ex prsn. Discs.

Quality Inn/ 3900 Tulane Av, New Orleans LA 70119. 504-486-5541.V,M, AE,DC. I-10 (Exit 232) to Tulane Av, E to mtl. Rstrnt/ lounge, pool, mtg rm, fax, sauna, whrlpool, cable TV, t pkng, laundry, n/s rms. Free bus/ train depot trans. AAA. $45-275/S or D; $10-20/ex prsn. Discs.

Rodeway Inn/ 1725 Tulane Av, New Orleans LA 70112. 504-529-5411. V,M,AE. I-10 (Exit 235B) W to mtl. Nrby rstrnt, pool, cable TV, t pkng, n/s rms. Free cont brfst. No pets. $45-125/S or D; $6-10/ex prsn. Discs.

Also see Gretna, Slidell.

Port Allen (Baton Rouge area)

Motel 6/ 2800 I-10 Frontage Rd, Port Allen LA 70767. 504-343-5945/ Fax: 389-5803. M,V,DC,D,AE. I-10 (Exit 151) to SR 415, S to Frontage Rd, turn rt. Cable TV, laundry, pool, n/s rms. Free local calls. $28/S; $34/D; $6/ex prsn. 5/23-12/20: Sun-Thurs: $32/S; $36/D. Fri, Sat, Holiday, spec event: $34/S; $40/D. Football wknds: $40/S; $46/D. Higher spec event rates. Disc.

Ruston

Super 8 Motel/ 1101 Cooktown (Tech Dr), Ruston LA 71270. 318-255-0588/ Fax: Ext 100. V,M,DC,CB,AE,D. I-20, Exit 84. B/f, n/s rms, pool, laundry, outlets, b/ small t pkng, cont brfst, copier, cable TV, micro-fridge. Free local calls. Pride Award. $40/S; $45-50/D; $5/ex prsn. Higher spec event rates. Discs.

Shreveport

Howard Johnson Lodge/ 1906 N Market St, Shreveport LA 71107. 318-424-6621. V,M,D,AE,DC,CB. I-20 (Exit 19A) to Spring St, N 2 mi. N/s rms, mtg rm, b/f, rstrnt/ lounge, pool, t pkng. $38-48/S; $48-58/D. Discs.

Motel 6/ 4915 Monkhouse Dr, Shreveport LA 71109. 318-631-9691/ Fax: 636-4514. M,V,DC,D,AE. I-20 to Arpt exit (Exit 13), N on Monkhouse Dr. Cable TV, pool, n/s rms. Free local calls. No pets. $28-30/S; $34-36/D; $4-6/ex prsn. Disc.

Also see Bossier City.

LOUISIANA / MAINE

Slidell (New Orleans area)
Budget Host Slidell/ 1662 Gause Blvd, Slidell LA 70458. 504-641-8800. V,M, AE,D,DC,CB,ER. I-10 (Exit 266) to US 190, W .2 mi. Cable TV, dd phone, n/s rms, pool, mtg rms, nrby rstrnt, t pkng, outlets, cot. Free crib. No pets. Mobil. $29-35/S; $35-50/D; $5/ex prsn. Spec events: $55-75. Discs.

Econo Lodge/ Box 1358, Slidell LA 70459. 504-641-2153. AE,V,M,DC. I-10 (Exit 266) & Gause Blvd (US 190). Nrby rstrnt, fax, b/f, cable TV, micro /fridges, n/s rms. Free cont brfst. AAA. $36-75/S; $41-75/D; $5/ex prsn. Discs.

Motel 6/ 136 Taos St, Slidell LA 70458. 504-649-7925/ Fax: 643-3567. M,V, DC,D,AE. I-10 (Exit 266) to US 190, W to frontage rd, lt between Taco Bell & Shoney's, lt on frontage rd. Nrby rstrnt, cable TV, laundry, pool, n/s rms. Free local calls. $33-34/S; $37-38/D; $4/ex prsn. 2/1-3/6: $46/S; $50/D. 3/7-9/6: $36/S; $40/D. Disc.

West Monroe
Super 8 Motel/ 1101 Glenwood Dr, W Monroe LA 71291. 318-325-6361/ Fax: 324-0534. V,M,DC,CB,AE,D. I-20 (Exit 114) to Thomas Rd, N to 2nd stoplight, rt on Glenwood Dr. B/f, n/s rms, pool, outlets, t/b/rv pkng, toast/ cereal bar, copier, cable TV, popcorn, cot. Free local calls. No pets. Pride Award. $39/S; $43/D; $5/ex prsn. Discs.

Maine

Augusta
Motel 6/ 18 Edison Dr, Augusta ME 04330. 207-622-0000/ Fax: 622-1048. V,M, AE,D,DC. I-95 (Exit 30) to US 202/

Western Av, W .3 mi. Cable TV, n/s rms, laundry, nrby rstrnt, t pkng. Free local calls. Premier Award. $30/S; $36/D; $6/ex prsn. 5/23-10/29: $36/S; $42/D. Disc.

Bangor
Bangor Motor Inn/ 701 Hogan Rd, Bangor ME 04401. 207-947-0355/ Fax: 947-0350. V,M,AE,D,DC,CB. I-95 at Hogan Rd, across from K-Mart. N/s rms, cable TV, VCR/ movies, arpt trans, TDD, tt/dd phone, fax, nwspr, micro-wave, cot, crib, outlets, b pkng, b/f. Free local calls, cont brfst. No pets. AA A. $41-44/S; $44-48/D. 7/2-10/15: $52/ S; $58/D; $8/ex prsn. Disc: Senior, bs ns, govt, family, milt. *Guaranteed rates.*

Econo Lodge/ 482 Odlin Rd, Bangor ME 04401. 207-942-6301. AE,V,M,DC. I-95 (Exit 45B) to US 2, lt at lights. Rstrnt/ lounge, fax, cable TV, t pkng, arpt trans, n/s rms. Free coffee, cont brfst. AAA. $29-39/S; $35-45/D; $5/ex prsn. 7/1-10/31: $35-45/S; $40-55/D. Discs.

Howard Johnson Lodge/ 336 Odlin Rd, Bangor ME 04401. 207-942-5251/ Fax: 942-4227. V,M,AE,D,DC. I-95, Exit 45B. Take US 2 from the W, or US 395 from the E. N/s rms, rstrnt/ lounge, pool, cable TV, fax. Free cont brfst. No pets. $36-50/S; $45-60/D. 7/1-10/31: $45-50/S; $65-70/D. Discs.

Motel 6/ 1100 Hammond St, Bangor ME 04401. 207-947-6921/ Fax: 941-8543. D,AE,M,V,DC. I-95 (Exit 45B) to SR 2, W to mtl. Nrby rstrnt, cable TV, laundry, pool, n/s rms. Free local calls. $28-30/S; $34-36/D; $6/ex prsn. 5/23-10/29: $36/S; $42/D. Disc.

Biddeford
Motel One-Eleven/ 470 Alfred Rd, Biddeford ME 04005. 207-284-2440. V,M, AE. ME Turnpike, Exit 4, lt onto Rte 111, 1/2 mi on lt. N/s rms, cable TV, TDD, tt/dd phone, refrig, cot, crib, outlets, t/b/rv pkng, b/f. Free local calls, coffee. No pets. AAA. $35/S; $39-44/D. 7/1-9/5: $49/S; $55-59/D. Disc: AAA. *Guaranteed rates.*

Boothbay
Hillside Acres Motor Court/ Adams Pond Rd, Box 300, Boothbay ME 04537. 207-633-3411. V,M. From Rte 1,

MAINE

turn onto Rte 27, S 8 mi, at Boothbay Info Center take sharp rt. Hillside Acres is directly behind info center. Pool, n/s rms, cable TV, cot, crib, eff. Free cont brfst 7/1-9/4. AAA/ Mobil. 5/15-6/3, 9/5-10/15: $35-55/S or D. 7/1-9/4: $40-68/S or D. CLOSED 10/16-5/14. *Guaranteed rates.*

White Anchor Motel/ RR 1, Box 438, Boothbay ME 04537. 207-633-3788. V,M,AE,D. Rte 27, 8 mi S of Rte 1. Cable TV. Free local calls, cont brfst. No pets. $35-39/S; $39-48/D; $6/ex prsn. *Guaranteed rates.*

Brunswick

Econo Lodge/ US 1 & I-95, Brunswick ME 04011. 207-729-9991. AE,D,M,V. I-95 (Exit 22) at US 1. Nrby rstrnt, pool, cable TV, laundry, n/s rms. No pets. AAA. $38-53/S; $46-53/D; $7/ex prsn. 5/1-6/30: $42-64/S; $49-64/D. 7/1-9/4: $60-83/S; $65-83/D. 9/5-10/31: $48-66/S; $53-66/D. Discs.

Ellsworth

Colonial Motor Lodge/ Bar Harbor Rd, Ellsworth ME 04605. 207-667-5548. V,M,AE. I-95 Bangor, Rte 1A to Ellsworth. On Bar Harbor Rd (Rte 3). Rstrnt, indr pool, whrlpool, n/s rms, satellite TV, tt/dd phone, refrig, cot, crib, t/b/rv pkng, eff, b/f. Free local calls, coffee. AAA. $42-78/S; $48-88/D; $4/ex prsn. 5/2-10/31: $48-58/S; $48-88/D; $6/ex prsn. Disc: Senior, AAA. *Guaranteed rates.*

Ellsworth Motel/ 24 High St, Ellsworth ME 04605. 207-667-4424. V,M. On rte 1 & 3, near jct with 1A. Nrby rstrnt, pool, n/s rms, cable TV, tt/dd phone, crib, conn rms. Free local calls. No pets, no smoking. AAA/ Mobil. 4/1-6/30, 9/3-12/31: $30-36/S; $32-44/D; $5/ex prsn. 7/1-9/2: $42-44/S; $45-56/D. CLOSED 1/1-3/30. *Guaranteed rates.*

Jasper's Motel & Restaurant/ 200 High St, Rte 1, Ellsworth ME 04605. 207-667-5318. V,M,AE,D. I-95, 26 mi from Bangor. Rstrnt, nrby lounge, n/s rms, cable TV, tt/dd phone, cot, crib, t/b/rv pkng. Free local calls. AAA. $30-42/S; $30-48/D; $8/ex prsn. 5/6-6/27, 9/3-10/13: $42-54/S; $42-55/D. 7/1-10/15, 12/31-1/1: $48-59/S; $72-79/D. Disc: Senior, family, AAA. *Guaranteed rates.*

Twilite Motel/ Rte 1 & 3, Ellsworth ME 04605. 207-667-8165. V,M,AE,D. In Ellsworth. N/s rms, cable TV, tt phone, nwspr, cot, crib, t/b pkng, conn rms. Free local calls, cont brfst. AAA. $30-34/S; $34-46/D; $5/ex prsn. 7/1-9/6: $46-54/S; $48-70/D. Disc: Family. *Guaranteed rates.*

Farmington

Mount Blue Motel/ Wilton Rd, RR 4, Box 5260, Farmington ME 04938. 207-778-6004/ 800-771-6004. V,M,AE,D. I-295 N to Rte 4 N. From W, Rte 2 NE. AAA/ Mobil. $39-$51/S or D; $5/ex prsn. Disc: Senior, L/s.

Lewiston

Motel 6/ 516 Pleasant St, Lewiston ME 04240. 207-782-6558/ Fax: 783-5270. M,V,DC,D,AE. I-495 (Exit 13) at Plourde Pkwy. NE of frwy, just off of Lisbon St. Nrby rstrnt, cable TV, n/s rms, t pkng. Free local calls. Premier Award. $30/S; $36/D; $6/ex prsn. 5/23-10/29: $36/S; $42/D. 10/30-12/20: $34/S; $40/D. Disc.

Ocean Park

Billow House Oceanfront Motel & Guesthouse/ 1 Temple Av, Box 7543, Ocean Park ME 04063. 207-934-2333. No credit cards. Main Trnpk (Exit 5) straight 3 mi to ocean front. Nrby rstrnt, n/s rms, cable TV, arpt trans, tt phone, laundry, refrig, microwave, cot, crib, eff, beach front. Free local calls, cont brfst. No pets, no smoking in rm. AAA. $40-50/S or D. 6/15-9/10: $65-115/S or D. Disc: L/s. *Guaranteed rates.*

Portland

Motel 6/ One Riverside St, Portland ME 04102. 207-775-0111/ Fax: 775-0449. V,M,AE,D,DC. I-95, Exit 8. After toll booth take lt at traffic signal to motel. Nrby rstrnt, cable TV, laundry, elevator, t pkng, n/s rms. Free local calls. Premier Award. $30/S; $36/D; $6/ex prsn. 5/23-10/29: $43/S; $49/D. Disc.

Saco

Lord's Motel/ 720 Portland Rd, Saco ME 04064. 207-284-4074/ Fax: 284-6453. V,M,AE,D. On US 1. Indr pool, cable TV, VCR/ movies, tt/dd phone, fax, copier, refrig, cot, crib, t/b/rv pkng, b/f. AAA. $35/S; $45/D; $5/ex

MAINE / MARYLAND

prsn. 7/1-9/2: $70/S; $90/D; $10/ex prsn. *Guaranteed rates*

Scarborough

Millbrook Motel/ 321 US Rte 1, Scarborough ME 04074. 207-883-6004/ 800-371-6005. V,M,D. ME Trnpk/ Rte 95 (Exit 6) to US 1, lt 1/2 mi. Nrby rstrnt, n/s rms, cable TV, tt/dd phone, b/f. Free local calls. No pets. AAA/ Mobil. $40/S; $45/D; $5/ex prsn. 7/1-9/7: $75/S; $80/D; $5-8/ex prsn.

Waterville

Budget Host Airport Inn/ 400 Kennedy Memorial Dr, Waterville ME 04901. 207-873-3366. V,M,AE,D. I-95 (Exit 33) to Kennedy Dr, E 1/4 mi. Cable TV, dd phone, n/s rms, cont brfst, rstrnt/ lounge, arpt trans, t pkng, cot, crib. AAA. $30-45/S; $33-60/D; $4-8/ex prsn. 3/1-6/30: $30-40/S; $35-50/D. 7/1-8/31: $40-50/S; $40-60/D. Discs.

Econo Lodge/ 455 Kennedy Memorial Dr, Waterville ME 04901. 207-872-5577. AE,D,M,V. I-95 (Exit 33) to SR 11 N/ 137 E. Mtl on NE side of I-95. Nrby rstrnt, pool, cable TV, t pkng, outlets, n/s rms. AAA. $32-35/S; $36-43/D; $5/ex prsn. 5/1-6/30: $36-40/S; $43-50/D. 7/1-9/15: $46-51/S; $53-66/D. 9/16-10/31: $39-46/S; $46-53/D. Discs.

Wilton

Whispering Pines Motel/ Box 649, Rte 2, Wilton ME 04294. 207-645-3721/ Fax: Ext 31/ 800-626-7463. V,M,AE,D. 1 mi W of jct Rtes 2 & 4. N/s rms, cable TV, playgrnd, tt/dd phone, fax, copier, refrig, microwave, cot, crib, outlets, eff, b/f, lake, swimming. Free coffee, tea, cocoa, use of boats. AAA. $36-66/S; $42-72/D; $6/ex prsn. Disc: Senior, bsns, l/s, family, AAA. *Guaranteed rates.*

Maryland

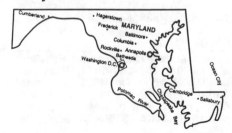

Aberdeen

Econo Lodge/ 820 W Bel Air Av, Aberdeen MD 21001. 410-272-5500. AE,V,M,DC. I-95 (Exit 85) at SR 22, turn S to Bel Air. Rstrnt, pool, fax, cable TV, t pkng, n/s rms. $30-38/S; $35-40/D; $4/ex prsn. 5/1-10/31: $38-43/S; $40-50/D. Discs.

Howard Johnson Lodge/ 793 W Bel Air Av, Aberdeen MD 21001. 410-272-6000/ Fax: 272-2287. V,M,D,AE,DC,CB. I-95 (Exit 85) to SR 22, W to mtl. N/s rms, mtg rm, b/f, pool, t pkng, fax, copier. Free cont brfst. $39-48/S; $47-56/D. Discs.

Baltimore

Howard Johnson Hotel/ 5701 Baltimore Ntl Pk, Baltimore MD 21228. 410-747-8900/ Fax: 744-3522. AE,V,M,DC,CB,D. I-695 (Exit 15A) at US 40. N/s rms, mtg rm, b/f, rstrnt, pool, t pkng, whrlpool, cable TV, VCR/ movies. $45-60/S; $45-70/D. Discs.

Motel 6/ 1654 Whitehead Ct, Baltimore MD 21207. 410-265-7660/ Fax: 944-0350. M,V,DC,D,AE. I-695 (Exit 17) to Security Blvd, E to Whitehead Ct, rt to mtl. Nrby rstrnt, cable TV, pool, n/s rms. Free local calls. $32-36/S; $38-42/D; $6/ex prsn. Higher spec event rates. Disc.

Also see Linthicum Heights.

Cambridge

Quality Inn/ Box 311, Cambridge MD 21613. 410-228-6900. V,M,D,AE. US 50 & Crusader Rd (Sunburst Hwy). Rstrnt/ lounge, fax, b/f, cable TV, t pkng, n/s rms. $41-46/S; $46-52/D; $6/ex prsn. Discs.

Camp Springs

Motel 6/ 5701 Allentown Rd, Camp Springs MD 20746. 301-702-1061/ Fax: 899-3478. M,V,DC,D,AE. I-95 (Exit 7A) to Hwy 5 (Branch Av), S to Allentown Rd, lt 1/2 mi to mtl. Cable TV, n/s rms. Free local calls. $40-46/S; $46-52/D; $6/ ex prsn. Higher spec event rates. Disc.

Capitol Heights

Motel 6/ 75 Hampton Park Blvd, Capitol Heights MD 20743. 301-499-0800/ Fax:

MARYLAND

808-7253. V,M,AE,D,DC. I-95 (Exit 15B) to SR 214 (Central Ave), W 1 blk to 1st traffic signal, lt on Hampton Park Blvd 1 blk. Nrby rstrnt, cable TV, laundry, elevator, n/s rms. Free local calls. $40-46/S; $46-52/D; $6/ex prsn. Higher spec event rates. Disc.

Clinton (Washington DC area)
Econo Lodge/ 7851 Malcolm Rd, Clinton MD 20735. 301-856-2800. V,M, AE,D,DC. I-95 (Exit 7A) to Branch Av, S 4 mi to mtl. Nrby rstrnt, fax, b/f, cable TV, t pkng, exerc equip, n/s rms, eff, laundry. Free cont brfst, nwspr, local calls. No pets. AAA. $45-80/S or D; $4/ex prsn. 1/25-4/30: $40-80/S or D. 1/21-1/24: $60-100/S or D. Discs.

Cockeysville (Timonium area)
Econo Lodge/ 10100 York Rd, Cockeysville MD 21030. 410-667-4900. V, M,AE,D,DC. Baltimore I-695 (Exit 26B) to York Rd (SR 45), N 4 mi. Rstrnt, pool, fax, cable TV, t pkng. Free cont brfst. $40-55/S; $45-60/D; $5/ex prsn. 3/1-4/30: $42-57/S; $47-62/D. Discs.

College Park (Washington DC area)
Quality Inn/ 7200 Baltimore Blvd, College Park MD 20740. 301-864-5820. V, M,D,AE. I-95 (Exit 25B) to US 1, 3 mi S to mtl. Rstrnt, pool, mtg rm, fax, b/f, cable TV, t pkng, n/s rms. Free cont brfst. No pets. AAA. $39-99/S or D; $10/ex prsn. Discs.

Easton
Econo Lodge/ 8175 Ocean Gateway, Easton MD 21601. 410-820-5555. V,M, AE. US 50 in tn. Meeting rm, fax, cable TV, t pkng, microwaves. Free cont brfst. $42-50/S; $44-52/D; $5-10/ ex prsn. 4/1-9/30: $48-69/S or D. Discs.

Elkridge
Econo Lodge/ 5895 Bonnie View Ln, Elkridge MD 21227. 410-796-1020. AE,V,M,DC. On US 1. From I-95: Nbnd, Exit 43 to SR 100, E to US 1, N 2 mi; Sbnd, Exit 47A to Hwy 195, E to (Exit 3) US 1, S 1/2 mi. Nrby rstrnt, pool, fax, cable TV, t pkng. $36-56/S; $40-60/D; $5/ex prsn. Discs.

Elkton
Econo Lodge/ 311 Belle Hill Rd, Elkton MD 21921. 410-392-5010. AE,V,M,DC. Jct of I-95 (Exit 109A) & SR 279, lt at light. Fax, b/f, cable TV, t pkng, outlets. Free local calls, coffee. $33-39/S; $39-45/D; $5/ex prsn. Discs.

Motel 6/ 223 Belle Hill Rd, Elkton MD 21921. 410-392-5020/ Fax: 398-1143. M,V,DC,D,AE. I-95 (Exit 109A) to SR 279, S 1 blk to Belle Hill Rd, turn rt. Nrby rstrnt, t pkng, cable TV, n/s rms. Free local calls. $28/S; $34/D; $6/ex prsn. Disc.

Gaithersburg (Washington DC area)
Econo Lodge/ 18715 N Frederick Av, Gaithersburg MD 20879. 301-963-3840. V,AE,M,DC. I-270 (Exit 11A) to Hwy 124 E (Montgomery Village Av), lt at 2nd light (Hwy 355, N Frederick Av), 3/4 mi on rt. Nrby rstrnt, mtg rm, fax, b/f, cable TV, t pkng, laundry, n/s rms. Free coffee, local calls. $38-49/S; $41-56/D; $6/ex prsn. Discs.

Grasonville
Friendship Inn/ 107 Hissey Rd, Grasonville MD 21638. 410-827-7272. V,M, AE,D,DC. US 50/301, E 7 1/2 mi past Bay Bridge (Exit 45B), lt onto overpass, lt to mtl. US 50/301 Wbnd, exit 45A. Rstrnt/ lounge, mtg rm, fax, b/f, cable TV, t pkng, n/s rms. $40-50/S; $48-60 /D; $8/ex prsn. 4/1-4/30: $40-60/S; $48-70/D. 5/1-11/15: $40-70/S; $48-80/D. Discs.

Hagerstown
Econo Lodge/ 18221 Mason-Dixon Rd, Hagerstown MD 21740. 301-791-3560. V,M,AE,D. I-81 (Exit 1) to SR 163 W (Mason Dixon Rd/ MD-PA line). Rstrnt, fax, b/f, cable TV, t pkng, exerc equip, outlets, n/s rms. AAA. $35-40/S; $38-43/D; $4/ex prsn. 3/15-11/14: $38-41/S; $43-46/D. Discs.

Motel 6/ 11321 Massey Blvd, Hagerstown MD 21740. 301-582-4445/ Fax: 582-0942. V,M,AE,D,DC. I-81 (Exit 5) to Halfway Rd, E 500 yds, turn rt on mall rd. Nrby rstrnt, cable TV, pool, n/s rms. Free local calls. Premier Award. $30-33/S; $36-39/D; $6/ex prsn. Disc.

Wellesley Inn/ 1101 Dual Highway, Hagerstown MD 21740. 301-733-2700/ Fax: 791-2106. AE,M,D,CB,V,DC. Cable TV, microwave. Free cont brfst.

MARYLAND

$40/S or D; $5/ex prsn. *Special rates - see discount section in front of book.

Hancock

Comfort Inn/ 118 Limestone Rd, Hancock MD 21750. 301-678-6101. V,M,DC,AE. I-70 (Exit 1B) to US 522, S to mtl. Nrby rstrnt, b/f, cable TV, n/s rms. Free cont brfst. No pets. $42-60/S; $45-60/D; $3/ex prsn. 5/1-11/31: $45-60/S; $48-60/D. Discs.

La Plata

Super 8 Motel/ 9400 Chesapeake St, La Plata MD 20646. 301-934-3465/ Fax: 934-3709. V,M,DC,CB,AE,D. US 30 at La Plata. B/f, n/s rms, outlets, t/b/rv pkng, cont brfst, copier, cable TV, suites, cot. Free local calls, crib. No pets. Prime Award. $36/S; $40-42/D; $4/ex prsn. Discs.

Laurel (Washington DC area)

Budget Host Valencia Motel/ 10131 Washington Blvd, Laurel MD 20723. 301-725-4200. AE,D,M,V. I-95 or Hwy 295, take Laurel exit to US 1 N. Family rms, dd phone, t pkng, cot. Free crib. No pets. AAA/ Mobil. $34/S; $34-39/D; $3/ex prsn. Discs.

Econo Lodge/ 9700 Washington Blvd, Laurel MD 20723. 301-776-8008. V,AE,M,DC. I-95 (Exit 38A) to SR 32, E 1 mi, turn rt on US 1, 2 mi on rt. Nrby rstrnt, fax, b/f, cable TV, n/s rms. Free coffee. No pets. AAA. $33-36/S; $36-46/D; $5/ex prsn. Discs.

Motel 6/ 3510 Old Annapolis Rd, Laurel MD 20724. 301-497-1544/ Fax: 317-8386. M,V,DC,D,AE. I-295 to Hwy 198 (Laurel exit), W to mtl. Cable TV, pool, n/s rms. Free local calls. $32-36/S; $38-42/D; $6/ex prsn. Higher spec event rates. Disc.

Linthicum Heights (Baltimore area)

Motel 6/ 5179 Raynor Av, Linthicum Heights MD 21090. 410-636-9070/ Fax: 789-0669. V,M,DC,D,AE. I-695: Ebnd, Exit 8 to Nursery Rd, E to Raynor Av; Wbnd, Exit 8, lt on Hammonds Ferry Rd, lt on Nursery Rd, rt on Raynor. Nrby rstrnt, cable TV, pool, elevator, n/s rms. Free local calls. $38-42/D; $6/ex prsn. Higher spec event rates. Disc.

Ocean City

Comfort Inn/ Box 1030 Ocean City MD 21842. 410-289-5155. AE,V,M,DC. US 50 E to Baltimore Av; N on Baltimore to 5th, rt to Broadwalk. 5th & Broadwalk. Oceanfront. Nrby rstrnt, pool, indr pool, b/f, cable TV, n/s rms. Free cont brfst. No pets. AAA. $39-89/S or D; $10/ex prsn. 5/1-6/22: $49-149/S or D. 6/23-8/20: $125-179/S or D. 8/21-9/24: $79-149/S or D. Discs.

Comfort Inn/ 11201 Coastal Hwy, Ocean City MD 21842. 410-524-3000. V,M,D,AE. US 113 to US 50. In N Ocean City across from beach. Rstrnt, indr pool, mtg rm, fax, whrlpool, cable TV, t pkng, microwave, refrig, n/s rms. No pets. Hospitality Award. AAA. $30-105/S or D; $10/ex prsn. 5/1-5/25, 9/4-10/28: $50-115/S or D. 5/26-9/3: $85-165/S or D. Discs.

Econo Lodge/ 14502 Coastal Hwy, Ocean City MD 21842. 410-250-1155. AE,D,M,V. US 50 E to US 90, to Coastal Hwy, N to 145th St. Rstrnt, pool, fax, b/f, cable TV, n/s rms. No pets. AAA. $45-79/S or D; $6/ex prsn. 5/1-6/15: $37-110/S or D. 6/16-10/4: $63-154/S or D. 10/5-10/17: $45-98/S or D. Discs.

Econo Lodge/ 6007 Coastal Hwy, Ocean City MD 21842. 410-524-6100. AE,D,M,V. SR 90, 61st St & bayside. Pool, mtg rm, fax, b/f, cable TV, t pkng, refrig, microwave, n/s rms. $29-44/S or D; $10/ex prsn. 5/1-9/4: $89-119/S or D. 9/5-10/2: $37-94/S or D. 10/3-10/31: $29-64/S or D. Discs.

Friendship Inn/ 32nd St & Baltimore Av, Ocean City MD 21842. 410-289-8136. V,M,AE. US 50 E to Ocean City, Baltimore Av N to 32nd St. Nrby rstrnt, pool, cable TV, n/s rms. No pets. $44-66/S or D; $6/ex prsn. 5/1-5/18: $42-64/S or D. 5/19-8/20: $78-120/S or D. 8/21-10/9: $80-102/S or D. Discs.

Quality Inn/ 1601 Boardwalk, Ocean City MD 21842. 410-289-4401. AE,V,M,DC. On the Boardwalk & Ocean at 17th St. Rstrnt, pool, indr pool, fax, b/f, sauna, whrlpool, cable TV, exerc equip, n/s rms, game rm, laundry, bikes. No pets. AAA. $39-84/S or D; $5-7/ex prsn. 5/1-6/22: $54-164/S or D. 6/23-9/3: $109-194/S or D. 9/4-10/28: $44-139/S or D. Discs.

MARYLAND

Quality Inn/ 5400 Beach Hwy, Ocean City MD 21842. 410-524-7200. AE,D, M,V. Oceanfront. Rstrnt/ lounge, pool, indr pool, fax, b/f, sauna, cable TV, exerc equip, n/s rms, laundry, kitchens, game rm. No pets. $38-119/S or D; $5/ex prsn. 5/1-6/15: $49-179/S; $54-179/D. 6/16-9/3: $119-214/S or D. 9/4-9/30: $52-154/S or D. Discs.

Rodeway Inn/ 2910 Baltimore Av, Ocean City MD 21842. 410-289-7291. V,M,D,AE. US 50 E to Ocean City, take Baltimore Av N to 29th St. Nrby rstrnt, indr pool, b/f, cable TV, n/s rms. $29-79/S or D; $10/ex prsn. 5/1-6/22: $29-115/S or D. 6/23-8/20: $95-160/S or D. 8/21-9/24: $69-129/S or D. Discs.

Pocomoke City

Quality Inn/ 825 Ocean Hwy, Box 480, Pocomoke City MD 21851. 410-957-1300. V,M,D,AE. US 13, 2 mi S of Pocomoke City. Rstrnt, pool, fax, cable TV, t pkng, n/s rms. Free cont brfst. AAA. $46-56/S or D; $6/ex prsn. 5/1-7/24: $44-69/S or D. 7/25-7/30: $75-86/S or D. 7/31-9/10: $56-69/S or D. Discs.

Princess Anne

Econo Lodge/ 10936 Market Ln, Princess Anne MD 21853. 410-651-9400/ Fax: 651-2868. AE,V,M,DC. US 13 N of SR 362 & 529. Nrby rstrnt/ lounge, pool, mtg rm, fax, b/f, cable TV, t pkng. Free coffee. AAA. $39-54/S or D; $5/ex prsn. 5/26-6/22: $49-75/S or D. 6/23-9/3: $60-75/S or D. Discs.

Salisbury

Budget Host Temple Hill Motel/ 1510 S Salisbury Blvd, Salisbury MD 21801. 410-742-3284/ Fax: 742-5343. AE,V,CB,DC,M,D. On US 13/ Salisbury Blvd, 2 mi S of Salisbury State Univ. Cable TV, dd phone, in-rm coffee, suites, nrby rstrnt, pool, cot. Free cont brfst. $34-38/S; $38-45/D; $5/ex prsn. 5/27-6/30: $36-40/S; $45-55/D. 7/1-9/5: $40-45/S; $55-65/D. Spec events: $65. Discs.

Comfort Inn/ 2701 N Salisbury Blvd, Salisbury MD 21801. 410-543-4666. V,M,D,AE. US 50 E to US 13, N to mtl. Nrby rstrnt, mtg rm, fax, b/f, cable TV, t pkng, outlets, n/s rms. Free cont brfst. $41-47/S; $43-49/D; $6/ex prsn. Discs.

Econo Lodge/ 712 N Salisbury Blvd, Salisbury MD 21801. 410-749-7155. V, M,D,AE. US 50, exit US Bsns 13; 2 blks from US 50 overpass. Nrby rstrnt, pool, fax, b/f, cable TV, t pkng, n/s rms. $36-45/S; $39-49/D; $5-8/ex prsn. 5/1-9/10: $39-89/S; $49-89/D. Discs.

Thurmont

Super 8 Motel Thurmont/ 300 Tippin Dr, Thur-mont MD 21788. 301-271-7888/ Fax: Ext 404. V,M,DC,CB,AE,D. US 15 to SR 806, turn W. B/f, n/s rms, toast bar, cable TV, suites, mtg rm, micro-refrig, cot. Free local calls, crib. Pride Award. $41-47/S; $46-51/D; $6/ex prsn. Higher spec event rates. Discs.

Upper Marlboro

Forest Hills Motel/ 2901 Crain Hwy, Upper Marlboro MD 20772. 301-627-3969. V,M,AE,D,DC. On US 301, 2 1/2 mi N SR 4. Refrig, tt phone, cot, crib. Free local calls, coffee, tea, cocoa. AAA/ Mobil. $41-44/S; $45-48/D; $4/ex prsn. Disc: Senior, l/s. *Guaranteed rates.*

Waldorf

Econo Lodge/ US 301, Acton Ln, Waldorf MD 20601. 301-645-0022. V, M, AE,D. I-95 (Exit 7A) to SR 5, S to US 301, SW to mtl. Nrby rstrnt, fax, b/f, cable TV, t pkng, microwave, refrig, game rm, laundry. Free cont brfst. AAA. $41-46/S; $46-51/D; $5/ex prsn. 33/1-10/31: $43-48/S; $48-53/D. Discs.

HoJo Inn/ 3125 Crain Hwy, Waldorf MD 20602. 301-932-5090/ Fax: Ext 109/ 800-826-4504. V,M,DC,AE. From beltway, Exit 7A to Hwy 301 to Waldorf. N/s rms, mtg rm, b/f, rstrnt, pool, t pkng, satellite TV, kitchenette. Free cont brfst. $39-46/S; $39-48/D. Higher spec event rates. Discs.

Super 8 Motel Waldorf/ 3550 Crain Hwy, Waldorf MD 20602. 301-932-8957/ Fax: Ext 403. V,M,DC,CB,AE,D. SR 5 to US 301 (Crain Hwy), S to mtl. B/f, n/s rms, b pkng, micro-refrig, cot. Free local calls, cont brfst, crib. $38-43 $44-49/D; $6/ex prsn. Higher spec event rates. Disc.

Massachusetts

Boston

See Framingham, Malden, Mansfield.

Centerville

Craigville Motel/ 8 Shoot Flying Hill Rd, Centervile MA 02632. 508-362-3401/ 800-338/5610. V,M,AE,D. US 6, Exit 6. Pool, cable TV, tt phone, cot, crib, conn rms. Free cont brfst, coffee, tea, cocoa. No pets. AAA. 3/1-11/30: $32/S; $36/D; $10/ex prsn. 6/1-9/30: $48/S or D. CLOSED DEC - FEB.

Chicopee (Springfield area)

Motel 6/ Burnett Rd, Chicopee MA 01020. 413-592-5141/ Fax: 592-0564. M,V,DC,D,AE. I-90 (Exit 6) to I-291, turn E on Burnett Rd. Nrby rstrnt, cable TV, laundry, pool, n/s rms, t pkng. Free local calls. Premier Award. $32-36/S; $38-42/D; $6/ex prsn. Disc.

Dalton

Inn at Village Square/ 633 Main St, Dalton MA 01226. 413-684-0860/ Fax: Ext 25. V,M,AE,D. MA Trnpk (Exit 2) to Rte 7, N to Pittsfield, Rte 8 S into Dalton. Rstrnt, cable TV, tt phone, fax, copier, crib. Free local calls, coffee, tea, cocoa. No pets. AAA. $45-55/S or D; $5/ex prsn. 6/1-9/15: $55-80/S; $65-90/D. 9/15-11/1: $55/S; $65/D. Disc: Senior, bsns.

East Wareham

Atlantic Motel/ 2859 Cranberry Hwy, E Wareham MA 02538. 508-295-0210. V,M,AE,D. Bet E & W lanes of US 6 & SR 28 at jct with SR 25. Nrby rstrnt/ lounge, pool, n/s rms, cable TV, tt phone, fax, refrig, cot, crib, outlets, t/b pkng. No pets. AAA. $36-45/S; $45-55/D; $5/ex prsn. 4/26-6/14, 9/8-10/13: $40-48/S; $48-60/D; $6/ex prsn. 6/15-9/7: $50-65/S; $60-75/D; $8/ex prsn. Disc: Senior, family, l/s. Guaranteed rates.

Framingham (Boston area)

Econo Lodge/ 1186 Worcester Rd, Framingham MA 01701. 508-879-1510. AE,D,M,V. I-90 (Exit 12) to SR 9, E past 2 lights, on rt. I-495 (Exit 23) to SR 9 E. Rstrnt/ lounge, cable TV, n/s rms. No pets. $35-85/S or D; $6/ex prsn. Discs.

Motel 6/ 1668 Worcester Rd, Framingham MA 01701. 508-620-0500/ Fax: 820-0868. V,M,AE,D,DC. I-90 (MA Trnpk) at (Exit 12) SR 9. From I-90, Exit 12 through toll booth to SR 9, W to traffic signal to "Y" in rd. Nrby rstrnt, cable TV, n/s rms. Free local calls. Premier Award. $40-43/S; $46-49/D; $6/ex prsn. 5/23-12/20: $36-38/S; $42-44/D. Higher spec event rates. Disc.

Gardner

Super 8 Motel/ N Pearson Blvd. Gardner MA 01440. 508-630-2888/ Fax: 630-1716. V,M,AE,D,DC. Rte 2, Exit 23, N to mtl. B/f, n/s rms, b pkng, cable TV, mtg rm. Free local calls, crib. No pets. $38-40/S; $44-50/D; $4/ex prsn. Discs.

Hyannis

Budget Host Hyannis Motel/ 614 Rte 132, Hyannis MA 02601. 508-775-8910/ Fax: 775-6476. V,AE,D,DC,M. Rte 6 (Exit 6) to Rte 132, S 2 1/2 mi to mtl. Nrby rstrnt/ lounge, pool, n/s rms, cable TV, tt/dd phone, fax, copier, refrig, cot, crib, eff, b/f. Free cont brfst, coffee, tea, cocoa. No pets. AAA/ Mobil. $35-39/S; $39-45/D; $5/ex prsn. 5/15-6/15, 9/1-10/15: $45/S; $45-55/D. 6/15-8/31: $55/S; $65-75/D; $8/ex prsn. Disc: Senior, l/s, TA, trkr, govt, milt.

Hyannis Center

HoJo Inn/ 447 Main St, Hyannis Center, MA 02601. 508-775-3000/ Fax: 771-1457. V,M,AE,D,DC. Hwy 132 to Arpt Rotary, rt onto Barnstable Rd to Main St., turn rt. (Cape Cod) N/s rms, mtg rm, lounge, indr pool, whrlpool. No pets. Gold Medal Winner. $32-95/S; $35-99/D. 5/1-6/30: $45-125/S; $49-130/D. 7/1-9/4: $89-130/S; $95-140/D.

9/5-10/31: $39-99/S; $45-109/D. Discs.

Lenox
Quality Inn/ 390 Pittsfield Rd, Box 755, Lenox MA 01240. 413-637-4244. AE, D,M,V. MA Trnpk (Exit 2) to US 20, W 5 mi to mtl. Rstrnt/ lounge, pool, fax, cable TV, t pkng. Free cont brfst. AAA. $45-55/S or D; $5/ex prsn. 5/1-6/1: $49-69/S or D. 6/2-6/29: $59-79/S or D. 6/30-10/21: $89-169/S or D. Discs.

Leominster (Worcester area)
Motel 6/ Commercial St, Leominster MA 01453. 508-537-8161/ Fax: 537-2082. M,V,DC,D,AE. Rte 2 to Rte 13, exit E to Searstown Mall. Nrby rstrnt, cable TV, laundry, pool, n/s rms, t pkng. Free local calls. Premier Award. $32-36/S; $38-42/D; $6/ex prsn. Disc.

Malden (Boston area)
Econo Lodge/ 321 Broadway, Malden MA 02148. 617-324-8500. V,M,D,AE. On SR 99, approx 1/4 mi N of SR 60. Nrby rstrnt, cable TV, t pkng, n/s rms. Free cont brfst. No pets. $45-85/S or D; $10/ex prsn. Discs.

Mansfield (Boston area)
Motel 6/ 60 Forbes Blvd, Mansfield MA 02048. 508-339-2323/ Fax: 337-6733. V,M,AE,D,DC. Jct I-95 & I-495 at SR 140. Nrby rstrnt, cable TV, pool, laundry, elevator, n/s rms, t pkng. Free local calls. $40/S; $46/D; $6/ex prsn. Higher spec event rates. Disc.

Milford
Tage Inn/ 24 Beaver St, Milford MA 01757. 508-478-8243/ Fax: 634-9936/ 800-322-8243. V,M,AE,D,DC. I-495, Exit 19, next to Burger King. Nrby rstrnt/ lounge, n/s rms, cable TV, tt/dd phone, mtg rm, fax, copier, nwspr, laundry, refrig, elevator, cot, crib, t/b pkng, conn rms, b/f. Free local calls, cont brfst, coffee, tea, cocoa. No pets. AAA. $40/S; $48/D. Space available. Disc: Bsns, family, trkr.

North Attleboro (Providence RI area)
Super 8 Motel/ 787 S Washington St, N Attleboro MA 02760. 508-643-2900. V, M,AE,D,DC. I-295 (Exit 1B) to N Attleboro/ US 1. I-95 (Exit 4) to I-295. B/f, n/s rms, cont brfst, cable TV, kitchenettes, suites. $36-44/S; $40-54/D; $5/ex prsn. Discs.

North Truro
Crow's Nest Motel/ Rte 6A, Box 177, N Truro MA 02652. 508-487-9031/ 800-499-9799. V,M,D. 1 mi off Rte 6. Nrby rstrnt, cable TV, cot, crib, eff. No pets. AAA/ Mobil. $48/S; $48-50/D; $7/ex prsn. Memorial Wknd, 6/21-9/2: $74/S; $74-78/D; $10/ex prsn. Columbus Wknd: $63/S; $63-65. *Guaranteed rates.*

Northborough
Friendship Inn/ SR 9 & US 20, Northborough MA 05132. 508-842-8941. AE,V,M,DC. I-495 (Exit 23B) to SR 9, W 5 mi to US 20 W. Rstrnt/ lounge, fax, cable TV, n/s rms. Free cont brfst. No pets. AAA. $42-56/S; $46-61/D; $5/ex prsn. 5/1-10/31: $46-61/S; $49-66/D. Discs.

South Deerfield
Motel 6/ US 5-10, S Deerfield MA 01373. 413-665-7161/ Fax: 665-7437. V,M,DC,D,AE. I-91 (Exit 24) to US 5, NE to mtl. Cable TV, nrby rstrnt, indr pool, n/s rms, t pkng. Free local calls. Premier Award. $36-40/S; $42-46/D; $6/ex prsn. 5/23-12/20: $32-34/S; $38-40/D. Higher spec event rates. Disc.

South Wellfleet
Even'tide Motel/ Rte 6, Box 41, S Wellfleet MA 02663. 508-349-3410/ Fax: 349-7804/ 800-368-0007. V, M,AE,D,DC,CB. On US 6 at mileage marker 98, 4 mi N of Eastham National Seashore Visitors Center. Nrby rstrnt, indr pool, n/s rms, cable TV, playgrnd, tt/dd phone, fax, laundry, refrig, microwave, cot, crib, t/b pkng, eff. Free coffee, tea. No pets. AAA/ Mobil. $40/S; $45-59/D; $7-10/ex prsn. 6/21-9-2: $72/S; $72-115/D. 9/3-10/6: $57/S; $62-79/D. Disc: Senior, l/s, AAA. No discounts summer season. *Guaranteed rates.*

South Yarmouth (Cape Cod area)
Econo Lodge/ 37 Neptune Ln, Box 530, S Yarmouth MA 02664. 508-394-9801. AE,V,M,DC. US 6 E to Exit 7, lt to Willow, lt to Higgens-Crowell Rd., 2 1/2 mi to SR 28, lt to mtl. Adj rstrnt, indr pool, mtg rm, b/f, whrlpool, cable TV, t pkng, n/s rms. No pets. $40-60/S or D; $5/ex

prsn. 6/30-9/3: $65-85/S or D. Discs.

Springfield
Friendship Inn/ 1356 Boston Rd, Springfield MA 01119. 413-783-2111. V,M, AE,D,DC. I-91 (Exit 8) to I-291, NE to (Exit 5A) US 20 (Indian Orchard Rd), E 3 mi to Boston Rd. I-90 (Exit 7) to SR 21, lt to US 20, turn rt. Nrby rstrnt/ lounge, pool, fax, cable TV,, n/s rms. $32-42/S; $38-46/D; $5/ ex prsn. 5/1-5/31, 7/1-10/15: $50-55/S; $55-60/D. 6/1-6/30: $42-46/S; $46-50/D. Discs. Also see Chicopee, West Springfield.

West Boylston (Worcester area)
Friendship Inn/ 90 Sterling St, W Boylston MA 01583. 508-835-6247. AE,M,V,DC. I-290 to SR 140, N to SR 12, N 2 mi to mtl. Nrby rstrnt, pool, fax, cable TV, t pkng, n/s rms. No pets. $33-50/S; $36-55/D; $5/ex prsn. Discs.

West Springfield (Springfield area)
Econo Lodge/ 1533 Elm St, W Springfield MA 01089. 413-734-8278. V,M,AE,D. I-91 (Exit 13B) to US 5 S. Nrby rstrnt, mtg rm, fax, cable TV, t pkng, outlets, n/s rms. $32-60/S; $35-65/D; $5/ex prsn. 5/1-9/14: $35-65/S; $40-70/D. 9/15-10/1: $45-75/S; $50-80/D. Discs.

Motel 6/ 106 Capital Dr, W Springfield MA 01089. 413-788-4000/ Fax: 781-3168. M,V,DC,D,AE. I-91 (Exit 13A) at Riverdale St/ Hwy 5, N to Ashley Av (1st light), rt to Capital Dr, rt. Nrby rstrnt, cable TV, n/s rms, t pkng. Free local calls. Premier Award. $30-36/S; $36-40/D; $6/ex prsn. Disc.

West Yarmouth
Mariner Motor Lodge/ 573 Main St, W Yarmouth MA 02673. 508-771-7887/ Fax: 711-2811/ 800-445-4050. V,M, AE,D. Rte 6 E, Exit 7, lt of ramp, next immediate lt to 2nd stoplight, lt on Rte 28; motel is 1/2 mi on rt. Nrby rstrnt/ lounge, pool, indr pool, sauna, whrlpool, n/s rms, cable TV, games, tt/dd phone, mtg rm, refrig, cot, crib, t/b/rv pkng, b/f. Free cont brfst. No pets. AAA/ Mobil. $32-48/S or D; $5/ex prsn. 6/21-9/8: $69-92/S or D. Wknds, holiday wknds, school vacation periods: $59-92/S or D. Disc: Senior. *Guaranteed rates.*

Williamstown
Willows Motel/ 480 Main St, Williamstown MA 01267. 413-458-5768. V, M,AE. On Main St, in Williamstown. Nrby rstrnt/ lounge, pool, n/s rms, cable TV, tt/dd phone, refrig, microwave, cot, crib, t/b/rv pkng, conn rms. Free local calls, coffee, tea, cocoa. AAA. $38-45/S; $42-55/D; $5/ex prsn. 5/26-11/7, Sun-Thurs: $42-45/S; $49-61/D. Fri-Sat 5/24-11/10: $62-66/S; $62-76/D; $7/ex prsn.

Worcester
Econo Lodge/ 531 Lincoln St, Worcester MA 01605. 508-852-5800. AE,D,M,V. I-290 (Exit 20) to SR 70, N 1/2 mi. Nrby rstrnt, t pkng, n/s rms. $36-46/S; $42-52/D; $5/ex prsn. Discs.

Also see Leominster, West Boylston.

Michigan

Allegan
Budget Host Sunset Motel/ 1580 Lincoln, Allegan MI 49010. 616-673-6622. V,M,D,AE. SR 40, 89, 1/2 mi N of tn. Cable TV, dd phone, t pkng, outlets, cot, crib. $30-75/S; $32-80/D; $5-10/ex prsn. Tulip time, spec events: $45-95.

Alma
Triangle Motel/ 131 W Lincoln, Alma MI 48801. 517-463-2296. V,M. Hwy 27: Nbnd, first Alma exit (SR 27) 1 blk W; Sbnd, State Rd exit, 1 blk S. Nrby rstrnt/ lounge, n/s rms, cable TV, tt/dd

phone, refrig, cot, outlets, t/b/rv pkng, b/f. Free local calls. $28/S; $30-35/D. Memorial Day wknd: $45-55/S; $55-65/D. Disc: Trkr, l/s. *Guaranteed rates.*

Alpena
Dew Drop Inn Motel/ 2469 French Rd, Alpena MI 49707. 517-356-4414. V, M,AE,D,DC,CB. Jct US 23 N & French Rd (1 mi N of hospital). N/s rms, cable TV, tt/dd phone, refrig, microwave, cot, crib, outlets, t/b/rv pkng. Free local calls. No pets. AAA. $32/S; $32-36/D; $3/ex prsn. 5/1-10/31: $36/S; $36-42/D. Disc: Senior, bsns, TA, govt, l/s, family, trkr, milt. *Guaranteed rates.*

Ann Arbor
Motel 6/ 3764 S State St, Ann Arbor MI 48104. 313-665-9900/ Fax: 665-2202. V,M,AE,D,DC. I-94 (Exit 177) to State St, S to mtl. Nrby rstrnt, cable TV, pool, n/s rms, Free local calls. $36/S; $42/D; $6/ex prsn. Higher spec event rates. Disc.

Auburn Hills (Detroit area)
Motel 6/ 1471 Opdyke Rd, Auburn Hills MI 48326. 810-373-8440/ Fax: 373-8642. M,V,DC,D,AE. I-75 (Exit 79) to University Dr, SW to Opdyke Rd, turn rt. Nrby rstrnt, cable TV, pool, n/s rms. Free local calls. $32/S; $38/D; $6/ex prsn. Disc.

Baraga
Lakeshore Cafe & Motel/ Rte 1, Box 233, Baraga MI 49908. 906-353-6256. V,M,AE,D. 6 mi N of Baraga on US 41. Rstrnt/ lounge, sauna, n/s rms, satellite TV, tt phone, crib. Free local calls, coffee, tea, cocoa. AAA. $28/S; $34-44/D; $4/ex prsn. *Guaranteed rates.*

Battle Creek
Comfort Inn/ 165 Capital Av SW, Battle Creek MI 49015. 616-965-3976. V,M, D,AE. I-94 (Exit 98B) N to SR 66, 3 mi to dntn (Exit 3) to Dickman Rd, lt 1/4 mi. Rstrnt/ lounge, pool, mtg rm, fax, cable TV, t pkng. Free cont brfst. $37-49/S; $47-66/D; $7/ex prsn. Discs.

Motel 6/ 4775 Beckley Rd, Battle Creek MI 49017. 616-979-1141/ Fax: 979-1733. V,M,D,AE,DC. I-94 (Exit 97) to Capital Av, S to mtl. Nrby rstrnt, cable TV, laundry, pool, n/s rms. Free local calls. $30-32/S; $36-38/D; $6/ex prsn. Disc.

Benton Harbor (St Joseph area)
Comfort Inn/ 1598 Mall Dr, Benton Harbor MI 49022. 616-925-1880. V,M,AE, D,DC. I-94 (Exit 29) to Pipestone Rd N, lt on Mall Dr to mtl. Nrby rstrnt, indr pool, fax, b/f, whrlpool, cable TV, n/s rms. Free cont brfst. AAA. $40-50/S; $46-56/D; $5/ex prsn. 5/26-9/3: $50-70/S; $56-76/D. Discs.

Motel 6/ 2063 Pipestone Rd, Benton Harbor MI 49022. 616-925-5100/ Fax: 934-8404. V,M,DC,D,AE. I-94 (Exit 29) to Pipestone Rd, NW to Mall Dr, rt to mtl. Nrby rstrnt, cable TV, pool, n/s rms, t pkng. Free local calls. $26-29/S; $32-35/D; $6/ex prsn. Disc.

Bridgeport (Frankenmuth area)
Motel 6/ 636 Dixie Hwy, Bridgeport MI 48722. 517-777-2582/ Fax: 777-9546. V,M,AE,D,DC. I-75 (Nbnd, Exit 144B; Sbnd, Exit 144) to Dixie Hwy. On W side of frwy. Nrby rstrnt, cable TV, n/s rms. Free local calls. Premier Award. $29-36/S; $35-42/D; $6/ex prsn. Disc.

Cadillac
Pine Chata Motel/ 5936 E M-55, Cadillac MI 49601. 616-775-4677/ Fax: 779-9560. V,M,D. 1/4 mi W on M-55; off 115 & M-55 jct. Nrby rstrnt, n/s rms, cable TV, tt phone, mtg rm, fax, copier, refrig, cot, outlets, t/rv pkng, lake. Free local calls, beach access. Only small pets. AAA. $32-48/S or D; $5/ex prsn. 9/1-12/25, 4/1-6/1: $28/S; $30-48/D. Spec event, holiday, wknd rates: $48/S; $58/D. Disc: Senior, bsns, govt, l/s, trkr, milt.

Canton (Detroit area)
Budgetel Inns/ 41211 Ford Rd, Canton MI 48187. 313-981-1808/ Fax: 981-7150. V,M,D,AE,DC,CB. I-275, Exit 25, W on Ford Road (Rte 153). N/s rms, b/f, fax, rstrnt. Free cont brfst, in-rm coffee, local calls. AAA. $36-50/S; $43-57/D. Spec rates may apply. Discs.

Super 8 Motel/ 3933 Lotz Rd, Canton MI 48188. 313-722-8880. V,M,DC,CB, AE,D. I-275 (Exit 22) to Michigan Av, turn E to Lotz Rd. B/f, n/s rms, suites, mtg rm, microwave, refrig, t pkng. Free

MICHIGAN

coffee, crib. $36/S; $42/D; $6/ex prsn. Higher spec event rates. Discs.

Canton Township (Detroit area)
Motel 6/ 41216 Ford Rd, Canton Township MI 48187. 313-981-5000/ Fax: 981-5432. M,V,DC,D,AE. I-275 (Exit 25) to Ford Rd, W to Bob Evans Rstrnt, turn rt to mtl. Nrby rstrnt, cable TV, pool, n/s rms. Free local calls. $30-32/S; $36-38/D; $6/ex prsn. Disc.

Cascade (Grand Rapids area)
Budgetel Inns/ 2873 Kraft Av SE, Cascade MI 49512. 616-956-3300/ Fax: 956-5561. V,M,D,AE,DC,CB. I-96, exit 43B E on 28th St. Take 28th St to Kraft Av & head S. N/s rms, b/f, fax, rstrnt. Free cont brfst, in-rm coffee, local calls. AAA. $37-48/S; $44-55/D. Discs.

Charlevoix
Sleep Inn/ 801 Petoskey Av, Charlevoix MI 49720. 616-547-0300. V,M,D,AE. On US 31 N in Charlevoix, adjacent to Charlevoix Golf Course. Nrby rstrnt, indr pool, mtg rm, fax, b/f, cable TV, n/s rms. Free cont brfst. $35-75/S; $38-80/D; $5/ex prsn. 5/16-10/31: $35-125/S; $38-130/D. 12/25-12/31: $75-125/S; $80-130/D. Discs.

Charlotte
Super 8 Motel/ I-69 & SR 50, Charlotte MI 48813. 517-543-8288. V,M,AE,D,DC. At jct of I-69 (Exit 90) & SR 50. B/f, n/s rms, toast bar, mtg rm, t/b pkng. Free local calls, crib. Pride Award. $40/S; $45/D; $5/ex prsn. Higher spec event rates. Discs.

Clare
Budget Host Clare Motel/ 1110 N McEwan, Clare MI 48617. 517-386-7201/ Fax: 386-2362. V,M,AE,D,DC,CB. On Bsns Rte 27, N of Bsns 10. Cable TV, dd phone, family rm, n/s rms, pool, whrlpool, t pkng, outlets, cot. Free crib. Mobil. $35-38/S; $38-62/D; $3/ex prsn. 5/15-9/15: $38-44/S; $44-53/D. Spec events: $52. Discs.

Coldwater
Econo Lodge/ 884 W Chicago Rd, Coldwater MI 49036. 517-278-4501. AE,V,M,DC. I-69 (Exit 13) to US 12, W 3 1/2 mi. Nrby rstrnt, fax, cable TV, t pkng, n/s rms. Free cont brfst, local calls. $30-36/S; $35-42/D; $6/ex prsn. 5/1-9/30: $33-38/S; $39-44/D. Discs.

Little King Motel/ 847 E Chicago Rd, Coldwater MI 49036. 517-278-6660. V,M,AE,D. US 12, 2 blks E of I-69 (US 12 Exit). Nrby rstrnt/ lounge, cable TV, dd phone, outlets, playgrnd, cot, crib. AAA/ IMA. $28/S; $32-40/D; $4/ex prsn. 5/1-10/31: $34/S; $38-46/D. Disc: TA, comm.

DeWitt
Sleep Inn/ 1101 Commerce Park Dr, DeWitt MI 48820. 517-669-8823. V,M,D,AE. I-69 to (Exit 87) Bsns US 127, N 1/2 mi to Commerce Park Dr. Nrby rstrnt, pool, mtg rm, fax, b/f, cable TV, t pkng, n/s rms. Free cont brfst. No pets. $44/S; $49-59/D; $5/ex prsn. 5/1-12/30: $43-53/S; $48-58/D. Discs.

Detroit
Budgetel Inns/ 30900 Van Dyke Rd, Detroit MI 48093. 810-574-0550/ Fax: 574-0750. V,M,D,AE,DC,CB. I-75, Exit I-696 E, N on Van Dyke Rd to 13 Mile Rd. N/s rms, b/f, fax, rstrnt, b pkng. Free cont brfst, in-rm coffee, local calls. AAA. $36-48/S; $43-55/D. 1/1-3/30: $34-46/S; $41-53/D. Spec rates may apply. Discs.

Also see Auburn Hills, Belleville, Canton, Canton Township, Roseville, Southfield, Southgate, Taylor, Warren.

Dundee
Comfort Inn/ 621 Tecumseh, Dundee MI 48131. 313-529-5505. V,M,D,AE. US 23 (Exit 17) to SR 50, E to Otter Dr. Nrby rstrnt, pool, mtg rm, fax, b/f, cable TV, t pkng, n/s rms. Free cont brfst. No pets. AAA. $36-54/S; $40-62/D; $5/ex prsn. 3/1-4/30, 9/1-10/31: $40-70/S; $54-76/D. 5/1-8/31: $48-70/S; $54-76/D. Discs.

Escanaba
Norway Pines Motel/ 7111 US 2, Escanaba/ Gladstone MI 49837. 906-786-5119. V,M,AE,D,DC,CB. On US 2, bet Escanaba & Gladstone. Nrby rstrnt, whrlpool, n/s rms, cable TV, playgrnd, tt/dd phone, refrig, outlets, t/b/rv pkng, conn rms. Free local calls, coffee. AAA. $28-33/S; $33-37/D. 6/23-9/7: $33-

MICHIGAN

40/S; $40-49/D. Disc: Senior, bsns, l/s, family, trkr, milt. *Guaranteed rates.*

Also see Gladstone.

Farmington Hills (Detroit area)
Motel 6/ 38300 Grand River Av, Farmington Hills MI 48335. 810-471-0590/ 471-2435. M,V,DC,D,AE. I-275/ I-96 or I-696, take Rte 102/ Farmington Hills exit to Grand River Av to mtl. Nrby rstrnt, cable TV, n/s rms. Free local calls. $30/S; $36/D; $6/ex prsn. Disc.

Flint
Econo Lodge/ 932 S Center Rd, Flint MI 48503. 810-744-0200. AE,V,M,DC. I-75 to I-69, E to Center Rd, N to mtl. Rstrnt/ lounge, indr pool, mtg rm, fax, b/f, cable TV, t pkng, n/s rms. No pets. $38-46/S; $41-46/D; $6/ex prsn. 6/16-11/2: $40-60/S; $42-60/D. Discs.

Howard Johnson Lodge/ G-3277 Miller Rd, Flint MI 48507. 810-733-5910/ Fax: 733-2713. V,M,AE,D,DC. I-75 (Nbnd, Exit 117B/ Sbnd, Exit 117) to Miller Rd. N/s rms, b/f, arpt trans, t pkng, cable TV, fax, kitchenettes, mtg rm, pool, nrby rstrnt. Free cont brfst, local call. No pets. $35-50/S; $40-55/D. 6/17-9/17: $40-60/S; $50-70/D. Discs.

Motel 6/ 2324 Austin Pkwy, Flint MI 48507. 810-767-7100/ Fax: 767-5702. M,V,DC,D,AE. I-75 at (Exit 117B) Miller Rd, E to Austin Pkwy, turn lt. Nrby rstrnt, cable TV, pool, n/s rms. Free local calls. $30/S; $36/D; $6/ex prsn. Disc.

Frankenmuth

See Bridgeport.

Gaylord
Downtown Motel/ 208 S Otsego Av, Gaylord MI 49735. 517-732-5010. V,M, AE,D,DC,CB. I-75 Exit 282, turn E, rt at first light past RR tracks. Nrby rstrnt/ lounge, n/s rms, cable TV, tt/dd phone, copier, cot, crib, outlets, t/b/rv pkng, eff. Free local calls, coffee, tea. AAA. $29-48/S; $29-52/D; $5/ex prsn. 5/1-10/31: $33-54/S; $33-58/D. 6/14-6/15, 9/1-9/2, 12/26-12/31: $48-52/S; $48-66/D.

Timberly Motel/ 881 S Otsego, Gaylord MI 49735. 517-732-5166. V,M,D,DC. I-75, Exit 279, rt 1 1/2 mi. Nrby rstrnt, n/s rms, cable TV, tt/dd phone, fax, nwspr, cot, crib, outlets, conn rms. Free local calls, coffee. AAA. $38-54/S; $38-60/D. Higher spec event/ holiday, wknd rates. Disc: Senior, bsns, l/s.

Gladstone (Escanaba area)
Bay View Motel/ 7110 US 2/ 41, SR 35, Gladstone MI 49837. 906-786-2843/ Fax: 786-6218/ 800-547-1201. V, M,AE,D. 4 1/2 mi N of US 2 & 41 & M-35. Nrby rstrnt, indr pool, sauna, n/s rms, cable TV, video games, playgrnd, tt phone, fax, copier, refrig, cot, crib, outlets. Free local calls, coffee. AAA/ Mobil. $30-40/S; $32-42/D; $5/ex prsn. 6/1-9/15: $45-55/S; $50-60/D. Higher spec event rates. Disc: Senior, bsns, govt, milt, l/s.

Budget Host Terrace Bay Inn & Resort/ 7146 P Rd, Box 453, Gladstone MI 49829. 906-786-7554. V,AE,CB,DC, D,M. US Hwys 2 & 41 bet Escanaba & Gladstone. Rstrnt/ lounge, indr pool, sauna, whirlpool, exerc equip, cable TV, VCR/ movies, video games, tt phone, mtg rm, fax, copier, nwspr, cot, crib, outlets, t/b/rv pkng, conn rms, tennis. No pets. Mobil. No pets. Mobil. $34/S; $48/D; $5/ex prsn. 5/1-9/30: $40/S; $58/D. Spec events, holidays, wknds 7/1-8/31: $48/S; $72/D. Disc: Senior, govt, l/s. *Guaranteed rates.*

Grand Marais
Budget Host Welker's Lodge/ Canal St, Box 277, Grand Marais MI 49839. 906-494-2361/ Fax: 494-2371. AE,V,M,D. End of SR 77 on Lake Superior. Cable TV, rstrnt, mtg rms, kitchens, indr pool, playgrnd, picnic area, sauna, whrlpool, laundry, babysitters, t pkng, cot, crib. Mobil. $37-55/S; $42-70/D; $5/ex prsn. Discs.

Grand Rapids
Econo Lodge/ 250 28th St SW, Grand Rapids MI 49548. 616-452-2131. AE,V,M,DC. US 131 at 28th St exit. Adj rstrnt, pool, fax, b/f, cable TV, t pkng, exerc equip, n/s rms. $44-48/S; $49-53/D; $5/ex prsn. 5/1-10/31: $42-46/S; $47-51/D. Discs.

MICHIGAN 140

Exel Inn/ 4855 28th St SE, Grand Rapids MI 49512. 616-957-3000/ Fax: 957-0194. M,V,AE,D,DC,CB I-96 (Exit 43A) to 28th St, go W 1/2 mi. On SE side of city. Nrby rstrnt, cable TV, game rm, laundry, fax, micro-fridge, n/s rms. Free cont brfst. AAA. $34-40/S; $40-49/D. Higher spec event rates. Discs.

Motel 6/ 3524 28th St SE, Grand Rapids MI 49508. 616-957-3511/ Fax: 957-4369. M,V,DC,D,AE. I-96 (Exit 43B) to 28th St, W 2.3 mi to mtl. Nrby rstrnt, cable TV, pool, n/s rms. Free local calls. $30/S; $36/D; $6/ex prsn. Disc.

Also see Cascade, Walker.

Harbor Beach

Train Station Motel/ 2044 N Lakeshore Dr, Harbor Beach MI 48441. 517-479-3215. V,M,AE,DC. 60 mi N of port Huron/Sarnia Ont on SR 25. Rstrnt/ lounge, n/s rms, satellite TV, tt/dd phone, copier, outlets, t/b/rv pkng. Free local calls, coffee. AAA. $40-62/S or D; $5/ex prsn. 12/1-4/1: $40-52/S or D. Disc: Senior, bsns, family. *Guaranteed rates.*

Holland

Budget Host Wooden Shoe Motel/ 465 US 31 & 16th St, Holland MI 49423. 616-392-8521. AE,V,D,M. On US 31 N, 3 mi W of Hwy 196, Exit 52. Family Rm, dd phone, cont brfst, nrby rstrnt/ lounge, pool, game rm, tanning salon, t pkng, outlets, cot, crib. AAA. $25-35/S; $35-40/D; $5/ex prsn. 5/1-9/30: $48-53/S; $56-60/D.

Houghton Lake

Rest All Inn/ 9580 W Lake City Rd, Houghton Lake MI 48629. 517-422-3119/ Fax: 422-5561/ 800-866-4322. V,M,D. Jct US 27 & SR 55. Whrlpool, n/s rms, cable TV, video games, TDD, tt/dd phone, fax, copier, laundry, refrig, cot, crib, outlets, t/b/rv pkng, conn rms, b/f. Free coffee. No pets. AAA. $37/S; $40/D; $5/ex prsn. 5/1-9/30: $41/S; $44/D. Last 2 wknds in Jan: $70/S; $75/D; $10/ex prsn. Disc: Senior, bsns, l/s, trkr. *Guaranteed rates.*

Indian River

Nor-Gate Motel/ 4846 S Straits Hwy, Indian River MI 49749. 616-238-7788. V,M,D. I-75, Exit 310, 2 blk W to Straits Hwy, S 1 1/2 mi. N/s rms, cable TV, dd phone, crib, eff. No pets. AAA/ Mobil. $30-34/S; $34-42/D; $3/ex prsn.

Iron Mountain

Howard Johnson/ 1609 S Stephenson Av, Iron Mountain MI 49801. 906-774-6220/ Fax: 774-6618. V,M,D,AE,DC, CB. On US 2, 2 mi W of US 141. N/s rms, mtg rm, b/f, t pkng, pool, hot tub, nrby rstrnt/ lounge. Free cont brfst. $35-46/S; $41-52/D. Discs.

Woodlands Motel/ N 3957 N US 2, Iron Mountain MI 49801. 906-774-6106. V, M,AE,D. On US 2, 1 mi N of city limits. N/s rms, cable TV, playgrnd, tt/dd phone, refrig, microwave, cot, crib, outlets, t pkng, eff. Free local calls. Mobil. $26-30/S; $30-40/D; $5/ex prsn. Disc: Senior, l/s, milt, family. *Guaranteed rates.*

Ironwood

Budget Host Cloverland Motel/ 447 W Cloverland Dr, Ironwood MI 49938. 906-932-1260. V,AE,DC,D,M. On US 2 W (Cloverland Dr). Nrby rstrnt, n/s rms, cable TV, arpt trans, tt phone, cot. Free local calls. AAA/ Mobil. $28-33/S; $33-45/D; $5/ex prsn. 10/15-12-20: $26-33/S; $33-40/D. 12/25-1/3: $65/S; $65-80/D. Disc: Senior, bsns, govt, l/s, family. *Guaranteed rates.*

Twilight Time Motel/ 930 E Cloverland Dr, Ironwood MI 49938. 906-932-3010/ 800-367-4775. V,M,AE,D,DC,CB. On US 2 (Cloverland Dr). Nrby rstrnt/ lounge, n/s rms, cable TV, dd phone, nwspr, refrig, cot, crib, t/b pkng. Free local calls, coffee. AAA. $26/S; $32-38/D; $5/ex prsn. 12/25-1/1: $60/S or D. Disc: Senior. *Guaranteed rates.*

Jackson

Motel 6/ 830 Royal Dr, Jackson MI 49204. 517-789-7186/ Fax: 789-5490. M,V,DC,D,AE. I-94 (Exit 138) to US 127, S to Andrew, lt to Royal Dr, turn lt. Nrby rstrnt, cable TV, pool, n/s rms. Free local calls. $30-32/S; $36-38/D; $6/ex prsn. Higher spec event rates. Disc.

Rodeway Inn/ 901 Rosehill Dr, Jackson

MI 49202. 517-787-1111/ Fax: 787-1119. V,M,AE. I-94 (Exit 141) to Elm Rd, N to Rosehill Dr, lt to mtl. Lounge, pool, mtg rm, cable TV, t pkng. Free cont brfst. AAA. $40-80/S; $45-100/D; $4/ex prsn. Spec events: $100-135/S or D. Discs.

Kalamazoo

Budgetel Inns/ 2203 S 11th St, Kalamazoo MI 49009. 616-372-7999/ Fax: 372-6095. V,M,D,AE,DC,CB. N from I-94 on US 131, exit 36B. N/s rms, b/f, fax. Free cont brfst, in-rm coffee, local calls. AAA. $38-50/S; $45-57/D. 1/1-3/30: $36-48/S; $43-55/D. Spec rates may apply. Discs.

Motel 6/ 3704 Van Rick Rd, Kalamazoo MI 49002. 616-344-9255/ Fax: 344-3014. M,V,DC,D,AE. I-94 (Exit 80) at Sprinkle Rd, turn S. Nrby rstrnt, cable TV, pool, n/s rms. Free local calls. $30/S; $36/D; $6/ex prsn. Disc.

Lake City

Northcrest Motel/ 1341 S Lakeshore Dr, Lake City MI 49651. 616-839-2075. V,M,D. I-75 N to Hwy 55, W to Hwy 66, lt 1 mi. Indr pool, whrlpool, cable TV, dd phone, cot, crib, b/f. Free local calls. AAA. $40-46/S or D; $2/ex prsn. *Guaranteed rates.*

Lansing

Howard Johnson/ 6741 S Cedar St, Lansing MI 48911. 517-694-0454/ Fax: 694-7087. AE,V,M,DC,CB,D. I-96 (Exit 104) at Cedar/ Pennsylvania exit. N/s rms, mtg rm, b/f, pool, t pkng, cable TV, suites, cont brfst, eff. $32-95/S; $37-95/D. Discs.

Motel 6/ 7326 W Saginaw Hwy, Lansing MI 48917. 517-321-1444/ Fax: 886-2024. V,M,AE,D,DC. I-69/ I-96 (Exit 93B) to Saginaw Hwy, E to mtl. Nrby rstrnt, cable TV, laundry, pool, n/s rms. Free local calls. $30-32/S; $36-38/D; $6/ex prsn. Discs.

Motel 6/ 112 E Main St, Lansing MI 48933. 517-484-8722/ Fax: 484-9434. V,M,AE,D,DC. I-496 at SR 27. Cable TV, laundry, pool, n/s rms. Free local calls. $26-27/S; $32-33/D; $6/ex prsn. Discs.

Mackinaw City

Budget Host Mackinaw City/ 517 N Huron Av, Box 672, Mackinaw City MI 49701. 616-436-5543. V,M,AE,D. From frwy, Exit 339: Nbnd, lt to stop sign, rt 2 blks; Sbnd, rt on Lovingy St to N Huron, rt 4 blks. Cable TV, pool, playgrnd, nrby rstrnt, beach access, crib. AAA. $28-72/S; $32-78/D; $5/ex prsn. 6/21-8/24: $48-125/S or D. 8/25-10/26: $36-68/S; $38-72/D. CLOSED NOV - MAR. Disc.

Comfort Inn/ 611 S Huron Av, Box 40, Mackinaw City MI 49701. 616-436-5057. V,M,D,AE. I-75 (Exit 338) to SR 108, N to Central, E to Huron, S to mtl. Nrby rstrnt, indr pool, b/f, whrlpool, cable TV, n/s rms. No pets. AAA. $48-98/S or D; $6/ex prsn. 6/23-9/3: $68-150/S or D. CLOSED 10/29-4/30. Discs.

Econo Lodge/ 519 S Huron, Box 566, Mackinaw City MI 49701. 616-436-7111. AE,D,M,V. I-75 N to (Exit 337) SR 108, N to US 31, E to Huron, N to mtl. Nrby rstrnt, indr pool, fax, b/f, sauna, whrlpool, cable TV, n/s rms. No pets. AAA. $35-79/S or D; $6/ex prsn. 5/1-6/22, 9/4-10/23: $39-111/S or D. 6/23-9/3: $60-141/S or D. Discs.

Econo Lodge/ 412 Nicolet St, Box 812, Mackinaw City MI 49701. 616-436-5026. AE,V,M,DC. I-75 (Exit 339) at bridge, lt 1 blk. Adj rstrnt/ lounge, mtg rm, fax, cable TV, t pkng, outlets, n/s rms. $31-59/S; $35-69/D; $6/ex prsn. 5/1-6/22: $31-53/S; $35-63/D. 6/23-9/5: $49-111/S; $53-121/D. Discs.

Friendship Inn/ 712 S Huron St, Box 282, Mackinaw City MI 49701. 616-436-5777. AE,M,V,DC. I-75 (Exit 337) to SR 131, E to Huron St (light), N 1 blk to mtl. Nrby rstrnt, indr pool, fax, b/f, sauna, whrlpool, cable TV, playgrnd, t pkng, n/s rms, refrig. Free AM coffee. No pets. 5/1-6/22, 9/5-10/22: $33-116/S or D; $5/ex prsn. 6/23-9/4: $50-150/S or D. CLOSED 10/23-4/30. Discs.

Quality Inn/ 917 S Huron Dr, Box 519, Mackinaw City MI 49701. 616-436-5051. V,M,D,AE. I-75 (N, Exit 337; S, Exit 338) to US 23, go to end of curve. Nrby rstrnt, indr pool, mtg rm, fax, b/f, sauna, whrlpool, cable TV, t pkng, n/s rms. $5/1-6/30: $35-85/S or D; $5/ex

MICHIGAN

prsn. 7/1-9/3: $59-149/S or D. 9/4-10/21: $39-79/S or C. 10/22-4/30: ClOSED. Higher spec event rates.

Rodeway Inn/ 619 S Nicolet St, Mackinaw City MI 49701. 616-436-5332. V,M,AE,D,DC. I-75: Sbnd, Exit 338; Nbnd, Exit 337. Nrby rstrnt, pool, cable TV, t pkng, refrig, playgrnd, n/s rms. $31-62/S; $40-71/D; $5/ex prsn. Discs.

Madison Heights (Detroit area)

Motel 6/ 32700 Barrington Rd, Madison Heights MI 48071. 810-583-0500/ Fax: 588-6945. M,V,DC,D,AE. I-75 (Exit 65A) at 14 Mile Rd, E to Barrington Rd, S to mtl. Nrby rstrnt, cable TV, n/s rms. Free local calls. $30/S; $36/D; $6/ex prsn. Disc.

Manistee

Days Inn/ 1462 US 31, Box 354, Manistee MI 49660. 616-723-8385. V,M,D,AE,DC,CB. US 31 & Merkey Rd. Fax, n/s rms, nrby rstrnt, indr pool, whrlpool, mtg rm, b/f, t pkng, arpt trans, cable TV, game rm, laundry. Free coffee. No pets. Chairman's Award. $34-70/S; $38-76/D; $6/ex prsn. 4/1-9/30: $42-80/S; $48-80/D. Discs.

Manistique

Best Western The Breakers/ Box 322, Manistique MI 49854. 906-341-2410/ Fax: 341-2207. V,M,AE,D,DC. I-75 to Mackinaw Bridge, 90 mi E of bridge on US 2, overlooking Lake MI. Rstrnt, indr pool, whrlpool, n/s rms, cable TV, VCR/ movies, tt/dd phone, fax, cot, crib, b pkng, conn rms. Free local calls, coffee. No pets. AAA/ Mobil. $40/S; $48/D; $5/ex prsn. 6/15-9/14: $60-65/S; $70-75/D. Disc: Senior, bsns, family, TA, govt, AAA. Guaranteed rates.

Budget Host Manistique Motor Inn/ Rte 1, Box 1505, Manistique MI 49854. 906-341-2552. V,M,AE,D,DC,CB.ER. On US 2, 3 mi E of tn. Cable TV, dd phone, n/s rms, nrby rstrnt/ lounge, pool, picnic area, arpt trans, t pkng, outlets, cot. crib. No pets. AAA/ Mobil. $30/S; $32-40/D; $4/ex prsn. Sum: $35-40/S; $45-53/D.

Econo Lodge/ E Lakeshore Dr, Box 184, Manistique MI 49854. 906-341-6014. V,M,D,AE. On US 2, just E of Manistique city limits. Nrby rstrnt, b/f, cable TV, exerc equip, outlets, n/s rms. Free cont brfst. $31-35/S; $38-48/D; $5/ex prsn. 5/1-6/19, 9/1-10/15: $38-42/S; $48-58/D. 6/20-8/31: $50-54/S; $60-70/D. Discs.

HoJo Inn/ 726 E Lake Shore Dr, Manistique MI 49854. 906-341-6981/ Fax: 341-6339. AE,V,M,DC,CB,D. SR 94 S to US 2, E on Lakeshore Dr. N/s rms, b/f, rstrnt, t pkng, fax, dd phone, whirlpool, laundry, outlets. $33-35/S; $38-65/D. 5/1-10/31: $38-60/S; $48-70/D. Discs.

Northshore Motor Inn/ Rte 1, Box 1967, Manistique MI 49854. 906-341-2420/ 800-297-7107. V,M,AE,D,DC,CB. On E US Hwy 2. Nrby rstrnt, n/s rms, cable TV, tt/dd phone, crib, t/b pkng. Free local calls. No pets. AAA/ Mobil. $25-39/S; $28-40/D; $4/ex prsn. 6/16- 9/15: $40-46/S; $42-50/D. Disc: Senior, bsns, govt, family, trkr, milt. Guaranteed rates.

Marquette

Budget Host Brentwood Motor Inn/ US 41 W, Marquette MI 49855. 906-228-7494. AE,DC,D,M,V. 1 mi W of tn on US 41. Cable TV, dd phone, family rms, n/s rms, kitchens, cont brfst, nrby rstrnt, b/f, picnic area, cot, crib. No pets. AAA. $28-37/S; $32-44/D; $3/ex prsn. Discs.

Tiroler Hof Motel/ 150 Carp River Hill, Marquette MI 49855. 906-226-7516/ 800-892-9376. V,M,AE,D. On US 41 S, overlooking Lake Superior. Seasonal rstrnt, sauna, n/s rms, satellite TV, playgrnd, tt/dd phone, laundry, cot, crib, b pkng, conn rms, hiking. Free local calls. AAA/ Mobil. $38-42/S; $42-46/D; $4/ex prsn. 5/16-10/15: $38-48/S; $48-52/D. Spec event rates: $42-46/S; $48-52/D. Guaranteed rates.

Munising

Terrace Motel/ 420 Prospect St, Munising MI 49862. 906-387-2735/ Fax: 387-2534. V,M,AE. SR 28 to Brook St, lt 2 blks, rt on Prospect St. Sauna, cable TV, fax, refrig, microwave, cot, crib, outlets, t/b/rv pkng. Free coffee. AAA. $34-44/S; $38-48/D; $5/ex prsn. 4/1-6/19, 9/7-11/30: $25-35/S; $28-38/D. Guaranteed rates.

MICHIGAN

New Baltimore
Lodge Keeper/ 29101 23 Mile Rd, New Baltimore MI 48047. 810-949-4520/ Fax: Ext 146. V,M,AE,D,DC,CB. I-94, Exit 243. Nrby rstrnt, n/s rms, cable TV, tt/dd phone, mtg rm, fax, copier, refrig, microwave, cot, crib, t/b/rv pkng, eff, conn rms. Free local calls, coffee. AAA. $40-50/S; $46-55/D. Higher spec event rates. Disc: Senior, bsns, TA, govt, l/s, family, trkr, milt, AARP.

Onekama
Budget Host Alpine Motor Lodge/ 8127 US 31, Box 366, Onekama MI 49675. 616-889-4281. V,M,D,AE. On US 31, 10 mi N of Manistee. Cont brfst, dd phone, in-rm coffee, pool, playgrnd, picnic area, n/s rms, cot, crib. Free mini golf. AAA/ Mobil. $30-40/S; $35-45/D; $5/ex prsn. 6/23-9/3: Sun-Thurs: $36-50/S; $40-55/D. Fri, Sat, Holiday: $50-65/S or D. CLOSED 11/19-4/27.

Oscoda
Rest All Inn/ 4270 N US 23, Oscoda MI 48750. 517-739-8822/ Fax: 739-0160/ 800-866-4322. V,M,D. I-75 N to Standish exit, 1 hour N (US 23). N/s rms, cable TV, games, playgrnd, TDD, tt/dd phone, fax, copier, laundry, cot, crib, outlets, t/b/rv pkng, eff, b/f. Free coffee. No pets. AAA. $37/S; $45/D; $3/ex prsn. 5/1-10/31, 1st wknd in Feb: $47/S; $55/D. Disc: Senior, bsns, TA, govt, l/s, trkr, milt, AAA.

Paradise
Howard Johnson Lodge/ SR 123 & Whitefish Point Rd, Paradise MI 49768. 906-492-3940/ Fax: 492-3943. V, AE,M,DC,D. I-75 N to SR 123 N (Tahquamenon Fall Exit); follow SR 123 into Paradise to jct of 123 & Whitefish Pt Rd. N/s rms, mtg rm, b/f, laundry, mtg rm, dd phone. Free cont brfst, coffee. No pets. Gold Medal Winner. $45-65/S; $45-75/D. Discs.

Petoskey
Econo Lodge/ 1858 US 131 S, Petoskey MI 49770. 616-348-3324. V,M, AE,D,DC. I-75 N to SR 32, W to US 131 N. Nearby rstrnt/ lounge, indr pool, fax, b/f, whrlpool, cable TV, t pkng, outlets. Free cont brfst. AAA. $41-75/S; $46-85/D; $5/ex prsn. 6/16-9/3: $46-75/S; $51-85/D. Discs.

Port Huron
Budget Host Inn/ 1484 Gratiot Blvd, Port Huron/ Marysville MI 48040. 810-364-7500/ Fax: 364-4423. AE,D,M,V. On I-94 bsns loop, 1 mi E of I-94, Exit 266, 4 mi S of Port Huron. Cable TV, dd phone, microwave, refrig, in-rm coffee, family rms, kitchens, n/s rms, pool, playgrnd, picnic area, t pkng, outlets, cot, crib. AAA. $35/S; $40-45/D; $5/ex prsn. 5/1-9/30: $40/S; $45-55/D. Spec events: $75-105. Discs.

Roseville (Detroit area)
Budgetel Inns/ 20675 13 Mile Rd, Roseville MI 48066. 810-296-6910/ Fax: 296-6073. V,M,D,AE,DC,CB. I-94, Exit 232, Little Mack Rd S, W on 13 Mile Rd. N/s rms, b/f, fax. Free cont brfst, in-rm coffee, local calls. AAA. $36-48/S; $43-55/D. 1/1-3/30: $34-46/S; $41-53/D. Spec rates may apply. Discs.

Saginaw
Knights Inn Saginaw North/ 2225 Tittabawassee Rd, Saginaw MI 48604. 517-791-1411/ Fax: 791-1325/ 800-843-5644. V,M,AE,D,DC,CB. Hwy 75 N to Hwy 675, Exit 6, Tittabawassee Rd. Pool, cable TV, VCR/ movies, games, tt phone, mtg rm, fax, copier, laundry, refrig, microwave, cot, crib, t/b/rv pkng, eff, b/f. Free local calls, coffee. AAA. $41/S; $47/D; $3/ex prsn. Disc: Senior, bsns, TA, govt, l/s, family, trkr, milt, AA, AARP, CAA. *Guaranteed rates.*

Quality Inn/ 3425 Holland Av, Saginaw MI 48601. 517-753-2461. AE,M,V,DC. I-75 (Exit 149B) to Holland Rd, W to mtl. Rstrnt/ lounge, pool, mtg rm, fax, cable TV, t pkng, n/s rms. $35-43/S; $43-50/D; $6/ex prsn. 5/1-11/1: $41-49/S; $50-60/D. Discs.

Saint Ignace
Budget Host Inn/ 700 N State St, St Ignace MI 49781. 906-643-9666/ Fax: 643-9126. V,AE,M,DC,CB,D. I-75 Bsns loop (Exit 344A) N 2 mi, on lt. Indr pool, whrlpool, n/s rms, cable TV, TDD, tt/dd phone, fax, copier, laundry, refrig, elevator, cot, crib, outlets, t/b/rv pkng, b/f. Free cont brfst, local calls, coffee. AAA/ Mobil. $40-92/S or D; $4/ex prsn. 6/19-9/3: $56-120/S or D. 6/20-6/23, 7/4: $70-150/S or D. Disc: Bsns, govt.

MICHIGAN

Comfort Inn/ 927 N State St, St Ignace MI 49781. 906-643-7733. V,M,D,AE. On Bsns I-75, 2 mi N of bridge. Nrby rstrnt, indr pool, mtg rm, fax, b/f, whrlpool, cable TV, exerc equip, n/s rms. Free cont brfst. No pets. AAA. 5/1-6/21, 9/4-10/31: $42-98/S or D; $5/ex prsn. 6/22-9/3: $78-155/S or D. 11/1-4/30: CLOSED. Discs.

Econo Lodge/ 1030 N State St, St Ignace MI 49781. 906-643-8060. AE,D,M,V. Bsns Loop I-75, Exit 344A. 2 1/2 mi N of bridge. Adj rstrnt, indr pool, whrlpool, cable TV, n/s rms. No pets. AAA. $46-82/S or D; $6/ex prsn. 6/22-8/26: $71-107/S or D. Discs.

Quality Inn/ 1021 N State St, St Ignace MI 49781. 906-643-7581. V,M,D,AE. I-75 bsns loop 2 mi N of Mackinac Bridge. Nrby rstrnt, indr pool, fax, b/f, whrlpool, cable TV, t pkng, n/s rms. AAA. $34-94/S; $38-98/D; $5/ex prsn. 6/26-8/31: $88-150/S; $94-160/D. 11/1-4/30: CLOSED. Discs.

Quality Inn/ 680 US 2, St Ignace MI 49781. 906-643-9688. AE,M,V,DC. 1 mi E of Bridge Tollgate on I-75 Bsns Rte & US 2. Nrby rstrnt, indr pool, mtg rm, fax, b/f, whrlpool, cable TV, b pkng, n/s rms. Free cont brfst. No pets. $38-70/S; $44-70/D; $6/ex prsn. 6/21-8/27: $65-95/S; $71-95/D. 8/28-10/31: $46-70/S; $49-70/D. Discs.

Rodeway Inn/ 750 W US 2, Box 651, St Ignace MI 49781. 906-643-8511. V,M,AE,D,DC. I-75 to US 2 Bsns, NE 1 mi. Nrby rstrnt, indr pool, whrlpool, cable TV, n/s rms. Free cont brfst. $38-125/S; $44-125/D; $6/ex prsn. 6/22-9/3: $54-125/S or D. 9/4-10/31: $43-110/S; $48-110/D. Discs.

Wayside Motel/ 751 N State St, St Ignace MI 49781. 906-643-8944. V,M. I-75 (Exit 344A) 2 mi N of bridge. N/s rms, cable TV, tt phone, cot, crib, outlets. Free local calls, coffee. AAA. $30/S; $35/D; $3/ex prsn. 5/1-10/31: $40/S; $45/D; $5/ex prsn. Last wknd in June: $80/S or D. Labor Day wknd: $75/S or D.

Sault Sainte Marie

Super 8 Motel/ 3826 I-75 Bsns Spur, Sault Ste Marie MI 49783. 906-632-8882/ Fax: 632-3766. V,M,AE,D,DC,CB. I-75 (Exit 392) to Bsns I-75, 4 blks N & E. B/f, n/s rms, b/t pkng, mtg rm, cont brfst, copier, outlets. Free local calls. Pride Award. $40/S; $45-47/D; $7/ex prsn. 6/1-10/21: $50/S; $56-60/D; $2/ex prsn. Discs.

Southfield (Detroit area)

Econo Lodge/ 23300 Telegraph Rd, Southfield MI 48034. 810-358-1800. V,M,D,AE. US 24 (Telegraph Rd) 2 mi S of I-696. Nrby rstrnt, pool, sauna, cable TV, t pkng, n/s rms. Free cont brfst. $38-47/S; $42-48/D; $5/ex prsn. Discs.

Southgate (Detroit area)

Budgetel Inns/ 12888 Reeck Rd, Southgate MI 48195. 313-374-3000/ Fax: 374-3010. V,M,D,AE,DC,CB. From dntn: I-75 S to Exit 37 (Northline Rd), W 1 blk to Reeck Rd. N/s rms, b/f, fax. Free cont brfst, in-rm coffee, local calls. AAA. $35-48/S; $42-55/D. 1/1-3/30: $33-46/S; $40-53/D. Spec rates may apply. Discs.

Taylor (Detroit area)

Super 8 Motel/ 15101 Huron St, Taylor MI 48180. 313-283-8830/ FAX: Ext 406. V,M,DC,CB,AE,D. I-75 to Eureka Rd, E 1/4 mi. B/f, n/s rms, outlets, micro-fridge, TDD, cot. Free crib. Pride Award. $37/S; $43/D; $6/ex prsn. Higher spec event rates. Discs.

Traverse City

Days Inn/ 420 Munson Av, Traverse City MI 49686. 616-941-0208/ Fax: 941-7521. V,M,D,AE,DC,CB. On US 31 N. Fax, n/s rms, rstrnt, indr pool, mtg rm, b/f, t pkng, data port, voice mail, mtg rm. Free trans, cont brfst. Chairman's Award. $41-73/D; $46-73/D; $5/ex prsn. 4/1-9/30: $44-95/S; $54-95/D. Discs.

Friendship Inn/ 1582 US 31 N, Traverse City MI 49686. 616-938-2080. V,M,D,AE. I-75 to SR 72, E to US 31, turn S. SR 37, take US 31 E to mtl. Nrby rstrnt, cable TV, t pkng, outlets, n/s rms. $33-45/S; $38-55/D; $5-10/ex prsn. 5/1-6/5: $38-55/S; $43-70/D. 6/6-9/4: $50-80/S; $55-100/D. 9/5-10/28: $33-45/S; $38-70/D. Discs.

Walker (Grand Rapids area)

Motel 6/ 777 Three Mile Rd, Walker MI 49504. 616-784-9375/ Fax: 784-7721. M,V,DC,D,AE. I-96, Exit 30A. Just S of I-96, at jct of Alpine Av and Three Mi Rd. Cable TV, laundry, pool, n/s rms. Free local calls. $30/S; $36/D; $6/ex prsn. Disc.

Warren (Detroit area)

Motel 6/ 8300 Chicago Rd, Warren MI 48093. 810-826-9300/ Fax: 979-4525. M,V,DC,D,AE. I-696 to US 53, N to Chicago/13 Mi Rd, E 1/8 mi to mtl. Nrby rstrnt, cable TV, n/s rms. Free local calls. $30/S; $36/D; $6/ex prsn. Disc.

Quality Inn/ 32035 Van Dyke, Warren MI 48093. 810-264-0100. V,M,D,AE. I-696 to Van Dyke, N 2 1/2 mi. Rstrnt, lounge, pool, mtg rm, fax, b/f, cable TV, t pkng, exerc equip, n/s rms. $37-41/S; $42-46/D; $5/ex prsn. 5/1-8/31: $39-42/S; $43-48/D. 12/30-1/1: $79/S or D. Discs.

West Branch

La Hacienda Motel/ 969 W Houghton Av, W Branch MI 48661. 517-345-2345. V,M,AE,D,DC,CB. I-75, Exit 215, E 1 1/4 mi on lt. Nrby rstrnt, n/s rms, cable TV, tt/dd phone, cot, t/b/rv pkng, eff. Free local calls, coffee. AAA. $28-42/S; $28-46/D; $5/ex prsn. 5/1-10/31: $30-46/S; $30-52/D. 7/19-7/20: $54-56/S; $54-62/D. Disc: Family.

West Springfield

Howard Johnson Hotel/ 1150 Riverdale St, W Springfield MI 01089. 413-739-7261/ Fax: 737-8410. V,M,D,AE,DC, CB. I-91 (Exit 13B) to MA Trnpk I-90 (Exit 4), turn E to US 5, S to mtl. N/s rms, mtg rm, rstrnt, pool, arpt trans, laundry. $40-65/S; $45-70/D. Discs.

Minnesota

Aitkin

Ripple River Motel/ 701 Minnesota Av S, Aitkin MN 56431. 218-927-3734/ Fax: 927-3540/ 800-258-3734. V,M,D. On Hwy 169, S edge of Aitkin. Whrlpool, n/s rms, cable TV, tt phone, fax, copier, refrig, micro-wave, cot, crib, t/b pkng, eff. Free local calls, cont brfst (wknd only). AAA. 35-37/S;

$40-90/D; $6/ex prsn. 5/31-9/1 Fri-Sat: $40-42/S; $45-90/D. Disc: Bsns, AAA, AARP.

Albert Lea

Countryside Inn/ 2102 E Main St, Box 782, Albert Lea MN 56007. 507-373-2446/ Fax: 373-3530. V,M,AE,D,DC, CB. I-35 (Nbnd, Exit 11; Sbnd, Exit 12) 1 1/4 mi toward tn. Nrby rstrnt/ lounge, cable TV, dd phone, outlets, b/f, n/s rms, cot, crib. AAA/ IMA. $33-36/S; $39-48/D; $4/ex prsn. Disc: Family, TA, senior.

Alexandria

"L" Motel/ 910 Hwy 27 W, Alexandria MN 56308. 612-763-5121/ 800-733-1793. V,M,D. 2nd stoplight turn lt, 2 blks. Nrby rstrnt, n/s rms, cable TV, tt phone, refrig, cot, outlets, t/b/rv pkng. Free cont brfst, coffee. $30/S; $35/D. 6/1-10/1: $35/S; $45/D. Disc: Family, l/s. Guaranteed rates.

Comfort Inn/ 507 - 50th Av W, Alexandria MN 56308. 612-762-5161. V,M,D,AE. I-94 to SR 29, N to 50th Av, W. Nrby rstrnt, indr pool, mtg rm, fax, whrlpool, cable TV, t pkng, n/s rms. Free cont brfst. No pets. AAA. $42-49/S; $48-55/D; $6/ex prsn. 5/1-9/30: $51-57/S; $57-61/D. Discs.

Anoka (Minneapolis/ St Paul area)

Super 8 Motel/ 1129 W Hwy 10 (Main St), Anoka MN 55303. 612-422-8000/ Fax: 422-4892. V,M,AE,DC,CB,D. US 10 & Thurston Ave. B/f, laundry, outlets, cont brfst, copier, satellite TV, cot, crib. Free local calls. Pride Award. $41/S; $47-51/D; $6/ex prsn. Discs.

Austin
Days Inn/ 700 16th Av NW, Austin MN 55912. 507-433-8600/ Fax: 433-8749. V,M,D,AE,DC,CB. I-90 (Exit 178A) at US 218. Fax, n/s rms, nrby rstrnt/ lounge, whrlpool, mtg rm, b/f, exerc equip, t pkng, arpt trans, cot. $40-56/S; $47-56/D; $7/ex prsn. 5/28-9/23: $43-56/S; $53-56/D. Discs.

Rodeway Inn/ 3303 Oakland Av W, Austin MN 55912. 507-437-7774. V,M,D,AE. I-90 & Oakland Av W. Nrby rstrnt, mtg rm, fax, b/f, whrlpool, cable TV, t pkng, n/s rms. Free cont brfst. AAA. $39-65/S; $45-71/D; $6/ex prsn. Discs.

Battle Lake
Nifty Nook Resort/ Rte 2, Box 271, Battle Lake MN 56515. 218-495-3479/ 800-545-4056. I-94, Exit Ashby, N on 78 (25 mi) W on Cty 72 (3 mi). On Otter Tail Lake. Lake front cottages, cable TV, refrig, crib. Free local calls. $40/S; $48/D; $5/ex prsn. Late Jun-Mid Aug: $50/S; $60/D. Disc: Family, l/s. *Guaranteed rates.*

Baxter (Brainerd area)
Super 8 Motel/ Box 2505, Baxter MN 56425. 218-828-4288/ Fax: Ext 200. V,M,AE,DC,CB,D. Hwy 371 N. B/f, n/s rms, game rm, cont brfst, outlets, b/t pkng, copier, cable TV, mtg rm. No pets. Pride Award. $37/S; $42-44/D; $2/ex prsn. 5/28-9/30: $44/S; $44-52/D. Higher spec event rates. Discs.

Bemidji
Bel Air Motel/ 1350 Paul Bunyan Dr NW, Bemidji MN 56601. 218-751-3222/ 800-628-3208. V,M,AE,D,DC,CB. 1/2 mi E of the NW jct of Hwys 2, 71, 197. Nrby rstrnt, n/s rms, cable TV, VCR, tt/dd phone, refrig, microwave, cot, crib, outlets, t/rv pkng. AAA. $26-42/S; $32-56/D; $4/ex prsn. 4/1-9/2: $42/S; $46-56/D; $6/ex prsn. Disc: Senior, bsns, govt, l/s, trkr, milt.

Bloomington (Minneapolis/ St Paul area)
Friendly Host/ 1225 E 78th St, Bloomington MN 55425. 612-854-3322/ Fax: 854-0245. V,M,AE,D,DC. On I-494, 12th Av Exit. Ebnd take Portland & 12th Av Exit, straight across Portland, take frontage rd to 12th Av. Nrby rstrnt, indr pool, cable TV, dd phone, arpt trans, outlets, whrlpool, cot, crib, n/s rms. AAA/ IMA. $40-45/S; $40-60/D; $5/ex prsn. Disc: Family, AAA, senior, AARP, TA.

Brainerd
Econo Lodge/ 2655 US 371 S, Brainerd MN 56401. 218-828-0027/ Fax: 828-0807. AE,V,M,DC. On US 317, S of Brainerd. Nrby rstrnt, fax, b/f, cable TV, t pkng, outlets, VCR, n/s rms. Free cont brfst. AAA. $30-35/S; $34-40/D; $5/ex prsn. 5/1-10/31: $35-40/S; $39-49/D. Higher spec event rates. Discs.

Also see Baxter, Nisswa.

Brooklyn Park (Minneapolis/ St Paul area)
Budget Host Inn/ Hwy 81 & 63rd Av N, Brooklyn Park MN 55428. 612-533-6455/ Fax: 533-1216. V,AE,CB,DC,D,M. Hwy 81 & 63rd Av N, 1/2 mi S of I-694, Exit 31. Cable TV, dd phone, microwave, refrig, in-rm coffee, n/s rms, fax, picnic area, family rms, laundry, crib, cot. No pets. AAA. $42/S; $46/D; $5/ex prsn. 6/1-8/31: $43/S; $49/D. Wknds, 6/1-8/31: $49/D. Spec events: $70-75. Discs.

Cambridge
Budget Host Imperial Motor Lodge/ 643 N Main, Cambridge MN 55008. 612-689-2200/ Fax: 689-1031. V,M,D,DC,AE,CB. I-95 to Old Hwy 65, N 6 blks at jct with Main. Cable TV, dd phone, mtg rm, indr pool, hot tub, sauna, nrby rstrnt/ lounge, arpt trans, t pkng, outlets, n/s rms, b/f, crib. Free cont brfst. No pets. $29-65/S or D; $4/ex prsn. Discs.

Chaska (Minneapolis/ St Paul area)
Super 8 Motel/ 830 Yellow Brick Rd, Chaska MN 55318. 612-448-7030. M,V,DC,D,CB,AE. 2 blks E of Hwy 41 on Hwy 212. B/f, n/s rms, cable TV, toast bar, refrig, microwave, cot. Free local calls. No pets. Pride Award. $39-42/S; $44-56/D; $4/ex prsn. Higher spec event rates. Discs.

Cloquet

Driftwood Motel/ 1413 Hwy 33 S, Cloquet MN 55720. 218-879-4638. V,M,D. 1 1/2 mi N of I-35, on Hwy 33. Nrby rstrnt, n/s rms, cable TV, playgrnd, tt phone, laundry, refrig, cot, outlets, t pkng, eff, conn rms, kitchenettes. $25/S; $30/D. 5/1-10/31: $35-44/S; $39-49/D. Disc: Senior, bsns, TA, govt, family, trkr, milt, l/s.

Super 8 Motel/ Hwy 33 & Big Lake Rd, Cloquet MN 55720. 218-879-1250. V, M,AE,D,DC,CB. I-35 to Hwy 33, N to Hwy 7 (Big Lake Rd), turn W 1/2 blk. B/f, n/s rms, game rm, t/b/rv pkng, toast bar. Pride Award. $39/S; $45-47/D; $3/ex prsn. Higher spec event rates. Discs.

Crosby

Lakeview Motel & Resort/ 426 Lakeshore Dr, Crosby MN 56441. 218-546-5924. V,M,D. Hwy 169 N to Garrison, Cty Rd 18 W to 6 N, Hwy 6 to 210 W. W end of Serpent Lake in Crosby. Nrby rstrnt, n/s rms, cable TV, playgrnd, tt/dd phone, refrig, microwave, cot, crib, outlets, t/b/rv pkng, lake. Free local calls. No pets. AAA. $32-46/S or D; $4/ex prsn. 5/9-6/20, 8/19-9/30: $35-51/S or D. 6/21-8/18: $37-56/S or D. Disc: Senior, bsns, l/s, AAA. *Guaranteed rates.*

Detroit Lakes

Budget Host Inn/ 895 Hwy 10 E, Detroit Lakes MN 56501. 218-847-4454/ Fax: 847-3326. D,V,M,AE,DC,CB. 1 1/2 mi SE on Hwy 10. Cable TV, dd phone, in-rm coffee, family rm, kitchens, t pkng, outlets. Free crib. AAA. $30-35/S; $36-48/D; $4-5/ex prsn. 5/1-9/30: $32-52/S; $36-62/D. Spec events: $57-72.

Dilworth

Howard Johnson Lodge/ 701 Center Av E, Dilworth MN 56529. 218-287-1212. V,M,D,AE,DC,CB. I-94 (Exit 6) to Cty Rd 11, N 2 mi to Hwy 10 (Center Av), W 2 mi to tn. N/s rms, mtg rm, b/f, t pkng, fax, micro-refrig. Free cont brfst, local calls, coffee. $28-49/S; $30-62/D. Discs.

Duluth

Allyndale Motel/ 510 N 66th Av W, Duluth MN 55807. 218-628-1061. V, M, AE,D,CB,DC. I-35: Nbnd, (Exit 251A) to Cody St; Sbnd, (Exit 252) to Central Av, rt 3 1/2 blks to Cody St, lt to mtl. Cable TV, dd phone, outlets, playgrnd, conn rms, cot, crib, refrig, microwave, n/s rms. IMA. $31-38/S; $36-48/D; $5/ex prsn. 6/21-6/22: $48/S; $53-58/D. Disc: TA.

Super 8 Motel/ 4100 W Superior St, Duluth MN 55807. 218-628-2241. M, V,AE,DC,CB,D. I-35 (Exit 253B) at 40th Av W. B/f, n/s rms, whrlpool, sauna, laundry, outlets, t/b/rv pkng, copier, cable TV, cot. Free local calls, crib. No pets. Pride Award. $43/S; $44-46/D; $2/ex prsn. 6/1-6/17, 9/7-9/30: $42/S; $49-56/D. 6/18-9/6: $44/S; $51-56/D. Higher spec event/ wknd rates. Discs.

Willard Munger Inn/ 7408 Grand Av, Duluth MN 55807. 218-624-4814/ Fax: 624-8097/ 800-982-2453. V,M,AE,D. I-35 to Cody St, follow signs to Lake Superior Zoo. 1 blk past zoo. Rstrnt, whrlpool, n/s rms, cable TV, tt phone, mtg rm, fax, nwspr, refrig, cot, crib, eff, kitchenette. Free coffee. $30-36/S; $40-46/D; $6/ex prsn. 4/1-10/15: $36-44/S; $50/D; $8/ex prsn. 6/21-6/22, 8/23-8/24: $50/S; $58/D. Disc: Bsns, govt, family, trkr, milt.

Eagan (Minneapolis/ St Paul area)

Budget Host Inn/ 2745 Hwy 55, Eagan MN 55121. 612-454-1211/ Fax: 686-7230. V,AE,CB,DC,D,M. On Hwy 55. Cable TV, dd phone, refrig, microwave, n/s rms, playgrnd, picnic area, t pkng, outlets, cot. $30-36/S; $35-45/D; $4/ex prsn. 6/1-8/31: $32-36/S; $36-48/D. Disc.

Ely

Budget Host Motel Ely/ 1047 E Sheridan St, Ely MN 55731. 218-365-3265. V,AE,CB,D,DC,M. Hwys 1 & 169. Cable TV, VCR, dd phone, n/s rms, playgrnd, arpt trans, t pkng, outlets, cot. Free brfst, crib. AAA/ Mobil. $34-45/S; $44-60/D, $56-80/3 bed rms.

Eveleth

Koke's Motel/ 714 Fayal Rd, Eveleth MN 55734. 218-744-4500/ 800-892-5107. V,M. 1/2 mi W on City route. Cable TV, tt/dd phone, cot, crib, outlets, t/b pkng. AAA. $26-42/S; $26-42/D; $3/ex prsn. Disc: Bsns, family,

MINNESOTA 148

l/s. *Guaranteed rates.*

Faribault
Lyndale Motel/ 904 Lyndale Av N, Faribault MN 55021. 507-334-4386/ Reserv: 800-559-4386. V,M,AE,D. I-35 (Exit 59) to Hwy 21, S 1 1/2 mi. Nrby rstrnt, n/s rms, cable TV, tt/dd phone, cot, crib, outlets, t pkng. Free coffee. No pets. AAA. $27-40/S; $31-40/D; $4/ex prsn. Wknds: $31-40/S or D. *Guaranteed rates.*

Fergus Falls
Comfort Inn/ 425 Western Av, Fergus Falls MN 56537. 218-736-5787. V,M, AE,D,DC. I-94 (Exit 54E) to Western Av, S to mtl. Nrby rstrnt, fax, b/f, whrlpool, cable TV, outlets, n/s rms. Free cont brfst. No pets. AAA. $38-85/S; $43-95/D; $5/ex prsn. Discs.

Finlayson (Banning Junction area)
Super 8 Motel/ I-35 & Hwy 23, Finlayson MN 55735. 612-245-5284/ Fax: 245-2233. V,M,AE,D,DC,CB. I-35, 10 min N of Hinckley at Finlayson Askov, Exit 195. B/f, n/s rms, nrby rstrnt/ lounge, whrlpool, game rm, outlets, t/b/rv pkng. $41/S; $45/D; $4/ex prsn. Higher spec event rates. Discs.

Fridley (Minneapolis/ St Paul area)
Budget Host Inn/ 6881 Hwy 65, Fridley MN 55432. 612-571-0420/ Fax: 572-8670. V,AE,CB,DC,D,M. Hwy 65, 1 1/2 mi N of I-694, Exit 38B. In-rm coffee, dd phone, refrig, microwave, kitchens, family rms, n/s rms, t pkng, outlets, cots. Free crib. No pets. AAA. $42-46/S; $42-52/D; $4/ex prsn. Spec events: $52-65. Disc.

Glenwood
Lake Reno Resort & Motel/ Rt 1, Box 65, Glenwood MN 56334. 612-283-5667/ 800-950-4696. I-94 (Exit 103) to Alexandria Glenwood exit, lt 7 mi to Lake Reno on Hwy 29 S. Nrby rstrnt/ lounge, playgrnd, refrig, microwave, cot, crib, outlets, t/rv pkng, eff, lakeshore. Free local calls, coffee. $40/S; $40-48/D; $7/ex prsn. Disc: L/s. *Guaranteed rates.*

Grand Marais
Wedgewood Motel/ HC 80, Box 100, Grand Marais MN 55604. 218-387-2944. V,M,D. On Hwy 61, 2 1/2 mi NE of Grand Marais. Free local calls, coffee. AAA/ Mobil. $25-30/S; $36/D; $3/ex prsn. Disc: Senior, l/s. *Guaranteed rates.*

Grand Rapids
Super 8 Motel/ 1902 S Pokegama Av, Box 335, Grand Rapids MN 55744. 218-327-1108/ Fax: Ext 101. M,V,AE, DC,CB,D. Jct SR 169 S & Arpt Rd. B/f, n/s rms, cont brfst, laundry, outlets, b/t pkng, copier, cable TV, mtg rm, cot, crib. No pets. Pride Award. $37/S; $42-44/D; $2/ex prsn. 5/28-9/30: $45/S; $44-53/D. Higher spec event/ wknd rates. Discs.

Granite Falls
Super 8 Motel/ 845 W US 212, Granite Falls MN 56241. 612-564-4075/ Fax: 564-4038. M,V,DC,D,CB,AE. On US 212, 3 blks W of jct 23/67 & 212. B/f, n/s rms, outlets, t/b/rv pkng, copier, mtg rm, cot. Free local calls, crib. Pride Award. Top Quality Award. $40/S; $43-47/D; $4/ex prsn. Discs.

Hastings (Minneapolis/ St Paul area)
Super 8 Motel/ 2450 Vermillion St, Hastings MN 55033. 612-438-8888/ Fax: Ext 100. V,M,AE,D,DC,CB. Hwy 61 & 25th St E. B/f, n/s rms, laundry, toast bar, t pkng, whrlpool, copier. Free local calls. No pets. Pride Award. $44/S; $50-54/D; $6/ex prsn. Higher spec event rates. Discs.

Hibbing
Days Inn Motel/ 1520 E Hwy 37, Hibbing MN 55746. 218-263-8306/ Fax: Ext 137. V,M,AE,D,DC,CB. At jct Hwys 169 & 37 E in Hibbing. N/s rms, cable TV, VCR/ movies, TDD, tt/dd phone, mtg rm, fax, copier, cot, crib, outlets, t/b/rv pkng, eff, b/f. Free cont brfst. AAA. $36-40/S or D; $3/ex prsn. 4/1-9/30: $40-44/S or D. Disc: Senior, bsns, TV, govt, milt, trkr, family. *Guaranteed rates.*

Super 8 Motel/ 1411 E 40th St, Hibbing MN 55746. 218-263-8982. AE,V,M,DC, CB,D. US 169 & SR 37 B/f, n/s rms, outlets, t/b/rv pkng, cable TV, cot, crib. Free local calls. No pets. Pride Award. $40/S; $48-53/D; $5/ex prsn. Higher

MINNESOTA

spec event rates. Discs.

International Falls
Budget Host International Motor Lodge/ 10 Riverview Blvd, International Falls MN 56649. 218-283-2577/ Fax: 285-3688. V,M,D,DC,AE,CB. Voyageur National Park area. US 71/ SR 11, just W of US 53. Cable TV, dd phone, in-rm coffee, n/s rms, mtg rm, playgrnd, picnic area, t pkng, outlets. Free crib. $30/S; $33-35/D; $5/ex prsn. 6/1-8/31: $36/S; $39-43/D. Disc.

Jackson
Budget Host Prairie Winds Motel/ 950 N Hwy 17, Jackson MN 56143. 507-847-2020/ Fax: 847-2022. V,M,AE,D, DC,CB. 2/3 mi S of I-90 on US 71. N/s rms, cable TV, tt phone, fax, cot, crib, t/b pkng. AAA/ Mobil. $31/S; $39-46/D; $4/ex prsn. Disc: TA. CLOSED 11/15-1/15. *Guaranteed rates.*

Lake City
Sunset Motel & Resort/ 1515 N Lakeshore Dr, Lake City MN 55041. 612-345-5331/ 800-945-0192. V,M,AE, D,DC. On Hwy 61. Pool, whrlpool, n/s rms, cable TV, tt phone, refrig, cot, crib, outlets, t/b pkng, eff, b/f. Free local calls, coffee. $38-44/S; $40-44/D; $2/ex prsn. 5/1-11/1: $48-52/S; $48-52/D. Wknd/ holidays 5/1-11/1: $56/S; $58-62/D. Disc: Senior, bsns, TA, govt, l/s, family, trkr. *Guaranteed rates.*

Lakeville (Minneapolis/ St Paul area)
Friendly Host/ 17296 I-35, Lakeville MN 55044. 612-435-7191/ Fax: 435-6620. V,M,AE,D,CB,DC. I-35 & Hwy 50; 12 mi S of Twin Cities & Bloomington. Nrby rstrnt, indr pool, cable TV, dd phone, game rm, outlets, whrlpool, b/f, playgrnd, cot, crib, kitchenette. AAA/ IMA. $40-50/S; $40-60/D; $5/ex prsn. Disc: Family, senior, l/s.

Motel 6/ 11274 210th St, Lakeville MN 55044. 612-469-1900/ Fax: 469-5359. M,V,DC,D,AE. I-35 (Exit 81) to Co Rd 70, E to 2nd entrance of McDonalds. Cable TV, n/s rms, t pkng. Free local calls. $30-32/S; $36-38/D; $6/ex prsn. Disc.

Litchfield
Scotwood Motel/ 1017 E Frontage Rd, Litchfield MN 55355. 612-693-2496. V,M,AE,D,DC,CB. E Hwy 12. Cable TV, dd phone, arpt trans, outlets, b/f, cot. Free cont brfst, crib. IMA. $36-45/S; $41-50/D. Disc: Senior, TA, family.

Long Prairie
Budget Host Inn/ 417 Lake St S, Long Prairie MN 56347. 612-732-6118. V,AE,DC,D,M. 5 blks S of jct US 71 & SR 27. N/s rms, cable TV, tt phone, fax, nwspr, refrig, microwave, cot, outlets, t/b/rv pkng. Free local calls, coffee. AAA. $30-36/S; $34-46/D; $3/ex prsn. Disc: Senior, bsns, govt, l/s, family, trkr.

Luverne
Comfort Inn/ 801 S Kniss, Luverne MN 56156. 507-283-9488. V,M,D,AE. I-90 (Exit 12) to US 75, N to mtl. Nrby rstrnt, indr pool, fax, b/f, whrlpool, cable TV, outlets, n/s rms. Free cont brfst. No pets. $43-56/S; $48-63/D. Discs.

Mankato
Budgetel Inns/ 111 W Lind Court, Mankato MN 56001. 507-345-8800/ Fax: 345-8921. V,M,D,AE,DC,CB. At jct Hwys 14 & 169. N/s rms, b/f, fax, rstrnt, sauna. Free cont brfst, in-rm coffee, local calls. AAA. $37-41/S; $44-48/D. 1/1-5/25: $34-38/S; $41-45/D. Spec rates may apply. Discs.

Super 8 Motel/ Box 390, Mankato MN 56001. 507-387-4041/ Fax: 387-4107. M,V,AE,DC,CB,D. On US 169, just N of jct 169 & 14. B/f, n/s rms, whrlpool, outlets, t/b/rv pkng, copier, fax, mtg rm, tt phone, cot, crib. Free local calls, coffee. No pets. Pride Award. $36-37/S; $42-45/D; $4/ex prsn. Higher spec event rates. Discs.

Milaca
Rodeway Inn/ 215 10th Av, Box 6, Milaca MN 56359. 612-983-2660. V,M, D,AE. E side of jct SR 23 & US 169 at the Milaca Jct Plaza. Nrby rstrnt, fax, b/f, t pkng, n/s rms. Free cont brfst. AAA. $39-51/S; $45-57/D; $6/ex prsn. Di

Minneapolis
See Anoka, Bloomington, Brooklyn Park, Chaska, Eagan, Fridley, Hastings, Richfield, Roseville.

MINNESOTA 150

Nisswa (Brainerd area)

Days Inn/ 45 N Smiley Rd, Nisswa MN 56468. 218-963-3500/ Fax: 963-4936. V,M,D,AE,DC,CB. Jct SRs 77, 13, 371. N 1 blk. Fax, n/s rms, nrby rstrnt, indr pool, whrlpool, b/f, t pkng, sauna, laundry, cable TV, cot. Free cont brfst. AAA. $36-68/S; $42-73/D; $5/ex prsn. 5/16-9/30: $49-68/S; $54-73/D. Discs.

Nisswa Motel/ Box 45, Nisswa MN 56468. 218-963-7611. V,M,AE,D. 15 mi N of Brainerd on Hwy 371. Turn E on County Rd 18 for 1 blk, lt 1 blk. Nrby rstrnt, cable TV, tt/dd phone, cot, crib, outlets, t/b pkng. Free local calls. AAA. $30-44/S or D; $3/ex prsn. 6/2-8/30, Mon-Thurs: $38-52/S or D. 5/24-9/3 Wknds, N Star Nationals: 56-64/S or D; $5/ex prsn. Discs. *Guaranteed Rates.*

Onamia

Econo Lodge/ 40993 US 169, Onamia MN 56359. 612-532-3838. V,M,D,AE. 4 mi S of Grand Casino, 7 mi N of Onamia. Nrby rstrnt, fax, b/f, whrlpool, sauna, cable TV, t pkng, outlets. Free cont brfst. $40-60/S; $44-64/D; $5/ex prsn. 3/2-4/30, 10/1-12/20: $36-50/S; $40-54/D. Discs.

Ortonville

Econo Lodge/ N US 75, Ortonville MN 56278. 612-839-2414. V,M,AE. US 12 to US 75, N 1/2 mi. Nrby rstrnt, mtg rm, fax, b/f, cable TV, t pkng, outlets. Free cont brfst. No pets. AAA. $30-70/S; $35-70/D; $5/ex prsn. 4/1-12/31: $35-80/S; $40-80/D. Discs.

Owatonna

Budget Host Inn/ 745 State Ave, Owatonna MN 55060. 507-451-8712/ Fax: 451-4456. V,M,D,AE. 1 blk E of I-35 (Exit 42A) on Hwy 14. N/s rms, cable TV, TDD, tt/dd phone, fax, copier, refrig, microwave, cot, crib, t/b/rv pkng, conn rms. Free local calls, coffee. AAA/ Mobil. $32-42/S; $40-50/D; $5/ex prsn. Disc: Senior, bsns, TA, govt, family, trkr, milt. *Guaranteed rates.*

Oakdale Motel/ 1418 S Oak Av, Owatonna MN 55060. 507-451-5480. V,M,AE,D. I-35, Exit 40. 1 mi on US 14 & 218, 1/2 mi on Cty Rd 45. Nrby rstrnt/ lounge, whrlpool, n/s rms, cable TV, tt/dd phone, fax, nwspr, refrig, microwave, cot, crib, eff. AAA. $25-30/S; $30-40/D; $3/ex prsn. 4/1-8/9, 8/20-9/30: $30-35/S; $30-45/D. 8/10-8/20: $35-40/S; $40-48/D. Discs. *Guaranteed rates.*

Super 8 Motel/ Box 655, Owatonna MN 55060. 507-451-0380/ Fax: Ext 236. M,V,AE,D,DC,CB. I-35 (Exit 42B) at Hwy 14, W. B/f, n/s rms, mtg rm, outlets, b/t pkng, cot, crib. Free local calls, coffee. Pride Award. $44/S; $47-52/D; $3/ex prsn. Discs.

Park Rapids

Super 8 Motel/ Box 388, Park Rapids MN 56470. 218-732-9704/ Fax: Ext 262. M,V,AE,DC,CB,D. Hwy 34 E. B/f, n/s rms, whrlpool, sauna, game rm, laundry, outlets, cont brfst, b/t pkng, cable TV, cot, crib. No pets. Pride Award. AAA. $36-38/S; $42-46/D; $8/ex prsn. Higher spec event rates. Discs.

Perham

Super 8 Motel/ 106 Jake St SE, Perham MN 56573. 218-346-7888/ Fax: 346-7880. M,V,DC,D,CB,AE. NW corner of jct Hwys 10 & 78. B/f, n/s rms, game rm, laundry, outlets, t/b/rv pkng, cont brfst, copier, VCR, mtg rm, cot, crib. Free local calls. No pets. Pride Award. $38/S; $46-50/D; $3/ex prsn. Higher spec event rates. Discs.

Pine River

Trailside Inn/ Box 466, Pine River MN 56474. 218-587-4499/ Fax: 587-4744. V,M,AE,D. On Hwy 371, 1 mi S of Pine River. Sauna, whrlpool, n/s rms, exerc equip, cable TV, TDD, tt phone, fax, laundry, cot, outlets, t pkng, b/f. Free local calls, cont brfst. AAA. $43-48/S or D; $5/ex prsn. 5/2-8/15, 8/18-9/4: $53-65/S or D. 8-16-8/17: $80/S or D. Disc: Senior, bsns, family, trkr, AAA. *Guaranteed rates.*

Pipestone

Super 8 Motel/ 605 8th Av SE, Pipestone MN 56164. 507-825-4217/ Fax: 825-4219. M,V,DC,D,CB,AE. Jct of Hwy 75, 23 & 30. B/f, n/s rms, nrby rstrnt/ lounge, laundry, outlets, t/b/rv pkng, copier, cable TV, cot, crib. Free local calls. Pride Award. AAA. $37/S; $43-46/D; $3/ex prsn. Higher spec event rates. Discs.

Red Wing

Days Inn Red Wing/ 955 E Seventh St, Red Wing MN 55066. 612-388-3568/ Fax: 385-1901/ 800-325-2525. V, M,AE,D,DC,CB. On Hwys 61 & 63, 1.5 mi S of Red Wing. Indr pool, whrlpool, n/s rms, cable TV, arpt trans, mtg rm, copier, refrig, cot, crib, outlets, t/b/rv pkng, b/f. Free local calls, cont brfst. AAA/ Mobil. $36-48/S; $41-48/D; $5/ex prsn. Spec event, holiday wknd rates: $68/S; $77/D. Disc: Senior, bsns, family, trkr.

Richfield (Minneapolis/ St Paul area)

Motel 6/ 7640 Cedar Av S, Richfield MN 55423. 612-861-4491/ Fax: 798-4366. M,V,DC,D,AE. I-494 to (Exit 3) Portland Av/ 12th Ave, N to 77th St, rt 1/2 mi to Cedar, turn lt to mtl. Cable TV, n/s rms. Free local calls. $39/S; $45/D; $6/ex prsn. Disc.

Rochester

Comfort Inn/ 111 SE 28th St, Rochester MN 55904. 507-286-1001. V,M,D,AE. Jct US 63 & US 52. Rstrnt/ lounge, fax, b/f, cable TV, t pkng, outlets, laundry, n/s rms. Free cont brfst. AAA. $42-52/S; $47-57/D; $5/ex prsn. 5/1-9/30: $47-57/S; $52-62/D. Discs.

Econo Lodge/ 519 Third Av SW, Rochester MN 55902. 507-288-1855. AE,V,M,DC. 3 blks W of US 63 at 6th St SW and 3rd Av, dntn. Nrby rstrnt, fax, cable TV, outlets, in-rm coffee, kitchenettes. Free cont brfst. $38-46/S; $41-49/D; $5/ex prsn. Discs.

Friendship Inn/ 116 Fifth St SW, Rochester MN 55902. 507-289-1628. AE,V,M,DC. I-90 to US 63, lt on 6th St, SW 1 blk to 1st Av, rt 1 blk to 5th St. Nrby rstrnt, indr pool, fax, sauna, cable TV, outlets, game rm, clinic trans, coffee, kitchenettes. Free cont brfst. $35-39/S; $42-45/D; $5/ex prsn. 5/1-7/31: $39-44/S; $44-49/D. 8/1-10/31: $37-42/S; $42-47/D. Discs.

Howard Johnson Lodge/ 111 SW 17th Av, Rochester MN 55902. 507-289-1617. V,M,D,AE,DC,CB. on US 52, just S of US 14 W. N/s rms, indr pool, nrby rstrnt, sauna, whrlpool, cable TV, laundry, arpt/ clinic trans. Free cont brfst. $36-51/S; $43-58/D. Discs.

Motel 6/ 2107 W Frontage Rd, Rochester MN 55901. 507-282-6625/ Fax: 280-7987. M,V,DC,D,AE. Located at US 52 & 19th St NW. Cable TV, pool, n/s rms. Free local calls, clinic/ hospital trans. $26-28/S; $32-34/D; $6/ex prsn. Disc.

Roseau

Super 8 Motel/ 318 West Side, Roseau MN 56751. 218-463-2196/ Fax: Ext 225. M,V,DC,D,CB,AE. On Hwy 11/89 just W of jct of Hwy 11 with Hwys 310 & 89. B/f, n/s rms, nrby rstrnt, outlets, t/b/rv pkng, cot, crib. Free local calls. Pride Award. AAA. $37/S; $40-47/D; $4/ex prsn. Higher spec event rates. Discs.

Roseville (Minneapolis/ St Paul area)

Motel 6/ 2300 Cleveland Av N, Roseville MN 55113. 612-639-3988/ Fax: 633-5748. M,V,DC,D,AE. I-35W to Co Rd "C," E to Cleveland Av, rt 1 1/2 mi to mtl. Nrby rstrnt, cable TV, pool, elevator, n/s rms. Free local calls. No pets. $32-35/S; $38-41/D; $6/ex prsn. Disc.

Saint Cloud

Budgetel Inns/ 70 S 37th Av, St Cloud MN 56301. 612-253-4444/ Fax: 259-7809. V,M,D,AE,DC,CB. I-94, Exit 167B N on Hwy 15 to Hwy 23, E to 37th Av, then S. N/s rms, b/f, fax, nrby rstrnt. Free cont brfst, in-rm coffee, local calls AAA. $34-44/S; $41-51/D. 1/1-5/25: $33-43/S; $40-50/D. Spec rates may apply. Discs.

Comfort Inn/ 4040 Second St, Box 7125, St Cloud MN 56302. 612-251-1500. V,M,DC,AE. I-94 (St Cloud Exit 167B) to SR 15 (Exit 167B), N to jct Second St, S 1 blk, turn W. Mtg rm, fax, b/f, sauna, whrlpool, cable TV, t pkng, n/s rms. Free cont brfst. AAA. $37-80/S; $42-85/D; $5/ex prsn. 3/1-9/30: $41-80/S; $46-85/D. 10/1-11/30: $40-80/S; $45-85/D. Discs.

Motel 6/ 815 First Av S, St Cloud MN 56387. 612-253-7070/ Fax: 253-0436. V,M,AE,D,DC. I-94: Ebnd, to Hwy 23,

MINNESOTA

turn lt on 10th Av S, go 1/2 blk, turn rt on 1st St S; Wbnd (Exit 167) to Hwy 15, lt on Hwy 23, to 10th Av S, rt 1/2 blk, rt on 1st. Nrby rstrnt, n/s rms. Free local calls. $27-29/S; $33-35/D; $6/ex prsn. Disc.

Saint Paul

Exel Inn/ 1739 Old Hudson Rd, St Paul MN 55106. 612-771-5566/ Fax: 771-1262. D,M,V,AE,DC,CB I-94, White Bear Av exit, turn N 1 blk to Old Hudson rd, lt 1/2 blk. E side of city. Nrby rstrnt, cable TV, game rm, laundry, fax, micro-fridge, n/s rms, elevator. Free cont brfst. AAA. $37-54/S; $44-59/D. Higher spec event rates. Discs.

Northernaire Motel/ 2441 Hwy 61, St Paul MN 55109. 612-484-3336/ Fax: 484-2063/ 800-899-7578. V,M,AE,D. At jct Hwy 61 & Hwy 36. Entrance to mtl 1 mi N of Hwy 36 at Cty Rd C, W 1 blk to Frontage Rd. Rstrnt, n/s rms, tt phone, fax, copier, microwave, cot. Free local calls, coffee. No pets. AAA. $43-47/S or D. Mar-Sept: $47-52/S or D. Higher wknd rates Sept-Nov. Disc: Senior, trkr, comm, l/s, AAA.

Also see Anoka, Bloomington, Brooklyn Park, Chaska, Eagan, Fridley, Hastings, Richfield, Roseville.

Sauk Centre

Econo Lodge/ Box 46, Sauk Centre MN 56378. 612-352-6581. AE,M,V,DC. I-94 at US 71. Rstrnt/ lounge, mtg rm, fax, cable TV, t pkng, outlets, copier, dd phones, n/s rms. Free AM coffee, cont brfst. AAA. $38-79/S; $43-85/D; $5/ex prsn. 5/1-6/15: $36-79/S; $41-85/D. Discs.

Gopher Prairie Motel/ 1222 S Getty, Sauk Centre MN 56378. 612-352-2275/ Fax: 352-5120. V,M,AE,D,DC,CB. I-94 (Exit 127) to W service rd. At NW corner I-94 & Hwy 71. N/s rms, cable TV, game rm, tt/dd phone, mtg rm, copier, refrig, cot, crib, outlets, t/b/rv pkng, eff, b/f. Free local calls, coffee. IMA. $28-33/S; $33-41/D; $4/ex prsn. Disc: Senior, bsns, govt, trkr. *Guaranteed rates*

Hillcrest Motel/ 965 Main St S, Sauk Centre MN 56378. 612-352-2215/ 800-858-6333. V,M,AE,D. I-94, exit Sauk Centre, 4 blk N on Hwy 71. Nrby rstrnt, n/s rms, cable TV, tt/dd phone, fax, copier, refrig, cot, crib, outlets, t/rv pkng. Free local calls, coffee. AAA. $24/S; $26-32/D; $4/ex prsn. Disc: Bsns, trkr, l/s. *Guaranteed rates.*

Shakopee

Budget Host Inn/ 1181 E First Av, Shakopee MN 55379. 612-445-9120/ Fax: 496-3546. V,AE,CB,DC,D,MC. Hwy 101 at Marschall. Cable TV, dd phone, in-rm coffee, n/s rms, cont brfst, rstrnt, mtg rm, fax, laundry, t pkng, outlets, cot. Free crib. AAA. $40/S; $44/D; $5/ex prsn. 5/1-9/14: $70/S or D. Wknds: $49/S or D. Spec events: $75. Discs.

Spicer

Cazador Inn/ 154 Lake Ave S, Box 310, Spicer MN 56288. 612-796-2091. V,M, AE,D,DC,CB. 10 minutes from Willmar. Across the beach from Green Lake. Indr pool, n/s rms, cable TV, dd phone, game rm, outlets, whrlpool, sauna, b/f, cot, crib, suites. Free cont brfst. IMA. Sun-Thurs: $34/S; $45/D; $8-10/ex prsn. Fri, Sat, Holiday, Spec Event: $65/S or D. Higher spec event rates. Disc: Senior, TA.

Thief River Falls

Super 8 Motel/ 1915 Hwy 59 SE, Thief River Falls MN 56701. 218-681-6205/ Fax: 681-7519. M,V,DC,D,CB,AE. US 59, E of jct with Hwy 32. B/f, n/s rms, outlets, b/t pkng, cont brfst, copier, cot. Free local calls. Pride Award. AAA. $39/S; $44-47/D; $3/ex prsn. Higher spec event rates. Discs.

Virginia

Ski View Motel/ 9th Av & 17th St N, Virginia MN 55792. 218-741-8918. V, M,AE,D,DC,CB. Hwy 53 to "H" exit, lt 8 blks at next traffic light. Nrby rstrnt, sauna, n/s rms, cable TV, tt phone, cot, crib, outlets, t/b pkng, conn rms. Free cont brfst, coffee. AAA/ Mobil. $30/S; $34-38/D; $4/ex prsn. Disc: Bsns, govt, family, trkr, milt. *Guaranteed rates.*

Lakeshor Motor Inn/ 404 N 6th Av, Virginia MN 55792. 218-741-3360/ Reserv: 800-569-8131. V,M,AE,D,DC, CB. Nbnd: take 1st bsns exit, follow to

2nd stoplight, turn lt, go 4 blks to 6th Av, rt 4 blks. Sbnd: Hwy 53 & 169, lt at 1st stoplight on Hwy 35, go to 2nd stoplight, rt on 6th Av, 4 blks. Cable TV, tt/dd phone, cot, crib, outlets. Free coffee. AAA/ Mobil. $31/S; $39-41/D; $4/ex prsn. 5/15-9/15: $34/S; $43-45/D. 3rd wknd in June: $55/S or D. Suite: $69-89. Discs.

Waterville
McWhirter's Lakeview Resort/ RR 2, Box 507, Waterville MN 56096. 507-362-4616/ Fax: 362-4180. Hwy 60 & 13. N 1 mi on 13. Cable TV, playgrnd, refrig, microwave, rv pkng. 5/1-10/15: $35-45/1-4 prsns; $3/ex prsn. Disc: L/s.

Worthington
Budget Host Inn/ 207 Oxford, Worthington MN 56187. 507-376-6155/ Fax: 376-3374. D,V,M,AE,DC,CB. I-90 (Exit 42) at Hwy 266, 1/2 mi S to Oxford St. Cable TV, dd phone, in-rm coffee, n/s rms, family, rm, nrby mtg rm, picnic area, t pkng, outlets. Free crib. AAA. $34/S; $40-44/D; $6/ex prsn. 6/7-9/21: $39/S; $44-46/D. Spec events: $65/1-4 prsns. Discs.

Mississippi

Biloxi
Econo Lodge/ 1776 Beach Blvd, Biloxi MS 39531. 601-374-7644. V,M,D,AE. I-10 (Exit 46A) to I-110, S (Exit 1B) to US 90, W 3 mi to mtl. Near Kessler AFB. Nrby rstrnt, pool, tennis, coffee, n/s rms. No pets. $45-110/S or D; $4/ex prsn. Discs.

Motel 6/ 2476 Beach Blvd, Biloxi MS 39531. 601-388-5130/ Fax: 388-8819. V,M,D,AE,DC. I-10 (Exit 34A) to Hwy 49, S 5 mi to Beach Blvd (US 90), E 7 mi to Beach Blvd & Briarfield Rd. Cable TV, pool, n/s rms, nrby rstrnt, laundry. Premier Award. $38/S; $44/D; $6/ex prsn. 5/23-12/20: Sun-Thurs: $36-42/S; $42-48/D. Fri, Sat, Holiday, Spec Events: $42-50/S; $48-56/D. Higher spec event rates.

Brandon
Days Inn/ US 80 Brandon MS 39042. 601-825-0894. V,M,D,AE,DC,CB. I-20 (Exit 56) to US 80, turn S. Fax, n/s rms, nrby rstrnt, pool, whrlpool, b/f, cot. No pets. $40-45/S; $45-50/D; $5/ex prsn. Discs.

Brookhaven
Howard Johnson Lodge/ 1210 Brookway Blvd, Box 850, Brookhaven MS 39601. 601-833-1341/ Fax: Ext 604. V, M,D,AE,DC,CB. I-55, Exit 40. N/s rms, mtg rm, b/f, rstrnt, pool, t/b pkng, kitchenette, cable TV. $32-37/S; $37-42/D. Discs.

Canton (Jackson area)
Econo Lodge/ I-55 & Frontage Rd, Canton MS 39046. 601-859-2643. V,M,AE. I-55 (Exit 119) to SR 22, E to mtl. Nrby rstrnt, pool, fax, cable TV, t pkng. No pets. AAA. $38-47/S; $42-55/D; $5/ex prsn. Discs.

Carthage
Econo Lodge/ Rte 8, Box 330, Carthage MS 39051. 601-267-7900/ Fax: 267-8083. AE,M,V,DC. On SR 25, E of jct with SR 35. Nrby rstrnt, pool, b/f, cable TV. No pets. AAA. $34-38/S; $38-42/D; $4/ex prsn. 2/1-11/30: $38-42/S; $42-44/D. Discs.

Cleveland
Comfort Inn/ 721 N Davis St, Cleveland MS 38732. 601-843-4060. AE,D,M,V. On US 61, 1 mi N of SR 8. Nrby rstrnt, pool, mtg rm, fax, b/f, cable TV, t pkng, exerc equip, n/s rms. Free cont brfst. No pets. AAA. $39-60/S; $41-65/D; $4/ex prsn. Discs.

Clinton
Days Inn/ 482 Springridge Rd, Clinton MS 39056. 601-924-7243/ Fax: 924-6028. V,M,D,AE,DC,CB. I-20, Exit 36.

Fax, n/s rms, nrby rstrnt, whrlpool, b/f, cot. Free cont brfst. $35-55/S; $40-65/D; $5/ex prsn. Discs

Corinth
Comfort Inn/ Box 540, Corinth MS 38834. 601-287-4421. V,M,D,AE. US 72 at US 45 Bypass. Nrby rstrnt, pool, mtg rm, fax, b/f, cable TV, t pkng, laundry, n/s rms. No pets. $38-56/S; $44-61/D; $4/ex prsn. 5/1-12/31: $37-55/S; $43-60/D. Discs.

Forest
Comfort Inn/ 1250 SR 35 S, Forest MS 39074. 601-469-2100. V,M,D,AE. I-20 (Exit 88) to SR 35, N to mtl. Nrby rstrnt, pool, fax, b/f, cable TV, n/s rms. Free cont brfst. AAA. $43-48/S; $48-52/D; $6/ex prsn. Discs.

Greenwood
Comfort Inn/ 401 US 82 W, Box 1701, Greenwood MS 38930. 601-453-5974. V,M,DC,AE. I-55 to US 82, W to mtl. Nrby rstrnt, pool, mtg rm, fax, b/f, cable TV, t pkng, in-rm coffee, refrig, microwave, n/s rms. Free cont brfst. AAA. $47-52/S; $47-54/D; $4/ex prsn. Discs.

Grenada
Comfort Inn/ 1552 Sunset Dr, Grenada MS 38901. 601-226-1683. V,M,DC,AE. I-55N (Exit 206) to SR 8, Frontage Rd E. Nrby rstrnt, pool, fax, b/f, whrlpool, cable TV, VCR, microwave, refrig, n/s rms. Free cont brfst. No pets. AAA. $42-72/S; $47-72/D; $5/ex prsn. 5/1-10/31: $47-90/S; $52-90/D. Higher spec event/ holiday rates. Discs.

Gulfport
Motel 6/ 9355 US 49, Gulfport MS 39503. 601-863-1890/ Fax: 868-2445. M,V,DC,D,AE. I-10 (Exit 34A) to Hwy 49, S to mtl. Nrby rstrnt, cable TV, laundry, pool, n/s rms, t pkng. Free local calls. $35/S; $41/D; $6/ex prsn. 5/23-12/20: Sun-Thurs: $32-38/S; $38-44/D; Fri, Sat, Holiday, Spec Events: $42-46/S; $48-42/D. Higher spec event rates. Disc.

Rodeway Inn/ 130 Teagarden Rd, Gulfport MS 39507. 601-896-7881. V,M,D,AE. I-10 (Exit 38) to Lorraine Rd, S to US 90, W 1/4 mi to mtl. Nrby rstrnt, pool, fax, cable TV, n/s rms. Free cont brfst. $40-95/S; $45-120/D; $5/ex prsn. Discs.

Hattiesburg
Econo Lodge/ 3501 Hardy St, Hattiesburg MS 39401. 601-264-0010. AE,V, M,DC. I-59 (Exit 65) to Hardy St, E. Nrby rstrnt, fax, b/f, cable TV, t pkng, refrig. Free cont brfst. No pets. $34-45/S; $38-45/D; $4/ex prsn. Discs.

Howard Johnson Lodge/ 6553 Hwy 49 N, Hattiesburg MS 39401. 601-268-2251/ Fax: 264-7283. AE,V,M,DC, CB,D. I-59 (Exit 67A) to Hwy 49, S. N/s rms, mtg rm, b/f, rstrnt, pool, t pkng, deluxe cont brfst, copier, coffee. $40-50/S; $40-58/D. Discs.

Motel 6/ 6508 US 49, Hattiesburg MS 39401. 601-544-6096/ Fax: 582-7743. M,V,DC,D,AE. I-59 (Exit 67A) to US 49, SE 1/2 mi to mtl. Cable TV, pool, nrby rstrnt, n/s rms, t pkng. Free local calls. $26-28/S; $30-32/D; $4/ex prsn. Disc.

Quality Inn 6528 US 49 N, Hattiesburg MS 39401. 601-544-4530. AE,V,M,DC. I-59 (Exit 67A) to US 49, S 1/2 mi to mtl. Nrby rstrnt, pool, mtg rm, fax, cable TV, t pkng, n/s rms. Free cont brfst. No pets. $37-44/S; $42-49/D; $5/ex prsn. 5/1-8/31: $44-51/S; $49-56/D. 9/1-10/31: $39-46/S; $44-51/D. Discs.

Hernando
Days Inn/ I-55 & US 304, Hernando MS 38632. 601-429-000. V,M,D,AE,DC,CB. Jct I-55 (Exit 280) and US 304. Fax, n/s rms, nrby rstrnt, pool, mtg rm, b/f, gas serv, cot. Free cont brfst. $39-89/S or D; $7-10/ex prsn. Discs.

Jackson
Econo Lodge/ 2450 US 80 W, Jackson MS 39204. 601-353-0340. AE,V,M,DC. I-20 (Exit 42B) to Ellis Av, N 2 blks to US 80, W to mtl. Nrby rstrnt, fax, cable TV, n/s rms, microwave, refrig. Free cont brfst, local calls. No pets. $33-55/S; $37-70/D; $5/ex prsn. Discs.

Econo Lodge/ 5925 I-55 N, Jackson MS 39213. 601-957-5500. V,M,AE. I-55 (Exit 103) to County Line Rd, S on frontage rd 1/2 mi to mtl. Nrby rstrnt/ lounge, pool, indr pool, mtg rm, fax, b/f, whrlpool, cable TV, t pkng, n/s rms.

MISSISSIPPI

Free cont brfst. AAA. $40-50/S; $45-55/D; $5/ex prsn. Discs.

Friendship Inn/ 3880 I-55 S, Jackson MS 39212. 601-373-1244. AE,V,M,DC. I-55 S, Exit 90A. Nrby rstrnt, pool, cable TV, t pkng, laundry, n/s rms. Free cont brfst. $29-36/S; $33-46/D; $4/ex prsn. Discs.

HoJo Inn/ 1065 S Frontage Rd, Jackson MS 39204. 601-354-4455. V,M, AE, D,DC. I-20 (Ebnd, Exit 45; Wbnd, Exit 45A), S on Gallatin St, 1 blk rt at Frontage Rd. N/s rms, rstrnt/ lounge, pool, t/b pkng, dd phone. Free local calls. No pets. $30-35/S; $35-40/D. Discs.

Motel 6/ 6145 I-55 N, Jackson MS 39213. 601-956-8848/ Fax: 956-1378. M,V,AE,D,DC. I-55 (Exit 103) to County Line Rd, turn S on frontage rd to mtl. Nrby rstrnt, cable TV, pool, elevator, n/s rms, t pkng. Free local calls. $31-32/S; $37-38/D; $6/ex prsn. Disc.

Sleep Inn/ 2620 US 80 W, Jackson MS 39204. 601-354-3900. V,M,DC,AE. I-20 (Exit 42B) to N Ellis Av, lt at 1st traffic light 2 blks, rt on US 80, W to mtl. Nrby rstrnt, cable TV, fax, n/s rms. Free local calls, cont brfst. No pets. $37-47/S; $41-51/D; $5/ex prsn. Discs.

Wilson Inn/ 310 Greymont Av, Jackson MS 39202. 601-948-4466/ Fax: Ext 157. AE,V,M,DC,D,CB. At jct High St & I-55, 2 mi from I-20. N/s rms, microwaves, refrig, desks, fax. Free cont brfst, local calls. AAA. $44/S; $44-70/D. Disc: TA, AARP, senior.

Also see Canton, Pearl.

McComb

Comfort Inn/ 107 Scott Dr, McComb MS 39648. 601-249-0080. V,M,DC,AE. I-55 (Exit 17) to Delaware Av E. Nrby rstrnt, pool, fax, b/f, cable TV, t pkng, n/s rms. Free cont brfst. No pets. AAA. $45-50/S; $45-60/D; $5/ex prsn. Discs.

Rodeway Inn/ Box 1366, McComb MS 39648. 601-684-8510. V,M,D,AE. Sbnd side of I-55 (Exit 13) at jct with Hwys 24, 48, 98. Rstrnt, cable TV, t pkng, n/s rms. No pets. $39-45/S; $43-49/D; $4/ex prsn. Discs.

Meridian

Budgetel Inns/ 1400 Roebuck Dr, Meridian MS 39301. 601-693-2300/ Fax: 485-2534. V,M,D,AE,DC,CB. I-59/20, Exit 153 S on US 45, W on Roebuck Dr. N/s rms, b/f, fax, rstrnt, pool. Free cont brfst, in-rm coffee, local calls. AAA. $36-47/S; $41-52/D. 1/1-6/8: $35-46/S; $40-51/D. Discs.

Comfort Inn/ 701 Bonita Lakes Dr, Meridian MS 39301. 601-693-1200. V,M,DC,AE. I-20 & I-59 (Exit 154A) at jct Hwys 19 & 39. Nrby rstrnt, pool, mtg rm, fax, b/f, cable TV, t pkng, outlets, exerc equip, n/s rms. Free cont brfst. $40-80/S; $45-85/D; $5/ex prsn. Discs.

Econo Lodge/ 2405 S Frontage Rd, Meridian MS 39301. 601-693-9393. AE,V,M,DC. I-20 & I-59 (Exit 153) at US 45, turn S to mtl. Nrby rstrnt, fax, b/f, cable TV, t pkng, outlets. Free cont brfst, local calls. AAA. $30-60/S; $35-65/D; $5/ex prsn. Discs.

Motel 6/ 2309 S Frontage Rd, Meridian MS 39301. 601-482-1182/ Fax: 483-9247. M,V,DC,D,AE. I-20 (Exit 153) to 22nd Av, go W on S Frontage Rd. Nrby rstrnt, cable TV, laundry, pool, n/s rms, t pkng. Free local calls. $25/S; $29/D; $4/ex prsn. Disc.

Sleep Inn/ 1301 Hamilton Av, Meridian MS 39301. 601-485-4646. V,M,DC,AE. I-20/59 to (Exit 153) US 45, S to mtl. Nrby rstrnt, pool, cable TV, t pkng, exerc equip, n/s rms. Free cont brfst. $35-50/S; $42-57/D; $5/ex prsn. Discs.

Natchez

Comfort Inn/ 337 Devereux Dr, Natchez MS 39120. 601-446-5500. V,M,DC,AE. US 61 N. Nrby rstrnt, pool, fax, b/f, cable TV, t pkng. Free cont brfst. No pets. AAA. $35-50/S; $40-55/D; $7/ex prsn. 2/16-4/30: $50-63/S; $58-69/D. 5/1-9/30: $40-55/S; $45-60/D. Higher spec event rates. Discs.

Howard Johnson Lodge/ 45 Seargent Prentiss Dr, Natchez MS 39120. 601-442-1691/ Fax: 445-5895. V,M,D,AE, DC,CB. Hwy 61, 1 blk S of jct with Hwys 65 & 84. N/s rms, mtg rm, rstrnt/ lounge, pool, t pkng, rm serv, valet. Free coffee. $42-46/S; $46-56/D. Discs.

MISSISSIPPI / MISSOURI

Pearl (Jackson area)
Econo Lodge/ 232 S Pearson Rd, Pearl MS 39208. 601-932-4226. V,M,AE,D. I-55 to I-20, E (Exit 48) to Pearson Rd, turn N to mtl. Nrby rstrnt, pool, fax, b/f, cable TV, t pkng, n/s rms, microwave, refrig. Free cont brfst, local calls. No pets. $42-75/S; $46-80/D; $4/ex prsn. Discs.

Sardis
Best Western Sardis Inn/ Box 279, Sardis MS 38666. 601-487-2424. V,M, AE,D,DC. I-55, Exit 252. Rstrnt/ lounge, pool, n/s rms, cable TV, tt phone, mtg rm, fax, copier, nwspr, laundry, refrig, cot, t/b/rv pkng, conn rms, b/f. Free local calls. $36-40/S; $40-45/D; $6/ex prsn. 4/1-9/7: $40-45/S; $45-49/D. Higher spec event rates. Disc: Senior, trkr, AARP.

Senatobia
Comfort Inn/ 513 E Main St, Senatobia MS 38668. 601-562-5647. V,M,D,AE. I-55 (Exit 265) to SR 4, W to mtl. Rstrnt, cable TV, n/s rms. Free cont brfst. $42-50/S; $46-55/D; $5/ex prsn. Discs.

Howard Johnson Lodge/ 501 E Main St, Senatobia MS 38668. 601-562-5241/ Fax: 562-4157. AE,V,M,DC, CB,D. I-55, Exit 265 at Senatobia. N/s rms, b/f, rstrnt, pool, rm serv, valet, fax. Free local calls. $38-70/S; $43-75/D. Discs.

Tupelo
Comfort Inn/ 1190 N Gloster St, Tupelo MS 38801. 601-842-5100. V,M,D,AE. Bsns US 78 (McCullough Blvd) to Bsns US 45, N to mtl. Nrby rstrnt, mtg rm, fax, b/f, cable TV, exerc equip, n/s rms. Free cont brfst. No pets. $43-49/S; $47-53/D; $4/ex prsn. Discs.

Econo Lodge/ 1500 McCullough Dr, Tupelo MS 38801. 601-844-1904. AE,V,M,DC. Jct of McCullough Blvd & SR 45. Nrby rstrnt, pool, fax, b/f, cable TV, t pkng. Free cont brfst. No pets. $40-55/S; $44-59/D; $5/ex prsn. 5/1-12/31: $39-54/S; $43-58/D. Discs.

Vicksburg
Econo Lodge/ Pemberton Blvd, Vicksburg MS 39180. 800-424-4777 — opening soon. V,M,AE,D. I-20 (Exit 1C) at Pemberton Blvd to mtl. Nrby rstrnt, pool, fax, b/f, cable TV, n/s rms. Free cont brfst. $49-65/S; $59-75/D; $6/ex prsn. 1/4-4/30: $32-45/S; $36-50/D. 5/1-9/15: $40-60/S; $45-65/D. Discs.

Missouri

Blue Springs (Kansas City area)
Motel 6/ 901 W Jefferson St, Blue Springs MO 64015. 816-228-9133/ Fax: 228-1619. M,V,DC,D,AE. I-70 (Exit 20) to Hwy 7, N to Shaw Pkwy, lt on Shaw, lt on Jefferson. Nrby rstrnt, cable TV, laundry, pool, n/s rms. Free local calls. $23-26/S; $29-32/D; $6/ex prsn. Disc.

Boonville
Comfort Inn/ I-70 & SR 5, Boonville MO 65233. 816-882-5317. V,M,D,AE. Rstrnt/ lounge, mtg rm, fax, b/f, sauna, whrlpool, cable TV, t pkng, n/s rms. Free cont brfst. AAA. $42-52/S; $47-57/D; $5/ex prsn. 5/1-9/15: $44-54/S; $49-59/D. Discs.

Branson
Corvair Resort & Motel/ HC 1, Box 1006, Branson MO 65616. 417-338-2231/ 800-577-0345. V,M,D. Hwy 76 to Cnty Rd 76-60, S 3 mi. Pool, cable TV, playgrnd, tt/dd phone, laundry, refrig, cot, crib, outlets, rv pkng, eff, conn rms. Free local calls. No pets, loud activities. AAA. $36-65/S or D; $5/ex prsn. 6/7-8/17: $45-80/S or D. CLOSED 12/24-2/28. Disc: L/s. *Guaranteed rates.*

Econo Lodge/ 230 S Wildwood Dr, Branson MO 65616. 417-336-4849. V, M,D,AE. US 65 to SR 76, W 2 mi to Wildwood Dr. Nrby rstrnt, pool, fax, b/f, whrlpool, cable TV, n/s rms. Free cont brfst. No pets. AAA. $35-55/S; $40-

MISSOURI

60/D; $5/ex prsn. 1/2-4/30: $30-45/S; $35-50/D. 5/1-8/31: $35-55/S; $40-60/D. 9/1-10/31: $50-70/S; $55-75/D. Discs.

Friendship Inn/ 3015 Green Mt Dr, Branson MO 65616. 417-335-4248. V, M,AE,D,DC. US 65 to SR 76 W, lt at Walmart (Green Mt Dr), 1/2 mi on rt. Nrby rstrnt, indr pool, b/f, cable TV, n/s rms. Free cont brfst. No pets. $39-59/S; $45-65/D; $6/ex prsn. Discs.

Lazy Valley Resort/ 285 River Lane, Branson MO 65616. 417-334-2397. No cr cds. Hwy 65 to Hwy 76 (Main St exit), 1 1/2 mi W to Fall Creek Rd, S 2 mi, follow signs. Pool, n/s rms, cable TV, playgrnd, copier, refrig, cot, crib, outlets, t pkng, eff, conn rms, b/f, fishing dock, boat marina. No pets. AAA. $48/S or D; $5/ex prsn. 2 bdrm condo: $100/4 prsns. Disc: L/s.

Quality Inn/ 3269 Shepherd Hills Expwy, Branson MO 65616. 417-335-6776. V,M,D,AE. SR 248 W, turn lt on Shepherd of the Hills Expwy. Nrby rstrnt, pool, indr pool, mtg rm, fax, b/f, whrlpool, cable TV, n/s rms. Free cont brfst. $39-75/S or D; $6/ex prsn. Discs.

Rodeway Inn/ 2422 Shepherd of the Hills Expwy, Branson MO 65616. 417-336-5577/ Fax: 337-7011. V,M,DC,AE, D. Hwy 65 to SR 248, W to Sh of Hills Expwy, lt approx 3 mi to mtl. 1 mi E of Hwy 76 & Shepherd of Hills Exprwy jct. Nrby rstrnt, pool, mtg rm, fax, b/f, whrlpool, cable TV, t pkng. Free cont brfst. No pets. $30-60/S; $30-65/D; $5/ex prsn. Discs.

Sleep Inn/ 210 Wildwood Dr S, Branson MO 65616. 417-336-3770. V,M,DC, AE. US 65 to SR 76, W 2 mi to Wildwood Dr, at Thousand Hills go S 2 blks to mtl. Across from Grand Palace. Nrby rstrnt, pool, b/f, cable TV, t pkng, n/s rms. Free cont brfst. No pets. $29-39/S; $34-49/D; $5/ex prsn. 5/1-8/31: $39-59/S; $44-64/D. 9/1-10/31: $49-69/S; $49-74/D. 11/1-12/31: $32-52/S; $42-62/D. Discs.

Also see Branson West, Hollister, Kimberling City.

Branson West

Lakeview Inn/ Box 2072, Branson W MO 65672. 417-272-8195/ Fax: 272-8271/ 800-343-2769. V,M,AE,D. 1 blk E of jct Hwy 76 & 13. Pool, n/s rms, cable TV, video games, tt/dd phone, fax, copier, laundry, cot, crib, t/b/rv pkng. Free local calls, coffee. No pets. AAA. $20-35/S; $20-40/D; $5/ex prsn. Disc: Senior, TA, family, AAA. *Guaranteed rates.*

White Oak Inn/ Box 1068, Branson W MO 65737. 417-272-8300/ Fax: 272-8221/ 800-822-6159. V,M,D,DC,CB. 8 mi W of Branson on Hwy 76, 3 mi W of Silver Dollar City. 2 blks from jcts Hwy 76 W & 13. Nrby rstrnt/ lounge, pool, n/s rms, cable TV, dd phone, fax, copier, nwspr, laundry, cot, crib, b pkng. Free local calls, coffee. No pets. AAA. $30/S; $35/D; $5/ex prsn. 5/17-10/26: $35/S; $40/D; $5/ex prsn. CLOSED 12/30-3/31. Disc: AAA, AARP. *Guaranteed rates.*

Bridgeton (St Louis area)

Econo Lodge/ 4575 N Lindbergh Blvd, Bridgeton MO 63044. 314-731-3000/ Fax: Ext 100. AE,V,M,DC. I-70, to Lindbergh Blvd, N 1/2 blk to Natural Bridge exit, S on Lindbergh. Nrby rstrnt/ lounge, pool, mtg rm, fax, cable TV, t pkng, trans. Free cont brfst. $30-36/S; $36-43/D; $4-5/ex prsn. 5/1-9/10: $34-40/S; $40-47/D. Discs.

Motel 6/ 3655 Pennridge Dr, Bridgeton MO 63044. 314-291-6100/ Fax: 291-3797. M,V,AE,D,DC. I-270 (Exit 20B) to St Charles Rock Rd, NW to Pennridge Dr, rt to mtl. Nrby rstrnt, cable TV, pool, laundry, elevator, n/s rms. Free local calls. $30-32/S; $36-38/D; $6/ex prsn. Disc.

Cameron

Budget Host Country Squire Inn/ 501 Northland Dr, Cameron MO 64429. 816-632-6623/ Fax: 632-5129. V,M, AE,D,DC,CB. I-35 (Exit 54) Cameron Hwy 36 W, lt on Jct 69, lt at Dairy Queen. Pool, n/s rms, cable TV, tt phone, fax, copier, microwave, cot, crib, t/b/rv pkng, conn rms, b/f. Free local calls, coffee. No alcohol. AAA. $30/S; $35/D; $5/ex prsn. 4/1-9/30: $33/S; $38/D. Disc: Senior, bsns, TA, govt, family, trkr, milt, AAA, AARP, l/s.

Super 8 Motel/ Hwy 69 & Hwy 36,

MISSOURI

Cameron MO 64229. 816-632-888. V, M,AE,D,DC,CB. I-35 (Exit 54) on Hwys 36 & 69. B/f, n/s rms, pool, whrlpool, outlets, t/b/rv pkng, cont brfst, cable TV, mtg rm. Free local calls. No pets. Pride Award. $38/S; $44-48/D; $2/ex prsn. Higher spec event rates. Discs.

Carthage
Econo Lodge/ 1441 W Central, Carthage MO 64836. 417-358-3900. AE,V, M,DC. E of jct of US 71 & SR 96. Nrby rstrnt, indr pool, fax, b/f, whrlpool, cable TV, t pkng, n/s rms. Free cont brfst, local calls. AAA. $40-50/S; $45-50/D; $5/ex prsn. 8/10-8/12: $85/S or D. Discs.

Cassville
Super 8 Motel/ Hwy 37, Cassville MO 65625. 417-847-4888. V,M,DC,CB, AE,D. Jct Hwy 37 & Hwys 76/86. B/f, n/s rms, pool, outlets, t/b/rv pkng, copier, cable TV, mtg rm, cot. Free local calls, crib. Pride Award. $37/S; $42-44/D; $4/ex prsn. Discs.

Charleston
Comfort Inn/ 102 Drake St, Charleston MO 63834. 314-683-4200. V,M,DC,AE. I-57 (Exit 10) at SR 105 N. Nrby rstrnt, pool, fax, b/f, cable TV, t pkng, n/s rms. Free cont brfst. AAA. $42-48/S; $48-54/D; $6/ex prsn. Discs.

Clarksville
Clarksville Motel/ Hwy 79, Box 57, Clarksville MO 63336. 314-242-3324. V,M. Across from Clarksville skylift. Nrby rstrnt, pool, cable TV, playgrnd, laundry, refrig, microwave, cot, crib, t pkng, conn rms. Free local calls, cont brfst. No pets. AAA. $31-45/S; $45-48/D; $5/ex prsn. Disc: Senior, bsns, govt, l/s. *Guaranteed rates.*

Collinsville (St Louis area)
Howard Johnson/ 301 N Hwy 157, Collinsville MO 62234. 618-345-1530/ Fax: 345-1321. V,M,D,AE,DC,CB. I-55/70 to Hwy 157, turn rt at light. N/s rms, rstrnt, lounge, pool, t pkng. $35-45/S; $45-65/D. Discs.

Columbia
Budget Host Inn/ 900 Vandiver Dr, Columbia MO 65202. 314-449-1065/ Fax: 442-6266. D,V,M,AE,DC,CB. I-70 (Exit 127) to SR 763, NW quadrant. Cable TV, VCR, dd/tt phone, microwave-fridge, n/s rms, pool, laundry, t pkng, outlets, cot, crib. Free cont brfst. AAA/ Mobil. $26-31/S; $30-45/D; $5/ex prsn. Spec events: $60. Discs.

Econo Lodge/ 900 I-70 Dr SW, Columbia MO 65203 314-442-1191. AE,V, M,DC. I-70 (Exit 125) at West Blvd. Rstrnt, indr pool, mtg rm, fax, sauna, whrlpool, cable TV, tennis crt, exerc equip, n/s rms. Free cont brfst, local calls. AAA. $34-50/S; $41-55/D; $5/ex prsn. Higher spec event rates. Discs.

Motel 6/ 1718 N Providence Rd, Columbia MO 65202. 314-442-9390/ Fax: 875-5477. M,V,DC,D,AE. I-70 (Exit 126) to Providence Rd, turn N. Nrby rstrnt, cable TV, pool, n/s rms. Free local calls. $22-26/S; $28-32/D; $6/ex prsn. Disc.

Motel 6/ 1800 I-70 Dr SW, Columbia MO 65203. 314-445-8433/ Fax: 446-1839. M,V,AE,D,DC. I-70 (Exit 124) to Stadium Blvd, turn S to I-70 Dr (frontage rd), lt for 3 blks. Nrby rstrnt, cable TV, indr pool, n/s rms, elevator. Free local calls. $24-26/S; $30-32/D; $6/ex prsn. Disc.

Cuba
Super 8 Motel/ Hwy 19 & I-44, Cuba MO 65453. 314-885-2087/ Fax: 885-2089. V,M,AE,D,DC,CB. Just NE of Jct I-44 & SR 19. B/f, n/s rms, laundry, brfst bar, t/b/rv pkng, elevator, cable TV, mtg rm, cot. Free local calls, crib. Pride Award. $39/S; $44-46/D; $3/ex prsn. Discs.

Doniphan
Days Inn of Doniphan/ 100 Oaktree Village, Doniphan MO 63935. 314-996-2400/ Fax: 996-5144. AE,V,M,DC, D, CB. At jct Hwy 160/ 142, just W of Hwy 67. Nrby rstrnt, pool, whrlpool, b/f, cable TV, cot. Free cont brfst. AAA. Chairman's Award. $39-49/S; $43-55/D; $5/ex prsn. Higher spec event, holiday, wknd rates.

Farmington
Days Inn/ 1400 Liberty St, Box 161, Farmington MO 63640. 314-756-8951.

MISSOURI

V,M,D,AE,DC,CB. US 67 at Liberty St. Fax, n/s rms, indr pool, whrlpool, mtg rm, exerc equip, t pkng, arpt trans, cable TV, video games, laundry, conn rms, cot. Free cont brfst. $40-42/S; $42-46/D; $3/ex prsn. Discs.

Super 8 Motel/ 930 Valley Creek Dr, Farmington MO 63640. 314-756-0344/ Fax: 760-0846. V,M,AE,D,DC. Jct Hwys 67 & 32. B/f, n/s rms, pool, laundry, outlets, b/t pkng, toast bar, copier, cable TV, cot. Free local calls, crib. No pets. Pride Award. $37/S; $42-44/D; $3/ex prsn. Higher spec event rates. Discs.

Fenton (St Louis area)

Motel 6/ 1860 Bowles Av, Fenton MO 63026. 314-349-1800/ Fax: 326-3456. V,M,DC,D,AE. I-44 (Exit 274) at Bowles Av, S to mtl. Nrby rstrnt, cable TV, pool, laundry, n/s rms. Free local calls. $36/S; $42/D; $6/ex prsn. Disc.

Fulton

Budget Host Westwoods Motel/ 422 Gaylord Dr, Fulton MO 65251. 314-642-5991. M,V,AE,CB,DC. Jct US 54 Bypass & F. Cable TV, dd phone, refrig, whrlpool, sauna, pool, nrby rstrnt, arpt trans, t pkng. AAA. $26-32/S; $32-50/D; $4/ex prsn. Discs.

Hannibal

Comfort Inn/ 123 Huckleberry Dr, Hannibal MO 63401. 800-221-2222 — opening soon. V,M,D,AE. US 61 S. Nrby rstrnt, pool, mtg rm, b/f, whrlpool, cable TV, exerc equip, n/s rms. Free cont brfst. $30-80/S or D. Discs.

Econo Lodge/ 612 Mark Twain Av, Hannibal MO 63401. 314-221-1490. AE, V,M,DC. US 61 to US 36, E 1 mi to mtl. Nrby rstrnt, pool, cable TV. Free cont brfst. No pets. $27-55/S; $30-65/D; $10-15/ex prsn. Discs.

Howard Johnson Lodge/ 3603 McMasters Av, Hannibal MO 63401. 314-221-7950. V,M,AE,D,DC. Jct of Hwy 36 & 61. N/s rms, mtg rm, b/f, rstrnt, pool, t pkng, laundry. $35-60/S; $40-75/D. Discs.

Sleep Inn/ 100 S Main, Hannibal MO 63401. 800-221-2222 — opening soon. V,M,D,AE. Main St near Broadway. 1 blk E of SR 79, 5 blks S of US 36, 1 mi E of US 61. Nrby rstrnt, pool, fax, b/f, cable TV, t pkng, n/s rms. Free cont brfst. No pets. $36-59/S; $46-72/D; $5/ex prsn. Discs.

Harrisonville

Slumber Inn/ 21400 E 275th St, Harrisonville MO 64701. 816-884-3100/ 380-1869. V,M,AE,D. US 71, Clinton Exit (SR 7 S). Nrby rstrnt, cable TV, rms, satellite TV, tt phone, fax, t/b/rv pkng, conn rms. Free local calls, cont brfst. AAA. $33/S; $34-38/D; $5/ex prsn. Disc: Senior, bsns, l/s, trkr, AAA, family.

Hollister (Branson area)

Econo Lodge/ Box 375, Hollister MO 65672. 417-334-2770. V,M,AE. On new US 65. Pool, b/f, cable TV, t pkng, n/s rms. $33/S; $37/D; $4/ex prsn. 5/1-10/1: $42/S; $46/D. Discs.

Jackson

Days Inn/ 517 Hwy 61 E, Jackson MO 63755. 314-243-3577/ Fax: 243-4384. V,M,D,AE,DC,CB. I-55 (Exit 99) to US 61, turn W. Fax, n/s rms, nrby rstrnt, whrlpool, b/f, t pkng. Free cont brfst. $40-45/S; $45-55/D; $5/ex prsn. Discs.

Jefferson City

Motel 6/ 1624 Jefferson St, Jefferson City MO 65109. 314-634-4220./ Fax: 635-5284. M,V,DC,D,AE. Hwy 54 at Stadium Blvd/ Jefferson St Exit. Nrby rstrnt, cable TV, n/s rms. Free local calls. $27-28/S; $33-34/D; $6/ex prsn. Disc.

Joplin

Best Inns/ 3508 S Rangeline Rd, Joplin MO 64804. 417-781-6776. AE,DC,CB, M,V,D. I-44, Exit 8B/ Rangeline N. Fax, pool, nrby rstrnt, dd/tt phone, b/f. Free cont brfst, coffee, crib, local calls. AAA. $39-42/S; $46-49/D; $6/ex prsn. Higher spec event rates. Disc: Senior, family.

Motel 6/ 3031 S Range Line Rd, Joplin MO 64804. 417-781-6400/ Fax: 781-5140. M,V,DC,D,AE. I-44 (Exit 8B) to US 71 (Range Line Rd), N to mtl. Nrby rstrnt, cable TV, laundry, pool, n/s rms. Free local calls. $29/S; $35/D; $6/ex prsn. Disc.

MISSOURI

Sleep Inn/ Box 2748, Joplin MO 64803. 417-782-1212. V,M,D,AE. I-44 (Exit 4) at SR 43, 4 mi E of dntn. Rstrnt, fax, b/f, cable TV, t pkng, n/s rms. Free cont brfst. No pets. AAA. $41-65/S; $47-65/D; $4/ex prsn. 5/1-9/30: $44-65/S; $50-65/D. Discs.

Kansas City

Econo Lodge/ 11300 NW Prairieview Rd, Kansas City MO 64153. 816-464-5082. V,M,AE. I-29 (Exit 12) & NW 112th St. Nrby rstrnt, fax, b/f, cable TV. Free coffee, local calls. AAA. $36-60/S; $45-80/D; $6/ex prsn. Higher spec event rates. Discs.

Econo Lodge/ 5100 E Linwood Blvd, Kansas City MO 64128. 816-923-7777. V,M,AE. I-70 (Exit 6) to VanBrunt, rt at light, 2 blks to mtl. Nrby rstrnt, pool, mtg rm, cable TV, t pkng, exerc equip, n/s rms. No pets. $30-45/S; $39-55/D; $5/ex prsn. Discs.

Econo Lodge/ 8500 E SR 350, Kansas City MO 64133. 816-353-3000. AE, V,M,DC. I-435 S (Exit 66) to Raytown/ SR 350 exit, SE 1/2 mi to mtl. Rstrnt/ lounge, pool, fax, b/f, whrlpool, cable TV, t pkng, n/s rms. $27-40/S; $28-52/D; $5/ex prsn. Discs.

Motel 6/ 6400 E 87th St, Kansas City MO 64138. 816-333-4468/ Fax: 333-7324. M,V,AE,D,DC. I-435 (Exit 69) to 87th St, E 1 blk. Nrby rstrnt, cable TV, n/s rms. Free local calls. $32/S; $38/S; $6/ex prsn. Disc.

Motel 6/ 8230 NW Prairie View Rd, Kansas City MO 64152. 816-741-6400/ Fax: 746-5378. M,V,DC,D,AE. I-29/US 71 (Exit 8) to Barry Rd, W at light to Hwy 9 (NW Prairie View Rd, lt to mtl. Cable TV, nrby rstrnt, laundry, pool, n/s rms. Free local calls. $29-30/S; $35-36/D; $6/ex prsn. Disc.

Also see Blue Springs, Kearney, Oak Grove.

Kearney (Kansas City area)

Econo Lodge/ 505 Shanks Av, Kearney MO 64060. 816-635-6000. V,M,AE. I-435 to I-35 N (Exit 26) to SR 92, turn W to mtl. Nrby rstrnt, pool, cable TV, t pkng, n/s rms. $27-42/S; $32-47/D; $5/ex prsn. Discs.

Kimberling City (Branson area)

Budget Host Wildwood Inn/ 26 Wildwood Ln, Kimberling City MO 65686. 417-739-4100/ Fax: 739-4332. V,AE,D,M. 5 mi S on Hwy 13. Pool, whrlpool, n/s rms, cable TV, playgrnd, tt/dd phone, fax, refrig, eff, conn rms, boat dock. Free local calls, coffee. No pets. AAA. $47/S or D; $6/ex prsn. 6/1-8/31: $50/S or D. Holidays, spec events: $60/S or D. Disc: Senior, family, l/s. *Guaranteed rates.*

Kingdom City

Days Inn/ I-70 at Mile Marker 148, Kingdom City MO 65262. 314-642-0050/ Fax: 642-5618. V,M,D,AE,DC, CB. Jct I-70 (Exit 184) and US 54. Fax, n/s rms, nrby rstrnt, whrlpool, b/f, t/rv pkng, cable TV, cot. Free cont brfst. Chairman's Award. $36-48/S; $39-51/D; $5/ex prsn. Discs.

Super 8 Motel/ I-70 & Hwy 54, Kingdom City MO 65262. 314-642-2888. V,M, AE,D,CB,DC. Jct of I-70 and Hwy 54. B/f, n/s rms, nrby rstrnt, toast bar, t/b/rv pkng, copier, cable TV, cot, crib. Free local calls. No pets. Pride Award. $40/S; $47-49/D; $3/ex prsn. Higher spec event rates. Discs.

Kirksville

Budget Host Village Inn/ 1304 S Baltimore, Box 673, Kirksville MO 63501. 816-665-3722/ Fax: 665-6334. D,V,M, AE,DC,CB On Hwy 63 S. Nrby rstrnt, n/s rms, cable TV, tt/dd phone, fax, copier, cot, crib, outlets, t/b/rv pkng. Free local calls, coffee. AAA. $34-36/S; $38-44/D; $4/ex prsn. Spec events: $40/S; $52/D. Disc: Senior, bsns, govt, trkr, milt.

Comfort Inn/ 2209 N Baltimore, Kirksville MO 63501. 816-665-2205. V, M,AE,D,DC. Jct US 63 & SR 6. Nrby rstrnt, fax, b/f, whrlpool, cable TV, outlets, n/s rms. Free cont brfst. AAA. $42-50/S; $47-60/D; $5/ex prsn. Discs.

Super 8 Motel/ 1101 Country Club Dr, Kirksville MO 63501. 816-665-8826. M, V,AE,DC,CB,D. Hwy 63 & Country Club Dr. B/f, n/s rms, outlets, cont brfst. cable TV, limited t pkng, cot, crib. Free local calls. No pets. Pride Award. $40/S; $47-49/D; $3/ex prsn. Higher spec event rates. Discs.

Lebanon

Econo Lodge/ 144 W Bsns Loop, Box 992, Lebanon MO 65536. 417-588-3226. AE,V,M,DC. I-44, Exit 127. Nrby rstrnt, cable TV, t pkng. $31-47/S; $35-51/D; $4/ex prsn. Discs.

Super 8 Motel/ 1831 W Elm, Lebanon MO 65536. 417-588-2574/ Fax: 588-2580. V,M,AE,D,CB,DC. N off I-44, Exit 127 at Bsns Loop Hwy 44. B/f, n/s rms, pool, laundry, outlets, t/b/rv pkng. toast bar, copier, cable TV, cot. Free local calls, crib. Pride Award. $37/S; $42-45/D; $3/ex prsn. Higher spec event rates. Discs.

Macon

Super 8 Motel/ 1420 N Rutherford St, #2A, Macon MO 63552. 816-385-5788/ Fax: Ext 400. V,M,AE,D,CB,DC. Jct of Hwy 36 & 63. B/f, n/s rms, outlets, t/b/rv pkng, copier, cable TV, mtg rm, cot. Free local calls, crib, popcorn. No pets. $39/S; $44-45/D; $4/ex prsn. Discs.

Maryville

Super 8 of Maryville/ 222 Summit Dr, Maryville MO 64468. 816-582-8088. V,M,AE,DC,CB,D. 1 blk E on US 71, in Maryville. N/s rms, rstrnt/ lounge, t/b/rv pkng, cable TV, mtg rm, conn rms, cot, crib. Free local calls. Pride Award. $36/S; $40-42/D; $1/ex prsn. Discs.

Mexico

Econo Lodge/ US 54 & Hamilton Pkwy, Mexico MO 65265. 314-581-1860. AE,V,M,DC. Hwy 54 S. Nrby rstrnt, sauna, cable TV, exerc equip. Free cont brfst. No pets. $35-39/S; $39-45/D; $5/ex prsn. Discs.

Moberly

Super 8 Motel/ 300 Hwy 24 E, Box 176, Moberly MO 65270. 816-263-8862. D, V,M,AE,DC,CB. Jct Hwys 24 and Bsns 63. B/f, n/s rms, outlets, t/b/rv pkng, toast bar, copier, cable TV, mtg rm, cot, crib. Free local calls. No pets. Pride Award. $39/S; $46-48/D; $3/ex prsn. Higher spec event rates. Discs.

Monroe City

Econo Lodge/ 3 Gateway Square, Monroe City MO 63456. 314-735-4200. V,M,AE. US 36 & SR 24. Nrby rstrnt, indr pool, fax, b/f, cable TV, t pkng. AAA. $29-40/S; $35-55/D; $5/ex prsn. 7/1-8/31: $29-45/S; $40-59/D. Discs.

Mount Vernon

Budget Host Ranch Motel/ Rte 1, Box 6B, Mount Vernon MO 65712. 417-466-2125/ Fax: 466-4440. AE,D,M,V. Jct I-44 & Hwy 39. Cable TV, dd phone, nrby rstrnt, n/s rms, pool, picnic area, cot, crib. AAA/ Mobil. $34-38/S; $38-52/D; $3/ex prsn.

Nevada

Comfort Inn/ 2345 Marvel Dr, Nevada MO 64772. 417-667-6777. AE,V,M,DC. US 71, exit Camp Clark W (Austin Blvd), turn W to mtl. Nrby rstrnt, indr pool, mtg rm, fax, b/f, whrlpool, cable TV, t pkng, outlets, laundry, n/s rms. Free cont brfst. AAA. $42-52/S; $45-60/D; $2/ex prsn. Discs.

North Kansas City

Days Inn/ 2232 Taney St, N Kansas City MO 64116. 816-421-6000/ Fax: 421-6675. V,M,D,AE,DC,CB. I-35/29 (Exit 6A) to SR 210, E to mtl. Fax, n/s rms, nrby rstrnt, b/f, cot. Free cont brfst, local calls. $35-55/S; $45-69/D; $6/ex prsn. Discs.

Oak Grove (Kansas City area)

Econo Lodge/ 410 SE 1st St, Box 178, Oak Grove MO 64075. 816-625-3681. AE,V,M,DC. I-70, Exit 28, at Oak Grove. Nrby rstrnt, fax, t pkng, outlets, n/s rms. AAA. $30-50/S; $35-60/D; $5 /ex prsn. Higher spec event rates. Discs.

Osage Beach

Comfort Inn/ Rte 2, Box 2585, Osage Beach MO 65065. 314-348-9555/ Fax: 348-6538. V,M,DC,AE. US 54 E, 4 mi past Glaize Bridge. US 54 W, 1 blk past KK jct. Nrby rstrnt, indr pool, mtg rm, fax, b/f, sauna, whrlpool, cable TV, n/s rms. Free cont brfst. No pets. AAA. $40-68/S; $45-70/D; $5/ex prsn. 5/1-5/25: $48-75/S; $54-75/D. 5/26-10/28: $48-80/S; $54-80/D. 10/2-12/17: $40-58/S; $45-60/D. Discs.

Ozark

Days Inn/ 900 N 18th, Ozark MO 67521. 417-581-5800/ Fax: 581-5807.

MISSOURI

V,M,D,AE,DC,CB. US 65 to SR 14, E to mtl. Fax, n/s rms, nrby rstrnt, indr pool, whrlpool, t pkng, cable TV, cot. Free cont brfst. Chairman's Award. $38-59/S; $42-64/D; $5/ex prsn. 4/1-10/31: $42-59/S; $45-64/D. Discs.

Perryville
Budget Host Inn/ 221 S Kings Hwy, Perryville MO 63775. 314-547-4516. AE,M,D,V. I-55, Exit 129, E 2 mi to Hwy 61, S 1 mi. Nrby rstrnt, cable TV, tt/dd phone, fax, refrig, cot, crib, t pkng. Free local calls, coffee. AAA. $26-38/S; $32-40/D; $6/ex prsn. Disc: Senior, family, trkr, AAA.

Popular Bluff
Super 8 Motel/ 2831 N Westwood Blvd, Poplar Bluff MO 63901. 314-785-0176/ Fax: 785-2865. M,V,AE,D,DC,CB. Hwy 60/67 N at Oakgrove Rd. B/f, n/s rms, outlets, cont brfst, copier, cable TV. Free local calls. No pets. $36/S; $40-46/D; $3/ex prsn. Discs.

Rockaway Beach
Eden Roc Resort/ 2652 Hwy 176, Box 674, Rockaway Beach MO 65740. 417-561-4163/ 800-955-3459. V,M,D. On SR 176, 5 mi E of Hwy 65 S; 4 mi N of Branson. Pool, n/s rms, cable TV, arpt trans, tt phone, refrig, microwave, cot, outlets, b/rv pkng, b/f. Free local calls, coffee. AAA. $25/S or D; $5/ex prsn. 4/1-10/31: $28/S; $32/D. Disc: Senior, bsns, TA, govt, milt, AARP, l/s. *Guaranteed rates.*

Rolla
Econo Lodge/ 1417 Martin Spring Dr, Rolla MO 65401. 314-341-3130. AE, V,M,DC. I-44 (Exit 184) to Martin Spring Dr, S to mtl. Rstrnt, pool, fax, cable TV, t pkng, outlets, n/s rms. Free cont brfst, local calls. $31-41/S; $38-48/D; $4/ex prsn. Discs.

Howard Johnson Lodge/ 127 HJ Dr, Rolla MO 65401. 314-364-7111/ Fax: Ext 200. AE,V,M,DC,CB,D. I-44 (Exit 184) to I-44 Bsns (Kings Hwy). N/s rms, b/f, rstrnt, indr pool, t pkng, Free cont brfst. $36-50/S; $44-60/D. Discs.

Saint Charles (St Louis area)
Econo Lodge/ 3040 W Clay, St Charles MO 63301. 314-946-9992. AE,V,M,DC. I-70 (Exit 227) at Zumbehl Rd, St Charles. Indr pool, fax, b/f, whrlpool, cable TV, t pkng, n/s rms. Free cont brfst. No pets. AAA. $32-40/S; $43-53/D; $3/ex prsn. 3/1-4/30: $37-43/S; $46-50/D. 5/1-10/31: $40-56/S; $50-60/D. Discs.

Saint James
Comfort Inn/ 110 N Outer Rd, St James MO 65559. 314-265-5005. V,M,D,AE. I-44 (Exit 195), 8 mi E of Rolla, MO. Nrby rstrnt, indr pool, mtg rm, fax, b/f, whrlpool, cable TV, t pkng, exerc equip, n/s rms. Free cont brfst. No pets. $39-54/S; $42-69/D; $5/ex prsn. 3/1-9/30: $44-59/S; $48-79/D. Discs.

Saint Joseph
Motel 6/ 4021 Frederick Blvd, St Joseph MO 64506. 816-232-2311/ Fax: 232-0254. M,V,DC,D,AE. I-29 (Exit 47) to Hwy 6 (Frederick Blvd), turn W to mtl. Nrby rstrnt, cable TV, pool, n/s rms, t pkng. Free local calls. $30-32/S; $36-38/D; $6/ex prsn. Disc.

Saint Louis
Bridgeport Inn/ 4199 N Lindbergh Blvd, St Louis MO 63044. 314-739-4600/ Fax: 770-1221/ 800-489-5656. V,M,AE, D,DC,CB. Just S of I-70, Exit 235 A; 1 mi from arpt. Nrby rstrnt/ lounge, n/s rms, cable TV, arpt trans, tt/dd phone, fax, copier, microwave, cot, crib, outlets, conn rms, b/f. Free cont brfst. $27-30/S; $29-34/D; $2/ex prsn. 6/1-8/31: $29-32/S; $31-36/D. Holidays: $40/S; $50/D. Discs. *Guaranteed rates.*

Econo Lodge/ 1351 Dunn Rd, St Louis MO 63138. 314-388-1500. V,M,D,AE. I-270 to Exit 32, bet Lilac Dr & Bellefontaine, E on Dunn Rd to mtl. Rstrnt/ lounge, pool, mtg rm, cable TV, t pkng, n/s rms. Free cont brfst. No pets. $30-39/S; $35-44/D; $5/ex prsn. Discs.

Howard Johnson/ 4530 N Lindbergh, St Louis MO 63044. 314-731-3800. V,M,D,AE,DC,CB. I-70 to Lindbergh N. N/s rms, mtg rm, rstrnt/ lounge, pool, fax, b/f, laundry. Free arpt trans. $45-55/S or D. Discs.

Motel 6/ 1405 Dunn Rd, St Louis MO 63138. 314-869-9400/ Fax: 869-8623. M,V,DC,D,AE. I-270 (Exit 32) to Bellefontaine Rd, N to Dunn Rd, E to mtl.

Nrby rstrnt, cable TV, laundry, pool, n/s rms. Free local calls. $30-32/S; $36-38/D; $6/ex prsn. Disc.

Motel 6/ 6500 S Lindbergh Blvd, St Louis MO 63123. 314-892-3664/ Fax: 892-1153. V,M,DC,D,AE. I-270/ I-255 N on I-55 to Lindbergh Blvd, NW 1 blk. Nrby rstrnt, cable TV, pool, n/s rms. Free local calls. $36/S; $42/D; $6/ex prsn. Disc.

Motel 6/ 4576 Woodson Rd, St Louis MO 63134. 314-427-1313/ Fax: 427-0826. M,V,DC,D,AE. I-70 (Exit 236) to Lambert Arpt, go 1/2 mi E to jct of Woodson Rd & Natural Bridge Rd. Nrby rstrnt, cable TV, pool, n/s rms. Free local calls. $36/S; $42/D; $6/ex prsn. Disc.

Also see Bridgeton, Collinsville, Fenton, St Charles, Wentzville, Collinsville IL.

Saint Robert

Howard Johnson Lodge/ 1083 Missouri Ave, St Robert MO 65583. 314-336-5115/ Fax: 336-3215. V,M,AE,D,DC. I-44 (Exit 161A) S on I-44 Spur 2 mi. N/s rms, mtg rm, b/f, rstrnt/ lounge, indr pool, t pkng, VCR/ movies. $42-46/S or D. Discs.

Also see Waynesville.

Sainte Genevieve

Econo Lodge/ Box 425, Ste Genevieve MO 63670. 314-543-2272. AE,V,M,DC. I-55, Ozora exit. On CR M/N at mi marker 143, 8 mi SW of Ste Genevieve. Rstrnt, pool, mtg rm, fax, b/f, cable TV, t pkng, outlets, n/s rms. Free local calls. $34-55/S; $40-60/D; $4/ex prsn. Discs.

Sikeston

Econo Lodge/ 110 S I-55, Sikeston MO 63801. 314-471-7400. AE,V,M,DC. I-55 (Exit 67) at jct with I-57. Nrby rstrnt, whrlpool, cable TV, t/rv/b pkng, n/s rms. Free local calls. $30-40/S; $35-50/D; $4/ex prsn. Discs.

Super 8 Motel/ 2609 E Malone, Box 1653, Sikeston MO 63801. 314-471-7944/ Fax: 471-7946. M,V,AE,DC, CB,D. I-55 (Exit 67) at E Malone Av. B/f, n/s rms, outlets, cont brfst, t pkng, copier, cable TV. Free local calls, crib. No pets. Pride Award. $39/S; $43-49/D; $3/ex prsn. Higher spec event rates. Discs.

Springfield

Best Inns/ 2355 N Glenstone, Springfield MO 65803. 417-866-6776. AE,DC, CB,M,V,D. I-44 S, Exit 80A/ Glenstone S. Pool, fax, nrby rstrnt, t pkng, dd/tt phone, b/f. Free cont brfst, coffee, crib, local calls. AAA. $39-42/S; $46-49/D; $6/ex prsn. Disc: Senior, family.

Budget Host Loveland Inn/ 2601 N Glenstone, Springfield MO 65803. 417-865-6565/ Fax: 865-9008. V,AE,CB,M,D,DC. 2 blks S of I-44, Exit 80A. Cable TV, dd phone, suites, kitchens, n/s rms, mtg rm, cot. No pets. AAA. $30-34/S; $36-46/D; $5/ex prsn. 5/11-10/31: $32-36/S; $38-48/D. Discs.

Comfort Inn/ 3330 E Battlefield Rd, Springfield MO 65804. 417-889-6300. V,M,AE,D,DC. I-44 to I-65 Bypass, S to Battlefield Rd. Nrby rstrnt, pool, fax, b/f, cable TV, n/s rms. Free cont brfst. No pets. AAA. $40-60/S; $45-65/D; $5/ex prsn. 5/1-10/31: $40-65/S; $45-70/D. 11/1-12/31: $35-50/S; $40-60/D. Discs.

Econo Lodge/ 2808 N Kansas, Springfield MO 65803. 417-869-5600. V,M,AE,D. I-44 (Exit 77) at SR 13, turn S to mtl. Nrby rstrnt, fax, b/f, cable TV, t pkng, outlets, n/s rms. Free cont brfst, popcorn. No pets. $35-55/S; $40-60/D; $5/ex prsn. Discs.

Econo Lodge/ 2611 N Glenstone Av, Springfield MO 65803. 417-864-3565. AE,V,M,DC. I-44 (Exit 80A) to Glenstone Av, S 1/4 mi to mtl. Nrby rstrnt, pool, fax, b/f, cable TV, t pkng, n/s rms, movies. Free cont brfst, nwspr, popcorn. No pets. AAA. $40-46/S; $45-50/D; $5/ex prsn. Discs.

Motel 6/ 3114 N Kentwood, Springfield MO 65803. 417-833-0880/ Fax: 833-5147. M,V,AE,D,DC. I-44, Exit 80B, N to 1st light, turn lt to Kentwood. Nrby rstrnt, cable TV, pool, elevator, n/s rms. Free local calls. $27-30/S; $33-36/D; $6/ex prsn. Disc.

Motel 6/ 2455 N Glenstone Av, Springfield MO 65803. 417-869-4343/

Fax: 869-5269. M,V,DC,D,AE. I-44 (Exit 80A) to Glenstone Av, S 2 blks. Nrby rstrnt, cable TV, pool, n/s rms. Free local calls. $25-26/S; $31-32/D; $6/ex prsn. Disc.

Strafford

Super 8 Motel/ 315 E Chestnut, Strafford MO 65757. 417-736-3883. V,M,AE,D,DC. I-44, Exit 88, S on 125 to Chestnut St, lt to mtl. N/s rms, laundry, outlets, t/b/rv pkng, toast bar, copier, cable TV, cot, crib. Free local calls. Prime Award. $36-37/S; $43-48/D; $5/ex prsn. Discs.

Waynesville (St Robert area)

Days Inn/ 14125 Hwy Z, Waynesville MO 65583. 314-336-5556/ Fax: 336-3918. C,M,AE,D,DC,CB. I-44, Exit 163 (Dixon). Pool, n/s rms, cable TV, VCR/ movies, tt/dd phone, fax, laundry, refrig, cot, crib, b/f. Free local calls, cont brfst. Chairman's Award. AAA. $37-46/S; $46-56/D; $5/ex prsn. Higher spec event/ holiday wknd rates. Disc: Senior, bsns, govt, milt, family.

Econo Inn/ HC6, Box 107B, Waynesville MO 65583. 314-336-7272. AE,D,M,V. I-44 (Exit 161A) at MO Av (to Ft L Wood), S across bridge, lt at first light to mtl. I-44 & Ft Leonard Wood. Nrby rstrnt, pool, fax, b/f, cable TV, t pkng, n/s rms. Free cont brfst. $34-54/S; $39-54/D; $5/ex prsn. Discs.

Wentzville (St Louis area)

Comfort Inn/ 1400 Continental Dr, Wentzville MO 63385. 314-327-5515. V, M,D,AE. I-70 (Exit 210B) to Pitman Av, 2 sharp rts to mtl. Nrby rstrnt, pool, mtg rm, fax, b/f, cable TV, t pkng, n/s rms. Free cont brfst. $30-37/S; $36-40/D; $4/ex prsn. 5/1-5/31: $33-43/S; $46-50/D. 6/1-8/31: $40-50/S; $46-66/D. 9/1-11/30: $33-37/S; $36-46/D. Discs.

Howard Johnson Lodge/ 1500 Continental Dr, Wentzville MO 63385. 314-327-5212/ Fax: 327-5516. V,M,D,AE,DC,CB. I-70 to Wentzville Exit 210B, turn N to Pitman Av, rt to service rd. N/s rms, b/f, t pkng. Free brfst buffet, local calls. $30-40/S; $36-43/D. Discs.

West Plains

Super 8 Motel/ 1210 Porter Wagoner Blvd, W Plains MO 65775. 417-256-8088. V,M,AE,DC,CB,D. Jct Bsns 63 & CC Hwy. B/f, n/s rms, outlets, t/b/rv pkng, toast bar, copier, cable TV, cot, crib. Free local calls. No pets. Pride Award. $40/S; $47-49/D; $3/ex prsn. Higher spec event rates. Discs.

Montana

Belgrade

Super 8 Motel/ 6450 Jackrabbit Ln, Belgrade MT 59714. 406-388-1493/ Fax: 388-2463. M,V,AE,DC,CB,D. I-90 (Exit 298) S side of Belgrade. B/f, n/s rms, indr pool, hot tub, cont brfst, cable TV, t/b/rv pkng, outlets, laundry, copier, fax, suites, mtg rm, arpt trans, cot, crib. Free local calls. Pride Award. $41/S; $45-49/D; $5/ex prsn. Discs.

Big Fork

Timbers Motel/ 8540 Hwy 35, Box 757, Big Fork MT 59911. 406-837-6200/ Fax: 837-6203/ 800-821-4546. V,M. On Hwy 35 at jct Hwy 209. Pool, sauna, whrlpool, n/s rms, cable TV, tt/dd phone, fax, copier, nwspr, cot, crib, t/b/rv pkng, conn rms. Free local calls, coffee. AAA. $30/S; $34-38/D; $5/ex prsn. 6/15-9/10: $44/S; $49-57/D.

Big Timber

Super 8 Motel/ I-90 & Hwy 10 W, Big Timber MT 59011. 406-932-8888/ Fax: 932-4103. V,M,DC,CB,AE,D. Just off I-90 (Exit 367) at Big Timber. B/f, n/s rms, laundry, copier, fax, cable TV, cot, crib, mtg rm, nrby rstrnt, outlets. $37-39/S; $40-48/D; $6/ex prsn. Higher spec event rates. Discs.

Billings

Cherry Tree Inn/ 823 N Broadway, Billings MT 59101. 406-252-5603/ 800-237-5882. V,M,AE,D,DC,CB. I-90/94 (Exit 450) to 9th Av N, 1/2 blk lt. Nrby rstrnt, n/s rms, cable TV, TDD, tt phone, mtg rm, laundry, refrig, elevator, cot, crib, outlets, eff, conn rms, b/f. Free cont brfst. AAA. $32-34/S; $36-42/D; $3/ex prsn. *Guaranteed rates.*

Days Inn/ 843 Parkway Ln, Billings MT 59101. 406-242-4007. V,M,D,AE,DC,CB. I-90: Wbnd, (Exit 447) to S Billings Blvd, lt on King Ave E, lt on Pkwy;

MONTANA

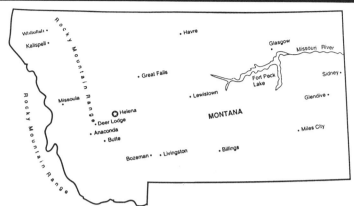

Econo Lodge/ 2601 Fourth Av N, Billings MT 59101. 406-245-6646. AE,V,M,DC. I-90 to 27th St, N to 4th Av, N to mtl. Nrby rstrnt, fax, cable TV, n/s rms. $36-40/S; $42-48/D; $4-5/ex prsn. 5/1-10/31: $38-44/S; $46-52/D. Discs.

Howard Johnson/ 27th St S, Billings MT 59101. 406-248-4656/ Fax: 249-7268. V,M,AE,D,DC. I-90/ 94 to Exit 450. N/s rms, mtg rm, b/f, trans, t/b pkng. Free cont brfst. $38-58/S; $42-62/D. Discs.

Kelly Inn/ 5425 Midland Rd, Billings MT 59101. 406-252-2700/ Fax: 252-1011. V,M,AE,D,DC,CB,ER. I-90, Exit 446, lt on King Av to Midland Rd. Pool, cable TV, dd phone, arpt trans, game rm, laundry, outlets, whrlpool, sauna, b/f, n/s rms, cont brfst, cot, crib, conn rms. AAA/ IMA. $34/S; $40-48/D; $4/ex prsn. 5/1-9/30: $38/S; $52-56/D. Disc: AARP, govt, corp, senior, TA, family.

Motel 6/ 5400 Midland Rd, RR 9, Billings MT 59101. 406-252-0093/ Fax: 245-1121. M,V,DC,D,AE. I-90 (Exit 446/ City Cntr) then take King Av exit to Mullowney Ln, S to Midland Rd, turn lt. Nrby rstrnt, cable TV, pool, n/s rms, t pkng. Free local calls. $28-33/S; $34-39/D; $6/ex prsn. Disc.

Motel 6/ 5353 Midland Rd, Billings MT 59102. 406-248-7551/ Fax: 245-7032. M,V,AE,D,DC. I-90 (Exit 446/ City Cntr) then King Av Exit to Mullowney Ln, S to Midland Rd, turn lt. Nrby rstrnt, cable TV, indr pool, n/s rms, t pkng. Free local calls. $28-33/S; $34-39/D; $6/ex prsn. Disc.

Sleep Inn/ 4904 Southgate Dr, Billings MT 59102. 605-229-0030. V,M,D,AE. I-90 (Exit 447) to S Billings Blvd, N to King Av, turn W to Southgate Dr. Nrby rstrnt, mtg rm, fax, b/f, cable TV, n/s rms. $43-58/S; $48-68/D; $5/ex prsn. Discs.

Bozeman

Econo Lodge/ 122 W Main St, Bozeman MT 59715. 406-587-4481. AE,V,M,DC. I-90 to 7th St, S to Main St, W to mtl. Nrby rstrnt, pool, fax, cable TV, n/s rms. Free coffee. $36-38/S; $44-47/D; $4/ex prsn. 4/1-9/30: $38-42/S; $44-47/D. Discs.

Royal 7 Motel/ 310 N 7th Av, Bozeman MT 59715. 406-587-3103/ 800-587-3103. V,M,AE,D. On I-90 bsns loop, 3/4 mi S of jct I-90, Exit 306. Rstrnt, whrlpool, n/s rms, cable TV, tt/dd phone, fax, copier, refrig, cot, crib, outlets, t pkng. Free local calls, cont brfst, coffee. AAA/ Mobil. $30/S; $40-45/D; $4/ex prsn. 6/1-10/31: $45/S; $45-55/D.

Sleep Inn/ 817 Wheat Dr, Bozeman MT 59715. 406-585-7888. V,M,D,AE. I-90 to (Exit 306) 7th Av, N to Wheat Dr, W 1 blk. Nrby rstrnt, indr pool, fax, b/f, sauna, whrlpool, cable TV, outlets, n/s rms. Free cont brfst. No pets. $41-59/S; $46-69/D; $4/ex prsn. 5/1-5/15: $45-65/S; $50-75/D. 5/16-9/30: $67-89/S; $72-99/D. Discs.

Western Heritage Inn/ 1200 E Main, Bozeman MT 59715. 406-586-8534/ Fax: 587-8729. V,M,AE,D,CB,DC. I-90, Exit 309. Cable TV, dd phone, laundry, outlets, whrlpool, sauna, b/f, n/s rms,

MONTANA

cot, crib, exerc equip, conn rms, kitchenettes. Free cont brfst. AAA/ IMA. $40/S; $47-49/D. 5/13-6/30: $46/S; $51-56/D. 7/1-9/30: $58/S; $65-70/D. Higher spec event rates. Disc: Family, AAA, senior, TA, AARP.

Culbertson

Kings Inn Motel/ 408 E 6th St, Culbertson MT 59218. 406-787-6277/ Fax: 787-6177/ 800-823-4407. V,M,AE,D,DC. On US 2, 1/4 mi E of jct SR 16. Nrby rstrnt/ lounge, n/s rms, cable TV, arpt trans, tt/dd phone, fax, cot, crib, outlets, t/b pkng. Free local calls, coffee. No pets. AAA. $30/S; $34-38/D; $5/ex prsn.

Cut Bank

Glacier Gateway Inn/ 1121 E Railroad St, Cut Bank MT 59427. 406-873-5544/ Fax: 873-5546/ 800-851-5541. V,M, AE,D,DC,CB. On US 2, 1/2 mi E from city center. Whrlpool, n/s rms, exerc equip, cable TV, VCR/ movies, tt/dd phone, mtg rm, copier, outlets, t/b/rv pkng, eff, b/f. Free local calls, cont brfst. AAA. $39/S; $44-48/D; $5/ex prsn. Disc: Govt, AAA.

Deer Lodge

Deer Lodge Super 8/ 1150 N Main, Deer Lodge MT 59722. 406-846-2370/ Fax: 846-2373. V,M,AE,DC,CB,D. I-90, Exit 184, S 1 blk. B/f, n/s rms, outlets, t/b/rv pkng, cable TV, VCR/ movies. Free local calls. Pride Award. AAA. $36-46/S; $40-46/D; $3-4/ex prsn. 6/1-9/30: $42-49/S; $47-52/D. Discs.

Ennis

Rainbow Valley Motel/ Box 26, Ennis MT 59729. 406-682-4264/ Fax: 682-5012. V,M,AE,D,DC,CB. 1 mi S of Ennis on US Hwy 287, adj to Madison River. 1 hr NW of Yellowstone Park. Pool, cable TV, dd phone, outlets, laundry, BBQ/ picnic area, cot, crib, kitchenettes. AAA/ IMA. $35/S; $45-50/D; $5/ex prsn. 6/1-11/30: $50/S; $60-65/D. Disc: TA.

Gardiner

Best Western by Mammoth Hot Springs/ Box 646, Gardiner MT 59030. 406-848-7311/ Fax: 848-7120/ 800-828-9080. C,M,AE,D,DC,CB. On Hwy 89, 1 mi from N entrance to Yellowstone Park. Indr pool, sauna, whrlpool, n/s rms, cable TV, mtg rm, copier, laundry, cot, crib, outlets, t/b/rv pkng, conn rms, b/f. Free local calls, coffee. AAA/ Mobil. 1/1-5/25, 10/7-12/31: $45-52/S or D; $5/ex prsn. 5/26-6/12: $50-55/S; $58-60/D. 6/13-10/6: $71-89/S or D. Discs.

Comfort Inn/ 107 Hell Roaring Av, Gardiner MT 59030. 406-848-7536. V,M, D, AE. On US 89 in Gardiner. Nrby rstrnt, mtg rm, fax, b/f, whrlpool, cable TV, t pkng, n/s rms. Free cont brfst. No pets. AAA. $40-80/S or D; $0-8/ex prsn. 5/1-6/15, 9/1-10/15: $55-135/S; $60-135/D. 6/16-8/31: $115-185/S or D. Discs.

Glendive

Budget Host Riverside Inn/ HC 44, Hwy 16, Glendive MT 59330. 406-365-2349/ Fax: 365-2340. AE,CB,DC,D,M,V. Jct I-94 & Hwy 16. Cable TV, dd phone, n/s rms, mtg rms, cot. Free crib. AAA. $37/S; $44-50/D; $4/ex prsn. 10/1-4/30: $32/S; $37-40/D. Discs.

Great Falls

Great Falls Inn/ 1400 28th St S, Great Falls MT 59405. 406-453-6000/ Fax: 453-6078/ 800-454-6010. V,M,AE,D. US 87/ 89 to 26th St, S 5 blks to 15th Av S, E 2 blks. N/s rms, cable TV, tt/dd phone, fax, laundry, refrig, elevator, cot, crib, outlets, t/b/rv pkng, b/f. Free local calls, cont brfst, coffee. AAA. $37-44/S; $41-44/D; $5/ex prsn. Disc: Senior, bsns, TA, govt, l/s, family, trkr, milt. *Guaranteed rates.*

Hamilton

Super 8 Motel/ 1335 N First, Hamilton MT 59840. 406-363-2940. V,M,AE,D, DC,CB. On US 93 N. B/f, n/s rms, outlets, t/b/rv pkng, copier, cable TV, mtg rm, cot. Free local calls, crib. Pride Award. $41/S; $45-49/D; $4/ex prsn. Higher spec event rates. Discs.

Hardin

American Inn/ 1324 N Crawford, Hardin MT 59034. 406-665-1870/ Fax: 665-1615. V,M,AE,D,CB,D. Cable TV, dd phone, arpt trans, game rm, laundry, outlets, b/f, pool, hot tub, exerc equip, cot, crib, n/s rms. Free cont brfst. AAA/ IMA. $32/S; $38-42/D; $4/ex prsn. 6/1-9/30: $45/S; $56-64/D. Disc: Senior, TA.

MONTANA

Helena

Days Inn/ 2001 Prospect Av, Helena MT 59601. 406-442-3280. V,M,D,AE,DC,CB. I-15 & Prospect Av. Fax, n/s rms, nrby rstrnt, mtg rm, b/f, copier. Free cont brfst, crib. $38-48/S; $46-61/D; $6/ex prsn. 5/1-9/30: $41-51/D; $50-65/D. Discs.

Econo Lodge/ 524 Last Chance Gulch, Helena MT 59601. 406-442-0600. AE, V,M,DC. I-15 to Cedar St, which becomes Main St then Last Chance Gulch. Nrby rstrnt, fax, cable TV, n/s rms. Free coffee. $37-59/S; $43-66/D; $4-10/ex prsn. Discs.

Motel 6/ 800 N Oregon St, Helena MT 59601. 406-442-9990/ Fax: 449-7107. M,V,DC,D,AE. I-15 to Capitol/ Prospect Exit, W to Fee St, N 3 blks to Missoula, E 2 blks to Oregon. Cable TV, pool, nrby rstrnt, n/s rms, t pkng. Free local calls. $28-34/S; $34-40/D; $6/ex prsn. Disc.

Kalispell

Motel 6/ 1540 US 93 S, Kalispell MT 59901. 406-752-6355/ Fax: 752-6358. M,V,DC,D,AE. US 2 (Idaho St) to US 93, S 1 mi to mtl. Nrby rstrnt, cable TV, laundry, pool, n/s rms, t pkng. Free local calls. $28-29/S; $34-35/D; $6/ex prsn. 5/23-9/27: $37/S; $43/D. Disc.

Lewistown

B & B Motel/ 520 E Main St, Lewistown MT 59457. 406-538-5496/ Fax: 538-4550. V,M,AE,D,DC. Nrby rstrnt/ lounge, cable TV, dd phone, arpt trans, n/s rms, outlets, cot, crib, kitchenettes. Free coffee. AAA/ IMA. $31-33/S; $35-41/D; $2/ex prsn. Disc: Family, TA.

Super 8 Motel/ 102 Wendell Av, Lewistown MT 59457. 406-538-2581/ Fax: 538-2702. V,M,AE,DC,CB,D. W side of tn on US 87. B/f, n/s rms, laundry, outlets, t pkng, cable TV, cot. Free local calls. $36/S; $39-42/D; $3/ex prsn. Discs.

Libby

Budget Host Caboose Motel/ Hwy 2 W, Box 792, Libby MT 59923. 406-293-6201/ Fax: 293-3621. D,V,M,AE,DC,CB. 2 blks W of dntn. Cable TV, dd phone, nrby rstrnt/ lounge, picnic area, arpt trans, t pkng, outlets, cot. Free crib. AAA. $28-40/S; $34-50/D; $5/ex prsn.

Livingston

Budget Host Parkway Motel/ 1124 W Park, Livingston MT 59047. 406-222-3840/ Fax: 222-7948. D,V,M,DC,CB,AE. I-90, Exit 333, 5 blks N. Cable TV, dd phone, in-rm coffee, family rms, kitchens, n/s rms, pool, rstrnt, laundry, t pkng, outlets, cot. Free crib. AAA. $28/S; $28-40/D; $4/ex prsn. 5/1-6/5, 9/12-11/1: $30-36/S; $36-48/D. 6/6-9/11: $46-48/S; $48-56/D. Spec events: $58/D. Disc.

Miles City

Budget Host Custer's Inn/ 1209 S Haynes, Box 1235, Miles City MT 59301. 406-232-5170. V,M,AE,DC,CB,D. 1 blk N of I-94, Broadus Frwy exit. Cable TV, dd phone, fax, nrby rstrnt, mtg rm, indr pool, sauna, picnic area, arpt trans, t pkng, outlets, cot crib. AAA. $26-29/S; $32-35/D; $4/ex prsn. 4/1-11/30: $29-31/S; $33-39/D. Discs.

Friendship Inn/ 501 Main St, Miles City MT 59301. 406-232-2450. AE,V,M,DC. I-94, Exit 135, 2 mi W. Rstrnt/ lounge, mtg rm, cable TV, t pkng, fax, coffee, n/s rms, b/f, trans. $33-65/S; $40-69/D; $4/ex prsn. Discs.

Motel 6/ 1314 Haynes Av, Rte 2, Box 3396, Miles City MT 59301. 406-232-7040/ Fax: 232-6540. M,V,DC,D,AE. I-94 (Exit 138) to Haynes Av, N 1 blk. Nrby rstrnt, cable TV, laundry, pool, n/s rms. Free local calls. $27-28/S; $33-34/D; $6/ex prsn. Disc.

Missoula

Days Inn/ RR 2, Missoula MT 59802. 405-721-9776/ Fax: 721-9781. V,M,D,AE,DC,CB. I-90 (Exit 96) at US 93. Fax, n/s rms, nrby rstrnt/ lounge, whrlpool, b/f, t pkng, arpt trans, satellite TV, laundry, cot. Free cont brfst. Chairman's Award. $43-61/S; $45-66/D; $5/ex prsn. Discs.

Econo Lodge/ 1609 W Broadway, Missoula MT 59802. 406-543-7231. AE,V,M,DC. I-90 (Exit 101) to Reserve St, E on Broadway to mtl. Rstrnt/ lounge, pool, whrlpool, cable TV, t pkng, n/s rms. $37-59/S; $43-66/D; $7/ex prsn. Discs.

MONTANA / NEBRASKA

Travelers Inn Motel/ 4850 N Reserve St, Missoula MT 59802. 406-728-8330/ Fax: 728-4435/ 800-862-3363. V,M, AE,D,DC,CB. I-90, Exit 101, S 1 blk to Reserve St. Rstrnt/ lounge, n/s rms, cable TV, tt/dd phone, fax, copier, refrig, cot, crib, conn rms. Free local calls, coffee, tea. AAA. $32/S; $39/D; $3/ex prsn. 4/16-5/31, 9/1-10/31: $38/S; $45/D. 6/1-8/31: $45/S; $48/D.

Polson

Days Inn/ 914 Hwy 93, Polson MT 59860. 405-883-3120. V,M,D,AE,DC, CB. On US 93 near jct with SR 35. Fax, n/s rms, nrby rstrnt, cable TV, cot. Free cont brfst. $30-65/S; $36-75/D; $5/ex prsn. Discs.

Shelby

O'Haire Manor Motel/ 204 2nd St S, Shelby MT 59474. 406-434-5555/ Fax: 434-2702/ 800-541-5809. V,M,AE,D, DC,CB. 2 blks S of Hwy 2 (Main St). Whrlpool, cable TV, arpt trans, tt/dd phone, fax, copier, laundry, refrig, microwave, crib, outlets. Free local calls, coffee. AAA. $26-29/S; $32-40/D; $3-4/ex prsn.

Sidney

Richland Motor Inn/ 1200 S Central Av, Sidney MT 59270. 406-482-6400/ Fax: 482-4743. V,M,AE,D,DC,CB. S side of Sidney on Central. Nrby rstrnt, cable TV, tt phone, mtg rm, fax, copier, microwave, crib, outlets, t/b pkng, b/f. Free local calls. AAA/ Mobil. $43/S; $46-48/D; $6/ex prsn. Disc: Senior, bsns, TA, govt, trkr.

Superior

Budget Host Big Sky Motel/ 103 4th Av E, Box 458, Superior MT 59872. 406-822-4831/ Fax: 822-4371. D,V,M. Just off I-90 at Superior Exit 47. Cable TV, dd phone, n/s rms, mtg rms, adj rstrnt, cot, crib, t pkng, outlets. AAA. $37/S; $40-42/D; $3/ex prsn. 6/1-10/31: $39/S; $42-45/D. Discs.

Three Forks

Broken Spur Motel/ 124 W Elm, Box 1009, Three Forks MT 59752. 406-285-3237/ Fax: 285-4133. V,M,AE,D. I-90, exit Three Forks, thru town on Hwy 2. N/s rms, cable TV, VCR, tt phone, fax, copier, cot, crib, outlets, t pkng. Free local calls, cont brfst, coffee. AAA/ Mobil. $34/S; $40/D; $6/ex prsn. 5/15-10/15: $38/S; $46/D. Disc: Bsns, govt, trkr, milt.

Whitefish

Comfort Inn/ 6390 S US 93, Whitefish MT 59937. 406-862-4020. V,M,AE,D, DC. On US 93 & W 18th St. Nrby rstrnt, indr pool, fax, whrlpool, cable TV, t pkng, outlets, n/s rms, waterslide. Free local calls, cont brfst. $29-299/S or D; $10/ex prsn. 5/1-6/8, 9/5-12/21: $29-199/S or D. 6/9-9/4: $59-229/S or D. Discs.

Nebraska

Alliance

McCarroll's Motel/ 1028 E 3rd St, Alliance NE 69301. 308-762-3680. V,M, AE,D,D,CB. E jct Hwy 2 & 385. Nrby rstrnt/ lounge, t pkng, cable TV, dd phone, arpt trans, outlets, b/f, n/s rms, cot, crib, conn rms. IMA. $34-35/S; $38-48/D; $3/ex prsn. Disc: TA.

Aurora

Budget Host Ken's Motel/ 1515 11th St, Aurora NE 68818. 402-694-3141. AE, D,M,V. I-80 (Exit 332) to Hwy 14, N 3 mi to US 34, W 5 blks. Nrby rstrnt, n/s rms, cable TV, dd phone, nwspr, refrig, cot, crib, outlets, t/b/rv pkng, conn rms. Free local calls. AAA/ Mobil. $26-28/S; $30-32/D; $6/ex prsn.

Bellevue (Omaha area)

Bellevue Super 8 Motel/ 303 S Ft Crook Rd, Bellevue NE 68005. 402-291-1518/ Fax: 292-1726. AE,M,V,D, DC,CB. Hwy 75 & Cornhusker Rd. Nrby rstrnt, whrlpool, n/s rms, cable TV, tt/dd phone, fax, nwspr, refrig, microwave, cot, crib, b pkng, eff. Free local calls, brfst, coffee. $35-45/S; $45-48/D; $6/ex prsn. 5/1-8/31: $45-55/S; $55-65/D. Disc: Senior, bsns, TA, govt, l/s, family, trkr, milt. *Guaranteed rates.*

NEBRASKA

Quality Inn/ SR 370 & Hillcrest, Bellevue NE 68005. 402-292-3800. V,M, AE,DC,D. US 75, I-29 or I-80 to SR 370. At the jct of US 76 & SR 370. Rstrnt/ lounge, indr pool, mtg rm, fax, b/f, whrlpool, cable TV, t pkng, n/s rms. Free full brfst. No pets. AAA. $39-48/S; $43-52/D; $4/ex prsn. 4/1-4/30: $40-49/S; $44-53/D. Discs.

Blair

Super 8 Motel/ 558 S 13th, Blair NE 68008. 402-426-8888/ Fax: 425-8889. V,M,AE,DC,D,CB. S of jct Hwys 30 & 75, on Hwy 75. B/f, n/s rms, rstrnt, cable TV, outlets, cot, crib, laundry. Free local calls. No pets. Pride Award. $42/S; $46-49/D; $3/ex prsn. 4/1-9/30: $35/S; $40-42/D. Discs.

Chadron

Super 8 Motel/ Hwy 20 W, Chadron NE 69337. 308-432-4471/ Fax: 432-3991. AE,CB,DC,M,V,D. Jct of Hwys 20, 385. B/f, n/s rms, nrby rstrnt, outlets, toast bar, cable TV, cot, crib. Free local calls. No pets. Pride Award. $37/S; $45-49/D; $2/ex prsn. Higher spec event rates. Discs.

Columbus

Econo Lodge/ 3803 23rd St, Columbus NE 68601. 402-564-9955. V,AE,M,DC. US 81 (23rd St) 5 blks W of jct US 81/ US 30 N. Nrby rstrnt, mtg rm, fax, b/f, cable TV, n/s rms. Free coffee. No pets. $36-51/S; $39-54/D; $4/ex prsn. Discs.

Sleep Inn/ 303 23rd St, Columbus NE 68601. 402-562-5200. V,M,AE,DC. On US 30, E part of Columbus. Nrby rstrnt, mtg rm, fax, b/f, cable TV, t pkng, outlets. Free cont brfst. No pets. $37-45/S; $42-50/D; $5/ex prsn. Discs.

Super 8 Motel/ 3324 20th St, Columbus NE 68601. 402-563-3456. AE,CB,DC, M,V,D. 20th St & US 30, 81. B/f, n/s rms, outlets, t/b/rv pkng, toast bar, copier, cable TV, cot. Free local calls. No pets. Pride Award. $39/S; $46-48/D; $3/ex prsn. Higher spec event rates. Discs.

Cozad

Budget Host Circle S Motel/ 440 S Meridian, Box 85, Cozad NE 69130. 308-784-2290. AE,D,M,V. I-80, Exit 222, N 1/2 mi. Rstrnt, n/s rms, cable TV, dd phone, nwspr, cot, crib, outlets, t/b/rv pkng, conn rms. Free local calls. AAA/ Mobil. $26-30/S; $30-32/D; $6/ex prsn.

Elm Creek

1st Interstate Inn/ Rte 2, Box 16-A, Elm Creek NE 68836. 308-856-4652. V, M,AE,D,DC. I-80 & Hwy 183, Exit 257. Nrby rstrnt, lounge, dd phone, outlets, crib, conn rms, n/s rms, mtg rm. AAA. $34/S; $38/D; $4/ex prsn. 5/1-10/31: $39/S; $41-43/D. 4/1-4/12: $39/S; $45/D. Disc: Comm, senior, TA, family.

Fremont

Comfort Inn/ 1649 E 23rd St, Fremont NE 68025. 402-721-1109. AE,DC,M,V. US 77 to US 30, E to Bell St, S to 23rd Av, E to mtl. Immediately S of US 30. Nrby rstrnt, indr pool, fax, b/f, whrlpool, cable TV, outlets, n/s rms. Free cont brfst. $40-60/S; $45-70/D; $5/ex prsn. Discs.

Motel 7/ 310 W 23rd St, Fremont NE 68025. 402-721-4310. V,M,AE,D. Jct Hwys 77 & 30 W. Nrby rstrnt/ lounge, n/s rms, cable TV, tt/dd phone, fax, cot, crib, conn rms. No pets. $31/S; $39/D; $3/ex prsn. Guaranteed rates.

Relax Inn Budget Host/ 1435 E 23rd, Fremont NE 68025. 402-721-5656. V,M,AE,D. On E Hwy 30 at jct Hwy 77. Nrby rstrnt/ lounge, n/s rms, cable TV, tt/dd phone, fax, cot, crib, outlets, t/b pkng. Free coffee. No pets. AAA/ Mobil. $33/S; $42/D; $4/ex prsn. Disc: Senior, bsns, govt, milt, trkr, l/s. Guaranteed rates.

Super 8 Motel/ 1250 E 23rd St, Fremont NE 68025. 402-727-4445. V, M,AE,DC,CB,D. Bet US 77 & US 275, on Hwy 30 (23rd St), E of dntn. B/f, n/s rms, outlets, t/b/rv pkng, copier, cable TV, cot. Free local calls, crib. $35/S; $41-45/D; $5/ex prsn. Higher spec event/ wknd rates. Discs.

Grand Island

Conoco Motel/ 2107 W 2nd, Grand Island NE 68803. 308-384-2700. V,M, AE,D,DC,CB. I-80, Exit 312 N 281, go to Hwy 30, turn rt. Over overpass, 1 1/2 blks on rt. Rstrnt/ lounge, pool,

NEBRASKA

n/s rms, cable TV, tt/dd phone, copier, refrig, cot, crib, t/b pkng, conn rms. Free local calls, coffee. No pets. AAA. $35/S; $42-47/D; $3/ex prsn. *Guaranteed rates.*

Budget Host Island Inn Motel/ 2311 S Locust, Grand Island NE 68801. 308-382-1815. V,M,AE,D. I-80 (Ebnd, Exit 312N; Wbnd, Exit 318) 1 mi N on S Locust from Jct Hwy 34 & S Locust. Nrby rstrnt, n/s rms, cable TV, dd phone, refrig, cot, crib, outlets, t/b pkng, conn rms. Free local calls. AAA/ Mobil. $26-32/S; $32-38/D; $6/ex prsn.

Comfort Inn/ 3535 W State St, Grand Island NE 68803. 308-381-7788. V, M,AE,DC,D. I-80 (Exit 312) to US 281 N. Nrby rstrnt, indr pool, fax, b/f, whrlpool, cable TV, t pkng, outlets, n/s rms. Free cont brfst. No pets. $41-51/S; $46-57/D; $4/ex prsn. Higher wknd rates. Discs.

Lazy V Motel/ 2703 E Hwy 30, Grand Island NE 68801. 308-384-0700. V,M,D. I-80 Wbnd, Exit 318 N 3 mi to Hwy 34, W 3 mi to Stuhr Rd, N 4 mi to Hwy 30, E 1/2 mi. Ebnd: Exit 312, N 4 mi to Hwy 34, E 4 mi to Stuhr Rd, N 4 mi to Hwy 30, E 1/2 mi. Cable TV, dd phone, outlets, pool, cot, crib, t pkng. Free in-rm coffee. AAA/ IMA. $24/S; $28-30/D; $4/ex prsn.

Motel 6/ 3021 S Locust St, Grand Island NE 68801. 308-384-4100/ Fax: 384-7035. M,V,DC,D,AE. I-80: Ebnd, (Exit 312) to Hwy 281, N approx 5 mi to Hwy 34, rt to Locust, turn lt; Wbnd, (Exit 318) to Hwy 34, follow prev dir. Cable TV, indr pool, n/s rms, t pkng. Free local calls. $28/S; $32-34/D; $4-6/ex prsn. Disc.

Hastings

Grand Motel/ 201 E "J"St, Hastings NE 68901. 402-463-1369/ Fax: 463-6906. V,M,AE,D,DC,CB. On US 6, 1/2 mi E of jct of Hwys 281 & 6. Pool, n/s rms, cable TV, tt/dd phone, fax, crib, outlets, t/b pkng. Free local calls, cont brfst, coffee. No pets. AAA. $27/S; $33/D; $4/ex prsn. Summer wknds, spec events: $31/S; $41/D. Disc: Senior, govt, milt.

Midlands Lodge/ 910 W "J" St, Hastings NE 68901. 402-463-2428/ 800-237-1872. V,M,AE,D,DC. Jct Hwys 6-34-281. Pool, n/s rms, cable TV, tt/dd phone, fax, copier, refrig, cot, crib, outlets, t/b/rv pkng, conn rms. Free local calls, coffee. AAA. $29/S; $34/D; $4/ex prsn. 5/1-9/1: $32/S; $37/D; $4/ex prsn. Disc: Family, l/s. *Guaranteed rates.*

Rainbow Motel/ Hwy 6/34/281 W, Hastings NE 68901. 402-463-7477/ Fax: 463-0657/ 800-825-7424. V,M,AE,D. I-80, turn onto Hwy 281 to Hwy 6/34. Nrby rstrnt/ lounge, n/s rms, cable TV, tt/dd phone, fax, laundry, refrig, microwave, cot, crib, conn rms. Free local calls, coffee. AAA/ Mobil. $27-29/S; $32-37/D; $5/ex prsn. *Guaranteed rates.*

Super 8 Motel/ 2200 N Kansas Ave, Hastings NE 68901. 402-463-8888. V, M,AE,DC,D,CB. I-80, Exit 312, 1/2 mi S. B/f, n/s rms, game rm, cont brfst, copier, t/b/rv pkng, cot. Free local calls, crib. Pride Award. $36/S; $42-44/D; $2/ex prsn. Discs.

X-L Motel/ Hwys 6, 34 & 281 W, Hastings NE 68901. 402-463-3148. V,M, AE,D,DC,CB. On Hwy 6, W of jct Hwys 281 & 34. 18 mi S of I-80. Pool, n/s rms, satellite TV, arpt trans, refrig, crib, outlets, tt phone, t/b pkng. Free local calls, cont brfst, coffee. No pets. AAA/ Mobil/ IMA. $27-29/S; $31-33/D; $5/ex prsn. 5/1-11/30: $30/S; $34/D.

Holdrege

Plains Motel/ 619 W Hwy 6, Holdrege NE 68949. 308-995-8646. V,M,D. 1 km W of jct of 183 & US 6 & 34. Nrby rstrnt, n/s rms, satellite TV, playgrnd, arpt trans, tt/dd phone, cot, crib, outlets, t/b/rv pkng, conn rms, b/f. Free local calls, coffee. IMA. $32-36/S; $40-46/D; $3/ex prsn. 11/1-11/15: $65/S or D. *Guaranteed rates.*

Kearney

Budget Host Western Inn/ 1401 2nd Av, Box 1903, Kearney NE 68847. 308-237-3153/ Fax: 234-6073. AE,M,V,D. 14 blks N of I-80, Exit 272. Rstrnt, pool, n/s rms, cable TV, dd/tt phone, fax. No pets. AAA/ Mobil. $32/S; $39-40/D. $4/ex prsn. 6/1-8/31: $36/S; $41-46/D. Disc: Senior.

Comfort Inn/ 903 2nd Av S, Kearney

NEBRASKA

NE 68847. 308-237-5858. AE,DC,M,V. I-80 (Exit 272) to 2nd Av, N 1/2 mi to W 8th St, take Frontage Rd N 1/2 blk. Rstrnt, fax, b/f, whrlpool, cable TV, outlets, exerc equip, n/s rms. Free cont brfst, local calls. No pets. AAA. $38-60/S; $42-70/D; $5/ex prsn. 11/2-3/31: $35-50/S; $38-60/D. Discs.

Ft Kearny 1st Inn/ 805 2nd Av, Kearney NE 68848. 308-234-2541/ 800-652-7245. V,M,AE,D,DC. I-80 & Hwy 10/ 44, Exit 272. Rstrnt/ lounge, mtg rm, pool, n/s rms. $36/S; $44/D. 5/16-10/31: $39-50/S; $50/D. Disc: Comm, senior, TA, family.

Kimball

1st Interstate Inn/ Rte 1, Box 136, Kimball NE 69145. 308-235-4601. V,M, AE,D,DC. I-80 & Hwy 71, Exit 20. Rstrnt, cable TV, dd phone, outlets, laundry, cot, crib, n/s rms, conn rms. AAA. $29/S; $34/D; $2/ex prsn. 5/1-10/31: $37/S; $42-44/D; $5/ex prsn. Spec events: $42/S; $47-49/D. Disc: Comm, family, senior, TA.

Super 8 Motel/ Box 117, Kimball NE 69145. 308-235-4888. AE,M,V,D,DC, CB. I-80 (Exit 20) at SR 71. B/f, n/s rms, outlets, toast bar, t/b/rv pkng, cable TV, cot, crib. Free local calls. Pride Award. $31/S; $33-36/D; $3/ex prsn. Higher spec event rates. Discs.

Lexington

Budget Host Minuteman Motel/ 801 S Plumb Creek Pkwy, Rt 2, Box 169A, Lexington NE 68850. 308-324-5544. AE,DC,M,V,CB,D. I-80 to Hwy 283, N 2 mi. Cable TV, dd phone, family rms, conn rm, n/s rms, nrby rstrnt, pool, arpt trans, t pkng. No cats. AAA/ Mobil. $30-34/S; $32-40/D; $4/ex prsn. Disc: AAA, Senior.

Econo Lodge/ Box 775, Lexington NE 68850. 308-324-5601/ Fax: 324-4284. V,AE,M,DC. I-80 to US 283, 4 blks N. Nrby rstrnt, fax, cable TV, t pkng, outlets, dd/tt phone, laundry, crib. Free cont brfst. AAA. $27-35/S; $31-41/D; $5/ex prsn. 5/1-10/31: $30-40/S; $36-46/D. Higher spec event rates. Discs.

Lincoln

Budget Host Great Plains Motel/ 2732 "O"St, Lincoln NE 68510. 402-476-3253/ Fax: 476-7540. AE,CB,DC,M, V,D. 27th & "O"St on US 6 & 34, dntn. Cable TV, dd phone, refrig, in-rm coffee, family rms, kitchens, nrby rstrnt, cot. Free crib. AAA/ Mobil. $32-36/S; $35-45/D; $4/ex prsn. Disc: Senior.

Comfort Inn/ 2940 NW 12th St, Lincoln NE 68521. 402-475-2200. V,M,DC,AE. I-80, Exit 399 (Arpt exit). On W side of frwy. Nrby rstrnt/ lounge, mtg rm, fax, b/f, sauna, whrlpool, cable TV, exerc equip, n/s rms, b/t pkng. AAA. $40-60/S; $45-70/D; $5/ex prsn. Higher spec event rates. Discs.

Econo Lodge/ 5600 Cornhusker Hwy, Lincoln NE 68529. 402-464-5971. V, AE,M,DC. I-80 (Exit 405) to US 77, S 2 1/2 mi to Cornhusker Hwy, rt 1 blk. Nrby rstrnt, cable TV, t pkng, outlets, n/s rms. Free local calls. $35-40/S; $38-49/D; $4/ex prsn. Discs.

Econo Lodge/ 2410 NW 12th St, Lincoln NE 68521. 402-474-1311. V,M,AE, DC,D. I-80 (Exit 399) at Cornhusker Hwy, SE side of I-80. Nrby rstrnt, pool, fax, cable TV, t pkng. $26-39/S; $31-50/D; $5/ex prsn. 5/1-9/30: $33-39/S; $40-50/D. Discs.

Motel 6/ 3001 NW 12th St, Lincoln NE 68521. 402-475-3211/ Fax: 475-1632. M,V,DC,D,AE. I-80, Exit 399. On W side of frwy. Nrby rstrnt, cable TV, pool, n/s rms, t pkng. Free local calls. $27-32/S; $33-38/D; $6/ex prsn. Disc.

Senate Inn/ 2801 W "O"St, Lincoln NE 68528. 402-475-4921. V,M,AE,D. I-80, Exits 396 or 397, S to "O"St. Pool, n/s rms, cable TV, outlets, t/b/rv pkng. Free cont brfst. coffee. Mobil. $34-44/S or D; $3/ex prsn.

Sleep Inn/ 3400 NW 12th St, Lincoln NE 68521. 402-475-1550. V,M,AE,DC. I-80 (Exit 399) to Arpt exit, turn toward arpt to mtl. Nrby rstrnt, pool, mtg rm, fax, b/f, cable TV, outlets, b pkng, n/s rms. Free cont brfst, arpt trans. No pets. AAA. $36-49/S; $42-55/D; $5-6/ex prsn. 5/1-5/26: $38-51/S; $42-55/D. 5/27-6/30: $43-55/S; $46-60/D. 7/1-10/31: $49-60/S; $52-69/D. Discs.

Town House Motel/ 1744 M St, Lincoln NE 68508. 402-475-3000/ 800-279-1744. V,M,AE,D,DC. I-80, Exit 401A to

NEBRASKA

I-180, approx 4 mi to M St, lt to 18th St. Nrby rstrnt/ lounge, n/s rms, cable TV, arpt trans, TDD, tt/dd phone, mtg rm, laundry, refrig, cot, crib, eff, b/f. Free local calls, coffee. AAA. $41-45/S; $46-50/D; $4/ex prsn. UNL Home Football games & 8/1-8/23: $59-64/1-4 prsns. Disc: Senior, TA, govt, milt, l/s. *Guaranteed rates.*

Nebraska City

Apple Inn/ 502 S 11th St, Nebraska City NE 68410. 402-873-5959/ Fax: 873-6640/ 800-659-4446. V,M,AE,D,DC,CB. I-29, exit Nebraska City, rt on Hwy 2 W 2 mi, cross Missouri River bridge, 1st rt after bridge, 1 mi to mtl. Pool, whrlpool, n/s rms, cable TV, TDD, mtg rm, copier, laundry, refrig, outlets, t/b pkng, b/f. Free local calls, cont brfst, coffee. AAA/ Mobil. $33/S; $37-41/D; $5/ex prsn. Disc: Senior, bsns, govt, family, milt, l/s. *Guaranteed rates.*

Norfolk

Days Inn/ 1001 Omaha Av, Norfolk NE 68701. 402-379-3035/ Fax: 371-1307. V,M,D,AE,DC,CB,JCB. Hwy 275, 2 blks E of Hwy 81. Fax, n/s rms, nrby rstrnt, indr pool, whrlpool b/f, exerc equip. Free cont brfst. $35-50/S; $40-55/D; $6/ex prsn. Discs.

North Platte

1st Interstate Inn/ Box 1201, N Platte NE 69101. 308-532-6980. V,M,AE,D,DC. I-80 & Hwy 83, Exit 177. Cable TV, dd phone, outlets, nrby rstrnt, b/f, n/s rms, cot, crib, conn rms. AAA. $30/S; $35/D; $2/ex prsn. 5/1-10/31: $36/S; $43-45/D. Spec events: $41/S; $46/D; $5/ex prsn.

Comfort Inn/ 2901 S Jeffers, N Platte NE 69103. 308-532-6144. V,AE,M,DC. I-80 (Exit 177) to US 83, S to mtl. Nrby rstrnt, indr pool, fax, b/f, whrlpool, cable TV, exerc equip, outlets, n/s rms. Free cont brfst. No pets. $38-40/S; $41-44/D; $2/ex prsn. 5/16-9/30: $47-50/S; $50-53/D. Higher spec event rates. Discs.

Motel 6/ 1520 S Jefferson St, N Platte NE 69101. 308-534-6200/ Fax: 532-5276. M,V,DC,D,AE. I-80 (Exit 177) to US 83 N to mtl. Nrby rstrnt, cable TV, pool, n/s rms, t pkng. Free local calls. $30/S; $36/D; $6/ex prsn. 5/25-10/25: $37/S; $43/D. Disc.

Travelers Inn/ 602 E 4th, N Platte NE 69101. 308-534-4020/ Fax: 534-7148/ 800-341-8000. V,M,AE,D,DC,CB. On Hwy 30 between Exits 177 & 179 on I-80. Pool, n/s rms, cable TV, arpt trans, tt/dd phone, fax, copier, cot, crib, outlets, t/b pkng, conn rms. Free local calls, coffee. AAA/ IMA. $30-34/S or D; $3/ex prsn. 6/1-9/4: $32-40/S or D. *Guaranteed rates.*

O'Neill

Golden Hotel/ 406 E Douglas, O'Neill NE 68763. 402-336-4436/ Fax: 336-3549/ 800-658-3148. V,M,AE,D. Dntn O'Neill, jct of Hwys 20-275 & 281. Sauna, n/s rms, cable TV, VCR/ movies, arpt trans, tt/dd phone, copier, laundry, refrig, cot, crib. Free local calls, cont brfst. AAA/ National 9. $21-27/S; $27-32/D; $5/ex prsn. Disc: Senior, bsns, govt, l/s, family, trkr, milt. *Guaranteed rates.*

Budget Host Carriage House/ 929 E Douglas, Box 151, O'Neill NE 68763. 402-336-3403/ Fax: 336-3409. M,V,D,AE. US 20 & 275, 6 blks E of stoplight. Cable TV, dd/tt phone, family rms, t pkng, cot. Free crib. Mobil. $23-26/S; $30-36/D; $2/ex prsn.

Capri Motel/ 1020 E Douglas, Box 306, O'Neill NE 68763. 402-336-2762/ Fax: 336-4365. V,M,AE,D,CB,DC. E Hwy 20 & 275. Nrby rstrnt, cable TV, dd phone, outlets, playgrnd, fax, t pkng, cot, crib, n/s rms. IMA $28/S; $35-38/D; $3/ex prsn. 3/15-3/16: $35/S; $38-45/D.

Elms Motel/ E Hwy 20/275, O'Neill NE 68763. 402-336-3800/ 800-526-9052. V,M,AE,D. SE edge of city limits. Nrby rstrnt, n/s rms, cable TV, playgrnd, arpt trans, tt/dd phone, copier, cot, crib, outlets, t pkng, conn rms. Free local calls, coffee. AAA/ Mobil. $25-30/S; $30-38/D; $3/ex prsn. Disc: L/s. *Guaranteed rates.*

Super 8 Motel/ E Hwy 20, O'Neill NE 68763. 402-336-3100. AE,CB,DC,M,V,D. 1 mi E of US 281 on US 20, 275. B/f, n/s rms, outlets, t/b/rv pkng, copier, cable TV, mtg rm, cot, crib. Free local calls. No pets. AAA. $39/S; $46-48/D; $3/ex prsn. Higher spec event rates. Discs.

NEBRASKA

Ogallala

Days Inn of Ogallala/ 601 Stagecoach Trail, Ogallala NE 69153. 308-284-6365/ Fax: 284-2351. V,M,AE,D,DC,CB. I-80 (Exit 126) to SR 61, turn NE. Nrby rstrnt, cable TV, tt/dd phone, fax, refrig, cot, crib, outlets, t/b/rv pkng, conn rms, b/f. Free local calls, cont brfst, coffee. No pets. AAA. $36-46/S; $45-48/D; $6/ex prsn. 6/1-9/30: $50-55/S; $60-65/D. Discs. *Guaranteed rates.*

Super 8 Motel/ 500 E "A"S, Ogallala NE 69153. 308-284-2076/ Fax: 284-2590. AE,CB,DC,M,V,D. I-80 (Exit 126) & SR 61. B/f, n/s rms, whrlpool, exerc equip, laundry, t pkng, outlets, copier, mtg rm, cot, crib. Free local calls. $32/S; $37-39/D; $2/ex prsn. 5/28-9/30: $37/S; $42-44/D. Higher spec event rates. Discs.

Omaha

Ben Franklin Motel/ 10308 Sapp Bros Dr, Omaha NE 68138. 402-895-2200/ Fax: 895-4625. V,M,AE,D,CB,DC. I-80 & 144th St, Exit 440. Pool, dd phone, game rm, laundry, outlets, refrig, VCR/ movies, lake access, picnic area, cot, crib, kitchenettes, conn rms, n/s rms. AAA/ IMA. $38/S; $40-42/D; $4/ex prsn. 3/1-11/30: $43/S; $43-47/D. Disc: Family, senior, TA, trkr, govt, milt, l/s.

Budgetel Inns/ 10760 "M"St, Omaha Nebraska 68127. 402-592-5200/ Fax: 592-1416. V,M,D,AE,DC,CB. I-80, Exit 445 "L"St (US 275) E, then S on 108th St. N/s rms, b/f, rstrnt, fax. Free cont brfst, in-rm coffee, local calls. AAA. $37-48/S; $44-55/D. 3/-9/2: $39-50/S; $46-57/D. Higher spec event summer wknd rates. Discs.

Comfort Inn/ 10919 "J"St, Omaha NE 68137. 402-592-2882. V,M,DC,AE. I-80 (Exit 445) to L St, E to 108th St, N to "J"St, W to mtl. Nrby rstrnt, indr pool, mtg rm, fax, b/f, sauna, whrlpool, cable TV, exerc equip, b pkng, n/s rms. Free cont brfst. $42-60/S; $47-70/D; $5/ex prsn. Discs.

Econo Lodge/ 3511 S 84th St, Omaha NE 68124. 402-391-4321. AE,DC,M,V. I-80 (Exit 448) at 84th St. Rstrnt, cable TV, t pkng, n/s rms. $35-45/S; $38-49/D; $5/ex prsn. Discs.

Econo Lodge/ 7833 W Dodge Rd, Omaha NE 68124. 402-391-7100. V, M, AE,DC,D. 2 mi E on W Dodge Rd (US 6) from I-680, Exit 3. Rstrnt, pool, fax, b/f, cable TV, t pkng, outlets, n/s rms. AAA. $38-45/S; $43-45/D; $5/ex prsn. 5/1-9/30: $40-47/S; $45-47/D. Discs.

Motel 6/ 10708 "M"St, Omaha NE 68127. 402-331-3161/ Fax: 597-0777. M,V,DC,D,AE. I-80 (Exit 445) to "L"St, E to traffic lights, turn rt on 108th, lt on "M"to mtl. In W Omaha. Nrby rstrnt, cable TV, laundry, pool, n/s rms. Free local calls. $30-33/S; $36-39/D; $6/ex prsn. Disc.

Sleep Inn/ 2525 Abbott Dr, Omaha NE 68110. 402-342-2525. V,M,DC,AE. I-480 to Eppley Airfield exit, follow arpt signs to mtl. Nrby rstrnt, mtg rm, fax, b/f, cable TV, t pkng, n/s rms. Free cont brfst. No pets. AAA. $40-45/S; $44-49/D; $4/ex prsn. Discs.

Super 8 Motel/ 10829 "M"St, Omaha NE 68137. 402-339-2250/ Fax: 339-6622. AE,CB,DC,M,V,D. 108th & "L"St at I-80. B/f, n/s rms, outlets, t/b/rv pkng, toast bar, copier, cable TV, mtg rm, cot, crib. Free local calls. No pets. AAA. Pride Award. $40/S; $47-49/D; $3/ex prsn. Higher spec event rates. Discs.

Also see Bellevue.

Saint Paul

Bel-Air Motel and RV Park/ 1158 Hwy 281, St Paul NE 68873. 308-754-4466. V,M,AE,D. 1/4 mi N of jct Hwys 281 & 92. N/s rms, satellite TV, tt/dd phone, refrig, cot, crib, outlets, t/b/rv pkng, conn rms, b/f. Free local calls. No pets. IMA. $30-35/S; $35-40/D; $5/ex prsn. Memorial Day wknd, 1st wknd in Nov, 2nd wk Sept: $35-40/S; $40-45/D. Disc: L/s, bsns, trkr, family. *Guaranteed rates.*

Scottsbluff

Lamplighter Motel/ 606 E 27th St, Scottsbluff NE 69361. 308-632-7108/ Fax: 632-7848. V,M,AE,D,CB,DC. 4 mi from Scottsbluff National Monument. Adj rstrnt, indr pool, cable TV, dd phone, outlets, conn rms, cot, crib, n/s rms. AAA/ IMA. $32/S; $35-40/D; $3/ex prsn. 6/1-9/1: $35/S; $38-43/D. Disc:

NEBRASKA

Senior, AARP, TA.

Sands Motel/ 814 W 27th St, Scottsbluff NE 69361. 308-632-6191. V,M,AE,D,DC. Hwy 71 N & Bsns Hwy 26 (corner Av I & 27th St) E 1/4 blk. Nrby rstrnt, n/s rms, cable TV, dd phone, fax, refrig, cot, t pkng. Free local calls. No pets. AAA. $27/S; $31-37/D; $4/ex prsn.

Super 8 Motel/ 2202 Delta Dr, Scottsbluff NE 69361. 308-635-1600/ Fax: 635-2483. AE,CB,DC,M,V,D. Jct Hwy 26 & 21st Av. B/f, n/s rms, pool, whrlpool, outlets, b/t pkng, toast bar, cable TV, cot. Free local calls. Pride Award. $38/S; $43-46/D; $3/ex prsn. Discs.

Sidney

Sidney Motor Lodge/ 2031 Illinois St, Sidney NE 69162. 308-254-4581/ Fax: 254-7273. V,M,AE,D,CB,DC. US Hwy 30 W. Nrby rstrnt/ lounge, cable TV, dd phone, arpt trans, outlets, micro-fridge, cot, crib, n/s rms, kitchenettes, family rms, conn rms. AAA/ IMA. $32/S; $34-42/D; $3/ex prsn. 7/16-8/17: $40/S; $42-50/D. Disc: TA.

Super 8 Motel/ 2115 Illinois St, Box 314, Sidney NE 69162. 308-254-2081. V,M,D,DC,CB,AE. Bsns I-80 (Exit 55 or 59). B/f, n/s rms, outlets, t/b/rv pkng, cable TV, mtg rm, cot, crib. Free local calls. $31/S; $33-36/D; $3/ex prsn. Higher spec event rates. Discs.

South Sioux City

Econo Lodge/ 4402 Dakota Av, S Sioux City NE 68776. 402-494-4114. V,AE,M,DC. I-29 N or S (Exit 144B) or US 20, W 1 mi to (Exit 2) Dakota Av. Nrby rstrnt, whrlpool, cable TV, t pkng, n/s rms. Free cont brfst. $35-40/S; $42-51/D, $4/ex prsn. Discs.

Park Plaza Motel/ 1201 1st Av, S Sioux City NE 68776. 402-494-2021/ Fax: 494-5998. V,M,AE,D,CB,DC. Rstrnt/ lounge, pool, cable TV, dd phone, outlets, laundry, cot, crib, n/s rms. AAA/ IMA. $35-41/S; $40-45/D; $3-4/ex prsn. Higher spec event rates. Disc: Comm, senior, TA.

Thedford

Rodeway Inn/ HC 58, Box 1D, Thedford NE 69166. 308-645-2284. V,M,AE, DC,D. Jct US 83 & SR 2. Rstrnt, fax, b/f, whrlpool, cable TV, t pkng, exerc equip, outlets, n/s rms. Free cont brfst. $38-48/S; $44-52/D; $5/ex prsn. 5/1-10/31: $42-52/S; $46-58/D. Discs.

Valentine

Comfort Inn/ 101 Main St, Valentine NE 69201. 402-376-3300. V,M,AE,DC,D. On US 83, 2 blks N of jct US 20 & US 83. Nrby rstrnt, indr pool, mtg rm, whrlpool, cable TV, exerc equip, n/s rms. Free cont brfst. $39-65/S; $46-75/D; $5/ex prsn. Discs.

Super 8 Motel/ Box 653, Valentine NE 69201. 402-376-1250/ Fax: 376-1211. V,M,AE,DC,CB,D. US 20 & US 83. B/f, n/s rms, indr pool, whrlpool, sauna, game rm, laundry, outlets, t/b/rv pkng, cable TV, mtg rm, cot, crib. Free local calls. No pets. Pride Award. $37/S; $45-49/D; $3/ex prsn. Higher spec event rates. Discs.

Trade Winds Lodge/ E Hwy 20 & 83, Valentine NE 69201. 402-376-1600. V, M,AE,D,DC,CB. On Hwys 20/83. Pool, n/s rms, cable TV, arpt trans, tt/dd phone, cot, crib, outlets, t/b/rv pkng, conn rms. Free local calls, coffee. AAA/ Mobil/ IMA. $25/S; $32/D; $3/ex prsn. 5/1-9/15: $30-40/S; $37-50/D; $4/ex prsn. Wknd rates highest. Disc: Senior.

Wayne

Super 8 Motel/ 610 Tomar Dr, Wayne NE 68787. 402-375-4898. V,M,DC,CB, AE,D. E Hwy 35. B/f, n/s rms, t/b/rv pkng, copier, cable TV, cot, crib. Free local calls. Pride Award. $40/S; $47-49/D; $3/ex prsn. Higher spec event rates. Discs.

York

Econo Lodge/ 3724 S Lincoln, York NE 68467. 402-362-1686. V,M,AE,D. 2 blks S of I-80 on US 81. Nrby rstrnt, indr pool, fax, b/f, whrlpool, cable TV. Free cont brfst. No pets. $38-60/S; $40-70/D; $5/ex prsn. Discs.

Super 8 Motel/ Box 532, York NE 68467. 402-362-3388/ Fax: 362-3604. V,M,D,DC,CB,AE. I-80 & US 81. B/f, n/s rms, pool, whrlpool, game rm, laundry, outlets, t/b/rv pkng, copier, cable TV, cot, crib. Free local calls.

Pride Award. $36/S; $41-43/D; $2/ex prsn. Higher spec event rates. Discs.

Nevada

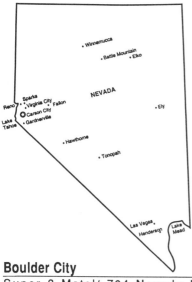

Boulder City

Super 8 Motel/ 704 Nevada Hwy, Boulder City NV 89005. 702-294-8888/ Fax: 293-4344. V,M,DC,CB,AE,D. On Bsns Rte 93 S. B/f, pool, kitchenettes, rstrnt/ lounge, game rm, mtg rm, laundry, elevator, boat pkng, microwave, crib. Free local calls, nwspr. $40/S; $40-48/D; $4/ex prsn. Higher spec event rates. Discs.

Carson City

Motel 6/ 2749 S Carson St, Carson City NV 89701. 702-885-7710/ Fax: 885-7671. M,V,DC,D,AE. S of town on Hwys 395/50 between Colorado & Sonoma Av. Nrby rstrnt, cable TV, pool, n/s rms. Free local calls. Sun-Thurs: $29/S or D. Fri, Sat, Holiday, spec events: $33/S or D. 5/25-9/27: $39/S or D. Higher spec event rates. Disc.

Elko

El Neva National 9 Inn/ 736 Idaho St, Elko NV 89801. 702-738-7152. V, M,AE,DC. I-80, Exit 301. Cable TV, dd phone. $29-38/S; $32-44/D. 5/16-9/11: $38/S; $38-54/D.

Motel 6/ 3021 Idaho St, Elko NV 89801. 702-738-4337/ Fax: 753-8381. M,V, DC,D,AE. I-80 to Exit 303, S to Idaho (SR 40), lt. Nrby rstrnt, cable TV, pool, laundry, n/s rms. Free local calls. $29-33/S; $33-37/D; $4/ex prsn. Disc.

Rodeway Inn/ 1349 Idaho St, Elko NV 89801. 702-738-7000/ Fax: 738-1216. V,AE,M,DC. I-80 (Exit 303) to Idaho St, rt to Elko Park. Rstrnt, pool, fax, b/f, cable TV, t pkng, exerc equip, n/s rms. No pets. AAA. $41-46/S; $46-56/D; $5/ex prsn. 6/6-9/5: $44-49/S; $49-59/D. 9/6-10/31: $38-43/S; $43-52/D. Discs.

Toppers Motel/ 1500 Idaho St, Elko NV 89801. 702-738-7254. V,M,AE,DC. Cable TV, adj rstrnt, refrig, cot. National 9. $28-36/S; $30-40/D; $4/ex prsn. 5/16-9/10: $32-44/S; $36-54/D.

Ely

Motel 6/ 7th St & Av "O," Ely NV 89301. 702-289-6671/ Fax: 289-4803. M,V,DC, D,AE. US 50 at US 93 S. Nrby rstrnt, cable TV, pool, laundry, n/s rms, t pkng. Free local calls. $28-30/S; $32-34/D; $4-6/ex prsn. Disc.

Fallon

Econo Lodge/ 70 E Williams Av, Fallon NV 89406. 702-423-2194. V,M,AE,DC, D US 95 to US 50, E 1 blk to mtl. Pool, fax, b/f, cable TV, t pkng, outlets, n/s rms. Free cont brfst. No pets. AAA. $40-65/S; $45-75/D; $5/ex prsn. 5/1-10/31: $48-78/S; $56-85/D. Spec events: $65-75/S; $85-105/D. Discs.

Fernley

Super 8 Motel/ 1350 Newlands Dr, Fernley NV 89408. 702-575-5555/ Fax: 575-6546. V,M,AE,DC,CB,D. I-80, Exit 48. B/f, n/s rms, b/t pkng, cable TV, cot. Free local calls. $10/S; $43-46/D; $3/ex prsn. Higher spec event rates. Discs.

Las Vegas

Econo Lodge/ 520 S Casino Center Blvd, Las Vegas NV 89101. 702-384-8211. AE,DC,M,V. I-15 N, exit Dntn Casino Cntr to mtl. Nrby rstrnt, fax. No pets. Discs. $35-75/S; $45-85/D; $8-10/ex prsn. Discs.

Friendship Inn/ 185 Albert Av, Las Vegas NV 89109. 702-735-1741. V,AE, M,DC. I-15 E, Flamingo Rd exit, E to mtl. 1 1/2 mi from arpt. Nrby rstrnt,

NEVADA

pool, fax, cable TV, laundry, eff, n/s rms. $37-85/S or D; $6/ex prsn. Discs.

Motel 6/ 195 E Tropicana Blvd, Las Vegas NV 89109. 702-798-0728/ Fax: 798-5657. M,V,DC,D,AE. I-15 (Exit 37) to E Tropicana Av, E to mtl, 2 blks off The Strip. Rstrnt, cable TV, laundry, pool, n/s rms. Free local calls. Sun-Thurs: $30-32/S; $36-38/D; $6/ex prsn. Fri, Sat, Holiday, Spec Events: $42-44/S; $48-50/D. Higher spec event rates. Disc.

Motel 6/ 5085 S Industrial Rd, Las Vegas NV 89118. 702-739-6747/ Fax: 736-5794. M,V,DC,D,AE. I-15 (Exit 37) to Tropicana Av, W to S Industrial Rd, turn lt. Pool, n/s rms. Free local calls. Sun-Thurs: $30-32/S; $36-38/D; $6/ex prsn. Fri, Sat, Holidays, Spec Events: $40-44/S; $46-50/D. Higher spec event rates. Disc.

Motel 6/ 4125 Boulder Hwy, Las Vegas NV 89121. 702-457-8051/ Fax: 457-0265. M,V,DC,D,AE. Hwy 93/95 between Desert Inn Rd & Sahara Av. Pool, n/s rms. Free local calls. Sun-Thurs: $30/S; $36/D; $6/ex prsn. Fri, Sat, Holidays, Spec Events: $40-44/S; $46-50/D. Higher spec event rates. Disc.

Quality Inn/ 377 E Flamingo Rd, Las Vegas NV 89109. 702-733-7777. V, AE,M,DC. I-15 to Flamingo Rd, E 1 1/2 mi to mtl. Rstrnt/ lounge, pool, mtg rm, fax, t pkng, n/s rms. No pets. $35-150/S or D; $8/ex prsn. Discs.

Lovelock

National 9 Motel/ 1390 Cornell Av, Lovelock NV 89419. 702-273-2224/ 800-562-2347. V,M,AE,DC. I-80 Bsns off ramp, from E, Exit 107 or 106, from W off ramp, Exit 105 or 106. N/s rms, dd phone, microwave, refrig. No pets. $25-30/S; $28-38/D; $4/ex prsn.

Reno

Motel 6/ 1400 Stardust St, Reno NV 89503. 702-747-7390/ Fax: 747-4527. M,V,DC,D,AE. I-80 to Keystone Av Exit, N to 7th St, lt onto Stoker, lt onto Stardust. Nrby rstrnt, cable TV, pool, n/s rms. Free local calls. Sun-Thurs: $25-29/S or D. Fri, Sat, Holidays, Spec Events: $34-42/S or D. Higher spec event rates. Disc.

Motel 6/ 1901 S Virginia, Reno NV 89502. 702-827-0255/ Fax: 827-4728. M,V,DC,D,AE. I-80 to Virginia St Exit, S to mtl. Nrby rstrnt, cable TV, pool, n/s rms. Free local calls. Sun-Thurs: $25-29/S or D. Fri, Sat, Holidays, Spec Events: $34-39/S or D. Higher spec event rates. Disc.

Motel 6/ 666 N Wells Av, Reno NV 89512 702-329-8681/ Fax: 329-2921. M,V,DC,D,AE. I-80 (Exit 14) at Wells Av, S to mtl. Nrby rstrnt, n/s rms. Free local calls. Sun-Thurs: $25-29/S or D. Fri, Sat, Holiday, Spec Events: $34-39/S or D. Higher spec event rates. Disc.

Motel 6/ 866 N Wells, Reno NV 89512. 702-786-9852/ Fax: 786-3162. M, V,DC,D,AE. I-80 (Exit 14) to Wells Av, N to mtl. Nrby rstrnt, cable TV, pool, n/s rms. Free local calls. Sun-Thurs: $25-29/S or D. Fri, Sat, Holidays, Spec Events: $34-39/S or D. Higher spec event rates. Disc.

Silver Chapparal/ 645 S Virginia Av, Reno NV 89411. 702-323-5411. V,M, AE,DC. I-80, S on Virginia. Dd phone, coffee, suites. No pets. National 9. $26-50/S; $26-60/D. $26-75/suites.

Also see Sparks.

Sparks (Reno area)

Motel 6/ 2405 Victorian Av, Sparks NV 89431. 702-358-1080/ Fax: 358-4883. M,V,DC,D,AE. I-80 (Exit 16) 4th St/Victorian Av, turn E to mtl. Nrby rstrnt, cable TV, n/s rms. Free local calls. Premier Award. Sun-Thurs: $26-32/S or D. Fri, Sat, Holidays, Spec Events: $35-42/S or D. Higher spec event rates. Disc.

Wells

Motel 6/ I-80, US 40 & US 93, Wells NV 89835. 702-752-2116/ Fax: 752-3192. M,V,DC,D,AE. I-80: Wbnd, Exit 352A, NW on US 40; Ebnd, Exit 352, lt on US 93, rt on US 40. Jct US 93 & 40. Nrby rstrnt, cable TV, laundry, pool, n/s rms, t pkng. Free local calls. $25-27/S; $31-33/D; $6/ex prsn. Disc.

Super 8 Motel/ 930 6th St, Wells NV

89835. 702-752-3384. V,M,AE,DC,D, CB. I-80, Exit 352, turn lt, then lt again at fourway crossing, 1/4 mi on lt. B/f, n/s rms, pool, nrby rstrnt, laundry, outlets, b/t pkng, cont brfst, cable TV, mtg rm, cot, crib. Free local calls. AAA. $40/S; $44-47/D; $4/ex prsn. Higher spec event wknd rates. Discs.

Winnemucca

Motel 6/ 1600 Winnemucca Blvd, Winnemucca NV 89445. 702-623-1180/ Fax: 623-4725. M,V,DC,D,AE. I-80, Exit 176. On E side of I-80. Cable TV, pool, n/s rms. t pkng. Free local calls. $28-36/S; $34-42/D; $6/ex prsn. Disc.

Super 8 Motel/ 1157 Winnemuca Blvd, Winnemucca NV 89445. 702-625-1818. V,M,D,DC,CB,AE. I-80 at Winnemucca Blvd. B/f, n/s rms, nrby rstrnt, t/rv pkng, copier, cable TV, cot. Free local calls, crib. $39/S; $43-46/D; $4/ex prsn. Higher spec event rates. Discs.

New Hampshire

Concord

Econo Lodge/ Gulf St, Concord NH 03301. 603-224-4011. V,M,AE,DC,D. I-93 (Exit 13) to Main St, N to Gulf St, immediate rt to mtl. Nrby rstrnt, pool, fax, cable TV, t pkng. Free cont brfst. AAA. $40-56/S; $48-63/D; $6/ex prsn. 5/1-10/31: $48-68/S; $56-85/D. Discs.

Dover

Days Inn/ 481 Central Av, Dover NH 03820. 603-742-0400/ Fax: 742-7790. V,M,D,AE,DC,CB,JCB. Hwy 108 at Dover. Fax, n/s rms, nrby rstrnt, pool, mtg rm, t pkng, arpt trans, cable TV, cot. Free cont brfst. $44-64/S; $48-68/D; $5-8/ex prsn.

Gorham

Royalty Inn/ 130 Main St, Gorham NH 03581. 603-466-3312/ Fax: 466-5802/ 800-437-3529. V,M,AE,D,DC,CB. On Main St. Indr pool, whrlpool, n/s rms, exerc equip, cable TV, games, tt/dd phone, mtg rm, copier, laundry, refrig, crib, outlets, t/b pkng, b/f. Free local calls. AAA. $42/S; $48/D; $5/ex prsn. 5/11-10/22: $61/S; $66/D. 12/27-12/31, 2/19-2/23 & wknds 1/1-3/31: $57/S; $62/D. Disc: Bsns. *Guaranteed rates.*

Hampton Beach

Hampton Harbor Motel/ 210 Ashworth Av, Hampton Beach NH 03842. 603-926-4432. V,M,AE,D. I-95, Exit 2 to 101, E (rt) on Ashworth Av. Nrby rstrnt, lounge, pool, n/s rms, cable TV, arpt trans, dd phone, refrig, cot, crib, eff. No pets. AAA. $39-49/S or D; $5/ex prsn. 5/1-10/15: $89-109/S or D; $10/ex prsn. Memorial Day & spec events: $69/S or D; $10/ex prsn. *Guaranteed rates.*

Lincoln

Parker's Motel/ Rte 3, Box 100, Lincoln NH 03251. 603-745-8341/ Fax: 745-4755/ 800-766-6835. V,M,AE,D. I-93, Exit 33, 2 mi N on Rte 3. Nrby rstrnt/ lounge, pool, sauna, whrlpool, n/s rms, cable TV, video games, dd phone, crib. AAA. $25-29/S; $29-48/D; $5/ex prsn. 6/21-10/20 & wknds 12/20-3/22: $47-65/S; $47-75/D. Holiday, spec event rates: $68-75/S; $68-90/D. *Guaranteed rates.*

Littleton

Eastgate Motor Inn/ 335 Cottage St, Littleton NH 03561. 603-444-3971. V,M,AE,D,DC,CB. I-93, Exit 41. Rstrnt/ lounge, pool, n/s rms, cable TV, playgrnd, dd phone, fax, cot, crib, t/b pkng, conn rms, b/f. Free local calls, cont brfst. AAA/ Mobil. $42/S; $48/D; $5/ex prsn. Disc: Bsns, TA, govt, family, trkr, milt. *Guaranteed rates.*

Nashua

Comfort Inn/ 10 St Laurent St, Nashua NH 03060. 603-883-7700. V,M,DC,AE. US 3, Exit 7E. Rstrnt/ lounge, pool, mtg

NEW HAMPSHIRE / NEW JERSEY

rm, fax, b/f, cable TV. Free local calls, cont brfst. No pets. $42-59/S $45-62/D; $7/ex prsn. 8/1-11/15: $45-70/S; $50-75/D. 11/16-2/29: $39-69/S; $42-72/D. Discs.

Motel 6/ 2 Progress Av, Nashua NH 03062. 603-889-4151/ Fax: 886-4721. V,AE,M,DC,D. From Rte 3 (Nbnd, Exit 5W; Sbnd, Exit 5E) to Rte 111, lt at light, lt at Main Dunstable Rd, 1/4 mi to mtl. Cable TV, pool, nrby rstrnt, n/s rms, t pkng. Free local calls. Premier Award. $36/S; $42/D; $6/ex prsn. 5/23-12/20: $30-32/S; $36-38/D. Disc.

Portsmouth

Port Motor Inn/ 505 US Hwy 1 Bypass, Portsmouth NH 03801. 603-436-4378/ Fax: Ext 200/ 800-282-PORT. V,M,AE, D,DC,CB. Pool, n/s rms, cable TV, tt/dd phone, fax, copier, refrig, crib, outlets, t/b pkng, eff, conn rms. Free cont brfst, coffee. AAA/ Mobil. $35-39/S; $38-48/D; $6/ex prsn. 5/1-10/31: $45-95/S; $48-110/D. Wknds, May-Oct, higher end. Disc: Senior, bsns, govt, family, trkr, milt, l/s.

Rochester

Friendship Inn/ 10 Farmington Rd, Rochester NH 03867. 603-332-1902. V,AE,M,DC. Spaulding Turnpike (Exit 15) to SR 11, W to mtl. Rstrnt, pool, cable TV, t pkng, n/s rms. Free cont brfst. No pets. $30-77/S; $40-77/D; $10/ex prsn. Discs.

West Ossipee

Wind Song Motor Inn/ Box 592, W Ossipee NH 03890. 603-539-4536/ Fax: 539-8159. V,M,AE,D. Jct Rte 16 & 25 W. Pool, sauna, n/s rms, exerc equip, satellite TV, VCR/ movies, games, tt/dd phone, mtg rm, copier, laundry, refrig, outlets, t/b/rv pkng, eff. Free local calls, coffee. AAA. $35-38/S; $38-58/D; $10/ex prsn. 6/15-10/15: $38-58/S; $44-88/D. Disc: Family. *Guaranteed rates.*

New Jersey

Absecon (Atlantic City area)

Friendship Inn/ 316 E White Horse Pike, Absecon NJ 08201. 609-652-0904. V,AE,M,DC. Garden State Pkwy (Exit 40) to White Horse Pike (US 30), E 1 mi. Rstrnt, pool, cable TV, n/s rms. No pets. $35-120/S or D; $5/ex prsn. 3/1-4/30, 10/1-11/30: $35-95/S or D. 5/1-9/30: $40-115/S; $40-120/D. Higher spec event rates. Discs.

Super 8 Motel/ 229 E Rte 30, Absecon NJ 08201. 609-652-2477/ Fax: 748-0666. AE,M,V,D,DC,CB. Garden State Pkwy (Exit 40) to US 30, E 1/2 mi. B/f, n/s rms, t/rv pkng, copier, cable TV, refrig. No pets. AAA. $30-35/S; $30-40/D; $5/ex prsn. 7/1-8/31: $45/S; $45-50/D. Higher spec event/ wknd/ holiday rates.

Atlantic City

Econo Lodge/ 117 S Kentucky Av, Atlantic City NJ 08401. 609-344-9093. V, M,AE,DC,D. Atlantic City Expressway or Black Horse Pike, lt at Pacific Av, rt at Kentucky Av. US 30, rt at Kentucky Av. Nrby rstrnt, pool, whrlpool, cable TV, n/s rms. Free cont brfst. No pets. $45-225/S or D; $10/ex prsn. Discs.

Econo Lodge/ 3001 Pacific Av, Atlantic City NJ 08401. 609-344-2925/ Fax: 344-3270. V,M,AE. Garden State Pkwy (Exit 38) to Pacific Av, turn rt. From US 40, lt at Pacific Av. Nrby rstrnt, fax, cable TV. Free cont brfst. No pets. $35-175/S or D; $10/ex prsn. Discs.

Howard Johnson/ Tennessee & Pacific Av, Atlantic City NJ 08401. 609-344-4193/ Fax: 348-1263. V,M,AE,DC,D, CB. Corner of Tennessee & Pacific Av. N/s rms, rstrnt, pool, rm serv, game rm. Free cont brfst. No pets. $45-195/S or D. Discs.

Also see Absecon, Pleasntville, West Atlantic City.

Bellmawr
Econo Lodge/ 301 S Black Horse Pike, Bellmawr NJ 08031. 609-931-2800. V, M,AE,DC,D. NJ Turnpike (Exit 3) to SR 168, N 1 blk. I-295 (Exit 28) to SR 168 S. Nrby rstrnt, mtg rm, fax, b/f, cable TV, outlets. Free coffee. No pets. AAA. $41-47/S; $47-57/D; $6/ex prsn. 12/31-1/1: $53-66/S; $66-81/D. Discs.

Bordentown
Econo Lodge/ US 130 & 206, Bordentown NJ 08505. 609-298-5000. V,M,AE,DC,D. NJ Turnpike (Exit 7) to US 206, N 1 mi to jct US 206 & US 130. Rstrnt/ lounge, pool, fax, b/f, cable TV, n/s rms. Free cont brfst. $44-135/S; $48-135/D; $6/ex prsn. 5/1-6/8: $44-99/S; $48-99/D. 6/9-9/4: $49-99/S; $55-99/D. Discs.

Cherry Hill
Econo Lodge/ SR 38 & Cuthbert Blvd, Cherry Hill NJ 08002. 609-665-3630. V,AE,M,DC. NJ Trnpk (Exit 4) to SR 73, N to SR 38, W to mtl. I-295 (Exit 34B) to SR 70, W to SR 38E sign. Rstrnt/ lounge, mtg rm, fax, cable TV, n/s rms. Free coffee. No pets. $37-41/S; $41-52/D; $6/ex prsn. 12/31: $70/S; $80/D. Discs.

Columbia
Daystop/ Box 305, Columbia NJ 07832. 908-496-8221/ Fax: 496-4809. V,M,D,AE,DC,CB,JCB. I-80 (Exit 4) & SR 94. Fax, n/s rms, rstrnt, t pkng, satellite TV, cot. Free local calls. $35=55/S; $40-60/D; $6/ex prsn. Discs.

East Brunswick
Motel 6/ 244 Rte 18, E Brunswick NJ 08816. 908-390-4545/ Fax: 390-5414. M,V,DC,D,AE. I-95 (Exit 9) at SR 18. Follow sign Edgeboro Rd, turn rt. Nrby rstrnt, cable TV, n/s rms, t pkng. Free local calls. Premier Award. $36-40/S; $42-46/D; $6/ex prsn. Higher spec event rates. Disc.

Lakehurst (Toms River area)
Econo Lodge/ 2016 SR 37 W, Lakehurst NJ 08733. 908-657-7100/ Fax: 657-1672. V,M,AE,DC,D,CB. Garden State Pkwy (Exit 82A) to Rte 37, W approx 5 mi. Nrby rstrnt, n/s rms, cable TV, VCR/ movies, TDD, tt/dd phone, mtg rm, fax, refrig, microwave, cot, crib, t/b pkng, b/f. Free coffee. No pets. AAA. $48-55/S or D; $6/ex prsn. 5/1-10/31: $55-95/S or D; $6-10/ex prsn. 11/21-11/23, 12/24, 25 & 31: $65-70/S or D. Discs.

Maple Shade (Mt Laurel area)
Motel 6/ Route 73, Maple Shade NJ 08052. 609-235-3550/ Fax: 439-9238. V,M,AE,DC,D. NJ Turnpike, Exit 4, N on Rte 73 3/4 mi; I-295, Exit 36B, N on Rte 73 to mtl. Nrby rstrnt, cable TV, pool, elevator, n/s rms. Free local calls. $33-36/S; $39-42/D; $6/ex prsn. Disc.

Marmora
Econo Lodge/ 119 US 9 S, Marmora NJ 08244. 609-390-3366. V,M,AE,D. Garden State Parkway (Exit 25) rt at first light, then lt on US 9 S. Nrby rstrnt, pool, mtg rm, cable TV, t pkng. Free cont brfst. $40-70/S; $45-75/D; $5-8/ex prsn. 7/1-8/31: $55-125/S; $60-135/D. Discs.

Mount Laurel
Econo Lodge/ 611 Fellowship Rd, Mt Laurel NJ 08054. 609-722-1919. V,M, AE,DC,D. NJ Turnpike (Exit 4) at SR 73, N to Fellowship Rd, turn lt (W) to mtl. I-295 (Exit 36A) to SR 73, S to Fellowship Rd, rt 1/4 mi. Nrby rstrnt, fax, b/f, cable TV, n/s rms. Free coffee. No pets. $42-50/S; $48-58/D; $6/ex prsn. 5/1-12/30 $40-48/S; $47-56/D. 12/31: $55/S; $65/D. Discs.

Also see Maple Shade.

New Brunswick (Princeton area)
Econo Lodge/ 26 US 1, New Brunswick NJ 08901. 908-828-8000. V,M,AE,DC, D. NJ Turnpike (Exit 9) to US 1, N 1 mi. Nrby rstrnt, pool, fax, cable TV, t pkng, laundry, n/s rms. Free coffee, cont brfst. $45-70/S; $47-70/D; $3-5/ex prsn. 5/1-5/17, 5/21-10/31: $49-75/S;

$51-75/D. 5/18-5/20: $74-125/S; $79-125/D. 12/31: $69-95/S or D. Discs.

North Plainfield
Howard Johnson Lodge/ US 22 W, N Plainfield NJ 07060. 908-753-6500/ Fax: 753-6791. V,M,AE,DC,D,CB. US 22 W at West End Av. N/s rms, b/f, rstrnt, pool, t pkng, rm serv, valet serv. Free cont brfst, nwspr. $45-75/S or D. Discs.

Piscataway
Motel 6/ 1012 Stelton Rd, Piscataway NJ 08854. 908-981-9200/ Fax: 562-0550. M,V,DC,D,AE. I-287 at US 27. Nrby rstrnt, cable TV, n/s rms, t pkng. Free local calls. Premier Award. $36-40/S; $42-46/D; $6/ex prsn. Higher spec event rates. Disc.

Pleasantville (Atlantic City area)
Comfort Inn/ 6817 Black Horse Pike, Pleasantville NJ 08232. 609-646-8880. V,AE,M,DC. Grdn St Pkwy to Atlantic City Expwy, E to Fire Rd, S to Black Horse Pike. Nrby rstrnt, pool, mtg rm, fax, b/f, cable TV, t pkng, n/s rms. Free cont brfst. No pets. $40-135/S or D; $10/ex prsn. Di

Princeton
See New Brunswick.

Somers Point
Econo Lodge/ 21 McArthur Blvd, Somers Point NJ 08244. 609-927-3220. V, AE,M,DC. Garden State Pkwy S to exit 30. Nrby rstrnt, fax, cable TV. Free cont brfst. No pets. $30-150/S or D; $5/ex prsn. Di

Toms River
See Lakehurst.

West Atlantic City
Comfort Inn/ 7095 Black Horse Pike (US 40), W Atlantic City NJ 08232. 609-645-1818. V,M,DC,AE. US 40 E to Atlantic City. Rstrnt, pool, mtg rm, fax, b/f, cable TV, t pkng, exerc equip, n/s rms. No pets. AAA. $29-120/S or D; $10/ex prsn. 5/1-6/30: $45-135/S or D. 7/1-8/31: $59-150/S or D. 9/1-12/31: $29-125/S or D. Discs.

Howard Johnson/ 1760 Tilton Rd, Atlantic City W NJ 08232. 609-641-3131/ Fax: 641-0555. V,M,AE,DC,D,CB. On Hwy 563 N of US 40. N/s rms, b/f, pool, trans, casino trans, cable TV, laundry. Free cont brfst, arpt trans. No pets. $39-150/S or D. Discs.

Wildwood
Knoll's Resort Motel/ 4111 Atlantic Av, Wildwood NJ 08260. 609-522-8211/ Fax: 522-0687/ 800-732-5665. V,M,AE,D. Garden State Pkwy S to Exit 4B, straight over bridge to Atlantic Av, lt 7 blks. Nrby lounge, pool, cable TV, tt/dd phone, fax, copier, refrig, microwave, cot, crib, t/b/rv pkng, conn rms. Free local calls. No pets. AAA. $44/S or D; $10/ex prsn. 7/1-9/15: $85-105/S or D. Memorial Day, 4th of Jul, Labor Day: $95-110/S or D. Disc: Senior, bsns, TA, govt, trkr, milt, l/s. *Guaranteed rates.*

New Mexico

Alamogordo
Days Inn/ 907 S White Sands Blvd, Alamogordo NM 88310. 505-437-5090/ Fax: 434-5667. V,M,D,AE,DC,CB,JCB. On US 54, 70 & 82, S side of tn. Fax, n/s rms, nrby rstrnt, pool, laundry, micro-fridge, cot. Free cont brfst. AAA. $38-45/S; $45-52/D; $5/ex prsn. Discs.

Motel 6/ 251 Panorama Blvd, Alamogordo NM 88310. 505-434-5970/ Fax: 437-5491. V,M,AE,DC,D. US 70/80 at

US 54. E on Panorama. Nrby rstrnt, cable TV, laundry, pool, n/s rms, t pkng. Free local calls. $26/S; $32/D; $6/ex prsn. Disc.

Super 8 Motel/ 3204 N White Sands, Alamogordo NM 88310. 505-434-4205. V,M,D,DC,CB,AE. N Hwys 54, 70 & 82. B/f, n/s rms, cont brfst, t pkng, cable TV, mtg rm, micro-fridge, copier, cot, crib. Free local calls. $32/S; $37/D; $2/ex prsn. Higher spec event rates. Discs.

Albuquerque

Comfort Inn/ 13031 Central Av, Albuquerque NM 87123. 505-294-1800.V, M,AE,DC,D. I-40 (Exit 167) to Tramway Blvd/ Central Blvd, 1/2 blk W on Central. Rstrnt, pool, mtg rm, fax, b/f, whrlpool, cable TV, t pkng, n/s rms, hot tub. Free full brfst. AAA. $41-47/S; $46-53/D; $6/ex prsn. 5/1-5/31: $43-49/S; $48-55/D. 6/1-10/31: $49-56/S; $52-59/D. Discs.

Econo Lodge/ 13211 Central Av NE, Albuquerque NM 87123. 505-292-7600. V,AE,M,DC. I-40 (Exit 167) at Central & Tramway. Rstrnt, indr pool, sauna, whrlpool, cable TV, t pkng. Free local calls, cot, cont brfst. $34-76/S; $35-96/D; $5/ex prsn. Discs.

Econo Lodge/ 10331 Hotel Av, Albuquerque NM 87123. 505-271-8500. AE,DC,M,V. I-40 to Eubank, N 1/10 mi, rt on Hotel Av. Nrby rstrnt, fax, b/f, cable TV, t pkng, n/s rms. Free cont brfst. No pets. AAA. $43-57/S; $47-63/D; $6/ex prsn. 9/1-9/30: $52-63/S; $57-72/D. 10/1-10/31: $52-85/S; $57-90/D. Discs.

Friendship Inn/ 717 Central Av NW, Albuquerque NM 87102. 505-247-1501/ Fax: 842-5067. V,AE,M,DC. I-25 to Central Av, W to mtl. Rstrnt, pool, mtg rm, fax, cable TV, n/s rms. $26-29/S; $29-34/D; $6/ex prsn. 6/1-8/30: $29-34/S; $39-45/D. 8/31-10/13: $45-55/S; $65-75/D. Discs.

Motel 6/ 1701 University Blvd NE, Albuquerque NM 87102. 505-843-9228/ Fax: 842-1757. M,V,DC,D,AE. I-40: Wbnd, (Exit 160) Carlisle Blvd N to Menaul, lt on Menaul to University, lt on Univ; Ebnd, (Exit 159A) N. Nrby rstrnt, cable TV, pool, n/s rms. Free local calls. $30-33/S; $36-39/D; $6/ex prsn. 5/23-10/25: $37/S; $43/D. Disc.

Motel 6/ 1000 Stadium Blvd SE, Albuquerque NM 87102. 505-243-8017/ Fax: 242-5137. M,V,DC,D,AE. I-25 at Stadium Blvd, turn E. Pool, n/s rms. Free local calls. $30-34/S; $36-40/D; $6/ex prsn. Disc.

Motel 6/ 13141 Central Av NE, Albuquerque NM 87123. 505-294-4600/ Fax: 294-7564. M,V,DC,D,AE. I-40 (Exit 167 to Tramway-Central Av, W on Central NE to mtl. Nrby rstrnt, cable TV, pool, n/s rms. Free local calls. $30-32/S; $36-38/D; $6/ex prsn. 5/23-10/25: $37/S; $43/D. Disc.

Motel 6/ 5701 Iliff Rd, NW, Albuquerque NM 87105. 505-831-8888/ Fax: 831-6296. V,AE,DC,M,D. I-40 (Exit 155) at Coors Rd; S 1 blk. Nrby rstrnt, cable TV, laundry, pool, elevator, n/s rms, t pkng. Free local calls. $30-33/S; $36-39/D; $6/ex prsn. 5/23-10/25: $37/S; $43/D. Disc.

Motel 6/ 3400 Prospect Av NE, Albuquerque NM 87107. 505-883-8813/ Fax: 883-6056. M,V,DC,D,AE. I-40 At Exit 160. I-25, Exit I-40, 2 mi E. Pool, n/s rms. Free local calls. $27-34/S; $33-40/D; $6/ex prsn. Disc.

Motel 6/ 6015 Iliff Rd NW, Albuquerque NM 87121. 505-831-3400/ Fax: 831-3609. M,V,DC,D,AE. I-40 (Exit 155) to Coors Rd, S to mtl. Nrby rstrnt, cable TV, pool, whrlpool, n/s rms. Free local calls. Premier Award. $30-33/S; $36-39/D; $6/ex prsn. 5/23-10/25: $37/S; $43/D. Disc.

Rodeway Inn/ 2108 Menaul Blvd NE, Albuquerque NM 87107. 505-884-2480. V,AE,M,DC. I-25 at Candelaria/ Menaul, go through light, lt 2 blks to mtl. I-40 to Carlisle Blvd, lt on Menaul to mtl. Nrby rstrnt, pool, fax, b/f, cable TV, t pkng, n/s rms. Free cont brfst. No pets. AAA. $30-40/S; $39-49/D; $5/ex prsn. 5/1-9/15: $43-53/S; $49-60/D. 9/16-10/31: $49-65/S; $59-75/D. Discs.

Rodeway Inn/ 12901 Central NE, Albuquerque NM 87108. 505-294-7515. V,M,AE,DC,D. I-40 (Exit 167) to Central Blvd, turn W to mtl. Nrby rstrnt, pool, fax, b/f, cable TV, t pkng, n/s rms. Free

NEW MEXICO

cont brfst. $29-34/S; $34-40/D; $10/ex prsn. 4/21-4/30: $41-46/S; $46-50/D. 5/1-9/30: $37-40/S; $41-47/D. 10/1-10/31: $61-66/S; $61-71/D. Discs.

Super 8 Motel/ 6030 Iliff NW, Albuquerque NM 87121. 505-836-5560 Fax: Ext 350. V,M,D,DC,CB,AE. I-40 (Exit 155) S to Coors Rd & Iliff. B/f, n/s rms, laundry, b/t pkng, copier, elevator, cable TV. Free local calls. Pride Award. $39-44/S; $45-51/D; $2/ex prsn. Higher spec event rates. Discs.

Belen

Budget Host Rio Communities Resort Motel/ 502 Rio Communities Blvd, Belen NM 87002. 505-864-4451/ Fax: 864-7264. V,AE,CB,DC,D,M. I-25 (Exit 195) at Belen, E across river on SR 47. Cable TV, dd phone, in-rm coffee, kitchens, adj rstrnt, pool, laundry, cot, crib. $30-34/S; $34-40/D; $3/ex prsn. Discs.

Bloomfield

Bloomfield Super 8 Motel/ 525 W Broadway, Bloomfield NM 87413. 505-632-8886. V,M,AE,D. Jct US 64 & SR 44. B/f, n/s rms, laundry, outlets. Free cont brfst. Pride Award. $38/S; $42-48/D; $2/ex prsn. Discs. *Guaranteed rates.*

Carlsbad

Motel 6/ 3824 National Prks Hwy, Carlsbad NM 88220. 505-885-0011/ Fax: 887-7861. M,V,DC,D,AE. S of town on US 62/180. Nrby rstrnt, cable TV, pool, n/s rms, t pkng. Free local calls. $26-32/S; $32-38/D; $6/ex prsn. Disc.

Clovis

Motel 6/ 2620 Mabry Dr, Clovis NM 88101. 505-762-2995/ Fax: 762-6342. M,V,DC,D,AE. E of town on US 60/70/84. Nrby rstrnt, cable TV, pool, n/s rms. Free local calls. $24-25/S; $30-31/D; $6/ex prsn. Disc.

Deming

Days Inn/ 1709 E Spruce St, Deming NM 88030. 505-546-8813/ Fax: 546-7095. V,M,AE,D,DC,CB. I-10, Exit 85, 1 1/2 mi on I-10 bsns loop. Rstrnt, pool, n/s rms, cable TV, tt/dd phone, mtg rm, fax, copier, cot, crib, t/b/rv pkng, conn rms. Free local calls, full brfst. AAA. $34/S; $42/D; $4/ex prsn. Discs. *Guaranteed rates.*

Motel 6/ Box 970, Deming NM 88031. 505-546-2623/ Fax: 546-0934. M,V,DC, D,AE. I-10 (Exit 85) to Motel Dr, turn S. Nrby rstrnt, cable TV, laundry, pool, n/s rms. Free local calls. $29/S; $35/D; $6/ex prsn. Disc.

Super 8 Motel/ 1217 W Pines, Deming NM 88030. 505-546-0481. AE,M,V,D, DC,CB. I-10, Deming exit 81. B/f, n/s rms, pool, outlets, b/t pkng, cable TV, cot. Free local calls. Pride Award. $38/S; $43-46/D; $3/ex prsn. Higher spec event rates. Discs.

Espanola

Comfort Inn/ 2975 S Riverside Dr, Espanola NM 87532. 505-753-2419. V, M,AE,DC,D. US 84/285, 25 mi N of Santa Fe. Nrby rstrnt, indr pool, whrlpool, cable TV, n/s rms. Free cont brfst. $39-62/S; $44-69/D; $5/ex prsn. Discs.

Farmington

Motel 6/ 1600 Bloomfield Hwy, Farmington NM 87401. 505-326-4501/ Fax: 326-3883. M,V,DC,D,AE. US 64 on E side of Farmington. Nrby rstrnt, cable TV, pool, laundry, n/s rms. Free local calls. $26-27/S; $32-33/D; $6/ex prsn. Disc.

Motel 6/ 510 Scott Av, Farmington NM 87401. 505-327-0242/ Fax: 327-5617. V,AE,DC,M,D. US 550 to Scott Av, turn S. Nrby rstrnt, cable TV, pool, elevator, n/s rms, t pkng. Free local calls. $27-29/S; $33-35/D; $6/ex prsn. Disc.

Super 8 Motel/ 1601 Bloomfield Hwy, Farmington NM 87401. 505-325-1813 Fax: Ext 199. V,M,D,DC,CB,AE. Hwy 64 at Carlton Av. /f, n/s rms, game rm, outlets, t/b/rv pkng, cont brfst, cable TV, cot, crib. Free local calls. $33/S; $39-45/D; $2/ex prsn. Higher spec event rates. Discs.

Fort Sumner

Super 8 Motel/ 1707 E Summer Av, Ft Sumner NM 88119. 505-355-7888. V, M,AE,DC,D,CB. Hwys 60/84 at 17th. B/f, n/s rms, cable TV, crib, cot, laundry. Free coffee. Pride Award.

$34/S; $40-41/D; $2/ex prsn. Higher spec event rates. Discs.

Gallup

Comfort Inn/ 3208 W US 66, Gallup NM 87301. 505-722-0982. V,M,AE,DC,D. I-40 (Exit 15 to US 66, W to mtl. Nrby rstrnt, indr pool, fax, b/f, cable TV, n/s rms. Free cont brfst. AAA. $40-45/S; $46-54/D; $5/ex prsn. 5/1-10/31: $50-60/S; $57-67/D. Discs.

Econo Lodge/ 3101 W US 66, Gallup NM 87301. 505-722-3800. V,AE,M,DC. I-40 (Exit 16) to US 66/ 666, E 1/2 mi. Nrby rstrnt, cable TV, t pkng, dd phone. Free in-rm coffee. $39-59/S; $39-65/D; $7/ex prsn. Discs.

HoJo Inn/ Drawer W, Gallup NM 87305. 505-863-6801/ Fax: 772-5106. V,M, AE, DC,D,CB. I-40, Exit 16, W on Old Rte 66. N/s rms, b/f, rstrnt, t pkng, laundry. Free cont brfst. Gold Medal Winner. $24-34/S; $30-40/D. Discs.

Motel 6/ 3306 W Rte 66, Gallup NM 87301. 505-863-4492/ Fax: 863-5849. M,V,DC,D,AE. -40 (Exit 16)to Frontage Rd. Nrby rstrnt, cable TV, pool, n/s rms. Free local calls. $28-33/S; $34-39/D; $6/ex prsn. 3/14-5/22: $37/S; $43/D. Disc.

Sleep Inn/ 3820 E Historic US 66, Gallup NM 87301. 800-221-2222 — opening soon. V,M,AE,DC. I-40 to Rte 66. Rstrnt, indr pool, fax, b/f, whrlpool, cable TV, t pkng, n/s rms. Free cont brfst. $35-45/S; $40-50/D; $4/ex prsn. 5/1-8/7, 8/14-10/31: $40-50/S; $45-55/D. 8/8-8/13: $60-80/S; $70-90/D. Discs.

Grants

Motel 6/ 1505 E Santa Fe Av, Grants NM 87020. 505-285-4607/ Fax: 285-6019. M,V,DC,D,AE. I-40, Exit 85, N to mtl. Nrby rstrnt, cable TV, laundry, pool, n/s rms. Free local calls. $30-36/S; $36-42/D; $6/ex prsn. Disc.

Super 8 Motel/ 1604 E Santa Fe Av, Grants NM 87020. 505-287-8811. AE,M,V,D,DC,CB. I-40 to E Grants exit (No 85 Grants Spur Hwy); take first rt turn. B/f, n/s rms, pool, whrlpool, laundry, toast bar, b/t pkng, cable TV, mtg rm, exerc equip, cot. Free local calls. Pride Award. $38/S; $42-46/D; $4/ex prsn. Higher spec event rates. Discs.

Las Cruces

Motel 6/ 235 LaPosada Ln, Las Cruces NM 88001. 505-525-1010/ Fax: 525-0139. V,M,AE,DC,D. I-10 at Main St, New Mexico State Univ exit. Nrby rstrnt, cable TV, laundry, pool, n/s rms. Free local calls. $32-35/S; $38-41/D; $6/ex prsn. Disc.

Lordsburg

Super 8 Motel/ 110 E Maple, Lordsburg NM 88045. 505-542-8882. AE,CB,DC, M,V,D. I-10 (Exit 22) at Main St, S to Maple, turn lt. N/s rms, outlets, t/b/rv pkng, cot, crib. No pets. AAA. $39/S; $43-45/D; $2/ex prsn. Higher spec event wknd rates. Discs.

Los Lunas

Comfort Inn/ 1711 Main St SW, Los Lunas NM 87031. 505-865-5100. V,M, AE,DC,D. I-25 E to SR 6 (W Main St), W to Grant St. Nrby rstrnt, fax, b/f, whrlpool, cable TV, t pkng, n/s rms. Free cont brfst. No pets. $41-65/S; $46-70/D; $5/ex prsn. 5/1-9/9: $40-65/S; $45-70/D. 9/10-10/15: $60-80/S; $65-85/D. Discs.

Moriarty

Howard Johnson Lodge/ 1316 Central Av, Box 1610, Moriarty NM 87035. 505-832-4457. M,V,AE,DC,D. On Hwy 66 between Exit 197 and Exit 194 on I-40. N/s rms, b/f, t/b/rv pkng. Free cont brfst. No pets. Gold Medal Winner. $30-34/S; $34-37/D. Discs.

Sunset Motel/ 501 Rte 66, Box 36, Moriarty NM 87035. 505-832-4234. V, M,D. 1/2 mi W on Rte 66, N side of rd. Nrby rstrnt, n/s rms, cable TV, dd phone, cot, t/b pkng. Free local calls. No alcohol. AAA. $35-41/S; $41-47/D; $7/ex prsn. Disc: Senior, milt, comm.

Raton

Motel 6/ 1600 Cedar St, Raton NM 87740. 505-445-2777/ Fax: 445-5359. M,V,DC,D,AE. I-25/US 85, Exit 451, W on Clayton Rd/ US 64/87 to Cedar, turn N. Nrby rstrnt, cable TV, laundry, pool, n/s rms, t pkng. Free local calls. $28/S; $34/D; $6/ex prsn. 5/23=12/20: $36/S;

NEW MEXICO

$42/D. Disc.

Roswell

Best Western El Rancho Palacio/ 2205 N Main St, Roswell NM 88201. 505-622-2721/ Fax: 622-2725. V,M,AE,D,DC,CB. On Hwy 285 & 70. Rstrnt, pool, whrlpool, n/s rms, cable TV, TDD, tt/dd phone, fax, copier, refrig, crib, outlets, t/b pkng, conn rms. Free local calls, coffee. AAA/ $38/S; $46/D; $3/ex prsn. Discs: Senior, bsns, TA, govt, l/s, family, trkr, milt.

Comfort Inn/ 2803 W 2nd St, Box 1415, Roswell NM 88202. 505-623-9440/ Fax: 622-9708. V,M,AE,D,DC,CB. W edge of Roswell on US 70/ 380. N/s rms, rstrnt, pool, mtg rm, fax, b/f, cable TV, t pkng, refrig. AAA. $38-75/S; $40-85/D; $5/ex prsn. 4/1-4/30: $45-85/S; $50-95/D. 5/1-10/31: $42-75/S; $45-85/D. Discs.

Days Inn Roswell/ 1310 N Main, Roswell NM 88201. 505-623-4021/ Fax: 623-0079. V,M,AE,D,DC,CB. On Hwy 285 N & 70 W in dntn. Pool, whrlpool, n/s rms, cable TV, TDD, tt/dd phone, mtg rm, copier, refrig, cot, crib, t/b pkng. Free local calls, cont brfst, coffee. AAA. $38/S; $48/D; $4/ex prsn. Discs.

Royal Motel/ 2001 N Main St, Roswell NM 88201. 505-622-0110 V,M,AE,DC. On Hwy 285 & 70, 1/2 mi N of town cntr. Adj rstrnt/ lounge, pool, cable TV, fax, kitchenettes. Free cont brfst. AAA/ Mobil/ National 9. $29-33/S; $33-40/D; $6/ex prsn. Higher spec event rates.

Super 8 Motel/ 3575 N Main St, Roswell NM 88201. 505-622-8886. V,M,AE,DC,D,CB. 3 mi N of dntn on US Hwy 70 285. B/f, n/s rms, pool, whrlpool, laundry, toast bar, t/b/rv pkng, cot, crib. Free local calls. No pets. Pride Award. $43/S; $48-52/D; $3/ex prsn. Discs.

Santa Fe

Howard Johnson Lodge/ 4044 Cerrillos Rd, Santa Fe NM 87501. 505-438-8950/ Fax: 471-9289. V,M,AE,D,DC,CB,JCB. I-25 (Exit 278) to Cerrillos Rd, N past Rodeo Rd 1/2 blk, E side of hwy. B/f, fax. Free cont brfst. No pets. Gold Medal Winner. $35-55/S; $44-65/D. Discs.

Motel 6/ 3007 Cerrillos Rd, Santa Fe NM 87505. 505-473-1380/ Fax: 473-7784. M,V,DC,D,AE. I-25: Nbnd, Exit 278/Cerrillos Rd; Sbnd, Exit St Francis Dr/ US 285, NW, lt on St Michaels, lt on Cerrillos. Nrby rstrnt, cable TV, pool, n/s rms. Free local calls. $35-40/S; $41-46/D; $6/ex prsn. Disc.

Motel 6/ 3695 Cerrillos Rd, Santa Fe NM 87505. 505-471-4140/ Fax: 474-4370. M,V,DC,D,AE. I-25 (Exit 278) to Cerrillos Rd, NW to mtl. Pool, n/s rms. Free local calls. $35-40/S; $41-46/D; $6/ex prsn. Disc.

Super 8 Motel/ 3358 Cerrillos Rd, Santa Fe NM 87501. 505-471-8811/ Fax: 471-3239. V,M,D,DC,CB,AE. I-25 (Exit 278) at US 84/285, N to Rodeo Rd, W to Cerrillos Rd, 3 1/2 mi NE to mtl. B/f, n/s rms, copier, elevator, cable TV. Free local calls. No pets. Pride Award. $36-41/S; $42-47/D; $4/ex prsn. Higher spec event rates. Discs.

Santa Rosa

Comfort Inn/ 3343 E Will Rogers Blvd, Santa Rosa NM 88435. 800-221-2222 — opening soon. V,M,AE,DC,D. 2 blks W of I-10 (Exit 277) on I-40 Bsns Rte (Will Rogers Blvd). Nrby rstrnt, pool, fax, b/f, sauna, whrlpool, cable TV, t pkng, n/s rms. Free cont brfst. $37-47/S; $45-55/D; $8/ex prsn. Discs.

Motel 6/ 3400 Will Rogers Dr, Santa Rosa NM 88435. 505-472-3045/ Fax: 472-5923. M,V,DC,D,AE. I-40 (Exit 277) to Will Rogers Dr, N to mtl. Nrby rstrnt, cable TV, laundry, pool, n/s rms, t pkng. Free local calls. $28-36/S; $34-42/D; $6/ex prsn. Disc.

Super 8 Motel/ 1201 Will Rogers Dr, Santa Rosa NM 88435. 505-472-5388/ Fax: Ext 233. V,M,D,DC,CB,AE. I-40 (Exit 275) to US 54/84 (W Rogers Dr), W to mtl. B/f, n/s rms, laundry, t/b/rv pkng, cable TV, cot, crib. Free local calls. $35/S; $41-43/D; $2/ex prsn. Higher spec event rates. Discs.

Socorro

Econo Lodge/ 713 California St NW, Box 977, Socorro NM 87801. 505-835-1500. V,M,AE. I-25 (Exit 147) to California St, NE to mtl. Nrby rstrnt, pool, fax, cable TV, t pkng. $40-48/S; $42-54/D; $3/ex prsn. Discs.

Motel 6/ 807 S US 85, Socorro NM 87801. 505-835-4300/ Fax: 835-3108. M,V,DC,D,AE. I-25 (Exit 147) Bsns I-25/60W, NW to mtl. Cable TV, pool, laundry, n/s rms. Free local calls. $26/S; $32/D; $6/ex prsn. Disc.

Tucumcari

Budget Host Royal Palacio Motel/ 1620 E Tucumcari Blvd, Tucumcari NM 88401. 505-461-1212. V,M,AE,D,DC, CB. I-40 (Exit 333) US 54 Bypass, W at traffic light. Cable TV, dd phone, n/s rms, nrby rstrnt, picnic area, laundry, arpt trans, t pkng, outlets. Free crib. AAA/ Mobil. $27/S; $35/D; $3/ex prsn. Disc: Senior.

Comfort Inn/ 2800 E Tucumcari Blvd, Tucumcari NM 88401. 505-461-4094. V,M,AE,DC,D. I-40 (Exit 335) at US 54, W 2/10 mi to mtl. Nrby rstrnt, pool, mtg rm, fax, b/f, cable TV, t pkng, n/s rms. Free full brfst. AAA. $40-58/S; $46-70/D; $6/ex prsn. 5/1-9/30: $52-60/S; $58-80/D. Discs.

Days Inn/ 2623 S First St, Tucumcari NM 88401. 505-461-3158/ Fax: 461-2205. V,M,AE,D,DC,CB. I-40, Exit 332. N/s rms, cable TV, tt/dd phone, fax, copier, crib, b/f. Free local calls, full brfst, coffee. AAA. $33-40/S; $44-50/D; $7/ex prsn. 5/1-9/30: $38-45/S; $48-56/D. Discs. *Guaranteed rates.*

Econo Lodge/ 3400 E Tucumcari Blvd, Tucumcari NM 88401. 505-461-4194. V,AE,M,DC. I-40 (Exit 335) to US 66, W 2 blks to mtl. Rstrnt, mtg rm, cable TV, t pkng, n/s rms. $21-32/S; $27-42/D; $6/ex prsn. Discs.

Friendship Inn/ 315 E Tucumcari Blvd, Tucumcari NM 88401. 505-461-0330. V,AE,M,DC. I-40 (Exit 332) to Tucumcari Blvd E. Rstrnt, pool, fax, b/f, cable TV, t pkng, n/s rms. $20-28/S; $29-39/D; $3-6/ex prsn. Discs.

Motel 6/ 2900 E Tucumcari Blvd, Tucumcari NM 88401. 505-461-4791/ Fax: 461-2283. M,V,DC,D,AE. I-40 (Exit 335) to Tucumcari Blvd, W to mtl. Nrby rstrnt, cable TV, laundry, pool, n/s rms, t pkng. Free local calls. $25-34/S; $31-40/D; $6/ex prsn. Disc.

Rodeway Inn/ 1023 E Tucumcari Blvd, Tucumcari NM 88401. 505-461-0360. V,M,AE,DC. I-40 (Wbnd, Exit 335; Ebnd, Exit 332) to 1st St, rt on Tucumcari Blvd. Nrby rstrnt, pool, fax, cable TV, t pkng, laundry, family rms, n/s rms. Free cont brfst. $29-45/S; $35-70/D; $6/ex prsn. Discs.

Rodeway Inn/ 1302 W Tucumcari Blvd, Tucumcari NM 88401. 505-461-3140. AE,DC,M,V. I-40 (Exit 332) to US 66, rt 2 blks to mtl. Rstrnt, pool, mtg rm, fax, cable TV, t pkng, n/s rms. Free cont brfst. AAA. $31-33/S; $41-46/D; $10/ex prsn. 5/1-10/31: $31-36/S; $48-55/D. Discs.

New York

Albany

Econo Lodge/ 1632 Central Av, Albany NY 12205. 518-456-8811. V,M,AE,DC, D. I-87 (Exit 2W) to SR 5, W 1/2 mi to mtl. Nrby rstrnt, fax, b/f, cable TV, n/s rms. Free coffee, cont brfst. $43/S; $47-54/D; $4/ex prsn. 6/1-7/20, 9/1-10/31: $51/S; $55-64/D. 7/21-8/31: $62/S; $68-77/D. Discs.

Howard Johnson Hotel/ 1614 Central Av, Albany NY 12205. 518-869-0281/ Fax: 869-9205. V,M,D,AE,DC,CB. NY St Thruway, Exit 24. N/s rms, mtg rm, rstrnt/ lounge, pool, t/b pkng, laundry, valet. No pets. $39-49/S; $45-55/D. Discs.

Motel 6/ 100 Watervliet Av, Albany NY 12206. 518-438-7447/ Fax: 438-0594. V,M,AE,D,DC. I-90: Ebnd, Exit 5, rt at Everett Rd to 1st traffic signal (Watervliet Av); Wbnd, Exit B-1 go to Exit 5/ Everett Rd, lt to Watervliet, lt. Cable TV, n/s rms. Premier Award. $40/S; $46/D; $6/ex prsn. 5/23-10/29: $44/S; $50/D. Disc.

Amherst (Buffalo area)

Motel 6/ 4400 Maple Rd, Amherst NY 14226. 716-834-2231/ Fax: 834-0872. V,M,AE,DC,D. I-90, Exit 50 (I-290), then take Exit 5B/ Millersport Hwy N to Maple Rd Exit, lt over I-290 to mtl. Nrby rstrnt, cable TV, n/s rms. Free local calls. Premier Award. Sun-Thurs:

NEW YORK

$36/S; $42/D; $6/ex prsn. Fri, Sat, Holidays, Spec Events: $40/S; $46/D. 5/23-12/20: $40-43/S; $46-49/D. Higher spec event rates.

Batavia
Friendship Inn/ 8212 Park Rd, Batavia NY 14020. 716-343-2311. V,M,AE, DC,D. I-90 (Exit 48) thru light, 3rd mtl on rt. Nrby rstrnt, fax, cable TV, t pkng, dd phone, n/s rms. Free cont brfst, local calls. AAA. $41-46/S; $46-51/D; $8/ex prsn. 5/1-6/14, 9/6-10/31: $51-57/S; $57-65/D. 6/15-9/5: $61-67/S; $69-79/D. Discs.

Binghamton
HoJo Inn/ 690 Front St, Binghamton NY 13905. 607-724-1341/ Fax: 773-8287. V,M,D,AE,DC,CB. I-81 (Exit 5) to Front St. N/s rms, mtg rm, b/f, pool, t pkng, valet serv. Free cont brfst. $40-60/S; $46-70/D. Higher spec event rates. Discs.

Motel 6/ 1012 Front St, Binghamton NY 13905. 607-771-0400/ Fax: 773-4781. M,V,DC,D,AE. I-81/I-88 between Exits 5 and 6 on Front St, on W side of frwy. Nrby rstrnt, cable TV, n/s rms. Free local calls. Premier Award. $33-38/S; $39-44/D; $6/ex prsn. Disc.

Super 8 Motel/ 650 Old Front St, Binghamton NY 13905. 607-773-8111/ Fax: Ext 138. AE,M,V,D,DC,CB. I-81 (Exit 5) to Hwy 11. Just W of frwy. B/f, n/s rms, nrby rstrnt, t/b/rv pkng, copier, microwave, cot. Free cont brfst. $40-43/S; $43-47/D; $5/ex prsn. Higher spec event rates. Discs.

Super 8 Motel/ Box ESS, Binghamton NY 13904. 607-775-3443/ Fax: 775-2368. V,M,AE,DC,D,CB. From I-81 take Exit 3, Exit 2 or Exit 2W S to Upper Court St. On Hwy 11/ Upper Court St. N/s rms, pool, cable TV, whrlpool, mtg rm, cot, VCR, t/b pkng. Free crib. $40-47/S; $43-53/D; $3/ex prsn. Higher spec event rates. Discs.

Also see Vesta.

Brockport
Econo Lodge/ 6575 4th Section Rd, Brockport NY 14420. 716-637-3157. V, M,AE,D. I-90 (Exit 47) to SR 19, N 9 mi to mtl. Nrby rstrnt, pool, cable TV, t pkng, n/s rms. Free cont brfst. AAA. $44-53/S; $48-68/D; $5/ex prsn. Discs.

Buffalo
Econo Lodge/ 4344 Milestrip Rd, Buffalo NY 14219. 716-825-7530. V,M,AE. I-90 (Exit 56) to SR 179, E 1/4 mi to mtl. Nrby rstrnt, fax, b/f, cable TV, t pkng, outlets, n/s rms. No pets. AAA. $36-68/S; $43-98/D; $7/ex prsn. Discs.

Wellesley Inn/ 4630 Genesee St, Buffalo NY 14225. 716-631-8966/ Fax: 631-8977. AE,M,D,CB,V,DC. Cable TV, microwave, refrig. Free cont brfst. $45/S or D; $5/ex prsn. *Special rates - see discount section in front of book.

Also see Amherst, Williamsville.

Canandaigua
Econo Lodge/ 170 Eastern Blvd, Canandaigua NY 14424. 716-394-9000. V,M,AE,DC,D. I-90 (Exit 44) to SR 332, S to SR 5 & US 20, E to mtl. Nrby rstrnt, fax, b/f, cable TV, t pkng, outlets, n/s rms. Free cont brfst. AAA. $42-50/S; $48-55/D; $6/ex prsn. 5/1-10/31: $50-58/S; $58-66/D. 11/1-12/31: $41-49/S; $47-54/D. Discs.

Also see Manchester.

Catskill
Red Ranch Motel/ 4555 Route 32, Catskill NY 12414. 518-678-3380/ 800-962-4560. V,M,AE,D,DC,CB. NYS Thruway Rte 87 (Exit 20) to Hwy 32, N

NEW YORK

9 mi. Pool, cable TV, video games, playgrnd, tt phone, refrig, cot, crib, outlets, t/b/rv pkng, conn rms, eff, b/f. No pets. AAA/ Mobil. $34-38/S; $34-48/D; $4/ex prsn. 6/16-9/4: $45-50/S; $45-68/D. Festival Wkns, holidays: $75/S or D; $5/ex prsn. Disc: TA, l/s. *Guaranteed rates.*

Clay
Friendship Inn/ 901 S Bay Rd, Clay NY 13041. 315-458-3510. V,M,AE,DC,D. I-81 N (Exit 29) to SR 481, (Exit 10) to Circle Dr, rt at 1st light, rt at next light. Nrby rstrnt, fax, cable TV, t pkng, outlets, kitchen, n/s rms. $35-45/S; $39-49/D; $10/ex prsn. Discs.

Corning
Evergreen Motel/ 135 E Corning Rd, Corning NY 14830. 607-937-5688/ Fax: 937-5753/ 800-553-8154. V,M,AE,D, DC,CB. Rte 17, Exit 47 or 48, 2 mi E of dntn Corning. Cable TV, playgrnd, arpt trans, tt/dd phone, fax, copier, laundry, refrig, microwave, crib, outlets, t/b pkng. Free cont brfst. No pets. $30/S; $39/D; $7/ex prsn. 5/16-10/31: $34/S; $42-95/D. Spec event, holiday wknds: $75/S; $95/D. Disc: Senior, bsns, TA, govt, trkr, milt, l/s. *Guaranteed rates.*

Cortland
Econo Lodge/ 3775 US 11 (Box 628, McGraw, NY 13101), Cortland NY 13045. 607-753-7594. V,M,AE,D. I-81 & US 11, Exit 10. Nrby rstrnt, fax, b/f, t pkng, outlets, n/s rms. Free cont brfst. AAA. $39-66/S; $44-71/D; $5/ex prsn. Discs.

Dansville
Daystop/ Commerce Dr, Dansville NY 14437. 715-335-6023/ Fax: 335-2090. V,M,D,AE,DC,CB,JCB. I-30, Exit 5, turn S. Fax, n/s rms, rstrnt, t pkng, cable TV, cot. $44-49/S or D.

Dunkirk
Friendship Inn/ 310 Lake Shore Dr, Dunkirk NY 14048. 716-366-2200. V, AE,M,DC. I-90 (NY Thruway) to (Exit 59) SR 60, lt on SR 5 W 1 mi. Nrby rstrnt, cable TV, t pkng, conn rms, n/s rms. Free coffee. $32-55/S; $38-70/D; $5/ex prsn. Higher spec event rates. Discs.

Quality Inn/ Vineyard Dr, Dunkirk NY 14048. 716-366-4400. V,M,AE,DC,D. 2 mi S of Dunkirk at Thruway exit 59. Rstrnt/ lounge, pool, mtg rm, cable TV, t pkng, n/s rms. $42-46/S; $46-50/D; $4/ex prsn. 5/1-6/30: $50-54/S; $56-60/D. 7/1-9/4: $52-54/S; $60-64/D. 9/5-10/31: $44-48/S; $48-52/D. Discs.

East Syracuse (Syracuse area)
Motel 6/ 6577 Court St Rd, E Syracuse NY 13057. 315-433-1300/ Fax: 437-2094. M,V,DC,D,AE. I-90, Exit 35 at Carrier Cir, go thru toll to 298E, 1st lt to College Pl, lt onto Court St. Nrby rstrnt, cable TV, n/s rms. Free local calls. Premier Award. $30-36/S; $36-42/D; $6/ex prsn. Higher spec event rates. Di

Elmira.
See Horseheads.

Fairport
Trail Break Motor Inn/ 7340 Pittsford - Palmyra Rd, Fairport NY 14450. 716-223-1710/ 800-927-2165. V,M,D,DC, CB,AE. 5 mi N of I-90 (Exit 45) on SR 31. Rstrnt, cable TV, tt/dd phone, refrig, crib, t/b/rv pkng, conn rms. Free local calls, coffee. AAA. $38/S; $42-47/D; $4/ex prsn. Disc: Senior, family. *Guaranteed rates.*

Falconer (Jamestown area)
Motel 6/ 1980 E Main St, Falconer NY 14733. 716-665-3670/ Fax: 664-7651. M,V,DC,D,AE. SR 17, Exit 13 at E Main St. Cable TV, n/s rms. Free local calls. Premier Award. $34-37/S; $40-43/D; $6/ex prsn. Disc.

Gates (Rochester area)
Motel 6/ 155 Buell Rd, Gates NY 14624. 716-436-2170/ Fax: 436-4814. M,V,DC,D,AE. I-390 (Exit 18B) at Brooks Av, W to 1st light (Buell Rd), rt 1/4 mi to mtl. N/s rms. Free local calls. Premier Award. $36-40/S; $42-46/D; $6/ex prsn. Disc.

Geneva
Motel 6/ 485 Hamilton St, Geneva NY 14456. 315-789-4050/ Fax: 781-2338. V,M,AE,D,DC. I-90 (Exit 42) to Rte 14, S 8 mi to Geneva, rt on Hwy 5/20 W/ Hamilton St. Nrby rstrnt, cable TV, n/s

NEW YORK

rms. Premier Award. $36-40/S; $42-46/D; $6/ex prsn. 5/23-10/29: $48/S; $54/D. Disc.

Glen Falls

Econo Lodge/ 29 Aviation Rd, Glen Falls NY 12804. 518-793-3491/ Fax: 793-8678. V,AE,M,DC. I-87, Exit 19. Nrby rstrnt, cable TV, fax, copier, n/s rms. No pets. $37-52/S; $47-57/D; $8/ex prsn. 5/1-6/29: $35-57/S; $40-67/D. 6/30-9/16: $42-82/S; $52-87/D. 9/17-10/29: $42-52/S; $47-62/D. Discs.

Hamburg

HoJo Inn/ 5245 Camp Rd, Hamburg NY 14075. 716-648-2000/ Fax: 648-9718. V,M,AE,D,DC,CB. I-90, Exit 57. Adj to toll booth on rt. N/s rms, b/f, pool, arpt trans, fax, copier, laundry, valet. Free local calls, cont brfst. $38-55/S; $43-65/D; $5/ex prsn. Higher spec event rates. Discs. and Buffalo Bills games. Discs.

Herkimer

Herkimer Motel/ 100 Marginal Rd, Herkimer NY 13350. 315-866-0490/ Fax: 866-0416. V,M,AE,D,DC,CB. 1 blk from Exit 30, I-90 NYS thruway. Rstrnt, pool, n/s rms, cable TV, tt/dd phone, mtg rm, copier, laundry, refrig, outlets, t/b/rv pkng, eff, b/f. Free local calls, coffee. AAA/ Mobil. $39-42/S; $42-50/D; $7/ex prsn. 7/1-9/2: $44-50/S; $50-64/D. Disc: Senior, govt, milt, AAA, family. *Guaranteed rates.*

Horseheads (Elmira area)

Motel 6/ 4133 Rte 17, Horseheads NY 14845. 607-739-2525/ Fax: 739-1051. M,V,DC,D,AE. On S side of Rte 17 at Horseheads, between jcts Rte 13 & 14. Nrby rstrnt, cable TV, n/s rms. Free local calls. Premier Award. $36-40/S; $42-46/D; $6/ex prsn. Disc.

Ithaca

Meadow Court Inn/ 529 S Meadow St, Ithaca NY 14850. 607-273-3885/ Fax: 277-0758/ 800-852-4014. V,M,AE,D, DC. On Rte 13 S, within the city of Ithaca. Rstrnt/ lounge, n/s rms, cable TV, tt phone, mtg rm, fax, copier, refrig, cot, crib, t/b pkng, conn rms, b/f. AAA/ Mobil. $40-95/S; $45-95/D; $5/ex prsn. College events, May thru Nov: $95/S or D. Disc: Bsns, govt, family, l/s.

Jamestown

Comfort Inn/ 2800 N Main St, Box 3296, Jamestown NY 14702. 716-664-5920. V,M,AE,DC. SR 17 (Exit 12) to SR 60 (N Main St), S to mtl. Nrby rstrnt/ lounge, mtg rm, fax, b/f, cable TV, n/s rms. Free cont brfst. AAA. $40-84/S or D; $5/ex prsn. 5/1-5/25, 9/6-10/31: $51-84/S; $56-84/D. 5/26-9/5: $58-84/S; $63-84/D. Discs.

Also see Falconer.

Lake George

Balmoral Motel/ 444 Canada St, Lake George NY 12845. 518-668-2673/ 800-457-2673. V,M,AE,D. Northway Rte I-87, Exit 22, rt on Rte 9, S 1 blk on lt. Pool, n/s rms, cable TV, video games, tt/dd phone, copier, laundry, cot, crib, outlets, t/b pkng, eff, conn rms, b/f. Free local calls, coffee. AAA. $32-50/S; $35-58/D; $7/ex prsn. 5/24-9/2: $58-75/S; $68-95/D. *Guaranteed rates.*

Comfort Inn/ I-87 & US 9N, Lake George NY 12845. 518-668-4141. V, M, AE,DC,D. I-87 (Exit 21) to SR 9, N 100 yds to mtl. Nrby rstrnt, cable TV. t pkng, n/s rms. Free cont brfst. No pets. $35-125/S; $40-125/D; $5/ex prsn. Discs.

Lake Placid

Quality Inn/ 122 Main St, Lake Placid NY 12946. 518-523-1818. V,M,AE,DC. On SR 73 in Lake Placid. Rstrnt, mtg rm, cable TV, n/s rms. Free cont brfst. $37-107/S or D; $10/ex prsn. Discs.

Latham

Microtel - Colonie/ 7 Rensselaer Av, Latham NY 12110. 518-782-9161/ Fax: 782-9162/ 800-782-9121. A,M,AE,D, DC,CB. NYS Thruway to Exit 24, 87 N to Exit 6 (Latham), 1/4 mi. N/s rms, cable TV, video games, tt/dd phone, mtg rm, fax, copier, refrig, microwave, crib, outlets, t/b/rv pkng, conn rms, b/f. Free coffee. AAA. $35/S; $39/D. 7/1-7/20, 9/1-10/31: $39/S; $43/D. 7/21-9/1: $46/S; $50/D. *Guaranteed rates.*

Liverpool (Syracuse area)

Econo Lodge/ 401 7th North St, Liverpool NY 13088. 315-451-6000. V,M, AE,DC,D. I-90 (Exit 36) to I-81, W to (Exit 25) to 7th North St, turn NW to mtl. Nearby rstrnt, fax, b/f, cable TV, n/s rms. Free cont brfst. $40-55/S; $47-65/D; $4/ex prsn. 5/1-10/31: $44-70/S; $52-80/D. Discs.

Maloane

Super 8 Motel/ US 11 & SR 30, Maloane NY 12953. 518-483-8123. V, M,D,AE,DC,CB. Jct Hwys 11, 30, 37, near Jons Plaza. N/s rms, b/f, fax, copier, cable TV. Free local calls. $45/S; $49/D; $4/ex prsn. Higher spec event rates. Discs.

Econo Lodge/ 227 W Main St, Malone NY 12953. 518-483-0500. V,AE,M,DC. SR 11, W of jct with SRs 30 & 37. Rstrnt/ lounge, pool, mtg rm, fax, b/f, t pkng, n/s rms. Free cont brfst. Pride Award. $40-48/S; $42-55/D; $5/ex prsn. Discs.

Manchester (Camandaigua area)

Friendship Inn/ SR 96 & 21, Manchester NY 14504. 716-289-3811. V,AE,M,DC. I-90 (Exit 43) to SR 21, S 1/2 mi to mtl. Nrby rstrnt, fax, cable TV, t pkng, outlets, n/s rms. No pets. AAA. $40-60/S; $40-70/D; $8/ex prsn. Discs.

Monticello

Econo Lodge/ 190 Broadway, Monticello NY 12701. 914-794-8800. V,M,AE, DC,D. NYS Thruway to Harriman (Exit 16) SR 17, W to (Exit 105A) Monticello Hwy 42, rt at 2nd traffic light. Nrby rstrnt, pool, mtg rm, fax, cable TV, VCR, eff. Free local calls, cont brfst. No pets. $40-75/S or D; $5-7/ex prsn. 5/26-9/6: $40-85/S; $46-95/D. Discs.

New Paltz

Econo Lodge/ 530 Main St, New Paltz NY 12561. 914-255-6200. V,AE,M,DC. I-87 (Exit 18) at SR 299, E 1/2 mi. Nrby rstrnt, pool, mtg rm, fax, cable TV, t pkng, outlets, n/s rms. Free cont brfst. No pets. $47-55/S or D; $6/ex prsn. 5/1-10/31: $51-65/S or D. Discs.

Newfane

Lake Ontario Motel/ 3330 Lockport-Olcott Rd, Newfane NY 14108. 716-778-5004/ 800-446-5767. V,M,AE,D. On Rte 78 at Newfane. N/s rms, cable TV, tt/dd phone, fax, copier, refrig, microwave, cot, t/b pkng, b/f. Free local calls. AAA. $37/S; $42-49/D; $6/ex prsn. Disc: Family, l/s. *Guaranteed rates.*

Niagara Falls

Budget Host Americana Motor Inn/ 9401 Niagara Falls Blvd, Niagara Falls NY 14304. 716-297-2660/ Fax: 297-7675. V,AE,CB,DC,D,M. I-90 Thruway to I-290, to Rt 62, N 12 mi. Cable TV, dd phone, family rms, kitchens, adj rstrnt/ lounge, pool, picnic area, laundry, b/f, cot, crib. No pets. AAA/ Mobil. $39/S; $45-49/D; $5-10/ex prsn. 6/23-9/5: $49/S; $65-69/D.

Econo Lodge/ 7708 Niagara Falls Blvd, Niagara Falls NY 14304. 716-283-0621. AE,DC,M,V. I-90 (Ebnd, Exit 50; Wbnd, Exit 53) at US 62. Nrby rstrnt, indr pool, fax, b/f, cable TV, t pkng, n/s rms. No pets. $39-99/S; $45-99/D; $10/ex prsn. Discs.

Hospitality Inn/ 6734 Niagara Falls Blvd, Niagara Falls NY 14304. 716-283-8611/ Fax: 283-6097/ 800-884-0684. V,M,AE,D. I-90 (Exit N22), W 1/4 mi on US 62. Nrby rstrnt, pool, n/s rms, cable TV, tt phone, fax, refrig, cot, crib, t/b pkng, conn rms. Free local calls. AAA. $26-49/S; $32-59/D; $6/ex prsn. 6/21-9/9: $36-59/S; $36-99/D. Higher holiday rates. Disc: Senior, l/s, AAA.

Howard Johnson Lodge/ 6505 Niagara Falls Blvd, Niagara Falls NY 14304. 716-283-8791/ Fax: 283-9313. V,M,D,AE,DC,CB. I-190, Exit 22. N/s rms, mtg rm, rstrnt, pool, arpt trans, t pkng, laundry, satellite TV, Falls tours. $35-59/S or D. Discs.

Niagara Rainbow Motel/ 7900 Niagara Falls Blvd, Niagara Falls NY 14304. 716-283-1760. V,M,AE,D. I-90 (Exit 22) to US 62, S 1 mi. Nrby rstrnt, pool, sauna, whrlpool, cable TV, VCR, tt phone, refrig, microwave, cot, outlets, t/b/rv pkng, conn rms, b/f. Free local calls, AAA. $25-69/S or D; $5/ex prsn. Higher holiday, spec event rates. Disc: Senior, bsns, TA, govt, milt, trkr, l/s.

Norwich

Super 8 Motel/ SR 12, Norwich NY 13815. 607-336-8880/ Fax: 336-2076. V,M, D,AE,DC,CB. On SR 12, N of Norwich. N/s rms, b/f, cont brfst, cable TV, cot. Free local calls. No pets. Pride Award. $43/S; $48/D; $5/ex prsn. Discs.

NEW YORK

Ogdensburg

Friendship Inn/ US 37 S, Riverside Dr, Ogdensburg NY 13669. 315-393-3730. AE,DC,M,V. I-81, N to SR 12, N to SR 37, N 4 mi. S of Ogdensburg. Nrby rstrnt, pool, cable TV, t pkng, n/s rms, fishing dock. $35-39/S; $35-55/D; $5/ex prsn. Discs.

Palantine Bridge (Canajoharie area)

Friendship Inn/ Box 130 Palantine Bridge NY 13428. 518-673-3233. V,M, AE,DC,D. I-90/ NY Thruway to (Exit 29) SR 10 Toll Plaza. Make 3 rt turns after paying toll. Take SR 5 E to mtl. Nrby rstrnt, fax, cable TV, outlets, n/s rms. $35-40/S; $40-45/D; $4/ex prsn. 5/1-6/30, 9/4-10/31: $40-50/S; $45-55/D. 7/1-9/3: $45-55/S; $55-100/D. Discs.

Pembroke

Econo Lodge/ 8493 SR 77, Pembroke NY 14036. 716-599-4681. V,M,AE,D. I-90 (Exit 48A) at Darien Lakes. Nrby rstrnt, fax, b/f, cable TV, t pkng, outlets, n/s rms. AAA. $39-60/S; $45-60/D; $5/ex prsn. 7/1-9/8: $50-75/S; $65-80/D. Discs.

Port Jervis

Comfort Inn/ Box 3159, Port Jervis NY 12771. 914-856-6611. V,M,AE,DC,D. I-84 (Exit 1) at SR 23. On Greenville Trnpk, just S of I-84 and W of SR 23. Rstrnt/ lounge, pool, mtg rm, b/f, cable TV, n/s rms. Free cont brfst. $38-75/S; $45-75/D; $7/ex prsn. 5/1-10/31: $48-95/S; $55-95/D. Discs.

Poughkeepsie

Econo Lodge/ 426 South Rd, Poughkeepsie NY 12601. 914-452-6600. V, M,AE,DC,D. NY Thruway (Exit 17) to I-84, E to US 9, N 13 mi. Thruway Exit 18 to 44/55, E to US 9 W, turn S across Mid-Hudson Bridge to US 9 S. Rstrnt/ lounge, mtg rm, fax, cable TV, t pkng, n/s rms. Free cont brfst. $43-58/S; $48-61/D; $3/ex prsn. Discs.

Friendship Inn/ 576 South Rd, Poughkeepsie NY 12601. 914-462-4400. V, M,AE,DC,D. I-84 to US 9, N 11 mi to mtl. Rstrnt/ lounge, pool, mtg rm, fax, cable TV, t pkng, n/s rms. No pets. $44-68/S; $47-95/D; $6/ex prsn. 5/18-5/29: $68/S; $68-95/D. Discs.

Ripley

Budget Host Colonial Squire Motel/ Shortman Rd, Ripley NY 14775. 716-736-8000. M,V,AE,D. I-90 (NY Thruway), Exit 61. Cable TV, dd phone, conn rms, rstrnt, mtg rm, pool, wading pool, t pkng, cot, crib. AAA. $36/S; $39/D; $4/ex prsn. 6/1-9/10: $49/S; $52/D. 9/10-10/31: $42/S; $45/D. Disc.

Rochester

Econo Lodge/ 940 Jefferson Rd, Rochester NY 14623. 716-427-2700. V, M,AE. I-390 to SR 252 (Jefferson Rd). Nrby rstrnt, mtg rm, fax, b/f, whrlpool, cable TV, t pkng, laundry, trans, n/s rms. Free cont brfst. AAA. $39-100/S or D; $5/ex prsn. 5/1-11/26: $43-100/S; $47-100/D. Discs.

Wellesley Inn/ 1635 W Ridge Rd, Rochester NY 14615. 716-621-2060/ Fax: 621-7102. AE,M,D,CB,V,DC. Cable TV, microwave, refrig. Free cont brfst. $46/S or D; $5/ex prsn. *Special rates - see discount section in front of book.

Wellesley Inn/ 797 E Henrietta Rd, Rochester NY 14623. 716-427-0130/ Fax: 427-0903. AE,M,D,CB,V,DC. Cable TV, microwave, refrig. Free cont brfst. $48/S or D; $5/ex prsn. *Special rates - see discount section in front of book.

Also see Gates.

Rock Hill Drive

Howard Johnson Lodge/ Box 469, Rock Hill Drive NY 12775. 914-796-3000. V, M,D,AE,DC,CB. SR 17 W, Exit 109, rt at stop sign. N/s rms, rstrnt, pool, exerc equip, in-rm coffee, rstrnt, steambath, micro-fridge, game rm. $49-99/S or D. Discs.

Suffern

Wellesley Inn/ 17 N Airmont Rd, Suffern NY 10901. 914-368-1900/ Fax: 368-1927. AE,M,D,CB,V,DC. Cable TV, microwave, refrig. Free cont brfst. $47/S or D; $5/ex prsn. *Special rates - see discount section in front of book.

Syracuse

John Milton Inn/ 6578 Thompson Rd, Syracuse NY 13206. 315-463-8555/

NEW YORK / NORTH CAROLINA

Fax: 432-9240/ 800-352-1061. V,M, AE,D,DC,CB. At NYS Thruway (I-90), Carrier Circle, Exit 35. N/s rms, cable TV, tt/dd phone, mtg rm, fax, copier, refrig, cot, crib, outlets, t/b/rv pkng, conn rms. Free local calls, cont brfst. AAA/ Mobil. $25-35/S; $32-40/D; $5/ex prsn. Disc: L/s.

Also see East Syracuse, Liverpool.

Tonawanda

Microtel/ One Hospitality Centre Way, Tonawanda NY 14150. 716-693-8100/ Fax: 693-8750/ 800-227-6346. V,M, AE,D,DC,CB. I-290 (Exit 1B) to Delaware Av, take 1st rd on rt (Crestmount Rd) to mtl. N/s rms, cable TV, tt phone, fax, copier, nwspr, crib, conn rms, b/f. AAA. $36/S or D; $4/ex prsn. 5/1-9/30: $40/S or D.

Utica

Howard Johnson Lodge/ 302 N Genesee St, Utica NY 13502. 315-724-4141/ Fax: Ext 195. AE,M,V,D,DC. I-90, Exit 31, over the bridge to Genesee St (dntn). N/s rms, rstrnt, pool, trans, b/t pkng, valet, fax, game rm, laundry. Free cont brfst. $35-75/S; $45-85/D. Discs.

Motel 6/ 150 N Genessee St, Utica NY 13502. 315-797-8743/ Fax: 797-1500. M,V,DC,D,AE. I-90, Exit 31 thru toll, follow Genessee St/Dntn Utica signs, rt on Genessee. Nrby rstrnt, cable TV, n/s rms. Free local calls. Premier Award. $36/S; $42/D; $6/ex prsn. 5/23-10/29: $46/S; $52/D. Disc.

Vesta (Binghamton area)

HoJo Inn/ 3601 Vestal Pkwy E, Vestal NY 13850. 607-739-6182/ Fax: 797-0309. V,M,AE,DC,D,CB. On Hwy 434 W. N/s rms, rstrnt/ lounge, pool, valet, mtg rm. Free cont brfst. $30-45/S; $35-55/D. 9/2-10/31:$35-45/S; $40-50/D. Discs.

Victor

Microtel - Victor/ 7498 Main St, Victor NY 14564. 716-924-9240/ Fax: 924-9241/ 800-278-8884. V,M,AE,D, DC,CB. NY St Thruway I-90 (Exit 45) thru toll booths, take immed rt (Exit 29, SR 96) lt onto 96, rt at 1st light, 1st driveway on rt. N/s rms, satellite TV, video games, TDD, tt/dd phone, fax, copier, refrig, microwave, crib, b pkng, eff, conn rms, b/f. Free coffee. AAA. $32-40/S; $35-45/D; $5/ex prsn. 6/21-10/31: $37-43/S; $40-48/D. Jul/Aug wknds: $40-46/S; $43-51/D. 7/12-7/13, 7/16-7/20, 5/17-5/18: $46-56/S or D. Disc: Family. *Guaranteed rates.*

Watkins Glen

Chieftain Motel/ 3815 State Rte 14, Watkins Glen NY 14891. 607-535-4759/ Fax: 535-4159. V,M,AE,D. 3 mi N of Watkins Glen on Rte 14, at jct of 14 & 14A. Pool, satellite TV, VCR/ movies, tt/dd phone, fax, copier, refrig, microwave, cot, crib, t/b/rv pkng, eff. Free local calls. No pets. AAA. $34-44/S; $34-49/D; $5/ex prsn. 5/25-9/5: $39-49/S; $39-54/D. Spec event wknds: $10 more per room. CLOSED NOV-APR. Disc: L/s.

Williamsville (Buffalo area)

Econo Lodge/ 7200 Transit Rd, Williamsville NY 14221. 716-634-1500. V, M,AE,D. I-90 (NY Thruway/ Exit 49) to SR 78, N to SR 5 (Transit Rd & Main). Rstrnt/ lounge, mtg rm, fax, b/f, cable TV, t pkng, outlets, n/s rms. No pets. AAA. $35-44/S or D; $5/ex prsn. 5/1-6/14, 9/5-12/31: $39-54/S; $39-59/D. 6/15-9/4: $54-74/S or D. Discs.

Howard Johnson Lodge/ 6619 Transit Rd, Williamsville NY 14221. 716-633-1011/ Fax: 633-1171. V,M,D,AE,DC,CB. I-90, Exit 49. N/s rms, b/f, fax. Free deluxe brfst. No pets. $40-100/S; $45-100/D. Discs.

North Carolina

Aberdeen (Pinehurst area)

Motel 6/ 1408 N Sandhills Blvd, Aberdeen NC 28315. 910-944-5633/ Fax: 944-1101. M,V,DC,D,AE. US 1 near jct US 15/501. Nrby rstrnt, cable TV, pool, n/s rms. Free local calls. Premier Award. $28-33/S; $32-37/D; $4/ex prsn. Higher spec event rates. Disc.

Albemarle

Rodeway Inn/ 200 Henson St, Albemarle NC 28001. 704-982-3939. V, M,AE,DC,D. On US 24/27 Bypass, 1 mi

NORTH CAROLINA

E of US 52. Nrby rstrnt, pool, cable TV, n/s rms. Free cont brfst. $46-60/S; $48-60/D; $6/ex prsn. Discs.

Asheville

Econo Lodge/ 190 Tunnel Rd, Asheville NC 28805. 704-254-9521. V,AE,M,DC. I-240 (Exit 6 or 7) at US 74 & 70. Nrby rstrnt, fax, b/f, cable TV, n/s rms, micro/fridge. Free cont brfst. AAA. $35-50/S; $40-55/D; $5/ex prsn. 6/2-9/30: $45-65/S; $50-70/D. 10/1-11/4: $50-70/S; $60-80/D. Discs.

Econo Lodge/ 1430 Tunnel Rd, Box 9676, Asheville NC 28815. 704-298-5519. V,AE,M,DC. I-40 (Exit 55) to US 70 E. Nrby rstrnt, pool, mtg rm, fax, b/f, cable TV, outlets. Free cont brfst. No pets. $31-36/S; $35-41/D; $5/ex prsn. 5/1-6/1: $35-46/S; $39-56/D. 6/2-10/5: $41-86/S; $46-91/D. 10/6-10/28: $51-91/S; $56-96/D. Discs.

Motel 6/ 1415 Tunnel Rd, Asheville NC 28805. 704-299-3040/ Fax: 298-3158. V,M,DC,D,AE. I-40, Exit 55, N to Hwy 70 (Tunnel Rd), turn lt. Nrby rstrnt, cable TV, pool, n/s rms. Free local calls. Premier Award. $28-34/S; $32-38/D; $4/ex prsn. Disc.

Also see Black Mountain, Fletcher.

Battleboro (Rocky Mount area)

Howard Johnson Lodge/ Rte 1, Box 161D, Battleboro NC 27809. 919-977-9595/ Fax: 977-9457. AE,M,V,D,DC. I-95 (Exit 145) at Gold Rock/Rocky Mount ramp. N/s rms, b/f, nrby rstrnt, pool, t pkng, tt phone, mtg rm. Free cont brfst. No pets. $30-55/S; $32-70/D. 5/1-6/25, 9/17-10/31: $30-40/S; $40-50/D; 6/26-9/16: $40-55/S; $40-65/D. Discs.

Motel 6/ Rte 1, Box 162A, Battleboro NC 27809. 919-977-3505/ Fax: 977-1770. M,V,DC,D,AE. I-95, Exit 145, E 1 blk to jct SR 4 & 48, rt on Gold Rock Rd. Nrby rstrnt, cable TV, pool, n/s rms, t pkng. Free local calls. $22/S; $26/D; $4/ex prsn. Disc.

Black Mountain (Asheville area)

Comfort Inn/ 585 SR 9, Black Mountain NC 28711. 704-669-0666. V,M,AE,DC. I-40 (Exit 64) to SR 9, S to mtl. Nrby rstrnt, pool, fax, b/f, cable TV, n/s rms.Free cont brfst. No pets. pets. $34-125/S; $34-139/D; $5/ex prsn. Discs.

Burlington

Motel 6/ 2155 Hanford Rd, Burlington NC 27215. 910-226-1325/ Fax: 570-9158. V,M,AE,DC,D. I-45, Exit 145/ Liberty Exit. Nrby rstrnt, cable TV, pool, n/s rms, t pkng. Free local calls. $30/S; $34/D; $4/ex prsn. Disc.

Super 8 Motel/ 802 Huffman Mill Rd, Burlington NC 27215. 910-584-8787/ Fax: 584-0594. M,V,AE,DC,CB,D. I-85 (Exit 141/ Elon College Exit) turn N on H Mill Rd. B/f, n/s rms, cable TV, cot, crib. Free local calls. No pets. $40/S; $40-44/D. Discs.

Also see Graham.

Canton

Comfort Inn/ Box 866, Canton NC 28716. 704-648-4881. V,M,DC,AE. I-40 (Exit 31) at Buckeye Cove Rd, 20 mi W of Asheville. Nrby rstrnt, pool, mtg rm, fax, b/f, cable TV, outlets, suites. Free cont brfst. No pets. Hospitality Award. AAA. $38-43/S; $48-53/D; $5/ex prsn. 5/1-6/15: $36-40/S; $45-50/D. 6/16-9/30: $50-55/S; $65-70/D. 10/1-10/31: $55-60/S; $70-75/D. Discs.

Econo Lodge/ 55 Buckeye Cove Rd, Canton NC 28716. 704-648-0300. AE, DC,M,V. I-40, Exit 31. Nrby rstrnt, pool, mtg rm, b/f, cable TV, t pkng. Free cont brfst. No pets. AAA. $31-34/S; $38-42/D; $5/ex prsn. 5/1-5/31: $35-39/S; $39-45/D. 6/1-9/30: $39-45/S; $45-58/D. 10/1-10/31: $39-45/S; $50-60/D. Discs.

Charlotte

Comfort Inn/ 5111 I-85 N Service Rd, Charlotte NC 28269. 704-598-0007. V, M,DC,AE. I-85 (Exit 41) at Sugar Creek

Rd. Nrby rstrnt, pool, mtg rm, fax, b/f, whrlpool, cable TV, t pkng, exerc equip. Free cont brfst. No pets. $40-125/S; $44-125/D; $6/ex prsn. Higher spec event rates. Discs.

Comfort Inn/ 4040 S I-85, Charlotte NC 28208. 704-394-4111. V,M,AE,DC,D. I-85 & Little Rock Rd. Nrby rstrnt/ lounge, pool, mtg rm, fax, b/f, cable TV, exerc equip, n/s rms. Free cont brfst, arpt trans. No pets. $44-105/S; $47-105/D; $5/ex prsn. Discs.

Comfort Inn/ 2721 E Independence Blvd, Charlotte NC 28205. 704-375-8444. V,M,DC,AE. US 74 to E Independence Blvd, across from Charlotte Old Coliseum. Nrby rstrnt, pool, mtg rm, fax, cable TV, t pkng, exerc equip. Free cont brfst. No pets. $40-65/S; $45-75/D; $6-10/ex prsn. Higher spec event rates. Discs.

Econo Lodge/ Box 668203 Charlotte NC 28266. 704-394-0172. V,M,AE,DC, D. I-85 & Little Rock Rd. Nrby rstrnt, pool, fax, b/f, cable TV, t pkng, eff, laundry, n/s rms. Free cont brfst. No pets. $32-95/S; $37-95/D; $5/ex prsn. Higher spec event rates. Discs.

Econo Lodge/ Box 26623, Charlotte NC 28213. 704-597-0470/ Fax: 597-0470. V,AE,M,DC. I-85 (Exit 41) Sugar Creek Rd S. 2 mi from I-77. Nrby rstrnt, pool, fax, b/f, cable TV, t pkng. Free cont brfst. No pets. $32-66/S or D; $6/ex prsn. Higher spec event rates. Discs.

HoJo Inn/ 6426 N Tryon St, Charlotte NC 28213. 704-596-0042. V,M,AE,DC, D,CB. On US 29/ Hwy 40. N/s rms, b/f, t pkng, cable TV, fax. Free cont brfst. No pets. Gold Medal Winner. $35-85/S; $38-95/D. Discs.

Howard Johnson Lodge/ 4419 Tuckaseegee Rd, Charlotte NC 28208. 704-393-9881. AE,M,V,D,DC. I-85: Nbnd, Exit 34, lt to stop sign, turn lt; Sbnd, exit at Hwy 27, E to light, turn rt. N/s rms, b/f, pool, cable TV, t/b pkng. Free cont brfst, local calls. No pets. $25-50/S; $33-50/D. Discs.

Motel 6/ 3430 St Vardell Ln, Charlotte NC 28210. 704-527-0144/ Fax: 522-9868. M,V,DC,D,AE. I-85 to I-77, S to Exit 7/Clanton Rd, E to St Vardell Ln,

turn lt. Cable TV, pool, laundry, n/s rms. Free local calls. $30-31/S; $34-35/D; $4/ex prsn. Higher spec event rates. Disc.

Rodeway Inn/ 1416 W Sugar Creek Rd, Charlotte NC 28256. 704-597-5074. V, AE,M,DC. I-85 (Exit 41) at Sugar Creek Rd. Nrby rstrnt, pool, fax, cable TV, n/s rms. Free cont brfst. No pets. $35-50/S; $40-55/D; $3/ex prsn. 5/19-5/29, 10/6-10/8: $70-80/S; $80-90/D. Discs.

Super 8 Motel/ 505 Clanton Rd, Charlotte NC 28217. 704-523-1404/ Fax: 525-6603. V,M,AE,DC,D,CB. I-77 S, Exit 7. B/f, n/s rms, pool, cont brfst, b pkng, copier, fax, cable TV. No pets. $38/S; $38-46/D; $4/ex prsn. Higher spec event rates. Discs.

Super 8 Motel/ 11300 Texland Blvd, Charlotte NC 28273. 704-588-8488 Fax: Ext 171. M,V,AE,DC,CB,D. I-77 (Exit 1) at Westinghouse Blvd, E to Texland Blvd. B/f, n/s rms, cable TV, t/b/rv pkng, mtg rm, TDD, cot. Free local calls, crib. No pets. $37/S; $43-46/D; $6/ex prsn. Discs.

Cherokee

Days Inn/ Box 1865, Cherokee NC 28719. 704-497-9171. V,M,D,AE,DC, CB,JCB. Hwy 19 N. Fax, n/s rms, nrby rstrnt, pool, playgrnd, cot. Chairman's Award. $39-69/S or D; $3/ex prsn. Disc.

Econo Lodge/ Box 2207, Cherokee NC 28719. 704-497-2226. V,M,AE. US 441N to jct Acquoni Rd & Big Cove Rd. Nrby rstrnt, pool, fax, b/f, cable TV, t pkng, n/s rms. Free cont brfst. No pets. AAA. $32-55/S; $37-60/D; $5/ex prsn. 5/1-8/31, 10/1-10/31: $55-85/S; $60-90/D. 9/1-9/30: $45-55/S; $50-60/D. Discs.

Quality Inn/ US 441, Cherokee NC 28719. 800-221-2222 — opening soon. V,M,AE,DC. Dntn Cherokee. Rstrnt, pool, mtg rm, b/f, cable TV, t pkng, n/s rms. Free cont brfst. No pets. $39-69/S; $44-69/D. 5/27-11/5: $49-99/S; $54-99/D. Discs.

Concord

Friendship Inn/ 2451 Kannapolis Hwy, Concord NC 28025. 704-788-8550.

NORTH CAROLINA

V,AE,M,DC. I-85 (Exit 58) at Concord. US 29 & 601 at US 29 Alt. Nrby rstrnt, fax, cable TV, t pkng, copier, refrig, n/s rms. No pets. AAA. $35-45/S; $39-59/D; $4/ex prsn. 3/1-10/31: $39-49/S; $42-54/D. Higher spec event rates. Discs.

Creedmoor

Econo Lodge/ 2574 Lyons Station Rd, Creedmoor NC 27522. 919-575-6451. V,AE,M,DC. I-85 (Exit 191) at Butner-Creedmoor, 15 mi N of Durham. Nrby rstrnt, cable TV, t pkng, n/s rms. Free local calls, AM coffee. No pets. $27-50/S; $33-60/D; $4/ex prsn. Discs.

Cushiers

Laurelwood Mountain Inn/ Box 188, Cushiers NC 28717. 704-743-9939/ 800-346-6846. V,M,AE. On Hwy 107 N at jct Hwy 64. N/s rms, cable TV, playgrnd, dd phone, fax, copier, refrig, microwave, cot, crib, eff. Free local calls, coffee. No pets. AAA. $41-53/S or D; $5/ex prsn. 5/20-9/31: $58-78/S or D. 10/1-10/31: $68-88/S or D. Disc: Senior, family, AAA, l/s. *Guaranteed rates.*

Dunn

Comfort Inn/ 1125 E Broad St, Dunn NC 28334. 910-892-1293/ Fax: 891-1038. V,M,DC,AE. I-95 S (Exit 73) at US 421, first rt to mtl. Rstrnt/ lounge, pool, mtg rm, fax, b/f, satellite TV, t pkng, laundry, n/s rms. Free cont brfst, local calls. $40-55/S; $40-66/D; $5/ex prsn. Discs.

Econo Lodge/ 513 Spring Branch Rd, Dunn NC 28334. 910-892-6181. V,AE,M,DC. I-95, Exit 72. Nrby rstrnt, pool, cable TV, t pkng, n/s rms. Free cont brfst. $36-46/S; $40-50/D; $5/ex prsn. Discs.

Durham

Econo Lodge/ 2337 Guess Rd, Durham NC 27705. 919-286-7746. V,AE,M,DC. I-85 at Guess Rd. Nrby rstrnt, cable TV, t pkng, n/s rms. No pets. $27-29/S; $34-39/D; $5/ex prsn. Discs.

Howard Johnson Lodge/ 1800 Hillandale Rd, Box 2992. Durham NC 27705. 919-477-7381/ Fax: 477-3857. AE, M, V,D,DC. I-85, Hillandale exit. N/s rms, b/f, rstrnt, pool, trans, valet, hospital/ clinic trans. $36-70/S; $40-80/D. Discs.

Super 8 Motel/ 507 E Knox St, Durham NC 27701. 919-688-8888 Fax: 683-2498. AE,M,V,D,DC,CB. I-85 at SR 55, Avondale. B/f, n/s rms, t/b/rv pkng, copier, laundry, elevator, cable TV, mtg rm. Free local calls. $35/S; $35-38/D; $5/ex prsn. 5/10-5/24: $38/S; $43-44/D. Higher spec event rates. Discs.

Fayetteville

Econo Lodge/ Box 65177, Fayetteville NC 28306. 910-433-2100. V,AE,M,DC. I-95, Exit 49. Nrby rstrnt/ lounge, pool, fax, b/f, cable TV, t pkng, n/s rms. Free cont brfst. Hospitality Award. AAA. $42-47/S; $47-57/D; $5/ex prsn. Discs.

Howard Johnson Plaza Hotel/ 1965 Cedar Creek Rd, Fayetteville NC 28302. 910-323-8282/ Fax: 323-4039. V,M,D,AE,DC,CB. I-95, Exit 49. N/s rms, mtg rm, b/f, rstrnt/ lounge, indr pool, sauna, hot tub, exerc equip, satellite TV. Gold Medal Winner. $45-65/S or D. Discs.

Motel 6/ 2076 Cedar Creek Rd, Fayetteville NC 28301. 910-485-8122/ Fax: 485-0701. M,V,DC,D,AE. I-95 (Exit 49) at SR 210/53, E to mtl. Nrby rstrnt, cable TV, pool, n/s rms. Free local calls. Premier Award. $27-29/S; $31-33/D; $4/ex prsn. Disc.

Quality Inn/ 2111 Cedar Creek Rd, Fayetteville NC 28301. 910-323-9850. V,M,DC,AE. I-95 (Exit 49) at SR 53/210 (Cedar Creek Rd). Rstrnt/ lounge, pool, fax, b/f, cable TV, t pkng, n/s rms. Free local calls, full brfst. No pets. $38-42/S; $42-51/D; $6/ex prsn. Discs.

Quality Inn/ Box 64166, Fayetteville NC 28306. 910-485-8135. V,M,AE,DC,D. I-95 Bsns & US 301 S. Rstrnt, pool, mtg rm, fax, cable TV, t pkng, n/s rms. No pets. Hospitality Award. AAA. $40-52/S; $48-52/D; $6/ex prsn. 3/1-4/30, 6/16-10/31: $40-62/S; $48-62/D. Discs.

Also see Spring Lake.

Fletcher (Asheville area)

Econo Lodge/ 196 Underwood Rd, Fletcher NC 28732. 704-684-1200/ Fax: 687-7861. V,M,AE. I-26, Exit 9, E to mtl. Nrby rstrnt, pool, fax, b/f, cable TV, t pkng, dd phone. Free AM coffee, local calls. No pets. AAA. $33-38/S; $33-43/D; $5/ex prsn. 5/1-6/15: $38-60/S; $50-60/D. 6/16-9/28: $50-81/S; $55-86/D. 9/29-10/28: $60-86/S; $60-91/D. Discs.

Gastonia

Econo Lodge/ 1601 Bessemer City Rd, Gastonia NC 28052. 704-867-1821. V, AE,M,DC. I-85 (Exit 14) to SR 274. Nrby rstrnt, pool, mtg rm, fax, b/f, cable TV, t pkng, n/s rms. Free AM coffee. No pets. $33-56/S; $38-66/D; $5/ex prsn. 5/27-5/30, 10/6-10/9: $56/S; $66/D. Discs.

Howard Johnson/ 800 W Franklin Blvd, Gastonia NC 28052. 704-865-3421. V,M,D,AE,DC,CB. I-85: Nbnd (Exit 10A) to Franklin Blvd, 6 mi to mtl; Sbnd to US 321, S to Franklin Blvd, rt to mtl. N/s rms, rstrnt/ lounge, pool, t pkng, fax, copier. No pets. $30-50/S; $36-56/D. Higher spec event rates. Discs.

Motel 6/ 1721 Broadcast St, Gastonia NC 28052. 704-868-4900/ 861-1603. V,M,AE,D,DC. I-85 N or S, Exit 17/ Hwy 321, lt (N) on Hwy 321/ Chester St, lt on Rankin Lake Rd, lt behind Hardy Pantry Shell on Broadcast St, turn rt to motel. Nrby rstrnt, pool, laundry. Premier Award. $28/S; $32/D; $4/ex prsn. Higher spec event rates. Disc.

Motel 6/ 1721 Broadcast St, Gastonia NC 28052. 704-868-4900/ Fax: 861-16 03. AE,D,V,M,DC. I-85 (Exit 17) to US 321, S to Rankin Ln, E to Broadcast St, turn N to mtl. Pool, laundry, nrby rstrnt. Premier Award. $28/S; $32/D; $4/ex prsn. Higher spec event rates. Disc.

Also see Kings Mountain.

Gerton

Mountain Meadows Motel/ Hwy 74A, Box 8, Gerton NC 28735. 704-625-1025. V,M,D. N/s rms, cable TV, refrig, microwave, cot, crib, outlets, eff, conn rms, fishing pond. Free coffee, tea. No pets. AAA. $28-45/S; $30-45/D; $5/ex prsn. 5/1-10/31: $35-50/S; $40-55/D. Disc: L/s. *Guaranteed rates.*

Goldsboro

Econo Lodge/ 704 US 70 Bypass E, Goldsboro NC 27534. 919-736-4510. V,AE,M,DC. US 70 Bypass E to Williams St. Nrby rstrnt, fax, cable TV, t pkng. Free AM coffee. No pets. $31-37/S; $34-43/D; $5/ex prsn. Discs.

Motel 6/ 701 Bypass 70 E, Goldsboro NC 27534. 919-734-4542/ Fax: 734-3503. M,V,DC,D,AE. At jct of US 70 Bypass & Bsns US 117. On service rd N of 70 & E of 117. Nrby rstrnt, cable TV, pool, n/s rms. Free local calls. $27/S; $31/D; $4/ex prsn. Disc.

Graham (Burlington area)

Econo Lodge/ 640 E Harden St, Box 852, Graham NC 27253. 910-228-0231/ Fax: 229-5873. V,AE,M,DC. Jct I-85/ 40 (Exit 148) to SR 54, N to mtl. Nrby rstrnt, fax, cable TV, t pkng. Free AM coffee. $33-43/S; $37-47/D; $5/ex prsn. 5/1-10/31: $35-45/S; $39-49/D. Spec events: $42-52/S; $47-57/D. Discs.

Greensboro

Microtel Greensboro/ 4304 Big Tree Way, Greensboro NC 27409. 910-547-7007/ Fax: 547-0450/ 800-956-7007. V,M,AE,D,DC,CB. I-40 to Wendover Av E exit, lt at 1st lt. Nrby rstrnt, n/s rms, cable TV, tt/dd phone, fax, copier, elevator, microwave, crib, conn rms, b/f. Free coffee. No pets. New. $37-46/S; $42-51/D; $5/ex prsn. 10/17-10/25: $74-78/S or D. 4/18-4/26: $72-76/S or D. Wknd rates may be higher.

Best Inns/ 6452 Burnt Poplar Rd, Greensboro NC 27409. 910-668-9400/ Fax: 668-9331. AE,DC,CB,M,V,D. I-40 or SR 68, Exit 210/ Regional Arpt Rd. Fax, dd/tt phone, b/f, t pkng. Free arpt trans, cont brfst, coffee, crib, local calls. AAA. $40-47/S; $47-54/D; $6/ex prsn. 4/1-12/31: $38-45/S; $45-52/D. Higher spec event rates. Disc: Senior, family.

Econo Lodge/ 3303 Isler St, Greensboro NC 27407. 910-852-4080. V,M, AE. I-40, Exit 217A, High Point Rd, rt at Veasley St, lt on Isler St. Nrby rstrnt, cable TV, n/s rms. Free cont brfst. $35-75/S; $40-75/D; $5/ex prsn. Discs.

Howard Johnson Lodge/ I-85 at Holden Rd, Greensboro NC 27407. 919-299-4612/ Fax: 855-3496. AE,M,V,D,DC. I-

NORTH CAROLINA 196

85, Exit 121. N/s rms, rstrnt/ lounge, pool, t pkng, playgrnd. Free in-rm coffee. No pets. $39-60/S; $45-65/D. Higher spec event rates. Discs.

Motel 6/ 831 Greenhaven Dr, Greensboro NC 27406. 910-854-0993/ Fax: 854-2431. M,V,DC,D,AE. I-85, Exit 122B/122C at Rehobeth Church Rd, E to Greenhaven Dr. Cable TV, pool, n/s rms, t pkng. Free local calls. $25-32/S; $29-36/D; $4/ex prsn. Higher spec event rates. Disc.

Motel 6/ 605 S Regional Rd, Greensboro NC 27409. 910-668-2085/ Fax: 454-6120. M,V,DC,D,AE. I-40 (Exit 210) at SR 68, turn S. Nrby rstrnt, cable TV, pool, n/s rms. Free local calls. Premier Award. $29/S; $33/D; $4/ex prsn. 10/17-10/27: $39/S; $43/D. Higher spec event rates. Disc.

Greenville

Comfort Inn/ 301 SE Greenville Blvd, Greenville NC 27858. 919-756-2792/ Fax: 321-0500. V,M,DC,AE. On US 264 Alt. Nrby rstrnt, pool, mtg rm, fax, b/f, cable TV, t pkng, n/s rms. Free cont brfst. $39-65/S; $45-65/D; $6/ex prsn. Spec events: $65/S or D. Discs.

Howard Johnson/ 702 S Memorial Dr, Greenville NC 27834. 919-758-6400/ Fax: 758-0643. V,M,D,AE,DC,CB. On US 264 at jct of Us 264 & US 13. N/s rms, rstrnt/ lounge, indr pool, rm serv, game rm, whrlpool, b/f. Free hot brfst, lounge coupon, arpt trans. $40-47/S; $47-52/D. Discs.

Super 8 Motel/ 1004 S Memorial Dr, Greenville NC 27834. 919-758-8888/ Fax: 758-0523. M,V,AE,DC,CB,D. On Memorial Dr (US 13) & SR 11, approx 1/4 mi S of Stantonburg Rd. B/f, n/s rms, t/b/rv pkng, cable TV, cot, crib. Free local calls. No pets. $32/S; $37/D; $5/ex prsn. Higher spec event rates. Discs.

Henderson

Budget Host Inn/ 1727 N Garnett St, Henderson NC 27536. 919-492-2013/ Fax: 492-7908. V,AE,CB,DC,D,M. I-85, Exit 215. Cable TV, dd phone, n/s rms, b/f, t pkng, cot. AAA. $32-36/S; $36-44/D; $4/ex prsn. Disc: Senior.

Howard Johnson Lodge/ Drawer F, Henderson NC 27536. 919-492-7001/ Fax: 438-2389. AE,M,V,D,DC. I-85 (Exit 215) at Parham Rd.. N/s rms, rstrnt, pool, t pkng, mtg rm, outlets. No pets. $43-55/S; $48-60/D. Discs.

Hendersonville

HoJo Inn/ Box 2498, Hendersonville NC 28793. 704-692-1446/ Fax: Ext 100. V,M,AE,DC,D,CB. US 25 & Hwy 191. N/s rms, rstrnt/ lounge, pool. No pets. $39-63/S; $43-67/D. Discs.

Quality Inn/ 201 Sugarloaf Rd, Hendersonville NC 28792. 704-692-7231. V,M,AE,DC,D. I-26 (Exit 18A) to US 64. Rstrnt/ lounge, indr pool, mtg rm, b/f, sauna, whrlpool, t pkng, n/s rms. No pets. AAA. $42-85/S or D; $6/ex prsn. 6/1-10/31: $50-95/S or D. Discs.

Hickory

Econo Lodge/ 325 US 70 SW, Box 1821, Hickory NC 28603. 704-328-2111. V,AE,M,DC. I-40 (Exit 125) to Lenoir-Rhyne Blvd, S 1/4 mi to US 70, rt 1 1/2 mi. Rstrnt/ lounge, pool, mtg rm, cable TV, t pkng, fax, n/s rms. Free coffee, nwspr. $33-44/S; $40-44/D; $6/ex prsn. Discs.

HoJo Inn/ 483 Hwy 70, Box 129, Hickory NC 28603. 704-322-1600/ Fax: 327-2041. V,M,AE,DC,D,CB. Hwy 70 & 321. N/s rms, rstrnt/ lounge, pool, exerc equip, trans, t pkng, cable TV, laundry. Free coffee, nwspr. $39-46/S; $46-60/D. Discs.

High Point

Howard Johnson Lodge/ 2000 Brentwood St, High Point NC 27263. 910-886-4141/ Fax: 886-5579. V,M, AE,DC,D,CB. I-85 Bsns Loop to Brentwood St, turn lt to mtl. Rstrnt, b/f, rstrnt/ lounge, pool, t/b pkng, copier, fax, rm serv, mtg rm, valet. $40-55/S; $45-60/D. 10/16-10/26: $140/S or D. Discs.

Motel 6/ 200 Ardale Dr, High Point NC 27260. 910-841-7717/ Fax: 841-7709. M,V,DC,D,AE. US 311 (Main St) to Greenview Terrace, NE to Ardale. Nrby rstrnt, cable TV, pool, n/s rms, t pkng. Free local calls. $25-32/S; $29-32/D; $4/ex prsn. Higher spec event rates. Disc.

NORTH CAROLINA

Jacksonville

Onslow Inn/ 201 Marine Blvd, Jacksonville NC 28540. 910-347-3151/ 346-4000/ 800-763-3151. V,M,AE,D,DC,CB. On Hwy 17 & 24. Pool, n/s rms, cable TV, playgrnd, tt/dd phone, mtg rm, fax, copier, cot, crib, t/b pkng, conn rms, b/f. Free local calls, coffee. Mobil. $38/S; $42/D; $4/ex prsn. Disc: Senior, bsns, TA, govt, trkr, milt, grp. *Guaranteed rates.*

Super 8 Motel/ 2149 N Marine Blvd, Jacksonville NC 28546. 910-455-6888 Fax: 455-3214. V,M,DC,CB,AE,D. On US Hwy 17, 1/2 mi N of Western Blvd. B/f, n/s rms, pool, cable TV, refrig, fax, copier, cot, crib. Free local calls. $43/S; $48-53/D; $5/ex prsn. Higher spec event rates. Discs.

Kenly

Econo Lodge/ Box 577, Kenly NC 27542. 919-284-1000. V,M,AE,DC,D. I-95, jct US 301, exit 107. Nrby rstrnt, pool, b/f, cable TV, t pkng, n/s rms. Free cont brfst. No pets. $36-38/S; $38-42/D; $5/ex prsn. 5/1-10/31: $42-48/S; $48-55/D. Discs.

Kernersville

Sleep Inn/ Heartland Dr, Kernersville NC 27284. 800-221-2222 — opening soon. V,M,AE,DC,D. Jct I-40 Bypass & SR 66. Nrby rstrnt, b/f, cable TV, t pkng, n/s rms, arpt trans. Free nwspr. $42/S; $47/D; $5/ex prsn. 4/25-4/30, 10/18-10/26: $65/S; $75/D. Discs.

Kill Devil Hills (Nags Head area)

Budget Host Inn/ 1003 S Croatan Hwy, Box 2695, MP-9, Kill Devil Hills NC 27948. 919-441-2503. V,M,AE. On Outer Banks approximately 100 mi S of Norfolk, VA. Nrby rstrnt, indr pool, n/s rms, cable TV, tt/dd phone, laundry, microwave, cot, crib, t/b/rv pkng, conn rms, b/f. Free coffee. $30-35/S; $35-55/D; $10/ex prsn. 6/1-8/31: $45/S; $65-75/D. Holidays: $50/S; $75-85/D. Disc: Senior, TA, milt. *Guaranteed rates.*

Comfort Inn/ 401 N Virginia Dare Trail, Drawer 3427, Kill Devil Hills NC 27948. 919-480-2600. V,M,AE,DC,D. Ocean front. Nrby rstrnt, pool, fax, b/f, cable TV, n/s rms, in-rm coffee. Free cont brfst. No pets. AAA. $35-90/S or D; $5/ex prsn. 5/1-5/28: $55-145/S or D. 5/29-9/30: $75-145/S or D. 10/1-10/15: $50-85/S or D. Discs.

Quality Inn/ US 158 Ocean front, Box 325, Kill Devil Hills NC 27948. 919-441-7126. V,M,AE,DC,D. Ocean front at Mi Post 7. Rstrnt/ lounge, indr pool, mtg rm, fax, cable TV, t pkng, exerc equip, refrig, microwave, n/s rms. No pets. $35-60/S or D; $10/ex prsn. 5/1-5/25: $50-75/S or D. 5/26-8/26: $70-120/S or D. 8/27-10/7: $50-100/S or D. Discs.

Kings Mountain (Gastonia area)

Comfort Inn/ 720-A York Rd,, Box 996, Kings Mountain NC 28086. 704-739-7070. V,M,DC,AE. I-85 (Exit 8) at SR 161. Nrby rstrnt, pool, mtg rm, fax, b/f, sauna, cable TV, t pkng, n/s rms. Free cont brfst. No pets. $38-70/S; $43-80/D; $5/ex prsn. Discs.

Lexington

Super 8 Motel/ 1631 Cotton Grove Rd, Lexington NC 27292. 704-352-6444. V,M,AE,DC,D,CB. I-85 (Exit 91) at SR 8, turn E to mtl. B/f, n/s rms, outlets, copier, cable TV, crib, cot. Free local calls. No pets. AAA. $39/S; $42-48/D; $3/ex prsn. Higher spec event rates. Discs.

Lumberton

Econo Lodge/ Box 693, Lumberton NC 28359. 910-738-7121. V,M,AE,D. I-95 (Exit 20) to SR 211, turn N to mtl. Nrby rstrnt, pool, fax, cable TV, t pkng, n/s rms. Free cont brfst, local calls. No pets. $30-59/S or D; $4/ex prsn. 5/1-10/16: $30-69/S or D. Discs.

Howard Johnson Lodge/ 3530 Capuano Dr, Lumberton NC 28358. 910-738-4281/ Fax: 738-1541. AE,M,V,DC. I-95 (Exit 20) to SR 211. N/s rms, b/f, rstrnt, pool, t pkng, mtg rm. Free coffee. No pets. gold Medal Winner. $35-52/S; $38-61/D. Discs.

Motel 6/ 2361 Lackey Rd, Lumberton NC 28358. 910-738-2410/ Fax: 738-8562. M,V,DC,D,AE. I-95 (Exit 19) to Carthage Rd, NE. Mrby rstrnt, cable TV, pool, n/s rms. Free local calls. $23-25/S; $27-29/D; $4/ex prsn. Disc.

NORTH CAROLINA

National 9 Inn/ 3621 Dawn Dr, Box 528, Lumberton NC 28358. 910-738-2481/ Fax: 738-8260. V,M,AE,DC. I-95 & SR 211, Exit 20. Cable TV, pool, adj rstrnt, dd phone, fax. Free cont brfst. $28-36/S; $30-70/D; $4/ex prsn. Higher spec event rates.

Super 8 Motel/ 150 Jackson Crt, Lumberton NC 28358. 910-671-4444. V,M,AE,DC,D,CB. I-95, Exit 22. B/s, n/s rms, copier, fax, nrby rstrnt, cont brfst, cot. Free local calls, crib, nwspr. $43/S; $46-53/D; $5/ex prsn. Higher spec event rates. Discs.

Maggie Valley

Comfort Inn/ 848 Soco Rd, Maggie Valley NC 28751. 704-926-9106. V,M,DC, AE. I-40, Maggie Valley exit, to US 19, S to mtl. Nrby rstrnt, pool, fax, cable TV, n/s rms. Free cont brfst. No pets. Hospitality Award. AAA. $35-55/S; $45-65/D; $8-10/ex prsn. 5/1-10/31: $55-75/S; $65-85/D. Discs.

Morehead City

Comfort Inn/ 3100 Arendell St, Morehead City NC 28557. 919-247-3434. V,M,AE,DC,D. On US 70 E, next to Morehead Plaza; across bridge from Atlantic Beach. Nrby rstrnt, pool, mtg rm, fax, b/f, cable TV, t pkng, n/s rms. Free deluxe cont brfst, local calls, nwspr. No pets. AAA. $29-50/S or D; $5/ex prsn. 3/1-4/30: $35-74/S; $39-74/D. 5/1-9/3: $43-90/S; $50-90/D. 9/4-11/22: $35-81/S; $39-81/D. Discs.

Econo Lodge/ 3410 Bridges St, Box 1229, Morehead City NC 28557. 919-247-2940. V,AE,M,DC. US 70 to 35th, N 1 blk to Bridges. Rstrnt, pool, mtg rm, fax, b/f, cable TV, t pkng, n/s rms. Free cont brfst, nwspr, local calls. No pets. AAA. $27-28/S; $27-33/D; $5/ex prsn. 3/1-4/30: $30-65/S; $35-65/D. 5/1-9/3: $39-82/S; $44-82/D. 9/4-11/22: $32-69/S; $35-69/D. Discs.

Morganton

Sleep Inn/ 2400A S Sterling St, Morganton NC 28655. 704-433-9000. AE,DC,M,V. I-40 (Exit 105) at SR 18. Nrby rstrnt, fax, b/f, cable TV, n/s rms. Free cont brfst. No pets. AAA. Sleep Inn of the Year. $35-39/S; $37-43/D; $5/ex prsn. Discs.

Murphy

Econo Lodge/ 100 Terrace St, Box 756, Murphy NC 28906. 704-837-8880. V, AE,M,DC. US 19/ 129 to US 64E dntn exit, turn N. Rstrnt, mtg rm, fax, cable TV, t pkng, outlets, n/s rms. Free cont brfst. No pets. AAA. $36-44/S; $40-48/D; $6/ex prsn. 5/1-5/25: $36-48/S; $40-52/D. 5/26-10/31: $40-64/S; $46-68/D. Discs.

Nags Head

Sea Foam Motel/ 7111 S Virginia Dare Tr, Nags Head NC 27959. 919-441-7320/ Fax: 441-7324. V,M. On SR 12 at Milepost 16.5. Nrby rstrnt, pool, cable TV, playgrnd, arpt trans, dd phone, fax, refrig, cot, crib, conn rms. Free coffee. No pets. AAA. $42-55/S or D; $5/ex prsn. 5/23-9/7: $72-88/S or D. CLOSED 12/15-2/38.

Comfort Inn/ 8031 Old Oregon Inlet Rd, Box 307, Nags Head NC 27959. 919-441-6315. V,M,AE,DC,D. US 158 Bypass to Milepost 17. Nrby rstrnt, pool, mtg rm, fax, b/f, cable TV, n/s rms. Free cont brfst. No pets. AAA. $35-100/S or D; $10/ex prsn. 5/1-6/8: $50-135/S or D. 6/9-9/2: $115-155/S or D. 9/3-10/28: $45-100/S or D. Discs.

Quality Inn/ 7123 S Virginia Dare Tr, Box 489, Nags Head NC 27959. 919-441-7191. V,M,AE,DC,D. On ocean front at Mi Post 16 1/2. Nrby rstrnt/lounge, pool, fax, cable TV, t pkng, n/s rms. AAA. $32-115/S or D; $8/ex prsn. 5/1-5/21: $45-110/S or D. 5/22-9/10: $50-125/S or D. 9/11-12/31: $32-105/S or D. Discs.

Also see Kill Devil Hills.

New Bern

Days Inn Historic New Bern/ 925 Broad St, New Bern NC 28560. 919-636-0150/ Fax: 636-0773. V,M,AE,D,DC, CB. Hwy 70, Exit Trent Woods to 17 & 55. Pool, n/s rms, cable TV, VCR/movies, games, tt phone, mtg rm, fax, copier, elevator, cot, crib, t/b/rv pkng. Free local calls, cont brfst, coffee. $32/S; $39/D. Discs. *Guaranteed rates*

Pinehurst

See Aberdeen.

NORTH CAROLINA

Raleigh
Econo Lodge/ 5110 Holly Ridge Dr, Raleigh NC 27612. 919-782-3201. V,AE,M,DC. Raleigh Beltline (I-440) to US 70, W 1 1/4 mi to mtl, behind Oak Park. Nrby rstrnt, cable TV, n/s rms. No pets. $34-44/S; $36-46/D; $2/ex prsn. Discs.

Friendship Inn/ 3500 Wake Forest Rd, Raleigh NC 27609. 919-872-9300. V,AE,M,DC. I-440 (Beltline) to Old Wake Forest Rd, N 2 blks to jct with St Albans Dr. Nrby rstrnt, cable TV, coffee. Free crib. No pets. $32/S; $34-38/D; $3/ex prsn. Discs.

Howard Johnson Lodge/ 3120 New Bern Av, Raleigh NC 27610. 919-231-3000/ Fax: 231-3138. V,M,AE,DC,D,CB. I-440 Beltline (Exit 13A) at US 64. On New Bern Av dntn. N/s rms, b/f, exerc equip, fax, cable TV, mtg rm. Free cont brfst. No pets. $44-69/S; $50-75/D. Discs.

Motel 6/ 1401 Buck Jones Rd, Raleigh NC 27606. 919-467-6171/ Fax: 469-8259. M,V,DC,D,AE. I-40, Exit 293 to US 1, S to mtl. Nrby rstrnt, cable TV, pool, n/s rms. t pkng. Free local calls. Premier Award. $34-37/S; $38-41/D; $4/ex prsn. Disc.

Motel 6/ 3921 Arrow Dr, Raleigh NC 27612. 919-782-7071/ Fax: 783-6259. M,V,DC,D,AE. I-440 Nbnd, Exit 7; Sbnd, Exit 7B. On SE side of Crabtree Mall. Cable TV, n/s rms. Free local calls. $32/S; $36/D; $4/ex prsn. Disc.

Roanoke Rapids
Comfort Inn/ Box 716, Roanoke Rapids NC 27870. 919-537-1011. V,M,AE,DC,D. I-95 at (Exit 176) SR 46, 6 mi S of VA state line. Rstrnt, pool, fax, b/f, cable TV, t pkng, exerc equip, n/s rms. Free cont brfst. No pets. AAA. $37-40/S; $48/D; $5/ex prsn. Discs.

Motel 6/ 1911 Weldon Rd, Roanoke Rapids NC 27870. 919-537-5252/ Fax: 537-9469. V,M,AE,D,DC. I-95: Nbnd, Exit 173/ Hwy 158, lt on Weldon Rd/ Hwy 158 (W); Sbnd, rt on Weldon Rd. Nrby rstrnt, pool, laundry, t pkng. $27/S; $31/D; $4/ex prsn. Disc.

Sleep Inn/ I-95 & US 158, Roanoke Rapids NC 27870. 919-537-3141. V,M,AE,DC. I-95 (Exit 173) at US 158. Nrby rstrnt, indr pool, mtg rm, fax, b/f, cable TV, t pkng, n/s rms. Free cont brfst. $40-49/S; $42-52/D; $5/ex prsn. Discs.

Rockingham
Super 8 Motel/ 416 S Hancock St, Rockingham NC 28379. 910-895-5231. V,M,AE,DC,D,CB. On US 1, N of US 74. N/s rms, b/f. $30-33/S; $30-41/D. Discs.

Rocky Mount
Super 8 Motel/ 307 Mosley Crt, Rocky Mount NC 27801. 919-977-2858 Fax: Ext 103. M,V,AE,DC,CB,D. I-95 (Exit 138) to US 64, E to Hwy 301 Bypass, turn N. B/f, n/s rms, toast bar, t/b/rv pkng, cable TV, TDD, cot. Free local calls, crib. No pets. $37/S; $42-50/D; $6/ex prsn. 4/1-9/30: $34/S; $39-41/D. Higher spec event rates. Discs.

Also see Battleboro.

Salisbury
Econo Lodge/ 1011 E Innes St, Salisbury NC 28144. 704-633-8850. V,AE,M,DC. I-85 (Exit 76B) at US 52, lt at 1st traffic light. Rstrnt, pool, cable TV, t pkng, n/s rms. $28-65/S; $36-85/D; $5/ex prsn. Discs.

Rodeway Inn/ 321-R Bendix Dr, Salisbury NC 28146. 704-636-7065. V,M,AE,DC,D. Corner I-85 & US 52 at Exit 76A. Rstrnt, pool, mtg rm, fax, cable TV, n/s rms. Free cont brfst. $42-100/S; $46-100/D; $5/ex prsn. Discs.

Sleep Inn/ 321 Bendix Dr, Salisbury NC 28146. 704-633-5961/ Fax: Ext 602. V,M,AE,D,DC,CB. I-85 (Exit 76A) at US 52. Rstrnt, pool, mtg rm, fax, b/f, cable TV. Free full brfst. $38-75/S; $42-75/D; $4/ex prsn. Discs.

Selma
Comfort Inn/ I-95, Exit 97, Selma NC 27576. 919-965-5200. V,AE,M,DC. I-95 (Exit 97) to Alt US 70, lt on Industrial Park Dr to mtl. Nrby rstrnt, pool, mtg rm, fax, b/f, cable TV, t pkng, exerc equip, outlets, outdoor hot tub. Free cont brfst. No pets. AAA. $42-85/S; $44-85/D; $4/ex prsn. Discs.

NORTH CAROLINA

Smithfield

Howard Johnson Lodge/ Box 1454, Smithfield NC 27577. 919-934-7176/ Fax: 934-6995. V,M,D,AE,DC,CB. I-95, Exit 95. N/s rms, b/f, rstrnt, pool, t pkng, valet serv. Free local calls. Gold Medal Winner. $40-50/S; $50-55/D. Discs.

Spring Lake (Fayetteville area)

Sleep Inn/ 102 Sleepy Dr, Spring Lake NC 28390. 910-436-6700. V,M,AE,DC. On SR 87 at Spring Lake. Nrby rstrnt, pool, mtg rm, fax, b/f, cable TV, t pkng, n/s rms. Free cont brfst. No pets. $40-50/S; $45-60/D; $5/ex prsn. 3/29-9/30: $42-52/S; $47-70/D. Discs.

Super 8 Motel/ 256 S Main St, Spring Lake NC 28390. 910-436-8588 Fax: Ext 171. M,V,AE,D,DC,CB. Hwy 87 (Main St) at jct with 210 (Bragg Blvd). 1 1/2 blks from main gate at Ft Bragg. B/f, n/s rms, cable TV, mtg rm, TDD, cot. Free local calls, crib. No pets. $38/S; $44-50/D; $6/ex prsn. Higher spec event rates. Discs.

Statesville

Best Western Statesville Inn/ 1121 Morland Dr, Statesville NC 28677. 704-873-4000/ Fax: 872-5056. V,M,AE,D, DC. 1 mi S on I-77 from I-40/I-77 jct. I-77, Exit 49A. Pool, cable TV, tt/dd phone, mtg rm, fax, copier, refrig, cot, crib, t/b/rv pkng, eff, conn rms, b/f. Free cont brfst, coffee. No pets. AAA/ Mobil. $43-45/S; $46-48/D. 5/1-10/31: $50/S; $54/D. Higher spec event rates.

Econo Lodge/ 725 Sullivan Rd, Statesville NC 28677. 704-873-5236. V,AE, M,DC. I-40 (Exit 151) at US 21. 1 1/4 mi W of I-77. Rstrnt, pool, fax, b/f, cable TV, t pkng, n/s rms. AAA. $27-41/S; $32-41/D; $5/ex prsn. 4/1-10/31: $34-59/S; $37-59/D. Discs.

Econo Lodge/ 1023 Salisbury Rd, Statesville NC 28687. 704-872-5215. V,AE,M,DC. I-77 (Exit 49B) & Salisbury Rd. Rstrnt/ lounge, pool, mtg rm, cable TV, t pkng, fax, copier, n/s rms. Free cont brfst. $29-41/S; $30-46/D; $5/ex prsn. Discs.

Wadesboro

Friendship Inn/ 1201 E Caswell St, Wadesboro NC 28170. 704-694-4616. V,AE,M,DC. US 74 & 52 S. Nrby rstrnt, fax, cable TV, outlets, n/s rms No pets. AAA. $39-49/S; $42-52/D; $4/ex prsn. 11/1-2/29: $35-45/S; $39-49/D. Discs.

Washington

Econo Lodge/ 1220 W 15th St, Washington NC 27889. 919-946-7781. V,AE,M,DC. US 17 (Ocean Hwy) & US 264, N side of tn. Nrby rstrnt, fax, cable TV, t pkng, n/s rms. Free cont brfst, nwspr. No pets. $33-35/S; $35-41/D; $5/ex prsn. 3/1-4/30: $33-36/S; $41-45/D. 5/1-6/30: $35-41/S; $41-45/D. 7/1-10/31: $36-49/S; $49-53/D. Discs.

Waynesville

Econo Lodge/ 1202 Russ Av, Waynesville NC 28786. 704-452-0353. V,AE, M,DC. Jct of US 276 & 19-74. Nrby rstrnt, pool, fax, b/f, cable TV, n/s rms. Free cont brfst. No pets. AAA. $28-36/S; $36-42/D; $5/ex prsn. 5/1-5/31: $34-37/S; $36-48/D. 6/1-10/31: $37-50/S; $45-59/D. Discs.

Wilkesboro

Quality Inn/ US 421, Wilkesboro NC 28697. 910-667-2176. AE,M,V,D,DC. US 421 & SR 268. Rstrnt/ lounge, pool, mtg rm, fax, b/f, cable TV, t pkng, n/s rms. No pets. $39-85/S; $44-85/D; $5/ex prsn. 3/1-10/31: $42-85/S; $47-85/D. Discs.

Wilmington

Motel 6/ 2828 Market St, Wilmington NC 28403. 910-762-0120/ Fax: 762-0426. M,V,DC,D,AE. I-40/SR 132 to US 17/74 Market St Exit, W to mtl. Nrby rstrnt, cable TV, pool, n/s rms, t pkng. Free local calls. $25-32/S; $29-36/D; $4/ex prsn. Disc.

Rodeway Inn/ 2929 Market St, Wilmington NC 28403. 910-763-3318. V,M,AE,D,DC. US 17 & US 74. Nrby rstrnt, pool, fax, b/f, cable TV, n/s rms. Free cont brfst. AAA. $36-49/S; $45-65/D; $5/ex prsn. 9/5-10/31: $34-40/S; $38-45/D. 11/1-2/29: $30-34/S; $36-42/D. Discs.

Super 8 Motel/ 3604 Market St, Wilmington NC 28403. 919-343-9778 Fax: Ext 100. M,V,AE,DC,CB,D. I-40 (Exit 74) to Hwy 17N (Market St), turn W past Kerr Av to mtl. B/f, n/s rms, b/rv pkng, cable TV, mtg rm, cot. Free local calls, crib. No pets. $34-40/S; $40-48/D; $5/ex prsn. Higher spec event rates. Discs.

Wilson
Comfort Inn/ 4941 US 264 W, Wilson NC 27894. 919-243-6160. V,M,AE,DC,D. I-95 to (Exit 121) US 264, E. 5 mi N of SR 42 on I-95, 6 mi S of US 97. Pool, mtg rm, fax, b/f, t pkng, exerc equip, outlets, n/s rms. Free full or cont brfst. No pets. $45-85/S or D; $6/ex prsn. Discs.

Winston-Salem
Motel 6/ 3810 Patterson Av, Winston-Salem NC 27105. 910-661-1588/ Fax: 767-8354. M,V,DC,D,AE. I-40 to US 52, N 3 1/2 mi, Patterson Av Exit, N to mtl. Cable TV, pool, n/s rms, t pkng. Free local calls. $25-32/S; $29-32/D; $4/ex prsn. Higher spec event rates. Disc.

Yadkinville
Sleep Inn/ Sharon Dr, Box 1175, Yadkinville NC 27055. 910-679-5000. V,M,AE,DC,D. I-77 (Exit 73) to US 421, SE to US 601. I-40 (Exit 188) to US 421, NW to US 601. At jct of US 421 & 601. Nrby rstrnt, pool, mtg rm, fax, b/f, cable TV, t pkng, exerc equip, n/s rms. Free cont brfst. No pets. AAA. $44-65/S; $48-70/D; $5/ex prsn. 4/1-4/30: $65-80/S; $70-85/D. 9/26-10/28: $60-80/S; $65-85/D. Discs.

North Dakota

Beulah
Super 8 Motel/ 720 Hwy 49 N, Beulah ND 58523. 701-873-2850/ Fax: 873-5453. M,V,AE,DC,CB,D. On SR 49, S of SR 200. B/f, n/s rms, outlets, b/t pkng, cable TV, cot. Free local calls,

crib. No pets. AAA. $31/S; $37-41/D; $5/ex prsn. Higher spec event rates. Discs.

Bismarck
Comfort Inn/ 1030 Interstate Av, Bismarck ND 58501. 701-223-1911. V,M,DC,AE. I-94, Exit 159. Nrby rstrnt, lounge, indr pool, mtg rm, b/f, whrlpool, cable TV, t pkng, outlets, game rm. Free cont brfst, trans. AAA. $37-45/S; $45-54/D; $2/ex prsn. Discs.

Expressway Inn/ 200 Bismarck Expressway, Bismarck ND 58504. 701-222-2900/ 800-456-6388. V,M,AE,D, DC. I-94 (Exit 161 or 156) to Bismarck Expressway. At jct 3rd. Pool, whrlpool, cable TV, games, playgrnd, arpt trans, TDD, tt/dd phone, mtg rm, fax, copier, laundry, refrig, elevator, crib, t/b/ pkng, b/f. Free cont brfst, coffee. AAA/ Mobil. $30/S; $39/D; $4/ex prsn. 6/1-10/1: $39/S; $46/D. Disc: Senior, govt, family, trkr, milt, l/s. *Guaranteed rates.*

Kelly Inn Bismrck/ 1800 N 12th St, Bismarck ND 58501. 701-223-8001/ 800-635-3559. V,M,AE,D,DC,CB. I-94, Exit 159, then S 2 blks. Indr pool, whrlpool, n/s rms, cable TV, games, arpt trans, TDD, tt/dd phone, mtg rm, fax, copier, refrig, cot, crib, outlets, t/b/rv pkng, b/f. Free coffee. AAA/ Mobil. $40-44/S; $46/D; $5/ex prsn. 6/1-9/30: $44/S; $51/D. Disc: Senior, bsns, TA, govt, l/s, family, trkr, milt. *Guaranteed rates.*

Motel 6/ 2433 State St, Bismarck ND 58501. 701-255-6878/ Fax: 223-7534. M,V,DC,D,AE. I-94, Exit 159 at US 83, turn N. Cable TV, pool, n/s rms. Free local calls. $26-29/S; $30-33/D; $4/ex prsn. Disc.

Bowman
Budget Host 4-U Motel/ 704 Hwy 12 W, Bowman ND 58623. 701-523-3243/ Fax: 523-3357. AE,M,V,D,DC. On Hwys 12 & 85, W end of tn. Nrby rstrnt, sauna, cable TV, tt/dd phone, fax, copier, nwspr, refrig, cot, crib, outlets, t/b pkng, conn rms. Free local calls. AAA/ Mobil. $22-26/S; $30-40/D; $4/ex prsn.

Super 8 Motel/ Box 675, Bowman ND 58623. 701-523-5613/ Fax: 523-5614. M,V,AE,DC,CB,D. US 12 & US 85. N/s

NORTH DAKOTA

rms, whrlpool, sauna, game rm, outlets, trans, t/b/rv pkng, cable TV, cot. Free local calls, crib. AAA. $29-33/S; $37-43/D; $4/ex prsn. Higher spec event rates. Discs.

Carrington

Super 8 Motel of Carrington/ Hwy 281, Carrington ND 58421. 701-652-3982/ Fax: 652-3984. V,M,AE,DC,D,CB. On Hwy 281, S of Hwy 281 & SR 200-52 exchange. B/f, n/s rms, laundry, outlets, cont brfst, cable TV, t/b/rv pkng, fax, copier, cot, crib. Free local calls. Pride Award. $30/S; $34-38/D; $4/ex prsn. Higher spec event rates. Discs.

Devils Lake

Comfort Inn/ 215 US 2 E, Devils Lake ND 58301. 701-662-6760. AE,DC,M,V. At US 2 & SR 20. Nrby rstrnt, indr pool, mtg rm, fax, b/f, whrlpool, cable TV, t pkng, outlets, game rm, tt phone, hot tub, t pkng, n/s rms. Free cont brfst. AAA. $36-46/S; $42-52/D; $5/ex prsn. Discs.

Days Inn/ Rte 5, Box 8, Devils Lake ND 58301. 701-662-5381/ Fax: 662-3578. V,M,D,AE,DC,CB,JCB. Hwy 20, S of jct of Hwys 2 & 20. Fax, n/s rms, rstrnt, whrlpool, b/f, cable TV, kitchens, cot. Free cont brfst. $34-38/S; $39-45/D; $5/ex prsn. Discs.

Super 8 Motel/ Hwy 2 E, Devils Lake ND 58301. 701-662-8656/ Fax: Ext 285. M,V,AE,DC,CB,D. US 2, E of jct SR 20. B/f, n/s rms, cable TV. Free local calls, cont brfst. $31/S; $40/D; $4/ex prsn. Higher spec event rates. Discs.

Dickinson

Comfort Inn/ 493 Elk Dr, Dickinson ND 58601. 701-264-7300. V,M,DC,AE. I-94 W to (Exit 61) SR 22, lt on Elk Dr to mtl. Nrby rstrnt, indr pool, fax, b/f, whrlpool, cable TV, n/s rms, t pkng, outlets. Free cont brfst. AAA. $28-31/S; $38-46/D; $3/ex prsn. Discs.

Friendship Inn/ 1000 W Villard, Dickinson ND 58601. 701-225-6703. V,AE,M,DC. I-94 (Ebnd, Exit 59; Wbnd, Exit 64) to City Center, follow rte to Villard Ave. Nrby rstrnt, pool, mtg rm, fax, cable TV, outlets, n/s rms. AAA. $27-36/S; $32-43/D; $4-5/ex prsn. 5/1-9/30: $29-40/S; $35-46/D. Discs.

Nodak Motel/ 600 E Villard, Dickinson ND 58601. 701-225-5119. V,M,AE,D. Nbnd, Hwy 22, turn rt after underpass, about 8 blks past Dairy Queen. Sbnd: turn lt before underpass at Hardy's about 8 blks E. Ebnd: Exit 59 to Villard St, about 3 mi on lt. Wbnd: Exit 64, approx 1-1/2 mi on rt. Nrby rstrnt/ lounge, cable TV, dd phone, arpt trans, outlets, b/f, playgrnd, n/s rms, cot, crib, kitchenettes, cont brfst. AAA/ IMA. $23/S; $28-32/D; $2/ex prsn.

Edgeley

Super 8 Motel/ Box 295, Industrial Pk, Edgeley ND 58433. 701-493-2075. V, M,DC,CB,AE,D. Jct US 281 & SR 13. B/f, n/s rms, laundry, outlets, t/b/rv pkng, cont brfst, cable TV, nrby mtg rm. Free local calls. No pets. Pride Award. Quality Award. $32/S; $37-39/D; $8/ex prsn. Higher spec event rates. Discs.

Fargo

Comfort Inn/ 3825 9th Av SW, Fargo ND 58103. 701-282-9596. V,M,AE,DC. I-29 (Exit 64) to 13th Av SW, turn W then N on 38th St to 9th Av SW. Nrby rstrnt, indr pool, fax, b/f, whrlpool, cable TV, outlets, n/s rms. Free cont brfst, arpt trans. AAA. $44-63/S; $47-69/D; $5/ex prsn. Discs.

Comfort Inn/ 1407 35th St S, Fargo ND 58103. 701-280-9666. V,M,DC,AE. I-29 to 13 Av S, E 2 blks to mtl. Nrby rstrnt, indr pool, fax, b/f, whrlpool, cable TV, outlets, n/s rms. Free cont brfst, arpt trans. AAA. $42-56/S; $47-70/D; $5/ex prsn. Discs.

Econo Lodge/ 1401 35th St S, Fargo ND 58103. 701-232-3412. V,AE,M,DC. I-29 (Exit 64) to 13th Av S, W to 34th St, S to 14th, E 1 blk on 35th. Nrby rstrnt, adj water slide, fax, b/f, cable TV, t pkng, outlets, n/s rms. Free cont brfst. AAA. $32-50/S; $37-60/D; $5/ex prsn. Discs.

Motel 6/ 1202 36th St S, Fargo ND 58103. 701-232-9251/ Fax: 239-4482. M,V,AE,D,DC. I-29, Exit 64, Nbnd: cross 13th Av to 36 St, rt to mtl; Sbnd: lt on 38th St, lt on 13th Av to 36th St, rt to mtl. Cable TV, indr pool, n/s rms. Free local calls. $25-27/S; $30-31/D;

NORTH DAKOTA

$4-6/ex prsn. Disc.

Sleep Inn/ 1921 44th St S, Fargo ND 58103. 701-281-8240. V,M,AE,DC,D. I-94 (Exit 348) to 45th St SW, 1 blk E to 44th St. Nrby rstrnt, mtg rm, fax, b/f, cable TV, t pkng, exerc equip, outlets, n/s rms. Free cont brfst. No pets. AAA. $39-59/S; $44-69/D; $4/ex prsn. Discs.

Super 8 Motel/ 3518 Interstate Blvd, Fargo ND 58103. 701-232-9202/ Fax: 232-4543. M,V,AE,DC,CB,D. I-29, Exit 64, turn E. N/s rms, pool, whrlpool, toast bar, mtg rm, laundry, cot, crib. Free local calls. Pride Award. $32-40/S; $39-50/D; $2/ex prsn. Higher spec event rates. Discs.

Grafton

Super 8 Motel/ 948 W 12th St, Grafton ND 58237. 701-352-0888 Fax: 352-0422. M,V,AE,DC,CB,D. W Hwy 17 (in the Pamida Shopping Center). B/f, n/s rms, nrby rstrnt, outlets, t/b/rv pkng, cable TV, mtg rm, cot. Free local calls, crib. No pets. $31/S; $37-40/D; $4/ex prsn. Higher spec event rates. Discs.

Grand Forks

Comfort Inn/ 3251 30th Ave S, Grand Forks ND 58201. 701-775-7503. V,M,AE,DC. I-29 (Exit 138) to 32nd Av (Bsns US 81), E to 34th St, N to 30th Av, E to mtl. Next to Columbia Mall. Nrby rstrnt, indr pool, fax, b/f, whrlpool, cable TV, outlets, n/s rms. Free cont brfst. AAA. $40-56/S; $45-66/D; $6/ex prsn. Discs.

Econo Lodge/ 900 N 43rd St, Grand Forks ND 58201. 701-746-6666. V,AE, M,DC. I-29 to US 2 E, rt on N 43rd to mtl. Nrby rstrnt, fax, b/f, cable TV, t pkng, outlets. Free cont brfst, local calls. AAA. $31-46/S; $36-51/D; $5/ex prsn. 4/1-10/31: $34-49/S; $39-54/D. Discs.

Plainsman Motel/ 2201 Gateway Dr, Grand Forks ND 58203. 701-775-8134. V,M,AE,D. 2 mi E of I-29 on Gateway Dr. Nrby rstrnt, n/s rms, cable TV,dd phone, laundry, refrig, outlets, microwave, cot. Free cont brfst. IMA. $29/S; $36/D; $5/ex prsn. Disc: Family.

Super 8 Motel/ 1122 N 43rd St, Grand Forks ND 58203. 701-775-8138. M, V,AE,DC,CB,D. I-29 (Exit 141) at US 2 (Gateway Dr), turn S on 43rd. B/f, n/s rms, outlets, t/b/rv pkng, copier, cable TV, cot. Free local alls, crib. $37/S; $43-47/D; $6/ex prsn. Higher spec event/ wknd rates. Discs.

Jamestown

Comfort Inn 811 20th St SW, Jamestown ND 58401. 701-252-7125. V,AE, M,DC. I-94 (Exit 258) to US 281, N 1 blk, lt to mtl. Rstrnt, indr pool, mtg rm, fax, b/f, whrlpool, cable TV, outlets, n/s rms. Free cont brfst. AAA. $39-50/S; $44-60/D; $5/ex prsn. Discs.

Mayville

Super 8 Motel/ 34 Center Av S, Mayville ND 58257. 701-786-9081. V, M,AE,DC,D,CB. On SR 18 (Center Av) 1 blk N of jct of Hwys 18 & 200. B/f, n/s rms, laundry, outlets, cont brfst, cable TV, mtg rm. Free local calls. $30/S; $36-38/D; $6/ex prsn. Discs.

Minot

Comfort Inn/ 1515 22nd Av SW, Minot ND 58701. 701-852-2201. V,M,DC,AE. US 2, 52 & US 83 Bypass W. Nrby rstrnt, indr pool, mtg rm, fax, b/f, whrlpool, cable TV, t pkng, outlets, n/s rms. Free cont brfst. $40-60/S; $45-65/D; $5/ex prsn. 9/5-12/31: $35-55/S; $40-60/D. Discs.

Select Inn of Minot/ 225 22nd Av NW, Minot ND 58701. 701-852-3411/ Fax: 852-3450/ 800-641-1000. V,M,AE,D, DC. N/s rms, cable TV, games, tt/dd phones, fax, copier, laundry, microwave, crib, outlets, t/b/rv pkng, eff. Free local calls, cont brfst, coffee. AAA. $29-37/S; $33-37/D; $4/ex prsn. Disc: Senior, bsns, TA, govt, family, trkr, milt, school. *Guaranteed rates.*

Super 8 Motel/ 1315 N Broadway, Minot ND 58701. 701-852-1817. M,V, AE,DC,CB,D. Hwy 83 N. B/f, n/s rms, laundry, outlets, t/b/rv pkng, copier, cable TV, cot. Free local calls, crib. $33/S; $40-45/D; $5/ex prsn. Higher spec event wknd rates. Discs.

Rugby

Econo Lodge/ Box 165, Rugby ND 58368. 701-776-5776. V,AE,M,DC. US 2 & SR 3. Rstrnt/ lounge, indr pool, mtg rm, fax, cable TV, t pkng, outlets, n/s rms. Free cont brfst, nwspr. AAA. $36-50/S; $44-60/D; $6/ex prsn. Discs.

Valley City

Mid Town Motel/ 906 Main St E, Valley City ND 58072. 701-845-2830. V,M. Exit 294, 1st motel in town. N/s rms, cable TV, tt phone, cot, crib, outlets, t pkng. Free coffee. AAA/ Mobil. $22/S; $25-31/D; $3/ex prsn.

Super 8 Motel/ 822 11th St SW, Rte 2, Box 1, Valley City ND 58072. 701-845-1140/ Fax: Ext 259. M,V,AE,DC,CB,D. I-94, Exit 292, lt at service station. N/s rms, outlets, t/b pkng, copier, cable TV, cot. Free local calls. $32-35/S; $38-41/D; $3/ex prsn. Higher spec event rates. Discs.

Wahpeton

Comfort Inn/ 209 13th St S, Wahpeton ND 58075. 701-642-1115. V,M,AE,D,DC,CB. I-29 (Exit 23) to US 81, E 10 mi to 13th St. Nrby rstrnt, indr pool, mtg rm, fax, b/f, whrlpool, cable TV, outlets. Free cont brfst. AAA. $39-56/S; $44-70/D; $5/ex prsn. Discs.

Super 8 Motel/ 995 21st Av N, Wahpeton ND 58075. 701-642-8731. V,M,DC,CB,AE,D. Hwy 210 Bypass. B/f, n/s rms, pool, nrby rstrnt/ lounge, mtg rm, whrlpool, game rm, laundry, copier, outlets, cable TV, exerc equip. Free local calls. Pride Award. AAA. $39/S; $44-48/D; $3/ex prsn. Higher spec event rates. Discs.

Washburn

Scot Wood Motel/ 1323 Frontage Rd, Box 1183, Washburn ND 58577. 701-462-8191. V,M,AE,D,DC. Nrby rstrnt, n/s rms, cable TV, tt phone, fax, copier, cot, crib, outlets, t/b pkng, conn rms, b/f. Free local calls, coffee. AAA/ Mobil. $29/S; $33-36/D; $5/ex prsn. Disc: L/s.

Williston

Super 8 Motel/ 2324 2nd Av W, Williston ND 58801. 701-572-8371/ Fax: 774-8048. M,V,AE,DC,CB,D. Bypass US 85/2. N/s rms, pool, whrlpool, game rm, outlets, t/b/rv pkng, cont brfst, copier, cable TV, cot. Free local calls, crib. AAA. $27/S; $37-40/D. Higher spec event rates. Discs.

Ohio

Akron

Comfort Inn/ 130 Montrose W Av, Akron OH 44321. 216-666-5050/ Fax: 668-2550. V,M,AE,DC. I-77 (Exit 137 B) to SR 18, W. Nrby rstrnt, indr pool, mtg rm, fax, b/f, cable TV, t pkng, n/s rms. Free cont brfst. No pets. AAA. $45-75/S; $45-85/D; $8/ex prsn. Discs.

Alpha (Beavercreek area)

Econo Lodge/ 2220 US 35, Box 108, Alpha OH 45301. 513-426-5822. AE,V,M,DC. On US 35 bet Dayton & Xenia. Cable TV, fax, t pkng, n/s rms. $33-37/S; $37-46/D; $5/ex prsn. Discs.

Amherst (Lorain area)

Motel 6/ 704 N Leavitt Rd, Amherst OH 44001. 216-988-3266/ Fax: 988-3283. M,V,DC,D,AE. OH Turnpike to SR 57 N (Lorain) 1 mi to SR 2 W to SR 58/ Leavitt Rd, rt to mtl. Nrby rstrnt, cable TV, pool, n/s rms. Free local calls. $30-36/S; $36-42/D; $6/ex prsn. Higher spec event rates. Disc.

Ashtabula

Ho Hum Motel/ 3801 N Ridge W, Ashtabula OH 44004. 216-969-1136/ 800-243-1136. V,M,AE,D. I-90, Exit 223 to Rte 45, N to Rte 20, E 1 mi. Cable TV, tt phone, cot, crib, t/b pkng, eff. Free local calls. AAA. $33-40/S; $35-50/D; $5/ex prsn. *Guaranteed rates.*

Athens

Budget Host Coach Inn/ 1000 Albany Rd, Athens OH 45701. 614-594-2294. V,M,AE,D,DC,CB. On Rte 50. N/s rms, cable TV, tt/dd phone, cot, crib, outlets, b pkng, conn rms. Free coffee. No pets. AAA. $34-50/S; $41-65/D;

$4/ex prsn. Spec events: $50/S; $65/D. Disc: Senior, bsns, TA, govt, AAA, AARP, I/s.

Botkins
Budget Host Inn/ Box 478, Botkins OH 45306. 513-693-6911/ Fax: 693-8202. V,M,AE,CB,DC,D. I-75 (Exit 104) at SR 219. Cable TV, dd phone, rstrnt/ lounge, mtg rm, pool, playgrnd, tennis, laundry, cot, t pkng. No pets. $26-31/S; $29-37/D; $3/ex prsn. 4/1-9/30: $29-34/S; $32-40/D. Disc: TA, senior.

Bryan
Plaza Motel/ 02-969 SR 15, Bryan OH 43506. 419-636-3159. V,M,AE,D,DC, CB. On SR 15. Cable TV, tt phone, copier, cot, crib. No pets. AAA. $30-48/S; $35-48/D; $5/ex prsn.

Canton
Comfort Inn/ 5345 Broadmoor Circle NW, Canton OH 44709. 216-492-1331. V,M,DC,AE. I-77 (Exit 109) to Everhard Rd, E to mtl. Nrby rstrnt, pool, mtg rm, fax, b/f, cable TV, t pkng, n/s rms. Free cont brfst. No pets. Hospitality Award. AAA. $45-85/S; $45-91/D; $4/ex prsn. Discs.

Also see North Canton.

Cincinnati
Budget Host Town Center Motel/ 3356 Central Pkwy, Cincinnati OH 45225. 513-559-1600/ Fax: 559-1616. AE,D,M,V. End of I-74 (Central Pkwy) or I-75 (Exit 3) at Hopple St. Cable TV, family rms, n/s rms, lounge, pool, game rm, t pkng, cot. $42-48/S; $43-63/D; $3/ex prsn. 4/1-5/16, 9/15-10/31: $39-44/S; $42-49/D. 11/1-3/31: $37-42/S; $40-47/D. Spec events: $74-81. Disc: Senior, AAA, AARP, trkr, milt, TA.

Howard Johnson Lodge/ 400 Glensprings Dr, Cincinnati OH 45246. 513-825-3129/ Fax: 825-0467. M,DC,D,V,AE, CB. I-275, Exit 41 at SR 4, S 1 mi to Glensprings Dr, rt 1/2 blk. Rstrnt/ lounge, mtg rm, b/f, pool. Free cont brfst, nwspr, coffee. $41-53/S; $48-60/D. Discs.

Motel 6/ 3960 Nine Mile Rd, Cincinnati OH 45255. 513-752-2262/ Fax: 753-3190. M,V,AE,DC,D. I-275, Exit 65, E on SR 125 to Nine Mile Rd, rt to mtl. Nrby rstrnt, cable TV, pool, n/s rms. Free local calls. $28-32/S; $34-38/D; $6/ex prsn. Disc.

Quality Inn/ 5589 Kings Mills Rd, Box 425, Cincinnati OH 45034. 513-398-8075. V,M,AE,DC. I-71 N (Exit 25) at Kings Mills, W to mtl. Across from Kings Island Amusement Pk. Rstrnt/ lounge, pool, mtg rm, cable TV, t pkng, n/s rms. $35-114/S or D; $8/ex prsn. Discs.

Quality Inn/ 1717 Glendale Milford Rd, Cincinnati OH 45215. 513-771-5252. V, M,AE,D,DC. I-75 (Exit 14) to Woodlawn/Evendale, turn W on SR 126 (Glendale Milford Rd) to mtl. Rstrnt/ lounge, pool, indr pool, mtg rm, fax, sauna, cable TV, n/s rms. No pets. AAA. $46-50/S; $48-56/D; $5/ex prsn. 5/1-5/25: $44-48/S; $46-53/D. 5/26-9/3: $59-68/S; $62-73/D. Discs.

Also see Sharonvi

Cleveland

See Macedonia, Middleburg Heights, Richfield.

Clyde
Winesburg Motel/ 214 E McPherson Hwy, Clyde OH 43410. 419-547-0531. V,M,AE,D. Us Rte 20, 1/2 blk E of jct SR 101. Nrby rstrnt/ lounge, n/s rms, cable TV, tt phone, refrig, t pkng. Free local calls. No pets. AAA. $28-45/S; $35-49/D; $5/ex prsn. 5/1-10/1: Sun-Thur: $35-55/S or D. Fri. Sat: $59-89/S or D. Disc: Senior, bsns, trkr.

Columbus
Cross Country Inn/ 6225 Zumstein Dr, Columbus OH 43229. 614-848-3918/ Fax: 848-6980. V,M,AE,D,DC. I-71, Exit 117. Pool, n/s rms, cable TV, TDD, tt/dd phone, mtg rm, fax, copier, elevator, crib, conn rms, b/f. Free local calls, coffee. No pets. AAA. $35-42/S; $42-49/D. Discs.

Cross Country Inn/ 4875 Sinclair Rd, Columbus OH 43229. 614-431-3670/ Fax: 431-7261. V,M,AE,D,DC. I-71, Exit 116. Pool, n/s rms, cable TV, TDD, tt/dd phone, fax, copier, crib, conn rms, b/f.

Free local calls, coffee. No pets. AAA. $35-42/S; $42-49/D. Discs.

Econo Lodge/ 920 Wilson Rd, Columbus OH 43204. 614-274-8581. AE,M,V,DC. I-70 (Exit 94) to Wilson Rd. I-270 (Exit 93) to I-70, E 1/2 mi. Adj rstrnt/ lounge, fax, b/f, cable TV, t pkng, outlets, n/s rms. Free coffee, cont brfst, nwspr. AAA. $33-41/S; $46-66/D; $5/ex prsn. 5/1-10/31: $36-46/S; $51-66/D. Discs.

HoJo Inn/ 1070 Dublin-Grandview Av, Columbus OH 43215. 614-486-4554. M,DC,D,V,AE,CB. I-70: Ebnd, Grandview Av Exit, rt 1 blk; Wbnd to 315 N, exit Dublin Rd, 1 mi on rt. Cable TV, movies, n/s rms, mtg rm, nrby rstrnt, t pkng. Free cont brfst. No pets. $40-47/S; $46-58/D. Discs.

Motel 6/ 1289 E Dublin-Granville Rd, Columbus OH 43229. 614-846-9860/ Fax: 846-6563. M,V,DC,D,AE. I-71, Exit 117 to Hwy 161, E to mtl. Nrby rstrnt, cable TV, n/s rms. Free local calls. $27-30/S; $33-36/D; $6/ex prsn. Disc.

Motel 6/ 5910 Scarborough Blvd, Columbus OH 43232. 614-755-2250/ Fax: 860-9090. M,V,DC,D,AE. I-70 to Brice Rd, S to Scarborough Blvd, rt 1/4 mi to mtl. Nrby rstrnt, cable TV, laundry, pool, n/s rms. Free local calls. $26-30/S; $32-36/D; $6/ex prsn. Disc.

Motel 6/ 5500 Renner Rd, Columbus OH 43228. 614-870-0993/ Fax: 870-3548. M,V,AE,DC,D. I-70, Exit 91B to Rome Hilliard Rd, N to Renner Rd, lt to mtl. Nrby rstrnt, cable TV, pool, n/s rms. Free local calls. $28-30/S; $34-36/D; $6/ex prsn. Disc.

Quality Inn/ 4801 E Broad St, Columbus OH 43213. 614-861-0321/ Fax: 861-8360. AE,V,M,DC. I-270 N (Exit 39) to Broad St, W to mtl. Rstrnt/ lounge, pool, mtg rm, fax, b/f, cable TV, n/s rms. Free arpt trans. AAA. $39-67/S; $45-75/D; $8/ex prsn. 5/1-9/30: $39-69/S; $47-77/D. Discs.

Also see Dublin, Grove City, Hilliard, Worthington.

Curtice

Econo Lodge/ 10530 Corduroy Rd, Curtice OH 43412. 419-836-2822. V, M,AE,D,DC. I-280 (Exit 7) to SR 2, E 10 mi, N on Teachout Rd to Corduroy Rd. Rstrnt/ lounge, fax, b/f, cable TV, t pkng, outlets. AAA. $35-45/S; $45-55/D; $6/ex prsn. 3/16-8/31: $49-55/S; $55-65/D. Discs.

Dayton

Econo Lodge/ 2221 Wagoner Ford Rd, Dayton OH 45414. 513-278-1500. AE,M,V,DC. I-75 (Exit 57B) at Wagoner Ford Rd. 3 mi S of I-70. Adj rstrnt, pool, cable TV, t pkng, game rm, n/s rms. $31-51/S; $35-61/D; $4/ex prsn. Discs.

Motel 6/ 7130 Miller Ln, Dayton OH 45414. 513-898-3606/ Fax: 890-3898. M,V,DC,D,AE. I-70 to I-75S, Exit 60/ Little York Rd, turn W, turn lt on Miller Ln 1/4 mi. Nrby rstrnt, cable TV, laundry, pool, n/s rms. Free local calls. $26-28/S; $32-34/D; $6/ex prsn. Disc.

Also see Englewood, Miamisburg.

Dublin

Budgetel Inns/ 6145 Park Center Circle, Dublin OH 43017. 614-792-8300/ Fax: 792-3333. V,M,D,AE,DC, CB. I-270, Exit 15 E on Tuttle Crossing Blvd, lt on Paul Blazer Pkwy, lt on Park Center Circle. N/s rms, b/f, fax. Free cont brfst, in-rm coffee, local calls. AAA. $37-49/S; $44-56/D. 3/29-9/2: $39-51/S; $46-58/D. Higher spec event rates. Discs.

Cross Country Inn/ 6364 Frantz Rd, Dublin OH 43017. 614-764-4545/ Fax: 764-0520. V,M,AE,D,DC. I-270, Exit 17A. Nrby rstrnt, pool, n/s rms, cable TV, TDD, tt/dd phone, mtg rm, fax, copier, crib, conn rms, b/f. Free local calls, coffee. No pets. AAA. $36-42/S; $42-49/D. Discs.

Eaton

Econo Lodge/ I-70 & US 127, Eaton OH 45320. 513-456-5959. M,V,AE,DC. I-70 (Exit 10) to US 127. Adj rstrnt, mtg rm, fax, cable TV, n/s rms. Free local calls, cont brfst. AAA. $33-36/S; $41-44/D; $4/ex prsn. Discs.

Elyria

Comfort Inn/ 739 Leona St, Elyria OH 44035. 216-324-7676. AE,V,M,DC. I-80 (Exit 8) to SR 57, N to Griswald Rd, turn W to mtl. I-90 (Exit 145A) to SR 57, S to Griswald Rd, W to mtl. Nrby rstrnt, mtg rm, fax, b/f, cable TV, t pkng, n/s rms. Free cont brfst. AAA. $40-60/S; $46-66/D; $6/ex prsn. 5/1-6/22: $44-80/S; $50-86/D. 6/23-8/31: $54-90/S; $60-96/D. Discs.

Econo Lodge/ 523 Griswold Rd, Elyria OH 44035. 216-324-3911. V,M,AE,D, DC. 1/4 mi N of OH Tnpk (I-80) & 1/4 mi S of SR 2 & 90, exit SR 57. Nrby rstrnt, pool, mtg rm, fax, b/f, cable TV. No pets. $29-37/S; $35-43/D; $6-10/ex prsn. 5/1-9/3: $36-80/S; $42-88/D. Discs.

Englewood (Dayton area)

Cross Country Inn/ 9325 N Main St, Englewood OH 45415. 513-836-8339/ Fax: 836-1772. V,M,AE,D,DC. I-70 & SR 48, Exit 29. Nrby rstrnt, pool, n/s rms, cable TV, TDD, tt/dd phone, fax, copier, crib, conn rms, b/f. Free local calls, coffee. No pets. AAA. $34-39/S; $41-46/D. Discs.

Motel 6/ 1212 S Main St, Englewood OH 45322. 513-832-3770/ Fax: 832-0128. M,V,AE,DC,D. I-70, Exit 29 to SR 48, N 1/4 mi, rt at Bob Evans Rstrnt to mtl. Nrby rstrnt, cable TV, pool, n/s rms. Free local calls. $26-29/S; $32-35/D; $6/ex prsn. Disc.

Findlay

Cross Country Inn/ 1951 Broad Av, Findlay OH 45840. 419-424-0466/ Fax: 424-1043. V,M,AE,D,DC. I-75 & SR 224, Exit 159. Nrby rstrnt, pool, n/s rms, cable TV, TDD, tt/dd phone, fax, copier, crib, conn rms, b/f. Free local calls, coffee. No pets. AAA. $36-42/S; $43-49/D. Discs.

Econo Lodge/ 316 Emma St, Findlay OH 45840. 419-422-0154. V,M,D,AE. I-75 (Exit 157) to SR 12 W. Nrby rstrnt, fax, cable TV, outlets, n/s rms. $28-55/S; $33-60/D; $5/ex prsn. Discs.

Franklin (Middletown area)

Comfort Inn/ 3458 Commerce Dr, Franklin OH 45005. 513-420-9378/ Fax: 422-4387. V,M,AE,DC. I-75 (Middletown Exit 32) to SR 122 E, lt to mtl. Nrby rstrnt, pool, fax, b/f, cable TV, t pkng, refrig, n/s rms. Free cont brfst. AAA. $36-58/S; $39-68/D; $5/ex prsn. 6/1-9/30: $48-79/S; $53-89/D. Discs.

Howard Johnson Lodge/ 6475 Culbertson Rd, Franklin OH 45005. 513-424-3551/ Fax: Ext 262. V,M,AE,D, DC,CB. I-75 (Ext 32) to SR 122, W to Culbertson Access Rd. Lounge, n/s rms, b/f, pool, t pkng, laundry, mtg rm, VCR, refrig. Free local calls, cont brfst, nwspr. No pets. $45-55/S; $48-55/D. Discs.

Fremont

Friendship Inn/ 3660 N SR 53, Fremont OH 43420. 419-332-5548. M,V,AE,DC. I-80 (Ohio Trnpk/ Exit 6) to SR 53, N 1/2 mi. Nrby rstrnt, cable TV, t pkng, n/s rms. Free cont brfst. No pets. $28-32/S; $28-38/D; $5/ex prsn. 5/1-6/1, 8/27-12/31: $32-58/S; $38-58/D. 6/2-8/26: $45-85/S; $55-85/D. Discs.

Gallipolis

Econo Lodge/ 260 Jackson Pike, Gallipolis OH 45631. 614-446-7071. V,M,AE,D,DC. US 35, exit SR 160, adj to Holzer Medical Ctr. Adj rstrnt, fax, b/f, cable TV, t pkng. Free cont brfst, coffee. No pets. $37-46/S; $46-56/D; $5/ex prsn. 10/12-10/15: $51-60/S; $60-70/D. Discs.

Girard (Youngstown area)

Econo Lodge/ 1615 E Liberty St, Girard OH 44420. 216-759-9820. AE,M,V,DC. I-80 to SR 193 (Belmont Av). At jct of Liberty & Belmont. Adj rstrnt, b/f, cable TV, t pkng, n/s rms. Free coffee, local calls. $30-38/S; $34-45/D; $5/ex prsn. 5/1-10/31: $34-42/S; $38-49/D. Discs.

Motel 6/ 1600 Motor Inn Dr, Girard OH 44420. 216-759-7833/ Fax: 759-0691. M,V,DC,D,AE. I-76 E take I-80 E to Exit 229/ Belmont Av/ SR 193, lt on Liberty St, rt on Motor Inn Dr. Nrby rstrnt, cable TV, pool, n/s rms. Free local calls. $24-26/S; $30-32/D; $6/ex prsn. Disc.

Grove City (Columbus area)

Comfort Inn/ 4197 Marlane Dr, Grove City OH 43123. 614-539-3500. V, M, AE,D,DC,CB. I-71 (Exit 100) to Stringtown Rd, turn W to Marlane. I-270 S to I-71 S. Nrby rstrnt, indr pool, mtg rm, fax, b/f, sauna, whrlpool, cable TV, exerc equip, n/s rms. Free cont brfst. No pets. $39-49/S; $44-54/D;

$5/ex prsn. 5/1-10/31: $49-54/S; $54-59/D. Discs.

Heath (Newark area)

Howard Johnson Lodge/ 775 Hebron Rd, Heath OH 43055. 614-522-3191/ Fax: 522-4396. M,DC,D,V,AE,CB. Wbnd 161 or 16 E, Exit Rte 79 S. Rte 40 or I-70 to Rte 79 N. Cable TV, n/s rms, mtg rm, rstrnt/ lounge, indr pool, exerc equip, refrig. Free cont brfst. $35-52/S; $43-63/D. 4/1-4/30: $44-70/S; $54-75/D. Discs.

Hilliard (Columbus area)

Motel 6/ 3950 Parkway Ln, Hilliard OH 43026. 614-771-1500/ Fax: 529-8259. M,V,AE,DC,D. I-270, Exit 13 to Hilliard-Cemetery Rd, W to Parkway Ln, lt to mtl. Nrby rstrnt, cable TV, pool, n/s rms, t pkng. Free local calls. $28-30/S; $34-36/D; $6/ex prsn. Disc.

Holland

Cross Country Inn/ 1201 E Mall Dr, Holland OH 43528. 419-866-6565/ Fax: 866-6608. V,M,AE,D,DC. I-475 & Airport Hwy/ SR 2 W, Exit 8. Nrby rstrnt/ lounge, pool, n/s rms, cable TV, TDD, tt/dd phone, fax, copier, crib, conn rms, b/f. Free local calls, coffee. No pets. AAA. $33-38/S; $40-45/D. Discs.

Huron (Sandusky area)

Comfort Inn/ 2119 W Cleveland Rd, Huron OH 44839. 419-433-5359. V,M,AE,DC. I-80 (Exit 7) to US 250, N to SR 2, turn E to mtl. Nrby rstrnt, pool, fax, cable TV, t pkng, outlets, n/s rms. Free cont brfst. No pets. AAA. $33/S; $39/D; $6/ex prsn. 5/1-6/30: $39-99/S or D. 7/1-8/26: $89-129/S or D. 8/27-9/30: $49-99/S or D. Discs.

Lebanon

Best Western Heritage Inn/ 674 N Broadway, Lebanon OH 45036. 513-932-4111/ Fax: 932-3333. V,M,AE,D,DC,CB. I-75, Exit 29, lt on Hwy 63, 7 mi, lt at T jct. I-71, Exit #28, rt on Hwy 48 3 mi, lt on Monroe, lt on Broadway. Pool, n/s rms, cable TV, satellite TV, tt/dd phone, mtg rm, fax, copier, refrig, cot, crib. Free local calls, coffee. AAA, Mobil. $35/S; $45/D; $5/ex prsn. 5/1-9/9: $55/S; $65/D. Discs. *Guaranteed rates.*

Lima

Comfort Inn/ 1210 Neubrecht Rd, Lima OH 45801. 419-228-4251. V,M,AE,D,DC,CB. I-75 (Exit 127) to SR 81, W to Neubrecht Rd. Rstrnt/ lounge, pool, mtg rm, fax, b/f, cable TV, t pkng, n/s rms. Free cont brfst. No pets. $43-47/S; $48-54/D; $5/ex prsn. Discs.

Days Inn/ 1250 Neubrecht Rd, Lima OH 45801. 419-227-6515/ Fax: 228-5378. AE,V,M,DC,D. I-75/ 81 W, Exit 127. Rstrnt/ lounge, pool, b/f, t pkng, game rm, picnic area, cot. Free local calls. AAA. $30-36/S; $39-44/D; $3/ex prsn. Discs.

Econo Lodge/ 1201 Neubrecht Rd, Lima OH 45801. 419-222-0596. V,M,AE,D,DC. I-75 (Exit 127) to SR 81, W to mtl. Rstrnt/ lounge, pool, mtg rm, fax, b/f, cable TV, t pkng, exerc equip. $42-43/S; $47-52/D; $5/ex prsn. Discs.

Motel 6/ 1800 Harding Hwy, Lima OH 45804. 419-228-0456/ Fax: 228-4630. M,V,DC,D,AE. I-75, Exit 125/125A to SR 309, E to mtl. Adj rstrnt, cable TV, n/s rms, t pkng. Free local calls. $26-30/S; $32-36/D; $6/ex prsn. Disc.

Macedonia (Cleveland area)

Motel 6/ 311 E Highland Rd, Macedonia OH 44056. 216-468-1670/ Fax: 467-9189. M,V,DC,D,AE. I-271 & SR 8, turn S to Highland. Nrby rstrnt, cable TV, pool, n/s rms. Free local calls. $32-36/S; $38-42/D; $6/ex prsn. Higher spec event rates. Disc.

Mansfield

Econo Lodge/ 1017 Koogle Rd, Mansfield OH 44903. 419-589-3333. V,M,D,AE. I-71 (Exit 176) to US 30, turn E to Koogle Rd. Rstrnt, pool, mtg rm, fax, cable TV, t pkng, outlets, n/s rms. AAA. $34-40/S; $38-44/D; $6/ex prsn. 5/1-10/15: $36-65/S; $42-72/D. Discs.

Marietta

Econo Lodge/ 702 Pike St, Marietta OH 45750. 614-374-8481. V,M,AE,D,DC,CB. I-77 (Exit 1) to SR 7, N 1 blk. Nrby rstrnt, pool, cable TV. Free cont brfst, local calls. $40-50/S; $44-54/D; $5/ex prsn. Discs.

Maumee

Cross Country Inn/ 1704 Tollgate Dr, Maumee OH 43537. 419-891-0880/ Fax: 891-1017. V,M,AE,D,DC. OH Turnpike & US 20, Exit 4. I-475, Exit 6. Nrby rstrnt, pool, n/s rms, cable TV, TDD, tt/dd phone, fax, copier, crib, conn rms, b/f. Free local calls. No pets. AAA. $30-38/S; $37-45/D. Discs.

Miamisburg (Dayton area)

Motel 6/ 8101 Springboro Pike, Miamisburg OH 45342. 513-434-8750/ Fax: 434-6734. M,V,DC,D,AE. I-75, Exit 44 to Hwy 725, E 2 blks to Hwy 741, rt 2 blks to mtl. Adj rstrnt, cable TV, pool, n/s rms, t pkng. Free local calls. $26-28/S; $32-34/D; $6/ex prsn. Disc.

Middleburg Heights (Cleveland area)

Motel 6/ 7219 Engle Rd, Middleburg Heights OH 44130. 216-234-0990/ Fax: 234-3475. M,V,DC,D,AE. I-71, Exit 235 to Bagley Rd, W 2 blks to Engle Rd, turn S. Nrby rstrnt, cable TV, n/s rms. Free local calls. $32-36/S; $38-42/D; $6/ex prsn. 12/21-5/22: $36-40/S; $42-46/D. Higher spec event rates. Disc.

Milan (Sandusky area)

Comfort Inn/ 11020 US 250, Milan OH 44846. 419-499-4681. V,M,AE,DC. I-80/I-90 (OH Trnpk/ Exit 7) to US 250 (Milan Rd), N 1 blk to mtl. Nrby rstrnt, pool, indr pool, fax, b/f, sauna, whrlpool, cable TV, t pkng, family rms, n/s rms. Free cont brfst. AAA. $36-46/S; $41-51/D; $3/ex prsn. 5/1-6/15: $41-150/S; $46-150/D. 6/16-9/10: $88-250/S or D. 9/11-10/14: $41-108/S; $46-108/D. Discs.

HoJo Inn/ 12110 US 250, Milan OH 44846. 419-499-4955/ Fax: 499-4091. M,V,AE,DC,D. I-90 (Exit 7) at US 250 S. Rstrnt/ lounge, n/s rms, pool, t pkng, mtg rm. No pets. Free local calls. $25-50/S; $35-55/D. 5/1-6/30: $45-75/S or D. 7/1-9/4: $80-125/S or D. 9/5-10/31: $25-65/S; $30-65/D. Discs.

Monroe

Cross Country Inn/ 1900 Welcome Way, Monroe OH 48161. 313-289-2330/ Fax: 289-3683. V,M,AE,D,DC. I-75 & SR 50, Exit 15. Nrby rstrnt, pool, n/s rms, cable TV, TDD, tt/dd phone, fax, copier, crib, conn rms, b/f. Free local calls, coffee. No pets. AAA. $35-40/S; $42-47/D. Discs.

New Philadelphia

Motel 6/ 181 Bluebell Dr SW, New Philadelphia OH 44663. 216-339-6446/ Fax: 339-7436. M,V,DC,D,AE. I-77, Exit 81/ New Philadelphia, E on SR 39, rt on Bluebell Dr. Nrby rstrnt, cable TV, pool, n/s rms. Free local calls. $30-32/S; $36-38/D; $6/ex prsn. 12/21-5/22: $36/S; $42/D. Disc.

North Canton (Canton area)

Motel 6/ 6880 Sunset Strip Av NW, N Canton OH 44720. 216-494-7611/ Fax: 494-5366. V,M,AE,DC,D. I-77, Exit 111 to Portage St, turn W. Nrby rstrnt, cable TV, pool, n/s rms. Free local calls. $30-34/S; $36-40/D; $6/ex prsn. Disc.

North Lima (Youngstown area)

Comfort Inn/ 10076 Market St, N Lima OH 44452. 216-549-2187/ Fax: 549-0275. V,M,AE,DC. I-76 (Ohio Turnpike/ Exit 16) to SR 7, N 1/4 mi to mtl. Rstrnt, pool, fax, b/f, cable TV, VCR, n/s rms, family rms. Free cont brfst, nwspr. AAA. $43-60/S or D; $4/ex prsn. 5/1-10/31: $49-65/S or D. Discs.

Norwalk

Econo Lodge/ 342 Milan Av, Norwalk OH 44857. 419-668-5656. AE,V,M,DC. I-80 (OH Trnpk, Exit 7) to I-250, S 4 mi. Adj rstrnt, pool, mtg rm, fax, b/f, cable TV, copier, n/s rms. Free cont brfst. No pets. AAA. $33-38/S; $38-48/D; $5/ex prsn. 5/19-6/29: $33-78/S; $38-88/D. 6/30-9/3: $48-88/S; $53-88/D. Discs.

Perrysburg (Toledo area)

Howard Johnson Lodge/ I-280 & Hanley Rd, Perrysburg OH 43551. 419-837-5245/ Fax: Ext 159. V,M,AE,D,DC,CB. OH Trnpk (80/90), Exit 5, N on I-280 to (Exit 1B) Hanley Rd. Rstrnt/ lounge, n/s rms, b/f, indr pool, t pkng, sauna, exerc area. $33-50/S; $39-50/D. Discs.

Piqua

HoJo Inn/ 902 Scot Dr, Piqua OH 45356. 513-773-2314/ Fax: 778-1763. M,V,AE,DC,D. I-75 (Exit 82) at US 36. On W side of I-75. Lounge, n/s rms, pool, mtg rm, fax. Free cont brfst. $29-

OHIO

39/S; $35-45/D. Discs.

Port Clinton

Comfort Inn/ 1723 E Perry St, Pt Clinton OH 43452. 419-732-2929. V,M,DC,AE. On waterfront. SR 2 to SR 163 (Perry St), W to mtl. Nrby rstrnt, pool, fax, b/f, whrlpool, cable TV, n/s rms. Free cont brfst. No pets. AAA. $40-90/S or D; $10/ex prsn. 5/1-5/18, 9/5-10/29: $60-100/S or D. 5/19-9/4: $100-150/S or D. Discs.

Richfield (Cleveland area)

Howard Johnson/ 5171 Brecksville Rd, Richfield OH 44286. 216-659-6116/ Fax: Ext 163. M,DC,D,V,AE,CB. OH Turnpike (Rte 80) E or W, take Exit 11 S toward Cleveland. Rstrnt/ lounge, exerc equip, t pkng, b/f, cable TV. Free cont brfst. Gold Medal Winner. $33-46/S; $41-56/D. Discs.

Sandusky

Comfort Inn/ 5909 Milan Rd, Sandusky OH 44870. 419-621-0200. V,M,DC,AE. US 250 & SR 2 jct at Sandusky/ Norwalk Exit. Nrby rstrnt, pool, indr pool, fax, sauna, whrlpool, cable TV, t pkng. Free cont brfst. No pets. AAA. $36-100/S; $36-140/D; $4/ex prsn. 5/1-6/8, 9/11-10/31: $36-150/S; $41-175/D. 6/9-9/10: $78-275/S or D. Discs.

Econo Lodge/ 1904 Cleveland Rd, Sandusky OH 44870. 419-627-8000. AE,M,V,D. I-80 (OH Tnpk, Exit 7) to US 250, N to US 6. Rstrnt/ lounge, pool, b/f, cable TV, n/s rms. Free coffee. No pets. AAA. $30/S or D; $5/ex prsn. 5/1-5/27: $30-90/S or D. 5/28-6/17: $50-98/S or D. 6/18-9/30: $70-115/S or D. Discs.

Friendship Inn/ 1021 Cleveland Rd, Sandusky OH 44870. 419-626-6852. AE,V,M,DC. US 6 & US 250, 1/2 mi W of Cedar Point entrance. Rstrnt, indr pool, cable TV, n/s rms. No pets. $25-40/S; $30-45/D; $5/ex prsn. 5/1-6/30: $40-80/S; $45-85/D. 7/1-9/3: $70-130/S; $75-130/D. 9/4-9/30: $25-65/S; $30-65/D. Discs.

Friendship Inn/ 3309 Milan Rd, Sandusky OH 44870. 419-626-8720. AE,V,M,DC. US 250, 2 mi S of Cedar Point entrance. Rstrnt, pool, cable TV, n/s rms. No pets. $25-45/S; $30-50/D;

$5/ex prsn. 5/1-6/30: $45-90/S; $50-90/D. 7/1-9/3: $80-140/S or D. 9/4-9/30: $25-65/S; $30-65/D. Discs.

HoJo Inn/ 2809 Milan Rd, Sandusky OH 44870. 419-626-3742. V,M,AE,D, DC,CB. On US 250, just N of jct with Hwy 2. Pool, n/s rms. No pets. Gold Medal Winner. $25-55/S; $30-55/D. 5/1-6/30: $39-69/S or D. 7/1-9/4: $75-125/S or D. Discs.

Howard Johnson Lodge/ 1932 Cleveland Rd, Sandusky OH 44870. 419-625-1333. V,M,AE,D,DC,CB. 1/2 mi E of SR 250 on SR 6. Adj rstrnt, cable TV, pool, n/s rms. Free cont brfst. No pets. $25-65/S; $30-65/D. 5/1-6/30: $45-75/S or D. 7/1-9/4: $80-125/S or D. Discs.

Quality Inn/ 3304 Milan Rd, Sandusky OH 44870. 419-626-2838. AE,V,M,DC. I-80/90 to US 250, N 8 mi to mtl. SR 2 to US 250, N 2 mi to mtl. Rstrnt, pool, fax, b/f, cable TV. No pets. $34-44/S; $38-48/D; $6/ex prsn. 5/1-6/8: $34-150/S or D. 6/9-9/10: $78-230/S or D. 9/11-10/31: $34-98/S or D. Discs.

Rodeway Inn/ 2905 Milan Rd, Sandusky OH 44870. 419-625-1291. M,V,AE, DC. I-80 & I-90 (Ohio Trnpk/ Exit 7) to US 250, N 8 mi to mtl. Rstrnt/ lounge, pool, fax, cable TV, n/s rms. $36-46/S; $41-51/D; $3/ex prsn. 5/1-6/8: $36-180/S; $41-180/D. 6/9-9/10: $78-250/S or D. 9/11-10/31: $36-108/S; $41-128/D. Discs.

Also see Huron, Milan.

Seville (Lodi area)

Comfort Inn/ 4949 Park Av W, Seville OH 44273. 216-769-4949. V,M,DC,AE. I-71 to I-76, E 1 1/2 mi to SR 3, N to mtl. Nrby rstrnt, indr pool, mtg rm, fax, b/f, cable TV, t pkng, exerc equip, whrlpool, family rm, n/s rms. Free cont brfst. No pets. AAA. $35-60/S; $40-60/D; $5/ex prsn. 5/1-9/30: $53-80/S; $58-80/D. Discs.

HoJo Inn/ Box 125, Seville OH 44273. 216-769-2053/ Fax: 769-4609. M,V,AE,DC,D. I-71 S (Exit 209) to I-76, W to US 224/ SR 19, turn N to mtl. Rstrnt, n/s rms, t pkng. $30-34/S; $35-39/D. Discs.

Sharonville (Cincinnati area)

Motel 6/ 2000 E Kemper Rd, Sharonville OH 45241. 513-772-5944. M,V,DC,D,AE. I-75 to I-275, E to Mosteller Rd, S to E Kemper Rd, turn rt to mtl. Nrby rstrnt, cable TV, laundry, pool, n/s rms. Free local calls. $26-30/S; $32-36/D; $6/ex prsn. Disc.

Motel 6/ 3850 Hauck Rd, Sharonville OH 45241. 513-563-1123/ Fax: 563-8242. AE,V,M,DC,D. I-275 (Exit 46) to US 42, N to Hauck Rd. Adj rstrnt, cable TV, pool, n/s rms. Free local calls. $28-32/S; $34-38/D; $6/ex prsn. Disc.

Sidney

Econo Lodge/ 2009 W Michigan St, Sidney OH 45365. 513-492-9164. AE, M,V,DC. I-75 (Exit 92) to US 47 (Michigan St) W. Rstrnt/ lounge, pool, mtg rm, fax, cable TV, t pkng, n/s rms. No pets. $32-36/S; $42-48/D; $5/ex prsn. Discs.

South Point

Comfort Inn/ 70 Private Rd, S Point OH 45680. 614-377-2786. V,M,AE,D,DC. US 52 at Delta Lane. Rstrnt/ lounge, pool, mtg rm, cable TV, t pkng, n/s rms. $35-55/S; $40-70/D; $5/ex prsn. 5/1-9/5: $40-60/S; $45-75/D. Discs.

Stow

Stow Inn/ 4601 Darrow Rd, Stow OH 44224. 216-688-3508. V,M,D. On SR 91. Rstrnt, pool, whrlpool, n/s rms, cable TV, playgrnd, TDD, tt phone, refrig, cot, crib, outlets, t/b/rv pkng, eff, b/f. Free local calls, coffee. AAA. $40-63/S; $47-63/D; $7/ex prsn. 5/16-9/14: $47-70/S; $54-70/D. Disc: Senior, bsns, family, milt, AAA, l/s.

Toledo

Motel 6/ 5335 Heatherdowns Blvd, Toledo OH 43614. 419-865-2308/ Fax: 868-6180. M,V,DC,D,AE. I-80/90, Exit 4 to US 20, N to Heatherdowns Blvd; turn W. Nrby rstrnt, cable TV, n/s rms. Free local calls. Premier Award. $26-30/S; $32-36/D; $6/ex prsn. Disc.

Upper Sandusky

Comfort Inn/ 105 Comfort Dr, Upper Sandusky OH 43351. 419-294-3891. V,M,AE,D,DC,CB. US 23 to US 30, W to mtl. Nrby rstrnt, mtg rm, fax, b/f, cable TV, n/s rms. Free cont brfst. No pets. $44-95/S; $48-99/D; $5/ex prsn. Discs.

Vandalia

Cross Country Inn/ 550 E National Rd, Vandalia OH 45377. 513-898-7636/ Fax: 898-0630. V,M,AE,D,DC. I-75 & SR 40, Exit 63. Nrby rstrnt, pool, n/s rms, cable TV, TDD, tt/dd phone, fax, copier, elevator, crib, conn rms, b/f. Free local calls, coffee. No pets. AAA. $36-41/S; $43-48/D. Discs.

Washington Court House

Knights Inn/ 1820 Columbus Av, Washington Court House OH 43160. 614-335-9133/ Fax: 333-7938. V, M,AE,D,DC,CB. Nrby rstrnt/ lounge, cable TV, tt/dd phone, mtg rm, fax, copier, refrig, microwave, crib, conn rms. Free local calls, coffee. No pets. AAA/ Mobil. $41/S; $47/D; $6/ex prsn. Disc: Senior, TA, govt, AAA, AARP. *Guaranteed rates.*

Westerville

Cross Country Inn/ 909 S State St, Westerville OH 43081. 614-890-1244/ Fax: 890-0983. V,M,AE,D,DC. I-270, Exit 29. Nrby rstrnt, pool, n/s rms, cable TV, TDD, tt/dd phone, fax, copier, crib, conn rms, b/f. Free local calls, coffee. No pets. AAA. $36-42/S; $42-49/D. Discs.

Winchester

Budget Host Inn/ 18760 State Rte 136, Winchester OH 45697. 513-695-0381. V,M,AE,D,DC,CB. Jct SR 136 & Hwy 32, N side turnoff. Nrby rstrnt, cable TV, fax, t pkng, cot. Free crib. No pets. $34/S; $39-42/D. Spec events: $30-40/S; $36-41/D. Disc: Senior.

Wooster

Econo Lodge/ 2137 Lincoln Way E, Wooster OH 44691. 216-264-8883. AE,M,V,DC. On US 30, 1 mi E of Wooster. Rstrnt, indr pool, mtg rm, fax, b/f, whrlpool, cable TV, t/b pkng, exerc equip, outlets, laundry, n/s rms. Free local calls, cont brfst. AAA. $32-39/S; $35-42/D; $4/ex prsn. 4/1-10/31: $35-42/S; $38-45/D. Discs.

Worthington (Columbus area)

Econo Lodge/ 50 E Wilson Bridge Rd, Worthington OH 43085. 614-888-3666. V,M,D,AE. I-270, exit US 23 S, lt at first light on Wilson Bridge Rd. Nrby rstrnt, cable TV, t pkng, n/s rms. Free coffee. No pets. $32-43/S; $41-56/D; $5/ex prsn. Di

Youngstown

See Girard, North Lima.

Oklahoma

Ardmore

Motel 6/ 120 Holiday Dr, Ardmore OK 73401. 405-226-7666/ Fax: 223-5710. M,V,DC,D,AE. I-35, Exit 31A E to US 70, immed lt at Holiday Dr. Nrby rstrnt, cable TV, laundry, pool, n/s rms. Free local calls. $25/S; $31/D; $6/ex prsn. Disc.

Broken Arrow

Econo Lodge/ 1401 N Elm Pl, Broken Arrow OK 74012. 918-258-6617/ Fax: 251-5660. AE,M,V,DC. SR 51 (Broken Arrow Expwy) at 161st St (N Elm). Nrby rstrnt, fax, cable TV, n/s rms. Free local calls, incoming fax, cont brfst, nwspr. AAA. $37-42/S; $40-46/D; $5/ex prsn. Discs.

Chandler

Econo Lodge/ 600 N Price, Chandler OK 74834. 405-258-2131/ Fax: 258-3090. AE,V,M,DC. I-44, Exit 18. Rstrnt, pool, mtg rm, fax, cable TV, t pkng, n/s rms. Free local calls. AAA. $36-42/S; $38-45/D; $5/ex prsn. Discs.

Checotah

Budget Host I-40 Inn/ I-40 & Hwy 69, Checotah OK 74426. 918-473-2331.
AE,D,M,V. I-40 (Exit 265) at Hwy 69, S 1 blk. Cable TV, dd phone, n/s rms, adj rstrnt, laundry, t pkng, outlets. $24-30/S; $28-38/D; $4/ex prsn.

Clinton

Comfort Inn/ 2247 Gary Frwy, Clinton OK 73601. 405-323-6840/ Fax: 323-4067. M,V,AE,DC. I-40, Exit 65. Rstrnt, pool, fax, b/f, cable TV, outlets, n/s rms. Free cont brfst. No pets. AAA. $35-47/S; $40-57/D; $5/ex prsn. 5/1-10/31: $35-52/S; $40-62/D. Discs.

Elk City

Budget Host Inn/ I-40 & Hwy 34, Elk City OK 73664. 405-225-4020. AE, D,M,V. I-40, Exit 41. Cable TV, dd phone, n/s rms, cafe, arpt trans, t pkng, cot, crib. $24/S; $29-31/D; $5/ex prsn. Disc: Senior.

Econo Lodge/ 108 Meadow Ridge, Elk City OK 73644. 405-225-5120/ Fax: 225-0908. AE,V,M,DC. I-40 (Exit 38) to SR 6 (2nd exit). Nrby rstrnt, cable TV, t pkng, dd phone, n/s rms. $29-32/S; $35-40/D; $4/ex prsn. Discs.

HoJo Inn/ 2604 E Hwy 66, Elk City OK 73644. 405-225-2241/ Fax: 225-2246. V,M,AE,D,DC,CB. I-40 (Exit 41) to Hwy 66, W to jct of Hwy 34 & Hwy 66. Fax, b/t pkng, n/s rms. Free cont brfst, nwspr. $28-30/S; $37-39/D. Discs.

Motel 6/ 2500 E Hwy 66, Elk City OK 73644. 405-225-6661/ Fax: 243-4201. M,V,DC,D,AE. I-40, Exit 41 to Bsns 40, W to mtl. Cable TV, laundry, pool, n/s rms, t pkng. Free local calls. $22-23/S; $28-29/D; $6/ex prsn. Disc.

Quality Inn/ 102 BJ Hughes Access Rd, Box 1025, Elk City OK 73648. 405-225-8140. M,V,AE,DC. I-40 (Exit 38) to SR 6, S 500 ft. Nrby rstrnt, indr pool, fax, b/f, cable TV, t pkng, n/s rms. Free cont brfst. AAA. $32-36/S; $40-52/D; $4/ex prsn. Discs.

Enid

Econo Lodge/ 2523 Mercer Dr, Enid OK 73701. 405-237-3090. AE,V,M,DC. US 81, 2 mi S of jct US 64 & US 60. Nrby rstrnt, fax, cable TV, t pkng, n/s rms. $31-35/S; $39-43/D; $3/ex prsn. Discs.

OKLAHOMA

Guymon
Econo Lodge/ 923 US 54E, Guymon OK 73942. 405-338-5431. V,M,AE,D, DC. Jct US 54, US 64 & SR 3. Nrby rstrnt, b/f, cable TV, n/s rms. $37-42/S; $42-46/D; $4/ex prsn. Discs.

Henryetta
HoJo Inn/ US 75 & Trudgeon Rd, Henryetta OK 74437. 918-652-4448. V,M, AE,D,DC,CB. On E side of US 75, 2/10 mi N of jct of I-40 & Indian Ntn Trnpk. I-40, Exit 240B. Pool, n/s rms, t pkng. Free cont brfst, local calls. No pets. $35-40/S; $40-50/D. Discs.

Lawton
Howard Johnson Hotel/ 1125 E Gore Blvd, Lawton OK 73501. 405-353-0200/ Fax: 353-6801. M,DC,D,V,AE,CB. I-44 N or S to Gore Blvd exit. Rstrnt/ lounge, indr pool, sauna, mtg rm, jog area, exerc equip, tennis. $41-61/S; $46-66/D. Discs.

McAlester
Comfort Inn/ 1215 George Nigh Expwy, Box 1532, McAlester OK 74502. 918-426-0115. V,M,DC,AE. US 69 S Bypass, 2 1/2 mi SW of US 270. Rstrnt, pool, fax, cable TV, t pkng, n/s rms. Free cont brfst. AAA. $38-75/S; $42-75/D; $4/ex prsn. Discs.

Also see Savannah.

Midwest City (Oklahoma City area)
Motel 6/ 6166 Tinker Diagonal, Midwest City OK 73110. 405-737-6676/ Fax: 737-2216. M,V,DC,D,AE. I-40, Exit 156A/156B to Hudiburg Dr, S to Tinker Diagonal. Cable TV, laundry, pool, n/s rms, t pkng. Free local calls. $25-27/S; $31-33/D; $6/ex prsn. Disc.

Moore (Oklahoma City area)
Motel 6/ 1417 N Moore Av, Moore OK 73160. 405-799-6616/ Fax: 799-5053. M,V,DC,D,AE. On W side of I-35, Exit 118, at N 12th St. Just S of I-40 jct with I-35. Nrby rstrnt, cable TV, laundry, pool, n/s rms. Free local calls. $23-24/S; $27-28/D; $4/ex prsn. Disc.

Muskogee
Econo Lodge/ 2018 W Shawnee Av, Muskogee OK 74401. 918-683-0101. AE,M,V,DC. From I-40, take SR 69 to SR 62/16, E 1 mi. Rstrnt, fax, cable TV, t pkng, outlets, n/s rms. Free cont brfst. No pets. $35-45/S; $45-60/D; $4/ex prsn. Discs.

Motel 6/ 903 S 32nd St, Muskogee OK 74401. 918-683-8369/ Fax: 683-9155. M,V,DC,D,AE. US 69 to Estelle St, W to mtl. Cable TV, laundry, pool, n/s rms, t pkng. Free local calls. $26/S; $32/D; $6/ex prsn. Disc.

Quality Inn/ 2300 E Shawnee Av, Muskogee OK 74403. 918-683-6551.V,M, DC,AE. US 69 or US 165 (Muskogee Trnpk) to US 62 at York St. E of dntn. Rstrnt/ lounge, pool, mtg rm, fax, cable TV, t pkng, n/s rms. $36-41/S; $42-47/D; $5/ex prsn. 6/1-9/30: $41-46/S; $47-52/S. Discs.

Oklahoma City
Econo Lodge/ 8200 W I-40, Oklahoma City OK 73128. 405-787-7051. AE,M, V,DC. S side of I-40, just W of Council Rd, Exit 142. Nrby rstrnt, pool, fax, b/f, cable TV, t pkng, outlets, n/s rms, eff. Free local calls. $30-40/S; $37-47/D; $6/ex prsn. Discs.

Econo Lodge/ 820 S MacArthur Blvd, Oklahoma City OK 73128. 405-947-8651. AE,DC,M,V. I-40 (Exit 144) to MacArthur, S 1/2 mi. Rstrnt/ lounge, pool, fax, b/f, cable TV, t pkng, n/s rms. $30-40/S; $35-45/D; $5/ex prsn. Discs.

Econo Lodge/ 7412 N Bryant, Oklahoma City OK 73111. 405-478-0205. AE,V,M,DC. I-35, N Wilshire Blvd exit to Bryant St. Nrby rstrnt, fax, b/f, cable TV, t pkng, n/s rms. $29-39/S; $34-44/D; $4/ex prsn. Discs.

Econo Lodge/ 1307 SE 44th St, Oklahoma City OK 73129. 405-672-4533. AE,V,M. I-35 S (Exit 123B) to SE 44th St. Rstrnt, n/s rms. No pets. $29-34/S; $34-46/D; $4/ex prsn. Discs.

Howard Johnson Lodge/ 5301 N Lincoln Blvd, Oklahoma City OK 73105. 405-528-7563/ Fax: 528-0425. M,V, AE,DC,D. I-44 to Lincoln Blvd, State Capitol Exit. Rstrnt/ lounge, n/s rms, pool, trans, t pkng, laundry, refrig, fax, copier, cable TV, mtg rm. Free cont brfst. $39-85/S or D. Discs.

OKLAHOMA

Howard Johnson/ 1629 S Prospect, Oklahoma City OK 73129. 405-677-0551/ Fax: 677-3417. V,M,AE,D,DC,CB. 1 blk S of jct of I-35 & I-40 on SE 15th and I-35. Cable TV, n/s rms, b/f, pool, fax, laundry. Free cont brfst. $42-52/S; $48-58/D. Discs.

Motel 6/ 11900 NE Expwy, Oklahoma City OK 73131. 405-478-8666/ Fax: 478-7442. M,V,DC,D,AE. I-35, Exit 137 to 122nd St. On frontage rd, E side of frwy. Nrby rstrnt, cable TV, laundry, pool, n/s rms, t pkng. Free local calls. $25-26/S; $31-32/D; $6/ex prsn. Disc.

Motel 6/ 820 S Meridian Av, Oklahoma City OK 73108. 405-946-6662/ Fax: 946-4058. V,M,AE,DC,D. I-40, Exit 145 to Meridian Av, S to mtl. Cable TV, laundry, pool, n/s rms. Free local calls. $30/S; $36/D; $6/ex prsn. Disc.

Motel 6/ 4200 W I-40, Oklahoma City OK 73108. 405-947-6550/ Fax: 947-0970. V,M,AE,DC,D. I-40, Exit 145, to access rd across Meridian 2 blks to mtl. Nrby rstrnt, cable TV, pool, elevator, n/s rms, t pkng. Free local calls. Premier Award. $32/S; $38/D; $6/ex prsn. Disc.

Motel 6/ 12121 NE Expwy, Oklahoma City OK 73131. 405-478-4030/ Fax: 478-4158. AE,V,M,DC,D. I-35, Exit 137, lt on NE 122nd St, lt on frontage rd to mtl. Nrby rstrnt, cable TV, laundry, pool, elevator, n/s rms, t pkng. Free local calls. $27-29/S; $33-35/D; $6/ex prsn. Disc.

Rodeway Inn/ 4601 SW 3rd St, Oklahoma City OK 73128. 405-947-2400/ 800-292-7929. AE,M,V,DC. I-40 (Exit 145) to Meridian Av, N 1 blk to SW 3rd, turn lt. Nrby rstrnt, pool, fax, b/f, cable TV, n/s rms. Free cont brfst. $36-65/S; $40-65/D; $4/ex prsn. Discs.

Also see Midwest City, Moore, Yukon.

Ponca City

Econo Lodge/ 212 S 14th St, Ponca City OK 74601. 405-762-3401/ Fax: 762-4550. AE,V,M,DC. I-35 N or S to SR 60, E 14 mi to SR 77 N, turn lt. Rstrnt, pool, mtg rm, fax, cable TV, t pkng, n/s rms. No pets. $27-30/S; $33-39/D; $4/ex prsn. Discs.

Purcell

Econo Lodge/ 2500 US 74 S, Purcell OK 73080. 405-527-5603. AE,V,M,DC. I-35 (Exit 91) to US 74 S. Rstrnt, cable TV, t pkng, outlets, n/s rms. Free coffee, local calls. AAA. $34-37/S; $40-45/D; $5/ex prsn. Discs.

Sallisaw

Econo Lodge/ 2403 E Cherokee, Sallisaw OK 74955. 918-775-7981. V,M, AE,D,DC. I-40, exit 311. Nrby rstrnt/ lounge, mtg rm, fax, b/f, cable TV, t pkng, n/s rms. $34-36/S; $39-41/D; $10/ex prsn. 5/1-8/31: $45-49/S; $48-53/D. Discs.

Savannah (McAlester area)

Budget Host Colonial Inn/ US Hwy 69, Savanna OK 74565. 918-548-3506/ Fax: 423-7565. V,AE,CB,DC,D,M. US 69 at Indian Nation Trnpk. Cable TV, dd phone, n/s rms, family rms, adj rstrnt, picnic area, arpt trans, t pkng, outlets. $24/S; $26-30/D; $2/ex prsn. Disc: Senior.

Shawnee

Budget Host Inn/ Hwy 177 & Acme Rd, Shawnee OK 74801. 405-275-8430. V, AE,CB,DC,D,M. I-40 (Exit 181) to Hwy 177, S 2 mi. Cable TV, dd phone, n/s rms, nrby rstrnt, t pkng. No pets. AAA. $30-32/S; $32-48/D; $4/ex prsn. Disc: Senior.

Econo Lodge/ 5107 N Harrison St, Shawnee OK 74801. 405-275-6720. AE,V,M,DC. I-40 (Exit 186) to SR 18; 1 blk N. Nrby rstrnt, cable TV, t pkng, outlets, n/s rms. No pets. AAA. $37-50/S; $43-60/D; $4/ex prsn. Discs.

Motel 6/ 4981 N Harrison St, Shawnee OK 74801. 405-275-5310/ Fax: 275-6370. M,V,AE,DC,D. I-40, Exit 186 to Shawnee-Meeker exit, N 1/4 mi on SR 18 (Harrison St), rt at Kettle Rstrnt. Nrby rstrnt, cable TV, pool, n/s rms, t pkng. Free local calls. Premier Award. $29/S; $35/D; $6/ex prsn. Disc.

Rodeway Inn/ 12510 Valley View Rd, Shawnee OK 74801. 405-275-1005. V, M,D,AE. I-40, Exit 192 (Earlsboro). Nrby rstrnt, fax, b/f, cable TV, t pkng, n/s rms. Free local calls. $30-34/S; $34-38/D; $3/ex prsn. 5/1-10/31: $32-

37/S; $35-41/D. 11/1-12/31: $27-30/S; $32-34/D. Discs.

Stillwater

Motel 6/ 5122 W 6th Av, Stillwater OK 74074. 405-624-0433/ Fax: 624-0315. M,V,DC,D,AE. I-35, Exit 174 to SR 51, E 12 mi to mtl. Nrby rstrnt, cable TV, laundry, pool, n/s rms, t pkng. Free local calls. $24-26/S; $30-32/D; $6/ex prsn. Disc.

Tulsa

Comfort Inn/ 4717 S Yale Av, Tulsa OK 74135. 918-622-6776/ Fax: 622-1809. V,M,DC,AE. I-44 (Exit 229) at Yale Ave. Nrby rstrnt, pool, mtg rm, fax, b/f, cable TV, t pkng, n/s rms. Free cont brfst. AAA. $39-45/S; $45-60/D; $5/ex prsn. Discs.

Days Inn/ 1016 N Garnett Rd, Tulsa OK 74116. 918-438-5050/ Fax: 438-8314. V,M,AE,D,DC,CB. I-244, Exit Garnett Rd, 1 1/2 blks. Nrby rstrnt/ lounge, n/s rms, cable TV, arpt trans, tt phone, fax, copier, cot, crib, conn rms, b/f. Free local calls, cont brfst, coffee. $29-34/S; $34-39/D; $5/ex prsn. Discs. *Guaranteed rates.*

Econo Lodge/ 11620 E. Skelly Dr, Tulsa OK 74128. 918-437-9200. AE,V,M. I-44 (Exit 235) at 11th St. Rstrnt/ lounge, indr pool, mtg rm, fax, b/f, cable TV, t pkng, n/s rms. Free cont brfst, arpt trans, nwspr. No pets. AAA. $34-43/S; $38-53/D; $5/ex prsn. 5/1-10/31: $36-50/S; $40-55/D. Discs.

Howard Johnson Plaza Hotel/ 17 W 7th St, Tulsa OK 74119. 918-585-5898/ Fax: Ext 108. V,M,AE,D,DC,CB. I-244, I-51 & 64, I-75 to dntn, off 7th St exit, at corner of 7th St & Boulder Av. Rstrnt/ lounge, n/s rms, pool, arpt trans, cable TV, mtg rm. $38-76/S; $38-80/D. Discs.

Howard Johnson/ 4724 S Yale, Tulsa OK 74135. 918-496-9300/ Fax: 495-1760. M,DC,D,V,AE,CB. I-44, Exit 229. Rstrnt, cable TV, mtg rm, b/f, laundry. Free cont brfst, local calls, nwspr. $37-50/S; $44-55/D. Discs.

Motel 6/ 1011 S Garnett Rd, Tulsa OK 74128. 918-234-6200/ Fax: 234-9421. M,V,DC,D,AE. I-44 Wbnd, Exit 235/ E 11th St, W to Garnett Rd. I-44 Ebnd,

Exit 234A. Nrby rstrnt, cable TV, laundry, pool, n/s rms, t pkng. Free local calls. $26-27/S; $30-31/D; $4/ex prsn. Disc.

Motel 6/ 5828 W Skelly Dr, Tulsa OK 74107. 918-445-0223/ Fax: 445-2750. M,V,DC,D,AE. I-44, Exit 222A/ 49th West Av, N to W Skelly, lt. Nrby rstrnt, cable TV, laundry, pool, n/s rms, t pkng. Free local calls. $25-26/S; $29-30/D; $4/ex prsn. Disc.

Quality Inn/ 222 N Garnett Rd, Tulsa OK 74116. 918-438-0780. AE,V,M,DC. I-244 at Garnett Rd. Rstrnt/ lounge, pool, mtg rm, fax, b/f, cable TV, t pkng, n/s rms. $40-48/S; $44-56/D; $4/ex prsn. Discs.

Weatherford

Econo Lodge/ Box 705, Weatherford OK 73096. 405-772-7711. AE,V,M,DC. I-40 (Exit 80) to SR 54. Nrby rstrnt, pool, fax, cable TV, t pkng, coffee, sandwiches, n/s rms, dd phone. No pets. $27-30/S; $33-41/D; $3/ex prsn. 5/1-10/31: $30-35/S; $41-46/D. Discs.

Yukon (Oklahoma City area)

Comfort Inn/ 321 N Mustang Rd, Yukon OK 73099. 405-324-1000. V,M,DC,AE. I-40 (Exit 138) at Mustang Rd. W of Oklahoma City. Nrby rstrnt, pool, mtg rm, fax, b/f, cable TV, t pkng, kitchenettes, n/s rms. Free cont brfst. $40-52/S; $45-57/D; $5/ex prsn. 4/1-4/30, 9/1-11/31: $42-54/S; $47-59/D. 5/1-8/31: $45-60/S; $50-65/D. Discs.

Oregon

Baker City

Friendship Inn/ 134 Bridge St, Baker City OR 97814. 503-523-6571. AE, V,M,DC. I-84: Nbnd, (Exit 304) to Campbell St, W to Resort St, S to Bridge St; Sbnd, (Exit 306) to US 30 (Elm St), NW until it curves into Bridge St. Nrby rstrnt, fax, cable TV, t pkng, outlets, n/s rms. $25-35/S; $29-39/D; $4/ex prsn. 2/11-4/1, 5/1-10/31: $36-46/S; $41-51/D. Discs.

Super 8 Motel/ 250 Campbell St, Baker City OR 97814. 503-523-8282/ Fax: 523-9137. M,V,AE,DC,CB,D. I-84 (Exit 304) to Campbell St, E toward OR In-

OREGON

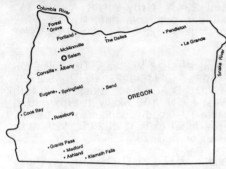

Interpretive Cntr. B/f, n/s rms, pool, whrlpool, cot, crib, exerc equip. Pride Award. $39/S; $45-49/D; $6/ex prsn. Higher spec event, wknd rates. Discs.

Boardman

Nugget Inn/ 105 Front St SW, Box 761, Boardman OR 97818. 503-481-2735/ Fax: 481-2600/ 800-366-4485. V, M,AE,D. I-84 at Exit 164. Pool, n/s rms, cable TV, tt phone, fax, refrig, microwave, cot, crib, t/b/rv pkng, conn rms. Free local calls, cont brfst. AAA. $38/S; $40-48/D; $5/ex prsn.

Burns

Motel 6/ 997 Oregon Av, Burns OR 97720. 503-573-3013/ Fax: 573-1428. M,V,DC,D,AE. E side of US 395/20 at SW edge of town. Nrby rstrnt, cable TV, laundry, pool, n/s rms, t pkng. Free local calls. $27-28/S; $33-34/D; $6/ex prsn. Disc.

Coos Bay

Motel 6/ 1445 Bayshore Dr, Coos Bay OR 97420. 503-267-7171/ Fax: 267-4618. AE,V,M,D,DC. On US Hwy 101 at Coos Bay Blvd. Cable TV, laundry, n/s rms, sauna, spa, exerc equip. Free local calls. Premier Award. $31-38/S; $37-44/D; $6/ex prsn. Disc.

Coquille

Myrtle Lane Motel/ 787 N Central, Coquille OR 97423. 503-396-2102. C,M,AE,D. Hwy 42 to Central Blvd, N 7-1/2 blks. N/s rms, cable TV, tt phone, refrig, microwave, cot, crib. Free local calls. AAA. $30-32/S; $35-40/D; $4/ex prsn. Disc: Family. *Guaranteed rates.*

Corvallis

Econo Lodge/ 101 NW Van Buren, Corvallis OR 97330. 503-752-9601. M, V,AE,DC. I-5 (Exit 228) to SR 34, W 10 miles, cross Willamette River, just past bridge. Rstrnt/ lounge, fax, b/f, whrlpool, cable TV, t pkng, n/s rms. $35-40/S; $38-42/D; $4/ex prsn. Discs.

Cottage Grove

Comfort Inn/ 845 Gateway Blvd, Cottage Grove OR 97424. 503-942-9747. V,M,AE,D,DC. I-5 (Exit 174) to Gateway Blvd, S 3 blks. Nrby rstrnt, pool, mtg rm, fax, b/f, whrlpool, cable TV, t pkng, n/s rms. Free cont brfst. AAA. $43-70/S; $48-70/D; $5/ex prsn. 6/1-10/31: $47-74/S; $52-74/D. Discs.

Eugene

Motel 6/ 3690 Glenwood Dr, Eugene OR 97403. 503-687-2395/ Fax: 687-6828. M,V,DC,D,AE. I-5, Exit 191, S to Glenwood Dr, lt 1 blk. Nrby rstrnt, cable TV, pool, n/s rms. Free local calls. $30-35/S; $36-41/D; $6/ex prsn. Disc.

Also see Springfield.

Florence

Park Motel/ 85034 Hwy 101 S, Florence OR 97439. 503-997-2634/ 800-392-0441. V,M,AE,D,DC,CB. 1.5 mi S of Florence, set back off Hwy 101, in the Dunes National Recreation Center. Rstrnt, cable TV, playgrnd, tt/dd phone, mtg rm, nwspr, refrig, microwave, cot, crib, outlets, t/b/rv pkng, eff. Free local calls. AAA. $37/S or D; $5/ex prsn. (rates for 1 bed.) 4/16-9/30: $49/S or D. Disc: Senior, bsns, TA, govt, milt, l/s. *Guaranteed rates.*

Gold Beach

Inn at Gold Beach/ 1435 S Ellensburg, Box 1036, Gold Beach OR 97444. 541-247-6606/ Fax: 247-7046/ 800-503-0833. V,M,AE,D,DC. N/s rms, cable TV, arpt trans, tt phone, fax, copier, refrig, microwave, cot, crib, t/b/rv pkng, conn rms. Free local calls, coffee. AAA. $32-42/S; $39-52/D; $6/ex prsn. 5/15-9/23: $55-59/S; $65-69/D. Disc: L/s. *Guaranteed rates.*

Grants Pass

Motel 6/ 1800 NE 7th St, Grants Pass OR 97526. 503-474-1331/ Fax: 474-0136. M,V,DC,D,AE. I-5, Exit 58, S on

OREGON

6th St, 2 blks. Nrby rstrnt, cable TV, laundry, pool, n/s rms. Free local calls. $30-36/S; $36-42/D; $6/ex prsn. Disc.

Klamath Falls

Econo Lodge/ 75 Main St, Klamath Falls OR 97601. 503-884-7735. AE,V,M. US 97 to Klamath Falls City Cntr exit, follow to Main St. Nrby rstrnt, fax, b/f, cable TV, t pkng, n/s rms. Free cont brfst. No pets. $33-37/S; $37-43/D; $4/ex prsn. 5/1-10/31: $37-41/S; $41-47/D. Discs.

Motel 6/ 5136 S 6th St, Klamath Falls OR 97603. 503-884-2110/ Fax: 882-3384. M,V,DC,D,AE. From US 97 Sbnd, follow Reno signs, take SR 39/140E/S 6th St to mtl. Nbnd, take Downtown Exit, E on S 6th St. Rstrnt, cable TV, pool, n/s rms. Free local calls. $30-35/S; $36-41/D; $6/ex prsn. Disc.

Lincoln City

Rodeway Inn/ 861 SW 51st St, Lincoln City OR 97367. 503-996-3996. V,M,D,AE. US 101, exit 51st S W. Rstrnt, mtg rm, cable TV, t pkng, n/s rms. Free cont brfst. $35-175/S; $45-175/D; $7/ex prsn. Discs.

Medford

Motel 6/ 2400 Biddle Rd, Medford OR 97504. 503-779-0550/ Fax: 857-9573. M,V,DC,D,AE. I-5, Crater Lake Exit 30 W; turn N (lt) on Biddle Rd. Nrby rstrnt, cable TV, pool, n/s rms. Free local calls. Premier Award. $34-39/S; $40-45/D; $6/ex prsn. Disc.

Motel 6/ 950 Alba Dr, Medford OR 97504. 503-773-4290/ Fax: 857-9574. M,V,DC,D,AE. I-5, Exit 27 to Barnett Rd, NE to Alba Dr. Just NE of frwy. Nrby rstrnt, cable TV, pool, n/s rms. t pkng. Free local calls. $26-32/S; $32-38/D; $6/ex prsn. Disc.

North Bend

Parkside Motel/ 1480 Sherman Av, N Bend OR 97459. 503-756-4124. V,M,AE,DC. On Hwy 101, N end of town, 2 hrs from Eugene. Cable TV, dd phone, fax, laundry, n/s rms, kitchens, coffee, suites. National 9. $28/S; $32-34/S; $6/ex prsn. $10 more per room for kitchens. $40-80/suites.

Ontario

Motel 6/ 275 NE 12th Av, Ontario OR 97914. 503-889-6617/ Fax: 889-8232. M,V,DC,D,AE. At jct of I-84 & US 30. I-84W to US 30/Payette Exit, E to Tapadera Av, turn lt. Nrby rstrnt, cable TV, laundry, pool, n/s rms. Free local calls. $27/S; $33/D; $6/ex prsn. Disc.

Pendleton

Chaparral Motel/ 620 SW Tutuilla, Pendleton OR 97801. 503-276-8654/ Fax: 276-5808. V,M,AE,D,DC. I-84, Exit 209, S 1 blk. Nrby rstrnt, n/s rms, cable TV, tt/dd phone, fax, refrig, microwave, cot, crib, t/b/rv pkng, eff, conn rms. Free local calls, coffee. AAA/ Mobil. $36/S; $43-46/D; $5/ex prsn. Pendleton Round-Up: $85/S; $95-125/D. Disc: Senior, bsns, govt, milt, family.

Motel 6/ 325 SE Nye Av, Pendleton OR 97801. 503-276-3160/ Fax: 276-7526. M,V,DC,D,AE. I-84, Exit 210 S to SE 3rd Dr, lt on SE Nye Ave to mtl. Nrby rstrnt, cable TV, laundry, pool, n/s rms. Free local calls. $29-33/S; $35-39/D; $6/ex prsn. Higher spec event rates. Disc.

Super 8 Motel/ 601 SE Nye Ave, Pendleton OR 97801. 503-276-8881. AE,V,M,D,DC,CB. I-84 (Exit 210) to SR 11, S. B/f, n/s rms, pool, nrby rstrnt, whrlpool, outlets, toast bar, t/b/rv pkng, copier, cable TV, cot. Free local calls, crib. Pride Award. $38/S; $42-46/D; $4/ex prsn. Higher spec event rates. Discs.

Portland

Friendship Inn/ 305 N Broadway, Portland OR 97227. 503-284-5181/ Fax: 287-9711. M,V,AE,DC. I-5, Exit 302A, SW on Broadway to mtl. Nrby rstrnt, cable TV, t pkng, n/s rms. No pets. $35-40/S; $40-49/D; $5/ex prsn. Discs.

HoJo Inn/ 3939 N E Hancock St, Portland OR 97212. 503-288-6891. M,DC,D,V,AE,CB. I-5 to I-84 E to Dalles, take 39th Av Exit (Hollywood Dist), turn off ramp, lt 2 blks. Nrby rstrnt, n/s rms, b/f, t pkng. Free cont brfst. No pets. $44-46/S; $46-48/D. Discs.

Motel 6/ 3104 SE Powell Blvd, Portland OR 97202. 503-238-0600/ Fax: 238-

OREGON

7167. M,V,DC,D,AE. Hwy 26 (Powell Blvd) bet I-5 & I-205. Cable TV, pool, n/s rms. Free local calls. $39/S; $45/D; $6/ex prsn. Disc.

Also see Tigard, Troutdale.

Redmond

Quality Hotel/ 521 S 6th St, Redmond OR 97756. 503-923-7378. V,M,AE,D, DC. On US 97 S (SW 6th St/ one-way going S) next to Sully's. Rstrnt/ lounge, mtg rm, whrlpool, cable TV, exerc equip, n/s rms, arpt trans. Free cont brfst. No pets. $44-70/S; $48-80/D; $5/ex prsn. 5/1-9/15: $48-70/S; $52-80/D. Discs.

Reedsport

Anchor Bay Inn/ 1821 Highway 101, Reedsport OR 97467. 541-271-2149/ Fax: 271-1802/ 800-767-1821. M,DC, D,V,AE,CB. Hwy 38 to Hwy 101, S 1 mi. Pool, n/s rms, cable TV, VCR, playgrnd, tt/dd phone, fax, laundry, refrig, cot, eff, conn rms. Free local calls, cont brfst, coffee. AAA/ Mobil. $33/S; $38-43/D; $5/ex prsn. 5/15-10/31: $39/S; $45-53/D. Disc: Senior, bsns, TA, govt, I/s. *Guaranteed rates.*

Roseburg

Howard Johnson Lodge/ 978 NE Stephens, Roseburg OR 97470. 503-673-5082/ Fax: 673-6594. V,M,AE,D, DC,CB. I-5 (Exit 125) Garden Valley Blvd to Stephens Av, rt. Rstrnt, b/f, n/s rms, laundry, tt phone, cable TV. Free cont brfst. $40-50/S; $45-65/D. 5/1-6/30, 9/16-10/31: $40-65/S; $50-75/D. 7/1-9/15: $50-85/S; $60-95/D. Discs.

Sycamore Motel/ 1627 S E Stephens St, Roseburg OR 97470. 503-672-3354/ Fax: 673-3455. V,M,AE,DC. I-5 to Exit 120, 3 mi N on Hwy 99 or Exit 124. Rt on Pine, 3/4 mi, across from Chin's Rstrnt. Cable TV, laundry, fax, kitchens. Free in-rm coffee. National 9. $26/S; $29-34/D; $4/ex prsn. Summer: $32-38/S; $34-48/D. $10 more per night for kitchens.

Salem

Motel 6/ 2250 Mission St SE, Salem OR 97302. 503-588-7191/ Fax: 588-0486. M,V,DC,D,AE. I-5, Exit 253, W on Mission St to mtl. Cable TV, pool, n/s rms. Free local calls. $30-34/S; $36-40/D; $6/ex prsn. Disc.

Motel 6/ 1401 Hawthorne Av NE, Salem OR 97301. 503-371-8024/ Fax: 371-7691. V,M,AE,DC,D. I-5, Exit 256 to Market St, turn W to Hawthorne, lt to mtl. Nrby rstrnt, cable TV, pool, n/s rms. Free local calls. $32-36/S; $38-42/D; $6/ex prsn. Disc.

Springfield (Eugene area)

Motel 6/ 3752 International Ct, Springfield OR 97477. 503-741-1105/ Fax: 741-6007. M,V,DC,D,AE. I-5, Exit 195 or 195A to Belt Line Rd, E to Gateway St, N to mtl. Cable TV, laundry, pool, n/s rms. Free local calls. $30-33/S; $36-39/D; $6/ex prsn. Disc.

Tigard (Portland area)

Motel 6/ 17950 SW McEwan Rd, Tigard OR 97224. 503-620-2066/ Fax: 639-7096. M,V,DC,D,AE. I-5, Exit 290 Durham/Oswego to Lower Boones Ferry Rd on E side of frwy, turn rt on McEwan. Nrby rstrnt, cable TV, pool, laundry, n/s rms, t pkng. Free local calls. $37/S; $43/D; $6/ex prsn. Disc.

Motel 6/ 17959 SW McEwan Rd, Tigard OR 97224. 503-684-0760/ Fax: 968-2539. M,V,AE,DC,D. I-5, Exit 290 to Lower Boones Ferry Rd, SW to SW McEwan Rd, turn rt to mtl. Cable TV, pool, n/s rms. Free local calls. Premier Award. $35-36/S; $41-42/D; $6/ex prsn. Disc.

Troutdale (Portland area)

Motel 6/ 1610 NW Frontage Rd, Troutdale OR 97060. 503-665-2254/ Fax: 666-1849. M,V,DC,D,AE. I-84, Exit 17/ Troutdale, rt. Mtl is on S side of I-84. Cable TV, laundry, pool, n/s rms. Free local calls. $30-33/S; $36-39/D; $6/ex prsn. Disc.

Winchester Bay

Friendship Inn/ 390 Broadway, Box 1037, Winchester Bay OR 97467. 503-271-4871. V,M,AE,D,DC. US 101, 4 blks N on Broadway. Nrby rstrnt, fax, b/f, cable TV, t pkng, kitchens, n/s rms. Free cont brfst. AAA. $48-58/S; $48-85/D; $5/ex prsn. Discs.

PENNSYLVANIA

Pennsylvania

Allentown

Allenwood Motel/ 1058 Hausman Rd, Allentown PA 18104. 610-395-3707. V,M,AE,D. 1/2 mi E on US 22 from Tnpk Exit 33, 3/4 mi S on SR 309, W on Tilghman St to light, 3/4 mi N on Hausman Rd to dead end, turn lt. Nrby rstrnt/ lounge, n/s rms, cable TV, tt/dd phone, nwspr, cot, crib, outlets, t pkng, conn rms. Free coffee. AAA. Sun-Thurs: $40/S or D; $5/ex prsn. Fri-Sat: $45/S or D. Higher holiday wknd rates. *Guaranteed rates.*

Howard Johnson Lodge/ 3220 Hamilton Blvd, Allentown PA 18103. 610-439-4000/ Fax: Exit 200. M,DC,D,V,AE,CB. I-78: Wbnd, Exit 16B to Hamilton Blvd, 1/2 mi on rt; Ebnd, Exit 16, lt at traffic light, 1/2 mi on rt. Rstrnt, cable TV, micro refrig, t pkng, b/f. Free cont brfst. No pets. $39-52/S; $44-65/D. Discs.

Microtel/ 1880 Steelstone Rd, Allentown PA 18103. 610-266-9070/ Fax: 266-0377. V,M,AE,D,DC,CB. Rte 22, Exit Arpt Rd S, rt to next light, rt again to mtl. N/s rms, cable TV, tt phone, copier, t/b/rv pkng, conn rms, b/f. Free coffee. AAA. $35-40/S; $40-44/D. 7/1-9/1: $37-41/S; $41-45/D. *Guaranteed rates.*

Altoona

Econo Lodge/ 2906 Pleasant Valley Blvd, Altoona PA 16601. 814-944-3555. V,M,DC,AE. US 220 Bypass to 17th St (US 220 Bsns), S 1/4 mi to mtl. Nrby rstrnt, mtg rm, fax, cable TV, t pkng, n/s rms. Free cont brfst. AAA. $38-48/S; $40-50/D; $5/ex prsn. 7/1-8/31: $40-50/S; $45-50/D. Discs.

HoJo Inn/ 1500 Sterling St, Altoona PA 16602. 814-946-7601/ Fax: 946-5162. M,V,AE,DC,D. US 220 N to Plank Rd, lt at end of exit ramp, rt at 2nd traffic light. Pool, mtg rm, nrby rstrnt, n/s rms, b/f, fax, pool. Free cont brfst. $36-47/S; $42-52/D. Discs.

Beaver Falls

Lark Motel/ Rte 18 N, Beaver Falls PA 15010. 412-846-6507. V,M,AE,D. PA Turnpike, Exit 2, 1/2 mi N on Rte 18. N/s rms, cable TV, playgrnd, tt/dd phone, refrig, cot, crib. Free local calls. No pets. AAA/ Mobil. $36-38/S; $40-44/D; $7/ex prsn. *Guaranteed rates.*

Bedford

Friendship Inn/ Transport St, RD 2, Box 28, Bedford PA 15522. 814-623-5174. AE,V,M,DC. PA Trnpk (Exit 11) to US 220, N 1/4 mi to mtl. Rstrnt/ lounge, fax, cable TV, t pkng, n/s rms. AAA. $30-36/S; $36-42/D; $6/ex prsn. 5/1-10/31: $34-40/S; $40-46/D. Discs.

Super 8 Motel/ US 220, Bedford PA 15522. 814-623-5880. M,V,AE,DC,CB, D. PA Trnpk/ I-70/ 76 (Exit 11) to Bsns 220. N of PA Trnpk. B/f, n/s rms, exerc equip, whrlpool, toast bar, b/rv pkng, copier, cable TV, mtg rm, refrig, cot. Free local calls, crib. Pride Award. $40/S; $44-46/D; $5/ex prsn. Higher spec event, wknd rates. Discs.

Belle Vernon

Budget Host Cheeper Sleeper Inn/ Rte 51 & I-70, Belle Vernon PA 15012. 412-929-4501/ Fax: 929-8792. V,M,AE,D, DC,CB. At jct Rte 51 & I-70. Nrby rstrnt/ lounge, pool, n/s rms, cable TV, dd phone, mtg rm, fax, copier, laundry, cot, crib, t/rv pkng, b/f, conn rms. Free local calls, cont brfst. No pets. $30/S; $33-37/D; $5/ex prsn. Disc: Senior.

Bethlehem

Econo Lodge/ US 22, Airport Rd S, Bethlehem PA 18018. 610-867-8681. V, M,AE,D,DC. US 22 to Airport Rd turn S to Catasauqua Rd, E 1/2 mi to mtl. Rstrnt/ lounge, pool, mtg rm, fax, t pkng, laundry, tennis, trans. Free cont brfst. AAA. $39-95/S; $46-125/D; $5/ex prsn. 5/1-7/31: $41-125/S; $49-125/D. 8/1-10/31: $44-125/S; $51-125/D. Discs.

PENNSYLVANIA 220

Budget Host Patriot Inn/ 6305 New Berwick Hwy, Bloomsburg PA 17815. 717-387-1776/ Fax: 387-9611. M,V,AE,CB,DC,D. I-80 at US 11. Cable TV, dd phone, conn rms, n/s rms, rstrnt/ lounge, t pkng, cot. Free crib. No pets. AAA. $39-85/S; $43-85/D; $5/ex prsn. Spec events: $50-65/D. Discs.

Breezewood

Econo Lodge/ Rte 1, Box 101-A, Breezewood PA 15533. 814-735-4341. AE,M,V,DC. PA Tnpk (Exit 12) to I-70/76 and US 30, rt on US 30. Nrby rstrnt, pool, cable TV, n/s rms, t pkng, n/s rms. Free coffee, local calls. No pets. AAA. $39-45/S; $39-49/D; $6/ex prsn. 5/1-10/31: $42-59/S; $42-65/D. Discs.

Quality Inn/ RD 1, Box 36, Breezewood PA 15533. 814-735-4311. AE,V,M,DC. On US 30 at PA Trnpk Interchange 12 & I-70. Nrby rstrnt, pool, cable TV, laundry, n/s rms. No pets. $38-50/S; $42-50/D; $5/ex prsn. 3/1-4/30: $40-52/S; $45-52/D. 5/1-6/10: $41-55/S; $46-55/D. 6/11-10/31: $43-60/S; $49-60/D. Discs.

Brookville

Budget Host Gold Eagle Inn/ 250 W Main St, Brookville PA 15825. 814-849-7344/ Fax: 849-7345. AE,M,V,D. I-80 (Exit 13) jct Hwys 28, 36 & 322. Rstrnt/ lounge, n/s rms, cable TV, tt/dd phone, mtg rm, cot, crib, t/b pkng, eff, conn rms. Free local calls, cont brfst. AAA. Sum: $30-38/S; $32-55/D; $5/ex prsn. Win: $28-37/S; $30-50/D. Spec events, up to $55. Disc: Senior.

HoJo Inn/ 245 Allegheny Blvd, Suite A, Brookville PA 15825. 814-849-3335/ Fax: 849-5259. M,V,AE,DC,D. I-80, Exit 13 to SR 36 N. Rstrnt, n/s rms, t pkng, laundry. Gold Medal Winner. $38-44/S; $43-49/D. 5/1-10/31: $32-50/S; $37-55/D. Discs.

Ramada Limited/ 235 Allegheny Blvd, Brookville PA 15825. 814-849-8381/ Fax: 849-8386. V,M,AE,D,DC,CB. I-80, Exit 13. Pool, n/s rms, cable TV, TDD, tt/dd phone, mtg rm, fax, copier, laundry, microwave, cot, crib, outlets, conn rms, b/f. Free cont brfst, coffee. AAA. $37-42/S; $42-48/D. 5/1-10/31: $42-48/S; $45-65/D; $5/ex prsn. 11/30-12/3: $52/S; $57/D. Discs. *Guaranteed rates.*

Campbelltown

Village Motel/ Rte 322, Box 76, Campbelltown PA 17010. 717-838-4761/ Fax: 838-1399. V,M,D. On Rte 322, 3 mi E of Hershey PA. Pool, n/s rms, cable TV, video games, playgrnd, tennis, dd phone, laundry, cot, crib, eff, conn rms. Free coffee. No pets. AAA. $32/S; $36-40/D; $4/ex prsn. 5/24-6/27: $44/S; $48-56/D. 6/28-9/1: $48/S; $52-60/D. *Guaranteed rates.*

Carlisle

Budget Host Coast-to-Coast Motel/ 1252 Harrisburg Pike, Carlisle PA 17013. 717-243-8585/ Fax: 243-9711. AE,M,V,D. Jct I-81 & US 11. Cable TV, dd phone, adj rstrnt/ mtg rm, t pkng, outlets, cot, crib. AAA. $30-36/S; $36-49/D; $4/ex prsn. Spec events: $60-80. Disc: AARP, AAA.

Econo Lodge/ 1460 Harrisburg Pike, Carlisle PA 17013. 717-249-7775. AE,V,M. I-81 (Exit 17) E to mtl. I-76 (Exit 16) N 1 mi. Adj rstrnt/ lounge, pool, fax, cable TV, t pkng. Free AM coffee. AAA. $38-65/S; $42-70/D; $5/ex prsn. 11/1-3/31: $38-40/S; $42-45/D. Discs.

Friendship Inn/ 1179 Harrisburg Pike, Carlisle PA 17013. 717-243-5504. V,M,AE,D,DC. PA Tnpk (I-76/ Exit 16) to US 11, N 1/2 mi on rt. I-81 (Exit 17) to US 11, S 1 mi on lt. Nrby rstrnt, b/f, cable TV, t pkng, n/s rms. Free cont brfst. No pets. $28/S; $30/D; $3/ex prsn. 5/1-10/31: $33/S; $35/D. Discs.

Rodeway Inn/ 1239 Harrisburg Pike, Carlisle PA 17013. 717-249-2800. V,M,AE,D,DC,CB. PA Trnpk (Exit 16) to US 11, N 1/4 mi to mtl. Nrby rstrnt, pool, fax, b/f, cable TV, t pkng, outlets. Free cont brfst. AAA. $38-49; $42-53/D; $5/ex prsn. 6/12-7/1: $42-53/S; $45-54/D. 7/2-9/12: $40-51/S; $43-52/D. Spec events: $50-65/D; $60-75/D. Discs.

Chambersburg

Econo Lodge/ 1110 Sheller Av, Chambersburg PA 17201. 717-264-8005. AE,M,V,DC. I-81 (Exit 5) at SR 316. Rstrnt/ lounge, mtg rm, fax, b/f, t pkng, exerc equip. Free cont brfst. No pets. AAA. $39-45/S; $42-45/D; $3/ex prsn. 4/1-10/31: $41-50/S; $44-50/D. Discs.

Friendship Inn/ 1620 Lincoln Way E, Chambersburg PA 17201. 717-264-4108. V,M,D,AE. I-81 (Exit 6) to US 30, E 2 mi on rt. Rstrnt, cable TV, t pkng, n/s rms. AAA. $30-37/S or D; $3/ex prsn. 5/1-11/1: $35-39/S; $37-42/D. Discs.

Clearfield

Friendship Inn/ RD 2, Box 297B, Clearfield PA 16830. 814-765-7587. M,V, AE,DC. I-80: Ebnd, (Exit 19) to SR 879, W 2 mi to US 322, E to mtl; Wbnd, (Exit 20) to SR 970, S 2 mi to US 322, W 3 mi. Rstrnt, fax, cable TV, n/s rms. Free cont brfst. AAA. $35-40/S; $40-50/D; $4-5/ex prsn. 5/1-11/30: $35-56/S; $40-68/D. Discs.

Danville

Howard Johnson Lodge/ 15 Valley W Rd, Danville PA 17821. 717-275-5100/ Fax: 275-1886. M,V,AE,DC,D. I-80, Exit 33. Jct of US 54 & I-80. Rstrnt, n/s rms, b/f, pool, t pkng, laundry, mtg rm, game rm, fax. $38-50/S; $43-56/D; 5/1-10/31: $45-65/S; $45-75/D. Higher spec event rates. Discs.

Drums (Hazleton area)

Econo Lodge/ Box 1470, Drums PA 18222. 717-788-4121. M,V,AE,DC. I-80 (Exit 39) at SR 309 N. I-81, Exit 42E to SR 309, S 3/4 mi. Nrby rstrnt, pool, fax, cable TV, t pkng, outlets, n/s rms. Free cont brfst, local calls, coffee. AAA. $35-37/S; $40-45/D; $5/ex prsn. 5/1-10/31: $43-48/S; $50-60/D. Discs.

Lookout Motor Lodge/ RR 2, Box 130, Drums PA 18222. 717-788-4131/ Fax: 788-5092. V,M,AE,D. I-80, Exit 38, Conyngham-Nescopeck, 1 mi N on Rte 93. I-81, Exit 41, W Hazleton, 5 mi N on Rte 93. Rstrnt/ lounge, n/s rms, cable TV, tt/dd phone, fax, cot. Free local calls, cont brfst. No pets. AAA. $36/S; $40/D; $5/ex prsn. 5/1-10/31: $42/S; $48/D. Disc: Senior, bsns. *Guaranteed rates.*

Essington (Philadelphia area)

Motel 6/ 43 Industrial Hwy, Essington PA 19029. 610-521-6650/ Fax: 521-8846. V,M,AE,D,DC. I-95, Exit 9A S to traffic signal, rt on Rte 291, 1/4 mi. Adj rstrnt, laundry, fax. Premier Award. $40/S; $46/D; $6/ex prsn. 12/21-5/22: $43-48/S; $49-54/D. Higher spec event rates. Disc.

Frackville

Econo Lodge/ 501 S Middle St, Frackville PA 17931. 717-874-3838. AE, M,V,DC. Jct of I-81 (Exit 36) & SR 61 W. Adj rstrnt/ theater, fax, cable TV, t pkng, n/s rms. Free coffee, cont brfst. No pets. AAA. $36-60/S; $40-70/D; $5/ex prsn. Discs.

Gettysburg

Blue Sky Motel/ 2585 Biglerville Rd, Gettysburg PA 17325. 717-677-7736/ Fax: 677-6794/ 800-745-8194. V,M,AE, D,DC,CB. On PA Rte 34. From Gettysburg town square, N on Carlisle St, approx 6 min from town. Pool, exerc equip, cable TV, playgrnd, tt/dd phone, fax, copier, refrig, cot, crib, t/b/rv pkng, eff. Free local calls, coffee. No pets. AAA/ Mobil. $29/S; $29-34/D; $4/ex prsn. 6/7 -9/2, Spec events: $49/S; $49-52/D. Disc: AARP, AAA, CAA. *Guaranteed rates.*

Comfort Inn/ 871 York Rd, Gettysburg PA 17325. 717-337-2400. V,M,AE,D, DC. On US 30, 1 mi W of jct US 30 & US 15. 1 mi E of Lincoln Sq in Gettysburg. Adj rstrnt, indr pool, mtg rm, fax, b/f, whrlpool, cable TV, t pkng, n/s rms. Free cont brfst, coffee, tea. No pets. AAA. $40-69/S; $46-79/D; $5-7/ex prsn. 5/1-5/31: $55-79/S; $65-89/D. 6/1-9/5: $69-89/S; $79-97/D. 9/6-10/31: $57-79/S; $69-89/D. Discs.

Econo Lodge/ 945 Baltimore Pike, Gettysburg PA 17325. 717-334-6715. V,M, AE,D,DC. US 15 to SR 97, SE to motel, adj to Natl Cemetery. Rstrnt/ lounge, two pools, mtg rm, fax, cable TV, t pkng, VCR. Free cont brfst. No pets. AAA. $33-55/S; $36-55/D; $4-5/ex prsn. 5/1-6/8: $48-62/S; $50-66/D. 6/9-9/4: $55-76/S; $58-76/D. 9/5-10/31: $48-66/S; $52-70/D. Discs.

Friendship Inn/ 1031 York Rd, Gettysburg PA 17325. 717-334-1804. AE, V,M,DC. On US 30 (York Rd), just N of Gettysburg. Nrby rstrnt, pool, fax, cable TV, t pkng. Free coffee. No pets. $33-

PENNSYLVANIA 222

36/S; $33-40/D; $4/ex prsn. 5/1-6/8: $45-56/S; $50-60/D. 6/9-9/5: $61-66/S; $61-70/D. 9/6-10/31: $46-62/S; $52-64/D. Discs.

Quality Inn/ 380 Steinwehr AV, Gettysburg PA 17325. 717-334-1103. V,M,AE,D,DC. Located in the heart of the museum area next to the Electric Map, Visitor Ctr & Wax Museum. Nrby rstrnt/ lounge, pool, mtg rm, fax, b/f, sauna, whrlpool, cable TV, t pkng, exerc equip, n/s rms, laundry. Free coffee, tea. $39-91/S; $48-97/D; $6/ex prsn. Discs.

Quality Inn/ 401 Buford Av, Gettysburg PA 17325. 717-334-3141. V,M,DC,AE. Hwy 30 & W Confederate Av, 8 blks W of center of town. Adj to National Park, General Lee's Headquarters/ Museum. Rstrnt/ lounge, pool, mtg rm, fax, cable TV, putting green, n/s rms. No pets. AAA. $38-72/S; $42-72/D; $5/ex prsn. 5/1-6/1, 9/4-10/28: $52-72/S; $56-72/D. 6/2-9/3: $60-78/S; $68-78/D. Discs.

Grantville

Econo Lodge/ Rte 1, Box 5005, Grantville PA 17028. 717-469-0631/ Fax: 469-0843. AE,M,V,DC. I-81 (Exit 28) to SR 743 S. Nrby rstrnt, mtg rm, fax, b/f, cable TV, t pkng, n/s rms. Free cont brfst. No pets. AAA. $35-48/S or D; $5/ex prsn. 3/1-4/30: $45-55/S or D. 5/1-10/31: $45-70/S or D. Discs.

Greencastle

Comfort Inn/ 50 Pine Dr, Greencastle PA 17225. 717-597-8164. V,M,AE,D,DC. I-81 (Exit 2) at SR 11 (Sbnd, lt 1/4 mi). Rstrnt, mtg rm, fax, cable TV, t pkng, on-site racquet/ health club, n/s rms. Free cont brfst. No pets. AAA. $43-51/S; $48-59/D; $6/ex prsn. Discs.

Econo Lodge/ 735 Buchanan Tr E, Greencastle PA 17225. 717-597-5255. AE,M,V,DC. I-81, Exit 3. Nrby rstrnt, b/f, cable TV, t pkng, n/s rms. Free coffee. No pets. $35-40/S; $47-51/D; $4/ex prsn. 5/1-9/30: $40-45/S; $45-49/D. 10/1-10/31: $42-46/S; $47-51/D. 11/1-11/30: $39-44/S; $44-49/D. Discs.

Friendship Inn/ 700 Buchanan Dr, 10835 John Wayne Dr, Greencastle PA 17225. 717-597-7762. AE,V,M,DC. I-81 N, exit US 11 N at Greencastle, 1 mi to mtl. Rstrnt, fax, b/f, cable TV, t pkng, n/s rms. No pets. $35-45/S; $40-50/D; $5/ex prsn. Discs.

Harrisburg

Friendship Inn/ 495 Eisenhower Blvd, Harrisburg PA 17111. 717-561-1885. AE,M,V. I-283, Exit 1. Nrby rstrnt, fax, cable TV, t pkng, n/s rms. No pets. AAA. $35-45/S; $38-55/D; $5/ex prsn. 9/26-10/9: $50-75/S; $65-85/D. Discs.

Sleep Inn/ 7930 Linglestown Rd, Harrisburg PA 17112. 717-540-9100. V,M, AE,D,DC. I-81 (Exit 27/ Hershey Exit) at SR 39, turn S to mtl. Nrby rstrnt, mtg rm, fax, b/f, cable TV, t pkng, n/s rms. Free cont brfst. $39-59/S or D; $7-10/ex prsn. 3/31-6/1: $46-56/S or D. 6/2-9/4: $49-69/S or D. Discs.

Super 8 Motel/ 4131 Executive Pk Dr, Harrisburg PA 17111. 717-564-7790/ Fax: Ext 165. M,V,AE,DC,D,CB. I-283 (Exit 1) to Eisenhower Blvd, N to Chambers Hill Rd, W to Exec Pk Dr, turn S to mtl. B/f, n/s rms, cable TV, cot, t pkng, adj swim club. Free local calls, crib, cont brfst. Pride Award. AAA. $38/S; $45/D; $5/ex prsn. 6/11-9/30: $44/S; $46-50/D. Higher spec event rates. Discs.

Also see Mechanicsburg, Middletown, New Cumberland, Wormleysburg.

Hershey

Friendship Inn/ 43 W Areba Av, Hershey PA 17033. 717-533-7054. V,M, AE,D,DC. 1/2 blk W of SR 743. 3 blks S of jct SR 422 & 743. Nrby rstrnt, fax, cable TV, b pkng, n/s rms, eff. Free coffee/ tea, local calls. No pets. AAA. $40-95/S; $45-100/D; $5/ex prsn. 5/1-5/25: $60-135/S; $75-145/D. 5/26-9/3: $65-145/S; $85-155/D. 9/4-10/31: $50-125/S; $60-130/D. Discs.

Indiana

Budget Host Inn Towner Motel/ R 886 Wayne Av, Indiana PA 15701. 412-463-8726/ Fax: 463-9560. AE,CB,DC,M,V,D. Near jct Hwy 119 & 422/ SR 286. Next to IUP University. Nrby rstrnt/ lounge, cable TV, dd phone, fax, copier, laundry, b/f. Free coffee. No pets. $34/S; $38/D; $4/ex prsn. Spec events, Parents wknd: $60/S or D. Disc: Senior, bsns, govt, family, trkr, milt, l/s.

King of Prussia (Philadelphia area)
Motel 6/ 815 W Dekalb Pike, King of Prussia PA 19406. 610-265-7200/ Fax: 265-7288. V,M,AE,D,DC. From 202 S, lt onto S Gulph Rd, rt into Howard Johnson's and follow road in back, through metal treadles to mtl. Rstrnt, t pkng. $40/S; $46/D; $6/ex prsn. 12/21-5/22: $40-46/S; $46-52/D. Higher spec event rates. Disc.

Kittanning
Friendship Inn/ RD 6, US 422 E, Kittanning PA 16201. 412-543-1100. V,M,AE,D,DC. 1 mi E of Kittanning on US 422, E of jct US 422, SR 66, 28. Nrby rstrnt, mtg rm, fax, b/f, cable TV, t pkng, outlets, n/s rms, kitchenettes. Free cont brfst. $42-46/S; $46-50/D; $12/ex prsn. 5/1-8/31: $44-50/S; $48-52/D. 9/1-10/31: $44-48/S; $46-50/D. Discs.

Lamar
Comfort Inn/ RR 3, Box 600, Lamar/ Mill Hall PA 17751. 717-726-4901. AE,V,M,DC. I-80 (Exit 25) to SR 64. Nrby rstrnt/ lounge, pool, mtg rm, fax, b/f, cable TV, t pkng, n/s rms. Free cont brfst. AAA. $39-59/S; $39-64/D; $5/ex prsn. Spec events: $75-95/S; $80-100/D. Discs.

Lancaster
Econo Lodge/ 2165 US 30 E, Lancaster PA 17602. 717-299-6900. AE,V,M,DC. US 222 to US 30 E. Nrby rstrnt, fax, b/f, cable TV, t pkng, n/s rms. Free coffee, local calls. No pets. AAA. $37-42/S; $41-48/D; $5/ex prsn. 5/1-6/15: $39-60/S; $41-60/D. 6/16-8/31: $59-75/S or D. 9/1-10/31: $44-75/S; $47-75/D. Discs.

Econo Lodge/ 2140 US 30 E, Lancaster PA 17602. 717-397-1900. AE,V,M,DC. PA Trnpk (Exit 21) to US 222, S to US 30, E to mtl. Nrby rstrnt, pool, b/f, whrlpool, cable TV, t pkng. Free coffee, local calls. No pets. AAA. $37-42/S; $41-48/D; $5/ex prsn. 5/1-6/15: $39-60/S; $41-60/D. 6/16-8/31: $59-75/S or D. 9/1-10/31: $44-75/S; $47-75/D. Discs.

Friendship Inn/ 2331 Lincoln Hwy E, Lancaster PA 17602. 717-397-4973. V,M,AE,D,DC. US 30, 4 mi E of Lancaster. Rstrnt/ lounge, pool, fax, cable TV, t pkng, n/s rms. No pets. $32-48/S or D; $6/ex prsn. 5/1-5/19: $48-58/S or D. 5/20-10/29: $58-75/S or D. 10/30-12/31: $35-48/S or D. Discs.

Howard Johnson Lodge/ 2100 US Hwy 30 E, Lancaster PA 17602. 717-397-7781/ Fax: 397-6340. M,DC,D,V,AE,CB. PA Turnpike to Exit 21, Rte 222 S for 20 mi to Rte 30 E (Coatesville exit), 3 mi on 30 E. Rstrnt/ lounge, b/f, indr pool, t pkng, game rm, cable TV. No pets. Gold Medal Winner. $36-67/S; $44-79/D. Discs.

Levittown (Philadelphia area)
Econo Lodge/ 6201 Bristol Pike, Levittown PA 19057. 215-946-1100. AE,V,M. PA Trnpk (Exit 29) to US 13, N 1 mi. Nrby lounge, mtg rm, fax, cable TV, t pkng, n/s rms. Free cont brfst. $40-55/S; $45-60/D; $5/ex prsn. Discs.

Lewisburg
Econo Lodge/ US 15, Box 651, Lewisburg PA 17837. 717-523-1106. V,M,AE,DC. US 15, 1/2 mi S of Lewisburg. Rstrnt/ lounge, cable TV, t pkng, outlets, n/s rms. Free coffee. $40-45/S or D; $5/ex prsn. 5/1-6/30: $45-50/S or D. 7/1-8/22: $50-55/S; $55-60/D. 8/23-8/31: $60-65/S; $70-75/D. Discs.

Manheim (Lebanon area)
Friendship Inn/ 2931 Lebanon Rd, Manheim PA 17545. 717-665-2755. AE,V,M,DC. PA Trnpk (Exit 20) to SR 72, S to mtl. Nrby rstrnt, pool, t pkng, n/s rms. $30-34/S; $36-40/D; $4/ex prsn. 5/1-6/30, 9/6-10/31: $30-42/S; $38-48/D. 7/1-9/5: $36-46/S; $42-52/D. Discs.

Meadville
Days Inn Conference Center/ 240 Conneaut Lake Rd, Meadville PA 16335. 814-337-4264/ Fax: 337-7304. V,M,AE,D,DC,CB. I-79, Exit 36A, 2 blks. Indr pool, whrlpool, n/s rms, cable TV, VCR/ movies, games, TDD, tt/dd phone, mtg rm, copier, laundry, refrig, elevator, cot, crib, t/b/rv pkng. AAA/ Mobil. $39-70/S; $39-75/S; $6/ex prsn. 4/1-9/30: $55-80/S; $65-90/D. Discs.

Mechanicsburg (Harrisburg area)
Amber Inn/ 1032 Audubon Rd, Mechanicsburg PA 17055. 717-766-

PENNSYLVANIA

9006. V,M,AE,D. US Rte 15, 1/2 mi N of PA Turnpike, Exit 17, (Wesley Dr), lt off ramp, lt at light, 1 blk to Audubon Rd, lt. Nrby rstrnt, n/s rms, cable TV, tt phone, cot, crib. Free local calls, coffee, tea. No pets. AAA. $32/S; $39/D; $5/ex prsn. 4/18-4/21, 7/26-7/28, 10/3-10/13: $40/S; $50/D.

Friendship Inn/ 650 Gettysburg Rd, Mechanicsburg PA 17055. 717-766-4728. AE,V,M,DC. Jct of US 15 (Exit 17) & PA Trnpk. Nrby rstrnt, pool, cable TV, t pkng, n/s rms. $28-38/S; $32-47/D; $5/ex prsn. Discs.

Middletown (Harrisburg area)

Rodeway Inn/ 800 Eisenhower Blvd, Middletown PA 17057. 717-939-4147/ Fax: 939-5291. V,M,AE,D,DC. PA Trnpk (Exit 19) to SR 283, S to mtl. Nrby rstrnt, mtg rm, b/f, cable TV, t pkng, outlets. Free cont brfst. Rodeway Inn of the Year. AAA. $38-68/S; $43-72/D; $5/ex prsn. 6/12-9/9: $43-73/S; $48-78/D. 9/10-10/15: $40-70/S; $45-75/D. Discs.

Mifflintown

Econo Lodge/ Box 202, Mifflintown PA 17059. 717-436-5981. M,V,AE,DC. US 322 & SR 35. Rstrnt, mtg rm, fax, b/f, cable TV, t pkng, n/s rms. No pets. AAA. $42-70/S; $44-70/D; $4/ex prsn. Discs.

Milford

Myer Motel/ Rtes 6 & 209, Milford PA 18337. 717-296-7223/ 800-764-MYER. V,M,AE,D,DC,CB. I-84, Exit 10, go to Milford, lt at light, 1/4 mi on rt. Nrby rstrnt, n/s rms, cable TV, tt/dd phone, refrig, cot, crib, eff. Free local calls. AAA/ Mobil. $40-55/S; $45-75/D; $7/ex prsn. Disc: Senior, govt, milt.

New Cumberland (Harrisburg area)

Motel 6/ 200 Commerce Dr, New Cumberland PA 17070. 717-774-8910/ Fax: 770-0433. M,V,DC,D,AE. I-83, Exit 18A, W on Limekiln Rd, rt on Commerce to mtl. Cable TV, pool, n/s rms. Free local calls. $27-32/S; $33-38/D; $6/ex prsn. Disc.N

Oakdale (Pittsburgh area)

Howard Johnson Lodge/ 2101 Montour Church Rd, Oakdale PA 15071. 412-923-2244/ Fax: 787-3625. M,V,AE,DC, D. I-79 to Rte 22/30, exit Montour Church Rd. Lounge, n/s rms, b/f, pool, t pkng, laundry, mtg rm. Free cont brfst. $38-49/S; $45-53/D. Di

Philadelphia

See Essington, King of Prussia, Levittown.

Pine Grove

Econo Lodge/ RD 1, Box 581, Pine Grove PA 17963. 717-345-4099/ Fax: 345-4984. AE,M,V,DC. I-81 (Exit 31) at SR 443, 1 blk E. Adj rstrnt, fax, b/f, cable TV, outlets. Free coffee. AAA. $40-45/S; $40-50/D; $5/ex prsn. 5/1-6/15, 10/16-10/31: $40-50/S; $45-55/D. 6/16-10/15: $40-75/S; $45-75/D. Discs.

Pine Grove Comfort Inn/ Box 327, Pine Grove PA 17963. 717-345-8031/ Fax: 345-2308. V,M,AE,D,DC,CB. I-81 (Exit 31) to SR 443 E. Next to McDonalds. Indr pool, n/s rms, exerc equip, games, TDD, tt/dd phone, fax, copier, elevator, cot, crib, t/b/rv pkng, b/f. Free coffee, discount coupons. AAA. $40-60/S; $45-65/D; $5/ex prsn. 5/1-10/8: $50-80/S; $56-86/D. 10/13-10/31: $45-65/S; $51-71/D. Discs. *Guaranteed rates.*

Pittsburgh

Econo Lodge/ 4800 Steubenville Pike, Pittsburgh PA 15205. 412-922-6900. AE,V,M. I-79 (Exit 16) to SR 60 (Steubenville Pike), E to mtl. Nrby rstrnt, pool, mtg rm, fax, cable TV, n/s rms. Free cont brfst, coffee, tea, popcorn, local calls. $35-45/S; $40-50/D; $6/ex prsn. 5/1-9/30: $40-50/S; $45-60/D. Discs.

Motel 6/ 211 Beecham Dr, Pittsburgh PA 15205. 412-922-9400/ Fax: 921-1725. M,V,DC,D,AE. I-79, Exit 16 to US 60 S; at first signal light turn lt on Lorish Rd to Beecham Dr. Nrby rstrnt, cable TV, n/s rms, t pkng. Free local calls. $28-30/S; $34-36/D; $6/ex prsn. Disc.

Also see Oakdale.

Pittston

Howard Johnson Lodge/ 307 Rte 315, Pittston PA 18640. 717-654-3301/ Fax:

883-0288. M,DC,D,V,AE,CB. Exit 37 off PA Turnpike NE extension. I-81 (Exit 48/ 48A) Pittston. Rstrnt, pool, b/f, mtg rm, cable TV. Free cont brfst. $42-50/S; $47-60/D. Discs.

Quakertown
Econo Lodge/ 1905 SR 663, Quakertown PA 18951. 215-538-3000/ Fax: 538-2311. V,M,AE,D,DC,CB. SR 633 (Exit 32) to PA Trnpk, NE. Nrby rstrnt, fax, b/f, cable TV, t pkng, n/s rms. Free cont brfst, coffee. $40-90/S; $40-100/D; $5/ex prsn. 5/1-9/30: $40-90/S; $45-100/D. Discs.

Reading
Wellesley Inn/ 910 Woodland Av, Reading PA 19610. 610-374-1500/ Fax: 374-2554. M,DC,D,V,AE,CB. Cable TV, microwave, refrig. Free cont brfst. $44/S or D; $5/ex prsn. *Special rates. See discount section at front of book.

Scranton
Econo Lodge/ 1175 Kane St, Scranton PA 18505. 717-348-1000/ Fax: 348-0683. V,M,AE,D,DC,CB. PA Turnpike, Exit 37. Rte 81 S or N, Exit 51. N/s rms, satellite TV, VCR/ movies, tt/dd phone, fax, copier, refrig, cot, crib, t/b/rv pkng, conn rms, b/f. Free local calls, cont brfst. AAA. $35/S; $40/D; $6/ex prsn. 5/1-10/31: $45/S; $50/D. Higher holiday, spec event rates. *Guaranteed rates.*

Selinsgrove
Comfort Inn/ Box 299, Selinsgrove PA 17870. 717-374-8880. M,V,AE,DC. On US 11 & 15, 1 blk S of Susquehanna Valley Mall. Rstrnt/ lounge, mtg rm, fax, b/f, cable TV, t pkng, outlets, n/s rms. Free cont brfst. AAA. $39-65/S; $39-80/D; $5/ex prsn. Discs.

Shippensburg
Budget Host Shippensburg Inn/ Hershey Rd, Box 349, Shippensburg PA 17257. 717-530-1234. AE,M,V. I-81, Exit 10. Cable TV, dd phone, n/s rms, nrby rstrnt, t pkng. Free crib. $34-38/S; $38-42/D. Spec events: $55-65.

Budget Host University Lodge/ 720 Walnut Bottom Rd, Box 349, Shippensburg PA 17257. 717-532-7311 Fax: 532-8872. M,V,AE. I-81 (Exit 10) to dntn. Cable TV, dd phone, n/s rms, mtg rms, t pkng, cot. Free crib. $34-38/S; $40-45/D. Spec events: $55-65.

Somerset
Budget Host Inn/ 799 N Central Av, Somerset PA 15501. 814-445-7988. V, M,AE,D,DC,CB. I-70/76, Exit 10 PA Trnpk. Cable TV, dd phone, n/s rms, adj rstrnt, cot, crib. AAA. $35-40/S; $35-42/D; $5/ex prsn. Wknds: $40-50/S; $45-70/D. Disc: Senior.

South Williamsport
King's Inn/ 590 Montgomery Pike, S Williamsport PA 17701. 717-322-4707/ Fax: 322-0946. V,M,AE,D,DC. On Rte 15 S, 1-1/2 mi from Williamsport. Rstrnt/ lounge, n/s rms, cable TV, tt/dd phone, fax, copier, crib, t/b/rv pkng, conn rms, b/f. Free cont brfst. AAA/ Mobil. $29-45/S; $34-52/D; $5/ex prsn. Higher spec event, holiday, wknd rates. Disc: Senior, bsns, TA, govt, family, trkr, milt, l/s.

State College
Friendship Inn/ 1040 N Atherton St, State College PA 16803. 814-238-6783. M,V,AE,DC. I-80 (Exit 24) to SR 26, 15 mi S to US 322 Bsns, rt, 3/4 mi. Nrby rstrnt, fax, cable TV, n/s rms. No pets. AAA. $36-64/S; $41-64/D; $5/ex prsn. Discs.

Sleep Inn/ 111 Village Dr, State College PA 16803. 814-235-1020. V,M,AE,D,DC. US 322 near Penn State Campus & dntn. Nrby rstrnt, mtg rm, fax, b/f, cable TV, n/s rms. Free cont brfst. $39/S; $45/D; $6/ex prsn. Spec events: $110/S; $130/D. Discs.

Washington
Motel 6/ 1283 Motel 6 Dr, Washington PA 15301. 412-223-8040/ Fax: 228-6445. V,M,AE,D,DC. I-70/ 79, Exit 7A/ Murtland Blvd Sbnd. At Texaco Station turn lt (North Av) up hill. Rstrnt, pool. Premier Award. $34-38/S; $40-44/D; $6/ex prsn. Higher spec event rates. Disc.

Waynesburg
Econo Lodge/ 350 Miller Ln, Waynesburg PA 15370. 412-627-5544. AE,M, V,DC. I-79 (Exit 3) at SR 21, rt at 1st light. Nrby rstrnt, mtg rm, fax, b/f, cable

PENNSYLVANIA / RHODE ISLAND

TV, t pkng. Free cont brfst. AAA. $41-50/S; $45-49/D; $4/ex prsn. Discs.

Wellsboro

Canyon Motel/ 18 East Av, Wellsboro PA 16901. 717-724-1681/ Fax: 724-5202/ 800-255-2718. V,M,AE,D,DC,CB. On US Rte 6. Pool, n/s rms, cable TV, playgrnd, TDD, tt/dd phone, fax, copier, refrig, crib, outlets, t/b pkng, b/f. Free local calls, cont brfst. AAA/ Mobil. $28-30/S; $45-49/D; $5/ex prsn.

Colton Point Motel/ RR 4, Box 138, Wellsboro PA 16901. 717-724-2155/ 800-829-4122. V,M,D. Nrby rstrnt/ lounge, n/s rms, cable TV, playgrnd, cot, crib, t/b/rv pkng. No pets. AAA. $30/S; $40-45/D; $5/ex prsn. Disc: Senior, bsns, TA, govt, l/s, family, trkr, milt. *Guaranteed rates.*

West Chester

Beechwood Motel/ 1310 Wilmington Pike, W Chester PA 19382. 610-399-0970. V,M,AE,D,DC. I-95, Exit 8, 10 mi on Rte 202. PA Turnpike, from W, Exit 23 to Rte 100S to Rte 202 S. Nrby rstrnt, n/s rms, cable TV, tt/dd phone, refrig, cot, crib, conn rms. Free local calls, cont brfst. No pets. AAA. $40-46/S or D; $5/ex prsn. Higher wknd rates, 4/1-10/31. Disc: Senior.

Williamsport

Ridgemont Motel/ RR 4, Box 536, Williamsport PA 17701. 717-321-5300. V,M,D. 2 mi S of Williamsport on Rte 15. Nrby rstrnt/ lounge, n/s rms, cable TV, dd phone, refrig, microwave, cot, crib, t/rv pkng. Free local calls. No pets. AAA/ Mobil. $33-35/S; $33-37/D; $1-3/ex prsn. *Guaranteed rates.*

Wormleysburg (Harrisburg area)

Friendship Inn/ 860 N Front St, Wormleysburg PA 17043. 717-763-7086. AE,V,M. I-81 (Exit 21) to US 11/ US 15, S to mtl. Rstrnt/ lounge, fax, cable TV, n/s rms. Free AM coffee. $28-30/S; $36-40/D; $5/ex prsn. 5/1-9/25: $30-36/S; $38-45/D. 9/26-10/9: $50-55/S; $60-70/D. Discs.

York

Chateau Motel/ 3951 E Market St, York PA 17402. 717-757-1714. V,M,D. I-83 (Exit 8) to Rte 462 (Market St), E 3 mi. Nrby rstrnt, n/s rms, cable TV, tt/dd phone, microwave, refrig, cot, crib, outlets, t pkng. Free local calls, coffee. No pets. AAA. $32-36/S; $36-43/D; $4/ex prsn. Spec events: $36-43/S; $40-45/D. Disc: Senior. *Guaranteed rates.*

Barnhart's Motel/ 3021 E Market St, York PA 17402. 717-755-2806/ Fax: 757-5475/ 800-882-7548. V,M,AE,D, DC. I-83, Exit 8 E, 1 mi on Hwy 462. Rte 30, Mt Zion Rd, 1/2 mi S, W 2 blks. N/s rms, cable TV, tt/dd phone, fax, copier, laundry, refrig, microwave, cot, crib, outlets, eff. Free cont brfst, coffee. No pets. AAA. $28-40/S; $34-40/D; $5/ex prsn. 5/1-10/30: $30-42/S; $36-42/D. Disc: Family. *Guaranteed rates.*

Budget Host Spirit of 76 Inn/ 1162 Haines Rd, York PA 17402. 717-755-1068/ Fax: 757-5571. AE,D,M,V. I-83 at Exit 7. Cable TV, movies, dd phone, n/s rms, adj rstrnt/ lounge, t pkng, cot, crib. AAA/ Mobil. $30-35/S; $35-40/D; $4/ex prsn. Spec events: $45.

Motel 6/ 125 Arsenal Rd, York PA 17404. 717-846-6260/ Fax: 845-5504. M,V,AE,DC,D. I-83 at US 30/Exit 9W/10. Nrby rstrnt, cable TV, laundry, elevator, n/s rms, t pkng. Free local calls. Premier Award. $28-30/S; $34-36/D; $6/ex prsn. 12/21-5/22: $32-36/S; $38-42/D. Higher spec event rates. Disc.

Rhode Island

Middletown (Newport area)

Howard Johnson Lodge/ 351 W Main Rd, Middletown RI 02842. 401-849-2000/ Fax: 849-6047. V,M,AE,D,DC, CB. Jct of Hwys 114 (W Main Rd) & 138 (E Main Rd). Rstrnt/ lounge, n/s rms, indr pool, t pkng, refrig, microwave, sauna. $34-59/S; $39-69/D. 5/1-6/30, 8/29-10/31: $44-94/S; $49-99/D. 7/1-8/27: $84-119/S; $89-124/D. Discs.

Newport

Comfort Inn/ 936 W Main Rd, Newport RI 02840. 401-846-7600. V,M,AE,D, DC. SR 138 to SR 114 (W Main Rd), N 2/10 mi to mtl. Nrby rstrnt, indr pool, mtg rm, fax, b/f, cable TV, n/s rms.

Free cont brfst. $40/S or D; $5/ex prsn. 5/1-5/15, 9/16-10/31: $80/S or D. 5/16-9/15: $110/S or D. Discs.

Harbor Base Pineapple Inn/ 372 Coddington Hwy, Newport RI 02840. 401-847-2600/ Fax: 847-5230. V,M,AE,D,DC,CB. I-38 E over Newport Bridge, at 1st light go rt, bear rt at traffic circle, 1 mi on rt. N/s rms, VCR/ movies, tt phone, fax, refrig, microwave, crib, eff. Free coffee. No pets. AAA. $20/S or D. 5/1-10/14 Sun-Thurs: $25-40/S or D. 5/1-10/14 Fri, Sat, holidays: $70-80/S or D.

Motel 6/ 249 J T Connell Hwy, Newport RI 02840. 401-848-0600/ Fax: 848-9966. M,V,AE,DC,D. From jct of Hwys 114 & 138, go W on 114 to JT Connell Hwy, turn S for 1/4 mi. Nrby rstrnt, cable TV, n/s rms, t pkng. Free local calls. Premier Award. $30-36/S; $36-42/D; $6/ex prsn. 5/25-10/29: $50/S; $56/D. Higher spec event rates. D

Also see Middletown.

Westerly

Pine Lodge Motel/ 92 Old Post Rd, Westerly RI 02891. 401-322-0333/ Fax: 322-2010/ 800-838-0333. V,M,AE,D,DC,CB. On US 1; 1-3/4 mi NE of jct SR 78. Fax, dd phone, copier, refrig, cot, crib, outlets, eff, conn rms. AAA/ Mobil. $45/S or D; $8/ex prsn. 6/16-9/14, Mem Day, Columbus Day wknds: $69/S or D. *Guaranteed rates.*

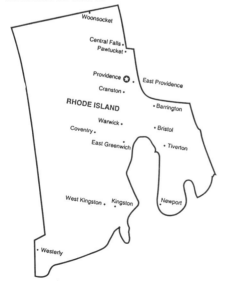

South Carolina

Aiken

Ramada Limited/ 1850 Richland Av W, Aiken SC 29801 803-648-6821/ Fax: 643-8546. V,M,AE,D,DC. I-20, Exit 22, Hwy 1 S, 7 mi, Exit Richland Av, rt 1-1/2 mi. Pool, n/s rms, cable TV, tt/dd phone, fax, copier, refrig, microwave, t/b/rv pkng, conn rms. Free cont brfst, coffee. No alcohol, parties. AAA. $25/S; $32/D; $4/ex prsn. Higher spec event rates. Discs. *Guaranteed rates.*

Comfort Suites/ 3608 Richland Av W, Aiken SC 29801. 803-641-1100. V,M,DC,AE. On US 1/78 near jct with SR 118. Nrby rstrnt, pool, mtg rm, whrlpool, cable TV, exerc equip, refrig, microwave, VCR, coffee, n/s rms. Free cont brfst. No pets. $39-160/S; $44-175/D; $5/ex prsn. Discs.

HoJo Inn/ 1936 Whiskey Rd S, Aiken SC 29803. 803-649-5000/ Fax: 641-4016. M,V,AE,DC,D. I-20 (Exit 18) to US 19 S. Just S of jct with Pine Log Rd. Rstrnt, n/s rms, b/f, t pkng, microwave, refrig, cable TV. Free cont brfst. No pets. $28-39/S; $28-43/D. Discs.

Beaufort

Howard Johnson Lodge/ US Hwy 21, Beaufort SC 29902. 803-524-6020/ Fax: 524-2027. M,DC,D,V,AE,CB. I-95 (Exit 33) to US Hwy 17 N to US Hwy 21, 18 mi on lt. Cable TV, b/f, pool. Free cont brfst. $45-50/S or D. Discs.

Bennettsville

Marlboro Inn/ 130 15-401 Bypass W, Bennettsville SC 29512. 803-479-4051/

SOUTH CAROLINA

Fax: 479-2275/ 800-214-3599. V,M, AE,D,DC,CB. N/s rms, cable TV, tt/dd phone, mtg rm, fax, refrig, microwave, crib, t/b/rv pkng, conn rms, b/f. Free local calls, cont brfst. No pets. AAA. $33/S; $40/D; $4/ex prsn. Spec event, holiday rates: $36/S; $44/D. *Guaranteed rates.*

Bishopville

Econo Lodge/ 1153 S Main St, Bishopville SC 29010. 803-428-3200. AE,V,M,DC. I-20 (Exit 116) at US 15. Adj rstrnt, fax, b/f, cable TV, t pkng. Free cont brfst. $32-38/S; $36-52/D; $5/ex prsn. Discs.

Charleston

Comfort Inn/ 5055 N Arco Ln, Charleston SC 29418. 803-554-6485. V,M, AE,D,DC. I-26 to Montague Av, NW to Arco Ln, turn lt. Nrby rstrnt, pool, mtg rm, fax, b/f, cable TV, n/s rms. Free cont brfst, arpt trans. AAA. $31-79/S or D; $6/ex prsn. Discs.

Econo Lodge/ 2237 Savannah Hwy, Charleston SC 29414. 803-571-1880/ Fax: 766-9351. AE,M,V,DC. US 17 (Savannah Hwy) at jct SR 7 & Mark Clark Expwy. Adj rstrnt, cable TV, n/s rms. Free cont brfst, local calls. No pets. $35-45/S; $39-45/D; $5/ex prsn. Discs.

HoJo Inn/ 3640 Dorchester Rd, Charleston SC 29405. 803-554-4140/ Fax: 554-4148. M,V,AE,DC,D. I-26 (Exit 215) at Dorchester Rd. Pool, n/s rms, b/f, t pkng, laundry, video games, cable TV, fax, copier, mtg rm. Free cont brfst. $29-45/S; $29-55/D. 5/1-6/30, 10/1-10/31: $39-49/S; $43-60/D. 7/1-9/30: $29-39/S; $39-49/D. Discs.

Motel 6/ 2058 Savannah Hwy, Charleston SC 29407. 803-556-5144/ Fax: 556-2241. V,M,AE,DC,D. I-26 Sbnd, Exit I-526 S, cross over SR 7 to US 17 to mtl. Nbnd: take SR 7 SW 6 mi, lt on Skylark Rd. Nrby rstrnt, cable TV, pool, n/s rms. Free local calls. $28-32/S; $32-36/D; $4/ex prsn. Higher spec event rates. Disc.

Motel 6/ 2551 Ashley Phosphate Rd, Charleston SC 29406. 803-572-6590/ Fax: 572-9026. V,M,AE,DC,D. I-26, Exit 209 to Ashley Phosphate Rd exit, turn W. Nrby rstrnt, cable TV, laundry, pool, n/s rms. Free local calls. $27-29/S; $31-33/D; $4/ex prsn. Disc.

Also see Goose Creek, North Charleston.

Clemson

Comfort Inn/ 1305 Tiger Blvd, Box 1496, Clemson SC 29633. 803-653-3600. V,M,AE,D,DC. I-85 (Exit 19) to US 76, N 14 mi to US 123 to mtl. Nrby rstrnt, pool, mtg rm, fax, b/f, whrlpool, cable TV, exerc equip, VCR, n/s rms. Free cont brfst. No pets. Hospitality Award. $47-155/S or D; $6-10/ex prsn. Higher rates for football wknds/ spec events. Discs.

Clinton

Comfort Inn/ Box 1058, Clinton SC 29325. 803-833-5558. AE,V,M,DC. I-385/ I-26 (Exit 52) to SR 56. Nrby rstrnt, pool, mtg rm, fax, b/f, cable TV, t/b pkng, outlets, laundry, VCR. Free cont brfst. No pets. AAA. $38-43/S; $40-50/D; $5-10/ex prsn. 3/1-4/30, 10/1-10/31: $50-60/S; $60-75/D. 5/1-9/30: $42-48/S; $45-60/D. Discs.

Columbia

Budgetel Inns/ 911 Bush River Rd, Columbia SC 29210 803-798-3222/ Fax: 731-5554. V,M,D,AE,DC,CB. I-26/126, Exit 108 Bush River Rd E. N/s rms, b/f, fax, pool. Free cont brfst, in-rm coffee, local calls. AAA. $35-46/S; $42-53/D. 3/1-12/31: $36-47/S; $43-54/D. Higher spec event rates. Discs.

Budgetel Inns/ 1538 Horseshoe Dr, Columbia SC 29223. 803-736-6400/ Fax: 788-7875. V,M,D,AE,DC,CB. Exit 74 to Two Notch Rd (US 1) E from I-20 to Horseshoe Dr. N/s rms, b/f, fax, pool. Free cont brfst, in-rm coffee, local calls. AAA. $33-45/S; $40-52/D. 3/1-12/31: $34-46/S; $41-53/D. Higher spec event rates.

Comfort Inn/ 2025 Main St, Columbia SC 29201. 803-252-6321. V,M,DC,AE. I-26 E into dntn. On corner of Main St & Elmwood Av. Nrby rstrnt, pool, mtg rm, fax, b/f, cable TV, exerc equip, n/s rms. Free cont brfst. AAA. $39-52/S; $44-57/D; $5/ex prsn. 9/1-3/31: $39-46/S; $44-51/D. Discs.

SOUTH CAROLINA

Comfort Inn/ 499 Piney Grove Rd, Columbia SC 29210. 803-798-0500. AE,V,M,DC. I-26 (Exit 104) at Piney Grove Rd. Nrby rstrnt, pool, mtg rm, fax, b/f, cable TV, t pkng, n/s rms. Free cont brfst. No pets. $39-58/S; $44-64/D; $5/ex prsn. Discs.

Comfort Inn/ 7700 Two Notch Rd, Columbia SC 29223. 803-788-5544. AE,V,M,DC. I-20 (Exit 74) to Two Notch Rd. I-77 (Exit 17) at US 1, rt 2 blks to mtl. Nrby rstrnt, pool, mtg rm, fax, b/f, cable TV, t pkng, n/s rms. Free cont brfst. No pets. AAA. $39-79/S; $45-99/D; $6/ex prsn. Higher spec event rates. Discs.

Econo Lodge/ 494 Piney Grove Rd, Columbia SC 29210. 803-731-4060. AE,V,M,DC. I-26 W (Exit 104) to Piney Grove Rd. Nrby rstrnt, mtg rm, fax, b/f, cable TV, t pkng, n/s rms. Free cont brfst. AAA. $29-34/S; $35-40/D; $5/ex prsn. 2/1-9/30: $34-39/S; $44-49/D. Discs.

HoJo Inn/ 494 Beltline Blvd, Columbia SC 29205. 803-738-1642. V,M,AE,D,DC,CB. US 76 & US 378, take Devine St, turn lt to Beltline Blvd. Rstrnt, n/s rm, b/f. Free cont brfst. No pets. $32-40/S; $40-49/D. Discs.

HoJo Inn/ 200 Zimalcrest Rd, Columbia SC 29210. 803-772-7200/ Fax: 772-6484. M,V,AE,DC,D. I-20 to (Exit 63) Bush River Rd N. I-26 to (Exit 108) Bush River Rd S. Rstrnt/ lounge, n/s rms, pool, t pkng, playgrnd, jog area, copier, fax, refrig. Free cont brfst. No pets. Gold Medal Winner. $30-65/S; $30-85/D. Discs.

Quality Inn/ 1029 Briargate Cir, Columbia SC 29212. 803-772-0270. V,M,DC,AE. I-20 (Exit 65) at Broad River Rd. Nrby rstrnt, pool, mtg rm, b/f, cable TV, t pkng, n/s rms. No pets. $41-60/S; $45-65/D; $5-6/ex prsn. Discs.

Dillon

Comfort Inn/ I-95 & SR 9, Dillon SC 29536. 803-774-4137. V,M,DC,AE. I-95 (Exit 193) to SR 9, E to mtl. Nrby rstrnt, pool, fax, b/f, cable TV, t pkng, n/s rms. Free cont brfst. No pets. AAA. $40-66/S; $43-76/D; $4/ex prsn. Higher rates during Darlington Race wknds & holidays. Discs.

Econo Lodge/ Rt 1, Box 76, Dillon SC 29536. 803-774-4181. M,V,AE,DC. I-95 (Exit 193) at SR 9. Adj rstrnt, cable TV, n/s rms. Free cont brfst, coffee. $31-60/S; $36-65/D; $4/ex prsn. 6/30-7/8: $51/S; $71/D. Rates higher on Darlington Race wknds & spec events. Discs.

Duncan (Spartanburg area)

Comfort Inn/ 1391 E Main St, Duncan SC 29334. 803-433-1333. V,M,DC,AE. I-85 (Exit 63) to SR 290, N 1 blk to mtl. Nrby rstrnt, pool, mtg rm, whrlpool, cable TV, t pkng, n/s rms. Free cont brfst. No pets. $35-40/S; $40-50/D. Discs.

Fair Play

Econo Lodge/ Box 186, Fair Play SC 29643. 803-972-9001. V,M,AE,D,DC. I-85 (Exit 2) at SR 59. Rstrnt, pool, cable TV, t pkng, n/s rms. $32-41/S; $37-57/D; $5/ex prsn. Discs.

Florence

Comfort Inn/ Box 5688, Florence SC 29501. 803-665-4558. V,M,DC,AE. I-95 (Exit 164) to US 52, S. Adj rstrnt, pool, mtg rm, fax, b/f, whrlpool, cable TV, exerc equip, n/s rms. Free cont brfst. No pets. Hospitality Award. AAA. $40-75/S; $45-90/D; $4/ex prsn. Higher spec event rates. Discs.

Econo Lodge/ 3932 W Palmetto St, Florence SC 29501. 803-662-7712. AE, M,V,DC. I-95 (Exit 157) at US 76. Rstrnt, pool, mtg rm, fax, b/f, cable TV, t pkng, n/s rms. AAA. $30-40/S; $35-55/D; $6/ex prsn. Higher spec event rates. Discs.

Econo Lodge/ Box 5688, Florence SC 29502. 803-665-8558. AE,M,V,DC. I-95 (Exit 164) at US 52, lt 1 blk. Nrby rstrnt, indr pool, fax, b/f, whrlpool, cable TV, t pkng, exerc equip, n/s rms. Free cont brfst. AAA. $33-45/S; $38-60/D; $4/ex prsn. Higher spec event rates. Discs.

Howard Johnson Lodge/ 3821 Bancroft Rd, Florence SC 29501. 803-664-9494/ Fax: 665-9125. V,M,AE,D,DC,CB. I-95 (Exit 157) at US 76. Pool, n/s rms, b/f, mtg rm, refrig, VCR/ movies, laundry. Free cont brfst. Gold Medal Winner. $29-49/S; $32-55/D. 12/22-1/6: $35-55/S; $42-75/D. Discs.

SOUTH CAROLINA

Motel 6/ 1834 W Lucas Rd, Florence SC 29501. 803-667-6100/ Fax: 673-9555. V,M,AE,D,DC. I-95, Exit 164/ Hwy 52. Nrby rstrnt, cable TV, pool, n/s rms. Free local calls. No truck parking. Premier Award. $27-30/S; $31-34/D; $4/ex prsn. Higher spec event rates. Disc.

Quality Inn/ 121 W Palmetto St, Drawer 2297, Florence SC 29503. 803-662-6341. V,M,DC,AE. US 301 & US 76, dntn. Rstrnt/ lounge, pool, mtg rm, fax, b/f, cable TV, n/s rms. No pets. $34/S; $38/D; $4/ex prsn. 3/21-3/31, 8/26-9/3: $60-75/S or D. Higher rates during Darlington Race wknds. Discs.

Quality Inn/ Box 1512, Florence SC 29503. 803-669-1715. V,M,DC,AE. I-95 (Exit 169) at TV Rd. 7 mi N of I-20/I-95 interchange. Rstrnt/ lounge, pool, mtg rm, fax, cable TV, t pkng, n/s rms, tennis, basketball. Free full brfst. AAA. $35-70/S; $45-70/D; $5/ex prsn. Higher rates during Darlington Race wknds. Discs.

Sleep Inn/ Box 5688, Florence SC 29502. 803-662-8558. M,V,AE,DC. I-95 (Exit 164) at US 52. Nrby rstrnt, pool, fax, b/f, cable TV, t pkng, n/s rms. Free deluxe cont brfst. No pets. Hospitality Award. AAA. $42-75/S; $47-90/D; $5/ex prsn. Discs.

Super 8 Motel/ 1832 W Lucas St, Florence SC 29501. 803-7267/ Fax: Ext 400. V,M,AE,DC. I-95 (Exit 164) to US 52, turn SE behind Texaco Mart. B/f, n/s rms, pool, t/b pkng, copier, cont brfst, cot. Free local calls, crib. Pride Award. $40/S; $46/D. Higher spec event rates. Disc.

Gaffney

Comfort Inn/ 143 Corona Dr, Gaffney SC 29341. 803-487-4200/ Fax: 487-4637. V,M,AE,D,DC,CB. I-85 (Exit) 92 at SR 11, N to mtl. Nrby rstrnt, pool, mtg rm, cable TV, t pkng, exerc equip, microwave, refrig. $37-65/S; $41-70/D; $5/ex prsn. Discs.

Goose Creek (Charleston area)

Econo Lodge/ 401 Goose Creek Blvd N, Goose Creek SC 29445. 803-797-8200. AE,M,V,DC. I-26: Wbnd, Exit 208 to US 52 W, 4 mi on lt; Ebnd, Exit 205 to US 52 W. Nrby rstrnt, pool, cable TV, t pkng, n/s rms. Free cont brfst, local calls. No pets. $36-43/S; $36-49/D; $5/ex prsn. Discs.

Greenville

Comfort Inn/ 540 N Pleasantburg Dr, Greenville SC 29607. 803-271-0060. V,M,AE,D,DC. I-385 at Pleasantburg Dr, turn S to mtl. Lounge, pool, mtg rm, fax, b/f, cable TV, n/s rms, laundry. Free hot buffet brfst, nwspr. No pets. AAA. $49-55/S or D; $5/ex prsn. 5/1-12/31: $48-54/S or D. Discs.

Comfort Inn/ 412 Mauldin Rd, Greenville SC 29605. 803-277-6730/ Fax: Ext 308. M,V,AE,DC. I-85 (Exit 46) at Mauldin Rd. Rstrnt, pool, mtg rm, fax, b/f, cable TV, t/b pkng, exerc equip. Free deluxe cont brfst. AAA. $39-75/S; $45-80/D; $5/ex prsn. 5/1-12/31: $37-72/S; $40-76/D. Discs.

Motel 6/ 224 Bruce Rd, Greenville SC 29605. 803-277-8630/ Fax: 299-1239. V,M,AE,DC,D. I-85, Exit 45A & Bsns US 25 Frontage Rd. Cable TV, pool, n/s rms. Free local calls. $26/S; $30/D; $4/ex prsn. Disc.

Greenwood

Econo Lodge/ 719 Bypass 25 NE, Greenwood SC 29646. 803-229-5329. AE,V,M,DC. From Hwy 72, take US 178 & 221 NW. Rstrnt, pool, fax, cable TV, t pkng, n/s rms. Free cont brfst. AAA. $31-37/S; $39-41/D; $5/ex prsn. Discs.

Greer

Comfort Inn/ 611 W Wade Hampton Blvd, Greer SC 29650. 803-848-4995. V,M,AE,D,DC. SR 14 & US 29, turn W on 29 (Wade Hampton Blvd). Nrby rstrnt, pool, mtg rm, fax, b/f, cable TV, exerc equip, n/s rms. Free cont brfst. No pets. $39-89/S; $44-99/D; $6/ex prsn. Discs.

Hardeeville

Comfort Inn/ Box 544, Hardeeville SC 29927. 803-784-2188. V,M,AE,D,DC, CB. I-95 (Exit 5) at US 17. Nrby rstrnt, pool, fax, b/f, whrlpool, cable TV, t pkng, exerc equip. Free cont brfst. No pets. AAA. $42-65/S; $45-80/D; $6/ex prsn. Higher spec event rates. Discs.

SOUTH CAROLINA

Howard Johnson Lodge/ Box 1107, Hardeeville SC 29927. 803-784-2271/ Fax: Ext 171. M,V,AE,DC,D. I-95, Exit 5. Rstrnt, n/s rms, b/f, pool, t pkng, cable TV, kiddie pool. $33-54/S; $37-69/D. Discs.

Hartsville

Days Inn/ 903 S Fifth St, Hartsville SC 29550. 803-383-0110/ Fax: 383-0428. V,M,AE,D,DC,CB. I-20 to Hwy 15 into Hartsville, 2 mi from traffic light on rt. Pool, n/s rms, exerc equip, cable TV, tt phone, mtg rm, fax, copier, cot, crib, t pkng, b/f. Free local calls, cont brfst, coffee. No pets. $37-42/S; $42-46/D; $5/ex prsn. 3/23-3/24, 8/31-9/1: $90/S or D. Discs. *Guaranteed rates.*

Hilton Head Island

Motel 6/ 830 William Hilton Pkwy, Hilton Head SC 29928. 803-785-2700/ Fax: 842-9543. V,M,AE,DC,D. On US 278 (Wm Hilton Pkwy), 2 blks S of Shelter Cove Marina. Nrby rstrnt, cable TV, pool, n/s rms. Free local calls. Premier Award. $30-33/S; $36-39/D; $6/ex prsn. 3/28-5/22: $36-40/S; $42-46/D. 5/25-12/21: $36/S; $42/D. Higher spec event rates. Disc.

Comfort Inn/ 2 Tanglewood Dr, Hilton Head Island SC 29928. 803-842-6662. AE,V,M,DC. US 278 at Pope Av. At 1st traffic circle take Pope Av, at 2nd circle take S Forest Beach Dr. Rstrnt/ lounge, pool, mtg rm, fax, b/f, cable TV, t pkng, n/s rms, in-rm coffee. Free cont brfst. AAA. $35-90/S; $35-100/D; $10/ex prsn. Discs.

Manning

Comfort Inn/ Box 57, Manning SC 29102. 803-473-7550. V,M,DC,AE. I-95 (Exit 119) at SR 261. Nrby rstrnt, pool, cable TV, t pkng, n/s rms. Free cont brfst. No pets. $30-45/S; $40-49/D; $5/ex prsn. Discs.

Marion

Comfort Inn/ Box 925, Marion SC 29571. 803-423-0516. V,M,AE,D,DC. Bet Marion & Mullins on US 76 & 501 Bypass exit. Nrby rstrnt, pool, mtg rm, fax, b/f, cable TV, t pkng, n/s rms. Free cont brfst. No pets. AAA. $41-71/S; $46-76/D; $5/ex prsn. Higher spec event/ holiday rates. Discs.

Myrtle Beach

Comfort Inn/ 2801 S Kings Hwy, Myrtle Beach SC 29577. 803-626-4444. V, M, DC,AE. I-95 to US 501, S to US 17 Bsns (Kings Hwy), S to 29th Ave S. Pool, b/f, cable TV, exerc equip, game rm, laundry, picnic area, n/s rms. Free cont brfst. No pets. AAA. $35-75/S; $40-80/D; $8/ex prsn. 5/1-6/15, 8/21-10/26: $50-75/S; $55-80/D. 6/16-8/20: $84-100/S; $89-105/D. Discs.

Grand Strand Motel/ 1804 S Ocean Blvd, Myrtle Beach SC 29577. 803-448-1461/ Fax: 626-2242/ 800-433-1461. V,M,AE,D. Nrby rstrnt, pool, cable TV, dd phone, fax, copier, laundry, elevator, microwave, cot, crib, eff. Free coffee. No pets. AAA. $22-56/S; $25-69/D; $6/ex prsn. Higher spec event, holiday, wknd rates. Disc: Senior.

Super 8 Motel/ 3450 US 17 S Bypass, Myrtle Beach SC 29577. 803-293-6100/ Fax: Ext 605. V,MC,AE,DC. US 501 to US 17 S Bypass, S 2 1/2 mi. Pool, n/s rm, b/f, game rm, outlets, t/b/rv pkng, cont brfst, copier, elevator, cable TV, cot. Free crib. $38/S or D; $5/ex prsn. 5/29-9/7: $65/S; $70/D. Higher spec event, holiday rates. Discs.

Also see North Myrtle Beach.

Newberry

Comfort Inn/ 1147 Wilson Rd, Newberry SC 29108. 803-276-1600. V,M,DC,AE. I-26 (Exit 76) to SR 219, W 3 mi to US 76 S. Nrby rstrnt, pool, mtg rm, fax, b/f, cable TV, t pkng, exerc equip, laundry, refrig, microwave, in-rm coffee. Free cont brfst. $38-60/S; $42-65/D; $4/ex prsn. 5/1-6/30: $39-60/S; $44-65/D. 7/1-8/31: $42-65/S; $48-70/D. 9/1-10/31: $40-55/S; $44-65/D. Discs.

North Charleston (Charleston area)

Budget Inn of Charleston/ 6155 Fain St, North Charleston SC 29406. 803-747-7691. V,M,AE. I-26, Exit 211A (Aviation Av), look for sign. Pool, n/s rms, satellite TV, games, arpt trans, tt phone, fax, copier, laundry, refrig, cot, crib, t/b/rv pkng. Free cont brfst, coffee. No pets. AAA. $28-35/S; $32-35/D; $4/ex prsn. Disc: Senior, bsns, TA, govt, l/s, milt.

SOUTH CAROLINA

Charleston Orchard Inn/ 4725 Saul White Blvd, North Charleston SC 29418. 803-747-3672/ Fax: 744-0953/ 800-368-4871. V,M,AE,D,DC. I-26, Exit 213A (Montague Av), lt side, next to Waffle House. Pool, cable TV, TDD, tt/dd phone, fax, copier, laundry, cot, crib, outlets, t/b/rv pkng, eff, conn rms, b/f. Free local calls, coffee. AAA. $38-45/S; $43-50/D; $5/ex prsn. Spec event, holiday, wknd rates: $45/S; $50/D. Disc: Senior, bsns, TA, govt, family, trkr, milt. *Guaranteed rates.*

Rodeway Inn/ 5020 Rivers Av, North Charleston SC 29418. 803-554-4982. V,M,AE,D,DC. I-26, exit 212C to I-526 E. Take exit 18 to US 52/78 (Rivers Av), 1 blk on lt. Nrby rstrnt, pool, fax, b/f, cable TV, kitchenettes, refrig, n/s rms. Free cont brfst. No pets. $31-37/S; $33-39/D; $6/ex prsn. Discs.

North Myrtle Beach

Comfort Inn/ 1755 US 17 N, North Myrtle Beach SC 29597. 802-249-2490. V,M,AE,D,DC. On US 17. Nrby rstrnt, pool, mtg rm, fax, b/f, cable TV, exerc equip, n/s rms. Free cont brfst. $35-70/S or D; $10/ex prsn. 3/1-4/30: $40-85/S or D. Discs.

Orangeburg

Sun Inn/ 885 Calhoun Dr, Orangeburg SC 28115. 803-531-1921/ Fax: 554-5368/ 800-488-5368. V,M,AE,D, DC. I-26, Exit 145A, follow Hwy 601 S 4 mi, Exit Hwy 301 lt 1/4 mi. Pool, n/s rms, cable TV, VCR/ movies, tt/dd phone, fax, copier, nwspr, t/b/rv pkng, conn rms. Free cont brfst. No alcohol, parties. AAA/ Mobil. $28/S; $34/D; $4/ex prsn. Disc: Senior, bsns, govt, I/s, family, trkr, milt. *Guaranteed rates.*

Richburg

Econo Lodge/ Rte 1, Box 182, Richburg SC 29729. 803-789-3000. AE,M,V,DC. I-77 (Exit 65) to SR 9. Adj rstrnt, fax, b/f, cable TV, t pkng, coffee. Free cont brfst. $30-37/S; $35-45/D; $5/ex prsn. Discs.

Ridgeland (Point South area)

Comfort Inn/ Drawer J, Ridgeland SC 29936. 803-726-2121. V,M,AE,D,DC. I-95 (Exit 21) at US 278. Nrby rstrnt, pool, indr pool, fax, cable TV, b/f, n/s rms. Free cont brfst. $40-80/S; $46-86/D; $6/ex prsn. Discs.

Econo Lodge/ 516 E Main St, Ridgeland SC 29936. 800-424-4777 — opening soon. V,M,AE,D,DC. I-95 (Exit 21) to US 278 W. Rstrnt, pool, b/f, cable TV, n/s rms. $40/S; $45/D; $5/ex prsn. Discs.

Point South Quality Inn/ Drawer AA, Ridgeland SC 29936. 803-726-8101/ Fax: Ext 311. V,M,AE,D,DC,CB. I-95 (Exit 33) at US 17. Rstrnt, indr pool, n/s rms, satellite TV, VCR/ movies, playgrnd, tt phone, mtg rm, fax, copier, laundry, cot, crib, t/b/rv pkng, eff. AAA. $36-44/S; $46-54/D; $6/ex prsn. Discs.

Rock Hill

Comfort Inn/ 875 Riverview Rd, Rock Hill SC 29730. 803-329-2171. V,M, AE,D,DC. I-77 (Exit 82B) & US 21, W to mtl. Nrby rstrnt, pool, fax, b/f, cable TV, t pkng, outlets, n/s rms. Free cont brfst. No pets. AAA. $36-42/S; $46-51/D; $5/ex prsn. 5/26-5/27: $55-60/S; $65-70/D. Discs.

Econo Lodge/ 962 Riverview Rd, Rock Hill SC 29730. 803-329-3232. AE,V,M,DC. I-77 (Exit 82 B) to Cherry Rd (US 21). Nrby rstrnt, fax, b/f, cable TV, t pkng, n/s rms. Free cont brfst. $32-45/S; $39-49/D; $5/ex prsn. Discs.

Rodeway Inn/ 656 Anderson Rd, Rock Hill SC 29730. 803-329-2100. V,M, D,AE. I-77, Exit 82, US 21 Bypass, 1 mi on rt at jct Mt Gallant & Anderson. Nrby rstrnt/ lounge, pool, mtg rm, fax, b/f, cable TV, t pkng, n/s rms, exerc equip. Free cont brfst. $30-70/S; $36-70/D; $5/ex prsn. 5/1-5/24: $32-70/S; $38-70/D. 5/25-5/30: $65/S or D. 5/31-9/4: $34-75/S; $40-85/D. Discs.

Saint George

Comfort Inn/ Box 654, Saint George SC 29477. 803-563-4180. V,M,DC,AE. Jct of I-95 (Exit 77) & US 78. Nrby rstrnt, pool, fax, b/f, cable TV, rv pkng, n/s rms. Free cont brfst. AAA. $38-48/S; $40-50/D; $5/ex prsn. 4/1-4/30: $42-52/S; $44-54/D. Discs.

Econo Lodge/ Box 132, Saint George SC 29477. 803-563-4027. AE,M,V,DC.

SOUTH CAROLINA

I-95 & US 78. Rstrnt, pool, fax, b/f, cable TV, t pkng, n/s rms. Free cont brfst. AAA. $21-35/S; $25-35/D; $4/ex prsn. Discs.

Santee

Comfort Inn/ 265 Britain St, Santee SC 29142. 803-854-3221. V,M,DC,AE. I-95, Exit 98. Adj rstrnt, pool, mtg rm, fax, b/f, cable TV, t pkng, n/s rms. Free cont brfst. $39-52/S; $40-75/D; $4/ex prsn. 5/1-8/1: $39-58/S; $42-95/D. 8/2-11/1: $39-58/S; $44-115/D. Discs.

Howard Johnson Hotel/ Box 130, Santee SC 29142. 803-478-7676/ 800-531-9438. V,M,AE,D,DC,CB. I-95 (Exit 102) to Road 400, turn rt. Rstrnt/ lounge, pool, n/s rms, t pkng, mtg rm. $30-45/S; $35-60/D. Discs.

Spartanburg

Comfort Inn/ 1353 Boiling Springs Rd, Spartanburg SC 29303. 803-585-5890. V,M,DC,AE. I-85, Exit 75 to mtl. Nrby rstrnt, pool, fax, b/f, cable TV, exerc equip, n/s rms. Free cont brfst. No pets. AAA. $40-60/S; $45-70/D; $5/ex prsn. Higher spec event rates. Discs.

Comfort Inn/ 2070 New Cut Rd, Spartanburg SC 29303. 803-576-2992. V,M,AE,D,DC,CB. I-26 W (Exit 17) at New Cut Rd to mtl. I-85 to I-26 NW towards Ashville, 1/2 mi to mtl. Nrby rstrnt, pool, fax, b/f, cable TV, t pkng, n/s rms. Free cont brfst. No pets. Hospitality Award. AAA. $39-75/S; $47-80/D; $6-10/ex prsn. 5/1-10/31: $45-75/S; $50-89/D. Higher spec event rates. Discs.

Econo Lodge/ 710 Sunbeam Rd, Spartanburg SC 29303. 803-578-9450. AE,V,M. I-85 (Exit 75) to Boiling Springs Rd. Nrby rstrnt, pool, fax, b/f, cable TV, t pkng, n/s rms. Free cont brfst. AAA. $32-45/S; $37-52/D; $4/ex prsn. Discs.

HoJo Inn/ 462 E Main St, Spartanburg SC 29302. 803-585-3621/ Fax: 585-6454. M,V,AE,DC,D. I-85 (Exit 73A) Hwy 585, SE to Main St & Pine St. Nrby rstrnt/ lounge, n/s rms, trans, cable TV. Free AM coffee. No pets. $30-38/S; $36-44/D. Discs.

Motel 6/ 105 Jones Rd, Spartanburg SC 29303. 803-573-6383/ Fax: 582-7060. V,M,AE,DC,D. I-85, Exit 78 to US 221 S. Nrby rstrnt, cable TV, pool, n/s rms. Free local calls. $28/S; $32/D; $4/ex prsn. Disc.

Also see Duncan.

Summerton

Econo Lodge/ Box 938, Summerton SC 29148. 803-485-2865. AE,V,M. I-95 (Exit 108) to SR 102 (Buff Blvd), N to mtl. Nrby rstrnt, pool, fax, b/f, cable TV, t pkng. Free cont brfst, local calls. $25-30/S; $25-36/D; $5/ex prsn. Discs.

Summerville

Econo Lodge/ 110 Holiday Inn Dr, Summerville SC 29483. 803-875-3022. AE,M,V,DC. I-26 & 17 Alt. Adj rstrnt/ lounge, fax, b/f, cable TV, t pkng, n/s rms. Free AM coffee. AAA. $40-45/S; $45-50/D; $4/ex prsn. Discs.

Sumter

Ramada Inn/ 226 N Washington St, Sumter SC 29151. 803-775-2323/ Fax: 773-9500. V,M,AE,D,DC,CB. 18 minutes W of I-95 & US 378 jct; 6 blks from Sumter City Hall. Pool, n/s rms, cable TV, TDD, tt/dd phone, mtg rm, fax, copier, laundry, elevator, cot, crib, b/rv pkng, b/f. Free local calls, coffee. AAA/ Mobil. $40-52/S; $40-56/D; $6/ex prsn. 4/15-12/31: $45-52/S; $48-56/D. 7/1-7-10, 9/1-9/2: $52-62/S; $56-66/D. Discs. Guaranteed rates.

Walterboro

Comfort Inn/ 1109 Sniders Hwy, Walterboro SC 29488. 803-538-5403. AE,V,M,DC. I-95 (Exit 53) at SR 63. Nrby rstrnt/ lounge, pool, mtg rm, fax, b/f, cable TV, playgrnd, kiddie pool, n/s rms. Free cont brfst. AAA. $32-50/S; $40-70/D; $6/ex prsn. Discs.

Days Inn Walterboro/ Rte 4, Box 890, Walterboro SC 29488. 803-538-2933/ Fax: 538-2158. V,M,AE,D,DC. I-95 at Exit 53. Pool, sauna, n/s rms, exerc equip, cable TV, tt phone, fax, cot, crib, outlets, conn rms, b/f. Free local calls, cont brfst. No pets. AAA. $38-65/S; $38-95/D; $5/ex prsn. Higher spec event rates. Disc: senior, bsns, TA, govt, milt, trkr, family.

Howard Johnson/ 1305 Bells Hwy, Walterboro SC 29488. 803-538-3948. V,M,AE,D,DC,CB. I-95, Exit 57. Rstrnt, n/s rms, b/f, pool, t pkng, cable TV. Free cont brfst, local calls. $25-45/S; $28-55/D. Discs.

South Dakota

Aberdeen

Super 8 Motel/ 714 S Hwy 281, Box 1593, Aberdeen SD 57401. 605-225-1711. AE,V,M,D,DC,CB. Jct of Hwys 12 & 281. Game rm, laundry, outlets, t/b/rv pkng, cont brfst, cable TV, arpt trans, TDD, eff, cot, n/s rms, b/f. Free local calls, crib. Pride Award. $31/S; $36-38/D; $5/ex prsn. Higher spec event rates. Dis

Arlington

Super 8 Motel/ Box 230, Arlington SD 57212. 605-983-4609. AE,V,M,D,DC,CB. US 14 Bypass. 22 mi W of I-29, Exit 133 at Brookings. Outlets, cont brfst, t/b/rv pkng, cable TV, mtg rm, kennel, n/s rms, b/f. Free local calls, crib. Pride Award. $30/S; $32-37/D; $5/ex prsn. 10/20-11/05: $40/S; $42-47/D. Higher spec event, wknd rates. Discs.

Belle Fourche

Sunset Motel/ HCR 30, Box 65, Belle Fourche SD 57717. 605-892-2508. V,M,AE,D. I-90, Exit 10. On Hwy 85. N/s rms, satellite TV, playgrnd, arpt, trans, dd phone, t/b/rv pkng. Free local calls, coffee. AAA. $25-50/S; $30-58/D. Higher spec event, holiday, wknd rates.

Brookings

Comfort Inn/ 514 Sunrise Ridge Rd, Brookings SD 57006. 605-692-9566. AE,V,M,DC. I-29 (Exit 132) at US 14, W to Service Rd & Sunrise Ridge Rd, S to mtl. Nrby rstrnt, fax, b/f, whrlpool, cable TV, t pkng, outlets, n/s rms. Free cont brfst. No pets. AAA. $37-89/S; $42-89/D; $5/ex prsn. Discs.

Buffalo

Tipperary Lodge Motel/ Box 247, Buffalo SD 57720. 605-375-3721/ 800-223-4666. V,M,AE,D,DC,CB. On N Hwy 85. N/s rms, cable TV, arpt trans, tt/dd phone, microwave, cot, crib, outlets, t/b pkng. Free local calls, cont brfst, coffee. AAA. $30/S; $34/D; $4/ex

Chamberlain

See Oacoma.

Deadwood

Super 8 Motel/ 196 Cliff St, Deadwood SD 57732. 605-578-2535/ Fax: 578-3604. AE,V,M,D,DC,CB. On Hwy 85 S, S of I-90. Pool, n/s rms, casino, whrlpool, t/b/rv pkng, cable TV, trolly. Free cont brfst, local calls. No pets. Pride Award. AAA. $40/S; $40-55/D. 4/30-5/31: $50/S; $50-60/D. 6/1-9/5: $65/S; $65-75/D. 9/1-9/30, 12/22-1/1: $55/S; $55-70/D. Higher wknd/ holiday rates. Discs.

Eagle Butte

Super 8 Motel/ Box 180, Eagle Butte SD 57625. 605-964-8888. AE,V,M,D,DC,CB. Hwy 212 W side of Cultural Ctr, straight S of Lindskor Car Dealership. Outlets, t/b/rv pkng, copier, elevator, cable TV, mtg rm, n/s rms, b/f. Free local calls. $35/S; $40/D; $6/ex prsn. Higher spec event, wknd/ holiday rates. Discs.

Faith

Prairie Vista Inn/ Box 575, Faith SD 57626. 605-967-2343/ Fax: 967-2653. V,M,AE,D,CB,DC. Hwy 212. Cable TV, dd phone, outlets, whrlpool, sauna, b/f, n/s rms, exerc equip, cot, crib, t pkng, outlets, mtg rm, fax, conn rms. Free coffee. AAA/ IMA. $35-39/S; $40-44/D; $5/ex prsn. 8/8-8/10, 10/4-10/6, 11/8-11/10: $49/S or D. Disc: Comm, family, senior, TA.

SOUTH DAKOTA

Gettysburg
Trail Motel/ 211 E Garfield, Gettysburg SD 57442. 605-765-2482. V,M,AE,D,DC. 15 minutes from Lake Oahe. Cable TV, dd phone, outlets, cot, crib, t pkng. IMA. $23/S; $29-32/D; $2-4/ex prsn. 4/1-11/30: $26/S; $30-35/D.

Super 8 Motel/ 719 E Hwy 212, Gettysburg SD 57442. 605-765-2373. V, M, AE,D,DC,CB. On US 212. Nrby rstrnt, whrlpool, laundry, outlets, t/b/rv pkng, cont brfst, copier, cable TV, mtg rm, cot, n/s rms. Free local calls. Pride Award. $35/S; $41-46/D; $6/ex prsn. Discs.

Hot Springs
Comfort Inn/ 737 S 6th St, Box 33, Hot Springs SD 57747. 605-745-7378. V,M,DC,AE. US 385/18 to US 18 Bypass, W to S 6th St, N to mtl. Nrby rstrnt, indr pool, mtg rm, fax, b/f, whrlpool, cable TV, t pkng, exerc equip, outlets. Free cont brfst. AAA. $36-99/S; $40-99/D; $6/ex prsn. 5/1-6/15, 9/5-10/31: $48-109/S; $52-109/D. 6/16-9/4: $82-149/S; $88-149/D. Dis

Kimball
Super 8 Motel/ Box 310, Kimball SD 57355. 605-778-6088/ Fax: Ext 202. V,M,AE,D,DC,CB. On Hwy 45, 2 blks N of I-90. Cable TV, copier, t/b pkng, cot, crib, n/s rms, b/f. Free local calls. Pride Award. $26-34/S; $36-44/D; $5/ex prsn. 10/19-11/12: $46/S; $51/D. Higher spec event rates. Discs.

Interior
Badlands Budget Host Motel/ HC54, Box 115, Interior SD 57750. 605-433-5335/ (Winter: 800-388-4643). M,V,D. I-90 (Exit 131) Badlands Loop N 240 to Hwy 377, then 2 mi S. Pool, playgrnd, picnic area, laundry, cot, crib, t/b pkng, conn rms. Free coffee. AAA. $37-45/S or D. Disc: Senior. CLOSED FALL & WINTER *Guaranteed rates.*

Badlands Inn/ Box 103, Interior SD 57750. 605-433-5401. V,M. On Hwy 377. I-90, Exit 131, 8-1/2 mi S. Pool, dd phone, cot. Free coffee, crib. IMA. $28/S; $34-39/D; $4/ex prsn. 6/1-9/5: $32/S; $41-45/D. Higher spec event/ holiday rates. Motel is closed 9/30-5/15. Disc: TA.

Kadoka
Sundowner Motor Inn/ Box 129, Kadoka SD 57543. 605-837-2296/ Fax: 837-2879/ 800-432-5682. V,M,AE,D,DC,CB. SD Hwy 73 & I-90, Exit 150, S 1/4 mi. Pool, n/s rms, cable TV, playgrnd, tt/dd phone, fax, copier, crib, outlets, t/b pkng, conn rms. Free local calls, coffee. No pets. AAA. $29-41/S; $33-48/D; $5/ex prsn. 6/10-7/31, 8/21-9/4: $33-58/S; $37-69/D. 8/1-8/20: $67-77/S; $73-88/D. Disc: Senior.

Kennebec
Budget Host Gerry's Motel/ Box 141, Kennebec SD 57544. 605-869-2210. D,M,V. I-90, Exit 235, N 1 blk. Cable TV, n/s rms, nrby rstrnt, adj lounge, cont brfst, t pkng, outlets, cot. No pets. AAA. $21/S; $25-29/D; $4/ex prsn. 5/25-6/30, 8/16-11/30: $28/S; $32-36/D. 7/1-8/15: $32/S; $36-44/D. Disc: Senior.

Keystone
Friendship Inn/ HC 33, Box 108, Keystone SD 57751. 605-666-4417. AE,V,M. SR 16A to SR 40, E 1 mi to mtl. Nrby rstrnt, pool, fax, whrlpool, cable TV, n/s rms. No pets. $29-69/S or D. 6/14-9/4: $59-109/S or D. Discs.

Kelly Inn/ Box 654, Keystone SD 57751. 605-666-4483/ Fax: 666-4883. V,M,AE,D,CB,DC,ER. Hwy 16A, S edge of Keystone. Cable TV, dd phone, outlets, whrlpool, sauna, b/f, microwave, exerc bike, mtg rm, cot, conn rms, family rms, n/s rms. Free coffee, crib. AAA/IMA. $30-43/S; $35-48/D; $5/ex prsn. 5/24-5/26, 6/10-9/1: $62/S; $67/D. 5/27-6/9: $53/S; $58/D. Discs.

Kimball
Travelers Motel/ Box 457, Kimball SD 57355. 605-778-6215. V,M,AE,D. On Hwy 45 & I-90, Exit 284. Nrby rstrnt, cable TV, tt/dd phone, outlets, t pkng, family rms, cot, crib, n/s rms. AAA/IMA. $32/S; $36/D; $3/ex prsn. 6/1-9/15, 10/14-11/15: $44/S or D. Disc: TA.

Lemmon
Prairie Motel/ 115 E 10th St, Lemmon SD 57638. 605-374-3304. V,M,AE,D,DC,CB. On US Hwy 12. Nrby rstrnt, n/s rms, cable TV, arpt trans, tt/dd phone,

SOUTH DAKOTA 236

copier, refrig, microwave, cot, crib, outlets, t/b/rv pkng. Free local calls, coffee. AAA. $23/S; $26-30/D; $4/ex prsn. Disc: Bsns, family, l/s.

Madison
Lake Park Motel/ Box 47, Madison SD 57042. 605-256-3524. V,M,AE,D,DC,CB. 2 blks W of Hwy 81 & 34 Jct. Pool, n/s rms, cable TV, arpt trans, tt/dd phone, refrig, cot, crib, outlets, t/b/rv pkng, b/f. Free local calls, coffee. No alcohol. AAA/ Mobil. $28/S; $35-38/D; $5/ex prsn. 10/15-12/1: $35/S; $48/D. Disc: Senior, bsns, TA, govt, l/s, family, trkr, milt. *Guaranteed rates.*

Martin
Cross Roads Inn/ Box 970, Martin SD 57551. 605-685-1070. V,M,D,AE,D,CB. Jct Hwy 18 & 73. Nrby rstrnt, cable TV, dd phone, arpt trans, outlets, b/f, mtg rm, cot, crib, n/s rms. AAA/ IMA. $36/S; $41-47/D; $5/ex prsn. 5/1-10/31: $38/S; $43-49/D. Disc: AAA, senior.

Milbank
Manor Motel/ Box 26, Milbank SD 57252. 605-432-4527. V,M,AE,D,CB, DC. E Hwy 12. Rstrnt, cable TV, dd phone, indr pool, arpt trans, outlets, whrlpool, sauna, t pkng, cot, crib, n/s rms, conn rms. AAA/ IMA. $30-32/S; $36-42/D; $4/ex prsn. Disc: Senior, AARP, family.

Miller
Dew Drop Inn/ HC 64, Box 140, Miller SD 57362. 605-853-2431/ 800-780-6996. V,M,AE,D,DC,CB. N Hwy 14 & 45. Nrby rstrnt/ lounge, cable TV, dd phone, arpt trans, outlets, b/f, t pkng, cont brfst, n/s rms, cot, crib, conn rms. Free local calls. IMA. $24/S; $30-34/D; $2/ex prsn. 5/16-10/31: $27/S; $33-38/D. Disc: Comm, senior, TA.

Mitchell
Anthony Motel/ 1518 W Havens St, Mitchell SD 57301. 605-996-7518/ Fax: 996-7251/ 800-477-2235. V,M,AE,D. I-90, Exit 330. Pool, cable TV, arpt trans, tt/dd phone, fax, copier, laundry, refrig, crib, outlets, eff, conn rms, b/f. Free coffee. No pets. AAA/ Mobil. $32-42/S; $32-46/D. Includes higher rates during summer.

Budget Host Inn/ 1313 S Ohlman, Mitchell SD 57301. 605-996-6647/ Fax: 996-7339. AE,V,M,D,DC,CB. I-90, Exit 330 N, 1st mtl on lt. N/s rms, cable TV, tt/dd phone, fax, laundry, cot, crib, outlets, t/b pkng. Free local calls, cont brfst. AAA. $32/S; $42/D; $6/ex prsn. 6/9-9/30: $36/S; $46/D. Disc: Senior, TA, trkr, milt.

Motel 6/ 1309 S Ohlman St, Mitchell SD 57301. 605-996-0530/ Fax: 995-2019. M,V,DC,D,AE. I-90, Exit 330 to Ohlman St, N to mtl. Cable TV, laundry, pool, n/s rms. Free local calls. $26-30/S; $32-36/D; $6/ex prsn. Disc.

Thunderbird Lodge/ Box 984, Mitchell SD 57301. 605-996-6645/ Fax: 995-5883. V,M,AE,D,DC,CB. I-90 & SR 37, Exit 332. Adj rstrnt, cable TV, dd phone, arpt trans, game rm, laundry, outlets, whrlpool, sauna, b/f, n/s rms, t pkng, cot, crib. AAA/ IMA. $36-38/S; $43-52/D; $2/ex prsn. 10/18-10/28: $62/S or D. Disc: AAA, senior, AARP,

Murdo
Super 8 Motel/ 604 E 5th, Murdo SD 57559. 605-669-2437. V,AE,M,DC, CB,D. I-90 (Exit 192) at US 83. Outlets, b/t pkng, cable TV, coffee, cot, crib, n/s rms, b/f. Free local calls. Pride Award. $27-34/S; $29-40/D; $2/ex prsn. 5/1-5/26, 9/8-10/31: $34/S; $36-40/D. 5/27-9/7: $45/S; $47-51/D. Higher spec event rates. Discs.

North Sioux City
Comfort Inn/ 115 Streeter Dr, Box 1220, North Sioux City SD 57049. 605-232-3366. V,M,D,AE. I-29 (Exit 2) to River Dr, W 1/10 mi. Nrby rstrnt/ lounge, indr pool, mtg rm, fax, b/f, whrlpool, cable TV, t pkng. Free cont brfst. $43-71/S; $48-76/D; $5/ex prsn. 5/1-5/31: $47-71/S; $52-76/D. 6/1-8/19: $52-76/S; $57-81/D. Discs.

Oacoma (Chamberlain area)
Oasis Inn/ Box 39, Oacoma SD 57365. 605-734-6061/ Fax: 734-4161. V,M,AE,D,CB,DC,ER. I-90 & Hwy 16, Exit 260. Cable TV, dd phone, arpt trans, laundry, outlets, whrlpool, sauna, b/f, playgrnd, cot, crib, n/s rms, t pkng, mini-golf, kids fishing pond. AAA/ IMA. $35-39/S; $39-45/D; $6/ex prsn. 5/24-9/15: $50/S; $60/D. 9/16-10/14: $42/S;

$48/D. 10/15-11/21: $60/S; $60-66/D. Disc: AAA, senior, AARP, TA, family.

Pickstown

Fort Randall Inn/ Box 108, Pickstown SD 57367. 605-487-7801/ Fax: 487-7802/ 800-340-7801. V,M,AE,D,DC,CB. At jct Hwys 18 & 281. Rstrnt/ lounge, n/s rms, cable TV, tt/dd phone, fax, copier, laundry, cot, crib, outlets, t/b/rv pkng. Free local calls. AAA. $36/S; $48/D; $5/ex prsn. Disc: Senior, trkr, l/s. *Guaranteed rates.*

Pierre

Budget Host State Motel/ 640 N Euclid, Pierre SD 57501. 605-224-5896/ Fax: 224-1815. V,AE,CB,D,DC,M. US Hwys 14 & 83 N. Cable TV, dd phone, family rms, kitchens, n/s rms, mtg rm, indr pool, whrlpool, sauna, exerc equip, b/f. AAA/ Mobil. Sum: $33/S; $43-45/D; $5/ex prsn. Win: $27/S; $33-40/D. Disc: Senior.

Comfort Inn/ 410 W Sioux Av, Pierre SD 57501. 605-224-0377. V,M,DC,AE. US 14/83 (Sioux Av). On E side of Missouri River. Nrby rstrnt, indr pool, mtg rm, fax, b/f, cable TV, outlets, n/s rms. Free cont brfst. $39-51/S; $43-55/D; $4-5/ex prsn. 5/1-8/31: $45-65/S; $49-69/D. Discs.

Governor's Inn/ 700 W Sioux Av, Pierre SD 57501. 605-224-4200. V,M,AE,D, DC,CB. Indr pool, cable TV, whrlpool, dd phone, laundry, outlets, b/f, cont brfst, microwave, refrig, mtg rm, rv pkng, exerc area, n/s rms, cot, crib, coffee. AAA/ IMA. $38/S; $43-49/D; $5/ex prsn. 4/1-12/31: $40/S; $45-51/D. Disc: Family, comm, senior,

Plankinton

Super 8 Motel/ 801 S Main, RR 3, Box 1C, Plankinton SD 57368. 605-942-7722. AE,V,M,D,DC,CB. I-90, Exit 308, 2 mi W of Hwy 281. N/s rms, b/f, b/t/rv pkng, outlets. Free local calls. Pride Award. $35/S; $40-45/D; $5/ex prsn. 10/20-11/05: $60/S; $66/D. Higher spec event, wknd rates. Discs.

Rapid City

Days Inn/ 1570 Rapp St, Rapid City SD 57701. 605-348-8410/ Fax: 348-3392. V,M,AE,D,DC,CB. I-90, Exit 59 (LaCrosse), 1 blk. **Indr pool, whrlpool, n/s rms, cable TV, VCR, games, arpt trans, tt/dd phone, mtg rm, copier, laundry, refrig, crib, outlets, t/b/rv pkng, b/f. Free local calls, cont brfst. No pets. AAA. $39-99/S; $49-129/D; $5/ex prsn. Discs.** *Guaranteed rates.*

Budget Host Bel Air Inn/ 2101 Mt Rushmore Rd, Rapid City SD 57701. 605-343-5126. AE,D,M,V. I-90 (Exit 57) to Hwy 16. Cable TV, dd phone, n/s rms, pool, babysitters, laundry, t pkng, outlets, crib. No pets. AAA. $27/S; $32-37/D. $5-6/ex prsn. 5/19-6/8, 8/27-9/17: $45/S; $50-55/D. 6/9-8/26: $62/S; $62-77/D. 9/18-10/14: $41/S; $46-51/D. Spec events: $103. Disc: Senior, AAA.

Comfort Inn/ 1550 N LaCrosse, Rapid City SD 57701. 605-348-2221. V,M,DC, AE. I-90 (Exit 59) to LaCrosse St, S to mtl. Nrby rstrnt, indr pool, fax, whrlpool, cable TV, outlets, n/s rms. $29-79/S; $34-89/D; $5/ex prsn. 6/9-8/19: $59-149/S; $64-149/D. 8/20-9/30: $39-79/S; $39-89/D. Discs.

Econo Lodge/ 625 E Disk Dr, Rapid City SD 57701. 605-342-6400. AE, V,M,DC. I-90 (Exit 59) at LaCrosse, N 1 blk, rt on Disk Dr. Nrby rstrnt, indr pool, fax, whrlpool, cable TV, t pkng, outlets, n/s rms. AAA. $29-199/S or D; $7/ex prsn. 7/1-8/5: $79-299/S or D. 8/6-8/12: $199-399/S or D. Discs.

Motel 6/ 620 E Latrobe St, Rapid City SD 57701. 605-343-3687/ Fax: 343-7566. M,V,DC,D,AE. I-90, Exit 59 to LaCrosse St, S to Rapp St, lt to mtl. Cable TV, laundry, pool, n/s rms. Free local calls. $26-27/S; $32-33/D; $6/ex prsn. 5/25-10/31: $48/S; $54/D. Disc.

Quality Inn/ 2208 Mt Rushmore Rd, Box 2047, Rapid City SD 57709. 605-342-3322. V,M,DC,AE. I-90 (Exit 57) to US 16 (Mt Rushmore Rd). Rstrnt/ lounge, pool, fax, b/f, cable TV, t pkng, outlets, n/s rms. $29-39/S; $34-44/D; $10/ex prsn. 5/1-6/30: $39-69/S; $49-89/D. 7/1-8/19: $89-119/S; $99-129/D. 8/20-9/30: $39-79/S or D. Discs.

Sunburst Inn/ 620 Howard St, Box 1451, Rapid City SD 57709. 605-343-5434/ 800-456-0061. V,M,AE,D. I-90, Exit 58 (Haines Av). On frontage rd,

SOUTH DAKOTA

620 Howard St. Nrby rstrnt/ lounge, pool, cable TV, tt/dd phone, fax, copier, cot, crib, b pkng. No pets. AAA. $24/S; $29-39/D; $5/ex prsn. 6/13-9/8: $59-79/S or D; $8/ex prsn. 8/1-8/11: $79-94/S or D; $8/ex prsn. Disc: Family, AAA, AARP.

Tip Top Motel/ 405 St Joseph St, Rapid City SD 57701. 605-343-3901. V,M, AE,D,CB,DC. Dntn near Civic Ctr. Nrby rstrnt/ lounge, cable TV, dd phone, laundry, pool, elevator, cot, crib, kitchenettes, family rms, n/s rms. AAA/ IMA. $22-27/S; $35-40/D; $5/ex prsn. 5/24-6/14, 8/12-9/3: $40/S; $48-56/D. 6/15-8/4: $50/S; $56-69/D. 9/4-10/15: $36/S; $41-50/D. Disc: AAA, senior, AARP. 8/5-8/11 rates higher, Cycle Rally.

Rockerville

Rockerville Trading Post Motel/ 13525 Main St, Rockerville SD 57701. 605-341-4880/ Fax: 341-7304. V,M,D. 12 mi S of Rapid City, 9 mi N of Mt Rushmore, on Hwy 16. Rstrnt, nrby lounge, pool, n/s rms, playgrnd, tt/dd phone, fax, copier, laundry, cot, crib, rv pkng, conn rms. Free coffee. AAA. $30-40/S; $39-65/D; $4/ex prsn. Spec event, holiday, wknd rates: $75/S; $95/D; $5/ex prsn. Disc: Senior.

Sioux Falls

Empire Inn/ 4208 W 41st St, Sioux Falls SD 57106. 605-361-2345/ 800-341-8000. V,M,AE,D,DC,CB. Corner of I-29 (Exit 77) & 41st St. Indr pool, sauna, whrlpool, cable TV, video games, tt phone, microwave, cot, crib, outlets, eff, conn rms. Free cont brfst. No pets. AAA/ IMA. $32-41/S; $37-41/D; $2/ex prsn. 6/1-8/31: $36-45/S; $40-45/D. Disc: Senior, family, trkr.

Brimark Inn/ 3200 W Russell, Sioux Falls SD 57107. 605-332-2000/ 800-658-4508. V,M,AE,D,DC,CB. I-29, Exit 81. Pool, whrlpool, n/s rms, cable TV, arpt trans, tt phone, mtg rm, fax, copier, laundry, cot, crib, outlets, t/b pkng, b/f. Free cont brfst. AAA. $36/S; $36-44/D; $6/ex prsn. Disc: Senior, trkr. *Guaranteed rates.*

Budget Host Plaza Inn/ 2620 E 10th St, Sioux Falls SD 57103. 605-336-1550/ Fax: 339-0616. AE,CB,DC,M,V,D. I-229 Bypass, Exit 6, Scenic Rte thru city. Cable TV, dd phone, pool, adj rstrnt, laundry, cot, crib. Mobil. Sum: $37/S; $39-43/D; $4/ex prsn. Win: $29/S; $37-40/D. Spec events: $39/S; $50/D. Disc: Senior.

Budgetel Inns/ 3200 Meadow Av, Sioux Falls SD 57106. 605-362-0835. V,M, D,AE,DC,CB. At Jct I-29 & 41st St, Exit 77. N/s rms, b/f, fax, indr pool, whrlpool. Free cont brfst, in-rm coffee, local calls. AAA. $35-54/S; $42-61/D. Spec rates may apply. Discs.

Exel Inn/ 1300 W Russell St, Sioux Falls SD 57104. 605-331-5800/ Fax: 331-4074. V,M,AE,DC,CB,D. I-29 to Russell St (Exit 81), 2 mi. I-90 to I-29, Exit 81. Nrby rstrnt, cable TV, game rm, laundry, fax, micro-fridge, n/s rms. Free cont brfst. AAA. $26-35/S; $30-43/D. Higher spec event wknd rates. Discs.

Motel 6/ 3009 W Russell St, Sioux Falls SD 57107. 605-336-7800/ Fax: 330-9273. M,V,DC,D,AE. I-29, Exit 81 to Russell St/ Hwy 38, E on Russell St 1/2 mi to mtl. Nrby rstrnt, cable TV, pool, n/s rms. Free local calls. $27-33/S; $33-39/D; $6/ex prsn. Disc.

Sleep Inn/ 1500 N Kiwanis Av, Sioux Falls SD 57107. 605-339-3992. AE,V,M,DC. I-29 (Exit 81) to SR 38, E 1 mi to Kiwanis Av. Nrby rstrnt, indr pool, mtg rm, fax, b/f, whrlpool, cable TV, t pkng, exerc equip, outlets, n/s rms. Free cont brfst. AAA. $39-59/S; $44-59/D; $5/ex prsn. Discs.

Super 8 Motel/ 4100 W 41st St, Sioux Falls SD 57106. 605-361-9719/ Fax: Ext 150. V,AE,M,DC,CB,D. I-29 (Exit 77) at 41st St, E 1 blk. Outlets, t/b/rv pkng, elevator, cable TV, mtg rm, cot, crib. Free local calls. No pets. Pride Award. $38/S; $42-47/D; $4/ex prsn. Higher spec event, wknd rates. Discs.

Spearfish

Comfort Inn/ 2725 1st Av, Box 1056, Spearfish SD 57783. 605-642-2337. V,M,DC,AE. I-90, Exit 14, S to 1st Av. Nrby rstrnt, indr pool, fax, b/f, whrlpool, cable TV, n/s rms, t pkng. Free cont brfst. $30-70/S; $45-70/D; $5/ex prsn. 5/21-9/30: $72-99/S; $80-99/D. Discs.

SOUTH DAKOTA

Fairfield Inn/ 2720 1st Av E, Spearfish SD 57783. 605-642-3500/ 800-228-2800. V,M,AE,D,DC. I-90, Exit 14, N of interstate. Pool, whrlpool, n/s rms, cable TV, video games, TDD, tt/dd phone, fax, copier, refrig, elevator, cot, crib, outlets, b/f. Free local calls, cont brfst. AAA. $40-45/S; $46-50/D; $5/ex prsn. 5/26-9/7: $61-74/S; $66-79/D. 7/18-7/20, 8/3-8/11: $110/S or D. 12/31: $51/S; $56/D. Disc: Senior, bsns, govt, milt, AARP, AAA.

Kelly Inn/ 540 E Jackson, Spearfish SD 57783. 605-642-7795. V,M,AE,D,DC. 1 blk W of I-90, Exit 12. Hot tub, sauna, cable TV, t pkng, outlets, n/s rms. Free coffee. AAA/ Mobil. $40-50/S or D. 5/15-9/15: $65-80/S or D.

Royal Rest Motel/ 444 Main, Spearfish SD 57783. 605-642-3842. V,M,AE,D,DC,CB. I-90, Exit 12 to 1st stoplight, 3-1/2 blks lt. Nrby rstrnt/ lounge, pool, n/s rms, cable TV, tt/dd phone, laundry, cot. Free local calls. AAA. $24-27/S or D; $5/ex prsn. 6/1-9/1: $42-45/S or D. Disc: Senior. *Guaranteed rates.*

Sturgis

National 9 Inn/ 2426 Junction Av, Sturgis SD 57785. 605-347-2506/ 800-524-9999. V,M,AE,D,DC,CB. At I-90, Exit 32. N/s rms, cable TV, playgrnd, arpt trans, tt/dd phone, mtg rm, fax, laundry, refrig, cot, crib, outlets, t/b/rv pkng, eff. Free local calls, cont brfst. AAA. $27/S; $31-35/D; $5/ex prsn. 6/1-9/30: $45/S; $58/D. 1st wk in Aug sold out for Sturgis Bike Rally. Disc: Senior, bsns, TA, govt, family, trkr, milt. *Guaranteed rates.*

Vermillion

Budget Host Tomahawk Motel/ 1313 W Cherry, Vermillion SD 57069. 605-624-2601/ Fax: 624-2449. M,V,AE,D,DC,ER,CB. Jct Bsns 50 & 19. Cable TV, dd phone, in-rm coffee, pool, wading pool, picnic area, cot, crib, arpt trans, t pkng. Free cont brfst. Mobil. $27/S; $33-44/D; $3/ex prsn. Spec events: $49. Disc: Senior.

Comfort Inn/ 701 W Cherry St, Vermillion SD 57069. 605-624-8333. M,V,AE,DC. I-29 (Exit 26) to SR 50, W 8 mi to mtl. Nrby rstrnt, fax, b/f, whrlpool, cable TV, t pkng, outlets, n/s rms. Free cont brfst. AAA. $37-57/S; $42-62/D; $5/ex prsn. 5/1-10/31: $39-59/S; $44-64/D. Discs.

Super 8 Motel/ 1208 E Cherry St, Vermillion SD 57069. 605-624-8005. V,AE,M,DC,CB,D. 6 mi W of I-29 on Bsns Rte 50 (Cherry St). B/f, n/s rms, whrlpool, indr pool, outlets, t/b/rv pkng, cont brfst, cable TV. Pride Award. $36/S; $40/D; $5/ex prsn. Higher spec event, wknd rates. Discs.

Wall

Sands Motor Inn/ 804 Glenn St, Box 426, Wall SD 57790. 605-279-2121. V,M,AE,D,DC. Nrby rstrnt, pool, cable TV, dd phone, outlets, in-rm coffee, cot, crib, n/s rms, conn rms. AAA/ IMA. $32-39/S; $35-45/D; $5/ex prsn. 6/8-6/21, 8/15-9/3: $49/S; $55/D. 6/22-8/1: $60/S; $68-70/D. 8/2-8/14: $73/S; $73-83/D. Disc: Senior, TA.

Watertown

Budget Host Inn/ 309 8th Av SE, Watertown SD 57201. 605-886-8455/ Fax: 886-6248. D,M,V. 1 blk W of jct US 212 & 81. Cable TV, dd phone, family rms, n/s rms, cont brfst, nrby rstrnt/ lounge, picnic area, cot, crib. $25-30/S; $30-40/D; $5/ex prsn. 6/1-8/31: $27/S; $32-37/D. Higher hunting season rates. Disc: Senior.

Super 8 Motel/ 503 14th Av SE, Watertown SD 57201. 605-882-1900/ Fax: Ext 420. V,AE,M,DC,CB,D. 3 blks S of Jct 212 & 81. Pool, n/s rms, b/f, whrlpool, sauna, laundry, copier, fax, cable TV, b/t pkng, outlets. Free local calls. Pride Award. AAA. $38/S; $45-47/D; $3/ex prsn. Higher spec event rates. Discs.

Winner

Buffalo Trail Motel/ W Hwy 18 & 44, Winner SD 57580. 605-842-2212. V,M,AE,D,DC. On the "Road to Rushmore." Nrby rstrnt/ lounge, cable TV, dd phone, pool, arpt trans, outlets, b/f, n/s rms, cot, crib. AAA/ IMA. $32/S; $36-38/D; $2/ex prsn. Higher rates Oct-Nov. Disc: TA.

Yankton

Comfort Inn/ 2118 Broadway, Yankton SD 57078. 605-665-8053. V,M,DC,AE.

SOUTH DAKOTA / TENNESSEE

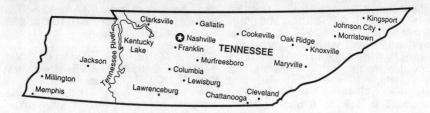

US 81 across from Yankton Mall, 2 mi N of dntn. Nrby rstrnt, fax, b/f, whrlpool, cable TV, t pkng, n/s rms. Free cont brfst. $38-49/S; $43-59/D; $4/ex prsn. Discs.

Tennessee

Alcoa (Knoxville area)

Quality Inn/ 2306 Airport Hwy, Box 477, Alcoa TN 37701. 615-970-3140. M,V,D,AE,DC. I-40 (Exit 386B) to US 129, S toward airport. Across st from Knoxville Arpt. Nrby rstrnt, pool, mtg rm, fax, cable TV, t pkng, n/s rms. Free deluxe cont brfst, arpt trans. $46-60/S; $59-65/D; $5/ex prsn. 5/1-10/31: $46-60/S; $46-70/D. Discs.

Brentwood

Travelers Rest Inn/ 107 Franklin Rd, Brentwood TN 37027. 615-373-3033/ Fax: 370-5709/ 800-852-0618. V,M, AE,D,DC,CB. I-65 S, Exit 74B. Pool, n/s rms, satellite TV, tt/dd phone, fax, laundry, refrig. Free local calls, cont brfst, coffee. No pets. AAA/ Mobil. $40/S; $48/D; $4/ex prsn. Disc: Senior. *Guaranteed rates.*

Bristol

Econo Lodge/ Box 1016, Bristol TN 37621. 615-968-9119. V,M,AE. I-81 (Exit 74A) to US 11, W to mtl. Rstrnt/ lounge, pool, mtg rm, fax, b/f, cable TV, t pkng, n/s rms. Free local calls, cont brfst. $38-44/S; $44-55/D; $5/ex prsn. Discs.

Bulls Gap (Greenville area)

Comfort Inn/ 50 Speedway Ln, Bulls Gap TN 37711. 615-235-9111. V,M, DC,AE. I-81 (Exit 23) at Andrew Johnson Hwy, to mtl. Nrby rstrnt, pool, mtg rm, fax, b/f, cable TV, t pkng, exerc equip, n/s rms. Free cont brfst, coffee. No pets. $40-79/S; $45-85/D; $5/ex prsn. 5/1-10/31: $49-85/S; $54-89/D. Discs.

Caryville

Budget Host Inn/ 115 Woods Av, Box 16, Caryville TN 37714. 423-562-9595/ Fax: 566-0515. V,M,AE,D. On I-75, Exit 134, jct US 25W & SR 63. Nrby rstrnt, cable TV, playgrnd, arpt trans, tt/dd phone, fax, copier, cot, crib, rv pkng. AAA/ Mobil. $25-35/S; $27-35/D; $5/ex prsn.

Lakeview Inn/ 276 John McGhee Blvd, Box 250, Caryville TN 37714. 423-562-9456/ Fax: 562-8346/ 800-431-6887. V,M,AE,D,DC,CB. I-75, Exit 134, rt at stoplight on John McGhee Blvd, 3rd motel on rt. Pool, n/s rms, cable TV, VCR/ movies, tt/dd phone, mtg rm, copier, laundry, refrig, cot, crib, t/b/rv pkng, conn rms, Free coffee. AAA. $26-32/S; $32-35/D; $5/ex prsn. 4/1-11/1: $26-32/S; $32-39/D. Disc: Senior, TA, family, milt. *Guaranteed rates.*

Chattanooga

Comfort Inn/ 7717 Lee Hwy, Chattanooga TN 37421. 615-894-5454. M,V,D,AE,DC. I-75: S, (Exit 7) to Lee Hwy, W to mtl; N, (Exit 7B) to Bonny Oaks Dr, W to Lee Hwy, rt to mtl. Nrby rstrnt, pool, fax, b/f, cable TV, n/s rms. Free cont brfst. $44-62/S; $48-64/D; $5/ex prsn. 5/1-8/31, 10/1-10/31: $48-64/S; $52-68/D. Discs.

Econo Lodge/ 1417 St Thomas St, Chattanooga TN 37412. 615-894-1417. M,V,AE,DC. On I-75: Sbnd, Exit 1, turn lt; Nbnd, Exit 1A. Nrby rstrnt, pool, cable TV, n/s rms. Free local calls, cont brfst. $27-40/S; $30-50/D; $4/ex prsn. Discs.

Econo Lodge/ 3655 Cummings Hwy, Chattanooga TN 37419. 615-821-2233.

TENNESSEE

AE,M,V,CB,DC,D. I-24, Exit 174. Nrby rstrnt, indr pool, fax, b/f, cable TV, n/s rms. Free cont brfst, local calls. No pets. AAA. $28-43/S; $36-50/D; $5/ex prsn. 5/1-9/3: $30-56/S; $38-68/D. Discs.

Friendship Inn/ 7725 Lee Hwy, Chattanooga TN 37421. 615-899-2288. AE,DC,M,V. I-75 S (Exit 7) to Lee Hwy. Nrby rstrnt, indr pool, fax, b/f, whrlpool, cable TV, t pkng, n/s rms. AAA. $34-42/S; $42-44/D; $5/ex prsn. 6/16-8/20: $42-44/S; $44-48/D. Discs.

Motel 6/ 7707 Lee Hwy, Chattanooga TN 37421. 423-892-7707/ Fax: 899-3818. V,M,AE,D,DC. I-75 at Exit 7/ 7B. Rstrnt, pool, t pkng, n/s rms. Free local calls. $26-28/S; $32-34/D; $6/ex prsn. Disc.

Quality Inn/ 2000 E 23rd St, Chattanooga TN 37406. 615-622-8353. V,M,DC,AE. I-24 (Exit 180) to 4th Av, lt to mtl. Nrby rstrnt, pool, mtg rm, b/f, whrlpool, cable TV, t pkng, n/s rms. Free cont brfst. $42-59/S or D; $5/ex prsn. Discs.

Quality Inn/ 6710 Ringgold Rd, Chattanooga TN 37412. 615-894-6820/ Fax: 490-0824. V,M,AE,D,DC,CB. I-75: (Sbnd, Exit 1; Nbnd, Exit 1A) to US 41 (Ringgold Rd), W to mtl. Rstrnt, pool, mtg rm, cable TV, t pkng. $44-59/S; $44-69/D; $5/ex prsn. Discs.

Super 8 Motel/ 20 Birmingham Rd, Chattanooga TN 37419. 615-821-8880. M,V,AE,DC,CB,D. I-24 (Exit 174) at Tiftonia. B/f, n/s rms, outlets, t/b/rv pkng, copier, cable TV, cot. Free local calls, crib. $39/S; $43-47/D; $5/ex prsn. Higher spec event rates. Discs.

Also see Ootewah.

Clarksville

Comfort Inn/ 111 Westfield Dr, Clarksville TN 37040. 615-647-6144. M,V,D,AE,DC. I-24 (Exit 4) to US 79/ SR 13, turn W to Westfield Dr. In back of Cracker Barrel. Nrby rstrnt, pool, fax, b/f, cable TV, n/s rms. Free cont brfst. $40-50/S; $45-55/D; $5/ex prsn. 5/1-6/4, 6/10-11/1: $50-60/S; $55-65/D. 6/5-6/9: $60-70/S; $65-75/D. Discs.

Comfort Inn/ 1112 SR 76, Clarksville TN 37043. 615-358-2020. V,M,DC,AE. I-24 (Exit 11) to SR 76 (1st Clarksville exit), turn W. Adj rstrnt, pool, fax, b/f, cable TV, t pkng, n/s rms. Free cont brfst. AAA. $30-45/S; $35-55/D; $4/ex prsn. 10/1-12/31: $27-37/S; $34-45/D. Discs.

Days Inn Clarksville/ 1100 Hwy 76, Connector Rd, Clarksville TN 37043. 615-358-3194/ Fax: 358-9869. AE, M,V,DC,D. I-24, Exit 11. Nrby rstrnt, pool, b/f, t pkng, arpt trans, cable TV, fax, n/s rms. Free cont brfst. $36-50/S; $40-60/D; $5/ex prsn. Discs.

Econo Lodge/ 201 Holiday Rd, Clarksville TN 37040. 615-645-6300. V, AE,M,DC. I-24, Exit 4. Nrby rstrnt, pool, mtg rm, fax, whrlpool, cable TV, exerc equip, n/s rms, microwave, refrig, laundry, copier. Free cont brfst. No pets. AAA. $30-50/S; $38-65/D; $6/ex prsn. Discs.

HoJo Inn/ 3080 Guthrie Hwy, Clarksville TN 37040. 615-648-8800. M,V,D,AE,DC,CB. Jct of I-24 (Exit 4) and Hwy 79. Pool, n/s rms, b/f, t pkng, cable TV. $35-60/S; $38-70/D. Discs.

Motel 6/ 881 Kraft St, Clarksville TN 37040. 615-552-0045/ Fax: 551-8516. V,M,DC,D,AE. On US 79 (Kraft St), 1 blk E of jct with US 41A. Nrby rstrnt, cable TV, pool, n/s rms. Free local calls. $24-25/S; $28-29/D; $4/ex prsn. Disc.

Quality Inn/ 803 N 2nd St, Clarksville TN 37040. 615-645-9084. V,M,AE,DC. I-24: Wbnd (Exit 11) to SR 76, SW 5 mi to mtl; Ebnd, (Exit 1) to SR 48 to Wilma Rudolph, rt to Kraft, rt to mtl. Lounge, indr pool, mtg rm, fax, b/f, sauna, whrlpool, cable TV, t pkng, n/s rms. Free deluxe cont brfst. $34-44/S; $40-50/D; $6/ex prsn. 5/1-7/31: $37-47/S; $43-55/D. 8/1-10/31: $35-45/S; $41-51/D. Discs.

Cleveland

Budgetel Inns/ 107 Interstate Dr NW, Cleveland TN 37312. 615-339-1000/ Fax: 339-2760. V,M,D,AE,DC,CB. I-75, Exit 25 W, lt onto Georgetown Rd. N/s rms, b/f, fax, rstrnt, pool, adj tennis/ golf/ skating. Free cont brfst, in-rm coffee, local calls. AAA. $42-56/S; $49-63/D. Special rates may apply. Discs.

TENNESSEE

Comfort Inn/ 153 James Asbury Dr, Cleveland TN 37312. 615-478-5265. V, M,DC,AE. I-75 (Exit 27) at Paul Huff Pkwy, turn W. Nrby rstrnt, pool, fax, b/f, cable TV, n/s rms. Free cont brfst. No pets. $28-43/S; $36-50/D; $5/ex prsn. 5/1-9/3: $30-55/S; $38-65/D. Discs.

Econo Lodge/ 2650 Westside Dr NW, Cleveland TN 37312. 615-472-3281. V,AE,M,DC. I-75 (Exit 25) SR 60. Nrby rstrnt, pool, mtg rm, fax, b/f, cable TV, t pkng, laundry, refrig, n/s rms. Free cont brfst, local calls. No pets. $38-50/S; $40-60/D; $4/ex prsn. 9/1-2/29: $34-46/S; $38-56/D. Discs.

Quality Inn/ 2595 Georgetown Rd, Cleveland TN 37311. 615-476-8511. M,V,D,AE,DC. I-75 (Exit 25) at SR 60, turn S to mtl. Nrby rstrnt, pool, mtg rm, fax, b/f, cable TV, t pkng, outlets, n/s rms. AAA. $40-55/S; $50-65/D; $5/ex prsn. 5/1-10/31: $40-45/S; $47-52/D. Discs.

Clinton

Super 8 Motel/ 2315 Andersonville Hwy, Clinton TN 37716. 615-457-0565. M,V,AE,DC,CB,D. I-75 (Exit 122) at SR 61. B/f, n/s rms, whrlpool, t pkng, cable TV, cot. Free local calls. Pride Award. $37/S; $42-45/D; $3/ex prsn. Higher spec event rates. Discs.

Columbia

Econo Lodge/ SR 99 & I-65, Columbia TN 38401. 615-381-1410. AE,M,DC,V. I-65 (Exit 46) at SR 99. Nrby rstrnt, fax, b/f, cable TV, n/s rms. Free cont brfst. AAA. $30-40/S; $40-45/D; $5/ex prsn. 3/1-12/31: $35-45/S; $40-50/D. Discs.

Ramada Inn/ 1208 Nashville Hwy, Columbia TN 38401. 615-388-2720/ Fax: 388-2360. V,M,AE,D,DC. SR 99 W of I-65. Pool, trans, n/s rms, rstrnt/ lounge, laundry, cable TV, suites, cot. Golden Key Award. $40-75/S or D; $5/ex prsn. Discs.

Cookeville

Comfort Inn/ 1100 S Jefferson Av, Cookeville TN 38501. 615-528-1040. AE,V,M,DC. I-40 (Exit 287) to SR 136, S to mtl. Nrby rstrnt, pool, fax, b/f, cable TV, t pkng, n/s rms. Free cont brfst. AAA. $35-37/S; $37-43/D; $5/ex prsn. 3/1-5/31: $37-40/S; $40-45/D. 6/1-10/31: $39-45/S; $43-50/D. Discs.

Executive Inn/ 897 S Jefferson Av, Cookeville TN 38501 615-526-9521/ Fax: 528-2285/ 800-826-2791 V,M,AE, D,DC,CB. I-40, Exit 287, 1 blk N of main Cookeville exit. Pool, n/s rms, cable TV, arpt trans, tt/dd phone, mtg rm, fax, copier, laundry, refrig, crib, outlets, t/b pkng. Free local calls, cont brfst. No pets. AAA. $38/S; $43/D; $5/ex prsn. 5/1-11/1: $40/S; $45/D. Spec event, holidays: $45/S; $50/D. *Guaranteed Rates.*

Howard Johnson Lodge/ 2021 E Spring St, Cookeville TN 38506. 615-526-3333/ Fax: 528-9036. AE,V,M,DC, D,CB. I-40 (Exit 290) at US 70. Adj lounge, pool, b/f, t pkng, refrig, cable TV, whrlpool. Free cont brfst. Gold Medal Winner. $34-40/S; $36-42/D. Discs.

Super 8 Motel/ 1330 Bunkerhill Rd, Cookeville TN 38501. 615-528-2020/ Fax: Ext 42. AE,M,V,DC,D,CB. I-40, Exit 287 behind Wendy's. N/s rms, pool, outlets, cont brfst, t/b/rv pkng, cable TV, cot, crib. Free local calls. AAA. $33/S; $39-40/D; $4/ex prsn. Higher spec event rates. Discs.

Cornersville

Econo Lodge/ 3731 Pulaski Hwy, Cornersville TN 37047. 615-293-2111. AE,M,DC,V. I-65 (Exit 22) to SR 31A. Nrby rstrnt, pool, b/f, cable TV, t pkng, n/s rms. AAA. $30-35/S; $40-45/D; $5/ex prsn. 3/1-12/31: $41-46/S; $45-50/D. Discs.

Denmark (Jackson area)

Econo Lodge/ 196 Providence Rd, Denmark TN 38391. 901-427-2778. AE,M,D,V. I-40, Exit 68. Fax, cable TV, t pkng, n/s rms. Free cont brfst. $28-36/S; $35-47/D; $4/ex prsn. 5/1-10/31: $30-38/S; $35-49/D. Discs.

Dickson

Comfort Inn/ 2325 SR 46 S, Dickson TN 37055. 615-446-2423. V,M,AE,DC. I-40 to SR 46, turn N. Adj rstrnt, pool, mtg rm, fax, fl, sauna, cable TV, t pkng, outlets, n/s rms. Free cont brfst. AAA. $37-44/S; $44-53/D; $5/ex prsn. 5/1-8/31: $40-66/S; $44-75/D. Higher spec event rates. Discs.

TENNESSEE

Econo Lodge/ 2338 SR 46, Dickson TN 37055. 615-446-0541. V,AE,M,DC. I-40 (Exit 172) & Hwy 46. Nrby rstrnt, pool, cable TV, t pkng, n/s rms. Free cont brfst, local calls, coffee. $32-62/S; $36-68/D; $5/ex prsn. Discs.

Dyersburg

Comfort Inn/ 815 Reelfoot Dr, Dyersburg TN 38024. 901-285-6951. M,V,D,AE,DC. I-155 (Exit 13) to US 412 & SR 78, turn S. Rstrnt, pool, mtg rm, fax, b/f, cable TV, t pkng, exerc equip, VCR/ movies, laundry, n/s rms. Free cont brfst. No pets. $42-46/S; $47-51/D; $6/ex prsn. 5/1-10/31: $45-58/S; $49-53/D. Discs.

Ramada Limited/ 2331 Lake Rd, Dyersburg TN 38024. 901-287-0044/ Fax: 287-1939. V,M,AE,D,DC. I-155, US 51, SR 78. B/f, n/s rms, sauna, fax. Free cont brfst, local calls, nwspr. $35-40/S; $40-50/D; $5/ex prsn. Discs.

Elizabethton

Comfort Inn/ 1515 US 19 E Bypass, Elizabethton TN 37643. 615-542-4466. V,M,AE,DC. On US 321/ 19E, just S of jct with SR 91 and Elk Av. Nrby rstrnt, pool, mtg rm, fax, b/f, cable TV, t pkng, exerc equip, n/s rms. Free cont brfst, coffee/ cider. Hospitality Award. AAA. $40-125/S or D; $6/ex prsn. Discs.

Franklin

Comfort Inn/ Franklin Common Court, Franklin TN 37064. 800-221-2222 — opening soon. M,V,D,AE,DC. I-65 (Exit 65) to Murfreesboro Rd, turn W to Carothers Rd, S to Franklin Common Crt. Adj rstrnt, pool, mtg rm, fax, b/f, cable TV, t pkng, n/s rms. Free cont brfst. $42-56/S; $47-68/D; $6/ex prsn. Discs.

Gatlinburg

Microtel/ 211 Airport Rd, Gatlinburg TN 37738. 423-436-0107/ Fax: 436-0273/ 800-266-3500. V,M,AE,D,DC,CB. Turn lt at traffic light #8 (Airport Rd) in dntn Gatlinburg. Nrby rstrnt/ lounge, n/s rms, cable TV, tt phone, mtg rm, fax, copier, elevator, crib, t/b/rv pkng, conn rms, b/f. Free coffee. AAA. $25/S; $30-50/D. 6/1-8/31, 10/1-10/31: $55/S; $60-75/D. Holidays: $55/S; $60-80/D. Disc. Senior, govt.

Comfort Inn/ 200 E Pkwy, Gatlinburg TN 37738. 615-436-5043/ 800-933-8679. V,M,DC,AE. Jct of US 321 & US 441. Cntr of tn at light #3. Rstrnt, pool, mtg rm, fax, whrlpool, cable TV, game rm, laundry, n/s rms. No pets. AAA. $45-93/S or D. Discs.

Comfort Inn/ Ski Mountain Rd, Box 138, Gatlinburg TN 37738. 615-436-7813. V,M,AE,DC. Hwy 441 to entrance of Great Smokey Mtn National Park, at traffic light #10. Nrby rstrnt, pool, fax, whrlpool, cable TV, family rms, n/s rms. Free full brfst. No pets. AAA. $40-150/S or D; $5/ex prsn. 5/12-9/30: $60-150/S or D. 10/1-10/29: $65-150/S or D. Discs.

Econo Lodge/ 247 Newton Ln, Gatlinburg TN 37738. 615-436-6626. V,M,AE. Hwy 441 to traffic light #6, turn lt 1 blk. Corner of Cherokee Rd & Newton Ln. Nrby rstrnt, pool, cable TV, microfridge, n/s rms. No pets. $38-75/S or D; $4/ex prsn. Higher spec event rates. Discs.

Econo Lodge/ 405 Airport Rd Gatlinburg TN 37738. 615-436-5836. AE, M,DC,V. Dntn at Light 8, S on Arpt Rd 1 1/2 blks to mtl. Nrby rstrnt, pool, cable TV, refrig, coffee, suites, n/s rms. No pets. $43-88/S or D; $5/ex prsn. Discs.

Rainbow Motel/ 390 E Parkway, Box 1397, Gatlinburg TN 37738. 423-436-5887/ 800-422-8922. V,M,D. From I-40, S on Rte 441/60 to Gatlinburg, turn lt at traffic light #3, go 3 blks to mtl. Pool, whrlpool, cable TV, VCR/ movies, tt phone, refrig, crib, eff. No pets. AAA/ Mobil. $30-45/S or D; $5/ex prsn. 7/1-11/1: $40-50/S or D. Jul 4, Labor Day, Oct wknds: $50-65/S or D.

Also see Kodak, Pigeon Forge, Sevierville.

Goodlettsville (Nashville area)

Comfort Inn/ 925 Conference Dr, Goodlettsville TN 37072. 615-859-5400. V,M,AE,DC. I-65 N (Exit 97) at Long Hollow Pike, turn E. Nrby rstrnt, indr pool, fax, b/f, cable TV, n/s rms. Free cont brfst. No pets. AAA. $35-55/S; $45-70/D; $5/ex prsn. 5/1-6/3: $40-60/S; $45-70/D. 6/4-6/11: $90/S or D. 6/12-

TENNESSEE

10/31: $45-75/S or D. Discs.

Econo Lodge/ 320 Long Hollow Pike, Goodlettsville TN 37072. 615-859-4988. AE,DC,M,V. I-65N (Exit 97) to Long Hollow Pk. Nrby rstrnt, pool, mtg rm, fax, b/f, cable TV, n/s rms. Free coffee. AAA. $31-39/S; $37-45/D; $5/ex prsn. 6/2-9/5: $39-50/S or D. Discs.

Friendship Inn/ 650 Wade Cir, Goodlettsville TN 37072. 615-859-1416. V,M, AE,DC. I-65 (Exit 96) turn toward Rivergate Mall, 1st light lt, behind Hooters rstrnt. Rstrnt/ lounge, pool, fax, cable TV, t pkng, n/s rms. Free cont brfst. AAA. $28-34/S; $32-38/D; $3/ex prsn. 5/1-8/31: $34-38/S; $36-42/D. Discs.

Motel 6/ 323 Cartwright St, Goodlettsville TN 37072. 615-859-9674/ Fax: 851-6115. V,M,DC,D,AE. I-65, Exit 97/ Long Hollow Pike. Motel is W of I-65 & N of Long Hollow Pike Rd. Nrby rstrnt, cable TV, pool, n/s rms. Free local calls. $27-33/S; $31-37/D; $4/ex prsn. Higher spec event rates. Disc.

Hermitage (Nashville area)

Comfort Inn/ 5768 Old Hickory Blvd, Hermitage TN 37076. 615-889-5060. V,M,AE,DC. I-40 E (Exit 221) at Old Hickory Blvd. Nrby rstrnt, pool, fax, b/f, cable TV, outlets, n/s rms. Free cont brfst. No pets. $35-60/S; $40-70/D; $5/ex prsn. 5/1-10/31: $35-70/S; $40-80/D. Discs.

Hermitage Inn/ 4144 Lebanon Rd, Hermitage TN 37076. 645-883-7444/ Fax: 889-9269. V,M,AE,D. I-40, Exit 221, N to Lebanon Rd, turn rt. Rstrnt, pool, cable TV, tt phone, fax, copier, refrig, microwave, cot, crib, t/b pkng, eff, conn rms. Free coffee. AAA. $30-35/S; $32-40/D; $4/ex prsn. 3/1-10/31: $35-42/S; $42-55/D. Disc: Senior, bsns, TA, family, milt. *Guaranteed Rates.*

Hurricane Mills

Best Western of Hurricane Mills/ I-40 & Hwy 13, Hurricane Mills TN 37078. 615-296-4251/ Fax: 296-9104. V,M,AE,D,DC,CB. I-40 & Hwy 13 exit. Pool, whrlpool, n/s rms, satellite TV, VCR/ movies, TDD, tt/dd phone, fax, copier, laundry, refrig, cot, crib, outlets, t/b pkng, b/f. Free local calls, cont brfst. No pets. AAA/ Mobil. $43/S; $46/D;

$4/ex prsn. 5/16-9/15: $55/S; $59/D. Disc: Senior, govt, family, trkr, milt. *Guaranteed rates.*

Jackson

Budgetel Inns/ 2370 N Highland Av, Jackson TN 38305. 901-664-1800/ Fax: 664-5456. V,M,D,AE,DC,CB. I-40, Exit 82A S on US 45, E on Ridgecrest Rd. N/s rms, b/f, fax, rstrnt, pool. Free cont brfst, in-rm coffee, local calls. AAA. $31-41/S; $37-47/D. 4/28-9/2: $33-43/S; $39-44/D. 9/3-12/31: $31-41/S; $37-47/D. Higher spec event rates.

Comfort Inn/ 1963 US 45 Bypass, Jackson TN 38305. 901-668-4100. V,M, DC,AE. I-40 (Exit 80A) at US 45 Bypass. Nrby rstrnt, pool, mtg rm, fax, b/f, cable TV, t pkng, exerc equip, n/s rms. Free cont brfst. No pets. AAA. $42-67/S; $47-72/D; $5/ex prsn. Discs.

Quality Inn/ 2262 N Highland Av, Jackson TN 38305. 901-668-1066. V,M, DC,AE. I-40 (Exit 82A) at Highland Av. Nrby rstrnt, pool, b/f, cable TV, t pkng, n/s rms. No pets. $36/S; $44/D; $5/ex prsn. 5/1-8/31: $38/S; $48/D. Discs.

Super 8 Motel/ 2295 N Highland, Jackson TN 38305. 901-668-1145/ Fax: 664-4442. V,M,DC,AE,D. I-40 (Exit 82A) to US 45, S to mtl. B/f, n/s rms, outlets, b/t pkng, cont brfst, trans, copier, elevator, cable TV, cot, crib. Free local calls. $33/S; $39-45/D; $4/ex prsn. Discs.

Also see Denmark.

Kimball

Budget Host Inn/ 395 Main St, Kimball TN 37347. 615-837-7185. AE,M,V,D, CB,DC. I-24, Exit 152. 24 mi W of Chattanooga. Cable TV, dd phone, n/s rms, fax, rstrnt, pool, laundry, cot, crib, t pkng. No pets. AAA. $30/S; $30-37/D; $5/ex prsn. 5/25-9/4: $30/S; $33-37/D.

Kingsport

Econo Lodge/ 1704 E Stone Dr, Kingsport TN 37660. 615-245-0286. V, AE,M,DC. On US 11 W, near SR 93 Bypass & Eastman Rd. Fax, cable TV, n/s rms. Free cont brfst. $32-36/S; $38-42/D; $4-5/ex prsn. Discs.

TENNESSEE

Kingston

Comfort Inn/ 905 N Kentucky St, Box 367, Kingston TN 37763. 615-376-4965/ Fax: 376-1005. V,M,AE,D,DC,CB. I-40 (Exit 352) at Kentucky St. Nrby rstrnt, fax, b/f, cable TV, exerc equip. Free cont brfst, local calls. No pets. AAA. $35-42/S; $42-52/D; $5/ex prsn. Discs.

HoJo Inn/ 1200 N Kentucky St, Kingston TN 37763. 615-376-3477. V,M,AE,DC,D. I-40 (Exit 352) at Kentucky St. Rstrnt, n/s rms, pool, cable TV. Free coffee. $30-38/S; $36-50/D. Discs.

Friendship Inn/ 123 Luyben Hills Rd, Box 260, Kingston Springs TN 37082. 615-952-2900. V,M,AE,DC. I-40 (Exit 188) to Kingston Springs. Nrby rstrnt, pool, cable TV, t pkng, n/s rms. $35-70/S; $40-75/D; $5/ex prsn. Discs.

Knoxville

Comfort Inn/ 7524 Strawberry Plains Pk, Knoxville TN 37924. 615-932-1217. V,M,AE,DC. E of Knoxville, on I-40, Exit 398. Nrby rstrnt, pool, mtg rm, fax, b/f, cable TV, t pkng, n/s rms. Free cont brfst. No pets. Hospitality Award. AAA. $39-44/S; $44-49/D; $5/ex prsn. 5/1-5/31: $39-54/S; $44-59/D. 6/1-10/31: $49-64/S; $54-69/D. Discs.

Comfort Inn/ 5334 Central Av Pike, Knoxville TN 37912. 615-688-1010. M,V,D,AE,DC. I-75 (Exit 108) at Merchant Dr, turn NE to Central Av Pk. Adj rstrnt, pool, fax, cable TV, n/s rms, exerc equip. Free cont brfst, in-rm coffee. AAA. $40-50/S; $46-60/D; $5/ex prsn. Discs.

Comfort Inn/ 7737 Kingston Pike, Knoxville TN 37919. 615-690-0034. M,V,D,AE,DC. I-75/ I-40 (Exit 380) at Vanosdale Rd/ Morrell Rd, turn rt at light. Nrby rstrnt, pool, mtg rm, fax, b/f, sauna, cable TV, exerc equip, n/s rms. Free cont brfst. No pets. $42-99/S; $46-105/D; $5/ex prsn. Discs.

Motel 6/ 402 Lovell Rd, Knoxville TN 37922. 423-675-7200/ Fax: 671-3339. V,M,DC,AE,D. I-40/75 at Exit 374/ Lovell Rd. Nrby rstrnt, cable TV, pool, n/s rms. Free local calls. Premier Award. $28-29/S; $32-33/D; $4/ex prsn. Disc.

Quality Inn/ 6712 Central Av Pike, Knoxville TN 37912. 615-689-6600. AE,DC,M,V. I-75 to Exit 110, E 1 blk to mtl. Rstrnt, indr pool, mtg rm, fax, b/f, cable TV, t pkng, n/s rms. Free full brfst. AAA. $40-70/S; $46-80/D; $6/ex prsn. 9/1-3/31: $40-43/S; $46-48/D. Discs.

Sleep Inn/ 5460 Central Av Pike, Knoxville TN 37912. 615-688-7300. AE,DC,M,V. I-75 (Exit 108) at Merchant Dr. Nrby rstrnt, pool, fax, b/f, whrlpool, cable TV, t pkng, n/s rms. Free cont brfst. AAA. $35-60/S; $40-65/D; $5/ex prsn. 5/1-10/31: $40-60/S; $50-70/D. Discs.

Super 8 Motel North/ 503 Merchant Dr, Knoxville TN 37912. 615-689-7666. V,M,AE,DC,D,CB. I-75 (Exit 108) at Merchant Dr, 1 blk W. N/s rms, cont brfst, b pkng, copier, fax, cable TV. Free crib. AAA. $35-45/S; $40-55/D; $5/ex prsn. Higher spec event rates. Discs.

Super 8 Motel/ 7585 Crosswood Blvd, Knoxville TN 37924. 615-524-0855. V,M,D,DC,CB,AE. I-40 (Exit 398) at Strawberry Plains Pk. B/f, n/s rms, pool, whrlpool, outlets, b/t pkng, cont brfst, cable TV, mtg rm, cot, crib. Free local calls. No pets. Pride Award. AAA. $35-40/S; $35-46/D; $5/ex prsn. 10/1-10/31; $46/S; $50-56/D. Higher spec event rates. Discs.

Econo Lodge/ 5505 Merchant Cntr Blvd, Knoxville, TN 37912. 615-687-5680. V,M,D,AE,DC. I-75 N, Exit 108, W to mtl. Nrby rstrnt, fax, b/f, cable TV, n/s rms. Free cont brfst. No pets. AAA. $37-66/S; $40-80/D; $5/ex prsn. 5/1-10/31: $40-80/S; $43-80/D. Discs.

Also see Alcoa, Powell.

Kodak (Gatlinburg area)

Econo Lodge/ 184 Dumplin Valley Rd, Kodak TN 37764. 615-933-8141. V,AE,M,DC. I-40, Exit 407. Nrby rstrnt, pool, cable TV, n/s rms. No pets. $30-80/S or D; $5/ex prsn. 5/1-5/23: $30-50/S; $40-50/D. 5/24-6/23: $40-60/S or D. 6/24-7/9: $60-80/S or D. Discs.

Lakeland

Super 8 Motel/ 9779 Huff 'N Puff Rd, Lakeland TN 38002. 901-372-4575.

TENNESSEE

AE,DC,MC,V. I-40 (Exit 20) to Canada Rd, N to Huff 'N Puff Rd, turn rt. B/f, n/s rms, pool, sauna, cont brfst, t/b/rv pkng, cont brfst, elevator, cable TV, cot. Free local calls, crib. AAA. $33/S; $38-43/D; $5/ex prsn. Discs.

Lebanon
Comfort Inn/ 829 S Cumberland St, Lebanon TN 37087. 615-444-1001. V,M,DC,AE. I-40 (Exit 238) to US 231 N. Nrby rstrnt, pool, fax, b/f, sauna, cable TV, t pkng, exerc equip, outlets, n/s rms. Free cont brfst. $29-36/S; $34-38/D; $5/ex prsn. 5/1-5/31, 6/17-10/31: $35-39/S; $39-56/D. 6/1-6/16: $42-55/S; $47-59/D. Discs.

Lenior City
Quality Inn/ 1110 N Hwy 321, Lenior City TN 37771. 615-986-2011. V,M,DC,AE. I-75 (Exit 81) at Scenic US 321. Rstrnt, pool, mtg rm, b/f, whrlpool, cable TV, n/s rms. Free cont brfst. No pets. $27-36/S; $31-40/D; $5/ex prsn. Discs.

Econo Lodge/ 1211 US 321 N, Lenoir City TN 37771. 615-986-0295. AE,M,V,DC. I-75 (Exit 81) at US 321/95. Nrby rstrnt, pool, fax, b/f, cable TV, n/s rms. Free cont brfst. No pets. AAA. $36-48/S; $42-60/D; $5/ex prsn. 6/1-8/20: $40-50/S; $45-65/D. Discs.

Madison (Nashville area)
Friendship Inn/ 625 Gallatin Rd, Madison TN 37115. 615-865-2323. V,M,AE,DC. I-65 (Exit 92) to Old Hickory Blvd, E 1 1/4 mi to US 31, N to Gallatin Rd, E to mtl. Nrby rstrnt, pool, fax, cable TV, n/s rms. Free cont brfst. $30-35/S; $35-40/D; $5/ex prsn. 4/1-10/31: $34-40/S; $40-45/D. Discs.

Manchester
Comfort Inn/ 2314 Hillsboro Blvd, Manchester TN 37355. 615-728-0800. V,M,DC,AE. I-24 (Exit 114) to US 41, W to mtl. Rstrnt, pool, mtg rm, fax, cable TV, t pkng, n/s rms. Free cont brfst. AAA. $33-35/S; $35-40/D; $5/ex prsn. Discs.

Econo Lodge/ Rte 8, Box 813, Manchester TN 37355. 615-728-9530. V,AE,M,DC. I-24 (Exit 114) & US 41. Pool, cable TV, t pkng, n/s rms. Free AM coffee. $25-27/S; $29-32/D; $5/ex prsn. Discs.

Martin
Econo Lodge/ 853 University St, Martin TN 38237. 901-587-4241/ Fax: 587-4649. V,M,AE,D,DC,CB. Jct of US 45E Bypass & SR 22, N on University St. Nrby rstrnt, pool, fax, b/f, cable TV, t pkng, outlets. Free cont brfst,local calls. No pets. AAA. $37-71/S; $41-71/D; $5/ex prsn. Higher spec event rates. Discs.

Memphis
Econo Lodge/ 3456 Lamar Av, Memphis TN 38118. 901-365-7335. V,AE,M,DC. I-240 (Exit 21) to Lamar Av, S to mtl. Nrby rstrnt, pool, fax, b/f, cable TV, t pkng, n/s rms. Free cont brfst, arpt trans. AAA. $34-51/S; $38-55/D; $4/ex prsn. Discs.

Howard Johnson Lodge/ 1541 Sycamore View, Memphis TN 38134. 901-388-1300/ Fax: Ext 247. AE,V,M,DC,D. I-40 E (Exit 12) at Sycamore View - Bartlett. Pool, n/s rms, b/f, t pkng, refrig, microwave, mtg rm, laundry, in-rm coffee. Free local calls, cont brfst, nwspr. Gold Medal Winner. $37-80/S; $45-80/D. Discs.

Motel 6/ 1321 Sycamore View Rd, Memphis TN 38134. 901-382-8572/ Fax: 385-0814. V,M,DC,D,AE. I-40, Exit 12C to Sycamore View Rd, S to mtl. Nrby rstrnt, cable TV, laundry, pool, n/s rms, t pkng. Free local calls. $28-32/S; $34-38/D; $6/ex prsn. Disc.

Motel 6/ 1117 E Brooks Rd, Memphis TN 38116. 901-346-0992/ Fax: 396-3264. V,M,DC,D,AE. I-55 to Elvis Presley Blvd Exit, turn rt on Brooks Av to mtl. Cable TV, pool, n/s rms, t pkng. Free local calls. $28-32/S; $34-38/D; $6/ex prsn. Disc.

Super 8 Motel/ 6015 Macon Cove Rd, Memphis TN 38134. 901-373-4888. M,V,AE,DC,CB,D. I-40 (Exit 12C) to Sycamore View Rd, S to Macon Cove Rd, immed rt. B/f, n/s rms, outlets, cable TV, copier, cot. Free local calls, crib. $42/S; $48-53/D; $5/ex prsn. Higher spec event rates. Discs.

Also see Millington.

TENNESSEE

Millington (Memphis area)
Econo Lodge/ 8193 US 51 N, Millington TN 38053. 901-873-4400. V,M,D,AE. I-240, Exit 2A to SR 51 N, 13 mi to mtl. Nrby rstrnt, pool, fax, b/f, cable TV, n/s rms. Free cont brfst. $36-51/S; $44-55/D; $4/ex prsn. Discs.

Morristown
Super 8 Motel/ 2430 E Andrew Johnson Hwy, Morristown TN 37814. 615-586-8880/ Fax: 585-0654. M,V,AE,DC, CB,D. I-81 (Exit 8) to US 25E, N 6 1/2 mi to Morristown, Hwy IIE, turn E. B/f, n/s rms, in-rm coffee, t pkng, copier. Free cont brfst. $36/S; $40-42/D; $2/ex prsn. Discs.

Murfreesboro
Comfort Inn/ 110 N Thompson Ln, Murfreesboro TN 37129. 615-890-2811. M,V,D,AE,DC. I-24 (Exit 78) at SR 96. Nrby rstrnt, pool, sauna, whrlpool, cable TV, n/s rms. Free cont brfst. No pets. $34-39/S; $39-45/D; $5/ex prsn. Discs.

Howard Johnson/ 2424 S Church St, Murfreesboro TN 37130. 615-896-5522/ Fax: 893-7216. M,DC,D, V,AE,CB. From Nashville or Chattanooga, Exit 81 A Shelbyville, off I-24. Rstrnt, pool, b/f, t pkng, cable TV, laundry. Free cont brfst. $30-65/S; $35-69/D. Higher spec event rates.

Motel 6/ 114 Chaffin Pl, Murfreesboro TN 37129. 615-890-8524/ Fax: 896-2924. V,M,DC,D,AE. I-24, Exit 78 or 78B to SR 96, E 1 blk on 96, then rt to mtl. Nrby rstrnt, cable TV, laundry, pool, n/s rms. Free local calls. $27-29/S; $31-33/D; $4/ex prsn. Disc.

Quality Inn/ 118 Westgate Blvd, Murfreesboro TN 37130. 615-848-9030. V,M,DC,AE. I-24 (E, Exit 81A: W, Exit 81) to US 231, S to mtl. On US 231 just S of jct with I-24. Nrby rstrnt, pool, mtg rm, fax, b/f, cable TV, n/s rms. Free cont brfst. $45-85/S; $50-90/D; $5-7/ex prsn. 5/1-10/31: $39-79/S; $45-85/D. Discs.

Nashville
Comfort Inn/ 2306 Brick Church Pike, Nashville TN 39207. 615-226-9560. V, M,AE,DC. I-65/ I-24 (Exit 87B) to Trinity Ln, W to mtl. Nrby rstrnt, pool, fax, b/f, cable TV, t pkng, n/s rms. Free cont brfst. AAA. $36-38/S; $38-52/D; $5/ex prsn. 5/1-6/1: $42-48/S; $46-55/D. 6/2-9/5: $42-55/S or D. 9/6-10/28: $42-50/S; $46-55/D. Discs.

Comfort Inn/ 97 Wallace Rd, Nashville TN 37211. 615-833-6860. V,M,DC,AE. I-24 (Exit 56) to Harding Pl, turn W, between Gameland and Shell Station. Nrby rstrnt, pool, mtg rm, fax, b/f, cable TV, t pkng, n/s rms. Free cont brfst. AAA. $37-45/S; $41-46/D; $5/ex prsn. 6/2-9/5: $40-55/S; $43-55/D. 9/6-10/28: $40-50/S; $43-50/D. Discs.

Econo Lodge/ 110 Maplewood Ln, Nashville TN 37207. 615-262-9193. M, V,D,AE,DC. I-65, exit 89, lt on Dickerson Pike, 1 blk to mtl. Nrby rstrnt, pool, fax, b/f, cable TV, n/s rms. Free cont brfst. AAA. $42-48/S; $46-60/D; $5/ex prsn. 11/1-3/3: $32/S; $38-42/D. Discs.

Econo Lodge/ 2460 Music Valley Dr, Nashville TN 37214. 615-889-0090. M,V,D,AE,DC. SR 155 (Briley Pkwy) towards Opryland, exit Music Valley Dr. Nrby rstrnt, pool, b/f, n/s rms. $36-43/S; $43-50/D; $5/ex prsn. 5/1-6/1, 9/6-10/28: $38-62/S; $48-62/D. 6/2-9/5: $62-70/S or D. Discs.

Econo Lodge/ 2403 Brick Church Pike, Nashville TN 37207. 615-226-9805. V, AE,M,DC. I-95 (Exit 87B) at Trinity Lane. Nrby rstrnt, b/f, cable TV, n/s rms. Free cont brfst. AAA. $30-36/S; $35-40/D; $5/ex prsn. 5/1-5/31: $32-39/S; $35-45/D. 6/1-9/15: $38-70/S; $48-80/D. Discs.

Econo Lodge/ 300 Interstate Dr, Nashville TN 37213. 615-242-9621. AE,DC,M,V. I-65 & I-24, bet Exit 84 and Exit 85. Adj rstrnt, pool, fax, cable TV, t pkng, n/s rms. Free cont brfst. No pets. AAA. $30-60/S; $33-99/D; $5/ex prsn. 3/1-4/30: $36-69/S; $39-80/D. 5/1-5/25: $39-69/S; $43-79/D. 5/26-10/29: $43-79/S; $49-89/D. Discs.

HoJo Inn/ 323 Harding Pl, Nashville TN 37211. 615-834-0570/ Fax: 831-2831. M,V,D,AE,DC,CB. I-24 to Nashville (Exit 56) E 1/4 mi. Pool, b/f, t pkng, arpt trans, fax, copier, mtg rm, laundry. Free local calls, cont brfst. $40-62/S; $48-70/D. Discs.

TENNESSEE / TEXAS

Howard Johnson Lodge/ 3414 Percy Priest Dr, Nashville TN 37214. 615-391-8074/ Fax: 391-8076. AE,V,M,DC, D. I-40 (Exit 219) Stewarts Ferry Pike exit. Adj rstrnt, pool, n/s rms, b/f, trans, VCR, t pkng. Free cont brfst, local calls. $35-60/S; $43-70/D. Discs.

Motel 6/ 95 Wallace Rd, Nashville TN 37211. 615-333-9933/ Fax: 832-7078. V,M,DC,D,AE. I-24, Exit 56 to Harding Pl, W 1 blk to Largo Rd, turn lt. Nrby rstrnt, cable TV, laundry, pool, n/s rms. Free local calls. $28-35/S; $32-39/D; $4/ex prsn. Higher spec event rates. Disc.

Motel 6/ 311 W Trinity Ln, Nashville TN 37207. 615-227-9696/ Fax: 650-0935. V,M,DC,D,AE. From I-24/I-65 take W Trinity Ln Exit, turn rt. Nrby rstrnt, cable TV, laundry, pool, n/s rms. Free local calls. $25-30/S; $29-34/D; $4/ex prsn. Higher spec event rates. Disc.

Motel 6/ 420 Metroplex Dr, Nashville TN 37211. 615-833-8887/ Fax: 831-2177. DC,M,V,AE,D. I-24, Exit 56 at Harding Pl, E to light, lt on Metroplex. Nrby rstrnt, cable TV, pool, n/s rms, elevator. Free local calls. $28-34/S; $32-38/D; $4/ex prsn. Higher spec event rates. Disc.

Super 8 Motel/ 412 Robertson Av, Nashville TN 37209. 615-356-0888/ Fax: Ext 118. M,V,AE,DC,CB,D. I-40 (Exit 204) at White Bridge Rd. B/f, n/s rms, toast bar, b/rv pkng, copier, elevator, cable TV, mtg rm, cot. Free local calls, crib. $42/S; $47-48/D; $6/ex prsn. Discs.

Super 8 Motel/ 3320 Dickerson Rd, Nashville TN 37207. 615-226-1897/ Fax: 228-9068. M,V,AE,DC,CB,D. I-65 (Exit 89) at Dickerson Pike. B/f, n/s rms, pool, b/rv pkng, elevator, cable TV, suites, mtg rm, cot. Free local calls, crib. No pets. $37/S; $43-45/D; $5/ex prsn. 5/1-9/30: $47/S; $54/D. 1st wk June: $55/S; $64/D. Discs.

Wilson Inn/ 600 Ermac, Nashville TN 37214. 615-889-4466/ Fax: 889-0484. V,M,AE,DC,D. I-40, Exit Briley Parkway to Elm Hill Pike, rt. T pkng, coffee, punch, popcorn, n/s rms. Free brfst. $45/S; $45-60/D. Disc: Corp, senior, family.

Also see Goodlettsville, Hermitage, Madison, Whites Creek.

Ooltewah (Chattanooga area)

Super 8 Motel/ 5111 Hunter Rd, Ooltewah TN 37363. 615-238-5951/ Fax: 238-5956. V,M,D,DC,CB,AE. I-75, Exit 11. B/f, n/s rms, indr pool, whrlpool, t/b/rv pkng, copier, cable TV, cot, crib. Free local calls. AAA. $35/S; $40/D; $5/ex prsn. Higher spec event rates. Discs.

Paris

Super 8 Motel/ 1309 E Wood, Paris TN 38242. 901-644-7008/ Fax: 642-8371. V,M,D,DC,CB,AE. On Hwy 79 (Wood St), just E of Hwy 641. B/f, n/s rms, pool, nrby rstrnt, whrlpool, laundry, b pkng, cable TV, mtg rm, cot. Free local calls. Pride Award. $36/S; $39-42/D; $3/ex prsn. 4/1-9/30: $39/S; $42-45/D. Higher spec event rates. Discs.

Pigeon Forge (Gatlinburg area)

Econo Lodge/ 2440 N Parkway, Box 1337 Pigeon Forge TN 37863. 615-428-1231. V,M,AE. I-40 E to SR 66 S to Sevierville exit/ US 441 S. Nrby rstrnt, pool, fax, b/f, whrlpool, cable TV, elevators, wading pool, n/s rms. Free cont brfst, coffee. AAA. $36-71/S; $41-76/D; $5/ex prsn. 2/1-4/30: $30-70/S; $35-75/D. 5/1-7/31: $50-91/S; $55-96/D. 8/1-10/31: $46-86/S; $51-101/D. Discs.

Howard Johnson Lodge/ 2826 Pkwy, Box 1110, Pigeon Forge TN 37868. 615-453-9151/ Fax: 428-4141. M,V,D,AE,DC,CB. On US 441, S of I-40 & I-81. Rstrnt, n/s rms, b/f, pool, kitchens, family rms, refrig, kiddie pool, elevator, laundry. No pets. $29-71/S or D. 11/1-11/25: $39-71/S or D. 10/1-10/31: $69-89. Discs.

Quality Inn/ Parkway at US 441, Pigeon Forge TN 37862. 800-221-2222 — opening soon. M,V,D,AE,DC. US 441 at Sevierville, Pigeon Forge boundary. Nrby rstrnt, pool, indr pool, mtg rm, fax, b/f, sauna, whrlpool, cable TV, exerc equip, n/s rms. Free cont brfst. $46-86/S or D; $10/ex prsn. 7/1-9/30: $66-100/S or D. 10/1-10/31: $76-116/S or D. Discs.

Quality Inn/ Parkway & Dollywood Ln,

TENNESSEE

Pigeon Forge TN 37863. 615-429-4494. M,V,D,AE,DC. I-40 (Exit 407 to SR 66, S to US 441 S. In Pigeon Forge at light #8. Rstrnt, pool, indr pool, mtg rm, fax, b/f, whrlpool, cable TV, n/s rms. Free cont brfst. No pets. $39-149/S or D; $5/ex prsn. 7/1-10/31: $49-149/S or D. Discs.

Rodeway Inn/ 4236 Parkway, Pigeon Forge TN 37863. 615-453-3530. M,V,D,AE. I-40 (Exit 407) to SR 66, S to US 441, S thru Pigeon Forge. Last mtl on rt before entering national park. Rstrnt, pool, cable TV, t pkng, n/s rms. Free cont brfst. No pets. $32-104/S or D; $6/ex prsn.

Portland

Budget Host Inn/ 5339 Long Rd, Portland TN 37148. 615-325-2005/ Fax: 325-7605. V,M,D,AE,DC,CB. I-65, Exit 117 to Hwy 52 W. Rstrnt, pool, n/s rms, VCR/ movies, tt/dd phone, fax, copier, laundry, refrig, microwave, cot, crib, t pkng, eff, b/f. Free coffee. AAA. $33/S; $38/D; $5/ex prsn. Disc: Senior, bsns, govt, family, trkr, milt, AAA, AARP.

Powell (Knoxville area)

Comfort Inn/ 323 E Emory Rd, Powell TN 37849. 615-938-5500. V,M,DC,AE. I-75 N (Exit 112) at Emory Rd. Nrby rstrnt, pool, fax, b/f, cable TV, t pkng, n/s rms, VCR, microwave, refrig. Free cont brfst. AAA. $38-82/S; $44-88/D; $6/ex prsn. 8/13-2/29: $36-84/S; $42-84/D. Discs.

Sevierville (Gatlinburg area)

Comfort Inn/ 860 Winfield Dunn Pkwy, Sevierville TN 37862. 615-428-5519/ Fax: 428-6700. V,M,DC,AE. On SR 66 bet I-40 & Gatlinburg. Nrby rstrnt, pool, indr pool, mtg rm, fax, b/f, whrlpool, cable TV, n/s rms. Free cont brfst. No pets. AAA. $35-120/S; $40-130/D; $5/ex prsn. 5/1-10/31: $35-130/S; $40-130/D. Discs.

Comfort Inn/ 155 Dumplin Valley Rd W, Sevierville TN 37764. 615-933-1719. V,M,AE,DC. I-40 (Exit 407) at Dumplin Valley Rd. Nrby rstrnt, pool, mtg rm, whrlpool, cable TV, exerc equip, n/s rms. Free cont brfst. No pets. Hospitality Award. $29-49/S; $37-59/D; $5/ex prsn. 5/1-9/11, 10/1-10/31: $39-59/S; $47-89/D. Discs.

Quality Inn/ I-40 & SR 66, Box 250, Sevierville TN 37764. 615-933-7378. M,V,D,AE,DC. I-40 (Exit 407) to SR 66, S to mtl. Rstrnt, indr pool, mtg rm, fax, b/f, cable TV, n/s rms. Free coffee bar. No pets. AAA. $28-58/S; $38-68/D; $5/ex prsn. 5/1-5/26: $34-64/S; $38-68/D. 5/27-8/19: $48-98/S or D. 8/20-11/4: $34-84/S; $38-88/D. Discs.

Sweetwater

Budget Host Inn/ Box 587, Sweetwater TN 37874. 615-337-9357/ Fax: 337-7436. M,V,D,AE,DC,CB. I-75 (Exit 60) to Hwy 68, W 1 blk. Cable TV, dd phone, n/s rms, rstrnt, laundry, t pkng, cot, crib. AAA. $25-35/S; $34-54/D; $5/ex prsn. Higher spec event rates. Discs.

Comfort Inn/ Box 48, Sweetwater TN 37874. 615-337-3353. V,M,DC,AE. I-75 N (Exit 60) at SR 68. Nrby rstrnt, indr pool, whrlpool, cable TV, n/s rms. Free cont brfst, nwspr. AAA. $34-65/S; $39-65/D; $4/ex prsn. Discs.

Comfort Inn/ 803 S Main St, Box 48, Sweetwater TN 37874. 615-337-6646. V,M,DC,AE. I-75 (Exit 60) to SR 68, E 2 mi. Nrby rstrnt, pool, fax, cable TV, n/s rms, fishing. Free cont brfst, nwspr. AAA. $32-55/S; $36-55/D; $4/ex prsn. Discs.

Quality Inn/ Rte 3, Box 6655, Sweetwater TN 37874. 615-337-3541. V,M,DC,AE. I-75 (Exit 60) at SR 68. Rstrnt, indr pool, mtg rm, fax, b/f, whrlpool, cable TV, t pkng, exerc equip, n/s rms, brfst bar. AAA. $39-48/S; $39-56/D; $6/ex prsn. 3/1-4/30: $40-52/S; $40-58/D. 5/1-9/2: $37-48/S; $39-52/D. Discs.

Union City

Super 8 Motel/ 1400 Vaden Av, Union City TN 38261. 901-885-4444. M, V,AE,DC,CB,D. Jct of Hwys 51 & SR 22. B/f, n/s rms, outlets, t/b/r pkng, copier, cable TV, cot. Free local calls, crib. $40/S; $46-50/D; $5/ex prsn. Higher spec event rates. Discs.

Whites Creek (Nashville area)

Super 8 Motel/ 7551 Old Hickory Blvd, Whites Creek TN 37189. 615-876-

3971/ Fax: 876-2021. V,M,D,DC, CB,AE. I-24 S (Exit 40) to Old Hickory Blvd, lt (E) 2 blks. I-65 S (Exit 92) to Old Hickory Blvd, rt (W) 4 mi. B/f, n/s rms, cont brfst, t/b/rv pkng, copier, cable TV, cot. Free crib. No pets. $35-40/S; $40-45/D; $5/ex prsn. Higher spec event rates. Discs.

Texas

Abilene

Econo Lodge/ 1633 W Stamford, Abilene TX 79601. 915-673-5424. AE,M,DC,V. I-20: Wbnd, Exit 285; Ebnd, Exit 286A. W to Grape St, mtl on lt. Nrby rstrnt, fax, cable TV, t pkng, n/s rms. Free cont brfst. AAA. $30-35/S; $35-45/D; $5/ex prsn. Discs.

Motel 6/ 4951 W Stamford St, Abilene TX 79603. 915-672-8462/ Fax: 672-3118. V,M,DC,D,AE. I-20, Exit 282 at Shirley Rd, follow frontage rd. Cable TV, pool, n/s rms. Free local calls. $25-26/S; $29-30/D; $4/ex prsn. Disc.

Super 8 Motel/ I-20 & Hwy 351, Abilene TX 79601. 915-673-5251/ Fax: 673-5314. V,M,D,DC,CB,AE. I-20 (Exit 288) at Hwy 351. B/f, n/s rms, pool, laundry, outlets, b/t pkng, cont brfst, cable TV, mtg rm, cot. Free local calls, crib. AAA. $35/S; $37-39/D; $4/ex prsn. Higher spec event rates. Discs.

Amarillo

Budget Host La Paloma Inn/ 2915 I-40 E, Amarillo TX 79104. 806-372-8101/ Fax: 374-5221. M,V,D,AE,DC,CB. I-40 (Exit 72A) at Nelson St/ Quarter Horse Dr. Cable TV, movies, dd phone, n/s rms, mtg rm, adj rstrnt/ lounge, indr pool, hot tub, arpt trans, t pkng, outlets, cot, crib. AAA/ Mobil. $30-50/S; $40-80/D; $10/ex prsn. Spec events: $78-100. Discs.

Econo Lodge/ Box 30338, Amarillo TX 79120. 806-335-1561. AE,M,V,CB, DC,D. I-40 at Lakeside Dr N. Rstrnt/ lounge, pool, fax, cable TV, n/s rms, eff. Free cont brfst. AAA. $37-52/S; $42-57/D; $5/ex prsn. Discs.

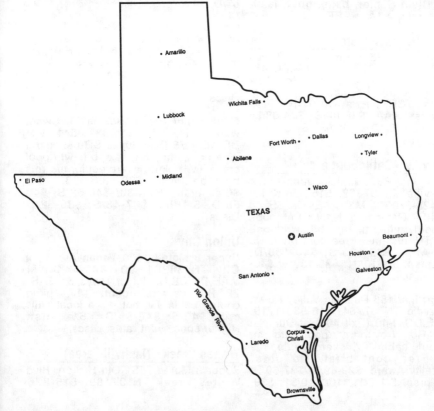

TEXAS

Friendship Inn/ 6005 Amarillo Blvd W, Amarillo TX 79106. 806-355-3321. V,M,AE,DC. I-40 (Exit 66) to Bell St, N 1 mi. Adj to Amarillo Medical Cntr. Nrby rstrnt, pool, fax, b/f, cable TV, n/s rms. AAA. $31-34/S; $33-38/D; $3/ex prsn. Discs.

Howard Johnson Lodge/ 2801 I-40 W, Amarillo TX 79109. 806-355-9171/ Fax: 355-0691. V,M,AE. I-40 (Exit 68B) at Georgia St. Rstrnt/ lounge, n/s rms, pool, t pkng. Free arpt trans, coffee. $39-44/S; $44-49/D. Discs.

Motel 6/ 4301 I-40 E, Amarillo TX 79104. 806-373-3045/ Fax: 373-0546. M,V,DC,D,AE. I-40: Ebnd, Exit 72B; Wbnd, Exit 73. On frontage rd on N side of frwy, between Bolton & Eastern St. Cable TV, pool, n/s rms, t pkng. Free local calls. $26-29/S; $32-35/D; $6/ex prsn. Disc.

Motel 6/ 3930 I-40 E, Amarillo TX 79103. 806-374-6444/ Fax: 371-0475. V,M,DC,D,AE. I-40, Exit 72B to Grand St, S to frontage rd, turn E. Nrby rstrnt, cable TV, pool, laundry, n/s rms, t pkng. Free local calls. $26-29/S; $32-35/D; $6/ex prsn. Disc.

Motel 6/ 6030 I-40 W, Amarillo TX 79106. 806-359-7651/ Fax: 359-0236. AE,M,V,DC,D. I-40 (Exit 66) at Bell St. On N side of frwy. Cable TV, laundry, pool, elevator, n/s rms. Free local calls. $28-30/S; $34-36/D; $6/ex prsn. Disc.

Motel 6/ 2032 Paramount Blvd, Amarillo TX 79109. 806-355-6554/ Fax: 355-5317. V,M,DC,D,AE. I-40, Exit 68A & Julian-Paramount Blvd S. Nrby rstrnt, cable TV, pool, n/s rms. Free local calls. $26-29/S; $32-35/D; $6/ex prsn. Disc.

Super 8 Motel/ RR 2, Amarillo TX 79101. 806-335-2836. M,V,AE,DC, CB,D. I-40 E (Exit 75) at Lakeside Dr. B/f, n/s rms, nrby rstrnt, outlets, t/b/rv pkng, cable TV, crib. No pets. $37/S; $41/D; $4/ex prsn. Higher spec event rates. Discs.

Anthony (El Paso area)

Super 8 Motel/ 100 Park N Dr, Anthony TX 79821. 915-886-2888/ Fax: 886-3888. V,M,DC,CB,AE,D. I-10, Exit "0." N/s rms, laundry, outlets, toast bar, satellite TV, refrig, nearby t/b/rv pkng, cot, crib. Free local calls. AAA. $40/S; $47-49/D; $4/ex prsn. Higher spec event, wknd rates. Discs.

Arlington (Dallas - Ft Worth area)

Comfort Inn/ 1601 E Division, Arlington TX 76011. 817-261-2300/ Fax: 861-8679. V,M,AE,DC. E of I-820, S of I-30, on Division St just E of Collins. Nrby rstrnt, pool, mtg rm, fax, b/f, cable TV, t pkng, exerc equip, n/s rms, game rm. Free cont brfst. AAA. $39-69/S; $44-74/D; $5/ex prsn. 3/1-4/30: $49-89/S; $54-94/D. 5/1-8/20: $59-109/S; $69-129/D. Discs.

Howard Johnson Lodge/ 117 S Watson, Arlington TX 76010. 817-633-4000/ Fax: 633-4931. M,DC,D,V,AE,CB. I-20 to 360 N to Abrams, stay on Service Rd (Watson Rd). Rstrnt/ lounge, indr pool, exerc equip, t pkng, mtg rm, n/s rms, b/f. $34-75/S; $39-75/D. 3/1-4/30: $45-78/S; $49-80/D.

Motel 6/ 2626 E Randol Mill Rd, Arlington TX 76011. 817-649-0147/ Fax: 649-7130. V,M,DC,D,AE. Hwy 360 at Randol Mill Rd, bet US 80 & I-30. Nrby rstrnt, cable TV, laundry, pool, n/s rms. Free local calls. $30-34/S; $36-40/D; $6/ex prsn. Disc.

Ramada Inn Arlington/ 700 E Lamar Blvd, Arlington TX 76011. 817-265-7711/ Fax: 861-9633. V,M,AE,D,DC. I-30 to SR 157, N to E Lamar Blvd, turn W. Pool, n/s rms, rstrnt/ lounge, mtg rm, cot. $44-49/S or D; $8/ex prsn. Discs.

Austin

Econo Lodge/ 6201 US 290 E, Austin TX 78723. 512-458-4759. AE,DC,M,V. US 290 1 blk E of I-35. Rstrnt, pool, fax, b/f, cable TV, t pkng, n/s rms. Free cont brfst. No pets. AAA. $37-80/S; $41-90/D; $5/ex prsn. Discs.

Exel Inn/ 2711 I-35 S, Austin TX 78741. 512-462-9201/ Fax: 462-9371. AE,V,M,CB,DC,D. I-35 N, exit Oltorf St SE; S, exit Woodward St to S Frontage Rd, N to mtl. Nrby rstrnt, pool, elevator, micro-fridge, n/s rms, cable TV, fax, laundry. Free coffee, cont brfst, crib, local calls. AAA. $35-40/S; $40-49/D; $4/ex prsn. Higher wknd/ spec event

TEXAS

rates. Discs.

Motel 6/ 9420 N I-35, Austin TX 78753. 512-339-6161/ Fax: 339-7852. V,M,DC,D,AE. I-35, Exit 241, W on Rundberg Ln. Cable TV, laundry, pool, n/s rms, t pkng. Free local calls. $34-36/S; $40-42/D; $6/ex prsn. Disc.

Motel 6/ 2707 Interregional Hwy S, Austin TX 78741. 512-444-5882/ Fax: 442-3759. V,M,DC,D,AE. I-35 Nbnd, Exit 232A/ Oltorf, E to mtl. I-35 Sbnd, Exit 231/ Woodward St/ St Edwards University, lt on Woodward, lt on frontage rd. Cable TV, pool, n/s rms. Free local calls. $34-36/S; $40-42/D; $6/ex prsn. Disc.

Motel 6/ 5330 N Interregional Hwy, Austin TX 78751. 512-467-9111/ Fax: 206-0573. V,M,DC,D,AE. I-35: Sbnd, Exit 238A, frontage rd past 51st st; Nbnd, Exit 238B, lt at 51st st, lt on frontage rd. Cable TV, pool, n/s rms. Free local calls. Premier Award. $36-38/S; $42-44/D; $6/ex prsn. Disc.

Motel 6/ 8010 N I-35, Austin TX 78753. 512-837-9890/ Fax: 339-3045. M,V,DC,D,AE. I-35: Nbnd, Exit 241; Sbnd, Exit 240A. At Rundberg Lane on W side of frwy. Pool, n/s rms, t pkng. Free local calls. $32-34/S; $38-40/D; $6/ex prsn. Disc.

Rodeway Inn/ 2900 N I-35, Austin TX 78705. 512-477-6395. M,V,AE,DC. I-35 (lower level/ Exit 236A) at 26th St. Nrby rstrnt, pool, fax, cable TV, n/s rms. Free cont brfst. No pets. AAA. $40-70/S or D; $5/ex prsn. Discs.

Rodeway Inn/ 5526 N I-35, Austin TX 78751. 512-451-7001. M,V,AE,DC. I-35 (Exit 238A/ 238B) at US 183. Nrby rstrnt, pool, mtg rm, fax, b/f, whrlpool, cable TV, n/s rms. Free cont brfst. AAA. $42-56/S; $46-75/D; $4/ex prsn. 10/1-1/15: $36-48/S; $40-52/D. Discs.

Bay City

Econo Lodge/ 3712 7th St, Bay City TX 77414. 409-245-5115. V,AE,M,DC. N side of SR 35 at Bay City. Nrby rstrnt, pool, fax, b/f, cable TV, t pkng, laundry, n/s rms. Free cont brfst, local calls. $33-36/S; $43/D; $5/ex prsn. Discs.

Baytown (Houston area)

Motel 6/ 8911 SR 146, Baytown TX 77520. 713-576-5777/ Fax: 576-2351. V,M,DC,AE,D. I-10, Exit 798 to SR 146, N to mtl. Nrby rstrnt, cable TV, laundry, pool, n/s rms, t pkng. Free local calls. Premier Award. $29-30/S; $33-34/D; $4/ex prsn. Disc.

Beaumont

Econo Lodge/ 1155 I-10 S, Beaumont TX 77701. 409-835-5913. V,AE,M,DC. I-10: Ebnd, take College St exit (851); Wbnd, take WA Blvd exit (850), then U-turn. Nrby rstrnt, pool, fax, b/f, cable TV, t pkng, copier, VCR, micro/frig, n/s rms. Free AM coffee, local calls. $35-50/S; $38-56/D; $5/ex prsn. Discs.

Quality Inn/ 1295 N 11th St, Beaumont TX 77702. 409-892-7722/ Fax: 892-6537. V,M,AE,DC. I-10 at 11th St. Rstrnt/ lounge, pool, mtg rm, fax, b/f, cable TV, t pkng, n/s rms. Free cont brfst. AAA. $38-52/S; $42-57/D; $6/ex prsn. Discs.

Super 8 Motel Beaumont/ 2850 I-10 E, Beaumont TX 77703. 409-899-3040/ Fax: Ext 100. M,V,AE,DC,CB,D. I-10 at 11th St. Pool, n/s rms, satellite TV, TDD, tt/dd phone, fax, copier, refrig, elevator, microwave, cot, crib, b pkng, b/f. Free local calls, coffee. No pets. AAA. $27-31/S; $32-37/D; $3/ex prsn. Spec events: $35/S; $42/D; $4/ex prsn. Discs. *Guaranteed rates.*

Bellmead (Waco area)

Motel 6/ 1509 Hogan Ln, Bellmead TX 76705. 817-799-4957/ Fax: 799-6183. V,M,DC,D,AE. I-35, Exit 338B at Behrens Circle exit. W side of frwy. Cable TV, laundry, pool, n/s rms, t pkng. Free local calls. $25/S; $29/D; $4/ex prsn. Disc.

Belton

Belton Inn Budget Host/ 1520 S I-35, Belton TX 76513. 817-939-0744/ Fax: 939-9238. V,M,AE,D,DC,CB. I-35 Sbnd, Exit 292, cross over & come back; Nbnd, Exit 293A. Pool, n/s rms, cable TV, VCR/ movies, tt/dd phone, fax, copier, refrig, cot, crib, outlets, t/b/rv pkng, eff, b/f. Free local calls, in-rm coffee. AAA. $35/S; $40/D; $5/ex prsn. Disc: Senior, bsns, TA, govt, l/s, family, trkr, milt, AAA.

Big Spring
Comfort Inn/ 2900 E I-20, Big Spring TX 79720. 915-267-4553. V,M,DC,AE. I-20, Exit 179, Bsns I-20. After exit make 1st lt. Nrby rstrnt, pool, mtg rm, cable TV, t pkng, n/s rms. Free cont brfst. No pets. $32-36/S; $40-42/D; $5/ex prsn. Discs.

Econo Lodge/ 804 I-20 W, Box 3007 Big Spring TX 79720. 915-263-5200. M,V,D,AE,DC. I-20 (Exit 177) to US 87. Mtl on N Service Rd. Rstrnt/ lounge, pool, fax, b/f, cable TV, t pkng, exerc equip, n/s rms. Free cont brfst. $43-65/S; $47-69/D; $4/ex prsn. 11/1-4/15: $39-65/S; $43-69/D. Discs.

Motel 6/ 600 W I-20, Box 2384, Big Spring TX 79720. 915-267-1695/ Fax: 267-4048. V,M,DC,D,AE. I-20/US 80, Exit 177 at US 87. Cable TV, laundry, pool, n/s rms, t pkng. Free local calls. $27/S; $31-33/D; $4-6/ex prsn. Disc.

Brownsville
Motel 6/ 2255 N Expressway, Brownsville TX 78520. 210-546-4699/ Fax: 546-8982. V,M,DC,D,AE. US 77/83 Nbnd, lt on FM 802 under freeway to lt on Central Blvd to mtl. Sbnd: Exit FM 802, stay on frontage rd. Cable TV, pool, n/s rms. Free local calls. $29/S; $35/D; $6/ex prsn. Disc.

Brownwood
Comfort Inn/ 410 E Commerce St, Brownwood TX 76801. 915-646-3511. M,V,D,AE,DC. On US 67, 377 & 84. Adj rstrnt/ lounge, pool, mtg rm, fax, b/f, sauna, cable TV, t pkng, n/s rms, in-rm coffee. Free cont brfst. AAA. $40-75/S; $44-75/D; $4/ex prsn. 5/1-9/30: $42-75/S; $46-75/D. Discs.

Channelview (Houston area)
Econo Lodge/ 17011 I-10 E, Channelview TX 77530. 713-457-2966. V,M,AE. I-10 (Exit 785), Magnolia. Rstrnt, pool, cable TV, t pkng, n/s rms. No pets. $30-90/S or D; $5/ex prsn. Discs.

Childress
Econo Lodge/ 1612 F N W, Childress TX 79201. 817-937-3695. M,V,D,AE, DC. US 287, 4 blks E of US 83 & US 287 jct. Rstrnt, pool, fax, cable TV, t pkng, n/s rms. Free full brfst. AAA. $48/S or D; $3/ex prsn. 5/1-8/31: $50/S or D. Discs.

Cleburne
Budget Host Sagamar Inn/ 2107 N Main, Cleburne TX 76031. 817-556-3631. V,M,DC,AE,D. On US 67, 20 mi S of Ft Worth, 12 mi S of I-35 W. Pool, n/s rms, cable TV, tt/dd phone, fax, microwave, cot, crib, t/b pkng, conn rms, b/f. Free local calls, cont brfst. AAA/ Mobil. $36/S; $42-48/D; $4/ex prsn. Discs. *Guaranteed rates.*

Days Inn/ 101 N Ridgeway Dr, Cleburne TX 76031. 817-645-8836/ Fax: 645-4813. V,M,AE,D,DC,CB. Hwy 67 S; 10 mi SW of I-35. Nrby rstrnt, pool, b/f, t pkng, refrig, microwave, cot. Free cont brfst. $36-43/S; $42-50/D; $5/ex prsn. Discs.

Clute (Freeport area)
Motel 6/ 1000 SR 332, Clute TX 77531. 409-265-4764/ Fax: 265-4758. V,M,DC,D,AE. On SR 332, W of Hwy 227. Nrby rstrnt, cable TV, laundry, pool, n/s rms, t pkng. Free local calls. $27/S; $31/D; $4/ex prsn. Disc.

Coldspring
San Jacinto Inn/ Box 459, Coldspring TX 77331. 409-653-3008/ Fax: 653-3009. C,M,AE,D,DC,CB. On Hwy 150 W, 26 mi from I-45, 10 mi from Hwy 59. Nrby rstrnt, n/s rms, tt/dd phone, fax, copier, microwave, cot, b/f. Free local calls, coffee. AAA. $34/S; $37/D; $5/ex prsn. Spec event, holiday, wknd rates: $40/S; $42/D.

College Station
Motel 6/ 2327 Texas Av, College Station TX 77840. 409-696-3379/ Fax: 693-6378. V,M,DC,D,AE. SR 6 Bsns at Brentwood Dr. Cable TV, laundry, pool, n/s rms, t pkng. Free local calls. $28-29/S; $32-33/D; $4/ex prsn. Disc.

Conroe
Motel 6/ 820 I-45 S, Conroe TX 77304. 409-760-4003/ Fax: 760-3159. V,M,DC,D,AE. I-45 Nbnd, take Exit 85/ Gladstell Rd, follow Nbnd frontage rd 1 1/2 mi, cross under I-45, lt onto Sbnd frontage rd. Sbnd: S on frontage rd.

TEXAS 254

Cable TV, laundry, pool, n/s rms, t pkng. Free local calls. $27-28/S; $31-32/D; $4/ex prsn. Disc.

Copperas Cove

HoJo Inn/ 302 W US 190, Copperas Cove TX 76522. 817-547-2345/ Fax: 547-5124. V,M,AE,DC,D. I-35 to Bsns 190, W. Pool, n/s rms, t/b pkng, cable TV, dd phone, fax, copier. Free cont brfst, local calls. No pets. Gold Medal Winner. $40-45/S; $42-52/D. Discs.

Corpus Christi

Days Inn Corpus Christi Airport/ 901 Navigation Blvd, Corpus Christi TX 78408. 512-888-8599/ Fax: 888-5746. V,M,AE,D,DC,CB. I-37 at Navigation. Pool, n/s rms, cable TV, playgrnd, TDD, tt/dd phone, mtg rm, fax, copier, laundry, refrig, microwave, cot, crib, b/f. Free local calls, coffee. AAA. $41/S; $46/D; $5/ex prsn. 6/16-9/5: $64/S; $74/D; $10/ex prsn. Discs. *Guaranteed rates.*

Motel 6/ 845 Lantana St, Corpus Christi TX 78408. 512-289-9397/ Fax: 289-0280. V,M,DC,D,AE. I-37 Sbnd: Exit 4B/ Lantana St. Nbnd: Exit 3B/ Mc-Bride-Lantana St, follow frontage rd. Cable TV, pool, n/s rms. Free local calls. $27-28/S; $31-32/D; $4/ex prsn. Disc.

Motel 6/ 8202 S Padre Island Dr, Corpus Christi TX 78412. 512-991-8858/ Fax: 991-1698. V,M,DC,D,AE. I-37 to S Padre Island Dr (SR 358) at Paul Jones Av. Cable TV, laundry, pool, n/s rms. Free local calls. $28-32/S; $34-38/D; $6/ex prsn. Disc.

Dalhart

Comfort Inn/ Rte 2, Box 22, Dalhart TX 79022. 806-249-8585. V,M,DC,AE. US 54, E of jct with US 87/ 385. Adj rstrnt, pool, fax, cable TV, t pkng, n/s rms. Free cont brfst. AAA. $36-56/S; $45-65/D; $5/ex prsn. Discs.

Days Inn of Dalhart/ 701 Liberal, Dalhart TX 79022. 806-249-5246/ Fax: 249-0805. V,M,AE,D,DC,CB. Jct Hwy 87, 385 & 54, E 4 blks. Indr pool, whrlpool, n/s rms, exerc equip, cable TV, VCR, arpt trans, copier, laundry, refrig, microwave, crib, outlets, t/b/rv pkng, b/f. Free local calls, cont brfst. AAA/ Mobil. $40/S; $45/D; $5/ex prsn. Spec event, holiday, wknd rates: $68/S; $74/D; $10/ex prsn. Discs. *Guaranteed rates.*

Econo Lodge/ 123 Liberal St, Dalhart TX 79022. 806-249-6464. V,AE,M,DC. US 54 & US 87. Nrby rstrnt, b/f, cable TV, t pkng, outlets, arpt trans. Free coffee, local calls. AAA. $28-34/S; $34-38/D; $4/ex prsn. 5/1-10/31: $30-34/S; $35-39/D. Discs.

Friendship Inn/ 400 Liberal St, Dalhart TX 79022. 806-249-4557. V,M,DC,D, AE. US 54, 2 blks E of US 87. Nrby rstrnt, pool, fax, cable TV, t pkng, copier, n/s rms. Free local calls, coffee. AAA. $28-38/S; $34-39/D; $4/ex prsn. 6/16-8/2: $30-36/S; $36-42/D. 8/3-8/5: $59/S; $69-79/D. Discs.

Super 8 Motel/ E Hwy 54, Box 1325, Dalhart TX 79022. 806-249-8526/ Fax: 249-5119. M,V,AE,DC,CB,D. From jct of Hwys 87 & 385, E 3/4 mi on Hwy 54. B/f, n/s rms, whrlpool, sauna, outlets, b/t pkng, toast bar, cable TV, cot, crib. Free local calls. $37/S; $40-43/D; $3/ex prsn. Higher spec event rates. Discs.

Dallas

Econo Lodge/ 2275 Valley View Ln, Dallas TX 75234. 214-243-5500/ Fax: 243-8738. V,AE,M,DC. I-35 E (Exit 441) at Valley View Ln, W 1 blk. Rstrnt, pool, mtg rm, fax, cable TV, t pkng, exerc equip, laundry, trans, n/s rms. Free coffee. $36-56/S; $36-66/D; $5/ex prsn. 3/1-9/30: $39-59/S; $39-69/D. Discs.

Exel Inn/ 8510 E RL Thornton Hwy, Dallas TX 75228. 214-328-8500/ Fax: 328-9701. AE,V,M,CB,DC,D. I-30, Jim Miller Rd Exit. Adj rstrnt, cable TV, elevator, pool, n/s rms, fax, laundry. Free coffee, cont brfst, crib, local calls. AAA. $29-40/S; $34-49/D; $4/ex prsn. Higher wknd/ spec event rates. Discs.

Howard Johnson/ 9386 LBJ Fwy, Dallas TX 75243. 214-690-1220/ Fax: 234-8903. M,V,D,AE,DC,CB. Hwy 635 at Abram Exit (East of I-75). Rstrnt, n/s rms, b/f, pool, cable TV, laundry, electronic locks. Free cont brfst. $44-49/S or D. Discs.

Motel 6/ 2660 Forest Ln, Dallas TX

TEXAS

75234. 214-484-9111/ Fax: 484-0214. V,M,DC,D,AE. I-635, Exits 26/ 27A bet Denton Dr & Josey Ln, S of frwy. Cable TV, pool, elevator, n/s rms. Free local calls. Premier Award. $32/S; $38/D; $6/ex prsn. Disc.

Motel 6/ 2753 Forest Ln, Dallas TX 75234. 214-620-2828/ Fax: 620-9061. V,M,DC,D,AE. Just S of I-635, bet Denton Dr & Josey Ln. Nrby rstrnt, cable TV, laundry, pool, n/s rms, t pkng, elevator. Free local calls. $30/S; $36/D; $6/ex prsn. Disc.

Motel 6/ 4325 Beltline Rd, Dallas TX 75244. 214-386-4577/ Fax: 386-4579. AE,V,M,DC,D. I-635 (Exit 23) to Midway Rd, N to Beltline Rd, turn rt. Nrby rstrnt, cable TV, laundry, pool, n/s rms, mtg rm, tennis ct. Free local calls. Premier Award. $36-38/S; $42-44/D; $6/ex prsn. Disc.

Motel 6/ 4220 Independence Dr, Dallas TX 75237. 214-296-3331/ Fax: 709-9438. M,V,DC,D,AE. I-20, Exit 463 at Cockrell Rd/ Camp Wisdom Rd. On N side of frwy. Pool, n/s rms. Free local calls. $27/S; $31/D; $4/ex prsn. Disc.

Also see Arlington, Duncanville, Euless, Garland, Grand Prairie, Irving, Mesquite, North Richland Hills, Plano.

Decatur

Comfort Inn/ 1709 SR 287, Decatur TX 76234. 817-627-6919. V,M,AE,DC. I-35 N to US 287, N to mtl. Bet Hwys 51 & 730 on US 287. Nrby rstrnt, pool, fax, whrlpool, cable TV, t pkng, n/s rms. Free cont brfst. No pets. AAA. $36-90/S; $46-90/D; $5/ex prsn. 5/1-8/31: $38-90/S; $49-100/D. 9/1-10/31: $37-90/S; $47-90/D. Discs.

Del Rio

Motel 6/ 2115 Av "F," Del Rio TX 78840. 210-774-2115/ Fax: 774-4878. V,M,DC,D,AE. On US Hwy 90/227/337/Ave F at Garner Drive. Nrby rstrnt, cable TV, laundry, pool, n/s rms, t pkng. Free local calls. $26-27/S; $30-33/D; $4-6/ex prsn. Disc.

Denton

Exel Inn/ 4211 I-35E N, Denton TX 76201. 817-383-1471/ Fax: 898-0329. AE,V,M,CB,DC,D. From I-35E, exit to Hwy 380W (University Dr), rt on Mesa. Nrby rstrnt, pool, cable TV, elevator, n/s rms, fax, t pkng, laundry. Free coffee, cont brfst, crib, local calls. AAA. $29-40/S; $34-49/D; $4/ex prsn. Higher wknd/ spec event rates. Discs.

Motel 6/ 4125 I-35 N, Denton TX 76207. 817-566-4798/ Fax: 591-0981. V,M,DC,D,AE. I-35, Exit 469 at US 380, W to N Mesa Dr, N to Los Colinas, rt to mtl. Nrby rstrnt, cable TV, pool, n/s rms. Free local calls. $28-29/S; $34-35/D; $6/ex prsn. Disc.

Dumas

Econo Lodge/ 1719 S Dumas Av, Dumas TX 79029. 806-935-9098/ Fax: 935-7483. V,M,AE. US 87 & US 287. Nrby rstrnt, pool, whrlpool, cable TV, t pkng, laundry, outlets, copier, fax, refrig, n/s rms. Free cont brfst M-Sat, local calls. $32-70/S; $34-70/D; $5/ex prsn. Discs.

Super 8 Motel/ 119 W 17th, Dumas TX 79029. 806-935-6222. V,M,DC,CB,AE,D. Hwy 287 (S Dumas Av) at 17th St. S of SR 152. B/f, n/s rms, outlets, t pkng, cable TV, refrig, cot, crib. Free local calls. AAA. $36-41/S; $41-46/D; $3-7/ex prsn. Higher spec event, wknd rates. Discs.

Duncanville (Dallas - Ft Worth area)

Motel 6/ 202 Jellison Rd, Duncanville TX 75116. 214-296-0345/ Fax: 296-7325. V,M,DC,D,AE. I-20 Ebnd: Exit 462A, S on Duncanville Rd, rt on Jellison; Wbnd: Exit 462B, rt on N Main, lt on Fairmeadows, lt on Duncanville, rt on Jellison. Cable TV, pool, n/s rms. Free local calls. $30/S; $34/D; $4/ex prsn. Disc.

Eastland

Budget Host Inn/ Box 108, Eastland TX 76448. 817-629-2655/ Fax: 629-1914. AE,M,V,CB,DC,D. I-20 (Exit 343) at FM 570. Cable TV, dd phone, rstrnt, mtg rm, lounge, pool, crib, t pkng. AAA/ Mobil. $32-40/S; $36-47/D; $4/ex prsn. Discs.

Econo Lodge/ 2001 I-20 W, Eastland TX 76448. 817-629-3324. V,AE,M,DC. I-20, Exit 343. Nrby rstrnt/ lounge, pool, cable TV, t pkng. Free cont brfst. $32/S; $40/D; $4/ex prsn. Discs.

TEXAS

Edinburg
Rodeway Inn/ 1400 W University Dr, Edinburg TX 78539. 210-381-5400. AE,DC,M,V. US 281 S to University Dr, W 2 1/2 mi to mtl. Nrby rstrnt, pool, mtg rm, t pkng, n/s rms. $38-44/S; $40-48/D; $5/ex prsn. Discs.

El Paso
Econo Lodge/ 6363 Montana Av, El Paso TX 79925. 915-778-3311. V,AE,M,DC. On Montana N of I-10; I-10: E, take Airway Dr, lt 3 blks to Montana; W, take Geronimo exit, to Montana, rt 3 blks. Nrby rstrnt, pool, fax, cable TV, t pkng, laundry, n/s rms. Free coffee, arpt trans. $32-50/S; $34-59/D; $5/ex prsn. Discs.

Motel 6/ 11049 Gateway Blvd W, El Paso TX 79935. 915-594-8533/ Fax: 592-6603. V,M,DC,D,AE. I-10 Ebnd, take Lomaland Exit 29, lt on Lomaland, lt on Gateway. I-10 Wbnd, Lee Trevino-Lomaland Exit 30. Nrby rstrnt, cable TV, laundry, pool, n/s rms. Free local calls. $30/S; $36/D; $6/ex prsn. Disc.

Motel 6/ 1330 Lomaland Dr, El Paso TX 79935. 915-592-6386/ Fax: 592-4416. M,V,DC,D,AE. I-10, Exits 29/30 at Lomaland Dr, N of frwy. Pool, n/s rms, t pkng. Free local calls. $29-30/S; $35-36/D; $6/ex prsn. Disc.

Motel 6/ 7840 N Mesa St, El Paso TX 79932. 915-584-2129/ Fax: 584-1643. V,M,DC,D,AE. I-10, Exit 11/ N Mesa St, W of frwy. Nrby rstrnt, cable TV, pool, n/s rms. Free local calls. $30/S; $36/D; $6/ex prsn. Disc.

Motel 6/ 4800 Gateway Blvd E, El Paso TX 79905. 915-533-7521/ Fax: 544-4904. V,M,AE,DC,D. I-10, Exit 23A/ Raynolds Rd exit. S of frwy. Rstrnt, cable TV, laundry, pool, elevator, n/s rms, t pkng. Free local calls. $30-32/S; $36-38/D; $6/ex prsn. Disc.

Also see Anthony.

Ennis
Quality Inn/ 107 Wagon Wheel Dr, Box 1149, Ennis TX 75119. 214-875-9641. V,M,DC,AE. Jct I-45 & SR 34. Rstrnt/ lounge, pool, mtg rm, fax, b/f, cable TV, t pkng, n/s rms. No pets. AAA. $42-58/S or D; $2/ex prsn. Discs.

Euless (Dallas - Ft Worth area)
Motel 6/ 110 W Arpt Frwy, Euless TX 76039. 817-545-0141/ Fax: 868-0584. M,V,DC,D,AE. Hwy 183/ Arpt Frwy at Main St/ Euless Rd Exit. Pool, n/s rms. Free local calls. $28-29/S; $34-35/D; $6/ex prsn. Disc.

Fort Stockton
Best Western Swiss Clock Inn/ 3201 W Dickinson, Ft Stockton TX 79735. 915-336-8521/ Fax: 336-6513. V,M,AE,D, DC,CB. I-10, Exit 256, 1/2 mi E. Pool, n/s rms, cable TV, arpt trans, TDD, tt phone, mtg rm, fax, copier, cot, crib, t/b pkng, b/f. Free local calls, coffee. AAA/ Mobil. $40/S; $48/D; $6/ex prsn. Discs. *Guaranteed rates.*

Econo Lodge/ 800 E Dickinson, Ft Stockton TX 79735. 915-336-9711/ Fax: 336-5815. AE,DC,M,V. US 290 E. Rstrnt/ lounge, pool, mtg rm, fax, b/f, cable TV, t pkng, n/s rms. Free full brfst. AAA. $36-44/S; $42-50/D; $4/ex prsn. Discs.

Motel 6/ 3001 W Dickinson Blvd, Ft Stockton TX 79735. 915-336-9737/ Fax: 336-8346. V,M,DC,D,AE. I-10, Exit 256/ Bsns I-10, E 2 blks. Cable TV, laundry, pool, n/s rms, t pkng. Free local calls. $26-27/S; $30-33/D; $4-6/ex prsn. Disc.

Fort Worth
Comfort Inn/ 8345 W Freeway, Ft Worth TX 76116. 817-244-9446 — opening soon. M,V,D,AE,DC. I-30 & Las Vegas Trail. Nrby rstrnt, pool, mtg rm, fax, b/f, whrlpool, cable TV, t pkng, n/s rms. Free cont brfst. No pets. $39-55/S; $45-65/D; $6/ex prsn. Discs.

HoJo Inn/ 4201 S Frwy, Ft Worth TX 76115. 817-923-8281/ Fax: 926-8756. V,M,AE,DC,D. I-35W to Seminary exit. Rstrnt, n/s rms, pool, trans, t pkng. No pets. $40-55/S; $45-60/D. Discs.

Motel 6/ 4433 S Frwy, Ft Worth TX 761 15. 817-921-4900/ Fax: 921-2702. V,M, DC,AE,D. I-35W: Sbnd, Exit 46A/ Felix St; Nbnd, Exit 46B/ Seminary Dr. Cable TV, pool, n/s rms. Free local calls. $29/S; $33-35/D; $4-6/ex prsn. Disc.

Motel 6/ 3271 I-35 W, Ft Worth TX 76106. 817-625-4359/ Fax: 625-8256.

TEXAS

V,M,DC,D,AE. On W side of I-35 (Exit 54B/ 54C) bet Papurt & 33rd/Long St, on Braswell. Cable TV, pool, n/s rms, t pkng. Free local calls. $27-28/S; $31-34/D; $4-6/ex prsn. Disc.

Motel 6/ 1236 Oakland Blvd, Ft Worth TX 76103. 817-834-7361/ Fax: 834-1573. M,V,DC,D,AE. I-30 to Oakland Blvd Exit, N 1 blk. Pool, n/s rms. Free local calls. $27-28/S; $33-34/D; $6/ex prsn. Disc.

Motel 6/ 8701 I-30 W, Ft Worth TX 76116. 817-244-9740/ Fax: 244-1697. V,M,DC,D,AE. I-30, Exit 6 at Las Vegas Tr. E of I-820. Adj rstrnt, cable TV, pool, n/s rms, t pkng. Free local calls. $28/S; $34/D; $6/ex prsn. Disc.

Motel 6/ 6600 S Frwy, Ft Worth TX 76134. 817-293-8595/ Fax: 293-8577. V,M,DC,AE,D. I-35W, Exit 44, Alta Mesa. Cable TV, laundry, pool, n/s rms, t pkng. Free local calls. $28/S; $32-34/D; $4-6/ex prsn. Disc.

Also see Arlington, Duncanville, Euless, Garland, Grand Prairie, Irving, Mesquite, North Richland Hills, Plano.

Fredericksburg

Budget Host Deluxe Inn/ 901 E Main, Fredericksburg TX 78624. 210-997-3344/ Fax: 997-4381. AE,M,V,CB, DC,D. Hwy 290 E. Cable TV, dd phone, family rms, kitchens, rstrnt, laundry, hot tub, cot, crib, arpt trans, t pkng. Free local calls. AAA. $32-50/S; $36-60/D; $5/ex prsn. Spec events: $46-90. Discs.

Gainesville

Budget Host Inn/ Rte 2, Box 120, Gainesville TX 76240. 817-665-2856. V,M,AE,D,DC,CB. N I-35, Exit 499, Frontage Rd. Cable TV, dd phone, n/s rms, nrby rstrnt, pool, cot, crib. AAA. $30-35/S; $30-40/D; $3/ex prsn.

Comfort Inn/ 1936 I-35 N, Box 76, Gainesville TX 76240. 817-665-5599. M,V,D,AE,DC. I-35 (N, Exit 499; S, Exit 498A) to US 82, exit Oklahoma City, N to mtl. On E side of fwy. Nrby rstrnt, pool, mtg rm, fax, b/f, cable TV, t pkng, n/s rms. Free cont brfst. $35-40/S; $42-47/D; $5/ex prsn. Discs.

Best Western Southwinds/ 2103 N I-35, Gainsville TX 76240. 817-665-7737/ Fax: 668-2651. V,M,AE,D,DC,CB. I-35: Sbnd, Exit 498B; Nbnd, Exit 499, stay on frontage road to underpass. Pool, n/s rms, cable TV, tt/dd phone, fax, copier, refrig, microwave, cot, crib, t/b pkng. Free local calls, cont brfst, coffee. Mobil. $35-37/S; $39-41/D; $5/ex prsn. Spec event, holiday, wknd rates: $39/S; $43/D. Discs. *Guaranteed rates.*

Galveston

Comfort Inn/ 2300 Seawall Blvd, Galveston TX 77550. 409-762-1166. M,V,D,AE,DC. I-45 S to Broadway, rt to 23rd St. Rstrnt/ lounge, pool, fax, b/f, cable TV, t pkng, n/s rms. Free cont brfst. No pets. $30-90/S; $35-99/D; $5/ex prsn. 2/1-2/29: $30-120/S; $30-130/D. 3/1-4/30: $40-65/S; $45-65/D. 5/1-9/30: $45-120/S or D. Discs.

Econo Lodge/ 2825 61st St, Galveston TX 77551. 409-744-7133. V,AE,M,DC. I-45 to 61st St, rt 1 1/2 mi to mtl. Nrby rstrnt, pool, cable TV, t pkng, n/s rms. Free local calls, coffee. No pets. $30-80/S; $35-90/D; $5-10/ex prsn. Discs.

Motel 6/ 7404 Av "J" Broadway, RR 4, Galveston TX 77554. 409-740-3794/ Fax: 740-4670. V,M,DC,D,AE. I-45, Exits 1A/B, N of frwy. Cable TV, laundry, pool, n/s rms. Free local calls. $28-34/S; $32-38/D; $4/ex prsn. Fri, Sat, holidays: $27-40/S; $31-44/D. Higher spec event rates. Disc.

Garland (Dallas - Ft Worth area)

Comfort Inn/ 3536 W Kingsley Rd, Garland TX 75041. 214-340-3501. M,V, D,AE,DC. I-635 (LBJ Fwy) at Kingsley-Jupiter Rd exit. Nrby rstrnt, indr pool, fax, b/f, sauna, whrlpool, cable TV, exerc equip, n/s rms. Free cont brfst. No pets. AAA. $46-52/S; $48-56/D; $4/ex prsn. 6/1-7/31: $48-54/S; $50-58/D. Discs.

Days Inn Garland/ 6222 Beltline Rd, Garland TX 75043. 214-226-7621/ Fax: 226-3617. V,M,AE,D,DC,CB. I-30 E, 2 mi from I-635 Exit Beltline/ Garland. Nrby rstrnt, pool, whrlpool, satellite TV, tt/dd phone, mtg rm, fax, copier, laundry, cot, t pkng, conn rms. Free local calls, cont brfst. AAA. $34/S; $39/D; $5/ex prsn. 3/1-10/31: $39/S;

TEXAS

$45/D. Discs. *Guaranteed rates.*

Motel 6/ 436 W I-30, Garland TX 75043. 214-226-7140/ Fax: 226-2416. V,M,DC,AE,D. I-30, Exit 58, at Beltline Rd. Nrby rstrnt, cable TV, laundry, pool, n/s rms, t pkng, elevator. Free local calls. $28/S; $32/D; $4/ex prsn. Disc.

Giddings

Econo Lodge/ US 290 E, Giddings TX 78942. 409-542-9666. AE,M,DC,V. SR 77, exit to US 290, E 2 mi to mtl. Nrby rstrnt, pool, mtg rm, fax, cable TV, t pkng, n/s rms. $39-42/S; $42-45/D; $5/ex prsn. 12/1-2/20: $36-39/S; $39-42/D. Discs.

Grand Prairie
(Dallas - Ft Worth area)

Motel 6/ 406 E Safari Blvd, Grand Prairie TX 75050. 214-642-9424/ Fax: 262-3482. V,M,DC,D,AE. I-30, Exit 34 to Beltline Rd, N to Safari Blvd. Cable TV, laundry, pool, n/s rms. Free local calls. $28-30/S; $34-36/D; $6/ex prsn. Disc.

Greenville

Motel 6/ 5109 I-30, Greenville TX 75402. 903-455-0515/ Fax: 455-8314. V,M,DC,D,AE. I-30, Exit 94A/B, S frontage rd. Nrby rstrnt, cable TV, laundry, pool, n/s rms, t pkng. Free local calls. $23-24/S; $29-30/D; $6/ex prsn. Disc.

Groom

Budget Host Chalet Inn/ Box 430, Groom TX 79039. 806-248-7524. AE,D,M,V. I-40, Exit 113 S 1/2 blk. Nrby rstrnt, n/s rms, cable TV, TDD, tt phone, cot, crib, b/f. Free local calls. No pets. AAA. $36/S; $48/D; $5/ex prsn. Disc: Senior, AAA. *Guaranteed rates.*

Groves

Motel 6/ 5201 E Pkwy, Groves TX 77619. 409-962-6611/ Fax: 962-8439. V,M,DC,AE,D. Hwy 73 at 39th St/Hwy 347. Cable TV, laundry, pool, n/s rms, t pkng. Free local calls. $25-26/S; $29-30/D; $4/ex prsn. Disc.

Harlingen

Motel 6/ 224 S US Expwy 77, Harlingen TX 78550. 210-421-4200/ Fax: 412-8159. V,M,DC,D,AE. US 77/ Bsns 83 at Tyler Av exit. On W side of 77. Cable TV, pool, n/s rms. Free local calls. $30-32/S; $36-38/D; $6/ex prsn. Disc.

Rodeway Inn/ 1821 W Tyler, Harlingen TX 78550. 210-425-1040. V,M,D,AE. US 77/ US 83 jct, E 2 blks, exit dntn. Rstrnt/ lounge, pool, fax, b/f, cable TV, t pkng, n/s rms. Free cont brfst. No pets. $44-56/S; $49-56/D; $5/ex prsn. 3/7-4/30: $52-68/S; $52-78/D. 5/1-12/31: $41-52/S; $45-52/D. Discs.

Super 8 Motel/ 1115 S Expressway 77/83, Harlingen TX 78550. 210-412-8873/ Fax: 407. V,M,D,DC,CB,AE. US 77 at "M" St. B/f, n/s rms, pool, toast bar, elevator, cable TV, mtg rm, TDD, cot. Free local calls, crib. $41/S; $46-51/D; $4/ex prsn. Higher spec event, wknd rates. Discs.

Houston

Econo Lodge/ 9535 Katy Frwy, Houston TX 77024. 713-467-4411. V,M,AE,DC. I-10 W, exit Bunker Hill Rd, make U-turn after exit, 1 blk to mtl. Rstrnt, pool, fax, cable TV, t pkng, n/s rms. Free cont brfst. $34-37/S; $36-39/D; $3/ex prsn. 5/1-9/2: $36-41/S; $43-46/D. Discs.

Grant Motor Inn/ 8200 S Main St, Houston TX 77025. 713-668-8000/ Fax: 668-7777/ 800-255-8904. V,M,AE,D,DC,CB. Near the jct of Main St and Kirby, on Main St. 5 mi S of dntn, 1 mi inside Loop 610 S. Whrlpool, n/s rms, satellite TV, VCR/ movies, tt/dd phone, fax, copier, laundry, microwave, cot, crib, conn rms, b/f. Free cont brfst, coffee. No pets. AAA. $32-39/S; $35-49/D; $4-6/ex prsn. Disc: Senior, l/s, bsns, family, govt, milt, medical. *Guaranteed rates.*

HoJo Inn/ 4602 Katy Frwy, Houston TX 77007. 713-861-9000/ Fax: Ext 300. V,M,AE,DC,D,CB. From dntn: I-10 W (Katy Frwy), exit N Shepard. From W: Loop to I-10 E, exit N Shepard, U turn on Peterson St (N side of Katy Frwy). N/s rms, mtg rm, fax, cable TV, b/f. Free cont brfst, local calls. Gold Medal Winner. $40-48/S; $45-52/D. Discs.

Howard Johnson Lodge/ 7777 Airport Blvd, Houston TX 77061. 713-644-

TEXAS

1261/ Fax: 644-1117. M,V,D,AE,DC,CB. I-45 to Arpt Blvd. Rstrnt/ lounge, n/s rms, pool, exerc equip, laundry, fax, arpt trans, Free cont brfst. $43-59/S; $43-65/D. Discs.

Howard Johnson Lodge/ 4225 N Frwy, Houston TX 77022. 713-695-6011/ Fax: 697-6404. V,M,AE,DC. One blk N of Loop 610/ I-45, at Crosstimbers, Exit 52B. Rstrnt/ lounge, n/s rms, pool, t pkng, cable TV, fax, mtg rm. $36-44/S; $42-48/D. 5/1-10/31: $44-48/S; $52-58/D. Discs.

Motel 6/ 3223 S Loop W, Houston TX 77025. 713-664-6425/ Fax: 666-8514. V,M,DC,D,AE. S Loop 610 at S Main. Nrby rstrnt, cable TV, pool, n/s rms, t pkng. Free local calls. $32-34/S; $36-38/D; $4/ex prsn. Disc.

Motel 6/ 5555 W 34th St, Houston TX 77092. 713-682-8588/ Fax: 681-8592. V,M,DC,D,AE. US 290 at 34th St. Nrby rstrnt, cable TV, laundry, pool, n/s rms. Free local calls. $35-36/S; $41-42/D; $6/ex prsn. Disc.

Motel 6/ 8800 Arpt Blvd, Houston TX 77061. 713-941-0990/ Fax: 944-5147. M,V,DC,D,AE. I-45 to Arpt Blvd. On W side of frwy. Nrby rstrnt, cable TV, pool, n/s rms. Free local calls. $32-34/S; $38-40/D; $6/ex prsn. Disc.

Motel 6/ 9638 Plainfield Rd, Houston TX 77036. 713-778-0008/ Fax: 771-2248. V,M,DC,D,AE. US 59, exit Bissonett Rd, W to Plainfield Rd, turn S. Cable TV, laundry, pool, n/s rms, t pkng. Free local calls. $32-34/S; $38-40/D; $6/ex prsn. Disc.

Motel 6/ 16884 NW Frwy, Houston TX 77040. 713-937-7056/ Fax: 849-5240. V,M,DC,AE,D. US 290 at Jones Rd. From 290, exit Senate Av to frontage rd on NE side of frwy. Nrby rstrnt, cable TV, laundry, pool, n/s rms, t pkng. Free local calls. $35-36/S; $41-42/D; $6/ex prsn. Disc.

Motel 6/ 14833 Katy Frwy, Houston TX 77094. 713-497-5000/ Fax: 497-1472 V,M,DC,AE,D. I-10 at US 6, Exit 751. Nrby rstrnt, cable TV, pool, n/s rms, t pkng. Free local calls. $34-36/S; $40-42/D; $6/ex prsn. Disc.

Rodeway Inn/ 1505 College Av, Houston TX 77587. 713-946-5900. M,V,D, AE,DC. I-45 to College Av/ Airport Blvd. Nrby rstrnt, pool, mtg rm, fax, b/f, cable TV, t pkng, n/s rms. Free cont brfst. No pets. AAA. $44-50/S; $48-56/D; $6/ex prsn. Discs.

Rodeway Inn/ 3135 Southwest Frwy, Houston TX 77098. 713-526-1071. M,V,D,AE,DC. US 59 (SW Frwy) to Buffalo Speedway. Across from Greenway Plaza. Rstrnt, pool, mtg rm, fax, cable TV, n/s rms. Free cont brfst, local calls, coffee. AAA. $46-55/S; $48-68/D; $6/ex prsn. Discs.

Rodeway Inn/ 5820 Katy Frwy, Houston TX 77007. 713-869-9211. V,M,AE,D, DC,CB. I-10, W at Washington/ Westcott exit. Rstrnt, pool, fax, cable TV, t pkng, laundry, copier, fax, n/s rms. Free cont brfst, local calls. No pets. AAA. $46-48/S; $48-55/D; $6/ex prsn. Discs.

Rodeway Inn/ 13611 Rankin Cir W, Houston TX 77073. 713-821-0410. V,M, DC,AE,D. I-45 to Rankin Cir/ Kuykendal Rd, rt at light, 1/2 mi along frwy to mtl. Nrby rstrnt, pool, mtg rm, b/f, sauna, whrlpool, t pkng, exerc equip, n/s rms. Free cont brfst. No pets. $42-47/S; $47-53/D; $6/ex prsn. Discs.

Sleep Inn/ JFK Blvd, Doubletree Plaza D, Houston TX 77032. 800-221-2222 — opening soon. V,M,DC,AE. Just N of Sam Houston Pkwy; 1/2 mi S of arpt. Nrby rstrnt, pool, fax, b/f, cable TV, n/s rms. Free cont brfst. No pets. $39-59/S or D; $5/ex prsn. 1/1-4/30: $49-69/S or D. Discs.

Super 8 Motel/ 4020 SW Freeway, Houston TX 77027. 713-623-4720/ Fax: 963-8526. V,M,D,DC,CB,AE. I-59 at Weslayan. N/s rms, pool, whrlpool, sauna, outlet, t/b/rv pkng, copier, elevator, satellite TV, exerc equip, mtg rm, cot. Free local calls, crib. $43/S; $50/D; $5/ex prsn. Discs.

Also see Baytown, Channelview, Pasaden, Spring, Webster.

Huntsville

Econo Lodge/ 1501 I-45 N, Huntsville TX 77340. 409-295-6401/ Fax: 291-6007. V,M,AE,D,DC,CB. I-45, Exit 116.

TEXAS

Nrby rstrnt, pool, fax, cable TV, t pkng. AAA. $35-40/S; $40-49/D; $6/ex prsn. Discs.

Motel 6/ 1607 I-45, Huntsville TX 77340. 409-291-6927/ Fax: 291-8963. V,M,DC,D,AE. I-45, Exit 116 at US 190. Adj rstrnt, cable TV, laundry, pool, n/s rms. Free local calls. $27-28/S; $31-32/D; $4/ex prsn. Disc.

Rodeway Inn/ 3211 I-45, Huntsville TX 77340. 409-295-7595. M,V,D,AE,DC. I-45 (Exit 114) at Lake Rd/ Hwy 1374. Nrby rstrnt, pool, b/f, whrlpool, cable TV, n/s rms. Free cont brfst. $30-60/S; $35-65/D; $5/ex prsn. Discs.

Irving (Dallas - Ft Worth area)

Howard Johnson/ 120 W Airport Fwy, Irving TX 75062. 214-579-8911/ Fax: 721-1846. M,V,D,AE,DC,CB. Hwy 183 to O'Connor Rd Exit. Rstrnt/ lounge, n/s rms, pool, t/b pkng, cable TV, mtg rm. No pets. $34-40/S; $40-46/D. Discs.

Motel 6/ 510 S Loop 12, Irving TX 75060. 214-438-4227/ Fax: 554-0048. M,V,DC,D,AE. I-30 to Loop 12, N to Irving Blvd (Hwy 356). N/s rms. Free local calls. $28-29/S; $34-35/D; $6/ex prsn. Disc.

Motel 6/ 7800 Heathrow Dr, Irving TX 75063. 214-915-3993 — Opening Soon. V,M,D,DC,AE. From DFW Arpt take N exit to Hwy 114 E. From Hwy 114 Ebnd, take Esters Blvd Exit, rt, rt again on Plaza. Hwy 114 Wbnd, Exit Esters, lt, rt on Plaza. Rstrnt, pool, laundry, elevator, arpt trans. $38/S; $44/D; $6/ex prsn. Disc.

Super 8 Motel/ 4245 W Airport Frwy, Irving TX 75062. 214-257-1810/ Fax: 257-1932. V,M,AE,D,DC. Hwy 183 (Arpt Frwy) at N Esters Rd exit. B/f, n/s rms, copier, fax, elevator, mtg rm, cable TV, cot, crib. Free local calls. No pets. Pride Award. $49/S; $56-58/D; $3/ex prsn. Higher spec event rates. Discs.

Killeen

Comfort Inn/ Trimmer Rd, Killeen TX 76541. 800-221-2222 — opening soon. M,V,D,AE,DC. Just S of Hwy 190. Nrby rstrnt, pool, fax, b/f, sauna, whrlpool, cable TV, t pkng, n/s rms. Free cont brfst, local calls. No pets. $40-55/S; $45-60/D; $5/ex prsn. Discs.

Days Inn/ 810 Central Texas Expwy, Killeen TX 76541. 817-634-6644/ Fax: 634-2751. AE,M,V,DC,D,CB. Hwy 190, exit Trimmier Rd to Service Rd at S side of frwy. Nrby rstrnt, pool, b/f, t pkng, cot. Free local calls, cont brfst, crib. Chairman's Award. $37-50/S; $45-60/D. Discs.

Friendship Inn/ 601 W Bsns US 190, Killeen TX 76541. 817-526-2232. V,M,AE,DC. US 190 to Bsns US 190. Nrby rstrnt, cable TV, laundry, n/s rms. Free cont brfst. No pets. $30-40/S; $33-49/D; $5/ex prsn. Discs.

Rodeway Inn/ 506 W Av F, Killeen TX 76511. 800-424-4777 — opening soon. M,V,D,AE,DC. US 90 to SR 195, N 1 mi, rt on Veterans Blvd to mtl. Nrby rstrnt, fax, b/f, cable TV, t pkng, n/s rms. Free cont brfst. No pets. $34-44/S; $39-49/D; $5/ex prsn. Discs.

Kingsville

Econo Lodge/ 2502 E Kennedy, Kingsville TX 78363. 512-595-7700. V,M,AE,DC. US 77 Bypass at SR 141 W. Nrby rstrnt, fax, b/f, cable TV, t pkng, n/s rms, micro/fridges. Free cont brfst. AAA. $37-47/S; $40-47/D; $6/ex prsn. 6/9-6/14: $59-69/S; $72-76/D. Discs.

Motel 6/ 101 N US 77, Kingsville TX 78363. 512-592-5106/ Fax: 592-6947. V,M,DC,D,AE. Just N of E King Ave on US 77. Do not take Bsns 77 exits. Cable TV, laundry, pool, n/s rms. Free local calls. $27/S; $31/D; $4/ex prsn. Disc.

Quality Inn/ 221 US 77 Bypass, Kingsville TX 78363. 512-592-5251. M, V,D,AE,DC. US 77 Bypass at SR 141 W. Nrby rstrnt/ lounge, pool, mtg rm, fax, b/f, cable TV, t pkng, exerc equip, n/s rms. Free cont brfst. $41-51/S; $44-51/D; $6/ex prsn. 6/9-6/14: $63-73/S; $76-80/D. Discs.

Laredo

Motel 6/ 5920 San Bernardo Av, Laredo TX 78081. 210-722-8133/ Fax: 725-8212. V,M,DC,D,AE. I-35, Exit 4 at Del Mar Blvd. W side of frwy. Adj rstrnt,

TEXAS

cable TV, laundry, pool, n/s rms, t pkng. Free local calls. Premier Award. $36-38/S; $42-44/D; $6/ex prsn. Disc.

Motel 6/ 5310 San Bernardo Av, Laredo TX 78041. 210-725-8187/ Fax: 725-0424. V,M,DC,D,AE. I-35 Sbnd: Exit 3B/ Mann Rd, follow frontage rd (San Bernardo Av), to mtl. Nbnd: Exit 3B, lt on Mann, lt on frontage rd & return to mtl. Nrby rstrnt, cable TV, pool, n/s rms. Free local calls. $33-36/S; $39-42/D; $6/ex prsn. Disc.

Livingston

Econo Lodge/ 117 US 59 Loop S, Livingston TX 77351. 409-327-2451. V,M,AE. US 190 to US 59, S to mtl. Nrby rstrnt, pool, fax, cable TV, t pkng, n/s rms. No pets. AAA. $32-38/S; $38-46/D; $6/ex prsn. Discs.

Longview

Econo Lodge/ 3120 Estes Pkwy, Longview TX 75602. 903-753-4884. V,AE,M,DC. I-20 & Estes Pkwy. Rstrnt, pool, mtg rm, fax, cable TV, t pkng, laundry, arpt trans, n/s rms. Free coffee. $34-36/S; $36-39/D; $4/ex prsn. Discs.

Motel 6/ 110 W Access Rd, Longview TX 75603. 903-758-5256/ Fax: 758-6940. V,M,DC,D,AE. Jct I-20 & Estes Pkwy (Exit 595/595A). Cable TV, pool, n/s rms. Free local calls. $27-28/S; $31-32/D; $4/ex prsn. Disc.

Ramada Ltd - Super 8, 3304 S Eastman Rd, Longview TX 75602. 903-758-0711/ Fax: Ext 296, V,M,AE, D,DC,CB. I-20 at Exit 596. Rstrnt, pool, sauna, n/s rms, exerc equip, cable TV, VCR, tt phone, mtg rm, laundry, cot, crib, t/b pkng, eff, conn rms. Free local calls, cont brfst. AAA. $36/S; $39-44/D; $7/ex prsn. Discs. *Guaranteed rates.*

Lubbock

Howard Johnson Lodge/ 4801 Av "Q," Lubbock TX 79412. 806-747-1671/ Fax: 747-4265. M,V,D,AE,DC,CB. I-27 to 50th St Exit, W to Ave "Q" N. Lounge, cable TV, nrby rstrnt, n/s rms, b/f, fax, whrlpool, mtg rm. Free cont brfst. $45-55/S; $60-75/D. 5/1-10/31: $30-45/S; $45-60/D. Discs.

Motel 6/ 909 66th St, Lubbock TX 79412. 806-745-5541/ Fax: 748-0889. V,M,DC,AE,D. I-27 at 66th St. Cable TV, laundry, pool, n/s rms. Free local calls. $27-28/S; $33-34/D; $6/ex prsn. Disc.

Rodeway Inn/ 6025 Avenue A, Lubbock TX 79404. 806-745-5111. V,M,D,AE. I-27 & US 84. Rstrnt/ lounge, indr pool, cable TV, t pkng, n/s rms. $25-31/S; $31-36/D; $5/ex prsn. Discs.

Super 8 Motel/ 501 Av "Q," Lubbock TX 79401. 806-762-8726. V,M,DC,AE,D. I-27: Sbnd, Exit Av "Q," SW on Q for 1 mi; Nbnd, turn lt on 4th St for 3/4 mi, lt on Q. B/f, n/s rms, outlets, satellite TV, crib. Free local calls. AAA. $38/S; $44-48/D; $4/ex prsn. Discs.

Lufkin

Motel 6/ 1110 S Timberland, Lufkin TX 75901. 409-637-7850/ Fax: 637-7649. V,M,DC,D,AE. US 59 (Timberland Dr) at S 1st St. Nrby rstrnt, cable TV, laundry, pool, n/s rms, t pkng. Free local calls. $24/S; $28/D; $4/ex prsn. Disc.

Marshall

Comfort Inn/ I-20 & US 59, Marshall TX 75670. 903-935-1135. V,M,AE,DC. Rstrnt, pool, fax, b/f, cable TV, t pkng, n/s rms, whrlpool. Free cont brfst. No pets. $40-45/S; $45-55/D; $5/ex prsn. 5/1-11/22: $42-48/S; $45-50/D. 11/23-12/31: $50-55/S; $55-70/D. Discs.

Motel 6/ 300 I-20 E, Marshall TX 75670. 903-935-4393/ Fax: 935-2380. V,M,DC,D,AE. I-20, Exit 617 at US 59. Cable TV, laundry, pool, n/s rms, t pkng. Free local calls. $27-28/S; $31-32/D; $4/ex prsn. Disc.

McAllen

Microtel Inn/ 801 E Expressway 83, McAllen TX 78501. 210-630-2727/ Fax: 630-0666. V,M,AE,D,DC,CB. I-83, Exit Jackson Av. Nrby rstrnt/ lounge, pool, cable TV, video games, tt phone, mtg rm, fax, copier, elevator, t/b/rv pkng, conn rms. Free cont brfst. No pets. AAA. $42-46/S; $47-51/D; $5/ex prsn. Disc: Senior, govt, milt. *Guaranteed rates.*

Motel 6/ 700 W Expwy 83, McAllen TX 78501. 210-687-3700/ Fax: 630-3180.

TEXAS

V,M,DC,AE,D. US 83 at 2nd St/10th St Exit. Nrby rstrnt, cable TV, pool, n/s rms. Free local calls. $35-36/S; $41-42/D; $6/ex prsn. Disc.

Rodeway Inn/ 1421 S 10th St, McAllen TX 78501. 210-686-1586. AE,DC,M,V. US 83 (Exit 336) to 2nd & 10th St. On Frontage Rd. Nrby rstrnt, pool, cable TV, t pkng, family rms, n/s rms. Free cont brfst. $36-45/S; $41-50/D; $5/ex prsn. Discs.

Mesquite (Dallas - Ft Worth area)

Motel 6/ 3629 Hwy 80, Mesquite TX 75150. 214-613-1662/ Fax: 613-1248. V,M,DC,D,AE. US 80 at Town E Blvd, bet I-635 & I-30. Nrby rstrnt, cable TV, pool, n/s rms. Free local calls. $24-26/S; $28-30/D; $4/ex prsn. Disc.

Midland

Motel 6/ 1000 S Midkiff Rd, Midland TX 79701. 915-697-3197/ Fax: 697-7631. V,M,DC,D,AE. I-20, Exit 134 at Midkiff Rd, N of frwy. Cable TV, pool, n/s rms. Free local calls. $24-25/S; $28-31/D; $4-6/ex prsn. Disc.

Rodeway Inn/ 3708 W Wall St, Midland TX 79703. 800-424-4777 — opening soon. V,M,D,AE. I-20 (Exit 136) to SR 349, N to Wall Av. Nrby rstrnt, pool, cable TV, n/s rms. Free cont brfst. $27/S; $30/D; $4/ex prsn. Discs.

Midlothian

Best Western Midlothian Inn/ 220 N Hwy 67, Midlothian TX 76065. 214-775-1891/ Fax: 723-1371. V,M,AE,D,DC,CB. Jct Hwy 67 & 287. Nrby rstrnt, pool, whrlpool, n/s rms, cable TV, VCR/ movies, tt/dd phone, mtg rm, fax, laundry, refrig, microwave, cot, b/f. Free cont brfst. AAA. $46-80/S; $48-90/D; $5/ex prsn. Discs. *Guaranteed rates.*

Mineral Wells

Budget Host Mesa Motel/ 3601 E Hwy 180, Mineral Wells TX 76067. 817-325-3377. M,V,D,AE,DC,CB. On Hwy 180 E of town. Nrby rstrnt/ lounge, cable TV, dd phone, kitchens, n/s rms, pool, playgrnd, picnic area, t pkng. AAA. $28/S; $30-34/D; $4/ex prsn.

HoJo Inn/ 2809 Hwy 180 W, Mineral Wells TX 76067. 817-328-1111/ Fax: Ext 200. M,V,D,AE,DC,CB. Hwy 180 at Mineral Wells. Rstrnt, n/s rms, pool, cable TV. Free cont brfst, local calls. $38-42/S; $42-48/D. Discs.

Nacogdoches

Econo Lodge/ 2020 NW Loop 224, Nacogdoches TX 75961. 409-569-0880. V,M,D,AE,DC. Loop 224 section of US 59, W of Nacogdoches. Rstrnt/ lounge, pool, mtg rm, fax, b/f, cable TV, t pkng, n/s rms. $34-60/S; $38-60/D; $4/ex prsn. 3/1-10/31: $38-60/S; $42-60/D. Discs.

New Braunfels

Budget Host Country Motor Inn/ 210 Hwy 81 E, New Braunfels TX 78130. 210-625-7373/ Fax: 629-2713. M,V,D,AE,DC,CB. I-35 & Exit 187. Cable TV, dd phone, family rms, kitchens, n/s rms, b/f, pool, wading pool. No pets. AAA. $39/S; $45/D. 5/31-8/31: $65/S; $65-75/D. Wknds: $75-125.

North Richland Hills (Dallas Ft Worth area)

Motel 6/ 7804 Bedford Euless Rd, N Richland Hills TX 76180. 817-485-3000/ Fax: 485-8936. M,V,DC,D,AE. I-820, Exit 22A to Hwy 26, N to Bedford Euless Rd, E to mtl. Nrby rstrnt, pool, n/s rms. Free local calls. $28-29/S; $34-35/D; $6/ex prsn. Disc.

Odessa

Best Western Garden Oasis/ 110 W I-20, Odessa TX 79761. 915-337-3006/ Fax: 332-1956. V,M,AE,D,DC,CB. Indr pool, sauna, whrlpool, n/s rms, cable TV, arpt trans, mtg rm, copier, laundry, cot, crib, outlets, t/b/rv pkng, b/f. Free local calls. AAA/ Mobil. $40-45/S; $48/D; $5/ex prsn. Disc: Senior, TA, govt, trkr, milt. *Guaranteed rates.*

Econo Lodge/ 1518 S Grant, Odessa TX 79761. 915-333-1486. AE,DC,M,V. I-20 (Exit 116) to US 385. Nrby rstrnt, fax, cable TV, t pkng, n/s rms. Free cont brfst. $30-38/S; $36-42/D; $5/ex prsn. Discs.

Motel 6/ 200 E I-20 Service Rd, Odessa TX 79766. 915-333-4025/ Fax: 333-2668. V,M,DC,D,AE. I-20, Exit 116 at US 385. S side of frwy. Cable TV, laundry, pool, n/s rms, t pkng. Free local calls. $25-26/S; $31-32/D; $6/ex prsn. Disc.

Rodeway Inn/ 2505 E 2nd St, Odessa TX 79761. 915-333-1528. V,M,D,AE. I-20 (Exit 121) to I-20 Bsns to mtl. Nrby rstrnt, mtg rm, fax, b/f, cable TV, n/s rms. Free cont brfst. No pets. $28-35/S; $32-39/D; $5/ex prsn. Discs.

Super 8 Motel/ 6713 E Hwy 80, Odessa TX 79762. 915-363-8281. V,M,DC,AE, D. I-20, Exit 121 to Loop 338, N 1/4 mi, E on Bsns 20 1/4 mi. B/f, n/s rms, brfst, b/t pkng, copier. Free local calls. AAA. $30/S; $34-35/D; $3/ex prsn. Discs.

Orange

Motel 6/ 4407 27th St, Orange TX 77632. 409-883-4891/ Fax: 886-5211. V,M,DC,D,AE. I-10, Exit 876/ 877 to Lutcher Dr N (N of frwy) to 27th St. Nrby rstrnt, cable TV, laundry, pool, n/s rms, t pkng. Free local calls. $24-26/S; $28-30/D; $4/ex prsn. Disc.

Paris

Comfort Inn/ 3505 NE Loop US 286, Paris TX 75460. 903-784-7481. V,M,DC,AE. US 82 to Loop 286; exit N. On E side of US 271. Nrby rstrnt, pool, fax, b/f, cable TV, t pkng, n/s rms, trans. Free cont brfst. No pets. $37-47/S; $41-51/D; $4/ex prsn. Discs.

Pasadena (Houston area)

Rodeway Inn/ 114 S Richey St, Pasadena TX 77506. 713-477-6871. M,V,AE,DC. Hwy 225 at Richey St. Rstrnt/ lounge, pool, mtg rm, t pkng, n/s rms. Free cont brfst. $32-49/S; $38-55/D; $6/ex prsn. Discs.

Pecos

Motel 6/ 3002 S Cedar, Pecos TX 79772. 915-445-9034/ Fax: 445-2005. V,M,DC,D,AE. I-20, Exit 42 at US 285 (Cedar St), N to mtl. Cable TV, laundry, pool, n/s rms, t pkng. Free local calls. $25-26/S; $29-32/D; $4-6/ex prsn. Disc.

Plano (Dallas - Ft Worth area)

Motel 6/ 2550 N Central Expressway, Plano TX 75074. 214-578-1626/ Fax: 423-6994. V,M,DC,D,AE. US 75, Exit 29A at 15th St. N of I-635. Nrby rstrnt, cable TV, pool, n/s rms. Free local calls. Premier Award. $33-34/S; $39-40/D; $6/ex prsn. Disc.

Sleep Inn/ 4801 W Plano Pkwy, Plano TX 75093. 214-867-1111. V,M,AE,DC. Dallas N Tollway to Plano Pkwy E to mtl. Nrby rstrnt, pool, fax, b/f, cable TV, n/s rms. Free cont brfst. No pets. AAA. $39-69/S; $45-79/D; $6/ex prsn. Discs.

Quanah

Quanah Parker Inn/ 1415 W 11th St, Quanah TX 79252. 817-663-6366/ Fax: 663-2593. V,M,AE,D. On Hwy 287 W. Nrby rstrnt, n/s rms, cable TV, tt/dd phone, fax, copier, crib, t/b pkng, conn rms. Free local calls, cont brfst. AAA. $33/S; $40/D; $6/ex prsn. Disc: Govt, trkr, AAA, AARP. *Guaranteed rates.*

Robstown

Econo Lodge/ 2225 US 77 S, Robstown TX 78380. 512-387-9444. V,AE,M,DC. On US 77, 2 mi S of jct with I-37. Nrby rstrnt, pool, fax, b/f, cable TV, t pkng, n/s rms. Free local calls, coffee, cont brfst. $39-43/S; $45-49/D; $4/ex prsn. 5/1-8/31: $43-49/S; $47-53/D. Discs.

Round Rock

Rodeway Inn/ I-35, exit 251, Round Rock TX 78681. 800-424-4777 — opening soon. M,V,D,AE,DC. I-35 (N, Exit 252; S, Exit 251) at Pflugerville Loop. On W side of frwy. Nrby rstrnt, pool, mtg rm, fax, b/f, whrlpool, cable TV, n/s rms. Free cont brfst. $40-90/S; $46-96/D; $6/ex prsn. Discs.

Salado

HoJo Inn/ Rte 2, Box 270A, Salado TX 76571. 817-947-5000/ Fax: Ext 233. AE,V,M,DC,CB,D. I-35: Sbnd, Exit 285; Nbnd, Exit 284. Pool, n/s rms, t pkng, cable TV. Free cont brfst. $28-38/S; $32-42/D. Discs.

San Angelo

Howard Johnson/ 333 Rio Concho, San Angelo TX 76903. 915-659-0747/ Fax: 659-0749. M,V,D,AE,DC,CB. Hwy 87, E on Concho Av. Rstrnt/ lounge, indr pool, t pkng, n/s rms, b/f, electronic locks, fax, mtg rm, game rm, hot tub, cable TV. Free cont brfst. $40-44/S; $44-48/D. Discs.

Motel 6/ 311 N Bryant, San Angelo TX 76903. 915-658-8061/ Fax: 653-3102. V,M,DC,D,AE. US 87/ 277 at 4th St, just S of US 67. Cable TV, laundry, pool, n/s rms. Free local calls. $26-27/S; $30-31/D; $4/ex prsn. Disc.

San Antonio

Comfort Inn/ 2635 NE Loop 410, San Antonio TX 78217. 210-653-9110. AE,M,V,DC,D. NE Loop 410 (Exit 25B) to Perrin Beitel, exit N. Rstrnt, pool, mtg rm, fax, cable TV, t pkng, n/s rms. Free cont brfst. No pets. AAA. $45-75/S or D. 5/1-8/31: $55-85/S or D. Discs.

Econo Lodge/ 11591 I-35 N, San Antonio TX 78233. 210-654-9111. V,M,D,AE. I-35 N at O'Conner Rd. Rstrnt, pool, fax, b/f, cable TV, t pkng, laundry, n/s rms. Free cont brfst. No pets. $35-90/S; $45-100/D; $5/ex prsn. Discs.

Econo Lodge/ 6735 US 90 W, San Antonio TX 78227. 210-674-5711. V,AE,M,DC. US 90 W to Military Dr exit. Nrby rstrnt, pool, cable TV, n/s rms. Free local calls. $31-43/S; $36-48/D; $5-6/ex prsn. Discs.

Econo Lodge/ 218 S W W White Rd, San Antonio TX 78219. 210-333-3346. V,M,AE. I-10 (Exit 580) at W W White Rd, S 1 blk to mtl. Nrby rstrnt, pool, mtg rm, fax, b/f, cable TV, copier, n/s rms. Free local calls, cont brfst. No pets. AAA. $27-69/S; $32-119/D; $5/ex prsn. Discs.

Howard Johnson Lodge/ 9603 I-35 N, San Antonio TX 78233. 210-655-2120. V,M,AE,DC,D. I-35 (Exit 167/N; Exit 167A/S) follow service rd S. I-35, just N of Bsns 410. Rstrnt, n/s rms, pool, t pkng, laundry, fax. $33-55/S; $40-70/D. Discs.

Motel 6/ 5522 N Pan Am Expwy, San Antonio TX 78218. 210-661-8791/ Fax: 666-5502. M,V,DC,D,AE. I-35/ I-410 at Rittiman Rd. Pool, n/s rms. Free local calls. $28-32/S; $34-38/D; $6/ex prsn. Disc.

Motel 6/ 211 N Pecos St, San Antonio TX 78207. 210-225-1111/ Fax: 222-1134. V,M,DC,D,AE. I-10/I-35, Exit 155B at Houston/Commerce St. W of frwy. Cable TV, pool, n/s rms. Free local calls. $39-42/S; $45-48/D; $6/ex prsn. Disc.

Motel 6/ 2185 SW Loop 410, San Antonio TX 78227. 210-673-9020/ Fax: 673-1546. V,M,DC,D,AE. I-410, Exit 7 at Marbach Rd. Bet Marbach Rd & US 90, W of frwy. Cable TV, laundry, pool, n/s rms. Free local calls. $32-38/S; $38-44/D; $6/ex prsn. Disc.

Motel 6/ 4621 E Rittiman Rd, San Antonio TX 78218. 210-653-8088/ Fax: 653-9690. DC,M,V,AE,D. I-35/I-410 at Rittiman Rd. Cable TV, pool, n/s rms, elevator. Free local calls. $30-34/S; $36-40/D; $6/ex prsn. Disc.

Motel 6/ 138 N WW White Rd, San Antonio TX 78219. 210-333-1850/ Fax: 333-1408. V,M,DC,D,AE. I-10, Exit 580 at WW White Rd. E of jct of I-10 & US 410. Cable TV, pool, laundry, n/s rms. Free local calls. $30-34/S; $36-40/D; $6/ex prsn. Disc.

Motel 6/ 9503 I-35 N, San Antonio TX 78233. 210-650-4419. Fax: 650-0118. V,M,AE,D,DC. I-35 at Exits 167/ 167B. Rstrnt, pool, n/s rms, laundry. Free local calls. $30-32/S; $36-38/D; $6/ex prsn. Disc.

Motel 6/ 16500 I-10 W, San Antonio TX 78257. 210-697-0731/ Fax: 697-0383. M,V,DC,D,AE. I-10 at Exits 555/ 556B. At Loop 1604. Cable TV, pool, n/s rms. Free local calls. $32-42/S; $38-48/D; $6/ex prsn. Disc.

Motel 6/ 9400 Wurzbach Rd, San Antonio TX 78240. 210-593-0013/ Fax: 593-0268. V,M,DC,D,AE. I-10 at Wurzbach Rd, SW of frwy. Nrby rstrnt, cable TV, pool, n/s rms. Free local calls. Premier Award. $36-42/S; $42-48/D; $6/ex prsn. Disc.

Quality Inn/ 10811 I-35 N, San Antonio TX 78233. 210-590-4646. M,V,D, AE,DC. I-35 to Weidner Rd, turn N to mtl. Nrby rstrnt/ lounge, pool, mtg rm, fax, b/f, whrlpool, cable TV, t pkng, n/s rms. Free cont brfst. No pets. AAA. $39-69/S or D; $6/ex prsn. 2/1-4/30: $46-119/S or D. 5/1-9/3: $46-99/S; $49-99/S. Discs.

Quality Inn/ 3817 N I-35, San Antonio TX 78219. 210-224-3030. V,M,AE,DC.

TEXAS

I-35 (Exit 161) near jct with I-410, 1/4 mi NE along frontage rd to mtl. Nrby rstrnt, pool, fax, b/f, whrlpool, cable TV, n/s rms. Free cont brfst. No pets. AAA. $40-90/S; $45-95/D; $5/ex prsn. 6/2-10/31: $45-95/S; $45-100/D. 11/1-12/31: $30-70/S; $35-75/D. Discs.

Rodeway Inn/ 1500 I-35 S, San Antonio TX 78204. 210-271-3334. M,V,D,AE,DC. I-35/I-10 (Exit 154B) at Laredo St. 1 mi S of dntn. Nrby rstrnt, pool, fax, b/f, cable TV, n/s rms. Free cont brfst, local calls, trans. $42-82/S; $48-88/D; $6/ex prsn. Discs.

Rodeway Inn/ 900 N Main Av, San Antonio TX 78212. 210-223-2951. M, V,D,AE,DC. I-35 at N Main St. Exit 157A or 157B. Rstrnt, pool, fax, b/f, cable TV, n/s rms, family rms. Free cont brfst. local calls, arpt trans. $42-82/S; $48-88/D; $6/ex prsn. Discs.

Rodeway Inn/ 19793 I-10 W, San Antonio TX 78257. 210-698-3991. M,V,D,AE,DC. I-10 at Camp Bullis. Rstrnt, pool, fax, b/f, cable TV, n/s rms. Free cont brfst. $42-82/S; $48-88/D; $6/ex prsn. Discs.

Scotsman Inn/ 211 N WW White, San Antonio TX 78219. 210-359-7268/ 800-677-7268. M,V,AE,DC,CB,D. I-10 & WW White. Cable TV, dd/tt phone, refrig, n/s rms, rstrnt, pool, laundry, t pkng, fax. Free local calls, coffee. $36/S; $41/D; $5/ex prsn. Discs.

Scotsman Inn/ 5710 Industry Park Dr, San Antonio TX 78218. 210-662-7400/ Reserv: 800-688-7268. M,V,AE,DC, CB,D. I-35 & Rittiman Rd. Nrby rstrnt, pool, dd/tt phone, n/s rms, refrig, laundry, cable TV, t/b pkng, elevator, fax. Free local calls, coffee. $30/S; $35-38/D; $2/ex prsn. Higher spec event rates. Discs.

Sleep Inn/ 8318 I-10 W, San Antonio TX 78230. 800-221-2222 — Opening soon. V,M,DC,AE. I-10, just NW of I-410. 6 mi S of arpt. Nrby rstrnt, pool, fax, b/f, cable TV, n/s rms. Free cont brfst. No pets. $49-69/S or D; $5/ex prsn. 5/1-1/1: $39-59/S or D. Discs.

Super 8 Motel I-35/ 11027 I-35 N, San Antonio TX 78233. 210-637-1033/ Fax: Ext 401. V,M,DC,AE,D. I-35 N (Exit 168) at Weidner Rd. B/f, n/s rms, pool, t/b/rv pkng, copier, cable TV, cot, crib. Free local calls. AAA. $35/S; $39/D; $4/ex prsn. 4/1-9/30: $47/S; $50/D; $5/ex prsn. Higher spec event rates.

Also see Universal City.

San Benito

Budget Host Motel/ 2055 W Hwy 77 Bsns, San Benito TX 78586. 210-399-6148. AE,M,V,D,DC,CB. Bsns 77 bet Harlingen & San Benito. Cable TV, dd phone, kitchens, pool, picnic area, sauna, whrlpool, laundry, arpt trans. AAA. Winter: $32-44/S; $32-44/D; $7/ex prsn. Summer: $29-42/S; $29-44/D. Disc: Senior.

San Marcos

Econo Lodge/ 811 S Guadalupe St, San Marcos TX 78666. 512-353-5300. V,M,AE. I-35 N (Exit 204A) at SR 123. Pool, fax, n/s rms, cable TV, eff. Free local calls, coffee, cont brfst. No pets. $35-60/S; $40-60/D; $5/ex prsn. 2/1-10/31: $35-70/S; $43-80/D. Discs.

Motel 6/ 1321 I-35 N, San Marcos TX 78666. 512-396-8705/ Fax: 396-7162. V,M,DC,D,AE. I-35, Exit 206/ Loop 82 to Aquarena Springs Dr. NW of frwy. Cable TV, laundry, pool, n/s rms, t pkng. Free local calls. $27-32/S; $33-38/D; $6/ex prsn. Disc.

Sequin

Econo Lodge/ 3013 N SR 123 Bypass, Sequin TX 78155. 210-372-3990. V, AE,M,DC. I-10 (Exit 610) to SR 123, N 1 blk. Adj rstrnt/ lounge, pool, fax, b/f, cable TV, t/rv pkng, n/s rms. Free local calls. No pets. $32-46/S; $40-50/D; $5/ex prsn. 3/1-4/30: $40-70/S; $46-80/D. 5/2-9/30: $46-70/S; $46-80/D. 10/1-10/31: $40-50/S; $46-60/D. Discs.

Shamrock

Econo Lodge/ 1006 E 12th St, Shamrock TX 79079. 806-256-2111. AE, M,DC,V. I-40: Ebnd, Exit 161, E 9 blks on Rte 66, past light; Wbnd, Exit 164, cross over to 66, go W 4 blks. Nrby rstrnt, pool, mtg rm, cable TV, t pkng. Free cont brfst. Hospitality Award. AAA. $31-41/S; $35-45/D; $4/ex prsn. 5/1-10/31: $35-45/S; $39-49/D. Discs.

TEXAS

Sherman
Super 8 Motel/ 111 Hwy 1417, Sherman TX 75090. 903-868-9325. V,M,DC,CB,AE,D. US 75 (Exit 56) at FM 1417. B/f, n/s rms, t/b/rv pkng, cot. Free local calls, crib. $32/S; $37-39/D; $4/ex prsn. Higher spec event rates. Discs.

South Padre Island
Motel 6/ 4013 Padre Blvd, S Padre Island TX 78597. 210-761-7911/ Fax: 761-6339. V,M,D,DC,AE. From US 77, E on US 100, 28 mi to the Island Causeway, N 3 1/2 mi on Padre Blvd. Cable TV, laundry, pool, n/s rms. Free local calls. $36/S or D. 2/1-5/22: $45/S or D. 5/25-9/6: $49/S or D. Disc.

Spring (Houston area)
Motel 6/ 19606 Cypresswood Ct, Spring TX 77388. 713-350-6400/ Fax: 353-6927. AE,M,V,DC,D. I-45 (Exit 68/69) at Holtzwarth, turn S to Cypresswood Dr, follow to Cypresswood Crt. Cable TV, laundry, pool, elevator, n/s rms. Free local calls. Premier Award. $34-36/S; $40-42/D; $6/ex prsn. Disc.

Sweetwater
Motel 6/ 510 NW Georgia, Sweetwater TX 79556. 915-235-4387/ Fax: 235-8725. V,M,DC,D,AE. I-20, Exit 244 at SR 70. N of frwy. Cable TV, laundry, pool, n/s rms, t pkng. Free local calls. $26-27/S; $30-32/D; $4-6/ex prsn. Disc.

Temple
Econo Lodge/ 1001 N General Bruce Dr, Temple TX 76504. 817-771-1688. V,AE,M,DC. I-35: Nbnd, Exit 301 (Adams Av); Sbnd, Exit 302 (Nugent Av). Nrby rstrnt, pool, fax, b/f, cable TV, laundry, n/s rms. Free cont brfst, local calls. $32-40/S; $38-50/D; $5/ex prsn. Discs.

HoJo Inn/ 1912 S 31st St, Temple TX 76504. 817-778-5521. AE,V,M,DC,CB,D. I-35 (Exit 299) to Hwy 3, W to 31st St, N to mtl. Pool, n/s rms, cable TV, fax, soft drinks, fax, kitchenette. Free cont brfst, local calls. $30-45/S; $35-50/D. Discs.

Motel 6/ 1100 N General Bruce Dr, Temple TX 76504. 817-778-0272/ 778-1839. V,M,DC,D,AE. I-35, Exit 302 at Nugent Av. W side of frwy. Cable TV, pool, n/s rms, t pkng. Free local calls. $26/S; $30-32/D; $4-6/ex prsn. Disc.

Super 8 Motel/ 5505 S General Bruce Dr, Temple TX 76502. 817-778-0962/ Fax: 778-1527. V,M,DC,AE,D. I-35, Exit 297. I-35 & Midway Dr. B/f, n/s rms, nrby rstrnt, pool, laundry, outlets, t/b/rv pkng, cont brfst, copier, cable TV, mtg rm. cot. Free local calls, crib. $40/S; $44-46/D; $4/ex prsn. Discs.

Terrell
Comfort Inn/ 1705 SR 34 S, Terrell TX 75160. 214-563-1511. V,M,DC,AE. I-20 to SR 34. On S side of I-20. Nrby rstrnt, pool, fax, whrlpool, cable TV, n/s rms. Free cont brfst. $40-45/S; $45-75/D; $5/ex prsn. 11/20-11/30: $46-60/S; $55-75/D. Discs.

Texarkana
Comfort Inn/ 5105 Stateline Av, Texarkana TX 75501. 903-792-6688. M,V,D,AE,DC. I-30 at US 59/ 71, Stateline Av. Nrby rstrnt, lounge, pool, fax, b/f, cable TV, t pkng, outlets, n/s rms. Free cont brfst. $40-46/S; $48-75/D; $6/ex prsn. Discs.

Econo Lodge/ 4505 N Stateline Av, Texarkana TX 75501. 903-793-5546. V,M,AE,DC. I-30 (Exit 223A) to Stateline Av, S 5 blks to mtl. Nrby rstrnt, fax, cable TV, t pkng, outlets. Free cont brfst. No pets. $34-37/S; $38-42/D; $5/ex prsn. Discs.

Motel 6/ 1924 Hampton Rd, Texarkana TX 75503. 903-793-1413/ Fax: 793-5831. V,M,DC,D,AE. I-30, Exit 222 & Summerhill Rd, turn N to Hampton. Cable TV, pool, n/s rms. Free local calls. $25/S; $31/D; $6/ex prsn. Disc.

Tyler
Econo Lodge/ 3209 W Gentry Pkwy, Tyler TX 75702. 903-593-0103. V, AE,M,DC. I-20 to US 69, N to mtl. Nrby rstrnt, pool, fax, cable TV, t pkng, laundry, VCR. AAA. $32-62/S; $36-62/D; $5/ex prsn. Discs.

Motel 6/ 3236 Brady Gentry Pkwy, Tyler TX 75702. 903-595-6691/ Fax: 595-5367. V,M,DC,D,AE. I-20 Ebnd, Exit 556/ Brady Gentry Pkwy (US 69) S 7 mi to htl. Wbnd, Exit 571A S to US 271, rt on Loop 323, lt on US 69 to mtl. Nrby rstrnt, cable TV, laundry, pool, n/s rms. Free local calls. $28-29/S; $32-33/D; $4/ex prsn. Disc.

Universal City (San Antonio area)
Comfort Inn/ 200 Palisades, Universal City TX 78148. 210-659-5851. V,M, AE,DC. I-35 to loop 1604 E to Palisades. Dntn. Nrby rstrnt, pool, mtg rm, fax, cable TV, t pkng, n/s rms, laundry. Free cont brfst. AAA. $39-89/S; $44-99/D; $5/ex prsn. 5/1-9/15: $39-124/S; $54-129/D. Discs.

Van Horn
Freeway Inn Motel/ 510 Van Horn Dr, Box 1059, Van Horn TX 79855. 915-283-2939. V,M. Jct I-10 & US 90, Exit 140A. Cable TV. No pets. AAA. $21/S; $25-29/D; $4/ex prsn. *Guaranteed rates.*

Comfort Inn/ 1601 W Broadway St, Box 669, Van Horn TX 79855. 915-283-2211. V,M,DC,AE. I-10 (Exit 138) to US 80 Bsns. 1/2 mi W of dntn. Nrby rstrnt, pool, fax, b/f, cable TV, t pkng, n/s rms. Free cont brfst. AAA. $38-48/S; $48-60/D; $4/ex prsn. 12/15-12/31: $48-60/S; $48-66/D. Discs.

Friendship Inn/ Box 821, Van Horn TX 79855. 915-283-2992. V,M,AE,DC. I-10 & US 80 W (Exit 138) at Golf Course Rd. Nrby rstrnt, pool, fax, cable TV, t pkng, b/f, n/s rms, tt/ dd phone, coffee. $38-50/S; $44-56/D; $4/ex prsn. Discs.

Howard Johnson Lodge/ 200 Golf Course Dr, Van Horn TX 79855. 915-283-2780/ Fax: 283-2804. M,V,D, AE, DC,CB. I-10 (Exit 138) & Golf Course Dr. Rstrnt/ lounge, pool, n/s rms, b/f, t pkng, cable TV, laundry, fax, arpt trans. Gold Medal Winner. $32-42/S; $37-47/D. Discs.

Super 8 Motel/ I-10 & Golf Course Rd, Van Horn TX 79855. 915-283-2282. AE,M,V,DC,D. I-10, Exit 138. B/f, n/s rms, outlets, t pkng, cont brfst, cable TV, cot, crib. Free local calls. $36-38/S; $39-42/D; $4/ex prsn. Discs.

Vernon
Econo Lodge/ 4100 SR 287 N W, Vernon TX 76384. 817-553-3384. V,M, D,AE. US 287, exit US 70 W toward Vernon. Rstrnt/ lounge, pool, fax, cable TV, t pkng, outlets, n/s rms. AAA. $32-36/S; $38-42/D; $5/ex prsn. 5/1-10/31: $38-44/S; $46-49/D. Discs.

Super 8 Motel/ 1829 Exp Hwy 287, Vernon TX 76384. 817-552-9321. V,M, DC,AE,D. Hwy 287 at Main St exit. B/f, n/s rms, outlets, t pkng, cont brfst, cable TV, cot, crib. Free local calls. $34/S; $36-38/D; $3/ex prsn. Higher spec event rates. Discs.

Western Motel/ 715 Wilbarger, Vernon TX 76384. 817-552-2531. V,M,AE,D, DC,CB. Hwy 287 to Laurie St, S 3 blks. Pool, cable TV, playgrnd, tt/dd phone, cot, crib, t pkng, conn rms. Free local calls, coffee. AAA/ Mobil. $24/S; $31/D; $2/ex prsn. Disc: Senior.

Victoria
Motel 6/ 3716 Houston Hwy, Victoria TX 77901. 512-573-1273/ Fax: 573-1831. V,M,DC,D,AE. US 59 on E end of town. From US 87/US 77 take US 59 N to mtl. Cable TV, pool, n/s rms. Free local calls. $27-28/S; $31-32/D; $4/ex prsn. Disc.

Waco
Econo Lodge/ 500 I-35, Waco TX 76704. 817-756-5371. M,V,D,AE,DC. I-35 S to Austin, exit 335 C, Lake Brazos Dr, past traffic light, under I-35 to mtl. Fax, cable TV, t pkng, n/s rms. $29-35/S; $33-40/D; $5/ex prsn. 5/15-9/30: $33-38/S; $35-42/D. Discs.

Motel 6/ 3120 Jack Kultgen Frwy, Waco TX 76706. 817-662-4622/ Fax: 662-6407. M,V,DC,D,AE. I-35 at Exits 331/ 333A, Valley Mills Rd. Cable TV, laundry, pool, n/s rms, t pkng. Free local calls. $28/S; $32/D; $4/ex prsn. Disc.

Also see Bellmead.

Waxahachie
Comfort Inn/ 200 I-35 E, Box 555, Waxahachie TX 75165. 214-937-4202. V,M,DC,AE. I-35 E at Bsns US 287. On frontage rd. Rstrnt, pool, mtg rm, fax, b/f, cable TV, n/s rms. Free cont brfst. AAA. $42-48/S; $44-50/D; $4/ex prsn. 2/1-4/30: $46-52/S; $48-54/D. 5/1-11/30: $44-50/S; $46-52/D. Discs.

Weatherford

Super 8 Motel/ 111 W I-20, Weatherford TX 76087. 817-594-8702/ Fax: 596-9766. V,M,DC,AE,D. I-20 (Exit 407) at jct with Hwys 171 & 51. N/s rms, pool, cont brfst, copier, laundry. $29/S; $32-37/D; $2/ex prsn. Discs.

Webster (Houston area)

Motel 6/ 1001 W NASA Rd 1, Webster TX 77598. 713-332-4581/ Fax: 332-0341. V,M,DC,D,AE. I-45, Exit 25, E on NASA Rd 1 to mtl. Nrby rstrnt, cable TV, pool, n/s rms, t pkng. Free local calls. Premier Award. $32-34/S; $36-38/D; $4/ex prsn. Disc.

Wichita Falls

Econo Lodge/ 1700 Fifth St, Wichita Falls TX 76301. 817-761-1889/ Fax: 761-1505. V,M,AE,D,DC,CB. On W Service Rd off I-44 & US 287 at 5th St. From S, exit at 8th St, go N to 5th & turn lt. Nrby rstrnt, pool, mtg rm, fax, b/f, cable TV, t pkng. Free cont brfst. No pets. $39-53/S; $43-53/D; $4/ex prsn. Discs.

Motel 6/ 1812 Maurine St, Wichita Falls TX 76304. 817-322-8817/ Fax: 322-5944. V,M,DC,D,AE. I-44/ US 287, Exit 2 at Maurine St. E side of frwy. Nrby rstrnt, cable TV, pool, n/s rms, t pkng. Free local calls. $30/S; $36/D; $6/ex prsn. Disc.

Ramada Limited/ 3209 US 287, Wichita Falls TX 75305. 800-2-RAMADA. V,M,AE,D,DC. US 287 at Mansor Dr, S. Pool, b/f, n/s rms, mtg rm. Free cont brfst, arpt trans. $39-45/S or D; $10/ex prsn. Discs.

Utah

Beaver

Quality Inn/ 1540 S SR 450 W, Box 1461, Beaver UT 84713. 801-438-5426. V,M,DC,AE. I-15 (Exit 109) at SR 160, W to mtl. Nrby rstrnt, indr pool, b/f, whrlpool, cable TV, t pkng, outlets, n/s rms. No pets. AAA. $38-54/S; $46-60/D; $6/ex prsn. Discs.

Bicknell

Aquarius Motel/ 240 W Main St, Bicknell UT 84715. 801-425-3835/ Fax: 425-3486/ 800-833-5379. V,M,AE,DC,D,CB. 8 mi W of jct SRs 12 & 24. N/s rms, cable TV, VCR/ movies, arpt trans, tt phone, fax, copier, laundry, refrig, cot, crib, outlets, t/b/rv pkng, b/f. Free local calls. AAA. $20-25/S; $32-36/D; $2-4/ex prsn. 4/1-10/31: $30-37/S; $39-43/D. *Guaranteed rates.*

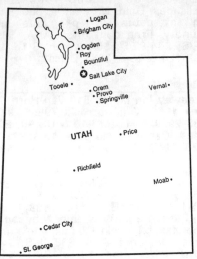

Bluff

Kokopelli Inn/ Box 27, Bluff UT 84512. 801-672-2322/ Fax: 672-2385/ 800-541-8854. V,M,AE,D. Center of Bluff on Hwy 191. Rstrnt, n/s rms, tt/dd phone, fax, copier, crib, t/b/rv pkng, picnic area. Free local calls, coffee. AAA. $36/S or D; $5/ex prsn. 3/15-4/30, 10/1-11/15: $40/S or D. 5/1-9/30: $48/S or D. Disc: Family.

Brigham City

Howard Johnson/ 1167 S Main, Brigham City UT 84302. 801-723-8511. V,M,AE,DC,D. I-15 & I-84 (Exit 364/ Brigham City) to Hwy 91, E 1.8 mi, rt at light. Rstrnt, n/s rms, b/f, indr pool, t pkng, whrlpool, fax. Free cont brfst. $40-48/S; $43-54/D; $4/ex prsn. Higher spec event rates. Discs.

Cedar City

Quality Inn/ 18 S Main St, Cedar City UT 84720. 801-586-2433. V,M,DC,AE. I-15 to 1st Cedar City exit, follow Main St to City Cntr. Nrby rstrnt, pool, fax, cable TV, t pkng, n/s rms. Free cont brfst, nwspr, local calls, arpt pick up. No pets. AAA. $37-60/S; $41-64/D; $4/ex prsn. 5/1-5/31, 9/6-10/31: $51-60/S; $55-64/D. 6/1-9/5: $62-70/S; $66-74/D. Discs.

Rodeway Inn/ 281 S Main St, Cedar City UT 84720. 801-586-9916. M,V, AE,DC. I-15 to 1st Cedar City exit. Rstrnt, pool, mtg rm, fax, sauna, whrlpool, cable TV, t pkng, n/s rms, game rm. AAA. $38-48/S; $40-48/D; $4/ex prsn. 5/1-6/15: $42-56/S or D. 6/16-9/3: $56-72/S; $58-74/D. Discs.

Super 8 Motel/ 145 N 1550 W, Cedar City UT 84720. 801-586-8880. V,M,D, DC,CB,AE. I-15, Exit 59. B/f, n/s rms, toast bar, t/b/rv pkng, elevator, cable TV, mtg rm. cot. Free local calls, crib. AAA. $40-44/S; $44-51/D. Higher spec event, wknd rates. Discs.

Clearfield

Super 8 Motel/ 572 N Main, Clearfield UT 84015. 801-825-8000. V,M,DC,CB, AE,D. I-15 (Exit 338) at 650 N. B/f, n/s rms, outlets, copier, cable TV, cot. Free local calls, crib. Pride Award. $36/S; $42-44/D; $4/ex prsn. Higher spec event rates. Discs.

Duchesne

Rio Damian Motel/ 23 W Main, Duchesne UT 84021. 801-738-2217. V, M,AE,DC. Downtown. Cable TV, nrby rstrnt. Free local calls. National 9. $38/S; $42-48/D. Summer: $42/S; $48-52/D. Family unit: $85.

Green River

Budget Host Book Cliff Lodge/ 395 E Main, Box 545, Green River UT 84525. 801-564-3406/ Fax: 564-8359. V,M,D, DC,CB,AE. I-70 to I-70 Bypass, 3 blks W of River. Cable TV, tt/dd phone, n/s rms, rstrnt, mtg rm, pool, arpt trans, t/b pkng, outlets, conn rms, cot, crib. Free local calls. AAA. $25-40/S; $30-65/D; $5/ex prsn. 5/1-9/30: $38-65/S; $45-85/D. Spec event, holiday, wknd rates: $45-70/S; $50-85/D. Disc: AARP, milt. *Guaranteed rates.*

Green River National 9 Inn/ 456 W Main St, Green River UT 84525. 801-564-8237. V,M,AE,DC. W Green River Exit, 1st mtl on lt. Adj rstrnt, t pkng, hot tub, cot, crib. AAA/ National 9. $30-40/S; $35-50/D.

Motel 6/ 946 E Main, Green River UT 84525. 801-564-3436/ Fax: 564-8272. M,V,DC,D,AE. I-70 at Bsns 70. N of I-70. Ebnd, Exit 158; Wbnd, Exit 162. Nrby rstrnt, cable TV, laundry, pool, n/s rms, t pkng. Free local calls. $27-35/S; $33-41/D; $6/ex prsn. 5/2-9/27: $32-35/S; $48-41/D. Disc.

Super 8 Motel/ 1200 E Main, Green River UT 84525. 801-564-8888. V,M, DC,AE,D. I-70 Bsns Loop. B/f, n/s rms, pool, outlets, t/b/rv pkng, copier, cable TV, mtg rm,cot. Free local calls, crib. $35-40/S; $40-45/D; $5/ex prsn. Higher spec event rates. Discs.

Hatch

Riverside Motel & Campground/ 594 US Hwy 89, Hatch UT 84735. 801-735-4223/ Fax: 735-4220/ 800-824-5651. V,M,D. On Hwy 89. Rstrnt, n/s rms, video games, playgrnd, fax, copier, laundry, refrig, microwave, cot, crib, outlets, t/b/rv pkng, river. Free coffee. AAA. $28/S; $30/D; $5/ex prsn. 5/1-10/31: $38/S; $42-45/D. Disc: Senior, family, l/s.

Heber City

High Country National 9 Inn/ 1000 S Main, Heber City UT 84032. 801-654-0201. V,M,AE,DC. S end of town. Rstrnt, pool, whrlpool, adj RV park, playgrnd, laundry, microwave, refrig, cable TV, cot, crib. AAA. $45/S; $45-55/D; $5/ex prsn. 4/22-11/20: $42/S; $44-46/D. Higher holiday/ spec event rates.

Hurricane

Park Villa Motel/ 650 W State St, Hurricane UT 84737. 801-635-4010/ Fax: 635-4025. V,M,AE,D. I-15, Exit Hwy 9, 9 mi. Pool, whrlpool, n/s rms, exerc equip, cable TV, arpt trans, tt/dd phone, fax, laundry, refrig, cot, crib, outlets, t/b/rv pkng, eff, b/f. Free local calls, coffee. AAA. $35-48/S or D; $4/ex prsn. 4/1-10/31: $45-48/S or D. Easter, Memorial Day, Labor Day wknds: $45-55/S; $48-55/D. Disc: Senior, bsns, TA, govt, family, milt. *Guaranteed rates.*

Rodeway Inn/ SR 9 & 2600 W, Hurricane UT 84737. 801-635-3500. M,V, D,AE,DC. I-15 (Exit 16) to SR 9, E 7 mi

UTAH

to mtl. Nrby rstrnt, indr pool, mtg rm, fax, b/f, cable TV, t pkng, n/s rms. Free cont brfst. $30-40/S; $35-45/D; $5/ex prsn. 2/1-4/30, 10/16-11/30: $35-50/S; $40-60/D. 5/1-10/15: $40-55/S; $50-70/D. Discs.

Kanab

Aiken's Lodge/ 79 W Center St, Kanab UT 84741. 801-644-2625/ 800-524-9999. V,M,AE,D,DC,CB. Cntr of town on Hwy 89. Nrby rstrnt, pool, n/s rms, cable TV, arpt trans, tt/dd phone, cot, crib, t/b/rv pkng, b/f. Free local calls, coffee. AAA/ National 9. $27/S; $29-36/D; $3/ex prsn. 5/1-10/30: $35/S; $37-47/D. *Guaranteed rates.*

Budget Host K Motel/ 330 S 100 E, Box 1301, Kanab UT 84741. 801-644-2611/ Fax: 644-2788. AE,M,V,DC,CB,D. S of Kanab, jct 89 & 89A. Cable TV, dd phone, kitchens, adj rstrnt, mtg rms, playgrnd, picnic area, laundry, cot, crib, babysitter, t pkng. $26-32/S; $32-44/D; $6/ex prsn. 3/1-11/30: $30-36/S; $36-48/D. Higher spec event/ holiday/ wknd rates.

Manti

Manti Country Village/ 145 N Main, Manti UT 84642. 801-835-9300/ Fax: 835-6286/ 800-452-0787. V,M,AE,D, DC. Rstrnt, whrlpool, n/s rms, cable TV, dd phone, fax, copier, cot, crib, b/f. Free local calls. AAA. $35/S; $38-41/D; $5/ex prsn. 7/9-7/20: $53/S; $53-63/D. Disc: Senior, bsns. *Guaranteed rates.*

Midvale (Salt Lake City area)

Motel 6/ 496 N Catalpa, Midvale UT 84047. 801-561-0058/ Fax: 561-5753. M,V,DC,D,AE. I-15 (Exit 301) to Midvale exit, turn E on 7200 S St, rt on Catalpa St. Nrby rstrnt, cable TV, laundry, pool, n/s rms, t pkng. Free local calls. $38-42/S; $42-48/D; $6/ex prsn. Higher spec event rates. Disc.

Moab

Red Rock Lodge Motel/ 51 N 100 W, Moab UT 84532. 801-259-5431. V,M, AE,D. 1 blk W of Hwy 191; from N, 1st stoplight; from S, 4th stoplight. Nrby rstrnt/ lounge, whrlpool, n/s rms, cable TV, tt/dd phone, refrig, cot. Free local calls, coffee. No pets. AAA. $45/S or D; $6/ex prsn. *Guaranteed rates.*

Monticello

Navajo Trails National 9 Inn/ 248 N Main St, Monticello UT 84535. 801-587-2251. V,M,AE,DC. Hwy 191. Cable TV, n/s rms, adj rstrnt, kitchenettes. No pets. AAA. $28/S; $32-39/D; $2/ex prsn. 5/1-10/31: $34/S; $39-52/D.

Nephi

Safari Motel/ 413 S Main St, Nephi UT 84648. 801-623-1071. V,M,AE. 3 mi NW of I-15, Exit 222. Nrby rstrnt, pool, cable TV, dd phone, cot, crib, t pkng. Free local calls. AAA. $30/S; $35/D; $3/ex prsn. *Guaranteed rates.*

Budget Host Roberta's Cove/ 2250 S Main, Box 268, Nephi UT 84648. 801-623-2629. M,V,AE,CB,DC,D I-15, Exit 222, S side of tn. Cable TV, dd phone, n/s rms, family rms, adj rstrnt, mtg rms, picnic area, laundry, cot, crib, t pkng, outlets. No pets. AAA/ Mobil. Winter: $29-34/S; $34-45/D; $5/ex prsn. Summer: $34-40/S; $40-50/D.

Super 8 Motel/ 1901 S Main, Nephi UT 84648. 801-623-0888/ Fax: 623-5025. V,AE,DC,CB,M,D I-15 (Exit 222) at Hwy 91. B/f, n/s rms, outlets, t pkng, satellite TV, cot. Free local calls. Pride Award. $36/S; $39-42/D; $3/ex prsn. Higher spec event rates. Discs.

Ogden

Motel 6/ 1500 W Riverdale Rd, Ogden UT 84405. 801-627-2880/ Fax: 392-1713. M,V,DC,D,AE. I-15: Nbnd (Exit 342) to Riverdale Rd, E 1 blk; Sbnd, exit on I-84 to 1st exit (Exit 81/ Riverdale), rt. Rstrnt, cable TV, laundry, pool, n/s rms, t pkng. Free local calls. Premier Award. $30-36/S; $36-42/D; $6/ex prsn. Disc.

Motel 6/ 1455 Washington Blvd, Ogden UT 84404. 801-627-4560/ Fax: 392-1878. M,V,DC,D,AE. I-15/84 (Exit 347) to 12th St, E 2 mi to Washington Blvd, turn rt 3 blks. Nrby rstrnt, cable TV, pool, laundry, n/s rms. Free local calls. $30-32/S; $36-38/D; $6/ex prsn. Disc.

Sleep Inn/ 1155 S 1700 W, Ogden UT 84404. 801-731-6500. V,M,AE,DC. I-15, Exit 347 to mtl. Nrby rstrnt, fax, b/f, whrlpool, cable TV, t pkng, n/s rms. Free cont brfst. AAA. $40-60/S; $45-60/D; $5/ex prsn. 6/15-9/15: $40-80/S;

$45-85/D. Discs.

Panguitch

Color Country Motel/ 526 N Main, Panguitch UT 84759. 801-676-2386/ Fax: 676-8484/ 800-225-6518. V,M, AE,D,DC. On Hwy 89, N end of town. Nrby rstrnt, pool, n/s rms, cable TV, dd phone, fax, copier, cot, crib, b pkng. Free local calls, coffee. AAA. $28/S; $32-35/D; $5/ex prsn. 5/1-10/31: $38/S; $48-52/D.

Panguitch Inn/ 699 N Main St, Panguitch UT 84759. 801-676-8871. V,M,AE,DC. On Utah Hwy 89 in Bsns district of Panguitch. Cable TV, in-rm coffee. No pets. National 9. $30-35/S; $35-45/D; $5/ex prsn.

Price

Budget Host Inn/ 145 N Carbonville Rd, Price UT 84501. 801-637-2424/ Fax: 637-4551. M,V,D,AE. Hwy 91, Exit 240 (Price), E 1/2 mi to Carbonville Rd, N 1/2 mi. Pool, n/s rms, cable TV, tt/dd phone, fax, copier, laundry, refrig, cot, crib, outlets, t/rv pkng. Free local calls, cont brfst, coffee. No pets. AAA. $29/S; $34/D; $5/ex prsn. 4/1-9/30: $34/S; $39/D. July 4, Labor Day wknds: $40/S; $45/D. Disc: Senior, bsns, govt, l/s, family, trkr, milt. *Guaranteed rates.*

Greenwell Inn & Restaurant/ 655 E Main St, Price UT 84501. 801-637-3520/ Fax: 637-4858/ 800-666-3520. V,M,AE,D,DC,CB. Hwy 6, Exit 243. Rstrnt/ lounge, n/s rms, cable TV, VCR/ movies, tt/dd phone, fax, copier, nwspr, laundry, refrig, cot, crib, t/b/rv pkng. Free cont brfst. AAA. $29-40/S; $31-49/D; $6/ex prsn. Disc: Senior, bsns, TA, govt, family, milt, AAA, AARP, l/s.

National 9 Inn/ 50 S 720 E, Box 4, Price UT 84501. 801-637-7980. V,M,AE,DC. 7 mi E on US 6. Cable TV, dd phone, pool, rstrnt, fax. AAA. $29/S; $35-40/D; $5/ex prsn. 4/15-10/15: $35/S; $40-45/D. Disc: AAA, AARP, comm.

National 9 Inn/ 641 W Price River Dr, Price UT 84501. 801-637-7000. V,M,AE. I-6, Exit 240. Cable TV, dd phone, nrby rstrnt, picnic area, fax. AAA. $29-34/S; $34-44/D; $5/ex prsn. Disc: Senior, AARP, AAA, TA.

Provo

Colony Inn Suites/ 1380 S University Av, Provo UT 84601. 801-374-6800. V, M,AE,DC. I-15, University Exit. Cable TV, pool, sauna, kitchenettes, adj rstrnt. AAA/ National 9. $24-36/S; $30-48/D; $5/ex prsn. 3/15-10/14: $28-46/S; $38-60/D. Disc: AARP, AAA, milt, comm, l/s.

Comfort Inn/ 1555 Canyon Rd, Provo UT 84604. 801-374-6020. M,V,D,AE, DC. I-15: N (Exit 264) to University Pkwy (Hwy 272), N to Canyon Rd; S (Exit 272) to University, S to Canyon Rd. Nrby rstrnt, indr pool, mtg rm, fax, b/f, cable TV, outlets, n/s rms. Free cont brfst, local calls, nwspr. AAA. $45-80/S; $48-85/D; $5/ex prsn. 6/1-8/31: $55-90/S; $60-95/D. Discs.

Howard Johnson Hotel/ 1292 S University Av, Provo UT 84601. 801-374-2500/ Fax: 373-1146. M,DC,D,V,AE, CB. I-15, Exit 266, N on University Av, 1/4 mi. Rstrnt, pool, exerc equip, cable TV, t pkng, whrlpool, game rm, trans, laundry, volleyball, picnic area. Free local calls. $35-55/S; $39-59/D.

Motel 6/ 1600 S University Dr, Provo UT 84601. 801-375-5064/ Fax: 374-0266. M,V,DC,D,AE. I-15 (Exit 266) to University Av, N to South St. Nrby rstrnt, cable TV, laundry, pool, n/s rms, t pkng. Free local calls. $30-33/S; $36-39/D; $6/ex prsn. Disc.

Uptown Motel/ 469 W Center St, Provo UT 84601. 801-373-8248. V,M,AE,D. E of I-15, Center St, Exit 268, straight 5 blks. Nrby rstrnt/ lounge, pool, satellite TV, playgrnd, tt/dd phone, cot, crib, outlets, t/b/rv pkng, conn rms. AAA. $26-36/S; $32-46/D; $4/ex prsn. 7/1-8/31: $32-42/S; $38-58/D. Disc: Senior, bsns, TA, l/s, trkr, milt. *Guaranteed rates.*

Richfield

New West Motel/ 447 S Main St, Richfield UT 84701. 801-896-4076/ Fax: 896-4520/ 800-278-4076. V,M,AE,D. On Bsns Loop; take either Richfield Exit & drive down Main St. Nrby rstrnt, n/s rms, cable TV, cot, rv pkng. Free local calls. AAA. $25/S; $30-35/D; $5/ex prsn. 4/1-10/31: $30/S; $35-40/D. Disc: Senior, family, govt, milt, AAA.

UTAH

Romanico Inn/ 1170 S Main, Richfield UT 84701. 801-896-8471/ 800-948-0001. V,M,AE,D,DC. I-70 S, Exit 37. Whrlpool, n/s rms, cable TV, dd phone, laundry, refrig, microwave, cot, crib, outlets, t pkng, conn rms. Free local calls, coffee. AAA. $40/S; $44/D; $4/ex prsn. 3/1-10/31: $50/D; $5/ex prsn. Disc: Senior, bsns, family, trkr. *Guaranteed rates.*

Budget Host Knights Inn/ 69 S Main St, Richfield UT 84701. 801-896-8228. AE,V,M,DC,CB,D. I-70, Exit 40 or 37, cntr of tn. Cable TV, dd phone, n/s rms, family rms, rstrnt, mtg rms, pool, arpt trans, cot, t pkng, outlets. AAA/ Mobil. $26-30/S; $32-38/D; $4/ex prsn. 5/1-10/31: $29-34/S; $37-46/D. Disc: Senior.

Quality Inn/ 540 S Main St, Richfield UT 84701. 801-896-5465. V,M,AE,DC. S end of Richfield. Rstrnt, pool, mtg rm, b/f, whrlpool, cable TV, t pkng, exerc equip, outlets, n/s rms, kitchenettes. Free full brfst. No pets. AAA. $40-98/S; $44-98/D; $6/ex prsn. Discs.

Super 8 Motel/ 1575 N Main St, Richfield UT 84701. 801-896-9204/ Fax: 896-9614. AE,M,V,DC,D. I-70 (Exit 40) to Main St. B/f, n/s rms, laundry, b/f pkng, satellite TV, cot. Free local calls. Pride Award. Quality Award. $38/S; $42-46/D; $4/ex prsn. Higher spec event rates. Discs.

Roosevelt

Frontier Motel/ 75 S 200 E, Roosevelt UT 84066. 801-722-2201/ 800-248-1014. V,M,AE,D,DC. Rstrnt, pool, sauna, n/s rms, cable TV, tt/dd phone, mtg rm, fax, cot, crib, outlets. Free local calls. AAA/ Mobil. $35/S; $39/D; $4/ex prsn. Disc: L/s.

Saint George

Comfort Inn/ 999 E Skyline Dr, St George UT 84770. 801-628-4271. M,V,D,AE,DC. I-15 (Exit 8) to St George Blvd, W to City Side, rt at Wendy's Restaurant. Nrby rstrnt, pool, fax, b/f, cable TV, t pkng, n/s rms. Free cont brfst. No pets. AAA. $42-48/S; $48-62/D; $6/ex prsn. Discs.

Econo Lodge/ 460 E St George Blvd, St George UT 84770. 801-673-4861. V,M,D,AE. I-15 S (Exit 8) to St George Blvd. Rstrnt, pool, mtg rm, fax, b/f, whrlpool, cable TV, t pkng, n/s rms. $34-54/S; $38-64/D; $5/ex prsn. 2/1-9/5: $36-58/S; $40-68/D. Discs.

Motel 6/ 205 N 1000 East St, St George UT 84770. 801-628-7979/ Fax: 674-9907. M,V,DC,D,AE. I-15 (Exit 8) at St George Blvd. W side of frwy. Nrby rstrnt, cable TV, laundry, pool, n/s rms. Free local calls. $30-32/S; $36-38/D; $6/ex prsn. Disc.

Sleep Inn/ 1481 S Sunland Dr, St George UT 84770. 801-673-7900. AE,M,V,DC. I-15 (Exit 6) E on Bluff St to Riverside Rd, Exit Sunland Dr N to mtl. Nrby rstrnt, pool, whrlpool, cable TV, t pkng, n/s rms. Free cont brfst. No pets. AAA. $30-45/S; $35-50/D; $5/ex prsn. Discs.

Salina

Budget Host Scenic Hills Motel/ 75 E 1500 S, Salina UT 84654. 801-529-7483/ Fax: 529-3616. M,V,AE,CB,DC,D. I-70, Exit 54. Cable TV, dd phone, kitchens, adj rstrnt, laundry, cot, crib, t pkng. AAA. $30-34/S; $34-42/D; $3-4/ex prsn. 5/15-10/15: $36-40/S; $40-50/D. Disc: Senior.

Salt Lake City

Motel 6/ 1990 W N Temple St, Salt Lake City UT 84116. 801-364-1053/ Fax: 596-9152. M,V,DC,D,AE. I-80 at N Temple/ Redwood exits. E side of frwy. Nrby rstrnt, cable TV, pool, laundry, n/s rms. Free local calls. $38-40/S; $42-46/D; $6/ex prsn. Higher spec event rates. Disc.

Motel 6/ 176 W Sixth S St, Salt Lake City UT 84101. 801-531-1252/ Fax: 359-2859. M,V,DC,D,AE. I-80/ I-15 (Exit 310) at 6th S St. E of frwy. Nrby rstrnt, cable TV, pool, n/s rms. Free local calls. $40-43/S; $46-49/D; $6/ex prsn. Higher spec event rates. Disc.

Also see Midvale, Tooele, Woods Cross.

Springdale

El Rio Lodge In Zion Canyon/ 995 Zion Pk Blvd, Springdale UT 84767. 801-772-3205. V,M,AE. Exit 16 off I-15 or SR 9 off Rte 89. Nrby rstrnt, cable TV, refrig, cot, crib, t/b/rv pkng, eff, conn rms. $35-40/S or D; $4/ex prsn. 3/7-10/31; Sun-Thur: $47-52/S or D. Wknds: $50-55/S or D. *Guaranteed rates.*

Tooele (Salt Lake City area)
Comfort Inn/ 491 S Main St, Tooele UT 84074. 801-882-6100. V,M,AE,DC. I-80 (Exit 99) to SR 36, S 12 mi to mtl. Nrby rstrnt, pool, fax, b/f, whrlpool, cable TV, t pkng, exerc equip, microwave, refrig, n/s rms. Free cont brfst, nwspr, coffee. No pets. AAA. $33-55/S; $35-57/D; $5/ex prsn. 11/16-2/29: $29-49/S; $32-54/D. Discs.

Tremonton
Sandman Motel/ 585 W Main, Tremonton UT 84337. 801-257-7149/ Fax: 257-3256. V,M,AE,D,DC,CB. From NW, I-84, Exit 40, lt 1 mi. From S I-84 & I-15, Exit 379 to 4-way stop, lt 1 mi. Nrby rstrnt, cable TV, tt/dd phone, nwspr, cot, crib, b/rv pkng. Free local calls. AAA. $34-36/S; $36-48/D; $5/ex prsn. Disc: Senior, bsns, TA, govt, milt, AARP, l/s. *Guaranteed rates.*

Western Inn/ 2301 W Main, Tremonton UT 84337. 801-257-3399/ Fax: 257-3256/ 800-528-7414. V,M,AE,D,DC,CB. I-84, Exit 40; I-15 Sbnd, Exit 382 loop to I-84 N, Exit 40. Nrby rstrnt, n/s rms, cable TV, tt/dd phone, fax, cot, crib, outlets, t/b/rv pkng, b/f. Free local calls. No pets. AAA. $42-45/S; $45-48/D; $3/ex prsn. Disc: Senior, trkr. *Guaranteed rates.*

Vernal
Econo Lodge/ 311 E Main St, Vernal UT 84078. 801-789-2000. V,AE,M,DC. US 40, 3 blks E of town cntr. Nrby rstrnt, fax, b/f, cable TV, t pkng, outlets, playgrnd, laundry, n/s rms. Free arpt trans, AM coffee. No pets. $37-47/S; $41-51/D; $4/ex prsn. 5/1-9/30: $39-49/S; $43-53/D. Discs.

Rodeway Inn/ 590 W Main St, Vernal UT 84078. 801-789-8172. V,M,D,AE. Hwy 40/ Main St. Rstrnt, mtg rm, cable TV, n/s rms. $36-65/S; $40-69/D; $4/ex prsn. Discs.

Wendover
Motel 6/ 561 Wendover Blvd, Box 190, Wendover UT 84083. 801-665-2267/ Fax: 665-2696. M,V,DC,D,AE. I-80: Ebnd (Exit 410) S to Wendover Blvd, E 1 mi; Wbnd (Exit 2) W on Wendover Blvd to mtl. Nrby rstrnt, cable TV, pool, laundry, n/s rms. Free local calls. Sun-Thurs: $28-30/S; $32-34/D; $4/ex prsn. Fri, Sat, Holiday, spec events: $37-40/S; $41-44/D. Higher spec event rates. Disc.

Woods Cross (Salt Lake City area)
Motel 6/ 2433 S 800 W, Woods Cross UT 84087. 801-298-0289/ Fax: 292-7423. V,M,DC,D,AE. I-15, Exit 318 turn W to 800 W, rt to mtl. Nrby rstrnt, cable TV, pool, n/s rms. Free local calls. $36-40/S; $42-46/D; $6/ex prsn. Higher spec event rates. Disc.

Vermont

Bennington
Harwood Hill Motel/ Historic Rte 7A, Bennington VT 05201. 802-442-6278. V,M,D,DC,CB. From center of Bennington, 3 mi N on Historic Rte 7A. Nrby rstrnt/ lounge, cable TV, cot, crib, t/b pkng, b/f. Free coffee. No pets. AAA/ Mobil. $40-58/S or D; $6/ex prsn. 2/1-4/30: $32-42/S or D. 9/27-10/23: $46-58/S or D.

Bennington Motor Inn/ 143 W Main St, Bennington VT 05201. 802-442-5479/ 800-359-9900. V,M,AE,D. VT 9, 3 blks W of US 7. Nrby rstrnt/ lounge, n/s rms,

VERMONT

cable TV, tt/dd phone, refrig, cot, crib, outlets. No pets. AAA/ Mobil. $46-48/S; $46-54/D; $5/ex prsn. 5/15-9/13: $54-56/S; $54-64/D. 9/14-10/31: $64-68/S; $68-76/D. Disc: Family.

Darling Kelly's Motel/ RR 1, Box 4400, Bennington VT 05201. 802-442-2322. V,M. On Rte 7, 1 mi S of Bennington. Lounge, pool, cable TV, tt/dd phone, cot, crib, conn rms. Free cont brfst. No pets. AAA. $38-42/S or D; $5/ex prsn.5/21-9/14, 10/25-10/31: $50-59/S or D. 9/15-10/24: $75-79/S or D; $8/ex prsn. Holidays: $67/S or D. Ski season wknds; Jan-Mar: $52/S or D. *Guaranteed rates.*

Knotty Pine Motel/ 130 Northside Dr, Bennington VT 05201. 802-442-5487/ Fax: 442-2231. V,M,AE,D,DC. Nrby rstrnt/ lounge, pool, cable TV, tt/dd phone, fax, copier, refrig, cot, crib, outlets, eff, conn rms. Free coffee. AAA/ Mobil. $38-44/S or D; $6/ex prsn. 5/17-9/12: $48-54/S or D. 9/13-10/26: $58-64/S or D. *Guaranteed rates.*

Brandon

Adams Motor Inn/ RR 1, Box 1142, Brandon VT 05733. 802-247-6644/ 800-759-6537. V,M. On US 7, 1 mi S of Brandon. Rstrnt/ lounge, pool, cable TV, playgrnd, mini-golf, cot, crib, outlets, t/b/rv pkng, conn rms. AAA/ Mobil. $45-60/S; $45-65/D; $5/ex prsn. 9/15-10/31: $50-65/S; $50-70/D. CLOSED 11/1-5/14. Disc: L/s. *Guaranteed rates.*

Brattleboro

Motel 6/ Putney Rd, Rte 5N, Brattleboro VT 05301. 802-254-6007/ Fax: 254-2508. V,M,AE,DC,D. I-91 (Exit 3/ Brattleboro-Keene, NH) to Hwy 9, E to Rte 5 (Putney Rd), N for 1/4 mi. Nrby rstrnt, cable TV, n/s rms, t pkng. Free local calls. Premier Award. Sun-Thurs: $36/S; $42/D; $6/ex prsn. Fri, Sat, Holiday, Spec Events: $40/S; $45/D. 5/23-12/20: $33-36/S; $39-42/D. Higher spec event rates. Disc.

Burlington

Friendship Inn/ 1860 Shelburne Rd, Burlington VT 05401. 802-862-0230. V,M,AE,DC. I-89 (Exit 13) to US 7, S 2 mi. Nrby rstrnt, pool, mtg rm, b/f, cable TV, t pkng, kitchen, n/s rms. Free cont brfst. $34-48/S; $39-48/D; $5-10/ex prsn. 5/1-6/22: $42-58/S; $48-58/D. 6/23-9/14: $48-80/S; $55-80/D. 9/15-10/21: $62-84/S; $68-98/D. Discs.

Also see Shelburne.

Ferrisburgh

Skyview Motel/ RR 1, Box 1370, Ferrisburgh VT 05456. 802-877-3410. V, M,AE,D. 22 mi S of I-89 on US Rte 7. Nrby rstrnt, n/s rms, cable TV, playgrnd, tt phone, refrig, cot, crib, outlets, t/b/rv pkng, eff, conn rms. Free coffee. AAA/ Mobil. $39/S; $44/D; $5/ex prsn. 6/1-10/31: $50/S; $55/D. *Guaranteed rates.*

Rutland

Econo Lodge Pico/ US 4, Box 7650, Rutland VT 05701. 802-773-6644/ Fax: 773-2193. AE,DC,M,V. On US 4, 5.5 mi E of US 7, 6 mi W of SR 100N. Nrby rstrnt, pool, mtg rm, fax, sauna, whrlpool, cable TV, n/s rms. Free cont brfst. AAA. $36-55/S; $43-75/D; $4-10/ex prsn. 9/15-12/22: $42-75/S; $45-100/D. 12/23-4/7: $45-110/S; $55-145/D. 4/8-4/30: $39-45/S; $43-65/D. Discs.

Howard Johnson/ S Main St, Rutland VT 05701. 802-775-4303/ Fax: 775-6840. M,V,D,AE,DC,CB. Hwy 4 or Hwy 103 to Hwy 7. Rstrnt/ lounge, mtg rm, cable TV, n/s rms, indr pool, sauna. Free cont brfst. $40-80/S; $48-88/D. Discs.

Tyrol Motor Inn/ Rte 4, Mendon, Rutland VT 05701. 802-773-7485/ 800-631-1019. V,M,AE,D. 5 mi from Killington access rd, 5 mi from Jct 7 & 4. Whrlpool, cable TV, tt phone, cot, crib, eff, conn rms. Free local calls, cont brfst. No pets. AAA/ Mobil. 4/1-9/14:$40/S; $48/D; $10/ex prsn. 9/15-10/15: $48-98/S or D. 10/16-3/31: wkdays: $48/S or D; wknds: $84/S or D. Holiday rates higher. Disc: Senior, bsns, l/s, family. *Guaranteed rates.*

Shaftsbury

Governor's Rock Motel/ RR 1, Box 282, Shaftsbury VT 05262. 802-442-4734. V,M. 7 mi N of Bennington on Historic Rte 7A; 3-1/4 mi from jct Scenic Rte 67. N/s rms, cable TV, refrig. Free cont brfst. No pets. AAA. $37-48/S; $48/D; $5/ex prsn. 9/1-11/1: $45-48/S; $48/D.

Disc: L/s. OPEN 5/1-11/1. *Guaranteed rates.*

Shelburne (Burlington area)

Econo Lodge/ 1961 Shelburne Rd, Shelburne VT 05482. 802-985-3377. M,V,D,AE,DC. I-89 (Exit 13) to I-189 S to US 7, turn S. 2 1/2 mi to mtl. Nrby rstrnt, pool, mtg rm, fax, b/f, cable TV, t pkng. Free cont brfst. $35-60/S; $40-60/D; $5/ex prsn. 5/1-5/31: $45-125/S; $50-125/D. 6/1-9/15: $50-95/S; $60-95/D. 9/16-10/17: $60-125/S; $75-125/D. Discs.

Springfield

Pa-Lo-Mar Motel/ 2 Linhale Dr, Springfield VT 05156. 802-885-4142. V,M,D. I-91, Exit 7, 6 mi W on Rte 11. Pool, n/s rms, cable TV, tt/dd phone, refrig, cot, crib, eff. Free local calls. AAA. $37/S; $45-48/D; $7/ex prsn. 2/15-2/28, 10/1-10/20, 12/21-1/2: $42/S; $56/D; $10/ex prsn.

Wilmington

Horizon Inn/ Box 817, Wilmington VT 05363. 802-464-2131/ Fax: 464-8302/ 800-336-5513. V,M,AE,D. I-91, Exit 2, Rte 9 W. Indr pool, sauna, whrlpool, n/s rms, exerc equip, cable TV, video games, tt/dd phone, mtg rm, fax, copier, cot, crib, b/rv pkng. Free coffee. No pets. AAA. $47-65/S or D. 1/2-3/31: $47-85/S or D; $10/ex prsn. 12/22-1/1, 1/12-1/14, 2/16-2/22: $95/S or D; $10/ex prsn.

Virginia

Abingdon

Super 8 Motel/ 298 Town Centre Dr, Abingdon VA 24210. 703-676-3329/ Fax: Ext 400. DC,CB,M,V,AE,D I-81 (Exit 17) NW toward Town Centre Mall. B/f, n/s rms, cont brfst, cable TV, mtg rm, cot. Free local calls, crib. No pets. AAA. $42/S; $47/D; $4/ex prsn. Higher spec event rates. Discs.

Alexandria (Washington DC area)

Comfort Inn/ 7212 Richmond Hwy, Alexandria VA 22306. 703-765-9000. V,M,D,AE,DC,CB. 2 1/2 mi S of Beltway on US 1. Nrby rstrnt, pool, mtg rm, fax, b/f, cable TV, t pkng, n/s rms. Free cont brfst. $45-70/S; $50-75/D; $7/ex prsn. 9/8-3/15: $40-55/S; $45-60/D. Discs.

Comfort Inn/ 6254 Duke St, Alexandria VA 22312. 703-642-3422. M,V,D,AE,DC. I-395 & SR 236 (Duke St W), 1st lt. Rstrnt/ lounge, pool, mtg rm, fax, b/f, cable TV, t pkng, n/s rms. Free cont brfst. No pets. $39-70/S; $39-76/D; $6/ex prsn. 3/15-9/10: $49-80/S; $49-86/D. Discs.

Arlington (Washington DC area)

Econo Lodge/ 6800 Lee Hwy, Arlington VA 22213. 703-538-5300. M,V,D,AE. I-66, Exit 69. I-495 N, E Exit 9B. I-495 S, E Exit 12A. Nrby rstrnt, fax, b/f, cable TV, eff, laundry, n/s rms, cont brfst. Free coffee. No pets. AAA. $40-60/S; $45-70/S; $5/ex prsn. 5/1-10/31: $50-70/S; $55-80/D. Discs.

Ashland (Richmond area)

Econo Lodge/ Box 308, Ashland VA 23005. 804-798-9221. V,AE,M,DC. I-95 (Exit 92) at SR 54, Ashland exit, turn rt at 1st light. Rstrnt, pool, fax, b/f, cable TV, n/s rms. Free cont brfst. No pets. AAA. $26-70/S; $30-70/D; $5/ex prsn. 5/1-6/8: $28-43/S; $32-50/D. 6/9-9/4: $39-70/S; $50-70/D. Discs.

HoJo Inn/ 101 S Carter Rd, Ashland VA 23005. 804-798-9291/ Fax: 798-1281. V,M,AE,DC,D. I-95 (Exit 92) to Rte 54. Rstrnt, n/s rms, b/f, pool, t/b pkng, cable TV. No pets. $29-45/S; $33-50/D. 5/1-9/30: $39-55/S; $45-59/D. Discs.

VIRGINIA

Baileys Crossroads (Washington DC area)

Econo Lodge/ 5666 Columbia Pike, Baileys Crossroads VA 22041. 703-820-5600. M,V,D,AE. I-395, exit Washington Blvd to Columbia Pike, W 2 mi. I-495, exit SR 7 E (Leesburg Pike) to Columbia Pike E to mtl. Rstrnt, pool, mtg rm, fax, cable TV, n/s rms. $39-59/S; $45-65/D; $6/ex prsn. 5/1-7/31: $59-79/S; $65-85/D. 8/1-10/31: $49-69/S; $55-75/D. Discs.

Big Stone Gap

Country Inn Motel/ Box 142, Big Stone Gap VA 24219. 540-523-0374/ Fax: 523-5043. V,M,AE,D,CB,DC. On US 23 Bsns. Cable TV, fax, tt phone, copier, cot, crib, t/b/rv pkng, b/f. AAA/ Mobil. $30/S; $32-35/D; $4/ex prsn. *Guaranteed rates.*

Blacksburg

Budget Host Inn/ 3333 S Main St, Blacksburg VA 24060. 703-951-4242/ Fax: 951-4189. M,V,D,AE,DC,CB. I-81 (Exit 118) 460 Bsns W, 7 1/2 mi. Cable TV, VCR/ movies, dd phone, n/s rms, copier, fax, laundry, t pkng, cot. AAA/ Mobil. $32-42/S; $38-48/D; $5/ex prsn. Spec event: $50-80. Discs.

Bristol

Budget Host Inn/ 1209 W State St, Bristol VA 24201. 540-669-5187/ Fax: 466-5848. M,V,AE,D,ER. Dntn on TN/VA state line. Cable TV, dd phone, n/s rms, nrby rstrnt, laundry, cot. No pets. AAA. Winter: $28-58/S; $32-60/D; $4/ex prsn. Summer: $29-58/S; $34-68/D. Higher spec event rates. Discs.

Econo Lodge/ 912 Commonwealth Av, Bristol VA 24201. 703-466-2112. V, AE,M,DC. I-81 to I-381 (Commonwealth), S 1 1/2 mi. Nrby rstrnt, fax, cable TV, n/s rms. Free AM coffee. No pets. $32-42/S; $36-46/D; $5/ex prsn. 5/1-10/31: $35-45/S; $40-50/D. Spec events: $65-75/S or D. Discs.

Buchanan

Wattstull Inn/ Rte 1, Box 21, Buchanan VA 24066. 540-254-1551. V,M. I-81, Exit 168. Rstrnt, pool, n/s rms, tt phone, cot, crib, conn rms. AAA/ Mobil. $38-45/S; $3/ex prsn. *Guaranteed rates.*

Charlottesville

Budget Inn/ 140 Emmet St, Charlottesville VA 22903. 804-293-5141/ Fax: 293-5143. V,M,D,AE. I-64 (Exit 118B) to 29 N Bsns, follow to mtl. Nrby rstrnt, n/s rms, cable TV, tt/dd phone, fax, copier, crib, conn rms. Free coffee. No pets. AAA. $32-36/S; $34-42/D; $5/ex prsn. 4/1-9/30: $34-38/S; $36-44/D. 10/1-10/31 & Spec events: $40-42/S; $42-48/D. *Guaranteed rates.*

Econo Lodge/ 400 Emmet St, Charlottesville VA 22903. 804-296-2104. V,AE,M,DC. I-64 (Exit 118B) to US 29, N to Bsns US 29. Rstrnt, pool, fax, cable TV, n/s rms. Free AM coffee. No pets. $37-47/S; $41-51/D; $5/ex prsn. 5/1-10/31: $40-53/S; $45-58/D. Spec events: $60-75/S or D. Discs.

Econo Lodge/ 2014 Holiday Dr, Charlottesville VA 22901. 804-295-3185. V,AE,M,DC. US 250 to 29, N to Holiday Dr, rt to mtl. Nrby rstrnt, fax, cable TV, n/s rms. Free cont brfst. $39-49/S; $43-53/D; $5/ex prsn. 5/1-10/31: $42-52/S; $46-56/D. Spec events: $50-70/S; $55-75/D. Discs.

Chesapeake (Norfolk area)

Comfort Inn/ 4433 S Military Hwy, Chesapeake VA 23321. 804-488-7900. V,M,AE,DC. I-264, I-64, I-664 to Bowers Hill exit, E to Military Hwy. Nrby rstrnt, pool, whrlpool, cable TV, t pkng, n/s rms. Free cont brfst. No pets. $46-65/S; $46-70/D; $5/ex prsn. Discs.

Days Inn Chesapeake/ 1439 N George Washington Hwy, Chesapeake VA 23323. 804-487-8861/ Fax: 485-1549. V,M,AE,D,DC,CB. I-64: (E, Exit 296A; W, Exit 296) to US 17N 2 1/2 mi on rt. N/s rms, cable TV, TDD, tt phone, fax, copier, refrig, microwave, cot, crib, outlets, t/rv pkng, b/f. Free local calls, cont brfst, coffee. No pets. AAA. $42-50/S; $46-56/D; $5/ex prsn. Discs. *Guaranteed rates.*

Econo Lodge/ 4725 W Military Hwy, Chesapeake VA 23321. 804-488-4963. V,AE,M,DC. I-64 at Bowers Hill/ Suffolk exit (299B), at light turn rt. Adj rstrnt, fax, cable TV, t pkng, n/s rms. $31-43/S; $34-46/D; $5/ex prsn. Discs.

VIRGINIA

Econo Lodge/ 3244 Western Branch Blvd, Chesapeake VA 23321. 804-484-6143. V,AE,M,DC. US 17 at Churchland. Nrby rstrnt, fax, cable TV, n/s rms. Free cot. $37-40/S; $42-45/D; $5/ex prsn. Discs.

Econo Lodge/ 2222 S Military Hwy, Chesapeake VA 23320. 804-543-2200. M,V,D,AE,DC. I-64 (Exit 291A) to I-464, N to 1st exit US 13, N 1/2 mi. From dntn Norfolk take I-464 S to US 13, N 1/2 mi. Nrby rstrnt, mtg rm, fax, b/f, cable TV, n/s rms, eff, VCR. Free coffee. $35-40/S or D; $5/ex prsn. 3/1-4/30: $40-45/S or D. 5/1-10/31: $50-65/S or D. Spec events: $56-70/S or D. Discs.

Motel 6/ 701 Woodlake Dr, Chesapeake VA 23320. 804-420-2976/ Fax: 366-9915. V,M,DC,AE,D. I-64 (Exit 289A) at Greenbrier Pkwy. Nrby rstrnt, cable TV, n/s rms. Free local calls. Premier Award. Sun-Thurs: $32/S; $38/D; $6/ex prsn. Fri, Sat, Holiday, Spec Events: $36/S; $42/D. 5/23-12/20: $30/S; $36/D. Higher spec event rates. Disc.

Super 8 Motel/ 3216 Churchland Blvd, Chesapeake VA 23321. 804-686-8888/ Fax: Ext 403. AE,M,V,DC,D,CB. I-664 to US 17, E 1 mi. B/f, n/s rms, toast bar, elevator, mtg rm, micro-refrig, cot. Free crib. Pride Award. $41/S; $47/D; $6/ex prsn. Higher spec event, wknd rates. Discs.

Christiansburg

Econo Lodge/ 2430 Roanoke St, Christiansburg VA 24073. 703-382-6161. V,AE,M,DC. I-81 (Exit 118) to Christiansburg/ Blacksburg exit, to US 460 & US 11. Rstrnt, pool, b/f, cable TV, t pkng, n/s rms. $35-45/S; $41-52/D; $4/ex prsn. 3/1-11/30: $37-47/S; $43-58/D. Discs.

HoJo Inn/ 100 Bristol Dr, Christiansburg VA 24073. 540-381-0150/ Fax: 381-0943. V,M,AE,DC,D. I-81 (Exit 118) at Hwy 400, W. Adj rstrnt, fax, n/s rms, b/f. Free coffee, local calls. $33-50/S; $33-60/D. Higher spec event rates. Discs.

Super 8 Motel/ 55 Laurel St, Christiansburg VA 24073. 540-382-5813/ Fax: Ext 400. M,V,AE,DC,CB,D. I-81 (Exit 118) to Hwy 460, W 5 mi to Hwy 114. B/f, n/s rms, outlets, b/rv pkng, cable TV, mtg rm, micro-refrig, TDD, cot. Free local calls, crib. Pride Award. $38-42/S; $44-48/D; $6/ex prsn. 4/1-9/30: $43/S; $49/D. Higher spec event rates. Discs.

Collinsville (Martinsville area)

Econo Lodge/ 800 S VA Av, Collinsville VA 24078. 703-647-3941. V,AE,M,DC. US 220 Bsns at Collinsville, 2 mi S of bypass. Do not take Bypass. Nrby rstrnt, fax, cable TV, t pkng, n/s rms, coffee. Free cont brfst, local calls. AAA. $31-41/S; $39-61/D; $5-10/ex prsn. Higher spec event rates. Discs.

Doswell

Econo Lodge/ Box 2001, Doswell, VA 23047. 804-876-3712. V,M,AE. I-95 (Exit 98) to US 30 E. Rstrnt, pool, mtg rm, fax, b/f, t pkng, outlets. No pets. $30/S or D; $5/ex prsn. 3/1-4/30: $30-75/S or D. 5/1-10/29: $30-95/S or D. Discs.

Dumfries

Econo Lodge/ 17005 Dumfries Rd, Dumfries VA 22026. 703-221-4176. V,AE,M,DC. I-95 (Exit 152) to SR 234, W 1/2 mi to mtl. Nrby rstrnt, mtg rm, fax, b/f, cable TV, t pkng, eff, n/s rms. Free coffee. No pets. $40-46/S; $42-52/D; $5/ex prsn. Discs.

Emporia

Comfort Inn/ 1411 Skippers Rd, Emporia VA 23847. 804-348-3282. V,M,AE,DC. I-95, Exit 8. Rstrnt/ lounge, pool, mtg rm, fax, b/f, cable TV, n/s rms, t pkng. Free cont brfst. AAA. $41-43/S; $43-49/D; $4/ex prsn. Discs.

Econo Lodge/ 3173 Sunset Dr, Emporia VA 23847. 804-535-8535. V,M,AE. I-95 (Exit 17) at US 301, turn lt to mtl. Nrby rstrnt, pool, b/f, cable TV, t pkng, n/s rms. AAA. $26-34/S; $30-42/D; $4/ex prsn. Discs.

Fairfax (Washington DC area)

Econo Lodge/ 9700 Lee Hwy, Fairfax VA 22031. 703-273-1160. V,M,AE. US 50, 3 mi W of Capital Beltway. Nrby rstrnt, fax, cable TV, n/s rms. Free in-rm coffee. No pets. $40-46/S; $40-52/D; $4/ex prsn. 3/16-10/31:

VIRGINIA

$40-53/S; $40-56/D. Discs.

Franklin

Comfort Inn/ 1620 Armory Dr, Franklin VA 23851. 804-569-0018. M,V,D,AE, DC. US 58 & SR 671. Nrby rstrnt, pool, mtg rm, fax, b/f, cable TV, t pkng, exerc equip, eff, microwave, refrig, n/s rms. Free cont brfst. $44-52/S; $46-56/D; $4/ex prsn. 5/1-10/31: $48-60/S; $50-62/D. Discs.

Super 8 Motel/ 1599 Armory Dr, Franklin VA 23851. 804-562-2888/ Fax: Ext 100. DC,CB,M,V,AE,D US 58, Franklin Bypass & Hwy 671. B/f, n/s rms, laundry, b/t pkng, suites, mtg rm, micro-refrig, cot. Free crib. $39/S; $45/D; $5/ex prsn. Higher spec event rates. Discs.

Fredericksburg

Comfort Inn/ 557 Warrenton Rd, Fredericksburg VA 22406. 703-371-8900/ 800-482-4888. V,M,AE,DC. I-95 (Exit 133) at US 17, N 1/4 mi to mtl. Nrby rstrnt, indr pool, sauna, whrlpool, cable TV, t pkng, exerc equip, n/s rms. Free cont brfst. No pets. $37-60/S; $40-70/D; $5/ex prsn. Discs.

Econo Lodge/ 5321 Jefferson Davis Hwy, Fredericksburg VA 22408. 703-898-5440/ Fax: 898-6172. V,AE,M,DC. I-95: (Sbnd, Exit 126; Nbnd, Exit 126A) take Massaponax exit, turn lt on US 1. Nrby rstrnt, pool, fax, b/f, n/s rms, cable TV, t pkng. Free full brfst. $31-43/S; $34-47/D; $5/ex prsn. 5/1-9/30: $33-47/S; $37-50/D. Discs.

Econo Lodge/ Box 36, Fredericksburg VA 22404. 703-786-8374. V,AE,M,DC. I-95 (Exit 130B) & SR 3 W, lt at 1st light, lt along service rd. Adj rstrnt, fax, b/f, n/s rms. Free cont brfst, local calls. AAA. $28-36/S; $33-40/D; $5/ex prsn. 6/16-9/3: $33-39/S; $38-44/D. Discs.

Howard Johnson Lodge/ 386 Warrenton Rd, Fredericksburg VA 22405. 540-371-6000/ Fax: 899-2740. M,DC, D,V,AE,CB. I-95 N or S, Exit 133 (Falmouth) to Rte 17, E. Rstrnt, pool, n/s rms, mtg rm, t pkng, cable TV. Free cont brfst. $30-60/S; $33-60/D. Discs.

Motel 6/ 401 Warrenton Rd, Fredericksburg VA 22405. 703-371-5443/ Fax: 371-7569. M,V,DC,D,AE. I-95 to US 17, E to mtl. Nrby rstrnt, cable TV, pool, n/s rms, t pkng. Free local calls. $26-28/S; $32-34/D; $6/ex prsn. Disc.

Front Royal

Budget Inn/ 1122 N Royal Av, Front Royal VA 22630. 540-635-2196/ Fax: 635-6986/ 800-766-6748. V,M,AE,D, DC,CB. I-66, Exit 6, 3 mi on Hwy 522/340 S. I-66, Exit 13, Hwy 522 N 2 mi. Nrby rstrnt/ lounge, n/s rms, cable TV, tt/dd phone, fax, laundry, refrig, cot, crib. Free local calls. No alcohol. AAA/ Mobil. $20-32/S; $24-36/D; $4/ex prsn. 5/1-10/31 Sun - Thurs: $26-40/S; $30-44/D; Fri, Sat: $29-44/S; $32-48/D. Discs. *Guaranteed rates.*

Hampton

Comfort Inn/ 1916 Coliseum Dr, Hampton VA 23666. 804-827-5052. M, V,D,AE,DC. I-64 (Exit 263B) to Mercury Blvd, Hampton Coliseum, turn E on Mercury, then rt on Coliseum. Nrby rstrnt, pool, fax, b/f, cable TV, t pkng, n/s rms. Free cont brfst. No pets. AAA. $40-70/S; $45-75/D; $5/ex prsn. 3/8-4/30: $45-70/S; $50-75/D. 5/1-6/15: $50-80/S; $55-85/D. 6/16-9/3: $60-105/S; $65-115/D. Discs.

Days Inn Hampton/ 1918 Coliseum Dr, Hampton VA 23666. 804-826-4810/ Fax: 827-6503. AE,M,V,DC,D. I-64 (Exit 263B) to Mercury Blvd, NE to Coliseum Dr SE. Rstrnt/ lounge, pool, mtg rm, t pkng, refrig, room safe, laundry, fax, n/s rms. $33-53/S; $38-58/D; $5/ex prsn. Discs.

Econo Lodge/ 2708 W Mercury Blvd, Hampton VA 23666. 804-826-8970. V, AE,M,DC. I-64 (Exit 263A) to W Mercury Blvd. Take Service Rd 1 mi W to mtl. Nrby rstrnt, fax, cable TV, t pkng, n/s rms. Free AM coffee. $30-43/S; $34-47/D; $5/ex prsn. 5/1-9/30: $34-46/S; $39-50/D. Spec events: $40-65/S; $50-70/D. Discs.

Econo Lodge/ 1781 N King St, Hampton VA 23669. 804-723-0741. V, AE,M,DC. I-64 (Exit 263B) at Coliseum, US 258 N to N King, turn lt. Nrby rstrnt, fax, cable TV, laundry, n/s rms. Free coffee. No pets. No pets. $30-37/S; $35-46/D; $5/ex prsn. 5/1-9/30: $35-40/S; $43-50/D. Discs.

Quality Inn/ 1809 W Mercury Blvd, Hampton VA 23666. 804-838-5011. M,V,D,AE,DC. I-64 (Exit 263B) at Mercury Blvd. Rstrnt/ lounge, indr pool, mtg rm, fax, b/f, cable TV, exerc equip, n/s rms. $39-89/S or D; $10/ex prsn. Spec events: $79-119/S or D. Discs.

Harrisonburg

Days Inn/ 1131 Forest Hill Rd, Harrisonburg VA 22801. 540-433-9353/ Fax: 433-5809. V,M,AE,D,DC. I-81, Exit 245 at Port Republic Rd. Fax, n/s rms, nrby rstrnt/ lounge, indr pool, whrlpool, mtg rm, b/f, exerc equip, t pkng, cable TV, laundry. Free cont brfst. $42-85/S; $48-85/D; $5/ex prsn. Discs.

Econo Lodge/ Box 1311, Harrisonburg VA 22801. 703-433-2576. V,AE,M,DC. I-81 (Exit 247A) to US 33, E for 1/10 mi. Adj rstrnt, pool, fax, b/f, cable TV, t pkng, exerc equip, cot, n/s rms. Free cont brfst. $36-66/S; $42-66/D; $5/ex prsn. Discs.

HoJo Inn/ 605 Port Republic Rd, Box 68, Harrisonburg VA 22801. 540-434-6771/ Fax: 434-0153. V,M,AE,DC,D. I-81 (Exit 245) at Port Republic Rd, turn rt. Across from James Madison Univ. Rstrnt, pool, trans. Free cont brfst. $40-50/S; $45-60/D. Discs.

Motel 6/ 10 Linda Lane, Harrisonburg VA 22801. 703-433-6939/ Fax: 564-0289. M,V,DC,D,AE. I-81 to US 33, E to Linda Av, lt to mtl. Nrby rstrnt, cable TV, pool, n/s rms. Free local calls. $30-32/S; $36-38/D; $6/ex prsn. Disc.

Super 8 Motel/ 3330 S Main, Harrisonburg VA 22801. 703-433-8888/ Fax: Ext 400. V,AE,DC,CB,M,D I-81, Exit 243. On W side of frwy. B/f, n/s rms, toast bar, mtg rm, micro-refrig, TDD, outlets, t/b/rv pkng, cot. Free local calls, crib. AAA. $40-42/S; $46-48/D; $6. ex prsn. 7/1-8/31 wknds: $46/S; $52/D. Discs.

Village Inn/ Rte 1, Box 76, Harrisonburg VA 22801. 540-434-7355/ 800-736-7355. V,M,AE,D,DC,CB. On Rte 11, 1-1/2 mi W of I-81, Exit 240. Pool, whrlpool, n/s rms, satellite TV, tt/dd phone, mtg rm, fax, copier, laundry, refrig, cot, crib, outlets, b/rv pkng, eff, b/f. Free local calls. AAA/ Mobil. $37/S; $43-53/D; $5/ex prsn. Spec events: $57/S; $57-72/D. *Guaranteed rates.*

Hillsville

Comfort Inn/ Rt 1, Box 350, Hillsville VA 24343. 703-728-4125. M,V,D,AE,DC. I-77 (Exit 14) to US 58 W. Nrby rstrnt, fax, cable TV, exerc equip, outlets, n/s rms. Free cont brfst. AAA. $47-79/S; $47-89/D; $6/ex prsn. 5/1-10/31: $47-85/S; $47-95/D. Discs.

Econo Lodge/ Box 1148, Hillsville VA 24343. 703-728-9118. V,AE,M,DC. I-77 (Exit 3) & US 58. Nrby rstrnt, cable TV, n/s rms, suites. $36-66/S; $43-87/D; $5/ex prsn. Discs.

Hot Springs

Roseloe Motel/ Rte 2, Box 590, Hot Springs VA 24445. 540-839-5373. V,M,AE,D,DC. On US 220, 3 mi N of Hot Springs. 25 mi N of I-64, Covington Exit, 55 mi W of I-81, Exit 225 Staunton. Cable TV, tt phone, refrig, microwave, crib, b pkng, eff, conn rms. Free local calls, coffee. AAA/ Mobil. $34/S; $44/D; $4/ex prsn.

Lexington

Econo Lodge/ RR 7, Box 81, Lexington VA 24450. 703-463-7371. M,V,D,AE,DC. Jct of I-64 (Exit 55) & US 11. I-81 (Exit 191) to I-64, NW to US 11. Entrance on US 11 Frontage Rd. Nrby rstrnt, cable TV, t pkng, n/s rms. Free cont brfst. $35-65/S; $45-70/D; $5/ex prsn. Higher spec event rates. Discs.

Howard Johnson Hotel/ US 11, Box 381 A, Lexington VA 24450. 540-463-9181/ Fax: 464-3448. V,M,AE,DC,D. I-81 at Exit 195; or from I-64, Exit 55, 3.5 mi N on US 11. Rstrnt, mtg rm, n/s rms, pool, t pkng, laundry, cable TV. $39-53/S; $45-60/D. 5/1-10/31: $39-58/S; $45-65/D. Higher spec event rates. Discs.

Lynchburg

Econo Lodge/ 2400 Stadium Rd, Lynchburg VA 24501. 804-847-1045. AE,M,V,DC. US 29 to Stadium Rd, turn W. Nrby rstrnt, n/s rms, cots. Free cont brfst. No pets. $35-81/S; $40-81/D; $5/ex prsn. Discs.

Ramada Limited/ 1500 Main St, Lynchburg VA 24504. 804-845-5975/ Fax: 845-8617. V,M,AE,D,DC. Hwy 29 Bypass at Main St Exit. Pool, b/f, n/s rms, cable TV, micro-fridge, mtg rm. $38-40/S; $45-48/D. Discs.

Manassas

Home Style Inn/ 9913 Cockrell Rd, Manassas VA 22110. 703-369-1603/ Fax: 369-6912/ 800-336-8312. V,M, AE,D,DC,CB. I-66 to 234 S, rt on Godwin Dr, lt on Ashton Av. Mtl on end. Nrby rstrnt, n/s rms, cable TV, tt/dd phone, fax, nwspr, laundry, refrig, microwave, t/b/rv pkng, eff, conn rms, b/f. No pets. $33/S; $36/D; $3/ex prsn. *Guaranteed rates.*

Marion

VA House Inn/ 1419 N Main St, Marion VA 24354. 540-783-5112/ Fax: 783-1007/ 800-505-5151. V,M,AE, D,DC. I-81, Exit 47, 1/4 mi on rt. Pool, kiddie pool, n/s rms, cable TV, tt/dd phone, fax, copier, cot, crib, t/b/rv pkng. Free local calls, cont brfst, coffee, tea. AAA. $37/S; $41/D; $5/ex prsn. 6/1-9/8: $37/S; $43/D. Race wknds Apr & Aug: $65/S or D. $70/5 prsns. Disc: Senior, AAA, l/s.

Budget Host Marion Motel/ 435 S Main St, Marion VA 24354. 703-783-8511/ Fax: 782-9656. V,M,AE. I-81 (Exit 44) to US 11. Cable TV, dd phone, kitchens, nrby rstrnt, cot, crib, t pkng. $24-36/S; $28-45/D; $5/ex prsn. 6/1-8/31: $25-39/S; $28-50/D. Spec events: $70. Disc: Senior.

Max Meadows (Wytheville area)

Comfort Inn/ SR 2, Box 426-B, Max Meadows VA 24360. 703-637-4141. V,M,AE,DC. I-77 or I-81, Exit 80. Nrby rstrnt, indr pool, fax, cable TV, t pkng, n/s rms. Free cont brfst. No pets. AAA. $38-43/S; $44-48/D; $5/ex prsn. 6/2-11/1: $40-61/S; $52-76/D. Discs.

New Market

Blue Ridge Motor Lodge/ 2251 Old Valley Pike, New Market VA 22844. 540-740-4136/ 800-545-8776. V,M,D. I-81, Exit 264 (New Market), 1 mi N on US 11. N/s rms, cable TV, playgrnd, tt/dd phone, refrig, bar-b-q, conn rms. Free local calls, coffee. No pets. AAA. $34/S; $38-44/D; $3/ex prsn. 5/1-10/31: $36/S; $44-50/D. Holidays & month of Oct: $40/D; $48-60/D. Disc: Senior, family, l/s.

Budget Inn/ 2192 Old Valley Pike, New Market VA 22844. 540-740-3105/ Fax: 740-3108/ 800-296-6835. V,M,AE,D, DC,CB. I-81, Exit 264, 1 mi N on US 11. N/s rms, cable TV, tt/dd phone, fax, copier, refrig, cot, crib, t/rv pkng, conn rms. Free local calls, coffee. No alcohol. AAA/ Mobil. $20-32/S; $24-36/D; $4/ex prsn. 5/1-10/31; Sun thru Thurs: $26-40/S; $30-44/D; Fri, Sat: $29-44/S; $32-48/D. Discs. *Guaranteed rates.*

Newport News

Days Inn/ 14747 Warwick Blvd, Newport News VA 23602. 804-874-0201. V,M,AE,D,DC,CB. Hwy 105 at Hwy 60 E. Rstrnt, pool, t pkng, arpt trans, picnic area, in-rm coffee, satellite TV, cot. $38-48/S; $42-54/D; $5/ex prsn. Discs.

Econo Lodge/ 15237 Warwick Blvd, Newport News VA 23602. 804-874-9244. V,AE,M,DC. US 60 E at Warwick Blvd. Nrby rstrnt, fax, b/f, cable TV, laundry, refrig, microwave, n/s rms. No pets. $33-61/S; $37-66/D; $5/ex prsn. 5/1-9/30: $41-61/S; $45-66/D. Discs. No pets.

Econo Lodge/ 11845 Jefferson Av, Newport News VA 23606. 804-599-3237. V,M,AE. I-64 (Exit 61A) at SR 143, S 2 mi. Nrby rstrnt, mtg rm, fax, b/f, cable TV, t pkng, microwave, refrig, laundry, n/s rms. Free coffee. No pets. $36-70/S or D; $4/ex prsn. Discs.

Howard Johnson Lodge/ 6069 Jefferson Av, Newport News VA 23605. 804-247-5330/ Fax: 245-3729. M,DC,D,V, AE,CB. I-64 E, exit J R Bridge-Mercury Blvd to Rte 258 S, 3 mi on lt at jct of 17, 258 & Rte 3. Rstrnt/ lounge, cable TV, t pkng, elevator, n/s rms. Free cont brfst. No pets. $40-45/S or D. Discs.

Motel 6/ 797 J Clyde-Morris Blvd, Newport News VA 23601. 804-595-6336/ Fax: 595-8124. AE,DC,D,M,V. I-64 (Exit 258A) to US 17 turn S to mtl. Nrby rstrnt, cable TV, pool, n/s rms, t pkng. Free local calls. $26-30/S; $32-36/D; $6/ex prsn. Higher spec event rates. Disc.

Norfolk

Comfort Inn/ 6360 Newtown Rd, Norfolk VA 23502. 804-461-1081. M,V,D, AE,DC. I-64 (Exit 284B) to Newtown

Rd S. Nrby rstrnt, pool, mtg rm, fax, cable TV, t pkng, exerc equip, n/s rms. Free cont brfst. No pets. $35-65/S; $40-75/D; $7/ex prsn. 3/1-4/30, 9/16-11/30: $40-75/S; $45-85/D. 5/1-9/15: $50-85/S; $55-95/D. Discs.

Econo Lodge/ 9601 4th View St, Norfolk VA 23503. 804-480-9611. AE,M,DC,V. I-64, Exit 273. 200 yds N of exit on US 60. Nrby rstrnt, mtg rm, fax, b/f, sauna, whrlpool, cable TV, t pkng, microwave, refrig, n/s rms. Free cont brfst. AAA. $35-44/S; $39-52/D; $4/ex prsn. 5/26-9/4: $46-56/S; $50-60/D. Discs.

Econo Lodge/ 3343 N Military Hwy, Norfolk VA 23518. 804-855-3116. M,V,D,AE,DC. I-64 (Exit 279) to arpt, 2nd lt, turn rt on Military Hwy, 1/4 mi. Nrby rstrnt, fax, cable TV, arpt trans, laundry, eff, n/s rms. $30-40/S; $33-49/D; $5/ex prsn. 3/1-4/30, 9/7-10/31: $33-49/S; $36-59/D. 5/1-9/6: $44-59/S; $49-89/D. Discs.

Econo Lodge/ 865 N Military Hwy, Norfolk VA 23502. 804-461-4865. AE,M,DC,V. On US 13 (Military Hwy) at Poplar Hall Dr. Nrby rstrnt, fax, b/f, cable TV, laundry, n/s rms. Free AM coffee. $31-40/S; $34-45/D; $5/ex prsn. 5/1-9/15: $32-46/S; $35-49/D. Spec events: $40-55/S; $50-65/D. Discs.

Econo Lodge/ 1850 E Little Creek Rd, Norfolk VA 23518. 804-588-8888. V,AE,M,DC. I-64, Exit 276C, (from E lt at 2nd light, from W rt) on E Little Creek Rd. Nrby rstrnt, pool, mtg rm, fax, cable TV, laundry, eff, refrig, microwave, n/s rms. Free cont brfst. $30-41/S; $33-46/D; $5/ex prsn. 6/1-9/16: $34-45/S; $40-50/D. Discs.

Econo Lodge/ 1111 E Ocean View Av, Norfolk VA 23503. 804-480-1111. V,AE,M,DC. On US 60, about 8 mi W of jct with US 13. Across from beach. Nrby rstrnt, fax, cable TV, t pkng, eff, microwave, n/s rms. Free cont brfst. No pets. $30-45/S; $35-50/D; $5/ex prsn. 3/1-4/30: $35-45/S; $40-50/D. 5/1-5/25: $35-80/S; $40-85/D. 6/16-9/3: $40-85/S; $45-90/D. Discs.

Motel 6/ 853 N Military Hwy, Norfolk VA 23502. 804-461-2380/ Fax: 461-5639. M,V,DC,D,AE. I-64 Ebnd, Exit 281/ Rte 13 S 1 1/2 mi; I-264, take Rte 13 N to mtl. Nrby rstrnt, cable TV, pool, laundry, n/s rms, t pkng. Free local calls. $28-30/S; $34-36/D; $6/ex prsn. Higher spec event rates. Disc.

Ramada Limited/ 515 N Military Hwy, Norfolk VA 23502. 804-461-1880/ Fax: Ext 286. V,M,AE,D,DC. I-264 to US 13 (Military Hwy),N to mtl. Pool, n/s rms. Free full brfst. $35-45/S or D; $10/ex prsn.

Rodeway Inn/ 7969 Shore Dr, Norfolk VA 23518. 804-588-3600. V,M,AE. I-64 (Ebnd, Exit 273; Wbnd, Exit 278) to US 60, E 5 mi to mtl. Nrby rstrnt, fax, b/f, cable TV, t pkng, microwave, n/s rms. Free cont brfst. No pets. $30-45/S; $35-50/D; $5/ex prsn. 3/1-4/30: $35-45/S; $40-50/D. 5/1-6/15: $35-80/S; $40-85/D. 6/16-9/3: $40-85/S; $45-90/D. Discs.

Also see Chesapeake, Portsmouth, Suffolk.

Petersburg

Comfort Inn/ 11974 S Crater Rd, Petersburg VA 23805. 804-732-2900. M,V,D,AE,DC. I-95 (Exit 45) to US 301. Rstrnt, pool, b/f, cable TV, t pkng, laundry, n/s rms. Free cont brfst. AAA. $37-60/S; $46-66/D; $5/ex prsn. Discs.

Econo Lodge/ 12002 S Crater Rd, Petersburg VA 23805. 804-732-2000. M,V,D,AE,DC. I-95 (Exit 45) at jct I-295, 6 mi S of Petersburg. Adj rstrnt, pool, fax, b/f, cable TV, t pkng, game rm, adj tennis, laundry, family rms. Free coffee, PM popcorn. AAA. $33-50/S or D; $5/ex prsn. 6/23-8/26: $35-60/S or D. Discs.

Econo Lodge/ 25 S Crater Rd, Petersburg VA 23803. 804-861-4680. M,V,D,AE,DC. I-95 Sbnd (Exit 52), lt on Whythe St, lt on Crater Rd. I-95/I-85 Nbnd (Exit 50) to SR 301, rt on Whythe St, lt on Crater Rd. Nrby rstrnt, fax, cable TV, AM coffee, refrig, laundry. $31-41/S; $33-43/D; $5/ex prsn. 5/1-10/31: $33-43/S; $37-49/D. Discs.

Econo Lodge/ 16905 Parkdale Rd, Petersburg VA 23805. 804-862-2717. V,AE,M,DC. I-95 (Exit 41) at SR 35. Rstrnt, pool, mtg rm, fax, b/f, cable TV, t pkng, playgrnd, n/s rms. Free local

VIRGINIA 282

calls, cont brfst. $29-66/S; $37-66/D; $5/ex prsn. Discs.

Howard Johnson Hotel/ 530 E Washington St, Petersburg VA 23803. 804-732-5950/ Fax: 862-9292. V,M, AE,DC,D. I-95 N to Exit 50D(Wythe St); I-95 S to Exit 52; I-85 N to Exit 69. Rstrnt, n/s rms, pool, t pkng, refrig, mtg rm, laundry, mtg rm, Ft Lee trans. $38-53/S; $41-56/D. Discs.

Quality Inn/ 12205 S Crater Rd, Box 1536, Petersburg VA 23805. 804-733-0600. V,M,AE,DC. I-95 (Exit 45) at I-295. 6 mi S of Petersburg. 9 mi from Ft Lee. Rstrnt/ lounge, pool, mtg rm, fax, b/f, cable TV, t pkng, n/s rms, tennis, basketball shuffleboard. $38-53/S or D; $5/ex prsn. 3/15-6/22: $38-60/S or D. 6/23-8/27: $38-70/S or D. Discs.

Portsmouth (Norfolk area)

Econo Lodge/ 1031 London Blvd, Portsmouth VA 23704. 804-399-4414. V,AE,M,DC. I-64, take I-264 (Norfolk/Portsmouth Exit), after dntn tunnel, Exit 7 on Effingham St, take lt on London Blvd, 2 blks to mtl. Nrby rstrnt, mtg rm, fax, b/f, cable TV, t pkng, exerc equip, microwave, refrig, VCR, n/s rms. Free cont brfst, Naval Base trans. No pets. AAA. $33-80/S; $35-90/D; $5/ex prsn. Discs.

Radford

Super 8 Motel/ 1600 Tyler Av, Radford VA 24141. 703-731-9355/ Fax: Ext 400. DC,CB,M,V,AE,D I-81 (Exit 109) to Hwy 177, N 2 mi. B/f, n/s rms, outlets, b/rv pkng, cable TV, mtg rm, micro-refrig, TDD, cot. Free local calls, crib. Pride Award. $38/S; $44/D; $6/ex prsn. 4/1-10/31: $42/S; $48-50/D. Higher spec event rates. Discs.

Richmond

Econo Lodge/ 2125 Willis Rd, Richmond VA 23237. 804-271-6031. V,AE,M,DC. I-95 (Exit 64) & Willis Rd. Nrby rstrnt, fax, cable TV, n/s rms. Free AM coffee. $31-41/S; $36-46/D; $5/ex prsn. 5/1-10/31: $34-46/S; $38-50/D. Spec events: $40-55/S; $45-60/D. Discs.

Econo Lodge/ 6523 Midlothian Trnpk, Richmond VA 23225. 804-276-8241. V,AE,M,DC. US 60 (Midlothian Trnpk), just E of SR 150. Adj rstrnt, fax, b/f, cable TV, t pkng, laundry, n/s rms. Free AM coffee. $31-43/S; $34-46/D; $5/ex prsn. Spec events: $35-50/S; $40-55/D. Discs.

HoJo Inn/ 801 E Parham Rd, Richmond VA 23227. 804-266-8753/ Fax: 261-1096. V,M,AE,DC,D. I-95 (Exit 83B) to Parham Rd W. Rstrnt, n/s rms, b/f, pool, t pkng, mtg rm. $40-45/S; $46-51/D. 5/1-9/11: $45-59/S; $60-69/D. Higher spec event rates. Discs.

Super 8 Motel/ 8260 Midlothian Trnpk, Richmond VA 23235. 804-320-2823. DC,CB,M,V,AE,D I-95N (Exit 67) Chippenham Pkwy to 60W; S Powhite Pkwy to US 60E. Elevator, t pkng, cable TV, mt rm, micro-refrig, TDD, cot, b/f, n/s rms. $38-40/S; $44-46/D; $6/ex prsn. Higher spec event, wknd rates. Discs.

Super 8 Motel/ 5110 Williamsburg Rd, Richmond VA 23231. 804-222-8008/ Fax: Ext 400. DC,CB,M,V,AE,D I-64 (Exit 195) to Williamsburg Rd, lt. Cable TV, microwave, refrig, TDD, cot, b/f, n/s rms. Pride Award. $40-42/S; $46-48/D; $5/ex prsn. Higher spec event rates. Discs.

Howard Johnson Lodge/ 1501 Robin Hood Rd, Richmond, VA 23220. 804-353-0116. AE,V,M,DC,CB,D. I-95 S/ I-64 E, Exit 78, rt onto Blvd, lt at 1st light to Robin Hood Rd; I-95 N/I-64 W, Exit 78, lt onto Hermitage then lt at light to R Hood Rd. Rstrnt/ lounge, n/s rms, pool, mtg rm, cable TV, t pkng, b/f. $30-39/S; $34-49/D. Discs.

Also see Ashland, Sandston.

Roanoke

Econo Lodge/ 308 Orange Av, Roanoke VA 24016. 703-343-2413. V,AE,M,DC. I-581 & US 460 (Orange Av) at Williamson Rd. Nrby rstrnt, fax, cable TV, t pkng, n/s rms. Free coffee, local calls. No pets. AAA. $35-37/S; $37-40/D; $5/ex prsn. 4/1-4/30: $43-47/S; $49-53/D. 5/1-10/31: $39-45/S; $47-50/D. Discs.

Friendship Inn/ 526 Orange Av NE, Roanoke VA 24016. 703-981-9341. AE,V,M,DC. US 460 & US 11. I-81 (Exit 143) to I-581, SE to (Exit 4) Orange Av, E 1 blk. Rstrnt, mtg rm, fax, cable TV, t pkng, n/s rms. $31-41/S; $35-45/D; $5/ex prsn. 5/1-10/31: $33-43/S; $37-51/D. Spec events: $40-60/S or D. Discs.

Also see Troutville.

Rocky Mount
Budget Host Inn/ Hwy 220 N, Rocky Mt VA 24151. 540-483-9757/ Fax: 337-0821. AE,D,M,V. 2 mi N on Hwy 220. Cable TV, dd phone, b/f, adj rstrnt, playgrnd, picnic area, cot, crib. $29/S; $32-95/D; $5/ex prsn. Special events: $20 higher. Discs.

Ruther Glen (Carmel Church area)
Comfort Inn/ Box 105 Ruther Glen VA 22546. 804-448-2828. M,V,D,AE,DC. I-95 (Exit 104) to SR 207, W to mtl. Rstrnt, pool, mtg rm, fax, b/f, cable TV, t pkng, n/s rms. AAA. $42-90/S; $47-90/D; $6/ex prsn. 5/1-5/25, 9/6-10/27: $46-90/S; $51-95/D. 5/26-9/5: $49-120/S; $54-125/D. Disc.

Howard Johnson/ 23786 Rogers Clark Blvd, Ruther Glen VA 22546. 804-448-2499/ Fax: 448-1052. M,DC,D,V,AE, CB. I-95, Exit 104 toward Bowling Green, Rte 207 E. Cable TV, whrlpool, t pkng, b/f, n/s rms. $38-48/S or D. Discs.

Salem
Budget Host Blue Jay Motel/ 5399 W Main St, Salem VA 24153. 540-380-2080. M,V,AE,D. I-81 (Exit 132) at US 11 & 460. Cable TV, dd phone, kitchens, n/s rms, rstrnt, pool, picnic area, arpt trans, cot, crib, t pkng. AAA. $25-34/S; $35-40/D; $5/ex prsn. 5/1-10/31: 34-42/S; $38-45/D. Spec events: $45-65. Discs.

Sandston (Richmond area)
Econo Lodge/ 5408 Williamsburg Rd, Sandston VA 23150. 804-222-1020. V, AE,M,DC. 1 mi off I-64 (Sandston/ Arpt Exit) on US 60, W of Sandston. Adj rstrnt, fax, cable TV, t pkng, laundry, n/s rms, refrig. Free AM coffee. $31-43/S; $35-47/D; $5/ex prsn. 5/1-10/31: $33-43/S; $37-47/D. Spec events: $40-55/S; $45-60/D. Discs.

Motel 6/ 5704 US 60, Sandston VA 23150. 804-222-7600/ Fax: 222-4153. M,V,DC,D,AE. 6 mi E of I-95 on I-64, Exit 197A, S 1 blk, rt on US 60, 1/2 blk. Nrby rstrnt, cable TV, pool, n/s rms, t pkng. Free local calls. $28-30/S; $34-36/D; $6/ex prsn. Disc.

Skippers
Econo Lodge/ Box 7, Skippers VA 23879. 804-634-6124. M,V,D,AE,DC. I-95 (Exit 4) at SR 629, 2 mi N of NC border. Rstrnt, pool, b/f, cable TV, t pkng, n/s rms. Free cont brfst, local calls. AAA. $29-56/S; $44-66/D; $5/ex prsn. Discs.

South Hill
Comfort Inn/ 918 E Atlantic St, S Hill VA 23970. 804-447-2600. V,M,AE,DC. I-85 (Exit 12/ old Exit 2) to SR 58 W. Nrby rstrnt, fax, b/f, cable TV, t pkng, exerc equip, outlets, n/s rms. Free cont brfst. No pets. $40-63/S or D; $6/ex prsn. Discs.

Econo Lodge/ 623 E Atlantic St, Box 550, S Hill VA 23970. 804-447-7116. V,AE,M,DC. Jct of I-85 (Exit 12) and US 58, E of tn. Rstrnt/ lounge, fax, cable TV, t pkng, outlets, n/s rms, TDD. Free local calls. AAA. $36-46/S; $43-53/D; $5/ex prsn. 2/1-4/30, 9/7-10/31: $37-47/S; $44-54/D. 5/1-9/6: $38-48/S; $46-66/D. Discs.

Staunton (Greenville area)
Econo Lodge/ 1031 Richmond Rd, Staunton VA 24401. 703-885-5158. V,AE,M,DC. I-81 (Exit 222) to US 250, W 1 mi to mtl. Rstrnt, fax, b/f, cable TV, n/s rms. Free full brfst. AAA. $34-46/S; $44-56/D; $5/ex prsn. Discs.

Econo Lodge/ Rte 2, Box 364, Staunton VA 24401. 703-337-1231. V,AE, M,DC. I-81/64 (Exit 213) to US 11/340 in Greenville, turn S to mtl. Nrby rstrnt, pool, fax, cable TV, wading pool, playgrnd, n/s rms. Free cont brfst. AAA. $30-34/S; $34/D; $5/ex prsn. 5/1-11/15: $30-35/S; $40-55/D. Discs.

Super 8 Motel/ 1015 Richmond Rd, Staunton VA 24401. 703-886-2888/ Fax: 886-7432. V,M,DC,CB,AE,D. I-81 (Exit 222) to US 250 (Richmond Rd), W .7 mi. B/f, n/s rms, brfst bar, cable TV, copier, mtg rm, t/b/rv pkng. Free nwspr, local calls, cot, crib. Pride Award. AAA. $41-44/S; $44-49/D; $5/ex prsn. Discs.

VIRGINIA

Suffolk (Norfolk area)

Comfort Inn/ 1503 Holland Rd, Suffolk VA 23434. 804-539-3600. M,V,D,AE, DC. On US 58 W. Nrby rstrnt, pool, fax, b/f, cable TV, t pkng, n/s rms. Free cont brfst. No pets. $35-45/S; $40-50/D; $5/ex prsn. 5/1-5/20: $40-50/S; $45-55/D. 5/21-9/10: $45-55/S; $50-60/D. Discs.

Econo Lodge/ 1017 N Main St, Suffolk VA 23434. 804-539-3451. AE,M,DC,V. US 58 to US 460, S on 460. Nrby rstrnt, fax, b/f, cable TV, microwave, refrig, laundry, n/s rms. No pets. $31-70/S; $35-70/D; $4/ex prsn. Discs.

Super 8 Motel/ 633 N Main, Suffolk VA 23434. 804-925-0992/ Fax: Ext 300. DC,CB,M,V,AE,D Jct US 460 & I-64 Bsns Rte 58. B/f, n/s rms, toast bar, elevator, suites, mtg rm, micro-refrig, cot. Free crib. Pride Award. $38/S; $44/D; $6/ex prsn. Higher spec event, wknd rates. Discs.

Troutville (Roanoke area)

Comfort Inn/ 2654 Lee Hwy S, Troutville VA 24175. 703-992-5600. M,V,D,AE,DC. I-81 (Exit 150A) at US 220. On E side of frwy. 6 mi N of Roanoke. Nrby rstrnt, pool, fax, b/f, cable TV, t pkng, in-rm coffee, n/s rms. Free cont brfst. AAA. $40-55/S; $45-60/D; $5/ex prsn. 5/1-10/31: $40-65/S; $45-70/D. Discs.

Howard Johnson Lodge/ Box 100, Troutville VA 24175. 703-992-3000. V,M,AE,DC,D. I-81 (Exit 150B) to US 220, N 1/4 mi. Rstrnt, n/s rms, b/f, pool, t pkng, cable TV, laundry, playgrnd, mtg rm. Free coffee. $38-64/S; $44-64/D. Discs.

Travelodge/ 2444 Lee Hwy S, Troutville VA 24175. 703-992-6700/ Fax: 992-3991. V,M,AE,D,DC. I-81, Exit 150A, rt at traffic signal, behind McDonalds. Nrby rstrnt, pool, n/s rms, satellite TV, playgrnd, TDD, mtg rm, fax, copier, nwspr, cot, crib, t/b pkng, eff. Free local calls, cont brfst. AAA. $40/S; $45/D; $6/ex prsn. Discs. *Guaranteed rates.*

Virgina Beach

Alamar Resort Motel/ 311 16th St, Virginia Beach VA 23451. 804-428-7582/ 800-346-5681. V,M. Rte 44, Exit Artic Av, rt 5 blks, lt on 16th. Pool, n/s rms, cable TV, video games, tt/dd phone, laundry, refrig, cot, crib, outlets, t/b/rv pkng, eff, b/f. Free coffee. No pets. AAA. $30/S or D; $8/ex prsn. 3/1-11/30: $30-48/S or D. *Guaranteed rates.*

Clarion Resort/ 501 Atlantic Av, Virginia Beach VA 23451. 804-422-3186. M, V,D,AE,DC. I-64 E, exit SR 44 E, exit Atlantic Av S to mtl. Rstrnt/ lounge, pool, mtg rm, sauna, whrlpool, exerc equip, n/s rms. No pets. Hospitality Award. $45-200/S or D; $10/ex prsn.

Comfort Inn/ 5189 Shore Dr, Virginia Beach VA 23455. 804-460-5566. M, V,D,AE,DC. US 13 toward jct with US 60, take 1st exit after tunnel, US 60 W 1 mi to mtl. Across from Little Creek Amphibious Base Gate 5. Nrby rstrnt, pool, fax, cable TV, eff, refrig, microwave, n/s rms. Free cont brfst. No pets. $40-55/S; $42-60/D; $6/ex prsn. 5/1-6/15: $45-80/S; $50-85/D. 6/16-9/4: $60-85/S; $70-85/D. 9/5-10/31: $42-55/S; $48-55/D. Discs.

Comfort Inn/ 2800 Pacific Av, Virginia Beach VA 23451. 804-428-2203. M, V,D,AE,DC. I-64 to SR 44, E to Pacific Av, N 7 blks to mtl. Nrby rstrnt, pool, indr pool, mtg rm, fax, b/f, whrlpool, cable TV, exerc equip, laundry, game rm, n/s rms. Free cont brfst, bicycles. No pets. Hospitality Award. AAA. $39-69/S or D; $8/ex prsn. 5/1-6/15: $47-99/S or D. 6/16-9/4: $81-144/S or D. 9/5-10/8: $45-94/S or D. Discs.

Comfort Inn/ 804 Lynnhaven Pkwy, Virginia Beach VA 23452. 804-427-5500/ Fax: 427-9230. V,M,AE,DC. SR 44 (Exit 5A) to Lynnhaven Pkwy, S 1 1/2 mi to mtl. Nrby rstrnt, mtg rm, fax, b/f, cable TV, t pkng, exerc equip, laundry, n/s rms. Free cont brfst. No pets. AAA. $40-70/S or D; $5/ex prsn. 6/16-9/23: $55-95/S or D. Discs.

Econo Lodge/ 3637 Bonney Rd, Virginia Beach VA 23452. 804-486-5711. V,AE,M,DC. SR 44 & Rosemont Rd (Exit 4), lt on Rosemont, lt on Bonney. Nrby rstrnt, fax, b/f, cable TV, laundry, n/s rms. Free AM coffee. $27-40/S; $35-50/D; $5/ex prsn. 5/1-10/31: $46-70/S; $56-80/D. Discs.

Econo Lodge/ 5819 Northampton Blvd,

Virginia Beach VA 23455. 804-460-1000. V,M,AE. I-64, Exit 282, N to mtl. Nrby rstrnt, mtg rm, fax, b/f, cable TV, t pkng, eff, conn rms, VCR. Free full brfst. AAA. $32-44/S; $34-46/D; $5/ex prsn. 6/1-9/16: $39-59/S; $43-63/D. Spec events: $60-80/S; $70-85/D. Discs.

Econo Lodge/ 1211 Atlantic Av, Virginia Beach VA 23451. 804-428-1183. V, M,D,AE. I-64, Exit 44 E to resort area, rt on Atlantic Av, 8 blks to mtl. Rstrnt/ lounge, indr pool, b/f, cable TV, n/s rms. No pets. $44-125/S or D; $8/ex prsn. 5/1-5/25: $59-125/S or D. 5/26-9/3: $84-155/S or D. 9/4-9/30: $69-125/S or D. Discs.

Friendship Inn/ 1909 Atlantic Av, Virginia Beach VA 23451. 804-425-0650. AE,DC,M,V. On Atlantic Av at 19th St. Nrby rstrnt, pool, fax, cable TV, n/s rms. $39-59/S or D; $10/ex prsn. 5/1-6/22: $65-140/S or D. 6/23-9/3: $100-160/S or D. 9/4-10/31: $59-80/S or D. Discs.

Friendship Inn/ 2802 Atlantic Av, Virginia Beach VA 23451. 804-428-3434. AE,DC,M,V. On Atlantic Av at 28th St. Nrby rstrnt, pool, fax, cable TV, n/s rms. $25-39/S or D; $8/ex prsn. 5/1-6/22: $39-90/S or D. 6/23-9/3: $65-90/S or D. 9/4-10/31: $35-44/S or D. Discs.

Howard Johnson Hotel/ 1801 Atlantic Av, Virginia Beach VA 23451. 804-437-9100/ Fax: 428-0827. M,V,D,AE,DC,CB. I-64 to Hwy 44, E to Atlantic Av, rt 3 blks. Rstrnt/ lounge, n/s rms, b/f, indr pool, whrlpool, mtg rm, micro, refrig. Free pkng garage. Gold Medal Winner. $39-69/S or D. 4/1-10/31: $69-99/S or D.

Howard Johnson Lodge/ 5173 Shore Dr, Virginia Beach VA 23455. 804-460-1151/ 800-882-3859. V,M,AE,DC,D,CB. From Chesapeake Bay Bridge Tunnel, take exit to US 60 W. Independence Blvd at Shore Dr (US 60). Nrby rstrnt, n/s rms, b/f, refrig. Free cont brfst. No pets. $35-40/S; $40-45/D. 5/1-10/31: $50-75/S; $55-85/D. Discs.

Quality Inn/ 2207 Atlantic Av, Box 328, Virginia Beach VA 23451. 804-428-5141. M,V,D,AE,DC. I-64 to SR 44, E to ocean front, N (lt) on Atlantic to 23rd & Atlantic. 2 blks on rt. Rstrnt/ lounge, indr pool, mtg rm, fax, b/f, whrlpool, cable TV, t pkng, n/s rms. Free local calls. No pets. AAA. $48-76/S or D; $8/ex prsn. 5/1-6/15: $55-105/S or D. 6/16-9/3: $125-151/S or D. 9/4-10/14: $85-115/S or D. Discs.

Rodeway Inn/ 2707 Atlantic Av, Virginia Beach VA 23451. 804-428-3970. V,M,D,AE. I-64 to SR 44 (Norfolk/ VA Beach Expressway), E to Atlantic Av, N (lt) to 28th St. US 13 to SR 60, E to Atlantic Av, S to 28th St. Nrby rstrnt, pool, fax, cable TV, refrig, n/s rms. Free cont brfst, bicycles. No pets. AAA. $39-69/S or D; $8/ex prsn. 5/1-6/15, 9/5-10/31: $54-119/S or D. 6/16-9/4: $99-154/S or D. Discs.

Warrenton

HoJo Inn/ 6 Broadview Av, Warrenton VA 22186. 703-347-4141/ Fax: 347-5632. M,V,D,AE,DC,CB. Jct of US 17/29 Bsns & Hwy 211. Rstrnt, n/s rms, pool, mtg rm, t pkng, outlets, fax, copier. Free AM coffee. $32-42/S; $39-49/D. Discs.

Waynesboro

Deluxe Budget Motel/ 2112 W Main St, Waynesboro VA 22980. 540-949-8253/ Fax: 943-3393/ 800-296-3393. V,M,AE,D. I-64 (Exit 94) to Hwy 340, N to Hwy 250, W to mtl. I-81 (Exit 222) to Hwy 250, E 7 mi to mtl. Rstrnt, pool, n/s rms, satellite TV, playgrnd, tt/dd phone, fax, copier, cot, crib, t pkng. Free local calls, coffee. No pets. AAA. $32/S; $38/D; $4/ex prsn. 5/15-5/31, 10/1-10/31: $38-50/S; $45-50/D. Disc: Senior, bsns, TA, govt, family, trkr, milt, l/s.

Super 8 Motel/ 2045 Rosser Av, Waynesboro VA 22980. 540-943-3888/ Fax: Ext 400. DC,CB,M,V,AE,D I-64 (Exit 94) at US 340. B/f, n/s rms, toast bar, suite, mtg rm, micro-refrig, TDD, outlets, t/b/rv pkng, cot. Free local calls, crib. Pride Award. $40/S; $46/D; $6/ex prsn. 4/1-9/30: $43/S; $49/D. Higher spec event, wknd rates. Discs.

Williamsburg

Motel Rochambeau/ 929 Capitol Landing Rd, Williamsburg VA 23185. 807-229-2851/ 800-368-1055. V,M,

VIRGINIA

AE,D. I-64, Exit 238, rt on Rte 5, 1 blk. Nrby rstrnt/ lounge, pool, cable TV, copier, nwspr, cot, crib, outlets, t/b/rv pkng, conn rms. No pets. AAA. $38-44/S or D; $5/ex prsn. 5/31-9/1: $44-48/S; $48/D. Holiday wknds: $38-58/S or D. CLOSED 11/1-4/30. Disc: Senior, AAA.

Red Carpet Inn/ 7224 Merrimac Trail, Williamsburg VA 23185. 804-229-0400/ Fax: 220-3075/ 800-251-1962. V,M,AE,D. I-64; Exit 242A, go 1/2 mi & exit to Rte 143, bear rt, 1/2 mi. Pool, n/s rms, cable TV, tt/dd phone, fax, refrig, microwave, cot, crib, t pkng, eff. Free coffee. No pets. AAA. $22-45/S or D; $5/ex prsn. 4/1-9/4: $36-79/S or D. Holiday wknds: $99/S or D. Suites: $60-160. Disc: Senior, bsns, TA, govt, family, trkr, milt, l/s. *Guaranteed rates.*

White Lion Motel/ 912 Capitol Landing Rd, Williamsburg VA 23185. 804-229-3931/ 800-368-1055. V,M,AE,D. I-64, Exit 238, rt on Rte 5, 3 blks on lt. Nrby rstrnt/ lounge, pool, n/s rms, cable TV, dd phone, copier, refrig, microwave, cot, crib, outlets, t/b/rv pkng, eff, conn rms. No pets. AAA. $38-44/S or D; $5/ex prsn. 5/31-9/1: $44-48/S; or D. Holiday wknds: $44-58/S or D. CLOSED 1/1-2/14. Disc: Senior, AAA, AARP. *Guaranteed rates.*

Bassett Motel/ 800 York St, Williamsburg VA 23185. 804-229-5175. V,M,DC. Exit 242A off 64 to Rte 199; Exit Rte 60, lt 1 1/2 mi. Nrby rstrnt/ lounge, n/s rms, cable TV, cot, crib, outlets, t/b pkng, conn rms. No pets. AAA. $34-39/S or D; $3/ex prsn. Mid June thru Labor Day: $44/S or D. CLOSED 11/15-3/15.

Budget Host Governor Spottswood Motel/ 1508 Richmond Rd, Williamsburg VA 23185. 804-229-6444/ Fax: 253-2410. M,V,AE,D,DC,CB. From W I-64, E to Exit 227 to US 60, E 12 mi on rt. Cable TV, dd phone, in-rm coffee, kitchens, b/f, adj rstrnt, mtg rms, pool, playgrnd, picnic area, laundry, cot. Free crib. AAA. Winter: $32/S; $34/D. Spring/Fall: $40/S; $44-48/D. Summer: $44/S; $48-52/D. Disc: Senior, Sept only.

Colonial America Inn/ 216 Parkway Dr, Williamsburg VA 23185. 804-253-6450/ Fax: 259-0342/ 800-296-STAY. V,M,AE,D. I-64, Exit 238, turn onto 143 towards Colonial Williamsburg. Stay in rt hand lane which becomes Rte 5 after 2 lights. At next light, turn lt onto 2nd St, then lt at Parkway Dr. Pool, n/s rms, cable TV, tt phone, fax, refrig, microwave, cot, outlets, t/b pkng, eff, conn rms, picnic area. Free coffee. No pets. AAA. $25-35/S; $30-48/D; $5/ex prsn. 6/15-9/15: $55-65/S; $65-79/D; $7/ex prsn. Holidays, spec events: $65/S; $75/D; $7/ex prsn. Disc: Senior, govt, family, govt, milt, trkr, AAA, l/s. *Guaranteed rates.*

Comfort Inn/ 706 Bypass Rd, Williamsburg VA 23185. 804-229-9230. V,M,AE,DC. SR 132 to US 60 Bypass, W to mtl. Rstrnt, pool, indr pool, fax, b/f, sauna, whrlpool, cable TV, exerc equip, n/s rms. No pets. $43-58/S; $48-63/D; $5/ex prsn. 5/1-6/12, 9/4-10/28: $50-65/S; $55-70/D. 6/13-9/3: $75-90/S or D. Discs.

Comfort Inn/ 2007 Richmond Rd, Williamsburg VA 23185. 804-220-3888. AE,M,V,DC. On US 60 (Richmond Rd), S of SR 646. Rstrnt, indr pool, fax, b/f, cable TV, t pkng, game rm, n/s rms. No pets. $30-45/S; $35-45/D; $5/ex prsn. 3/22-4/30, 9/4-12/31: $35-65/S or D. 5/1-9/3: $39-69/S; $45-75/D. Discs.

Comfort Inn/ 120 Bypass Rd, Williamsburg VA 23185. 804-229-2000. M,V,D,AE,DC. On US 60 Bypass, just S of jct with US 60. Nrby rstrnt, pool, fax, b/f, cable TV, t pkng, n/s rms. Free cont brfst. AAA. $35-59/S or D; $5/ex prsn. 5/1-6/15, 9/6-10/31: $49-79/S or D. 6/16-9/5: $59-89/S or D. Discs.

Comfort Inn/ 5611 Richmond Rd, Williamsburg VA 23188. 804-565-1100. V,M,DC,AE. I-64 (Exit 234) to SR 646 to Lightfoot, W to US 60, S (lt) on US 60, 2 mi to mtl. Rstrnt, pool, mtg rm, fax, b/f, cable TV, game rm, n/s rms. Free cont brfst. No pets. $40-80/S or D; $6/ex prsn. Discs.

Econo Lodge/ 442 Parkway Dr, Williamsburg VA 23185. 804-229-7564. V,M,AE. I-64 (Exit 238) to SR 143, E to SR 5, to Hwy 31 W. Rstrnt, fax, b/f, cable TV, t pkng, refrig, microwave, n/s rms. Free coffee. No pets. AAA. $33-

50/S or D; $5/ex prsn. 5/1-6/15: $50-60/S or D. 6/16-9/5: $66-75/S or D. 9/6-12/31: $45-53/S or D. Discs.

Econo Lodge/ 7051 Richmond Rd, Williamsburg VA 23188. 804-564-3341. M,V,D,AE,DC. On US 60 W. I-64, Exit 231A, S 1 mi to US 60, lt to mtl. Nrby rstrnt, fax, cable TV, t pkng, n/s rms. $25-45/S; $30-50/D; $5/ex prsn. 4/1-5/31, 10/1-11/30: $40-56/S; $46-60/D. 6/1-9/30: $56-80/S; $60-80/D. Discs.

Econo Lodge/ 1900 Richmond Rd, Williamsburg VA 23185. 804-229-6600. AE,DC,M,V. I-64 (Exit 234) to SR 646, rt to US 60 (Richmond Rd), E 4 mi. Rstrnt, pool, fax, cable TV, t pkng. Free coffee. $40-55/S or D; $5/ex prsn. 5/1-6/10: $45-65/S or D. 6/11-9/9: $55-65/S or D. Discs.

Friendship Inn/ 7247 Pocohontas Trail, Williamsburg VA 23185. 804-220-2000. V,M,AE,DC. I-64 (Exit 242A, Williamsburg/ Busch Gardens), lt on US 60, W 1/4 mi to mtl. Rstrnt, pool, mtg rm, fax, whrlpool, cable TV, t pkng, picnic area, n/s rms. Free coffee. $25-75/S; $29-79/D. 5/1-6/15: $35-75/S; $39-79/D. 6/16-8/19: $55-95/S; $59-99/D. Discs.

Motel 6/ 3030 Richmond Rd (US 60), Williamsburg VA 23185. 804-565-3433/ Fax: 565-1013. M,V,DC,D,AE. I-64 to SR 646 (Lightfoot Exit 234), SW 1 mi to US 60, E 2 1/2 mi. Nrby rstrnt, cable TV, laundry, pool, laundry, n/s rms, t pkng. Free local calls. $30-40/S; $36-46/D; $6/ex prsn. Higher spec event rates. Disc.

Quality Inn/ 300 Bypass Rd, Williamsburg VA 23185. 804-229-6270. M, V,D,AE,DC. On US 60 Bypass, bet US 60 & SR 132. Rstrnt, pool, mtg rm, fax, b/f, whrlpool, cable TV, n/s rms, brfst. $35-90/S or D; $5/ex prsn. 5/1-6/14: $45-90/S or D. 6/15-9/3: $55-120/S or D. 9/4-10/31: $40-90/S or D. Discs.

Quality Inn/ 1700 Richmond Rd, Williamsburg VA 23185. 804-229-2401. M,V,D,AE,DC. In city at jct of US 60 & US 60 Bypass. Rstrnt, pool, fax, b/f, cable TV, t pkng, n/s rms. No pets. AAA. $40-45/S; $40-49/D; $5/ex prsn. 5/1-9/30: $59-65/S; $59-69/D. Discs.

Quality Inn/ 6493 Richmond Dr, Williamsburg VA 23185. 804-565-1111. M,V,D,AE,DC. I-64 to SR 646, SE (rt) to US 60 (Richmond Rd), NW (rt) to mtl. Rstrnt, pool, fax, b/f, cable TV, t pkng, n/s rms. Free cont brfst. No pets. AAA. $45-65/S or D; $5/ex prsn. 6/11-9/9: $55-75/S or D. Discs.

Rodeway Inn/ 1420 Richmond Rd, Williamsburg VA 23185. 804-229-2981.V, M,D,AE. At jct of US 60 (Richmond Rd) and US 60 Bypass. N of Williamsburg. Rstrnt, pool, fax, b/f, cable TV, t pkng, n/s rms. AAA. $30-70/S or D; $5/ex prsn. 5/1-6/16: $40-80/S or D. 6/17-9/5: $45-90/S or D. 9/6-10/31: $35-80/S or D. Discs.

Winchester

Econo Lodge/ 1593 Martinsburg Pike, Winchester VA 22603. 703-662-4700. V,AE,M,DC. I-81 (Exit 317) at US 11. Nrby rstrnt, fax, b/f, cable TV, t pkng. Free cont brfst, local calls. No pets. AAA. $37-45/S; $43-51/D; $5/ex prsn. 5/1-5/3: $37-43/S; $40-49/D. 5/4-5/6: $53-57/S; $60-65/D. Discs.

Quality Inn/ 603 Millwood Av, Winchester VA 22601. 703-667-2250. M,V,D,AE,DC. I-81 (Exit 313) to US 50 W, stay in rt lane. Adj rstrnt, pool, fax, sauna, cable TV, n/s rms. Free cont brfst. $46-52/S or D; $6/ex prsn. 5/1-5/2, 5/6-10/31: $48-60/S; $50-65/D. 5/3-5/5: $55-65/S; $55-70/D. Discs.

Woodbridge (Washington DC area)

Econo Lodge/ 13317 Gordon Blvd, Woodbridge VA 22191. 703-491-5196. M,V,D,AE. I-95: Sbnd,(Exit 161) to Woodbridge, exit lt, turn rt on SR 123; Nbnd, (Exit 160) to Woodbridge/ Occoquan, turn rt on SR 123. Adj rstrnt, fax, cable TV, t pkng, n/s rms, AM coffee. $44-54/S; $46-56/D; $5/ex prsn. 5/1-10/31: $46-60/S $49-65/D. Discs.

Friendship Inn/ 13964 Jefferson Davis Hwy, Woodbridge VA 22191. 703-494-4144. M,V,D,AE,DC. I-95 (S, Exit 161; N, Exit 160) to SR 123, S to US 1, rt to mtl. Nrby rstrnt, cable TV, n/s rms, AM coffee. $38-48/S; $40-50/D; $5/ex prsn. 5/1-10/31: $40-55/S; $43-58/D. Discs.

Woodstock

Budget Host Inn/ Rte 2, Box 78,

VIRGINIA / WASHINGTON

Woodstock VA 22664. 540-459-4086/ Fax: 459-4043. V,AE,CB,DC,D,M. On Rte 11 S. Cable TV, dd phone, n/s rms, b/f, rstrnt, pool, picnic area, laundry, cot, crib, t pkng. AAA. $30/S; $34-40/D; $4/ex prsn.

Wytheville

Johnsons Motel/ 1910 W Lee Hwy, Box 443, Wytheville VA 24382. 540-228-4812/ Fax: 228-5999/ 800-776-4812. V,M,AE,D,DC. On US Rte 11. I-77, Exit 41. I-81, Exit 70, 73 or 67 Nbnd. N/s rms, cable TV, tt/dd phone, fax, copier, refrig, microwave, cot, crib, outlets, t/b/rv pkng, eff. Free local calls, coffee. Mobil. $26-28/S; $32-36/D; $5/ex prsn. Spec events: $40/S; $48/D; $8/ex prsn. Disc: Senior, milt, l/s. *Guaranteed rates.*

Days Inn/ 150 Malin Dr, Wytheville VA 24382. 540-228-5500/ Fax: 228-6301. V,M,AE,D,DC. I-81 & I-77, Exit 73. Fax, n/s rms, nrby rstrnt, b/f, game rm, cot. $36-54/S; $42-58/D; $5/ex prsn. Discs.

Econo Lodge/ 1190 E Main St, Wytheville VA 24382. 703-228-5517. V,AE, M,DC. I-81 S (Exit 73) to US 11. I-77: Sbnd, (Exit 41) to 1st light, turn lt then second lt onto Main St; Nbnd,(Exit 73) to US 11. Nrby rstrnt, fax, cable TV, t pkng, n/s rms. Free AM coffee. $31-41/S; $35-45/D; $5/ex prsn. 5/1-10/31: $33-51/S; $37-56/D. Spec events: $50-65/S or D. Discs.

Motel 6/ 220 Lithia Rd, Wytheville VA 24382. 703-228-7988/ Fax: 223-1860. M,V,DC,D,AE. I-77/ I-81 to (Exit 73) Main St, W to mtl. Cable TV, pool, n/s rms. Free local calls. $26-28/S; $32-34/D; $6/ex prsn. Disc.

Washington

Auburn

Nendels Auburn/ 102 15th St NE, Auburn WA 98002. 206-833-8007/ Fax: 931-1113/ 800-547-0106. V,M,AE,D, DC,CB. I-5 to Hwy 18 E to Hwy 167 N, Exit 15th St NW, rt 4 blks. Nrby rstrnt/ lounge, n/s rms, satellite TV, tt/dd phone, fax, refrig, microwave, crib, b/f. Free local calls, cont brfst, coffee. AAA. $48-56/S or D; $5/ex prsn. Disc:

Senior, bsns, govt, trkr, milt, AAA. *Guaranteed rates.*

Bellingham

Coachman Inn/ 120 Samish Way, Bellingham WA 98225. 360-671-9000/ Fax: 738-1984/ 800-962-6641. V,M, AE, D. I-5 to Exit 252 (Samish Way), Exit 3 blks on rt, across from McDonalds. Approx 3 mi from WWU. Pool, sauna, n/s rms, cable TV, tt phone, fax, copier, refrig, microwave, cot, crib, conn rms, b/f. Free local calls, cont brfst, coffee. No alcohol. AAA. $32-40/S; $38-42/D; $5/ex prsn. 3/1-9/30: $40-45/S; $45-50/D; $7/ex prsn. Disc: Senior, bsns, TA, govt, l/s, family, trkr, milt, AAA, AARP,BCA. *Guaranteed rates.*

Motel 6/ 3701 Byron Av, Bellingham WA 98225. 360-671-4494/ Fax: 734-7367. M,V,DC,D,AE. I-5 (Exit 252) to Samish Way, NW to Byron, rt. Nrby rstrnt, cable TV, pool, n/s rms. Free local calls. $29-36/S; $35-42/D; $6/ex prsn. Disc.

Rodeway Inn/ 3710 Meridian St, Bellingham WA 98225. 360-738-6000. M,V,D,AE,DC. I-5 (Exit 256) to Meridian, S to mtl. Nrby rstrnt, fax, b/f, whrlpool, cable TV, t pkng, n/s rms. Free cont brfst. AAA. $42-58/S; $42-64/D; $6/ex prsn.

Bremerton

Super 8 Motel/ 5068 Kitsap Way, Bremerton WA 98310. 360-377-8881/ Fax: 373-8755. V,M,AE,D,DC. SR 3, Kitsap Way exit. B/f, n/s rms, laundry, cable TV, mtg rm. Free local calls, crib. Manager Award. $43/S; $47-51/D; $5/ex prsn. Higher spec event rates. Discs.

WASHINGTON

Centralia
Motel 6/ 1310 Belmont Av, Centralia WA 98531. 360-330-2057/ Fax: 330-2066. M,V,DC,D,AE. I-5/ US 99 (Exit 82) at Harrison Av, W to Belmont, rt 2 blks to mtl. Nrby rstrnt, cable TV, laundry, pool, n/s rms. Free local calls. $27-30/S; $33-36/D; $6/ex prsn. Disc.

Chelan
Apple Inn Motel/ 1002 E Woodin Av, Box 1450, Chelan WA 98816. 509-682-4044. V,M,AE,D,DC. On 97A. Nrby rstrnt/ lounge, pool, whrlpool, n/s rms, cable TV, tt phone, refrig, cot, crib, t/b pkng. Free local calls, coffee. No pets. AAA. $30-34/S or D; $5/ex prsn. 5/25-9/14: $49-59/S or D. Disc: Bsns, trkr, AAA. *Guaranteed rates.*

Chewelah
Nordlig Motel/ 101 W Grant St, Chewelah WA 99109. 509-935-6704. V,M,AE,D. 1 blk W of Hwy 395. N/s rms, cable TV, tt phone, mtg rm, refrig, microwave, crib, outlets, t pkng, b/f. Free local calls, coffee. AAA. $36/S; $42/D; $5/ex prsn. Disc: Senior, l/s. *Guaranteed rates.*

Clarkston
Motel 6/ 222 Bridge St, Clarkston WA 99403. 509-758-1631. V,M,DC,AE,D. SR 12 & Bridge St, immed W of bridge connecting Clarkston with Lewiston, ID. Rstrnt, cable TV, laundry, pool, n/s rms. Free local calls. Premier Award. $30-36/S; $36-42/D; $6/ex prsn. Disc.

Everett (Seattle - Tacoma area)
Comfort Inn/ 1602 SE Everett Mall Way, Everett WA 98208. 206-355-1570. M,V,D,AE,DC. I-5 (Exit 189) to Everett Mall Way. Nrby rstrnt, whrlpool, cable TV, n/s rms. Free cont brfst. No pets. $42-53/S; $46-64/D; $6/ex prsn. Discs.

Motel 6/ 224 128th St SW, Everett WA 98204. 206-353-8120/ Fax: 347-2269. M,V,DC,AE,D. I-5 (Exit 186) to 128th St, W to 4th Ave W. Nrby rstrnt, cable TV, n/s rms. Free local calls. $30-34/S; $36-40/D; $6/ex prsn. Disc.

Motel 6/ 10006 Evergreen Way, Everett WA 98204. 206-347-2060/ Fax: 347-1529. M,V,DC,AE,D. I-5 (Exit 189) to Mukilteo Ferry-Paine Field (SR 526W), W to Evergreen Way, lt 1/4 mi to mtl. Nrby rstrnt, cable TV, pool, n/s rms, t pkng. Free local calls. $28-33/S; $34-39/D; $6/ex prsn. Disc.

Fife (Tacoma area)
Econo Lodge/ 3518 Pacific Hwy E, Fife WA 98424. 206-922-0550. V,AE,M,DC. I-5, Exit 136B, rt at 1st light. Nrby rstrnt, fax, cable TV, t pkng, n/s rms. Free cont brfst. AAA. $30-37/S; $36-42/D; $4/ex prsn. 5/1-10/1: $33-42/S; $42-55/D. Discs.

Motel 6/ 5201 20th St E, Fife WA 98424. 206-922-1270/ Fax: 926-3662. M,V,DC,AE,D. I-5, Exit 137/ Fife-Milton, S on 54th Av, E to 1st light, rt on 20th. Rstrnt, cable TV, pool, n/s rms, t pkng. Free local calls. $28-33/S; $34-39/D; $6/ex prsn. Disc.

Forks
Pacific Inn Motel/ 352 S Forks Av, Box 1997, Forks WA 98331. 360-374-9400/ Fax: 374-9402/ 800-235-7344. V,M, AE, D,DC,CB. Rstrnt, n/s rms, cable TV, tt/dd phone, copier, laundry, cot, crib, t/b/rv pkng, b/f. Free local calls, coffee. No pets. AAA. $38/S; $43-47/D; $5/ex prsn. 5/15-9/30: $43/S; $48-52/D. Disc: Bsns, govt, family, trkr, milt.

Greenacres
Alpine Motel & RV Park/ Box 363, Greenacres WA 99016. 509-928-2700. V,M. I-90, Exit 293. Nrby rstrnt, pool, n/s rms, cable TV, video games, playgrnd, tt/dd phone, nwspr, laundry, microwave, outlets, b/rv pkng, b/f. Free local calls. AAA. $40-44/S; $44-47/D; $6/ex prsn. 4/1-9/30: $46-56/S; $52-59/D. Disc; Oct thru Mar: Senior, bsns, trkr, milt, govt, AAA.

Issaquah (Seattle area)
Motel 6/ 1885 15th Pl NW, Issaquah WA 98027. 206-392-8405/ Fax: 557-6465. M,V,DC,AE,D. I-90 (Exit 15) to Lk Sammamish State Pk, N on 17th Av to SE 56th St, turn lt. Rstrnt, cable TV, laundry, pool, n/s rms, arpt trans. Free local calls. $34-37/S; $40-33/D; $6/ex prsn. Disc.

Kelso
Kelso Budget Inn/ 505 N Pacific Av, Kelso WA 98626. 360-636-4610/ Fax:

WASHINGTON

636-4773. V,M,AE. I-5, Exit 40, approx 1 mi. N/s rms, cable TV, tt/dd phone, fax, cot, t/b pkng, eff, conn rms. Free local calls. AAA. $30/S; $39/D; $5/ex prsn. 5/1-9/30: $33/S; $42/D. Disc: Senior, AAA, l/s.

Motel 6/ 106 Minor Rd, Kelso WA 98626. 360-425-3229/ Fax: 423-4650. M,V,DC,D,AE. I-5, Kelso Exit 39 to Allen St, E to Minor Rd. Nrby rstrnt, cable TV, pool, n/s rms. Free local calls. $34-37/S; $40-43/D; $6/ex prsn. Disc.

Kirkland (Seattle area)

Motel 6/ 12010 120th Place NE, Kirkland WA 98034. 206-821-5618/ Fax: 821-7459. M,V,DC,D,AE. I-405 to 124th St exit, E to 120th Pl NE, turn rt. Nrby rstrnt, cable TV, pool, elevator, n/s rms. Free local calls. $34-37/S; $40-43/D; $6/ex prsn. Disc.

Long Beach

Our Place at the Beach/ Box 266, Long Beach WA 98631. 360-642-3793/ Fax: 642-3896/ 800-538-5107. V,M,AE,D,DC,CB. Sauna, whrlpool, exerc equip, cable TV, dd phone, mtg rm, fax, copier, refrig, microwave, cot, crib, outlets. Free local calls, coffee. AAA/Mobil. $37-45/S; $37-50/D; $5/ex prsn. 5/15-9/30: $45-54/S or D. Disc: Senior, bsns, govt. *Guaranteed rates.*

Lynden

Windmill Inn Motel & RV Park/ 8022 Guide Meridian Rd, Lynden WA 98264. 360-354-3424. V,M,AE,D. 1/4 mi S of Lyden on SR 539. Cable TV, tt/dd phone, refrig, cot, crib, t/b/rv pkng, eff. Free local calls, coffee, tea. AAA. $35-37/S; $45-47/D; $4/ex prsn. Disc: Senior, *Guaranteed rates.*

Moses Lake

Motel 6/ 2822 Wapato Dr, Moses Lake WA 98837. 509-766-0250/ Fax: 766-7762. M,V,DC,D,AE. I-90 (Exit 176) turn rt on Wapato Dr to mtl. Nrby rstrnt, cable TV, laundry, pool, n/s rms, t pkng. Free local calls. $27-31/S; $33-37/D; $6/ex prsn. Disc.

Oak Harbor

Acorn Motor Inn/ 8066 State Hwy 20, Oak Harbor WA 98277. 360-675-6646/ Fax: 679-1850/ 800-280-6646. V,M,AE,D,DC,CB. N/s rms, cable TV, arpt trans, tt/dd phone, fax, copier, nwspr, refrig, microwave, cot, crib, t pkng, b/f. Free local calls, cont brfst. AAA. $41-52/S; $44-56/D; $4/ex prsn. 6/15-9/15: $48-58/S; $52-64/D; $6/ex prsn. Spec events: $58/S; $62/D. Disc: Senior, bsns, govt, l/s, family, milt. *Guaranteed rates.*

Okanogan

Ponderosa Motor Lodge/ 1034 S 2nd Av, Okanogan WA 98840. 509-422-0400/ Fax: 422-4206/ 800-732-6702. V,M,AE,D,DC. Hwy 97 Nbnd, 1st Okanogan exit, 1/2 mi to stop, rt 3 blks. Hwy 97 Sbnd, 1st exit, lt at blinking light, 4 blks on Hwy 20/215 from N Cascades. Pool, n/s rms, cable TV, tt/dd phone, mtg rm, copier, laundry, refrig, cot, crib, outlets, t/b/rv pkng, eff, b/f. Free local calls, coffee. AAA. $28/S; $37-42/D. 2nd wknd Aug: $75/S; $75-85/D; $10/ex prsn. Disc: Senior, bsns, TA, govt, l/s, family, trkr, milt. *Guaranteed rates.*

Omak

Leisure Village Motel/ 630 Okoma Dr, Box 2055, Omak WA 98841. 509-826-4442. V,M,AE,D. I-97 to Main St, lt to Okoma Dr. Indr pool, sauna, whrlpool, n/s rms, cable TV, tt/dd phone, refrig, microwave, cot, crib, t/b/rv pkng, eff. Free local calls, cont brfst. AAA. $33/S; $38-48/D. 5/1-10/14: $35/S; $40-50/D. 2nd wknd Aug: $70/S; $80/D. Disc: Senior, bsns, TA, govt, trkr, milt, AAA, AARP. *Guaranteed rates.*

Pasco

Motel 6/ 1520 N Oregon St, Pasco WA 99301. 509-546-2010/ Fax: 544-0279. V,M,DC,AE,D. On Oregon St, just S of jct of US 395 & US 12. Cable TV, laundry, pool, n/s rms, t pkng. Free local calls. $28-31/S; $34-37/D; $6/ex prsn. Disc.

Port Angeles

Super 8 Motel/ 2104 E 1st St, Port Angeles WA 98362. 360-452-8401/ Fax: 452-4406. V,AE,DC,CB,M,D Hwy 101 at S end of Port Angeles. B/f, n/s rms, laundry, copier, cable TV, mtg rm. Free local calls, crib. $42/S; $46-50/D; $4/ex prsn. 5/21-9/30: $55/S; $60-65/D.

WASHINGTON

Higher spec event rates. Discs.

Port Townsend
Waterstreet Hotel/ 635 Water St, Port Townsend WA 98368. 360-385-5467/ 800-735-9810. V,M,AE. SR 20, Port Townsend Exit, follow to corner of Water & Quincy Sts. Nrby rstrnt/ lounge, n/s rms, cable TV, playgrnd, laundry, refrig, crib, eff. Free local calls, cont brfst. AAA. $45-100/S or D; $8/ex prsn. 5/1-10/31: $50-125/S or D. Disc: Senior, I/s. AAA. *Guaranteed rates.*

Ritzville
Colwell Motor Inn/ 501 W 1st St, Ritzville WA 99169. 509-659-1620. V,M,AE,D,CB,DC. I-90, Exit 220, Nbnd 395 to downtown. Nrby rstrnt/ lounge, pool, cable TV, dd phone, laundry, outlets, sauna, in-rm coffee, nearby t pkng, cot, crib, conn rms, family rms. AAA/ IMA. $38-46/S; $42-58/D; $2/ex prsn. Disc: Milt.

Seattle
Motel 6/ 18900 47th Av S, Seattle WA 98188. 206-241-1648/ Fax: 244-3614. M,V,DC,D,AE. I-5, Exit 152, W on S 188th St, lt on 47th Av, S to mtl. Cable TV, pool, n/s rms. Free local calls. $30-34/S; $36-40/D; $6/ex prsn. Disc.

Motel 6/ 16500 Pacific Hwy S, Seattle WA 98188. 206-246-4101/ Fax: 244-3764. M,V,DC,D,AE. I-5 to 188th St, W to 47th Av S. On W side of frwy between Hwy 518 and 167th. Cable TV, n/s rms. Free local calls. $33/S; $39/D; $6/ex prsn. Disc.

Motel 6/ 20651 Military Rd, Seattle WA 98198. 206-824-9902/ Fax: 870-3842. M,V,DC,D,AE. I-5 (Exit 151) S on Military Rd to mtl. Cable TV, pool, n/s rms, t pkng, whrlpool. Free local calls. $33-36/S; $39-42/D; $6/ex prsn. Disc.

Also see Everett, Issaquah, Kirkland.

Silverdale
Cimarron Motel/ 9734 NW Silverdale Way, Silverdale WA 98383. 360-692-7777/ Fax: 692-0961. V,M,AE,D,DC, CB. I-5 to Hwy 16, N on Hwy 3 to "Hood Canal Bridge" sign, veer lt, stay on Hwy 3 to Anderson Hill exit, rt 4 blks. N/s rms, cable TV, arpt trans, tt phone, fax, copier, laundry, refrig, cot, crib, rv pkng, eff, b/f. Free cont brfst, local calls. No pets. AAA/ Mobil. $45/S or D. Disc: Bsns, govt, milt, AAA.

Spokane
Friendship Inn/ 4301 W Sunset Blvd, Spokane WA 99204. 509-838-1471. M,V,D,AE,DC. 2 mi W of dntn on Sunset Hwy (US 2) W. Rstrnt/ lounge, pool, mtg rm, fax, b/f, sauna, whrlpool, cable TV, n/s rms. $40-100/S; $44-100/D; $5/ex prsn. 5/1-10/31: $44-125/S or D. Discs.

Motel 6/ 1508 S Rustle St, Spokane WA 99204. 509-459-6120/ Fax: 747-1857. M,V,DC,D,AE. I-90, Exit 277/ 277A to Rustle St, N to mtl. Nrby rstrnt, cable TV, pool, n/s rms. Free local calls. $27-36/S; $33-42/D; $6/ex prsn. Disc.

Rodeway Inn/ W 827 1st Av, Spokane WA 99204. 509-838-8271. M,V,D,AE, DC. I-90 (Exit 280) to Lincoln St, N to 1st Av. Nrby rstrnt, pool, mtg rm, fax, sauna, whrlpool, cable TV, n/s rms. Free cont brfst. AAA. $39-49/S; $43-53/D; $10/ex prsn. 6/1-9/15: $45-55/S; $49-59/D. Spec events: $55-65/S; $61-71/D. Discs.

Super 8 Motel/ 2020 Argonne Rd, Spokane WA 99212. 509-928-4888. V, M,DC,AE,D. I-90 (Exit 287) at Argonne Rd. B/f, n/s rms, game rm, laundry, outlets, b/t/rv pkng, toast bar, copier, elevator, satellite TV, mtg rm, cot. Free local calls, crib. $38-42/S; $44-56/D; $5/ex prsn. Higher spec event rates. Discs.

Sunnyside
Friendship Inn/ 724 Yakima Valley Hwy, Sunnyside WA 98944. 509-837-4721. V,AE,M,DC. I-82 (E, Exit 63; W, Exit 69/ Vernita Bridge) follow Sunnyside signs past 2 lights to mtl. Nrby rstrnt, pool, cable TV, t pkng, outlets, n/s rms. Free cont brfst. $34-64/S; $40-71/D; $4/ex prsn. 5/1-10/31: $38-68/S; $44-75/D. Discs.

Tacoma
Motel 6/ 1811 S 76th St, Tacoma WA 98408. 206-473-7100/ Fax: 472-7952. V,M,DC,AE,D. I-5 (Exit 128/ 129) to 72nd St, E to Hosmer St, rt 1/4 mi.

WASHINGTON

Rstrnt, cable TV, pool, n/s rms, whrlpool. Free local calls. $40/S; $46/D; $6/ex prsn. Disc.

Also see Everett, Fife.

Tumwater
Motel 6/ 400 W Lee St, Tumwater WA 98501. 360-754-7320/ Fax: 705-0655. M,V,DC,D,AE. I-5, Exit 102/ Black Lk & Olympia, E on Trosper Rd, rt on Capitol, rt on W Lee. Nrby rstrnt, cable TV, pool, n/s rms, t pkng. Free local calls. $30-33/S; $36-39/D; $6/ex prsn. Disc.

Wenatchee
Travelodge/ 1004 N Wenatchee Av, Wenatchee WA 98801. 509-662-8165/ Fax: 662-8165/ 800-578-7878. V,M, AE,D,DC,CB. On Hwys 2 & 97 (Wenatchee Av). 1/4 blk N of 9th St. Indr pool, sauna, whrlpool, n/s rms, exerc equip, cable TV, tt/dd phone, copier, laundry, refrig, crib, t/b/rv pkng, eff, b/f. Free local calls, cont brfst. No pets. AAA. $35/S; $41/D. 5/1-10/14: $41/S; $45/D. Disc: Senior, govt, family, I/s, AAA. *Guaranteed rates.*

Avenue Motel/ 720 N Wenatchee Av, Wenatchee WA 98801. 509-663-7161/ 800-733-8981. V,M,AE,D,DC,CB. 2 mi from N end of town. Nrby rstrnt/ lounge, pool, whrlpool, n/s rms, cable TV, tt/dd phone, fax, cot, crib, eff, conn rms. Free local calls, coffee. AAA. $42/S or D; $5/ex prsn. 5/1-10/31: $45/S or D. Disc: Senior, bsns, govt, trkr.

Yakima
Red Carpet Motor Inn/ 1608 Fruitvale Blvd, Yakima WA 98902. 509-457-1131/ Fax: 457-1391/ 800-457-5090. V,M,D. Hwy 12 to 16th Av, rt at 1st traffic light. Pool, sauna, n/s rms, cable TV, tt phone, fax, copier, laundry, refrig, microwave, cot, crib, b pkng, b/f. Free local calls, coffee. AAA. $30-34/S; $34-38/D; $6/ex prsn. 4/1-9/30: $32-37/S; $36-41/D. Disc: Senior, bsns, TA, govt, I/s, family, trkr, milt, AAA, AARP.

Motel 6/ 1104 N 1st St, Yakima WA 98901. 509-454-0080/ Fax: 452-2241. M,V,DC,D,AE. US 12 or I-82 to N 1st St/ Exit 31, S 1 mi to mtl. Nrby rstrnt, cable TV, laundry, pool, n/s rms. Free local calls. $35-38/S; $41-44/D; $6/ex prsn. Disc.

Quality Inn/ 12 Valley Mall Blvd, Yakima WA 98903. 509-248-6924. M,V,D,AE,DC. I-82, Exit 36 to mtl. Nrby rstrnt, pool, mtg rm, fax, b/f, cable TV, t pkng, n/s rms. Free cont brfst. $42-48/S; $48-57/D; $8/ex prsn. Discs.

West Virginia

Beaver
Sleep Inn/ 1124 Airport Rd, Box 250, Beaver WV 25813. 304-255-4222. V, M,AE,D,DC. I-64 (W, Exit 125; E, Exit 125B) to E Airport Rd, 1/5 mi N to mtl. N/s, nrby rstrnt, mtg rm, b/f, cable TV, t pkng, fax. Free cont brfst. No pets. AAA. $43-53/S; $48-58/D; $5/ex prsn. 4/1-4/30: $46-56/S; $51-61/D. Discs.

Bluefield
Econo Lodge/ 3400 Cumberland Rd, Bluefield WV 24701. 304-327-8171. V,AE,M,DC. US 52, N of US 460. Nrby rstrnt, fax, cable TV, t pkng, n/s rms. Free AM coffee. $33-43/S; $36-46/D; $5/ex prsn. 5/1-10/31: $37-47/S; $40-53/D. Discs.

Bridgeport (Clarksburg area)
Econo Lodge/ SR 2, Box 168 Bridgeport WV 26330. 304-842-7381. M,V,D,AE,DC. I-79, Exit 121 at Meadowbrook Rd. Nrby rstrnt, fax, b/f, cable TV, t pkng, n/s rms, copier. Free local calls, coffee. $41-61/S; $48-71/D; $5/ex prsn. Discs.

Chapmanville

Friendship Inn/ SR 10 & US 119, Chapmanville WV 25508. 304-855-7182. V, AE,M,DC. US 119 at SR 10. Nrby rstrnt, mtg rm, fax, b/f, cable TV, t pkng, outlets, conn rms, coffee. $43-48/S; $48-53/D; $3/ex prsn. Discs.

Charleston

Budget Host Inn/ 3313 E Kanawha Blvd, Charleston WV 25306. 304-925-2592. AE,D,M,V. I-77 & 64, Exit 96. Cable TV, dd phone, n/s rms, b/f. $30/S; $33-36/D.

Motel 6/ 6311 MacCorkle Av SE, Charleston WV 25304. 304-925-0471/ Fax: 926-8489. V,M,DC,D,AE. I-64/I-77 (Exit 95) to MacCorkle Av, turn rt. Nrby rstrnt, cable TV, n/s rms, elevator. Free local calls. $31-33/S; $37-39/D; $6/ex prsn. Disc.

Sleep Inn/ 2772 Pennsylvania Av, Charleston WV 25302. 800-221-222 — Opening soon. V,M,AE,D,DC. I-79 (Exit 1) at Mink Shoals. N/s, rstrnt, mtg rm, fax, b/f, cable TV. Free cont brfst. $38-52/S; $43-57/D; $5/ex prsn. Spec events: $45-60/S; $48-64/D. Discs.

Also see Cross Lanes.

Cross Lanes (Charleston area)

Comfort Inn/ 102 Racer Dr, Cross Lanes WV 25313. 304-776-8070. V,M,AE,DC. I-64, Exit 47. Nrby rstrnt/ lounge, pool, mtg rm, fax, b/f, whrlpool, cable TV, t pkng, n/s rms. Free cont brfst. No pets. AAA. $35-45/S; $40-55/D; $5/ex prsn. 5/1-10/31: $45-55/S; $45-60/D. Discs.

Motel 6/ 330 Goff Mountain Rd, Cross Lanes WV 25313. 304-776-5911/ Fax: 776-7450. V,M,DC,D,AE. I-64, exit Goff Mountain Rd, NE to mtl. Adj rstrnt, cable TV, pool, n/s rms. Free local calls. $30-32/S; $36-38/D; $6/ex prsn. Disc.

Davis

Budget Host Highlander Village/ Box 587, Davis WV 26260. 304-259-5551/ Fax: 636-5419. AE,D,M,V. On Williams Av, bet Hwy 93 & 90. Cable TV, dd phone, mtg rms, nrby rstrnt, t pkng. $30/S; $36/D; $6/ex prsn. 12/15-3/15, Wknds, 6/16-6/30: $43/S; $49/D. Disc: Senior.

Mountain Aire Lodge/ Star Rte 32, Box 493, Davis WV 26260. 304-259-5211/ Fax: 259-5214/ 800-553-0724. V, M,AE,D. I-68 at Keyser Ridge MD; S on US 219 to Thomas WV; at Thomas, 2 mi S on SR 32 to Davis, N end of town. Nrby rstrnt/ lounge, n/s rms, cable TV, tt phone, crib, conn rms. Free local calls. No pets. AAA. 1/1-2/28: Wknds, 12/24 - 1/2: $43-49/S; $49-55/D. 1/1-2/28 Mon-Thurs, 5/1-11/30: $33-39/S; $39-45/D. 3/1-4/30, 12/1-12/23: $27-33/S; $33-39/D. Disc: Senior, bsns, l/s.

Elkins

Econo Lodge/ Rte 1, Box 15, Elkins WV 26241. 304-636-5311. V,AE,M,DC. On US 33, E side of city. Nrby rstrnt/ lounge, indr pool, mtg rm, cable TV, t pkng, playgrnd, picnic area, eff, b/f, n/s rms. Free cont brfst, in-rm coffee. $37-50/S; $38-53/D; $3/ex prsn. Higher holiday, spec event rates. Discs.

Super 8 Motel/ Rte 3, Box 284, Elkins WV 26241. 304-636-6500. V,M,D,DC, CB,AE On US 219-250 S. B/f, n/s rms, suite, mtg rm, microwave-refrig, suite, mtg rm, TDD, outlets, t/b/rv pkng, cot. Free local calls, crib. Pride Award. $39-42/S; $45-48/D; $6/ex prsn. Higher spec event rates. Discs.

Fairmont

Country Club Motor Lodge/ 1499 Locust Av, Fairmont WV 26554. 304-366-4141/ Fax: 367-1882/ 800-CALLWVA. V,M,AE,D,DC,CB. I-79, Exit 132 to Rte 250 N, 3 mi, lt at 1st stoplight, 1 mi on Country Club Rd. Nrby rstrnt/ lounge, n/s rms, cable TV, tt phone, fax, microwave, copier, cot. No pets. AAA. $23-27/S; $27-30/D. Spec event, holiday rates: $25-29/S; $29-33/D. Disc: Bsns, TA, family, l/s. *Guaranteed rates.*

Ghent

Econo Lodge/ Box 370, Ghent WV 25843. 304-787-3250. V,M,D,AE,DC. I-77 (Exit 28) bet Princeton & Beckley, WV. Nrby rstrnt, cable TV, t pkng, n/s rms. Free cont brfst. No pets. $37-50/S; $45-57/D; $6/ex prsn. 4/1- 12/7: $35-42/S; $39-50/D. Discs.

WEST VIRGINIA

Huntington

Econo Lodge/ 3325 US 60 E, Huntington WV 25705. 304-529-1331. V,AE,M,DC. I-64 (Exit 15) to US 60. 1 mi W on US 60. Rstrnt/ lounge, pool, mtg rm, fax, b/f, cable TV, t pkng, n/s rms. Free local calls, hot brfst. AAA. $35-39/S; $39-46/D; $4/ex prsn. 5/1-11/30: $37-42/S; $42-48/D. Discs.

Ramada Inn/ 5600 US 60 E, Huntington WV 25705. 304-736-3451/ Fax: Ext 706. V,M,AE,D,DC. 1 mi E of I-64 (Exit 15) on US 60 E. Pool, trans, b/f, n/s rms, rstrnt/ lounge, mtg rm, exercise equip. $40-54/S; $45-59/D; $5/ex prsn. Discs.

Keyser

Econo Lodge/ US 220, Box 160, Keyser WV 26726. 304-788-0913. V,M,D,AE. US 50 to US 220 N, 3 mi to Keyser. Nrby rstrnt/ lounge, fax, b/f, cable TV, t pkng, outlets, n/s rms. Free cont brfst. AAA. $43-69/S; $45-79/D; $4/ex prsn. 5/1-10/31: $43-64/S; $45-69/D. Discs.

Kingwood

Heldreth Motel & Restaurant/ Rte 26 S, Box 564, Kingwood WV 26537. 304-329-1145/ Fax: 329-1147. V,M,AE, D,DC,CB. I-68 W, Exit 23, 15 mi on Rte 26 S to mtl. I-68 E, Exit 4, 20 mi on Rte 7 E, turn rt on Rte 26 S. Rstrnt/ lounge, cable TV, dd phone, mtg rm, fax, outlets, t/b pkng, b/f. Free local calls. No pets. $27/S; $33/D; $5/ex prsn. Disc: Senior, bsns, TA, govt, l/s, trkr, milt. *Guaranteed rates.*

Lewisburg

Budget Host Fort Savannah Inn/ 204 N Jefferson St, Lewisburg WV 24901. 304-645-3055/ 800-678-3055. V,M,AE, D,DC,CB. 1-1/4 mi S of I-64, Exit 169, dntn. Pool, whrlpool, n/s rms, cable TV, VCR, arpt trans, tt phone, mtg rm, fax, copier, laundry, cot, crib, t/b/rv pkng, conn rms, b/f. AAA/ Mobil. $30-38/S; $38-45/D; $5/ex prsn. 4/1-11/1: $40-50/S; $60/D. 2nd wk Aug: $70-90/S or D. Disc: Senior, bsns, govt, family, milt, AAA, l/s. *Guaranteed rates.*

Martinsburg

Thriftlodge/ 1193 Winchester Av, Martinsburg WV 25401. 304-267-2994/ Fax: 267-2232/ 800-525-9055. V,M, AE,D,DC,CB. I-81, Exit 12, turn rt at 2nd light (US 11 S), 3 blks on rt. Nrby rstrnt/ lounge, pool, n/s rms, cable TV, dd phone, fax, refrig, cot, crib, t/b pkng. Free coffee. No pets. AAA/ Mobil. $30-34/S; $32-40/D; $4/ex prsn. Holidays & Oct wknds: $34-42/S; $36-54/D; $6/ex prsn. Discs: Senior, bsns, govt, trkr, milt, AAA, l/s. *Guaranteed rates.*

Morgantown

Econo Lodge/ 15 Commerce Dr, Morgantown WV 26505. 304-296-8774. M,V,D,AE,DC. I-79 (Exit 152) to US 19, N to mtl. Rstrnt, fax, b/f, cable TV, t pkng, n/s rms. Free local calls. No pets. AAA. $42-44/S; $48-50/D; $5/ex prsn. Discs.

Friendship Inn/ 452 Country Club Rd, Morgantown WV 26505. 304-599-4850. V,M,AE,DC. I-79 (Exit 155) to US 19, S to SR 705, E to University, S to McDonalds, lt 2 blks. Nrby rstrnt, fax, b/f, cable TV, n/s rms. $30-38/S; $35-43/D; $5/ex prsn. Discs.

Parkersburg

Econo Lodge/ I-77 & US 50, Parkersburg WV 26101. 304-422-5401. V,AE,M,DC. I-77 (Exit 176) at US 50. Rstrnt/ lounge, pool, mtg rm, fax, cable TV, n/s rms. No pets. $38-43/S; $41-46/D; $4/ex prsn. 5/1-10/31: $43-49/S; $46-55/D. Spec events: $61-76/S; $66-81/D. Discs.

Princeton

Budget Host Inn/ 1115 Oakvale Rd, Box 5473, Princeton WV 24740. 304-425-8711/ Fax: 487-9785. AE,D,M,V. I-77 & US 460 Service Rd. Cable TV, dd phone, conn rms, picnic area, game rm, t pkng, n/s rms, cot. Free crib. $36/S; $42-48/D; $5/ex prsn. 4/1-9/30: $48/S; $53-58/D. Discs.

Ripley

Econo Lodge/ 1 Hospitality Dr, Ripley WV 25271. 304-372-5000. V,AE,M,DC. I-77 (Exit 138), N on W side of I-77. Bet Charleston & Parkersburg. Nrby rstrnt, fax, cable TV, n/s rms. Free cont brfst, coffee. No pets. AAA. $38-45/S; $41-

48/D; $4/ex prsn. Discs.

Super 8 Motel/ 102 Duke Dr, Ripley WV 25271. 304-372-8880. V,M,D,DC, CB,AE I-77 (Exit 138) to Hwy 33, E 1 blk. Outlets, toast bar, t/b/rv pkng, cable TV, mtg rm, b/f, n/s rms. Free local calls, crib. Pride Award. $38/S; $43-48/D; $5/ex prsn. Higher spec event rates. Discs.

Summersville

Best Western Summersville Lake Motor Lodge/ 1203 S Broad St, Summersville WV 26651. 304-872-6900/ Fax: 872-6908. V,M,AE,D,DC,CB. On US 19, 55 mi N of I-77, 30 mi S of I-79. Rstrnt/ lounge, n/s rms, cable TV, tt phone, fax, copier, nwspr, elevator, t pkng, conn rms. Free cont brfst. AAA/ Mobil. $36/S; $41/D; $5/ex prsn. 4/1-10/31: $41-45/S; $46-50/D. Discs. *Guaranteed rates.*

Comfort Inn/ 903 Industrial Dr N, Summersville WV 26651. 304-872-6500. M,V,D,AE,DC. On US 19, S of jct with SR 41. Rstrnt, pool, mtg rm, fax, b/f, sauna, cable TV, t pkng, exerc equip, n/s rms. Free cont brfst. Hospitality Award. AAA. $40-47/S; $45-52/D; $5/ex prsn. 4/1-4/30, 11/1-12/31: $43-49/S; $48-54/D. 5/1-10/31: $46-59/S; $51-64/D. Discs.

Sleep Inn/ 701 Professional Park Dr, Summersville WV 26651. 304-872-4500. V,M,DC,AE. I-79 (Exit 57) SR 19 S, 30 mi. Nrby rstrnt, mtg rm, fax, b/f, cable TV, t pkng, outlets, n/s rms. Free cont brfst. AAA. $38/S; $43/D; $5/ex prsn. 6/1-11/30: $41-48/S; $46-53/D. Discs.

Teays

Days Inn Teays/ Putnam Village Dr, Teays WV 25569. 304-757-8721/ Fax: 757-0630. AE,M,V,DC,D. I-64 to SR 34, turn N, 1/2 mi. Nrby rstrnt, pool, cable TV, tt phone, mtg rm, fax, copier, cot, crib, eff, conn rms. Free local calls, cont brfst, coffee. AAA. $34-38/S; $40-48/D; $4/ex prsn. Discs. *Guaranteed rates.*

Weston

Comfort Inn/ Box 666, Weston WV 26452. 304-269-7000. M,V,D,AE,DC. I-79 (Exit 99) to US 33 E. Rstrnt/ lounge, pool, fax, cable TV, t pkng, n/s rms. Free cont brfst. $36-44/S; $42-50/D; $5-6/ex prsn. 5/1-10/31: $40-52/S; $48-60/D. Discs.

Super 8 Motel/ 12 Market Pl, Weston WV 26452. 304-269-1086. DC,CB,M, V,AE,D I-79 (Exit 99) at Hwy 33. Toast bar, suite, micro-refrig, mtg rm, TDD, outlets, t/b/rv pkng, cot, b/f, n/s rms. Free local calls, crib. Pride Award. $40-44/S; $46-50/D; $6/ex prsn. Higher spec event rates. Discs.

Wisconsin

Appleton

Exel Inn/ 210 Westhill Blvd, Appleton WI 54914. 414-733-5551/ Fax: 733-7199. AE,V,M,CB,DC,D. US 41, exit to College Av, E 1 blk, turn lt on Westhill Blvd. Nrby rstrnt, cable TV, n/s rms, fax, laundry. Free coffee, cont brfst, crib, local calls. AAA. $35-40/S; $40-49/D; $4/ex prsn. Higher wknd/ spec event rates. Discs.

Roadstar Inn/ 3623 W College Av, Appleton WI 54914. 414-731-5271/ Fax: 731-0227. V,A,AE,D,DC,CB. From Hwy 41, Exit College Av. Nrby rstrnt/ lounge, n/s rms, satellite TV, tt phone, fax, crib, t pkng, eff, conn rms. Free local calls, cont brfst. AAA. $33-39/S; $39-44/D; $6/ex prsn. EAA, Spec events: $65/S or D. Discs.

Ashland

Anderson's Chequamegon Motel/ 2200 W Lakeshore Dr, Ashland WI 54806. 715-682-4658/ 800-727-2776. V,M,D, DC,CB,AE. W edge of Ashland on US Hwy 2. N/s rms, cable TV, VCR movies, tt phone, copier, refrig, microwave, cot, crib, outlets, t/b pkng. Free local calls, coffee. No pets. AAA. $26-40/S; $28-42/D; $4/ex prsn. 6/15-10/15: $42-48/S; $42-49/D. Disc: Senior, bsns, govt, l/s. *Guaranteed rates.*

Ashland Motel/ 2300 W Lakeshore Dr, Ashland WI 54806. 715-682-5503. V,M, AE,D. On Hwy 2 & 13 W. Rstrnt, n/s rms, cable TV, tt/dd phone, nwspr, cot, crib, outlets. Free local calls. AAA/ Mobil. $27-33/S; $31-45/D; $5/ex prsn. 5/15-10/10: $35-45/S; $39-59/D. Disc: Family. *Guaranteed rates.*

Lake Aire Motor Inn/ 104 N Ellis Av, Ashland WI 54806. 715-682-4551. V,M,AE,D,DC. Corner US 2 and WI Hwy 13. Sauna, whrlpool, n/s rms, exerc equip, cable TV, fax, refrig, cot, crib, outlets, t/b/rv pkng, eff, b/f. Free local calls, cont brfst. AAA. $28-50/S; $32-50/D. 5/24-10/4: $45/S; $45-75/D. Disc: Bsns, govt, family, trkr. *Guaranteed rates.*

Baraboo

HoJo Inn/ 750 W Pine, Baraboo WI 53913. 608-356-8366/ Fax: 356-8824. AE,V,M,DC,CB,D. I-90/94 to Exit 92 or Hwy 12 E. Lounge, n/s rms, b/f, pool, exerc equip, mtg rm, refrig, t/b pkng, sauna. Free cont brfst. $32-150/S; $42-175/D. Discs.

Spinning Wheel Motel/ 809 8th St, Baraboo WI 53913. 608-356-3933. V,M,D. 2 mi E of Hwy 12 on Hwy 33. Nrby rstrnt, n/s rms, cable TV, tt/dd phone, cot, crib, conn rms. Free local calls, coffee. AAA/ Mobil. $33-40/S; $35-45/D; $6/ex prsn. 6/9-9/5, 5/24-27: $53/S; $57-63/D. Disc: Senior, trkr, AAA, AARP. *Guaranteed rates.*

Beloit

Econo Lodge/ 2956 Milwaukee Rd, Beloit WI 53511. 608-364-4000. V,M,D,AE. I-90 (Exit 185), I-43 to mtl. Rstrnt/ lounge, pool, mtg rm, fax, b/f, cable TV, t pkng, outlets, laundry, n/s rms. No pets. $33-45/S; $39-51/D; $6/ex prsn. 5/1-10/31: $37-49/S; $43-55/D. Discs.

Super 8 Motel/ 3002 Milwaukee Rd, Beloit WI 53511. 608-365-8680/ Fax: 365-2411. AE,M,V,DC,D,CB. I-90 (Exit 185) at I-43 W. N/s rms, nrby rstrnt, cable TV, mtg rm, cot, crib. Free local calls. Pride Award. $42/S; $47-52/D; $5/ex prsn. Higher spec event rates. Discs.

Black River Falls

Pines Motor Lodge/ Rte 4, Box 297, Black River Falls WI 54615. 715-284-5311/ Fax: 284-7002/ 800-345-PINE. V,M,AE,D. I-94 (Exit 115) at Hwy 12 & 27. Indr pool, sauna, n/s rms, satellite TV, tt phone, mtg rm, fax, copier, cot, crib, outlets, t/rv pkng, conn rms. Free coffee. AAA. $28-36/S; $36-43/D. Disc: Senior, bsns, family, trkr.

American Budget Inn/ 919 Hwy 54 E, Black River Falls WI 54615. 715-284-4333. V,M,AE,D,DC. I-94 at Hwy 54. Pool, whrlpool, sauna, cable TV, n/s rms, conn rms, laundry, t/rv pkng, outlets, game rm. $40-48/S; $46-54/D. Higher spec event rates. Discs.

Brookfield (Milwaukee area)

Motel 6/ 20300 W Bluemound Rd, Brookfield WI 53045. 414-786-7337/ Fax: 789-0510. M,V,DC,D,AE. I-94, Exit 297/ Bluemound Rd, N. Nrby rstrnt, cable TV, laundry, pool, n/s rms. Free local calls. $28-30/S; $34/D; $4-6/ex prsn. Disc.

Cameron

Viking Motel/ 201 S 1st St, Cameron WI 54822. 715-458-2111. V,M. On US Hwy 8, 1-1/2 mi E of Hwy 53. Nrby rstrnt/ lounge, n/s rms, cable TV, tt phone, cot, crib, outlets, t pkng, conn rms. Free local calls. No pets. AAA. $35/S; $40/D; $5/ex prsn. Summer wknds, Holidays, spec events: $40/S; $45/D. Disc: Senior, bsns, trkr.

Camp Douglas

K & K Motel/ 219 Hwys 12 & 16, Camp Douglas WI 54618. 608-427-3100/ Fax: 427-3824. V,M,AE,D,DC,CB. I-90/ 94 (Exit 55) to Hwys 12 & 16, 1/4 mi E. N/s rms, cable TV, tt/dd phone, fax, copier, laundry, refrig, cot, crib, t/b pkng, b/f. Free local calls, coffee. AAA/ Mobil. $30-33/S; $37-43/D; $5/ex prsn. 5/1-9/30: $33-39/S; $38-47/D. Higher spec event, holiday, wknd rates.

Chippewa Falls

Indianhead Motel/ 501 Summit Av, Chippewa Falls WI 54729. 715-723-9171/ Fax: 723-6142. V,M,AE,D,DC, CB. On SR 29 & 124. N/s rms, cable TV, TDD, tt/dd phone, fax, copier, laundry, refrig, microwave, cot, crib, outlets, t pkng, b/f. Free coffee. AAA/ IMA. $33/S; $35-40/D; $5/ex prsn. 6/27-6/30, 7/18-7/21: $47/S; $57/D. Disc: Trkr. *Guaranteed rates.*

Eau Claire

Days Inn/ 6319 Truax Ln, Eau Claire WI 54703. 715-874-5550/ Fax: 874-6101. V,M,AE,D,DC. Jct Hwy 12 & I-94, Exit 59. Fax, n/s rms, nrby rstrnt, b/f, t pkng, cable TV, laundry, VCR/ movies, cot. Free cont brfst, local calls, crib. $42-52/S; $47-57/D; $10/ex prsn. Discs.

Exel Inn/ 2305 Craig Rd, Eau Claire WI 54701. 715-834-3193/ Fax: 839-9905. AE,V,M,CB,DC,D. I-94 to Hwy 37; N to Craig Rd, lt 2 blks. Nrby rstrnt, n/s rms, cable TV, fax, laundry, t pkng, outlets. Free coffee, cont brfst, crib, local calls. AAA. $32-38/S; $38-44/D; $4/ex prsn. Higher wknd/ spec event rates. Discs.

Roadstar Inn/ 1151 MacArthur Rd, Eau Claire WI 54701. 715-832-9731/ Fax: 832-0690. V,M,AE,D,DC,CB. I-94, Exit Hwy 37. Nrby rstrnt/ lounge, n/s rms, satellite TV, tt phone, fax, crib, conn rms. Free local calls, cont brfst. AAA. $30-37/S; $37-43/D; $7/ex prsn. 5/1-10/31 wknds: $35-42/S; $42-48/D. Music Festivals: $60/S or D. Discs.

Fond du Lac

Friendship Inn/ 649 W Johnson St, Fond du Lac WI 54935. 414-923-2020. V,AE,M,DC. US 41 to SR 23, E 3 blks. Nrby rstrnt, indr pool, fax, whrlpool, cable TV, t pkng, outlets, n/s rms. Free cont brfst. No pets. Hospitality Award. AAA. $34-49/S; $40-54/D; $5/ex prsn. 5/26-9/2: $39-49/S; $44-54/D. Discs.

Motel 6/ 738 W Johnson St, Fond du Lac WI 54935. 414-923-0678/ Fax: 923-0915. M,V,DC,D,AE. US 41 at SR 23 (Johnson St) turnoff, turn E. Rstrnt, cable TV, pool, n/s rms. Free local calls. $24/S; $30/D; $6/ex prsn. Higher spec event rates. Disc.

Northway Motel/ 301 S Pioneer Rd, Fond du Lac WI 54935. 414-921-7975/ Fax: 921-7983. V,M,AE,D. E Frontage Rd off Hwy 41, bet Hwy 23 & Hwy 151. Rstrnt, n/s rms, cable TV, tt/dd phone, fax, refrig, microwave, cot, crib, t/b pkng, conn rms. Free local calls, coffee. No pets. AAA/ Mobil. $25-36/S; $36-42/D; $5/ex prsn. Higher spec event, holiday wknd rates. Disc: Senior, bsns, govt, family, trkr, milt, l/s.

Super 8 Motel/ 391 N Pioneer Rd, Fond du Lac WI 54935. 414-922-1088. V,M,DC,CB,AE,D. US 41 to SR 23, exit E Johnson St, N to Pioneer Rd. B/f, n/s rms, outlets, t/b/rv pkng, laundry, cont brfst, cot. Pride Award. $37/S; $42-47/D; $3/ex prsn. 4/1-9/30: $44/S; $49-54/D. Higher spec event rates. Discs.

Glendale (Milwaukee area)

Exel Inn/ 5485 N Port Washington Rd, Glendale WI 53217. 414-961-7272/ Fax: 961-1721. AE,V,M,CB,DC,D. From I-43, exit Silver Spring Dr E, turn S on Port Washington. Nrby rstrnt, cable TV, elevator, n/s rms, fax, laundry. Free coffee, cont brfst, crib, local calls. AAA. $38-44/S; $43-53/D. $4/ex prsn. Higher wknd/ spec event rates. Discs.

Green Bay

Exel Inn/ 2870 Ramada Way, Green Bay WI 54304. 414-499-3599/ Fax: 498-4055. AE,V,M,CB,DC,D. SW side of city. Hwy 41, exit Oneida St. Hwy 43, Exit 172 W to Hwy 41 S, exit Oneida St. Adj rstrnt, cable TV, n/s rms, fax, laundry. Free coffee, cont brfst, crib, local calls. AAA. $37-42/S; $42-51/D; $4/ex prsn. Higher wknd/ spec event rates. Discs.

Motel 6/ 1614 Shawano Av, Green Bay WI 54303. 414-494-6730/ Fax: 494-0474. M,V,DC,D,AE. US 41 to Hwy 29/32 exit, E 1 mi to mtl. Cable TV, pool, n/s rms. Free local calls. $26-28/S; $32/D; $4-6/ex prsn. Disc.

Roadstar Inn/ 1941 True Lane, Green Bay WI 54304. 414-497-2666/ Fax:

WISCONSIN

497-4754. V,M,AE,D,DC,CB. Hwy 41, Exit Lombardi Av. Nrby rstrnt/ lounge, n/s rms, satellite TV, tt phone. AAA. $32-37/S; $38-43/D; $6/ex prsn. 5/1-10/31 wknds: $37-42/S; $43-48/D. Packer games: $70/S; $80/D; $10/ex prsn. Discs.

Hurley

American Budget Inn/ 850 N 10th Av, Hurley WI 54534. 715-561-3500. M,AE,V,D,DC,CB. Hwy 51 (10th Av). Pool, whrlpool, sauna, n/s rms, conn rms, laundry, t/rv pkng, outlets, game rm. AAA. $40-48/S; $46-54/D; $5/ex prsn. Higher wknd/ spec event rates. Discs.

Janesville

Motel 6/ 3907 Milton Av, Janesville WI 53546. 608-756-1742/ Fax: 754-4493. M,V,DC,D,AE. I-90 at SR 26/ Milton Av Exit, turn N, lt on frontage rd to mtl. Cable TV, laundry, n/s rms. Free local calls. $27-29/S; $33-35/D; $6/ex prsn. Disc.

LaCrosse

Exel Inn/ 2150 Rose St, LaCrosse WI 54603. 608-781-0400/ Fax: 781-1216. AE,V,M,CB,DC,D. N side of city. From I-90, exit Hwy 53 S, S 1/2 mi. Nrby rstrnt, cable TV, n/s rms, fax, laundry. Free coffee, cont brfst, crib, local calls. AAA. $32-38/S; $38-44/D; $4/ex prsn. Higher wknd/ spec event rates. Discs.

Roadstar Inn/ 2622 Rose St, LaCrosse WI 54603. 608-781-3070/ Fax: 781-5114. V,M,AE,D,DC,CB. 1 blk S of I-90, Hwy 35 S. N/s rms, satellite TV, tt/dd phone, mtg rm, fax, refrig, crib, outlets, t/b/rv pkng, conn rms. Free local calls, cont brfst, coffee. Mobil. $36-41/S; $42-48/D; $5/ex prsn. Wknds: $41-46/S; $47-53/D. Oktober Fest Wknd: $65/1-4 prsns. Discs. *Guaranteed rates.*

Lake Geneva

Budget Host Diplomat Motel/ 1060 Wells St, Lake Geneva WI 53147. 414-248-1809. M,V,D,AE. Hwy 50 to Wells St, S 1 mi. Satellite TV, dd phone, n/s rms, b/f, pool, picnic area, t pkng. No pets. AAA. $34-41/S; $41-51/D; $10/ex prsn. May-Oct: $41-81/S; $51-101/D. Disc: Senior.

Lancaster

Pine Grove Motel/ 1415 S Madison, Lancaster WI 53813. 608-723-6411. V,M,D. 2 mi N of jct Hwy 61 & Hwy 81, S edge of town. Nrby rstrnt, n/s rms, cable TV, TDD, tt/dd phone, cot, crib, outlets, t/b/rv pkng. Free local calls, coffee. No pets. AAA. $27-44/S; $29-44/D; $4/ex prsn. Disc: Senior, bsns, TA, govt, AAA, l/s, family, trkr, milt. *Guaranteed rates.*

Madison

Budget Host Inn/ 3177 E Washington, Madison WI 53704. 608-249-7667/ Fax: 249-7669. V,M,AE,D,DC,CB. 3 mi S of I-90/94 on Hwy 151. Rstrnt, indr pool, sauna, whrlpool, n/s rms, cable TV, tt/dd phone, fax, cot, crib, outlets, conn rms. Free local calls, cont brfst. No pets. AAA. $34-36/S; $37-41/D; $5/ex prsn. 6/1-10/1: $36-41/S; $37-43/D. Discs. *Guaranteed rates.*

Econo Lodge/ 4726 E Washington Av, Madison WI 53704. 701-572-4242. V,M,D,AE. I-35A & US 151 S, off I-90/94. Nrby rstrnt, cable TV, n/s rms. Free cont brfst. $35-40/S; $40-45/D; $4/ex prsn. Discs.

Edgewood Motel/ 101 W Broadway, Madison WI 53716. 608-222-8601/ Fax: 222-4070/ 800-341-8000. V,M,AE,D. Hwy 12 & 18, Exit Monona Dr. Cable TV, VCR, playgrnd, TDD, tt phone, fax, copier, refrig, microwave, cot, crib, outlets, t pkng. Free local calls, cont brfst, coffee. AAA/ IMA. $33/S; $37-39/D; $2/ex prsn. 10/1-10/5: $38/S; $45/D; $3/ex prsn.

Exel Inn/ 4202 E Towne Blvd, Madison WI 53704. 608-241-3861/ Fax: 241-9752. AE,V,M,CB,DC,D. 1/2 mi S of I-90/94 on US 151. Nrby rstrnt, cable TV, n/s rms, fax, laundry. Free coffee, cont brfst, crib, local calls. AAA. $34-42/S; $42-50/D; $4/ex prsn. Higher wknd/ spec event rates. Discs.

Motel 6/ 1754 Thierer Rd, Madison WI 53704. 608-241-8101/ Fax: 241-0740. DC,M,V,AE,D. I-90/94, Exit 135 to E WA (Hwy 151), SW about 1 mi. Cable TV, laundry, indr pool, n/s rms. Free local calls. $30-32/S; $36-38/D; $6/ex prsn. Disc.

WISCONSIN

Motel 6/ 6402 E Broadway, Madison WI 53704. 608-221-0415/ Fax: 221-0970. M,V,DC,D,AE. I-90, Exit 142B/ Cambridge to US 12/ 18, E 1/4 mi. Cable TV, pool, n/s rms, t pkng. Free local calls. $27/S; $31/D; $4/ex prsn. Disc.

Roadstar Inn West/ 6900 Seybold Rd, Madison WI 53719. 608-274-6900. V,M,AE,D,DC,CB. I-90, take Hwy 12/18 W, Exit Gammon Rd. Nrby rstrnt/ lounge, n/s rms, satellite TV, tt phone, fax, laundry, crib, conn rms. Free local calls, cont brfst. AAA. $36/S; $47/D; $7/ex prsn. Wknds, Feb-Oct: $41/S; $52/D. Spec event, holiday rates: $51/S; $62/D. Discs.

Manitowoc

Westmoor Motel/ 4626 Calumet Av, Manitowoc WI 54220. 414-684-3374/ Fax: 684-9464. V,M,AE,D. Jct I-43 & Hwy 151. Nrby rstrnt, cable TV, dd phone, outlets, t pkng, cot, crib, n/s rms. IMA. $30-32/S; $32-40/D; $5/ex prsn. 5/1-9/30: $36/S; $45-48/D. Disc: Family, senior, comm.

Marinette

Chalet Motel/ 1301 Marinette Av, Marinette WI 54143. 715-735-6687/ Fax: 732-3912. V,M,D,DC,AE,CB. On US 41, 4 blks S of Hwy 64. Nrby rstrnt, n/s rms, cable TV, arpt trans, cot, crib, t pkng, outlets, dd phone.AAA/ IMA. $28/S; $36-44/D; $3/ex prsn. Disc: AAA, senior, family, comm, govt.

Super 8 Motel/ 1508 Marinette Av, Marinette WI 54143. 715-735-7887/ Fax: 735-7455. V,M,DC,CB,AE,D. On Hwy 41, 1/2 mi S of Hwy 64. B/f, n/s rms, whrlpool, sauna, outlets, b/t pkng, mtg rm, copier, cot. Free local calls, crib. $38-41/S; $42-46/D; $4/ex prsn. Discs.

Marshfield

Marshfield Inn/ 116 W Ives, Marshfield WI 54449. 715-387-6381/ 800-851-8669. V,M,AE,D,DC,CB. Jct of N Central Av & Ives St. Nrby rstrnt, whrlpool, n/s rms, satellite TV, tt/dd phone, copier, laundry, cot, crib, b/f. Free local calls, cont brfst, coffee. AAA. $41-48/S; $47-53/D; $5/ex prsn. Disc: Senior, bsns, l/s, govt, milt.

Milwaukee

Exel Inn/ 1201 W College Av, Milwaukee WI 53221. 414-764-1776/ Fax: 762-8009. AE,V,M,CB,DC,D. S side of city. I-94, exit 319, College Av. Adj rstrnt, cable TV, n/s rms, fax, t pkng, laundry. Free coffee, cont brfst, crib, local calls, arpt trans. AAA. $34-41/S; $41-50/D; $4/ex prsn. Higher wknd/ spec event rates. Discs.

Motel 6/ 5037 S Howell Av, Milwaukee WI 53207. 414-482-4414/ Fax: 482-1089. M,V,DC,D,AE. I-94, Exit 318/ Arpt to Hwy 38 (Howell Av), N 1/2 mi. Nrby rstrnt, cable TV, pool, n/s rms, t pkng. Free local calls. $27-30/S; $31-34/D; $4/ex prsn. Disc.

Also see Brookfield, Glendale, Wauwatosa.

Monroe

Alphorn Inn/ 250 N 18th Av, Monroe WI 53566. 608-325-4138/ Fax: 329-4804/ 800-948-1805. V,M,AE,D,DC,CB. Hwy 69 & Hwy 11 Bypass to 18th Av. Nrby rstrnt/ lounge, n/s rms, cable TV, VCR, tt phone, fax. Free local calls, cont brfst. No pets. AAA/ Mobil. $29-40/S; $38-47/D; $3/ex prsn. Disc: Senior, bsns, TA, l/s, family.

Gasthaus Motel/ 685 30th St, Monroe WI 53566. 608-328-8395. V,M,AE,D. On Hwy 69 S, in Monroe. N/s rms, cable TV, VCR/ movies, tt/dd phone, cot, crib, outlets, t/b/rv pkng, conn rms, b/f. Free local calls, coffee. No pets. AAA. $27/S; $31-36/D; $3/ex prsn. Disc: Senior, l/s, family, milt. *Guaranteed rates.*

Nekoosa

Shermalot Motel/ 1148 Queensway, Nekoosa WI 54457. 715-325-2626. V,M,AE,D. 12 mi S of WI Rapids on State Hwy 13. Nrby rstrnt/ lounge, n/s rms, cable TV, dd phone, cot, crib, t/b pkng, conn rms, b/f. Free local calls. AAA/ Mobil. $40/S; $47/D; $5/ex prsn. CLOSED 11/1-3/31. Disc: Senior, l/s. *Guaranteed rates.*

Oconto

Ramada Limited/ 600 Brazeau Av, Oconto WI 54153. 414-834-5559/ Fax: 834-5619. V,M,AE,D,DC. US 41 at

WISCONSIN

Oconto. Indr pool, trans, b/f, n/s rms, whrlpool, cable TV, cot. Free cont brfst, local calls. $40-55/S; $44-60/D; $8/ex prsn. Discs.

Oshkosh

Howard Johnson Lodge/ 1919 Omro Rd, Oshkosh WI 54901. 414-233-1200. V,M,AE,DC,D. Jct US 41 & SR 21, W of US 45. Rstrnt/ lounge, n/s rms, b/f, indr pool, t pkng. Free coffee. $30-60/S; $32-75/D. Discs.

Motel 6/ 1015 S Washburn St, Oshkosh WI 54901. 414-235-0265/ Fax: 235-1664. M,V,DC,D,AE. US 41 at 9th Av. W of 41. Nrby rstrnt, cable TV, pool, n/s rms, t pkng. Free local calls. $25/S; $31/D; $6/ex prsn. Higher spec event rates. Disc.

Super 8 Motel/ Box 3168, Oshkosh WI 54903. 414-426-2885/ Fax: 426-5488. V,M,DC,CB,AE,D. US 41 at Hwy 44. Laundry, outlets, t pkng, cont brfst, trans, copier, cable TV, mtg rm, nwspr, TDD, cot, b/f, n/s rms. Free local calls. Quality Award. AAA. $41/S; $47-51/D; $5/ex prsn. Higher spec event rates. Discs.

Osseo

Budget Host Ten Seven Inn/ 1994 E 10th, Osseo WI 54758. 715-597-3114. V,M,D,AE. I-94 & Hwy 10. Satellite TV, dd phone, b/f, playgrnd, cot, arpt trans, t pkng, outlets. Free crib. AAA. $28-35/S; $33-55/D; $5 ex prsn. Spec events: $55. Discs.

Friendship Inn Alan House/ Box 7, Osseo WI 54758. 715-597-3175/ Fax: Ext 135. V,M,AE,D,DC,CB. At jct I-94 & US 10. Rstrnt/ lounge, indr pool, mtg rm, b/f, cable TV, t pkng, outlets, n/s rms. No pets. AAA. $36-47/S; $46-55/D; $8/ex prsn. Discs.

Pembine

Grand Motel/ Box 67, Pembine WI 54156. 715-324-5417. V,M,D. Jct of Hwys 141 & 8 W. Cable TV, playgrnd, tt/dd phone, copier, refrig, microwave, cot, crib, outlets, t/b pkng, eff, b/f. Free local calls, coffee. AAA/ Mobil. $25-32/S; $30-42/D; $4/ex prsn. Disc: Bsns, trkr, trkr, govt. *Guaranteed rates.*

Portage

Days Inn/ N 5800 Kinney Rd, Portage WI 53901. 608-742-1554/ Fax: 742-1725. V,M,AE,D,DC. I-90/94 at SR 78 S. Fax, n/s rms, nrby rstrnt, whrlpool, exerc equip, t pkng, cot. Free cont brfst. AAA. $35-80/S; $45-75/D; $5/ex prsn. Discs.

Prairie du Sac

Skyview Motel/ S 9645 US Hwy 12, Prairie du Sac WI 53578. 608-643-4344. V,M,AE,D. US Hwy 12 jct PF. Satellite TV, dd phone, outlets, playgrnd, fax, t pkng, nrby rstrnt, cot, crib, n/s rms. AAA/ IMA. $28/S; $34-38/D; $5/ex prsn. 5/12-9/24, 11/21-11/30: $37/S; $42-50/D. Disc: Family, senior, TA.

Prentice

Countryside Motel/ Box 286, Prentice WI 54556. 715-428-2333/ Fax: 428-2349. V,M,AE,D,DC. 2 blks E of Hwy 13, turn S on Granberg Rd. Nrby rstrnt, n/s rms, satellite TV, VCR, tt phone, fax, copier, refrig, microwave, cot, outlets, t/b/rv pkng, b/f. Free local calls, coffee. AAA. $34/S; $40/D; $6/ex prsn. Disc: Trkr.

Racine

Rodeway Inn/ 910 S Sylvania Av, Racine WI 53172. 414-886-0385. M,V,D,AE,DC. I-94 (Exit 333) to SR 20, W to Frontage Rd, lt 1000 ft to mtl. Nrby rstrnt, indr pool, whrlpool, cable TV, n/s rms. Free cont brfst. $39-75/S; $44-80/D; $5/ex prsn. Discs.

Reedsburg

Copper Springs Motel/ E 7278 Hwy 23/33, Reedsburg WI 53959. 608-524-4312/ Fax: 524-9767. V,M,AE,D. On Hwy 23/33. Nrby rstrnt, picnic area, crib, n/s rms, dd phone, arpt trans, outlets. Free coffee. AAA/ IMA. $29/S; $35-42/D; $5/ex prsn. 6/1-9/15: $33/S; $39-48/D. Disc: AAA, senior, family.

Super 8 Motel/ 1470 E Main St, Reedsburg WI 53959. 608-524-2888/ Fax: 524-9658. V,M,AE,D,DC,CB. SR 23 & 33, across from Viking Village. Whrlpool, laundry, outlets, t/v/rv pkng, cont brfst, copier, cable TV, cot, crib, b/f, n/s rms, pool. Free local calls. Pride Award. $40/S; $45-55/D; $5/ex

WISCONSIN

prsn. Higher spec event rates. Discs.

Rice Lake
Currier's Lakeview Resort Motel/ 2010 E Sawyer St, Rice Lake WI 54868. 715-234-7474/ 800-433-5253. V,M, AE,D. I-53, Exit 140, rt 1 mi to Cnty Rd "SS," lt 1-1/2 mi to Sawyer. N/s rms, cable TV, playgrnd, tt phone, refrig, cot, crib, outlets, eff, lake, boat rental. Free local calls, cont brfst. AAA/ Mobil. $32-39/S; $39-44/D; $4/ex prsn. 5/19-9/5: $39-49/S; $48-55/D. Spec event, holiday, wknd rates: $69/S; $69-75/D.

River Falls
Best Western Motor Inn/ 708 N Main St, River Falls WI 54022. 715-425-6707/ Fax: 425-6464. V,M. E on I-94, Exit 3 on WI 35, 8 mi S to River Falls Exit. I-94 W, Exit 10 on WI 65, 9 mi S. Nrby rstrnt/ lounge, n/s rms, cable TV, dd phone, fax, microwave, cot, outlets. Free local calls, cont brfst. No pets. $48/S; $48-60/D; $5/ex prsn. Discs.

Saint Croix Falls
Dalles House Motel/ 728 Vincent S, Box 664, St Croix Falls WI 54024. 715-483-3206/ Fax: 483-3207. V,M,AE, D,CB. Jct US hwy 8 & WI 35 S. Rstrnt/ lounge, indr pool, cable TV, dd phone, laundry, outlets, sauna, tanning salon, cot, crib. IMA. $46/S; $46-53/D; $5/ex prsn. Disc: TA, comm, govt.

Sheboygan
Parkway Motel/ 3900 Motel Rd, Sheboygan WI 53081. 414-458-8338/ Fax: 459-7470. V,M,AE,D,DC,CB. I-43 Country Trunk V & OK Exit 120. Satellite TV, tt/dd phone, fax, copier, refrig, cot, crib, outlets, t/b/rv pkng, eff, b/f. Free local calls, coffee. AAA/ Mobil/ IMA. $36-41/S or D; $3/ex prsn. 6/1-9/30: $41-45/S or D. Some summer wknds $10 higher. Disc: Bsns, family, trkr, AAA.

Ramada Inn Harbor Centre/ 724 Center Av, Sheboygan WI 53081. 414-458-1400/ Fax: 458-6767. V,M,AE,D,DC. I-43 (Exit 126) to Hwy 23E, E to 8th St, S to Center Av. Trans, b/f, n/s rms, rstrnt/ lounge, mtg rm. Free cont brfst. $42-65/S or D; $6/ex prsn. Higher spec event rates. Discs.

Super 8 Motel/ 3402 Wilgus Rd, Sheboygan WI 53081. 414-458-8080/ Fax: 458-8013. V,M,DC,CB,AE,D. I-43 (Exit 126) to 23E (Kohler Dr), E to Taylor Dr, lt to Wilgus, lt. Cable TV, mtg rm, cot, crib, b/f, n/s rms, fish freezer. Free local calls. Pride Award. $36/S; $41-46/D; $4/ex prsn. 3/1-11/30: $40/S; $45-48/D. Higher spec event rates. Discs.

Shell Lake
Aqua Vista Resort Motel/ Hwy 63 & Co Rd B, Shell Lake WI 54871. 715-468-2256/ 800-889-2256. V,M,AE,D. Hwy 53 to County Rd B, W 4-1/2 mi. N/s rms, cable TV, VCR, arpt trans, tt/dd phone, copier, refrig, microwave, cot, crib, outlets, b pkng, eff. Free local calls. No pets. AAA. $30/S; $34-39/D; $3/ex prsn. 5/24-9/9: $45/S; $45-50/D. Spec events, summer wknds: $55/S; $55-59/D. Disc: Bsns, govt. *Guaranteed rates.*

Sparta
Best Nights Inn/ 303 W Wisconsin St, Sparta WI 54656. 608-269-3066/ Fax: 269-3175. V,M,AE,D,DC,CB. I-90, Exit 25, 1/2 mi into town, at stoplight go rt, 5 blks. N/s rms, satellite TV, tt/dd phone, fax, copier, refrig, microwave, cot, crib, outlets, t/b/rv pkng, eff. Free local calls, cont brfst. AAA/ Mobil. $35-38/S; $38-48/D; $7/ex prsn. 5/20-10/15: $69-72/S; $69-79/D. Spec event, holiday wknd rates: $79-89/S or D. Disc: Senior, bsns, govt, family, trkr, milt, l/s.

Stevens Point
Budgetel Inns/ 4917 Main St, Stevens Point WI 54481. 715-344-1900/ Fax: 344-1254. V,M,D,AE,DC,CB. US 51, Exit 158 onto US 10, W to Country Club Dr. From US 10, S on Country Club Dr. N/s rms, b/f, fax, pool. Free cont brfst, in-rm coffee, local calls. AAA. $35/S; $42/D. 5/24-9/2: $39-48/S; $46-55/D. 9/3-12/31: $35-44/S; $42-51/D. Higher spec event rates.

Point Motel/ 209 Division St, Stevens Point WI 54481. 715-344-8312/ 800-344-3093. V,M,D,DC,AE,CB. Bsns 51 N, Exit 161 to 2nd stoplight. Nrby rstrnt/ lounge, n/s rms, cable TV, playgrnd, tt/dd phone, mtg rm, cot, crib, outlets, conn rms. Free local calls, cont brfst.

WISCONSIN

AAA/ Mobil. $36-38/S; $42-44/D; $2-4/ex prsn. Disc: Senior, l/s, bsns, trkr.

Roadstar Inn/ 159 N Division St, Stevens Point WI 54881. 715-341-9090. V,M,AE,D,DC,CB. Hwy 51 to Bsns 51, near Perkins Rstrnt. Nrby rstrnt/ lounge, n/s rms, satellite TV, tt phone. AAA. $33-36/S; $36-39/D; $3/ex prsn. Wknds: $38-41/S; $41-44/D. Discs.

Traveler Motel/ 3350 Church St, Stevens Point WI 54481. 715-344-6455. V,M,AE,D. Bsns 51 S. Cable TV, outlets, conn rms, n/s rms, cot, crib. AAA/ IMA. $28/S; $30-33/D; $4/ex prsn. 5/1-10/31: $34/S; $37-41/D. Disc: AAA, senior, AARP, TA, comm, family.

Sturgeon Bay

Comfort Inn/ 923 Greenbay Rd, Sturgeon Bay WI 54235. 414-743-7846. M,V,D,AE,DC. Jct SR 42, SR 57 & County Rd S. Nrby rstrnt, indr pool, fax, b/f, whrlpool, cable TV, t pkng, outlets, n/s rms. Free cont brfst. $35-53/S; $42-61/D; $7/ex prsn. 5/1-6/30: $53-71/S; $60-79/D. 7/1-9/4: $79-97/S; $86-104/D. 9/5-10/31: $59-77/S; $66-85/D. Discs.

Tomah

Budget Host Daybreak Motel/ Hwy 12 & 16 E, Tomah WI 54660. 608-372-5946/ Fax: 372-5947. AE,M,V,CB,DC,D. I-90/ I-94, 3 exits. Satellite TV, dd phone, n/s rms, mtg rms, b/f, fax, nrby rstrnt, arpt trans, cot, crib, t pkng, outlets. AAA/ Mobil. $30-36/S; $40-48/D; $5/ex prsn. 5/16-10/15 Sun-Thur: $32-36/S; $45-53/D. 5/16-10/15 Fri-Sat: $48/S; $48-58/D. Discs.

Econo Lodge/ 2005 N Superior, Tomah WI 54660. 608-372-9100. V,AE,M,DC. I-94 (Exit 143) at US 12 & SR 21. Nrby rstrnt, indr pool, fax, whrlpool, cable TV, t pkng, outlets, n/s rms. Free cont brfst. AAA. $41-52/S; $44-57/D; $5/ex prsn. 5/1-9/14: $41-56/S; $44-61/D. Discs.

HoJo Inn/ I-90 & Hwy 131, Tomah WI 54660. 608-372-4500. AE,V,M,DC, CB,D. I-90 & Hwy 131, Exit 41. Cable TV, n/s rms, b/f, t/b pkng. Free local calls, cont brfst. Gold Medal Winner. $33-48/S; $40-50/D. 6/2-9/15: $39-50/S; $46-60/D. Discs.

Park Motel/ 1515 Kilbourn Av, Tomah WI 54660. 608-372-4655. V,M,D. 1 mi N of I-90, Exit 43, or 3-1/2 mi S of I-94, Exit 143. Nrby rstrnt/ lounge, n/s rms, cable TV, cot, crib, outlets. AAA. $28/S; $32-38/D; $4/ex prsn. 5/15-10/15: $32-42/S; $36-52/D. Disc: Senior. *Guaranteed rates.*

Waukesha

Comfort Inn/ 2111 E Moreland Blvd, Waukesha WI 53186. 414-547-7770. M,V,D,AE,DC. I-94 (Exit 297) to US 18, W 3/4 mi to mtl. Nrby rstrnt, mtg rm, fax, b/f, sauna, whrlpool, cable TV, exerc equip, outlets, n/s rms. Free cont brfst. No pets. $35-49/S; $39-53/D; $6/ex prsn. 7/1-8/31: $45-70/S; $50-76/D. 9/1-10/31: $37-49/S; $41-53/D. Discs.

Wausau

Budgetel Inns/ 1910 Stewart Av, Wausau WI 54401. 715-842-0421/ Fax: 845-5096. V,M,D,AE,DC,CB. US 51, Exit 192 E to Stewart Av. N/s rms, b/f, fax, rstrnt, pool. Free cont brfst, in-rm coffee, local calls. AAA. $35/S; $42/D. 5/24-9/2: $41-45/S/ $48-52/D. 9/3-43/S; $46-50/D. Higher spec event rates. Discs.

Exel Inn/ 116 S 17th Av, Wausau WI 54401. 715-842-0641/ Fax: 848-1356. AE,V,M,CB,DC,D. W side of city. Hwy 51 Nbnd, Exit Hwy 52 E, lt at 17th Av. Hwy 51 Sbnd, exit lt on Bridge St, rt on 17th Av. Nrby rstrnt, cable TV, n/s rms, fax. Free coffee, cont brfst, crib, local calls. AAA. $34-41/S; $41-50/D; $4/ex prsn. Higher wknd/ spec event rates. Discs.

Marlene Motel/ 2010 Stewart Av, Wausau WI 54401. 715-845-6248/ Fax: 842-7419/ Reserv: 800-835-0180. V,M,AE,D. Hwy 51, Exit 192, 3 blks. Nrby rstrnt/ lounge, cable TV, tt/dd phone, fax, nwspr, refrig, cot, crib, outlets, t/b pkng, conn rms. Free coffee. AAA. $30/S; $33-36/D; $3/ex prsn.

Wautoma

Super 8 Motel/ Box 578, Wautoma WI 54982. 414-787-4811/ Fax: 787-4305. AE,M,V,DC,D,CB. US 21 & 73 E. Cont brfst, whrlpool, sauna, mtg rm, cable

WISCONSIN / WYOMING

TV, t pkng, b/f, n/s rms, pool. Free local calls. Quality Award. $40/S; $45-50/D; $5/ex prsn. 6/1-9/30: $45/S; $50-52/D. Higher spec event, wknd rates. Discs.

Wauwatosa (Milwaukee area)

Exel Inn/ 115 N Mayfair Rd, Wauwatosa WI 53226. 414-257-0140/ Fax: 475-7875. AE,V,M,CB,DC,D. From I-94, exit 304B/ Hwy 100 N/ Mayfair Rd. Nrby rstrnt, cable TV, n/s rms, fax, laundry. Free coffee, cont brfst, crib, local calls. AAA. $36-46/S; $41-51/D; $4/ex prsn. Higher wknd/ spec event rates. Discs.

Westfield

Westfield Pioneer Motor Inn/ 242 Pioneer Rd, Westfield WI 53964. 608-296-2135/ Fax: 296-3933. V,M,AE,D. Hwy 51, Exit 113 to Frontage Rd N, 1 blk. Whrlpool, n/s rms, exerc equip, cable TV, VCR/ movies, games, TDD, mtg rm, fax, copier, cot, crib, outlets, t/b/rv pkng, b/f. Free local calls, coffee. No pets. AAA. $36-41/S; $41-46/D; $5/ex prsn. 5/1-9/30: $41-44/S; $46-49/D. Disc: Senior, bsns, govt, family, trkr, l/s.

Wisconsin Dells

Days End Motel/ N604 Hwy 12-16, Wisconsin Dells WI 53965. 608-254-8171. V,M,AE,D,DC. I-90/ 94 (Exit 85), 1 mi W on Hwy 12-16. Pool, n/s rms, playgrnd, dd phone, refrig, microwave, cot, crib, outlets, t/b pkng, conn rms, b/f. Free coffee. No pets. AAA/ IMA. $28-49/S or D; $5/ex prsn. 6/14-9/1: $45-80/S or D. Spec event, holiday, wknd rates: $33-54/S or D. *Guaranteed rates.*

Comfort Inn/ 703 Frontage Rd N, Wisconsin Dells WI 53965. 608-253-3711. M,V,D,AE,DC. I-90/ I-94 (Exit 87) to SR 13, E to mtl. Nrby rstrnt, indr pool, fax, b/f, whrlpool, cable TV, t pkng, n/s rms. Free cont brfst. No pets. AAA. $41-67/S; $47-67/D; $6/ex prsn. 7/1-9/5: $79-99/S; $85-99/D. Discs.

Days Inn/ 944 Hwys 12 & 13, Box 381, Wisconsin Dells WI 53965. 608-254-6444/ Fax: Ext 106. V,M,AE,D,DC,CB. I-94, Exit 87, straight to 2nd light, turn lt. Pool, indr pool, sauna, whrlpool, n/s rms, cable TV, games, mtg rm, fax, copier, refrig, cot, crib, t/b/rv pkng, eff, b/f. Free local calls, cont brfst. No pets. $44/S; $48/D; $5-10/ex prsn. 5/1-9/25: $77-90/S or D. 5/24-5/27: $78-82/S; $82-87/D. 6/28-7/6: $85-95/S; $105-135/D. Discs. *Guaranteed rates.*

Wisconsin Rapids

Econo Lodge/ 3300 8th St S, Wisconsin Rapids WI 54494. 715-423-7000. M,V,D,AE,DC. On SR 13 in central Wisconsin. Rstrnt, mtg rm, b/f, cable TV, n/s rms. No pets. $38-43/S; $44-50/D; $3/ex prsn. Discs.

Wyoming

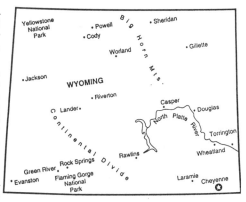

Afton

Corral Motel/ 161 Washington, Box 442, Afton WY 83110. 307-886-5424. V,M,AE,D,DC,CB. On Hwy 89. Log cabins, cable TV, tt phone, cot, crib, eff, conn rms. AAA/ Mobil. $30-34/S; $34-42/D; $5/ex prsn. CLOSED NOV THRU MAR.

Buffalo

Canyon Motel/ 997 Fort St, Box 56, Buffalo WY 82834. 307-684-2267/ 800-231-0742. V,M,AE,D. I-90 or I-25, Exit Hwy 16 W (Buffalo), 2 mi. Cable TV, playgrnd, arpt trans, tt phone, refrig, cot, crib, outlets, t/b/rv pkng, eff, conn rms, b/f. Free local calls, coffee. AAA/ Mobil. $20/S; $24-28/D; $3/ex prsn. 5/1-10/31: $32/S; $35-44/D. Disc: Senior, family, l/s. *Guaranteed rates.*

Comfort Inn/ 65 US 16 E, Buffalo WY 82834. 307-684-9564. V,M,AE,DC. I-90 (Exit 58) to US 16, W 1 mi to mtl. I-25 (Exit 299), US 16, E 1 blk to mtl. Nrby

WYOMING

rstrnt, b/f, whrlpool, cable TV, n/s rms. Free cont brfst. $19-59/S; $24-64/D; $5/ex prsn. 5/1-6/15, 8/21-10/31: $29-79/S; $34-89/D. 6/16-8/20: $59-99/S; $64-99/D. Discs.

Crossroads Inn/ 75 N By-Pass, Buffalo WY 82834. 307-684-2256/ 800-852-2302. I-25, Exit 299, W on US 16. I-90, Exit 58, 1/4 mi W. Rstrnt/ lounge, pool, n/s rms, cable TV, TDD, tt phone, mtg rm, fax, copier, cot, crib, outlets, t/b pkng, b/f. AAA. $30-40/S or D; $6/ex prsn. 4/16-5/31, 9/1-11/30: $40-52/S or D. 6/1-6/30, 7/1-8/31: $53-63/S; $63-78/D. Disc: Senior, bsns.

Econo Lodge/ 333 Hart St, Buffalo WY 82834. 307-684-2219. AE,M,DC,V. I-25 to US 16, W to mtl. Nrby rstrnt, b/f, cable TV, t pkng, outlets, n/s rms. AAA. $31/S; $35-37/D; $5/ex prsn. 5/1-9/10: $50-70/S; $55-70/D. 9/11-10/31: $39-55/S; $43-55/D. Discs.

Casper

1st Interstate Inn/ Box 9047, Hilltop Station, Casper WY 82609. 307-234-9125. V,M,AE,D,DC. 20 SE WY Blvd. Nrby rstrnt, cable TV, dd phone, outlets, laundry, cot, crib, conn rms, n/s rms. AAA. $29/S; $34/D; $2/ex prsn. 5/1-10/31: $36/S; $41-43/D. Spec events: $40/S; $45/D; $5/ex prsn. Disc: Comm, senior, TA, family.

AAA Westridge Motel/ 955 Cy Av & S Poplar St, Casper WY 82601. 307-234-8911/ 800-356-6268. V,M,AE,D, DC,CB. I-25, Exit 188B, 1.7 mi. Rstrnt, nrby lounge, n/s rms, cable TV, playgrnd, arpt trans, tt/dd phone, cot, crib, t/b pkng, conn rms. AAA. $38/S; $38-42/D; $4/ex prsn. 5/1-10/1: $42/S; $43-48/D; $4/ex prsn. Disc: Senior, bsns, TA, govt, family, trkr, milt, l/s.

Kelly Inn/ 821 N Poplar, Casper WY 82601. 307-266-2400/ Fax: 266-1146. V,M,AE,D,DC,ER. I-25 at N Poplar, 1/4 mi from Casper Events Center. Adj rstrnt, cable TV, dd phone, arpt trans, outlets, whrlpool, sauna, b/f, n/s rms, cot, crib, laundry. AAA/ IMA. $38-43/S; $43-50/D; $5/ex prsn. Disc: AAA, senior, TA, comm, govt, family.

Motel 6/ 1150 Wilkins Circle, Casper WY 82601. 307-234-3903/ Fax: 234-8359. M,V,DC,D,AE. I-25, Exit 188B to N Poplar, N 1/2 mi to Wilkins Circle, lt to mtl. Cable TV, laundry, pool, n/s rms, t pkng. Free local calls. $27/S; $33/D; $6/ex prsn. Disc.

National 9 Inn Showboat/ 100 W "F" St, Casper WY 82601. 307-235-2711. V,M,AE,DC. I-25, Exit Center St. Cable TV, dd phone, adj rstrnt, VCR, fax, cont brfst. AAA. $29-34/S; $34-45/D; $5/ex prsn.

Super 8 Motel/ 3838 Cy Av, Casper WY 82604. 307-266-3480. V,M,D,DC, CB,AE On Hwy 220 (Cy Av) SW of I-25 (Nbnd, Exit 185, Sbnd, Exit 188B). B/f, n/s rms, laundry, outlets, cont brfst, t/b/rv pkng, suite, mtg rm. Free local calls. Pride Award. $33-35/S; $39-45/D; $4/ex prsn. 5/1-11/1: $38/S; $46/D. Discs.

Cheyenne

Comfort Inn/ 2245 Etchepare Dr, Cheyenne WY 82007. 307-638-7202. V,M,AE,DC. I-80 to I-25, S to College Dr (Exit 7), turn W. Rstrnt, pool, mtg rm, fax, b/f, cable TV, t pkng, n/s rms. Free cont brfst. $40-46/S; $40-50/D; $5/ex prsn. 5/1-7/20, 7/31-9/30: $44-50/S; $49-55/D. 7/21-7/30: $160-180/S or D. Discs.

Days Inn/ 2360 Lincolnway, Cheyenne WY 82001. 307-778-8877/ Fax: 778-8697. V,M,AE,D,DC. I-25 & us 30. Fax, n/s rms, nrby rstrnt, whrlpool, b/f, exerc equip, t pkng, sauna, hot tub. Free cont brfst. $36-49/S; $39-54/D; $5/ex prsn. Discs.

Luxury Inn/ 1805 Westland Rd, Cheyenne WY 82001. 307-638-2550/ Fax: 778-8113. V,M,AE,D,DC,CB. I-25, Exit 10 (Missile Dr) Ebnd, 1st st to rt. Indr pool, whrlpool, n/s rms, exerc equip, cable TV, fax, copier, cot, crib, t/b/rv pkng, b/f. Free local calls, cont brfst. No pets. AAA. $41/S; $47/D. 11/1-11/30: $36/S; $38/D. 12/1-2/29: $27/S; $30/D. Frontier Days: $111/S or D; $10/ex prsn. *Guaranteed rates.*

Motel 6/ 1735 Westland Rd, Cheyenne WY 82001. 307-635-6806/ Fax: 638-3017. M,V,DC,D,AE. I-25 (Exit 9) at W Lincolnway, E 1 mi to Westland Rd, lt to mtl. Cable TV, laundry, pool, n/s rms, t pkng. Free local calls. $27-36/S; $33-

WYOMING

42/D; $6/ex prsn. Higher spec event rates. Disc.

Quality Inn/ 5401 Walker Rd, Cheyenne WY 82001. 307-632-8901. V,M,DC,AE. I-25 (Exit 12) at Central Av to mtl. Rstrnt/ lounge, pool, fax, b/f, cable TV, t pkng, n/s rms. $29-36/S; $35-42/D; $5/ex prsn. 6/16-9/30: $32-42/S; $39-48/D. Discs.

Ramada Ltd/ 2512 W Lincolnway, Cheyenne WY 82001. 307-632-7556/ Fax: 635-9141. V,M,AE,D,DC,CB. I-25, Exit 9 to W Lincolnway. I-80, take Casper exit to I-25. Indr pool, hot tub, n/s rms, cable TV, arpt trans, copier, refrig, microwave, cot, crib, outlets, t/b/rv pkng, b/f. Free local calls, cont brfst. No pets. AAA. $33-39/S; $40-48/D; $6/ex prsn. 6/1-9/30: $43/S; $66/D. Disc: Senior, bsns, govt, family, trkr, milt. *Guaranteed rates.*

Cody

Trout Creek Inn/ Northfork Rte, Cody WY 82414. 307-587-6288. M,V,D,AE. Just W of Buffalo Bill Reservoir, 12 mi W of Cody on US Hwys 14, 16 & 20, 30 miles E of Yellowstone Pk. Pool, n/s rms, satellite TV, VCR/ movies, playgrnd, arpt trans, tt/dd phone, mtg rm, copier, laundry, refrig, microwave, cot, crib, ranch brfst, outlets, t/b/rv pkng, eff, b/f, private pond, river. Free cont brfst. IMA. $34/S; $38-42/D; $4-8/ex prsn. 5/1-6/14, 8/21-10/20: $44/S; $48/D; $8/ex prsn. 6/15-8/20: $59/S; $53-38/D. Disc: Senior, bsns, TA, govt, family, trkr, milt, l/s.

Comfort Inn/ 1601 Sheridan Ave, Cody WY 82414. 307-587-5556. V,M,AE,DC. Jct US 14, 14A, 16, 20 & SR 120. Rstrnt/ lounge, pool, mtg rm, fax, cable TV, t pkng, outlets, trans, n/s rms. No pets. AAA. $36-60/S; $40-65/D; $6/ex prsn. 5/1-5/31: $36-75/S; $40-80/D. 6/1-8/31: $75-115/S; $85-125/D. 9/1-9/30: $50-85/S; $55-90/D. Discs.

Holiday Motel/ 1807 Sheridan Av, Cody WY 82414. 307-587-4258/ Fax: 527-6990. V,M,AE,D. One blk from main hwy. Nrby rstrnt/ lounge, cable TV, dd phone, arpt trans, laundry, outlets, n/s rms, cot, crib. AAA/ IMA. $24-27/S; $27-38/D; $3/ex prsn. 6/8-8/24: $39/S; $42-52/D. Disc: Senior.

Rainbow Park Motel/ 1136 17th St, Cody WY 82414. 307-587-6251. V,M,AE,D,CB,D. On Hwy 14, 16, 20 & 120, 3 blks from dntn. Rstrnt/ lounge, cable TV, dd phone, outlets, playgrnd, laundry, cot, crib, n/s rms, kitchenettes. AAA/ IMA. $25/S; $28-32/D; $3/ex prsn. 6/10-8/31: $39/S; $42-56/D. 9/1-10/31: $31/S; $34-40/D.

Diamondville

Energy Inn Motel/ Box 494, Diamondville WY 83116. 307-877-6901. V,M,AE,D,DC,CB. At jct Hwys 30 & 189. Nrby rstrnt/ lounge, n/s rms, cable TV, TDD, tt/dd phone, fax, copier, refrig, microwave, cot, crib, t/b/rv pkng, eff, b/f. Free local calls, coffee. AAA/ Mobil. $34/S; $42/D; $8/ex prsn. *Guaranteed rates.*

Douglas

1st Interstate Inn/ 2349 E Richards, Box 151, Douglas WY 82633. 307-358-2833. V,M,AE,D,DC. I-25 & Hwy 59, Exit 135. Nrby rstrnt, lounge, cable TV, dd phone, arpt trans, outlets, laundry, cot, crib, conn rms, n/s rms. AAA. $29/S; $34/D; $2/ex prsn. 4/30-10/31: $34/S; $39-41/D. Spec event rates: $39/S; $44/D; $5/ex prsn. Disc: Family, senior, TA, comm.

Chieftain Motel/ 815 Richards St, Douglas WY 82633. 307-358-2673. V,M,AE,D,DC,CB. I-25: Nbnd, Exit 135; Sbnd, Exit 140. 1 mi from I-25. N/s rms, cable TV, arpt trans, tt/dd phone, refrig, crib, t pkng. AAA. $31/S; $36-42/D; $5/ex prsn. 5/1-8/9, 8/20-10/31: $34/S; $43-48/D. Disc: Senior, bsns, family, trkr, l/s. *Guaranteed rates.*

Dubois

Black Bear Country Inn/ 505 W Ramshorn, Box 595, Dubois WY 82513. 307-455-2344/ 800-873-BEAR. V,M, AE,D,DC,CB. Gateway to Teton & Yellowstone National Parks. Nrby rstrnt/ lounge, n/s rms, cable TV, playgrnd, arpt trans, tt phone, mtg rm, copier, refrig, microwave, cot, crib, t/b/rv pkng, conn rms. Free local calls, coffee. AAA. $30-50/S; $32-55/D. Disc: L/s.

Branding Iron Motel/ 401 W Ramshorn, Box 705, Dubois WY 82513. 307-455-2893/ Fax: 455-2446. V,M,AE,D,CB,

WYOMING

DC. Hwy 26 & 287. Cable TV, dd phone, outlets, t pkng, nrby rstrnt, cot, crib, n/s rms, conn rms, kitchenettes. AAA/ IMA. $26-30/S; $32-41/D; $4/ex prsn.

Stagecoach Motor Inn/ 103 Ramshorn St, Box 216, Dubois WY 82513. 307-455-2303/ Fax: 455-3903/ 800-455-5090. V,M,AE,D,DC. Pool, n/s rms, cable TV, arpt trans, tt/dd phone, fax, copier, refrig, cot, crib, outlets, t/b pkng, b/f. Free local calls, coffee. AAA. $30-34/S; $38-46/D; $5/ex prsn. 5/1-9/30: $34-38/S; $44-54/D. *Guaranteed rates.*

Evanston

Whirl Inn Motel/ 1724 Harrison Dr, Evanston WY 82930. 307-789-9610/ 800-621-9610. V,M,AE,DC. 1 blk off Wbnd Exit 3, 4 blks off Ebnd Exit 3. Cable TV, dd phone, conn rms. No pets. AAA/ National 9. $20-27/S; $27-35/D; $4/ex prsn. $46/suite.

Gillette

Motel 6/ 2105 Rodgers Dr, Gillette WY 82716. 307-686-8600/ Fax: 682-1938. M,V,DC,D,AE. I-90 at Exit 124/ US Hwy 14/16. N 1 blk to Rodgers, W 1 blk. Nrby rstrnt, cable TV, laundry, n/s rms, t pkng, indr whrlpool, sauna. Free local calls. Premier Award. $26/S; $30/D; $4/ex prsn. 5/23-12/20: $37/S; $43/D; $6/ex prsn. Disc.

National 9 Inn/ 1020 E Hwy 14-16, Gillette WY 82716. 307-628-5111. V,M,AE,DC. 1/4 mi W of Jct I-90, Exit 128. Rstrnt, pool, fax, sauna, lounge, cable TV. AAA. $36-49/S; $39-57/D; $5/ex prsn.

Jackson

Elk Refuge Inn/ Box 2834, Jackson WY 83001. 307-733-3582/ 800-544-3582. V,M,AE. 1 1/2 mi N of Jackson on Hwy 89, across from National Elk Refuge. N/s rms, cable TV, tt/dd phone, nwspr, refrig, outlets, t pkng, eff. Free local calls, coffee. No pets. AAA. $46-62/S; $48-62/D; $5/ex prsn. 5/1-6/14, 9/15-10/31: $49-69/S; $55-69/D. 6/15-9/14: $70-89/S; $74-89/D; $8/ex prsn. Disc: Senior, family, l/s. Discounts only in winter. *Guaranteed rates.*

Motel 6/ 600 S Hwy 89, Jackson WY 83001. 307-733-1620/ Fax: 734-9175. M,V,DC,D,AE. US 89/ 191/ 26, 1/2 mi S of SR 390/22. Cable TV, laundry, pool, n/s rms, t pkng. Free local calls. $30/S; $36/D; $6/ex prsn. 5/2-9/28: $40-45/S; $46-51/D. Disc.

Jackson Hole

Trapper Inn/ 235 N Cache Dr, Box 1712, Jackson Hole WY 83001. 307-733-2648/ Fax: 739-9351. V,M,AE,D, CB,DC. Hwys 191, 89, 26 & 187. Nrby rstrnt/ lounge, cable TV, dd phone, laundry, outlets, b/f, mtg rm, hot tubs, cot, crib, n/s rms. AAA/ IMA. $45-58/S or D; $6/ex prsn. 3/22-3/23, 5/12-6/14, 9/2-10/15, 12/21-1/1 $68-78/S; $68-85/D. 5/15-9/1: $85/S; $95-101/D. Disc: Family, senior, TA.

Lander

Budget Host Pronghorn Lodge/ 150 E Main St, Lander WY 82520. 307-332-3940/ Fax: 332-2651. AE,CB,DC, D,M,V. Jct US 287 & 789. Cable TV, dd phone, kitchens, n/s rms, rstrnt, mtg rms, picnic area, hot tub, laundry, arpt trans, cot, crib, t pkng, outlets. AAA/ Mobil. $30/S; $33-40/D; $5/ex prsn. 5/15-10/15: $39/S; $42-48/D.

Holiday Lodge/ 210 McFarlane Dr, Lander WY 82520. 307-332-2511. V,M, AE,DC. Jct 191-297. Cable TV, dd phones, whrlpool, outlets. Free local calls. AAA/ National 9. $30-35/S; $32-45/D.

Silver Spur Motel/ US 287 N, Lander WY 82520. 307-332-5189/ Fax: 332-9251/ 800-922-7831. V,M,AE,D,DC. 1 mi N of Hwys 287 & 789. Nrby rstrnt/ lounge, pool, cable TV, tt/dd phone, fax, copier, nwspr, cot, crib, outlets, t/b/rv pkng, b/f. Free local calls, coffee. AAA. $30/S; $34-40/D; $4/ex prsn. 6/1-9/30: $37/S; $40-48/D. *Guaranteed rates.*

Laramie

Econo Lodge/ 1370 McCue St, Laramie WY 82070. 307-745-8900. M,V,D, AE,DC. I-80 (Exit 310) to Curtis St, E 1 blk to McCue, S 1/2 blk. Nrby rstrnt, indr pool, fax, b/f, cable TV, t pkng, outlets, n/s rms. $39-199/S or D; $10/ex prsn. 5/1-5/25: $29-199/S or D. 5/26-9/4: $49-199/S or D.

WYOMING

Motel 6/ 621 Plaza Ln, Laramie WY 82070. 307-742-2307/ Fax: 742-3897. M,V,DC,D,AE. I-80, Exit 313 to 3rd St exit. Just off of Service rd S of frwy. E of US 287. Cable TV, pool, laundry, n/s rms, t pkng. Free local calls. $23-29/S; $29-35/D; $6/ex prsn. Disc.

Travel Inn/ 262 N 3rd St, Laramie WY 82070. 307-745-4853/ Fax: 721-4943/ 800-227-5430. V,M,AE,D. I-80, snowy Range Exit (311) E 1 mi. Pool, n/s rms, cable TV, tt/dd phone, copier, refrig, cot, crib, outlets, t/b/rv pkng, b/f. Free local calls, coffee. No pets. AAA. $31-34/S; $34-38/D; $3/ex prsn. 5/1-10/31: $41-45/S; $45-60/D; $4/ex prsn. 7/15-7/31: $50-55/S; $60-72/D; $5/ex prsn. Disc: Senior, family. *Guaranteed rates.*

Lovell

Cattlemen Motel/ 470 Montana Av, Lovell WY 82431. 307-548-2296/ 800-845-2296. V,M,AE,D. 1/2 blk S of Main, ctr of town. Nrby rstrnt/ lounge, cable TV, tt/dd phone, cot, crib, outlets, t/b/rv pkng. Free local calls, coffee. AAA. $36/S; $39-44/D; $3/ex prsn. 5/15-11/30: $38/S; $41-46/D; $5/ex prsn. Disc: Senior, bsns, TA, govt, trkr, milt, AAA. *Guaranteed rates.*

Pinedale

Sun Dance Motel/ 148 E Pine St, Pinedale WY 82941. 307-367-4336. V, M,AE,D. On Hwy 191. Nrby rstrnt, cable TV, arpt trans, tt phone, refrig, cot, crib, outlets, conn rms. Free local calls, coffee. AAA. $35/S; $40-49/D; $5/ex prsn. 6/15-9/1: $40/S; $48-54/D. *Guaranteed rates.*

Powell

Super 8 Motel/ 845 E Coulter, Powell WY 82435. 307-754-7231/ Fax: Ext 118. M,V,AE,DC,CB,D Alt 14, 3 blks from center of tn. Outlets, t/b/rv pkng, copier, cable TV, cot, b/f, n/s rms. Free local calls, crib. Pride Award. $31/S; $37-39/D; $4/ex prsn. 6/10-9/30: $44/S; $48-51/D. Higher spec event, wknd rates. Discs.

Rawlins

Days Inn of Rawlins/ 2222 E Cedar, Rawlins WY 82301. 307-324-6615. V,M,AE,D,DC. I-80, Exit Cedar St, approx 1/8 mi on lt. Indr pool, n/s rms, cable TV, games, arpt trans, mtg rm, fax, copier, laundry, refrig, cot, crib, t/b/rv pkng, b/f. Free local calls, cont brfst. AAA. $40/S; $45/D; $5/ex prsn. 6/1-9/30: $50/S; $55/D. Disc: Senior, bsns, govt, family, milt.

Sleep Inn/ 1400 Higley Blvd, Rawlins WY 82301. 307-328-1732. V,M,AE,DC. I-80 (Exit 214) to Higley Blvd, S to mtl. Rstrnt, fax, b/f, sauna, cable TV, t pkng, n/s rms. AAA. $41-46/S; $46-51/D; $5/ex prsn. 5/1-9/30: $46-51/S; $51-56/D. Discs.

Riverton

Tomahawk Motor Lodge/ 208 E Main St, Riverton WY 82501. 307-856-9205. V,M,AE,D,DC. Downtown. Cable TV, dd phone, outlets, arpt trans, in-rm coffee/ tea. cot, crib. n/s rms. Free local calls, family rms, conn rms. AAA/ IMA. $32-34/S; $37-44/D; $5/ex prsn. 7/1-9/30: $37/S; $42-47/D. Higher spec event rates. Disc: AAA, senior, TA, family.

Rock Springs

American Family Inn/ 1635 Elk St, Rock Springs WY 82901. 307-382-4217/ Fax: 362-4150/ 800-548-6621. V,M,AE,D,DC. I-80, Exit 104 (Elk St), N 1 blk. Pool, whrlpool, n/s rms, cable TV, mtg rm, fax, copier, laundry, refrig, microwave, crib, outlets, t/b/rv pkng. Free local calls, cont brfst. AAA. $34/S; $40/D; $5/ex prsn. 5/1-5/31, 9/1-9/30: $38/S; $46/D. 6/1-8/31: $45/S; $55/D. Disc: Senior, bsns, govt, family, trkr, milt, AAA, AARP.

Friendship Inn/ 1004 Dewar Dr, Rock Springs WY 82901. 307-362-6673. V,M,AE,DC. I-80 (Exit 102) to Dewar Dr, S 1 mi to mtl. Nrby rstrnt, fax, cable TV, t pkng, outlets, n/s rms. AAA. $33-57/S; $37-57/D; $6/ex prsn. 5/1-10/31: $36-63/S; $40-63/D. Discs.

Motel 6/ 2615 Commercial Way, Rock Springs WY 82901. 307-362-1850/ Fax: 362-5998. M,V,DC,D,AE. I-80, Exit 102 to I-80 Business/Rock Springs (Ebnd) or Dewar Dr (Wbnd), go NW on Dewar to Foothill, turn rt. Nrby rstrnt, cable TV, laundry, pool, n/s rms. Free local calls. $28-32/S; $34-38/D; $6/ex prsn. Disc.

Sheridan

Mill Inn/ 2161 Coffeen Av, Sheridan WY 82801. 307-672-6401. V,M,AE,D. I-90, Exit 25, rt 2 blks. Nrby rstrnt/ lounge, n/s rms, exerc equip, cable TV, tt/dd phone, fax, elevator, cot, crib, outlets, t/b/rv pkng, eff, conn rms. Free local calls, cont brfst. No pets. AAA. $29-52/S; $32-65/D; $5/ex prsn. Spec event, holiday rates: $59/S; $64-74/D. Disc: L/s.

Comfort Inn/ 1450 Brundage Ln, Sheridan WY 82801. 800-221-2222 — opening soon. M,V,D,AE,DC. I-90 (Exit 25) to Brundage Lane, E to mtl. Nrby rstrn, b/f, whrlpool, cable TV, outlets, n/s rms. Free cont brfst. $29-79/S; $39-89/D; $5/ex prsn. 6/16-8/20: $49-99/S; $54-99/D. Discs.

Guest House Motel/ 2007 N Main St, Sheridan WY 82801. 307-674-7496/ Fax: 674-7687. V,M,AE,D. I-90, Exit 20, 3/4 mi S on Main St. Adj rstrnt/ lounge, cable TV, dd phone, arpt trans, laundry, outlets, in-rm coffee, cot, crib, n/s rms, conn rms. AAA/ IMA $26/S; $32-38/D; $4/ex prsn. 5/1-8/31: $33/S; $39-44/D. Disc: Family, govt.

Rock Trim Motel/ 449 Coffeen Av, Sheridan WY 82801. 307-672-2464. V, M,AE,D. I-90, Exit 25, rt on US 14 & Bsns loop 87, 3/4 mi. N/s rms, cable TV, tt/dd phone, laundry, refrig, microwave, cot, crib, outlets, eff. Free local calls, coffee. AAA. $26-30/S; $28-32/D; $4-5/ex prsn. 5/1-9/30: $30-33/S; $36-39/D. Disc: Senior, bsns, TA, govt, trkr, milt, AAA, l/s. *Guaranteed rates.*

Sundance

Bear Lodge/ 218 Cleveland, Box 912, Sundance WY 82729. 307-283-1611. V, M,AE,D,DC,CB. I-90, Exit 189, lt 1 mi; I-90 Exit 185, rt 1 mi. Nrby rstrnt/ lounge, whrlpool, n/s rms, cable TV, tt/dd phone, cot, crib, outlets, conn rms. Free local calls, coffee. AAA/ IMA. $32-36/S; $32-44/D; $4/ex prsn. 6/1-6/15, 8/21-11/30: $36-40/S; $36-46/D. 6/16-8/20: $48-52/S; $48-58/D.

Budget Host Arrowhead Motel/ 214 Cleveland, Box 191, Sundance WY 82729. 307-283-3307. AE,M,V,D,CB, DC Cntr of tn. Cable TV, dd phone, adj rstrnt, mtg rms, arpt trans, cot, crib, t pkng, outlets. AAA/ Mobil. $26-30/S; $28-40/D; $4/ex prsn. May-Nov: $40-45/S; $45-50/D. Higher spec event rates.

Torrington

Maverick Motel/ Rte 1, Box 354, Torrington WY 82240. 307-532-4064/ Fax: 532-5846. 1-1/2 mi W of Main jct, on US 26 & 85. N/s rms, cable TV, tt phone, fax, cot, crib. Free local calls. AAA. $29/S; $33/D; $2/ex prsn.

Super 8 Motel/ 1548 S Main, Torrington WY 82240. 307-532-7118. V,AE,DC, CB,M,D US 85 at US 26. Outlets, toast bar, t/b pkng, cable TV, b/f, n/s rms. Free local calls. No pets. $39/S; $45-50/D; $4/ex prsn. Higher spec event rates. Discs.

Wheatland

Vimbo's Motel/ 203 16th, Box 188, Wheatland WY 82201. 307-322-3242/ 800-577-3842. V,M,AE,D. Take exit at mi marker 78, turn to stop sign, then lt towards town. Rstrnt/ lounge, n/s rms, cable TV, arpt trans, tt phone, mtg rm, cot, crib, outlets, t/b/rv pkng, conn rms, b/f. Free local calls. AAA. $36/S; $43/D; $3/ex prsn. 7/15-8/15: $56/S; $63/D; $6/ex prsn.

Canada

All prices are in Canadian dollars unless otherwise indicated.

Alberta

Calgary

Budget Host Motor Inn/ 4420 16th Ave NW, Calgary AB T3B 0M4. 403-288-7115/ Fax: 286-4899. AE,M,V,ER. On Trans-Canada Hwy 1 W. Nrby rstrnt/ lounge, satellite TV, dd phones, n/s rms, b/f, laundry, cot, crib, t pkng. CAA. $54/S; $59-64/D; $5/ex prsn. 6/15-9/30: $64/S; $69-74/D. Stampede 7/4-7/14: $85/S; $95-100/D. Higher spec event rates. Discs.

Comfort Inn/ 2363 Banff Trail NW, Calgary AB T2M 4L2. 403-289-2581. AE,M,V,DC. SR 1 (16th Ave) in Motel Village. Hwy 2 to Glenmore Tr, W to Crowchild Tr, N to 23rd Av. Nrby rstrnt, indr pool, fax, sauna, whrlpool, cable TV, t pkng, outlets. Free cont brfst. No pets. CAA. $50-60/S; $60-70/D; $5/ex prsn. 5/1-6/1: $70-90/S or D. 6/2-7/16: $80-100/S; $80-119/D. 7/17-9/30: $70-80/S or D. Discs.

Econo Lodge/ Box 7, Site 12, SS 1, Calgary AB T2M 4N3. 403-288-4436. AE,M,V. Trans-Canada Hwy 1 at 101 St. Nrby rstrnt, pool, fax, sauna, whrlpool, cable TV, t pkng, exerc equip, outlets, n/s rms. $35-59/S; $40-59/D; $5/ex prsn. 3/1-4/30, 9/6-10/31: $40-59/S; $45-69/D. 5/1-9/5: $49-99/S; $59-119/D. Discs.

Econo Lodge/ 5307 MacLeod Trail S, Calgary AB T2H 0J3 403-258-1064. V, M,AE,D,DC. Deerfoot Trail to Glenmore Trail, W to MacLeod Trail, N to 53rd Av. From US, N on Hwy 2, becomes MacLeod Tr, lt at 53 Av. Nrby rstrnt, cable TV, t pkng, n/s rms. Free cont brfst. $44-80/S; $44-90/D; $8/ex prsn. Discs.

Econo Lodge/ 2440 16 Av NW, Calgary AB T2M 0M5. 403-289-2561. V,M,AE,D,DC. On Hwy 1 in city. Rstrnt, cable TV, exerc equip, n/s rms. Free cont brfst. $49-68/S; $58-78/D; $10/ex prsn. 5/1-9/30: $58-78/S; $68-99/D. Spec events: $90-99/S; $99-110/D. Discs.

Howard Johnson/ 4510 Macleod Trail S, Calgary AB T2G 0A4. 403-243-1700/ Fax: 243-4719. M,DC,D,V,AE,CB. From N: Hwy 2 to Glenmore Trail W, exit at MacLeod Trail N, go to 45 Av. From S: Hwy 2 becomes MacLeod Trail. Rstrnt/ lounge, cable TV, n/s rms, t pkng, mtg rm, in-rm coffee, fax. $49-89/S; $49-99/D. Discs.

Quality Inn/ 2359 Banff Trail NW, Calgary AB T2M 4L2. 403-289-1973. M,V,DC,D,AE. Trans Canada Hwy, SR 1 & Banff Trail. Rstrnt/ lounge, indr pool, mtg rm, fax, b/f, whrlpool, cable TV, exerc equip, outlets. CAA. $59-79/S; $69-89/D. $5/ex prsn. 5/1-9/5: $74-109/S; $79-119/D. 9/6-3/30: $59-69/S; $64-74/D. Discs.

Edmonton

Comfort Inn/ 4009 Calgary Trail N, Edmonton AB T6J 5H2. 403-435-4877. M,V,DC,D,AE. On Calgary Trail. Rstrnt, fax, cable TV, t pkng, outlets, n/s rms. $35/S; $39/D; $5/ex prsn. 5/1-10/31: $42/S; $45/D. Discs.

Comfort Inn/ 17610 100th Av, Edmonton AB T5S 1S9. 403-484-4415/ Fax: 481-4034. M,V,DC,D,AE. Yellowhead Hwy to 184th St, S to 100th Av, E to 176 St. Rstrnt, fax, b/f, cable TV, t pkng, outlets, n/s rms. Free local calls. $55-89/S; $55-99/D; $4/ex prsn. 7/1-9/30: $63-89/S; $71-99/D. 10/1-12/31: $55-85/S; $55-93/D. Discs.

Howard Johnson Plaza Hotel/ 10010 104 St, Edmonton AB T5J 0Z1. 403-423-2450/ Fax: 426-6090. M,DC,D,V, AE,CB. From W: Hwy 16 to Stoney Plain Rd to Jasper Av to 104 St, 1 blk S. Rstrnt/ lounge, mtg rm, indr pool, cable TV, whrlpool, sauna, weight rm, in-rm coffee. Gold Medal Winner. $59-129/S or D. Discs.

Quality Hotel/ 10815 Jasper Av, Edmonton AB T5J 2B1. 403-423-1650. M,V,AE,D,DC. Hwy 2 N from Calgary or Yellowhead to city centre. Rstrnt/ lounge, mtg rm, sauna, cable TV, exerc equip. $54-89/S or D; $10/ex prsn. Discs.

CANADA

Quality Inn/ 10209 100th Av, Edmonton AB T5J 0A1 403-428-6442. AE,M,V,DC. Hwy 2 N (Calgary Trail) to dntn, turn on Jasper Av, lt on 102 St to 100th Av. Hwy 16 & Yellow Head Trail, follow signs to dntn. Rstrnt/ lounge, mtg rm, fax, cable TV, outlets, arpt trans. Free pkng, brfst. $49-100/S; $54-125/D; $4/ex prsn. Discs.

Sandman Hotel/ 17635 Stony Plain Rd, Edmonton AB T5S 1E3. 403-483-1385/ Fax: 489-0611. M,V,AE. Rstrnt/ lounge, mtg rm, movies, sauna, pool, whrlpool, kitchenette. $60/S; $65-70/D. Disc: Corp, senior, l/s.

Medicine Hat

Super 8 Motel/ 1280 Trans-Canada Hwy, Medicine Hat AB T1B 1J5. 403-528-8888/ Fax: 526-4445. AE,M,V,DC, CB,D. Trans-Canada Hwy E #1 to 13th Ave SE Exit. Nrby rstrnt, b/f, n/s rms, pool, copier, cable TV, b/t/rv pkng, cot. Free cont brfst, local calls. $40-46/S; $43-56/D; $6/ex prsn. Higher spec event rates. Discs.

Red Deer

Friendship Inn/ 4124 Gaetz Av, Red Deer AB T4N 3Z2. 403-342-6969. V, M,AE,D,DC. At jct of Gaetz Av & 42 St, in Red Deer. Nrby rstrnt, cable TV, t pkng, n/s rms. $39-48/S; $44-53/D; $5/ex prsn. 5/1-8/31: $43-52/S; $48-57/D. Discs.

British Columbia

Blue River

Sandman Hotel/ Hwy 5, Box 31, Blue River BC V0E 1J0. 604-673-8364/ Fax: 673-8440. M,V,AE. Rstrnt, sauna, kitchenette. $54/S; $59-64/D. Disc: Corp, senior, l/s.

Cache Creek

Sandman Hotel/ Hwy 1, Box 278, Cache Creek BC V0K 1H0. 604-457-6284/ Fax: 457-9674. M,V,AE. Rstrnt, sauna, kitchenette. $48/S; $53-58/D. Disc: Corp, senior, l/s.

Cranbrook

Sandman Hotel/ 405 Cranbrook St, Cranbrook BC V1C 3R5. 604-426-4236/ Fax: 426-3905. M,V,AE. Rstrnt, mtg rm, movies, sauna, pool, kitchenette. $55/S; $60-65/D. Disc: Corp, senior, l/s.

McBride

Sandman Hotel/ Hwy 16, Box 548, McBride BC V0J 2E0. 604-569-2285/ Fax: 569-2440. M,V,AE. Rstrnt, mtg rm, sauna, kitchenette. $53/S; $58-63/D. Disc: Corp, senior, l/s.

Prince George

Sandman Hotel/ 1650 Central St, Prince George BC V2M 3C2. 604-563-8131/ Fax: 563-8613. M,V,AE. Rstrnt, movies, sauna, pool, kitchenette. $60/S; $65-70/D. Disc: Corp, senior, l/s.

Princeton

Sandman Hotel/ Hwy 3, Box 421, Princeton BC V0X 1W0. 604-295-6923/ Fax: 295-6625. M,V,AE. Rstrnt, mtg rm, sauna, kitchenette. $52/S; $57-62/D. Disc: Corp, senior, l/s.

Smithers

Sandman Hotel/ Hwy 16 W, Box 935, Smithers BC V0J 2N0. 604-847-2637/ Fax: 847-3709. M,V,AE. Movies, sauna, kitchenette. $49/S; $54-59/D. Disc: Corp, senior, l/s.

Terrace

Sandman Hotel/ 4828 Hwy 16 W, Terrace BC V8G 1L6. 604-635-9151/ Fax: 635-6225. M,V,AE. Rstrnt, mtg rm, movies, pool, kitchenette. $58/S; $63-68/D. Disc: Corp, senior, l/s.

Vernon

Sandman Hotel/ 4201 32nd St, Vernon BC V1T 5T3. 604-542-4325/ Fax: 542-8379. M,V,AE. Rstrnt, mtg rm, movies, sauna, pool, kitchenette. $52/S; $57-62/D. Disc: Corp, senior, l/s.

Victoria

Quality Inn/ 455 Belleville St, Victoria BC V8V 1X3. 604-386-2421. V,M,AE. From Swartz Bay Ferry Terminal take Hwy 17, 30 km to mtl. Rstrnt/ lounge, indr pool, mtg rm, fax, b/f, sauna, whrlpool, exerc equip. No pets. $49-79/S or D; $15/ex prsn. 5/1-6/30, 9/16-10/15: $49-99/S or D. 7/1-9/15: $99-138/S or D. Discs.

Rodeway Inn/ 2915 Douglas St, Victoria BC V8T 4M8. 604-385-6731. V,M,AE. From Vancouver Ferry take Hwy 17 until turns into Blanshard St, rt at Topaz St to mtl. Rstrnt/ lounge, mtg rm, fax, cable TV, t pkng, n/s rms. CAA. $39-59/S; $49-69/D; $10/ex prsn. 5/1-9/30: $39-59/S; $49-89/D. Discs.

Williams Lake

Sandman Hotel/ 664 Oliver St, Williams Lake BC V2G 1N6. 604-392-6557/ Fax: 392-6242. M,V,AE. Rstrnt, mtg rm, movies, sauna, pool, kitchenette. $57/S; $62-67/D. Disc: Corp, senior, l/s.

Manitoba

Brandon

Comfort Inn/ 925 Middleton Av, Brandon MB R7C 1A8. 204-727-6232/ Fax: 727-2246. AE,M,V,DC. Hwy 1 (Trans Canada Hwy) at Middleton Av, turn N. Nrby rstrnt, fax, b/f, cable TV, t pkng, outlets, cont brfst. Free local calls. $45-79/S; $45-86/D; $4/ex prsn. 6/1-9/30: $47-78/S; $47-86/D. Discs.

Winnipeg

Clarion Hotel/ 222 Broadway, Winnipeg MB R3C 0R3. 204-942-8251/ 800-665-8088. M,V,DC,D,AE. Hwy 75 to mtl. Rstrnt/ lounge, indr pool, mtg rm, sauna, cable TV, exerc equip. $59-99/S or D; $10/ex prsn. Discs.

Comfort Inn/ 3109 Pembina Hwy, Winnipeg MB R3T 4R6. 204-269-7390/ Fax: 261-7565. V,M,AE. Trans Canada Hwy to Perimeter Hwy (Hwy 100), exit on Rte 42 N (Pembina Hwy) to mtl. Rstrnt, fax, b/f, cable TV, outlets, cont brfst. Free local calls. $42-70/S; $47-78/D; $4/ex prsn. 6/1-9/30: $48-78/S; $53-86/D. Discs.

Comfort Inn/ 1770 Sargent Av, Winnipeg MB R3H 0C8. 204-783-5627. M,V,DC,D,AE. Hwy 1 E (Trans Can Hwy) or Hwy 100 W, exit Portage Av (Rte 85), lt at Berry St, rt on Sargent Av. Nrby rstrnt, fax, b/f, cable TV, t pkng, outlets, cont brfst. Free local calls. $52-80/S; $59-88/D; $4/ex prsn. 5/1-6/16: $49-74/S; $56-82/D. 6/17-9/17: $57-79/S; $64-87/D. 9/18-12/31: $51-76/S; $58-84/D. Discs.

New Brunswick

Bathurst

Comfort Inn/ 1170 St Peter Av, Bathurst NB E2A 2Z9. 506-547-8000. M,V,DC,D,AE. Hwy 11 (Exit 310) to Vanier Blvd, N to Hwy 134 (St Peter Av), turn S. Nrby rstrnt, fax, b/f, cable TV, t pkng, outlets, cont brfst. Free local calls. $57-64/S; $65-72/D; $4/ex prsn. 5/1-6/15: $54-66/S; $62-74/D. 6/16-9/15: $55-62/S; $63-70/D. 9/16-12/31: $56-62/S; $64-71/D. Discs.

Campbellton

Howard Johnson Hotel/ 157 Water St, Campbellton NB E3N 3H2. 506-753-4133/ Fax: 753-6386. V,M,AE,D,DC, CB. Hwy 11, Exit 412, at intersection turn rt, go to 2nd intersection, lt on Ramsay St to Salmon Blvd. Hotel on lt. Rstrnt, n/s rms, b/f, t pkng. Free local calls. Gold Medal Winner. $54-71/S; $59-76/D. Discs.

Edmundston

Comfort Inn/ 5 Bateman Av, Edmundston NB E3V 3L1. 506-739-8361. M,V,DC,D,AE. Trans-Canada Hwy 2 (Exit 18) to Hebert Blvd, N to Carrier Rd, lt to Bateman Av, lt to mtl. Nrby rstrnt, fax, b/f, cable TV, t pkng, outlets, cont brfst. Free local calls. $56-68/S; $64-74/D; $4/ex prsn. 5/1-6/16: $55-63/S; $63-71/D. 6/17-9/4: $63-70/S; $71-78/D. 9/5-10/31: $56-64/S; $64-72/D. Discs.

Fredericton

Keddy's Inn/ 368 Forest Hill Rd, Fredericton NB E3B 5G2. 506-454-4461/ Fax: 452-6915/ 800-561-7666. V,M,AE,D,DC. Trans Canada Hwy 2, Exit 295, Forest Hill Rd. Indr pool, sauna, n/s rms, cable TV, VCR/ movies, games, tt/dd phone, mtg rm, copier, laundry, refrig, cot, crib, outlets, t/b/rv pkng, eff. Free local calls. CAA. $40/S or D; $8/ex prsn. 6/15-9/30: $50/S or D. *Guaranteed rates - subject to space available.*

Moncton

Comfort Inn/ 2495 Mountain Rd, RR 8, Moncton NB E1C 8K2. 506-384-3175. M,V,DC,D,AE. Hwy 2 (Trans Canada Hwy/ Exit 488) to Rte 126 (Mountain

CANADA

Rd), S to mtl. Nrby rstrnt, fax, b/f, cable TV, t pkng, outlets, cont brfst. Free local calls. $57-69/S; $65-77/D; $4/ex prsn. 5/1-9/17: $56-68/S; $64-74/D. 9/18-12/31: $56-66/S; $64-74/D. Discs.

Howard Johnson Hotel/ Box 5005, Moncton NB E1C 8R7. 506-384-1050/ Fax: 859-6070. M,DC,D,V,AE,CB. Trans-Canada Hwy 2 at jct Mountain Rd (Magnetic Hill exit), Exit 488 A & B. Rstrnt/ lounge, indr pool, mtg rm, satellite TV, laundry, game rm, whrlpool. $55-82/S; $61-92/D. Discs.

Keddy's Motor Inn/ RR 6, Shediac Rd, Moncton NB E1C 8K1. 506-854-2210/ Fax: 857-9960. 800-561-7666. V,M,AE, D,DC. Trans Can Hwy, Exit 502. Indr pool, sauna, cable TV, VCR/ movies, tt phone, mtg rm, fax, copier, laundry, cot, crib, outlets, t/b/rv pkng, eff. Free local calls. CAA. $45/S or D. Disc: Senior, bsns, TA, govt, family, trkr, milt. *Guaranteed rates.*

Saint John

Comfort Inn/ 1155 Fairville Bvd, Box 3935, Station B, St John NB E2M 5E5. 506-674-1873. M,V,DC,D,AE. St John Thwy (Hwy 1): E, Exit 107 (Catherwood), NW on Fairville Blvd to mtl; W, Exit 104 to Hwy 7, NE on Fairville Blvd. Nrby rstrnt, fax, b/f, cable TV, t pkng, outlets. $56-64/S; $64-72/D; $4/ex prsn. 5/1-6/15: $55-62/S; $63-70/D. 6/16-9/15: $68-75/S; $76-83/D. Discs.

Howard Johnson Hotel/ 400 Main St at Chesley Dr, St John NB E2K 4N5. 506-642-2622/ Fax: 658-1529. V,M,AE,D, DC,CB. Exit 112 from Rte 1 W, Follow Rte 100 along Main St, lt at Chesley. Rte 1 E from the States, cross Harbour Bridge, exit on Chesley Dr. Rstrnt, indr pool, exerc equip, n/s rms, b/f, laundry, arpt trans, baby sitting. Free cont brfst, M-F. $55-82/S; $55-92/D. 5/1-10/31: $59-92/S; $59-102/D. Discs.

Sussex

Quality Inn/ Rte 2, Trans Canada Hwy, Sussex NB E0E 1P0. 506-433-3470. M,V,DC,D,AE. Rstrnt/ lounge, indr pool, mtg rm, sauna, whrlpool. $50-60/S; $55-65/D; $5-6/ex prsn. 5/1-9/15: $55-62/S; $60-75/D. Discs.

Nova Scotia

Amhurst

Comfort Inn/ 143 S Albion St, Amherst NS B4H 2X2. 902-667-0404. M,V,DC, D,AE. Hwy 104 (Trans Canada Hwy/ Exit 4) to Hwy 2 (S Albion St), N to mtl. Nrby rstrnt, fax, b/f, cable TV, outlets, cont brfst. Free local calls. $57-64/S; $65-72/D; $4/ex prsn. 5/1-6/15: $55-62/S; $63-70/D. 6/16-9/15: $68-75/S; $75-82/D. 9/16-12/31: $56-63/S; $64-71/D. Discs.

Bridgewater

Comfort Inn/ 49 North St, Bridgewater NS B4V 2V7. 902-543-1498. M,V,DC,D, AE. Hwy 103 (Exit 12/ Bridgewater) to Hwy 10, E on North St to mtl. Nrby rstrnt, fax, b/f, cable TV, outlets, cont brfst. Free local calls. $56-63/S; $64-71/D; $4/ex prsn. 5/1-6/15: $55-62/S; $63-70/D. 6/16-9/17: $64-71/S; $72-79/D. Discs.

Dartmouth (Halifax area)

Best Western Mic Mac Hotel/ 313 Prince Albert Rd, Dartmouth NS B2Y 1N3. 902-469-5850/ Fax: 469-5859. V,M,AE,D,DC. Hwy 118 to Exit 4, Hwy 111, Exit 6A. Rstrnt/ lounge, n/s rms, cable TV, VCR/ movies, tt/dd phone, mtg rm, fax, copier, elevator, cot, crib. No pets. CAA. $47-52/S or D; $5/ex prsn. 7/1-10/31: $62-67/S; $67-72/D. Disc: Senior, govt, milt, trkr. *Guaranteed rates.*

Comfort Inn/ 456 Windmill Rd, Dartmouth NS B3A 1J7. 902-463-9900/ Fax: 466-2080. V,M,DC,D,AE. AM MacKay Bridge or Hwy 111 W, exit Shannon Pk to Princess Margaret Blvd, lt to Windmill Rd. Nrby rstrnt, fax, b/f, cable TV, outlets, cont brfst. Free local calls. $56-68/S; $64-76/D; $4/ex prsn. 5/1-6/30: $58-68/S; $66-76/D. 7/1-9/30: $72-82/S; $80-90/D. Discs.

Howard Johnson Hotel/ 739 Windmill Rd, Dartmouth NS B3B 1C1. 902-468-7117/ Fax: 468-1770. V,M,AE,D,DC, CB. Halifax Arpt: Hwys 102, Exit Rte 118 to Akerley Blvd. Dntn Halifax: take Murray MacKay Bridge, exit to Bedford onto Windmill Rd. Rstrnt/ lounge, n/s rms, b/f, satellite TV, in-rm coffee, picnic area, mtg rm. No pets. $55-60/S or

CANADA

D. 5/1-10/31: $55-70/S; $65-85/D. Discs.

Halifax
Econo Lodge/ 560 Bedford Hwy, Halifax NS B3M 2L8. 902-443-0303. AE,M,V. SR 102 merges into SR 2, 8 km to mtl on rt side. Rstrnt, indr pool, fax, cable TV, n/s rms. CAA. $43-49/S; $49/D; $7/ex prsn. 6/16-10/15: $51-58/S; $68/D. Discs.

Also see Dartmouth.

New Glasgow
Comfort Inn/ 740 Westville Rd, New Glasgow NS B2H 2J8. 902-755-6450/ Fax: 752-6680. M,V,DC,D,AE. Hwy 104 (Trans Canada Hwy/ Exit 23) to Westville Rd, N to mtl. Nrby rstrnt, fax, b/f, cable TV, t pkng, outlets, cont brfst. Free local calls. $57-64/S; $65-72/D; $4/ex prsn. 5/1-6/15: $54-61/S; $62-69/D. 6/16-10/15: $67-74/S; $74-81/D. 10/16-12/31: $55-62/S; $63-70/D. Discs.

Sydney
Keddy's Motor Inn/ 600 Kings Rd, Sydney NS B1S 1B9. 902-539-1140/ Fax: 539-2258/ 800-561-7666. V,M,AE,D,DC,CB. Trans Can Hwy, Exit 6 (Sydney, via Kings Rd). Indr pool, sauna, whrlpool, n/s rms, cable TV, games, tt phone, mtg rm, fax, copier, elevator, cot, crib, t/b pkng, b/f. Free local calls. CAA. $48/S or D; $10/ex prsn. *Guaranteed rates.*

Truro
HoJo Inn/ 165 Willow St, Truro NS B2N 4Z9. 902-893-9413/ Fax: 897-9937. V,M,AE,D,DC,CB. Off Hwy 102 to Halifax Exit 13, lt at stop sign, lt at lights onto Willow St, 1/4 mi on rt. Rstrnt, b/f, n/s rms, cable TV, b/t pkng, mtg rm, kitchenettes. $46-80/S or D. 3/1-4/30: $51-86/S or D. Discs.

Yarmouth
Comfort Inn/ 96 Starrs Rd, Yarmouth NS B5A 2T5. 902-742-1119. M,V,DC,D,AE. Jct Hwy 101 & Starrs Rd. Nrby rstrnt, fax, b/f, cable TV, t pkng, outlets, cont brfst. Free local calls. $57-65/S; $65-73/D; $4/ex prsn. 5/1-6/15: $55-63/S; $64-71/D. 6/16-9/15: $68-76/S; $76-83/D. 9/16-10/31: $60-68/S; $68-76/D. Discs.

Ontario

Atikokan
Radisson Motel/ 310 Mackenzie Av, Atikokan ON P0T 1C0. 807-597-2766/ Fax: 597-2729. V,M,AE,D,DC. Hwy 11 to Hwy 11B, N. (Mackenzie Av) Nrby rstrnt, n/s rms, cable TV, tt/dd phone, fax, refrig, cot, outlets, t/b pkng. Free local calls. No pets. CAA. $49-55/S or D; $3/ex prsn. Disc: Senior, l/s. *Guaranteed rates.*

Barrie
Comfort Inn/ 210 Essa Rd, Barrie ON L4N 3L1. 705-721-1122/ Fax: 721-8547. V,M,AE. Hwy 400 to Essa Rd, rt to mtl. Nrby rstrnt, mtg rm, fax, b/f, cable TV, t pkng, outlets. Free cont brfst. No pets. CAA. $58-64/S; $66-74/D; $6/ex prsn. 5/1-10/31: $56-64/S; $64-74/D. Discs.

Belleville
Howard Johnson Lodge/ 325 N Front St, Belleville ON K8P 3C6. 613-968-5353/ Fax: 968-6474. V,M,AE,D,DC,CB. Hwy 401, Exit 543 (Hwy 62) S. Lounge, exerc equip, mtg rm, t pkng, n/s rms, fax, cable TV. Free cont brfst. No pets. $45-75/S; $51-79/D. Discs.

Brantford
Comfort Inn/ 58 King George Rd, Brantford ON N3R 5K4. 519-753-3100/ Fax: 753-8138. AE,M,V,DC. Hwy 403 to Hwy 24, S to King George Rd. From Cambridge & Hwy 401, take Hwy 24 S to mtl. Rstrnt/ lounge, fax, b/f, cable TV, outlets. Free local calls. $53-75/S; $61-79/D; $4/ex prsn. 5/1-9/30: $56-82/S; $64-86/D. Discs.

Brockville
Comfort Inn/ 7777 Kent Blvd, Brockville ON K6V 6N7. 613-345-0042. M,V,DC,D,AE. Hwy 401 (Exit 696) to Hwy 29, NW on 29 to Jefferson, S to Kent. Nrby rstrnt, fax, cable TV, outlets, n/s rms. Free cont brfst, local calls. $54-56/S; $62-64/D; $4/ex prsn. 5/1-9/5: $56-58/S; $64-66/D. Discs.

Burlington
Comfort Inn/ 3290 S Service Rd, Burlington ON L7N 3M6. 905-639-1700/

Fax: 639-8968. AE,M,V,DC. QEW to Guelph Line, S to Harvester Rd, NE (lt) lt onto S Serv Rd. Nrby rstrnt, fax, b/f, cable TV, t pkng, outlets, cont brfst. Free local calls. $57-150/S; $65-150/D; $4/ex prsn. 5/1-6/30: $59-150/S; $67-150/D. 7/1-9/30: $62-150/S; $70-150/D. Discs.

Chatham

Comfort Inn/ 1100 Richmond St, Chatham ON N7M 5J5. 519-352-5500/ Fax: 352-2520. M,V,DC,D,AE. Hwy 401 (Exit 81) to Bloomfield Rd, N to Richmond, rt to mtl. Nrby rstrnt, fax, b/f, cable TV, t pkng, outlets, cont brfst. $57-77/S; $65-85/D; $4/ex prsn. 5/1-5/31: $54-71/S; $62-79/D. 6/1-12/31: $55-72/S; $63-80/D. Discs.

Cornwall

Comfort Inn/ 1755 Vincent Massey Dr, Cornwall ON K6H 5R6. 613-932-7786. AE,M,V,DC. Hwy 401 to Power Dam Dr, S to Hwy 2 (Vincent Massey), E to mtl. Rstrnt, mtg rm, b/f, cable TV, t pkng, outlets. Free cont brfst. No pets. CAA. $58-83/S; $63-88/D; $5/ex prsn. 5/1-10/31: $59-84/S; $64-89/D. Discs.

Econo Lodge/ 1750 Vincent Massey Dr, Cornwall ON K6H 5R8. 613-932-1271. V,M,AE,DC. Hwy 401 (Exit 789) to Brookdale Av, S to Vincent Massey Dr (Hwy 2), W to mtl. Rstrnt, indr pool, fax, whrlpool, cable TV, t pkng, refrig, microwave. Free cont brfst. $46-80/S; $50-80/D; $6/ex prsn. 5/1-7/27, 8/1-9/30: $46-100/S; $50-100/D. 7/28-7/31: $65-100/S; $90-100/D. Discs.

Dryden

Comfort Inn/ 522 Government Rd, Dryden ON P8N 2P5. 807-223-3893/ Fax: 323-5627. V,M,AE. Trans Canada Hwy (Govt Rd) 1 blk E of Hwy 601. Nrby rstrnt, mtg rm, fax, b/f, cable TV, t pkng, outlets, playgrnd, cont brfst, n/s rms. Free local calls. $57-88/S; $57-96/D; $4/ex prsn. 5/1-12/31: $55-86/S; $55-94/D. Discs.

Fort Erie

Super 8 Motel/ 1 Journey's End Dr, Ft Erie ON L2A 6G1. 905-871-8500/ Fax: 871-9388. V,M,AE,DC,CB. QEW (Exit 1B) to Concession Rd S, rt on Walden Ave, rt on Journey's End Dr. N/s rms, cable TV, VCR/ movies, tt/dd phone, fax, copier, microwave, cot, crib, outlets, t/b/rv pkng, conn rms, b/f. Free local calls, coffee. CAA. $55-60/S; $63-68/D; $8/ex prsn. Holidays, spec event rates: $80/S or D. Discs.

Gananoque

Econo Lodge/ 785 King St E, Gananoque ON K7G 1H4. 613-382-4728. AE,M,V. Hwy 401 (Exit 648) to 1000 Islands Pkwy, exit at Hwy 2, follow rte into tn. Nrby rstrnt, pool, b/f, whrlpool, cable TV, t pkng, n/s rms, in-rm coffee. No pets. CAA. $49-149/S or D; $7/ex prsn. 6/30-9/3: $59-159/S or D. Discs.

Haliburton

Lakeview Motel/ Box 485, Haliburton ON K0M 1S0. 705-457-1027. V,M. On Hwy 121. Nrby rstrnt, pool, n/s rms, cable TV, tt/dd phone, cot, crib, outlets. Free local calls, coffee. No pets. CAA. $50/S; $60/D; $10/ex prsn. 6/21 thru 9/2: $58/S; $68/D. *Guaranteed rates.*

Hamilton

Days Inn Hamilton/ 1187 Upper James, Hamilton ON L9C 3B2. 905-575-9666/ Fax: 575-1098. V,M,AE,D,DC. QEW Toronto to 403 Hamilton to Mohawk Rd to Upper James. N/s rms, exerc equip, cable TV, VCR, games, mtg rm, copier, cot, crib, outlets, t/b/rv pkng. Free local calls, cont brfst, coffee. CAA/ Mobil. $47/S or D; $7/ex prsn. 5/1-10/31 wknds: $55/S; $59/D. Discs. *Guaranteed rates.*

Howard Johnson Plaza Hotel/ 112 King St E, Hamilton ON L8N 1A8. 905-546-8111/ Fax: 546-8144. V,M,AE,D,DC,CB. From Toronto, QEW to 403 to Hwy 8 (East Main St). From Niagara, QEW to Centennial Pkwy (Hwy 20) to Queenston Rd, W to King St. Rstrnt, indr pool, n/s rms, b/f, exerc equip, whrlpool, sauna, mtg rm. Gold Medal Winner. $59-109/S; $59-129/D. Discs.

Quality Hotel/ 55 Catharine St S, Hamilton ON L8N 4E8. 905-546-1800. V,M,AE. QEW to Burlington St, lt on Wellington, rt on King St, lt on Catharine to mtl. Rstrnt/ lounge, mtg rm, fax, b/f, cable TV, t pkng, outlets. Free local calls. $49-99/S; $49-130/D; $4/ex prsn. Discs.

Huntsville

Highland Court Motel/ 208 Main St W, Huntsville ON P1H 1Y1. 705-789-4424. V,M,AE,D. From Hwy 11, Exit Muskoka Rd 3 S. N/s rms, cable TV, dd phone, refrig, outlets, eff, conn rms. Free local calls, coffee. CAA. $40-45/S; $44-56/D; $5/ex prsn. 7/1-9/15: $45-58/S; $52-64/D. Disc: L/s. *Guaranteed rates.*

Kapuskasing

Comfort Inn/ 172 Government Rd E, Kapuskasing ON P5N 2W9. 705-335-8583. M,V,DC,D,AE. Hwy 11 (Government Rd) at Brunelle. Nrby rstrnt, fax, cable TV, outlets, cont brfst, n/s rms. Free local calls. $57-76/S; $65-84/D; $8/ex prsn. 6/1-12/31: $58-77/S; $66-85/D. Discs.

Kenora

Comfort Inn/ 1230 Hwy 17 E, Kenora ON P9N 1L9. 807-468-8845/ Fax: 468-1588. V,M,AE. On Hwy 17. Nrby rstrnt, fax, b/f, cable TV, outlets, cont brfst. Free local calls. $60-77/S; $60-86/D; $4/ex prsn. 5/1-5/31: $55-81/S; $55-89/D. 6/1-9/30: $65-91/S; $65-99/D. Discs.

Kirkland Lake

Comfort Inn/ 445 Government Rd W, Kirkland Lake ON P0K 1A0. 705-567-4909. M,V,DC,D,AE. Hwy 11, 112 to Hwy 66 (Government Rd), E to mtl. Nrby rstrnt, fax, cable TV, t pkng, outlets, n/s rms. $54-70/S; $64-80/D; $8/ex prsn. 5/1-9/15: $56-72/S; $66-82/D. Discs.

Kitchener

Howard Johnson Hotel & Conference Centre/ 1333 Weber St E, Kitchener ON N2A 1C2. 519-893-1234/ Fax: 893-2100. V,M,AE,D,DC,CB. Hwy 401 to Hwy 8, exit towards Kitchener, exit at Weber St, lt. Rstrnt/ lounge, indr pool, t pkng, n/s rms, in-rm coffee, sauna, whrlpool, mtg rm, VCR. $59-79/S; $61-81/D. Discs.

Rodeway Suites/ 55 New Dundee Rd, Kitchener ON N2G 3W5. 519-895-2272. V,M,AE,D,DC. Hwy 401 (Exit 275) to Homer Watson Blvd, N 1 blk. Nrby rstrnt, mtg rm, fax, outlets, n/s rms, refrig, microwave. $39-49/S; $49-69/D; $6/ex prsn. CLOSED 9/1-4/30. Discs.

London

Comfort Inn/ 1156 Wellington Rd, London ON N6E 1M3. 519-685-9300/ Fax: 685-0081. V,M,AE. Hwy 401 (Exit 186) to Wellington Rd, N 1 km to mtl. Nrby rstrnt, cable TV, t pkng, cont brfst, n/s rms. Free local calls. $45-59/S; $45-67/D; $4/ex prsn. Discs.

Econo Lodge/ 1170 Wellington Rd S, London ON N6E 1M3. 519-681-1550. V,M,AE,D,DC. Hwy 401 (Exit 186) to Wellington Rd, N 5 km to mtl. Rstrnt, mtg rm, fax, b/f, cable TV, t pkng, n/s rms, brfst bar. Free local calls. $45-50/S; $49-61/D; $5/ex prsn. 3/1-11/30: $48-53/S; $60-65/D. Discs.

Markham (Toronto area)

Comfort Inn/ 8330 Woodbine Av, Markham ON L3R 2N8. 905-477-6077/ Fax: 477-9667. V,M,AE. Hwy 401 (Exit 375) to Hwy 404, N to Hwy 7, E (rt) to Woodbine Av, S to mtl. Nrby rstrnt, mtg rm, fax, b/f, cable TV, t pkng, outlets, game rm, laundry, cont brfst, n/s rms. Free local calls, coffee. $49-86/S; $49-94/D; $4/ex prsn. 5/1-8/31: $54-87/S; $54-96/D. Discs.

Howard Johnson/ 555 Cochrane Dr, Markham ON L3R 8E3. 905-479-5000/ Fax: 479-1186. AE,M,V,DC,CB,D. Hwy 404 to Hwy 7, E to Valhalla Dr, rt to Cochrane, rt to mtl. Rstrnt, n/s rms, laundry, mtg rm, in-rm coffee, cont brfst, t pkng. Free local calls. $59-89/S; $59-99/D. Discs.

Massey

Mohawk Motel/ 335 Sauble St, Box 429, Massey ON P0P 1P0. 705-865-2722/ Fax: 865-3370. V,M,AE. On Trans Can Hwy 17. N/s rms, cable TV, dd phone, fax, refrig, microwave, cot, crib, outlets, t/b/rv pkng, eff, conn rms. Free local calls, coffee. CAA. $38/S; $44/D; $4/ex prsn. 5/15-10/15: $44/S; $48/D. Disc: Senior, l/s. *Guaranteed rates.*

Mississauga (Toronto area)

Howard Johnson/ 2420 Surveyor Rd, Mississauga ON L5N 4E6. 905-858-8600/ Fax: 858-8574. V,M,AE,D,DC, CB. Hwy 401 to Erin Mills Pkwy, S to

CANADA

Millcreek Dr. Hwy 403 to Erin Mills Pkwy, N to Millcreek Dr. Rstrnt, n/s rms, in-rm coffee, mtg rm, game rm, laundry, t pkng. Free local calls, cont brfst. $59-69/S; $64-79/D. Discs.

Morrisburg

Howard Johnson Hotel/ Hwy 2, Box 1140, Morrisburg ON K0C 1X0. 613-543-3788/ Fax: 543-3160. V,M,AE,D,DC,CB. Hwy 401, Exit 750, S on Rt 31 to Hwy 2, E 1 km. Rstrnt/ lounge, pool, exerc equip, n/s rms, mtg rm, game rm, whrlpool, sauna, golf, t pkng. $62-89/S or D. 5/1-10/31: $72-90/S or D. Discs.

Niagara Falls

Holiday Inn By The Falls/ 5339 Murray St, Niagara Falls ON L2G 2J3. 905-356-1333/ Fax: 356-7128. V,M,AE,D,DC,CB. Hwy 420, Exit Stanley Av S to Murray St. Pool, indr pool, sauna, whrlpool, n/s rms, satellite TV, tt/dd phone, fax, copier, elevator, cot, crib, b pkng, conn rms. CAA/ Mobil. $48-78/S or D; $10/ex prsn. 4/12-10/13: $68-155/S or D. Holidays, wknds: $75-155/S or D. Disc: Senior.

Comfort Inn/ 4009 River Rd, Niagara Falls ON L2E 3E9. 905-356-0131. AE, M,V,DC. 1 1/2 mi N of the falls on Niagara Pkwy. Rstrnt, pool, t pkng, family rms, attraction trans, n/s rms. $39-79/S or D; $5/ex prsn. 4/1-4/30: $39-149/S or D. 5/1-9/30: $49-189/S or D. 10/1-12/31: $39-99/S or D. Discs.

Comfort Inn/ 5657 Victoria Av, Niagara Falls ON L2G 3L5. 905-356-2461. AE, M,V,DC. I-90 to I-190, N to Robert Moses Pkwy to Rainbow Bridge, exit Victoria Av. Rstrnt/ lounge, pool, mtg rm, fax, sauna, whrlpool, cable TV, n/s rms. No pets. $40-140/S; $40-150/D; $10/ex prsn. 6/16-9/30: $50-220/S or D. Discs.

Comfort Suites/ 5851 Victoria Av, Niagara Falls ON L2G 3L6. 905-356-2648. AE,M,V,DC. QEW Hwy 420 to Stanley Av, S to Ferry St, N to mtl. Rstrnt/ lounge, indr pool, mtg rm, fax, b/f, whrlpool, n/s rms. No pets. CAA. $49-129/S; $59-139/D; $10/ex prsn. 5/1-6/22, 8/28-10/21: $59-129/S; $69-139/D. 6/23-8/27: $99-139/S; $109-149/D. Discs.

Econo Lodge/ 7514 Lundy's Ln, Niagara Falls ON L2H 1G8. 905-354-1849. V,AE,M,DC. Rainbow bridge 420 to Hwy 20 (Lundy's Lane), lt to mtl. QEW to McCloud Rd, exit to Lundy's Ln, lt to mtl. Nrby rstrnt, pool, t pkng, outlets, n/s rms, picnic tables. Free local calls. No pets. $30-45/S or D; $5/ex prsn. 5/1-6/29, 9/6-10/31: $30-75/S or D. 6/30-9/5: $40-99/S or D. Discs.

Econo Lodge/ 5781 Victoria Av, Niagara Falls ON L2G 3L6. 905-356-2034. V,AE,M,DC. Hwy 420 to Stanley Av, S to Ferry St, N to mtl. Rstrnt, indr pool, whrlpool, t pkng, outlets, n/s rms. Free local calls. No pets. $35-50/S or D; $5-10/ex prsn. 5/1-6/29, 9/6-10/10: $35-75/S or D. 6/30-9/5: $45-110/S or D. Discs.

HoJo Inn/ 8100 Lundy's Ln, Niagara Falls ON L2H 1H1. 905-358-9777. AE, M,V,DC,D,CB. QEW, exit Lundy's Ln, rt. Rstrnt, n/s rms, pool, satellite TV, t pkng. $30-50/S or D. 5/1-6/23, 9/5-10/31: $40-70/S or D. 6/24-9/4: $65-140/S or D. Higher spec event/ holiday wknd rates. Discs.

Howard Johnson Hotel/ 5905 Victoria Av, Niagara Falls ON L2G 3L8. 905-357-4040/ Fax: 357-6202/ 800-565-4656 (US & CN). V,M,AE,D,DC,CB. QEW to Rte 420, rt on Stanley Av, lt on Ferry St (Victoria Av). E: Rainbow Bridge to Falls Av, lt, rt onto Clifton Hill (Victoria Av). Rstrnt, indr pool, n/s rms, fax, sauna, whrlpool, laundry. No pets. $40-150/S or D. Discs.

Howard Johnson Hotel/ 4357 River Rd, Niagara Falls ON L2E 3E8. 905-358-5555/ Fax: 358-0140/ 800-465-6027. V,M,AE,D,DC,CB. Whirlpool bridge, turn rt off bridge. Rainbow bridge, lt on River Rd, 3/4 mi. From N or S Hwy 420 to River Rd, lt 3/4 mi. Rstrnt, indr pool, b/f, n/s rms, whrlpool, sauna, sundeck, t pkng. No pets. Gold Medal Winner. $38-78/S or D. 5/1-6/24, 9/6-10/31: $40-100/S or D. 6/25-9/5: $60-130/S or D. Discs.

Quality Hotel/ 5257 Ferry St, Niagara Falls ON L2G 1R6. 905-356-2842. AE, M,V,DC. QEW 420 to Stanley Av, S to Ferry St, lt to mtl. I-90 to I-190 N, exit Robert Moses Pkwy to Rainbow Bridge.

Rstrnt, indr pool, mtg rm, fax, sauna, whrlpool, cable TV, t pkng. No pets. CAA. $50-150/S or D; $8-50/ex prsn. 7/1-9/3: $90-190/S or D. Discs.

Quality Inn/ 4946 Clifton Hill, Box 60, Niagara Falls ON L2E 6S8. 905-358-3601. AE,M,V,DC. QEW to Hwy 420, rt on Stanley Av, lt at Ferry St, rt at Clifton Hill. From US, Rainbow Bridge, exit 3, rt on River Rd, rt at Clifton Hill. Rstrnt, pool, indr pool, fax, whrlpool, cable TV, playgrnd, family rms. No pets. $49-99/S or D; $6/ex prsn. 5/1-6/30, 9/1-10/31: $59-139/S or D. 7/1-8/31: $69-139/S or D. Discs.

North Bay

Howard Johnson Hotel/ 425 Fraser St, N Bay ON P1B 3X1. 705-472-8200/ Fax: 472-0656. V,M,AE,D,DC,CB. Hwy 17 or Hwy 11, Exit Fisher St, rt on McIntyre. Rstrnt/ lounge, n/s rms, b/f, laundry, mtg rm, fax. $49-73/S; $57-83/D. Discs.

Oshawa

Rodeway Suites/ 1910 Simcoe St N, Oshawa ON L1G 4Y3. 905-404-8700. V,M,AE,D,DC. Hwy 401 at Simcoe St N. On Simcoe between Hwys 3 & 4, E of Hwy 401. Nrby rstrnt, mtg rm, fax, b/f, cable TV, t pkng, n/s rms, refrig, microwave. Free cont brfst. No pets. CAA. $52-63/S; $61-72/D; $7/ex prsn. 5/1-9/1: $54-65/S; $63-74/D. Discs.

Ottawa

Econo Lodge/ 475 Rideau St, Ottawa ON K1N 5Z3. 613-789-3781. V,M,AE, D,DC. Hwy 417 (Queensway), take Nicholas exit 118 to Laurier, rt 2 km to Chapel, lt on Chapel to Rideau, rt. Rstrnt, mtg rm, sauna, cable TV, exerc equip, n/s rms. $58-65/S; $60-75/D; $6/ex prsn. Discs.

Owen Sound

Diamond Motel/ 713 9th Av E, Owen Sound ON N4K 3E6. 519-371-2011/ Fax: 371-9460/ 800-461-7849 (Ontario). V,M,AE. On Hwy 6 & 10; 3 lights S of Hwy 26, 2 blks S of Hwy 21. Pool, sauna, n/s rms, cable TV, arpt trans, mtg rm, fax, copier, refrig, cot, crib, outlets, t/b/rv pkng, eff. Free local calls, coffee. No pets. CAA. $45/S; $48-55/D. 5/1-6/14, 9/10-10/15: $50/S; $55-65/D. 6/15-9/9: $55/S; $65-75/D. Disc: Senior, bsns, govt, family, trkr, l/s. *Guaranteed rates.*

Pembroke

Colonial Fireside Inn/ 1350 Pembroke St W, Pembroke ON K8A 7A3. 613-732-3623/ Fax: 732-4232/ 800-265-2559. V,M,AE,D. Trans Can Hwy 17, Exit Forest Lea Rd to Pembroke St. Pool, cable TV, VCR, playgrnd, tt/dd phone, fax, refrig, microwave, cot, crib, outlets, t/b pkng, eff, conn rms. Free local calls, cont brfst. CAA. $42-60/S; $48-75/D; $5/ex prsn. 4/1-9/30: $44-60/S; $56-80/D. *Guaranteed rates.*

Comfort Inn/ 959 Pembroke St E, Pembroke ON K8A 3M3. 613-735-1057. M,V,DC,D,AE. Pembroke St E (Old Hwy 17) to mtl. Nrby rstrnt, fax, cable TV, t pkng, outlets, cont brfst, n/s rms. Free local calls. $52-57/S; $60-65/D; $4/ex prsn. 2/1-4/30: $53-58/S; $61-66/D. 5/1-7/31: $58-64/S; $66-72/D. 8/1-10/31: $57-63/S; $65/71/D. Discs.

Perth

Friendship Inn/ 125 Dufferin St, Perth ON K7H 3A5. 613-267-3300. AE,M,V. Hwy 7 & 511. Rstrnt, pool, fax, cable TV, t pkng, outlets. Free local calls. No pets. CAA. $39-49/S; $49-59/D; $7/ex prsn. 5/1-6/13, 9/8-11/21: $49-59/S; $59-69/D. 6/14-9/7: $59-69/S; $79-89/D. Discs.

Peterborough

Comfort Inn/ 1209 Lansdowne St, Peterborough ON K9J 7M2. 705-740-7000/ Fax: 745-0506. M,V,DC,D,AE. From Toronto Hwy 401 E (Exit 436) to Hwy 115, N to The Parkway, N to Lansdowne St. From Ottawa, Hwy 7 becomes Lansdowne St. Rstrnt/ lounge, indr pool, mtg rm, fax, b/f, cable TV, t pkng, n/s rms. Free local calls, cont brfst. CAA. $55-135/S or D; $5/ex prsn. 5/1-9/30: $52-129/S; $62-129/D. Discs.

Quality Inn/ 1074 Lansdowne St, Peterborough ON K9J 1Z9. 705-748-6801. M,V,DC,D,AE. Hwy 401 E, exit 436, Hwy 115 N to The Parkway, lt on Lansdowne St. Hwy 401 W, exit 464, Hwy 28 N to Hwy 115. Nrby rstrnt, mtg

CANADA

rm, fax, b/f, whrlpool, cable TV, t pkng, exerc equip, cont brfst. Free local calls. $54-64/S; $62-72/D; $4/ex prsn. Discs.

Rexdale (Toronto area)
Carlingview Airport Inn/ 221 Carlingview Dr, Rexdale ON M9W 5E8. 416-675-3303/ Fax: 675-6524/ 800-263-6100 (Canada only). V,M,AE,D, DC. Ebnd on 401, take Renforth N to Carlingview, lt. Wbnd; 401, take Carlingview cut-off. Hwy 427, Exit Dixon E to Carlingview S. Rstrnt/ lounge, pool, n/s rms, cable TV, arpt trans, tt phone, fax, copier, elevator, cot, crib, b/rv pkng, conn rms. CAA. $58/S or D; $6/ex prsn. *Guaranteed rates.*

Richards Landing (St Joseph Island)
Clansmen Motel/ RR 2, Richards Landing ON P0R 1J0. 705-246-2581. Personal cheques. On St Joseph Island, 6 mi from jct of Hwy 548 & Hwy 17E (Trans Canada). 28 mi E of Sault Ste Marie. N/s rms, cable TV, VCR/ movies, fax, copier, refrig, microwave, cot, crib, outlets, eff. Free local calls, coffee. CAA. $45/S; $55/D; $5/ex prsn. *Guaranteed rates.*

Saint Catharines
Comfort Inn/ 2 Dunlop Dr, St Catharines ON L2R 1A2. 905-687-8890/ Fax: 687-4033. V,M,AE. QEW (Exit 46) to Lake St, S to Dunlop Dr, lt on S Service Rd. Rstrnt, fax. b/f, cable TV, n/s rms. $56-76/S; $64-84/D; $4/ex prsn. 5/1-9/30: $60-81/S; $68-89/D. Discs.

Saint Thomas
Comfort Inn/ 100 Centennial Av, St Thomas ON N5R 5B2. 519-633-4082/ Fax: 633-8294. M,V,DC,D,AE. Hwy 401 (Exit 186) to Wellington Rd, E on Hwy 3 (St Thomas Expwy), S (rt) on Centennial Av. Nrby rstrnt, fax, b/f, cable TV, t pkng, cont brfst, n/s rms. Free local calls. $58-70/S; $66-78/D; $4/ex prsn. 5/1-10/31: $57-69/S; $65-77/D. 11/1-12/31: $56-68/S; $64-76/D. Discs.

Sault Ste Marie
Comfort Inn/ 333 Great Northern Rd, Sault Ste Marie ON P6B 4Z8. 705-759-8000/ Fax: 759-8538. V,M,AE. Hwy 17 E to Black Rd (bypass), N to Hwy 17, W (lt) to Great Northern Rd, N to mtl.

Nrby rstrnt, fax, b/f, cable TV, t pkng, outlets, cont brfst, n/s rms. Free local calls. No pets. $56-80/S; $64-90/D; $4/ex prsn. 5/1-6/16: $60-80/S; $68-90/D. 6/17-9/8: $72-88/S; $80-96/D. 9/9-10/9: $79-92/S; $87-105/D. Discs.

Scarborough (Toronto area)
Quality Inn/ 22 Metropolitan Rd, Scarborough ON M1R 2T6. 416-293-8171. M,V,DC,D,AE. Hwy 401, exit Warden Av S, lt on Metropolitan Rd. Rstrnt/ lounge, pool, indr pool, mtg rm, whrlpool, exerc equip. $55-75/S; $65-99/D; $6/ex prsn. 6/16-9/30: $60-79/S; $70-99/D. Discs.

Simcoe
Comfort Inn/ 85 The Queensway E, Simcoe ON N3Y 4M5. 519-426-2611/ Fax: 426-0053. M,V,DC,D,AE. Hwy 403 to Hwy 24, S (Rest Acres Rd) 37 km, to Hwy 3 (The Queensway), lt to mtl. Nrby rstrnt, fax, b/f, cable TV, t pkng, outlets, cont brfst, n/s rms. Free local calls. $49-59/S; $57-67/D; $4/ex prsn. 5/1-10/31: $52-67/S; $60-75/D. 11/1-12/31: $48-58/S; $56-66/D. Discs.

Sudbury
Howard Johnson Hotel/ 390 Elgin St S, Sudbury ON P3B 1B4. 705-675-1273/ Fax: 671-1766. M,DC,D,V,AE,CB. Hwy 17, S on Paris St, dntn. Hwy 69, turn rt on Paris. Rstrnt, indr pool, mtg rm, in-rm coffee, fax, copier, whrlpool, t pkng. Free cont brfst. $49-82/S; $59-92/D. Discs.

Thunder Bay
Comfort Inn/ 660 W Arthur St, Thunder Bay ON P7E 5R8. 807-475-3155/ Fax: 475-3816. V,M,AE. Trans Canada Hwy (Hwy 11/17) to Arthur St, E to mtl. Nrby rstrnt, fax, b/f, cable TV, outlets, cont brfst, n/s rms. Free local calls. $60-92/S; $60-100/D; $4/ex prsn. 6/17-9/17: $62-97/S; $62-99/D. 9/18-12/31: $55-91/S; $55-99/D. Discs.

Toronto
Beverley Place/ 235 Beverley St, Toronto ON M5T 1Z4. 416-977-0077/ Fax: 599-2242. V,M,AE. QEW E to Spadina Exit, N to Queen, rt to Beverley St. Free full brfst. No pets. CAA. $45-55/S; $60-70/D; $15/ex prsn. 5/1-12/31: $50-65/S; $65-85/D. *Guaran-*

teed rates.

Comfort Inn/ 240 Belfield Rd, Toronto ON M9W 1H3. 416-241-8513. V,M,AE. QEW to Hwy 427, N to Hwy 27, N 3 km to Belfield. Nrby rstrnt, mtg rm, fax, b/f, cable TV, arpt trans, n/s rms. Free cont brfst, pkng. No pets. CAA. $50-57/S; $57-63/D; $6/ex prsn. 6/1-9/15: $57-63/S; $63-75/D. Discs.

Friendship Inn/ 2095 Lake Shore Blvd W, Toronto ON M8V 1A1. 416-255-4433. AE,M,V. QEW at Parklawn Rd, S to mtl. Nrby rstrnt, pool, mtg rm, fax, cable TV, tennis, coffee, refrig. Free cont brfst. No pets. CAA/ Mobil. $52/S; $52-75/D; $5/ex prsn. Discs.

Comfort Inn/ 68 Monogram Pl, Trenton ON K8V 6E6. 613-965-6660. M,V,DC,D,AE. Hwy 401 (Exit 526) to Glen Miller Rd, S to Sidney St, lt on Monogram Pl to mtl. Nrby rstrnt, mtg rm, fax, b/f, cable TV, t pkng, cont brfst, n/s rms. Free local calls. $53-61/S; $61-69/D; $4/ex prsn. 6/1-9/30: $55-63/S; $63-71/D. Discs.

Also see Markham, Mississagua, Rexdale, Scarborough.

Wawa

Kinniwabi Pines Motel & Cottages/ PO Box 1429, Wawa ON P0S 1K0 705-856-7302/ Fax: 856-2772/ 800-434-8240. M,DC,D,V,AE,CB. On Lake Superior side of Trans Can Hwy 17, 5.2 km S of Hwy 101. Nrby rstrnt/ lounge, n/s rms, cable TV, playgrnd, arpt trans, dd phone, fax, refrig, cot, outlets, t/b/rv pkng, eff. Free local calls, coffee. CAA. $35/S; $40/D; $3/ex prsn. 6/1-10/14: $40/S; $48/D. Disc: Senior. *Guaranteed rates.*

Welland

Super 8 Motel/ 870 Niagara St, Welland ON L3C 1M3. 905-732-4811/ Fax: 732-9654. AE,M,V,DC,D,CB. QEW, exit Hwy 406 to Welland (20 km), lt on Niagara St (Hwy 58) to mtl. N/s rms, cable TV, VCR/ movies, tt/dd phone, fax, copier, cot, crib, outlets, t/b/rv pkng, conn rms, b/f. Free local calls, coffee. CAA. $52-58/S; $58-64/D; $6/ex prsn. Holidays, spec events: $80/S or D. Discs.

Prince Edward Island

Summerside

Quality Inn/ 618 Water St E, Summerside PE C1N 2V5. 902-436-2295 Fax: 436-6277. AE,M,V,DC. Rte 11, 2 km off Rte 1A from Borden. Rstrnt/ lounge, pool, indr pool, mtg rm, fax, b/f, cable TV, exerc equip, n/s rms, t pkng, outlets. CAA. $55-94/S or D; $7/ex prsn. 5/1-5/31: $52-89/S or D. 6/1-9/30: $72-130/S; $79-130/D. Discs.

Quebec

Alma

Comfort Inn/ 870 av du Pont Sud, Alma PQ G8B 2V8. 418-668-9221. M,V,DC, D,AE. Hwy 170 to Hwy 169, rt 10 km to mtl. Hwy 172 to Hwy 169 (Chemin du Pont-Tache'), lt to mtl. Nrby rstrnt, fax, b/f, cable TV, t pkng, outlets, cont brfst, n/s rms. Free local calls. $57-65/S; $65-75/D; $4/ex prsn. 5/1-6/15: $55-61/S; $63-69/D. 6/16-9/19: $62-68/S; $70-76/D. Discs.

Brossard (Montreal area)

Comfort Inn/ 7863 boul Taschereau, Brossard PQ J4Y 1A4. 514-678-9350. M,V,DC,D,AE. Hwy 10, exit boul Taschereau W, 2 km, U-turn before boul Napoleon, to mtl. Rstrnt, fax, b/f, cable TV, t pkng, exerc equip, outlets, cont brfst. Free local calls. $60-70/S; $65-82/D; $4/ex prsn. 5/1-6/16: $56-66/S; $64-72/D. 6/17-9/30: $58-68/S; $60-80/D. Discs.

Quality Inn/ 6680 Taschereau Blvd, Brossard PQ J4W 1M8. 514-671-7213. M,V,DC,D,AE. Hwy 10 & 15 on Hwy 134. Rstrnt, pool, mtg rm, fax, b/f, cable TV, t pkng, shuttle. Free cont brfst. CAA. $56-70/S; $60-76/D; $10/ex prsn. 5/1-10/31: $60-80/S; $70-91/D. Discs.

Drummondville

Comfort Inn/ 1055 rue Hains, Drummondville PQ J2C 5L3. 819-477-4000. M,V,DC,D,AE. Trans Canada Hwy (Hwy 20), exit Hwy 143 S (dntn Drummondville), rt at rue Hains to mtl. Nrby rstrnt, fax, b/f, cable TV, t pkng, outlets, cont brfst. Free local calls. $56-64/S;

$64-72/D; $4/ex prsn. 5/1-9/30: $62-70/S; $70-78/D. Dis

Montreal

See Brossard.

Rimouski

Comfort Inn/ 455 boul St Germain ouest, Rimouski PQ G5L 3P2. 418-724-2500. M,V,DC,D,AE. Rte 132 (boul St Germain), mtl E of rue de Lausanne. Nrby rstrnt, fax, b/f, cable TV, outlets, cont brfst. Free local calls. No pets. $56-62/S; $64-70/D; $4/ex prsn. 5/1-6/16: $54-60/S; $62-68/D. 6/17-9/4: $61-69/S; $69-79/D. 9/5-10/31: $55-61/S; $63-69/D. Discs.

Riviere du Loup

Comfort Inn/ 85 boul Cartier, Riviere Du Loup PQ G5R 4X4. 418-867-4162. M,V,DC,D,AE. Trans Canada Hwy (Hwy 20), exit 507 S on boul Cartier. Nrby rstrnt, fax, b/f, cable TV, outlets, cont brfst. Free local calls. $56-62/S; $64-70/D; $4/ex prsn. 5/1-5/31: $54-60/S; $62-68/D. 6/1-9/4: $61-69/S; $69-79/D. 9/5-12/31: $55-61/S; $63-69/D. Discs.

Rock Forest (Sherbrooke area)

Comfort Inn/ 4295 boul Bourque, Rock Forest PQ J1N 1S4. 819-564-4400. M,V,DC,D,AE. Hwy 10, exit 128 (boul Bourque) to mtl. Hwy 55, exit 140 (Hwy 410), exit 4 (Rock Forest) to boul Bourque. Nrby rstrnt, fax, b/f, cable TV, outlets, cont brfst. Free local calls. $55-65/S; $63-68/D; $4/ex prsn. 5/1-6/23: $53-58/S; $61-66/D. 6/24-7/31: $55-65/S; $63-73/D. 8/1-8/31: $58-68/S; $66-76/D. Discs.

Saint Jean sur Richelieu

Auberge Mirifik Inn Harris/ 576 Champlain St, St Jean Sur Richelieu PQ J3B 6X1. 514-348-3821/ Fax: 348-7725/ 800-668-3821. V,M,AE. Hwy 10 to Hwy 35, Exit boul Seminar up to the river. Pool, whrlpool, n/s rms, exerc equip, cable TV, mtg rm, copier, laundry, refrig, elevator, outlets, b pkng, eff. Free local calls, cont brfst. CAA. $40/S; $48/D; $10/ex prsn. 5/1-9/30: $48/S; $58/D. Disc: Bsns, TA, govt, milt. *Guaranteed rates.*

Comfort Inn/ 700 rue Gadbois, St Jean Sur Richelieu PQ J3A 1V1. 514-359-4466. AE,M,V,DC. Hwy 133 to Hwy 35, Exit 9 to mtl. Nrby rstrnt, fax, b/f, cable TV, t pkng, outlets, cont brfst. Free local calls. $50-58/S; $58-66/D; $4/ex prsn. 6/17-9/4: $52-67/S; $60-77/D. Discs.

Saint Laurent

Econo Lodge/ 6755 Cote de Liesse, St Laurent PQ H4T 1E5. 514-735-5702. V,M,AE,D,DC. From arpt, take 520 E, exit Hickmore, 1st rt, lt at stop, underpass, rt on Griffith, mtl on rt. Rstrnt/ lounge, pool, fax, cable TV, t pkng, outlets, n/s rms. No pets. $59/S or D; $8/ex prsn. 5/1-10/31: $59-75/S; $65-85/D. Discs.

Howard Johnson Hotel/ 6600 Cote de Liesse, St Laurent PQ H4T 1E3. 514-735-7788/ Fax: 735-8515. V,M,AE,D,DC,CB. Cote de Liesse Wbnd, exit Hickmore, lt, go under overpass, rt onto Cote de Liesse E Service Rd, go past Hickmore, mtl on rt. Rstrnt/ lounge, indr pool, n/s rms. Free shuttle. $59-99/S or D. Discs.

Sainte Adele

Motel Spa Excelsior Rustique/ 280 Montee Seraphin, Ste Adele PQ J0R 1L0. 514-229-2022/ Fax: 229-3661/ 800-990-2732. V,M,AE. Hwy 15 N, Exit 67, continue straight 6 kilometers. Nrby rstrnt/ lounge, pool, indr pool, sauna, whrlpool, cable TV, tt phone, mtg rm, fax, copier, cot, conn rms. Free local calls. No pets. CAA. $40/S; $48/D; $10/ex prsn. Spec events, holidays, wknds: $59/S or D. *Guaranteed rates.*

Sainte Foy

Auberge Laurier/ 3125 Avenue des hotels, Ste Foy PQ G1W 3Z6. 418-653-7221/ Fax: 653-2307. Nrby rstrnt/ lounge, pool, tt/dd phone, fax, copier, nwspr, cot, crib, outlets, t/b pkng, conn rms. CAA. $48/S or D; $6/ex prsn. 1/26-2/12, 5/16-10/14: $69/S or D. Disc: Senior.

Sept Iles

Comfort Inn/ 854 boul Laure, Sept-Iles PQ G4R 1Y7. 418-968-6005. M,V,DC,D,AE. On Hwy 138. Nrby rstrnt, fax, b/f, cable TV, outlets, cont brfst. Free local calls. $57-63/S; $65-71/D; $8/ex prsn. 5/1-6/16: $56-62/S; $64-70/D. 6/17-

9/18: $62-70/S; $69-78/D. Discs.

Thetford Mines

Comfort Inn/ 123 boul Smith S, Thetford Mines PQ G6G 7S7. 418-338-0171. M,V,DC,D,AE. Hwy 20 E, exit 228 S (Hwy 263) to Hwy 116 E to Hwy 165 S to Hwy 112 to Thetford Mines. From Quebec City Hwy 73 to Hwy 112. Nrby rstrnt, fax, b/f, cable TV, t pkng, outlets, cont brfst. Free local calls. $56-68/S; $64-76/D; $4/ex prsn. Discs.

Saskatchewan

Prince Albert

Comfort Inn/ 3863 2nd Av W, Prince Albert SK S6W 1A1. 306-763-4466/ Fax: 764-2210. AE,M,V,DC. Hwy 11, exit Hwy 2 N, W on Marquis Rd to mtl. Nrby rstrnt, fax, b/f, cable TV, t pkng, outlets, cont brfst. Free local calls. $50-75/S; $50-83/D; $4/ex prsn. 5/1-6/30, 10/1-12/31: $45-75/S; $45-83/D. 7/1-9/30: $45-77/S; $49-85/D. Discs.

Regina

Comfort Inn/ 3221 E Eastgate Dr, Regina SK S4Z 1A4. 306-789-5522/ Fax: 789-5522. AE,M,V,DC. Trans Canada Hwy W, exit Fleet St N, rt on Eastgate Dr to mtl. Trans Canada Hwy E, exit Prince of Wales Dr N, lt on Eastgate Dr. Nrby rstrnt, fax, b/f, cable TV, t pkng, outlets, cont brfst. Free local calls. $45-75/S; $45-83/D; $4/ex prsn. 7/1-9/30: $55-77/S; $55-85/D. Discs.

Howard Johnson Hotel/ 1717 Victoria Av, Regina SK S4P 0P9. 306-569-4656/ Fax: 569-4977. M,DC,D,V, AE,CB. From E: Trans-Canada Hwy (turns into Victoria Av) to Broad St. From W: Trans Canada Hwy to Albert St, N to Victoria Av, E to Broad St. Rstrnt/ lounge, mtg rm, exerc equip, in-rm coffee. $65-90/S; $65-95/D. Discs.

Saskatoon

Comfort Inn/ 2155 Northridge Dr, Saskatoon SK S7L 6X6. 306-934-1122/ Fax: 934-6539. AE,M,V,DC. Hwys 11, 12 & 16, exit Circle Dr E, lt on Northridge Dr to mtl. Nrby rstrnt, fax, b/f, cable TV, t pkng, outlets, cont brfst. Free local calls. $50-75/S; $50-83/D;

$4/ex prsn. 5/1-6/30, 10/1-12/31: $45-75/S; $45-83/D. 7/1-9/30: $45-77/S; $49-85/D. Discs.

Swift Current

Comfort Inn/ 1510 S Service Rd E, Swift Current SK S9H 3X6. 306-778-3994/ Fax: 773-9312. AE,M,V,DC. Trans Canada Hwy, exit Hwy 4 S, rt on S Serv Rd to mtl. Nrby rstrnt, fax, b/f, cable TV, t pkng, outlets, cont brfst. Free local calls. $49-63/S; $50-83/D; $4/ex prsn. 5/1-9/30: $45-63/S; $45-83/D. 10/1-12/31: $45-58/S; $45-66/D. Discs.

Friendship Inn/ 160 Begg St W, Swift Current SK S9H 0K4. 306-773-4668. V, M,AE,D,DC. On Hwy 1. Rstrnt, pool, fax, cable TV, t pkng, outlets, n/s rms, coffee, kitchenettes, cots, suites. No pets. $38-46/S: $44-52/D; $2/ex prsn. 5/1-11/15: $40-48/S; $46-54/D. Discs.

ORDER NOW!

Before you travel,
save money! Save time!

1997
State by State
Guide to
Budget Motels

Published in January of each year, the **State by State Guide to Budget Motels** tells you where to find the best buys and best locations! It's the only guide that's become the standard of the travel industry for budget motels. The **State by State Guide to Budget Motels** is totally revised and updated each year, with all new typesetting, many new listings, and money-saving facts!

Yes! Send me the
1997 State by State Guide to Budget Motels

Only **$12.95**
Plus $3.00 for Postage and Handling

Send to:

Name _____

Address _____

City _____ State _____ Zip _____

Telephone (___) _____

I enclose a check for: _____

Please charge to my   Visa   Mastercard

Card Number _____ Expiration Date ____

My signature _____

MARLOR PRESS, INC.

4304 Brigadoon Drive Saint Paul, MN 55126
FAX (612) 490-1182